FOR REFERENCE

Do Not Take From This Room

THE REPUBLICS AND REGIONS
of the
RUSSIAN FEDERATION

EastWest Institute
New York Prague Moscow Kyiv Brussels Košice

The EastWest Institute serves as a leading values-based action network facilitating communication and cooperation among Europe, Eurasia, and North America. EWI is an independent European-American non-profit organization that was founded in 1981 to help bring about an end to the Cold War. EWI today brings together a multinational staff of 75 with a global network of more than 4,000 professionals in 51 countries to:

- Defuse tensions that threaten peace and stability;
- Facilitate practical cooperation across borders and between neighbors;
- Support demand-driven reform efforts which strengthen the rule-of-law and create favorable conditions for economic development including local and foreign investment;
- Identify, nourish, and connect public, private and NGO sector leaders for dealing with 21st century challenges.

In pursuit of these goals, we concentrate our efforts on those regions where help is most needed and where we can be useful—Russia, Ukraine, and Southeastern Europe, as well as Central Europe, the Caucasus, and Central Asia. The strength of the partnership between Europe and North America is vital to the success of our work. By bridging ideas, boundaries, and societies, EWI strives to contribute to a more peaceful and democratic world.

For more information, please contact us at:

EastWest Institute
700 Broadway, Second Floor
New York, NY 10003
Tel (212) 824-4100, Fax (212) 824-4149
Website: http://www.iews.org
E-mail: iews@iews.org

168090

THE REPUBLICS AND REGIONS
of the
RUSSIAN FEDERATION

A Guide to Politics, Policies, and Leaders

EDITED BY

ROBERT W. ORTTUNG

WITH DANIELLE N. LUSSIER AND
ANNA PARETSKAYA

EASTWEST INSTITUTE

M.E.Sharpe
Armonk, New York
London, England

Library of Congress Cataloging-in-Publication Data

The republics and regions of the Russian Federation: a guide to politics, policies, and
leaders / by EastWest Institute ; edited by Robert W. Orttung with Danielle N. Lussier
and Anna Paretskaya.
    p. cm.
Includes bibliographical references and index.
ISBN 0-7656-0559-7
  1. Russia (Federation)—Administrative and political divisions. 2. Local officials and
employees—Russia (Federation)—Directories. 3. Russia (Federation)—Politics and
government—1991– I. Orttung, Robert W. II. Lussier, Danielle N. III. Paretskaya, Anna.
IV. EastWest Institute (New York, N.Y.)

JN6699.A88 R47 2000
914.7′003—dc21

                                             00-020489

Contents

Preface

The republics and regions of the Russian Federation are playing an increasingly important role in the life of the country. Each region elects its own regional executive, and regional elites have a definite influence on national executive and legislative elections. Between elections, the regions play a crucial role in defining the country's political, economic, and social policies and in determining how these policies are implemented. As power in Russia has been decentralized, it has become increasingly important to know who has taken it and how they hope to use it. Familiarity with Russia's regions and the people who rule them will be crucial for an understanding of Russian developments for the foreseeable future.

This reference guide offers comprehensive but concise portraits of Russia's 89 regions. Each profile features:

- a brief overview of the region,
- key demographic, economic, and electoral statistics,
- a guide to regional political institutions,
- the regional leadership's political and economic platform and alliances,
- key policy initiatives,
- relations with Moscow,
- an overview of important regional politicians, businessmen, and enterprises,
- relations with other regions,
- foreign policy,
- attitudes toward business development,
- career history of the regional executive,
- contact information for the regional leadership,
- and information about the most important regional WWW sites.

The compilers of this book hope that you enjoy using it as much as we have enjoyed working on it. The situation in Russia's regions is always changing, but we hope that this book provides a baseline for further study.

Robert Orttung, Danielle Lussier,
and Anna Paretskaya

Acknowledgments

The profiles in this book draw heavily on material gathered by the EastWest Institute's network of correspondents throughout the Russian regions.

Altai Krai: ASI-Altai
Arkhangelsk Oblast: Gleb Tiurin, Tatyana Barandova
Bashkortostan: Fidail Shayakhmetov
Bryansk Oblast: Nikolai Gorelov, Aleksandr Levinsky, Jean-Charles Lallemand
Buryatia: Andrei Khodoev
Chelyabinsk Oblast: Igor Stepanov
Chukotka Autonomous Okrug: Varvara Litovka, Yurii Prygov
Dagestan: Nabi Abdullaev, Polina Sanaeva
Gorno-Altai Republic: Svetlana Tyukhteneva
Irkutsk Oblast: Maksim Bakanovich, Svetlana Burdinskaya, Natalia Michurina, Sergey Safronov, Galina Solonina, Elena Veselkova, Yekaterina Vorobieva, Yekaterina Vyrupaeva, Svetlana Batutene
Kaliningrad Oblast: Yekaterina Vasileva, Aleksei Ignatev
Karelia: Boris Matveev
Kirov Oblast: Marina Bakhtina
Khabarovsk Krai: Sergei Shilo
Komi Republic and Komi-Permyak Autonomous Okrug: Yurii Shabaev
Krasnodar Krai: Sergei Kuzmin, Nikolay Semenenko
Krasnoyarsk Krai: Pavel Avramov, Sergey Bondarev
Kursk Oblast: Sergei Sarychev
Moscow City: Vasilii Filippov, Dmitrii Grushkin, Olga Komarova, Aleksei Pyatkovskii, Vasilii Treskov
Moscow Oblast: Denis Makarov
Nizhnii Novgorod Oblast: Yury Rodygin
Novgorod Oblast: Ivan Novgorodskii
Novosibirsk Oblast: Stanislav Okhvat
Omsk Oblast: Valery Chukhlomin, Marina Chukhlomina
Orenburg Oblast: Dmitrii Goncharov
Penza Oblast: Irina Rodina, Yelena Zateeva
Perm Oblast: Oksana Oracheva, Andrei Suslov
Primorskii Krai: Yevgenii Popravko, Andrei Ivlev, Vladimir Oshchenko
Pskov Oblast: Andrei Shcherkin
Rostov Oblast: Marina Svetlova, Andrei Miroshnichenko

Ryazan Oblast: Sergei Postnov
St. Petersburg: Lyudmila Bogomolova, Yurii Bryukvin, Marina Makova, Daniel Tsygankov, John Varoli, Ravil Zotov
Sakha Republic (Yakutia): Oleg Yemelyanov
Samara Oblast: Andrei Perla, Lyudmila Lipunova
Saratov Oblast: Yuliya Yeliseeva
Smolensk Oblast: Arsentii Ledovskii
Stavropol Krai: Kharon Deniev, Irina Morozova
Sverdlovsk Oblast: Tatiana Barannikova, Olga Gorchakova, Natalia Mints, Sergei Pushkarev, Dmitry Strovsky, Gerald Easter
Tatarstan: Midkhat Faroukshine
Tomsk Oblast: Andrei Bondarenko, Nikolai Kashcheev
Tver Oblast: Boris Goubman
Ulyanovsk Oblast: Sergey Gogin
Volgograd Oblast: Ivan Kurilla
Voronezh Oblast: Andrei Muchnik
Yaroslavl Oblast: Ilya Kravchenko, Anton Mavrin

Andrei Muchnik, who was an intern at the Institute during the summer of 1998, helped draft several of the first profiles.

The maps of the Russian Federation appearing throughout this volume were designed by M.E. Sharpe, Inc. and the EastWest Institute. The inset maps of each region were adapted by the EastWest Institute from maps issued by Goskomstat in *Regiony Rossii*, Moscow, 1997.

This book was made possible partly through generous funding from Morgan Stanley Dean Witter. Additionally, part of the funds for this work were provided by the National Council for Eurasian and East European Research (NCEEER), under authority of a Title VIII grant from the U.S. Department of State. Neither Morgan Stanley Dean Witter, NCEEER, nor the U.S. Government is responsible for the views expressed within this text. Naturally, all mistakes of omission or commission are the responsibility of the editors.

List of Abbreviations

BG	Boston Globe	OG	Obshchaya Gazeta
BR	Bryanskii Rabochii	OMRI DD	Open Media Research Institute Daily Digest
CSM	Christian Science Monitor	OMRI RRR	Open Media Research Institute Russian
DP	Delovoe Povolzhie		Regional Report
EWI RRR	EastWest Institute Russian Regional Report	OV	Omskii Vestnik
FI	Finansovye Izvestiya	PG	Priokskaya Gazeta
FR	Finansovaya Rossiya	PR	Panorama Respubliki
GV	Gorodskie Vesti	PS	Politicheskaya Sreda
IG	Ivanovskaya Gazeta	RFE/RL	Radio Free Europe/Radio Liberty Newsline
JFP	Jamestown Foundation Prism	RFR	Radio Free Europe/Radio Liberty Russian
KD	Kommersant Daily		Federation Report
KP	Komsomolskaya Pravda	RG	Rossiiskaya Gazeta
KV	Kommersant Vlast	RK	Rabochii Krai
KW	Kommersant Weekly	RT	Russkii Telegraf
LG	Literaturnaya Gazeta	RTA	Respublika Tatarstan
LI	Lipetskie Izvestiya	RV	Rossiiskie Vesti
MK	Moskovskii Komsomolets	SP	Stavropolskaya Pravda
MN	Moskovskie Novosti	SPT	St. Petersburg Times
MT	Moscow Times	SPV	Sankt-Peterburgskie Vedomosti
NC	Nefte Compass	SR	Sovetskaya Rossiya
NG	Nezavisimaya Gazeta	TI	Tulskie Izvestiya
NI	Novye Izvestiya	UP	Ulyanovskaya Pravda
NNS	National News Service	UR	Uralskii Rabochii
NV	Naryana Vynder	VSP	Vostochno-Sibirskaya Pravda
NYT	New York Times	VU	Vechernyaya Ufa
		WP	Washington Post

English–Russian Translation of Russian Political Parties and Movements

Agrarian Party of Russia	Agrarnaya partiya Rossii
All Russia	Vsya Rossiya
Bloc of Ivan Rybkin	Blok Ivana Rybkina
Cedar	Kedr
Communist Party of the Russian Federation (KPRF)	Kommunisticheskaya Partiya Rossiiskoi Federatsii (KPRF)
Communist Party of the Soviet Union (CPSU)	Kommunisticheskaya Partiya Sovetskogo Soyuza (CPSU)
Communists–Workers' Russia–For the Soviet Union	Kommunisty–Trudyashchiesya Rossii –Za Sovetskii Soyuz
Congress of Russian Communities (KRO)	Kongress russkikh obshchin (KRO)
Democratic Party of Russia	Demokraticheskaya partiya Rossii
Fatherland	Otechestvo
For the Motherland!	Za Rodinu!
Forward, Russia!	Vpered, Rossiya!
Great Power	Derzhava
Liberal Democratic Party of Russia (LDPR)	Liberalno-Demokraticheskaya Partiya Rossii (LDPR)
My Fatherland	Moe Otechestvo
National Patriotic Union of Russia (NPSR)	Natsionalno Patrioticheskii Soyuz Rossii (NPSR)
Muslim Movement Nur	Musulmanskoe dvizhenie "Nur"
Our Home Is Russia (NDR)	Nash Dom Rossiya (NDR)
Pamfilova-Gurov-Lysenko Bloc	Pamfilova-Gurov-Lysenko
Party of Russian Unity and Concord	Partiya Rossiiskogo yedinstva i soglasiya (PRES)
Party of Workers' Self-Government	Partiya samoupravleniya trudyashchikhsya
Pensioners' Party	Partiya pensionerov
Power to the People!	Vlast—narodu!
Right Cause	Pravoe delo
Russia's Choice	Vybor Rossii
Russian Movement for Democratic Reforms	Rossiiskoe dvizhenie demokraticheskikh reform
Trade Unions and Industrialists of Russia—Union of Labor	Profsoyuzy i promyshlenniki Rossii—Soyuz truda
Transformation of the Fatherland	Preobrazhenie Otechestva
Transformation of the Urals	Preobrazhenie Urala
Union of Right Forces	Soyuz pravykh sil
Unity	Yedinstvo
Voice of Russia	Golos Rossii
Women of Russia	Zhenshchiny Rossii
Yabloko	Yabloko
Zhirinovsky Bloc	Blok Zhirinovskogo

Russian–English Translation of Russian Political Parties and Movements

Agrarnaya partiya Rossii	Agrarian Party of Russia
Blok Ivana Rybkina	Bloc of Ivan Rybkin
Blok Zhirinovskogo	Zhirinovsky Bloc
Demokraticheskaya partiya Rossii	Democratic Party of Russia
Derzhava	Great Power
Golos Rossii	Voice of Russia
Kedr	Cedar
Kommunisticheskaya Partiya Rossiiskoi Federatsii (KPRF)	Communist Party of the Russian Federation (KPRF)
Kommunisticheskaya Partiya Sovetskogo Soyuza (CPSU)	Communist Party of the Soviet Union (CPSU)
Kommunisty–Trudyashchiesya Rossii–Za Sovetskii Soyuz	Communists–Workers' Russia–For the Soviet Union
Kongress russkikh obshchin (KRO)	Congress of Russian Communities (KRO)
Liberalno-Demokraticheskaya Partiya Rossii (LDPR)	Liberal Democratic Party of Russia (LDPR)
Moe Otechestvo	My Fatherland
Musulmanskoe dvizhenie "Nur"	Nur Muslim Movement
Nash Dom Rossiya (NDR)	Our Home Is Russia (NDR)
Natsionalno Patrioticheskii Soyuz Rossii (NPSR)	National Patriotic Union of Russia (NPSR)
Otechestvo	Fatherland
Pamfilova–Gurov–Lysenko	Pamfilova–Gurov–Lysenko Bloc
Partiya pensionerov	Pensioners' Party
Partiya Rossiiskogo yedinstva i soglasiya	Party of Russian Unity and Concord
Partiya samoupravleniya trudyashchikhsya (PRES)	Party of Workers' Self-Government
Pravoe delo	Right Cause
Preobrazhenie Otechestva	Transformation of the Fatherland
Preobrazhenie Urala	Transformation of the Urals
Profsoyuzy i promyshlenniki Rossii—Soyuz truda	Trade Unions and Industrialists of Russia—Union of Labor
Rossiiskoe dvizhenie demokraticheskikh reform	Russian Movement for Democratic Reforms
Soyuz pravykh sil	Union of Right Forces
Vlast—narodu!	Power to the People!
Vpered, Rossiya!	Forward, Russia!
Vsya Rossiya	All Russia
Vybor Rossii	Russia's Choice
Yabloko	Yabloko
Yedinstvo	Unity
Za Rodinu!	For Motherland!
Zhenshchiny Rossii	Women of Russia

Introduction

Robert W. Orttung

Russia's Federal Structure

Russia has an extremely complicated federal structure. The 89 constituent units do not have equal rights and powers as they do in the United States. Instead the Constitution adopted in 1993 provides for a confusing, asymmetrical distribution of power to units whose jurisdictions are poorly defined and, in some cases, overlapping. Regions vary enormously in terms of size, population, natural resource endowment, political freedoms, and economic performance.

The federation is divided into two federal cities, 21 ethnic republics, 55 oblasts and krais, one autonomous oblast, and 10 autonomous okrugs. The capital city Moscow and the former Czarist capital St. Petersburg are the only metropolises in Russia designated as *federal cities*, giving them status as two of the country's 89 regions. All other cities are subordinate to regional governments.

Moscow City is by far the most privileged region in the country. Many of Russia's most powerful and richest companies are registered there and pay taxes into the city's coffers rather than the regions where they actually operate. Moscow's ability to tap into this tax revenue generates enormous tensions with the other regions, which believe that much of Moscow's contemporary glitter and success were achieved at their expense. Moscow also once controlled the vast majority of the country's banking capital and foreign investment, but by the end of the 1990s this situation was starting to change. Moscow suffered more than other regions from the economic crisis of 1998, since its banks had invested heavily in suddenly worthless state bonds. Additionally, toward the end of the decade, a greater share of foreign direct investment began flowing into the regions rather than the capital. St. Petersburg runs a distant second to Moscow, but its sheer size and imperial past give it numerous advantages.

The regional units of the federation are organized on two principles: territorial and ethnic. Russia's 49 *oblasts* and 6 *krais* are territorial units and there is no apparent difference among them in terms of constitutional rights (the krais are simply territories that once stood on the farthest boundary of the country). With a few exceptions, the governors of these regions were appointed by President Boris Yeltsin until 1996–97, since which time governors have been elected.

The remaining 32 units of the federation are defined ethnically. The 21 *republics* provide territorial homes to some of Russia's most significant ethnic minorities. However, not all of Russia's minorities have their own republic and not all members of a group that has a republic live on its territory. Moreover, in many cases the "titular" group for which a republic is named does not make up a majority of the population. Data gathered in the 1989 census shows that the titular population exceeded 50 percent in six republics: Chuvashia, Kabardino-Balkaria, North Ossetia, Checheno-Ingushetia (then one unit, now two), Tyva, and Dagestan (where the Avars, Dargins, Kumyks, Lezgins, and Laks made up 73 percent of the population). In eight republics ethnic Russians make up more than 50 percent of the population: Karelia, Komi, Mordovia, Udmurtia, Adygeya, Gorno-Altai, Buryatia, and Khakassia. In the remaining six republics, Tatarstan, Bashkortostan, Karachaevo-Cherkessia, Sakha (Yakutia), Marii El, and Kalmykia, no group has an absolute majority.

Republics enjoy several advantages over other regions in terms of their relationship with the federal government in Moscow. They were empowered to elect their regional executives (presidents) much earlier than the krais and oblasts were. The 1993 Russian Constitution entitles them to regional constitutions, while the oblasts and krais have only charters. Starting with Tatarstan in 1994, several republics have signed power-sharing treaties with the federal government, giving them extensive control of the natural resources located on their territory, special tax advantages, and increased abilities to conduct foreign policies. Oblasts and krais began to sign such treaties only later.

Chechnya stands as an exception because it is the only region that has refused to accept its status as a part of the Russian Federation. Chechnya declared its independence toward the end of 1991. Russia fought an unsuccessful war in 1994–96 to return Chechnya to the Russian Federation, but ended up signing a humiliating treaty in 1996 which postponed a decision on independence for five years. Following Chechen rebel attacks on Dagestan in August 1999 and terrorist bombings that killed more than 200 people in September, Russian troops again invaded the republic, taking control of Grozny by February 2000. The heavily bombed city was by then virtually uninhabitable, and most of the population fled. Although the eventual outcome of the conflict cannot be predicted, protracted guerrilla warfare seems likely.

In addition to the republics, there are two other classes of ethnically defined units in Russia. The 1993 Constitution includes contradictory statements about the 10 *autonomous okrugs*. On one hand, Article 5 says that they are equal to the other 89 units of the federation. On the other hand, Article 66 subordinates them to the oblast or krai on whose territory they are located. The Russian Constitutional Court refused to clarify these ambiguities in a ruling issued on 14 July 1997. Some of the okrugs, like West Siberia's Khanty-Mansi and Yamal-Nenets, have extensive natural resource endowments, while others are extremely poor. The resource-rich okrugs, particularly the two in Western Siberia, have long sought absolute independence from the region of which they are a part. However, only the autonomous okrug of Chukotka, in the northernmost corner of the Far East, has won its independence, separating from Magadan Oblast in June 1992.

All of the okrugs are designated for specific ethnic groups, but the titular nationality makes up a majority only in Komi-Permyak and Agin-Buryatia. Elsewhere Russians predominate.

The last ethnically defined unit is the Jewish Autonomous Oblast, the only autonomous oblast in the federation. (There were five autonomous oblasts in the Soviet Union, but the other four were upgraded to republican status after the Union was dissolved.) The Jewish Autonomous Oblast won its independence from Khabarovsk Krai on 25 March 1991. It is one of the most unusual of the Russian regions because it was set up by Stalin in the Far East as a homeland for the Soviet Union's Jews, most of whom lived in the western part of the country and few of whom chose to resettle in the new region. The Jewish population in the area was never large and today Jews number only four percent of the total. On the eve of the 2000 presidential election, the governors of both the Jewish Autonomous Oblast and Khabarovsk Krai announced a desire to reunite the two regions within the framework of a larger Far Eastern region.

Who Are Russia's Governors?

By any standards, Russia's 89 regional executives are a motley collection of individuals. Several are well known internationally. Moscow Mayor Yurii Luzhkov once seemed likely to be Yeltsin's successor until his Fatherland party performed poorly in the 1999 State Duma elections and Yeltsin resigned the presidency in favor of his prime minister, Vladimir Putin. Krasnoyarsk Governor Aleksandr Lebed, who had ended the 1994–96 Chechen war and came in third in the 1996 presidential campaign, also seemed like a potential president until his career was sidetracked by the numerous scandals plaguing his Siberian region's energy and metals industry. (His brother Aleksei is the governor of Khakassia, making them the only two governors who are related.) Kursk Governor Aleksandr Rutskoi served as Yeltsin's vice president until 1993, when he was imprisoned after leading an insurrection against the president. His notoriety made him a hero in his hometown, which duly elected him in 1996. Kalmykia President Kirsan Ilyumzhinov is also president of the World Chess Federation (FIDE) and built a Chess City to host international tournaments in one of Russia's poorest regions.

Others are well known nationally. Tula Governor Vasilii Starodubstev was one of the 1991 coup leaders against USSR President Mikhail Gorbachev. Moscow Oblast Governor Boris Gromov led Soviet troops out of Afghanistan in 1989. Samara Governor Konstantin Titov entered the 2000 campaign for Russia's presidency, as did Kemerovo's Aman Tuleev, who also ran for the top job in 1991 and 1996. Neither performed well.

Several governors have gained prominence for widely noted accomplishments. Tatarstan President Mintimer Shaimiev signed the first power-sharing agreement between a region and the federal government in 1994, giving his region substantial autonomy in tax collections, control of natural resources, and foreign policy. Novgorod Governor Mikhail Prusak has excelled in bringing foreign direct investment to his region. Orel Governor Yegor Stroev is the first among equals as the chairman of the Federation Council, making him one of Russia's top politicians. Primorskii Krai Governor Yevgenii Nazdratenko beat back a 1997 Kremlin attempt to remove him from office and remains firmly entrenched, even though electricity blackouts are frequent in his Far Eastern outpost. Saratov Governor Dmitrii Ayatskov became famous by pushing land privatization at the local level. Krasnodar Governor Nikolai Kondratenko drew attention for his numerous anti-Semitic statements.

The average governor is about 53.5 years old. In early 2000, the youngest governor was Ust-Orda Buryatia's 36-year-old Valerii Maleev. Other governors in their thirties were Pskov's Yevgenii Mikhailov, 37, and Ilyumzhinov, 38. The oldest governor was Dagestan's 70-year-old Magomedali Magomedov.

With one exception, Russia's governors are male. The lone woman was Koryak Autonomous Okrug Governor Valentina Bronevich. Her region is in a remote corner of the Russian Pacific coast and she does not play a prominent role on the national stage.

Just over half of the governors have backgrounds as economic managers (see Table 1). Twenty-one governors (24 percent) began their professional lives in the agricultural sector, the worst-performing sector of the Russian economy. Sixteen (18 percent) are industrialists, six worked in the construction industry, and three in transportation. These backgrounds partially explain the governors' strong preference to avoid political labels and pursue pragmatic policies in their relations with the Kremlin and within their regions.

A significant number of the governors cut their political teeth working for the Communist Party of the Soviet Union (CPSU) before the collapse of the USSR. Twenty-two (25 percent) of the 89 governors made their careers in the CPSU, with two of them reaching the party's Politburo (Orel's Stroev and North Ossetia's Aleksandr Dzasokhov). Overall, at least 44 governors (49 percent) had significant experience in the CPSU ranks.

As a group, the governors have held numerous elective offices. Many of them were elected to the national legislatures that have been created in Russia since 1989—the USSR Congress of People's Deputies and the RSFSR Congress of People's Deputies,

Table 1

Professional Background of Russian Governor

Career	Number of governors
CPSU	22
Agriculture	21
Industry	16
Military	7
Construction	6
Regional administration, economics	5
Legal	4
Transportation	3
Business	2
Journalism	1
Diplomacy	1
LDPR activism	1

and, since 1993, the Russian State Duma and the Federation Council (Council members were elected in 1993, but currently hold seats by virtue of their local elective office, although this is being changed). Governors have also been active in regional legislatures and several served as mayors before being elected governor. Pskov Governor Mikhailov is unique in that he worked his way up through the ranks of one of post-perestroika Russia's new parties, the Liberal Democratic Party of Russia headed by Vladimir Zhirinovsky.

Seven of the governors (8 percent) are military men, usually with significant experience in hot spots such as Afghanistan and Moldova. These governors by no means represent a unified bloc among Russia's regional elite. The Lebed brothers have focused on managing the economic resources of their regions, perhaps hoping thereby to win support for another presidential bid by Aleksandr. Moscow Oblast's Gromov came to power with the support of Mayor Luzhkov, while Kursk's Rutskoi was an early supporter of the pro-Kremlin Unity party, which saw Luzhkov as its arch-rival. Ingushetia's Ruslan Aushev and Karachaevo-Cherkessia's Vladimir Semenov are more concerned with managing the numerous ethnic conflicts in their North Caucasus regions than anything else. Chechnya's President Aslan Maskhadov led Chechen rebels in their victorious battle against Russian troops in the republic's 1994–96 battle for independence. After launching a military assault to reimpose order on the republic in September 1999, the Kremlin effectively withdrew its recognition of Maskhadov's legitimacy, arguing that he did not control the territory that was supposed to be under his jurisdiction.

Only two governors built their pre-political careers as what might be considered businessmen working in the shifting sands of Russia's post-communist economy: Kalmykia's Ilyumzhinov and the Nenets Autonomous Okrug's Vladimir Butov. Both of these leaders, however, have reputations as rather unscrupulous operators and certainly would not be considered worthy examples of successful capitalist enterprise. After making a fortune as the head of a trading company, Ilyumzhinov has brought lots of money to his region by setting up a free economic zone, which allows companies to avoid taxes in other regions by registering there. He is considered one of Russia's most eccentric governors. The Nenets regional legislature has accused Butov of using his position to favor his own companies. He is also locked in a ongoing struggle with LUKoil, Russia's largest oil company, which would like to develop the region's resources itself.

Nine of the governors made careers as professional economists or urban managers, while four come from a legal background. One was a diplomat and one worked as a journalist.

Since Yeltsin authorized all regions to elect their governors in 1996, there has been enormous turnover among the country's cadre of regional executives. At the beginning of 2000, 52 governors (58 percent) were serving their first term and had been in office less than four years. Many of them faced reelection campaigns in 2000. The Russian Duma adopted a law in October 1999 allowing governors to serve five-year terms, but no more than two in a row, so future turnover should be more muted. Most incumbent governors were elected for four-year terms. Sixteen (18 percent) governors have been in office between five and eight years.

Twenty-one governors (24 percent) have ruled their regions for more than eight years, with the longest incumbents serving in office continually since 1989. Leaders like Tatarstan's Shaimiev or Komi's Yurii Spiridonov headed up their region's CPSU organization and have managed to hang on to power since then through two sets of elections. Since the new law regulating the terms of the governors does not fully come into effect until the fall of 2001, many of these ex-

ecutives may be able to secure a third term before being forced from office.

Several governors have more executive experience than this listing suggests. Kabardino-Balkaria's Valerii Kokov resigned as CPSU republican first secretary after democratic activists criticized him for supporting the 1991 coup. He was soon elected to the presidency, however. Dzasokhov and Stroev had served as first party secretaries in their regions in the 1980s before moving to national jobs. Other governors had initially been appointed and then fired by Yeltsin in the early 1990s, including Bryansk's Yurii Lodkin and Sverdlovsk's Eduard Rossel. Former Novosibirsk Governor Vitalii Mukha, who lost a 1999 reelection bid, had been appointed and removed by Yeltsin before winning a term from the voters. Tambov Governor Oleg Betin served as a Yeltsin appointee from March to December 1995, but then lost a campaign to hold the office through popular election. Four years later he came back to win office by defeating Aleksandr Ryabov in a rematch of the 1995 race.

The Governors' Platforms

Russia's governors are mainly pragmatists—or, in a more cynical interpretation, opportunists. The vast majority of them do not consistently support any particular political ideology. Rather they like to keep their options open so that they can build alliances with whomever is politically, economically, or personally useful to them at any given time. Once Yeltsin resigned his office and named Vladimir Putin as acting president and his preferred successor, nearly all the governors announced that they too supported Putin, even if they had been backing Putin's rivals just a few weeks before. No matter what a governor really thinks, it is always better to have a friend than an enemy in the Kremlin. In almost every case, expedience is more important than personal loyalty or ideological consistency.

In the period leading up to the December 1999 State Duma elections, with Yeltsin apparently sick and no longer in control of the country, Russia's regional executives started to place bets on who they thought could win the 2000 presidential campaign (see Table 2, p. xviii). Many, such as Nizhnii Novgorod's Ivan Sklyarov, bet on Luzhkov and joined his Fatherland party. Others, like Tatarstan's Shaimiev and Bashkortostan's Rakhimov, who thought a Luzhkov victory was inevitable but were not happy about it, set up All Russia to form an arms-length alliance with Luzkhov. When it became clear that former Prime Minister Yevgenii Primakov had a better shot at the presidency, Luzhkov threw his support behind him. At that point All Russia made a formal alliance with Fatherland but made clear that it supported Primakov over Luzhkov as the presidential candidate. The All Russia governors favored Primakov because they thought he would make a weaker president than Luzhkov and therefore would leave greater power in their regions. All these calculations proved to be irrelevant after Fatherland–All Russia's poor performance in the December 1999 elections, leaving Yeltsin an opening to virtually name his own successor as president.

Many of the weaker governors, who remained heavily dependent on the Kremlin, were left out of the Fatherland–All Russia alliance. They joined up with a last-minute pro-Kremlin party, Unity, which went on to take a large share of Duma seats. This party included such figures as Kursk's Rutskoi and Tver's Vladimir Platov, who barely won reelection at the January 2000 polls. Although they may have seemed like a motley group in September, a few months later, the Unity governors appeared to have brighter prospects because they had picked the right horse in the parliamentary and presidential campaigns.

The 1999 State Duma elections marked the end of Our Home Is Russia, which had been the "party of power" in 1995. It did not cross the five-percent barrier, and its members, such as Novgorod's Prusak, dispersed into the pro-Putin majority. The Union of Right Forces, the latest reincarnation of Russia's Choice, the party of power in 1993, became respectable again when, with Putin's backing, it won eight percent of the vote in the 1999 Duma elections. But when Samara's Titov decided to pursue a quixotic presidential campaign against Putin, he drove a wedge in the party between the ideological purists, who wanted a more consistent reformer in the Kremlin and did not support Putin's prosecution of the war in Chechnya, and the more pragmatic elements who wanted to be associated with the campaign's likely winner.

Ideologically, it is hard to distinguish major differences between parties like Our Home Is Russia, Fatherland, and Unity. For a governor, the only reason to be affiliated with one is a desire to secure better ties to the Kremlin. These parties represent a muddled, centrist segment of the political spectrum signifying support for a market economy, although one that has strong state intervention, and for strengthening the Russian state, although without defining exactly how to achieve this end. They oppose NATO expansion and want Russia to compete better globally, but are not hidebound enemies of the West.

While the Communist Party of the Russian Federation has been the only sizable opposition to the Kremlin since 1991, its inability to win more than 30 percent of the vote makes it a relatively toothless threat. The leftist governors are a weak link in this already weak group because they find it more important to maintain good relations with the Kremlin than with their party comrades. Many of them, such as Volgograd's Nikolai Maksyuta and Stavropol's Aleksandr Chernogorov, have poor relations with local party leaders, who constantly criticize them for implementing policies that are not consistent with the party's platform. Altai Krai Governor Aleksandr Surikov openly defied the party to support Putin. Kemerovo's Aman Tuleev, who ran for the State Duma on the Communist party list in 1999 (without formally being a member of the party), served in Yeltsin's cabinet and ran against Communist party leader Gennadii Zyuganov in the 1996 and 2000 presidential campaigns.

The Lebed brothers are political outsiders who seem increasingly peripheral. Pskov's Yevgenii Mikhailov was the only member of Zhirinovsky's Liberal Democratic party to serve as governor, but as his popularity waned, he left the LDPR and appointed himself head of the regional Unity branch. Several governors, like Sverdlovsk's Eduard Rossel and Ulyanovsk's Yurii Goryachev, have formed their own parties, which are important within their regions, but have little influence beyond regional boundaries. As Federation Council speaker, Stroev likes to stay above the fray.

Relations with Moscow

Despite the enormous amount of decentralization in Russian politics since 1991, the governors' relationship with Moscow remains extremely important. The Russian president has an extensive set of tools he can use to keep the regions in line. The following discussion roughly groups these implements in the order of their usefulness, starting with the most useful and proceeding to the least useful.

Table 2

The Governors' Political Affiliation on the Eve of the 1999 State Duma Elections

Unity:

Adygeya President Aslan Dzharimov (former member of All Russia)

Arkhangelsk Governor Anatolii Yefremov (former member of Fatherland)

Buryatia President Leonid Potapov

Chelyabinsk Governor Petr Sumin (former member of Voice of Russia and All Russia)

Chukotka Governor Aleksandr Nazarov (former member of Voice of Russia)

Dagestan President Magomedali Magomedov (unofficial supporter)

Evenk Governor Aleksandr Bokovikov

Ivanovo Governor Vladislav Tikhomirov

Kaliningrad Governor Leonid Gorbenko (former member of Voice of Russia)

Kalmykia President Kirsan Ilyumzhinov

Kamchatka Governor Vladimir Biryukov

Koryak Governor Valentina Bronevich

Kostroma Governor Viktor Shershunov

Kursk Governor Aleksandr Rutskoi

Leningrad Governor Valerii Serdyukov

Magadan Governor Valentin Tsvetkov (former member of Voice of Russia)

Nenets Governor Vladimir Butov

Omsk Governor Leonid Polezhaev (former member of All Russia)

Orenburg Governor Vladimir Yelagin

Primorskii Krai Governor Yevgenii Nazdratenko

Rostov Governor Vladimir Chub (former member of Voice of Russia and All Russia)

Sakha President Mikhail Nikolaev

Sakhalin Governor Igor Farkhutdinov

Smolensk Governor Aleksandr Prokhorov

Tver Governor Vladimir Platov (former member of Voice of Russia)

Fatherland*:

Karelia Prime Minister Sergei Katanandov

Kirov Governor Vladimir Sergeenkov

Komi President Yurii Spiridonov

Mordovia President Nikolai Merkushkin

Moscow Mayor Yurii Luzhkov

Moscow Oblast Governor Anatolii Tyazhlov

Murmansk Governor Yurii Yevdokimov

Nizhnii Novgorod Governor Ivan Sklyarov

Novosibirsk Governor Vitalii Mukha

Udmurtia State Council Chairman Aleksandr Volkov

*Fatherland united with All Russia to compete in the elections.

All Russia*:

Bashkortostan President Murtaza Rakhimov

Belgorod Governor Yevgenii Savchenko

Chuvashia President Nikolai Fedorov

Ingushetiia President Ruslan Aushev

Irkutsk Governor Boris Govorin

Khabarovsk Governor Viktor Ishaev

Khanty-Mansi Governor Aleksandr Filipenko

North Ossetia President Aleksandr Dzasokhov

Penza Governor Vasilii Bochkarev

Perm Governor Gennadii Igumnov

St. Petersburg Governor Vladimir Yakovlev

Tatarstan President Mintimer Shaimiev

*All Russia united with Fatherland to compete in the elections.

Our Home Is Russia:

Astrakhan Governor Anatolii Guzhvin

Jewish Autonomous Oblast Governor Nikolai Volkov

Novgorod Governor Mikhail Prusak

Saratov Governor Dmitrii Ayatskov

Tomsk Governor Viktor Kress

Tyumen Governor Leonid Roketskii

Tyva President Sherig-Ool Oorzhak

Ust-Orda Buryatia Governor Valerii Maleev

Union of Right Forces (*Right Course, Voice of Russia, Novaya Sila*):

Gorno-Altai Republic President Semen Zubakin

Marii El President Vyacheslav Kislitsyn

Samara Governor Konstantin Titov

Vologda Governor Vyacheslav Pozgalev

Communists:

Altai Krai Governor Aleksandr Surikov

Amur Governor Anatolii Belonogov

Bryansk Governor Yurii Lodkin

Kemerovo Governor Aman Tuleev

Krasnodar Governor Nikolai Kondratenko

Ryazan Governor Vyacheslav Lyubimov

Stavropol Governor Aleksandr Chernogorov

Tambov Governor Aleksandr Ryabov

Tula Governor Vasilii Starodubtsev

Vladimir Governor Nikolai Vinogradov

Volgograd Governor Nikolai Maksyuta

Voronezh Governor Ivan Shabanov

Lebed:

Krasnoyarsk Governor Aleksandr Lebed

Khakassia Prime Minister Aleksei Lebed (also a signatory to Voice of Russia)

Zhirinovsky:

Pskov Governor Yevgenii Mikhailov

Unaffiliated with Major Blocs:

Orel Governor Yegor Stroev

Sverdlovsk Governor Eduard Rossel

Ulyanovsk Governor Yurii Goryachev

Yaroslavl Governor Anatolii Lisitsyn

The most important tool is psychological. Yeltsin came to power, in part, by telling the regions to "take as much sovereignty as you can swallow." Putin, in contrast, built his political popularity on his campaign to prevent Chechnya from winning independence. The difference in the way the governors perceive the intentions of the two presidents and their estimation of the presidents' ability to impose their will is quite substantial. From the beginning of his rule until 1996, Yeltsin seemed to bestow federal largesse on the regions that complained the loudest or had the most economic resources to deploy against the Kremlin. Regions therefore had incentives to exercise their autonomy. Since the 1996 presidential election, the Kremlin has seemed more to favor regions that are politically loyal. Judging by Putin's campaign tactics, he too seems more interested in rewarding his allies than appeasing his opponents. The governors have taken note.

A second tool the Kremlin can exploit to maintain its authority over the regions is the disunity among the regions themselves. The regions are divided along several cleavages. Russia's main revenue-producing assets, whether natural resources, such as oil, or proximity to Moscow or another major urban area, are unevenly distributed among regions. Many of the rich regions resent that they have to effectively subsidize poorer regions through their contributions to the federal budget. Regions are also divided on the basis of the privileges assigned them in the Constitution, with the republics enjoying more advantages than the oblasts and krais. So far, the regional elites have failed to organize in any effective and consistent way against the Kremlin.

A third tool of Kremlin control is the ability to offer or deny backing to help governors win reelection. On the eve of the 1999 State Duma elections, for example, First Deputy Presidential Chief of Staff Igor Shabdurasulov barnstormed the country, offering governors whatever they needed to win reelection in exchange for supporting Unity in the parliamentary elections and Putin in the presidential elections. In particular, the Kremlin can offer media exposure on important national networks, expertise from Moscow-based political consultants, and financial aid timed to increase popular support for the governor just before the election.

A fourth lever the Kremlin has in its relations with the governors is its control over the appointment of law-enforcement personnel in the regions. In Russia the law is applied selectively and the Kremlin can use it to reward loyal governors or punish uppity ones. The federal government controls the appointment of the top officials in the Federal Security Service (FSB). However, the federal and regional government both have a say in appointing regional police chiefs (Ministry of Internal Affairs) and regional procurators. Until summer 2000, the governors also had a voice in removing police chiefs, but now this power is solely in the hands of the federal government. By appointing officials friendly or hostile to the governor, the Kremlin can influence the way the governor behaves. Moreover, if the Kremlin wants to crack down on a specific region, it can call for the revocation of regional laws that violate the Russian Constitution or federal legislation. Putin used this power extensively during his first months in office. In cases where the Kremlin is generally pleased with a local executive's performance, it can ignore inconsistencies between regional and federal legislation.

A fifth form of influence is the distribution of federal funds. This power clearly declined following the devaluation of the ruble in August 1998, but rose again in 1999 when oil prices were climbing. Since federal budgets are often unrealistic and not all projects listed in the official document are actually funded, the Ministry of Finance has wide discretion in determining which regions receive the money designated for them. The federal government can also grant lucrative export-import privileges and tax breaks to specific enterprises that can dramatically help some regions. In 1998 the Kremlin introduced a treasury system in each region to enhance its control over the way tax revenues are divided among government entities. Since many regions are in debt, the local manager of Sberbank, which controls the vast majority of the banking system's assets, can make life easy or hard for governors by restructuring debt loads or demanding immediate payment.

Sixth, the natural monopolies—Unified Energy System (which controls electricity generation and distribution), Gazprom (natural gas extraction and distribution), the Railroads Ministry, and Transneft (oil distribution pipeline)—also have powerful influence over the regions since they set prices for and control access to vital energy supplies or transportation routes. Many regions owe significant sums to these organizations and are therefore beholden to them. By putting pressure on the heads of these concerns, the Kremlin can indirectly ratchet up pressure on the regions.

Finally, the federal government has signed treaties with 46 regions, the most recent being a 16 June 1998 treaty with Moscow City. Yeltsin used the early treaties with Tatarstan and Bashkortostan to offer them strong incentives to remain within the Russian Federation, specifically ceding them control over their natural resources, lucrative tax breaks, and greater control over their relations with foreigners. Some of the treaties give the regions an enhanced voice in federal appointments of top law-enforcement officers in their regions. According to a law on center-periphery relations adopted in June 1999 (*Parlamentskaya gazeta*, 30 June), all of the existing treaties must be brought into compliance with the Russian Constitution by 2002. These treaties were signed between Yeltsin (or in some cases, the RF prime minister) and the regional executive, and were never approved by the federal or regional legislatures. Often, key provisions in the treaty were not published. It remains unclear what the practical effect of the new law will be since the Constitution itself suffers from a number of internal contradictions. On one hand, it asserts that all regions should be treated equally, while other sections clearly favor some regions over others. The Russian president could use the new law to radically restructure the relationship between the federal government and the regions—a concern that was palpable in Tatarstan at the beginning of 2000 because the republic's leader had backed Luzhkov over Putin in the December 1999 Duma elections. All new treaties, if any new ones are signed, must now be approved by the relevant regional legislature and the Federation Council.

Once Putin was inaugurated as Yeltsin's successor he began a concerted campaign to strengthen the ability of the central government to influence the regions, unleashing a string of initiatives to strengthen federal state capacity. Initially the governors expressed cautious support for these plans, but by summer 2000 they had moved into explicit and vocal opposition.

Beyond trying to force regions to bring their legislation into compliance with federal norms, Putin's first major initiative was to make the presidential representatives in the regions more effective. Yeltsin established the institution of presidential representatives in 1991 so that he would have an official in each region to serve as his eyes and ears. Ultimately Yeltsin had representatives in more than 80 regions, though

exceptional regions like Tatarstan never had a presidential representative assigned to them. In practice, however, the presidential representatives were captured by the very governors they were supposed to be monitoring. In effect the representatives began to function as regional advocates at the federal level rather than federal advocates at the regional level. Yeltsin recognized this failing and tried to strengthen their powers in 1997, but this reform ended in failure. In the test case of Primorskii Krai, Yeltsin tried to transfer some of Governor Nazdratenko's powers to his representative in the region, Viktor Kondratov. However, Kondratov proved incapable of countering Nazdratenko, and the governor eventually won his removal.

On 13 May 2000, Putin effectively abolished the office of presidential representative. Instead he divided Russia into seven federal districts, and appointed "governors-general" to rule over these larger units. The main idea behind the reform was that, because the new presidential representatives would be responsible for several regions, they would stand above the governors and therefore be less susceptible to being "captured." Each representative was responsible for coordinating the work of the federal agencies in his federal district and ensuring that the regions under his purview brought their legislation into line with federal norms.

The way Putin implemented this reform suggested that his main goal was to impose better top-down control over the regions. Improving the economy was only a second priority. The seven districts Putin created were based on Russia's military districts rather than the eight interregional associations that functioned during the 1990s (compare Table 3 and Table 5). Likewise, five of the seven men appointed as presidential representatives had backgrounds in Russia's military or law enforcement agencies. All of the representatives joined the national Security Council. Additionally, Putin used the reform as a new way of institutionalizing the usual "divide and conquer" policy. Putin named a capital city in each of the seven districts where his representative would be based. Doing this clearly gave seven regions privileged access to the new, and presumably powerful, representatives that the other regions did not have. By summer 2000, it was too soon to tell whether the new representatives would be effective. However, they clearly faced an enormous task in dealing with the numerous regions included under their jurisdiction.

Putin's second initiative was to seek the removal of the governors and regional legislative chairmen from the upper house of the federal legislature, the Federation Council. Holding seats in the national legislature made the governors national politicians and theoretically gave them a way to organize themselves to support the collective interests of the regions against the federal government. Perhaps most importantly, the governors used the Federation Council's monthly meetings as an excuse to come to Moscow and lobby the federal ministries to secure funding for projects in their regions. In seeking to change the way members for the Federation Council are chosen, Putin clearly sought to reduce the stature of the governors and curtail their access to Moscow and to the national media. According to Putin's plan, the governors would no longer walk the halls of power in the capital, but would have to appeal for support to the presidential representatives in the seven federal districts. Although the State Duma, the lower chamber of the national parliament, gave this proposal overwhelming support, the regional leaders in the Federation Council soundly vetoed it. Subsequently, a committee worked out a compromise by which the regional leaders would no longer sit in the upper chamber, but they would have strong control over the representatives who replaced them. The new reforms should be fully in effect by 1 January 2002.

Additionally, Putin introduced a bill to the State Duma which would give him the power to remove governors accused of committing a crime and to disband regional legislatures. Again, the Duma supported this proposal and the Federation Council rejected it. In this case, the Duma was ultimately able to override the upper house veto. According to this legislation, once the president removed a governor, new elections would have to be held in six months. Of course there is no guarantee that the Kremlin would be any happier with the new governor than the old one under this system. Putin's proposal did not seek the right for the president to appoint governors directly, the system that had largely been in place until 1996. Prime Minister Yevgenii Primakov famously floated this idea in February 1999. When he was still acting president, Putin ruled out such an option in his comments during a meeting with the Siberian Accord Interregional Association in February 2000. In any case, implementing this idea would necessitate changing the Constitution, since Article 11 requires that the regions themselves define how they choose their leadership. Additionally, electing executives was a key part of a federal law on regional political institutions adopted in October 1999 (*Rossiiskaya gazeta*, 19 October 1999). The Federation Council had strongly opposed Yeltsin's attempt to remove Nazdratenko in 1997 precisely because it sensed that the membership's collective power was at stake.

Despite the apparently growing antagonism between the president and the governors in the summer of 2000, the president has a powerful arsenal that he can use to keep the governors in line. Even though they are elected by their constituents, the governors must maintain good relations with the Kremlin in order to assure that these weapons are not used against them. They also must maintain good ties with the Kremlin so that they can secure federal backing for their own initiatives and simply conduct day-to-day business. Of course, having especially good relations with the Kremlin can help them secure preferential treatment, which will always make their lives easier. Under President Yeltsin, Sverdlovsk Governor Eduard Rossel discovered that it was possible to build a powerful political base in his home region (and coincidentally Yeltsin's) by pursuing an antagonistic policy toward the Kremlin. He also discovered, however, that having an enemy in the Kremlin made it difficult to get things done. Thus, it is no surprise that once Yeltsin stepped down, Rossel announced that he would work hard to build a good relationship with Putin, a position publicly endorsed almost unanimously by the governors.

The Governors in Their Districts

While the Kremlin enjoys significant leverage in its relations with the regional executives, the governors also have considerable resources that they can use against the Kremlin as well as their local adversaries. First, in the wake of the August 1998 financial crisis, the regions inevitably became more self-sufficient and less prone to assume that the federal government would always bail them out. According to a 1999 study produced by Aleksei Lavrov's team at the Finance Ministry, about 25 of the 89 regions contribute more to the federal budget than they receive in federal spending. The conventional wisdom has been that there are only between 10 and 12 "donor" regions, but the Lavrov finding suggests that there are many more self-sufficient regions than is widely believed.

Table 3

Leadership and Composition of the Seven Federal Districts

CENTRAL FEDERAL DISTRICT

Georgii Poltavchenko (b. 1953) served in the KGB, St. Petersburg Federal Tax Police, and as presidential representative in Leningrad Oblast.

Capital: Moscow City
  Belgorod
  Bryansk
  Ivanovo
  Kaluga
  Kostroma
  Kursk
  Lipetsk
  Moscow Oblast
  Orel
  Ryazan
  Smolensk
  Tambov
  Tver
  Tula
  Vladimir
  Voronezh
  Yaroslavl

NORTH-WEST FEDERAL DISTRICT

General Viktor Cherkesov (b. 1950) served in the KGB and is known for prosecuting dissidents in the 1980s. He is married to Nataliya Chaplina, the editor of the pro-reform newspaper *Chas Pik*.

Capital: St. Petersburg
  Arkhangelsk
  Kaliningrad
  Karelia
  Komi
  Leningrad Oblast
  Murmansk
  Nenets Autonomous Okrug
  Novgorod
  Pskov
  Vologda

SOUTHERN FEDERAL DISTRICT

Army General Viktor Kazantsev (b. 1946) was a career military officer who served as the commander of the federal troops in Chechnya before his appointment.

Capital: Rostov-na-Donu
  Adygeya
  Astrakhan
  Chechnya
  Dagestan
  Ingushetia
  Kabardino-Balkaria
  Kalmykia
  Karachaevo-Cherkessia
  Krasnodar
  North Ossetia-Alania
  Rostov
  Stavropol
  Volgograd

VOLGA FEDERAL DISTRICT

Sergei Kirienko (b. 1962) worked in the Komsomol, Garantiya Bank, and Norsi-oil. Yeltsin then appointed him first deputy fuel and energy minister, then minister, and ultimately prime minister. He was elected to the State Duma in 1999 when he lost a bid to oust Moscow Mayor Yurii Luzhkov.

Capital: Nizhnii Novgorod
  Bashkortostan
  Chuvashia
  Kirov
  Komi-Permyak Autonomous Okrug
  Marii El
  Mordovia
  Nizhnii Novgorod
  Orenburg
  Penza
  Perm
  Samara
  Saratov
  Tatarstan
  Udmurtia
  Ulyanovsk

What is most important is that the governors often have extensive control over the local economy and the resources located inside the regions they govern. In many cases, the regions own controlling stakes in local enterprises. Luzhkov, for example, controls extensive holdings throughout the capital, including large car factories, an oil company, hotels, and stores. The presidents of Tatarstan and Bashkortostan control the key energy companies in their regions and can use company resources for their own benefit.

Second, the governors can use their institutional resources to shape the outcome of federal, regional,

URAL FEDERAL DISTRICT

Petr Latyshev (b. 1948) long served in the Perm and then Krasnodar Ministry of Internal Affairs (MVD). From 1900 to 1993, he was a member of the Russian Congress of People's Deputies. From 1994 to 2000, he served as deputy minister of internal affairs, where, among other duties, he led a corruption investigation into St. Petersburg Governor Vladimir Yakovlev.

Capital: Yekaterinburg
  Chelyabinsk
  Khanty-Mansii Autonomous Okrug
  Kurgan
  Sverdlovsk
  Tyumen
  Yamal-Nenets Autonomous Okrug

FAR EASTERN FEDERAL DISTRICT

Lieutenant General Konstantin Pulikovskii (ret.) served as the deputy commander of the North Caucasus Military District July-August 1996 and as acting commander of federal troops in Chechnya, where he was famous for issuing an ultimatum to Grozny residents in 1996, giving them 48 hours to leave the city.

Capital: Khabarovsk
  Amur
  Chukotka Autonomous Okrug
  Jewish Autonomous Oblast
  Kamchatka
  Khabarovsk
  Koryak Autonomous Okrug
  Magadan
  Primorskii Krai
  Sakha
  Sakhalin

SIBERIAN FEDERAL DISTRICT

Leonid Drachevskii (b. 1942) is a former world champion in rowing, who served in the RSFSR State Committee on Physical Education and Sport. He was also Russian general counsel in Barcelona, head of the Ministry of Foreign Affairs Department for the CIS, ambassador to Poland, and Minister for the CIS. He is considered a moderate reformer and is well-liked by the intelligentsia.

Capital: Novosibirsk
  Agin-Buryatia
  Altai Krai
  Buryatia
  Chita
  Evenk Autonomous Okrug
  Gorno-Altai Republic
  Irkutsk
  Kemerovo
  Khakassia
  Krasnoyarsk
  Novosibirsk
  Omsk
  Taimyr Autonomous Okrug
  Tomsk
  Tyva
  Ust-Ordyn Buryat Autonomous Okrug

and local elections conducted in their region. In presidential campaigns, the governor can often, but not always, deliver votes for one of the candidates. Presidential candidates thus make extensive efforts to win the support of as many governors as possible. Most important in these efforts is the governors' ability to control some or all of the significant local media.

The governors also have a powerful voice in State Duma elections, in both the party-list and single-member-district votes. In 1999, the regional executives played a major role in the campaign, having themselves set up several of the parties, such as Fatherland and All Russia, that worked against the Kremlin. Other governors helped to organize the pro-Kremlin Unity party. In the single-member-district races, the governor-backed candidate won in about 75 percent of the contests. As a result, members of the State Duma elected in 1999 from both parts of the

ballot are more closely allied to the governors than their predecessors. However, when forced to choose between the president and the governors in summer 2000, the deputies chose the president.

Through their control of the media and other institutional resources, the governors have powerful advantages in their reelection campaigns, but these do not necessarily ensure their ability to win reelection. In fact, until the elections of 1999, governors were more likely to lose to a challenger than win (see Table 4). However, in 1999, governors discovered the technique of rescheduling elections to an earlier date as a way of throwing the opposition off balance. In the elections held from fall 1999 to summer 2000 their performance was much improved.

The governors have generally had success in influencing the election of a regional legislature that is sympathetic to their policies, though there are several exceptions here as well. In the Federation Council, the chairperson of the regional legislature usually stands in the shadow of the region's governor, as in the case of Saratov Oblast. In a few regions, however, executive-legislative relations are extremely conflictual. Governor Yakovlev of St. Petersburg is in constant battle with the city's Legislative Assembly, to the point where the legislature could not elect a chairman for more than a year after it was seated in December 1998. In the Nenets Autonomous Okrug, the executive and legislative branches have been battling over how to develop the region's extensive oil and gas deposits.

The governors often argue with the mayors of their regional capitals over the regional budget. The governor generally wants to use some of the tax money collected in the city to subsidize programs that benefit the region's poorer rural areas, while mayors want revenues generated in the city to be used for projects that benefit its residents. Complicating the picture is the fact that the federal government often sides with the mayors to increase its leverage over the governors.

Third, the governors often are able to capture or circumvent federal agencies working in their districts. Federal agencies are often dependent on the governors for their office space and other resources, so they may be reluctant to buck the governors as much as their Moscow-based superiors would like. Although Moscow has established a federal treasury system to gain better control over budgetary expenditures, governors like Ulyanovsk's Goryachev have been able to circumvent the treasury by forcing large local enterprises to pay their taxes directly to the oblast rather than through the federal system.

Fourth, the governors can use the prevalence of barter, tax write-offs, and other forms of soft budget constraints to hide how they are actually spending their money and other resources. The governors take advantage of the lack of fiscal transparency to pursue their own goals while evading oversight from the federal government and the public.

Finally, the regional executives can block the implementation of federal policies in their regions. The most prominent example of such an effort was Moscow Mayor Luzhkov's successful campaign to prevent Anatolii Chubais's federal privatization policy from being implemented in the capital and instead imposing his own program.

Thus, while the Russian president has a powerful

Table 4

The Role of Incumbency in Gubernatorial Elections

Year	No. of elections	Incumbent winners	Incumbent winners
1999	17	12	71%
1998	11	5	45%
June 1996–March 1997	48	21	44%

arsenal, the governors remain a significant lobbying group at the federal level and somewhat autonomous players at the regional level. While the president can issue decrees from the Kremlin, he has to intimidate or entice the governors to actually implement them. Yeltsin often seemed powerless precisely because he had bought the governors' political loyalty by decentralizing power to them. Putin seems to be in a much stronger position, but it is too early to tell how his relationship with the governors will ultimately evolve.

Relations Between Governors

As mentioned above, the numerous divisions among the governors have given the Kremlin useful leverage over them. In established democracies, political parties often serve to aggregate political interests. In Russia, the governors' attempts to form regionally based political parties have not proven effective. For example, the 1999 efforts to establish blocs based on the expectation that a Luzhkov-Primakov alliance could win the presidency fell apart when Yeltsin resigned and gave his prime minister the incumbent's advantage. The rapid dissolution of the Fatherland–All Russia party suggests that there were few real bonds beyond temporary political advantage holding it together.

Despite these failures, the governors have been able to organize some forms of collective action through the Federation Council, the eight existing interregional associations, and other means. Following an agreement worked out between the State Duma and Yeltsin at the end of 1995, the upper house of Russia's legislature was made up of the country's 89 governors and the 89 chairmen of the regional legislatures, with the governor usually the dominant of the two representatives from each region. Putin's reforms have now removed the governors and regional legislative chairmen from the upper house, with the last regional leaders set to leave by 1 January 2002. Until Putin's reform, the regional leaders effectively served as "senators," giving them a direct voice in federal policy-making. According to the 1993 Constitution, the Federation Council must approve or reject legislation adopted by the State Duma. In the area of security policy, it must confirm changes in borders between Russian regions, confirm presidential introductions of emergency rule, and ratify the use of force beyond Russia's borders. In terms of political appointments, the Federation Council must confirm the nomination of the procurator general, judges of the highest courts, half the members of the Audit Chamber, and one-third of the Central Electoral Commission. It also must approve the impeachment of the president by a two-thirds vote. Until Putin's reform, however, the body met for only a few days each month and its sessions were relatively poorly attended because the governors were busy with their numerous other responsibilities. Its potential for organizing the regional elite was thus effectively limited.

The Federation Council's first collective assertion of power against the Kremlin came in 1997, when it opposed the president's efforts to remove Governor Nazdratenko from office. In 1999, the Federation Council also stood up to the Kremlin by voting to continue anti-corruption investigations against Kremlin insiders and refusing to accept Yeltsin's decision to fire Procurator General Yurii Skuratov. In 2000, however, the upper house failed to prevent Putin from implementing the core of his reforms because the regional leaders did not want to declare total war on the president. In general, governors find that it is easier to resolve their differences with the federal government one-on-one and in secret. Since they are pursuing a variety of differing interests, they prefer to avoid intervening in each other's affairs. Moreover, the fact that all governors were equal in the Federation Council diluted the possibility of strong regional leaders (heads of the republics or rich regions, for example) from banding together, as Nikolai Petrov has pointed out. Thus, except in a few key cases, the Federation Council proved of little use in organizing collective action among the governors.

Another institutionalized form of cooperation between regions are the eight interregional associations (see Table 5). These groups meet several times a year and often serve as a forum for the Russian president to address several governors at once. The meetings usually focus on specific issues of concern to re-gional politicians, such as the forestry industry or road building. However, these associations have never provided an effective base for collective action because political differences among the governors prevent them from achieving potential mutually beneficial economic cooperation. Saratov Governor Dmitrii Ayatskov has complained, for example, that the Volga association has squandered opportunities to press the interests of the aviation and automobile industries because it was distracted by political issues.

Outside of the Federation Council and the interregional associations, the governors work together through multilateral large-scale investment projects, bilateral ties, and participation in interregional trade exhibitions. Directed federal programs, focused on such topics as the development of the Far East or protecting the environment of the Urals, provide a basis for regional cooperation. Bilateral agreements between regions provide the basis for cooperation between enterprises, developing infrastructure, establishing regional trade representatives, and organizing conferences, as political scientist Vladimir Klimanov has pointed out. By November 1999, for example, Moscow City had signed 73 such bilateral agreements. Large nationally and regionally based enterprises that seek to preserve a unified Russian market also work to promote linkages between regions.

Foreign Policy

Many of Russia's regions now seek and maintain relations with foreign countries, regional governments within foreign countries, transnational corporations, non-governmental organizations, and international institutions. Most of these ties are economic in nature and do not elicit any particular protest from the federal government as a whole or the Ministry of Foreign Affairs in particular. In fact, in most cases the federal government encourages the regions to seek outside investments because it reduces the pressure on tight federal resources.

There have, of course, been occasions when regional leaders have contradicted the federal government on political and national security questions. Primorskii Krai Governor Yevgenii Nazdratenko unsuccessfully fought against the adoption of a treaty between Russia and China. Nazdratenko and Sakhalin

Table 5

Membership of the Eight Interregional Associations

North-West	Black Earth	North Caucasus	Siberian Accord	Far East
Karelia	Belgorod	Adygeya	Gorno Altai	Buryatia
Komi	Bryansk	Dagestan	Buryatia	Sakha (Yakutia)
Arkhangelsk	Voronezh	Ingushetiya	Tyva	Primorskii Krai
Vologda	Kursk	Kabardino-Balkaria	Khakassia	Khabarovsk
Kaliningrad	Lipetsk	Kalmykia	Altai Krai	Amur
Kirov	Novgorod	Karachaevo-Cherkessia	Krasnoyarsk	Kamchatka
Leningrad Oblast	Orel	North Ossetia	Irkutsk	Magadan
Murmansk	Tambov	Krasnodar	Kemerovo	Sakhalin
Novgorod	Tula	Stavropol	Novosibirsk	Chita
Pskov		Rostov	Omsk	Jewish AO
St. Petersburg			Tomsk	Agin Buryatia AO
Nenets AO			Tyumen	Koryak AO
			Chita	Chukotka AO

Central Russia	Greater Volga	Greater Ural	Agin Buryatia AO
Bryansk			Taimyr AO
Vladimir	Marii El	Bashkortostan	Ust-Orda Buryatia AO
Ivanovo	Mordovia	Udmurtia	Khanty-Mansii AO
Kaliningrad	Tatarstan	Kurgan	Evenk AO
Kaluga	Chuvashia	Orenburg	Yamal Nenets AO
Kostroma	Astrakhan	Perm	
Moscow Oblast	Volgograd	Sverdlovsk	
Ryazan	Nizhnii Novgorod	Chelyabinsk	
Smolensk	Penza	Komi-Permyak AO	
Tver	Samara		
Tula	Saratov		
Yaroslavl	Ulyanovsk		
Moscow			

Note: Eight regions are members of two associations.

Governor Igor Farkhutdinov have protested against any potential attempts by Russia to return disputed Sakhalin territory to Japan. Luzhkov criticized the federal government's policy toward Ukraine, arguing that the Crimean Peninsula rightfully belonged to Russia. Several regions have established closer ties to Belarus's Aleksandr Lukashenko than the federal government seemed to support. And some of Russia's Turkic regions have lent more support to Turkey than the federal government has. While these exceptions are important, they should not be exaggerated, because the regions play a negligible role in the formation of Russia's foreign policy generally.

Several regions have enjoyed the international spotlight. Through much of the 1990s, foreign attention was showered on Moscow City because of its key position in a centralized state. Popular regional executives like St. Petersburg Mayor Anatolii Sobchak (1991–96) and Nizhnii Novgorod Governor Boris Nemtsov (1991–97) earned foreign plaudits. Moscow, St. Petersburg, and Nizhnii Novgorod were the only local governments to successfully issue eurobonds on international markets before the August 1998 crash prevented more regions from doing so. Under Mikhail Prusak, Novgorod Oblast attracted relatively large amounts of direct foreign investment because it set up a system for helping foreign businesses navigate the difficult Russian bureaucracy to realize their projects. Additionally, regions like Novgorod, Samara, Khabarovsk, Sakhalin, and Tomsk were able to gain support from the U.S. government's Regional Initiative aid program. Several other organizations, such as the

European Union's Technical Assistance–Commonwealth of Independent States (TACIS), George Soros's Open Society Institute, the European Bank for Reconstruction and Development (EBRD), and the World Bank, are giving direct aid to the regions. Numerous regions have set up their own trade representation in foreign countries.

The increased foreign outreach by regions is not surprising, since 46 Russian regions now have an external border (up from 29 during the Soviet era). The Russian Foreign Ministry has begun to set up regional offices to coordinate Russian foreign policy with local actors. Not wanting to be left behind, many regions maintain their own home pages on the World Wide Web, affording them quick and inexpensive direct contact with outsiders.

Attitudes Toward Business

With the exception of a few staunchly Communist areas, most Russian regions are interested in attracting outside investment. Many offer a variety of incentives for investors, including tax breaks, and at least claim to support such worthy goals as the development of small business. However, Russia is a very poor competitor on the international market and has been able to attract only a tiny fraction (1–2 percent) of the vast sums of transnational capital. Most regions lack a well-developed legal system capable

of protecting investors' rights. Moreover, while governors support foreign investment, they usually want to maintain strict control over the way the money is used, a condition that is usually not acceptable to potential investors. Additionally many in the regions are suspicious of the intentions of foreign investors, fearing that they will fall victim to the machinations of supposedly rapacious multinational corporations.

While Moscow once won the vast majority of the money that did come into Russia (more than 78 percent in 1997), in 1998 the picture began to shift. During that year, while about 24 percent went to Moscow City, more money began to flow to Moscow Oblast, Krasnodar Krai, Leningrad Oblast, Irkutsk Oblast, and Sverdlovsk Oblast. In 1998, the regions that won more than $100 million in foreign investments were Moscow City, St. Petersburg, Moscow Oblast, Samara, Novosibirsk, Krasnodar, Sakhalin, and Sverdlovsk.

The major international ratings agencies, such as Moody's, Standard & Poor's, and IBCA, issue reports on the most important regions. Additionally, Bank Austria and the Russian journal *Ekspert* provide regular rankings of the regions' investment climate. Bank Austria takes into account political, economic, social, and environmental factors as well as the regions' track records, while *Ekspert* uses a similarly wide range of variables. The cumulative scores are listed in each of the regional profiles that follow.

THE REPUBLICS AND REGIONS
of the
RUSSIAN FEDERATION

REPUBLIC OF ADYGEYA

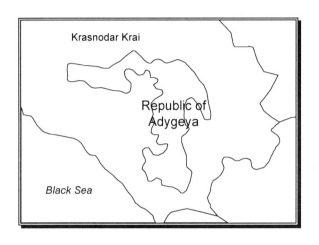

Territory: 7,600 km^2
Population (as of 1 January 1998): 450,000
Distance from Moscow: 1,669 km

Major Cities:
Maikop, *capital* (pop. 166,200)
Adygeisk (12,500)

Basic Facts

Population (as of 1 Jan. 1998): 450,000 (0.31% of Russian total)

Ethnic breakdown (1989 census): Russians 68.0%, Adygei 22.1%, Ukrainians 3.2%, Armenians 2.4%

Urban population (as of 1 Jan. 1998): 53.9% (Russia overall: 73.1%)

Student population (as of 1 Sept. 1997): 263 per 10,000 (Russia overall: 208/10,000)

Pensioner population (1997): 27.56% (Russia overall: 25.96%)

Percent of population with higher education (1989 census): 9.1% (Russia overall: 11.3%)

Percent of population working in (1997): Industry: 16.6% (Russian average: 23.0%); Agriculture: 17.4% (13.7%); Trade: 17.0% (13.5%); Culture: 14.4% (13.3%)

Average monthly personal income in July 1998: 507.9 new rubles (Russian average: 891.7 new rubles)

Average monthly personal expenses in July 1998: 328.1 new rubles (Russian average: 684.9 new rubles)

Average monthly subsistence requirement in 1998: 319 new rubles (Russian average: 438 new rubles)

Consumer price index (as of July 1998): 87 (Russia overall = 100)

Budgetary revenues (1997): 857.4 billion rubles (Russia overall: 433,378.2 billion rubles)

Budgetary expenditures (1997): 910.3 billion rubles (Russia overall: 468,111.6 billion rubles)

Industrial production as percentage of all Russian production (Jan.–Aug. 1998): 0.05%

Proportion of loss-making enterprises (as of July 1998): 57.5% (Russia overall: 50.4%)

Number of enterprises which have wage arrears (as of 1 Sept. 1998): 331 (0.24% of Russian total)

Agricultural production as percentage of all Russian production (1997): 0.31%

Number of private farms (as of 1 Jan. 1998): 1,523 (0.56% of Russian total)

Capital investment (1997): 285.6 billion rubles (Russia overall: 408,797 billion rubles)

Sources of investment (1997): federal budget: 21.9% (Russian average: 10.2%); regional budget: 11.2% (10.5%); extra-budgetary funds: 66.9% (79.3%)

Foreign investment (1997): 25,000 USD (Russia overall: 12,294,734,000 USD)

Number of joint ventures (1997): 21 (0.14% of Russian total)

Fixed capital investment in joint ventures and foreign companies (1997): 8,785 million rubles (Russia overall: 16,265.4 billion rubles)

Number of small businesses (as of 1 July 1998): 2,200 (0.25% of Russian total)

Number of telephones per 100 families (1997): in cities: 43.9 (Russian average: 49.2); in villages: 17.7 (19.8)

Brief Overview

The Republic of Adygeya is located on the northern slope of the Caucasus Mountains and is surrounded by Krasnodar Krai, of which it was a part until 1991. Maikop, the republican capital, is located 1,670 km south of Moscow and 160 km from the city of Krasnodar. Members of over 50 ethnic groups reside in the republic, with the Adygei making up 22.1 percent of the total population.

The republic's territory is rich in mineral resources, including gas, oil, rare metals, silver, gold, precious stones, and construction materials. Agriculture is the major regional specialization. Local farms cultivate grain and vegetables, and breed cattle. Yet much of the region's agricultural output is wasted because regional processing plants have insufficient capacity. The republic's industrial complex specializes in food processing (50% of regional GDP), lumber and cellulose production (18%), and machine building and metal processing (14%). The republic is the 17th poorest region in the country: less than half of its expenses are covered by its own budgetary revenues.

According to the republican administration, the region offers numerous investment possibilities but ethnic conflict in neighboring republics dissuades most investors from working in the area. The republican legislature has approved some benefits for foreign investors. According to a 1998 survey by *Ekspert* magazine, the republic ranked 74th among Russia's 89 regions in terms of investment potential and 55th in terms of investment risk. A 1998 survey by Bank Austria ranked the republic 68th in terms of investment climate.

Electoral History

2000 Presidential Election
Putin: 44.74%
Zyuganov: 44.51%
Yavlinskii: 2.97%
Tuleev: 1.77%
Zhirinovsky: 1.71%
Turnout: 65.81% (Russia overall: 68.64%)

1999 Parliamentary Elections
Communist Party of the Russian Federation: 39.42%
Unity: 22.61%
Fatherland–All Russia: 8.34%
Yabloko: 4.63%
Zhirinovsky Bloc: 4.52%
Union of Right Forces: 3.92%
In a single-mandate district: 1 Communist Party of the Russian Federation
Turnout: 61.73% (Russia overall: 61.85%)

1997 Republican Presidential Election
Dzharimov (incumbent): 57.80%
Sovmiz: 19.51%
Tsiku (State Duma deputy, KPRF): 15.76%
Turnout: 56.77%

1996 Presidential Election
Zyuganov: 51.50%/60.53% (first round/second round)
Yeltsin: 20.02%/34.48%
Lebed: 13.99%
Yavlinskii: 5.29%
Zhirinovsky: 5.07%
Turnout: 66.97%/64.85% (Russia overall: 69.67%/68.79%)

1995 Parliamentary Elections
Communist Party of the Russian Federation: 41.12%
Liberal Democratic Party of Russia: 9.60%
Communists–Worker's Russia: 5.70%
Party of Workers' Self-Government: 5.08%
Yabloko: 4.50%
Our Home Is Russia: 4.13%
Congress of Russian Communities: 4.10%
In a single-mandate district: 1 Communist Party of the Russian Federation
Turnout: 64.23% (Russia overall: 64.37%)

1993 Constitutional Referendum
"Yes"—38.3 "No"—60.1%

1993 Parliamentary Elections
Communist Party of the Russian Federation: 28.87%
Liberal Democratic Party of Russia: 18.11%
Yabloko: 10.88%
Party of Russian Unity and Concord: 9.96%
Russia's Choice: 8.15%
Women of Russia: 7.13%
Agrarian Party of Russia: 5.49%
Democratic Party of Russia: 5.24%
In a single-mandate district: 1 independent
From electoral associations: 1 Communist Party of the Russian Federation
Turnout: 61.73% (Russia overall: 54.34%)

1991 Presidential Election
Yeltsin: 51.22%
Ryzhkov: 22.96%
Zhirinovsky: 10.36%
Tuleev: 7.81%
Makashov: 2.37%
Bakatin: 2.25%
Turnout: 73.23% (Russia overall: 76.66%)

Regional Political Institutions

Executive:
President, 5-year term
Aslan Alievich Dzharimov, elected January 1992,
January 1997
   Ul. Zhukovskaya, 22; Maikop, 352700
   Tel 7(877–22) 2–19–01;
   Fax 7(877–22) 2–19–00
   Federation Council in Moscow:
   7(095) 292–12–61, 926–64–83

Legislative:
Unicameral
Khase—45 members, 5-year term, elected 1995
Chairman—Yevgenii Ivanovich Salov, elected
January 1996

Regional Politics

First Republican President—Dzharimov

Aslan Dzharimov became the first president of the Republic of Adygeya in January 1992. Adygeya achieved the status of republic only in 1991, having been an autonomous region inside Krasnodar Krai for nearly sixty years. Dzharimov was reelected on 12 January 1997, winning 58 percent of the vote in an election dogged by controversy after two candidates were denied registration. The republican electoral commission rejected Valentin Lednev, one of the presidential hopefuls, because he did not speak the Adygeyan language and had not been living in the republic for the previous ten years. The Adygeyan Constitution requires that candidates meet these criteria even though mandating such qualifications violates Russian legislation.

Adygeya is one of the safest and most stable regions in the North Caucasus. Surrounded by Krasnodar Krai on all sides, the republic is shielded from the ethnic warfare and disorder that plague much of the North Caucasus. Nevertheless, the republic's proximity to such chaos has hindered economic development and thwarted attempts to attract investment for local industry.

Executive Platform: Gorbachev-Style Social Politics

Dzharimov launched his political career at an early age by joining the Communist Party when he was only 16.

He backed Gorbachev's economic policies, arguing that if market reforms were the only way to bring the country out of its economic crisis, then the party should take the lead in implementing these policies (NNS). While serving in the USSR Congress of People's Deputies, Dzharimov spoke out strongly against annulling Article 6, the constitutional provision that ensured the Communist Party's leading role in the country. Nevertheless, Dzharimov is not a devoted Communist. He did not join the resurrected Communist Party of the Russian Federation (KPRF), and supported Yeltsin during his clash with the parliament in 1993. In 1999 Dzharimov joined the All Russia party organized by Tatarstan President Mintimer Shaimiev, then switched his support to the Kremlin's new Unity bloc.

In his 1993 campaign for election to the Federation Council, Dzharimov stated that his greatest accomplishments as president of Adygeya had been to bring social and political stability to Adygeya and establish civil peace and inter-ethnic accord as a basis for the socioeconomic and cultural development of the republic (NNS). Dzharimov stresses the need to reform legislative bodies and local government in order to improve the state's administrative apparatus (NNS). He particularly emphasizes expanding Adygeya's economic and cultural ties with its neighboring regions, especially Krasnodar Krai.

Policies: Economic Reforms

Despite the region's economic difficulties, Dzharimov has been willing to stick with economic reforms such as privatization and land reform. He is particularly interested in developing a program to combat unemployment in the republic and provide support for the most needy strata of society. Dzharimov has also spoken in favor of creating a special program for supporting small and medium-sized businesses and establishing conditions for cooperating with foreign firms. He argues that the federal government should pay more attention to social issues (NNS). The president is an advocate of agricultural reform, supporting both private farmers and the restructuring of collective farms (NNS).

Relationships Between Key Players: Ethnic Imbalance

Ethnic Adygei make up only 22 percent of the republic's 450,000 people. The largest ethnic group is the Russians, at 68 percent. Ethnic representation in the regional government is basically consistent with these proportions for ministerial positions and government committees, services, and agencies. However, the "power" agencies such as the police, the local Federal Security Service (FSB), the Federal Agency for Governmental Communication and Information (FAPSI), and the procurator's office are 80 percent ethnic Russians (*EWI RRR*, 24 November 1998).

Ties to Moscow: Ambiguous Relations

Since Dzharimov has not been actively involved with any particular party throughout his tenure as president, his relationship with Moscow varies according to the issue at hand. Although he supported Yeltsin in his October 1993 standoff with the parliament, various other issues found the two at opposite ends of the spectrum. In August 1996 Dzharimov protested the federal Interior Ministry's attempt to send some of its Adygeya-based units to Chechnya.

In November 1997 Dzharimov suspended the issue of new Russian passports in his region on the grounds that the new identity documents were written exclusively in Russian, while Adygeya has two official languages, Russian and Adygeyan (*RFE/RL*, 18 November 1997).

In January 1998 Yeltsin signed a decree annulling several directives that had been issued by Adygeyan authorities in December 1997. The directives involved tasks to be carried out by various collective farms and companies in the agrarian sector, putting raion officials and the Adygeyan Agriculture Ministry in charge of monitoring these tasks. Yeltsin's decree charged that these directives violated the Russian Constitution, the civil code, and various other federal laws by limiting the economic freedom of the respective enterprises (*RFE/RL*, 27 January 1998).

Relations with Other Regions: Peaceful Relations with Neighbors

Although Adygeya seceded from Krasnodar Krai, it necessarily maintains good relations with it. Dzharimov has quipped that the republic simultaneously "left the krai and remained in it," contributing to Russia's complicated federal system (*EWI RRR*, 24 November 1998). Most ethnic Adygei have well-developed business ties to the krai, which is only 1.5 hours away by car from the republican capital of Maikop. Adygeyans buy food in Krasnodar and rely on its importers for foreign food products and consumer goods. Adygeyans also supply the Krasnodar market with their own food products for cash. Given the pervasive wage and pension arrears that Adygeya experiences along with the rest of the country, the Krasnodar connection is a vital lifeline for the landlocked republic.

Adygeya has managed to stay out of the ethnic conflicts prominent throughout the North Caucasus, allowing Dzharimov to remain on good terms with the other leaders in the area. In July 1997 Adygeya joined Kabardino-Balkaria and Karachaevo-Cherkessia in forming an Interparliamentary Assembly. The assembly seeks to facilitate collective efforts among its members in addressing issues of federalism, and hopes to strengthen the friendship and cooperation among neighboring regions (*Vesti*, 24 July 1997).

Adygeya has also participated in the North Caucasus Congress of Chambers of Industry and Trade, which includes chambers from Rostov, Krasnodar, Stavropol, Dagestan, Karachaevo-Cherkessia, and North Ossetia. The assembly hopes to influence the federal government to change its investment priorities to focus on the development of the small business sector rather than supporting unprofitable state sector enterprises.

Adygeya belongs to the Association of Cooperation of Republics, Krais, and Oblasts of the North Caucasus. The other member regions are the republics of Dagestan, Ingushetia, Kabardino-Balkaria, Karachaevo-Cherkessia, North Ossetia, and Kalmykia, Krasnodar and Stavropol krais, and Rostov Oblast.

Foreign Relations: Participation in Abkhaz Conflict

Dzhamirov has supported the participation of Adygeyan volunteers in the war in Abkhazia, yet he also spoke in favor of finding a peaceful solution to the conflict (NNS).

Attitudes Toward Business: Pro-Investment

Dzharimov's main economic priority is combating the republic's high unemployment. The President's administration has identified numerous investment opportunities in the region, but ethnic conflict and

Aslan Alievich Dzharimov

7 November 1939—Born in Egerukhai aul (a North Caucasian mountain village) in the Koshekhabl raion of Adygeya

1956—Joined the CPSU

1957—Began working at the Path to Communism collective farm

1964—Graduated from Kuban Agricultural Institute and began work as an agrarian, then as a senior economist for the Koshekhabl raion agricultural administration

1967–1968—Graduate student in agricultural economics at the Kuban Agricultural Institute

1968–1975—Head of economic planning for the agricultural management department of the Adygeyan regional executive committee, then deputy manager of the agriculture department of the Adygeyan regional committee of the CPSU and director of the Adygeyan region experimental agriculture station

1975—Defended his candidate of sciences dissertation entitled, "The Economic Effectiveness of Applying Mineral Fertilizers in the Collective Farms of the Adygeya Autonomous Oblast"

1975–1984—Manager of the agricultural department and secretary of the Adygeyan oblast committee of the CPSU for agriculture

1984–1987—Manager of the department of agriculture and food industry for the Krasnodar Krai committee of the CPSU

1985—Finished the Academy of General Sciences of the Central Committee of the CPSU

1987–1989—Secretary of the Krasnodar Krai committee of the CPSU for the agro-industrial complex

January 1989—First secretary of the Adygeya regional committee of the CPSU and elected to the USSR Congress of People's Deputies

1990—Elected to the Adygeya Council of People's Deputies and was elected chairman in March 1990; served as a delegate to the XXVIII Party Congress of the CPSU

1990–August 1991—Member of the Central Committee of the RSFSR Communist Party 5 January 1992—Elected President of the Republic of Adygeya and simultaneously held the post of chairman of the republic's Council of Ministers

December 1993—Elected to the Federation Council

1994—Participated in a government delegation pilgrimage to Mecca

January 1996—Appointed to the second session of the Federation Council, serving on the Committee on Security and Defense Questions

12 January 1997—Reelected President of Adygeya

instability in Adygeya's neighbors have deterred most potential investors. Nevertheless, the republican legislature has passed some investment incentives for foreign firms. Adygeya has economic ties with over 20 foreign countries, including the UK, USA, France, Japan, Germany, Turkey, Syria, and the Czech Republic. There are 17 joint-stock companies in Adygeya, including the Russian-British Mavel, Russian-Cypriot AO KAD, and Russian-American Intergas. Dzharimov signed a cooperation agreement with LUKoil President Vagit Alekperov in May 1997 under which LUKoil will supply oil products to Adygeya's industries, agriculture, and individual consumers (*KD*, 23 May 1997).

Agin-Buryat Autonomous Okrug

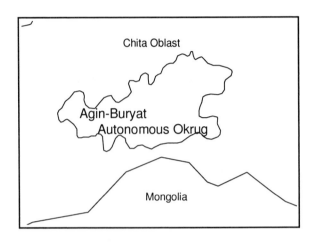

Territory: 19,000 km²
Population (as of 1 January 1998): 78,000
Distance from Moscow: 6,286 km

Major Cities:
Aginskoe, *capital* (pop. 9,300)

Basic Facts

Population (as of 1 Jan. 1998): 78,000 (0.05% of Russian total)

Ethnic breakdown (1989 census): Buryats 53.8%, Russians 41.5%, Ukrainians 1.1%

Urban population (as of 1 Jan. 1998): 32.2% (Russia overall: 73.1%)

Student population (as of 1 Sept. 1997): 21 per 10,000 (Russia overall: 208/10,000)

Pensioner population (1997): 19.23% (Russia overall: 25.96%)

Percent of population with higher education (1989 census): 9.9% (Russia overall: 11.3%)

Average monthly personal income in July 1998: 265.0 new rubles (Russian average: 891.7 new rubles)

Average monthly personal expenses in July 1998: 108.1 new rubles (Russian average: 684.9 new rubles)

Average monthly subsistence requirement in 1998: 551 new rubles (Russian average: 438 new rubles)

Consumer price index (as of July 1998): 116 (Russia overall = 100)

Budgetary revenues (1997): 123.5 billion rubles (Russia overall: 433,378.2 billion rubles)

Budgetary expenditures (1997): 167.1 billion rubles (Russia overall: 468,111.6 billion rubles)

Industrial production as percentage of all Russian production (Jan.–Aug. 1998): 0.002%

Proportion of loss-making enterprises (as of July 1998): 100% (Russia overall: 50.4%)

Number of enterprises which have wage arrears (as of 1 Sept. 1998): 61 (0.05% of Russian total)

Agricultural production as percentage of all Russian production (1997): 0.01%

Number of private farms (as of 1 Jan. 1998): 392 (0.14% of Russian total)

Capital investment (1997): 44.6 billion rubles (Russia overall: 408,797 billion rubles)

Sources of investment (1997): federal budget: 42.6% (Russian average: 10.2%); regional budget: 2.2% (10.5%); extra-budgetary funds: 52.2% (79.3%)

Foreign investment (1997): 0 (Russia overall: 12,294,734,000 USD)

Number of joint ventures (1997): 1 (0.007% of Russian total)

Number of telephones per 100 families (1997): in cities: 23.6 (Russian average: 49.2); in villages: 13.4 (19.8)

Brief Overview

The Agin-Buryat Autonomous Okrug is located in the southern part of East Siberia about 6,200 km from Moscow. It is situated within the territory of Chita Oblast.

Although there are few geological studies of the okrug, some gold, tin, coal, copper and other metals have been discovered. Seventy percent of the region's GDP comes from agriculture, which is mostly oriented toward cattle-breeding. Local industries include non-ferrous metallurgy, mining, forestry and timber work-

ing, as well as food-processing and light industry. The only large industrial enterprise, which produces 40 percent of the region's total industrial output, is the Orlovskii Mining and Processing Works. Agin-Buryat AO is the second poorest region in the country—its own budgetary revenues cover slightly more than 10 percent of its expenditures.

According to a 1998 survey by *Ekspert* magazine, the okrug ranked 85th among Russia's 89 regions in terms of investment potential and 85th in terms of investment risk. A 1998 survey by Bank Austria ranked the okrug 86th in terms of investment climate.

Electoral History

2000 Presidential Election
Putin: 62.80%
Zyuganov: 26.35%
Tuleev: 3.15%
Zhirinovsky: 2.78%
Yavlinskii: 1.28%
Turnout: 73.16% (Russia overall: 68.64%)

1999 Parliamentary Elections
Fatherland–All Russia: 37.42%
Unity: 21.80%
Communist Party of the Russian Federation: 20.75%
Zhirinovsky Bloc: 5.08%
Yabloko: 2.84%
Union of Right Forces: 1.88%
In a single-mandate district: 1 independent
Turnout: 69.52% (Russia overall: 61.85%)

1997 Gubernatorial Election
Zhamsuev (State Duma deputy): 44.56%
Dondokov: 33.03%
Abiduev: 9.39%
Zhambalov: 8.71%
Chimitdorzhin: 0.38%
Turnout: 64.83%

1996 Presidential Election
Yeltsin: 44.73%/49.16% (first round/second round)
Zyuganov: 35.74%/47.23%
Zhirinovsky: 5.68%
Lebed: 5.34%
Yavlinskii: 2.60%
Turnout: 69.06%/66.24% (Russia overall: 69.67%/ 68.79%)

1995 Parliamentary Elections
Agrarian Party of Russia: 32.32%
Communist Party of the Russian Federation: 18.02%
Liberal Democratic Party of Russia: 8.94%
Communists–Workers' Russia: 7.25%
Women of Russia: 4.45%
Our Home Is Russia: 3.76%
Power to the People: 3.06%
Party of Workers' Self-Government: 1.56%
Russia's Democratic Choice: 1.42%

Yabloko: 1.20%
Trade Unions and Industrialists of Russia–Union of Labor: 1.19%
Derzhava: 1.08%
In a single-mandate district: 1 independent
Turnout: 71.14% (Russia overall: 64.37%)

1993 Constitutional Referendum
"Yes"—67.8% "No"—29.2%

1993 Parliamentary Elections
Agrarian Party of Russia: 21.49%
Party of Russian Unity and Concord: 19.22%
Liberal Democratic Party of Russia: 14.38%
Communist Party of the Russian Federation: 9.75%
Russia's Choice: 9.50%
Women of Russia: 9.02%
Democratic Party of Russia: 5.65%
Yabloko: 4.00%
In a single-mandate district: 1 independent
Turnout: 63.27% (Russia overall: 54.34%)

1991 Presidential Election
Ryzhkov: 47.58%
Yeltsin: 17.45%
Tuleev: 10.86%
Zhirinovsky: 6.11%
Bakatin: 3.93%
Makashov: 2.91%
Turnout: 79.91% (Russia overall: 76.66%)

Regional Political Institutions

Executive:
Governor, 4-year term
Bair Bayaskhalanovich Zhamsuev, elected February 1997
Agin Buryat Autonomous Okrug Administration; Bazar Rinchino, 92; Aginskoe, 674460; Agin-Buryat Autonomous Okrug, Chita Oblast
Tel: 7(302–39) 3–41–52;
Fax: 7(302–39) 3–49–84
Federation Council in Moscow: 7(095) 292–23–03, 926–64–67
Legislative:
Unicameral
Okrug Duma—15 members, 4-year term, elected October 1996
Chairman—Dashi Dugarov, elected November 1996

Regional Politics

Young Komsomol Director Turned Independent Manager

Bair Zhamsuev was elected governor of the Agin-Buryat Autonomous Okrug on 23 February 1997. Zhamsuev spent most of his career climbing the Komsomol and Communist party ladders. He also gained valuable management experience as the okrug's deputy governor before being elected to the State Duma in 1993. While in the Duma, Zhamsuev was elected deputy chair of the Duma Committee on Nationality Affairs and chair of the sub-committee on national minorities and indigenous peoples. His experience there and as the okrug's representative in Moscow gave him the opportunity to build strong contacts in the capital. Zhamsuev has written about a dozen articles on ethnic issues of federalism and youth affairs. He is not affiliated with a political party, and during his Duma career he took positions that both supported and opposed the government.

Executive Platform: Socially Oriented Federalism

Zhamsuev's Duma campaign platform stressed federalism as the basis for Russian unity. He emphasized that economics should be socially oriented, and that a region's specific features should be considered while conducting reform. Zhamsuev rejected shock therapy and encouraged cooperation between all political groups and branches of power.

Zhamsuev was elected governor of Agin-Buryatia after the okrug's first attempt to elect a leader via popular mandate in October 1996 was unsuccessful since no candidate managed to win 50 percent of the vote. The okrug Duma then amended the law to hand victory to the candidate who had won a simple majority, and Zhamsuev was elected with 44 percent of the vote. During the gubernatorial campaign, Zhamsuev promised to resolve the okrug's social problems and pay off back salaries, pensions, and student stipends in one and a half to two years.

Relationships Between Key Players: Communist and Agrarian Centered

Political activity in the okrug is essentially limited to the Agrarian Party and the Communist Party. Our Home Is

Russia has a branch in the region, yet as in many other regions, the movement's activity has declined.

Ties to Moscow: Former Duma Deputy

In March 1995 Zhamsuev joined the pro-Yeltsin Stability faction in the Duma. However, during the 1995 Duma campaign, he disassociated himself from Our Home Is Russia. Upon his reelection to the Duma in 1995, Zhamsuev joined the Russian Regions faction.

After Zhamsuev left the State Duma to become governor his seat was filled by the nationally famous singer Iosif Kobzon. Zhamsuev and Kobzon work closely together and Kobzon played a key role in securing an advantageous loan for conducting investment projects in Agin-Buryatia. In addition to being a Russian celebrity, Kobzon chairs the Moskovit firm, which deals in oil, sugar, metals, and show business. The region has been so happy with Kobzon's ability to secure advantages that other small and usually overlooked regions are seeking celebrities to represent them in the State Duma as well.

Zhamsuev feels strongly that regional constitutions and laws should comply with federal legislation. He believes that the federal government should take a more aggressive stance in dealing with regions that adopt laws in violation of federal norms.

Relations with Other Regions: Close to Siberian Neighbors

Agin-Buryatia is the only Siberian region aside from the Tyva Republic in which the indigenous populations exceed the non-indigenous populations (Ian Bremmer and Ray Taras, eds., *New States, New Politics: Building the Post-Soviet Nations*, New York: Cambridge University Press, 1997, 193). Ethnic Buryats span three of Russia's regions. In addition to the Agin-Buryat Autonomous Okrug, there is the Ust-Orda Buryat Autonomous Okrug and the Republic of Buryatia, which is the largest Buryat region. Agin-Buryatia and Ust-Orda Buryatia were separated from the Buryat-Mongol ASSR (the present-day Republic of Buryatia) in 1937 when the Soviet leadership reduced the Buryat-Mongol titular territory in an attempt to suppress alleged nationalist sentiment (Bremmer and Taras, p. 209). During the Gorbachev era, Buryatia demanded that its pre-1937 borders be restored, but eventually recognized the constitutional status of the two autonomous okrugs.

Bair Bayaskhalanovich Zhamsuev

29 January 1959—Born in the village of Agin, Chita Oblast

1980—Graduated from Chita State Pedagogical Institute as a history teacher

1980–1981—School teacher in Chita Oblast

1981–1985—Instructor and then deputy director of the Chita Oblast Komsomol Department of Sport and Defense Preparation

1985–1988—Second and then first secretary of the Agin-Buryat Komsomol

1988–1990—Second secretary of the Chita Oblast Komsomol

1990–1991—Second secretary of the Agin-Buryat CPSU Okrug Committee

1991–12 December 1993—Deputy governor of the Agin-Buryat Okrug; permanent representative of the Agin-Buryat AO to the Russian government

1993—Graduated from the Russian Government's Academy of Management as a jurist

12 December 1993—Elected to the Duma as an independent from the Agin-Buryat single-member district, winning 52.8% of the vote; joined the New Regional Policy faction; served as chairman of the Committee on Nationalities

14 March 1995—Joined the pro-Yeltsin Stability Duma faction

17 December 1995—Re-elected to the Duma; served as deputy chairman of the Committee on Nationalities; was a member of the Russian Regions faction

23 February 1997—Elected governor with 44.5% of the vote

5 March 1997—Became a member of the Federation Council

In 1991 Agin-Buryatia participated in an all-Buryat congress in Ulan-Ude, resulting in the creation of an all-Union association of Buryat culture. The goal of the association is to establish a national-cultural autonomy to consolidate the Buryat people.

As an autonomous okrug, Agin-Buryatia has the ambiguous status of simultaneously being an equal subject of the Russian Federation and subordinate to Chita Oblast. Like other autonomous okrugs, its own economic health depends on the strength of its host oblast. Agin-Buryatia has not done as well economically as Ust-Orda Buryatia, which is in Irkutsk Oblast, partly because Irkutsk has traditionally been richer than Chita (*EWI RRR*, 21 January 1999).

The okrug belongs to the Siberian Accord Association, which includes Buryatia, Gorno-Altai, and Khakassia republics; Altai and Krasnoyarsk krais; Irkutsk, Novosibirsk, Tomsk, Tyumen, and Kemerovo oblasts; and Taimyr, Ust-Orda Buryat, Khanty-Mansi, Evenk, and Yamal-Nenets autonomous okrugs.

Foreign Relations: Focused on China

Agin-Buryat's largest foreign trade partner is China. In fact, all of the okrug's exports, 98 percent of which are raw materials, are shipped to China. The other 2 percent is made up of equipment.

Attitudes Toward Business: Low Economic Potential

The Agin-Buryat administration is open for outside investment, but the region has little actual economic potential. The okrug relies primarily on agriculture and has only one large industrial enterprise, the Orlovskii Mining and Processing Works.

ALTAI KRAI

Territory: 169,100 km^2
Population (as of 1 January 1998):
2,672,000
Distance from Moscow: 3,419 km

Major Cities:
Barnaul, *capital* (pop. 586,200)
Biisk (225,300)
Rubtsovsk (165,100)

Basic Facts

Population (as of 1 Jan. 1998): 2,672,000 (1.81% of Russian total)

Ethnic breakdown (1989 census): Russians 89.5%, Germans 4.8%, Ukrainians 2.9%

Urban population (as of 1 Jan. 1998): 52.6% (Russia overall: 73.1%)

Student population (as of 1 Sept. 1997): 170 per 10,000 (Russia overall: 208/10,000)

Pensioner population (1997): 25.86% (Russia overall: 25.96%)

Percent of population with higher education (1989 census): 8.2% (Russia overall: 11.3%)

Percent of population working in (1997): Industry: 21.2% (Russian average: 23.0%); Agriculture: 23.5% (13.7%); Trade: 12.7% (13.5%); Culture: 12.4% (13.3%)

Average monthly personal income in July 1998: 399.6 new rubles (Russian average: 891.7 new rubles)

Average monthly personal expenses in July 1998: 312.9 new rubles (Russian average: 684.9 new rubles)

Average monthly subsistence requirement in July 1998: 383 new rubles (Russian average: 438 new rubles)

Consumer price index (as of July 1998): 93 (Russia overall = 100)

Budgetary revenues (1997): 5,051.4 billion rubles (Russia overall: 433,378.2 billion rubles)

Budgetary expenditures (1997): 5,893.0 billion rubles (Russia overall: 468,111.6 billion rubles)

Industrial production as percentage of all Russian production (Jan.–Aug. 1998): 0.73%

Proportion of loss-making enterprises (as of July 1998): 60.8% (Russia overall: 50.4%)

Number of enterprises which have wage arrears (as of 1 Sept. 1998): 5,112 (3.78% of Russian total)

Agricultural production as percentage of all Russian production (1997): 2.38%

Number of private farms (as of 1 Jan. 1998): 6,118 (2.23% of Russian total)

Capital investment (1997): 2,594.1 billion rubles (Russia overall: 408,797 billion rubles)

Sources of investment (1997): federal budget: 16.9% (Russian average: 10.2%); regional budget: 9.6% (10.5%); extra-budgetary funds: 73.5% (79.3%)

Foreign investment (1997): 19,283,000 USD (Russia overall: 12,294,734,000 USD)

Number of joint ventures (1997): 92 (0.62% of Russian total)

Fixed capital investment in joint ventures and foreign companies (1997): 60,390 million rubles (Russia overall: 16,265.4 billion rubles)

Number of small businesses (as of 1 July 1998): 10,800 (1.24% of Russian total)

Number of enterprises privatized in 1997: 39 (1.42% of Russian total), including those which used to be municipal property: 79.5% (Russian average: 66.4%); regional property: 5.1% (20.0%); federal property: 15.4% (13.6%)

Number of telephones per 100 families (1997): in cities: 43.5 (Russian average: 49.2); in villages: 28.7 (19.8)

Brief Overview

Altai Krai is located in the southern part of Western Siberia in the basin of the upper Ob River, an area colonized by the Russians in the 18th century. It borders Novosibirsk and Kemerovo oblasts, Gorno-Altai Republic, and Kazakhstan. Russians (90.5% of the population) are by far the region's largest ethnic group, with Germans (3.8%) a distant second.

The region's rolling plains and the foothills of the Altai Mountains, once covered by steppe, are almost entirely under cultivation, producing wheat, corn, oats, sunflower, and beets. However, soils in the region have suffered from nuclear tests at Semipalatinsk in adjacent Kazakhstan, the main nuclear test site for the former Soviet Union.

The region is quite rich in various mineral resources, mainly non-ferrous and precious metals. The chemical, metal-processing, and machine-building industries play an important role in the regional economy. Over 60 percent of the region's 400 industrial enterprises are located in the cities of Barnaul, Biisk, and Rubtsovsk.

According to a 1998 survey by *Ekspert* magazine, the krai ranked 24th among Russia's 89 regions in terms of investment potential and 48th in terms of investment risk. A 1998 survey by Bank Austria ranked the krai 44th in terms of investment climate.

Electoral History

2000 Presidential Election
Putin: 44.57%
Zyuganov: 40.48%
Zhirinovsky: 4.01%
Yavlinskii: 3.40%
Tuleev: 3.27%
Turnout: 71.20% (Russia overall: 68.64%)

2000 Gubernatorial Election
Surikov (incumbent, NPSR): 77.22%
Raifikesht: 10.91%
Sannikov: 4.14%
Turnout: 71.15%

1999 Parliamentary Elections
Communist Party of the Russian Federation: 36.79%
Unity: 23.21%
Zhirinovsky Bloc: 7.13%

Union of Right Forces: 6.77%
Yabloko: 5.71%
Fatherland–All Russia: 4.45%
In single-mandate districts: 2 Communist Party, 1 Our Home Is Russia, 1 independent
Turnout: 65.95% (Russia overall: 61.85%)

1996 Gubernatorial Election
Surikov (krai legislature chairman, NPSR): 46.92%/ 49.36% (first round/second round)
Korshunov (incumbent): 43.39%/46.14%
Akelkin (local legislature deputy): 3.18%
Turnout: 48.3%/55.86%

1996 Presidential Election
Zyuganov: 41.97%/55.52% (first round/second round)
Yeltsin: 21.80%/38.56%
Lebed: 19.39%
Zhirinovsky: 7.38%
Yavlinskii: 5.05%
Turnout: 70.67%/67.08% (Russia overall: 69.67%/ 68.79%)

1995 Parliamentary Elections
Communist Party of the Russian Federation: 25.98%
Liberal Democratic Party of Russia: 15.59%
Agrarian Party of Russia: 12.38%
Our Home Is Russia: 4.96%
Communists–Workers' Russia: 4.70%
Women of Russia: 4.48%
Yabloko: 3.58%
Party of Workers' Self-Government: 3.55%
Derzhava: 3.08%
In single-mandate districts: 2 Communist Party of the Russian Federation, 1 Agrarian Party of Russia, 1 independent
Turnout: 66.95% (Russia overall: 64.37%)

1993 Constitutional Referendum
"Yes"—50.1% "No"—47.8%

1993 Parliamentary Elections
Liberal Democratic Party of Russia: 27.75%
Agrarian Party of Russia: 23.40%
Russia's Choice: 10.81%
Communist Party of the Russian Federation: 9.86%
Women of Russia: 8.58%
Party of Russian Unity and Concord: 5.47%
Democratic Party of Russia: 4.71%

Yabloko: 3.19%
In single-mandate districts: 1 Russian Movement for
    Democratic Reforms, 1 Russia's Choice,
    1 Agrarian Party of Russia, 1 independent
From electoral associations: 1 Russia's Choice,
    1 Agrarian Party of Russia
Turnout: 54.25% (Russia overall: 54.34%)

1991 Presidential Election
Yeltsin: 46.38%
Ryzhkov: 23.59%
Zhirinovsky: 11.59%
Tuleev: 9.11%
Bakatin: 2.73%
Makashov: 2.45%
Turnout: 77.21% (Russia overall: 76.66%)

Regional Political Institutions

Executive:
    Governor, 4-year term
    Aleksandr Aleksandrovich Surikov, elected
    December 1996
        Prospekt Leninskii, 59; Barnaul, 656035; Altai Krai
        Tel 7(385–2) 22–68–14, 22–88–05;
        Fax 7(385–2) 22–85–42
        Federation Council in Moscow:
        7(095) 292–75–41, 926–64–18

Legislative:
    Unicameral
    Legislative Assembly (Zakonodatelnoe Sobranie)—
    50 members, 4-year term, elected March 1996
    Chairman—Aleksandr Grigorevich Nazarchuk,
    elected March 1996

Regional Politics

Communist Who Longs for Soviet Days

Aleksandr Surikov is not afraid to admit his longing
for the Soviet past. The Siberian governor entered
politics in 1985, yet has spent most of his post-Soviet
political career trying to rebuild the glory of the country that was lost. Surikov sticks to a protectionist economic platform and maintains close ties to the opposition. Nevertheless, he has tried to present himself as
a centrist with strong diplomatic skills. These skills,
however, have not been successful in neutralizing op-

posing forces in regional politics as the Communists
continue to lose their political clout in Altai Krai.

Executive Platform: Economic Protectionist

Aleksandr Surikov was elected governor of Altai Krai
on 1 December 1996, narrowly defeating the incumbent
by a 3 percent margin in the runoff, and was reelected in
a first-round March 2000 victory of 77.22 percent.
Surikov's electoral bid was supported by the National
Patriotic Union of Russia (NPSR), an umbrella group of
nationalist and Communist parties led by the Communist Party of the Russian Federation. Surikov, in many
ways, is a very traditional Communist. He feels that the
country's most productive development occurred before
the 1990s and that the Soviet Union was successful at
"achieving full industrialization and the institutionaliza-
tion of the welfare state" (Panorama Research Group,
Labyrint Electronic Database, Moscow). Nevertheless,
when campaigning for the 1993 Federation Council elections, Surikov announced that he considered himself a
centrist. He was in favor of maintaining Russia within
its current borders and granting political and economic
equality to all Federation subjects (NNS).

Still, Surikov's platform is generally consistent with
that of the Communist Party. He has spoken in favor of
regulating inflation and maintaining a fixed exchange
rate in order to support domestic producers. Surikov
advocates state support for industrial and agricultural
enterprises and compensation for the population's financial losses. He also believes it is necessary to support small and medium enterprises and farmers, and to
reexamine privatization bearing in mind the interests
of workers' collectives.

Surikov claims that one of Altai Krai's most severe problems is its inability to stimulate economic
growth without the aid of the federal government
(*NG*, 18 February 1999). The krai lacks the resources
to invest in its own industry. As economic production continues to drop, the krai experiences a further
decline in the standard of living, at least according
to official statistics. Yet, even though the krai
economy is slow in its development, Altai is home
to some successful joint ventures (see Attitudes Toward Business).

Despite what the official numbers say, at least one
visitor who saw the krai in the mid-1980s and the
summer of 1999 noted an interesting paradox. During the 1980s when all the factories were working,
the population seemed relatively poor in compari-

son with living standards in Moscow. By 1999, even though the factories stood idle, the population seemed much better off. Apparently, the factories were in fact hurting the local economy and their closure has improved the situation.

Relationships Between Key Players: Struggle with Split Legislature

Unlike many other regional governors who are involved in heated conflict with the local mayors, Surikov has developed good working relationships with the local executives in Altai Krai. However, Surikov has had difficulty dealing with the presidential representative in the krai, Vladimir Raifikesht (*NG*, 18 February 1999). Raifikesht had served as the krai's governor from August 1991 until January 1994, when he resigned for personal reasons.

The legislature in Altai Krai is about evenly split between the Communists and a centrist bloc of Our Home Is Russia and Yabloko deputies. Since the region has traditionally been a Communist stronghold, Surikov's narrow victory in 1996 and the lack of a Communist majority in the regional parliament meant that Surikov faced considerable opposition to his plans.

Ties to Moscow: Critical of Yeltsin and Cabinets

Surikov was a longstanding critic of President Boris Yeltsin and a staunch supporter of the opposition. He felt that Yeltsin's various cabinets were responsible for the harsh economic decline afflicting Russia during the post-Soviet era.

Like all governors, Surikov likes to claim that he has considerable political clout in Moscow. Instead of influencing the executive branch, however, he claims more influence over the legislature. For example, he once asserted that he personally persuaded key members of the State Duma to pass a law benefiting teachers (*OMRI RRR*, 1 December 1996).

As a regional executive, Surikov is automatically given a seat in the Federation Council, the upper chamber of the federal legislature. However, Surikov feels that the current method of forming the upper chamber is not the best way to choose the members of the national parliament, and that members to the Federation Council should be popularly elected as are members of the lower house, the State Duma (*NG*, 18 February 1999). When the Federation Council was first formed in 1993 it was through popular mandate, and Surikov served in the Council as an elected deputy.

Surikov is very critical of Federation Council speaker and Orel Oblast Governor Yegor Stroev. He has called for Stroev to resign as the upper chamber's speaker and has suggested that the assembly's leadership should rotate among its members.

Surikov felt that the Primakov government's approach to solving the country's financial crisis was vague. He believes that the state should help only private sector banks that finance production in the real economy (*EWI RRR*, 8 December 1998).

In the 1999 parliamentary elections Surikov backed the Communists.

Relations with Other Regions: Siberian Collaborator

Surikov has been active in working with other Siberian leaders to address issues of common interest. In April 1998 Surikov met with Novosibirsk Governor Vitalii Mukha, Tomsk Governor Viktor Kress, speaker of the Novosibirsk legislature Viktor Leonov, and Altai Krai Legislative Assembly speaker Aleksandr Nazarchuk to develop a program for overcoming the economic crisis, which was presented to Prime Minister Sergei Kirienko. Their suggestions included lifting tariffs on rail cargo shipments, expanding road construction, pursuing anti-monopoly policies, developing protectionist trade policies in the interests of domestic producers, and strengthening state regulation of foodstuffs (*EWI RRR*, 16 April 1998).

Altai Krai belongs to the Siberian Accord Association, which also includes the republics of Buryatia, Gorno-Altai, and Khakassia; Krasnoyarsk Krai; Irkutsk, Novosibirsk, Omsk, Tomsk, Tyumen, and Kemerovo oblasts; and Agin-Buryat, Taimyr, Ust-Orda Buryat, Khanty-Mansi, Evenk, and Yamal-Nenets autonomous okrugs.

Foreign Relations: Cultural Ties to Germany

Since 1989 the German government has prioritized improving living conditions for ethnic Germans in Russia in the hope of reducing emigration to Germany. There are about 25,000 ethnic Germans in Altai Krai, making up nearly 5 percent of the krai's population. Germany gave the region $17 million in 1997 to build food-processing facilities, housing, and social amenities in several krai districts that are home to ethnic Germans.

In April 1998 Surikov joined leaders from

Aleksandr Aleksandrovich Surikov

15 August 1940—Born in Murmansk

1957–1959—Worked at the Kuibyshevtransstroi trust

1959–1966—Studied at the Saratov polytechnical institute and obtained a degree in bridge and tunnel construction

1966–1969—Worked as a foreman and director of the Zavyalov construction division

1969–1976—Director of construction authority N3 in Altaisk

1976–1985—Director of the association Altaiavtodor

1985–1990—Deputy chairman of the Altai Krai executive committee

November 1990—Became the general director of the Altaistroi building-industrial organization

August 1991—Elected chairman of the Altai Krai Council

December 1993—Elected to the first session of the Federation Council

13 March 1994—Elected to the Altai Krai Legislative Assembly and on 29 March was elected chair

January 1996—Ex officio became a member of the Federation Council where he serves as deputy chair of the Committee on the Budget, Tax Policies, Finance, Currency, and Customs Regulations

1 December 1996—Elected governor of Altai Krai

Married with two sons

Kemerovo, Saratov, Yaroslavl, and Moscow in calling for an end to the import and sale of Latvian goods in Altai Krai and urged that all contracts with Latvian enterprises be revised (*RFE/RL*, 14 April 1998). The boycott was initiated in response to the Latvian authorities' decision to disperse a 3 March demonstration of Russian-speaking pensioners in Riga.

Additionally, the regional capital Barnaul is participating in a World Bank housing project, receiving $18 million for building cottages and townhouses.

Attitudes Toward Business: Small, Successful Foreign Ventures

Altai Krai has historically been a strong agro-industrial region for Siberia. Although the region does not have as much foreign investment as other Siberian regions, it is home to some successful joint ventures involving foreign partners. In 1997 Altai Krai won a $3 million credit from Germany company WAQTI Interconsulting and from Ezra Holding Co. in the United States to build gas pipelines in the region. In Barnaul, Andsart & Co. is assembling South Korean Hyundai Galloper jeeps. In January 1998 Switzerland's Nestlé bought a controlling stake in the Altai

and Kamskaya Confectionery Factories located in Barnaul and in Perm Oblast.

In March 1999 Almazy Rossii-Sakha (ALROSA), Russia's main diamond producer, and Lazare Kaplan International Inc. signed an agreement for producing $1 billion in diamonds at the Kristall factories in Barnaul and Moscow.

Internet Sites in the Region

http://arw.dcn-asu.ru/econ/altai/soc-econ.htm
This website offers specific information on the region's economic development and potential, privatization results, and banking system.

http://arw.dcn-asu.ru/econ/normativ/da10/altaireg.htm
This website lists the text of more than 450 krai laws.

http://arw.dcn-asu.ru/regioninfo/economy/firms/
This is a list of firms in Altai, grouped by economic category.

http://arw.dcn-asu.ru/nko/index.ru/html
This is a list of more than fifty nonprofit organizations operating in Altai. The groups cover a wide range of interests, but most are social in nature.

AMUR OBLAST

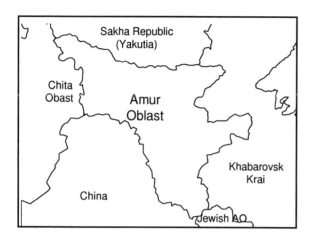

Territory: 363,700 km²
Population (as of 1 January 1998):
1,023,000
Distance from Moscow: 7,985 km

Major Cities:
Blagoveshchensk, *capital* (pop. 217,200)
Svobodnyi (72,500)
Belogorsk (74,500)
Tynda (50,000)

Basic Facts

Population (as of 1 Jan. 1998): 1,023,000 (0.7% of Russian total)

Ethnic breakdown (1989 census): Russians 86.8%, Ukrainians 6.7%, Belarusans 1.7%

Urban population (as of 1 Jan. 1998): 65.0% (Russia overall: 73.1%)

Student population (as of 1 Sept. 1997): 161 per 10,000 (Russia overall: 208/10,000)

Pensioner population (1997): 19.84% (Russia overall: 25.96%)

Percent of population with higher education (1989 census): 11.2% (Russia overall: 11.3%)

Percent of population working in (1997): Industry: 15.4% (Russian average: 23.0%); Agriculture: 10.8% (13.7%); Trade: 17.3% (13.5%); Culture: 11.9% (13.3%)

Average monthly personal income in July 1998: 899.7 new rubles (Russian average: 891.7 new rubles)

Average monthly personal expenses in July 1998: 678.2 new rubles (Russian average: 684.9 new rubles)

Average monthly subsistence requirement in 1998: 497 new rubles (Russian average: 438 new rubles)

Consumer price index (as of July 1998): 124 (Russia overall = 100)

Budgetary revenues (1997): 2,991.2 billion rubles (Russia overall: 433,378.2 billion rubles)

Budgetary expenditures (1997): 3,293.2 billion rubles (Russia overall: 468,111.6 billion rubles)

Industrial production as percentage of all Russian production (Jan.–Aug. 1998): 0.27%

Proportion of loss-making enterprises (as of July 1998): 68.1% (Russia overall: 50.4%)

Number of enterprises which have wage arrears (as of 1 Sept. 1998): 993 (0.73% of Russian total)

Agricultural production as percentage of all Russian production (1997): 0.95%

Number of private farms (as of 1 Jan. 1998): 1,936 (0.7% of Russian total)

Capital investment (1997): 2,241.7 billion rubles (Russia overall: 408,797 billion rubles)

Sources of investment (1997): federal budget: 25.4% (Russian average: 10.2%); regional budget: 9.5% (10.5%); extra-budgetary funds: 65.1% (79.3%)

Foreign investment (1997): 505,000 USD (Russia overall: 12,294,734,000 USD)

Number of joint ventures (1997): 63 (0.43% of Russian total)

Fixed capital investment in joint ventures and foreign companies (1997): 1,032 million rubles (Russia overall: 16,265.4 billion rubles)

Number of small businesses (as of 1 July 1998): 3,700 (0.43% of Russian total)

Number of enterprises privatized in 1997: 2 (0.07% of Russian total), including those which used to be municipal property: 50.0% (Russian average: 66.4%); regional property: 0% (20.0%); federal property: 50.0% (13.6%)

Number of telephones per 100 families (1997): in cities: 18.9 (Russian average: 49.2); in villages: 18.9 (19.8)

Brief Overview

Amur Oblast is situated in the southwest part of Russia's Far East, near the Amur River. It borders Khabarovsk Krai, the Sakha Republic, the Jewish Autonomous Oblast, Chita Oblast, and China.

Forests cover about 73 percent of the region's territory. Amur's complex geological composition offers coal and charcoal, gold, iron, titanium, copper, and precious stones. The region is the country's fourth-largest producer of gold. As a result of the oblast's rich mineral resources, major industries are gold and coal mining, non-ferrous metallurgy, metal processing and machine building, forestry and timber production, energy, and food processing.

Amur Oblast, which encompasses more than half the cultivated land in the Far East, is also an important producer of agricultural products. It is Russia's largest producer of soybeans (65 percent of the country's total) and the largest grain exporter in the area.

According to a 1998 survey by *Ekspert* magazine, the oblast ranked 54th among Russia's 89 regions in terms of investment potential and 47th in terms of investment risk. A 1998 survey by Bank Austria ranked the oblast 66th in terms of investment climate.

Electoral History

2000 Presidential Election
Putin: 49.40%
Zyuganov: 33.50%
Zhirinovsky: 5.94%
Yavlinskii: 3.08%
Tuleev: 3.07%
Turnout: 68.27% (Russia overall: 68.64%)

1999 Parliamentary Elections
Unity: 36.21%
Communist Party of the Russian Federation: 24.33%
Zhirinovsky Bloc: 11.29%
Union of Right Forces: 4.48%
Fatherland–All Russia: 3.47%
Yabloko: 3.32%
In a single-mandate district: 1 independent
Turnout: 62.49% (Russia overall: 61.85%)

1997 Gubernatorial Election
Belonogov (oblast legislature chairman): 60.51%
Lyashko (incumbent): 24.41%
Sebina (LDPR): 2.32%

Surat (first deputy governor): 2.07%
Simonov: 1.69%
Khakhin: 1.04%
Turnout: 52.13%

1996 Presidential Election
Zyuganov: 41.85%/53.07% (first round/second round)
Yeltsin: 26.60%/40.67%
Lebed: 11.84%
Zhirinovsky: 7.91%
Yavlinskii: 6.06%
Turnout: 68.58%/65.59% (Russia overall: 69.67%/ 68.79%)

1995 Parliamentary Elections
Communist Party of the Russian Federation: 34.89%
Liberal Democratic Party of Russia: 12.90%
Women of Russia: 5.86%
Communists–Workers' Russia: 5.79%
For the Motherland: 5.02%
Our Home Is Russia: 3.54%
Yabloko: 3.35%
Party of Workers' Self-Government: 3.05%
In a single-mandate district: 1 independent
Turnout: 67.43% (Russia overall: 64.37%)

1993 Constitutional Referendum
"Yes"—49.4% "No"—48.9%

1993 Parliamentary Elections
Liberal Democratic Party of Russia: 24.90%
Communist Party of the Russian Federation: 16.23%
Russia's Choice: 12.51%
Women of Russia: 10.31%
Agrarian Party of Russia: 9.78%
Party of Russian Unity and Concord: 7.08%
Democratic Party of Russia: 5.01%
Yabloko: 4.68%
In a single-mandate district: 1 independent
Turnout: 59.44% (Russia overall: 54.34%)

1991 Presidential Election
Yeltsin: 37.72%
Ryzhkov: 31.19%
Zhirinovsky: 9.05%
Tuleev: 7.20%
Makashov: 5.74%
Bakatin: 4.72%
Turnout: 74.71% (Russia overall: 76.66%)

Regional Political Institutions

Executive:

Governor, 4-year term
Anatolii Nikolaevich Belonogov, elected March 1997
    Ul. Lenina, 135; Blagoveshchensk, 675023
    Tel 7(416–2) 44–03–22;
    Fax 7(416–2) 44–62–01
    Federation Council in Moscow:
    7(095) 292–30–17, 926–67–20

Legislative:

Unicameral
Council of People's Deputies—30 members,
4-year term, elected March 1997
Chairman—Viktor Vasilevich Martsenko, elected
April 1997

Regional Politics

Amur's Sixth Governor Outlasts the Rest

Anatolii Belonogov is the sixth executive to govern Amur Oblast since President Boris Yeltsin introduced the institution of governor in 1991. Power has changed hands more in Amur than in any other Russian region. Yeltsin first appointed Albert Krivchenko to the post at its inception. Then, in April 1993, Aleksandr Surat was popularly elected to the office. A few months later, in October, Yeltsin removed Surat from power after he refused to implement the president's decree on constitutional reform. Two months later Yeltsin appointed Vladimir Polevanov to the job, but less than a year later Polevanov left to become Deputy Prime Minister and Chairman of the State Property Committee. Yeltsin then appointed Vladimir Dyachenko to the post, but removed him a year and a half later, right before the 1996 Russian presidential elections. At this point Yeltsin put Yurii Lyashko in the governor's seat and hoped for his success in the September elections.

However, Amur's gubernatorial election proved to further complicate the region's political situation. Anatolii Belonogov beat out Lyashko, but only by a 0.08 percent margin of 189 votes. Lyashko challenged the results in court, claiming that numerous electoral law violations invalidated the elections. In particular, residents of northern regions claimed that they were unable to vote because of bad weather, while helicopters did not pick up some ballot boxes for counting. The presidential administration, which had supported

Lyashko's candidacy, backed the allegations and demanded an investigation. The regional procurator's office found that many voters' signatures had been falsified, and in November, the oblast court annulled the results of the September poll. Lyashko's victory turned out to be short-lived, however. In the March 1997 repeat elections Belonogov's victory was far more convincing than his initial win in September. Belonogov pulled in more than 60 percent of the vote, while incumbent Lyashko earned only 24 percent.

Executive Platform: Communist Longing for Soviet Days

Belonogov is a devoted Communist. Throughout his various positions in the early 1990s he remained loyal to the opposition and actively participated in launching the Communist Party of the Russian Federation (KPRF) in 1993. During the 1996 Russian presidential campaign, Belonogov served as an aide to Communist candidate Gennadii Zyuganov. Zyuganov returned the favor by coming to Amur prior to the 1997 gubernatorial elections to campaign for Belonogov, which helped contribute to his impressive victory.

Belonogov does not display much sympathy for his opponents. He strongly disagrees with both the liberal approaches of reformers like Yegor Gaidar and Grigorii Yavlinskii and the national-patriotic policies of Vladimir Zhirinovsky and Aleksandr Lebed. Belonogov is more supportive of bygone political leaders such as Vladimir Lenin and Yurii Andropov, and considers the development of the CIS in place of the USSR to be a national catastrophe (Panorama Research Group, Labyrint Electronic Database, Moscow).

Ties to Moscow

In spite of his loyalty to the opposition, Belonogov has tried to stay on the good side of the party in power. In 1997 when he attended the KPRF annual congress he told the presidential administration that it should not take his affiliation with the opposition too seriously (*EWI RRR*, 8 May 1997).

On 20 May 1998 Belonogov signed a power-sharing agreement with the federal government. In the December 1999 parliamentary elections he backed the Communists.

Relations with Other Regions

Amur Oblast is home to the Svobodnyi cosmodrome, which is located at a former strategic nuclear missile base

Anatolii Nikolaevich Belonogov

24 February 1939—Born in the village of Ust-Umlekan, Amur Oblast

1962—Graduated from the Blagoveshvechsk Agricultural Institute

March 1963—Joined the Communist Party

September 1956–September 1957—Worked for the Far Eastern Railroad

1962–1970—Director of collective farm, then head zoo technician

1970–1975—Second secretary, then first secretary of the Oktyabr district committee of the CPSU

1975–1985—Assistant manager and manager of agricultural department, manager of department of agriculture and food industry, secretary of Amur Oblast committee of the CPSU

1985–1990—First deputy chair of the Amur Oblast executive committee, chair of the Amur Oblast agro-industrial committee, chair of Amur Oblast executive committee

18 March 1990—Elected to the RSFSR Congress of People's Deputies

Spring 1990—Elected to the Congress of People's Deputies of Amur Oblast and became chair

1993—Participated in the restoration of the Communist Party of the Russian Federation

13 October 1994—Elected to the oblast council, and on 23 October, elected chair

22 September 1996—Elected governor of Amur Oblast, but the vote was overturned

23 March 1997—Elected governor in repeat elections

15 January 1998—Joined the United Commission for Coordinating Legislation

and set to become Russia's top space center. The Soviet Union had launched many of its rockets from Kazakhstan, at a base the Russians must now pay to use. Svobodnyi cosmodrome's activities, which are controlled by the Russian Defense Ministry, have spurred protests from the neighboring Sakha Republic. Sakha is concerned about the environmental hazards caused by debris dropped on its territory from cosmodrome rocket launches. Sakha's complaints, however, are directed primarily to Russia's Defense Ministry rather than to Amur officials.

Amur Oblast belongs to the Far East and Baikal Association, which also includes the republics of Buryatia and Sakha (Yakutia); Primorskii and Khabarovsk krais; Kamchatka, Magadan, Chita, and Sakhalin oblasts; the Jewish Autonomous Oblast; and Koryak and Chukotka autonomous okrugs. One of the association's goals is to increase contacts with Asian countries, particularly in the economic sphere. Amur has already built successful trade partnerships with several Asian companies. (See Foreign Relations.)

Foreign Relations: Increased Ties with Asia

Belonogov has a very Russo-centric approach to the successor states of the USSR. He has actively supported the creation of a Russian-Belarusan union, appearing as one of fourteen signatories on a support letter published by *Rossiiskaya Gazeta* in 1997. Belonogov feels that Latvian citizenship laws violate the rights of the Russian nation, and believes that Russia should defend the interests of Russians outside of Russia's borders. He is also against transferring the Kuril Islands to Japan.

In spite of Belonogov's visible longing for aspects of the Soviet era, Amur's foreign relations have benefited from more open borders. The region is now taking greater advantage of its proximity to Asia to develop relations with Asian enterprises. The cities of Blagoveshchensk, Poyarkovo, Dzhalinda, and Konstantinovka have become centers of intense trade with companies from China, Taiwan, Hong Kong, Japan, and South Korea. Regional exports are mostly composed of forestry products (36%) and metals (17%), while major import items are food products and consumer goods.

Attitudes Toward Business: Heavily Invested Agricultural Region

One would expect that a region ruled by such a devout Communist would lag behind in market economic structures, but in fact, Amur has been labeled "overinvested" by an *Ekspert* magazine survey. The region has a high representation of both Russian and foreign investors. The Amur administration has adopted special investment legislation for domestic investors and has developed more than 50 investment projects in transportation, mineral resource extraction, hydro-energy, and agriculture that are open to foreign investors.

ARKHANGELSK OBLAST

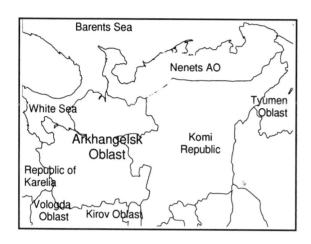

Population (as of 1 January 1998):
1,492,000
Distance from Moscow: 1,133 km

Major Cities:
Arkhangelsk, *capital* (pop. 368,900)
Severodvinsk (239,000)
Kotlas (66,800)
Novodvinsk (48,700)
Koryazhma (44,500)

Basic Facts

Population (as of 1 Jan. 1998): 1,492,000 (1.01% of Russian total)

Ethnic breakdown (1989 census): Russians 92.6%, Ukrainians 3.5%, Belarusans 1.3%

Urban population (as of 1 Jan. 1998): 74.1% (Russia overall: 73.1%)

Student population (as of 1 Sept. 1997): 121 per 10,000 (Russia overall: 208/10,000)

Pensioner population (1997): 26.74% (Russia overall: 25.96%)

Percent of population with higher education (1989 census): 8.8% (Russia overall: 11.3%)

Percent of population working in (1997): Industry: 28.3% (Russian average: 23.0%); Agriculture: 11.0% (13.7%); Trade: 12.2% (13.5%); Culture: 11.9% (13.3%)

Average monthly personal income in July 1998: 667.1 new rubles (Russian average: 891.7 new rubles)

Average monthly personal expenses in July 1998: 400.0 new rubles (Russian average: 684.9 new rubles)

Average monthly subsistence requirement in 1998: 497 new rubles (Russian average: 438 new rubles)

Consumer price index (as of July 1998): 114 (Russia overall = 100)

Budgetary revenues (1997): 3,545.2 billion rubles (Russia overall: 433,378.2 billion rubles)

Budgetary expenditures (1997): 4,091.1 billion rubles (Russia overall: 468,111.6 billion rubles)

Industrial production as percentage of all Russian production (Jan.–Aug. 1998): 0.73%

Proportion of loss-making enterprises (as of July 1998): 69.1% (Russia overall: 50.4%)

Number of enterprises which have wage arrears (as of 1 Sept. 1998): 1,565 (1.16% of Russian total)

Agricultural production as percentage of all Russian production (1997): 0.77%

Number of private farms (as of 1 Jan. 1998): 1,166 (0.43% of Russian total)

Capital investment (1997): 2,508.4 billion rubles (Russia overall: 408,797 billion rubles)

Sources of investment (1997): federal budget: 9.7% (Russian average: 10.2%); regional budget: 4.6% (10.5%); extra-budgetary funds: 85.7% (79.3%)

Foreign investment (1997): 94,270,000 USD (Russia overall: 12,294,734,000 USD)

Number of joint ventures (1997): 43 (0.29% of Russian total)

Fixed capital investment in joint ventures and foreign companies (1997): 72,645 million rubles (Russia overall: 16,265.4 billion rubles)

Number of small businesses (as of 1 July 1998): 4,100 (0.47% of Russian total)

Number of enterprises privatized in 1997: 126 (4.59% of Russian total), including those which used to be municipal property: 34.1% (Russian average: 66.4%); regional property: 37.3% (20.0%); federal property: 28.6% (13.6%)

Number of telephones per 100 families (1997): in cities: 44.9 (Russian average: 49.2); in villages: 28.4 (19.8)

Brief Overview

Arkhangelsk Oblast is located in the north of the Eastern European Plain and borders the republics of Komi and Karelia, as well as Vologda, Kirov, and Tyumen oblasts. The northern boundary of the oblast is defined by three Arctic Ocean seas: the White Sea, Barents Sea, and Karsk Sea. Over a third of Arkhangelsk's territory is covered by forests, another 24 percent is pastures, 19 percent is islands (including Novaya Zemlya, Zemlya Frantsa Iosifa, the Solovetskie islands), while lakes, rivers, and swamps occupy 16 percent of the space. Only 1.3 percent of Arkhangelsk's land is suitable for agriculture.

The oblast is fairly rich in mineral resources, particularly in oil and gas in the Timan-Pechora Field—the 14th largest repository of hydrocarbon reserves in the country (0.71 percent of the country's total resources). It also has a diamond field, but development will only occur in the future. Nevertheless, the oblast is mostly known for its forestry resources and is one of the country's biggest suppliers of timber and cellulose. Regional timber-processing enterprises annually produce 180,000–300,000 tons of paper, 550,000–700,000 tons of cellulose, and about 400,000 tons of pasteboard. The oblast boasts a highly developed fishing industry, with the annual haul reaching 135,000 tons.

The city of Arkhangelsk is the oldest sea harbor in Russia, founded in the late 16th century, and is now the major hub in the country's European North. It processes up to 2,000 ships annually. The oblast's second largest city, Severodvinsk, hosts construction facilities for Russia's nuclear fleet.

According to a 1998 survey by *Ekspert* magazine, the oblast ranked 47th among Russia's 89 regions in terms of investment potential and 44th in terms of investment risk. A 1998 survey by Bank Austria ranked the oblast 15th in terms of investment climate.

Electoral History

2000 Presidential Election
Putin: 59.80%
Zyuganov: 20.27%
Yavlinskii: 6.22%
Zhirinovsky: 3.72%
Tuleev: 2.78%
Turnout: 69.15% (Russia overall: 68.64%)

1999 Parliamentary Elections
Unity: 27.56%
Communist Party of the Russian Federation: 15.32%
Union of Right Forces: 10.77%
Zhirinovsky Bloc: 9.16%
Fatherland–All Russia: 7.67%
Yabloko: 6.80%
In single-mandate districts: 1 Fatherland–All Russia, 1 independent
Turnout: 62.49% (Russia overall: 61.85%)

1996 Gubernatorial Election
Yefremov (incumbent): 34.54%/58.67% (first round/second round)
Guskov (State Duma deputy): 28.85%/33.24%
Pozdeev: 21.35%
Ivanov (oblast legislature member): 5.42%
Turnout: 47.5%/41.03%

1996 Presidential Election
Yeltsin: 40.85%/63.91% (first round/second round)
Zyuganov: 18.32%/27.74%
Lebed: 17.28%
Yavlinskii: 10.79%
Zhirinovsky: 6.55%
Turnout: 66.79%/66.29% (Russia overall: 69.67%/68.79%)

1995 Parliamentary Elections
Communist Party of the Russian Federation: 14.09%
Liberal Democratic Party of Russia: 10.84%
Women of Russia: 8.85%
Party of Workers' Self-Government: 8.30%
Our Home Is Russia: 7.98%
Yabloko: 7.72%
Russia's Democratic Choice: 4.99%
Pamfilova–Gurov–Lysenko Bloc: 3.35%
Congress of Russian Communities: 3.08%
In single-mandate districts: 1 Communist Party of the Russian Federation, 1 independent
Turnout: 65.99% (Russia overall: 64.37%)

1993 Constitutional Referendum
"Yes"—71.6% "No"—26.2%

1993 Parliamentary Elections
Liberal Democratic Party of Russia: 22.22%
Russia's Choice: 21.83%
Women of Russia: 12.85%

Yabloko: 8.20%
Party of Russian Unity and Concord: 6.63%
Communist Party of the Russian Federation: 6.44%
Agrarian Party of Russia: 6.39%
Democratic Party of Russia: 5.74%
In single-mandate districts: 2 independent
From electoral associations: 1 Communist Party of
    the Russian Federation, 1 Russia's Choice
Turnout: 58.20% (Russia overall: 54.34%)

1991 Presidential Elections
Yeltsin: 56.34%
Ryzhkov: 19.15%
Zhirinovsky: 6.57%
Tuleev: 6.20%
Bakatin: 5.17%
Makashov: 2.62%
Turnout: 74.41% (Russia overall: 76.66%)

Regional Political Institutions

Executive:
    Governor, 4-year term
    Anatolii Antonovich Yefremov, elected
    December 1996
        Troitskii Prospekt, 49; Arkhangelsk, 163004
        Tel 7(818–2) 65–30–41, 65–31–02;
        Fax 7(818–2) 43–21–12
        Federation Council in Moscow:
        7(095) 292–61–04, 926–60–29

Legislative:
    Unicameral
    Council of People's Deputies—39 members,
    4-year term, elected June 1996
    Chairman—Vyacheslav Ivanovich Kalyamin,
    elected June 1996

Regional Politics

Impatient Yeltsin Loyalist

Anatolii Yefremov is known for his loyalty to President Boris Yeltsin's administration. However, given the severity of the country's economic crisis, even the most reliable of the president's supporters became impatient with the federal government's inability to pay its debts. In March 1997, Yefremov announced that he wanted to sell two nuclear submarines to "friendly countries" to pay off the government's then

1.1 trillion ruble ($190 million) debt to the Severodvinsk Russian State Center for Atomic Shipbuilding that produced them. He claimed that the debt would never be repaid unless such extraordinary measures were taken. The town's population of 239,000 is highly dependent on the shipyards for revenue.

President Yeltsin appointed Anatolii Yefremov governor on 4 March 1996. He replaced Pavel Balakshin, whom Yeltsin had fired for abuse of office. Other members of the Federation Council initially blocked Yefremov's membership in the upper house because they believed that Balakshin had been sacked illegally. In December 1996, Yefremov won a popular mandate for his office, receiving 58 percent of the vote, and removing any doubts about the legitimacy of his tenure in the position.

Executive Platform: Technocratic Consensus Builder

Yefremov's offer to sell submarines abroad was an unusual episode for a man who usually pursues technocratic solutions. Shortly before the gubernatorial elections in 1996, he put together a 300-member committee of experts to address the region's economic problems. In addition, he called on all citizens to suggest ways of bringing the oblast's economy out of its crisis. The plan his team developed sought to reduce the plunging standard of living for the oblast's residents and the declining levels of production by the unimaginative means of optimizing the oblast's budget policy, mobilizing domestic resources, and improving the oblast's overall managerial approach. The plan also included tax breaks for the oblast's forestry industry. However, since the regional government is only collecting about half of the taxes due, it has extremely limited means to make much of an improvement in the situation. Yefremov has been able to win additional support from Moscow, but such subsidies are not a long-term solution. There has been some talk of establishing a free economic zone, but this plan has not been realized.

In the run-up to the 1999 State Duma elections, Yefremov joined up with Moscow Mayor Yurii Luzhkov's Fatherland movement, but in the end he endorsed Unity.

Policies: Economic Development

The situation in the oblast is as extreme as the cold can be in the winter. The infrastructure of roads, gas pipelines, and electricity is poorly developed, there has been little real economic restructuring, and many of the region's workers lack the skills to succeed in the new economy. However, the region could potentially generate enormous wealth from its still unmeasured and untapped reserves of oil, gas, and diamonds.

Yefremov believes that one of Russia's greatest problems is the lack of qualified personnel in the fields of marketing, management, business analysis, and other professions connected with the development of a market economy. Although Yeltsin sponsored a program to let young people study abroad to gain this kind of knowledge, Yefremov argued that it is too expensive to meet all the country's needs through foreign study programs. Accordingly, he declared Arkhangelsk a Free Territory of Culture and Education in order to train specialists. While the details of the program have yet to be worked out, the "free" means that participants in the program will be granted various tax and other benefits to carry out their projects (*NG*, 27 November 1998).

Yefremov is very concerned with tax collection in his oblast. At one point the governor himself even traveled throughout the region to collect taxes from enterprises that had not paid up. In January 1998, before the August financial crisis hit, the region's enterprises owed 2.5 trillion rubles ($415 million) to the oblast and local budgets (*EWI RRR*, 8 January 1998).

In January 1999 the oblast assembly passed a law creating a regional free enterprise zone providing tax holidays for businesses. The main goal of the zone is to develop Arkhangelsk's transportation infrastructure, in particular by reactivating the Northern Sea Route and the Arkhangelsk seaport. Businesses operating in the zone are freed from property and profit taxes (*EWI RRR*, 22 January 1999).

The Keston Institute reported on 4 June 1997 that Arkhangelsk Oblast had passed a harsh law on religious practices that discriminates against religions other than Russian Orthodoxy, labeling such religions "sects." The law prevents non-recognized religions from renting space in state-owned buildings, a provision that effectively prevents them from meeting.

Following the 17 August 1998 financial crisis, Yefremov, like many other governors, introduced price controls to stem the rising cost of living for local residents (*RT*, 9 September 1998).

Relationships Between Key Players: Mayor Is Old Rival

Former Governor Balakshin won election as mayor of the city of Arkhangelsk in December 1996. Among his first actions was ordering a review of the former mayor's financial operations. Balakshin's predecessor, Vladimir Gerasimov, had served as mayor from 1991 to 1996. In June 1997 the local procurator filed a suit against him for abusing his office. Balakshin considers local government to be completely powerless. He argues that the federal government is not interested in strengthening local government because effective local governments would weaken federal power. To make local government a reality, Balakshin says federal laws must define how much tax revenue local governments should receive. Currently, the oblast governments determine those tax issues. He has also advocated giving local governments the right to own land (*EWI RRR*, 2 April 1998).

Ties to Moscow: Wavering Yeltsin Supporter

Yefremov tended to support President Yeltsin on most political and economic issues. He initially played an active part in the pro-governmental Our Home Is Russia movement and in April 1997 was elected to its political council. However, as Yeltsin gradually faded from the political spotlight, Yefremov aligned himself with presidential hopeful Moscow Mayor Yurii Luzhkov (see Executive Platform and Relations with Other Regions), and then signed on to support the Kremlin's new Unity bloc.

Relations with Other Regions: Difficulties with Its Resource-Rich Okrug

Nenets Autonomous Okrug is officially a part of Arkhangelsk Oblast. However, the Nenets government has demonstrated separatist tendencies on several occasions (for additional information, see profile of Nenets Autonomous Okrug). Following the protests of the Yamal-Nenets and Khanty-Mansi autonomous okrugs against Tyumen Oblast, the Nenets Autonomous Okrug voted on 29 October 1996 not to participate in the Arkhangelsk Oblast gubernatorial and legislative elections set for 8 December 1996.

Autonomous okrugs have a relatively ambiguous status under Russia's 1993 constitution. On one hand, they are defined as independent members of the federation with their own governors. On the other, they are subordinate to the oblasts on whose territory they are located. Nenets authorities are hoping to gain greater control over the revenue generated from the exploitation of the area's rich hydrocarbon resources.

Yefremov has enjoyed good relations with Moscow City Mayor Yurii Luzhkov, who harbored presidential ambitions in the last Yeltsin years. Luzhkov signed a treaty of cooperation with Arkhangelsk in November 1996, just in time to boost Yefremov's standing before the gubernatorial elections.

The ability of South Africa's De Beers to gain control of Arkhangelsk's main diamond deposit was a blow to Almazy Rossii-Sakha (ALROSA), Russia's main diamond producer, which is based in the Republic of Sakha (Yakutia) (see Attitutudes Toward Business).

Arkhangelsk Oblast is part of the NorthWest Association. The other members of this Association are the republics of Karelia and Komi; Vologda, Kaliningrad, Kirov, Leningrad, Murmansk, Novgorod, and Pskov oblasts; Nenets Autonomous Okrug; and St. Petersburg.

Foreign Relations: Seeking Help from Northern Neighbors

Arkhangelsk Oblast is interested in greater cooperation with the Northern European countries, such as Finland, Sweden, and Norway. These countries are helping Arkhangelsk deal with its mounting social and economic problems. They view aid to Russia's North as a strategic issue, for it is in their interest to prevent these Russian regions from slipping further into poverty and instability. As it is, Russia's Nordic neighbors suffer from higher radiation levels (since the Northern Fleet has turned the Kola Peninsula into a nuclear dump) and from higher levels of atmospheric pollution (*Itogi*, 21 October 1997).

Finland is actively promoting the idea of developing a northern transport route linking the Finnish region of Oulu with Karelia, Arkhangelsk, and Komi. The link would reroute Northwest Russian cargo traffic to Finnish ports. The Arkhangelsk Oblast administration fully supports the project and even suggested publicizing the idea through a motor race in March 1998 (*EWI RRR*, 26 February 1998). Komi has also supported the idea (*EWI RRR*, 22 December 1998).

In May 1998 Yefremov participated in the G-8 conference in Birmingham, England.

Attitudes Toward Business: Open to Some, But Not All, Foreign Investors

Direct foreign investment in Russia's north is still very low. According to the Arkhangelsk tax service, there are only 120 joint ventures in the whole region, of which three-fourths exist solely on paper. The remaining joint ventures specialize in resource extraction only, be it oil, fish, timber, or, more recently, diamonds (*Itogi*, 21 October 1997). For instance, South Africa's De Beers, working with a Russian partner, won the right to mine the diamonds in Arkhangelsk's Lomonosov deposit, but they gave it up in May 2000.

Arkhangelsk depends on its forestry industry for approximately 50 percent of its overall output. The oblast has two large pulp factories that produce pulp, paper, and cardboard, exporting approximately 200,000 tons of paper products a year. Four years ago, the region had a network of small logging and paper mills that were engaged in collecting, sawing, drying, and packaging lumber products which were then shipped to the main river port. They shipped 3.5 million tons of timber a year. Many of these plants are now closed.

During the late 1990s, the forestry industry experienced a severe crisis because of a drop in prices on the international market, the prevalence of obsolete equipment in local plants, the generally low level of technology, poor product quality, and a general lack of financing to improve conditions. During the Soviet era, many workers were attracted to the North because the state offered them relatively high wages. Now, however, the factories must try to maintain these special salary supplements. The high cost of supporting workers in the far north raises the price of products produced there, making them uncompetitive. Approximately two-thirds of the production facilities are now sitting idle.

The Lomonosov diamond deposit, 100 kilometers from the city of Arkhangelsk, is one example of the incredible sluggishness in Russia's development of its natural resources. Surveyors believe that the deposit holds an estimated $12 billion worth of precious stones which can be extracted over 40 years, with an annual take of $300 million. Overall, developing the deposit will require an estimated $745 million investment. If these figures prove correct, the site will produce 20–25 percent of the output of the Republic of Sakha (Yakutia), Russia's major diamond-producing region (*KD*, 3 December 1997). The scale of the project requires foreign investment, since this much domestic funding is not available.

During the Soviet era, the lack of development was attributed to resource conservation. After market reforms were launched, Severalmaz was created to develop the Lomonosov deposit but its application for a mining license was delayed. After about ten years of

---

Anatolii Antonovich Yefremov

30 January 1952—Born in the Maloe Toinokur village in the Primore district of Arkhangelsk

1975—Graduated from the Arkhangelsk Forestry Institute as a transportation engineer-mechanic

1975–1984—Worked as a Komsomol functionary, rising to become second secretary of the oblast Komsomol committee

1984–1990—Supervisor and then director of a regional freight transport company

1990—Elected deputy chairman of the oblast executive committee

1991–1994—Deputy governor, heading the Committee on Industry, Transport, Communication, and Road Construction

1994–1996—Director of Arkhangelsk Oblast's mission in Moscow

4 March 1996—Appointed Governor of Arkhangelsk Oblast

22 December 1996—Elected Governor of Arkhangelsk Oblast

---

exploratory work, the company announced in late 1997 that the only way to further develop the mine and proceed with extracting diamonds was to build a quarry. Archaic regulations listing diamond extraction as a classified project discouraged foreign investors. An extraordinary meeting of shareholders in the Severoalmaz diamond mining company on 28 February 1998 brought sensational news: the company had its first strategic investor, a Moscow-based company called Soglasie which was working closely with De Beers (*EWI RRR*, 12 March 1998). In June 1998 Prime Minister Kirienko removed the closed zone status of Arkhangelsk's Lomonosov diamond deposit, giving De Beers and Soglasie direct access to the site (*EWI RRR*, 23 July 1998). By the end of 1998, De Beers was strengthening its grip in the region. Unfortunately for the region, however, Arkhangelsk is not a high priority for De Beers and the company agreed to sell its stake in May 2000. DeBeers probably left because of new laws that prevent diamonds from being exported.

Port operations have declined five-fold in recent years, dropping from 6 million tons in 1989 to 1.6 million tons in 1995. Export cargo dropped from 2.7 million tons in 1989 to 1.1 million tons in 1994. Ice breakers are required from November through May, significantly adding to the cost of using the port. (Murmansk's port, in contrast, is ice free.) Port authorities cannot afford to dredge the port properly because the federal government is not maintaining its payments to the region.

The government tried to privatize Arkhangelsk's port, but retained 45 percent of its stock, and barred foreign investors from participating in the sale. As a result, 20 percent of the port's equity remains unclaimed. Meanwhile, the government, though the largest shareholder, has failed to invest a single ruble in the port's development.

The situation is the same in the fishing and fish-processing industries: the government bars foreign investment, despite the desperate need for capital. Because of the unreasonably high taxes they must pay in the Russian ports, Russian fishermen prefer to sell fish to Norwegian processing plants. Consequently, even the successful Russian fish processing plants are denied raw fish.

In April 1999 Yefremov signed a cooperation agreement with Gazprom Chairman Rem Vyakhirev, which calls for building a $400 million gas pipeline between the village of Nyuksenitsa, Vologda Oblast, and Arkhangelsk, installing gas in populated areas, and opening up the oblast's mineral resources. Gazprom agreed to become a stockholder in the local company Severgaz, which Yefremov believes will help the company attract credit and investment for building the pipeline and developing mineral deposits. Arkhangelsk is also inviting Gazprom to invest in the Lomonosov diamond deposit.

ASTRAKHAN OBLAST

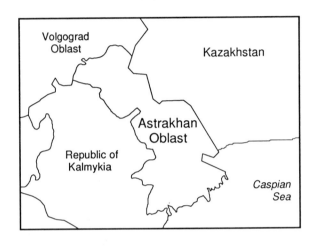

Territory: 44,100 km^2
Population (as of 1 January 1998):
1,029,000
Distance from Moscow: 1,534 km

Major Cities:
Astrakhan, *capital* (pop. 485,800)
Akhtubinsk (49,900)
Znamensk (35,900)

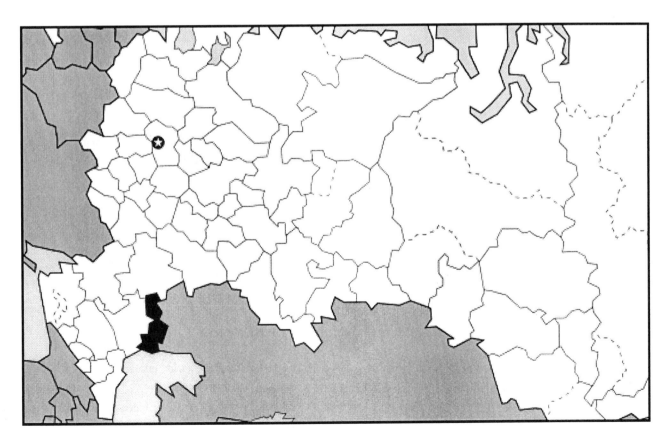

Basic Facts

Population (as of 1 Jan. 1998): 1,029,000 (0.70% of Russian total)

Ethnic breakdown (1989 census): Russians 72.0%, Kazakhs 12.8%, Tatars 7.2%, Ukrainians 1.9%

Urban population (as of 1 Jan. 1998): 66.8% (Russia overall: 73.1%)

Student population (as of 1 Sept. 1997): 146 per 10,000 (Russia overall: 208/10,000)

Pensioner population (1997): 23.32% (Russia overall: 25.96%)

Percent of population with higher education (1989 census): 9.7% (Russia overall: 11.3%)

Percent of population working in (1997): Industry: 17.2% (Russian average: 23.0%); Agriculture: 13.1% (13.7%); Trade: 14.1% (13.5%); Culture: 13.1% (13.3%)

Average monthly personal income in July 1998: 547.1 new rubles (Russian average: 891.7 new rubles)

Average monthly personal expenses in July 1998: 349.0 new rubles (Russian average: 684.9 new rubles)

Average monthly subsistence requirement in 1998: 430 new rubles (Russian average: 438 new rubles)

Consumer price index (as of July 1998): 88 (Russia overall = 100)

Budgetary revenues (1997): 1,994.5 billion rubles (Russia overall: 433,378.2 billion rubles)

Budgetary expenditures (1997): 2,347.9 billion rubles (Russia overall: 468,111.6 billion rubles)

Industrial production as percentage of all Russian production (Jan.–Aug. 1998): 0.27%

Proportion of loss-making enterprises (as of July 1998): 42.9% (Russia overall: 50.4%)

Number of enterprises which have wage arrears (as of 1 Sept. 1998): 1,190 (0.88% of Russian total)

Agricultural production as percentage of all Russian production (1997): 0.47%

Number of private farms (as of 1 Jan. 1998): 1,757 (0.64% of Russian total)

Capital investment (1997): 1,912.4 billion rubles (Russia overall: 408,797 billion rubles)

Sources of investment (1997): federal budget: 6.3% (Russian average: 10.2%); regional budget: 5.6% (10.5%); extra-budgetary funds: 88.1% (79.3%)

Foreign investment (1997): 980,000 USD (Russia overall: 12,294,734,000 USD)

Number of joint ventures (1997): 106 (0.72% of Russian total)

Fixed capital investment in joint ventures and foreign companies (1997): 6,608 million rubles (Russia overall: 16,265.4 billion rubles)

Number of small businesses (as of 1 July 1998): 3,600 (0.41% of Russian total)

Number of enterprises privatized in 1997: 23 (0.84% of Russian total), including those which used to be municipal property: 91.4% (Russian average: 66.4%); regional property: 4.3% (20.0%); federal property: 4.3% (13.6%)

Number of telephones per 100 families (1997): in cities: 41.2 (Russian average: 49.2); in villages: 22.3 (19.8)

Brief Overview

The oblast is located in the Caspian lowland at the mouth of the Volga River. It borders Volgograd Oblast, Kalmykia, and Kazakhstan. Astrakhan Kingdom was conquered by Ivan the Terrible and integrated into the Russian state in 1556. It then began its rapid development as an industrial and trade center. The region's economy peaked during the first decade of the 20th century following the construction of the Trans-Caspian Railroad and the development of the Baku oil fields.

During Soviet times, the regional economy was mostly dominated by fishing and the fish processing industry, shipbuilding, and freight handling. Now, due to environmental problems, the fishing industry is in decline and the regional administration is attempting to reorient the oblast economy toward the extraction of raw materials, in particular oil, gas, and sulfur. The hydrocarbon reserves of Astrakhan oblast are the third largest in the country and account for 4.43 percent of the country's total deposits.

According to a 1998 survey by *Ekspert* magazine, the oblast ranked 61st among Russia's 89 regions in terms of investment potential and 19th in terms of investment risk. A 1998 survey by Bank Austria ranked the oblast 48th in terms of investment climate. Since 1997, investments in the oblast have jumped considerably.

Electoral History

2000 Presidential Election
Putin: 60.99%
Zyuganov: 26.66%
Tuleev: 3.04%
Zhirinovsky: 2.56%
Yavlinskii: 2.56%
Turnout: 67.66% (Russia overall: 68.64%)

1999 Parliamentary Elections
Unity: 32.28%
Communist Party of the Russian Federation: 26.51%
Zhirinovsky Bloc: 6.66%
Union of Right Forces: 5.37%
Fatherland–All Russia: 5.36%
Yabloko: 4.64%
In a single-mandate district: 1 independent
Turnout: 61.26% (Russia overall: 61.85%)

1996 Gubernatorial Election
Guzhvin (incumbent): 52.45%
Zvolinskii (State Duma deputy, KPRF): 39.79%
Turnout: 56.89%

1996 Presidential Election
Zyuganov: 36.54%/47.79% (first round/second round)
Yeltsin: 29.52%/46.85%
Lebed: 16.14%
Zhirinovsky: 7.16%
Yavlinskii: 6.04%
Turnout: 69.27%/66.50% (Russia overall: 69.67%/ 68.79%)

1995 Parliamentary Election
Communist Party of the Russian Federation: 24.05%
Liberal Democratic Party of Russia: 16.36%
Our Home Is Russia: 12.47%
Communists–Workers' Russia: 6.00%
Women of Russia: 5.52%
Yabloko: 4.01%
Party of Workers' Self-Government: 3.81%
Derzhava: 3.10%
Russia's Democratic Choice: 2.22%
Congress of Russian Communities: 2.05%
In a single-mandate district: 1 independent
Turnout: 62.02% (Russia overall: 64.37%)

1993 Constitutional Referendum
"Yes"—57.1% "No"—40.5%

1993 Parliamentary Elections
Liberal Democratic Party of Russia: 17.25%
Communist Party of the Russian Federation: 16.61%
Russia's Choice: 13.73%
Agrarian Party of Russia: 11.90%
Women of Russia: 9.99%
Party of Russian Unity and Concord: 8.16%
Yabloko: 7.92%
Democratic Party of Russia: 5.36%
In single-mandate districts: 2 independent
From electoral associations: 1 Communist Party of the Russian Federation, 1 Russia's Choice
Turnout: 51.42% (Russia overall: 54.34%)

1991 Presidential Election
Yeltsin: 56.41%
Ryzhkov: 15.27%
Tuleev: 11.58%

Zhirinovsky: 5.71%
Makashov: 3.55%
Bakatin: 3.43%
Turnout: 74.72% (Russia overall: 76.66%)

Regional Political Institutions

Executive:
Governor, 4-year term
Anatolii Petrovich Guzhvin, elected
December 1996
Sovetskaya ul., 15; Astrakhan, 414008
Tel 7(851–2) 22–85 -19;
Fax 7(851–2) 22–95–14
Federation Council in Moscow:
7(095) 292–58–56, 926–65–53

Legislative:
Unicameral
Representative Assembly (Predstavitelnoe
Sobranie)—29 members, 4–year term, elected
October 1997
Chairman—Pavel Petrovich Anisimov, elected
November 1997

Regional Politics

Yeltsin-Appointee Rules Underdeveloped Caspian Region

Astrakhan Governor Anatolii Guzhvin is one of the few governors in power who were originally appointed to the post by President Boris Yeltsin in 1991 when the institution was created. Guzhvin was popularly elected to the position in December 1996, defeating his only opponent, Communist State Duma Deputy Vyacheslav Zvolinskii by a margin of about 12 percent. Guzhvin had the backing of Viktor Chernomyrdin's Our Home Is Russia movement and Grigorii Yavlinskii's Yabloko.

Guzhvin and Astrakhan are largely unnoticed on the Russian stage. Guzhvin was a strong Yeltsin supporter who maintained good relations with all of his prime ministers. Nevertheless, his region usually does not draw Moscow's attention, in spite of its wealth of underdeveloped natural resources and potential for developing stronger international transportation links. Although Guzhvin appears to be open to business initiatives and economic development, foreign investment in Astrakhan is small in comparison to other regions with similar assets.

Executive Platform: Critical Liberal Reformer

Guzhvin was a strong ally of President Boris Yeltsin and he has followed a pro-reform platform, in particular regarding privatization, education, and public health. The governor belonged to Our Home Is Russia (NDR) and chaired the Astrakhan Oblast branch of the movement, but he has been distancing himself from NDR and in 1999 he joined the All Russia regional party.

After being appointed governor in 1991, Guzhvin began promoting democratic initiatives in such spheres as land reform, privatization, education, public health, and culture. Guzhvin backed former Prime Minister Yegor Gaidar's reforms, although he suggested corrections to minimize their negative impact in the social sphere. Guzhvin feels that the most important condition for successful reform is economic stability, especially as it relates to the population.

Despite Guzhvin's ties to Moscow, his loyalty to Astrakhan is greater than any sense of obligation he feels toward the federal government. Guzhvin is critical of the federal government's fiscal policies toward the regions. He believes that the federal government is unjust in its allocation of subsidies to the regions and that it does not consider strongly enough which regions are successful at collecting and paying taxes to the federal budget when deciding on the distribution of federal funds (*RG*, 20 September 1997). Guzhvin is highly critical of Russia's tax collecting procedures and has stated that if he were able to halt payments to the federal government, he would stop payments immediately (*MN*, 1 September 1998).

Policies: Maintaining Status Quo

Guzhvin believes that he has accomplished a great deal in his tenure as governor, particularly in revitalizing industry and production (*RG*, 20 September 1997). He also takes credit for the oblast's relative success at paying pensions and promoting the social sphere. Although Astrakhan has managed to sustain Russia's turbulent transition without any major catastrophes, the region has relied primarily on its wealth of natural resources. However, there is plenty of work to be done in this area. The regional energy and mineral industries are underdeveloped and lack the kind of foreign investment and partnerships present in regions with similar resource endowments.

Relationships Between Key Players: Independent

Elections to the Astrakhan Oblast legislature were held in October 1997, yielding an assembly dominated by independents with a small representation of Communists. Even though Guzhvin was active in Our Home Is Russia and chaired the oblast branch of the movement, he did not attempt to establish an NDR faction in the oblast legislature. The oblast administration encompasses individuals of various political views.

Ties to Moscow: Behind Individuals in Power

Guzhvin had a close and long-standing relationship to President Yeltsin. Guzhvin joined Yeltsin in the defense of the White House during the August 1991 coup attempt. For his bravery, Yeltsin rewarded Guzhvin with the governor's seat in Astrakhan. Guzhvin was also flexible enough to support Yeltsin's string of prime ministers. He was a strong supporter of Yegor Gaidar and his liberal economic reforms. After Gaidar was dismissed, Guzhvin developed a relationship with Viktor Chernomyrdin, viewing him as an experienced practitioner, in contrast to Gaidar. Similarly, Guzhvin backed the appointment of former prime minister Yevgenii Primakov.

In November 1997 Guzhvin signed a power-sharing agreement with Yeltsin. Guzhvin has been highly critical of the federal center's relationship to the regions, particularly concerning tax payments and transfer allocations. (See Executive Platform.)

Relations with Other Regions: Cooperation with Volgograd

Astrakhan and Volgograd oblasts are trying to encourage greater interregional trade, though the effort has not turned a profit yet. The cooperation began after Guzhvin and Volgograd Governor Nikolai Maksyuta signed a treaty promoting trade at a midnight airport meeting during the summer of 1998, when they were returning from a Federation Council session in Moscow. The two governors sat together on the flight, an opportunity that gave them their first chance to speak about common interests, according to reports in Volgograd newspapers. Guzhvin had to change planes in Volgograd, so the governors decided not to wait until the next meeting in Moscow but to sign an agreement in the airport. Since then both governors have encour-

aged local producers, primarily of food products, to sell in the neighboring region. Guzhvin has pushed Astrakhan producers to sell rice in Volgograd at prices lower than they charge at home (*DP*, November 1998, n. 47). Volgograd businessmen believe that the initial efforts have little more than publicity value.

Astrakhan is a member of the Greater Volga Association, which also includes the republics of Tatarstan, Mordovia, Chuvashia, and Marii El; and Volgograd, Nizhnii Novgorod, Penza, Samara, Saratov, and Ulyanovsk oblasts.

Foreign Relations: Seeks Cooperation

In September 1997 Guzhvin signed a cooperation agreement with the Slovak minister of economy. The agreement sought cooperation in the areas of mutual interest—Slovakia's production technology and Astrakhan's fish, meat, and crops (*Volga*, 23 September 1997).

Astrakhan has been trying to reassert its position in foreign trade via its Caspian Sea port. A new seaport was opened in 1997, with the capacity to handle 300,000 tons of cargo a year. The port hopes to double its capacity in the near future.

Attitudes Toward Business: Assertive of Regional Interests

There is tremendous investment potential in Astrakhan's natural resources. The oblast is home to the largest European natural gas field, which is capable of providing 50 billion cubic meters of gas annually for 100 years. However, the sulfur content in the gas makes exploiting it environmentally risky. The oblast also possesses vast oil deposits, which are handled by LUKoil. Gazprom has designs on dominating Astrakhan's fuel industry. It has been focused on searching for gas, but has also begun its own oil exploration. In April 1998 the Stroigaz company and the Astrakhan state properties fund joined forces to form the oil company Astrakhannefteprom, which intends to invest up to $500 million in prospecting and producing hydrocarbons in Astrakhan.

Guzhvin is intent on ensuring that the oblast, rather than Moscow, reaps the rewards that come from exploiting Astrakhan's natural resources. He has focused on building relationships with LUKoil, Gazprom, Rosneft, and Stroitransgaz that are independent of

Anatolii Petrovich Guzhvin

25 March 1946—Born in the city of Akhtubinsk in Astrakhan Oblast

1970—Graduated from the Astrakhan Technical Institute of Fishing and Economics as an electro-mechanical engineer

1972—Began working for the Komsomol and in 1975 became the first secretary of the Astrakhan Oblast Komsomol committee

1980–1985—First secretary of the Kamyzyak district committee of the CPSU

1985–1987—Second secretary of the oblast committee of the CPSU

1987–1991—Chairman of the executive committee of the Astrakhan Oblast Council of People's Deputies

1988–1990—Deputy to the RSFSR Supreme Soviet

28 August 1991—Appointed Governor of Astrakhan Oblast by order of President Boris Yeltsin

1995—Joined Our Home Is Russia (NDR)

January 1996—Appointed to the Federation Council and joined the FC Committee for CIS affairs

8 December 1996—Elected Governor of Astrakhan Oblast

Activities: enjoys hunting and fishing

Married, with a son, daughter, and two grandchildren

Moscow intermediaries. Guzhvin's priority of ensuring Astrakhan's interests makes him mindful of the usefulness of foreign investment. He encourages investment and invites cooperative relationships with foreign businesses. One such example was Guzhvin's participation in the Russian delegation to the "Business and Investment Opportunities in the Russian Federation" conference in California in February 1998.

Another of Astrakhan's economic assets is its access to the Caspian Sea, which has not been maximized. In March 1998 Guzhvin signed an agreement with a group of Swiss businessmen to continue talks on the second part of the Caspian Sea port in Olya. Guzhvin has also discussed the possibility of gaining financial support for port construction with Transstroi President V. Brezhnev and LUKoil President Vagit Alekperov. An Iranian delegation has visited Astrakhan to discuss establishing a Russian-Iranian joint venture in Olya.

Similarly, Astrakhan is also likely to benefit from the construction of Russia's leg of an international transportation corridor that will go from northern Europe through Finland, St. Petersburg, Moscow, Novorossiisk, and Astrakhan.

In an attempt to heed Yeltsin's requests to support domestic industry, in spring 1998 the oblast administration opened a supermarket called "Astrakhan Without America," which sells only domestically produced items. The supermarket was met with overwhelming enthusiasm, leading the store to double its staff. Guzhvin hopes to open similar stores throughout the city and other parts of the oblast.

Internet Sites in the Region

http://www.astrakhan.su/
This website features basic information about the oblast, its history, and its culture. It displays a variety of demographic maps and photographs of points of interest.

REPUBLIC OF BASHKORTOSTAN

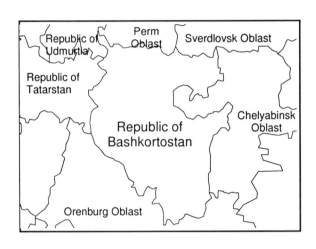

Territory: 143,600 km²
Population (as of 1 January 1998): 4,111,000
Distance from Moscow: 1,519 km

Major Cities:

Ufa, *capital*
  (pop. 1,084,000)
Sterlitamak (261,900)
Salavat (156,800)
Neftekamsk (118,300)

Oktyabrskii (111,400)
Beloretsk (73,100)
Ishimbai (71,100)
Kumertau (69,700)
Sibai (56,500)

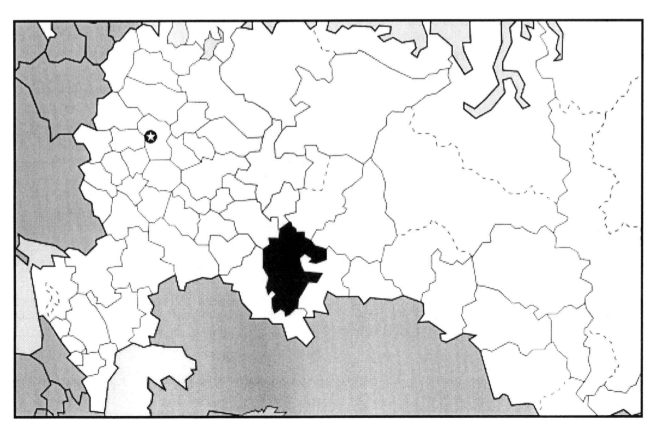

Basic Facts

Population (as of 1 Jan. 1998): 4,111,000 (2.79% of Russian total)

Ethnic breakdown (1989 census): Russians 39.3%, Tatars 28.4%, Bashkirs 21.9%, Chuvash 3.0%, Marii 2.7%, Ukrainians 1.9%

Urban population (as of 1 Jan. 1998): 64.8% (Russia overall: 73.1%)

Student population (as of 1 Sept. 1997): 147 per 10,000 (Russia overall: 208/10,000)

Pensioner population (1997): 25.13% (Russia overall: 25.96%)

Percent of population with higher education (1989 census): 7.6% (Russia overall: 11.3%)

Percent of population working in (1997): Industry: 25.9% (Russian average: 23.0%); Agriculture: 17.1% (13.7%); Trade: 10.2% (13.5%); Culture: 13.9% (13.3%)

Average monthly personal income in July 1998: 560.5 new rubles (Russian average: 891.7 new rubles)

Average monthly personal expenses in July 1998: 488.0 new rubles (Russian average: 684.9 new rubles)

Average monthly subsistence requirement in 1998: 333 new rubles (Russian average: 438 new rubles)

Consumer price index (as of July 1998): 88 (Russia overall = 100)

Budgetary revenues (1997): 12,468.7 billion rubles (Russia overall: 433,378.2 billion rubles)

Budgetary expenditures (1997): 12,583.4 billion rubles (Russia overall: 468,111.6 billion rubles)

Industrial production as percentage of all Russian production (Jan.–Aug. 1998): 2.61%

Proportion of loss-making enterprises (as of July 1998): 53.1% (Russia overall: 50.4%)

Number of enterprises which have wage arrears (as of 1 Sept. 1998): 6,090 (4.51% of Russian total)

Agricultural production as percentage of all Russian production (1997): 4.14%

Number of private farms (as of 1 Jan. 1998): 3,066 (1.12% of Russian total)

Capital investment (1997): 11,939 billion rubles (Russia overall: 408,797 billion rubles)

Sources of investment (1997): federal budget: 1.5% (Russian average: 10.2%); regional budget: 11.7% (10.5%); extra-budgetary funds: 86.8% (79.3%)

Foreign investment (1997): 12,025,000 USD (Russia overall: 12,294,734,000 USD)

Number of joint ventures (1997): 132 (0.90% of Russian total)

Fixed capital investment in joint ventures and foreign companies (1997): 213 million rubles (Russia overall: 16,265.4 billion rubles)

Number of small businesses (as of 1 July 1998): 14,200 (1.64% of Russian total)

Number of enterprises privatized in 1997: 44 (1.60% of Russian total), including those which used to be municipal property: 50.0% (Russian average: 66.4%); regional property: 50.0% (20.0%); federal property: 0% (13.6%)

Number of telephones per 100 families (1997): in cities: 40.9 (Russian average: 49.2); in villages: 17.7 (19.8)

Brief Overview

The first mentions of Bashkortostan in written sources occurred in the 9th and 10th centuries. Then, Bashkirs were a nomadic, pagan tribe. By the end of 14th century they were mostly converted to Islam. In 1557, Bashkiria joined the Russian state. Now, the republic's population includes 70 nationalities: Russians make up the largest group, followed by Tatars and Bashkirs.

The republic lies on the border of Europe and Asia and encompasses the eastern end of the Eastern European Plain, part of the Southern Ural Mountains, and some plateaus beyond the Urals. The republic boasts over 70 kinds of mineral resources, including oil, gas, coal, copper, iron, and several precious metals. The extraction and processing of raw materials, particularly oil, gas, and coal, account for most of the republic's industry. Bashkortostan has one of the highest concentrations of chemical, petrochemical, and military industries in the Russian Federation. Fuel and energy make up over 50 percent of its exports, while the chemical industry comprises another 30 percent.

According to a 1998 survey by *Ekspert* magazine, the republic ranked 12th among Russia's 89 regions in terms of investment potential and 38th in terms of investment risk. A 1998 survey by Bank Austria ranked the republic 38th in terms of investment climate. Since 1997, both investment potential and investment risk has grown in the republic—by 8 points (4th biggest increase in the country) and 21 points (8th biggest), respectively.

Electoral History

2000 Presidential Election
Putin: 60.25%
Zyuganov: 28.09%
Yavlinskii: 3.27%
Tuleev: 2.36%
Zhirinovsky: 1.51%
Turnout: 79.46% (Russia overall: 68.64%)

1999 Parliamentary Elections
Fatherland–All Russia: 35.20%
Communist Party of the Russian Federation: 23.88%
Unity: 14.31%
Union of Right Forces: 6.04%
Yabloko: 3.95%
Zhirinovsky Bloc: 3.12%

In single-mandate districts: 4 Fatherland–All Russia, 1 Our Home Is Russia, 1 independent
Turnout: 73.60% (Russia overall: 61.85%)

1997 Republican Presidential Election
Rakhimov (incumbent): 70.2%
Kazakulov: 9.0%
Turnout: 68.1%

1996 Presidential Election
Yeltsin: 34.19%/51.01% (first round/second round)
Zyuganov: 41.86%/43.14%
Lebed: 8.93%
Yavlinskii: 6.78%
Zhirinovsky: 2.87%
Turnout: 79.03%/80.49% (Russia overall: 69.67%/ 68.79%)

1995 Parliamentary Elections
Communist Party of the Russian Federation: 25.52%
Agrarian Party of Russia: 15.42%
Our Home Is Russia: 15.32%
Communists–Workers' Russia: 6.06%
Women of Russia: 5.39%
Liberal Democratic Party of Russia: 4.63%
Yabloko: 4.33%
In single-mandate districts: 2 Communist Party of the Russian Federation, 2 Agrarian Party of Russia, 2 independent
Turnout: 73.81% (Russia overall: 64.37%)

1993 Constitutional Referendum
"Yes"—40.8% "No"—56.3%

1993 Parliamentary Elections
Agrarian Party of Russia: 24.76%
Communist Party of the Russian Federation: 15.08%
Party of Russian Unity and Concord: 13.06%
Liberal Democratic Party of Russia: 12.56%
Women of Russia: 9.23%
Russia's Choice: 8.51%
Democratic Party of Russia: 4.45%
Yabloko: 3.88%
In single-mandate districts: 4 independent, 1 Agrarian Party of Russia, 1 Party of Russian Unity and Concord
From electoral associations: 1 Communist Party of the Russian Federation
Turnout: 63.74% (Russia overall: 54.34%)

1991 Presidential Elections

Yeltsin: 45.93%
Ryzhkov: 23.64%
Zhirinovsky: 7.53%
Tuleev: 6.54%
Makashov: 5.14%
Bakatin: 2.97%
Turnout: 76.13% (Russia overall: 76.66%)

Regional Political Institutions

Executive:
  President, 5-year term
  Murtaza Gubaidullovich Rakhimov, elected June 1998
    Bashkortostan Republic Administration;
    Ul. Tukaeva, 46; Ufa, 450101
    Tel 7(347–2) 50–24–06;
    Fax 7(347–2) 50–02–81
    Federation Council in Moscow:
    7(095) 292–58–23, 926–64–91

Legislative:
  Bicameral
  State Assembly (Gosudarstvennoe Sobranie),
  4-year term, elected March 1999
  Legislative Chamber—150 members
  House of Representatives—40 members
  Joint chairman—Konstantin Tolkachev, elected
  March 1999

Regional Politics

President Maintains Complete Control

Bashkortostan President Murtaza Rakhimov handily won reelection on 14 June 1998. In the fall of 1997 he had announced that he would not run for reelection, but would allow the republic's youth to take the reins of the administration. That statement was most likely a feint designed to encourage a well-spring of popular support for the leader, who subsequently decided to stand for another term. In an interview with *Nezavisimaya gazeta*, Rakhimov claimed that the reason for his reversal was that there was no certainty in Russia's future, and that the existing policies seeking to ensure a secure economic and political future for the country were insufficient (*NG*, 3 June 1998). He claimed that the center was not at all interested in the regions and their political and economic concerns (*NG*, 3 June 1998).

Rakhimov's reelection was allegedly blemished with numerous violations of the electoral law (*BG*, 16 June 1998). Rakhimov received 70 percent of the vote and his only competitor, Rif Kazakulov, took only 9 percent. Kazakulov, who is the forestry minister in Rakhimov's cabinet, made statements suggesting that it would be in Bashkortostan's best interests if Rakhimov won the election, inspiring suspicions that his campaign was planned by the administration so that the election would have two candidates and thus be legal (*BG*, 16 June 1998). Candidates who posed a serious threat to Rakhimov's victory were all expelled from the election on the grounds that the signatures they had collected for nomination were falsified (*MT*, 16 June 1998). A Russian Supreme Court order demanded that two of the candidates be reinstated, but this decree was ignored. The electorate had little knowledge of these events, since the local media offered one-sided support for Rakhimov (*RFE/RL*, 15 June 1998). The independent newspaper and radio station had been shut down, and the station director arrested (*BG*, 16 June 1998). The treatment of the independent media prompted protests in Ufa, involving several thousand people (*RFE/RL*, 15 June 1998).

The candidates barred from the election were Duma deputy Aleksandr Arinin from Our Home Is Russia, former premier of the Baskortostan government Marat Migraziamov, and the well-known banker Rafis Kadyrov. The latter two candidates were considered serious contenders for the position. They accused the president of running Bashkortostan as a personal fiefdom, exploiting the region's oil resources for private gain (*Monitor*, 10 June 1998).

The election had a 68.3 percent voter turnout. The protest vote against all candidates was 17 percent, the highest ever in an election at the regional level (*RT*, 16 June 1998). In Ufa, the capital of Bashkortostan and a region of high sympathy for Duma member Arinin, only 53.4 percent of the voters participated in the election, and of those who did, 34.6 percent voted against both the candidates (*MT*, 16 June 1998). Arinin appealed the election results to the Russian Supreme Court, but they were not overturned.

The results were not the only controversial part of the presidential elections in Bashkortostan. In the fall of 1997 a republican code was passed stating that a candidate could become president only if he spoke Bashkir (although it was not specified how well) (*RT*, 4 June 1998). The titular language is not the official language of the republic, and is spoken by less than 20 percent of the population. Thus, under such a law, the number of potential candidates would be greatly reduced. The Constitutional Court of the Russian Federation found this law in violation of the Russian Constitution, yet the Bashkortostan parliament retained it on the books. However, the implied ramifications of such a law did not play into the dynamic of the most recent elections. Rakhimov was supported by all ethnic groups.

Executive Platform: Strengthening Republican Autonomy

Rakhimov's primary goal since the beginning of his political career has been to gain as much sovereignty as possible for his republic. He has achieved this on many levels, perhaps most successfully by simply ignoring federal policies with which he does not agree. His battle is not for nationalist goals, but simply greater autonomy. Under Yeltsin, the center ignored such defiance in order to maintain stability in a potentially troublesome region. Even after the dismissal of Prime Minister Viktor Chernomyrdin, Rakhimov remained a member of the Our Home Is Russia (NDR) political council (*RT*, 16 June 1998). However, in 1999 he joined the All Russia party founded by Tatarstan's President Mintimer Shaimiev.

Policies: Pro-Business

President Rakhimov plays an active role in adopting most of the republic's policies, and guiding local and regional politics and economics. In his pursuit of sovereignty he has sought to build up republican banks and promote financial autonomy from Moscow. The administration participated in the establishment of the first Russian regional investment and credit bank, Bashkredit bank (*OMRI RRR*, 4 September 1996). In December 1996 Rakhimov signed a decree allowing local companies to pay their debts to the local budget via additional share issues, increasing the government's stake in companies' equity capital (*OMRI RRR*, 18 December 1996). A few months later, in March 1997, the government became further involved in regional business, allocating $3.5 million from the local budget for mortgage lending in the region (*KD*, 19 March 1997). In December 1997 the president reduced taxes on all deliveries of raw materials to petrochemical processing plants by one-third, allowing suppliers to save up to $17 a ton (*KD*, 17 March 1997).

Relationships Between Key Players: Presidential Control over Republican and Local Government

President Rakhimov has direct control over the republic's local government since the republican constitution gives him the power to appoint mayors. This provision goes against the federal constitution, which specifies that local officials must be elected. The Russian Supreme Court ruled the Bashkortostan law on local government unconstitutional in March 1998, a ruling the republic ignored (*KD*, 28 March 1998). Under Yeltsin, Moscow did not take action against the republic, and Rakhimov continued to determine the character of local as well as regional politics.

Elections for Bashkortostan's State Assembly were held in March 1999. No parties gained substantial representation in the assembly's lower chamber, and the Communist Party did not win any seats. The upper chamber is dominated by heads of local administrations and prominent business and social institutions. Since Rakhimov appoints local executives, he has considerable control over the upper chamber.

Ties to Moscow: Compatible Interests

Under Yeltsin, Rakhimov was considered a strong regional leader whose sovereignty campaign was annoying but within the limits of propriety (*NG*, 16 June 1998). On 13 August 1992 Rakhimov, together with Sakha (Yakutia) President Mikhail Nikolaev and Tatarstan President Mintimer Shaimiev, issued a statement charging the federal authorities with "ignoring the legal interests of the republics." The conflict revolved around the Russian Federation's new budget. Rakhimov and other leaders met with Yeltsin on 23 October 1992, forming the President's Council of Republican Leaders (Panorama). Slightly over a year later Tatarstan signed the first power-sharing agreement with Moscow. Bashkortostan, on 3 August 1994, was the third Russian region to sign a similar agreement. Bashkortostan's agreement gave the republic exclusive rights over its property and mineral resources, special privileges regarding foreign trade, and an independent system of legislative and legal institutions.

In the second round of the 1996 presidential elections, Bashkortostan overwhelmingly supported Yeltsin. Rakhimov expressed his loyalty to Yeltsin on several occasions (*KD*, 16 June 1998). President Yeltsin also called Rakhimov and spoke of his support for the republican president during his reelection bid (*NG*, 16 June 1998).

Yet, there were clear limits to Rakhimov's allegiance to Yeltsin. Rakhimov determined his own course of action, following only the presidential decrees with which he agreed. Rakhimov considered Gaidar's government as working against the country's interests and destroying its economy (Panorama). He also opposed Yeltsin's policy toward Chechnya, stating that Russia "should not have tried to hold on to Chechnya by force and organize a mass grave there as an example (*RFE/RL*, 17 January 1996)." In February 1998 Rakhimov tested his power further by claiming the right to appoint republican Supreme Court judges, a right held by the federal government (*KD*, 27 February 1998).

The delicate balance of power between the two presidents is representative of the relationship between the republic and the central government. As the example of Chechnya shows, autonomous republics like Bashkortostan have the potential to destabilize the country. Yeltsin's tolerance for Rakhimov was the sacrifice he made in order to maintain relative peace and order between the republic and the center. It is important for the central government to maintain good relations with the ethnically defined republics, particularly those which expressed their desire for autonomy from the center. As a result, if the republics demonstrated electoral support for the central government, Yeltsin tended to turn his back on their legal violations and challenges for power. It is probably for this reason that the federal government did not probe too deeply into the allegations of fraud in Rakhimov's reelection. Controversial elections of a similar nature in Orel and Mordovia also were not challenged by Yeltsin.

Relations with Other Regions: Popular with Other Regional Executives

President Rakhimov enjoyed good relations with several other presidents and governors of Russia's regions. Leaders who have openly stated their support for him are the President of Ingushetia Ruslan Aushev, President of Kalmykia Kirsan Ilyumzhinov, President of the Komi Republic Yurii Spiridonov, President of Tatarstan Mintimer Shaimiev, Kursk Governor Aleksandr Rutskoi, and Sverdlovsk Governor Eduard Rossel.

Rakhimov is particularly close to Shaimiev. Their relationship is based not only on similar political and economic interests, but also on common approaches to

Moscow. In June 1997 they signed a cooperation treaty with Ingushetia President Ruslan Aushev (*EWI RRR*, 19 June 1997). On 28 August 1997 Rakhimov and Shaimiev signed an agreement to more closely integrate the economies of their respective republics. Specifically, the economic cooperation would match Tatarstan's oil with Bashkir refining facilities (*EWI RRR*, 4 September 1997). The two republics are complementary because Tatarstan produces oil but has no refining facilities, while Bashkortostan has surplus refining capabilities.

Bashkortostan is a member of the Urals Regional Association, headed by Sverdlovsk Governor Eduard Rossel. The other members of the association are Udmurtia; Komi-Permyak AO; and Kurgan, Orenburg, Perm, Sverdlovsk, and Chelyabinsk oblasts.

Foreign Relations: Big Stick in Foreign Contacts

Bashkortostan has rather extensive foreign economic relations. Germany is the republic's primary trading partner and is also involved in 20 joint venture projects in the region. In November 1996 Deutsche Bank agreed to open a credit line to Bashkreditbank to finance local companies' long-term export-import operations, primarily to help Bashkir enterprises purchase German manufactured equipment and technology (*KD*, 30 November 1996).

Bashkortostan has signed trade cooperation agreements with the governments of Hungary, Bulgaria, Poland, Romania, Finland, Austria, Saxony, Spain, Turkey, India, China, France, Slovakia, Thailand, and the Canadian province of Alberta, among others (*VU*, 14 October 1997). Bashkortostan trades with 71 different countries, and exports contribute to one-fifth of the republic's gross domestic product. Sixty percent of the exports are mineral products (*VU*, 14 October 1997).

Bashkortostan has a representative office in Austria, and would like to open others but believes that it could not handle the financial responsibility (*EWI RRR*, 18 September 1997). Therefore, Rakhimov has granted representative authority to Bashkir companies that have foreign offices. These include Salavatnefteorgsintez in China and Bashneftekhim in Ukraine. A similar tactic may be used in India, with which Bashkortostan signed a cooperation treaty in 1995.

The federal government has tried to impose greater control over the regions' foreign dealings. Rakhimov has opposed these attempts as too restrictive in terms of foreign policy divisions between the center and the regions (*EWI RRR*, 24 April 1997).

Murtaza Gubaidullovich Rakhimov

7 February 1934—Born in the village Tavakanovo in the Kugarchinsk raion of Bashkortostan

1952–1956—Student at the Ufa Oil Technical School

1956–1960—Operator at Ufa's Order of Lenin oil processing factory

1964—Graduated from the Ufa Oil Institute via correspondence, as an engineer-technician

1960–1976—Unit chief, deputy shop chief, deputy factory chief, deputy to the senior engineer for starting up new production at Ufa's 22nd Congress of the CPSU oil processing factory

1974—Joined the CPSU

1976–1978—Senior chemist, deputy senior engineer

1978–1986—Senior Engineer

1986–1990—Director of Ufa's 22nd Congress of the CPSU oil processing factory

1989–1991—Member of the USSR Congress of People's Deputies and the Supreme Soviet

4 March 1990—Elected to the Supreme Soviet of Bashkortostan Autonomous Soviet Socialist Republic, and on 6 April was chosen as chairman

1990–1993—Chairman of the Bashkortostan Supreme Soviet

11 October 1990—Declared Bashkir state sovereignty

August 1991—Left the Communist Party

12 December 1993—Elected president of Bashkortostan, also elected to the Federation Council, and serves as head of the Bashkortostan Presidential Council and the Bashkortostan Security Council

January 1994–January 1996—Member of the Federation Council's committee on federation affairs, agreements, and regional politics

1994—Completed a pilgrimage to Mecca in a government delegation

1995—Joined Our Home Is Russia Council

January 1996—Became a member of the Federation Council by appointment and joined the Committee on Federal Issues, the Federation Treaty, and Regional Issues

March 1997—Joined the federal commission on problems in Chechnya

14 June 1998—Reelected president of the Republic of Bashkortostan

---

Attitudes Toward Business: Development Not on Par with Economic Needs

Although Rakhimov claims to be interested in further developing Bashkortostan's mineral resources and improving its oil processing industry, the projects that have materialized are marginal in comparison to the region's potential and need for restructuring. In 1997 the French engineering company Technip offered a $190 million technical reconstruction loan to two of the republic's oil processing plants—Ufaneftekhim and Novo-Ufimskii (*EWI RRR*, 24 April 1997). These were two of the enterprises that took advantage of Rakhimov's December 1996 policy of repaying local debts with additional share issues.

In May 1998 Bashkortostan signed an agreement with LUKoil stating that the company would prioritize investment in the republic (*Izvestiya*, 27 May 1998). LUKoil will help modernize the republic's refineries and supply them with oil.

In fall 1998 Rakhimov combined five major energy sector companies into the Bashkir Fuel Company, under his control. This measure was taken even though Bashkortostan owned controlling stakes only in two of the firms—Bashkir Petrochemical Company and Bashneft. The other three companies are Bashkirenergo, Ural-Siberian Pipeline, and Uraltransnefteprodukt. The Unified Energy System (EES), controlled by Anatolii Chubais, owns 21.3 percent of Bashkirenergo and has long been in confrontation with the regional authorities.

In late 1996 President Rakhimov issued a decree aimed at reducing the number of cash transactions in Bashkortostan and increasing the use of bank cards (*EWI RRR*, 8 May 1997). This decree had far-reaching results. A Republican Processing Center was established, the capital for which was provided by Moscow's International Industrial Bank (Mezhprombank) and the Bahkortostan administration. Bashkir banks would like to limit the influence of Mezhprombank and have thus agreed to create a single payments system (*EWI RRR*, 8 May 1997). The primary bank is Bashkreditbank, which issues the Bashcard. The other banks, Sotsinvestbank, Agroprombank Bashkiriya, Bashinvestbank, and Bashekonombank, issue and service the cards at their 70 local branches (*EWI RRR*, 8 May 1997).

Internet Sites in the Region

http://bashinform.ru/win/

This website provides an in-depth look into a wide variety of the republic's offerings. One of the most impressive features is a who's who list supplying contact, biographical, and other information for 628 of the region's leaders. This site also provides links to an impressive list of regional websites including those of companies and educational institutions.

http://www.bashstat.ru/

The website of the Bashkir branch of Goskomstat provides extensive information about the republic and its neighbors.

http://www.bashnet.ru/

Extensive information about the republic.

BELGOROD OBLAST

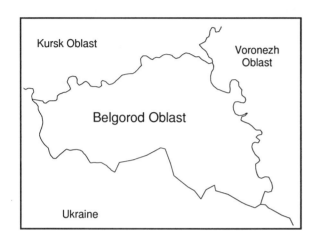

Territory: 27,100 km²
Population (as of 1 January 1998):
1,484,000
Distance from Moscow: 695 km

Major Cities:
Belgorod, *capital* (pop. 332,800)
Staryi Oskol (208,200)
Gubkin (85,100)
Shebekino (46,100)
Alekseevka (38,500)
Valuiki (35,100)

Basic Facts

Population (as of 1 Jan. 1998): 1,484,000 (1.0% of Russian total)

Ethnic breakdown (1989 census): Russians 92.9%, Ukrainians 5.5%

Urban population (as of 1 Jan. 1998): 65.5% (Russia overall: 73.1%)

Student population (as of 1 Sept. 1997): 194 per 10,000 (Russia overall: 208/10,000)

Pensioner population (1997): 29.38% (Russia overall: 25.96%)

Percent of population with higher education (1989 census): 8.4% (Russia overall: 11.3%)

Percent of population working in (1997): Industry: 22.5% (Russian average: 23.0%); Agriculture: 19.1% (13.7%); Trade: 11.4% (13.5%); Culture: 12.0% (13.3%)

Average monthly personal income in July 1998: 656.6 new rubles (Russian average: 891.7 new rubles)

Average monthly personal expenses in July 1998: 474.3 new rubles (Russian average: 684.9 new rubles)

Average monthly subsistence requirement in 1998: 329 new rubles (Russian average: 438 new rubles)

Consumer price index (as of July 1998): 93 (Russia overall = 100)

Budgetary revenues (1997): 2,405.1 billion rubles (Russia overall: 433,378.2 billion rubles)

Budgetary expenditures (1997): 2,457.5 billion rubles (Russia overall: 468,111.6 billion rubles)

Industrial production as percentage of all Russian production (Jan.–Aug. 1998): 0.97%

Proportion of loss-making enterprises (as of July 1998): 41.3% (Russia overall: 50.4%)

Number of enterprises which have wage arrears (as of 1 Sept. 1998): 2,058 (1.52% of Russian total)

Agricultural production as percentage of all Russian production (1997): 1.6%

Number of private farms (as of 1 Jan. 1998): 1,620 (0.59% of Russian total)

Capital investment (1997): 3,683.1 billion rubles (Russia overall: 408,797 billion rubles)

Sources of investment (1997): federal budget: 5.8% (Russian average: 10.2%); regional budget: 15.1% (10.5%); extra-budgetary funds: 79.1% (79.3%)

Foreign investment (1997): 122,048,000 USD (Russia overall: 12,294,734,000 USD)

Number of joint ventures (1997): 144 (0.98% of Russian total)

Fixed capital investment in joint ventures and foreign companies (1997): 19,304 million rubles (Russia overall: 16,265.4 billion rubles)

Number of small businesses (as of 1 July 1998): 6,500 (0.45% of Russian total)

Number of enterprises privatized in 1997: 38 (1.39% of Russian total), including those which used to be municipal property: 73.6% (Russian average: 66.4%); regional property: 13.2% (20.0%); federal property: 13.2% (13.6%)

Number of telephones per 100 families (1997): in cities: 49.9 (Russian average: 49.2); in villages: 19.0 (19.8)

Brief Overview

Belgorod Oblast is located in southwestern Russia in the basin of the Vorskla, Severskii Donets, and Oskol rivers. It borders Kursk and Voronezh oblasts and Ukraine. The administrative center, Belgorod city, was founded in 1593 as a fortress against Tatar attacks and is now an important industrial center.

Once covered by forest-steppe, the rich soils (one third of which are black-earth soils) are extensively used for agriculture—grain, sugar beets, sunflower seeds, and fruit being the main crops. Some of the local soil has suffered, however, from radioactive contamination as a result of the 1986 accident at the Chernobyl nuclear power station.

The oblast's economy is based on the huge deposits of iron ore in the Kursk Magnetic Anomaly, which accounts for 40 percent of all iron reserves in Russia. The site, located near Belgorod city, holds approximately 40 billion tons of ore that has more iron content (56–66 percent) and fewer harmful by-products than any other in Europe or Russia. The oblast's territory is also rich in other mineral resources, such as chalk, sand, and clay, as well as some rare and precious metals. Over half of the regional industrial product comes from ferrous metallurgy, concentrated at the Lebedinskii Iron Ore Works at Staryi Oskol, followed by food processing (16%), energy generation (11%), and machine-building (9.6%).

Until recently, the oblast was a favorable place to invest. Companies from Panama, Yugoslavia, Great Britain, and Bulgaria established joint ventures there. However, according to a 1998 survey by *Ekspert* magazine, since 1997 the oblast had seen almost the largest decline of investment potential in Russia—by 11 points—and ranked 20th among Russia's 89 regions in terms of investment potential and 3rd in terms of investment risk. A 1998 survey by Bank Austria ranked the oblast 16th in terms of investment climate.

Electoral History

2000 Presidential Election
Putin: 47.54%
Zyuganov: 39.78%
Yavlinskii: 3.42%
Zhirinovsky: 2.70%
Tuleev: 1.51%
Turnout: 73.53% (Russia overall: 68.64%)

1999 Parliamentary Elections
Unity: 27.01%
Communist Party of the Russian Federation: 27.86%
Fatherland–All Russia: 11.07%
Zhirinovsky Bloc: 5.86%
Union of Right Forces: 4.93%
Yabloko: 4.20%
In single-mandate districts: 2 independent
Turnout: 66.83% (Russia overall: 61.85%)

1999 Gubernatorial Election
Savchenko (incumbent): 53.46%
Beshmelnitsyn: 19.71%
Zhirinovsky (LDPR): 17.72%
Turnout: 71.33%

1996 Presidential Election
Zyuganov: 46.35%/58.57% (first round/second round)
Yeltsin: 22.87%/36.28%
Lebed: 16.95%
Yavlinskii: 5.75%
Zhirinovsky: 4.31%
Turnout: 75.71%/75.36% (Russia overall: 69.67%/ 68.79%)

1995 Parliamentary Elections
Communist Party of the Russian Federation: 31.59%
Liberal Democratic Party of Russia: 14.60%
Our Home Is Russia: 6.69%
Agrarian Party of Russia: 5.63%
Communists–Workers' Russia: 4.91%
Women of Russia: 4.34%
Yabloko: 3.79%
In single-mandate districts: 1 Communist Party of the Russian Federation, 1 Power to the People
Turnout: 75.49% (Russia overall: 64.37%)

1993 Constitutional Referendum
"Yes"—44.2% "No"—54.1%

1993 Parliamentary Elections
Liberal Democratic Party of Russia: 37.07%
Communist Party of the Russian Federation: 15.90%
Agrarian Party of Russia: 10.23%
Russia's Choice: 10.02%
Women of Russia: 7.12%
Party of Russian Unity and Concord: 4.70%
Democratic Party of Russia: 4.64%
Yabloko: 4.57%
In single-mandate districts: 2 independent
Turnout: 67.03% (Russia overall: 54.34%)

1991 Presidential Election

Yeltsin: 50.08%

Ryzhkov: 21.91%

Zhirinovsky: 10.44%

Tuleev: 5.25%

Makashov: 5.08%

Bakatin: 2.99%

Turnout: 85.43% (Russia overall: 76.66%)

Regional Political Institutions

Executive:

    Governor, 4-year term

    Yevgenii Stepanovich Savchenko, elected

    December 1995, June 1999

        Belgorod Oblast Administration,

        Ploshchad Revolyutsii, 4; Belgorod, 308005

        Tel 7(072–2) 22–42–47, 22–45–77;

        Fax 7(072–2) 22–33–43

        Federation Council in Moscow:

        7(095) 292–57–27, 926–65–40

        Fax: 7(095) 292–64–03

Legislative:

    Unicameral

    Oblast Duma—35 members, 4-year term,

    elected October 1997

    Chairman—Anatolii Yakovlevich Zelikov,

    elected November 1997

Regional Politics

Pragmatic Yeltsin Appointee

Despite the leftist politics of his region, Yevgenii Savchenko is a pragmatic Yeltsin appointee who won election as governor in 1995. Yeltsin only allowed a handful of governors to run at that time, the crucial run-up to the 1996 presidential elections. These governors had to be loyal to the president and likely to win a popular mandate from their constituents.

By 1999, however, Savchenko's plummeting popularity prompted him to move up Belgorod's gubernatorial elections from December to 30 May, giving his opponents little time for campaigning and thus ensuring his reelection. Savchenko's successful reelection convinced many other governors that they should move up their elections as well in order to ensure victory. As a result, in 1999, the governors of Novgorod, Tomsk, and Omsk also moved up their elections.

Changing the rules of the game like this is definitely a dangerous precedent for Russian democracy.

Savchenko was educated as an agronomist and spent his early career working in Belgorod's agricultural sector. In 1983, when he was 33, he began working his way up the party ladder, serving both at home and in Moscow, as was typical for party functionaries. He spent the early 1990s consulting for the Russian Agriculture Ministry and then for private firms in Moscow.

Executive Platform: Strong State Influence

Savchenko supports a strong role for the state in social development. He has spoken out against the monetarist policies of the federal government and particularly criticizes the liberalization of foreign trade and the increase in foreign and domestic debt. The governor denounced the introduction of the ruble corridor in 1995 as hurting Belgorod exporters. He supports market reforms in principle, but criticizes the forced disbanding of collective farms. Savchenko also backs the integration of industrial and agricultural enterprises into the so-called APK (agro-industrial complex) entities.

In campaigning for reelection in 1999, Savchenko listed maintaining political stability in the region as one of his main accomplishments during his first term as governor. He asserted that this stability has enabled the region to work at solving social and economic problems. Savchenko also reasserted his support for increasing state regulation of the economy (*RF*, no. 9, 1999).

Savchenko became a member of the council of Our Home Is Russia (NDR) in May 1995. In 1999 he joined the All Russia regional party.

Policies: Anti-Reform

Savchenko is pursuing a policy of regional autarky. In July 1994 he tried to limit the sales of goods produced in Belgorod beyond the region's borders in order to satisfy the needs of the region's population with domestic goods, rather than products imported from abroad. In late 1996 and early 1997 Savchenko issued several decrees to further this goal, but these edicts were later ruled unconstitutional. One of them prohibited the import of American chicken ("Bush legs"). The others introduced special procedures requiring all products from outside Belgorod Oblast to undergo extensive quality control checks (*Izvestiya*, 4 January 1997). As a result of Savchenko's efforts, imported food products have not exceeded 10 percent of the oblast's total consumption.

Savchenko has also made several attempts to put

the oblast's industry under his personal control. In July 1996, for instance, he declared a "regional order" in the oblast and then issued several mandatory instructions to enterprises and organizations, regardless of whether they were privately or state owned (*Trud*, 1 July 1996).

In January 1997, Savchenko began to crack down on illegal alcohol imports into Belgorod so that the oblast could collect taxes on legalized trade.

Despite these anti-reform measures, Belgorod was one of the first oblasts to implement housing reform. In the first five years of the reform, 9,736 homes were built from the housing construction fund and an average of 9 families per week were moving into new homes. Additionally, the number of homes equipped with natural gas has risen 4.5 times, and 90 percent of all village houses are now outfitted (*RF*, no. 9, 1999). When housing reform was fashionable in the early part of 1998, under First Deputy Prime Minister Boris Nemtsov, Savchenko declared that by 2003 every resident of Belgorod would pay for 100 percent of their municipal services.

Belgorod is also one of the few regions in Russia to pass laws on veterans and the handicapped, which grant benefits to one-fifth of the oblast's population (*RF*, no. 9, 1999). Savchenko also boasted that Belgorod is one of only four regions that pays children's benefits on time.

Relationships Between Key Players

The chairman of the oblast Duma is Anatolii Zelikov, who was elected to the position after the October 1997 elections. In October 1997, Communists won 13 of 35 seats in the elections to the Belgorod Oblast Duma, increasing their representation five times (*EWI RRR*, 16 October 1997). Independents won the rest of the seats.

Taxes from the Lebedinskii Iron Ore Works and the Oskolskii Electro-Metallurgical Plant make up 70 percent of the revenue for the Oblast (*Izvestiya*, 30 April 1998). Governor Savchenko has tried to influence policy at the plants, with little success (see Attitudes Toward Business).

Ties to Moscow

Yeltsin appointed Savchenko as governor in October 1993. At the time, Savchenko was loyal to Yeltsin and sufficiently popular in his district that Yeltsin allowed him to run for governor in December 1995. Only a select few governors were allowed to stand for popular election prior to the presidential elections in June 1996.

Savchenko's loyalty to Yeltsin was well received in the federal government. Former Russian Prime Minister Sergei Stepashin asked Savchenko to join his cabinet as deputy prime minister for agriculture, but Savchenko declined, citing his desire to continue working in Belgorod.

Relations with Other Regions

Belgorod's leadership is a part of the Black Earth Association, headed by Orel Governor and Federation Council Speaker Yegor Stroev, which also includes Voronezh, Belgorod, Kursk, Lipetsk, Orel, and Tambov oblasts.

Foreign Relations: Proponent of Slavic Unity

Savchenko supports a strong union among Russia, Ukraine, and Belarus. He has said that "the border between Russian and Ukraine is a national disgrace" (*RF*, no. 9, 1999). In 1995 Savchenko proposed that the presidents of Russia, Ukraine, and Belarus meet in Belgorod to discuss ways to build greater unity among the Slavic peoples (*OMRI RRR*, 6 March 1997). Savchenko and Belgorod have joined a group bringing together leaders from several southern Russian regions and Ukrainian regions, including the Russian oblasts Kursk and Voronezh, and Lugansk, Kharkov, and Sumsk oblasts in Ukraine.

There are strong ties between Belgorod Oblast and Belarus. Belarusan officials frequently visit the oblast's administration. Belgorod exports metallurgical and agricultural products to Belarus. Belarus, in turn, sends Belgorod agricultural machinery.

Attitudes Toward Business: Metal Is Key

Sitting on top of Belgorod's enormous resources, the Lebedinskii Iron Ore Works (LGOK) at Staryi Oskol supplies about a quarter of Russia's iron-ore concentrate and pellets and is one of Europe's largest metals plants. The plant has been the subject of a ferocious ownership battle for several years. In 1997 it changed hands four times. The conflict began in 1994 when one of LGOK's major shareholders, Rossiiskii Kredit bank (at that point owning 23.3 percent of the stock), disagreed over policy matters with Director Anatolii Kalashnikov (*Izvestiya*, 31 October 1997; *MT*, 28 October 1997). The bellicose director used local police to kick the shareholders off the plant's premises, and fired workers who sold their shares to the bank when the latter attempted to beef up its share to the 25 percent necessary for influencing company poli-

Yevgenii Stepanovich Savchenko

8 April 1950—Born in Krasnaya Yaruga, Belgorod Oblast

1969—Graduated from the Starooskolskii Technical College with major geophysics

1976—Graduated from the Timiryazev Academy of Agriculture in Moscow, with a degree in agronomy

1976–78—Chief Agronomist of Sverdlov Collective Farm in Belgorod Oblast

1978–79—Senior Agronomist in the Rakityan Raion Ispolkom

1979–83—Director of an elite seed farm

1983–85—Headed Agriculture Administration in Rakityan region

1985–88—First Secretary of the Shebekino CPSU City Committee

1988–89—Instructor of the CPSU Central Committee, Moscow

1989–90—Deputy Chairman of the Belgorod Oblast Executive Committee (Ispolkom)

1991–92—General director of the firm Russian Seeds (Moscow)

1992–93—Worked in the Ministry of Agriculture in Moscow

October 1993—Appointed Belgorod governor by Yeltsin

12 May 1995—Joined NDR council

17 December 1995—Elected Belgorod governor

January 1996—Joined Federation Council, serves as chairman of the Committee on Agricultural Policy

1996—Awarded State Medal of Honor

30 May 1999—Reelected governor of Belgorod

cies. When the bank persisted in its efforts, Kalashnikov illegally issued 100 million more shares, diluting the despised bank's holdings to a mere 5 percent.

Governor Savchenko saw this conflict as an opportunity and offered to serve as a mediator in April 1997. Kalashnikov immediately turned against him (even though he had helped to finance Savchenko's election campaign), but this time law-enforcement agencies were not on his side. They began harassing him the way they used to harass his enemies, while the regional arbitration court declared the 100-million-share issue illegal and confiscated 15 percent of the stock that Kalashnikov had personally bought. Ultimately, the governor ended up with 15 percent of LGOK's shares, which, combined with Rossiiskii Kredit's 36 percent, became enough to fire Kalashnikov and replace him with Deputy Governor Nikolai Kalinin at a 2 November shareholders' meeting (*Segodnya*, 4 November 1997).

Once Rossiiskii Kredit gained control of the plant, it raised prices for the plant's output of unfinished steel products. The price hike caused the nearby Oskolskii Electro-Metallurgical Plant, which relies heavily on Lebedinskii products as inputs, to begin buying up Lebedinskii stock. The battle grew heated by the summer of 1998, because at that point Rossiiskii Kredit held 46 percent of the stock and Oskolskii owned 41 percent. The federal government was set to auction off a decisive ten percent stake, but in July the sale was postponed indefinitely as the actual ownership of the stake was in dispute.

Desperate for cash in the weeks before 17 August 1998, Rossiiskii Kredit sold its stake to Nakosta AG (Switzerland), a partner of Oskolskii, and the team gained complete control of Lebedinskii. Whether Nakosta and the Oskolskii plant have been able work effectively together remains unclear. Certainly, the raging ownership battles at Lebedinskii have taken their toll, and profits in 1998 were significantly lower than in the previous year. Production dropped 2.5 percent in the first eight months of 1998, reflecting slumping domestic consumption, reduced prices internationally, and the adoption of protectionist measures in key export markets. The conflicts have also postponed a $1 billion investment program that would allow Lebedinskii to build a hot briquetting iron plant whose products are in great demand internationally. Partly as a result of the conflict, Belgorod showed one of the greatest drops in *Ekspert*'s 1998 annual survey of regional investment potential.

The Oskolskii plant is a key exporter which sends 70 percent of its product abroad. Its production processes and product line are comparable to advanced US mini-mills. Since 1996 it has been upgrading its equipment with help from Siemens and the EBRD.

BRYANSK OBLAST

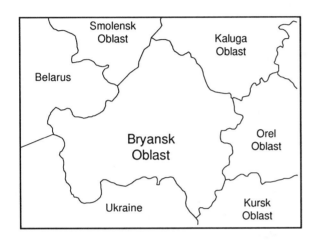

Territory: 34,900 km²
Population (as of 1 January 1998):
1,465,000
Distance from Moscow: 379 km

Major Cities:
Bryansk, *capital* (pop. 459,000)
Klintsy (69,000)
Novozybkov (43,400)
Dyadkovo (34,700)

Basic Facts

Population (as of 1 Jan. 1998): 1,465,000 (1.00% of Russian total)

Ethnic breakdown (1989 census): Russians 96.0%, Ukrainians 1.8%, Belarusans 0.8%

Urban population (as of 1 Jan. 1998): 68.6% (Russia overall: 73.1%)

Student population (as of 1 Sept. 1997): 115 per 10,000 (Russia overall: 208/10,000)

Pensioner population (1997): 30.65% (Russia overall: 25.96%)

Percent of population with higher education (1989 census): 7.7% (Russia overall: 11.3%)

Percent of population working in (1997): Industry: 23.6% (Russian average: 23.0%); Agriculture: 14.6% (13.7%); Trade: 15.5% (13.5%); Culture: 12.5% (13.3%)

Average monthly personal income in July 1998: 536.6 new rubles (Russian average: 891.7 new rubles)

Average monthly personal expenses in July 1998: 372.3 new rubles (Russian average: 684.9 new rubles)

Average monthly subsistence requirement in 1998: 330 new rubles (Russian average: 438 new rubles)

Consumer price index (as of July 1998): 86 (Russia overall = 100)

Budgetary revenues (1997): 1,765.8 billion rubles (Russia overall: 433,378.2 billion rubles)

Budgetary expenditures (1997): 1,984.8 billion rubles (Russia overall: 468,111.6 billion rubles)

Industrial production as percentage of all Russian production (Jan.–Aug. 1998): 0.32%

Proportion of loss-making enterprises (as of July 1998): 53.6% (Russia overall: 50.4%)

Number of enterprises which have wage arrears (as of 1 Sept. 1998): 4,520 (3.34% of Russian total)

Agricultural production as percentage of all Russian production (1997): 1.26%

Number of private farms (as of 1 Jan. 1998): 1,236 (0.45% of Russian total)

Capital investment (1997): 947.9 billion rubles (Russia overall: 408,797 billion rubles)

Sources of investment (1997): federal budget: 21.9% (Russian average: 10.2%); regional budget: 8.0% (10.5%); extra-budgetary funds: 70.1% (79.3%)

Foreign investment (1997): 1,821,000 USD (Russia overall: 12,294,734,000 USD)

Number of joint ventures (1997): 82 (0.01% of Russian total)

Fixed capital investment in joint ventures and foreign companies (1997): 2,133 million rubles (Russia overall: 16,265.4 billion rubles)

Number of small businesses (as of 1 July 1998): 3,700 (0.43% of Russian total)

Number of enterprises privatized in 1997: 12 (0.44% of Russian total), including those which used to be municipal property: 58.3% (Russian average: 66.4%); regional property: 0% (20.0%); federal property: 41.7% (13.6%)

Number of telephones per 100 families (1997): in cities: 32.8 (Russian average: 49.2); in villages: 11.3 (19.8)

Brief Overview

Bryansk Oblast is located in the broad basin of the Desna River and borders Smolensk, Kaluga, Orel, and Kursk oblasts; Belarus; and Ukraine. Local soil was badly contaminated by the 1986 accident at the Chernobyl nuclear power station and much of the land cannot be cultivated.

The oblast is one of the poorest in the country in terms of mineral resources, though it has some reserves of peat and materials for the construction, glass, and chemical industries. The oblast is one of the largest machine-building centers in Central Russia, with most of the enterprises concentrated around the city of Bryansk. Many of these enterprises used to belong to the defense industry, which has shrunk significantly in recent years, further damaging the oblast's economic situation.

Nevertheless, the oblast is a significant producer of machines and equipment for various industries, some of which are exported. Although the oblast passed investment legislation, it has attracted few international investors. The oblast ranked 39th among Russia's 89 regions in terms of investment potential and 68th in terms of investment risk, according to a 1998 survey by *Ekspert* magazine. A 1998 survey by Bank Austria ranked the oblast 63rd in terms of investment climate.

Electoral History

2000 Presidential Election
Zyuganov: 45.90%
Putin: 42.97%
Zhirinovsky: 3.17%
Yavlinskii: 2.20%
Tuleev: 1.54%
Turnout: 70.41% (Russia overall: 68.64%)

1999 Parliamentary Elections
Communist Party of the Russian Federation: 40.78%
Unity: 25.23%
Zhirinovsky Bloc: 7.34%
Union of Right Forces: 4.97%
Fatherland–All Russia: 4.32%
Yabloko: 2.53%
In single-mandate districts: 2 Communist Party of the Russian Federation
Turnout: 63.77% (Russia overall: 61.85%)

1996 Gubernatorial Election
Lodkin (State Duma deputy, NPSR): 54.54%

Semernev (incumbent): 25.81%
Barabanov (former governor, 1991–93, 1995–96): 5.57%
Simutin: 4.12%
Fedorov (oblast legislature deputy): 2.07%
Yakovlev: 1.82%
Khramchenkov (LDPR): 0.57%
Zuikov: 0.48%
Turnout: 50.61%

1996 Presidential Election
Zyuganov: 49.58%/59.23% (first round/second round)
Yeltsin: 26.23%/36.29%
Lebed: 11.60%
Zhirinovsky: 5.09%
Yavlinskii: 3.48%
Turnout: 72.20%/70.86% (Russia overall: 69.67%/ 68.79%)

1995 Parliamentary Elections
Communist Party of the Russian Federation: 35.44%
Liberal Democratic Party of Russia: 19.82%
Our Home Is Russia: 5.91%
Communists–Workers' Russia: 4.15%
Forward, Russia: 3.17%
Women of Russia: 2.66%
Party of Workers' Self-Government: 2.58%
Yabloko: 2.40%
In single-mandate districts: 2 Communist Party of the Russian Federation
Turnout: 69.37% (Russia overall: 64.37%)

1993 Constitutional Referendum
"Yes"—41.6% "No"—56.6%

1993 Parliamentary Elections
Liberal Democratic Party of Russia: 27.23%
Communist Party of the Russian Federation: 20.18%
Russia's Choice: 12.57%
Agrarian Party of Russia: 10.80%
Women of Russia: 7.66%
Democratic Party of Russia: 5.70%
Party of Russian Unity and Concord: 4.86%
Yabloko: 4.46%
In single-mandate districts: 1 Agrarian Party of Russia, 1 Communist Party of the Russian Federation
From electoral associations: 1 Agrarian Party of Russia
Turnout: 65.89% (Russia overall: 54.34%)

1991 Presidential Election
Yeltsin: 53.78%
Ryzhkov: 19.31%
Zhirinovsky: 9.41%
Tuleev: 5.75%
Makashov: 4.53%
Bakatin: 3.72%
Turnout: 81.89% (Russia overall: 76.66%)

Regional Political Institutions

Executive:
Governor, 4-year term
Yurii Yevgenevich Lodkin, elected December 1996
Leninskii Prospekt, 33; Bryansk, 241002
Tel 7(083–2) 46–26–11;
Fax 7(083–2) 41–38–95
Federation Council in Moscow:
7(095) 292–58–02, 926–64–47

Legislative:
Unicameral
Oblast Duma—50 members, 4–year term, elected December 1996 and March 1997
Chairman—Stepan Nikolaevich Ponasov, elected October 1995, December 1996

Regional Politics

Popular Yeltsin Opponent

Yurii Lodkin is the fourth governor to head the Bryansk administration since Yeltsin established the office in 1991 (www.admin.bryansk.ru). He is the second of the four governors to hold this position twice. Vladimir Barabanov was the initial Yeltsin appointee, but Lodkin defeated him in unusual elections held in April 1993. Yeltsin removed Lodkin from this elected position by presidential decree in September 1993 because the governor backed the Supreme Soviet in its battle with the president. Vladimir Karpov replaced Lodkin after his dismissal, but fell to Yeltsin's ax in the summer of 1995. At that point, Yeltsin returned Barabanov to office. But a year later, Yeltsin dismissed Barabanov and replaced him with Aleksandr Semernev (*OMRI RRR*, 27 November 1996). Lodkin defeated Semernev in the election held on 8 December 1996 (in which Barabanov also participated) by a 53—26 percent margin, achieving a second gubernatorial victory. Of the four governors who have served in Bryansk,

Lodkin is the only one to have attained the post via popular elections, a feat he accomplished twice.

Executive Platform: Communist

Lodkin is a traditional Communist both politically and economically, and he had the support of Gennadii Zyuganov and the KPRF in his second gubernatorial campaign. The governor's rhetoric emphasizes the ideals of social justice and the possibility of genuinely carrying out populist economic reforms (NNS). Lodkin has made health care and education priorities. He spoke out against Yeltsin's reforms for having driven up prices, impoverished large numbers of people, increased unemployment, destroyed the country's collective farms, reduced industrial output, failed to reorient unwanted defense enterprises, and sold off the state's riches (*NNS*).

The governor claims that the most important issue is the region's struggling economy and its impact on social services and the population's living standards. Lodkin prioritizes food processing and light industry over heavy industry, which he believes it is impossible to support in the country's currently poor economic conditions (*OMRI RRR*, 27 November 1996). In terms of agricultural policy, Lodkin wants to create a retail network for foodstuffs and goods that is not reliant on middlemen, who traditionally take a large share of the profits. He believes that tax and credit policies should benefit productive manufacturing firms and agricultural enterprises.

Policies: Unsuccessful Economic Approaches

Lodkin has not been successful in pulling Bryansk out of its economic turmoil. The oblast lacks the resources necessary to help support regional industry. Agricultural production has decreased, unemployment has increased, and the volume of trade is declining. Economic conditions in Bryansk are considerably worse than in the oblast's neighboring Communist regions. Essentially, for the Bryansk administration, it has been easier to criticize Moscow than to implement a successful economic program (*EWI RRR*, 9 April 1998).

The oblast's 1999 budget assumed an 11 percent budget deficit, which is perhaps a slight improvement over the oblast's 1998 budget which had a nearly 30 percent planned deficit. Nevertheless, the gain is only superficial since the level of revenue actually collected is a third less than planned.

Bryansk citizens have expressed dissatisfaction with Lodkin's performance, claiming that he has failed to deliver the social reforms promised in his campaign, specifically in regard to wage arrears in the social service sector (Aleksandr Levinskii, "Uchastniki aktsii protesta kritikovali ne tol'ko Moskvu no i gubernatora-kommunista," unpublished manuscript). Lodkin became particularly unpopular among teachers and other workers in the social sphere when, in 1997, he approved an increase in the salaries of oblast bureaucrats.

Lodkin has also been accused of violating the freedom of the press by authorizing the removal of Vladimir Pronin, editor-in-chief of the popular weekly newspaper *BK-Fakt*. Pronin was dismissed for "playing political games," but the real controversy involved several anti-administration articles that he had published. Lodkin claimed that Pronin was acting on behalf of anti-administration interests, based locally and in Moscow (*EWI RRR*, 30 April 1998).

Relationships Between Key Players: Communist Party Dominance

The Communist Party apparatus (KPRF Obkom) is heavily integrated into the power structures and decision-making apparatus. (This analysis is taken from Jean-Charles Lallemand, "Bryansk and Smolensk: Two Rather Different 'Red Belt' Regions," *EWI RRR*, 22 July 1999.) Bryansk boasts no noticeably prosperous companies. Therefore, the new business elite, as a social group, has less influence than in nearby Smolensk. Here, the KPRF Obkom sometimes serves as a referee in political disputes between the regional and municipal executive authorities. The Communists and their allies occupy two-thirds of the seats in the Oblast Duma, 28 of 32 seats in the Bryansk City Council, and similar majorities in the other district (raion) soviets. The KPRF Obkom claims to have around 10,000 permanent members, many more than other political organizations (5,000 for Zhirinovsky's party, 3,500 for Fatherland, and 200–400 for each of the "pro-reform" organizations). The decision-making power among Bryansk's ruling elite is divided according to a triangle: Governor Lodkin at the top; Aleksandr Shulga, the First Secretary of the KPRF obkom and deputy chairman of the oblast assembly; and Aleksandr Blakitny, the Bryansk City Council chairman.

Since March 1999, regional leaders have effectively abolished the concept of local self-government in the region. All elected mayors and rural leaders have been removed from office by local soviets (councils), which have themselves arbitrarily appointed new, or sometimes confirmed former, leaders. The oblast administration, the KPRF obkom, and the local soviets claimed that they had to take these steps in order to reduce the amount of money spent on elections. The appointment of a new Bryansk mayor (a member of the KPRF who directed the Bryansk branch of the Rossiiskii Kredit Bank between 1994 and 1997) by the city council following the resignation of his predecessor sparked a noisy scandal in spring 1999. Several candidates from non-Communist parties who were interested in the job, complained. Moreover, the oblast elite likes to promote "territorial civil communitarian self-government," as a means of undermining any real municipal self-government. They also intend to merge cities with the surrounding districts (such as Bryansk, Klintsy, or Novozybkov), in order to "simplify provincial management."

In Bryansk, control of the mass media is more in dispute than it is in Smolensk, and the dispute remains unresolved for the moment. The local elite's desire to expand its control over the mass media has been stimulated not only by the 1999 and 2000 federal elections, but also, and maybe above all, by the upcoming gubernatorial elections in December 2000. Governor Lodkin has used all possible means of pressure (fiscal, economic, legal) against independent papers which criticize his leadership. He has barred some papers' access to the region's only printing plant, which the oblast administration owns. While the independent papers are dying, each branch of authority(the regional administration, regional assembly, mayor's office, Bryansk city council, Bryansk urban districts, etc.) has been publishing its own newspaper or bulletin. The provincial leadership in Bryansk is even more politicized (if not ideologized) than in Smolensk and tries harder to "conquer" public opinion, using such classic means as party propaganda. The weekly *Bryanskoe Vremya*, which for years has been learning to live in market conditions without subsidies from governors, is actually the last independent sociopolitical newspaper left.

Despite the de facto one-party monopoly in the Bryansk regional leadership, the political landscape is not completely monolithic. The total dominance of the Communists stimulated the opposition parties and civil society organizations into a new wave of political activism in the summer of 1999. Even Lodkin began to distance himself from the KPRF leadership and to impose his own views.

An interesting example of Lodkin's tactics was the establishment of a regional branch of Moscow Mayor Yurii Luzhkov's Fatherland party in Bryansk. Lodkin suggested to Luzhkov that his ally Aleksandr Salov set up the regional branch. Actually, Salov, who was a member of the Bryansk KPRF until the end of 1998, is the director of the only private firm which obtained in December 1997 the governor's special accreditation to sell all alcoholic beverages imported to Bryansk within the province. Moreover Governor Lodkin and the "vodka oligarch" Salov had founded a regional private radio station ("Chistie Klyuchi"). They celebrated the radio station's first birthday in mid-June 1999 in Bryansk, organizing a large public show. As a result, in Bryansk, the KPRF and Fatherland seem to be two parts of the same regional elite. Nevertheless, one of the Communist Party leaders, Valentin Kuptsov, came to Bryansk in the middle of June to remind the local Communist elite that Luzhkov's movement had to be considered the main opponent to Zyuganov's KPRF in the next federal elections.

The reformist opposition parties (Russia's Democratic Choice, Yabloko, Our Home Is Russia, etc.) were experiencing a kind of revival in summer 1999. Despite their lack of permanent members, they hoped to capture protest votes cast against Lodkin. According to several leaders of these organizations, Lodkin has been losing legitimacy as a leader. While their liberal and democratic mottoes sounded too abstract and idealistic during the 1990s, they now present themselves more concretely as defending all citizens against the abuse of power by Lodkin's administration. They have gained support from several businessmen who are angry about the unfair regulations adopted by the oblast administration. Therefore, the leader of Bryansk's Russia's Democratic Choice, Lyudmila Komogortseva, has acquired a good reputation in the central Moscow apparatus of her party for leading the struggle against the Communists. She ran the Right Cause campaign for the "Red Belt" provinces. Moreover, a handful of independent members in the Bryansk municipal soviet have joined the Yabloko branch, which did not exist when they were elected in December 1996.

The Bryansk leadership of All Russia presents itself as moderate, even if firmly opposed to Lodkin's leadership. The chairman is Oleg Shenkarev, the former first secretary of the KPRF Obkom (until 1996), who resigned after the central KPRF apparatus decided to endorse Lodkin's candidacy (and not his) in the gubernatorial elections. He was twice elected to the State Duma in a single-mandate constituency, with Communist support, in 1993 and 1995. He had good ties with Semago in the State Duma and hoped to hold onto his Duma seat, but now as one of Lodkin's main opponents (see *EWI RRR*, 8 July). Sergei Maslov, the deputy chairman of All Russia's Bryansk chapter, is also a well-known local figure. He runs an organization of retired officers

that criticizes the way the oblast administration handles its relations with veterans.

The leaders of these opposition organizations aimed to set up a large alliance to put forward a joint candidate in the single-member districts to compete against the candidate from the pro-Communist bloc. They assert that they now have enough members to control the electoral processes not only in the large cities, but also in most parts of the Bryansk countryside as well.

Ties to Moscow: Conflict with Federal Powers

Consistent with his Communist ideology, Lodkin is anti-reform, and thus tends to blame Moscow for all of the oblast's difficulties. He claims that the country's overall financial troubles inhibit the oblast's development. Clearly, the blame for all of the oblast's economic problems cannot be placed on Moscow. Bryansk's neighboring regions, many of which are also ruled by Communist governors, are doing much better than Bryansk, yet when this is pointed out to Lodkin, he declares the rulers of the regions "Gaidar's lackeys" (*EWI RRR*, 18 June 1998). In fact, accusing someone of being a Gaidar supporter seems to be the governor's favorite insult, and he uses it for all those who are in opposition to him.

Moscow holds Lodkin in equally low esteem. After Yeltsin's October 1993 clash with the parliament, the president issued a decree granting himself the power to appoint and dismiss regional authorities. Yeltsin used this decree to immediately dismiss Lodkin, who opposed him during the stand-off. Lodkin brought a suit against Yeltsin to finish out his original term, which would have ended in 1998. However, his subsequent reelection made the case moot.

Lodkin's second election, in 1996, was also not welcomed by Moscow. Then Presidential Administration First Deputy Chief of Staff Aleksandr Kazakov singled out Lodkin as an incorrigible representative of the opposition. Nevertheless, after his victory, Lodkin stressed that he would cooperate with the federal government since it is necessary for a regional leader to do so (*OMRI RRR*, 11 December 1996). Lodkin has succeeded in obtaining federal subsidies from Moscow, primarily due to the fact that Bryansk Oblast has suffered from the Chernobyl disaster more than has any other region in Russia.

Lodkin has made some attempt to downplay his opposition affiliation. In April 1997, before attending the Communist Party of the Russian Federation's annual congress, Lodkin, as well as five other regional executives, informed the presidential administration

Yurii Yevgenevich Lodkin

26 March 1938—Born in the town of Dyatkov in Bryansk Oblast

1958—Finished the Dyatkov Industrial Technical School and the Central Committee Higher Party School

1958—Started work as a shift operator at a glass factory. He served in the Soviet Army for three years and then worked as a mechanic and technician in a closed enterprise

1967–1968—Became a member of the city committee of the Komsomol and assistant editor of the raion newspaper. He then received a higher education in journalism and worked as an editor at the oblast newspaper, *Bryansk Worker*, starting as a correspondent and then assistant to the department on industry, transportation, and trade connections

1984–1987—Worked for the oblast committee of the CPSU, then as a correspondent for the Soviet Telegraph Agency (TASS); earned recognition for coverage of the Chernobyl catastrophe

1990—Elected to the RSFSR Congress of People's Deputies and joined the Supreme Soviet's Committee on Ecological Questions and the Rational Use of Natural Resources

April 1993—Elected governor of Bryansk Oblast

25 September 1993—Removed from this position by Yeltsin

3–4 October 1993—Was in the White House supporting the opposition during stand-off with Yeltsin

12 December 1993—Elected to the Federation Council and served on the Social Politics Committee and Mandate Commission. Became one of the leaders of the regional block of Communists and the national-patriotic People's Unity

17 December 1995—Elected to the State Duma on the Communist party ticket; served on the Duma committee for veterans' issues

7 August 1996—Elected to the Coordinating Council of the National-Patriotic Union of Russia (NPSR)

8 December 1996—Elected governor of Bryansk

Member of the Communist Party

Married, with one son

---

of their decision to attend the Communist congress instead of a meeting organized by Our Home Is Russia and requested that the administration not take their affiliation with the opposition too much to heart (*EWI RRR*, 8 May 1997).

Although Moscow and Gaidar-style reformers are Lodkin's favorite scapegoats, he does try to command an independent, authoritative position for Bryansk in relation to the center. In his campaign, Lodkin emphasized the need for signing a power-sharing agreement with the center, which was eventually concluded on 4 July 1997 (*OMRI RRR*, 27 November 1996). This agreement was part of the presidential administration's plan to earn the support of opposition governors.

Despite his conflict with the Yeltsin administration, the governor stressed that the oblast benefits from his connections in Moscow. During his gubernatorial campaign, Lodkin emphasized that his experience in the Federation Council from 1993 to 1995 and his subsequent service in the State Duma enabled him to build strong ties in both the legislative and the executive branches of power that would help him to promote the oblast's interests (*OMRI RRR*, 27 November 1996).

Relations with Other Regions: Pro-Stroev, Anti-Luzhkov

Lodkin expressed early support for Orel Governor Yegor Stroev as a potential candidate for the presidential election in 2000 (*EWI RRR*, 9 October 1997). Stroev is the chairman of the Black Earth regional association, of which Bryansk is a member. The other regions in the association are Belgorod, Kursk, Lipetsk, Tula, Tambov,

Novgorod, and Voronezh. Although there is almost no Black Earth in Bryansk, the governor likes to participate in the association's meetings because of its collegial relations. Lodkin has stated that "we are all equal here," as opposed to the Central Russia Association, of which Bryansk is also a member (*EWI RRR*, 9 October 1997). Moscow Mayor Yurii Luzhkov, another one-time aspirant for the 2000 presidential election, is also a member of the Central Russia Association, representing the wealthy capital which is surrounded by poor oblasts. The other members of the Central Russia Association are Vladimir, Ivanovo, Kaluga, Kostroma, Moscow, Ryazan, Smolensk, Tver, Tula, and Yaroslavl oblasts, and the association is officially headed by the liberal Yaroslavl Governor Anatolii Lisitsyn.

Attitudes Toward Business: Small-Scale Foreign Investment

Although pro-market reforms are not high on Lodkin's agenda, he has promoted some international investment in the region. One specific project venture involves the Bryansk firm Elikson and South Korea's Samsung Electronics, which will invest $30 million in a new wireless phone system for the oblast, creating 50,000 new numbers. Only Lodkin and the region's acting representative in Moscow knew about this agreement, while oblast officials and the Bryansk city phone station were not informed about it, sparking a protest over the plans (*EWI RRR*, 23 April 1998).

One successful business venture in Bryansk has been the Bryansk international airport. The airport has been handling an increased amount of international cargo, allowing it to compete for business with Moscow and St. Petersburg. In October 1997, at Lodkin's urging, the construction of a new runway began. Once complete, this new airstrip will allow the airport to accommodate jumbo jets from all continents (*BR*, 10 February 1998).

Lodkin has also discussed the possibility of assembling Daewoo vehicles at the Bryansk Automotive Works, a suggestion made to him by former First Deputy Prime Minister Anatolii Chubais (*EWI RRR*, 30 October 1997).

Internet Sites in the Region

http://www.admin.bryansk.ru/
This website provides information about various aspects of the region, including news, museums, history, and an administration home page. It also has a search mechanism and links to other Russian sites. The site hosts the pro-administration newspaper *The Provincial* (which is the web version of *Bryanskaya Nedelya*).

REPUBLIC OF BURYATIA

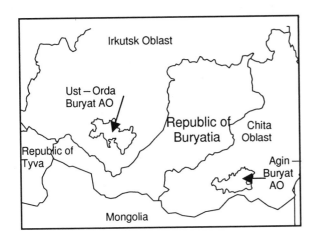

Territory: 351,300 km²
Population (as of 1 January 1998): 1,046,000
Distance from Moscow: 5,532 km

Major Cities:
Ulan-Ude, *capital* (pop. 370,100)
Gusinoozersk (32,500)
Severobaikalsk (27,900)

Basic Facts

Population (as of 1 Jan. 1998): 1,046,000 (0.71% of Russian total)

Ethnic breakdown (1989 census): Russians 69.9%, Buryats 24%, Ukrainians 2.2%, Tatars 1%

Urban population (as of 1 Jan. 1998): 59.7% (Russia overall: 73.1%)

Student population (as of 1 Sept. 1997): 196 per 10,000 (Russia overall: 208/10,000)

Pensioner population (1997): 21.70% (Russia overall: 25.96%)

Percent of population with higher education (1989 census): 11.8% (Russia overall: 11.3%)

Percent of population working in (1997): Industry: 20.5% (Russian average: 23.0%); Agriculture: 14.1% (13.7%); Trade: 14.2% (13.5%); Culture: 14.8% (13.3%)

Average monthly personal income in July 1998: 545.1 new rubles (Russian average: 891.7 new rubles)

Average monthly personal expenses in July 1998: 468.3 new rubles (Russian average: 684.9 new rubles)

Average monthly subsistence requirement in 1998: 399 new rubles (Russian average: 438 new rubles)

Consumer price index (as of July 1998): 126 (Russia overall = 100)

Budgetary revenues (1997): 2,166.6 billion rubles (Russia overall: 433,378.2 billion rubles)

Budgetary expenditures (1997): 2,826.8 billion rubles (Russia overall: 468,111.6 billion rubles)

Industrial production as percentage of all Russian production (Jan.–Aug. 1998): 0.30%

Proportion of loss-making enterprises (as of July 1998): 76.6% (Russia overall: 50.4%)

Number of enterprises which have wage arrears (as of 1 Sept. 1998): 875 (0.65% of Russian total)

Agricultural production as percentage of all Russian production (1997): 0.81%

Number of private farms (as of 1 Jan. 1998): 2,877 (1.05% of Russian total)

Capital investment (1997): 1,851.3 billion rubles (Russia overall: 408,797 billion rubles)

Sources of investment (1997): federal budget: 17.4% (Russian average: 10.2%); regional budget: 4.2% (10.5%); extra-budgetary funds: 78.4% (79.3%)

Foreign investment (1997): 214,000 USD (Russia overall: 12,294,734,000 USD)

Number of joint ventures (1997): 64 (0.43% of Russian total)

Fixed capital investment in joint ventures and foreign companies (1997): 21,821 million rubles (Russia overall: 16,265.4 billion rubles)

Number of small businesses (as of 1 July 1998): 4,700 (0.54% of Russian total)

Number of enterprises privatized in 1997: 21 (0.77% of Russian total), including those which used to be municipal property: 23.8% (Russian average: 66.4%); regional property: 61.9% (20.0%); federal property: 14.3% (13.6%)

Number of telephones per 100 families (1997): in cities: 32.3 (Russian average: 49.2); in villages: 25.7 (19.8)

Brief Overview

The Republic of Buryatia, with a territory of 351,300 sq km, is located in a mountainous part of southeast Siberia and borders the Republic of Tyva, Irkutsk and Chita oblasts, and Mongolia. The Buryats, the indigenous ethnic group, now make up less than a third of the republic's total population. They speak the Buryat language, but Russian and Mongolian are also widespread in the republic. The Buryats living east of Lake Baikal are Buddhists, while western Buryats mostly practice Orthodoxy with borrowings from shamanism.

The republic is one of the country's richest in mineral resources. It has extensive deposits of gold, coal, various non-ferrous metals, and other minerals. However, not all deposits are well explored and developed. The republic is one of the largest energy producers in the area and exports energy to neighboring Chita Oblast and Mongolia, but in general it is not highly developed. Buryatia also must import agricultural products even though over 13 percent of the republic's territory is devoted to agricultural uses and slightly less than half of its population is employed in the agricultural sector. In general, the republic is considered to be one of the poorest in the country: in 1997, less than half (49 percent) of its expenditures were covered by its own budgetary revenues.

The republic hosts two important railroads, the Trans-Siberian and Baikal-Amur, which connect the central part of Russia with the Far East and countries of southwest Asia (China, Japan, Mongolia, and North Korea). These Asian countries are the republic's main trade partners. Mongolia, North Korea, the United States, and South Korea are the largest investors in Buryatia's economy. According to a 1998 survey by *Ekspert* magazine, the republic had experienced the country's 10th largest decrease in investment potential since 1997. In 1998, *Ekspert* ranked the republic 57th among Russia's 89 regions in terms of investment potential and 53rd in terms of investment risks. A 1998 survey by Bank Austria ranked the republic 67th in terms of investment climate.

Electoral History

2000 Presidential Election
Putin: 42.16%
Zyuganov: 40.32%
Tuleev: 3.77%
Yavlinskii: 3.70%
Skuratov: 3.30%

Zhirinovsky: 2.55%
Turnout: 61.67% (Russia overall: 68.64%)

1999 Parliamentary Elections
Communist Party of the Russian Federation: 27.06%
Unity: 25.46%
Fatherland–All Russia: 10.05%
Union of Right Forces: 8.36%
Zhirinovsky Bloc: 7.01%
Communists–Workers' Russia: 3.49%
Yabloko: 3.14%
In a single-mandate district: 1 Fatherland–All Russia
Turnout: 57.06% (Russia overall: 61.85%)

1998 Republican Presidential Election
Potapov (incumbent): 63.3%
Saganov: 6.5%
Turnout: 53.8%

1996 Presidential Election
Zyuganov: 40.22%/49.50% (first round/second round)
Yeltsin: 30.59%/45.30%
Lebed: 10.57%
Yavlinskii: 7.59%
Zhirinovsky: 4.84%
Turnout: 64.02%/61.73% (Russia overall: 69.67%/ 68.79%)

1995 Parliamentary Elections
Communist Party of the Russian Federation: 27.88%
Liberal Democratic Party: 8.62%
Communists–Workers' Russia: 7.87%
Women of Russia: 6.55%
Agrarian Party of Russia: 6.29%
Our Home Is Russia: 5.57%
Party of Workers' Self-Government: 4.09%
Power to the People: 3.69%
Yabloko: 2.76%
Russia's Democratic Choice: 2.48%
In a single-mandate district: 1 independent
Turnout: 63.76% (Russia overall: 64.37%)

1993 Constitutional Referendum
"Yes"—55.5% "No"—40.3%

1993 Parliamentary Elections
Party of Russian Unity and Concord: 17.39%
Liberal Democratic Party of Russia: 17.32%
Communist Party of the Russian Federation: 15.58%

Russia's Choice: 13.24%
Women of Russia: 11.96%
Yabloko: 5.76%
Agrarian Party of Russia: 5.47%
Democratic Party of Russia: 4.79%
In a single-mandate district: 1 Agrarian Party of Russia
Turnout: 56.17% (Russia overall: 54.34%)

1991 Presidential Elections
Yeltsin: 34.53%
Ryzhkov: 25.03%
Tuleev: 20.15%
Zhirinovsky: 11.44%
Bakatin: 2.54%
Makashov: 2.35%
Turnout: 77.79% (Russia overall: 76.66%)

Regional Political Institutions

Executive:
President, 4-year term
Leonid Vasilevich Potapov, elected February
1994, June 1998
    Buryatia Republic Adminstration;
    Sukhe-Bator, 9; Ulan-Ude, 670001
    Tel 7(301–2) 21–46–52, 21–51–86;
    Fax 7(301–2) 21–25–55
    Federation Council in Moscow:
    7(095) 292–76–07, 926–63–44

Legislative:
Unicameral
Narodnii Khural—65 members, 4–year term,
elected June 1998
Chairman—Mikhail Innokentevich Semenov,
elected July 1994, July 1998

Regional Politics

Republican President at Center of Scandals

Buryatia President Leonid Potapov is best known for
the variety of scandals that have followed him through
his career. The first major scandal unfolded during his
first presidential campaign. In December 1993 the local newspaper *Buryatiya* printed two stories accusing
Potapov of using one-third of the money that had been
allocated by the Supreme Soviet for eliminating floods
in the republic to finance his campaign (Panorama Research Group, Labyrint Electronic Database, Moscow).
Potapov, who had the backing of several minor parties,

including Social Justice, the Union of Manufacturers
and Employers, the Agrarian Union, and the Union of
Women, denied all allegations, and went on to secure a
presidential victory on 30 June 1994.

He won a second term as president on 21 June 1998,
beating out nine other candidates and securing 63 percent of the vote. The second-place finisher was Vladimir
Saganov, the chairman of the budget committee of the
Buryatian legislature, who received 6.5 percent. Potapov's
strong electoral finish was attributed in part to the fact
that his main competitor, the president of Buryatia's Union
of Industrialists and Entrepreneurs, Aleksandr Korinev,
withdrew from the race three days before the election,
throwing his support to the incumbent.

Whether his victory was coerced or not, Potapov possesses attributes attractive to the diverse electorate of the
republic. An ethnic Russian, Potapov learned to speak
the Buryat language while living in a Buryat village as a
child during World War II (*NG*, 16 June 1998). He has
also expressed a deep respect for Buddhism, claiming
that it is the most democratic religion (*NG*, 16 June 1998).

Such comments are ironic, given the scandal
surrounding Potapov's use of about 100 troops to
disperse a demonstration by Buddhist monks in May
1998. The monks were protesting the removal of a rare,
17th-century Tibetan medical atlas for a U.S. tour. Thirty
of the protestors were beaten, fifteen were detained, and
three were arrested. A spokesperson for the president
remarked that Potapov felt that the use of force was
justified (*MT*, 7 May 1998). Officials in Buryatia claim
that the protest was planned to discredit Potapov before
the June election (*MT*, 7 May 1998). These allegations
seem plausible given the context in which the monks'
protest took place. The Dalai Lama wrote a letter to
Potapov supporting the exhibit, and the president offered
the monks the opportunity to accompany the atlas on
the tour, but they refused (*MT*, 7 May 1998). The atlas
was returned undamaged in the summer of 1999.

Executive Platform: Regulated Economy

In his 1994 campaign, Potapov spoke in favor of maintaining control of prices and greater state direction of
Russia's transition to capitalism. He believes that lib-
eralizing prices was a mistake that hurt farmers, an
important issue to the president since 40 percent of
the republic's population live in the countryside. The
agrarian sector of Buryatia's economy has experienced
considerable difficulties adapting to market conditions.

Potapov is against the sale of farmland, and organized

a referendum on this question that was held 5 July 1998. The referendum was invalid since only 40 percent of the electorate participated, short of the necessary 50 percent voter turnout. Nevertheless the results suggest widespread opposition to private property since 83 percent of those who did vote supported the moratorium.

Potapov feels that state subsidies are crucial in financing economic reform in Buryatia (NNS). The collapse of the local timber industry, which relied on markets in Central Asia, is one of the region's greatest problems (NNS). He believes that for Buryatian industry to successfully adapt to market economics, widespread qualitative restructuring is necessary. However, Potapov is vague about how to achieve this restructuring, claiming that federal measures are necessary, but also that the republic needs to become more self-sufficient and independent.

With Lake Baikal straddling Buryatia's western border, Potapov has spoken out strongly in favor of protecting the environment. Nevertheless, these ecological concerns are balanced by an interest in attracting investment and developing new markets for the republic's mineral resources.

Policies: Industrial Protectionist

Many of the president's policies have been focused on protecting the republic's industries and furthering economic development. In September 1996, Potapov signed a decree that made it difficult to sell vodka from other regions in Buryatia (Panorama). In November 1996 he set up a temporary special economic regime aimed at improving Buryatia's economic and social situation without using additional federal funds (OMRI RRR, 13 November 1996). The plan included deferring some tax privileges, issuing republican securities, and temporarily suspending some federal programs financed from the republican budget.

The Buryatia budget contributed nearly 300 million old rubles for the preservation of Lake Baikal in 1997 (NG, 16 June 1998).

Relationships Between Key Players: Supportive Home Legislature, Controversial Court

Like many regional executives, Potapov has come into conflict with powerful local executives. Potapov removed the former mayor of Buryatia's capital Ulan-Ude, Valerii Shapovalov, from office and had him arrested in October 1996 and January 1997 on various criminal charges. Shapovalov subsequently won the right to run for reelection as mayor, but did not emerge victorious. He also ran unsuccessfully against Potapov in the 1998 presidential election.

The regional and republican courts ruled that Potapov's removal of Shapovalov from his position was unlawful. In October 1997 the Constitutional Court ruled that the regions have the right to remove elected local officials who have been found guilty of violating federal and regional laws (RG, 23 October 1997). However, no court had found Shapovalov guilty of a crime prior to Potapov's action to remove him from office; therefore, although he was in jail facing accusations, he was still formally mayor.

Elections to Buryatia's parliament, the Narodnii Khural, took place in June and July 1998. Essentially, an entirely new assembly has been formed that appears to share Potapov's views (NG, 7 July 1998).

Ties to Moscow: Critical of Yeltsin

Potapov supported Yeltsin in the 1996 elections because he believed there were no reasonable alternatives (NG, 16 June 1998). He had not always stood behind Russia's president. When Yeltsin was in conflict with the Supreme Soviet in March–April 1993, Potapov supported the legislature. He also condemned Yeltsin for the October 1993 storming of the White House. Potapov was highly critical of Yeltsin's approach to transition and blamed Yeltsin for Russia's economic problems (NG, 16 June 1998).

On 29 August 1995 Potapov signed a power-sharing agreement with Yeltsin. Potapov claims that relations between the center and Buryatia are good, although he has criticized the Kremlin in the past for ignoring the needs of the regions.

Potapov announced in a Buryat newspaper that Boris Yeltsin supported his candidacy in the 1998 republican presidential election. In his reelection campaign, Potapov also tried to secure support from Chernomyrdin, Zyuganov, and Zhirinovsky, yet received it only from Zhirinovsky.

In July 1999, Potapov called presidential rule the optimal form of government for contemporary Russia, emphasizing the historical orientation of the people toward a strong personification of power. Nevertheless he was strongly critical of the way presidentialism had been implemented under Yeltsin. Potapov charged that the main problem with this model is the arbitrary use of power that is permitted by the Constitution of the Russian Federation. He emphasized that he did not support this constitution from the start. Moreover, he argued, "If the prime minister is confirmed by the State Duma, then the Duma should dismiss him. Prime ministers should never be changed so impetuously, as they were during the last years of Yeltsin's rule." Potapov further stated, "I believe that the Duma should confirm not only the candidate for prime minister, but also candidates for the power ministries. Only then will it be a truly representative organ. Now, the public sees the arbitrary rule of one person who possesses an enormous amount of power, and it can do nothing. What kind of democracy is this? It is distorted" (*Pyatnitsa*, 8 July 1999).

Like many other republican presidents, in 1999 Potapov joined the All Russia movement founded by Tatarstan President Mintimer Shaimiev, then signed on to support the Kremlin's new Unity bloc.

Relations with Other Regions: Strong Relations in Siberia and Far East

Ethnic Buryats span three of Russia's regions. In addition to the Republic of Buryatia, two autonomous okrugs, Agin Buryat and Ust-Orda Buryat, are also Buryat regions. These two okrugs were separated from the Buryat-Mongol ASSR (present day Buryatia) in 1937 when the Soviet government reduced the Buryat-Mongol titular territory in an attempt to suppress alleged nationalist sentiment (Ian Bremmer and Ray Taras, eds., *New States, New Politics: Building the Post-Soviet Nations*, New York: Cambridge University Press, 1997, 209). During the Gorbachev era, Buryatia demanded that its pre-1937 borders be restored, but eventually recognized the constitutional status of the two autonomous okrugs. In 1991 an all-Buryat congress was held in Ulan-Ude, resulting in the creation of an all-Union association of Buryat culture. The goal of the association is to establish a national-cultural autonomy, to consolidate the Buryat people.

Buryatia's strongest relations are with Irkutsk. In December 1997 the two regions signed an economic and social cooperation agreement that included provisions to protect Lake Baikal and work on a joint energy development program (Radio Rossii, 9 January 1998). In February 1999 Buryatia, Irkutsk, and Chita prepared to sign an agreement regulating timber exports from their regions. The regions hoped to organize a competition for exporting timber that would ultimately result in a syndicate and a regulated price policy (*EWI RRR*, 11 February 1999).

Although Buryatia, Irkutsk, and Chita are intensifying their cooperation in the timber industry, the regions are at odds regarding the creation of a special economic zone along the Baikal-Amur Railway (BAM) to help spark industrial development in the depressed areas around the rail line. Buryatia and Chita support the draft law for the special economic zone, since it would induce economic growth in their regions, but Irkutsk is against it since the oblast will lose tax revenue for the exploitation of mineral deposits in the BAM zone (*EWI RRR*, 7 April 1999).

In August 1997 Potapov signed an agreement with Moscow Mayor Yurii Luzhkov. The agreement stated that the Moscow government would develop an investment partnership with Buryatia, specifically in ore mining, tourism, bottling Baikal water, and pharmacology. Under this arrangement, in which Luzhkov pledged to invest up to $8.6 million, Moscow agreed to finance the reconstruction of the Ulan-Ude airport under the guarantee of the Buryatia government. The goal of this project is to raise the airport to international standards so that transport between Moscow and Asian-Pacific countries can be increased. Luzhkov and Potapov are in agreement that the chief economic task right now in Russia is to revive industry, and that all anti-crisis measures will be only mildly effective without such a revival. Moscow and Buryatia would also like to provide supplementary free medical services to their citizens. Part of this project includes the creation of a cooperative pharmacological enterprise that would produce conventional drugs as well as medicines from Tibetan recipes (*NG*, 16 June 1998).

Buryatia is a member of both the Far East and Baikal and the Siberian Accord regional associations. The Far East and Baikal Association includes Sakha (Yakutia) Republic; Primorskii Krai; Amur, Kamchatka, Magadan, Chita, and Sakhalin oblasts; the Jewish Autonomous Oblast; and Koryak and Chukotka autonomous okrugs. Buryatia is the only member of the Far East and Baikal Association that also belongs to the Siberian Accord Association. The other members of the Siberian Accord Association are Gorno-Altai and Khakassia republics; Altai and Krasnoyarsk krais; Irkutsk, Novosibirsk, Tomsk, Tyumen, and Kemerovo oblasts; and Agin-Buryat, Taimyr, Ust-Orda Buryat, Khanty-Mansi, Evenk, and Yamal-Nenets autonomous okrugs.

Foreign Relations: Eastern Foreign Interests

Buryatia's top economic priorities are in the Asia-Pacific region, specifically in the area of cross-border trade with China and Mongolia. China is Buryatia's main trading partner. In 1997 turnover between the two sides reached $50.6 million, with exports from Buryatia accounting for $41.2 million of the total. Mongolia is Buryatia's second largest partner, with exchanges be-

---

Leonid Vasilevich Potapov

4 July 1935—Born in the village Uakit in the Bauntovskii raion of Buryatia

1959—Graduated from the Khabarovsk Institute of Railroad Engineers

1965—Graduated from the Irkutsk Institute of Economics

1959–1976—Worked as a master craftsman, shop head, and starting in 1968, chief engineer of the Ulan-Ude Motorcar Repair Factory

1964—Joined the CPSU

1976—Moved into party work

1978—Became secretary of the Buryatia regional committee of the CPSU

1979—Awarded a Candidate of Science degree in Economics

1987–1990—Appointed chairman of the Maryiskii regional executive committee in Turkmenistan

January 1990—Elected to the Supreme Soviet of Turkmenistan

April 1990—Chosen as First Secretary of the Buryatia regional committee of the CPSU

1990—Elected to the Supreme Soviet of Buryatia, where he organized and headed the Communist faction

July 1990—Selected as a delegate to the 28th Congress of the CPSU

1990–1991—Member of the CPSU Central Committee; after August 1991 he carried out the duties of the Chairman for the Committee on budget, financial, and economic reforms in Buryatia

21 October 1991—Elected chairman of the republic's Supreme Soviet

June 1993—Elected to the RSFSR Congress of People's Deputies for the Baikal national-territorial region

12 December 1993—Elected to the Federation Council

30 June 1994—Elected president of the Republic of Buryatia

21 June 1998—Reelected president for a second term

Married, with two children

---

tween the two sides totaling $18.8 million, of which $17.4 million were exports from Buryatia. Trade with these two top partners has been increasing over the past few years, along with the volume of Buryat exports to them (*EWI RRR*, 14 January 1999).

Attitudes Toward Business: Working for Business Cooperation

In 1996 Buryatia adopted a comprehensive program for stimulating domestic and foreign investments, particularly in increasing the region's export of high-tech products. As of January 1999 Buryatia boasted 103 joint ventures with foreign partners representing 22 different countries, and foreign investment had reached $10.4 million. Of the total foreign investment, 56.6 percent comes from the Asia-Pacific region. The majority of their investment lies in the production of consumer goods, as well as retail and food service. China has the greatest number of joint ventures (40) in the region. There are 14 joint ventures with partners from European countries, concentrated largely in the region's timber industry and consumer goods (*EWI RRR*, 14 January 1999).

The timber industry is traditionally an important economic sector for Buryatia. Over 64.5 percent of the republic's territory is covered with forests. However, the collapse of the Soviet system cut Siberia off from its former partners in the other Soviet republics, reduciing the competitiveness of Siberian timber products on the world market. In Buryatia, the volume of production in the timber sector dropped to 25 percent of its previous level, decreasing from 3.3 million cubic meters in 1991 to 800,000 cubic meters by 1997 (*EWI RRR*, 22 December 1998). The region uses only 25–30 percent of its timber resources every year, yet Buryatia is exporting timber products at a higher rate, primarily to countries in the Asia-Pacific region. The problems plaguing Buryatia's timber industry, 98 percent of which is privatized, include the deterioration of productive capacities, lack of capital, underdeveloped marketing systems, and the absence of processing enterprises that can add value to the raw materials. The republic's three largest companies, Baikal Timber Company, Arig Us-Les, and Zabaikal-Les, together owe $23 million to the government in back taxes (*EWI RRR*, 22 December 1998).

To confront the problems ailing this extremely important economic sector, the republican government decided to take on the role of middleman by forming a state timber export company. In 1998 Potapov ordered the republican Chamber of Commerce and Trade to create a special export center to evaluate the quality and prices of export timber. The economics and industry ministries are developing plans for timber export companies and a raw timber exchange. A single state timber export company will be in charge of monitoring the world market, seeking out potential clients, selling the timber, transporting and insuring it, and paying customs duties. Even though such a structure would alleviate many of the problems the private sector faces, private producers are not pleased with the republican government's decision. They fear that the new structure will be allowed to set export quotas and price limits, control hard currency flows, and distribute revenues. Thus, the republican budget is the only party that will truly benefit from the new organizational structure (*EWI RRR*, 22 December 1998). In

February 1999, Buryatia combined efforts with the governments of Irkutsk and Chita to establish an agreement for regulating timber exports from their regions, instituting additional constraints on private developers (*EWI RRR*, 11 February 1999) (see Relations with Other Regions).

Potapov has also been actively trying to promote Buryatia's timber industry abroad. In April 1999 he traveled to Italy, where he held negotiations on developing a joint-venture lumber complex in northern Buryatia along the Baikal-Amur railway. A consortium of Italian firms and the Severobaikalsk company Sebal will construct a lumber processing plant in the Severobaikalsk raion, the most plentiful wood source in Buryatia. The financial insurance company Sache will serve as the guarantor for the Credito Italiano bank, which will issue an estimated $26.3 million credit (*EWI RRR*, 16 April 1999).

In October 1997 the republic signed a cooperation agreement with the oil company Sidanko. The goals of the agreement are to guarantee the stability of Buryatia's oil enterprises; clean up the region's environment, particularly in the Baikal zone; and create favorable conditions for the development of the enterprise Buryatnefteprodukt (*FI*, 30 October 1997).

Internet Sites in the Region

http://www.buriatia.ru/
This website offers detailed information about the republic's culture, cities, sciences, economy, business developments, and investment projects. A "yellow pages" feature is currently under construction.

http://www.region.rags.ru/texts/02.txt
The Constitution of the Republic of Buryatia can be found at this location.

http://www.region.rags.ru/texts/f burat.txt
The text of Buryatia's power-sharing agreement with the Russian Federation.

REPUBLIC OF CHECHNYA (ICHKERIA)

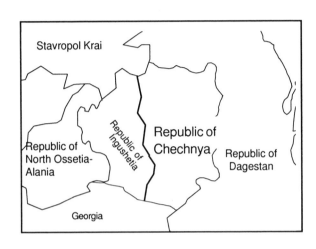

Territory: 15,000 km²
Population (as of 1 January 1998): 797,000
Distance from Moscow: 2,007 km

Major Cities:
Grozny, *capital*

Basic Facts

Population (as of 1 Jan. 1998): 797,000 (0.54% of Russian total)

Ethnic breakdown (1989 census): Chechens 66%, Russians 24.8%, Ingush 2.3%, Armenians 1.4%, Ukrainians 1.1%

Urban population (as of 1 Jan. 1998): 33.6% (Russia overall: 73.1%)

Pensioner population (1997): 18.70% (Russia overall: 25.96%)

Budgetary revenues (1997): 163.2 billion rubles (Russia overall: 433,378.2 billion rubles)

Budgetary expenditures (1997): 445.0 billion rubles (Russia overall: 468,111.6 billion rubles)

Brief Overview

The Chechen Republic is located on the northern slopes of the Caucasus Mountains and on the adjoining Chechen Plain and borders Stavropol Krai and the republics of North Ossetia, Ingushetia, and Dagestan, as well as Georgia. The Russians conquered the Chechen territory at the end of the nineteenth century despite stiff resistance by the Chechens. The territory was included in the Checheno-Ingush Autonomous Republic between 1934 and 1944, when both Ingush and Chechens were relocated to Central Asia for alleged collaboration with the Nazis. In 1957, both peoples were rehabilitated and their republic was restored, but within revised borders. In 1992, Checheno-Ingushetia split, forming two independent republics.

At the end of the 1994–96 war with Russia, the population of Chechnya was about 800,000. The renewed fighting in 1999 caused an additional outflow of refugees. Much of the ethnic Russian population, many of whom worked in the key oil sector, left even before the fighting began in 1994 (*Izvestiya*, 21 July 1998).

Chechnya boasts considerable supplies of natural resources, including construction materials, mineral waters, and most importantly, oil and gas. Oil and gas extraction and processing, as well as the petrochemical industry, were once the most important and well-developed industries in the republic. However, most oil and gas fields have been exhausted, and many refineries were damaged during the 1994–96 war.

Agriculture has also played a significant role in the republican economy. Fertile soils and favorable climatic conditions allowed for rich crops of grapes, tobacco, grain, beets, sunflowers, fruit, and vegetables, mostly cultivated on the plains. Sheep and goat breeding was well developed in the republic's mountainous areas.

The republic is located at the juncture of important highways and railroads, as well as gas and oil pipelines. Some observers believe that the war between the Russian Federation and Chechnya largely grew out of conflicts among various oil companies over control of the Chechen pipeline.

Today, there is little legitimate economic activity in the republic. There are no major foreign investment projects underway and it is unlikely that any will begin in the immediate future since the investment situation continues to deteriorate. The republic ranked 86th among Russia's 89 regions in terms of investment potential and 89th in terms of investment risk, according to a 1998 survey by *Ekspert* magazine. A 1998 survey by Bank Austria ranked the republic 89th in terms of investment climate.

Electoral History

2000 Presidential Election*
Putin: 50.63%
Zyuganov: 22.76%
Yavlinskii: 9.28%
Dzhabrailov: 5.89%
Zhirinovsky: 2.62%
Pamfilova: 1.19%
Tuleev: 0.89%
Turnout: 78.48% (Russia overall: 68.64%)

1997 Republican Presidential Election

Maskhadov: 63.6%
Basaev: 21.1%
Turnout: 72.2%

1996 Presidential Election*

Yeltsin: 64.76%/73.38% (first round/second round)
Zyuganov: 16.23%/21.54%
Yavlinskii: 4.23%
Lebed: 2.53%
Gorbachev: 1.76%
Zhirinovsky: 1.40%
Turnout: 73.04%/74.53% (Russia overall: 69.67%/
    68.79%)

1995 Parliamentary Elections*

Our Home Is Russia: 48.03%
Nur: 13.00%
Communist Party of the Russian Federation:
    11.43%
Agrarian Party of Russia: 4.59%
Derzhava: 4.34%
Women of Russia: 2.85%
Liberal Democratic Party of Russia: 1.50%
Yabloko: 1.42%
In a single-mandate district: 1 independent
Turnout: 62.06% (Russia overall: 64.37%)

Although these are the official results, their validity is highly suspect.

Regional Politics

Fierce Warrior and Peacemaker Seeks to Defend Republic Again

Aslan Maskhadov was the brilliant chief-of-staff who led the irregular Chechen troops to victory over the much better armed Russian forces during the 1994–96 war in the separatist republic. He was also the Chechen representative in the peace talks that brought that round of fighting to an end. As president, he has supported Chechen independence from Russia; however, his views on attaining Chechen sovereignty are more moderate than those of the Chechen extremists whose actions continue to impede the region's political and economic development.

Although Moscow once considered Maskhadov the best Chechen leader for working with the Rus-

sian government, this view quickly changed when Russian forces renewed their attack on Chechnya in October 1999. The Kremlin declared Maskhadov's presidency illegitimate and refused to negotiate with his government. Seeking retribution for alleged Chechen terrorist acts on Russian territory, in particular the string of apartment building bombings that occurred in September 1999, Moscow demanded that the Chechen government hand over the field commanders it accused of setting off the bombs. However, Maskhadov's control over the warlords, particularly his main rival in the presidential campaign, Shamil Basaev, has always been limited. The renewed fighting in the fall of 1999 further weakened Maskhadov's already tenuous grip over the republic and the once great peacemaker found himself battling both Russian invaders and domestic guerrillas.

Following the end of the 1994–96 conflict, Maskhadov joined Aleksandr Lebed, Russian Security Council Secretary, in signing the Khasavyurt agreement that formally enacted a cease-fire and postponed a decision on whether Chechnya would remain a part of the Russian Federation until the end of 2001. (Lebed is now the governor of Krasnoyarsk Krai.) Although Maskhadov demonstrated a willingness to negotiate with Moscow following the Khasavyurt agreement, the widespread support for independence among other Chechen leaders left him little room to make concessions (*NG*, 29 January 1997).

Maskhadov won the Chechen presidential election on 27 January 1997 in the wake of two years of war that leveled most of the republic's buildings and destroyed much of its basic infrastructure. Although the vote did not take place in ideal conditions, its results were considered to reflect the will of the Chechen people.

Executive Platform: Pragmatic, Independence Fighter

Maskhadov is a plainsman from the Nadterechnii Region with a quiet and reserved personality. His dignified and modest style appeals to the conservative Chechen society (Carlotta Gall and Thomas de Waal, *Chechnya: Calamity in the Caucasus*, New York: New York University Press, 1998, 366). Maskhadov worked his way up in the Soviet military and served in Vilnius when the Soviets led a botched attempt to crack down on the rebellious republic in January 1991. He was regarded as one of the best artillery officers at the time and his men described him as strict but fair (Gall and deWoal, 188).

Maskhadov disagreed with the late Chechen leader Dzhokhar Dudaev's policy of fighting for independence to the death of the last Chechen, taking a more realistic and pragmatic approach to the 1994–96 war. In particular, he tried to distance himself from the terrorist attacks conducted by the field commanders Shamil Basaev and Salman Raduev in neighboring Russian regions. Nevertheless, he shares their goal of winning unqualified independence from Russia. Because of his disagreements with the field commanders, Maskhadov has had little success in imposing his authority over the republic. By the end of 1999, invading Russian troops and the local warlords controlled much of Chechnya's territory.

Policies: Efforts to Impose Control over Unruly Republic

Prior to the October 1999 Russian invasion, which inflicted further devastation on the republic, Chechnya's undefined status as neither a Russian republic nor an independent country greatly hindered its reconstruction effort. Every Chechen citizen who lost his home during the 1994–96 war was entitled to compensation from the Russian government to rebuild, under the terms of the 12 May 1997 treaty signed by President Boris Yeltsin and Maskhadov. Yet, by the time the new war started, no one had received any compensation. Nearly all of the buildings of the republic's three universities were destroyed and had not been rebuilt, leaving young people without any opportunity to acquire an education. Unemployment is widespread, as much of the region's industry has been leveled. Schoolteachers go unpaid, relying on donations from students' families. Approximately 15 percent of the region's arable land is mined, greatly hampering one of the few means of healthy economic activity. These conditions mean that Chechens often have to resort to a life of crime to support themselves (talk by Musa Muradov, EastWest Institute, New York, 23 June 1999). The republic has been at a virtual standstill since the renewed conflict began. Much of the population has fled, and those remaining are simply trying to survive.

Chechens elected Maskhadov because they thought that he could deliver peace and stability. His main goals were to restore the Chechen economy and repair the infrastructure that was extensively damaged during the 1994–96 war. Maskhadov had hoped to attract outside investment that could kick-start the rebuilding process, but that proved to be an impossible task. The Chechen president has tried to reduce the rampant crime in the region and, in particular, end the numerous hostage-takings that have effectively isolated Chechnya from much of the outside world. Six Red Cross workers were murdered in December 1996, prompting all international aid agencies to withdraw. In December 1998, four foreign telecom workers (three British and one New Zealander) were beheaded by captors who feared that they were about to be apprehended.

Maskhadov sought to impose order through a number of means. He declared Chechnya an Islamic Republic on 5 November 1997, and on 3 September 1997 carried out a public execution of convicted murderers. When Russia invaded Chechnya in October 1999, the republic was in the process of completing a new constitution based on Islamic Sharia law, fulfilling a 3 February 1999 Maskhadov decree. The new constitution, if it survives the present conflict, should go into effect in 2001, when the terms of the region's current president and parliament members expire. The old constitution was adopted in March 1992 under Dudaev. It declared Chechnya a secular state and gave the parliament considerable powers. Maskhadov wanted a constitution that enshrined Chechnya's Islamic status and concentrated power in the presidency (*RFE/RL*, 3 February 1998). The new constitution drew on the Koran, Sharia law, Sunni prophets, and Chechen customs and traditions as well as the constitutions of several Islamic states, including Pakistan, Egypt, Iran, and Syria. If implemented, the new constitution will introduce governance by a "mekhkda" or "father of the nation" and a "council of the nation," which will replace the parliament and ensure that all the republic's laws are in accordance with the Koran. Additionally, only Muslims will be allowed to vote or run for office, leaving non-Muslims without any electoral rights or representation.

The day before Maskhadov issued the February 1999 decree calling for the creation of an Islamic state in Chechnya, he allowed opposition field commanders to form a Shura council. The Shura is headed by Shamil Basaev. The establishment of the Shura was clearly an attempt by Maskhadov to neutralize his opposition and essentially did little to threaten his own power since the new form of government places nearly all power in the presidency.

Maskhadov introduced a state of emergency on 23 June 1998, following a battle between his troops and field commander Salman Raduev's men in Gudermes, where Chechen Security Minister Lechi Khultygov was killed. The state of emergency mainly entailed increased police patrols and restrictions on the use of private transportation. Its purpose was to prevent Maskhadov from being overthrown (*RFE/RL*, 1 July 1998). He introduced another state of emergency on 15 December 1998, following the brutal murder of the four telecom workers (*KD*, 16 December 1998). Maskhadov also has banned all rallies in the republic since 19 February 1998 and the bearing of arms since 25 February 1998 (*KD*, 30 June 1998).

Relationships Between Key Players: Powerful Enemies Seek Maskhadov's Removal

Even before the October 1999 Russian invasion, Chechnya had been slipping into anarchy and chaos. If the Chechens had not faced a common enemy in the Russians, the republic might have degenerated into civil war. As it is, presenting a united front against the Russians is proving difficult since there is so much discord among the various Chechen factions.

Industrial and agricultural output began to plunge as early as 1992. Prior to the October 1999 Russian invasion, Maskhadov probably controlled the situation on less than 50 percent of the territory, while various field commanders controlled the rest. Maskhadov's authority has diminished even further since October 1999. Small military groups have easy access to weapons, and kidnapping for ransom is widespread. Maskhadov himself has survived numerous assassination attempts since March 1996.

Before Chechen forces were mobilized to defend the republic against the October 1999 invasion, Maskhadov's army was estimated to include 8,530 men arrayed against 300 groups including about 2,500 individuals. Despite his apparent strength, Maskhadov tried to avoid direct confrontation with his opponents within the republic. Any blood spilled in an attempt to take Raduev, for example, would lead his supporters to seek revenge. In any case, the alliances of his opponents and friends are constantly shifting.

Even former President Dudaev was able to hold the various groups and clans together only when they faced a common enemy in the Russians (for an analysis of Chechen politics up to the beginning of the 1994 war, see John B. Dunlop, *Russia Confronts Chechnya: Roots of a Separatist Conflict*, Cambridge: Cambridge University Press, 1998). In the period between 1996 and 1999, Maskhadov's key opponents were Salman Raduev, the commander of the army of General Dudaev, the largest of the militias, with a base 60 km southeast of Grozny; Shamil Basaev, who twice served as Maskhadov's acting prime minister (resigning 9 July 1998) and advocated unifying Chechnya and Dagestan as an independent country; and former field commander Khunkar Israpilov.

Between 1996 and 1999, Raduev held a number of rallies at which he denounced Maskhadov's policies. During that time Raduev controlled Kadi-Yurt, and Basaev controlled Vedeno and Dargo (C. W. Blandy, *Chechnya: A Beleaguered President*, Conflict Studies Research Centre, Occasional Brief 61, p. 9). Basaev was Maskhadov's main opponent in the 1997 presidential elections, winning about 21 percent of the vote. On 29 September 1998, they began advocating Maskhadov's impeachment on the grounds that he had violated the constitution by endangering Chechnya's sovereignty as he continued talks with Moscow. They also claimed that he had embezzled profits gained from the sale of Chechen oil. Chechnya's Sharia court ruled on 24 December 1998 that while Maskhadov had violated some provisions of the constitution, the crimes did not warrant impeachment (*RFE/RL*, 28 December 1998). Basaev and his allies vowed to keep fighting for Maskhadov's removal, although the two seem to have found common ground once again, at least temporarily, in combating the Russians.

Maskhadov also opposes the Wahhabis and on 16 July 1998 banned them from the republic (*RT*, 24 July 1998 and *RFE/RL*, 17 July 1998). They have support from former Chechen Minister of Foreign Affairs Movladi Udugov and his Islamic Path party, founded in the summer of 1997; former acting President Zelimkhan Yandarbiev; Vice President Vakha Arsanov, and the Jordanian-born warlord Khattab, who controls Serzhen-Yert and Aleroy. The Wahhabis are seeking to unify many of the regions of the North Caucasus, and have stirred up trouble in Dagestan, where they invaded and took control of several villages in August 1999, greatly angering Russia, and leading to the second invasion. This sect of extremists is said to have links to the leadership of Saudi Arabia. They are also opposed by Raduev, who sees them as a threat. The Russians are fearful of this outside threat as well, and the Wahhabis' presence reduces their desire to let Chechnya become independent.

Maskhadov's inability to control these various groups contributed significantly to the republic's deteriorating social conditions. Even prior to Russia's most recent attacks, the vast majority of people in Chechnya had lost confidence in Maskhadov's government, and many had come to believe that the only solution was a return to the previous leadership of the republic, which was largely Russian. Moscow was able to impose a relative sense of order and harmony in the republic, and the population had secured a minimal standard of living—a stark contrast to the situation under the rule of Dudaev and Maskhadov.

The bombing attacks Russia began in September 1999 and the subsequent invasion in October 1999 caused thousands of Chechens to flee their homes. According to official statistics issued by the Russian Ministry of Internal Affairs, more than 237,000 refugees had crossed the Russian border by the end of November 1999. However, the real number of refugees is likely higher, as those who have settled with family members in Russia or have moved outside the North Caucasus region are not necessarily accounted for in the official figures. The magnitude of the refugee crisis and casualties remains unclear. Official Russian reports on casualties do not always separate deaths from injuries, or military from civilian casualties. Anecdotal evidence suggests that the real number of deaths is much higher. Likewise, no one is certain how many civilians remain in the republic.

Ties to Moscow: Kremlin Refuses to Acknowledge Maskhadov

The Russian federal government has drastically altered its position toward Maskhadov since the Chechen president first came to power. In the earlier part of his tenure, Moscow viewed Maskhadov as a man it could work with and the person most likely to pacify the region. Yeltsin met with the Chechen president twice, on 12 May and 18 August 1997.

Yet, in spite of its finding common ground with Maskhadov, Moscow has never implemented many of the agreements that it has signed with Chechnya, including the "Fig Leaf Treaty" of 12 May 1997 (Blandy, 5), nor has it carried out one of the more than fifty agreements signed during the negotiation process following the 1994–96 conflict. Faced with its own financial problems, Russia is unlikely to make substantial sums available for rebuilding Chechnya. In any case, much of the aid that Moscow has sent has not been used for the purposes for which it was intended. Former Grozny Mayor Beslan Gantemirov was jailed in Moscow on charges of embezzling 57 million rubles sent as economic aid (*RFE/RL*, 22 December 1998). In late 1999, however, Moscow released him to help lead a pro-Russian government in the parts of the republic occupied by Russian troops.

Despite its support for Maskhadov, Moscow had effectively blockaded Chechnya by placing a circle of troops around the republican border. Governors in nearby regions felt these troops were necessary to prevent the Chechen chaos from spilling into their territories. Moscow's policies in this regard are completely understandable. After all, Yeltsin's personal emissary to Chechnya, Valentin Vlasov, was kidnapped on 1 May 1998 and released only six months later.

It appeared for awhile that the Kremlin's policy toward the breakaway region was becoming more realistic. On 22 September 1997 Yeltsin signed a decree ordering the preparation of a power-sharing treaty with Chechnya, as if it were any other Russian region. On 1 December 1998, Yeltsin officially recognized that his previous decree lacked standing (*NG*, 3 December 1998). On 1 August 1998 Maskhadov met with then Prime Minister Sergei Kirienko, who offered to turn Chechnya into a "free or special economic zone." Shortly thereafter, however, Yeltsin sacked Kirienko. On 29 October 1998 Maskhadov met with Prime Minister Yevgenii Primakov in North Ossetia. Neither side made any substantive concessions. Primakov offered money to cover wage and pension arrears and to finance some investment projects, but he did not mention Kirienko's idea of the special economic zone. Later Maskhadov announced his willingness to continue discussions with Primakov, describing him as a "practical man" (*Segodnya*, 4 December 1998).

Shortly after Primakov was dismissed in May 1999

and replaced by Sergei Stepashin, Russian helicopters attacked camps on the Terek River belonging to field commander Khattab. Stepashin was a strong advocate of force from the Russian side during the Russian-Chechen war. Though Stepashin remained in the prime minister's seat for a very brief time, his tenure marked Moscow's renewed interest in using force to address its grievances with Chechnya.

In August 1999 a group of Wahhabi fighters commanded by Basaev and Khattab invaded and occupied several mountain villages in Dagestan. Russians managed to regain control of the regions over the course of the next several weeks, but this conflict served as a springboard for a renewed attack on the republic. Explosions in two Moscow apartment buildings and one in Volgodonsk as well as smaller-scale terrorist assaults in the North Caucasus created a sense of panic about Chechen terrorism throughout Russia.

In September 1999 Russia began a bombing campaign against Chechnya, followed by an invasion, with the stated goal of fighting terrorism. From the outset of the invasion Maskhadov demanded negotiations with Yeltsin, but the Russian president refused to meet with his Chechen counterpart. Maskhadov proposed mediation through both Georgian President Eduard Shevardnadze and NATO. Maskhadov even appealed to Pope John Paul II to intervene to protect the Chechen people from genocide.

The fighting that began in the fall of 1999 put Maskhadov in an extremely difficult situation. He was being forced to repel Russian attacks and defend his republic, without having any real leverage to bring the conflict to an end. Though Moscow is allegedly fighting terrorism, Maskhadov's government has also been under attack. The Kremlin claims that Maskhadov was not elected to his post in accordance with Russian legal norms and no longer recognizes him as Chechnya's legitimate president. Moscow even went so far as to try and establish its own puppet government by reviving the Chechen parliament elected in 1994, an attempt that proved unsuccessful.

Russian Prime Minister Putin and Minister of Emergency Situations Sergei Shoigu announced in December 1999 that the Russian side would agree to meet with Maskhadov, but only if he released all foreign and Russian hostages and handed over the Chechen terrorists responsible for various crimes throughout Russia. Maskhadov was in no position to meet these demands. Nevertheless, pressure from international organizations, such as the Organization for Security and Cooperation with Europe (OSCE), which recognizes Maskhadov as Chechnya's legitimate president, may provide the ultimate pressure for negotiations between the two sides.

Prior to the 1999 conflict, Maskhadov was pursuing apparently contradictory objectives in relation to Russia. He was simultaneously working for Chechen independence from Moscow and seeking financial support from the Russians. Although his election entitled him to a seat in the upper house of the Russian parliament, Maskhadov refused to participate in Federation Council sessions since he considered it part of a foreign legislature. Chechnya has not paid federal taxes since 1992. On 29 December 1998, Maskhadov reiterated his demand that Moscow recognize Chechen independence, claiming it was the only way to reduce crime in the region. On the other hand, Maskhadov wants Moscow to make war reparations and contribute to the rebuilding of the Chechen economy. He was also pursuing other initiatives such as securing Moscow's agreement to transport Caspian oil through Chechnya to ports in Novorossiisk. Moscow is very unlikely to agree to such a proposal, since no one can offer solid guarantees that uncontrolled criminal groups would not simply steal the oil.

There are several further ironies in the Maskhadov-Moscow relationship. Though Russian leaders generally supported him until recently, the hard-working and pragmatic Maskhadov seemed the person most likely to win the republic's independence (Blandy, 15–16). Of course, even with a leader like Maskhadov, Chechnya's chances of thriving as an independent country are virtually nonexistent. A further irony is that every time the Kremlin expressed its backing for Maskhadov, it undermined his support base among Chechens.

Relations with Other Regions: Has Support of Ethnic Republican Leaders

What happens in Chechnya has a powerful impact on other regions of the North Caucasus. In particular, President of Ingushetia Ruslan Aushev and North Ossetia President Aleksandr Dzasokhov have supported Maskhadov, describing him as one of the key factors preventing the situation in his republic from becoming even worse. Aushev and Dzasokhov have spoken out against Moscow for its refusal to meet with Maskhadov and seek a peaceful solution to the republic's problems. Ingushetia has been dramatically affected by the 1999–2000 conflict, receiving more than 226,000 refugees, nearly doubling its regional population of 313,000. Tatarstan President Mintimer Shaimiev, who heads the Russian republic that has managed to secure more autonomy from Moscow than any other region, has sharply criticized the federal government for bringing troops into Chechnya without first holding negotiations with Maskhadov (*EWI RRR,* 21 October 1999).

Maskhadov arguably has the closest ties to Krasnoyarsk Governor Aleksandr Lebed, with whom he signed the Khasavyurt treaty. Although the treaty has questionable legal status and signaled Russia's capitulation in the war, it made Lebed a hero as a peacemaker. Chechens would have been happy to see him as Russian president (Dzhebrail Khaizov, "Kavkazskie plenniki," *Kommersant Vlast,* 11 August 1998).

Foreign Relations: Fruitlessly Seeking International Recognition

Maskhadov's government strenuously sought international recognition of its independence, but without success. Moscow even closed the Grozny airport to foreign flights, forcing Maskhadov to travel abroad through Russia on a Russian passport.

Maskhadov's goal has been to build an Islamic government and he hoped to maintain close ties to the Arab world. However, his conflict with the Wahhabis complicated his links with the Middle East. When Maskhadov and Basaev (who were allies in the first half of 1998) fought with the clans of Yandarbiev and Udugov, official Grozny had a falling out with Saudi Arabia, Jordan, and the United Arab Emirates, which until the summer of 1998, had supported an independent Chechnya. The Saudis had apparently paid for the use of cellular phones in the republic, but then cut off the funds, leading the Moscow telecom companies to cancel service to the region for lack of payment (*Segodnya,* 6 August 1998).

Chechnya has received virtually no international aid in rebuilding and developing its economy. Until hostage-taking and murders forced the foreigners out, international presence in the region had been limited largely to humanitarian aid. The International Red Cross provided pensioners with free loaves of bread, and the OSCE conducted a humanitarian aid mission. Yet much humanitarian assistance designated for Chechnya was channeled through Russia, and often did not make it to the republic. Some Islamic states have offered assistance to Chechnya, but these resources are directed to the Wahhabis, who comprise a very small but powerful part of the region's population and are responsible for the majority of the violence in the region. For example, Saudi Arabia financed the establishment of Islamic schools, which paid students $50 each month for attendance. This was an attractive offer for many unemployed youth (Muradov).

Western governments have condemned Russia's brutal 1999 Chechen campaign, but are hesitant to adopt sanctions against Russia. The West has strong interests in Chechnya because further destabilization there could have a negative impact on nearby Georgia and Azerbaijan. Both are important to the development of Caspian oil reserves. Maskhadov has tried to raise funds in the UK, Turkey, and the U.S., but politicians and potential foreign investors there are generally more interested in recovering hostages held on Chechen territory and the republic's ability to get along with Moscow than discussing the details of any investment projects.

The Chechen leadership said that it would recognize the Taliban, the militant Islamic group that controls much of Afghanistan. Russia, however, indicated that such relations would be illegal, arguing that part of a state cannot establish relations with another state (*RFE/RL,* 24 August 1998).

Attitudes Toward Business: Violence Scares off Potential Investors

Before the 1994–96 Chechen war, the republic served as an enormous arms bazaar, and weapons merchants were able to set up their trade after that war ended (Gall and de Wahl, 370). But the region's reputation for violence keeps most investors out. In theory, Chechnya could once again become involved in the oil business. In addition to transporting Caspian oil, Chechnya could rebuild its refining capacity to revive its economy. Before the 1999 Russian invasion, Chechnya extracted about 5,000

Aslan Alievich Maskhadov

21 September 1951—Born in Kazakhstan to a Chechen family that had been deported there

1957—Family moved back to Chechnya

1969—Began serving in the Soviet military

1969—Graduated from the Tbilisi Higher Military School

1981—Graduated from Moscow's Kalinin Higher Artillery School and proceeded to serve as a platoon commander in the Russian Far East and as a regiment commander in Seged, Hungary

Fall 1990—Chief of staff of the rocket and artillery forces and the deputy commander of the 7th Division in Vilnius, Lithuania

January 1991—Participated in the Soviet troops' storming of the television tower in Vilnius

Fall 1992—Following a conflict with his new commander on the eve of his division's move to the Leningrad Military District, resigned from the military

November 1992—Returned to Chechnya

1992–1994—Served as chief of Chechnya's civil defense, deputy chief of Chechnya's armed forces

March 1994—Named chief of staff of Chechen armed forces; participated in raids against the anti-Dudaev opposition in Urus-Martanov, Nadterech, and Gudermes raions

11 December 1994—Russian invasion of Chechnya begins

December 1994–January 1995—Following the Russian invasion, headed the defense of the presidential palace in Grozny

February 1995—Promoted to rank of general by Chechen President Dzhokhar Dudaev

June 1995—Participated in peace talks

April 1996—Dudaev assassinated

August 30–31, 1996—Signed Khasavyurt agreement with Russian Security Council Secretary Aleksandr Lebed postponing a decision on Chechnya's status with regard to Russia until 31 December 2001

17 October 1996—Became Chechen prime minister under interim President Zelimkhan Yandarbiev

23 November 1996—Signed an agreement with Prime Minister Viktor Chernomyrdin defining relations between Russia and Chechnya

27 January 1997—Elected president of Chechnya with 59.3% of the vote

12 May 1997—Met with Yeltsin

18 August 1997—Met with Yeltsin

23 June 1998—Declared state of emergency

23 July 1998—Survived assassination attempt

15 December 1998—Declared second state of emergency

tons of petroleum a day, but 2,000 tons never reached its refineries because they were either stolen, dumped on the ground, or burned in the republic's numerous fires (*NG*, 2 December 1998). Overall output was much less than before the col-lapse of the Soviet Union. Since four foreign telecom company workers were beheaded in December 1998, other potential investors would be unlikely to enter the market any time soon.

Ultimately, working with the Chechen diaspora

may provide opportunities for establishing international business ties. But even this possibility is in doubt. The Chechen-Mokhadzhirs who live in Turkey do not support Maskhadov's clan.

Internet Sites in the Region

http://www.amina.com/chechens/
This site has extensive information about Chechnya, including daily news reports, maps of the republic, photographs, biographic information, and other materials.

http://src-home.slav.hokudai.ac.jp/eng/server-e-fr1.html
This site contains numerous links to web pages with information about Chechnya.

CHELYABINSK OBLAST

Territory: 87,900 km^2
Population (as of 1 January 1998): 3,681,000
Distance from Moscow: 1,919 km

Major Cities:
Chelyabinsk, *capital* (pop. 1,084,100)
Magnitogorsk (425,000)
Zlatoust (199,600)
Miass (166,200)
Ozersk (89,000)
Troitsk (85,100)
Kopeisk (72,900)

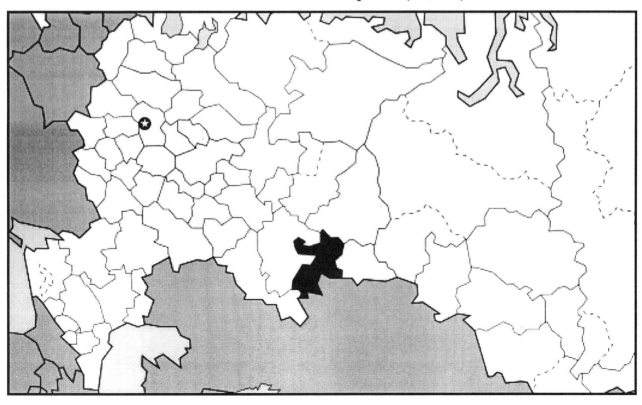

Basic Facts

Population (as of 1 Jan. 1998): 3,681,000 (2.5% of Russian total)

Ethnic breakdown (1989 census): Russians 81%, Tatars 6.2%, Bashkirs 4.5%, Ukrainians 3.0%, Germans 1.1%

Urban population (as of 1 Jan. 1998): 81.3% (Russia overall: 73.1%)

Student population (as of 1 Sept. 1997): 184 per 10,000 (Russia overall: 208/10,000)

Pensioner population (1997): 26.0% (Russia overall: 25.96%)

Percent of population with higher education (1989 census): 9.0% (Russia overall: 11.3%)

Percent of population working in (1997): Industry: 31.6% (Russian average: 23.0%); Agriculture: 9.2% (13.7%); Trade: 13.2% (13.5%); Culture: 12.9% (13.3%)

Average monthly personal income in July 1998: 694.9 new rubles (Russian average: 891.7 new rubles)

Average monthly personal expenses in July 1998: 487.6 new rubles (Russian average: 684.9 new rubles)

Average monthly subsistence requirement in 1998: 363 new rubles (Russian average: 438 new rubles)

Consumer price index (as of July 1998): 96 (Russia overall = 100)

Budgetary revenues (1997): 8,330.2 billion rubles (Russia overall: 433,378.2 billion rubles)

Budgetary expenditures (1997): 8,557.1 billion rubles (Russia overall: 468,111.6 billion rubles)

Industrial production as percentage of all Russian production (Jan.–Aug. 1998): 2.89%

Proportion of loss-making enterprises (as of July 1998): 45.6% (Russia overall: 50.4%)

Number of enterprises which have wage arrears (as of 1 Sept. 1998): 1,499 (1.11% of Russian total)

Agricultural production as percentage of all Russian production (1997): 2.25%

Number of private farms (as of 1 Jan. 1998): 5,957 (2.17% of Russian total)

Capital investment (1997): 8,362.1 billion rubles (Russia overall: 408,797 billion rubles)

Sources of investment (1997): federal budget: 9.8% (Russian average: 10.2%); regional budget: 18.4% (10.5%); extra-budgetary funds: 71.8% (79.3%)

Foreign investment (1997): 40,275,000 USD (Russia overall: 12,294,734,000 USD)

Number of joint ventures (1997): 217 (1.47% of Russian total)

Fixed capital investment in joint ventures and foreign companies (1997): 95,659 million rubles (Russia overall: 16,265.4 billion rubles)

Number of small businesses (as of 1 July 1998): 17,700 (2.04% of Russian total)

Number of enterprises privatized in 1997: 32 (1.17% of Russian total), including those which used to be municipal property: 96.9% (Russian average: 66.4%); regional property: 0% (20.0%); federal property: 3.1% (13.6%)

Number of telephones per 100 families (1997): in cities: 41.4 (Russian average: 49.2); in villages: 17.6 (19.8)

Brief Overview

Chelyabinsk Oblast is situated in the southern Urals bordering Kazakhstan; Bashkortostan; Sverdlovsk, Kurgan, and Orenburg oblasts. The city of Chelyabinsk, the oblast's administrative center, was founded as a fortress in 1736.

The region is rich in mineral resources such as coal, iron and copper ores, graphite, and clays. The oblast also possesses a highly developed industry, mainly ferrous and non-ferrous metallurgy, ore mining, mechanical engineering, and machine building. It ranks fifth nationally in terms of industrial production.

Major industrial centers are Magnitogorsk, with iron and steel plants, and Chelyabinsk, on the Miass River. The oblast also houses large nuclear industry centers in the cities of Snezhinsk and Ozersk and important manufacturers of space equipment and rockets. Until 1992, the region was closed to foreigners since nuclear weapons were produced at its militarized industrial cities. The area suffers greatly from radioactive contamination caused by nuclear waste and nuclear accidents in 1949, 1957, and 1967. Today, it has one of the highest pollution rates in the country (282.3 kg of waste per capita), according to *Ekspert* magazine.

The oblast's financial situation has been rather stable. For instance, in 1997 it generated one of the highest proportions of regionally based budget revenues—93.3 percent. According to a 1998 survey by *Ekspert* magazine, the oblast ranked 15th among Russia's 89 regions in terms of investment potential and 60th in terms of investment risk. A 1998 survey by Bank Austria ranked the oblast 10th in terms of investment climate.

Electoral History

2000 Presidential Election
Putin: 49.00%
Zyuganov: 32.46%
Yavlinskii: 7.80%
Zhirinovsky: 2.85%
Tuleev: 1.82%
Turnout: 68.08% (Russia overall: 68.64%)

1999 Parliamentary Elections
Communist Party of the Russian Federation: 22.58%
Unity: 19.83%
Union of Right Forces: 11.61%
Yabloko: 10.33%
Fatherland–All Russia: 8.61%
Zhirinovsky Bloc: 6.21%
In single-mandate districts: 1 Communist Party of the Russian Federation, 4 independent
Turnout: 60.82% (Russia overall: 61.85%)

1996 Gubernatorial Election
Sumin (State Duma Deputy): 50.79%
Solovev (incumbent, Chelyabinsk Oblast Union of Industrialists and Entrepreneurs): 15.99%
Grigoriadi (State Duma deputy): 8.58%
Golovlev (State Duma deputy): 6.49%
Kichedzhi: 3.64%
Kostromin (National-State party): 3.52%
Belishko: 1.42%
Ubozhko (Conservative party): 0.84%
Vlasov: 0.45%
Yalovenko (LDPR): 0.42%
Turnout: 53.48%

1996 Presidential Election
Yeltsin: 36.60%/58.52% (first round/second round)
Zyuganov: 24.73%/34.96%
Lebed: 19.82%
Yavlinskii: 8.77%
Zhirinovsky: 5.23%
Turnout: 70.29%/69.31% (Russia overall: 69.67%/ 68.79%)

1995 Parliamentary Elections
Communist Party of the Russian Federation: 14.70%
Liberal Democratic Party of Russia: 10.06%
Yabloko: 9.89%
Our Home Is Russia: 7.94%
Congress of Russian Communities: 7.33%
Russia's Democratic Choice: 6.72%
Communists–Workers' Russia: 5.79%
Women of Russia: 5.75%
Party of Workers' Self-Government: 4.80%
In single-mandate districts: 2 Russia's Democratic Choice, 3 Congress of Russian Communities
Turnout: 62.80% (Russia overall: 64.37%)

1993 Constitutional Referendum
"Yes"—75.6% "No"—22.3%

1993 Parliamentary Elections
Russia's Choice: 23.58%
Liberal Democratic Party of Russia: 20.38%
Yabloko: 11.34%
Women of Russia: 8.52%
Communist Party of the Russian Federation: 7.49%
Party of Russian Unity and Concord: 6.77%
Democratic Party of Russia: 4.69%
Agrarian Party of Russia: 4.06%
In single-mandate districts: 3 Russia's Choice,
    2 independent
Turnout: 51.43% (Russia overall: 54.34%)

1991 Presidential Elections
Yeltsin: 77.20%
Ryzhkov: 8.14%
Zhirinovsky: 5.77%
Makashov: 2.75%
Tuleev: 2.02%
Bakatin: 1.74%
Turnout: 80.31% (Russia overall: 76.66%)

Regional Political Institutions

Executive:
Governor, 4-year term
    Petr Ivanovich Sumin, elected December 1996
    Ul. Tsvillinga, 27; Chelyabinsk, 454089
    Tel 7(351–2) 33–92–41
    Fax 7(351–2) 36–25–90
    Federation Council in Moscow:
    7(095) 292–41–16, 926–68–24

Legislative:
Unicameral
    Legislative Assembly (Zakonodatelnoe
    Sobranie)—41 members, 4-year term, elected
    December 1996
    Chairman—Viktor Fedorovich Davydov,
    elected December 1995, January 1997

Regional Politics

Moderate Oppositionist Tackles Economic Depression

Petr Sumin has been prominent in Ural politics since
the early 1990s when he became the chairman of
the Chelyabinsk Oblast Council of People's Deputies. In 1993 Sumin formed his own regional political movement, the Revival of the Urals, which exhibits a rather Communist coloring. The same year,
he was popularly elected governor of Chelyabinsk
but did not take office because the Constitutional
Court declared the election illegal. In 1995 Sumin
was elected to the State Duma, and one year later
he won election as governor of Chelyabinsk Oblast,
earning 53.92 percent of the vote.

Sumin's Revival of the Urals movement enjoys
considerable popularity in Chelyabinsk but has little
influence outside the oblast. Sumin has sampled various oppositionist parties and movements, supporting both Aleksandr Lebed and Gennadii Zyuganov
at various times. The majority of Sumin's policies,
however, are dark pink—state regulation of enterprise activities, media censorship, and a strong emphasis on the social consequences of reform. As
governor of Chelyabinsk, Sumin has been confronted
with a depressing economic situation offering bleak
prospects for development. Though he has actively
sought foreign investment in the region, the results
of his efforts have not proven sufficient for maintaining a healthy economy.

Sumin has demanded that the federal government take responsibility for the impact of its actions on the region's welfare. He comfortably rejects the federal government's authority in circumstances when he feels it is acting unjustly. Sumin's
primary ally in the Russian government was former
Prime Minister Viktor Chernomyrdin, whom he relied on to gain needed subsidies for the region.

Executive Platform: Moderately Communist

Petr Sumin follows a primarily oppositionist plat-
form, and is frequently described as moderately
Communist even though he is not an official mem-
ber of the Communist party. In April 1995 he joined
General Aleksandr Lebed's Congress of Russian
Communities (KRO) as a member of the National
Council. A few months later he was elected to the
State Duma on the KRO ticket. Yet, his loyalty to
Lebed was shallow, and in the 1996 presidential
campaign he backed Gennadii Zyuganov over
Lebed. In the 1999–2000 elections he backed the
pro-Kremlin Unity ticket.

Policies: Unsuccessful Economic Salvation

The primary focus of Sumin's governance has been
economic policy. Sumin is actively involved in try-

ing to prevent the region's bleak economic situation from falling into complete collapse. However, the governor has not had much success in finding lasting solutions to Chelyabinsk's problems. In July 1998 Sumin signed a decree allowing oblast taxes to be paid with promissory notes from branches of six Moscow commercial banks and four oblast banks. The financial crisis and effective ruble devaluation that occurred shortly thereafter presumably made collecting on the promissory notes extremely difficult, thus leaving a void in the oblast budget. While this was happening, oblast miners blockaded the Trans-Siberian railway for more than a month, placing an additional strain on regional industries and oblast resources. In order to end the blockade, the oblast administration took out a short-term 15-million-ruble loan at five percent annual interest from the Promstroi Bank, adding to its financial burden. (For more details on the blockade, see Relationships Between Key Players.)

After Russia's economy collapsed in August, Sumin established a special rapid response task force for dealing with the situation in the oblast. Emphasizing that the oblast was in no position to bail out regional banks, he asked Acting Prime Minister Viktor Chernomyrdin to pressure the Central Bank to help regional banks. He also suggested that organizations transfer their accounts from branches of Moscow affiliates to local banks. With help from Chernomyrdin, Sumin managed to secure 900 million rubles for pension payments in Chelyabinsk and got the federal government to forgive 236 million rubles in loans the oblast received for agricultural production.

Then, to ensure the maintenance of the region's industrial base and prevent further uprisings like the miners' blockade, Sumin told the directors of the ten largest enterprises in the oblast that he would personally coordinate their relations with the regional railroad, as well as electricity and natural gas providers, until the economic situation became more stable. Sumin's goal was to alleviate conflicts that could destabilize and shut down Chelyabinsk's enterprises. Sumin demanded that the enterprise and monopoly directors report to him about their progress in improving relations and about the plants' situation in regard to electricity, gas, and cargo shipments (*EWI RRR*, 15 October 1998).

Although Sumin prioritizes economic policy above all else, his approaches to solving the region's problems tend to be short-term. The only major new initiative he has enacted is a sales tax, which went into effect on 1 October 1998. The tax is expected to generate 750 million rubles a year, 40 percent of which will go to the oblast budget, and 60 percent to local governments. This alone, however, will not solve the region's economic problems.

Relationships Between Key Players: Strong Support

In spite of the region's economic difficulties, Sumin enjoys strong support in Chelyabinsk. The Chelyabinsk Oblast legislature is dominated by members of Sumin's Revival of the Urals movement. In Chelyabinsk Oblast's 1997 legislative elections the movement was also reportedly supported by current Krasnoyarsk Krai Governor Aleksandr Lebed and by members of the Communist Party and Yabloko (*RFE/RL*, 16 December 1997). Two of Chelyabinsk's representatives to the 1995–1999 State Duma, Aleksandr Chershintsev and Vladimir Gorbachev, were backed by the Revival of the Urals, providing Sumin with legislative support at the federal level (*RFE/RL*, 16 December 1997).

The media in Chelyabinsk generally give Sumin and his administration favorable coverage. However, in early 1998 a radio report quoted a local human rights defender severely criticizing Chelyabinsk Prime Minister Vladimir Utkin. Four days later the chair of the Chelyabinsk Oblast State Television and Radio Company, Vitalii Ponurov, ordered that any news reports on top officials in the region must be cleared by the company's first deputy chairman, Boris Durmanov, essentially reestablishing censorship in Chelyabinsk's mass media (*RFE/RL*, 29 January 1998).

One of the greatest challenges Sumin has encountered in his region was the 31-day blockade of the Trans-Siberian railroad by Chelyabinsk miners in July and August 1998, after they had been on strike since the end of June to protest wage arrears. Throughout the stand-off, Sumin warned that he might declare a state of emergency, especially as the fuel shortages threatened to shut down the oblast's Mayak nuclear storage facility, presenting an immense environmental hazard. To resolve the situation, a tripartite agreement was concluded between Sumin, the management of Chelyabinskugol, and union leaders. Money to cover the back wages came primarily from the federal defense ministry and power and heat producers in the oblast, all of which had run up sizable debts to Chelyabinskugol. The oblast administration took out a short-term 15 million ruble loan at five percent annual interest from the Promstroi Bank in order to pay the miners in full (*EWI RRR*, 27 August 1998).

In the sphere of regional development, one of the big construction projects in the oblast is the building of a subway system in the capital city, Chelyabinsk. Sumin considers this one of the most important projects in the region. It is being financed through federal subsides and by the tax debt of construction companies to the federal, oblast, and local budgets.

Ties to Moscow: Former Chernomyrdin Supporter

Sumin has an active relationship with the federal government, and has frequently looked to Moscow to help Chelyabinsk out of various difficulties. Sumin had cultivated a good relationship with former Prime Minister Viktor Chernomyrdin and was pleased when Chernomyrdin was re-appointed as acting Prime Minister following the dismissal of Sergei Kirienko in August 1998. Sumin felt that Chernomyrdin would be supportive of the regions' interests and would help improve the country's difficult economic and financial situation. Chernomyrdin had the support of several regional executives because of his ability to secure federal subsidies for them.

Sumin is not afraid to play hardball with the federal government. One example was the situation regarding federal tax debts and Chelyabenergo, the regional subsidiary of the Unified Energy System (EES). On 26 June 1998 the Federal Tax Service notified all regional subsidiaries of EES that they had to pay their tax debts in full by 1 July or tax authorities reserved the right to freeze bank accounts and confiscate their property. Sumin sent a telegram to then Prime Minister Sergei Kirienko and the federal tax authorities stating that Chelyabenergo would not pay any federal taxes until the federal authorities paid their debt to the company. The federal government owed Chelyabenergo 2.5 times the amount the enterprise owed to the federal budget. Sumin further declared that he was taking personal responsibility for relieving Chelyabenergo of its

federal tax obligation (*EWI RRR*, 2 July 1998).

In June 1998 Sumin signed an agreement between Chelyabinsk and then Deputy Prime Minister Viktor Khristenko on improving the oblast's financial situation. Chelyabinsk resolved to follow federal standards in credit agreements, housing issues, wage levels, and restructuring tax debts. The goal of the agreement was to help the oblast pay wage arrears to public sector employees and avoid such problems in the future.

Khristenko and Sumin also signed an agreement stating their respective rights in regard to international economic relations and investment policies. The agreement states that all of Russia's international agreements affecting the economic interests of Chelyabinsk Oblast must be approved by the oblast administration before signing. The agreement also gives Chelyabinsk jurisdiction over the region's foreign economic relations, development and implementation of foreign economic and investment programs, regulation of activities of foreign nationals and entities on oblast territory, and borrowing on foreign markets using the oblast budget as collateral (*EWI RRR*, 2 July 1998). Both the oblast and Moscow are responsible for coordinating Chelyabinsk's exports, drafting Russia's international agreements that affect the oblast's interests, formulating and implementing federal, regional, and inter-regional programs regarding foreign economic relations and foreign investment in the oblast economy, and coordinating activities concerning the establishment of free economic zones in Chelyabinsk. Other stipulations of the agreement include a federal transfer of state shares in publicly owned enterprises to the oblast government under a trust management arrangement and the creation of free economic zones in the oblast to attract foreign investment. This agreement more clearly defines Chelyabinsk's relations to Moscow, building on the power-sharing agreement the region signed with President Boris Yeltsin in July 1997.

Relations with Other Regions: Courted by Luzhkov

Moscow Mayor Yurii Luzhkov has proposed several cooperative projects between Moscow and Chelyabinsk—in particular, initiatives to help closed cities in the region (*EWI RRR*, 22 October 1998).

Nevertheless, Sumin declined to join Luzhkov's Fatherland party in favor of the Voice of Russia political bloc, which was founded by Samara Governor Konstantin Titov. By the time of the December 1999 parliamentary elections, however, Sumin had signed on with the Kremlin's new Unity bloc.

Chelyabinsk belongs to the Urals Regional Association, which includes the republics of Bashkortostan and Udmurtia; Komi-Permyak Autonomous Okrug; and Kurgan, Orenburg, Perm, and Sverdlovsk oblasts.

Foreign Relations: Building Economic Ties

Sumin has been active promoting Chelyabinsk on the international scene and has developed economic relationships with several foreign countries. In early 1998 Chelyabinsk signed a cooperation agreement with Bulgaria's Plovdiv region (*EWI RRR*, 9 April 1998). One part of the agreement is to create a loading machine joint building venture. The two regions are also contemplating opening a Russian-Bulgarian Business Center in Chelyabinsk, which would act as a dealer for the venture. Another joint venture involves building a Russian-Bulgarian tobacco factory in Chelyabinsk that is capable of processing 5,000 tons of tobacco per year. In July 1997 the Chelyabinsk Oblast administration signed a $5 million contract with the government of Turkmenistan to supply Turkmenistan with cars and tractors in exchange for Turkmen cotton and textile products.

In 1998, 22 Chelyabinsk agricultural enterprises hired 604 Chinese peasants to work on their land. The Chinese workers received 17.25 percent of the overall harvest. In comparing harvests over the previous several years, the Ovoshchi Association had found that Chinese workers produced a yield three to four times higher than that of the Russian agricultural workers, and thus the hiring of Chinese workers instead of Russians had proven more profitable for the region's agricultural sector.

Sumin has been very concerned about the United States' anti-dumping campaign against Russian metal enterprises. He met with then Prime Minister Primakov regarding this issue in November 1998, requesting that the prime minister address the issue with American leaders. Half of Chelyabinsk's GDP comes from the region's steel mills, particularly the giant plant at Magnitogorsk, and Russian producers made close to $1 billion in 1998 by exporting steel to the United States (*EWI RRR*, 19 November 1998). In 1998 the U.S. bought about 70 percent of Russian steel since its price was considerably lower than that of domestic steel (*EWI RRR*, 5 November 1998). However, in February 1999 the U.S. imposed import restrictions on Russian exports that effectively lowered Russian exports in 1999 to about 15 percent of what they were in 1998. The U.S. was concerned about protecting the jobs of American workers. The Russian steel makers have reduced the sting of this loss by finding new customers on the domestic market and in the rebounding Asian economies.

Attitudes Toward Business: Wants FDI

Sumin has concentrated considerable attention on Chelyabinsk's industrial base, attempting to attract investment in order to improve the region's depressed economy. In January 1998 Sumin participated in the second annual U.S.-Russian Investment Symposium held at Harvard University, and in March 1998 he engaged in a meeting of the Gore-Chernomyrdin summit in Washington. At the meeting Sumin signed a $62 million agreement with the American firm AGKO Limited to create a joint venture for producing 200 combines per year. The joint venture was not very successful and was regarded by many as simply another attempt by Sumin to take control of the Chelyabinsk Tractor Factory (*KD*, 20 March 1998).

Sumin's administration has tried several ways to take over the Chelyabinsk Tractor Factory, which was declared bankrupt in 1997 (*KD*, 20 March 1998). However, the oblast has yet to successfully revitalize the once prominent enterprise. An auction to sell off the plant was held in early 1999, but no one offered a bid in the competition. The asking price was 3 billion rubles, the amount owed to the plant's creditors; yet a much higher investment in the plant would be necessary to turn it into a profitable enterprise. The factory was considered one of the Soviet Union's great industrial achievements, producing 30,000 tractors annually during the 1960s–1980s. In the 1990s production fell to below 10 percent of its previous levels, and by now most of the factory's valuable equipment has been

Petr Ivanovich Sumin

21 June 1946—Born in the village Verkhnyaya Sanarka in Chelyabinsk Oblast

1969—Graduated from the metallurgy department of the Chelyabinsk Polytechnic Institute

1969–1971—Worked in the Chelyabinsk Metallurgy Factory

1971–1973—Deputy secretary, secretary of the Komsomol committee of the Chelyabinsk Metallurgy Factory

1972—Joined the Communist Party

1973–1978—First secretary of the Metallurgy district committee of the Komsomol, then second secretary and first secretary of the Chelyabinsk city committee of the Komsomol

1978–1980—Assistant shop director of the Chelyabinsk Metallurgy Factory

1980–1984—Second, then first, secretary of the CPSU Metallurgy district committee

1984–1987—Chair of the Chelyabinsk City Executive Committee

1987–1989—First deputy chair of the Chelyabinsk Oblast Executive Committee

1989–1990—Second secretary of the Chelyabinsk CPSU Oblast Committee

18 March 1990—Elected to the RSFSR Congress of People's Deputies

Spring 1990—Elected to the Chelyabinsk Oblast Soviet

1990–1991—Chairman of the Chelyabinsk Oblast Executive Committee

January 1991—Elected chair of the Chelyabinsk Soviet

25 April 1993—Elected governor of Chelyabinsk Oblast, but did not take office (elections were ruled invalid)

1993—Founded the Revival of the Urals movement

1993–1995—Vice President of the Ural Investment Holding Company, Vybor

April 1995—Elected member of the National Council of the Congress of Russian Communities (KRO)

17 December 1995—Elected to the Duma

22 December 1996—Elected governor of Chelyabinsk Oblast

---

stolen and the remaining workers frequently report to work drunk (*KD*, 2 February 1999).

One of the region's most important enterprises is Chelyabenergo, the oblast's top power producer, providing 87 percent of Chelyabinsk's electricity supply. In May 1998 the enterprise signed a credit agreement with Siemens corporation, Germany's Hermes insurance group, and two foreign banks to provide a loan for financing the final part of Chelyabenergo's heating station plant. The credit is being delivered over a 12–year period, and Chelyabenergo will begin paying back the loan two years after the station is completed.

In July 1998 Koelgamramor, the largest marble quarrying and processing enterprise in the CIS, located in Koelga, Chelyabinsk Oblast, opened a $1.5 million Italian-made production line. Koelgamramor supplied the marble fixtures that went into the reconstructed Christ the Savior Cathedral in Moscow.

In April 1999 Sumin announced that he was granting political protection from possible bankruptcy to the 200 firms deemed most important to Chelyabinsk's economy. The governor believed that as many as 2,000 firms could be declared bankrupt in Chelyabinsk. He thought that the oblast law on bankruptcy must be amended since it allowed every creditor, regardless of how small, to initiate bankruptcy proceedings against large enterprises. To address this problem, the oblast administration created a special committee to determine whether it makes sense to bankrupt specific firms, thus preventing the bankruptcy of enterprises that are vital to the oblast economy (*EWI RRR*, 21 April 1999).

Internet Sites in the Region

http://www.gubern.chel.su
This is the official home page of the Chelyabinsk Oblast administration, featuring a governor's page, contact details for administration officials, and an economic survey of the oblast. You can also send e-mail messages to Sumin and the oblast's presidential representative Nikolai Sudenkov. The site also includes some useful official documents, such as the text of Chelyabinsk's power-sharing agreement with the federal government.

http://www.chel.com.ru/chelyabinsk/
This site features the city of Chelyabinsk and provides detailed information on local policy, the economic situation, business initiatives, and links to regional newspapers and magazines.

CHITA OBLAST

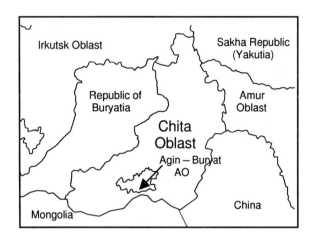

Territory: 431,500 km²
Population (as of 1 January 1998):
1,277,000
Distance from Moscow: 6,074 km

Major Cities:
Chita, *capital* (pop. 313,000)
Krasnokamensk (56,800)
Borzya (32,200)

Basic Facts

Population (as of 1 Jan. 1998): 1,277,000 (0.87% of Russian total)

Ethnic breakdown (1989 census): Russians 91.0%, Ukrainians 3.0%, Buryats 2.8%, Tatars 1.0%

Urban population (as of 1 Jan. 1998): 62.8% (Russia overall: 73.1%)

Student population (as of 1 Sept. 1997): 105 per 10,000 (Russia overall: 208/10,000)

Pensioner population (1997): 20.75% (Russia overall: 25.96%)

Percent of population with higher education (1989 census): 10.3% (Russia overall: 11.3%)

Percent of population working in (1997): Industry: 16.4% (Russian average: 23.0%); Agriculture: 12.8% (13.7%); Trade: 13.6% (13.5%); Culture: 14.3% (13.3%)

Average monthly personal income in July 1998: 516.3 new rubles (Russian average: 891.7 new rubles)

Average monthly personal expenses in July 1998: 338.1 new rubles (Russian average: 684.9 new rubles)

Average monthly subsistence requirement in 1998: 521 new rubles (Russian average: 438 new rubles)

Consumer price index (as of July 1998): 161 (Russia overall = 100)

Budgetary revenues (1997): 2,477.9 billion rubles (Russia overall: 433,378.2 billion rubles)

Budgetary expenditures (1997): 2,987.3 billion rubles (Russia overall: 468,111.6 billion rubles)

Industrial production as percentage of all Russian production (Jan.–Aug. 1998): 0.23%

Proportion of loss-making enterprises (as of July 1998): 79.2% (Russia overall: 50.4%)

Number of enterprises which have wage arrears (as of 1 Sept. 1998): 827 (0.61% of Russian total)

Agricultural production as percentage of all Russian production (1997): 0.88%

Number of private farms (as of 1 Jan. 1998): 1,873 (0.68% of Russian total)

Capital investment (1997): 1,844.0 billion rubles (Russia overall: 408,797 billion rubles)

Sources of investment (1997): federal budget: 19.2% (Russian average: 10.2%); regional budget: 3.7% (10.5%); extra-budgetary funds: 77.1% (79.3%)

Foreign investment (1997): 281,000 USD (Russia overall: 12,294,734,000 USD)

Number of joint ventures (1997): 30 (0.2% of Russian total)

Fixed capital investment in joint ventures and foreign companies (1997): 6,242 million rubles (Russia overall: 16,265.4 billion rubles)

Number of small businesses (as of 1 July 1998): 4,000 (0.46% of Russian total)

Number of enterprises privatized in 1997: 16 (0.58% of Russian total), including those which used to be municipal property: 56.2% (Russian average: 66.4%); regional property: 12.5% (20.0%); federal property: 31.3% (13.6%)

Number of telephones per 100 families (1997): in cities: 29.2 (Russian average: 49.2); in villages: 14.3 (19.8)

Brief Overview

The territory that makes up today's Chita Oblast was first explored by Cossacks led by Petr Beketov in 1653. People began to move into and develop the area in order to strengthen Russia's border with China and Mongolia, extract mineral resources, and build the Trans-Siberian railroad. In 1920, Chita became the capital of the Far East Republic, which merged with the Russian Federation in November 1922, a month before the Soviet Union was constituted. This southeast Siberian oblast has extensive international borders with China (998 km) and Mongolia (868 km) and internal borders with Irkutsk and Amur oblasts and the republics of Buryatia and Sakha (Yakutia).

The oblast's territory is rich in ferrous, non-ferrous, rare, and precious metals (6 percent of Russia's total gold and 16 percent of its silver reserves), coal, charcoal, and mineral waters. Forests cover about 60 percent of its territory. As a result, the oblast's main industries are metallurgy, fuel, and timber. However, the decades of exploiting regional natural resources have created environmental problems that threaten the safety and health of Chita's residents. High rates of uranium and thorium production have contaminated groundwater, damaged agricultural land, and created waste sites near apartment buildings. The uranium processing plant in Krasnokamensk produces a waste steam with the highest level of radioactivity of any uranium production site in the world. The oblast also has advanced light and food industries. Local agriculture focuses on cattle, reindeer, and sheep breeding. Chita Oblast accounts for over 40 percent of wool production in Eastern Siberia.

In addition to a grim ecological situation, Chita Oblast has suffered one of the worst economic declines in the country. According to a survey by *Ekspert* magazine, in 1997 its industrial production was under 25 percent of the 1991 output (16th worst in the country), while real per capita income slightly exceeded 10 percent of 1991 levels. That is why, aside from ecological problems, there are no major international investment projects underway in the region, although it has extensive border trade with China.

According to the same study by *Ekspert*, the oblast ranked 52nd among Russia's 89 regions in terms of investment potential and 82nd in terms of investment risks. A 1998 survey by Bank Austria ranked the oblast 62nd in terms of investment climate.

Electoral History

2000 Presidential Election
Putin: 49.14%
Zyuganov: 35.48%
Zhirinovsky: 5.87%
Tuleev: 2.43%
Yavlinskii: 2.07%
Turnout: 64.57% (Russia overall: 68.64%)

1999 Parliamentary Elections
Unity: 30.33%
Communist Party of the Russian Federation: 29.39%
Zhirinovsky Bloc: 12.68%
Union of Right Forces: 4.09%
Fatherland–All Russia: 3.35%
Communists–Workers' Russia: 3.09%
Women of Russia: 2.32%
Yabloko: 2.20%
In single-mandate districts: 2 independent
Turnout: 59.36% (Russia overall: 61.85%)

1996 Gubernatorial Election
Geniatulin (incumbent): 30.76%
Shvyryaev: 22.89%
Bogatov (State Duma deputy, LDPR): 19.55%
Kurochkin (State Duma deputy, KPRF): 10.98%
Kolesnikov (State Duma Deputy, APR): 7.14%
Turnout: 46.17%

1996 Presidential Election
Zyuganov: 39.12%/52.50% (first round/second round)
Yeltsin: 24.54%/40.89%
Zhirinovsky: 12.95%
Lebed: 11.70%
Yavlinskii: 5.49%
Turnout: 64.36%/62.01% (Russia overall: 69.67%/ 68.79%)

1995 Parliamentary Elections
Communist Party of the Russian Federation: 21.56%
Liberal Democratic Party of Russia: 20.59%
Communists–Workers' Russia: 8.29%
Agrarian Party of Russia: 6.10%

Women of Russia: 5.76%
Our Home Is Russia: 4.25%
Party of Workers' Self-Government: 4.14%
In single-mandate districts: 1 Agrarian Party of
    Russia, 1 independent
Turnout: 64.02% (Russia overall: 64.37%)

1993 Constitutional Referendum
"Yes"—55.3% "No"—42.1%

1993 Parliamentary Elections
Liberal Democratic Party of Russia: 30.49%
Communist Party of the Russian Federation: 11.54%
Russia's Choice: 10.92%
Women of Russia: 9.96%
Agrarian Party of Russia: 8.40%
Democratic Party of Russia: 7.61%
Party of Russian Unity and Concord: 6.72%
Yabloko: 4.50%
In single-mandate districts: 2 independent
Turnout: 49.33% (Russia overall: 54.34%)

1991 Presidential Elections
Yeltsin: 36.56%
Ryzhkov: 31.53%
Zhirinovsky: 10.65%
Tuleev: 6.57%
Makashov: 4.91%
Bakatin: 4.40%
Turnout: 75.28% (Russia overall: 76.66%)

Regional Political Institutions

Executive:
    Governor, 4–year term
    Ravil Faritovich Geniatulin, elected
    October 1996
        Chita Oblast Administration;
        Ul. Tchaikovskaya, 8; Chita-21, 672021
        Tel 7(302–22) 3–34–93, 3–21–84;
        Fax 7(302–22) 6–33–19
        Federation Council in Moscow:
        7(095) 292–57–70, 926–65–32

Legislative:
    Unicameral
    Oblast Duma—39 members, 4–year term,
    elected October 1996
    Chairman—Vitalii Yevgenevich Vishnyakov,
    elected March 1994, November 1996

Regional Politics

Yeltsin Appointee in Environmental Disaster Zone

President Boris Yeltsin appointed Ravil Geniatulin governor of Chita Oblast in February 1996, and he won election to the office in October of that year. The region he now governs is one of the poorest in Russia, but it also has considerable potential.

Chita possesses rich deposits of gold, silver, thorium, and uranium. The gold-mining potential around the town of Balei is attracting the greatest international attention. An estimated $2.8 billion worth of gold ore is located in and around Balei's existing mines (www.earthisland.org). Foreign investors equipped with modern technology hope to capitalize on these resources. Residents welcome this development, which will inevitably improve the region's struggling economy. In Balei, dangerously high indoor radiation levels have caused numerous health problems. Many city residents pass diseases from generation to generation, and 95 percent of the children in affected areas have been diagnosed with chronic problems (www.earthisland.org). Regional authorities hope to review proposed operations to ensure that international standards for responsible mining are maintained and environmental standards enforced.

Executive Platform: Reformer in Oppositionist Stronghold

Yeltsin appointed Geniatulin to replace Boris Ivanov shortly before the region's first gubernatorial elections. Geniatulin won election to the post of governor a few months later, in October. He received only 31 percent of the vote in the oblast's first-past-the-post elections. Geniatulin's closest rival received 23 percent of the vote, so the ultimate outcome might have been different if the electoral law had required a runoff. The opposition's vote was split between the KPRF and the Agrarian party, allowing Geniatulin to win in a traditionally leftist region.

Policies: Economic and Environmental Emergencies

Geniatulin's main policy initiatives address the region's economic and ecological challenges. On

31 October 1997 Geniatulin declared a state of emergency in Chita Oblast to deal with the region's energy crisis. Unpaid workers at Chita's largest power plant had gone on strike almost three weeks before, causing massive power cuts since the plant was forced to operate at half capacity. The situation became graver as temperatures dropped, threatening to freeze the heating systems in the oblast capital. The workers agreed to end the strike after the Chita administration allocated $1.7 million to pay half of the strikers' wage arrears.

In May 1998 the administrations of Chita and Khabarovsk Krai announced a state of emergency in connection with forest fires, prohibiting people from visiting the woods. Fires destroyed more than 150 thousand hectares of forest in Chita (*KD*, 21 May 1998).

Relationships Between Key Players

In August 1997 the Chita Oblast Administration, the Federation of Trade Unions, and the Union of Employers of Chita Oblast signed a trilateral agreement. The agreement focuses on cutting unemployment, stabilizing the labor market, and providing social guarantees. Similar agreements have been established in the past, but none have yielded successful results.

Ties to Moscow: Debt Defaulter

Given its poverty and remote location in southeastern Siberia on the Mongolian border, Moscow pays little attention to Chita. In June 1998 Chita Oblast became the first of several regions to default on payments of its agrobonds. Oblast officials claimed they were awaiting a $7.5 million transfer from the federal government to cover the debts, but the money never arrived. The default, combined with Russia's overall problems, will make it even more difficult for Chita to obtain credits.

Relations with Other Regions: Contributor to Alliance Group

In May 1998 Geniatulin joined with ten other governors to contribute funds to the Alliance Group, a foundation providing crisis support to enterprises in Russia and the CIS. The other founders are Saratov, Leningrad, Novgorod, Murmansk, Irkutsk,

Magadan, Novosibirsk, and Voronezh oblasts, and the republics of Udmurtia and Buryatia. The heads of these regions feel that close cooperation between regional administrations and enterprises provides the most effective aid (*FI*, 21 May 1998). Clearly it is in the governors' interests to revive enterprises, since administrations will benefit from the increased tax base.

Chita Oblast belongs to the Far East and Baikal Association, which is headed by Khabarovsk Krai Governor Viktor Ishaev. The association includes the republics of Buryatia and Sakha (Yakutia); Primorskii and Khabarovsk krais; Amur, Kamchatka, Magadan, and Sakhalin oblasts; the Jewish Autonomous Oblast; and the Koryak and Chukotka autonomous okrugs. In April 1997 the association agreed that it should increase cooperation with countries in the Asian-Pacific Region (APR). The Far Eastern regions intend to export machinery and raw materials to Asia and offer the APR countries opportunities to participate in joint ventures to extract far eastern mineral resources.

Foreign Relations: China Is Most Important

Geniatulin signed an accord with the deputy chairman of China's Inner Mongolia Autonomous Region on 22 November 1997. The agreement called for the construction of a 12-kilometer pipeline that would transport petroleum products to China. The pipeline will run from Zabaikalsk to Manchuria and will be able to carry 2,000 tons a day (*RFE/RL*, 24 November 1997).

In April 1996 the oblast Duma voted to restrict visits by foreigners to Chita to a maximum of fifteen days and to require all foreigners staying more than three days to register with the police. The law also states that local residents can rent apartments to foreigners only if there are at least 12 square meters of living space for each guest. This law was probably meant to discourage visitors from China (*RFE/RL*, 24 April 1996). The oblast has trouble with Chinese traders smuggling goods across the border to be sold in Russia.

International economic difficulties have also had negative consequences on Chita's economy. The Priargunsky Chemical Mining Union, which manages mining operations in Krasnokamensk, has been affected by the financial losses associated with the bankruptcy of Oren Benton, the former leader

Ravil Faritovich Geniatulin

20 December 1955—Born in Chita

1973–1974—After finishing school, Geniatulin worked at PATP-2, where he fixed automobiles

1974–1976—Served in the army in Ulan-Ude, Buryatia

1976–1980—Entered the history-philosophy department of the Chita Pedagogical Institute

1980–1982—Worked as a lecturer in the history department and served as the secretary of the institute's Komsomol committee

1982–1985—First secretary of the Chita city Komsomol committee

1985–1986—Instructor in the Chita city Party committee

1987–1990—Deputy chairman of the Chita city executive committee

1990–1991—First Secretary of the Chita city Party committee

14 November 1991—Elected chairman of the Chita city executive committee

24 December 1991—Appointed mayor of Chita city by order of the president

1 February 1996—Appointed governor of Chita Oblast by order of the president

27 October 1996—Elected governor of Chita Oblast

Married, with one son and two daughters; loves the waltz and pelmeni

in uranium trading. Krasnokamensk officials claim that they are owed $600 million from unfulfilled contracts with Benton's Concord Oil Company (www.earthisland.org).

Chita's environmental problems have attracted the attention of international scientists. There is strong potential that U.S. and non-Russian environmental scientists will work cooperatively with Russian scientists and technicians in Chita to develop and implement environmental management programs (www.earthisland.org).

Attitudes Toward Business

In October 1997 Geniatulin signed a general cooperation agreement with the president of Sidanko (*FI*, 28 October 1997). According to the agreement, the oblast administration will ensure the company favorable conditions to develop projects that increase the supply of fuel to the oblast. In return, Sidanko will guarantee that oblast enterprises are supplied with oil products. The administration also promised to give Sidanko priority in participating in the Eastern Transit project, which will supply gasoline and diesel fuel to China.

Internet Sites in the Region

http://www.chita-russia.org/
This colorful site provides lots of general political and economic information about the oblast.

CHUKOTKA AUTONOMOUS OKRUG

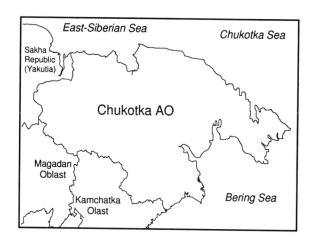

Territory: 737,700 km²
Population (as of 1 January 1998): 81,000
Distance from Moscow: 8,635 km

Major Cities:
Anadyr, *capital* (pop. 13,200)

Basic Facts

Population (as of 1 Jan. 1998): 81,000 (0.06% of Russian total)

Ethnic breakdown (1989 census): Russians 66.1%, Ukrainians 16.8%, Chukchi 7.3%, Belarusans 1.9%, Tatars 1.4%

Urban population (as of 1 Jan. 1998): 69.3% (Russia overall: 73.1%)

Pensioner population (1997): 17.28% (Russia overall: 25.96%)

Percent of population with higher education (1989 census): 14.9% (Russia overall: 11.3%)

Percent of population working in (1997): Industry: 22.0% (Russian average: 23.0%); Agriculture: 7.0% (13.7%); Trade: 7.5% (13.5%); Culture: 14.6% (13.3%)

Average monthly personal income in July 1998: 1,753.3 new rubles (Russian average: 891.7 new rubles)

Average monthly personal expenses in July 1998: 862.9 new rubles (Russian average: 684.9 new rubles)

Average monthly subsistence requirement in 1998: 1,701 new rubles (Russian average: 438 new rubles)

Consumer price index (as of July 1998): 323 (Russia overall = 100)

Budgetary revenues (1997): 1,511.8 billion rubles (Russia overall: 433,378.2 billion rubles)

Budgetary expenditures (1997): 1,995.2 billion rubles (Russia overall: 468,111.6 billion rubles)

Industrial production as percentage of all Russian production (Jan.–Aug. 1998): 0.06%

Proportion of loss-making enterprises (as of July 1998): 63.6% (Russia overall: 50.4%)

Number of enterprises which have wage arrears (as of 1 Sept. 1998): 179 (0.13% of Russian total)

Agricultural production as percentage of all Russian production (1997): 0.04%

Number of private farms (as of 1 Jan. 1998): 36 (0.01% of Russian total)

Capital investment (1997): 216.1 billion rubles (Russia overall: 408,797 billion rubles)

Sources of investment (1997): federal budget: 51.3% (Russian average: 10.2%); regional budget: 29.5% (10.5%); extra-budgetary funds: 19.2% (79.3%)

Number of small businesses (as of 1 July 1998): 100 (0.01% of Russian total)

Number of enterprises privatized in 1997: 5 (0.18% of Russian total), including those which used to be municipal property: 0% (Russian average: 66.4%); regional property: 20.0% (20.0%); federal property: 80.0% (13.6%)

Number of telephones per 100 families (1997): in cities: 53.8 (Russian average: 49.2); in villages: 24.5 (19.8)

Brief Overview

Chukotka Autonomous Okrug is located on the Chukotka peninsula, the easternmost point of Eurasia, and borders Magadan Oblast and the Koryak Autonomous Okrug.

Economic development of the okrug began in the 1930s with increased air and sea traffic in the region. The discovery of tin and gold fields in the 1940s brought additional interest. Since World War II, the okrug has been one of the country's main suppliers of industrial gold. Reindeer breeding dominates the region's agriculture. The region is one of the poorest in the entire country. In 1997, per capita income was 3.93 percent of the 1991 level, the worst ratio in the country. In addition, Chukotka's budgetary revenues cover less than 40 percent of its expenditures. The okrug also has the fifth worst air pollution in Russia—about 700 kg of toxic waste per capita.

In 1997, Chukotka AO had the largest investment risk increase—51 points—and ranked 80th among Russia's 89 regions in terms of investment potential and 76th in terms of investment risk, according to a 1998 survey by *Ekspert* magazine. A 1998 survey by Bank Austria ranked the okrug 74th in terms of investment climate.

Electoral History

2000 Presidential Election
Putin: 67.24%
Zyuganov: 15.33%
Yavlinskii: 4.61%
Zhirinovsky: 3.88%
Tuleev: 3.07%
Turnout: 73.92% (Russia overall: 68.64%)

1999 Parliamentary Elections
Unity: 43.44%
Communist Party of the Russian Federation: 11.13%
Zhirinovsky Bloc: 8.06%
Union of Right Forces: 7.60%
Yabloko: 7.00%
Fatherland–All Russia: 3.24%
In a single-mandate district: 1 independent
Turnout: 69.04% (Russia overall: 61.85%)

1996 Gubernatorial Election
Nazarov (incumbent): 65.18%
Yetylin: 21.04%
Broitman: 2.31%
Turnout: 59.42%

1996 Presidential Election
Yeltsin: 48.49%/74.29% (first round/second round)
Lebed: 17.06%
Zyuganov: 13.50%/19.14%
Zhirinovsky: 7.56%
Yavlinskii: 6.37%
Turnout: 73.10%/76.55% (Russia overall: 69.67%/68.79%)

1995 Parliamentary Election
Our Home Is Russia: 17.40%
Liberal Democratic Party of Russia: 13.32%
Communist Party of the Russian Federation: 11.03%
Women of Russia: 7.60%
Party of Workers' Self-Government: 6.73%
Yabloko: 6.51%
Congress of Russian Communities: 3.58%
Communists–Workers' Russia: 2.74%
Kedr: 2.55%
Forward, Russia: 2.34%
Common Cause: 2.01%
In a single-mandate district: 1 independent
Turnout: 66.82% (Russia overall: 64.37%)

1993 Constitutional Referendum
"Yes"—74.3%   "No"—23.6%

1993 Parliamentary Elections
Liberal Democratic Party of Russia: 23.32%
Russia's Choice: 14.40%
Yabloko: 12.25%
Women of Russia: 11.42%
Party of Russian Unity and Concord: 9.49%
Democratic Party of Russia: 8.70%
Communist Party of the Russian Federation: 6.60%
Agrarian Party of Russia: 0.97%
In a single-mandate district: 1 independent
Turnout: 54.00% (Russia overall: 54.34%)

1991 Presidential Elections
Yeltsin: 57.65%
Ryzhkov: 12.53%
Zhirinovsky: 9.48%
Tuleev: 8.86%
Bakatin: 5.21%

Makashov: 3.08%

Turnout: 75.86% (Russia overall: 76.66%)

Regional Political Institutions

Executive:

Governor, 4-year term
Aleksandr Viktorovich Nazarov, elected
December 1996
   Chukotka Autonomous Okrug Administration;
   Lenin St., 27; Anadyr, 686710
   Tel: 7(13) 4–21–26, 4–25–77;
   Fax: 7(13) 4–24–66, 4–29–19
   Federation Council in Moscow:
   7(095) 292–68–45, 926–69–31,
   Fax: 7(095) 292–57–35

Legislative:

Unicameral
Duma—13 members, 4-year term,
elected December 1996
Chairman—Vasilii Nikolaevich Nazarenko,
elected January 1997

Regional Politics

Introduction: Low-Profile Developer

Aleksandr Nazarov has quietly maneuvered a place for himself in Moscow politics, placating the party of power skillfully enough that the federal government generally takes a "hands-off" approach to his region. He has drawn no negative attention to himself at the national level, while tirelessly promoting the development potential that lies untapped in his region.

Executive Platform

Aleksandr Nazarov was elected governor in December 1996 with 63 percent of the vote. Then, he was a regional leader of the Our Home Is Russia movement. Along with other regional executives, Nazarov was elected to the political council of the movement in April 1998 (*EWI RRR*, 30 April 1998). In 1999, however, he joined the Voice of Russia party headed by Samara Governor Konstantin Titov, but then became a prime mover, with Emergency Minister Sergei Shoigu, in organizing the Kremlin's Unity bloc.

Nazarov immigrated to Chukotka in 1981. Until 1987, he was in the periphery of the periphery, serving as the vice-chairman of the executive committee of Bilibino, one of Chukotka's eight districts. He shifted to okrug-level politics in 1987, and was elected chairman of the executive committee of the okrug only in April 1990. With the collapse of the Soviet Union in 1991, Yeltsin began redesigning regional government by appointing governors directly, and he chose Nazarov to lead Chukotka (*EWI RRR*, 5 February 1998). Having survived in the governor's chair since 1991, Nazarov, is in the company of a handful of other regional executives who have lasted as long.

Policies: Regional Protectionism

Although he makes much of his commitment to democracy, Nazarov has established a border regime that rather creatively interprets the federal Constitution's provision for a 5-kilometer-wide border zone and prohibits movement anywhere in the region without special administrative permission. These restrictions are selectively enforced primarily to target "foreigners" (including anyone from outside of Chukotka, even Russians). Such intense regulations are probably due to Nazarov's concern over protecting Chukotka's natural resources. When the okrug was still part of Magadan Oblast much of the wealth generated from natural resources went to the oblast, rather than the okrug.

Nazarov pays a lot of attention to the problems connected with customs and the fur industry. He says that it is impossible for Chukotka to make a profit under the current customs regime. Nazarov believes that the problem would be solved if Chukotka were granted special status as a "presidential territory," allowing the Chukotka administration to keep the sales tax collected on the sale of fish and sea products (*Segodnya*, 16 January 1998).

For centuries, the main trade of the indigenous people of Chukotka has been in furs. However, Nazarov says that the shooting of animals for their fur should be monitored by the state authorities.

Before the August 1998 crisis, Nazarov was pushing to obtain supplies of necessary goods in the most efficient way possible. For example, rather than rely on shipments of vegetables from central Russia, which take a long time to reach Chukotka, thus making them more expensive,

Nazarov had begun to import more food from the United States, which was transported across the Pacific Ocean (*Business in Russia*, no. 8, 1998). Unfortunately, the precipitous decline in the value of the ruble at the end of 1998 made this strategy less effective.

Nazarov wants to create what he calls a "Golden Arctic Ring," a sea lane open throughout the year, which would connect the Arctic and the Pacific oceans. Such a link would help support the local gold mining industry.

Relationships Between Key Players: Aspires for Absolute Control

Chukotka was the first region to attempt to promote its status within Russia's hierarchical federal system when it declared itself a republic in 1990. Immediately after the region took this step, official documents and newspaper articles began to carry the designation "ChSAR" (Chukotka Soviet Autonomous Republic), although eventually the region dropped its pretensions to republic status. Chukotka is no longer subordinate to Magadan Oblast as it was until 1992. It is a fully independent region and the only autonomous okrug with this standing. Other okrugs are subordinate to the oblast or krai on whose territory they are located.

Chukotka, like most of the Far Eastern regions, is very poor and can barely sustain itself on the scarce money it gets from Moscow. Even the federal subsidies are not sufficient. According to Nazarov, 1998 was no exception. By June of that year, the government had only paid out 12.3 percent of the 323.8 million rubles ($54 million) authorized for supplying the north and had transported only about 75 percent of food and fuel that had been supplied by that time the previous year (*FI*, 23 June 1998). People are fleeing Chukotka, moving to the regions closer to the center. The capital city of the okrug, Anadyr, is among the most expensive cities in Russia in terms of basic food prices (*RFE/RL*, 25 August 1997). The governor does not try to cover up his problems. In January 1999, he told the *New York Times* that "the northern territories are in terrible shape" (*NYT*, 6 January 1999).

Nazarov clearly wishes to have absolute control of the region, and has systematically persecuted the one independent federal agency in Chukotka that is not woven into his patronage system: the local branch of the Academy of Sciences.

Ties to Moscow: Strong Connections

Chukotka has surprisingly close ties to Moscow, and visitors note the cosmopolitan sophistication of Anadyr's residents. Nazarov himself is undeniably a Moscow insider.

There are also strong financial ties between Moscow and Chukotka. In April 1998 the Russian Fuel and Energy Ministry signed an agreement on cooperation with the Chukotka Autonomous Okrug as well as ancillary documents designed to facilitate implementation of the accord. The agreement provides for the ministry and Anadyr to work together over a period of five years to ensure steady supplies of fuel and energy to Chukotka (*Interfax*, 25 April 1998). LUKoil signed an exclusive contract with the Chukotka administration in 1996 and opened a subsidiary in Chukotka in fall 1997 (*KD*, 3 October 1997).

Relations with Other Regions: Cooperation with Moscow City

Moscow Mayor Yurii Luzhkov paid a three-day visit to Chukotka in August 1996, during which he and Nazarov signed an agreement on Moscow's promised assistance to Chukotka. In November 1996, Nazarov pulled off a spectacle called "Chukotka Days in Moscow," for which dozens of native Chukchi artists, dancers, and singers were sent to Moscow to perform in theaters and in Gorky Park, while Chukchi businessmen put on their own road show aimed at attracting investment.

Chukotka is a member of the Far East and Baikal Association, which also includes the republics of Buryatia and Sakha (Yakutia); Primorskii and Khabarovsk krais; Amur, Kamchatka, Magadan, Chita, and Sakhalin oblasts; the Jewish Autonomous Oblast; and Koryak Autonomous Okrug (*OMRI/DD*, 15 January 1997).

Foreign Relations: Alaskan Interests

Chukotka once had its own branch office in Anchorage, Alaska, and Nazarov is said to have invested government funds in a proposed tunnel under the Bering Strait.

Aleksandr Viktorovich Nazarov

1951—Nazarov was born in Pavlodar Oblast, Kazakhstan, to the family of a collective farmer

1972—After serving on a Soviet submarine, he worked for a year as an electrician at a submarine repair works in Arkhangelsk Oblast. Then the Komsomol sent him to the far north, where he helped build the Bilibino Nuclear Power Plant and the Magadan, Arkagalinsk, and Luchegorsk thermal power plants. During this time, Nazarov graduated from the Makeevsk Engineering Construction Institute and completed correspondence work from the Khabarovsk Communist Party School. He was a member of the CPSU until August 1991

1981—Worked in the industrial-transportation department of the Bilibinskii Raion Committee of the CPSU

1983—Elected to the Bilibinskii Raion Soviet

1987—Elected to the Chukotka Okrug Executive Committee

1990—Elected to the Chukotka Okrug and Magadan Oblast Soviets. In his election cam-paign Nazarov borrowed from the platform of the local CPSU and the platform of the political organization Alternative. He spoke against Magadan Oblast interfering in Chukotka's affairs

25 April 1990—Elected chairman of the Chukotka Okrug Executive Committee

23 August 1991—Nazarov, while in Moscow, declared that he had quit the CPSU and blamed Politburo for the coup

11 November 1991—Nazarov was appointed governor of the Chukotka Autonomous Okrug

January 1995—Elected to the Federation Council

1995—Joined the Our Home Is Russia movement

23 December 1996—Elected governor of Chukotka Autonomous Okrug

Nazarov is currently the Chairman of the Federation Council's Committee on Northern Affairs and Minority Peoples

The governor's apparent eagerness to establish close ties with Alaska seems to contradict his generally hostile attitude toward outsiders. Even stranger is the fact that the administration-controlled newspaper schizophrenically runs stories that celebrate foreign ties alongside articles that express suspicion about the activities of foreigners in the region, accusing them of being cultural imperialists. It may simply be a way for the administration to continue to demand exorbitant "license" fees from foreigners for the privilege of allowing them to work in the region.

Attitudes Toward Business:
Unused Potential

Chukotka has huge oil deposits, rich gold mines, tin-bearing soil, mercury deposits, and precious stones. But when it became cheaper to buy those resources on the world markets than to extract them, the mines were abandoned. Nazarov hopes that when prices rebound, foreign investors will send capital to the region to exploit its natural wealth. He admits, however, that the region's northern conditions will make any operations difficult.

CHUVASH REPUBLIC (CHUVASHIA)

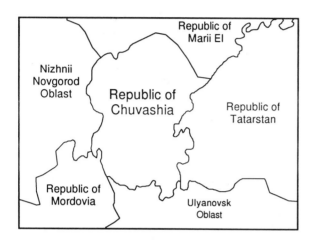

Territory: 18,300 km²
Population (as of 1 January 1998):
1,359,000
Distance from Moscow: 768 km

Major Cities:
Cheboksary, *capital* (pop. 456,300)
Novocheboksarsk (124,300)
Kanash (55,000)

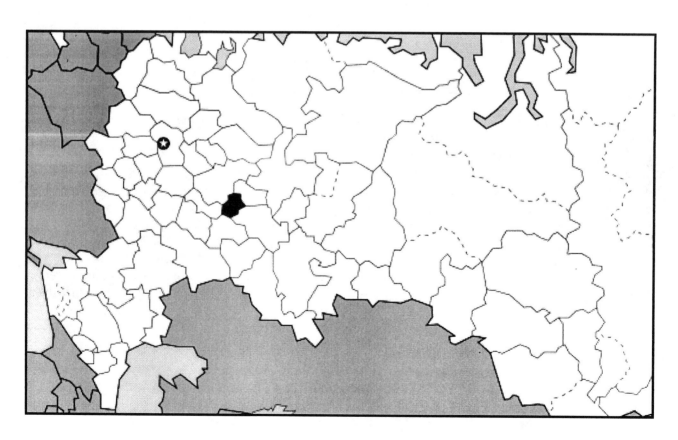

Basic Facts

Population (as of 1 Jan. 1998): 1,359,000 (0.92% of Russian total)

Ethnic breakdown (1989 census): Chuvash 67.8%, Russians 26.7%, Tatars 2.7%, Mordvins 1.4%

Urban population (as of 1 Jan. 1998): 60.9% (Russia overall: 73.1%)

Student population (as of 1 Sept. 1997): 199 per 10,000 (Russia overall: 208/10,000)

Pensioner population (1997): 24.72% (Russia overall: 25.96%)

Percent of population with higher education (1989 census): 7.9% (Russia overall: 11.3%)

Percent of population working in (1997): Industry: 26.7% (Russian average: 23.0%); Agriculture: 18.8% (13.7%); Trade: 11.0% (13.5%); Culture: 13.2% (13.3%)

Average monthly personal income in July 1998: 383.1 new rubles (Russian average: 891.7 new rubles)

Average monthly personal expenses in July 1998: 353.3 new rubles (Russian average: 684.9 new rubles)

Average monthly subsistence requirement in 1998: 344 new rubles (Russian average: 438 new rubles)

Consumer price index (as of July 1998): 80 (Russia overall = 100)

Budgetary revenues (1997): 2,716.1 billion rubles (Russia overall: 433,378.2 billion rubles)

Budgetary expenditures (1997): 2,899.8 billion rubles (Russia overall: 468,111.6 billion rubles)

Industrial production as percentage of all Russian production (Jan.–Aug. 1998): 0.44%

Proportion of loss-making enterprises (as of July 1998): 46.9% (Russia overall: 50.4%)

Number of enterprises which have wage arrears (as of 1 Sept. 1998): 2,558 (1.89% of Russian total)

Agricultural production as percentage of all Russian production (1997): 1.14%

Number of private farms (as of 1 Jan. 1998): 1,106 (0.4% of Russian total)

Capital investment (1997): 2,236.6 billion rubles (Russia overall: 408,797 billion rubles)

Sources of investment (1997): federal budget: 7.3% (Russian average: 10.2%); regional budget: 18.3% (10.5%); extra-budgetary funds: 74.4% (79.3%)

Foreign investment (1997): 1,560,000 USD (Russia overall: 12,294,734,000 USD)

Number of joint ventures (1997): 42 (0.29% of Russian total)

Fixed capital investment in joint ventures and foreign companies (1997): 0 (Russia overall: 16,265.4 billion rubles)

Number of small businesses (as of 1 July 1998): 4,500 (0.52% of Russian total)

Number of enterprises privatized in 1997: 2 (0.07% of Russian total), including those which used to be municipal property: 100% (Russian average: 66.4%); regional property: 0% (20.0%); federal property: 0% (13.6%)

Number of telephones per 100 families (1997): in cities: 44.1 (Russian average: 49.2); in villages: 13.8 (19.8)

Brief Overview

Chuvashia is located in the eastern part of European Russia, occupying an area of 18,300 sq. km (about one-fourth the size of Nizhnii Novgorod Oblast), most of which is located on the right bank of the middle Volga River and forms a slightly raised plateau (the Chuvash Plateau). The republic's capital city, Cheboksary, a Volga port and major industrial center of the republic, lies between Nizhnii Novgorod and Tatarstan's capital, Kazan. Chuvashia borders the republics of Marii El, Tatarstan, and Mordovia, and Ulyanovsk and Nizhnii Novgorod oblasts.

The Chuvash, a Turkic people, make up the majority of the republic's population (68 percent), while Russians comprise less than 30 percent. Their language differs considerably from other Turkic languages, and the exact place occupied by the Chuvash language within the Uralo-Altaic language family is still debated. In contrast to most other Turkic peoples living in Eurasia, the majority of Chuvash are Christians. Most of them converted to Russian Orthodoxy in the 18th and 19th centuries, following the annexation of their territory by Ivan the Terrible in the 16th century.

The republic is fairly poor in natural resources. While some clays and peat are being extracted, its major wealth comes from the woods that cover about one-third of its territory. The economy is dominated by agriculture, with crops of grain, potatoes, hemp, tobacco, and hops (Chuvashia accounts for about 80 percent of the hops grown in Russia). Industry, which developed considerably after World War II, includes machine-building, metal-processing, energy, chemicals, consumer goods, and food processing. The republic enjoys a favorable geographic location at the junction of important railroads, highways, and river routes that connect the Central, Volga, and Urals economic regions of the country.

Chuvashia has trade relations with over 60 foreign countries, including China, Germany, the United States, the Netherlands, Italy, Syria, and Hungary. It exports chemicals, machines, consumer goods, secondary resources, and agricultural products.

To attract investment, republican authorities have introduced several tax breaks for manufacturing companies both domestic and foreign. It has become less dangerous to invest in the republican economy: investment risk decreased by 29 points (fourth largest decrease in the country) in 1997–1998 The republic ranked 48th among Russia's 89 regions in terms of investment potential and 33rd in terms of investment risk, according to a 1998 survey by *Ekspert* magazine. A 1998 survey by Bank Austria ranked the republic 57th in terms of investment climate.

Electoral History

2000 Presidential Election
Putin: 44.28%
Zyuganov: 42.88%
Yavlinskii: 3.05%
Zhirinovsky: 2.05%
Tuleev: 1.84%
Turnout: 70.77% (Russia overall: 68.64%)

1999 Parliamentary Elections
Communist Party of the Russian Federation: 35.60%
Fatherland–All Russia: 14.97%
Unity: 13.15%
Union of Right Forces: 6.53%
Zhirinovsky Bloc: 5.89%
Yabloko: 3.83%
In single-mandate districts: 1 Communist Party of the Russian Federation, 1 independent
Turnout: 56.00% (Russia overall: 61.85%)

1997 Republican Presidential Election
Fedorov (incumbent): 56.7%
Shurchanov (republican legislature chairman): 34.9%
Turnout: 60.0%

1996 Presidential Election
Zyuganov: 53.93%/62.59% (first round/second round)
Yeltsin: 20.55%/31.82%
Lebed: 7.65%
Yavlinskii: 4.57%
Zhirinovsky: 4.25%
Turnout: 67.16%/67.26% (Russia overall: 69.67%/68.79%)

1995 Parliamentary Elections
Communist Party of the Russian Federation: 33.12%
Liberal Democratic Party of Russia: 12.17%
Party of Workers' Self-Government: 11.57%
Agrarian Party of Russia: 5.73%

Communists–Workers' Russia: 5.17%
Our Home Is Russia: 4.72%
Women of Russia: 2.51%
Yabloko: 1.72%
In single-mandate districts: 1 Party of Workers' Self-
Government, 1 independent
Turnout: 61.00% (Russia overall: 64.37%)

1993 Constitutional Referendum
"Yes"—40.0% "No"—56.2%

1993 Parliamentary Elections
Liberal Democratic Party of Russia: 22.53%
Communist Party of the Russian Federation:
19.73%
Agrarian Party of Russia: 12.75%
Democratic Party of Russia: 9.11%
Russia's Choice: 8.90%
Women of Russia: 8.50%
Party of Russian Unity and Concord: 4.83%
Yabloko: 3.43%
In single-mandate districts: 2 independent
Turnout: 63.56% (Russia overall: 54.34%)

1991 Presidential Election
Yeltsin: 52.29%
Ryzhkov: 21.86%
Tuleev: 6.54%
Makashov: 6.04%
Zhirinovsky: 5.55%
Bakatin: 2.54%
Turnout: 78.43% (Russia overall: 76.66%)

Regional Political Institutions

Executive:
President, 4-year term
Nikolai Vasilevich Fedorov, elected December 1997
Presidential Administration and the Cabinet of
Ministers
Dom Sovetov, Cheboksary, 428004
Tel 7(835–2) 62–46–87
Federation Council in Moscow:
7(095) 292–58–18, 926–60–66

Legislative:
Unicameral
State Council (Gosudarstvennyi Sovet)—47
members, 4-year term, elected July 1998
Chairman—Lev Panteleimonovich Kurakov,
elected July 1998

Regional Politics

Beer-Loving Reformer

Nikolai Fedorov is a "young reformer" who managed to win two presidential terms in a republic that usually has voted strongly in favor of the Communist Party. In the early 1990s, he served under Yeltsin as the Russian justice minister, but he broke with the president over the use of force against the parliament in 1993. Fedorov presents himself as a pragmatic leader with "democratic conservative-progressive" views (Panorama Research Group, Labyrint Electronic Database, Moscow).

At the beginning of 1998, he summed up his record during his first term; focusing on concrete results: "In Chuvashia neither capitalism nor socialism is being built, but rather schools, hospitals, and roads. The results of the past four years, in my opinion, are apparent. There is economic and political stability and interethnic and civil harmony in society" (*Izvestiya*, 13 January 1998).

Fedorov was reelected president of the Republic of Chuvashia on 28 December 1997, commanding 57 percent of the vote. He defeated the Communist chairman of the republican parliament, Valentin Shurchanov, a long-standing rival, who pulled in 34 percent of the vote. This was a vast improvement over Fedorov's first election in 1993, in which he received less than 30 percent. Fedorov, who joined the Beer Lovers' Party in 1994, was backed in 1997 by Our Home Is Russia, and enjoyed strong support from the rural areas (*RG*, 16 December 1997). In 1999 he joined the All Russia regional party founded by Tatarstan President Mintimer Shaimiev.

Executive Platform: Locomotive Economics and Cultural Defense

Fedorov presents himself as an advocate of reform, but, as is often fashionable today, stresses that the population's social needs are more important than the speed of the changes. He claims to be building a society in which the state provides free healthcare, education, and strong social support for pensioners and children. Fedorov credits himself for promoting "locomotive" economics in the republic (*Ekspert*, 29 June 1998). Although Chuvashia is not among the wealthiest of Russia's regions, it does not exhibit signs of decay, depression, or neglect, and it pays state pensions on time.

Fedorov is critical of the federal government, which he feels has abandoned the republic. He has asserted: "The less you depend on the center, and the more taxes you collect, the more they demand from you, the more they cut back transfers, and the less they plan for the following year. There is no point in searching for handouts. Only one option is left: to work well, but not show this to the center." He considers it necessary to develop new taxes and a better legal system that is favorable to competitive market enterprises (NNS).

Fedorov also believes it is important to defend the Chuvash language, culture, and national influence (NNS).

Policies: Concrete Results

Fedorov's achievements as the republican president include a number of policy initiatives. He is credited with launching the first local oil exploration; building houses, roads, and schools; and paying pensions on time. During Fedorov's first presidential term, thirty new hospitals, many of European quality, were built in the republic (*Izvestiya*, 13 January 1998). Part of Fedorov's economic strategy has been to allocate 200 million rubles annually from the republican budget to build homes. The construction industry benefits from the payments in real money, and Fedorov claims that people are willing to pay for the new homes. Additionally, gas was installed in twice as many homes over the four years of Fedorov's first term as during the entire Soviet period (*Izvestiya*, 13 January 1998). In January 1995 Fedorov signed a decree allowing the citizens of Chuvashia to refuse to participate in military activities in Chechnya, greatly increasing Fedorov's popularity in the republic (Panorama). In October 1996, Fedorov's government launched a program to support small businesses in the consumer goods and services sector, hoping that it would create 10,000 jobs over the next year. These social reforms boosted his reputation and clinched his reelection in a region that has been traditionally a bastion of pro-Communist sentiment (*MT*, 30 December 1997).

In January 1997 the State Council of Chuvashia decided to reduce tax rates for financial institutions in order to increase the financing of local companies and organizations by banks and to stimulate housing construction (*OMRI RRR*, 15 January 1997). Fedorov also tried to levy additional taxes on alcoholic beverages, tobacco products, and jewelry, but local procurators blocked the initiatives (*RG*, 11 March 1998). This incident is just one of many instances in which Fedorov's proposals were blocked by the republican legislature during Fedorov's first term.

Relationships Between Key Players: Improving Relations with the Legislature

During his first term and into the beginning of his second, Fedorov had very poor relations with the Communist-dominated republican legislature, the State Council, which relentlessly sought to reduce his power and block his initiatives. The tense relations between reform-minded Fedorov and the Communist majority resulted in a variety of constitutional and legislative power struggles.

Following the 12 July 1998 elections to the republican legislature, the situation had changed in Fedorov's favor. Only eight members of the Communist Party were elected to the 87-seat legislature whereas Communists previously held more than 30 seats in the old 47-member house. One member of Our Home Is Russia and 55 independents were also elected. Elections in the remaining 23 districts were not valid because turnout was less than the required 25 percent. The independent deputies are more pragmatic than the Communists had been, and therefore more cooperative with the president.

Before the 1998 elections, executive-legislative elections had been highly conflictual. In 1995 Fedorov appealed to the Constitutional Court regarding the November 1994 election of 14 deputies to the Chuvash State Council. Fedorov's complaint was that these deputies had been elected in districts with less than 25 percent voter turnout, violating federal electoral legislation. Fedorov attempted to use this violation as an excuse to dissolve the council, which had been staunchly opposed to his reforms. Considering that Fedorov appealed the legitimacy of the 14 deputies a full seven months after the elections, Fedorov's personal interests appeared to be the main motivation for the court appeal rather than a concern for preserving the sanctity of the law (*OMRI DD*, 20 July 1995). However, Fedorov's attempt to dismiss the council was unsuccessful. The court's decision stated that the ruling did not affect the legitimacy of the deputies who had been elected with sufficient voter turnout, and only the suspect 14 needed to resign (*OMRI DD*, 14 July 1995, 20 July 1995). The Communist legislature then retaliated by holding a referendum in December 1995 that nearly succeeded in abolishing the presidency.

One point of contention between Fedorov and the legislature concerned charters for cities and local governments (*OMRI RRR*, 13 November 1996). Fedorov's draft allowed the republican president to appoint and remove local administrators, a violation of federal legislation that requires elections for local officials.

On 19 January 1997 Fedorov tried to fire republican Procurator Sergei Rusakov for criminal activities in the republic. This act had no legal basis since only the Russian procurator can fire his regional subordinates. In response, the Russian procurator ordered Fedorov to rescind his decree. The Chuvash legislature also asked Fedorov to revoke this order (*OMRI RRR*, 3 February 1997). Clearly, the former justice minister supports federal laws when they are to his advantage, and ignores them when they are not.

Ties to Moscow: Critcal of Yeltsin, Putin

After winning election to the USSR Congress of People's Deputies, Fedorov became Russian Justice Minister in June 1990. He maintained this post in Yegor Gaidar's cabinet after November 1991 but resigned in March 1993, protesting Yeltsin's intention to use force to close the Russian parliament (*Panorama*). Fedorov also opposed Yeltsin's use of force in Chechnya, stating that the right of the Chechen people to self-determination should have priority over Russia's territorial integrity (*OMRI DD*, 28 June 1996).

Despite this earlier break with the Russian president, Fedorov campaigned for Yeltsin during the 1996 presidential campaign; but Gennadii Zyuganov won an overwhelming 62.59 percent of the vote in the second round in Chuvashia. After Zyuganov's strong showing, Fedorov offered his

resignation to Yeltsin, but was not called upon to leave. In July 1997 Yeltsin invited Fedorov to join the federal government as a deputy prime minister (*KD*, 4 July 1997). Fedorov declined the offer, stating that he intended to serve out the remainder of his presidential term.

On 27 May 1996 Fedorov signed a power-sharing agreement with Yeltsin. In the summer of 2000, Fedorov was one of the most critical opponents of Putin's federal reforms.

Relations with Other Regions: Dispute with Marii El

In January 1995 Fedorov organized a meeting of the Consent for the Sake of the Fatherland committee with leaders from seven national republics of the Russian Federation, demanding a peaceful solution to the conflict in Chechnya and a restoration of the Council of Republican Heads, which had existed until October 1993 (*Panorama*).

On 10 June 1998 Fedorov signed a framework agreement with Yamal-Nenets Autonomous Okrug Governor Yurii Neelov to increase trade between the two regions (*Izvestiya*, 11 June 1998). Their trade transactions will involve barter operations rather than cash, because monetary exchanges have proven difficult between regions.

Chuvashia has been arguing with neighboring Marii El over the $33,000 in tax revenues that are generated by the Volga River islands between them. The islands are generally believed to be a part of Chuvashia, whose residents use the islands to grow hay. Yet, Marii El officials claim that a 1925 All-Russian Central Executive Committee order gave it the right to the land and the resulting taxes (*Izvestiya*, 16 June 1998).

Chuvashia is a member of the Greater Volga Association, which includes Tatarstan, Mordovia, and Marii El republics, and Astrakhan, Volgograd, Nizhnii Novgorod, Penza, Saratov, and Ulyanovsk oblasts. In March 1998 the association met to discuss the state of the petrochemical processing industry. The result was a statement of intent to form a cartel agreement. The cartel's goals are to coordinate prices, control competition among members, and eliminate outside competition. This joint effort illustrates how the Greater Volga association presents a united front of regional participants. A June

Nikolai Vasilevich Fedorov

9 May 1958—Born in the village Chedino in the Mariinsko-Posadskii raion of Chuvashia

1980—Graduated from the Kazan State University Legal Department, candidate's degree

1980–1982—Instructor and legal consultant at the Chuvash State University

1982—Joined the Communist Party

1982–1985—Graduate student at the USSR Academy of Sciences Institute of State and Law

1985–1989—Senior instructor of scientific communism at Cheboksary University

1989–1991—USSR Congress of People's Deputies, member of the USSR Supreme Soviet Council of Nationalities, chaired subcommittee on legislation

1989–1990—Participated in the development of several democratic laws, including the Law on the Press

1990—Declined Mikhail Gorbachev's offer to join the USSR Constitutional Oversight Committee, stating that he wanted "to work in real politics"

1992—Became the chairman of the committee for rehabilitating repressed people from Karachaevo-Cherkessia and vice-chairman of the interregional committee for Soviet security in the North Caucasus

1990–1993—Russian Justice Minister, member of the State Council, member of the Security Council

March 1993—Resigned from the cabinet in protest over Yeltsin's proposed decree establishing presidential rule

1993—Chairman of the Moscow Lawyers' Board

August 1993—Became chairman of the committee, Consent for the Sake of the Fatherland which spoke out against the fetishism of reforms

12 December 1993—Elected to State Duma as #4 on the Democratic Party of Russia ticket

26 December 1993—Elected president of Chuvashia in a 7-man race

1994—Joined the Beer Lovers' Party

January 1996—Became a member of the Federation Council; vice-chairman of the Committee on International Affairs

1994—Joined the United Commission for the coordination of legislative appointments

28 December 1996—By the order of the President, was approved as a member of Russia's Interdepartmental Committee for Council of Europe affairs

28 December 1997—Elected to a second term as president of Chuvashia

Member of the International Russian Club

Enjoys boxing and karate; loves to read (his favorite author is Dostoevsky)

Speaks Russian and Chuvash equally well, and also has a command of German

Married, with a son and a daughter

1998 association conference demonstrated that a collective approach put the regions in a better position to solve their economic problems and perhaps to more successfully lobby in Moscow.

Attitudes Toward Business: Development a Lower Priority

The region has strong business potential and possesses a highly developed infrastructure. Chuvashia also possesses considerable mineral resources including gypsum, clay, loam, tripoli, peat, and phosphor.

The majority of Fedorov's reforms have been socially oriented, and business development has ranked lower on the president's list of priorities. Nevertheless, Fedorov has directed some successful business initiatives in his "locomotive" economics, the most notable of which was the republic's first local oil exploration. Several investment projects have been successfully realized in cooperation with foreign firms such as Siemens and ABB (*Expert*, 29 June 1998). The republic has economic relations with more than 60 countries, including Australia, Belgium, Germany, Italy, France, Finland, the United States, Argentina, Brazil, India, Mexico, Syria, and Turkey.

The town of Novocheboksarsk is the site of a $10 million joint venture project between the U.S. company Dupont and its Russian counterpart Khimiprom (*MT*, 16 September 1997). The project concerns the formulation and packaging of the herbicide sulfonylurea. This product, which should have been available for the 1999 growing season, will most likely be used on Russia's grain fields, but future products could be used for sugar-beet, corn, flax, rice, and other crops.

Fedorov, who joined the Beer Lovers' Party in 1994, has not focused on developing the region's potential in beer production (although, coincidentally, the first Russian beer museum was opened in the capital, Cheboksary, in 1997). Although 40 million German marks have gone toward building a new beer factory in the republic, most of the region's beer enterprises are idle (*Ekspert*, 29 June 1998). Only four of the republic's nine breweries are operating. Eighty percent of Russia's hops are grown in Chuvashia.

Fedorov served on the board of directors of Anatolii Chubais's electricity monopoly Unified Energy System in 1998 (*RG*, 13 February 1998). St. Petersburg Governor Vladimir Yakovlev and Rostov Governor Vladimir Chub were also on the board that year.

The tax rate for banks functioning in Chuvashia is 43 percent, 13 percent to the federal budget and 30 percent to the republican budget. However, banks have certain privileges in the region: if a bank directs at least 90 percent of its credit resources to aid enterprises and organizations in Chuvashia, it is subjected to only a 10 percent republican tax. Commercial banks granting loans and credits to Chuvash citizens for constructing and purchasing homes only have to pay 5 percent ("Chuvashia: The First Acquaintance," unpublished manuscript prepared by the Office of the President of the Chuvash Republic, November 1998).

The president announced in 1999 that he is ready to present the republic for an audit on international standards, seeking to demonstrate that he is serious about attracting foreign investors.

Internet Sites in the Region

http://www.cap.ru/cap/start.htm
This website offers detailed information about the republic's various industries and features extensive comments by President Nikolai Fedorov on economics, education, social services, etc.

http://www.chuvashia.ru/
This site does not offer any information on the administration of Chuvashia, but it does provide a significant amount of material about the region's economic development, including a search engine for acquiring information about the republic's investors and investment projects.

REPUBLIC OF DAGESTAN

Territory: 50,300 km²
Population (as of 1 January 1998):
2,095,000
Distance from Moscow: 2,166 km

Major Cities:
Makhachkala, *capital* (pop. 344,200)
Derbent (89,000)
Khasavyurt (85,500)
Kaspiisk (66,600)
Buinaksk (58,500)

Basic Facts

Population (as of 1 Jan. 1998): 2,095,000 (1.42% of Russian total)

Ethnic breakdown (1989 census): Avars 27.5%, Dargins 15.6%, Kumyks 12.9%, Lezgins 11.3%, Russians 9.2%, Laks 5.1%, Tabasarans 4.3%, Azeris 4.2%, Chechens 3.2%, Nogais 1.6%, Rutuls 0.8%, Aguls 0.8%, Tats 0.7%, Jews 0.5%, Ukrainians 0.5%, Armenians 0.4%, Tsakhurs 0.3%

Urban population (as of 1 Jan. 1998): 41.5% (Russia overall: 73.1%)

Student population (as of 1 Sept. 1997): 199 per 10,000 (Russia overall: 208/10,000)

Pensioner population (1997): 20.43% (Russia overall: 25.96%)

Percent of population with higher education (1989 census): 8.3% (Russia overall: 11.3%)

Percent of population working in (1997): Industry: 10.9% (Russian average: 23.0%); Agriculture: 31.2% (13.7%); Trade: 11.1% (13.5%); Culture: 15.0% (13.3%)

Average monthly personal income in July 1998: 370.2 new rubles (Russian average: 891.7 new rubles)

Average monthly personal expenses in July 1998: 169.7 new rubles (Russian average: 684.9 new rubles)

Average monthly subsistence requirement in 1998: 308 new rubles (Russian average: 438 new rubles)

Consumer price index (as of July 1998): 88 (Russia overall = 100)

Budgetary revenues (1997): 2,860.4 billion rubles (Russia overall: 433,378.2 billion rubles)

Budgetary expenditures (1997): 3,389.4 billion rubles (Russia overall: 468,111.6 billion rubles)

Industrial production as percentage of all Russian production (Jan.–Aug. 1998): 0.09%

Proportion of loss-making enterprises (as of July 1998): 56.3% (Russia overall: 50.4%)

Number of enterprises which have wage arrears (as of 1 Sept. 1998): 606 (0.45% of Russian total)

Agricultural production as percentage of all Russian production (1997): 0.67%

Number of private farms (as of 1 Jan. 1998): 18,286 (6.67% of Russian total)

Capital investment (1997): 3,298.8 billion rubles (Russia overall: 408,797 billion rubles)

Sources of investment (1997): federal budget: 17.8% (Russian average: 10.2%); regional budget: 4.0% (10.5%); extra-budgetary funds: 78.2% (79.3%)

Foreign investment (1997): 8,398,000 USD (Russia overall: 12,294,734,000 USD)

Number of joint ventures (1997): 6 (0.04% of Russian total)

Fixed capital investment in joint ventures and foreign companies (1997): 8,694 million rubles (Russia overall: 16,265.4 billion rubles)

Number of small businesses (as of 1 July 1998): 1,400 (0.16% of Russian total)

Number of enterprises privatized in 1997: 6 (0.22% of Russian total), including those which used to be municipal property: 33.3% (Russian average: 66.4%); regional property: 66.7% (20.0%); federal property: 0% (13.6%)

Number of telephones per 100 families (1997): in cities: 33.0 (Russian average: 49.2); in villages: 10.3 (19.8)

Brief Overview

Dagestan is located in the eastern part of the Caucasus Mountains, along the Caspian Sea. It borders Kalmykia, Stavropol Krai, Chechnya, Georgia, and Azerbaijan. Dagestan is the largest republic of the North Caucasus in terms of territory and population. Over 30 ethnic groups reside there.

The republic is rich in oil, gas, copper, sulfur, sands (about 15% of the country's total reserves), and mineral waters. Regional industry specializes in oil and gas extraction, machine building, chemicals, food processing, and light industries. Traditional crafts, such as jewelry and rug weaving, are of great importance. Republican farms produce grapes and other fruits and vegetables, and breed cattle. Yet, the republic is one of the poorest in the country, with only about 15 percent of its expenditures covered by its own budgetary revenues (fourth worst in the country), and per capita income in 1997 that was only 6.58 percent of what it was in 1991.

The republic exports oil, ferrous metals, sulfur, cement, copper, timber, wool, leather, and equipment. Its major imports are: petroleum products, machines, equipment, and consumer goods. Dagestan trades with over 40 foreign countries, including Iran, Turkey, Norway, Great Britain, United Arab Emirates, China, Azerbaijan, Ukraine, Belarus, Kazakhstan, and Georgia.

According to a 1998 survey by *Ekspert* magazine, the republic ranked 55th among Russia's 89 regions in terms of investment potential and 88th in terms of investment risk. A 1998 survey by Bank Austria ranked the republic 84th in terms of investment climate.

Electoral History

2000 Presidential Election
Putin: 81.04%
Zyuganov: 16.35%
Yavlinskii: 0.52%
Zhirinovsky: 0.28%
Dzhabrailov: 0.26%
Tuleev: 0.21%
Turnout: 83.60% (Russia overall: 68.64%)

1999 Parliamentary Elections
Communist Party of the Russian Federation: 37.56%
Unity: 28.91%
Fatherland–All Russia: 28.09%
Union of Right Forces: 1.22%
Communists–Workers' Russia: 0.48%
Zhirinovsky Bloc: 0.40%
Yabloko: 0.39%
In single-mandate districts: 2 independent
Turnout: 76.63% (Russia overall: 61.85%)

1996 Presidential Election
Yeltsin: 28.52%/52.65% (first round/second round)
Zyuganov: 63.23%/44.81%
Yavlinskii: 1.70%
Lebed: 1.34%
Zhirinovsky: 1.12%
Turnout: 68.94%/74.07% (Russia overall: 69.67%/ 68.79%)

1995 Parliamentary Elections
Communist Party of the Russian Federation: 43.57%
Our Home Is Russia: 14.55%
Russia's Democratic Choice: 13.49%
Agrarian Party of Russia: 7.18%
Transformation of the Fatherland: 2.48%
Nur: 2.02%
In a single-mandate district: 1 independent
Turnout: 76.47% (Russia overall: 64.37%)

1993 Constitutional Referendum
"Yes"—20.5%   "No"—77.8%

1993 Parliamentary Elections
Communist Party of the Russian Federation: 54.00%
Agrarian Party of Russia: 18.36%
Party of Russian Unity and Concord: 6.82%
Democratic Party of Russia: 4.32%
Liberal Democratic Party of Russia: 3.38%
Yabloko: 3.27%
Women of Russia: 2.34%
Russia's Choice: 2.03%
In single-mandate districts: 2 independent
From electoral associations: 1 Communist Party of the Russian Federation
Turnout: 57.58% (Russia overall: 54.34%)

1991 Presidential Elections
Yeltsin: 65.86%
Ryzhkov: 11.39%
Makashov: 6.95%
Tuleev: 5.74%
Bakatin: 5.58%
Zhirinovsky: 2.99%
Turnout: 78.73% (Russia overall: 76.66%)

Regional Political Institutions

Executive:
 Chairman of the Republican State Council,
 4-year term
 Magomedali Magomedovich Magomedov,
 elected July 1994, June 1998
  Dom Sovetov; Pl. Lenina, 2;
  Makhachkala, 367012;
  Republic of Dagestan
  Tel 7(872–2) 67–30–60, 67–30–59;
  Fax 7(872–2) 67–20–17
  Federation Council in Moscow:
  7(095) 292–45–82, 926–62–74

Legislative:
 Unicameral
 People's Assembly (Narodnoe Sobranie)—121
 members, 4–year term, elected March 1999
 Chairman—Mukhu Gimbatovich Aliev, elected
 March 1995, March 1999

Regional Politics

Regional Executive Elected via Constitutional Assembly

Magomedali Magomedov was one of two Russian regional executives not to earn his position via popular elections (the other until 2000 was Udmurtia's Aleksandr Volkov). In July 1994 Magomedov was elected Chairman of the Dagestan Republican State Council by the Constitutional Assembly. Uniquely among the regions, Dagestan employs a parliamentary system of government that enshrines a delicate political balance of power among the republic's various ethnic groups. In drafting Dagestan's constitution, the borders of constituencies were drawn in order to prevent mono-ethnic units and promote cross-national voting. If the results of popular elections do

not provide representation to certain ethnic groups, the government reserves the authority to intervene in electoral proceedings to allocate seats. No nationality is allowed to have more than one member in the State Council. To be considered for a position on the Council, a candidate must be among the three representatives of his ethnic group who has gained the most nominations from the Assembly. These guidelines are meant to ensure that those in power are representatives of their nationalities and to safeguard against extremists.

The precautions help maintain the peace among the more than thirty ethnic groups in the republic. The most prominent are the Avars, Dargins, Kumyks, Lezgins, Russians, Laks, Tabasarans, Azeris, Chechens, and Nogais. The populace also has attachments to clan identities, as well as a sense of being part of a larger Dagestani and North Caucasus group. In the early 1990s Dagestan was noted for the relative peace among its ethnic groups and the absence of the ominous nationalist tendencies that have threatened to reduce the North Caucasus to a region of unstable nation states.

However, some aspects of Dagestan's experiment in balancing ethnic powers were short lived. Until March 1998, its Constitution forbade representatives of the same ethnic minority from holding the position of Chairman of the State Council for two consecutive terms. An amendment adopted in March allows one individual to serve as chairman for two consecutive terms and removes all nationality restrictions. Thus, the revised Constitution permitted Magomedov, an ethnic Dargin, to run for reelection as Chairman of the Dagestan Republican State Council, and he won a second term on 25 June 1998. Magomedov has tried to transform himself from the State Council Chairman to the republic's directly elected president. The republic has held three referendums on creating the presidency, in June 1991, December 1993, and March 1999. So far, the republic's voters are unwilling to replace collective leadership with a president.

Executive Platform: Ensure Subsidy Flow from Moscow

Magomedov, a member of Our Home Is Russia, was a strong supporter of Russian President Boris Yeltsin, and in 1999 gave his support to the new pro-Kremlin Unity bloc. He is adamant that Dagestan remain part of the Russian Federation. Unlike many of Russia's ethnic republics, Dagestan is not trying to usurp as much sovereignty as possible from the central government. Rather, the republic is interested in obtaining as many subsidies as possible from federal coffers. Now 85 percent of Dagestan's budget comes from Moscow (*EWI RRR*, 2 April 1998). In fact, securing such subsidies also appears to be Magomedov's main economic platform. Given current conditions, Dagestan could not survive without federal aid.

Relationships Between Key Players: Chaos Verging on Civil War

Given its proximity to war-torn Chechnya, the increasing number of clashes between armed groups, and the continuing economic collapse, the political climate in Dagestan is extremely turbulent. Many leaders, including Magomedov, fear the onset of civil war. Kidnappings of rich Dagestanis and foreigners for ransoms of $25,000 are common (*EWI RRR*, 17 May 1998). Gun battles between well-armed gangs and exploding bombs have also become a part of daily life.

The violence has directly affected the highest levels of the republic's political leadership. On 21 May 1998, over two hundred armed men seized the republican administrative building in Dagestan's capital Makhachkala. The confrontation was led by State Duma member Nadir Khachilaev, who is also the head of the Union of Muslims of Russia. During the demonstration, thousands of people in the central square demanded the government's resignation and free presidential elections. When the stand-off was over Magomedov appeared on television, blaming the police for the conflict (*EWI RRR*, 21 May 1998).

The federal authorities eventually stepped in and arrested Nadir's brother, Magomed Khachilaev, the leader of the Lak national movement and a member of the Dagestani Popular Assembly, in Makhachkala on 9 September. In his house, they found 13 submachine guns, 28 grenade launchers with 90 grenades, and seven heavy machine guns, including one stolen from the government building during the riots on 21 May. On 18 September the State Duma voted to strip his brother Nadir Khachilaev, of his parliamentary immunity. On the following day Nadir ac-

cused the entire leadership of Dagestan of using federal bayonets to prop up the republic's fragile regime and do away with political opposition. In many ways, the public saw the events from Khachilaev's point of view, as the government's press service seem powerless to do anything. As a result, Khachilaev's supporters managed to portray a criminal investigation as a case of political persecution against the legitimate opposition. Khachilaev was ultimately arrested in October 1999 in Chechnya.

In one of the most prominent politically motivated murders, killers assassinated the spiritual leader of Dagestani Muslims, 39-year-old Mufti Saiid-Mukhamad Abubakarov, in the center of Makhachkala on 20 August 1998. On 25 August 1998, a large group of Avars gathered in Makhachkala to demand the resignation of the government. They demanded better representation of ethnic groups in government, free elections of the republic's top leadership, and prosecution of the men who assassinated Abubakarov (*EWI RRR*, 1 September 1998).

In March 1999 Dagestan held elections for the republican People's Assembly. Magomedov retained control over the assembly by essentially conducting the campaign in his favor, overlooking electoral violations involving his supporters. According to the republic's Constitution, officials working for the republican or local governments cannot simultaneously hold seats in the legislature, yet several bureaucrats, including 15 heads of local government, won election to the assembly. Many opposition candidates to Magomedov's leadership were denied registration for the elections.

It is absolutely clear that Magomedov's hold on power is safe with the current political establishment, which he tightly controls. However, Dagestanis' increasingly direct criticism of their government cannot simply be ignored. People are not demanding economic reforms anymore; they are protesting the wave of lawlessness that has engulfed Dagestan. The public can clearly see the connection between criminal elements and the authorities, as illustrated by numerous high-profile investigations that have been shut down by decree from above as "politically undesirable."

Dagestani Wahhabis are also in opposition to the republic's leadership. Traditional Islamic groups in the region view Wahhabis with suspicion since orthodox interpretation of Islam challenges the adaptations of Islam to local Dagestani traditions over the centuries. Wahhabism is the official Muslim ideology in Saudi Arabia and is widespread in India, Afghanistan, and Indonesia. It also became popular in Chechnya after the collapse of the Soviet Union.

During the summer of 1998, a group of 400 Wahhabis residing in three villages in the southern Buinaksk raion of Dagestan (Karamakhi, Chabanmakhi, and Kadar), many with military training from Chechnya, clashed with the police, killing several officers, and successfully expelled law enforcement and government officials from their land (*EWI RRR*, 27 August 1998). Thus, a portion of Dagestani territory and, more significantly, a key highway connecting the highlands with the valley, came under the control of the separatist rebels. Moreover, the residents of the rebellious territory established their own form of government. Over 7,000 people came under the jurisdiction of Shariah law, and according to Islamic tradition, men began wearing beards and women started to cover their faces. By mid-August, law enforcement agencies began concentrating their forces on the borders of the rebellious territory. In response, the Wahhabis strengthened their outposts and their leaders proclaimed the creation of an "independent Islamic territory" in the very heart of Dagestan. At the 19 August joint emergency session of the State Council (collective executive), the cabinet, and the People's Assembly, Dagestani leaders passed a resolution warning of the impending danger of religious extremism and civil war in the republic. The resolution called for further dialogue with the extremists, but, at the insistence of Mufti Saiid-Mukhamad Abubakarov, emphasized readiness to use force if necessary to solve the problem.

However, the problem remained of who exactly was going to disarm the Wahhabis? The police were obviously powerless, and using the Russian army would immediately incite anti-Russian nationalist sentiment, only helping the extremists. The day after the 21 August murder of the mufti, thousands of his followers came to Makhachkala, armed and demanding revenge. They staged a rally on the city's central square and expressed their willingness to help the republican government punish the guilty. The mufti had consistently criticized the Wahhabis, rejecting any chance of compromise. He even openly advocated armed persecution of the Wahhabis, especially when he said in one interview,

"Every Muslim killed by a Wahhabi will be in paradise, as will any Muslim who kills a Wahhabi." His death, has made it possible to channel the wrath of his spiritual followers toward the Wahhabis, thus pulling Dagestan toward the brink of civil war.

In the growing chaos, Dagestani authorities have redoubled their efforts to censor the press. In October 1998 the republican Ministry for Nationalities and External Affairs was transformed into the Ministry of National Policy, Information, and External Relations, with Magomedsalikh Gusaev at the helm. The new ministry has engaged in several attempts to control reporters, forcing the Moscow-based NTV to be more circumspect in its reporting from the republic and effectively removing financial support for the critical newspaper *Molodezh Dagestana*.

Ties to Moscow: Dependent on Subsidies

Because of Dagestan's extreme dependence on the federal budget, Magomedov constantly seeks to curry favor in Moscow. Good relations with the republican president were also important to Moscow, which depends on pro-Kremlin leaders to help achieve stability in the North Caucasus. Magomedov is one of the most active supporters of maintaining Russia's territorial integrity, and always consults the Kremlin before making decisions on key issues (*Monitor*, 26 June 1998). Additionally, Dagestan's strategic location is important to Moscow for economic reasons. About 70 percent of Russia's Caspian seashore and its main seaport, Makhachkala, are located in Dagestan. The republic also controls the main pipeline taking Caspian oil west through Russia.

Moscow is trying to use its power to counter the violent attacks against the Dagestani leadership and to root out corruption within the existing authorities. Russian Deputy Interior Minister Vladimir Kolesnikov stated that his agency had launched a ruthless campaign against criminals, regardless of their official status and rank, at a 9 September 1998 emergency meeting of the State Council. His investigators found evidence of massive embezzlement from the republican pension fund, even though its head, Sharapudin Musaev, and his armed bodyguards managed to resist arrest and escaped into the safety of his clan's highland village. They had targeted several individuals. The mayor of Kaspiisk, Ruslan Gadzhibekov, was arrested on 14

September 1998 on charges of masterminding the murder of Arsen Baymarov, the owner of the largest private construction company in Kaspiisk. The mayor was also accused of embezzling large amounts of money from the city treasury. Kolesnikov was also investigating Dagestani Deputy Prime Minister Gadzhi Makhachev, the head of the Dagneft oil company and the Avar ethnic movement, who was rumored to be hiding in the United States. Overall, in 1998 Kolesnikov's team filed 80 criminal cases, arrested 67 individuals, and freed 33 hostages.

Magomedov had very close relations with former Prime Minister Viktor Chernomyrdin, and the prime minister's downfall was a disappointment to the Dagestani leader. During his brief tenure, Prime Minister Sergei Kirienko promised real economic aid to the republic (*KD*, 16 July 1998). However, shortly after Kirienko's ouster, Magomedov said that during his tenure, not a single government program for social and economic development in Dagestan had been financed or executed.

Dagestan's economic problems may be reducing popular support for staying within the Russian Federation. Even before the slump of the past few years, perhaps 40 percent of the labor force had gone north as seasonal workers during the summer. The reduction in this seasonal work, plus the end of subsidies for federally sponsored industries (such as defense plants), has left Dagestan's economy in dire straits. Recorded cash incomes are among the lowest of any Russian region. Although some groups in Chechnya aspire to separate Dagestan from Russia, and even invaded the republic in the fall of 1999, secession seems unlikely.

Relations with Other Regions: Chechen Chaos Is the Main Concern

The war in neighboring Chechnya and the subsequent chaos there has had a devastating impact on Dagestan. Dagestan has been supportive of Chechnya's secessionist aspirations and deals with Chechnya as if it were a separate state and not another republic in the Russian Federation. Yet Magomedov is careful not to develop the kind of relations that would aggravate Moscow (*EWI RRR*, 21 May 1998).

A group of parliamentary deputies from Dagestan, Ingushetia, Georgia, and Azerbaijan met in Makhachkala in June 1997 to establish a common Caucasian legislative body that would be analogous to the European Parliament. The assembly's main goals would be to promote the economic growth, political development, and cultural revival of the Caucasian peoples (*EWI RRR*, 26 June 1997). Other regions in the North Caucasus were skeptical of the assembly, and conflicting interests among them cast serious doubt over the creation of such an organization.

Dagestan belongs to the North Caucasus Congress of Chambers of Industry and Trade. Chambers from Rostov, Krasnodar, Stavropol, Adygeya, Karachaevo-Cherkessia, and North Ossetia have participated in the congress. The main goal of this assembly is to affect federal investment policy so that more emphasis will be placed on developing the small business sector rather than continuing to support unprofitable enterprises in the state sector.

Dagestan is a member of the Association of Co-operation of Republics, Krais, and Oblasts of the North Caucasus. This association includes the republics of Adygeya, Ingushetia, Kabardino-Balkaria, Karachaevo-Cherkessia, North Ossetia, and Kalmykia; Krasnodar and Stavropol krais; and Rostov Oblast.

Foreign Relations: Fragmented Republic Pursues Fragmented Goals

Dagestan's foreign policy encompasses a variety of goals that reflect the diversity of the republic's populace and administration. Various groups representing Islamic interests have had relations with Saudi Arabia, and the notorious former State Duma member Nadir Khachilaev (now on the run) has met with Libya's Muammar Qaddafi and Iraqi President Saddam Hussein.

Turkey is very eager to develop cultural and economic relations with Dagestan. Turkish consumer goods are abundant in the republic, and the Turkish government pays for several hundred Dagestani students to study in Turkish universities (*EWI RRR*, 21 May 1998). A joint college staffed with Turkish faculty has also opened in the Dagestani capital, Makhachkala.

Dagestan has official representations in Azerbaijan, Ukraine, and Chechnya. Dagestan's approach to foreign policy is greatly determined by Moscow's approval. It is for this reason that official Dagestani

Magomedali Magomedovich Magomedov

15 June 1930—Born in Levashi village in Dagestan

1952—Graduated from Dagestan Pedagogical Institute

1952–1957—Worked as a school director

1954—Joined the CPSU

1957—Became chair of the Komintern collective farm

1966—Named management director of agriculture for Levashi raion

1968—Graduated from the Dagestan Agricultural Institute via correspondence

1969—Elected chair of the Levashi raion executive committee

December 1970—Became first secretary of the Levashi raion committee of the CPSU

September 1975—Named manager of the agricultural department of the Dagestan oblast committee of the CPSU

January 1979—Became First Deputy Chairman of the Dagestani Council of Ministers and in 1982 began to serve simultaneously as the chairman of the republican council on agro-industrial unification

May 1983—Became Chairman of the Dagestan Council of Ministers

August 1987—Elected Chairman of the Dagestan Supreme Soviet

1989–1991—Served in the USSR Congress of People's Deputies

1990—Elected to the RSFSR Congress of People's Deputies

March 1990—Elected to the Dagestani Congress of People's Deputies and chosen as chairman of the Dagestan Supreme Soviet on 24 April

12 December 1993—Elected to the Federation Council

26 July 1994—Elected Chairman of the Dagestan Republican State Council

March 1997—Joined the federal commission for problems in Chechnya

25 June 1998—Reelected Chairman of the Dagestan Republican State Council, Member of the second session of the Federation Council, serving on the Committee for Federation Issues, Federal Treaties, and Regional Politics

Married, with six children

groups chose not to participate in the April 1998 Congress of the Peoples of Chechnya and Dagestan even though Dagestan has served a crucial role in the Congress's development and the republican Ministry of Nationalities and External Relations participated in its planning (*EWI RRR*, 21 May 1998).

During the last quarter of 1998, Dagestani villagers entered into several border conflicts with their neighbors in Azerbaijan. Farmers on both sides of the border fought over access to water and disputed plots of land (*EWI RRR*, 8 December 1998).

Attitudes Toward Business: Violence Prevents Most Activity

The violence in the area prevents all but the bravest businessmen from working in the North Caucasus region. Nevertheless, a few projects are underway in Dagestan. In October 1997 the republican government approved a proposal by the Italian firm Simon and the joint stock company Maksi to establish a shoe factory in Dagestan (*EWI RRR*, 16 October 1997). In May 1997 Dagestan signed a cooperation agreement with LUKoil President Vagit Alekperov. The agreement states that the company will participate in tenders for extracting oil on Dagestan's territory and in areas of the Caspian Sea (*KD*, 29 May 1997). Additionally, the Dutch company Philips has formed a partnership with former defense enterprise Elektrosignal to produce color television sets. The sets are produced in Derbent using European production technology (*EWI RRR*, 14 May 1998).

One of the region's most promising projects is restructuring the Makhachkala sea port, the only warm-water Russian port on the Caspian Sea. Makhachkala's oil facilities have been operating for 110 years and are among the largest in the country. They include 153 reservoirs with an overall capacity of 543,000 tons, and can transship up to 10 million tons of oil annually. In the fourth quarter of 1998 Makhachkala firms received, stored, and transshipped 400,000 tons of petroleum products, and the republic has contracts for 2.8 million tons for 1999 (*EWI RRR*, 18 March 1999). In early 1999 Mobil began transporting 70,000 tons of fuel oil per week through Makhachkala.

Perhaps the greatest business issue involving Dagestan is its role in a major Russian pipeline proposal. The Ministry of Fuel and Energy would like to build a new pipeline crossing Dagestan that would transport oil from Azerbaijan across Russia without crossing Chechnya. The pipeline would be economically beneficial to Dagestan, yet the republic's close proximity to Chechnya raises questions of security.

In November 1998, Dagestan's Ministry of State Property made public a list of enterprises to be privatized by the end of the year. Both the composition of the list and the prices for each enterprise raised a host of questions, none of which were answered by Usman Usmanov, who heads the ministry. The list contained nine large state enterprises in spheres ranging from timber processing to food industries. One of the most successful companies on the list was the yeast plant in Makhachkala, which has boosted its usually profitable operations even further during the August crisis, when many competing, imported products dropped out of the market. The plant was privatized for 14.5 million rubles ($900,000). Not counting the value of the land on which the plant stands, the worth of its buildings and equipment greatly exceeded the asking price (*EWI RRR*, 12 November 1998).

Internet Sites in the Region

http://www.caspian.net/dagestan.html
This site provides an extensive overview of the republic, including a useful ethnic map.

EVENK AUTONOMOUS OKRUG

Territory: 767,600 km²
Population (as of 1 January 1998): 20,000
Distance from Moscow: 5,738 km

Major Cities:
Tura, *capital* (pop. 5,900)

Basic Facts

Population (as of 1 Jan. 1998): 20,000 (0.01% of Russian total)

Ethnic breakdown (1989 census): Russians 67.5%, Evenks 14.1%, Ukrainians 5.3%, Yakuts 3.8%, Tatars 1.4%, Belarusans 1.1%

Urban population (as of 1 Jan. 1998): 29.2% (Russia overall: 73.1%)

Pensioner population (1997): 20.00% (Russia overall: 25.96%)

Percent of population with higher education (1989 census): 11.6% (Russia overall: 11.3%)

Average monthly personal income in July 1998: 938.6 new rubles (Russian average: 891.7 new rubles)

Average monthly personal expenses in July 1998: 588.8 new rubles (Russian average: 684.9 new rubles)

Average monthly subsistence requirement in 1998: 736 new rubles (Russian average: 438 new rubles)

Consumer price index (as of July 1998): 274 (Russia overall = 100)

Budgetary revenues (1997): 407.5 billion rubles (Russia overall: 433,378.2 billion rubles)

Budgetary expenditures (1997): 429.2 billion rubles (Russia overall: 468,111.6 billion rubles)

Industrial production as percentage of all Russian production (Jan.–Aug. 1998): 0.0003%

Proportion of loss-making enterprises (as of July 1998): 42.9% (Russia overall: 50.4%)

Number of enterprises which have wage arrears (as of 1 Sept. 1998): 44 (0.03% of Russian total)

Agricultural production as percentage of all Russian production (1997): 0.01%

Number of private farms (as of 1 Jan. 1998): 55 (0.02% of Russian total)

Capital investment (1997): 23.4 billion rubles (Russia overall: 408,797 billion rubles)

Sources of investment (1997): federal budget: 43.4% (Russian average: 10.2%); regional budget: 49.5% (10.5%); extra-budgetary funds: 7.1% (79.3%)

Number of telephones per 100 families (1997): in cities: 35.9 (Russian average: 49.2); in villages: 33.4 (19.8)

Brief Overview

The Evenk Autonomous Okrug was founded in 1930. It is a part of Krasnoyarsk Krai and borders Taimyr Autonomous Okrug, the Republic of Sakha (Yakutia), and Irkutsk Oblast. Despite its designation as an ethnic region, Russians make up the majority of the population.

Major industries are hunting, fishing, reindeer breeding, and forestry, which fail to bring much profit to the regional budget—only about 20 percent of the okrug's expenditures are covered by its own budgetary revenues. Yet the okrug is rich in mineral resources, particularly oil and graphite. Geologists believe that diamond fields also will be discovered in the region in the near future.

According to a 1998 survey by *Ekspert* magazine, the okrug ranked 89th among Russia's 89 regions in terms of investment potential and 83rd in terms of investment risk. A 1998 survey by Bank Austria ranked the okrug 87th in terms of investment climate.

Electoral History

2000 Presidential Election
Putin: 61.99%
Zyuganov: 21.47%
Tuleev: 4.44%
Zhirinovsky: 3.49%
Yavlinskii: 3.13%
Turnout: 57.33% (Russia overall: 68.64%)

1999 Parliamentary Elections
Unity: 39.51%
Communist Party of the Russian Federation: 12.10%
Zhirinovsky Bloc: 8.13%
Union of Right Forces: 5.64%
Fatherland–All Russia: 5.48%
Yabloko: 4.50%
In a single-mandate district: 1 independent
Turnout: 62.18% (Russia overall: 61.85%)

1997 Gubernatorial Election
Bokovikov: 49.00%
Yakimov (incumbent): 40.45%
Uodai: 3.17%
Turnout: 59.85%

1996 Presidential Election
Yeltsin: 43.42%/65.76% (first round/second round)
Zyuganov: 20.00%/28.33%
Lebed: 16.41%
Zhirinovsky: 7.05%
Yavlinskii: 6.29%
Turnout: 65.50%/62.39% (Russia overall: 69.67%/ 68.79%)

1995 Parliamentary Election
Communist Party of the Russian Federation: 13.73%
Liberal Democratic Party of Russia: 13.02%
Women of Russia: 10.48%
Congress of Russian Communities: 8.52%
Our Home Is Russia: 6.66%
Party of Workers' Self-Government: 5.84%
Yabloko: 4.97%
Communists–Workers' Russia: 3.62%
Kedr: 2.20%
Russia's Democratic Choice: 2.17%
Power to the People: 2.09%
In a single-mandate district: 1 independent
Turnout: 61.96% (Russia overall: 64.37%)

1993 Constitutional Referendum
"Yes"—67.4%   "No"—30.3%

1993 Parliamentary Elections
Liberal Democratic Party of Russia: 20.94%
Women of Russia: 17.39%
Russia's Choice: 15.36%
Party of Russian Unity and Concord: 10.48%
Yabloko: 7.94%
Communist Party of the Russian Federation: 7.45%
Democratic Party of Russia: 7.32%
Agrarian Party of Russia: 3.58%
In a single-mandate district: 1 independent
Turnout: 59.66% (Russia overall: 54.34%)

1991 Presidential Election
Yeltsin: 39.11%
Ryzhkov: 19.64%
Tuleev: 17.48%
Zhirinovsky: 16.33%
Bakatin: 2.84%
Makashov: 1.66%
Turnout: 74.35% (Russia overall: 76.66%)

Regional Political Institutions

Executive:
Governor, 4-year term
Aleksandr Aleksandrovich Bokovikov, elected March 1997
Evenk Autonomous Okrug Administration;
Ul. Sovetskaya, 4; Tura, 663370;
Evenk Autonomous Okrug, Krasnoyarsk Krai
Tel 7(391–13) 2–21–35;
Fax 7(391–13) 2–26–55
Federation Council in Moscow:
7(095) 292–56–31, 926–62–51

Legislative:
Unicameral
Zakonodatelnii Suglan—23 members, 4-year term, elected December 1996
Chairman—Anatolii Yegorovich Amosov, elected January 1997

Regional Politics

Electoral Violations Surround First Victory

Aleksandr Bokovikov was elected governor of Evenk Autonomous Okrug on 16 March 1997 after almost four months of election controversy. Bokovikov had initially been announced the victor in gubernatorial elections held 22 December 1996, yet inconsistencies in the results of the elections caused them to be annulled. The preliminary results of the election showed that Bokovikov had defeated the incumbent Anatolii Yakimov by fewer than 100 votes, but the final tally had Yakimov leading by 550 votes. After the cancellation, Bokovikov filed a lawsuit against the okrug electoral commission, but the decision was not overturned, and new elections had to be held.

Bokovikov, who served previously as the chairman of the okrug legislative assembly, the Sulgan, had the support of the Communist Party and the National Patriotic Union of Russia. Sergei Filatov's All-Russia Coordinating Council backed Yakimov, and Prime Minister Viktor Chernomyrdin sent federal money to the okrug before the first elections.

Executive Platform: Leftist

Bokovikov belongs to the leftist camp, having represented the Communist party and the National Patriotic Union of Russia in the 1996 gubernatorial campaign. He opposes the sale of land.

Relationships Between Key Players

Evenk Autonomous Okrug has a very small population of approximately 20,000. Even though it is designated as an ethnic region, ethnic Russians make up 67.5 percent of the okrug population, while the Evenks are only 14 percent. The interests of the indigenous peoples are represented by the local Association of Indigenous Peoples of the North, which also participates in political negotiations and decisions.

Ties to Moscow

On 1 November 1997 Bokovikov signed a power-sharing agreement with President Yeltsin and the governors of Krasnoyarsk Krai and Taimyr Autonomous Okrug. Both Evenk and Taimyr are simultaneously part of Krasnoyarsk Krai and equal subjects of the Russian Federation, creating various legal ambiguities. This treaty outlines the delineation of authority between the federal, krai, and okrug governments. Bokovikov signed a similar treaty with then Krasnoyarsk Krai Governor Valerii Zubov a few months prior to this agreement (see Relations with Other Regions).

Relations with Other Regions: Krasnoyarsk Supporter

The governor appears to have good relations with his Siberian neighbors. In June 1997 Bokovikov signed an agreement with then Krasnoyarsk Krai Governor Valerii Zubov stating that Evenk Autonomous Okrug is a constituent part of the krai and that its residents can vote in the krai's gubernatorial and legislative elections. At the time, the two regions were set to sign an additional 12 agreements regarding economic issues. Bokovikov wants the Evenk Okrug to remain part of Krasnoyarsk, unlike the leadership of the Taimyr Autonomous Okrug, which has threatened to secede from the krai. Bokovikov is also in favor of regulated relations with neighboring Yakutia and Taimyr.

The Evenk Autonomous Okrug belongs to the Siberian Accord Association. The other member regions are: the republics of Buryatia, Gorno-Altai, and Khakassia; Altai and Krasnoyarsk krais; Irkutsk, Novosibirsk, Omsk, Tomsk, Tyumen, and Kemerovo oblasts; and Agin-Buryat, Taimyr, Ust-Orda Buryat, Khanty-Mansi, and Yamal-Nenets autonomous okrugs. The association is headed by Omsk Governor Leonid Polezhaev.

Foreign Relations: Northern Forum Member

In 1994 Evenk became a member of the Northern Forum, a non-profit organization composed of regional governments in northern countries. The Northern Forum represents the interests of its members in Arctic policy groups such as the Arctic Council and the Barents Euro Arctic Regional Council, and in scientific groups like the United States Arctic Research Commission. The Northern Forum members include regions from Canada, China, Japan, Mongolia, Korea, Finland, Sweden, Norway, and the

Aleksandr Aleksandrovich Bokovikov

7 September 1956—Born

1978—Graduated from Krasnoyarsk Polytechnical Institute as an engineer-mechanic and was sent to work in the Kuibyshev factory in Irkutsk

1979–1983—Worked as a government purveyor for the Evenk Okrug fishing collective and the deputy chairman of procurement

1983–1992—Worked as a government purveyor, deputy director, and then director for the Ilimpi hunting collective; During this period Bokovikov also worked as the director of the Kislokanski state farm and chairman of the Evenk agroindustrial association. He also completed 5 years of study in the hunting faculty of Irkutsk Agricultural Institute, yet did not receive a diploma

1992–1994—General director of the firm Kontrakt and director of the Ilimpi municipal fur enterprise

6 March 1994—Elected to the Legislative Sulgan of the Evenk Autonomous Okrug, and on 17 June, elected chairman

January 1996—Appointed to the Federation Council, serving on the Committee for Northern Affairs and Minority Peoples

22 December 1996—Elected governor of Evenk Autonomous Okrug

January 1997—Election results annulled due to "multiple electoral violations"

16 March 1997—Elected governor of Evenk Autonomous Okrug

United States. Ten Russian regions are involved, including Evenk Autonomous Okrug.

Attitudes Toward Business

Geologists believe that Evenk might be sitting on a diamond mine, which could transform the region's economy, now based primarily on hunting and trapping. In March 1998 the firm Almazy Rossii-Sakha (ALROSA) announced its intentions to look for diamonds there. Two Canadian companies, Siberian Pacific Resource and Nord-West Industrial Inc., are already working in the area.

GORNO-ALTAI REPUBLIC

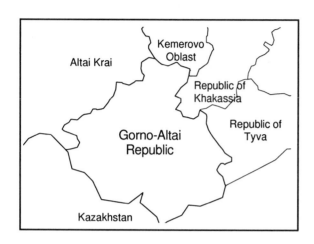

Territory: 92,600 km²
Population (as of 1 January 1998): 202,000
Distance from Moscow: 3,641 km

Major Cities:
Gorno-Altaisk, *capital* (pop. 49,000)

Basic Facts

Population (as of 1 Jan. 1998): 202,000 (0.14% of Russian total)

Ethnic breakdown (1989 census): Russians 60.4%, Altai 31%, Kazakhs 5.6%

Urban population (as of 1 Jan. 1998): 24.4% (Russia overall: 73.1%)

Student population (as of 1 Sept. 1997): 228 per 10,000 (Russia overall: 208/10,000)

Pensioner population (1997): 22.77% (Russia overall: 25.96%)

Percent of population with higher education (1989 census): 10.6% (Russia overall: 11.3%)

Percent of population working in (1997): Industry: 9.8% (Russian average: 23.0%); Agriculture: 24.6% (13.7%); Trade: 11.9% (13.5%); Culture: 20.2% (13.3%)

Average monthly personal income in July 1998: 469.3 new rubles (Russian average: 891.7 new rubles)

Average monthly personal expenses in July 1998: 242.3 new rubles (Russian average: 684.9 new rubles)

Average monthly subsistence requirement in 1998: 400 new rubles (Russian average: 438 new rubles)

Consumer price index (as of July 1998): 98 (Russia overall = 100)

Budgetary revenues (1997): 402.8 billion rubles (Russia overall: 433,378.2 billion rubles)

Budgetary expenditures (1997): 474.4 billion rubles (Russia overall: 468,111.6 billion rubles)

Industrial production as percentage of all Russian production (Jan.–Aug. 1998): 0.002%

Proportion of loss-making enterprises (as of July 1998): 88.9% (Russia overall: 50.4%)

Number of enterprises which have wage arrears (as of 1 Sept. 1998): 192 (0.14% of Russian total)

Agricultural production as percentage of all Russian production (1997): 0.21%

Number of private farms (as of 1 Jan. 1998): 1,202 (0.44% of Russian total)

Capital investment (1997): 155.9 billion rubles (Russia overall: 408,797 billion rubles)

Sources of investment (1997): federal budget: 44.0% (Russian average: 10.2%); regional budget: 15.6% (10.5%); extra-budgetary funds: 40.4% (79.3%)

Foreign investment (1997): 0 (Russia overall: 12,294,734,000 USD)

Number of joint ventures (1997): 2 (0.01% of Russian total)

Fixed capital investment in joint ventures and foreign companies (1997): 0 (Russia overall: 16,265.4 billion rubles)

Number of small businesses (as of 1 July 1998): 600 (0.07% of Russian total)

Number of enterprises privatized in 1997: 0

Number of telephones per 100 families (1997): in cities: 33.9 (Russian average: 49.2); in villages: 19.6 (19.8)

Brief Overview

The Gorno-Altai Republic, with a territory of 92,600 sq km, is situated in the southwestern part of Siberia, in the Altai Mountains. The republic, which was formed in 1991 after the region seceded from Altai Krai, borders the republics of Tyva and Khakassia, Kemerovo Oblast, Altai Krai, Kazakhstan, Mongolia, and China.

The highest Siberian mountain, Belukha (4,506 meters) is located on the republic's territory. A quarter of the territory is covered with forests, mostly cedar and larch. Flora and fauna are very diverse due to the republic's location at the intersection of the Kazakh steppe, Siberian taiga, and Mongolian semi-desert. The republic has over 7,000 lakes; the largest and deepest (230.8 sq km and 325 meters deep), Terletskoe Lake, is bigger than Liechtenstein. Most of the rivers in the republic are not suitable for navigation.

Though the republic is rich in raw materials, such as coal, charcoal, mercury, marble, granite, and semi-precious stones, the extracting and processing industries are underdeveloped. Nevertheless, the republic houses the country's only mercury works, Aktash. Agriculture is the dominant industry: 60 percent of GDP comes from farming, which is mostly concentrated in stock breeding. The republic is one of the least urbanized territories of the Russian Federation, which allows it to preserve its natural landscape and environment.

According to a 1998 survey by *Ekspert* magazine, the republic ranked 82nd among Russia's 89 regions in terms of investment potential and 79th in terms of investment risk. A 1998 survey by Bank Austria ranked the republic 73rd in terms of investment climate.

Electoral History

2000 Presidential Election
Zyuganov: 42.72%
Putin: 37.89%
Tuleev: 9.32%
Zhirinovsky: 3.01%
Yavlinskii: 2.63%
Turnout: 68.59% (Russia overall: 68.64%)

1999 Parliamentary Elections
Unity: 27.51%
Communist Party of the Russian Federation: 25.63%
Fatherland–All Russia: 10.25%
Zhirinovsky Bloc: 5.99%
Union of Right Forces: 5.40%
Yabloko: 3.38%
In a single-mandate district: 1 Fatherland–All Russia
Turnout: 71.17% (Russia overall: 61.85%)

1997 Republican Executive Election
Zubakin (State Duma deputy): 23.5%
Antradonov: 23.3%
Volkov (incumbent): 12.0%
Turnout: 71.2%

1996 Presidential Election
Zyuganov: 43.61%/51.68% (first round/second round)
Yeltsin: 28.77%/40.04%
Lebed: 13.03%
Zhirinovsky: 4.83%
Yavlinskii: 3.46%
Turnout: 74.10%/70.94% (Russia overall: 69.67%/ 68.79%)

1995 Parliamentary Elections
Communist Party of the Russian Federation: 25.95%
Agrarian Party of Russia: 11.37%
Liberal Democratic Party of Russia: 9.34%
Communists–Workers' Russia: 7.64%
Women of Russia: 5.63%
Our Home Is Russia: 4.96%
Party of Workers' Self-Government: 3.10%
In a single-mandate district: 1 Russia's Democratic Choice
Turnout: 75.50% (Russia overall: 64.37%)

1993 Constitutional Referendum
"Yes"—54.0%   "No"—42.5%

1993 Parliamentary Elections
Party of Russian Unity and Concord: 26.55%
Liberal Democratic Party of Russia: 17.04%
Women of Russia: 12.47%
Communist Party of the Russian Federation: 11.02%
Russia's Choice: 9.31%
Agrarian Party of Russia: 8.74%
Democratic Party of Russia: 4.83%
Yabloko: 3.16%
In a single-mandate district: 1 independent
Turnout: 66.67% (Russia overall: 54.34%)

1991 Presidential Elections

Ryzhkov: 32.03%
Tuleev: 24.36%
Yeltsin: 22.39%
Zhirinovsky: 10.21%
Makashov: 3.53%
Bakatin: 2.20%
Turnout: 81.84% (Russia overall: 76.66%)

Regional Political Institutions

Executive:
 President, 4-year term
 Semen Ivanovich Zubakin, elected December 1997
  Government of the Republic of Altai;
  Ul. Kirova, 16; Gorno-Altaisk, 659700
  Tel 7(38541) 9–34–56

Legislative:
 Unicameral
 El Kurultai—41 members, 4-year term, elected
 December 1997
 Chairman—Daniil Ivanovich Tabaev, elected
 January 1998

Regional Politics

Gaidar Follower Governs Chaotic Siberian Region

Gorno-Altai is one of the poorest regions in Siberia, and Semen Zubakin came to power in the midst of a dire political and economic crisis. The republic, which receives 85 percent of its budget from federal subsidies, had long been politically unstable. In January 1997 the republican parliament sacked the region's government and its head Vladimir Petrov. Valerii Chaptynov was appointed to head the republic, but he passed away in August, at which point the chairman of the republican legislature, Vladilen Volkov, took over temporarily until new elections could be held. Zubakin was elected republican president on 14 December 1997, winning a narrow victory by only 0.2 percent. Zubakin is the only regional executive who is a member of Yegor Gaidar's Russia's Democratic Choice party.

Thus, the Gorno-Altai Republic has witnessed several changes of power in its short history. The republic was formed in 1991 when the region seceded from Altai Krai. A new constitution was adopted in 1997, establishing the office of a directly elected president serving simultaneously as the republican prime minister. This consolidation of power in a unified executive while the republican leadership kept changing only exacerbated the political chaos. In late 1997 the newspaper *Trud* reported that the levels of corruption in Altai were absurdly high and secessionist tendencies were strong among the republic's population (*Trud*, 29 October 1997).

Executive Platform: Liberal and Democratic

Zubakin is a strong supporter of Yegor Gaidar, and has been a member of Gaidar's party Russia's Choice since it was founded just before the December 1993 State Duma elections. Prior to joining this party, Zubakin belonged to the Democratic Party of Russia, which was founded by Nikolai Travkin. Zubakin characterizes his political views as democratic and liberal. He is critical of the Communist Party and the Liberal Democratic Party of Russia (LDPR) and of their leaders, Gennadii Zyuganov and Vladimir Zhirinovsky (Panorama).

Zubakin's economic views are generally liberal. He is against the state regulation of prices and was an advocate of voucher privatization. However, he supports indexing salaries for public sector employees. In the political sphere, he strongly supports the integrity of Russia's current borders. Zubakin believes that the Kuril Islands should remain part of Russia, while Ukraine is entitled to maintain its current possession of Crimea.

Policies: Tariff-Free Zone

Promoting economic development in the Gorno-Altai Republic is a formidable task. With his razor-thin electoral victory, Zubakin does not have widespread public support, and he has failed to establish a concrete plan of action for governing the republic. The region's political stratification hinders the adoption of comprehensive initiatives (see Relationships Between Key Players).

The republic has a tariff-free zone to attract more trade activity to the region. Nevertheless, the level of trade in the republic remains very low, even though the republic straddles the borders of Mongolia, Kazakhstan, and China, a location that seemingly offers great trade potential.

Relationships Between Key Players: Tense Relations with Legislature

Altai's intense political discord has hindered Zubakin's attempts to lead from the start. Since the republican electoral law requires that a candidate win only a plurality rather than a majority of votes, Zubakin was able to gain office with only 23.5 percent of the vote (70 percent voter turnout). The fact that Altai's political leadership changed three times in 1997 prior to Zubakin's election certainly contributed to the region's economic instability and political chaos.

In August 1998, just a few months after Zubakin took over as head of the republic, ten of the region's largest parties began prodding him to resign. The regional legislature, El Kurultai, which is dominated by the local branch of Our Home Is Russia, then considered a motion to remove Zubakin, but ultimately voted in favor of the president at its 23–25 September 1998 session (*EWI RRR*, 17 December 1998).

In June 1999 the El Kurultai voted 26 to 6 to express no confidence in Zubakin. The legislature also voted no confidence in Zubakin's ministers for social protection and for science and education. Zubakin was not obliged to resign as a result of the vote; however, at the same session, the El Kurultai passed a law on recalling the head of the republic and government (*RFR*, 9 June 1999)

The main opposition leader in the region is Yurii Antaradonov, who lost to Zubakin by 0.2 percent in the 1997 presidential elections. Antaradonov, a leader of the region's indigenous people, stepped down as head of an organization called Altai's Ecological-Economic Region in the fall of 1998 and announced his voluntary resignation as the republic's deputy prime minister because he felt it was not possible to work under pressure. He believes that the personal and business relations between the current leaders have a negative impact on inter-ethnic relations. Moreover, he asserts that only the tolerance of the indigenous people prevents conflict in the region.

In May 1998 Agrarian Party Chairman Mikhail Lapshin won the State Duma seat Zubakin vacated when he was elected president of Altai. Lapshin narrowly defeated Zubakin's preferred candidate, Andrei Vavilov. Vavilov was nearly barred from the race for having begun his campaign activities before officially registering as a candidate, and Lapshin accused Zubakin of "openly using all acceptable and unacceptable measures" to support Vavilov's campaign (*RFE/RL*, 29 May 1998).

In March 1999, 20 various public organizations in Gorno-Altai presented an appeal to Zubakin and El Kurultai Chairman Daniil Tabaev protesting the construction of a Catholic church on the banks of Terletskoe Lake. Zubakin has pledged not to allow the construction of a Catholic church in the republic (*RFE/RL*, 15 March 1999).

Ties to Moscow: Looks to Right-Center Bloc

Zubakin was generally supportive of President Boris Yeltsin. In the lead-up to the 1999 parliamentary election he was involved in setting up the right-center political bloc, Union of Right Forces led by former acting Prime Minister Yegor Gaidar, former First Deputy Prime Minister Boris Nemtsov, and Unified Energy System head Anatolii Chubais.

Among Russia's ethnic republics, Gorno-Altai is one of the most heavily dependent on transfers from the federal budget. Discussions between Zubakin and then Prime Minister Yevgenii Primakov at the end of 1998 regarding possible financial help from the center to Gorno-Altai as a depressed region ended on a positive note. However, workers in the agrarian sector (more than 70 percent of the population) had by mid-1999 still not received their 1997 salaries as promised by Zubakin. The plight of the agricultural territories is particularly acute as 90 percent of the region's unemployed reside in rural areas. In mid-1999 public sector employees had not been paid since March 1998.

On 5 November 1998 republican radio announced that cattle belonging to a collective farm in the republic's Kosh-Agachsk district bordering Mongolia, China, Kazakhstan, and Tyva were being seized in order to pay off the farm's debts to the federal budget. The cattle are the only property that could be taken away from the collective farmers and sold for profit as meat. Collective farm workers had no way to make tax payments. Given the desperate nature of the situation, the republican legislature decided to halt such practices.

Relations with Other Regions

The Gorno-Altai Republic is part of the Siberian Accord Association, which includes the republics

Semen Ivanovich Zubakin

4 May 1952—Born in Verkh-Uimon village of the Gorno-Altai Republic

1969–1972—Studied at the Toguchinsk Forestry Technical College as a technician-forester and then began work in forestry

1975—Worked as a state insurance agent in the Ust-Koksinsk district

1976–1985—Worked as an inspector, senior economist, and deputy director of the State Insurance Agency for Gorno-Altai

1980–1985—Studied finance at the All-Union Finance and Economics Correspondence Institute

1986–1991—Worked as an inspector and then deputy director for the department of state revenues, and then worked in the republican finance department

1991–October 1993—Member of the Democratic Party of Russia

1992–1993—Chairman of the Altai Republic Supreme Soviet Committee for Issues of Economic Reform and Property

October 1993—Joined Yegor Gaidar's Russia's Choice (which later became Russia's Democratic Choice)

1994–1995—Head controller-inspector of the Finance Ministry in the Gorno-Altai Republic and a member of the republican assembly (El Kurultai)

17 December 1995—Elected to the State Duma, where he served on the Committee for the Budget, Taxes, Banking, and Finances

14 December 1997—Elected president of the Gorno-Altai Republic

January 1998—Joined the Federation Council

of Buryatia and Khakassia; Altai and Krasnoyarsk krais; Irkutsk, Novosibirsk, Omsk, Tomsk, Tyumen, and Kemerovo oblasts; and Agin-Buryat, Taimyr, Ust-Orda Buryat, Khanty-Mansi, Evenk, and Yamal-Nenets autonomous okrugs.

Foreign Relations

The 1998 economic crisis in Southeast Asia affected the economy of Gorno-Altai Republic in a very direct way: South Korea was the main buyer of stag antlers, which can be used to make medicinal products. These exports were the primary source of hard currency for the republic's budget. The yield for antler products was low in 1997 and hardly any antlers were sold in 1998. As a result, the republic's hard currency reserves were depleted at the beginning of 1999.

Attitudes Toward Business: Behind in Development

Zubakin is pro-business and hopes to develop the region's depressed economy. However, he has not been successful at establishing concrete initiatives nor actively involved in attracting investment to the republic. Investment and industrial development are absolutely crucial to reduce Altai's reliance on federal transfers.

REPUBLIC OF INGUSHETIA

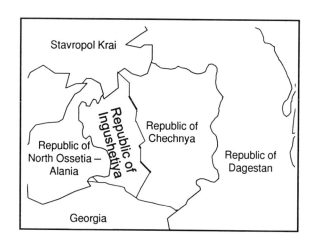

Territory: 4,300 km²
Population (as of 1 January 1998): 313,000

Major Cities:
Nazran, *capital* (pop. 76,200)
Malgobek (35,700)
Karabulak (18,700)

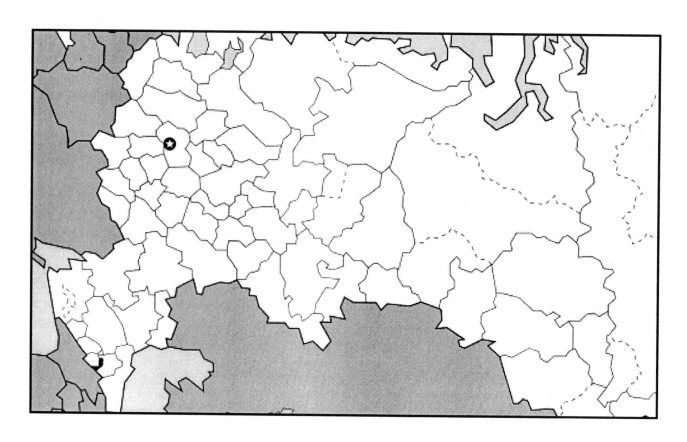

Basic Facts

Population (as of 1 Jan. 1998): 313,000 (0.21% of Russian total)

Ethnic breakdown (1989 census): Ingush 74.5%, Russians 13.3%, Chechens 10.3%

Urban population (as of 1 Jan. 1998): 41.8% (Russia overall: 73.1%)

Student population (as of 1 Sept. 1997): 88 per 10,000 (Russia overall: 208/10,000)

Pensioner population (1997): 16.29% (Russia overall: 25.96%)

Percent of population working in (1997): Industry: 18.1% (Russian average: 23.0%); Agriculture: 21.7% (13.7%); Trade: 4.5% (13.5%); Culture: 16.5% (13.3%)

Average monthly personal income in July 1998: 370.7 new rubles (Russian average: 891.7 new rubles)

Average monthly personal expenses in July 1998: 142.9 new rubles (Russian average: 684.9 new rubles)

Average monthly subsistence requirement in 1998: 363 new rubles (Russian average: 438 new rubles)

Consumer price index (as of July 1998): 130 (Russia overall = 100)

Budgetary revenues (1997): 326.9 billion rubles (Russia overall: 433,378.2 billion rubles)

Budgetary expenditures (1997): 414.7 billion rubles (Russia overall: 468,111.6 billion rubles)

Proportion of loss-making enterprises (as of July 1998): 66.7% (Russia overall: 50.4%)

Number of enterprises which have wage arrears (as of 1 Sept. 1998): 109 (0.08% of Russian total)

Agricultural production as percentage of all Russian production (1997): 0.10%

Number of private farms (as of 1 Jan. 1998): 1,130 (0.41% of Russian total)

Capital investment (1997): 665.4 billion rubles (Russia overall: 408,797 billion rubles)

Sources of investment (1997): federal budget: 68.6% (Russian average: 10.2%); regional budget: 11.1% (10.5%); extra-budgetary funds: 20.3% (79.3%)

Number of joint ventures (1997): 0

Fixed capital investment in joint ventures and foreign companies (1997): 0 (Russia overall: 16,265.4 billion rubles)

Number of small businesses (as of 1 July 1998): 1,900 (0.22% of Russian total)

Number of enterprises privatized in 1997: 6 (0.04% of Russian total), including those which used to be municipal property: 33.3% (Russian average: 66.4%); regional property: 66.7% (20.0%); federal property: 0% (13.6%)

Number of telephones per 100 families (1997): in cities: 22.2 (Russian average: 49.2); in villages: 0 (19.8)

Brief Overview

The Republic of Ingushetia is located on the northern slope of the Caucasus Mountains and the adjoining Tersko-Kumsk lowland. Its neighbors are North Ossetia, Chechnya, and Georgia, though most of its actual borders are not clearly defined. Ingushetia voluntarily joined the Russian Empire in the beginning of the nineteenth century. Its territory is rich in oil, gas, and mineral waters.

Agriculture forms the basis of the republican economy. Benefiting from a favorable climate and rich soil, republican farms grow high-quality grain, vegetables, fruits, and grapes. Small-scale electric, petrochemical, and food processing companies comprise the industrial sector. Ingushetia could potentially extract oil and gas, but its lack of capital and its outdated equipment prevent the republic from developing these resources. Now, the republic is the poorest in the country, with only about 12 percent of expenditures covered by its own budgetary revenues.

According to a 1998 survey by *Ekspert* magazine, the republic ranked 77th among Russia's 89 regions in terms of investment potential and 87th in terms of investment risk. Investment risk had increased by 46 points since 1997, the third largest increase in the country. A 1998 survey by Bank Austria ranked the republic 88th in terms of investment climate.

Electoral History

2000 Presidential Election
Putin: 85.42%
Zyuganov: 4.63%
Yavlinskii: 4.45%
Dzhabrailov: 2.05%
Tuleev: 0.77%
Pamfilova: 0.32%
Zhirinovsky: 0.29%
Turnout: 92.76% (Russia overall: 68.64%)

1999 Parliamentary Elections
Fatherland–All Russia: 87.98%
Yabloko: 2.90%
Communist Party of the Russian Federation: 1.82%
Unity: 1.04%
Zhirinovsky Bloc: 0.52%
Bloc of Nikolaev-Fedorov: 0.41%

Communists–Workers' Russia: 0.38%
Union of Right Forces: 0.38%
Our Home Is Russia: 0.38%
In a single-mandate district: 1 Liberal Democratic Party of Russia
Turnout: 68.30% (Russia overall: 61.85%)

1998 Republican Presidential Election
Aushev (incumbent): 66.5%
Kostoev: 13.3%

1996 Presidential Election
Yeltsin: 46.26%/79.80% (first round/second round)
Zyuganov: 24.49%/15.52%
Yavlinskii: 15.19%
Gorbachev: 4.45%
Lebed: 2.24%
Zhirinovsky: 1.74%
Turnout: 70.03%/83.40% (Russia overall: 69.67%/ 68.79%)

1995 Parliamentary Elections
Our Home Is Russia: 34.11%
Nur: 23.71%
Russia's Democratic Choice: 5.52%
Yabloko: 5.33%
Communist Party of the Russian Federation: 5.12%
Liberal Democratic Party of Russia: 2.08%
In a single-mandate district: 1 independent
Turnout: 57.16% (Russia overall: 64.37%)

1993 Constitutional Referendum
"Yes"—56.2%   "No"—42.5%

1993 Parliamentary Elections
Democratic Party of Russia: 71.07%
Communist Party of the Russian Federation: 6.44%
Party of Russian Unity and Concord: 4.90%
Liberal Democratic Party of Russia: 3.20%
Women of Russia: 2.76%
Yabloko: 2.11%
Russia's Choice: 1.65%
Agrarian Party of Russia: 0.69%
In a single-mandate district: 1 independent
Turnout: 46.09% (Russia overall: 54.34%)

Regional Political Institutions

Executive:
President, 5-year term
Ruslan Sultanovich Aushev, elected February
1993, February 1994, March 1998
Bulvarnaya St., 1; Nazran, 366720
Tel 7(873–22) 2–33–07, 2–33–85
Federation Council in Moscow:
7(095) 292–75–18, 926–61–44, 925–23–69
Fax 7(095) 334–20–39

Legislative:
Unicameral
People's Assembly (*Narodnoe sobranie*)—21
members, 4-year term, elected February 1999
Chairman—Ruslan Sultanovich Pliev, elected
June 1995, March 1999

Regional Politics

Elected President Three Times

Ruslan Aushev has been the only leader to rule over
the Republic of Ingushetia, Russia's youngest administrative region. The territory of the republic had
been part of the Republic of Checheno-Ingushetia
since 1934. In 1988–89, 60,000 Ingush citizens
signed a petition calling for the formation of a separate Ingush republic, and in 1992 the Chechen parliament announced the restoration of the 1934 border between the two regions. Thus, the formation
of the Republic of Ingushetia has been the one major
territorial question in the North Caucasus that has
been settled without conflict.

The struggle for an Ingush territorial identity has
been long and painful. In 1944 the entire Ingush
population was deported from the North Caucasus,
as were the Karachai, Balkar, and Chechen populations. Stalin relocated these groups to areas in
Central Asia, Kazakhstan, and Siberia, claiming that
they had conspired with the Germans during World
War II. The territories inhabited by these peoples
were then assimilated into other North Caucasian
regions. In 1956 Khrushchev granted the deported
peoples the right to return to their homelands, and
the names of their former regions were restored.
However, one Ingush region, Prigorodnyi Raion,
was not returned to the Ingush and remained part

of North Ossetia, initiating a longstanding conflict
between the two regions.

Aushev, as president of this young republic located in an area of great strategic importance, has
been confronted with numerous challenges. He assumed the leadership of Ingushetia after the official division of the Chechen-Ingush Autonomous
Republic in November 1992 when he was appointed
to lead the provisional government. A month later
he resigned from the position out of dissatisfaction
with the policies of the Russian government in the
region and its ineffectiveness at resolving the
Prigorodnyi Raion conflict. Aushev was elected the
first Ingush president in an unopposed election in
February 1993 with 99.8 percent of the vote, and
reelected the following year with 94.2 percent of
the vote. In his most recent reelection, on 1 March
1998, Aushev took 66.5 percent of the vote, with
his closest opponent pulling in 13 percent. Although
this victory margin was considerably lower than in
his previous two elections, suggesting a more legitimate proceeding, the fairness of the elections is
still questionable. Aushev's opponents complained
that he usurped all media access and prevented
them from gaining air time (*RT*, 28 February 1998).

Aushev is an important politician in this politically chaotic region. His recent victory was considered important to the stability of the North
Caucasus, since Aushev has played the crucial political role of bridging the gap between separatist
Chechnya and pro-Russian North Ossetia.

Executive Platform: Conflict Resolution

Aushev's main priority has been to solve the conflict with North Ossetia regarding the Prigorodnyi
Raion. Armed conflict between the Ingush and the
Ossetians who had migrated into the area has been
frequent since the Ingush returned to Prigorodnyi
in 1957. It climaxed in the 1990s when Ingushetia
demanded the reacquisition of its former territory.
In a week of extraordinary violence in October
1992, over 600 people were killed and thousands
of homes were destroyed, resulting in 34,000–
64,000 Ingush refugees.

Aushev has been critical of the federal government's handling of the Ingush-Ossetian conflict. He
claims that the government has failed to enforce its
law on restoring territory, "On the Rehabilitation of

Repressed Peoples," and has been unable to ensure that Ingush refugees are returned peacefully to the Prigorodnyi Raion (Jane Ormrod, "The North Caucasus: Confederation in Conflict," in Ian Bremmer and Ray Taras, eds., *New States, New Politics: Building the Post-Soviet Nations*, 108). Aushev is a strong supporter of keeping Ingushetia in the Russian Federation, yet he has claimed that if Russia fails to solve the problem of Prigorodnyi Raion, the secession of Ingushetia is inevitable, and that as president he is prepared to pass a referendum on secession (Panorama Research Group, Labyrint Electronic Database, Moscow). However, it seems unlikely that Aushev would ever make good on this threat. He would not want to jeopardize the republic's alliance with Russia.

In his most recent campaign, Aushev listed his top priorities as helping the refugees from North Ossetia and Chechnya, finishing the construction of the regional airport, and completing other infrastructure projects (*EWI RRR*, 5 March 1998). The refugee situation is probably the greatest problem confronting Ingushetia. The republic shelters hundreds of thousands of refugees from Chechnya and the Prigorodnyi Raion. As a result, well over 50 percent of the region's population is unemployed or medically unable to work.

Aushev believes it is necessary to create a market economy, develop small and medium-sized businesses, rebuild agriculture, and create self-sufficient cooperatives (NNS).

Aushev is in favor of asymmetric federalism, and feels that each region should make its own deal with the center, taking into consideration the region's national and geographic peculiarities. Regarding the possibility of decreasing the number of regions in Russia, Aushev feels that regions should unite voluntarily if they so wish and that the borders of ethnically defined regions should not be disturbed (*EWI RRR*, 11 March 1999).

In 1999 Aushev joined the All Russia regional party founded by Tatarstan President Mintimer Shaimiev.

Policies: Seeking Security

Aushev, who is very dissatisfied with the level of security provided by Moscow to Ingushetia, has campaigned to have responsibility for some police functions devolve to the regions (*Monitor*, 29 June 1998).

In 1998, he led an experiment to establish municipal level police units. The experiment involved the creation of police subunits that were responsible to the municipal government rather than to the Russian interior ministry in Moscow.

Ingushetia's charter grants the republic's president more power than most other regional executives, allowing Aushev's policymaking to take on a rather authoritarian character. Aushev has the right to dictate foreign policy and introduce states of emergency, rights which violate federal legislation. The republic's constitution also states that republican laws supersede federal legislation—a clear violation of the federal constitution (*EWI RRR*, 24 November 1998).

In both 1998 and 1999, Aushev tried to hold a referendum on whether the republic should have the right to appoint its own police chiefs, legalize bride-kidnapping, allow residents to carry daggers, and permit the republican president to pardon those involved in blood feuds, in which the relatives of a murder victim kill the murderer. In 1998 federal authorities barred the referendum from taking place, and in 1999 Aushev voluntarily canceled it after gaining concessions from Moscow (see Ties to Moscow).

In January 1997 President Aushev issued a decree to ban the sale of alcohol in Ingushetia for the holy month of Ramadan.

Relations Between Key Players: Strong Support for the President

In February 1999 Ingushetia held elections to the People's Assembly. As required by law, two Chechens were elected to the 21-person body. Since no Russians were elected to the legislature, Aushev removed the ethnic Ingush winner with the smallest number of votes and replaced him with a Russian. Following the elections, Aushev said that he would not allow the parliament to intervene in the political life of the republic. He threatened to use his power to disband the parliament if it stepped out of line (*EWI RRR*, 11 March 1999). Chairman of the Ingush parliament Ruslan Pliev is very supportive of Aushev. When the president announced his plan to run for reelection in 1998, Pliev commented that Aushev was the only candidate who could oppose the belligerent forces in the Caucasus (*EWI RRR*, 18 December 1997).

Over the past several years Aushev has tried to reform Ingushetia's power structure by introducing a Congress of the Peoples of Ingushetia, and in April 1999 he signed a law establishing the body, which became the highest representative political institution in the republic (*Segodnya*, 13 April 1999). It will be elected every five years and meets annually to discuss internal issues regarding the republican constitution. Aushev chairs the Congress which includes legislators, members of the government appointed by them and the president, and republican judges. Critics of the Congress claim that its creation ends the division of power in the region.

Aushev and Chechen President Aslan Maskhadov opened Ingushetia's new capital, Magas, on 31 October 1998 (*KD*, 3 November 1998). Like St. Petersburg, the new capital was built on barren ground. At the time of the official opening, the Turkish firm Entes had only completed the presidential palace, and buildings for the parliament and the government were under construction. Aushev said that he built the new capital to demonstrate that he had no claims to North Ossetian territory, particularly the right bank of Vladikavkaz. By his own account, he has spent 10 billion rubles on the project since 1995. The money came from the off-shore free trade zone that existed in Ingushetia until 1997, various business centers, registration of off-shore businesses in the republic, and a four-year, $80 million loan from Turkey. He claimed that he built himself a palace because "if the president does not build a palace for all the Ingush, what will become of them?"

Ties to Moscow: Critical of Moscow, but Backs Russian Unity

Aushev's relationship to Moscow is complex. Although he is highly critical of the way the federal government handles North Caucasian issues, his own clashes with Moscow have been limited. Aushev believes that Moscow does not have a coherent regional policy and that federal agreements lack sufficient implementation mechanisms (Panorama). Yet, Moscow and Aushev seem to share a mutually beneficial relationship—Moscow needs Aushev's diplomacy and Ingushetia needs Moscow's help in developing its republic.

Aushev is known in Moscow for his mediation skills. After President Yeltsin's decree to dismiss the

parliament in September 1993, Aushev and Kalmykian President Kirsan Ilyumzhinov attempted to mediate the conflict and find a peaceful solution. More importantly, Aushev was against using force to resolve the Chechen conflict and repeatedly in 1994–95 offered to mediate with the goal of ending the war. The Ingush have strong cultural and historical ties to the Chechens, and Aushev is close friends with Chechen president Aslan Maskhadov. This relationship provided Moscow with an informal mediator between the federation and the rebel region.

Aushev had hoped that Moscow would reciprocate his mediation efforts in Chechnya by playing a similar role in resolving the conflict between Ingushetia and North Ossetia. However, Aushev has been disappointed with Moscow's involvement in this process. President Yeltsin met with Aushev and North Ossetian President Aleksandr Dzasokhov on 24 February 1998 to discuss the return of Ingush refugees to Prigorodnyi Raion, yet the problem remains far from solved. Aushev has asserted that Russian federal authorities are not taking adequate measures to protect the Ingush in North Ossetia, and that the administration in North Ossetia has ignored the rulings of federal bodies (*EWI RRR*, 26 February 1998). In September 1997 the Congress of the Peoples of Ingushetia blamed the federal government for the lack of resolution to the Ingush-Ossetian dispute and voted no confidence in the president's representative in the area, Aleksandr Kovalev (*EWI RRR*, 2 October 1997).

Aushev's dissatisfaction with Moscow is not limited to the government's handling of the Prigorodnyi Raion conflict. The Ingush president has also been at odds with the central government regarding the appointment of officials. It is for this reason that Aushev refused to sign a power-sharing agreement with then Prime Minister Viktor Chernomyrdin on 6 March 1998. The treaty was supposed to resolve the dispute between Ingushetia and the federal authorities over Aushev's interest in appointing officials in Ingushetia's procurator's office and the republican office of the Ministry of Internal Affairs. Aushev wanted to hold a referendum on these issues, but withdrew the proposal under pressure from the Russian Supreme Court (*EWI RRR*, 12 March 1998).

In February 1999 Aushev won a victory over Moscow when he signed an agreement with then Presidential Chief of Staff Nikolai Bordyuzha giving Ingushetia a larger voice in the appointment of police and other legal authorities in the region. Aushev also received the power to pardon some crimes that are connected with local traditions. The center finally conceded these powers to the republican government after Aushev tried twice to hold a referendum on the issue.

On 3 July 1997 the federal government announced that it was stripping Ingushetia of its free economic zone status. This status had allowed the republic to remain exempt from federal taxes, providing some funding used to support the numerous refugees in the region. As a result of this loss, unemployment has increased, pushing joblessness among youth as high as 80 percent (*Izvestiya*, 25 February 1998).

On 9 January 1997, Aushev, a Muslim, received the order of Prince Daniil of Moscow from the Russian Orthodox Church in recognition of his peace efforts in settling the Chechen conflict of 1994–96 (*OMRI RRR*, 15 January 1997). Aushev was presented the award by Metropolitan Gedeon of Stavropol and Vladikavkaz.

Relations with Other Regions: Continuing Tension with North Ossetia

In January 1999 Aushev and North Ossetian President Aleksandr Dzasokhov signed an agreement on returning Ingush refugees to the Prigorodnyi Raion in North Ossetia. The prime ministers of the two republics signed an additional agreement in March 1999 stating that all refugees should be returned to their former homes by December 1999. According to Aushev the agreement guarantees the refugees their choice of housing (either returning to their apartment or receiving a plot of land in an ethnic Ingush region); security; credits to repair their homes; and local aid in obtaining water, gas, and heat. It is unclear how many refugees will return. The Ingush claim 20,000, but North Ossetia says this number is exaggerated (*EWI RRR*, 4 March 1999).

This agreement is a considerable accomplishment given the tense relations between the two leaders. Dzasokhov's victory over incumbent Akhsarbeck Galazov in January 1998 was initially welcomed in

Ingushetia, where there was hope that a new president would bring an agreeable settlement to the Ingush-Ossetian conflict. However, in June 1998, the kidnapping of six Ingush by Ossetians provoked hostility between the two presidents, with Aushev directly accusing Dzasokhov of failing to control and ameliorate the region's violent conditions.

Many leaders from different regions were on hand for the celebration of Ingushetia's fifth anniversary as a republic in 1997, including Chechen President Aslan Maskhadov, North Ossetian Prime Minister Yurii Biragov, Tatarstan President Mintimer Shaimiev, and Bashkortostan President Murtaza Rakhimov. Shaimiev and Rakhimov signed a cooperation treaty with Aushev and discussed the possibility of establishing a "chamber of nationalities" inside or parallel to the Federation Council to increase the influence of Russia's ethnic republics.

Ingushetia is a member of the Association of Cooperation of Republics, Krais, and Oblasts of the North Caucasus. The other members are the republics of Adygeya, Dagestan, Kabardino-Balkaria, Karachaevo-Cherkessia, North Ossetia, and Kalmykia; Krasnodar and Stavropol krais; and Rostov Oblast. Aushev feels that such interregional associations are useless and that no real work is being done within the groups (*EWI RRR*, 11 March 1999).

Aushev has good relations with Kursk Oblast Governor Aleksandr Rutskoi.

Attitudes Toward Business: Undeveloped Potential

Although Aushev would like to see business growth and development in Ingushetia, the plethora of other problems confronting the region have made it impossible for him to prioritize such policies. Ingushetia has the potential to extract oil and gas, but lacks the capital and technology to develop these natural resources.

In May 1998 the U.S. firm Pacific Petroleum formed the first joint venture in Ingushetia. The project will refine oil and gas for the region, most of which will be sold on Russian and Western markets. The venture will be called South-Pacific Petroleum, 55 percent of which will be owned by Pacific Petroleum.

Ruslan Sultanovich Aushev

29 October 1954—Born in Volodar village, Kokchetav Oblast, Kazakhstan

1971—Began serving in the Soviet Army

1975—Graduated from the Ordzhonikidze Military Training School

1975–1985—Commander of an infantry platoon

1977—Joined the CPSU

1980—Volunteered to serve in Afghanistan; after two years he became head of an infantry battalion

7 May 1982—Awarded the Gold Star Hero of the Soviet Union for his service in Afghanistan

1982–1985—Graduated from the Frunze Military Academy and returned to service in Afghanistan, where he was severely wounded in 1986

1987–1989—Lieutenant-colonel and commander of an infantry regiment in the Far East

March 1989—Elected to the USSR Congress of People's Deputies from Primorskii Krai and served on the Supreme Soviet Committee on Military Service Issues

August 1991—Promoted to general-major and named chairman of the USSR Cabinet of Ministers Committee for Military-Internationalist Affairs

March 1992—Became chairman of the Committee for Military-Internationalist Affairs for the council of CIS heads of government

10 November 1992—Named acting head of the provisional administration of the Republic of Ingushetia

28 February 1993—Elected president of the Republic of Ingushetia, winning 99.8% of the vote

12 December 1993—Elected to the Federation Council, where he served on the Committee for Security and Defense Issues

27 February 1994—Elected as president of the Republic of Ingushetia in new presidential elections, winning 94.2% of the vote

January 1995—Appointed to the Federation Council, serving on the Committee for Security and Defense Issues

March 1997—Became a member of the federal commission on problems in Chechnya

1 March 1998—Reelected president of the Republic of Ingushetia, pulling in 66.5% of the vote

IRKUTSK OBLAST

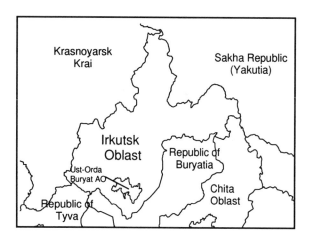

Territory: 767,900 km²
Population (as of 1 January 1998):
2,774,000
Distance from Moscow: 5,042 km

Major Cities:
Irkutsk, *capital* (pop. 590,500)
Angarsk (266,800)
Bratsk (255,600)
Ust-Ilimsk (108,300)
Usole-Sibirskoe (104,300)

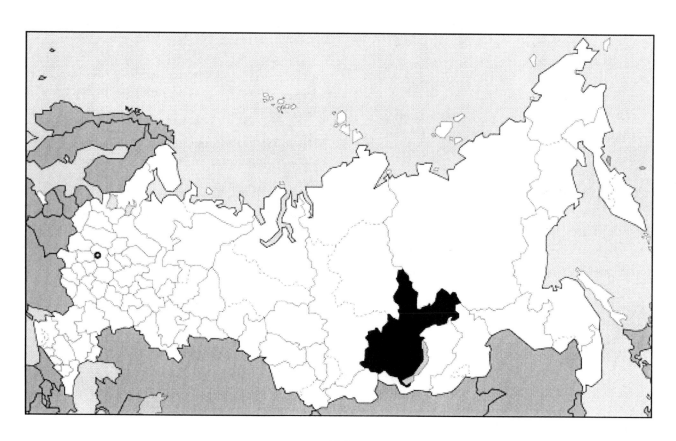

Basic Facts

Population (as of 1 Jan. 1998): 2,774,000 (1.55% of Russian total)

Ethnic breakdown (1989 census): Russians 90.1%, Ukrainians 3.5%, Tatars 1.3%, Buryats 1.1%

Urban population (as of 1 Jan. 1998): 79.6% (Russia overall: 73.1%)

Student population (as of 1 Sept. 1997): 211 per 10,000 (Russia overall: 208/10,000)

Pensioner population (1997): 23.25% (Russia overall: 25.96%)

Percent of population with higher education (1989 census): 10.1% (Russia overall: 11.3%)

Percent of population working in (1997): Industry: 26.7% (Russian average: 23.0%); Agriculture: 8.1% (13.7%); Trade: 14.1% (13.5%); Culture: 13.2% (13.3%)

Average monthly personal income in July 1998: 968.3 new rubles (Russian average: 891.7 new rubles)

Average monthly personal expenses in July 1998: 703.5 new rubles (Russian average: 684.9 new rubles)

Average monthly subsistence requirement in 1998: 453 new rubles (Russian average: 438 new rubles)

Consumer price index (as of July 1998): 139 (Russia overall = 100)

Budgetary revenues (1997): 6,839.4 billion rubles (Russia overall: 433,378.2 billion rubles)

Budgetary expenditures (1997): 7,907.5 billion rubles (Russia overall: 468,111.6 billion rubles)

Industrial production as percentage of all Russian production (Jan.–Aug. 1998): 1.61%

Proportion of loss-making enterprises (as of July 1998): 68.9% (Russia overall: 50.4%)

Number of enterprises with wage arrears (as of 1 Sept. 1998): 1,100 (0.81% of Russian total)

Agricultural production as percentage of all Russian production (1997): 0.2%

Number of private farms (as of 1 Jan. 1998): 3,225 (1.18% of Russian total)

Capital investment (1997): 5,617.0 billion rubles (Russia overall: 408,797 billion rubles)

Sources of investment (1997): federal budget: 8.6% (Russian average: 10.2%); regional budget: 12.5% (10.5%); extra-budgetary funds: 78.9% (79.3%)

Foreign investment (1997): 61,154,000 USD (Russia overall: 12,294,734,000 USD)

Number of joint ventures (1997): 87 (0.59% of Russian total)

Fixed capital investment in joint ventures and foreign companies (1997): 131,774 million rubles (Russia overall: 16,265.4 billion rubles)

Number of small businesses (as of 1 July 1998): 12,000 (1.38% of Russian total)

Number of enterprises privatized in 1997: 75 (2.73% of Russian total), including those which used to be municipal property: 93.3% (Russian average: 66.4%); regional property: 4.0% (20.0%); federal property: 2.7% (13.6%)

Number of telephones per 100 families (1997): in cities: 36.7 (Russian average: 49.2); in villages: 11.1 (19.8)

Brief Overview

Irkutsk Oblast is located in the center of Asia, and the southern part of Eastern Siberia, stretching from the northwestern shores of Lake Baikal and the western Sayan Mountains, northward into the hilly Central Siberian Plateau, and eastward to the Patom Mountains. The region borders Krasnoyarsk Krai; the republics of Tyva, Buryatia, and Sakha (Yakutia); and Chita Oblast. The land is largely covered by dense taiga, with some mixed forest and steppe in the south.

The oblast is rich in raw materials such as coal, iron ore, gold, rare metals, and precious stones, and has some oil and gas as well as forest and water resources that supply three hydroelectric plants providing cheap electricity. Forestry, paper and cellulose production, and coal, ore, and gold mining dominate the oblast economy. Irkutsk also accounts for a high share of Russia's aluminum production. There is a nuclear fuel enrichment facility in the city of Angarsk. Most of the population and industry of the region are concentrated along the Trans-Siberian Railroad and in the Angara valley. There is little agriculture, due to the severe climate. The oblast is among the 20 largest air polluting regions in the country (190.4 kg per capita).

The region has commercial ties with over 90 foreign countries, exporting aluminum, oil and petroleum products, cellulose, and timber. It imports alumina, machines and equipment, and consumer goods.

According to a 1998 survey by *Ekspert* magazine, the oblast ranked 16th among Russia's 89 regions in terms of investment potential and 62nd in terms of investment risk. A 1998 survey by Bank Austria ranked the oblast 9th in terms of investment climate.

Electoral History

2000 Presidential Election
Putin: 50.11%
Zyuganov: 33.03%
Yavlinskii: 5.05%
Zhirinovsky: 3.91%
Tuleev: 2.35%
Turnout: 65.15% (Russia overall: 68.64%)

1999 Parliamentary Elections
Unity: 33.13%
Communist Party of the Russian Federation: 23.60%
Zhirinovsky Bloc: 7.57%
Union of Right Forces: 7.07%
Yabloko: 5.82%
Fatherland–All Russia: 5.29%
In single-mandate districts: 1 Fatherland–All
    Russia, 1 Our Home Is Russia, 2 independent
Turnout: 54.56% (Russia overall: 61.85%)

1997 Gubernatorial Election
Govorin: 50.31%
Levchenko: 18.92%
Mashinskii: 13.97%
Shchadov: 7.27%
Shuba: 1.02%
Seredyuk: 0.97%
Shaburov: 0.74%
Ten: 0.67%
Turnout: 45.8%

1996 Presidential Election
Yeltsin: 32.2%/52.64% (first round/second round)
Zyuganov: 27.57%/39.77%
Lebed: 16.29%
Yavlinskii: 8.86%
Zhirinovsky: 8.48%
Turnout: 62.78%/60.96% (Russia overall: 69.67%/
    68.79%)

1995 Parliamentary Elections
Communist Party of the Russian Federation: 15.68%
Liberal Democratic Party of Russia: 15.61%
Our Home Is Russia: 8.26%
Women of Russia: 6.97%
Yabloko: 6.57%
Party of Workers' Self-Government: 5.98%
Communists–Workers' Russia: 5.54%
Agrarian Party of Russia: 3.37%
In single-mandate districts: 1 Our Home Is Russia,
    1 Agrarian Party of Russia, 3 independent
Turnout: 58.43% (Russia overall: 64.37%)

1993 Constitutional Referendum
"Yes"—72.6%   "No"—25.3%

1993 Parliamentary Elections

Liberal Democratic Party of Russia: 21.48%
Russia's Choice: 16.85%
Women of Russia: 13.24%
Communist Party of the Russian Federation: 9.50%
Party of Russian Unity and Concord: 8.88%
Yabloko: 6.71%
Democratic Party of Russia: 6.13%
Agrarian Party of Russia: 4.95%
In single-mandate districts: 4 independent
Turnout: 50.37% (Russia overall: 54.34%)

1991 Presidential Election

Yeltsin: 52.75%
Ryzhkov: 14.53%
Zhirinovsky: 12.47%
Tuleev: 10.45%
Bakatin: 3.66%
Makashov: 2.16%
Turnout: 71.48% (Russia overall: 76.66%)

Regional Political Institutions

Executive:
　　Governor, 4-year term
　　Boris Aleksandrovich Govorin, elected July 1997
　　　Irkutsk Oblast Administration;
　　　Ul. Lenina, 1a; Irkutsk, 664027
　　　Tel 7(395–2) 27–64–15, 27–67–60;
　　　Fax 7(395–2) 24–33–40
　　　Federation Council in Moscow:
　　　7(095) 292–68–21

Legislative:
　　Unicameral
　　Legislative Assembly (*Zakonodatelnoe Sobranie*)—45 members, 4-year term, elected June 1996
　　Chairman—Ivan Zigmundovich Zelent, elected March 1994, July 1996

Regional Politics

Native Irkutsk Man

Boris Govorin describes himself as a "native Irkutsk man" who values decency above all else. He was elected on 29 July 1997 to fill the vacancy left by Yurii Nozhikov, who resigned on 21 April 1997 (Nozhikov was only the second elected Russian governor to resign, following Moscow Mayor Gavriil Popov, who quit in June 1992). Govorin, who was mayor of Irkutsk at the time of his election, defeated seven other candidates, winning just over 50 percent of the vote with a 43 percent voter turnout. Nozhikov had a very high approval rating (70 percent) at the time he quit, but had clashed with the federal government after calling for and then abandoning an attempt to get Irkutsk to withhold its taxes. Nozhikov claimed that his main motive for resigning was to move up the election date, which had originally been set for March 1998 (*EWI RRR*, 30 April 1997). He asserted that the Communist Party was prepared to spend huge amounts of money to win the election, and that it would be successful if given until March 1998 to campaign but would not capture the post if elections were held immediately (*EWI RRR*, 30 April 1997). Nozhikov supported Govorin's campaign.

Irkutsk has enormous potential, especially if it is able to develop its energy export market to South Korea and China, whose growing economies could use more resources. However, the region is having trouble escaping Moscow's control. Moreover, it is saddled with inefficient Soviet-era plants such as the Angarsk oil refinery, which are a drain on local resources. Another curse is local government officials who have been using state funds in inappropriate ways.

Executive Platform: Reform-Minded Patriot

Even though the Kremlin claimed Govorin's victory a success for the president, Govorin distanced himself from Our Home Is Russia (NDR) and relied on his own personal resources during the campaign. No federal authorities traveled to the oblast to campaign on his behalf even though Communist Party leader Gennadii Zyuganov and former Security Council Secretary Aleksandr Lebed visited Irkutsk to campaign for their respective candidates. Govorin secured victory by presenting himself as a reform-minded patriot, with statements such as "I am a native Irkutsk man, and that means something" (*VSP*, n. 23, 1997), and "The most important quality that I value in people is decency. The other important quality is love for your country. It is really very dangerous for a country if the people in power are indifferent" (*VSP*, n. 23, 1997). Thus,

Govorin appealed to the oblast as a reformer interested in what was best for Irkutsk Oblast, not as a puppet for Moscow's interests in the region.

In his campaign, Govorin strove to project an image that he would not become a local Chubais (*EWI RRR*, 21 August 1997). He called attention to his accomplishments as mayor of Irkutsk, such as introducing new bus routes, constructing a veterans' hospital, and commissioning a new building for the central market (*EWI RRR*, 21 August 1997).

In spite of his general reform position, statements Govorin made during his campaign challenged the depth of his pro-market orientation. While speaking to a group of workers at Irkutsk Cable, a firm that lost half of its workforce after being bought by Moscow investors, Govorin said that it might be necessary to "deprivatize" the plant in order to "remove an owner who throws people on the street" (*VSP*, n. 22, 1997). He further suggested that the oblast administration could help keep the plant in operation by increasing purchases from it.

In 1999 Govorin joined the All Russia regional party set up by Tatarstan President Mintimer Shaimiev and St. Petersburg Governor Vladimir Yakovlev.

Policies: Restructure Public and Private Sectors

During a 15 January 1998 meeting with regional enterprise directors, bankers, and other members of the Chamber of Commerce and Industry, Govorin claimed that the policies of the previous administration, supported by the region's industrial managers, were responsible for the oblast's economic decline. As a result, the oblast administration announced its intention to more actively use its shareholder's rights to influence company policies. In the fall of 1997 Govorin had served as the personal coordinator and decisionmaker for all privatization packages and issues involving oblast administration property (*Segodnya*, 16 September 1997). The administration also hoped to establish a coordinating council under Govorin with the goal of synchronizing the activities of government agencies and firms (*EWI RRR*, 22 January 1998). These examples show that Govorin takes a personal involvement in overseeing the institution of market reforms.

On 12 January 1998, when the federal government was pushing this issue, Govorin signed a decree reforming the oblast's public housing complex. Approximately 2.5 million new rubles ($417,000 at the time) of federal and regional money were to be spent from 1998 to 2003 to implement the reform program. The oblast planned to launch five pilot projects in the cities of Irkutsk, Bratsk, Ust-Ilimsk, and Shelekhov. The goal of the program is to increase the quality and efficiency of the oblast's public housing and municipal services. The oblast administration predicted that 80 percent of the residents would be able to afford their utility bills for 1998, and the rest would receive housing subsidies (*EWI RRR*, 22 January 1998). The August 1998 crisis put these plans on hold.

In October 1998 the Irkutsk Oblast administration approved a program to support and develop small businesses in the region. The program provides information and legal advice, helps locate potential employees, and advises on the restructuring and downsizing of large businesses.

Relationships Between Key Players: Conflict over Crime and Mismanagement

On 11 May 1998 Govorin met with regional law-enforcement officials to discuss the conflict between the procurator's office and the oblast police. A few weeks prior to the meeting, the procurator's deputy was severely critical of the police's economic crime unit, claiming that it spent too much time chasing small businesses, and paid inadequate attention to the multiple crimes occurring in the large business sector (*EWI RRR*, 21 May 1998). Only about one-eighth of the economic criminal cases launched in 1997 made it to court. Govorin warned law-enforcement officials against hiding the real state of affairs behind statistics (*EWI RRR*, 21 May 1998).

In the March 1998 mayoral contests in Irkutsk Oblast, only 7 of about 30 incumbents won reelection. The mayors' municipal mismanagement was the cause of their demise. Govorin had criticized the executives several times for using oblast money for purposes other than those for which it had been intended, and warned that people would not tolerate such behavior (*EWI RRR*, 9 April 1998). Thus Govorin was probably content to see a fresh force of local executives who might work more efficiently than their predecessors.

Ties to Moscow: Stands Up
for Regional Interests

Although Govorin is reform minded and is supported by Moscow, the interests he promotes for Irkutsk sometimes lead to conflict with the center. Most of the friction concerns the economic and business development of the oblast. Irkutsk has been pushing to sell its vast natural and mineral resources on the Asian market. In 1996, 43 percent of the region's exports, including aluminum, timber products, and oil, went to China, Japan, and Singapore. However, Moscow hopes to capitalize on Irkutsk's wealth by serving as middleman between the region and its Asian interests. The issue concerning Irkutskenergo and Unified Energy System is one such example.

Irkutskenergo is one of the few Russian power companies not under the control of the monopoly Unified Energy System of Russia. Irkutskenergo was privatized before the 1992 presidential decree that created Unified Energy System. Since then, Unified Energy System has been trying to bring Irkutskenergo under its wing. The various laws, court rulings, and decrees that have enabled Irkutskenergo to remain independent of Unified Energy System have allowed the 40 percent state stake to remain in the hands of the oblast government. Moscow believes that it should control these shares. Govorin is clearly on the side of Irkutskenergo and would like to minimize Moscow's influence over the firm. The ownership struggle is compounded by the fact that Irkutskenergo won the right to export electricity to Mongolia and is now planning to enter the lucrative Chinese market as well. In October 1997 Govorin met with First Deputy Prime Minister Boris Nemtsov to discuss the situation. A working group was established to find a solution to the problem, and Irkutskenergo's Chinese project (see Foreign Relations) probably will not proceed until the issue is resolved.

Another example of conflicting interests between Govorin and the center is the creation of a special economic zone around the Baikal Amur Railroad (BAM) including parts of Irkutsk, Chita, Buryatia, and Sakha. The leaders of these regions agree that something needs to be done to revitalize the depressed BAM region, yet feel that the draft law proposed by the State Duma is seriously flawed. In particular, Govorin stressed that the legislation does not explain how the federal, regional, and local governments will work together to make the BAM a profitable enterprise. Govorin is also concerned about the impact a special economic zone will have on the region's tax base since Irkutsk acquires significant income from the exploitation of precious resources within the BAM region, including the Kovytka gas field and Sukhoi Log gold deposit (*EWI RRR*, 7 April 1999).

Other negotiations involving Irkutsk resources and foreign markets have been handled directly by the Russian prime minister. In June 1997 Prime Minister Viktor Chernomyrdin signed several agreements opening up oil and gas fields in Irkutsk and other Far Eastern regions to China. In July 1998, then Prime Minister Sergei Kirienko met with Japanese businessmen in Tokyo to offer them the opportunity to participate in the Kovytka gas field, as well as other projects in Russia (*RFE/RL*, 14 July 1998).

Govorin disagreed with President Yeltsin's March 1998 decision to dissolve the cabinet and dismiss Prime Minister Viktor Chernomyrdin, claiming that these actions resembled the events of 1991 and 1993. Govorin stated that civilized countries do not implement such policies, and that this is just one example of how sick Russian society is (*EWI RRR*, 2 April 1998). His disapproval seemed to stem from the executive's lack of predictability, and the lack of confidence that such events instill in the populace.

On 27 May 1996, before Govorin came to power, Irkutsk signed a power-sharing agreement with Moscow and the Ust-Orda Buryat Autonomous Okrug, which is located in Irkutsk (*OMRI DD*, 28 May 1996).

Relations with Other Regions: Close to
Siberian Neighbors, Stroev

Govorin appears to have amicable relations with neighboring governors. Irkutsk has strong ties with the Republic of Buryatia, which lies along its southeastern border. In January 1998 Irkutsk signed a cooperation agreement with Buryatia regarding provisions to protect Lake Baikal. The two regions also intend to establish a joint energy development program. Irkutsk signed a similar agreement with Sakha (Yakutia) in December 1997.

On 9–12 March 1998 Govorin led a high-level regional delegation to Orel Oblast to learn about the region's success in agricultural reform. Orel Oblast Governor and Federation Council Speaker Yegor Stroev hosted the delegation.

Govorin was scheduled to join Krasnoyarsk Governor Aleksandr Lebed on a demonstration flight over the North Pole in July 1998 but cancelled, perhaps because he had supported Lebed's opponent, former Governor Valerii Zubov, in Krasnoyarsk's most recent election (*EWI RRR*, 9 July 1998).

Govorin belongs to the group of eleven governors who have agreed to contribute funds to the Alliance Group, a foundation that will provide crisis support to enterprises in Russia and in countries of the CIS. The other founder regions are Saratov, Leningrad, Novgorod, Murmansk, Magadan, Chita, Novosibirsk, and Voronezh oblasts, and the republics of Udmurtia and Buryatia. These regional executives feel that close cooperation between the regional administrations and enterprises will provide the most effective aid to needy enterprises.

Irkutsk belongs to the Siberian Accord Association, which includes the republics of Buryatia, Gorno-Altai, and Khakassia; Altai and Krasnoyarsk krais; Novosibirsk, Tomsk, Tyumen, and Kemerovo oblasts; and Agin-Buryat, Taimyr, Ust-Orda Buryat, Khanty-Mansi, Evenk, and Yamal-Nenets autonomous okrugs.

Foreign Relations: Eastward Economic Expansion

Both Irkutskenergo and Vostsibugol have been forced to look for external markets since many of the firms that were their traditional customers in the oblast have gone out of business. The project stipulates the construction of a 2,600-km-high voltage transmission line between Bratsk and Beijing at a cost of $1.5 billion within four years. In the next 25–30 years the line will transmit 18 billion kilowatt-hours of electricity to China per year. Chinese and Russian government officials agreed to create a special international company to undertake the construction project. The project will include several investment firms and banks providing credit and loans guaranteed by the Canadian, U.S.,

and Swedish governments (*EWI RRR*, 11 June 1998).

The first joint Russian-U.S. faculty for training managers opened in Irkutsk in 1991 under the auspices of Irkutsk University and the University of Maryland. Govorin completed course work in the program.

In January 1998 Govorin participated in the third session of the joint Russian-Austrian commission on trade and economic cooperation.

Attitudes Toward Business: Strong Promoter of Business Development

Irkutsk is home to several investment projects and joint ventures involving international partners. In addition to the Irkutskenergo electricity export project discussed above, several other major investment projects involving natural resources are underway: the Angarsk refinery, the Kovytka gas field, and the Sukhoi Log mineral deposit. Govorin has not always supported the objectives of investors, worrying about social consequences for the region's population.

Most prominently, the governor has opposed Sidanko's plans to make the Angarsk refinery profitable. Vladimir Potanin's Oneksimbank gained control of the refinery in 1997 from the state and tried to increase its efficiency by laying off thousands of employees. Govorin opposed this plan because the regional government would eventually have to care for the newly unemployed. By the end of 1998, Potanin wanted the Russian government to renationalize the refinery because he claimed it was worthless. The giant enterprise was originally built to supply low-octane gasoline, diesel, and other fuels to troops located between the Urals and the Far East. There is currently little demand for these products. Oneksimbank's Sidanko oil company was supposed to supply the refinery with 170,000 tons of oil for processing on 1 November 1998, but refused to do so because the regional government had blocked the reorganization plans and the refinery had not paid off its debts for oil that had been delivered earlier. Govorin threatened that if the plant did not succeed in paying its debts to the regional budget, the governmnet would seize some of the company's assets (*EWI RRR*, 22 January 1998).

The Sidanko oil company is starting to develop the Kovytka gas field, which is expected to contain

Boris Aleksandrovich Govorin

1947—Born in the city of Irkutsk; later, graduated from the Irkutsk Polytechnical Institute night school as an energy specialist

1970–1972—Served in the army, stationed at Komsomolsk-na-Amure in Khabarovsk Krai

1972–1980—Worked in the enterprise Southern Electrical Systems as an engineer and group director

1980–1983—Deputy director of the enterprise

1983—Began working in executive branch agencies in Irkutsk as deputy chairman of the Sverdlovsk district executive committee and then as chairman of the district executive committee

July 1987– First deputy chairman of the city executive committee

25 May 1990—Elected chairman of the city executive committee

13 January 1992–Appointed mayor of Irkutsk by Yeltsin

1993–1995—Vice President of the Association of Siberian and Far Eastern Mayors

1995—Representative of the Russian Federation at the Council of Europe's Congress of Local and Regional Powers

27 March 1994—Elected mayor of Irkutsk, winning 78.8% of the vote, and also elected to the first session of the Irkutsk Oblast Legislative Assembly

1996—President of the Association of Siberian and Far Eastern Mayors

16 June 1996—Elected to the second session of the Irkutsk Oblast Legislative Assembly

May 1997—Joined the President's Council on Local Self-Government in the Russian Federation

27 July 1997—Elected governor of Irkutsk Oblast

15 August 1997—Became part of the government's Council of Local Government Leaders to address Socioeconomic Reforms

January 1998—Joined the government commission for reforming communal apartments in the Russian Federation

March 1998—Became a member of the Board of Directors of Irkutskenergo

---

870 billion cubic meters of gas and 83 million tons of gas condensate. Kovytka is expected to yield 30 billion cubic meters of gas per year (*MT*, 28 October 1997). The consortium for developing the field is made up of Sidanko (60.5 percent), the Irkutsk Oblast administration (19 percent), and Irkutskenergo (14 percent). British Petroleum is participating as a partner of Oneksimbank, which owns Sidanko. Sidanko in turn owns RUSIA Petroleum, which holds the license to the field. The main draw to the project is a proposed 3,360 km pipeline that will carry gas from Irkutsk to Beijing and possibly to South Korea and Japan as well. China could use the energy supplies to power its surging economy. The estimated cost of the pipeline is $8–10 billion, and gas production is expected to begin in 2000 or shortly thereafter. The directors of the consortium side with the Irkutsk administration in demanding that the consortium be allowed to control production at Kovytka, but Moscow has an interest in strengthening its role in the project (*MT*, 28 October 1997).

Sukhoi Log, the most valuable mine in Russia, has been the subject of a long, complicated development struggle involving the oblast administration, courts, and multiple foreign companies. The deposit contains an estimated 1,100 metric tons of gold and other precious metals, yet requires a $2 billion investment to extract them. Many firms have been involved in the competition for extraction rights, with a final decision on the tender still pending. Several firms have demonstrated strong interest in the deposit's development, including two Canadian companies, Plaser Dome and Barrick Gold; the U.S.'s Newmont Gold Company; Britain's RTZ; and a consortium of South Africa's JCI and the U.S. firms Golden Fields, High River Gold, and TECH. Russian companies and banks interested in the project are Rossiiskii Kredit, Menatep, Oneksimbank, Yevrozoloto, Almazy Rossii-Sakha, and Lanta-Bank. Oneksimbank already has control of the Kovytka gas deposit, so if it gains control of Sukhoi Log it will have considerable leverage over the oblast administration (*KD*, 3 April 1998). Barrick Gold has been lobbying intensely to win the new tender, and has developed friendly ties with the local administration (*MT*, 30 October 1998).

Some other investment projects and possibilities in Irkutsk Oblast are:

- The package delivery service DHL plans to invest $5 million to build up infrastructure and increase its local partnerships with airlines in Russia, including opening a representative office in Irkutsk.
- The firm Your Financial Guardian is seeking financing for building a third aluminum plant in the oblast. The plant will cost about $1.5 billion and will have the capacity to produce 200,000 to 300,000 tons of aluminum per year.

In June 1997 the East Siberian Center for Investment Policy opened in Irkutsk. The center works under the auspices of the Federal Securities Commission and supplies information about the Russian stock market to local businesses and individuals.

Internet Sites in the Region

http://www.admirk.ru/
This is the website of the Irkutsk Oblast Administration. It features basic information about the oblast and relatively detailed descriptions of the region's investment projects and interests.

http://www.express.irk.ru/index.htm
This website features an updated news server and detailed information about the oblast's history and various offerings.

http://www.vsp.ru/
The website of the newspaper *Vostochno-Sibirskaya Pravda*, which is updated daily, has extensive information about the region's politics and economy. The newspaper published the full text of Moscow Mayor Yurii Luzhkov's address to the founding congress of his Fatherland party.

IVANOVO OBLAST

Territory: 21,800 km²
Population (as of 1 January 1998):
1,246,000
Distance from Moscow: 318 km

Major Cities:
Ivanovo, *capital* (pop. 463,800)
Kineshma (99,900)
Shuya (67,600)
Vichuga (46,400)
Furmanov (42,200)

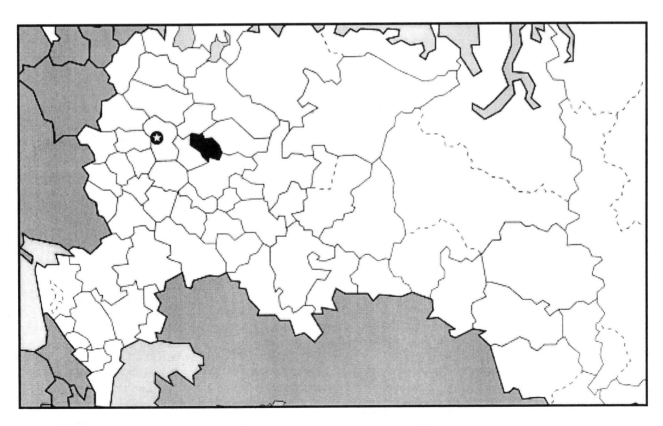

Basic Facts

Population (as of 1 Jan. 1998): 1,246,000 (0.85% of Russian total)

Ethnic breakdown (1989 census): Russians 95.8%, Ukrainians 1.2%

Urban population (as of 1 Jan. 1998): 82.4% (Russia overall: 73.1%)

Student population (as of 1 Sept. 1997): 224 per 10,000 (Russia overall: 208/10,000)

Pensioner population (1997): 29.78% (Russia overall: 25.96%)

Percent of population with higher education (1989 census): 8.9% (Russia overall: 11.3%)

Percent of population working in (1997): Industry: 32.7% (Russian average: 23.0%); Agriculture: 8.9% (13.7%); Trade: 15.2% (13.5%); Culture: 12.0% (13.3%)

Average monthly personal income in July 1998: 475.2 new rubles (Russian average: 891.7 new rubles)

Average monthly personal expenses in July 1998: 377.3 new rubles (Russian average: 684.9 new rubles)

Average monthly subsistence requirement in 1998: 316 new rubles (Russian average: 438 new rubles)

Consumer price index (as of July 1998): 123 (Russia overall = 100)

Budgetary revenues (1997): 2,443.5 billion rubles (Russia overall: 433,378.2 billion rubles)

Budgetary expenditures (1997): 2,510.3 billion rubles (Russia overall: 468,111.6 billion rubles)

Industrial production as percentage of all Russian production (Jan.–Aug. 1998): 0.37%

Proportion of loss-making enterprises (as of July 1998): 60.0% (Russia overall: 50.4%)

Number of enterprises which have wage arrears (as of 1 Sept. 1998): 614 (0.45% of Russian total)

Agricultural production as percentage of all Russian production (1997): 0.62%

Number of private farms (as of 1 Jan. 1998): 907 (0.33% of Russian total)

Capital investment (1997): 878.6 billion rubles (Russia overall: 408,797 billion rubles)

Sources of investment (1997): federal budget: 11.6% (Russian average: 10.2%); regional budget: 6.7% (10.5%); extra-budgetary funds: 81.7% (79.3%)

Foreign investment (1997): 5,486,000 USD (Russia overall: 12,294,734,000 USD)

Number of joint ventures (1997): 14 (0.10% of Russian total)

Fixed capital investment in joint ventures and foreign companies (1997): 30,052 million rubles (Russia overall: 16,265.4 billion rubles)

Number of small businesses (as of 1 July 1998): 5,200 (0.60% of Russian total)

Number of enterprises privatized in 1997: 22 (0.80% of Russian total), including those which used to be municipal property: 13.6% (Russian average: 66.4%); regional property: 36.4% (20.0%); federal property: 50.0% (13.6%)

Number of telephones per 100 families (1997): in cities: 35.4 (Russian average: 49.2); in villages: 18.0 (19.8)

Brief Overview

Founded in 1929, Ivanovo Oblast is located in the center of European Russia, about 300 km east of Moscow, and borders Vladimir, Yaroslavl, Kostroma, and Nizhnii Novgorod oblasts.

Historically, the oblast was an industrial center. It lacked rich mineral resources and soil suitable for fruitful agriculture. In earlier centuries, peasants unable to feed themselves by cultivating the land became involved in crafts—icon painting, weaving, and carving. Later, when the region had established economic ties with Central Asia and started to receive cotton from there, it became the center of the country's textile and light industries. Today, Ivanovo's 70 textile factories produce over half of the country's cotton fabrics.

Machine building is another significant regional industry. Ivanovo enterprises manufacture equipment for the textile industry and others as well. The regional chemical industry produces dyes and acids for the local textile manufacturers. The oblast also has a well-developed timber industry, since about a half of its territory is covered by forests. Lumber plants and textile factories are the region's major exporters.

According to a 1998 survey by *Ekspert* magazine, the oblast ranked 58th among Russia's 89 regions in terms of investment potential and 40th in terms of investment risk. Since 1997, regional investment potential had grown by 6 points, the 10th largest gain in the country. A 1998 survey by Bank Austria ranked the oblast 65th in terms of investment climate.

Electoral History

2000 Presidential Election
Putin: 53.13%
Zyuganov: 30.26%
Yavlinskii: 4.67%
Zhirinovsky: 3.61%
Tuleev: 2.24%
Turnout: 68.76% (Russia overall: 68.64%)

1999 Parliamentary Elections
Unity: 26.53%
Communist Party of the Russian Federation: 23.55%
Zhirinovsky Bloc: 9.49%
Fatherland–All Russia: 9.46%
Union of Right Forces: 7.36%
Yabloko: 4.39%
In single-mandate districts: 1 Unity, 1 Communist Party of the Russian Federation
Turnout: 62.18% (Russia overall: 61.85%)

1996 Gubernatorial Election
Tikhomirov (incumbent): 50.12%
Sirotkin (LDPR): 23.86%
Lobaev: 9.41%
Pimenov (NPSR): 7.71%
Turnout: 47.36%

1996 Presidential Election
Yeltsin: 29.60%/53.20% (first round/second round)
Lebed: 29.59%
Zyuganov: 23.22%/39.06%
Zhirinovsky: 7.00%
Yavlinskii: 6.08%
Turnout: 71.99%/68.61% (Russia overall: 69.67%/ 68.79%)

1995 Parliamentary Elections
Communist Party of the Russian Federation: 17.48%
Liberal Democratic Party of Russia: 17.48%
Trade Unions and Industrialists of Russia—Union of Labor: 9.60%
Our Home Is Russia: 6.88%
Yabloko: 5.49%
Women of Russia: 4.21%
Russia's Democratic Choice: 3.99%
Communists–Workers' Russia: 3.42%
Party of Workers' Self-Government: 3.14%
Congress of Russian Communities: 3.04%
In single-mandate districts: 1 Communist Party of the Russian Federation, 1 independent
Turnout: 67.00% (Russia overall: 64.37%)

1993 Constitutional Referendum
"Yes"—62.4% "No"—35.1%

1993 Parliamentary Elections
Liberal Democratic Party of Russia: 28.24%
Russia's Choice: 16.60%
Women of Russia: 8.85%
Communist Party of the Russian Federation: 8.67%
Party of Russian Unity and Concord: 7.16%
Agrarian Party of Russia: 6.82%
Yabloko: 6.82%
Democratic Party of Russia: 5.07%

In single-mandate districts: 1 Russia's Choice,
   1 independent
Turnout: 57.78% (Russia overall: 54.34%)

1991 Presidential Elections
Yeltsin: 53.67%
Ryzhkov: 19.83%
Zhirinovsky: 7.18%
Tuleev: 7.12%
Makashov: 4.23%
Bakatin: 2.97%
Turnout: 78.03% (Russia overall: 76.66%)

Regional Political Institutions

Executive:
   Governor, 4-year term
   Vladislav Nikolaevich Tikhomirov, elected December 1996
      Ul. Baturina, 5; Ivanovo, 153002
      Tel 7(093–2) 41–77–05, 41–77–08;
      Fax 7(093–2) 37–24–85
      Federation Council in Moscow:
      7(095) 292–19–73, 926–61–48

Legislative:
   Unicameral
   Legislative Assembly (*Zakonodatelnoe
   Sobranie*)—35 members, 4-year term, elected
   December 1996
   Chairman—Valerii Grigorevich Nikologorskii,
   elected March 1994, December 1996

Regional Politics

Agrarian Struggling to Support Depressed Textile Region

"We are not yet giving up" has become Vladislav Tikhomirov's mantra in reponse to the devastated state of Ivanovo's textile industry (*RK*, 6 March 1996). The industry's collapse threw the region into an economic depression that continued throughout the 1990s. In 1996 the unemployment rate in Ivanovo was double the national average, placing Ivanovo, along with its neighbors, Vladimir and Yaroslavl, among the regions with the highest unemployment rates. The oblast's unemployment problem is a direct result of the textile industry's

inability to adapt to market conditions, in which it has lost its main supply of Uzbek cotton and faces tough foreign competition in selling its products.

Until Yeltsin appointed Tikhomirov to his position in February 1996, the governor was a member of the Communist-aligned Agrarian Party of Russia. Yeltsin appointed him to make the best of a bad situation since no ideological ally of the president would be able to win the upcoming popular vote on 1 December 1996. Tikhomirov served the president's purpose in the sense that he was able to win a popular mandate in the region with 50.12 percent of the vote. However, in contrast to his patron, Tikhomirov has conservative views on land reform and maintains close ties to his former party. After several years under Tikhomirov's leadership, the region has not shown any real improvement or signaled that a turnaround is likely soon.

Executive Platform: Populist

Tikhomirov built his support base from a variety of constituencies. As the Yeltsin-appointed incumbent, he had access to the resources available to the party of power. Tikhomirov could also draw on his extensive ties to the opposition. Although Tikhomirov resigned from the Agrarian party following his appointment as governor, he publicly continued to support party positions (*IG*, 7 September 1996). Like the Agrarian party leadership, the governor is against selling farm land, a position that likely increased his support among conservative collective farmers. Taking such a stand in Ivanovo is politically popular since the rural electorate, which tends to back the Communists, turned out strongly in the gubernatorial elections (*OMRI DD*, 4 December 1996).

Tikhomirov has given top priority to social programs and supporting the poverty-stricken strata of society (*RK*, 2 March 1996). In his 1996 gubernatorial campaign he stressed measures to help veterans, the handicapped, and children, and to pay pension arrears (*RK*, 19 September 1996). Tikhomirov's main economic interest was to revitalize the region's textile industry. He hoped to attract investors and establish links with commercial banks and organizations in order to help ensure the supply of fiber to the mills. Tikhomirov also advocated greater state support for regional collective farms, since no other form of agriculture then existed that could support the farming community

(*RK*, 19 September 1996). In the campaign he also expressed a desire to lower taxes, increase oblast revenues, find a solution to the unemployment crisis, and change the relations between the oblast and the Ivanovo city government (*RK*, 19 September 1996). However, the governor did not outline specific measures for accomplishing these tasks.

He stated that Russia should have a national idea, even if it is capitalism, because the country will not become a great power unless it believes in something (www.ivadm.ivanovo.ru).

Ties to Moscow: Yeltsin Appointee

Despite his Agrarian party background, Tikhomirov was appointed by Yeltsin and was on friendly terms with the president. He used this connection to try to establish policies that would benefit the region's depressed textile industry, but his efforts have produced little concrete aid. On 20 May 1998, Ivanovo signed a power-sharing treaty with Yeltsin.

Tikhomirov sees the center and regions as being on different sides of the barricades and charges that the president has too much power. He would like to see treaties signed between Moscow and all the regions delegating additional powers to the regions (www.ivadm.ivanovo.ru).

Relations with Other Regions: Supported by Krasnoyarsk Governor Lebed

While he was serving briefly as secretary of the Russian Security Council, Aleksandr Lebed (now governor of Krasnoyarsk) offered his support to Tikhomirov's gubernatorial campaign (*RK*, 20 November 1996). Tikhomirov invited Lebed to visit the oblast in spring of 1996, during which Lebed asked about the political situation in the oblast and requested that Ivanovo show support for the families of those who had been killed in the Chechen conflict.

Ivanovo is a member of the Central Russia Association, which is headed by the governor of neighboring Yaroslavl Oblast, Anatolii Lisitsyn. The association also includes Bryansk, Vladimir, Kaluga, Kostroma, Moscow, Ryazan, Smolensk, Tver, and Tula oblasts as well as the city of Moscow.

Foreign Ties: Fears "Economic Occupation"

Philosophically, Tikhomirov seems to fear outsiders, as suggested in his comment that "our great country will be able to avoid the worst of evils—economic occupation" (www.ivadm.ivanovo.ru). However, he would like Russia to take better advantage of its position between Europe and Asia to promote trade. But he proposes trade barriers to shield domestic production and the lifting of the value-added tax on raw materials, spare parts, and technologies that boost local production.

In practical terms, though, Tikhomirov's relations with other countries revolve around Ivanovo's textile industry. During the Soviet era, Ivanovo received the cotton necessary for its textile industry from Central Asia, primarily Uzbekistan, via the central planning system. After the collapse of the Soviet Union, Ivanovo continued to receive Central Asian cotton, yet it was obtained through barter deals, which were phased out when the republics began to demand advance payment in hard currency for cotton supplies (*MT*, 9 September 1997). The loss of Uzbek cotton provoked the collapse of Ivanovo's textile industry, and thus Ivanovo's relations with Uzbekistan are particularly strained. This situation has turned into a tense triangle since the UK became involved as a creditor for many Ivanovo textile industries, providing the mills with cotton, ironically from Uzbekistan.

Ivanovo has also suffered from the sometimes tense economic relations between Russia and the European Union. From 1993 to 1996 the EU limited Russian textile imports to $140 million per year and Russia limited EU imports to $750 million. In 1997 Russia suggested gradually removing all quotas by 2005. These quotas contributed greatly to Ivanovo's textile crisis by severely limiting the oblast's foreign market while leaving local producers to compete with European imports in addition to the very cheap imports from Southeast Asia on the domestic market. In 1997 the EU imported $140 million in Russian textile products, yet Russia imported $900 million (*KD*, 13 January 1998). The EU finally agreed to drop all quotas when Russia threatened to retaliate starting 1 May 1998 (*Ekspert*, 6 April 1998). This agreement should certainly help Ivanovo's textile exports and contribute to improving the region's economic health.

Attitudes Toward Business: Textile Revitalization

Tikhomirov's main business concern has been to revitalize the oblast's textile industry. His concerns

Vladislav Nikolaevich Tikhomirov

14 August 1939—Born in Kukoba village in Yaroslavl Oblast. Later, graduated from the Ivanovo Agricultural Institute as an agronomist. He worked as an economist for the Kineshemskii sovkhoz and was elected secretary of the Komsomol district committee. Tikhomirov then went on to head the Komsomol and the Gavrilovo-Posadskii district committee of the CPSU

1987–1990—Chairman of the regional executive committee

4 March 1990—Elected to the RSFSR Congress of People's Deputies

March 1990—Elected chairman of the Ivanovo Oblast Council of People's Deputies

June-August 1990—First secretary of oblast Communist party committee

12 December 1993—Elected to the Federation Council from Ivanovo, member of the Agricultural Committee

27 March 1994—Elected to the Ivanovo Legislative Council, and chosen as chairman

January 1996—Became an ex-officio member of the Federation Council, where he holds the position of deputy chairman of the Agricultural Committee

February 1996—Appointed by Yeltsin to the position of governor of Ivanovo Oblast

1 December 1996—Elected governor of Ivanovo Oblast, winning 50.12% of the vote in the first round

---

are justifiable—the textile industry in 1997 contributed less than 2 percent of the oblast budget, whereas before 1990 it contributed 26 percent (*KD*, 13 January 1998). Ivanovo's textile mills once employed 70 percent of the local work force and produced one-third of Russia's cotton fabric (*MT*, 9 September 1997). In 1996, industrial output fell to less than 30 percent of its 1990 level, reaching an all-time low (*EWI RRR*, 5 June 1997).

Presently, the majority of Ivanovo's textile industry operates on tolling contracts with Russian and international trading firms. The factories are given a set amount of cotton for fabric production and then return part of the finished product as payment to the firms. The remainder is sold in an attempt (which is never successful) to cover production costs and wages (*MT*, 9 September 1997).

In the first half of 1997, 60 percent of the oblast's textile enterprises were unprofitable (*KD*, 13 January 1998). Yet, in the spring, the region experienced a boost in textile production. This was primarily due to a $40 million agreement between the Ivanovo administration and the British commodities trader A. Meredith Jones & Co. This deal required the federal

government to ensure a loan from a commercial bank to the Ivanovo administration. Once such a credit line was established, Meredith Jones would ship cotton to 23 of the oblast's textile mills and accept payment six months later. It took considerable time to find a commercial bank supportive of the project, but eventually Menatep offered the loan at a 16 percent interest rate (*MT*, 9 September 1997).

This arrangement is preferable to tolling contracts since it allows the factories to directly sell the cloth that is produced. As a result of this agreement, several factories, which would have otherwise been idle, operated in 1997. Yet, although the English credit has enabled flagging textile mills to produce cloth, it does not offer a long-term solution to the industry's problems and is insufficient for bringing them back to a profitable level.

Essentially, for Ivanovo's textile industries to experience a significant turnaround, new markets must be found. The region's industry does have some potential, inspiring the measured optimism Tikhomirov expresses. The mills have some modern equipment and are capable of producing basic cloth for an export market (*MT*, 9 September 1997).

Yet, the textile industry needs better marketing and working capital to purchase cotton. Tikhomirov has not offered any suggestions on how to improve these aspects of the industry.

Nevertheless, Tikhomirov has used the oblast administration to help enterprises regulate their links with commercial organizations in other oblasts (*Budin-2*, #38, October 1996). He has also invited the head of Central Bank to set up a branch in Ivanovo (*RK*, 6 March 1996).

Outside of the textile industry, a handful of other enterprises are establishing themselves in the oblast. In December 1997 Sun Brewing company, which operates breweries in several regions, announced plans to invest $150 million to reconstruct a brewery in Ivanovo (*KD*, 16 December 1997). Additionally, the Samara telephone company Smarts, which has embarked on a joint venture with the German-Italian firm ITALTEL, is working to set up branches of its company in Ivanovo as well as in Orenburg, Astrakhan, Saratov, Penza, Volgograd, Ulyanovsk, and Chuvashia (*KD*, 22 November 1997).

Internet Sites in the Region

http://ivadm.ivanovo.ru/
Website of the Ivanovo Oblast Administration. The site has extensive and up-to-date press releases from the oblast administration. It also includes an oblast encyclopedia with a who's who in Ivanovo and maps.

http://www.ivanovo.ru/
One of the main web servers in the region, with extensive links.

JEWISH AUTONOMOUS OBLAST

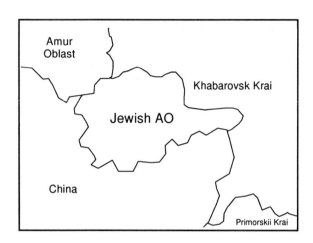

Territory: 36,000 km²
Population (as of 1 January 1998): 205,000
Distance from Moscow: 8,361 km

Major Cities:
Birobidzhan, *capital* (pop. 81,500)

Basic Facts

Population (as of 1 Jan. 1998): 205,000 (0.14% of Russian total)

Ethnic breakdown (1989 census): Russians 83.2%, Ukrainians 7.4%, Jews 4.2%, Belarusans 1.0%

Urban population (as of 1 Jan. 1998): 67.6% (Russia overall: 73.1%)

Student population (as of 1 Sept. 1997): 89 per 10,000 (Russia overall: 208/10,000)

Pensioner population (1997): 20.98% (Russia overall: 25.96%)

Percent of population with higher education (1989 census): 7.8% (Russia overall: 11.3%)

Percent of population working in (1997): Industry: 16.0% (Russian average: 23.0%); Agriculture: 12.3% (13.7%); Trade: 11.0% (13.5%); Culture: 15.3% (13.3%)

Average monthly personal income in July 1998: 530.9 new rubles (Russian average: 891.7 new rubles)

Average monthly personal expenses in July 1998: 374.0 new rubles (Russian average: 684.9 new rubles)

Average monthly subsistence requirement in 1998: 462 new rubles (Russian average: 438 new rubles)

Consumer price index (as of July 1998): 129 (Russia overall = 100)

Budgetary revenues (1997): 480.4 billion rubles (Russia overall: 433,378.2 billion rubles)

Budgetary expenditures (1997): 619.5 billion rubles (Russia overall: 468,111.6 billion rubles)

Industrial production as percentage of all Russian production (Jan.–Aug. 1998): 0.03%

Proportion of loss-making enterprises (as of July 1998): 75.9% (Russia overall: 50.4%)

Number of enterprises which have wage arrears (as of 1 Sept. 1998): 297 (0.22% of Russian total)

Agricultural production as percentage of all Russian production (1997): 0.1%

Number of private farms (as of 1 Jan. 1998): 325 (0.12% of Russian total)

Capital investment (1997): 418.8 billion rubles (Russia overall: 408,797 billion rubles)

Sources of investment (1997): federal budget: 45.0% (Russian average: 10.2%); regional budget: 4.1% (10.5%); extra-budgetary funds: 50.9% (79.3%)

Foreign investment (1997): 452,000 USD (Russia overall: 12,294,734,000 USD)

Number of joint ventures (1997): 8 (0.05% of Russian total)

Fixed capital investment in joint ventures and foreign companies (1997): 61 million rubles (Russia overall: 16,265.4 billion rubles)

Number of small businesses (as of 1 July 1998): 400 (0.05% of Russian total)

Number of enterprises privatized in 1997: 2 (0.07% of Russian total), including those which used to be municipal property: 100% (Russian average: 66.4%); regional property: 0% (20.0%); federal property: 0% (13.6%)

Number of telephones per 100 families (1997): in cities: 37.5 (Russian average: 49.2); in villages: 30.0 (19.8)

Brief Overview

Russian colonization of the oblast's current territory began in the second half of the 19th century. Cossacks, the first migrants, settled along the Amur River, on the border with China. In 1928, the Soviet government established a Jewish administrative unit on the sparsely populated territory north of the Amur, with a center in Birobidzhan. Although the Soviet government financed Jewish migration to the region, Jews now make up only about 4 percent of the population.

The oblast is situated in the southern part of the Russian Far East and borders Amur Oblast in the west, Khabarovsk Krai in the north and east, and China in the south. The oblast has one of the most favorable climates in the Far East. About half the territory lies on a plain suitable for agriculture, and the rest is rich in mineral resources. Tin extraction, metal processing, machine construction, and light industry are among the main types of activity in the oblast. Since forests occupy about 40 percent of the oblast's territory, forestry, and lumber and cellulose industries are also highly developed and produce over 10 percent of the oblast's industrial output.

According to a survey by *Ekspert* magazine, the oblast is the 10th poorest in the country: it can cover only 35.4 percent of its budget from its own revenues, gaining the rest in federal subsidies. Its population is also among the poorest—per capita income in 1997 amounted to 10.66 percent of 1991 average earnings.

Since 1991, when the oblast became a free economic zone, it has actively pursued economic and cultural ties with Asian-Pacific nations, the United States, and Israel. The region is constantly expanding its cooperation with China.

According to the same study by *Ekspert*, the oblast ranked 79th among Russia's 89 regions in terms of investment potential and 41st in terms of investment risk. A 1998 survey by Bank Austria ranked the oblast 70th in terms of investment climate.

Electoral History

2000 Presidential Election
Putin: 42.87%
Zyuganov: 39.73%
Yavlinskii: 5.20%
Zhirinovsky: 4.11%
Tuleev: 1.91%
Turnout: 68.88% (Russia overall: 68.64%)

2000 Gubernatorial Election
Volkov (incumbent): 56.76%
Korsunskii: 25.71%
Sirotkin: 4.27%
Turnout: 68.81%

1999 Parliamentary Elections
Communist Party of the Russian Federation: 34.01%
Unity: 21.14%
Zhirinovsky Bloc: 8.72%
Union of Right Forces: 6.85%
Fatherland–All Russia: 6.35%
Yabloko: 5.09%
In a single-mandate district: 1 Communist Party of the Russian Federation
Turnout: 59.99% (Russia overall: 61.85%)

1996 Gubernatorial Election
Volkov (incumbent): 70.09%
Leskov: 16.28%
Turnout: 42.48%

1996 Presidential Election
Yeltsin: 30.36%/49.43% (first round/second round)
Zyuganov: 32.84%/43.68%
Lebed: 15.30%
Zhirinovsky: 7.99%
Yavlinskii: 6.45%
Turnout: 67.59%/65.49% (Russia overall: 69.67%/68.79%)

1995 Parliamentary Election
Communist Party of the Russian Federation: 23.42%
Liberal Democratic Party: 11.58%
Communists–Workers' Russia: 8.46%
Women of Russia: 7.05%
Party of Workers' Self-Government: 6.09%
Our Home Is Russia: 5.06%
Yabloko: 4.56%
Agrarian Party of Russia: 3.48%
In a single-mandate district: 1 Communist Party of the Russian Federation
Turnout: 63.92% (Russia overall: 64.37%)

1993 Constitutional Referendum
"Yes"—62.9% "No"—34.1%

1993 Parliamentary Elections

Liberal Democratic Party of Russia: 24.96%

Russia's Choice: 15.38%

Women of Russia: 14.92%

Communist Party of the Russian Federation: 12.26%

Party of Russian Unity and Concord: 6.41%

Democratic Party of Russia: 5.92%

Agrarian Party of Russia: 5.01%

Yabloko: 4.86%

In a single-mandate district: 1 Agrarian Party of Russia

Turnout: 48.39% (Russia overall: 54.34%)

1991 Presidential Election

Yeltsin: 42.89%

Ryzhkov: 29.37%

Zhirinovsky: 7.52%

Makashov: 6.72%

Tuleev: 5.24%

Bakatin: 3.66%

Turnout: 70.76% (Russia overall: 76.66%)

Regional Political Institutions

Executive:

Governor, 4-year term

Nikolai Mikhailovich Volkov, elected October 1996

60–letiya USSR Prospekt, 18;

Birobidzhan, 682200

Tel 7(426–22) 6–02–42;

Fax 7(426–22) 4–07–25

Federation Council in Moscow:

7(095) 292–31–76, 926–62–49

Legislative:

Unicameral

Legislative Assembly (*Zakonodatelnoe Sobranie*)—15 members, 4-year term, elected October 1997

Chairman—Stanislav Vladimirovich Vavilov, elected March 1994, November 1997

Regional Politics

Quiet Leader of Soviet Zion

Nikolai Volkov, a moderate reformer, has quietly ruled over the Jewish Autonomous Oblast since December 1991, when he was appointed to the post by Russian President Boris Yeltsin. Although Volkov attracts little attention beyond his home district, he is quite popular in the region and was elected governor in October 1996, winning 72 percent of the vote. He was reelected in March 2000, winning 56.76 percent of the vote.

The Jewish Autonomous Oblast has one of the most unusual histories of all of Russia's regions. The territory was founded in 1928 as part of the Soviets' plan for simultaneously assimilating Soviet Jews into a socialist Zion and populating the area near the Sino-Soviet border (for a detailed history of the Jewish Autonomous Oblast, see Robert Weinberg, *Stalin's Forgotten Zion*, Berkeley and Los Angeles: University of California Press, 1998). In 1934 the area was given the status of an autonomous oblast within Khabarovsk Krai. In a concerted effort to bring the country's Jews (which then constituted the largest Jewish population in the world) into the ranks of the socialist revolution, the Soviet government financed Jewish migration to the region and established Yiddish schools, newspapers, and cultural institutions there that promoted the same Soviet goals as the country's Russian-language institutions. The idea of creating a Jewish homeland attracted international attention, and foundations around the world, particularly in the United States, raised money for the settlements to buy tools, seed, and other supplies. Over one thousand foreign Jews moved to the region in the first ten years of its existence.

The Jewish Autonomous Oblast never served as a Russian Jewish homeland, however. There was no Jewish population living near the region when it was established, and the majority of the Soviet Union's Jews were not interested in leaving their homes in the western part of the country to settle undeveloped land in the Far East. In the first few years thousands of Jews moved to the region, but the Stalinist regime of the 1930s visited anti-Semitic repression on the settlements. Despite a slight burst of interest after World War II, the region soon lost its sense of cultural distinction, becoming just another part of Russia. During the Gorbachev era the oblast, like many of Russia's ethnic regions, experienced a cultural revitalization. Nevertheless, many Jews from the oblast have followed Russian Jews from the rest of the country in immigrating to Israel or the United States. The region's Jewish population is experiencing a steady decline, and at present, Jews comprise less than 4 percent of the population. Most of the region's inhabitants are Russian and Ukrainian.

Executive Platform: Yeltsin Loyalist

Volkov was a devoted ally of President Boris Yeltsin and a strong supporter of former Prime Minister Viktor Chernomyrdin. The governor joined Chernomyrdin's Our Home Is Russia (NDR) movement, and in 1997 was elected to NDR's political council. In his gubernatorial bid, Volkov received a wide range of support from the region's political organizations including the Communist party, the Liberal Democratic Party of Russia, and Our Home Is Russia. He is pro-market, but opposed to shock therapy. Volkov is also in favor of state support for agriculture. The region's agricultural enterprises have suffered tremendously in recent years, lacking sufficient finances and technology to cultivate the fields. As a result, much of the oblast's lands remain fallow.

Policies: Protectionist, Reformist

Volkov seems to follow a reformist track, but favors some forms of state intervention. For example, he introduced price controls in the region following the financial crisis that shook Russia in August 1998.

Volkov is preparing a law on the buying and selling of land in the Jewish Autonomous Oblast that is similar to the liberal land law adopted in Saratov Oblast, which allows Russian citizens to purchase land and foreigners to sign 99-year leases on it. In 1998 he allowed Chinese peasants to lease 3,000 hectares of arable land in the oblast (see Foreign Relations).

Relationships Between Key Players: Supportive Legislature

The majority of the Jewish Autonomous Oblast's legislature belongs to NDR. Thus Volkov, who is an active member of the NDR political council, presumably receives strong support in the legislature for his initiatives.

In March 1999 the oblast's legislative assembly passed a budget bill with a record 48 percent deficit. (In 1998 the region's deficit was 35 percent). The bleak economic situation worsened by the shrinking of federal subsidies (*RFR*, 17 March 1999).

Ties to Moscow

Volkov was a strong supporter of President Yeltsin, who was quite popular in the region. Volkov is not overly assertive, and unlike many leaders in the Far East, did not challenge Yeltsin's authority.

Relations with Other Regions: Calm Relations with Khabarovsk

The Jewish Autonomous Oblast is simultaneously subordinate to Khabarovsk Krai and an equal subject of the Russian Federation. Although there was brief discussion in the early 1990s about the oblast's becoming an independent ethnic republic, the proposal was withdrawn and the issue has not surfaced again. Essentially, the small number of Jews living in the region, coupled with their high emigration rate, give the region little basis for defining itself as an ethnic republic. Volkov is on friendly terms with Khabarovsk Governor Viktor Ishaev, and the two regions have a good relationship In fact in 2000, Volkov suggested that the oblast should rejoin Khabarovsk Krai.

The Jewish Autonomous Oblast belongs to the Far East and Baikal Association, which also includes the republics of Buryatia and Sakha (Yakutia); Primorskii and Khabarovsk krais; Amur, Kamchatka, Magadan, Chita, and Sakhalin oblasts; and Koryak and Chukotka autonomous okrugs. The regions in the Far East and Baikal Association are trying to enhance their relations with countries in the Asian-Pacific region, specifically regarding trade and participation in joint ventures.

Foreign Relations: Active Relations with China

The oblast shares a long border with China and has extensive relations with this southern neighbor. The Sino-Russian border agreement, which was renegotiated in 1997, led to numerous protests in the Jewish Autonomous Oblast. The border demarcation agreement signed in late 1997 provided for the transfer of several Amur River islands from the Jewish Autonomous Oblast to China. The main cause for objection was that about 50 kilometers of the border coincided with the Russian bank of the Amur River, provoking protests from the region's fishermen and farmers.

In spite of the bitterness regarding the region's

Nikolai Mikhailovich Volkov

19 December 1951—Born in the village Krasnoe in Orel Oblast

1973—Graduated from the Odessa Engineering-Building Institute as an engineer-hydrotechnician

1973–1991—Worked for Birobidzhantselinstra construction company in various technical positions

March 1990—Elected unopposed to the Jewish Autonomous Oblast Council

14 December 1991—Appointed governor of the Jewish Autonomous Oblast

12 December 1993—Elected to the first session of the Federation Council and became a member of the Committee on Federation Affairs, Federal Agreements, and Regional Policies

May 1995—Joined Our Home Is Russia (NDR)

January 1996—Appointed to the Federation Council and joined the Committee for International Affairs

20 October 1996—Elected governor of the Jewish Autonomous Oblast

26 March 2000—Reelected governor

Married, with a daughter

Enjoys fishing

---

lost territory, Volkov continues to develop and expand the region's ties to China. In 1998 Chinese farmers rented nearly 3,000 hectares of land from the oblast. The agreement established between the oblast and Chinese farm enterprises stipulated that half of all proceeds from the crops would be used to pay rent. The Chinese brought their own workers, equipment, seeds, and fertilizer to farm the land rather than making use of Russian resources. Nevertheless, this arrangement was still beneficial to the oblast since local farmers lacked the resources and equipment to cultivate the land themselves.

Attitudes Toward Business: Free Economic Zone

The Jewish Autonomous Oblast has considerable economic potential given its location and natural resources. The oblast has a very favorable climate for the Far East, and much of its territory lies on a plain making it fit for agriculture. The region also has considerable mineral deposits and sizable for-

ests. Furthermore, in fall 1998 the oil exploration company Irkutskgenfizika announced that it thought it had discovered large oil deposits in the oblast.

However, much of the region's natural wealth is untapped or underdeveloped. The oblast is in need of advanced technology for further developing its natural resources. In 1991 the oblast became a free economic zone and has since pursued economic and cultural ties with countries in the Asian-Pacific region, the United States, and Israel. Development is proceeding, albeit slowly.

Internet Sites in the Region

http://www.eao.ru/
This is the official website of the Jewish Autonomous Oblast. It offers information on the region's legislative assembly, investment projects, and mass media. The site also allows you to e-mail the oblast's government.

REPUBLIC OF KABARDINO-BALKARIA

Territory: 12,500 km2
Population (as of 1 January 1998): 792,000
Distance from Moscow: 1,873 km

Major Cities:
Nalchik, *capital* (pop. 231,800)
Prokhladnyi (59,700)

Basic Facts

Population (as of 1 Jan. 1998): 792,000 (0.54% of Russian total)

Ethnic breakdown (1989 census): Kabardins 48.2%, Russians 32.0%, Balkars 9.4%, Ukrainians 1.7%, Ossetians 1.3%, Germans 1.1%

Urban population (as of 1 Jan. 1998): 57.5% (Russia overall: 73.1%)

Student population (as of 1 Sept. 1997): 189 per 10,000 (Russia overall: 208/10,000)

Pensioner population (1997): 22.22% (Russia overall: 25.96%)

Percent of population with higher education (1989 census): 10.1% (Russia overall: 11.3%)

Percent of population working in (1997): Industry: 23.9% (Russian average: 23.0%); Agriculture: 14.1% (13.7%); Trade: 11.5% (13.5%); Culture: 16.3% (13.3%)

Average monthly personal income in July 1998: 550.9 new rubles (Russian average: 891.7 new rubles)

Average monthly personal expenses in July 1998: 326.2 new rubles (Russian average: 684.9 new rubles)

Average monthly subsistence requirement in 1998: 357 new rubles (Russian average: 438 new rubles)

Consumer price index (as of July 1998): 100 (Russia overall = 100)

Budgetary revenues (1997): 1,777.5 billion rubles (Russia overall: 433,378.2 billion rubles)

Budgetary expenditures (1997): 1,965.6 billion rubles (Russia overall: 468,111.6 billion rubles)

Industrial production as percentage of all Russian production (Jan.–Aug. 1998): 0.12%

Proportion of loss-making enterprises (as of July 1998): 59.8% (Russia overall: 50.4%)

Number of enterprises which have wage arrears (as of 1 Sept. 1998): 582 (0.43% of Russian total)

Agricultural production as percentage of all Russian production (1997): 0.67%

Number of private farms (as of 1 Jan. 1998): 728 (0.27% of Russian total)

Capital investment (1997): 1,031.7 billion rubles (Russia overall: 408,797 billion rubles)

Sources of investment (1997): federal budget: 18.4% (Russian average: 10.2%); regional budget: 26.2% (10.5%); extra-budgetary funds: 55.4% (79.3%)

Foreign investment (1997): 254,000 USD (Russia overall: 12,294,734,000 USD)

Number of joint ventures (1997): 22 (0.15% of Russian total)

Fixed capital investment in joint ventures and foreign companies (1997): 8,523 million rubles (Russia overall: 16,265.4 billion rubles)

Number of small businesses (as of 1 July 1998): 2,300 (0.26% of Russian total)

Number of enterprises privatized in 1997: 6 (0.22% of Russian total), including those which used to be municipal property: 50.0% (Russian average: 66.4%); regional property: 50.0% (20.0%); federal property: 0% (13.6%)

Number of telephones per 100 families (1997): in cities: 45.8 (Russian average: 49.2); in villages: 29.7 (19.8)

Brief Overview

Kabardino-Balkaria is located in the central part of the northern Caucasus Mountains and adjoining plain. It borders Georgia, Stavropol Krai, North Ossetia, Karachaevo-Cherkessia, and Ingushetia. Its population is composed of more than 100 different ethnic groups, the largest of which are Kabardins (48.2 percent), followed by Russians (32 percent), and Balkars (9.4 percent). During World War II, the Balkars were deported to Central Asia because Stalin accused them of collaborating with the Nazis. Although they were allowed to return to their land in 1957, there are still disputes over that issue with the Kabardins.

The mountainous part of the republic is rich in various mineral resources, including tin, copper, iron ore, gold, limestone, coal, charcoal, and clay. Most of the republic's GDP (70 percent) comes from machine building, food processing, and textile manufacturing. Agricultural products include grains, fruits, vegetables, and beef. The republic is also rich in mineral waters, which, along with its unique climatic conditions, allowed it to become one of the country's most famous resort and tourism centers.

Although the republic is one of the regions with the most favorable legislative conditions for foreign and domestic investors, both Russian and international businesses are generally fearful of working there. In 1997 the region experienced the second-largest increase in investment risk—by 51 points—according to a 1998 survey by *Ekspert* magazine which ranked the republic 71st among Russia's 89 regions in terms of potential and 42nd in terms of risk. A 1998 survey by Bank Austria ranked the republic 72nd in terms of investment climate.

Electoral History

2000 Presidential Election
Putin: 74.87%
Zyuganov: 19.65%
Yavlinskii: 1.56%
Tuleev: 1.04%
Zhirinovsky: 0.47%
Turnout: 88.50% (Russia overall: 68.64%)

1999 Parliamentary Elections
Fatherland–All Russia: 34.71%
Communist Party of the Russian Federation: 23.85%
Unity: 20.62%
Our Home Is Russia: 9.86%
Yabloko: 1.39%
Zhirinovsky Bloc: 1.33%
Union of Right Forces: 1.30%
In a single-mandate district: 1 independent
Turnout: 78.42% (Russia overall: 61.85%)

1997 Republican Presidential Election
Kokov (incumbent): 99.35%
Turnout: 97.72%

1996 Presidential Election
Yeltsin: 43.75%/63.61% (first round/second round)
Zyuganov: 37.25%/33.18%
Lebed: 9.80%
Yavlinskii: 3.36%
Zhirinovsky: 1.43%
Turnout: 73.84%/79.45% (Russia overall: 69.67%/ 68.79%)

1995 Parliamentary Elections
Our Home Is Russia: 24.96%
Communist Party of the Russian Federation: 23.67%
Agrarian Party of Russia: 15.30%
Women of Russia: 4.74%
Communists–Workers' Russia: 4.16%
Congress of Russian Communities: 3.30%
Liberal Democratic Party of Russia: 3.08%
In a single-mandate district: 1 Our Home Is Russia
Turnout: 68.08% (Russia overall: 64.37%)

1993 Constitutional Referendum
"Yes"—62.0%   "No"—36.0%

1993 Parliamentary Elections
Party of Russian Unity and Concord: 31.53%
Communist Party of the Russian Federation: 20.08%
Agrarian Party of Russia: 12.87%
Liberal Democratic Party of Russia: 8.79%
Russia's Choice: 6.62%
Democratic Party of Russia: 5.23%
Women of Russia: 4.62%
Yabloko: 4.24%
In a single-mandate district: 1 independent
Turnout: 58.75% (Russia overall: 54.34%)

1991 Presidential Elections

Yeltsin: 63.88%

Ryzhkov: 15.08%

Tuleev: 8.17%

Zhirinovsky: 5.80%

Bakatin: 2.74%

Makashov: 1.95%

Turnout: 74.43% (Russia overall: 76.66%)

Regional Political Institutions

Executive:

President, 5-year term

Valerii Mukhamedovich Kokov, elected
January 1997

Leninskii Prospekt, 27; Nalchik, 360028

Tel 7(866–22) 2–20–64;

Fax 7(866–22) 7–61–74

Federation Council in Moscow:
7(095) 292–59–93, 926–63–19

Legislative:

Bicameral

Parliament—4-year term, elected
December 1997

Republican Council (*Sovet respubliki*)—
36 members

Chairman—Z. Nakhushev, elected December
1993, December 1997

Representative Council (*Sovet predstavitelei*)—
36 members

Chairman—Ilyas Borisovich Bechelov, elected
December 1997

Regional Politics

Ethnic Kabardin Maintains United Republic

Valerii Kokov dominates Kabardino-Balkaria almost
completely, having wiped out almost the entire opposition. After initially being elected on 5 January
1992, he won a second term on 12 January 1997
with nearly unanimous support. Of the republic's
500,000 voters, 97.53 percent participated in the
elections, giving Kokov 99.37 percent of the vote.

His election violated federal law, however, since
he ran unopposed. In spite of this major electoral
violation, then presidential chief of staff Anatolii
Chubais and Deputy Prime Minister Vladimir

Babichev attended Kokov's inauguration, bringing
him warm greetings from President Yeltsin (*OMRI
RRR*, 29 January 1997). Moscow Mayor Yurii
Luzhkov was also present for the festivities. The
presidential administration was presumably relieved by Kokov's reelection since he had successfully defused a Balkar secessionist attempt just
weeks before (*OMRI RRR*, 15 January 1997).

Although Kabardino-Balkaria belongs to the
relatively peaceful and stable western section of
the North Caucasus, Kokov must work carefully to
prevent the outbreak of inter-ethnic violence. The
Kabardino-Balkar Republic, which was founded
in 1922, brings together two very distinct ethnic
groups indigenous to the Caucasus. The Kabardins
comprise 48 percent of the republic's population,
while the Balkars make up only 9 percent. Russians represent 32 percent, and all other nationalities combined make up about 10 percent. The
Kabardin and Balkar cultural, linguistic, and historical identities differ significantly. The Kabardins
are more closely related to the neighboring Cherkes,
while the Balkars share ties with the Karachai. One
important distinction between the two groups is that
the Balkars were among the groups deported from
the North Caucasus in 1944, and their territories
were turned over to the Kabardin ASSR and re-
settled. Although the Balkars were permitted to return to their homeland in 1956, they were not always allowed to rebuild their homes on their former
territory. This issue, and the feelings of victimiza-
tion and discrimination that characterize Balkar national consciousness, have created a tense foundation for Kabardin-Balkar relations.

Throughout the 1990s Balkars have become more
assertive in their complaints against Kabardins and
demands for recognition of their territorial and political rights. These tense relations have hindered the
development of constitutional and legislative reforms, yet it is unlikely that these conflicts will es-
calate to a violent confrontation. Some steps have
been taken to ease these tensions. On 3 March 1994
Yeltsin signed a decree rehabilitating the Balkars,
reviving their cultural heritage, providing special
pensions to deportees, and repatriating those still living abroad. Kokov then proceeded to reinstate the
region's pre-1944 territorial divisions.

On 17 November 1996, a congress of Balkars
announced the group's intention to secede from
the republic and establish an independent Balkar

Valerii Mukhamedovich Kokov

18 October 1941—Born in Tyrnyauz village of Kabardino-Balkaria

1964—Graduated from the economics department of Kabardino-Balkar State University

1964—Began working as the head agronomist for the Working Mountain-Dwellers collective farm in the Balkar raion of Kabardino-Balkaria

1966—Joined the CPSU

1966–1970—Received a candidate's degree in economics at the All-Union Scientific Research Institute of Agriculture

1970—Began working as a senior economist and head of the labor and salary department for the Kabardino-Balkaria Agricultural Ministry

1972—Became the director of the Lenin collective farm in the Urvan Raion of Kabardino-Balkaria

1974–1983—Served as the first secretary of the Urvan CPSU district committee

1975—Joined the Supreme Soviet of Kabardino-Balkaria

1978—Graduated Rostov Higher Party School

1983—Was named Chairman of the Kabardino-Balkaria State Committee for the Industrial-Technical Protection of Agriculture

1985—Became secretary of the Kabardino-Balkar CPSU oblast committee on agriculture

1988—Became the second secretary of the Kabardino-Balkar CPSU Oblast Committee Agrarian Commission

February 1990—Became first secretary of the Kabardino-Balkar CPSU oblast committee, yet left the post shortly thereafter when elected to the USSR Congress of People's Deputies

4 March 1990—Elected to the Russian Congress of People's Deputies and to the Kabardino-Balkar Supreme Soviet; on 30 March elected chairman of the Supreme Soviet

July–August 1990—Member of the CPSU Central Committee

31 January 1991—Through Kokov's initiative, the republican Supreme Soviet adopted a Declaration of State Sovereignty relinquishing Kabardino-Balkaria's status as an autonomous republic and proclaiming the region a subject of the Soviet Union

1991—Appointed first deputy chairman of the Kabardino-Balkaria Council of Ministers

Republic within the Russian Federation. The separatist movement was led by retired Lt.-Gen. Sufyan Beppaev, formerly the head of the Transcaucasus Military District. Kokov denounced the attempt as violating the republican constitution, and threatened to start a new war in the region. In June 1998 Beppaev declared that this attempt was a mistake, and placed blame on the local Balkar nomenklatura who had hoped that a radical action would strengthen their positions (*NG*, 3 June 1998; for an account of a meeting with Beppaev, see Mark Taplin, *Open Lands: Travels Through Russia's*

Once Forbidden Places, South Royalton, VT: Steerforth Press, 1997, 180–183).

Executive Platform: Defending Sovereignty

Kokov supports a strongly authoritarian brand of politics. He is in favor of strengthening executive powers throughout the country. Kokov believes that defending state sovereignty and maintaining Russian and republican territorial integrity are among the most important functions of the government (*NG*, 17 September 1997). Kokov's current posi-

29 August 1991—Resigned from his positions in the Council of Ministers and the Supreme Soviet after the Democratic Kabardino-Balkar movement demanded that he resign; began working as the first deputy to the chairman of the republic's Council of Ministers

5 January 1992—Elected president of the Kabardino-Balkar Republic

12 October 1993—Elected to the Federation Council, where from January 1994 to January 1996 he served on the Committee for International Affairs

1994—Completed pilgrimage to Mecca as part of a government delegation organized by the Russian Islamic Cultural Center

January 1996—Appointed to the second session of the Federation Council and on 24 January was elected one of four deputy chairs

May 1996—Became a member of the National Economic Council

12 January 1997—Reelected president of the Kabardino-Balkar Republic in an unchallenged election

7 March 1997—Became deputy chairman of the Federal Commission on Problems in Chechnya

16 April 1997—Joined the presidential commission on relations between the federal executive and the regions regarding constitutional-legal reforms in the regions

October 1997—Member of the presidential commission for opposition to political extremism

6 March 1998—Joined a government commission charged with drafting a position paper on state national politics

Kabardin

Married, with a son, daughter, and granddaughter

tion regarding the Kabardino-Balkaria Republic is that it should remain a united republic that is part of the Russian Federation (NNS). The fact that Kokov holds such views given the turmoil surrounding territorial issues in the North Caucasus is important to Moscow, and most certainly explains why the Kremlin has overlooked Kokov's more disagreeable actions.

Kokov advocates state support for business undertakings that seek to expand production and create new jobs (NNS). He believes that agricultural reforms in the republic should be enacted taking into account the republic's ethnic history and mountainous conditions, in particular, the shortage of land (NNS). The president has permitted various forms of land relations, although he generally is opposed to private ownership in the republic. Kokov emphasizes that there are possibilities in the

republic for the development of lease-based small farms (NNS).

Kokov was deputy chairman of Our Home Is Russia (NDR), but resigned from this position after Viktor Chernomyrdin was dismissed from his post as prime minister (*RFE/RL*, 7 May 1998). He claimed to be stepping down because the republican constitution did not permit him to belong to political parties and movements; however, this provision did not prevent him from remaining on board while Chernomyrdin was prime minister.

Policies

When Georgian troops invaded Abkhazia in August–September 1992, Kokov dispatched medical supplies and food to the region and allowed volunteers to go and help the Abkhazi, increasing his popularity among the Kabardin national-radicals. However, Kokov prohibited the formation of volunteer detachments, once again straining relations with the Kabardins (Panorama Research Group, Labyrint Electronic Database, Moscow).

Kabardino-Balkaria has the status of a free economic zone, which has aided the republican administration in offering various tax incentives to foreign investors and further developing the region's industry.

Relationships Between Key Players: Economic Elite Control Local Parliament

The Kabardino-Balkar legislature is dominated by the republic's economic elite. Eighty percent of the new members elected in December 1997 are local factory directors and businessmen. This parliamentary make-up suggests a strong support base for Kokov.

Ties to Moscow: Yeltsin Loyalist

Kokov was fairly loyal to Yeltsin. In May 1993 Kokov announced that the "power structures and the majority of the republic's inhabitants support the federal government's course of reforms" (Panorama). The Kremlin was well-disposed to Kokov since he never claimed independence for Kabardino-Balkaria, and has prevented others from doing so.

On 1 July 1994 Kokov signed a power-sharing agreement with President Yeltsin. This was the second treaty to be concluded in the Russian Federation. Approximately half of Russia's regions have entered into similar agreements with the Kremlin.

In August 1997 the Moscow-based International Industrial Bank (MPB) loaned $5.2 million to Kabardino-Balkaria to cover the region's budget deficit and help reduce social tensions. The bank also intended to invest $34.5 million annually in local industry (*Segodnya*, 29 August 1997) although these plans have since collapsed.

Relations with Other Regions: Peaceful Relations with North Caucasian Leaders

Kabardino-Balkaria has a much larger population than Adygeya and Karachaevo-Cherkessia and so it plays a leading role in the western part of the North Caucasus. In July 1997 Kokov joined the leaders of

Karachaevo-Cherkessia and Adygeya to form an Interparliamentary Assembly of the three republics. The assembly is pro-Russian with the intention of strengthening Russian federalism, and deepening the bonds of friendship and cooperation among the member regions (*Vesti*, 24 July 1997).

The Kabardino-Balkar Republic belongs to the Association of Cooperation of Republics, Krais, and Oblasts of the North Caucasus. The other member regions include the republics of Adygeya, Dagestan, Ingushetia, Karachaevo-Cherkessia, North Ossetia, and Kalmykia; Krasnodar and Stavropol krais; and Rostov Oblast.

In May 1997 the Kabardino-Balkar Republic passed a decision to return Chechen migrants to Chechnya (*EWI RRR*, 19 June 1997). This decision was passed after several months of accepting large numbers of Chechen refugees into the region with virtually no money from Moscow or Chechnya to help support them.

Foreign Ties: Republic Gains Larger International Presence

Although Kokov himself has not established any significant foreign relations, the Kabardino-Balkar Republic is moving onto the international scene. The airport in the republican capital Nalchik connects Kabardino-Balkaria with Turkey, Syria, Jordan, and the United Arab Emirates. The republican administration hopes that a new airport complex of modern international standards will be built in the near future. The republic is searching for international partners to help in the realization of this project (www.kbsu.ru).

More than half of the republic's exports go to western countries: Turkey, the United States, Germany, Finland, and the Netherlands. The republic's most important exports are artificial diamonds, tungsten, molybdenum, oil products, medical and wood manufacturing equipment, cable, artificial leather, leather and fur products, and agricultural goods.

Attitudes Toward Business: Free Economic Zone Encourages Investment

Kabardino-Balkaria's free economic zone status grants the republic several advantages in developing industries and businesses. Foreign investment in the republic is protected by the Law on Foreign Investments in the Kabardino-Balkar Republic, international treaties, and other legislative and legal acts passed by the RF and the Kabardino-Balkar Republic (www.kbsu.ru).

To stabilize and develop the republic's economy, the administration has prepared a complete set of measures to increase the attractiveness of investing in the region and improve work conditions for foreign investors. The gist of the reforms are tax breaks. Tax incentives began in 1996 when a law was passed stating that non-resident enterprises in the republic were granted tax privileges on the republican and local levels (www.kbsu.ru). The administration hopes to extend complete republican and local tax exemptions to investors (www.kbsu.ru). Kabardino-Balkaria's status as a free economic zone has made it possible to establish a customs-free production zone on the territory of the Elbrus-AVIA state aviation enterprise (www.kbsu.ru).

There are several investment projects for which the republican administration would like to find foreign capital. Agricultural projects include the production of mineral water, starch, meat and poultry, and confectionery products. Potential industrial undertakings include the production of gas water-heaters and stoves, pharmaceutical enterprises, electro-technical wares and many other products. The republic also hopes to secure foreign investors for several construction projects.

Internet Sites in the Region

http://www.kbsu.ru/kbr/Ealt1ru.htm
This website offers detailed information about the republic, including its history, industry, trade relations, and investment projects. It also outlines the specifics of Kabardino-Balkaria's status as a free economic zone.

KALININGRAD OBLAST

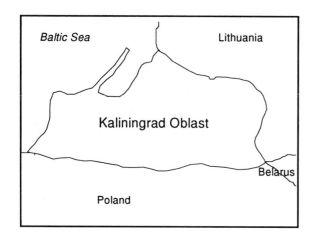

Territory: 15,100 km²
Population (as of 1 January 1998):
943,000
Distance from Moscow: 1,289 km

Major Cities:
Kaliningrad, *capital* (pop. 425,600)
Sovetsk (44,000)
Chernyakhovsk (43,000)
Baltiisk (31,200)
Gusev (28,100)

Basic Facts

Population (as of 1 Jan. 1998): 943,000
(0.64% of Russian total)

Ethnic breakdown (1989 census): Russians
78.5%, Belarusans 8.5%, Ukrainians 7.2%,
Lithuanians 2.1%

Urban population (as of 1 Jan. 1998): 77.7%
(Russia overall: 73.1%)

Student population (as of 1 Sept. 1997): 161
per 10,000 (Russia overall: 208/10,000)

Pensioner population (1997): 22.8% (Russia
overall: 25.96%)

**Percent of population with higher education
(1989 census):** 12.4% (Russia overall: 11.3%)

Percent of population working in (1997):
Industry: 19.9% (Russian average: 23.0%);
Agriculture: 10.5% (13.7%); Trade: 18.7%
(13.5%); Culture: 11.7% (13.3%)

**Average monthly personal income in July
1998:** 578.3 new rubles (Russian average:
891.7 new rubles)

**Average monthly personal expenses in July
1998:** 491.2 new rubles (Russian average:
684.9 new rubles)

**Average monthly subsistence requirement in
1998:** 381 new rubles (Russian average: 438
new rubles)

Consumer price index (as of July 1998): 89
(Russia overall = 100)

Budgetary revenues (1997): 1,825.7 billion
rubles (Russia overall: 433,378.2
billion rubles)

Budgetary expenditures (1997): 2,087.1
billion rubles (Russia overall: 468,111.6
billion rubles)

**Industrial production as percentage of all
Russian production (Jan.–Aug. 1998):** 0.21%

**Proportion of loss-making enterprises (as of
July 1998):** 47.5 % (Russia overall: 50.4%)

**Number of enterprises which have wage
arrears (as of 1 Sept. 1998):** 335 (0.25%
of Russian total)

**Agricultural production as percentage of all
Russian production (1997):** 0.4%

Number of private farms (as of 1 Jan. 1998):
4,280 (1.6% of Russian total)

Capital investment (1997): 1,129.4 billion
rubles (Russia overall: 408,797 billion rubles)

Sources of investment (1997): federal budget:
12.8% (Russian average: 10.2%); regional
budget: 4.0% (10.5%); extra-budgetary funds:
83.2% (79.3%)

Foreign investment (1997): 11,292,000 USD
(Russia overall: 12,294,734,000 USD)

Number of joint ventures (1997): 317 (2.2%
of Russian total)

**Fixed capital investment in joint ventures and
foreign companies (1997):** 114,576 million
rubles (Russia overall: 16,265.4 billion rubles)

**Number of small businesses (as of 1 Jan.
1997):** 9,200 (1.06% of Russian total)

Number of enterprises privatized in 1997: 20
(0.73% of Russian total), including those which
used to be municipal property: 70.0% (Russian
average: 66.4%); regional property: 25.0%
(20.0%); federal property: 5.0% (13.6%)

Number of telephones per 100 families (1997):
in cities: 33.6 (Russian average: 49.2); in villages:
15.1 (19.8)

Brief Overview

Kaliningrad Oblast is the westernmost part of the Russian Federation, an exclave situated 600 km away from the rest of the country. It is sandwiched between Poland and Lithuania on the southern coast of the Baltic Sea. The region is 1,100 km from the closest Russian port, St. Petersburg, while only 500–800 km from the ports of Western Europe. The oblast is the smallest administrative unit of Russia but has the highest population density in the area and one of the highest in the Russian Federation. The City of Kaliningrad was founded in 1255 as Koenigsberg when the Germans expanded eastward. After World War II, it was assigned to the USSR and received its current name. Most of the German population was deported from the oblast in the years immediately following the war.

The region, which includes the Amber Free Economic Zone, is rich in various raw materials, including oil, peat, charcoal, and salt. It also claims 95 percent of world amber supplies. The main industries are machine building, metal processing, fisheries, and cellulose. Over half of the region's fish and cellulose is exported abroad, while the machine building and metal processing plants produce for the domestic market. Kaliningrad's seaports are of crucial importance for the economy of the region and the country at large—they can process up to 8 million tons of cargo annually, which is about 40 percent of Russia's total capacity in the Baltic region.

According to a 1998 survey by *Ekspert* magazine, the oblast is ranked 41st among Russia's 89 regions in terms of investment potential and 15th in terms of investment risk. The investment risk had grown by 14 points since 1997. A 1998 survey by Bank Austria ranked the oblast 39th in terms of investment climate.

Electoral History

2000 Presidential Election
Putin: 60.16%
Zyuganov: 23.48%
Yavlinskii: 6.26%
Zhirinovsky: 3.63%
Tuleev: 1.65%
Turnout: 67.09% (Russia overall: 68.64%)

1999 Parliamentary Elections
Unity: 33.45%
Communist Party of the Russian Federation: 19.75%
Fatherland–All Russia: 8.30%
Union of Right Forces: 8.29%
Zhirinovsky Bloc: 8.00%
Yabloko: 5.91%
In a single-mandate district: 1 independent
Turnout: 56.92% (Russia overall: 61.85%)

1996 Gubernatorial Election
Gorbenko: 22.29%/49.56% (first round/second round)
Matochkin (incumbent): 31.33%/40.44%
Semenov (oblast legislature deputy chairman, KPRF): 21.65%
Vasilev (oblast legislature deputy): 5.41%
Syrovatko: 4.81%
Makurov: 4.15%
Timofeev: 1.27%
Turnout: 43.9%/43.63%)

1996 Presidential Election
Yeltsin: 33.46%/57.69% (first round/second round)
Zyuganov: 23.08%/35.34%
Lebed: 19.31%
Yavlinskii: 12.85%
Zhirinovsky: 7.2%
Turnout: 71.71%/69.18% (Russia overall: 69.67%/68.79%)

1995 Parliamentary Elections
Communist Party of the Russian Federation: 19.30%
Liberal Democratic Party of Russia: 11.44%
Congress of Russian Communities: 9.18%
Our Home Is Russia: 8.55%
Yabloko: 8.16%
Party of Workers' Self-Government: 4.78%
Women of Russia: 4.68%
Communists–Workers' Russia: 3.37%
Russia's Democratic Choice: 3.26%
In a single-mandate district: 1 independent
Turnout: 63.77% (Russia overall: 64.37%)

1993 Constitutional Referendum
"Yes"—64.8%   "No"—32.9%

1993 Parliamentary Elections

Liberal Democratic Party of Russia: 29.96%

Russia's Choice: 19.96%

Communist Party of the Russian Federation: 10.40%

Women of Russia: 7.98%

Yabloko: 7.94%

Democratic Party of Russia: 7.58%

Party of Russian Unity and Concord: 5.21%

Agrarian Party of Russia: 3.03%

In a single-mandate district: 1 New Regional Policy

From electoral associations: 1 Liberal Democratic Party of Russia

Turnout: 59.81% (Russia overall: 54.34%)

1991 Presidential Election

Yeltsin: 39.09%

Ryzhkov: 23.76%

Zhirinovsky: 12.93%

Tuleev: 7.54%

Makashov: 4.56%

Bakatin: 4.09%

Turnout: 74.12% (Russia overall: 76.66%)

Regional Political Institutions

Executive:

Governor, 4-year term

Leonid Petrovich Gorbenko, elected October 1996

Ul. Dmitrii Donskoi, 1; Kaliningrad, 236007

Tel. 7(011–2) 46–75–45, 46–42–31;

Fax 7(011–2) 46–38–62

Federation Council in Moscow:

7(095) 292–12–87, 926–65–08

Legislation:

Unicameral

Oblast Duma—32 members, 4-year term, elected October 1996

Chairman—Valerii Nikolaevich Ustyugov, elected March 1994, October 1996

Regional Politics

Shadowy Figure Rules Russia's Exclave

Kaliningrad Oblast is the only Russian region that is not connected to the rest of the country. It borders countries that are developing faster and are likely soon to enter the European Union (EU). In fact, it could ultimately find itself an island of Russia within the EU. It is also not far from Aleksandr Lukashenko's Belarus. Kaliningrad Governor Leonid Gorbenko presents the image of a conservative, authoritarian manager. He is rumored to have connections with criminal circles, and will disappear for up to two weeks without any explanation, causing many residents to believe that Deputy Governor Mikhail Karetnii is the one really running the oblast.

In July 1998, *Izvestiya* reported that Gorbenko had created an atmosphere of suspicion and fear in Kaliningrad. The newspaper claimed that the governor's appointees lacked professionalism or moral sensibility. The article also asserted that Gorbenko had changed local customs regulations to impede the Kia automobile assembly venture in the oblast, and ruin Volkswagen's hopes to assemble cars in Kaliningrad. Gorbenko governs Kaliningrad according to his wishes, with little concern about Moscow's approval. He has insisted on limiting imports to the region and antagonized most of the region's Baltic neighbors.

Executive Platform: Self-Defined Authoritarian

Leonid Gorbenko has flirted with a variety of political positions. Both Aleksandr Lebed and Moscow Mayor Yurii Luzhkov supported his candidacy for governor in 1996. After coming in second to incumbent Yurii Matochkin in the first round, Gorbenko also picked up the support of Communist candidate Yurii Semenov. The Communist backing allowed Gorbenko to coast to a second-round triumph with a 10 percent victory margin. Gorbenko has also been lumped with governors known as "strong managers." These governors ran as independents with solid support from the business community. Their campaigns focused heavily on economic issues, and they tended to support Russian President Boris Yeltsin in political matters. In 1999 Gorbenko joined Samara Governor Konstantin Titov's Voice of Russia movement, but then became an early supporter of the Kremlin's new Unity bloc.

Although Gorbenko sided with Yeltsin on many issues, he constantly challenged Moscow's authority (see Ties to Moscow). Kaliningrad's exclave status greatly impacts political dynamics on regional, federal, and international levels. In many respects Gorbenko has ruled over the oblast as if it were a entity separate from Russia. Due to its location, Kaliningrad relies on imports much more than any other Russian region. Foreign policy is thus a vital component of the governor's job, and Gorbenko has tried to keep his relations with other states independent of Moscow—more so than Moscow would prefer. Kaliningrad is also treated as a special case in Russian domestic policy. Gorbenko has tried to take advantage of the region's exceptional status to govern the oblast as if it were exempt from many aspects of federal control.

Gorbenko's profiteering image evolved before he came to power. During his gubernatorial campaign, Gorbenko's opponents accused him of connections to Moscow's "criminal-political circles." Gorbenko also allegedly profited from corrupt business dealings during his decade-long tenure as head of the Kaliningrad port. He supposedly owned a $1 million house even though he received only a small salary as a state employee. Gorbenko's son has also been accused of selling oil on the black market with the help of the oblast administration.

In spite of the shady areas of Gorbenko's past, his career in management and his authoritative stature have served as assets in addressing social concerns. Gorbenko actively fights the problem of wage arrears, which has made him extremely popular among workers who are paid from the local budget. Kaliningrad experienced no widespread social unrest in response to the economic crisis following the August 1998 crash, which hit the import-reliant oblast particularly hard.

Policies: Protectionist

Most of Gorbenko's policies have focused on protecting the region's industries. He possesses a strong anti-trade sentiment, which is usually not beneficial for Kaliningrad, a region that relies on imports to fulfill basic consumer needs. Many of Gorbenko's import restrictions, particularly those limiting the amount of grain brought into the oblast, have hurt regional producers and increased prices for consumers (see also Attitudes Toward Business).

Gorbenko took his protectionism to the extreme following Russia's August 1998 financial crisis and subsequent panic. On 8 September 1998 he declared a state of emergency in the oblast, announcing that

he was assuming "complete responsibility for political and economic decisions." In making such a move, Gorbenko greatly overstepped his power, since only the president of the Russian Federation has the right to declare a state of emergency.

In spite of his protectionist tendencies, Gorbenko has also exhibited some sense of liberalism. In early 1998 he put forward a law calling for the sale and purchase of land in the oblast (see Relationships Between Key Players).

Gorbenko has also been active in addressing the problem of AIDS in Kaliningrad. Kaliningrad has the highest rate of HIV infection in the Russian Federation. Gorbenko suggested legalizing a few brothels and requiring medical check-ups for the prostitutes they employ in order to curtail the spread of AIDS. Yet, brothels are outlawed in the Russian Federation Criminal Code, and thus it is unlikely that Gorbenko's proposal will be adopted. However, the oblast did open up Russia's first needle exchange center, allowing drug users to exchange used needles for new ones free of charge. The exchange center also provides free AIDS tests and other medical services.

Relationships Between Key Players: Tense Relations with Oblast Duma

Gorbenko's relationship with the oblast Duma is tense, partially due to the governor's conflict with Duma Speaker Valerii Ustyugov. During one heated speech before the Duma, Gorbenko called the assembly a place where "all riffraff congregate" (*EWI RRR*, 11 September 1997). Thus it was no surprise that the Duma voted down a bill calling for the sale and purchase of land in January 1998. The bill was more radical than the law adopted in Saratov in November 1997 since it allowed agricultural land to be used for other purposes five years after it was sold. Gorbenko had ordered his staff to prepare a draft land law after the presidential administration had shown its support for the measure. President Yeltsin also expressed support for permitting new buyers to change the function of the land they purchased. An amended draft law passed its first reading in the oblast Duma in November 1998 (*EWI RRR*, 3 December 1998).

The Duma was in conflict with the governor regarding the use of budget funds in addressing the crisis that began on 17 August 1998, and appealed to President Yeltsin to send a commission to the oblast to intervene in the conflict.

Yurii Savenko was elected Mayor of Kaliningrad in October 1998. He is known for promoting stability and did not make any grandiose campaign promises. Savenko and the Kaliningrad city council are at odds with Gorbenko because he sought to put 50 percent of the income tax collected in Kaliningrad city into the oblast budget. Traditionally only 30 percent of this tax has gone into oblast coffers and Mayor Savenko thinks that even this amount is too much. Such battles between governors and mayors are typical throughout Russia.

In spite of this conflict, it seems that anyone would be more pleasing to Gorbenko than Kaliningrad's previous mayor, Igor Kozhemyakin. Gorbenko, as well as a number of city and oblast leaders, attempted to usurp power from the mayor in March 1998, claiming that the mayor had been sick "too often." Kozhemyakin died shortly thereafter, paving the way for Savenko's election.

More recently Gorbenko came into conflict with Kaliningrad port director Vladimir Boichenko and the presidential representative in Kaliningrad, Aleksandr Orlov, regarding the construction of an oil refinery in the region. Since oil products in Kaliningrad cost 80–130 percent more than they do in the rest of Russia, the region is in desperate need of its own refinery. Gorbenko wants to build a refinery separate from the port and withdraw the existing oil storage facilities from the port, while Boichenko and Orlov wanted to build a refinery as an integral part of the port, which belongs to the federal government. The oblast Duma also opposed Gorbenko's port proposition. Orlov claimed that the governor had no intention of actually building a refinery but intended to use the new legal entity to export oil abroad at a considerable profit. Both sides have had some success at lobbying their arguments and it remains uncertain which side will prevail.

Ties to Moscow

Gorbenko is in a constant struggle with the federal government to seize more power. Although Gorbenko was considered a Yeltsin supporter, he clearly dictates his own course of action and is not afraid to act outside of his authority.

Relations with Other Regions: Relatively Isolated

Kalinigrad's distant location and Gorbenko's independent-authoritative style of governance have caused the oblast to remain relatively isolated from other regions. During his campaign, Gorbenko struck a deal with Moscow Mayor Yurii Luzhkov for Kaliningrad to supply Moscow with fish and transport imported goods to the capital while Moscow would invest in several trawlers. However, this arrangement was more a campaign attempt to drum up additional electoral support than the beginning of a lasting economic initiative. Gorbenko also seems to admire the policies of Saratov Governor Dmitrii Ayatskov, choosing to model Kaliningrad's land reform bill on Ayatskov's initiative.

Kaliningrad belongs to the North-West Association, which includes the republics of Karelia and Komi; Arkhangelsk, Vologda, Kirov, Leningrad, Murmansk, Novgorod, and Pskov oblasts; Nenets Autonomous Okrug; and the city of St. Petersburg.

Foreign Relations: Baltic Antagonism

Due to Kaliningrad's exclave position, foreign relations play a greater role in Gorbenko's governance than do inter-regional affairs. However, Gorbenko is more focused on domestic issues than his predecessor Yurii Matochkin. He removed the entire international department of Matochkin's administration. Matochkin was a former minister who had many personal contacts in Moscow, but Gorbenko has a poor network outside of the oblast. He is also anti-trade, avoiding strong ties with the Baltic states. This policy has complicated the region's relations with Poland and Lithuania. Additionally, the signing of a free trade agreement between Lithuania and Poland and the establishment of a free economic zone in the Lithuanian region of Klaipeda are causing Kaliningrad to lose much of its shipping revenue from Poland.

In August 1997 Gorbenko banned the import of wheat, flour, and bread products from Lithuania and set new, higher prices for grain in order to protect local producers. Lithuania was greatly disturbed by this action. Although this measure was meant to help the oblast's bread producers, it has actually raised the prices they must pay for grain, thus increasing consumer prices as well.

In October 1997 President Yeltsin and Lithuanian President Algirdas Brazaukas signed a treaty delimiting the Russian-Lithuanian border, which consists solely of Kaliningrad's eastern border. Gorbenko had urged Yeltsin to proceed slowly with this agreement. The main point of contention was

Lake Vistytis, part of which was claimed by both Lithuania and Kaliningrad.

Brazaukas suggested multiple times that Lithuania should supply energy to Kaliningrad as a cheaper alternative to shipping it from Leningrad Oblast across the Baltic states. Russian authorities in Moscow object to this idea because they fear that it would make Kaliningrad dependent on its neighbor. After Gorbenko threatened to buy electricity from Lithuania, Russia's electricity monopoly, Unified Energy System, agreed to lower the rates it charged Kaliningrad by 50 percent.

Despite these tensions, relations between Lithuania and Kaliningrad appear to be improving. In summer 1998 at a meeting of the Baltic Council, Lithuania called for holding an international conference on Kaliningrad to discuss strengthening trade and other economic ties with the oblast. Lithuania hopes to improve cooperation between the Baltic countries and Kaliningrad. The character of such relations is becoming increasingly important as Kaliningrad's neighbors prepare to enter the European Union and the EU has designated Lithuania to develop relations with the Russian exclave. Gorbenko demonstrated his interest in improving Kaliningrad/Lithuanian relations by visiting Vilnius in October 1998. Lithuania also supplied Kaliningrad with food aid to help with the region's shortages in winter 1998–99.

Gorbenko also has disagreements with Latvia. In March 1998, following an incident considered threatening to Latvia's Russian minority, he requested that then-acting Prime Minister Sergei Kirienko impose economic sanctions against Latvia. Ninety percent of the cargo that comes through Latvian ports is from Russia, and Gorbenko would like to redirect that traffic through ports in St. Petersburg, Murmansk, and Kaliningrad.

Despite the obvious tensions, there are also signs that cooperation is possible. In February 1998 Kaliningrad Oblast signed an agreement with regions from five other countries aimed at establishing a "Baltic Euro-region." Representatives from regions in Poland, Denmark, Latvia, Lithuania, and Sweden also signed the accord, which promotes cooperation in economics, agriculture, transportation, environmental protection, and education.

In September 1997 the World Bank approved an overall $60 million credit for ecological programs in the forestry industry for Kaliningrad, Krasnoyarsk, and Khabarovsk.

In the wake of Russia's financial crisis, which was particularly devastating for import-reliant Kaliningrad, Gorbenko emphasized developing a program for economic cooperation with Belarus. He has suggested that Kaliningrad might play a role in settling debts between Russia and Belarus. This is an important step for Gorbenko, who in August 1997 refused to see Belarusan President Aleksandr Lukashenko after the arrest in Belarus of journalists from Russia's ORT television network.

Some parts of the oblast became quite desperate for help following the financial crisis of August 1998. Two oblast cities, Kaliningrad and Baltiisk, asked the Polish town of Elblag for humanitarian aid. Military units based in the region also requested food aid from Lithuania.

Attitudes Toward Business: Protectionism Turned Sour

Kaliningrad's isolated location has tremendously impacted its economic development. Kaliningrad was home to a free economic zone from 1991 to 1995 that sought to convert Kaliningrad into a Russian economic gateway. It is unclear why the free economic zone ended, yet some observers have suggested that the free economic zone's replacement with a special economic zone sent a signal to potential investors that Kaliningrad had not yet achieved a stable investment climate (*EWI RRR*, 9 April 1998). The creation of a special economic zone lowered prices on most goods, but has not served to attract investment that will revive the region's enterprises. Thus, most of the goods imported to the region duty-free, primarily alcohol and tobacco, are transshipped to the rest of Russia. In March 1998 the federal government issued a directive limiting the import of 35 different goods through Kaliningrad Oblast, thus weakening this privileged form of trade. Kaliningrad had been requesting such limitations for two years, reflecting Gorbenko's critical attitude toward trade. However, the import limitations fall below the actual needs of the oblast, thus hurting Kaliningrad consumers. Further import limitations were added in July 1998.

Many of Gorbenko's protectionist measures have served to hurt regional producers. Russia's largest chicken factory, Pribezhnaya, located in Kaliningrad, is on the verge of bankruptcy because of the high tariff imposed on the imported eggs needed to grow its chickens. The factory imports eggs from Holland since they yield saleable chickens after 40–42 days,

Leonid Petrovich Gorbenko

20 June 1939—Born in the village of Shenderovka in the Cherkas Oblast of Ukraine

1958—Graduated from the Kaliningrad Nautical School as a radio navigator

1958–1963—Worked as a hydro-acoustician and then as a radio navigator at the Atlantic Scientific Producers' Service

1970—Graduated from Kaliningrad Technical Institute with a degree in mechanics

1973–1980—Head engineer at a fishing seaport

1980–1986—Deputy general director of Kaliningradrybprom

1983—Graduated from the Moscow Institute of National Economy, Department of Industrial Production Organization

1986—Became head of the Kaliningrad Fishing Seaport

20 October 1996—Elected governor of Kaliningrad Oblast

13 November 1996—Appointed to the Federation Council

16 April 1997—Joined the Presidential Commission on improving federal relations

20 May 1998—Appointed deputy chair representing the Russian Federation in the chamber of regions of the Congress of Local and Regional Powers of Europe

Married with one son

---

whereas domestically produced eggs take 54–56 days to produce market-ready chickens. The longer turn-around from using domestic eggs significantly reduces the firm's profit margin.

The region has been only moderately successful at establishing relationships with foreign investors. Kaliningrad's Avtotor plant had been assembling cars for South Korea's Kia until the car manufacturer went bankrupt in summer 1998. Kia's project collapsed after the tax police seized two subsidiaries of Avtotor for failing to pay federal and oblast taxes. In fall 1998 the Kia-Baltika plant in Kaliningrad began restructuring its main production line to assemble BMWs. The plant produced the first BMW on 5 July 1999. Ultimately, the plant could assemble up to 20,000 BMW-523i and BMW-528i cars a year as well as some off-road Land Rovers. The Kaliningrad cars should cost about $40,000, 20 percent less than cars imported from Germany. So far, the Kaliningrad workers are only adding a few details in assembly kits shipped from Germany, but should do more in the future. Full-scale production was scheduled to start in September 1999 (*Kommersant Daily*, 6 July 1999).

The region is involved in some significant Russian projects. Gazprom is planning to build a pipeline connecting Kaliningrad with Tver Oblast.

Gazprom also intends to build a power station and underground gas facility at the pipeline's end point in Kaliningrad. In June 1997 LUKoil was granted permission to develop two oil fields in Kaliningrad Oblast. The fields are about 2,500 square km each, bordering Poland and Lithuania. They are estimated to contain 8 and 5.4 million tons of oil respectively.

One underdeveloped resource in Kaliningrad is the amber industry. Kaliningrad experts have estimated that the oblast holds 90 percent of the world's amber.

Internet Sites in the Region:

http://www.enet.ru/koi/city firms.html
This website offers a detailed list of firms and organizations working in Kaliningrad Oblast and their phone numbers. It is also possible to e-mail several of the officials listed straight from the website.

http://www.region.rags.ru/rus85.htm
This website provides basic information about foreign investment in Kaliningrad Oblast. However, the information has not been updated since 1996.

http://www.kp.koenig.su/
This is the home page for the weekly *Kaliningradskaya Pravda*. It features news stories, advertisements, and an archive. However, the site had not been updated since January 1998 in summer 1999.

REPUBLIC OF KALMYKIA (KHALMG TANGCH)

Territory: 76,100 km²
Population (as of 1 January 1998): 317,000
Distance from Moscow: 1,836 km

Major Cities:
Elista, *capital* (pop. 99,900)
Lagan (15,400)
Gorodovikovsk (10,600)

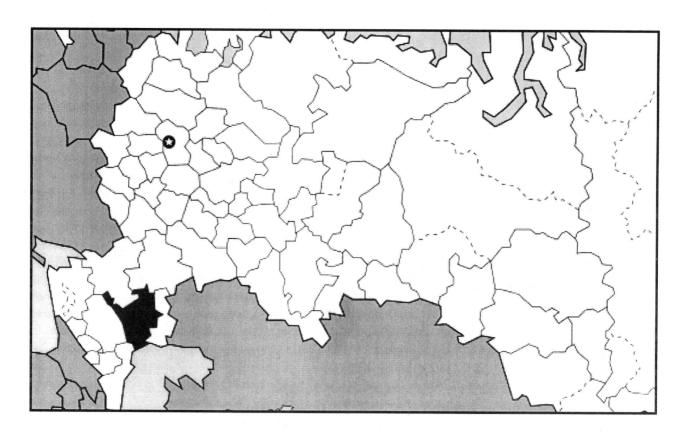

Basic Facts

Population (as of 1 Jan. 1998): 317,000 (0.22% of Russian total)

Ethnic breakdown (1989 census): Kalmyks 45.4%, Russians 37.7%, Dargins 4.0%, Chechens 2.6%, Kazakhs 2.0%, Germans 1.7%

Urban population (as of 1 Jan. 1998): 39.7% (Russia overall: 73.1%)

Student population (as of 1 Sept. 1997): 193 per 10,000 (Russia overall: 208/10,000)

Pensioner population (1997): 20.5% (Russia overall: 25.96%)

Percent of population with higher education (1989 census): 9.2% (Russia overall: 11.3%)

Percent of population working in (1997): Industry: 8.7% (Russian average: 23.0%); Agriculture: 29.4% (13.7%); Trade: 10.2% (13.5%); Culture: 16.6% (13.3%)

Average monthly personal income in July 1998: 406.1 new rubles (Russian average: 891.7 new rubles)

Average monthly personal expenses in July 1998: 187.1 new rubles (Russian average: 684.9 new rubles)

Average monthly subsistence requirement in 1998: 349 new rubles (Russian average: 438 new rubles)

Consumer price index (as of July 1998): 86 (Russia overall = 100)

Budgetary revenues (1997): 826.9 billion rubles (Russia overall: 433,378.2 billion rubles)

Budgetary expenditures (1997): 972.7 billion rubles (Russia overall: 468,111.6 billion rubles)

Industrial production as percentage of all Russian production (Jan.–Aug. 1998): 0.02%

Proportion of loss-making enterprises (as of July 1998): 76.8% (Russia overall: 50.4%)

Number of enterprises which have wage arrears (as of 1 Sept. 1998): 243 (0.18% of Russian total)

Agricultural production as percentage of all Russian production (1997): 0.25%

Number of private farms (as of 1 Jan. 1998): 1,662 (0.6% of Russian total)

Capital investment (1997): 347.3 billion rubles (Russia overall: 408,797 billion rubles)

Sources of investment (1997): federal budget: 49.3% (Russian average: 10.2%); regional budget: 2.8% (10.5%); extra-budgetary funds: 47.9% (79.3%)

Foreign investment (1997): 0 (Russia overall: 12,294,734,000 USD)

Number of joint ventures (1997): 2 (0.01% of Russian total)

Fixed capital investment in joint ventures and foreign companies (1997): 0 (Russia overall: 16,265.4 billion rubles)

Number of small businesses (as of 1 July 1998): 1,300 (0.15% of Russian total)

Number of enterprises privatized in 1997: 5 (0.18% of Russian total), including those which used to be municipal property: 100% (Russian average: 66.4%); regional property: 0% (20.0%); federal property: 0% (13.6%)

Number of telephones per 100 families (1997): in cities: 64.1 (Russian average: 49.2); in villages: 37.8 (19.8)

Brief Overview

The Republic of Kalmykia lies in the southeast of European Russia in the North Caspian Depression and borders Volgograd, Astrakhan, and Rostov oblasts, Stavropol Krai, and the Republic of Dagestan. Its western border parallels the lower reaches of the Volga River (with a small corridor providing access to the river at Tsagan-Aman), stretching further southward along the shores of the Caspian Sea to the Kuma River. To the east, the republic reaches the Yergeni hills. Except for these hills, where irrigation farming is possible, the steppes, semi-deserts and deserts, which cover the republic's territory, allow only livestock breeding.

The economy is therefore dominated by the production and partial processing of wool, leather, and meat. However, the republic also houses some machine building, metal processing, and construction materials industries. The Kalmyk part of the Caspian Sea shelf is thought to contain oil. Uranium mining ended in the southwest part of the republic 20 years ago, and has left seriously contaminated soils.

The Kalmyks, who account for about 45 percent of the republic's population and continue to grow, came to the territory as a nomadic people from Central Asia in the 17th century. They established the famous Khanate of Chan Ayuki, a loyal ally of the Russian state. However, those living on the eastern bank of the Volga left again in 1771 for Dsungaria in what is now northwest China as a consequence of the increasing Russian settlement. Those who stayed gained an autonomous oblast in 1920 and an ASSR in 1935. In 1943, the Kalmyk population was deported to Siberia for alleged collaboration with the German occupiers. About one-third of them died between that time and 1957, when they were allowed to return and reestablish the ASSR. The Kalmyks constitute a western branch of the Mongols both linguistically and ethnically, and practice a Tibetan, Lamaist form of Buddhism. Buddhists were persecuted during the Soviet era, but recently the religion has experienced a revival.

The republic is one of the most heavily subsidized in the federation. In 1997, Kalmykia's own revenues covered only 32.2 percent of its budget, according to a survey by *Ekspert* magazine. According to the same survey, the investment climate in the republic has been consistently getting worse:

the republic in 1998 ranked 81st among Russia's 89 regions in terms of investment potential and 80th in terms of investment risk. A 1998 survey by Bank Austria ranked the republic 81st in terms of investment climate.

Electoral History

2000 Presidential Election
Putin: 56.26%
Zyuganov: 32.21%
Tuleev: 3.73%
Yavlinskii: 1.75%
Zhirinovsky: 1.25%
Turnout: 69.76% (Russia overall: 68.64%)

1999 Parliamentary Elections
Unity: 34.91%
Communist Party of the Russian Federation: 25.81%
Fatherland–All Russia: 10.27%
Communists–Workers' Russia: 4.00%
Union of Right Forces: 3.80%
Zhirinovsky Bloc: 3.19%
Yabloko: 3.07%
In a single-mandate district: 1 Unity
Turnout: 64.33% (Russia overall: 61.85%)

1996 Presidential Election
Yeltsin: 58.49%/70.27% (first round/second round)
Zyuganov: 25.72%/26.71%
Lebed: 5.42%
Zhirinovsky: 3.57%
Yavlinskii: 2.50%
Turnout: 75.66%/73.36% (Russia overall: 69.67%/ 68.79%)

1995 Parliamentary Elections
Our Home Is Russia: 24.00%
Communist Party of the Russian Federation: 17.92%
Agrarian Party of Russia: 15.46%
Liberal Democratic Party of Russia: 9.62%
Communists–Workers' Russia: 6.48%
Women of Russia: 2.83%
Yabloko: 2.50%
Party of Workers' Self-Government: 1.75%
In a single-mandate district: 1 Agrarian Party of Russia
Turnout: 67.45% (Russia overall: 64.37%)

1995 Republican Presidential Election
Ilyumzhinov (incumbent): 86.23%
Turnout: 77.33%

1993 Constitutional Referendum
"Yes"—48.7% "No"—45.9%

1993 Parliamentary Elections
Liberal Democratic Party of Russia: 20.30%
Communist Party of the Russian Federation:
   14.18%
Agrarian Party of Russia: 11.63%
Women of Russia: 10.51%
Russia's Choice: 10.24%
Party of Russian Unity and Concord: 8.91%
Democratic Party of Russia: 8.13%
Yabloko: 4.78%
In a single-mandate district: 1 independent
Turnout: 57.76% (Russia overall: 54.34%)

1991 Presidential Elections
Yeltsin: 31.06%
Ryzhkov: 27.70%
Tuleev: 18.68%
Zhirinovsky: 10.36%
Makashov: 4.48%
Bakatin: 2.68%
Turnout: 77.65% (Russia overall: 76.66%)

Regional Political Institutions

Executive:
   President, 7-year term
   Kirsan Nikolaevich Ilyumzhinov, elected 1993,
   October 1995
      Republic of Kalmykia Presidential Administration;
      Dom Pravitelstva; Elista, 358000;
      Republic of Kalmykia
      Tel 7(847–22) 5–06–55, 6–13–88;
      Fax 7(847–22) 6–28–80
      Federation Council in Moscow:
      7(095) 292–42–27, 926–67–92

Legislative:
   Unicameral
   Narodnyi Khural—27 members, 4-year term,
   elected October 1998
   Chairman—Vyacheslav Anatolevich
   Bembetov, elected February 1999

Regional Politics

Eccentric Leader Stresses Chess and Buddhism

Although the Republic of Kalmykia is relatively obscure, President Kirsan Ilyumzhinov has made a big name for himself at home and abroad. Ilyumzhinov combines his state duties with the presidency of the International Chess Federation (FIDE). He amassed a multi-million-dollar fortune in the early 1990s as the head of a trading company. He then converted his wealth into political power, winning the republican presidency in 1993. Ilyumzhinov's core political philosophy is that Kalmykia should work like a giant corporation, and he does not shy away from ostentatiously displaying his wealth to demonstrate his personal financial acumen. He claimed that his 1997 earnings were 5,799,570,394 rubles ($1 million) and that he had paid taxes on the full amount. While the tax service did not question the source of his income, *Izvestiya*, which reported the immodest gains, did (*EWI RRR*, 8 January 1998). Ilyumzhinov drives around Elista, the republic's capital, in one of his four white Rolls Royces. Overall, he owns 36 cars which are garaged in a variety of cities around the world so that the president can use them when he travels (*Izvestiya*, 21 July 1998).

Chess is Ilyumzhinov's main obsession. He has decreed that chess should be taught in Kalmykia's schools and children must play the game at least twice a week. Government bureaucrats usually keep a set conspicuously handy in their offices. Critics claimed that Ilyumzhinov deprived mothers of welfare subsidies for their children in order to complete the construction of an expensive Chess City—the site for the Chess Olympiad in September 1998. Leading up to the Olympiad, 2,500 construction workers worked 12-hour days, 6-days a week to complete as much of the $150 million city as possible before the games began (*Izvestiya*, 21 July 1998.)

The president's other obsession is Buddhism, the traditional religion of the Kalmyks. While residents of his poor republic struggle to make ends meet, Ilyumzhinov has spent lavish sums building a new temple complete with a gold-plated statue of Buddha. Ilyumzhinov pays for the temples out of his own pocket, but it is not clear where the money initially came from. He has also invited the Dalai Lama to make his permanent residence in Kalmykia, but the exiled Tibetan leader has agreed only to pay a visit.

Beyond Ilyumzhinov's eccentric flamboyance, there is a more sinister side to his reputation. Ilyumzhinov represses all opposition parties and media in the republic. On 8 June 1998, Kalmykia's most outspoken opposition journalist, Larisa Yudina, was found murdered with multiple stab wounds and a fractured skull not far from the Chess City construction site. Several close associates of Ilyumzhinov have been arrested under suspicion of committing the crime, though no one has been convicted of the murder yet. One suspect, Tyurbya Boskhomdzhiev, was the president's personal representative in Volgograd and the other, Sergei Vaskin, was one of his aides (*NG*, 16 June 1998). At the time of her death, Yudina had been investigating the corrupt business practices of regional officials.

Executive Platform: Promoting Kalmykia Through Chess

Already a multi-millionaire, 30-year-old Ilyumzhinov was first elected president on 11 April 1993. The young president became rich in the early nineties through his diversified trading company, San. His campaign slogan in 1993 was that he would make everyone in his impoverished republic rich since he had already acquired successful experience accumulating his own personal fortune. In keeping with that philosophy, he declared that Kalmykia should become one gigantic firm, "Corporation Kalmykia."

During the republican presidential election campaign, Ilyumzhinov used his own resources to provide a special 50 percent discount on bread and milk for the residents of Elista. He also gave a Mercedes-Benz to the local police and a Zhiguli (popular Russian car) to the head priest of the main Russian Orthodox church. Additionally, Ilyumzhinov promised to give every Kalmyk $100. At the same time, there were rumors that several million dollars had disappeared from the republic's treasury.

Ilyumzhinov believes that chess is the market niche Kalmykia can fill to succeed in the global economy. He was elected president of the International Chess Federation (FIDE) in November 1995 and put Kalmykia on the map by hosting the 1996 world championships between Anatolii Karpov and Gata Kamsky. Ilyumzhinov has sought to turn Kalmykia into a world center for chess, building a Chess City complete with a chess palace and hotel facilities to host international competitions. The region's hosting of the 1998 Chess Olympiad generated substantial media attention.

Policies: Preserving Personal Power

The common thread to Ilyumzhinov's unusual political philosophy and seemingly wacky policy initiatives is the preservation of his own political power. Among Ilyumzhinov's first moves in office was disbanding the republican legislature. The next legislature voted in August 1995 to extend his term until the year 2000. The next day, however, Ilyumzhinov decided that the legislature's support was insufficient for a leader of his stature, and he called pre-term presidential elections for 15 October 1995. Running unopposed, Ilyumzhinov won 85 percent of the vote for a seven-year term. Russia's Central Electoral Commission said that the elections were not valid because there had been no alternative candidate, but the federal authorities dropped their complaint against him in January 1997 when it became inconvenient to pursue it. When it comes to regional leaders, the Kremlin values stability over observing the fine points of electoral democracy and Ilyumzhinov was doing a good job diffusing any potential trouble.

On 16 February 1998 Ilyumzhinov issued a decree abolishing his government. He explained the move as an attempt to restructure the executive branch, making it better able to address issues of economic reform (*Segodnya*, 17 February 1998).

In March 1999 the Kalmykia legislature passed a law seeking to develop the regional gaming business. The law establishes easy licensing requirements to open casinos and eliminates regional taxes on the businesses. Additionally, it makes Kalmykia the first region to make it possible to set up a casino on the Internet that is accessible to anyone with access to the international computer network (*FI*, 16 March 1999).

Relationships Between Key Players: Khanate

Ilyumzhinov is a proponent of strong presidential rule and effectively controls the local elite. The October 1998 Narodnyi Khural elections produced a pro-Ilyumzhinov legislature. Such loyalty is not surprising since Ilyumzhinov personally appointed one-third of the parliament's members. The Republic of Kalmykia does not have a constitution as such. Its basic law is the *Stepnoye Ulozheniye* (which means "the law of the steppes" and implicitly refers to laws that were used during the period of Kievan Rus). Ten out of fourteen paragraphs of this document contradict the Russian Constitution.

In January 1999 the Narodnyi Khural dismissed the republic's prime minister, Viktor Baturin. Baturin, who had been appointed by Ilyumzhinov to the post just over two months before, is the brother-in-law of Moscow Mayor Yurii Luzhkov. The legislature, the mayor of Kalmykia's capital city Elista, and the leaders of the republic's rural areas stormed out against Baturin because he was trying to force greater fiscal discipline on the republic. This event left Ilyumzhinov in an awkward position. He felt that it was important to support the local leaders, yet clearly wanted to maintain his good relationship with Luzhkov. Baturin had helped considerably in the construction of the republic's Chess City. Ultimately Ilyumzhinov accepted the Khural's decision, and proceeded to appoint Baturin as his state advisor. This position had been held by Ilyumzhinov's older brother (*EWI RRR*, 28 January 1999).

The people of Kalmykia often call Ilyumzhinov the "khan." He does not mind, but prefers to be called *khozyain* (master). In his speeches he often makes references to the centuries of the khans' rule in Kalmykia.

The murder of Larisa Yudina focused attention on the issue of press freedom and also brought a lot of negative attention to Ilyumzhinov. Yudina was the editor of the only independent paper left in the republic, *Sovetskaya Kalmykia*. The president effectively controls the rest of the local media. In August 1994 the republic registered a second newspaper under the name *Sovetskaya Kalmykia* and took away much of the property belonging to Yudina's paper. In the summer and fall of 1994, republican kiosks sold both newspapers, forcing the salesmen to ask customers which of the two they wanted. In 1995, the authorities banned sales of Yudina's paper. Following that crackdown, the paper was printed in Volzhskii (Volgograd Oblast) with a print-run of 4,000 because that was as many as fit into a Zhiguli, the car Yudina used to distribute her publication. Initially, the publisher printed

the newspaper without any guarantee that it would be paid, but since 1997 the Yabloko party has financed the costs. The paper ultimately had to change its name to *Sovetskaya Kalmykia Segodnya* in order to win registration. Yudina's paper carried negative reports on Ilyumzhinov, drawing attention to alleged corruption and misused finances in the republican administration. The fact that Yudina's body was found near the site of the Chess City further implicated Ilyumzhinov in connection with her death. Yabloko's national leaders have worked hard to bring attention to the case.

In October 1998 Russia's Deputy Procurator General Vladimir Ustinov and Kalmykia Procurator Yurii Dzhapov sent a declaration to Kalmykia's Supreme Court requesting that the republic's October 1998 legislative elections be declared invalid. The procurators' claim was that the republic lacks legitimate local government, and since the local government formed the electoral committees, the elections were not legitimate (*Izvestiya*, 30 October 1998).

Ecological issues are high on Kalmykia's agenda. The republic is home to Europe's first desert. Desertification affects 82 percent of the republic's territory and is severe over 43 percent of the land. The crisis is a result of over-grazing, primarily by sheep, and the introduction of irrigation-based farming (*Interpress*, 10 June 1997).

Ties to Moscow: Support May Be Evolving Toward Opposition

While maintaining tight control at home, Ilyumzhinov assiduously courted the favor of Yeltsin's administration. In the early 1990s Ilyumzhinov vigorously supported the integrity of the Russian Federation and opposed "the madness of sovereignties" (NNS). After appearing to side with Russian Supreme Soviet Speaker Ruslan Khasbulatov in the September–October 1993 showdown, Ilyumzhinov later renounced his republic's sovereignty in an apparent attempt to curry favor with the president. Other republican leaders in Russia strongly protested the move since they feared that it would infringe on their prerogatives. Additionally, election observers say that Ilyumzhinov carried out massive fraud in the 1996 Russian presidential election to win greater support from Yeltsin.

Just as the Moscow media were filled with stories

about the murder of journalist Yudina, Ilyumzhinov announced on 14 June 1998 that he would compete in the Russian presidential elections in 2000. (In the end he supported Unity.) Then in November 1998 Ilyumzhinov raised considerable concern in Moscow when he told Russian Public Television (ORT) that Kalmykia considered itself "de facto, outside of the Russian Federation" since Moscow failed to send money to the republic. The State Duma condemned Ilyumzhinov for his statement, prompting rumors that the republican president would be removed from power (*RFE/RL*, 19 November 1998). Ilyumzhinov quickly retracted his remarks, claiming that the statements were simply meant to draw attention to the region's plight.

Relations with Other Regions: Off Shore Zone Antagonizes Neighbors

The Republic of Kalmykia does not get along with its neighbors. One of the main points of dispute is the republic's special economic zone which gives companies registered in the republic special tax breaks. Numerous businesses from neighboring regions register in Elista thereby depriving the regions where they actually operate of considerable tax revenue. Volgograd Governor Nikolai Maksyuta denounced this law in June 1998, complaining that his region lost 170 million new rubles ($28 million) in taxes during the first five months of the year. Maksyuta's determination to dismantle the zone was strengthened after he learned that 50 regions suffer from Kalmykia's tax laws (*EWI RRR*, 25 June 1998). Federal authorities have not objected to this law because Kalmykia paid its taxes on time. But if other governors oppose the offshore zone, it might soon disappear.

There have been other disputes with neighboring regions as well. For instance, Kalmykia is trying to steal the initiative from Astrakhan by building its own seaport in Lagan for a railway-and-ferry connection to the Iranian port of Amir-Abad. Construction was to be complete at the end of 1999, setting up possible competition with Astrakhan/ Olya. However, the Lagan port will operate in a shallow area of the Caspian Sea, a constraint that may prove problematic in the future (*EWI RRR*, 19 March 1998).

Ilyumzhinov has good relations with Moscow Mayor Yurii Luzhkov. Luzhkov provided considerable financial resources as well as construction workers for Ilyumzhinov to build his Chess City. Ilyumzhinov also won support from Tatarstan President Mintimer Shaimiev, who helped to soothe Ilyumzhinov's relations with the center in the fall of 1998, following his apparently separatist remarks.

Foreign Relations

Ilyumzhinov is fluent in English and Japanese; he also understands Chinese, Korean, and Turkish (*RG*, 25 April 1996).

Attitudes Toward Business: Grand Schemes, Few Results

Ilyumzhinov hopes that the chess games will give the republic wide international publicity that will attract western businessmen to invest in everything from oil processing plants to a port on the Caspian to public videophones on the streets of the capital. None of the plans are likely to be implemented any time soon, however. Kalmykia currently produces 350,000 tons of oil a year, but it would need to produce at least one million to make building the processing plant worthwhile. This goal may not be completely unrealistic. Some estimates suggest that Kalmykia has reserves of between 400 and 800 million tons of oil (including up to 400 million tons from the Caspian Sea).

To foster investment in Kalmykia and register offshore companies, Ilyumzhinov created ARIS— the Agency for Development and Cooperation. Journalist Yudina was investigating the conduct of ARIS when she was murdered.

Internet Sites in the Region:

http://kirsan.kalmykia.ru/epigr.htm
President Ilyumzhinov's personal home page offers his biography in comics, a photo album, and some of the few articles that say something positive about him. You can also find a link to the FIDE site. Kalmykia is presented as a paradise on earth. Under the link "friends" you will find pictures of the Pope John Paul II and the famous psychic Vanga.

http://www.infoline.ru/g23/3525/index.htm
This site describes the Chess City. You can check out models of palaces and residential buildings in development. You can also see the heroes of

Kirsan Nikolaevich Ilyumzhinov

5 April 1962—Born in Elista

1976—Won Kalmykia's chess championship

1979—Finished school with high honors

1979–1980—Working at "Zvezda" plant in Elista

1980–1982—Served in the Soviet Army

1982–1983—Worked as a youth brigade-leader at "Zvezda"

1989—Graduated from MGIMO in Moscow (International Relations Institute—the elite school for Soviet and Russian diplomats); became a specialist in international trade with Asian countries and Japanese affairs

1989–1990—Chief manager of the Soviet-Japanese joint venture "Raduga" (Rainbow)

1990–1993—President of "San" corporation

1991—Quit the CPSU

1991–1993—Deputy of the Supreme Soviet of the Russian Federation; Ilyumzhinov was a member of the Committee on Foreign Relations and Foreign Trade and the faction Smena (New Politics)

1992—Elected president of the Russian Federation Chamber of Entrepreneurs

11 April 1993—Elected president of the Republic of Kalmykia (Khalmg-Tangch)

November 1993—Became a deputy of the Federation Council winning a landslide victory with 75.3 percent of the vote

September–October 1993—During the clash between Yeltsin and the Russian parliament, Ilyumzhinov tried to mediate; Ilyumzhinov was inside the Supreme Soviet building as Yeltsin's tanks shelled it.

15 October 1995—Reelected president for a seven-year term with 85 percent of the vote

Ethnic Kalmyk

Married, with one child

Kalmykia—the president and his favorite ministers—and read their biographies written in the best traditions of socialist realism and *Pionerskaya Pravda*. There is also some information about Kalmykian history and chess playing in Kalmykia.

http://www.yabloko.ru/news/judina.html
The Yabloko party site provides the latest developments in the Yudina murder investigation. There is also a lot of information about Ilyumzhinov and politics in Kalmykia.

KALUGA OBLAST

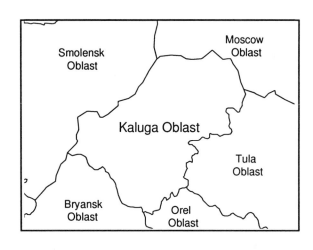

Territory: 29,900 km²
Population (as of 1 January 1998): 1,094,000
Distance from Moscow: 188 km

Major Cities:
Kaluga, *capital* (pop. 345,000)
Obninsk (109,900)
Lyudinovo (44,200)
Kirov (40,500)
Maloyaroslavets (29,300)

Basic Facts

Population (as of 1 Jan. 1998): 1,094,000 (0.74% of Russian total)

Ethnic breakdown (1989 census): Russians 93.8%, Ukrainians 2.8%

Urban population (as of 1 Jan. 1998): 74.4% (Russia overall: 73.1%)

Student population (as of 1 Sept. 1997): 107 per 10,000 (Russia overall: 208/10,000)

Pensioner population (1997): 25.78% (Russia overall: 25.96%)

Percent of population with higher education (1989 census): 11.1% (Russia overall: 11.3%)

Percent of population working in (1997): Industry: 26.9% (Russian average: 23.0%); Agriculture: 10.3% (13.7%); Trade: 11.3% (13.5%); Culture: 13.8% (13.3%)

Average monthly personal income in July 1998: 581.2 new rubles (Russian average: 891.7 new rubles)

Average monthly personal expenses in July 1998: 426.4 new rubles (Russian average: 684.9 new rubles)

Average monthly subsistence requirement in 1998: 352 new rubles (Russian average: 438 new rubles)

Consumer price index (as of July 1998): 95 (Russia overall = 100)

Budgetary revenues (1997): 2,092.6 billion rubles (Russia overall: 433,378.2 billion rubles)

Budgetary expenditures (1997): 2,322.0 billion rubles (Russia overall: 468,111.6 billion rubles)

Industrial production as percentage of all Russian production (Jan.–Aug. 1998): 0.32%

Proportion of loss-making enterprises (as of July 1998): 47.5% (Russia overall: 50.4%)

Number of enterprises which have wage arrears (as of 1 Sept. 1998): 2,423 (0.14% of Russian total)

Agricultural production as percentage of all Russian production (1997): 0.87%

Number of private farms (as of 1 Jan. 1998): 1,986 (0.72% of Russian total)

Capital investment (1997): 1,690.8 billion rubles (Russia overall: 408,797 billion rubles)

Sources of investment (1997): federal budget: 18.0% (Russian average: 10.2%); regional budget: 5.1% (10.5%); extra-budgetary funds: 76.9% (79.3%)

Foreign investment (1997): 994,000 USD (Russia overall: 12,294,734,000 USD)

Number of joint ventures (1997): 26 (0.18% of Russian total)

Fixed capital investment in joint ventures and foreign companies (1997): 11,313 million rubles (Russia overall: 16,265.4 billion rubles)

Number of small businesses (as of 1 July 1998): 6,200 (0.71% of Russian total)

Number of enterprises privatized in 1997: 31 (1.13% of Russian total), including those which used to be municipal property: 83.9% (Russian average: 66.4%); regional property: 0% (20.0%); federal property: 16.1% (13.6%)

Number of telephones per 100 families (1997): in cities: 54.6 (Russian average: 49.2); in villages: 16.2 (19.8)

Brief Overview

Kaluga Oblast is located in central Russia and borders Moscow, Tula, Orel, Bryansk, and Smolensk oblasts. The oblast center, the city of Kaluga, is located 190 km southwest of Moscow. Until 1917, the region was one of the most industrially backward areas in the country; however, it was industrialized during the first decades of the Soviet regime.

Almost half (49 percent) of regional GDP comes from machine-building and metal-processing industries, followed by food processing (20.1 percent) and light industries (16.6 percent). Most of the machine-building industry is concentrated in Kaluga city, Ludinovo, and Kirov and specializes in energy, transport, aerospace and electronic equipment, and machine-tool construction. Nonferrous metals, steam locomotives, electric transformers, and steam turbines are exported from the region to over 40 foreign countries. The second largest city in the area, Obninsk, houses Russia's first nuclear power plant as well as many research institutes. Over 100 regional companies have won foreign investment from 22 countries.

Although the oblast lacks special legislation offering investment incentives, investment risk declined there by 13 points between 1997 and 1998. According to a 1998 *Ekspert* survey, the oblast is ranked 40th among Russia's 89 regions in terms of investment potential and 23rd in terms of risk. A 1998 survey by Bank Austria ranked the oblast 47th in terms of investment climate.

Electoral History

2000 Presidential Election
Putin: 50.98%
Zyuganov: 33.80%
Yavlinskii: 5.56%
Zhirinovsky: 2.26%
Tuleev: 1.92%
Turnout: 69.38% (Russia overall: 68.64%)

1999 Parliamentary Elections
Communist Party of the Russian Federation: 29.44%
Unity: 20.89%
Fatherland–All Russia: 12.62%
Union of Right Forces: 7.62%

Yabloko: 5.93%
Zhirinovsky Bloc: 5.73%
In single-mandate districts: 2 Communist Party of the Russian Federation
Turnout: 62.82% (Russia overall: 61.85%)

1996 Gubernatorial Election
Sudarenkov (oblast legislature chairman): 63.51%/ 45.76% (first round/second round)
Savchenko (incumbent): 30.48%/39.63%
Pushkin (LDPR): 3.57%
Vasilkov: 0%
Turnout: 43.1%/40.96%

1996 Presidential Election
Yeltsin: 31.43%/48.59% (first round/second round)
Zyuganov: 35.42%/45.58%
Lebed: 15.60%
Yavlinskii: 7.46%
Zhirinovsky: 5.11%
Turnout: 72.85%/71.26% (Russia overall: 69.67%/ 68.79%)

1995 Parliamentary Elections
Communist Party of the Russian Federation: 25.99%
Liberal Democratic Party of Russia: 10.01%
Our Home Is Russia: 9.02%
Congress of Russian Communities: 6.56%
Yabloko: 5.33%
Agrarian Party of Russia: 4.42%
Communists–Workers' Russia: 4.42%
In single-mandate districts: 1 Agrarian Party of Russia, 1 Pamfilova–Gurov–Lysenko bloc
Turnout: 68.17% (Russia overall: 64.37%)

1993 Constitutional Referendum
"Yes"—49.6%   "No"—48.4%

1993 Parliamentary Elections
Liberal Democratic Party of Russia: 28.06%
Russia's Choice: 16.58%
Communist Party of the Russian Federation: 14.31%
Agrarian Party of Russia: 10.13%
Yabloko: 6.97%
Women of Russia: 6.80%
Democratic Party of Russia: 5.30%
Party of Russian Unity and Concord: 4.62%

In single-mandate districts: 1 Russia's Choice, 1 Agrarian Party of Russia
From electoral associations: 1 Women of Russia
Turnout: 63.74% (Russia overall: 54.34%)

1991 Presidential Election
Yeltsin: 54.77%
Ryzhkov: 19.23%
Zhirinovsky: 8.58%
Tuleev: 5.98%
Makashov: 3.86%
Bakatin: 3.75%
Turnout: 82.55% (Russia overall: 76.66%)

Regional Political Institutions

Executive:
Governor, 4–year term
Valerii Vasilevich Sudarenkov, elected November 1996
Kaluga Oblast Administration;
Pl. Staryi Torg, 2; Kaluga, 248661
Tel 7(084–22) 56–23–57;
Fax 7(084–22) 53–13–09
Federation Council in Moscow:
7(095) 292–59–03, 926–65–49,
Fax 7(095) 292–59–03

Legislative:
Unicameral
Legislative Assembly (*Zakonodatelnoe Sobranie*)—40 members, 4-year term, elected August and October 1996
Chairman—Viktor Mikhailovich Kolesnikov, elected November 1996

Regional Politics

Communist with Presidential Support

Valerii Sudarenkov, the former Communist chairman of the oblast legislature, beat out Yeltsin appointee Oleg Savchenko on 9 November 1996 with a 63–31 percent margin to secure the governor's seat in Kaluga Oblast. Although Sudarenkov was supported by the Communists during the election, he also maintained good relations with the presidential administration. Then First Deputy Presidential Chief of Staff Aleksandr Kazakov described Sudarenkov as a reasonable and experienced politician.

Executive Platform: Mix of Liberal and Conservative Ideas

Sudarenkov subscribes to a left-of-center ideology. Although he is not a Communist party member and does not adhere to a consistent Communist platform, the local Communists have plenty of reasons to support him. After his election, Sudarenkov fired the key officials responsible for agriculture, industry, social policy, and health care, and replaced them with old party comrades. The governor has spoken out against importing foreign goods into Russia, and in favor of protecting Russian industries involved in foreign trade (NNS). He hopes to revive the region's economy without the aid of foreign investors. Sudarenkov claims that if Kaluga could keep 70 percent of the tax revenues collected in the oblast while sending 30 percent to Moscow, rather than the current 50/50 arrangement, the region's financial difficulties would be solved (*FR*, 16 January 1998). The governor has suggested increasing federal subsidies to the agro-industrial complex, evening out the income gap between urban and rural areas, and establishing standards for controlling the purchase and sale of land (NNS). He has also expressed a strong desire to eliminate unemployment in the oblast. Unlike many governors, he stresses the need to develop local government.

Sudarenkov's conservative side also came to the fore in regard to the controversial law "On Freedom of Conscience and Religious Associations" which was approved on 4 July 1997 by the Federation Council. This law limits the activities of missionaries and the rights of religious associations that are not included under the rubric of "all-Russia religious organizations" (Orthodoxy, Islam, Judaism, and Buddhism). Sudarenkov supported the law as necessary to "protect society from the massive expansion of pseudo-religious cults and organizations that through their proselytizing endanger individual rights and freedoms, and the health of citizens" (*RFE/RL*, 7 July 1997).

Policies: Economically Based

One of Sudarenkov's first priorities after his election was to examine the privatization deals made in Kaluga and overturn those in which state property had been sold at very low prices.

Valerii Vasilevich Sudarenkov

13 June 1940—Born in the village Nizhnie Gorki in the Maloyaroslavetskii Raion of Kaluga Oblast

1960–1963—Served in the Pacific Ocean Fleet

1963—Joined the Communist Party and remained a member until it was disbanded in August 1991

1964–1972—Worked at the Kaluga Oblast technical school, as an engineer-technician of a turbine factory, as a senior engineer, office head, and head of the shop of a motor factory

1969—Graduated from the Kaluga branch of the Moscow Higher Technical School

1972–1984—Worked as an instructor, assistant department manager, and manager of the defense industry department of the Kaluga Oblast CPSU Committee

1979—Graduated from the Moscow Higher Party School

1984–1986—First secretary of the Kaluga CPSU City Committee

1986–1990—Assistant to the Chairman of the Uzbek Republic Council of Ministers

27 February 1990–August 1991—First secretary of the CPSU Kaluga Oblast Committee

March 1990—Elected to the Kaluga Oblast Council of People's Deputies, serving as the chairman from April 1990 to December 1993

July 1990–August 1991—Member of the CPSU Central Committee

1990—Resigned as the First Secretary of the CPSU Kaluga Oblast Committee

October 1993—Participated in the Federation Council

12 December 1993—Elected to the first assembly of the Federation Council and served on the Committee for Science, Culture, and Education from January 1994 to January 1996

March 1994– Elected to the Kaluga Obast Legislative Assembly; April 1994, became chairman; August 1996, lost seat in elections

January 1996—Appointed to the second assembly of the Federation Council and became chairman of the Committee for Science, Culture, Education, Public Health, and Ecology

March 1996—Became a member of the Russian delegation to annual sessions of the Council of Europe

9 November 1996—Elected governor of Kaluga Oblast

Married, with two daughters and two grandsons

Sudarenkov signed an arrangement with directors of regional banks, the "agreement on cooperative intentions in the cultivation and realization of investment policies in Kaluga Oblast," in 1997 (*Delovaya Provintsiya*, 1–7 July 1997). This agreement attempted to establish guidelines for introducing lucrative credit projects with bank guarantees in the region (*Vest*, 14 June 1997).

Ties to Moscow

Although Sudarenkov beat out former presidential representative and Yeltsin appointee Oleg Savchenko to win the Kaluga governor's seat, he has maintained relatively good relations with the federal government. This is most likely due to his more centrist political approach, which serves to bridge the conflicting interests and positions of the local Communist party with the Kremlin. Yeltsin's team was always aware that Sudarenkov was much more likely to cooperate with them than were some of Kaluga's other possible leaders.

Relations with Other Regions

Kaluga is a member of the Central Russia Association, which is headed by Yaroslavl Governor Anatolii Lisitsyn. The other members include Bryansk, Vladimir, Ivanovo, Kostroma, Moscow, Ryazan, Smolensk, Tver, and Tula oblasts, and the city of Moscow.

Foreign Relations: Anti-Foreign Investment

Sudarenkov would like to see Kaluga stabilize its economy without the help of foreign investors, and thus has not enacted any policies intended to attract business to the region.

In June 1997 the World Bank announced its intention to provide a $66 million loan for the Health Reform Pilot Project, which will help improve family planning and reproductive and cardiovascular health care in Kaluga and Tver oblasts (*EWI RRR*, 12 June 1997).

Attitudes Toward Business: Lack of Concrete Plans

Sudarenkov believes that Kaluga's industrial recession is the result of a combination of factors, including mutual non-payments between firms, insufficient capital flow, low liquidity, lack of competition, high prices for goods, and the inadequate conversion of defense enterprises (*Vest*, 14 June 1997). The governor also faults the lack of know-how exhibited by individual enterprise directors in adapting to market conditions, restructuring their enterprises, and coordinating the production and sale of competitive products. Unfortunately, he has not succeeded in establishing a program to address these issues.

Nevertheless, some foreign investors are working in the region. South African Breweries began producing the Zolotaya Bochka beer in Kaluga in April 1999. The firm is the fourth largest brewer in the world and is the latest foreign company trying to enter the Russian market, where per capita beer consumption is 20 liters a year, much less than in many other countries. The firm invested $40 million in renovating the half-finished beer factory in Kaluga in 1998. The plant has the capacity to produce 100 million bottles a year. The company expects to be profitable in three years (*Moscow Times*, 16 July 1999). Starting in 2000, the plant was also slated to produce the Czech Staropramen beer (*Kommersant Daily*, 16 July 1999).

In 1998, following a $10.8 million investment in foreign equipment, Kaluga's Transvok enterprise became the first plant in Russia capable of producing fiber optic cable. Initially, the plant was to produce 6,000 km of cable to fulfill an order from the Railroads Ministry. The Finnish firm Nokia was the main partner in setting up the new plant, which plans to buy the materials required to make the cable from Corning, Lucent Technologies, DuPont, and other firms. Credit Suisse First Boston provided the financing (*Finansoviye izvestiya*, 11 August 1998).

Internet Sites in the Region

http://www.kaluga.ru/kaluga/
This website offers information about the history, culture, and industry of Kaluga city and oblast. It provides several links to other websites in the region, as well as to other sources of mass media information.

KAMCHATKA OBLAST

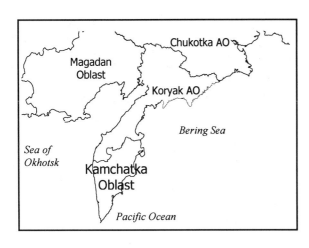

Territory: 472,300 km²
Population (as of 1 January 1998):
396,000
Distance from Moscow: 11,876 km

Major Cities:
Petropavlovsk-Kamchatskii, *capital*
(pop. 201,900)
Elizovo (39,300)
Vilyuchinsk (35,500)
Klyuchi (10,100)

Basic Facts

Population (as of 1 Jan. 1998): 396,000 (0.27% of Russian total)

Ethnic breakdown (1989 census): Russians 81%, Ukrainians 9.1%, Northern peoples 2.6%, Belarusans 1.6%, Tatars 1.2%

Urban population (as of 1 Jan. 1998): 80.6% (Russia overall: 73.1%)

Student population (as of 1 Sept. 1997): 144 per 10,000 (Russia overall: 208/10,000)

Pensioner population (1997): 18.94% (Russia overall: 25.96%)

Percent of population with higher education (1989 census): 15.5% (Russia overall: 11.3%)

Percent of population working in (1997): Industry: 23.8% (Russian average: 23.0%); Agriculture: 4.5% (13.7%); Trade: 18.2% (13.5%); Culture: 13.1% (13.3%)

Average monthly personal income in July 1998: 1,433.5 new rubles (Russian average: 891.7 new rubles)

Average monthly personal expenses in July 1998: 803.6 new rubles (Russian average: 684.9 new rubles)

Average monthly subsistence requirement in 1998: 854 new rubles (Russian average: 438 new rubles)

Consumer price index (as of July 1998): 208 (Russia overall = 100)

Budgetary revenues (1997): 2,117.6 billion rubles (Russia overall: 433,378.2 billion rubles)

Budgetary expenditures (1997): 3,026.3 billion rubles (Russia overall: 468,111.6 billion rubles)

Industrial production as percentage of all Russian production (Jan.–Aug. 1998): 0.26%

Proportion of loss-making enterprises (as of July 1998): 59.7% (Russia overall: 50.4%)

Number of enterprises which have wage arrears (as of 1 Sept. 1998): 312 (0.23% of Russian total)

Agricultural production as percentage of all Russian production (1997): 0.38%

Number of private farms (as of 1 Jan. 1998): 523 (0.19% of Russian total)

Capital investment (1997): 983.8 billion rubles (Russia overall: 408,797 billion rubles)

Sources of investment (1997): federal budget: 22.3% (Russian average: 10.2%); regional budget: 10.1% (10.5%); extra-budgetary funds: 67.6% (79.3%)

Foreign investment (1997): 34,014,000 USD (Russia overall: 12,294,734,000 USD)

Number of joint ventures (1997): 41 (0.28% of Russian total)

Fixed capital investment in joint ventures and foreign companies (1997): 42,615 million rubles (Russia overall: 16,265.4 billion rubles)

Number of small businesses (as of 1 July 1998): 2,100 (0.24% of Russian total)

Number of enterprises privatized in 1997: 6 (0.22% of Russian total), including those which used to be municipal property: 83.3% (Russian average: 66.4%); regional property: 0% (20.0%); federal property: 16.7% (13.6%)

Number of telephones per 100 families (1997): in cities: 60.8 (Russian average: 49.2); in villages: 52.7 (19.8)

Brief Overview

Kamchatka Oblast is located in the extreme north-east of Russia. Its territory includes the Kamchatka peninsula, the neighboring part of the mainland, the Kommandor Islands, and the Koryak Autonomous Okrug. It borders Magadan Oblast and Chukotka Autonomous Okrug in the north, the Okhotsk Sea in the west, and the Bering Sea and the Pacific Ocean in the east. Two-thirds of the territory is mountainous and a significant part is covered by permafrost. It includes 29 active volcanoes and is seismically active. The oblast is one of the most inaccessible in the country. Over half of the region's population lives in its administrative center, Petropavlovsk-Kamchatskii.

The oblast's territory has large mineral resource deposits, such as gas, coal, and metals including gold and silver, but current levels of extraction barely meet local needs. Key industries include fishing and fish processing, which account for over 70 percent of regional industrial output, and forestry. These industries make up all of the oblast's exports. Additionally, the region is rich in fur, medicinal plants, and berries, the exploitation of which, along with reindeer breeding, provides a living for the northern indigenous people residing in the oblast.

The oblast is one of the poorest in the country. According to a 1998 survey by *Ekspert* magazine, Kamchatka covers only 40 percent of its financial needs from its own budgetary revenues. The same survey showed that Kamchatka had seen the sixth largest investment potential decrease in the country (by 6 points) since 1997, while investment risk increased by 24 points (7th largest) over the same period: the oblast ranked 72nd among Russia's 89 regions in terms of investment potential and 69th in terms of investment risk. A 1998 survey by Bank Austria ranked the oblast 37th in terms of investment climate. Although the regional administration aspires to attract foreign investment to the region to develop its natural resources, fisheries, and tourist potential, no major investment projects are currently underway.

Electoral History

2000 Presidential Election
Putin: 48.79%
Zyuganov: 28.15%

Yavlinskii: 6.32%
Zhirinovsky: 6.10%
Tuleev: 3.73%
Turnout: 63.74% (Russia overall: 68.64%)

1999 Parliamentary Elections
Unity: 29.87%
Communist Party of the Russian Federation: 17.84%
Zhirinovsky Bloc: 10.92%
Union of Right Forces: 9.59%
Yabloko: 6.15%
Fatherland–All Russia: 6.04%
In a single-mandate district: 1 independent
Turnout: 59.69% (Russia overall: 61.85%)

1996 Gubernatorial Election
Biryukov (incumbent): 47.67%/60.96 (first round/ second round)
Oleinikov: 10.65%/27.80%
Kulak: 9.36%
Tokmantsev: 8.02%
Grigoreva: 5.79%
Fatnev (oblast legislature deputy): 2.97%
Yekimov (LDPR): 1.70%
Sverdlov: 0.99%
Turnout: 42.1%/34.25%

1996 Presidential Election
Yeltsin: 34.29%/61.81% (first round/second round)
Zyuganov: 18.69%/29.47%
Yavlinskii: 17.28%
Lebed: 14.06%
Zhirinovsky: 9.96%
Turnout: 61.41%/58.86% (Russia overall: 69.67%/ 68.79%)

1995 Parliamentary Elections
Yabloko: 20.43%
Liberal Democratic Party of Russia: 16.02%
Communist Party of the Russian Federation: 11.31%
Our Home Is Russia: 7.03%
Women of Russia: 4.11%
Party of Workers' Self-Government: 3.96%
Communists–Workers' Russia: 3.51%
In a single-mandate district: 1 Yabloko
Turnout: 61.44% (Russia overall: 64.37%)

1993 Constitutional Referendum
"Yes"—69.6% "No"—28.4%

1993 Parliamentary Elections
Liberal Democratic Party of Russia: 27.16%
Yabloko: 17.61%
Russia's Choice: 15.51%
Party of Russian Unity and Concord: 8.64%
Women of Russia: 8.21%
Democratic Party of Russia: 6.40%
Communist Party of the Russian Federation: 5.05%
Agrarian Party of Russia: 1.13%
In a single-mandate district: 1 independent
Turnout: 44.09% (Russia overall: 54.34%)

1991 Presidential Election
Yeltsin: 60.18%
Ryzhkov: 16.48%
Zhirinovsky: 5.31%
Makashov: 4.75%
Tuleev: 4.42%
Bakatin: 3.46%
Turnout: 72.77% (Russia overall: 76.66%)

Regional Political Institutions

Executive:
Governor, 4-year term
Vladimir Afanasevich Biryukov, elected
December 1996
   Pl. Lenina, 1; Petropavlovsk-
   Kamchatskii, 683040
   Tel 7(415–22) 11–20–96, 11–20–91;
   Fax 7(415–22) 27–38–43
   Federation Council in Moscow:
   7(095) 292–62–27, 926–62–52

Legislative:
Unicameral
Council of People's Deputies—49 members,
4-year term, elected November 1997
Chairman—Lev Nikolaevich Boitsov, elected
December 1997

Regional Politics

Yeltsin Appointee Remains in Far Eastern Oblast

President Boris Yeltsin appointed Vladimir Biryukov as Kamchatka's governor in November 1991. Biryukov won the region's first election in December 1996, taking 61 percent of the vote in the runoff. He had won 48 percent in the first round, just 2 percent short of what he needed to win the election outright. His large victory margin can be partially attributed to the Communists' failure to nominate a candidate, and an endorsement by the oblast branch of Yabloko, which has a strong following in Kamchatka.

Since his election, however, Biryukov has become extremely unpopular in his region because of his inability to solve the region's chronic energy problems. During the summer of 1999, NTV showed repeated reports from the region with angry demonstrators demanding Biryukov's removal because they only had electricity in their apartments for a few hours a day.

At the time of the election, Yabloko's Mikhail Zadornov represented the region in the State Duma and was Kamchatka's best known politician on the national stage. Zadornov ultimately left the legislature to serve as Russia's finance minister, a decision that cost him his membership in the Yabloko party. He lost that job following the sacking of Prime Minister Yevgenii Primakov. In December 1999, Zadornov was elected to the Duma from a district in Moscow

Executive Platform: Reformist

Biryukov is strongly in the reformist camp. Not only was he appointed by Yeltsin to govern Kamchatka, but in May 1995, he became the leader of the Kamchatka Oblast branch of Our Home Is Russia (NDR). Grigorii Yavlinskii's Yabloko party also backed his electoral bid, one of the few instances in which Yavlinskii and then Prime Minister Viktor Chernomyrdin's parties worked together.

Policies

The most important problem in Kamchatka is its severe lack of energy, which is crippling the regional economy. For most of the 1990s Kamchatka's output has continued to shrink. During the winter of 1998–99 and during the summer of 1999, many apartments and factories only received electricity for one or two hours a day every two to three days. To make matters worse, when the electricity came on, people would turn on their lights, heaters, computers, and other appliances at once. The system was then overwhelmed and if the voltage spiked, it sometimes destroyed their electrical appliances.

Fuel oil and coal for local electric power generation must be shipped to the region by boat, and often the shipping companies in the Far East cannot meet the needs of the region. Moreover, in June 1999, the Kamchatka electricity utility owed the fuel suppliers 1.5 billion rubles, while the federal government owed the region more than one billion rubles. These energy problems have plagued the region since the early 1990s (*Nezavisimaya Gazeta Regiony*, no. 11, June 1999).

Reducing the region's reliance on ship-borne fuel will not be easy. The region has some coal, but mining it would cause ecological problems. Installing gas pipelines would be expensive and spills would be inevitable because of the numerous earthquakes in the region. One possible alternative would be the construction of small-scale nuclear power plants but these also would be vulnerable to tremors.

Relationships Between Key Players: Struggle with Opposition

The Kamchatka Oblast legislature, which was elected in November 1997, has an eclectic array of deputies. No one party controls a clear majority in the assembly: Communists hold 10 of the 49 seats, Yabloko holds 9, and several seats belong to "new Russians." Prior to the election, *Nezavisimaya Gazeta* claimed that the number of legislative candidates in the oblast with criminal pasts was unprecedented (*NG*, 28 November 1997).

The numerous political fault lines in the legislature have not worked to Biryukov's advantage. In fall 1998, Communists and members of Vladimir Zhirinovsky's Liberal Democratic Party of Russia began procedures to remove the governor from office. They held him responsible for the oblast's numerous problems, including wage arrears, inadequate funding for health care and education, insufficient fuel, and poor preparation for winter. The opposition hoped to persuade the electoral committee to hold a referendum on the governor's removal from office.

Ties to Moscow: Aid Recipient

Biryukov's negotiating skills have proven strong enough to secure some emergency aid for the re-

gion in winter. In December 1998 Kamchatka received an emergency fuel shipment from the federal government when the region's energy supply had reached a dangerously low level. The regional legislature even appealed directly to the United Nations for humanitarian assistance in the form of fuel during the winter of 1998–99. Federal representatives have visited Kamchatka and tried to solve the region's energy crisis, with little success.

Relations with Other Regions: Cooperation with Koryak Autonomous Okrug

In May 1999 Biryukov signed a cooperation agreement with Koryak Autonomous Okrug Governor Valentina Bronevich. The agreement was the result of long negotiations between the two regions, whose relationship has been strained by legal ambiguities. As an autonomous okrug, Koryak is simultaneously subordinate to Kamchatka and an equal subject of the Russian Federation in accordance with the Constitution. In 1991 the Koryak Okrug Soviet tried to secede from Kamchatka in hopes of establishing a Koryak republic within the RSFSR. Bronevich, however, is intent on keeping the Koryak Autonomous Okrug within Kamchatka and feels that her okrug would benefit from increasing its ties with Kamchatka.

Kamchatka belongs to the Far East and Baikal Association, which includes the republics of Buryatia and Sakha (Yakutia); Primorskii and Khabarovsk krais; Amur, Magadan, Chita, and Sakhalin oblasts; the Jewish Autonomous Oblast; and the Chukotka Autonomous Okrug.

Foreign Relations: Credit from EBRD

In December 1997 the EBRD offered a $100 million credit for the first stage of construction of the Mutnov Geothermal Station in Kamchatka. The energy that the plant could ultimately produce would remove the need to ship 120,000 tons of fuel to Kamchatka (*Segodnya*, 30 October 1997).

Attitudes Toward Business: Interested in Investment

One of Kamchatka's greatest assets is its fish supply, providing the remote region with a successful food industry that meets local needs as well as ex-

Vladimir Afanasevich Biryukov

19 October 1933—Born in Astrakhan

1956—Graduated from the Astrakhan Fishing Industry and Economics Institute

1956–1977—Worked in various fish combines in Kamchatka

January 1977—Appointed General Director of the Kamchatrybprom fishing industry

1979–1980—Chair of the Kamchatka Oblast executive committee

1980–1987—Worked as the chief specialist of the Kamchatka department of the Giprorybprom institute

1987–1989—Deputy chair of the agro-industrial committee of Kamchatka Oblast

March 1990—Elected to the Kamchatka Oblast Council

April 1990—Elected chair of the Kamchatka Oblast executive committee

16 November 1991—Appointed governor of Kamchatka Oblast

May 1995—Elected chair of the regional branch of Our Home Is Russia (NDR)

January 1996—Appointed to the Federation Council and became a member of the Committee for the Budget, Tax Policies, Finance, Currency, and Customs Regulations

December 1996—Elected governor of Kamchatka Oblast

Married, with two children

ports. Biryukov worked several years for the region's fish industry before entering politics and thus is very familiar with this sector.

Biryukov would like to attract foreign investment to the region to further develop the region's natural resource extraction, fish industry, and tourism. Although Kamchatka is Russia's third largest gold producer, the amounts produced are extremely small. In 1997, just over 7,000 foreign tourists visited the region, mostly rich people interested in exotic hunting experiences. Given the extreme conditions and energy problems, no major investment projects are currently underway.

Internet Sites in the Region

http://www.kamchatka.ru/kam/
This site provides a general overview of the region, including a section on its volcanoes.

KARACHAEVO-CHERKESSIA (REPUBLIC)

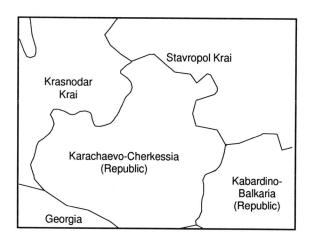

Territory: 14,100 km²
Population (as of 1 January 1998): 436,000
Distance from Moscow: 1,674 km

Major Cities:
Cherkessk, *capital* (pop. 120,500)
Ust-Dzheguta (31,500)
Karachaevsk (15,500))

Basic Facts

Population (as of 1 Jan. 1998): 436,000 (0.30% of Russian total)

Ethnic breakdown (1989 census): Russians 42.4%, Karachai 31.2%, Cherkes 9.7%, Abazins 6.6%, Nogais 3.1%, Ukrainians 1.5%

Urban population (as of 1 Jan. 1998): 44.4% (Russia overall: 73.1%)

Student population (as of 1 Sept. 1997): 194 per 10,000 (Russia overall: 208/10,000)

Pensioner population (1997): 25.00% (Russia overall: 25.96%)

Percent of population with higher education (1989 census): 22.2% (Russia overall: 11.3%)

Percent of population working in (1997): Industry: 9.8% (Russian average: 23.0%); Agriculture: 16.4% (13.7%); Trade: 13.2% (13.5%); Culture: 15.0% (13.3%)

Average monthly personal income in July 1998: 436.3 new rubles (Russian average: 891.7 new rubles)

Average monthly personal expenses in July 1998: 283.5 new rubles (Russian average: 684.9 new rubles)

Average monthly subsistence requirement in 1998: 345 new rubles (Russian average: 438 new rubles)

Consumer price index (as of July 1998): 91 (Russia overall = 100)

Budgetary revenues (1997): 709.5 billion rubles (Russia overall: 433,378.2 billion rubles)

Budgetary expenditures (1997): 787.5 billion rubles (Russia overall: 468,111.6 billion rubles)

Industrial production as percentage of all Russian production (Jan.–Aug. 1998): 0.07%

Proportion of loss-making enterprises (as of July 1998): 50.0% (Russia overall: 50.4%)

Number of enterprises which have wage arrears (as of 1 Sept. 1998): 541 (0.40% of Russian total)

Agricultural production as percentage of all Russian production (1997): 0.37%

Number of private farms (as of 1 Jan. 1998): 959 (0.35% of Russian total)

Capital investment (1997): 535.9 billion rubles (Russia overall: 408,797 billion rubles)

Sources of investment (1997): federal budget: 15.9% (Russian average: 10.2%); regional budget: 7.4% (10.5%); extra-budgetary funds: 76.7% (79.3%)

Foreign investment (1997): 78,000 USD (Russia overall: 12,294,734,000 USD)

Number of joint ventures (1997): 12 (0.08% of Russian total)

Fixed capital investment in joint ventures and foreign companies (1997): 7,294 million rubles (Russia overall: 16,265.4 billion rubles)

Number of small businesses (as of 1 July 1998): 2,300 (0.26% of Russian total)

Number of enterprises privatized in 1997: 15 (0.55% of Russian total), including those which used to be municipal property: 20.0% (Russian average: 66.4%); regional property: 73.3% (20.0%); federal property: 6.7% (13.6%)

Number of telephones per 100 families (1997): in cities: 56.1 (Russian average: 49.2); in villages: 29.9 (19.8)

Brief Overview

Karachaevo-Cherkessia was established as an autonomous oblast within Stavropol Krai in 1922 and became an independent republic within the Russian Federation in July 1991. It is situated on the northern slope of the Caucasus Mountains and borders Kabardino-Balkaria, Stavropol and Krasnodar krais, and Georgia. Like many other North Caucasus republics, it is home to numerous ethnic groups. More than half of the republic's territory is mountainous. Many major rivers, such as the Kuban, Urun, and the Big and Small Zelenchuks, pass through its territory. The region is rich in various raw materials—gas, oil, copper, coal, granite, marble, and clays—and mineral and thermal waters.

Major regional industries are chemicals and petrochemicals (29 percent of total industrial output); production of construction materials (24.2 percent); machine building (23.9 percent); food processing (14.7 percent); and light industry (14.3 percent). A majority of industrial enterprises are located in the republican center, the city of Cherkessk, and in the city of Karachaevsk.

The republic's main foreign trade partners are the CIS countries (76.7 percent of the republic's imports), the European Community (5.4 percent), and the countries of Eastern and Central Europe (1.5 percent).

According to a 1998 survey by *Ekspert* magazine, the republic ranked 76th among Russia's 89 regions in terms of investment potential and 81st in terms of investment risk. A 1998 survey by Bank Austria ranked the republic 77th in terms of investment climate.

Electoral History

2000 Presidential Election
Putin: 58.10%
Zyuganov: 34.76%
Yavlinskii: 1.78%
Tuleev: 1.16%
Zhirinovsky: 0.99%
Turnout: 69.92% (Russia overall: 68.64%)

1999 Parliamentary Elections
Communist Party of the Russian Federation: 40.84%
Fatherland–All Russia: 15.44%
Unity: 14.91%
Communists–Workers' Russia: 4.75%

Yabloko: 4.17%
Union of Right Forces: 2.94%
Zhirinovsky Bloc: 2.69%
In a single-mandate district: 1 independent
Turnout: 63.39% (Russia overall: 61.85%)

1999 Republican Presidential Election
Semenov: 17.9%/75.5% (first round/ second round)*
Derev: 40.1%/25%
Khubiev (incumbent): 6.4%
Turnout: 77%/62.8%

*The results for the second round are not official; official results could not be obtained.

1996 Presidential Election
Yeltsin: 25.82%/49.89% (first round/second round)
Zyuganov: 55.42%/46.09%
Lebed: 8.77%
Yavlinskii: 3.07%
Zhirinovsky: 2.49%
Turnout: 72.46%/74.23% (Russia overall: 69.67%/ 68.79%)

1995 Parliamentary Elections
Communist Party of the Russian Federation: 40.03%
Our Home Is Russia: 12.67%
Derzhava: 7.86%
Communists–Workers' Russia: 7.10%
Liberal Democratic Party of Russia: 6.91%
Congress of Russian Communities: 6.56%
Nur: 2.20%
Agrarian Party of Russia: 2.01%
Women of Russia: 2.00%
In a single-mandate district: Communist Party of the Russian Federation
Turnout: 61.63% (Russia overall: 64.37%)

1993 Constitutional Referendum
"Yes"—27.5%   "No"—70.8%

1993 Parliamentary Election
Communist Party of the Russian Federation: 38.58%
Liberal Democratic Party of Russia: 20.19%
Agrarian Party of Russia: 10.80%
Party of Russian Unity and Concord: 7.54%
Democratic Party of Russia: 4.61%
Women of Russia: 4.41%

Russia's Choice: 4.30%
Yabloko: 3.40%
In a single-mandate district: 1 independent
Turnout: 71.90% (Russia overall: 54.34%)

1991 Presidential Election
Yeltsin: 61.76%
Ryzhkov: 12.78%
Zhirinovsky: 8.05%
Tuleev: 7.39%
Makashov: 4.13%
Bakatin: 2.42%
Turnout: 85.68% (Russia overall: 76.66%)

Regional Political Institutions

Executive:
President, 4-year term
Vladimir Semenov, elected May 1999
Dom Pravitelstva; Pl. Lenina;
Cherkessk, 357100;
Republic of Karachaevo-Cherkessia
Tel 7(878–22) 5–40–40, 5–40–11
Fax 7(878–22) 5–29–80

Legislative:
Unicameral
People's Assembly (*Narodnoe Sobranie*)—73
members, 4-year term, elected June 1995
Chairman—Igor Vladimirovich Ivanov,
elected June 1995

Regional Politics

Elections Spark Republican Divide

Karachaevo-Cherkessia was the last Russian region
to elect its leader. In January 1992 President Yeltsin
appointed Vladimir Khubiev head of the newly established Karachaevo-Cherkes Republic. Khubiev
had already long ruled the region during the Soviet
era. Yeltsin reappointed Khubiev to this position in
April 1995. In spring 1996 a new republican constitution was adopted which stipulated that the president should be popularly elected, but Khubiev
postponed the vote. Finally, on 22 September 1998,
the Legislative Assembly, under pressure from
crowds protesting in the streets, adopted legislation providing for the direct election of the republi-

can president. Those elections took place on 25
April and 16 May 1999.

In the first round, on 25 April, Cherkessk Mayor
Stanislav Derev led with 40.1 percent of the vote.
Former commander of the Russian ground troops
Vladimir Semenov came in second with 17.9 percent. Khubiev finished fifth with 6.4 percent. Overall there were 15 candidates in the race with a 77
percent voter turnout. Derev is an ethnic Cherkes, a
group that makes up 9.7 percent of the republic's
population. Semenov, like Khubiev, is an ethnic
Karachai, (31.2 percent of the population). Even
though Derev won more than twice as many votes
as Semenov in the first round, Semenov was expected
to have a considerably better showing in the runoff
since many of the republic's ethnic Karachai voted
for the six other Karachai candidates, including
Khubiev, in the first round. Many predicted that the
republic's Russian majority would be the deciding
factor in the election's outcome.

However, the second round was marked with so
much chaos and controversy that it was left to the
Russian Supreme Court to decide the outcome. A
string of explosions rocked the region in the days
between the two rounds. Preliminary results suggested that Semenov had won more than 70 percent of the vote, yet numerous electoral violations
challenged the validity of the election. Many of the
residents could not even vote since several polling
stations did not open. This situation angered Derev's
supporters, who gathered in the republican capital
demanding that the results be overturned. After the
election results remained unconfirmed for nearly two
weeks and the political situation in the republic continued to deteriorate, Russian President Boris Yeltsin
dismissed Khubiev and republican Prime Minister
Anatolii Ozov and appointed the chairman of the
Karachaevo-Cherkes People's Assembly, Igor
Ivanov, to serve as acting president. This action was
taken following the recommendation of then Prime
Minister Sergei Stepashin and presidential Chief of
Staff Aleksandr Voloshin, who visited the region and
decided that neither Semenov nor Derev could calm
the intense ethnic passions the elections had un-
leashed. Stepashin argued that appointing an ethnic
Russian to the position would help to calm the tension between the Karachai and Cherkes.

Approximately three weeks after the runoff, the
Karachaevo-Cherkes Supreme Court finally confirmed Semenov's victory. He pulled in 75 percent

of the vote while Derev earned 18 percent. However, the more than 1,500 reported electoral violations and the continued state of instability in the republic meant that the long-awaited results brought virtually no peace to the region, and the case moved immediately on to the Russian Supreme Court without Semenov taking power. On 23 July the Russian Supreme Court overturned the Karachaevo-Cherkes Supreme Court's decision and ruled that a more thorough investigation of the reported violations was necessary. Russian President Boris Yeltsin appointed first deputy chairman of the Central Electoral Commission and former plenipotentiary presidential representative in Chechnya Valentin Vlasov to serve as acting president until a final decision could be made regarding the region's elections. (Vlasov had been held hostage for six months by Chechen kidnappers in 1998.) He simultaneously retained his post in the Central Electoral Commission.

The Russian Supreme Court's ruling in this instance was interpreted as a cancellation of the May election, since further investigation of the issue would almost inevitably lead to that end. Stepashin stated that a new election should be held in the republic. Derev and his supporters welcomed the Russian Supreme Court's ruling, and Derev reconfirmed his intentions to run again. This time it was Semenov's followers who took to the streets in outrage. Demonstrations took place throughout the republic's Karachai territories demanding that Semenov be allowed to take office. In the city of Karachaevsk people stopped going to work as a form of political protest, completely idling the city's industries. Even state employees, except for police and emergency medical units, went on strike. In particular, Semenov's supporters were angered by Vlasov's appointment and the appointment of Aleksandr Volkodav, head of internal affairs for Astrakhan Oblast, as the Minister of Internal Affairs for Karachaevo-Cherkessia. Volkodav had served in this capacity before and was dismissed in 1995. The Karachai opposed the appointments on the grounds that they violated the Constitution.

In August 1999 the republican Supreme Court ruled once again that the results of the elections were indeed valid and that Semenov was the legitimate victor. Immediately following this decision, the International Cherkes Association demanded the establishment of a separate Cherkes Republic. Shortly after, Semenov was inaugurated, but chose

to hold the ceremony not in the republican capital of Cherkessk, but in the town of Ust-Dzheguta to avoid Cherkes demonstrations. By the end of September Cherkes demonstrators had blockaded the republican government building to prevent Semenov's government from entering their offices. Finally, in October 1999 then Prime Minister Vladimir Putin met with Semenov and Derev to find a solution to the republic's political crisis. According to the agreement they reached, Semenov would be allowed to work as the republic's president, but he would have to stand for a referendum on 22 October 2000, one year after the Russian Supreme Court certified his 16 May election victory. If the voters find his performance unacceptable, new elections will be held. On 22 October, the republic's citizens should also vote on whether to split the republic into Karachai and Cherkes units.

Executive Platform: Seeks to Retain Republican Unity

Semenov and Derev remain divided on the future of their North Caucasus republic. Semenov said that dividing it in two would set a "precedent that could blow up Russia." He vaguely called for eliminating ethnic divisions altogether. Derev, on the other hand, thought it was time to "divide up the communal apartment." He would also split Kabardino-Balkaria (which has been relatively peaceful), but only after the 2000 presidential elections.

Policies: Restoring Order

By the time that Semenov ultimately took power, the longstanding political crisis in the region had left it largely ungovernable. Semenov has been working to establish order in the chaotic republic. Shortly after receiving confirmation of his legitimacy from the Russian Supreme Court, Semenov issued a decree banning demonstrations and protests in Karachaevo-Cherkessia. The ban was clearly targeted at the Cherkes community.

Relationships Between Key Players: Presidential Elections Bring Tension to a Head

Prior to the 1999 republican presidential elections and subsequent controversy, Karachaevo-Cherkessia had been one of the most calm and stable regions in the rather turbulent North Caucasus. One of the reasons Khubiev managed to stay in power for so long was because of his ability to maintain order in the region. Khubiev openly backed most of Yeltsin's policies. Thus, Moscow felt little reason to challenge his authority and open up the possibility of ethnic tensions.

Khubiev, an ethnic Karachai, had opposed calls from some Karachai groups to divide the region into respective Karachai and Cherkes republics. Under Khubiev's rule the two groups had relatively peaceful relations, even though their cultural, linguistic, and historical identities are distinctly different. The Karachai were among the North Caucasian nationalities deported by Stalin in 1944, and now share a republic with the Cherkes, who were not subjected to exile. Prior to the collapse of the Soviet Union, ethnic Karachai tended not to hold politically sensitive positions in the region, even in the largely Karachai territories. Thus the Karachai, in spite of the fact that their population is three times as large as that of the Cherkes, continue to perceive themselves as the victims of discriminatory practices and feel that outsiders have hindered their professional and educational development (Jane Ormrod, "The North Caucasus: Confederation in Conflict," in Ian Bremmer and Ray Taras, eds., *New States, New Politics: Building the Post-Soviet Nations*, New York: Cambridge University Press, 1997, 112.). However, their complaints had not been targeted at the Cherkes but rather at the Russians, who make up the largest ethnic group in the republic (42 percent).

Khubiev's grasp on the republic was challenged when Derev was elected mayor of the republic's capital, Cherkessk, in October 1997. In the election, Derev won 75 percent of the vote, putting him in a strong position to challenge Khubiev in the presidential elections. At the time of his election, Derev was the director of the Merkurii plant, which produces vodka and mineral water and sells its products throughout Russia. The taxes from Merkurii contribute 25 percent of the republican budget, and 50 percent of the city's budget. Derev's business has also made him one of the area's richest men. However, in December 1997, the authorities halted production at the plant and filed charges against management for not paying taxes after a truck carrying 10,000 bottles of "underground" vodka, allegedly from Merkurii, was detained in Stavropol

Krai. Protesters who demanded Khubiev's resignation at a Cherkessk rally in January 1998 believed that these actions were undertaken to discredit Derev (*EWI RRR*, 29 January 1998).

As mayor of Cherkessk, Derev has actively tried to secure allies among the Russians and the Karachai. Many of the workers at Merkurii are Russian and Derev's first deputy mayor is an ethnic Russian. The Muslim mayor also contributed a large sum to the local Russian Orthodox church, which honored him for helping to build a new church, increasing his popularity among the republic's Russian population. He also began to build a monument to the repressed Karachai in the center of Cherkessk. Prior to the republican presidential elections, the republic's Karachai population had shown support for Derev. When he ran for Cherkessk mayor in 1997, 35 percent of the city's Karachai voted for him in spite of President Khubiev's open opposition to his candidacy. However, the conflict between the Karachai and Cherkes over the presidential elections makes future Karachai support for Derev unlikely.

The presidential race that shook this previously calm region was characterized by mounting ethnic tensions and violence culminating in one of the most controversial elections in Russia's regions. Following the first electoral round in April 1999, which sent Semenov and Derev to the runoff, there were terrorist acts against both candidates throughout the region. Derev's campaign headquarters was set on fire, and an explosion went off at Semenov's headquarters in Cherkessk. The homes of several of Derev's supporters were targeted with grenades and Molotov cocktails.

Derev supporters began gathering in front of the republican government's building in Cherkessk on the afternoon of the runoff, demanding that it be declared invalid due to multiple violations. At 8 o'clock in the morning, when voting was supposed to begin, only 5 of the 52 polling stations in the republic's Cherkes territories were open. By evening, republican officials had managed to open 43 more stations. Yet, in the Adyge-Khabl and Khabez raions, where a large number of Cherkes live, only one station was open. Due to all of the confusion, nearly one-third of the republic's residents were unable to cast their votes (*Izvestiya*, 18 May 1999). The day after the runoff, Derev's demonstrators grew to more than 15,000. They demanded that the federal government take control of the republic and stated that if the election results were not canceled, then the Cherkes and Karachai could no longer live in the same republic.

Grigorii Kazankov, Derev's campaign manager, charged that the election results should be nullified since many of the ballots submitted were invalid, including votes by people who had died before the polling, residents of other regions, and children under the age of 18. He also claimed that the number of voters in Cherkessk had suspiciously increased by 10 percent between the two rounds, from 20,000 to 22,500. According to the newspaper *Vremya MN*, prior to the first round there were 289,000 registered voters in the republic, yet 305,000 ballots were counted. The second round had 313,000 registered voters. Kazankov further charged that Semenov supporters terrorized many of Derev's ethnic Russian voters, who were then afraid to participate in the runoff (*EWI RRR*, 10 June 1999).

The situation in the region turned violent on 22 May when Karachaevo-Cherkessia's presidential representative, Magomed Kaitov, an ethnic Karachai who participated in the first electoral round, was allegedly shot by Derev supporters who were angry that Kaitov endorsed Semenov in the second round. It was shortly thereafter that Moscow established a provisional government in the republic headed by the chairman of the Karachaevo-Cherkes People's Assembly, Igor Ivanov.

In June 1999 the Karachaevo-Cherkes Supreme Court ratified Semenov's victory, but the Russian Supreme Court overturned the decision in July and called for further investigation into the alleged voting violations. Immediately following the republican Supreme Court's decision, Derev's supporters called for a separation of the Cherkes lands from the republic. They wanted to join neighboring Stavropol Krai as an autonomous region, leaving the rest of present-day Karachaevo-Cherkessia to form an independent Karachai Republic. Semenov claimed that these demands were unconstitutional and threatened the territorial integrity of the Russian Federation. Derev insisted that Moscow name an interim president for the next four years. He believed that the interim president should be an ethnic Russian with knowledge of Karachaevo-Cherkessia. Derev explained that during the period of the interim presidency, the region's Cherkes population would decide whether to proceed with their secessionist demands

(*NG*, 22 June 1999). After the Russian Supreme Court ruling, Derev said that he would run in the next elections for the republic's presidency, yet would still try to have the Cherkes secede from the republic if he did not win (*MT*, 24 July 1999).

The Russian Ministry of Federal Affairs and Nationalities has suggested that Karachaevo-Cherkessia adopt a governing system like that of Dagestan, in which the chief executive is elected by the state council, a representative assembly organized to reflect the region's exact ethnic composition (*KD*, 27 July 1999).

Ties to Moscow: Kremlin Intervenes to Preserve Order

Although the federal government did not openly support Semenov, he was clearly Moscow's preferred candidate. Having held various positions in the Russian armed forces, Semenov has good relations with Moscow. In his campaign, he presented himself as an advocate of law and order who would work hard to fight crime and corruption. Semenov promised to strengthen the economy and agriculture and to bring order to the republic (*NG Regiony*, 13 April 1999). However, Semenov has been unable to assert any effective control under the present circumstances and has criticized Moscow's approach to the problem. Following the inconclusive voting, the Russian procurator for the North Caucasus filed charges against Cherkessk Electoral Commission Chairman Aleksei Gavrilenko of trying to disrupt the conduct of the elections. At 4 a.m. on the day of the runoffs, Gavrilenko quit his job, just as the polling stations were about to open. Eight other members of the commission followed suit. Gavrilenko allegedly resigned because he did not like the preliminary results of the absentee balloting. He then shut down 38 of the 52 polling places controlled by the commission. This partially explains the vast drop in Derev's support between the two voting rounds (*EWI RRR*, 1 July 1999).

Prior to Moscow's intervention and the establishment of a provisional government, then Prime Minister Sergei Stepashin had warned that if law and order could not be maintained in the republic during the elections, and if the violent outbreaks continued after the elections, the federal government would have to take control of the region. He stated, "We cannot allow a second Chechnya in

Vladimir Magomedovich Semenov

8 June 1940—Born in the village of Khurzuk in Karachaevo-Cherkessia

—Graduated from the Bakinsk training school, the Frunze Military Academy, and the USSR Military Academy

1958–1986—Served in the Soviet army working his way through the ranks as first deputy commander and then commander of the Transcaucasus Military District (1986–1991)

1989–January 1992—Member of the USSR Congress of Peoples' Deputies

August 1991–December 1991—Chief commander of ground forces and deputy defense minister

March 1992–August 1992—Commander of the CIS forces

August 1992—Became chief commander of Russian Federation ground forces and served as the Russian Federation's representative for issues regarding Russian troops in Moldova

11 April 1997—Dismissed by presidential decree following various controversies and accusations of alleged criminal acts

June 1998—Appointed chief military consultant to the Russian Federation Defense Ministry

16 May 1999—Elected president of Karachaevo-Cherkessia

10 June 1999—Karachaevo-Cherkes Supreme Court confirmed Semenov's victory

23 July 1999—Russian Supreme Court overturned republican court's decision on the election results

27 August 1999—Karachaevo-Cherkes Supreme Court confirmed the May election results a second time

Karachai

Married to a Chechen woman, has one daughter

---

the North Caucasus" (*EWI RRR*, 6 May 1999). The appointment of a provisional government to prevent the situation in Karachaevo-Cherkessia from escalating into massive violence suggested a change in Moscow's approach to addressing conflict in the North Caucasus, emphasizing conflict prevention rather than conflict resolution. Prior to this incident the federal government had only intervened in conflicts in the North Caucasus after they had escalated to large-scale violence, most notably in Chechnya, Ingushetia, and North Ossetia.

Eventually, it was the center's influence that brought the conflict under control. Putin apparently threatened Semenov and Derev, declaring that if they did not agree to a compromise, he would use all of the central government's force against them. Since the republic is heavily reliant on Moscow for subsidies, an accommodation was quickly found.

Relations with Other Regions: Khubiev Had Good Ties

Khubiev had good relations with the other executives in the North Caucasus, and entered into various cooperative organizations and agreements with them. Karachaevo-Cherkessia has participated in the North Caucasus Congress of Chambers of Industry and Trade. This assembly was created by chambers from Rostov, Krasnodar, Stavropol, Adygeya, Dagestan, and North Ossetia, and its main goal is to influence federal investment priorities. Presently, the majority of federal money goes to unprofitable enterprises in the state sector. The North Caucasus Congress would like to see more federal money directed toward increasing the size of the small business sector.

In July 1997 Khubiev joined the leaders of

Kabardino-Balkaria and Adygeya to form an Inter-parliamentary Assembly of the three republics. The organization is pro-Russian, with the goals of assisting in the development of state rights and federalism and strengthening the friendship and cooperation among their regions (*Vesti,* 24 July 1997). It is unclear what role Karachaevo-Cherkessia's new executive will play in the assembly.

In November 1997 Khubiev signed an inter-governmental agreement with the head of Komi Republic, Yurii Spiridonov. The agreement secures a mutually favorable regimen of market activity for the two regions. Small businesses in Karachaevo-Cherkessia can provide Komi with agricultural goods and products from chemical and light industries without a middleman, thus keeping prices low for Komi customers.

The republic belongs to the Association for Cooperation among the Republics, Krais, and Oblasts of the North Caucasus. The other association members are the republics of Adygeya, Dagestan, Ingushetia, Kabardino-Balkaria, North Ossetia, and Kalmykia; Krasnodar and Stavropol krais; and Rostov Oblast.

REPUBLIC OF KARELIA

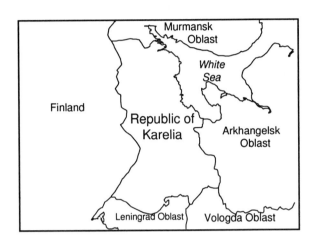

Territory: 172,400 km²
Population (as of 1 January 1998):
776,000
Distance from Moscow: 925 km

Major Cities:
Petrozavodsk, *capital* (pop. 282,400)
Kondopoga (36,600)
Segezha (34,900)
Kostomuksha (32,200)
Sortavala (20,800)

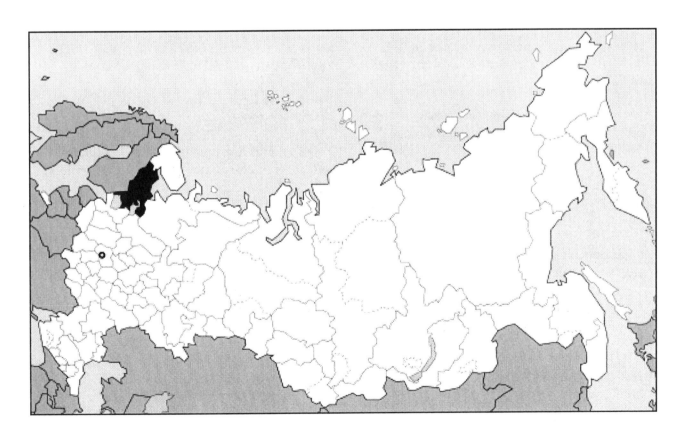

Basic Facts

Population (as of 1 Jan. 1998): 776,000 (0.53% of Russian total)

Ethnic breakdown (1989 census): Russians 73.6%, Karelians 10.1%, Belarusans 7.0%, Ukrainians 3.6%, Finns 2.3%, Veps 0.8%

Urban population (as of 1 Jan. 1998): 73.8% (Russia overall: 73.1%)

Student population (as of 1 Sept. 1997): 143 per 10,000 (Russia overall: 208/10,000)

Pensioner population (1997): 27.19% (Russia overall: 25.96%)

Percent of population with higher education (1989 census): 9.6% (Russia overall: 11.3%)

Percent of population working in (1997): Industry: 25.9% (Russian average: 23.0%); Agriculture: 5.4% (13.7%); Trade: 13.5% (13.5%); Culture: 14.0% (13.3%)

Average monthly personal income in July 1998: 1,025.2 new rubles (Russian average: 891.7 new rubles)

Average monthly personal expenses in July 1998: 617.4 new rubles (Russian average: 684.9 new rubles)

Average monthly subsistence requirement in 1998: 520 new rubles (Russian average: 438 new rubles)

Consumer price index (as of July 1998): 111 (Russia overall = 100)

Budgetary revenues (1997): 2,038.8 billion rubles (Russia overall: 433,378.2 billion rubles)

Budgetary expenditures (1997): 2,538.5 billion rubles (Russia overall: 468,111.6 billion rubles)

Industrial production as percentage of all Russian production (Jan.–Aug. 1998): 0.43%

Proportion of loss-making enterprises (as of July 1998): 62.7% (Russia overall: 50.4%)

Number of enterprises which have wage arrears (as of 1 Sept. 1998): 572 (0.42% of Russian total)

Agricultural production as percentage of all Russian production (1997): 0.31%

Number of private farms (as of 1 Jan. 1998): 654 (0.24% of Russian total)

Capital investment (1997): 1,155.6 billion rubles (Russia overall: 408,797 billion rubles)

Sources of investment (1997): federal budget: 15.0% (Russian average: 10.2%); regional budget: 8.9% (10.5%); extra-budgetary funds: 76.1% (79.3%)

Foreign investment (1997): 4,299,000 USD (Russia overall: 12,294,734,000 USD)

Number of joint ventures (1997): 121 (0.82% of Russian total)

Fixed capital investment in joint ventures and foreign companies (1997): 11,580 million rubles (Russia overall: 16,265.4 billion rubles)

Number of small businesses (as of 1 July 1998): 3,800 (0.44% of Russian total)

Number of enterprises privatized in 1997: 52 (1.90% of Russian total), including those which used to be municipal property: 66.7% (Russian average: 66.4%); regional property: 0% (20.0%); federal property: 32.4% (13.6%)

Number of telephones per 100 families (1997): in cities: 50.3 (Russian average: 49.2); in villages: 27.8 (19.8)

Brief Overview

The republic of Karelia is located in European Russia's northwest and borders Finland (and the European Union) and Arkhangelsk, Vologda, Leningrad, and Murmansk oblasts. In the 9th century, the territory of modern Karelia was part of Kievan Rus. During the 11th and 12th centuries, the area was part of the Novgorod Republic.

The region is rich in mineral resources, including iron ores, granite, marble, and various metals. The republican economy specializes in processing local mineral and forestry resources. The republic produces about 10 percent of the country's iron ore; 25 percent of its paper; 10 percent of its cellulose; and 42 percent of tractors for the forestry industry.

Over 400 regional enterprises are involved in foreign trade, generally exporting raw materials such as forestry products; cellulose; metals; and seafood (fish and shrimp). The republic's main foreign partners are Great Britain, Finland, and Germany. The republican government is actively seeking investment in the forestry and transportation industries.

The investment situation in the republic degenerated 1997 to 1998: investment potential has decreased by 15 points, the largest in the country. According to a 1998 survey by *Ekspert* magazine, the republic ranked 64th among Russia's 89 regions in terms of investment potential and 26th in terms of investment risk. A 1998 survey by Bank Austria ranked the republic 42nd in terms of investment climate.

Electoral History

2000 Presidential Election
Putin: 64.27%
Zyuganov: 17.04%
Yavlinskii: 7.35%
Zhirinovsky: 3.41%
Tuleev: 2.28%
Turnout: 68.26% (Russia overall: 68.64%)

1999 Parliamentary Elections
Unity: 31.19%
Communist Party of the Russian Federation: 13.58%
Union of Right Forces: 10.25%
Yabloko: 9.67%
Fatherland–All Russia: 8.80%
Zhirinovsky Bloc: 8.55%
In a single-mandate district: 1 independent
Turnout: 61.59% (Russia overall: 61.85%)

1998 Republican Executive Election
Katanandov: 37.8%/49.5% (first round/second round)
Stepanov (incumbent): 35.1%/43.2%
Turnout: 56.9%/47.9%

1996 Presidential Election
Yeltsin: 42.36%/66.21% (first round/second round)
Zyuganov: 16.99%/26.39%
Yavlinskii: 14.27%
Lebed: 12.04%
Zhirinovsky: 8.48%
Turnout: 67.74%/65.31% (Russia overall: 69.67%/ 68.79%)

1995 Parliamentary Elections
Communist Party of the Russian Federation: 15.43%
Liberal Democratic Party of Russia: 13.62%
Our Home Is Russia: 10.93%
Women of Russia: 7.65%
Yabloko: 7.47%
Russia's Democratic Choice: 5.93%
Party of Workers' Self-Government: 5.15%
In a single-mandate district: 1 independent
Turnout: 63.43% (Russia overall: 64.37%)

1993 Constitutional Referendum
"Yes"—69.1% "No"—28.4%

1993 Parliamentary Elections
Russia's Choice: 21.80%
Liberal Democratic Party of Russia: 21.09%
Women of Russia: 12.69%
Yabloko: 11.21%
Party of Russian Unity and Concord: 9.05%
Communist Party of the Russian Federation: 7.32%
Democratic Party of Russia: 5.43%
Agrarian Party of Russia: 2.60%
In a single-mandate district: 1 Russia's Choice
Turnout: 54.74% (Russia overall: 54.34%)

1991 Presidential Election
Yeltsin: 53.31%
Ryzhkov: 18.07%
Tuleev: 9.22%
Zhirinovsky: 8.08%
Bakatin: 3.84%
Makashov: 2.87%
Turnout: 73.43% (Russia overall: 76.66%)

Regional Political Institutions

Executive:
Prime Minister, 4-year term
Sergei Leonidovich Katanandov, elected May 1998
    Ul. Kuibysheva, 5; Petrozavodsk, 185610
    Tel 7(8148–22) 7–24–34, 7–28–65

Legislative:
Bicameral
Legislative Assembly (Zakonodatelnoe
sobranie), 4-year term, elected May 1998
Republican Chamber—25 members
Chairman—Vladimir Vasilevich Shilnikov,
elected January 2000
House of Representatives (*Palata
Predstavitelei*)—36 members
Chairman—Nikolai Ivanovich Levin, elected
February 2000

Regional Politics

Emotional Mayor Becomes Youngest Karelian Leader

Karelian Prime Minister Sergei Leonidovich Katanandov, an ethnic Russian who was elected to office on 17 May 1998 at the age of 43, is Karelia's youngest leader since revolutionary times. He is known as a strong manager who believes that the state should play a large role in guiding the republic's economy.

During the eight years he served as mayor of Petrozavodsk, observers became very familiar with his style. Katanandov has a strong, assertive character. At weekly meetings, he often became extremely angry with aides who did not meet his expectations and sometimes fired them on the spot. However, in some cases, his haste led him to dismiss the wrong person and he had to apologize for his mistake. Local journalists recall that during a meeting with the republic's finance minister in December 1997, Mayor Katanandov became involved in a heated argument about how the city and republic should divide the income tax. In the end Katanandov gave the minister the rude Russian gesture *figa*, a clenched fist with the thumb thrust between the index and middle fingers, as an argument for why the city should keep the income tax collected on its territory (this story and several others recounted here were originally published by

Boris Matveev, a journalist for Petrozavodsk's *Severnyi Kuryer*, in *EWI RRR*, 18 June 1998).

Among Petrozavodsk residents Katanandov is most famous for a comment he made regarding fountains: "No matter what happens in the republic or the country, no matter how difficult life gets, while I am mayor, Petrozavodsk will have a new fountain every year. Our city should be beautiful and clean." Some criticized him for building fountains while the city's poorest residents did not have bread, but most appreciated his initiative. Of course, he did not stop at fountains. He also reconstructed the embankment and ensured that the city center looked good.

Executive Platform: Building a Strong, Non-Communist Karelia

Katanandov's platform marks a sharp break from that of his immediate predecessor, former Prime Minister Viktor Stepanov. Stepanov was a Communist politician who was supported by the republic's Communist Party and other leftist groups. Katanandov, in contrast, is a pragmatic manager who does not formally belong to any political party. Katanandov was born in 1955 in Petrozavodsk to the family of a well-known builder (*NG*, 2 April 1998). Following family tradition, Katanandov worked his way up in the construction industry to become the head of an association that builds large pre-fabricated panel buildings. He was elected to the city council in 1990 and then was appointed head of the city executive committee, effectively serving as Petrozavodsk mayor. He was directly elected to that position in 1994.

Katanandov won the gubernatorial race on 17 May 1998 by a margin of 49.48–43.16 percent with the backing of Our Home Is Russia (NDR) and the local political group (Concord) Soglasie. Yeltsin's presidential administration also indirectly supported him. Although some Communist members of the State Duma charged that there were numerous irregularities during the campaign, Stepanov emphasized that a new election would not change the results (*EWI RRR*, 21 May 1998).

One of Katanandov's main goals is to establish the republic's financial independence. He wants to put an end to "blaming Moscow and begging for money from the federal government." He believes that a series of small, short-term, profitable projects will help the economy recover and will be more effective than long-term programs that are difficult to implement (*RT*, 7 April 1998).

Katanandov was one of the first regional executives to join Moscow Mayor Yurii Luzhkov's Fatherland movement in November 1998. When the results of the 1999 State Duma elections were clear, he quickly lined up behind Putin.

Relationships Between Key Players: Unusually Active Legislature

Until October 1999, when a federal law required a separation between regional executive and legislative branches, Karelia was a special case. The prime minister is directly elected, but he is formally the chairman of the Legislative Assembly. Because of this institutional arrangement, the republican parliament played a greater role in political life than do similar institutions in other regions.

The newly elected premier seems to be on good terms with most of the local leaders. Andrei Demin, 34, was elected mayor of Petrozavodsk on 26 April 1998. He was the youngest mayor in the history of the Karelian capital, giving him a strong link with the prime minister (*EWI RRR*, 14 May 1998). During his campaign Katanandov mentioned that he and Demin maintained a close and cordial relationship. He also noted that he was happy to see many young deputies and heads of local governments being elected to the republican Legislative Assembly.

On 8 April 1997 President Boris Yeltsin named Vladimir Zlobin, a former Federal Security Service (FSB) colonel, as his personal representative in the republic of Karelia. Although Yeltsin also had an FSB man representing his interests in Primorskii Krai, the appointment of a secret police representative was highly unusual.

Ties to Moscow: Improving

During his election campaign Katanandov went to Moscow and met with the federal government and the Moscow city government. The federal officials did not support the incumbent Stepanov, thus implying that Katanandov was the preferable candidate. The Moscow city government expressed a strong interest in working with Karelia's precious stone extraction and processing industry.

Relations with Other Regions

Katanandov was one of the small group of governors who helped Moscow Mayor Yurii Luzhkov organize his Fatherland party in late 1998.

Karelia is a part of the Northwest Association. This association also includes the Komi Republic; Arkhangelsk, Vologda, Kaliningrad, Kirov, Leningrad, Murmansk, Novgorod, and Pskov oblasts; Nenets Autonomous Okrug; and St. Petersburg.

Foreign Relations: AssiDoman Left in Disgust

Some foreign investors have had a tough time working in Karelia and left in disgust. In June 1996 Sweden's AssiDoman bought what ultimately became a 57 percent stake in the Segezha Paper Mill (Segezhabumprom) and announced a $100 million investment program. Karelia lacks the funds to modernize the plant itself. But the Swedes shut down production at the plant in March 1997. They cited problems working with the federal and regional governments, including supplying fuel to the city of Segezha, allocating timber licenses, and paying taxes and contributions to the pension fund. According to AssiDoman, Segezhabumprom's debt to the federal budget and the pension fund topped 80 billion old rubles (then $14 million). The company's attempts to spread the repayment of this debt over three years were unsuccessful. The conflict continued for more than a year, until AssiDoman announced that it would sell its stake in February 1998. AssiDoman believes that its share of the plant is worth $52 million, although the firm was reportedly willing to sell it in spring 1998 for as low as $20 million.

Katanandov maintains that the only way to save Segezhabumprom is to find a new owner or for the government to step in and assume control. Katanandov also proposed instituting rigid government oversight of timber production and support of local industry. He gained popularity during the electoral campaign by criticizing then Prime Minister Stepanov's handling of the relationship with AssiDoman. After a campaign swing through Segezha, Katanandov immediately petitioned Stepanov to create an emergency commission to deal with the situation. Interestingly, while Katanandov

Sergei Leonidovich Katanandov

21 April 1955—Born in Petrozavodsk to the family of a famous builder; his father for many years headed Glavsevzapstroi, which handled all construction work in the republic

1972–1978—Studied in the department of Civil and Industrial Construction at Petrozavodsk University

1978–1982—Worked on various construction sites

1982—Became the head engineer of the Petrozavodsk Construction Department where he built the Vanguard Shipbuilding Factory, a dairy and meat packing plant, bread factory, and numerous apartment buildings

1984—Named chief engineer in the Petrozavodskstroi Trust

1989—Named head of an association that built large pre-fabricated buildings

1990—Elected to the Petrozavodsk City Soviet and gave up work in the construction industry. Two to three years after he left the field, the economic crisis forced the closure of most

construction companies in Karelia, including those that Katanandov had headed. He was elected chairman of the soviet and quickly gained control of the city's executive branch as well.

August 1991—Strongly backed Yeltsin against the hard-line coup

1993—Graduated from the Academy of State and Municipal Service with degrees as a manager and jurist

1994—Won Petrozavodsk's first mayoral election and became a member of the republic's House of Representatives

1995—Joined President Yeltsin's Council on Local Government

1995—Won an award in the Russian Mayor–95 contest

1996—Named to the Russian delegation on local government to the Council of Europe

17 May 1998—Elected prime minister of Karelia

criticized Stepanov for relying too much on Moscow, he also called on the federal center for more help. During the campaign, Katanandov tried to procure additional loans from then First Deputy Prime Minister Boris Nemtsov and others in the Russian Government. Katanandov's assertion that it was necessary to "take drastic measures" on the republican level to deal with the problem has so far left his exact intentions unclear.

Italy's FATA Group is planning to open a $70 million food processing plant in Karelia. The Karelian project envisages developing a full spectrum of agricultural producers—from bread and dairy shops to fish and meat plants to a distillery. According to FATA's chief representative in the Commonwealth of Independent States, a total of about 1,000 new jobs will be created (*MT*, 31 January 1998).

Finland's ENSO, the largest forestry products company in the world is building a modern sawmill factory worth $30–$40 million in Karelia. The deal, concluded in January 2000, is the largest investment project in the region in the past several years.

Attitudes Toward Business: Supportive of Economic Revival

Small and medium-sized businesses prevail in the region due to the lack of concentrated capital necessary for large enterprises. The previous premier tended to ignore them, while Katanandov has expressed support. This helped him to win his current office (*RT*, 7 April 1998).

Forestry is Karelia's leading industry, and the republic exports about 1.5 million cubic meters of lumber annually to neighboring Finland. The republic derives 60 percent of its budgetary income from logging (*EWI RRR*, 26 June 1997). Timber working is also very important. In an interview with *Russkii Telegraf*, Katanandov said that the revival of the forestry products processing sector was crucial since it has always been the most important industry in Karelia. In 1998 the only operating timber enterprise in Karelia was the Kondopozhskii Combine, which cuts and exports timber. Other such plants were then currently idle (*RT*, 7 April 1998).

There is no clash between large financial groups in Karelia, because they are not deeply involved in this region. This is mainly why the battle over Segezhabumprom, which involved only several million dollars, became such an important issue in Karelia.

Internet Site in the Region

http://www.gov.karelia.ru/info/
This is the official webpage of the Republic of Karelia's administration. It includes basic information about the republic and its geography, culture, and economy.

http://www.karelia.ru
Provides a general introduction to the numerous Internet resources in Karelia. The section on the governor has extensive information.

KEMEROVO OBLAST

Territory: 95,500 km²
Population (as of 1 January 1998):
3,023,000
Distance from Moscow: 3,482 km

Major Cities:
Kemerovo, *capital* (pop. 495,500)
Novokuznetsk (566,200)
Prokopevsk (240,800)
Leninsk-Kuznetskii (116,100)
Kiselevsk (111,600)
Mezhdurechensk (104,000)
Anzhero-Sudzhensk (96,600)

Basic Facts

Population (as of 1 Jan. 1998): 3,023,000 (2.05% of Russian total)

Ethnic breakdown (1989 census): Russians 90.5%, Ukrainians 2.1%, Tatars 2%, Germans 1.5%

Urban population (as of 1 Jan. 1998): 86.8% (Russia overall: 73.1%)

Student population (as of 1 Sept. 1997): 152 per 10,000 (Russia overall: 208/10,000)

Pensioner population (1997): 26.66% (Russia overall: 25.96%)

Percent of population with higher education (1989 census): 8.0% (Russia overall: 11.3%)

Percent of population working in (1997): Industry: 33.1% (Russian average: 23.0%); Agriculture: 5.4% (13.7%); Trade: 12.3% (13.5%); Culture: 11.2% (13.3%)

Average monthly personal income in July 1998: 912.7 new rubles (Russian average: 891.7 new rubles)

Average monthly personal expenses in July 1998: 557.1 new rubles (Russian average: 684.9 new rubles)

Average monthly subsistence requirement in 1998: 405 new rubles (Russian average: 438 new rubles)

Consumer price index (as of July 1998): 109 (Russia overall = 100)

Budgetary revenues (1997): 9,502.1 billion rubles (Russia overall: 433,378.2 billion rubles)

Budgetary expenditures (1997): 12,378.9 billion rubles (Russia overall: 468,111.6 billion rubles)

Industrial production as percentage of all Russian production (Jan.–Aug. 1998): 2.27%

Proportion of loss-making enterprises (as of July 1998): 55.6% (Russia overall: 50.4%)

Number of enterprises which have wage arrears (as of 1 Sept. 1998): 7,584 (5.61% of Russian total)

Agricultural production as percentage of all Russian production (1997): 1.75%

Number of private farms (as of 1 Jan. 1998): 1,936 (0.7% of Russian total)

Capital investment (1997): 8,855.0 billion rubles (Russia overall: 408,797 billion rubles)

Sources of investment (1997): federal budget: 19.0% (Russian average: 10.2%); regional budget: 9.1% (10.5%); extra-budgetary funds: 71.9% (79.3%)

Foreign investment (1997): 15,994,000 USD (Russia overall: 12,294,734,000 USD)

Number of joint ventures (1997): 74 (0.5% of Russian total)

Fixed capital investment in joint ventures and foreign companies (1997): 70,032 million rubles (Russia overall: 16,265.4 billion rubles)

Number of small businesses (as of 1 July 1998): 10,300 (1.19% of Russian total)

Number of enterprises privatized in 1997: 131 (4.78% of Russian total), including those which used to be municipal property: 92.3% (Russian average: 66.4%); regional property: 3.1% (20.0%); federal property: 4.6% (13.6%)

Number of telephones per 100 families (1997): in cities: 35.4 (Russian average: 49.2); in villages: 18.0 (19.8)

Brief Overview

Kemerovo Oblast, a region often called Kuzbas after the Kuznetsk Coal Basin, is located in southwestern Siberia, where the West Siberian Plain meets the South Siberian mountains. The oblast, 95,700 sq km, borders Tomsk Oblast in the north, Krasnoyarsk Krai and Khakassia in the east, Altai Krai in the west, and Novosibirsk Oblast and Gorno-Altai Republic in the south. The oblast's oldest city, Kuznetsk (after 1961, Novokuznetsk), was founded in 1618, soon after Cossack Ataman Yermak's push into Siberia. It remains the largest city in the region, exceeding even the oblast capital, Kemerovo. The region is one of the country's most urbanized. Over seventy percent of the population lives in nine regional industrial centers.

The Kuznetsk Coal Basin is one of the largest in the world. The oblast accounts for over 30 percent of Russia's total coal production. The Kuzbas is the main fuel and energy base for the eastern part of Russia, and its significance has grown since the Soviet Union collapsed. The region's other industries, such as machine construction, chemicals, and metallurgy, are based on coal mining. Despite the fact that the mining industry has been suffering greatly over the past few years, it still brings the oblast considerable profits, placing the region 14th in the country in terms of its budgetary revenues (in absolute figures). In 1998, Kemerovo was among five regions that jointly contributed over 50 percent of the payments to the federal budget, with its share being 4.5 percent.

Despite the solid investment the oblast had received, its investment potential had decreased by 6 points in 1998, according to a survey by *Ekspert* magazine. On the other hand, the same survey pointed out that investment risk in the region also had fallen by 11 points since 1997. The oblast ranked 11th among Russia's 89 regions in terms of investment potential and 57th in terms of investment risk. A 1998 survey by Bank Austria ranked the oblast 8th in terms of investment climate.

Electoral History

2000 Presidential Election
Tuleev: 51.57%
Putin: 25.01%
Zyuganov: 14.93%
Yavlinskii: 3.06%
Zhirinovsky: 2.22%
Turnout: 65.18% (Russia overall: 68.64%)

1999 Parliamentary Elections
Unity: 33.67%
Communist Party of the Russian Federation: 28.91%
Union of Right Forces: 7.69%
Zhirinovsky Bloc: 5.45%
Yabloko: 4.62%
Fatherland–All Russia: 4.47%
In single-mandate districts: 2 Unity, 1 Communist Party of the Russian Federation, 1 independent
Turnout: 55.29% (Russia overall: 61.85%)

1997 Gubernatorial Election
Tuleev (incumbent): 94.5%
Medikov (State Duma deputy): 2.1%
Turnout: 54.3%

1996 Presidential Election
Zyuganov: 38.88%/51.54% (first round/second round)
Yeltsin: 23.02%/41.54%
Lebed: 15.29%
Zhirinovsky: 11.63%
Yavlinskii: 5.34%
Turnout: 66.62%/62.99% (Russia overall: 69.67%/ 68.79%)

1995 Parliamentary Elections
Communist Party of the Russian Federation: 48.05%
Liberal Democratic Party: 12.65%
Party of Workers' Self-Government: 7.06%
Women of Russia: 3.54%
Our Home Is Russia: 3.51%
Yabloko: 2.89%
Russia's Democratic Choice: 2.78%
In single-mandate districts: 2 independent, 2 Communist Party of the Russian Federation
Turnout: 61.11% (Russia overall: 64.37%)

1993 Constitutional Referendum
"Yes"—60.3% "No"—36.5%

1993 Parliamentary Elections
Liberal Democratic Party of Russia: 29.42%
Russia's Choice: 13.74%
Women of Russia: 10.65%
Communist Party of the Russian Federation: 9.57%
Democratic Party of Russia: 7.45%
Yabloko: 6.83%
Russian Movement for Democratic Reforms: 6.47%
Party of Russian Unity and Concord: 5.71%

Agrarian Party of Russia: 5.61%

In single-mandate districts: 1 Women of Russia, 3 independent

From electoral associations: 1 Agrarian Party of Russia

Turnout: 50.79% (Russia overall: 54.34%)

1991 Presidential Elections

Tuleev: 44.71%

Yeltsin: 39.63%

Zhirinovsky: 5.80%

Ryzhkov: 5.07%

Makashov: 1.31%

Bakatin: 1.03%

Turnout: 69.74% (Russia overall: 76.66%)

Regional Political Institutions

Executive:

Governor, 4-year term

Aman Gumirovich Tuleev, elected October 1997

Sovetskii Prospekt, 62; 650099, Kemerovo

Tel. 7(384–2) 36–43–33

Fax 7(384–2) 23–31–56

Federation Council in Moscow:

7(095) 292–64–10, 926–63–65

Legislative:

Unicameral

Council of People's Deputies—35 members, 4-year term, elected April 1999

Chairman—Gennadii Timofeev Dyudyaev, elected April 1999

Regional Politics

Populist Patriot Rules Over Kuzbas Miners

Aman Tuleev is a well-known figure on Russia's political scene. Before becoming governor of Kemerovo Oblast, Tuleev held multiple regional and federal political positions, and even ran for president of Russia in 1991 and abortively in 1996 and again in March 2000. An ethnic Kazakh, Tuleev uses populist, patriotic rhetoric to play to his constituents. Consistent with his style as a people's leader, Tuleev frequently addresses people by the familiar "you" form *ty* instead of the polite form *vy*. According to Tuleev: "When I address a person as *ty*, I mean

it as an expression of confidence. In my opinion *ty* is more simple and heartfelt. If this is offensive to someone, then I beg pardon since I do not intend to degrade or insult anyone by using *ty*" (V. S. Kladchikhir, *Ne poslednie pyat' let iz zhizni nesoglasnogo politika*, Kemerovo: AO Kemerovskoe Knizhnoe Izdatelstvo, 1994, 145).

Kemerovo Oblast has suffered tremendously from the collapse of its coal mining industry, and this has fueled social unrest. Although Tuleev had served in Yeltsin's cabinet and Yeltsin had appointed him governor, Tuleev has been in constant conflict with Moscow regarding the federal government's responsibility to the region and its workers. He has been working to increase his control over the coal industry.

Executive Platform: Leftist Populist

Tuleev came to power in the midst of widespread social unrest. Local miners had been planning a general strike for 11 July 1997, at which they would demand back pay and funding for the regional mining industry as well as the resignation of President Boris Yeltsin and the entire federal government. To prevent the situation from getting out of control, on 1 July Yeltsin dismissed Governor Mikhail Kislyuk and replaced him with the more popular Tuleev. The federal government was confident of Tuleev's loyalty in spite of his Communist ties and leftist ideas. According to Sergei Samoilov, then head of the Presidential Administration's Territorial Department, the government had been negotiating with Tuleev for some time about the possibility of his becoming governor, and Tuleev affirmed his cooperation (*EWI RRR*, 3 July 1997). Although a demonstration did take place on 11 July, the anticipated massive protest did not materialize. Nevertheless, the participants criticized the government's reforms and demanded that Yeltsin and his cabinet step down. Tuleev attended the rally but did not support the demands for the president's resignation. Rather, he promised to publish information about the spending of budgetary funds and ordered tough public oversight of regional deputies, local administrators, and enterprise managers (*EWI RRR*, 17 July 1997). This event was just Tuleev's first experience as governor at calming disgruntled workers in economically depressed Kemerovo. Conflict between the mining community and the federal government has been the defining characteristic of Tuleev's tenure.

Although he is not formally a member of the Communist party, Tuleev has strong ties to the leftist opposition. He considers himself more of a left social democrat than a communist. Yeltsin, however, was not bothered by Tuleev's communist affiliations. Tuleev served in the president's cabinet as Minister of CIS Affairs for nearly a year before Yeltsin appointed him governor. Tuleev's style of governance is determined less by a specific political ideology and more by his interest in addressing social demands by employing whatever tactics are necessary, regardless of their political coloring. He is a charismatic leader whose political approaches are highly populist.

In spring 1995 Tuleev created a regional electoral union, called People's Power, that reflected Tuleev's inclination toward a traditional Soviet imperialist patriotism rather than Gennadii Zyuganov's nationalist-patriotic ideas. Although he is supportive of a market economy, Tuleev argues that the transition should have been introduced gradually and that the state should have maintained stability by protecting the fundamental elements of the economy (Kladchikhir, 115). Tuleev blames the federal government for Kemerovo's economic problems because it did not provide the region with enough support to withstand the devastation inflicted on the coal-mining industry.

In June 1999 Tuleev founded a new political party, Revival and Unity. The party called for a new regional policy that recognizes the real responsibility of the regions for their own economic and social development and also strengthens the federal government's economic policy. The party has also expressed support for small business, agricultural enterprises, and reforming the process of fiscal federalism by reworking the procedure for issuing federal subsidies to the regions. But the real aim of the party was to mobilize leftist supporters at the expense of the Communists. As a candidate for the Russian presidency in the 2000 election, Tuleev used his media opportunities (which were plentiful, reportedly thanks to Kremlin backing) to criticize the Communist party leadership. The well-funded campaign was not a success: Tuleev won less than 3 percent of the presidential vote, making hardly a dent in Zyuganov's second-place showing (*RFE/RL Russian Election Report*, 7 April 2000).

Tuleev did win a majority in Kemerovo, however.

Tuleev's populist appeal resonates strongly in economically depressed Kemerovo. Until Tuleev was elected governor on 19 October 1997, Kemerovo was the only Russian oblast that had not held popular elections for governor, due to the absence of electoral legislation. After serving as an appointed governor for a little over three months, Tuleev won one of the most lopsided victories in Russia, receiving 95 percent of the vote.

In contrast to many other governors, Tuleev has backed the suggestion of consolidating Russia's regions and reducing the number of federation subjects. He stated that the ideal number of regions would be between 25 and 35 (*RFE/RL*, 25 September 1998).

Policies: Pro-Regional

Tuleev is extremely active in addressing regional problems and concerns, although he rarely takes responsibility for botched policy. Instead of intervening at the onset of a problem, it seems that Tuleev jumps in as the hero at the climax of a situation. For example, in April 1998 Tuleev introduced direct government rule in the city Prokopevsk, something that had never been done in Russia. Protesters in the city had been requesting that Tuleev take action for more than six months, blaming Mayor Yevgenii Golubev for the city's hardships. Tuleev transferred responsibility for solving the city's problems to oblast administration officials, with no protest from Golubev (*KD*, 8 April 1998). Tuleev also refuses to take any responsibility for the difficulties the region's mining industry continually faces. He has complained multiple times that Moscow is failing to keep its promises to pay back wages to the region's coal miners. In June 1998 he announced plans to institute criminal proceedings against 50 local officials who he alleged were responsible for not paying local workers in the past (*RFE/RL*, 5 June 1998).

Tuleev followed his own course of action in dealing with the country's post–August 1998 economic crisis. He slashed the profit tax by 40 percent for local processing enterprises and cut electricity rates without consulting Moscow. Tuleev also set out immediately to revoke the licenses of firms that raised prices "artificially" (*EWI RRR*, 10 September 1998). The oblast decided to establish its own gold reserve, in violation of federal law. Tuleev complained that "the Finance Ministry is not recognizing previous agreements." He also stated that "the threat of a split in the federation will become more real every day" if federal authorities did not change their approach to the regions (*RFE/RL*, 9 September 1998).

Tuleev has been trying to enact a policy for land privatization in Kemerovo. In January 1998 he promised that every oblast resident would be allotted a plot of land for permanent lease, free of charge, by spring 1998. Priority in land distribution would be given to laid-off miners, recent college graduates suffering from downsizing, young families, families of military servicemen, and forced migrants (www.kemerovo.su). It seems, however, that no concrete policy for implementing such land allocation has yet been adopted.

Relationships Between Key Players: Consolidated Power

Tuleev has managed to consolidate all power in the region, since he essentially controls the oblast legislature. He was chairman of the Legislative Assembly from 1990 until March 1996, and his People's Power bloc won a majority of the seats in the December 1996 election. In April 1999 the legislature was renamed the Kemerovo Oblast Council of People's Deputies, and Tuleev supporters won 34 of the council's 35 seats. The elections were plagued by controversy, and many candidates complained of severe violations of the electoral law involving the registration and activities of the bloc supporting Tuleev. Non-Tuleev candidates claimed that contenders from Tuleev's bloc demanded that they give up their candidacy, threatening them with unemployment. One of Tuleev's most vocal opponents was former Legislative Assembly Chairman Aleksandr Filatov, who prior to the elections announced, "If I had a gun, I would shoot Tuleev" (*KD*, 13 April). Filatov was not reelected to the legislature, and Tuleev supporter Gennadii Dyudyaev became the new chairman.

There have been several problems regarding the leadership of the oblast's cities. Before the gubernatorial elections in October 1997, the Russian Procurator General filed criminal charges against Leninsk-Kuznetskii Mayor Gennadii Konyakhin for abuse of power following an investigation of corruption in the city. After a year-long trial, the court released Konyakhin from jail, giving him a suspended four-year sentence, but banned him from holding public office for three years (*KD*, 19 November 1998).

Tuleev has been in constant conflict with Prokopevsk Mayor Yevgenii Golubev since Golubev came to power in 1997. The two were also rival candidates in the region's gubernatorial election. In April 1998 Tuleev initiated direct government rule in the city at the request of city residents, essentially usurping all of Golubev's power (see Policies). In May 1999 mayoral elections were held in Prokopevsk even though Golubev still had 2 years left to serve in his term. Golubev boycotted the election on these grounds, and Tuleev supporter Valerii Garanin was elected mayor of Prokopevsk. Tuleev's influence over local structures continues to increase, and in the April 1999 elections all 11 of the candidates Tuleev supported in oblast mayoral elections emerged victorious.

Ties to Moscow: Struggle for Power

Tuleev has had a long, turbulent relationship with the Moscow authorities. His own national political aspirations—as a presidential candidate in 1991, a Duma contender in 1995, a presidential candidate in 1996, a minister in 1996–97, another presidential campaign in 2000—brought him into conflict with Moscow. He was highly critical of Yeltsin during the 1991 presidential campaign and has repeatedly blasted Yeltsin's various governments. In 1992 Tuleev accused the Gaidar government of "deliberate actions which led to the destruction of the state's economic foundation" (Panorama Research Group, Labyrint Electronic Database, Moscow). In March 1993 he called the president's advisers "collective Rasputins," referring to the eccentric monk who was rumored to have had considerable control over Russian Tsar Nicholas II. This comment was directed in particular at Sergei Filatov, Vladimir Shumeiko, Sergei Shakhrai, Anatolii Chubais, and Andrei Kozyrev. In an interview with ITAR-TASS in February 1996, Tuleev said, "Boris Yeltsin is dangerous for Russia, and the existing regime in this country is rooted in violence and robbery" (NNS). Yet, in spite of all the criticism and reproaches he directed toward Yeltsin's regime, Tuleev proved willing to compromise. In April 1998 Tuleev and Volgograd Governor Nikolai Maksyuta published an open letter to Communist leader Gennadii Zyuganov, asking him to back Sergei Kirienko's confirmation as prime minister. Tuleev and Maksyuta cited the need to preserve stability in the country, viewing Kirienko as a compromise candidate (*EWI RRR*, 16 April 1998).

However, as a regional politician, in his roles as chairman of the oblast Duma and as governor, Tuleev's relationship with Moscow has been characterized by a constant struggle for power. Tuleev has blamed the plight of the regions on the federal government, claiming that the federal government has robbed the regions of both power and money (*RFE/RL*, 11 September 1998). After Yeltsin dismissed the parliament in 1993, Tuleev suggested forming a united Siberian republic, which would remain in the Russian Federation as an autonomous republic. He also suggested transferring the capital of Russia to Novosibirsk.

Power and responsibility are at the center of the conflict between Kemerovo's mining industry and the federal government. Tuleev spent most of 1998 intervening in miners' strikes and blockades. In May 1998, miners held a 10-day blockade of the Trans-Siberian railroad. Six days after the blockade began Tuleev declared a state of emergency in the oblast. The blockade was lifted after several days of negotiations between then Deputy Prime Minister Oleg Sysuev and the Kemerovo miners. The government promised to spend $6.3 million on creating new jobs for employees of closing mines, and the Railroad Ministry promised to provide 53 million rubles for helping miners find new jobs. Tuleev promised to act as a "guarantor"—to ensure that the government fulfilled its obligations to the miners (*RFE/RL*, 26 May 1998).

The miners were not satisfied that the federal government fulfilled its protocols. In July 1998 they organized a 25-day blockade of the Trans-Siberian railroad at three different points in the oblast. The miners demanded the fulfillment of protocols signed by Sysuev on 24 May 1998 and Yeltsin's resignation. Tuleev demanded that President Yeltsin and then Prime Minister Sergei Kirienko take action to end the blockades. The government claimed that it had fulfilled its obligations to the miners since the 10-day blockade of the Trans-Siberian in May 1998.

This incident made clear the need for a definitive agreement between federal and regional authorities regarding the coal industry in Kemerovo. Tuleev has long hoped to sign a power-sharing agreement with Moscow, yet finding an agreeable balance of power between the oblast and center has been quite a challenge. Tuleev has constantly sought more power from the federal government. One treaty was drafted in fall 1997 and sent on to the regional legislature for approval. However, Kemerovo Oblast lawyers, who claimed that the agreement gave too much power to the region, ensured that it was not adopted (*KD*, 31 October 1997). On 30 January 1998, in response to a miners' strike, Tuleev signed a protocol with then Minister of Fuel and Energy Sergei Kirienko to influence how federal aid was distributed among individual coal-mining operations. How the actual devolution of power was to be implemented was left ambiguous (*RT*, 12 February 1998), and given the subsequent blockades in May and July, the agreement must be judged unsuccessful. In July 1998 Tuleev stated that he would not sign a power-sharing treaty with the federal government if it refused to hand over its shares in Kemerovo enterprises to the oblast government and continued to prevent the region from selling coal. Tuleev wanted the state to buy the region's coal rather than force producers to find customers (*NI*, 31 July 1998).

Finally, in August 1998, right before the dismissal of Kirienko's government, it appeared that an agreement had finally been reached, and Tuleev signed a protocol on a power-sharing treaty with the federal government. According to the agreement, all sides would cooperate to develop a stabilization program for Kemerovo. The oblast was to reduce its 49 percent budget deficit by 13 percent and turn 76 percent of the taxes and pension fund contributions collected in the region over to the federal government. The federal government would in turn reduce the number of bureaucrats employed in the region and appoint regional representatives to 50 percent of the seats it holds on the boards of directors of regional firms owned by the federal government. This agreement was viewed as a victory for both sides, since Tuleev finally secured a treaty from the federal government, but also agreed to accept some responsibility for the region's difficulties (*EWI RRR*, 27 August 1998). The agreement was never formally adopted, however, following the dismissal of the Kirienko government.

Given his strategy of blaming the region's problems on the federal government, it may be that Tuleev does not really want to sign an agreement with Moscow. Federal officials consistently complain that he is not willing to take responsibility for the problems affecting his region.

Aman Gumirovich (Moldagazyevich) Tuleev

13 May 1944—Born in the city Krasnovodsk in Turkmenistan

1964—Moved to Kemerovo Oblast

1964–1973—Worked on the railroad

1968—Joined the CPSU
Graduated from the Tikhoretsk Railroad Institute, and then from the Novosibirsk Institute of Railway Engineers in
1973 via correspondence

1973—Appointed head of the Mezhdurechensk station of the Western Siberian railroad

1978–1985—Deputy director, and then director of the Novokuznetsk section of the Kemerovo railroad

1985–1988—Manager of the department of transport and communications for the Kemerovo Oblast Committee of the CPSU

1988—Graduated from the CPSU Central Committee Academy of General Sciences

1988—Became director of the Kemerovo railroad

1990—Elected to the Congress of People's Deputies of the RSFSR and to the Kemerovo Oblast Congress of People's Deputies, where he was elected chairman

January–August 1991—Served as chairman of the Kemerovo Oblast executive committee

1991—Ran for president of the RSFSR

12 December 1993—Elected to the Federation Council

April 1994—Elected to the Legislative Assembly of Kemerovo Oblast and chosen as chairman at the first session

17 December 1995—Elected to the State Duma from the Communist party list, but chose to remain chairman of the Kemerovo Council rather than join the Duma

22 August 1996—Appointed Minister for CIS Affairs

9 September 1996—Joined the Government's Commission on Strategic Questions

18 January 1997—Appointed to the Inter-governmental Commission for Economic Cooperation between Russia and Armenia

March 1997—Confirmed Chairman of the Russian section of the Inter-governmental Cooperation Commission on Trade, Economics, and Scientific-Technology between Russia, Argentina, and Brazil

1 July 1997—Appointed governor of Kemerovo Oblast

19 October 1997—Elected governor of Kemerovo Oblast

26 March 2000—Won less than 3% of vote in Russian presidential election

Kazakh

Married, with two sons

Relations with Other Regions: Cooperation with Novosibirsk

Despite a generally conflictual relationship, in April 1999 Tuleev signed an agreement with then Novosibirsk Governor Vitalii Mukha to create a cooperative enterprise for extracting coal from the eastern part of the Kuznets basin. More than 200 million rubles will go into developing the enterprise, which expects to extract 1.7 million tons of coal per year.

Kemerovo belongs to the Siberian Accord Association, which includes the republics of Buryatia, Gorno-Altai, and Khakassia; Altai and Krasnoyarsk krais; Irkutsk, Novosibirsk, Omsk, Tomsk, and

Tyumen oblasts; and Agin-Buryat, Taimyr, Ust-Orda Buryat, Khanty-Mansi, Evenk, and Yamal-Nenets autonomous okrugs.

Foreign Relations: Sanctions Against Latvia

Having served as Minister of CIS Affairs in the federal government and on several inter-governmental committees, Tuleev is no stranger to foreign relations. He is a member of the Federation Council Commission on Protecting the Rights of Russian-Speakers in Latvia. Tuleev called for an end to the import of Latvian products to Kemerovo Oblast, in protest of Latvia's policies toward Russian-speakers. He also requested that managers of enterprises in Kemerovo cease deliveries of goods to Latvia. Other regional leaders such as Dmitrii Ayatskov from Saratov, Anatolii Lisitsyn of Yaroslavl, and Moscow Mayor Yurii Luzhkov have also called on the Russian government to increase pressure on Latvia.

In March 1998 Ukrainian President Leonid Kuchma met with Tuleev in Kemerovo and signed several trade agreements. The agreements provided that Kemerovo would ship coking coal, rail tracks, chemical and electrical goods to Ukraine and receive cars and buses, light industry goods, and foodstuffs in return (*RFE/RL*, 2 March 1998).

In October 1997 Tuleev flew to France to receive a government credit of $200 million for purchasing equipment for open coal mining and support programs to create new jobs (Radio Mayak, 27 October 1997).

Kemerovo has also received substantial support from the World Bank to reform its coal industry. However, it is not clear how effective the program has been or if all the money was spent for the intended purpose. *Business Central Europe* has noted that "there are strong suspicions that more targeted loans—such as a half-disbursed $400 million World Bank program aimed at the coal industry—have disappeared into the pockets of officials and businessmen" (*Business Central Europe*, November 1998).

Attitudes Toward Business: Protectionist

Tuleev is very interested in stimulating business in Kemerovo and protecting the region's industries.

However, it seems that he feels this would be best accomplished by playing an active role in mergers and transferring ownership shares of many large enterprises in the region over to the oblast administration. In February 1998 Tuleev announced his intention to merge the Kuznetsk and West Siberian metallurgical plants (*KD*, 25 February 1998). In March 1998 Tuleev moved to block the new owners of Yuzhnyi Kuzbass, the Sibir Central Concentrating Factory, and Uglemetkorporatsiya, from appointing their general director Valentin Neidenov. Tuleev sent a letter to the prime minister requesting that the results of the auction for ownership of the factory be overturned and that the oblast receive 50 percent of the proceeds rather than 10 percent. This would threaten the disbursal of World Bank funds intended to help the coal region since one of the preconditions for transferring money is the privatization of coal enterprises. Not long before this incident Tuleev signed a deal with Moscow to exchange shares in the firm for fuel from Moscow's Central Fuel Company (*Ekspert*, 23 March 1998).

In April 1998 Tuleev signed a cooperation agreement for improving the region's financial systems and starting a program for making Daewoo tractors and other products.

Internet Sites in the Region

http://www.kemerovo.su/

This is the Kemerovo Administration's home page. It offers basic information about the oblast and its main cities, and displays both the oblast and Russian Federation constitutions. Some of the other features of this site include recent press clippings from the administration, a list of the top enterprises in the region, and information about the oblast's investment climate.

http://www.kemsc.ru/

This is the website for the Kemerovo Scientific Center, which includes considerable information on the region's coal industry.

KHABAROVSK KRAI

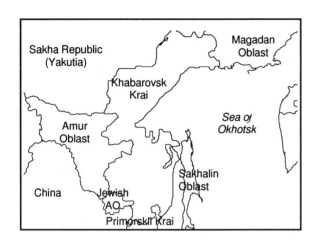

Territory: 788,600 km²
Population (as of 1 January 1998): 1,546,000
Distance from Moscow: 8,533 km

Major Cities:
Khabarovsk, *capital* (pop. 612,000)
Komsomolsk-na-Amure (298,500)
Amursk (55,400)
Nikolaevsk-na-Amure (33,500)

Basic Facts

Population (as of 1 Jan. 1998): 1,546,000 (1.05% of Russian total)

Ethnic breakdown (1989 census): Russians 86%, Ukrainians 6.2%, Northern peoples 1.3%

Urban population (as of 1 Jan. 1998): 80.6% (Russia overall: 73.1%)

Student population (as of 1 Sept. 1997): 285 per 10,000 (Russia overall: 208/10,000)

Pensioner population (1997): 22.05% (Russia overall: 25.96%)

Percent of population with higher education (1989 census): 13.3% (Russia overall: 11.3%)

Percent of population working in 1997: Industry: 22.1% (Russian average: 23.0%); Agriculture: 3.7% (13.7%); Trade: 17.8% (13.5%); Culture: 12.7% (13.3%)

Average monthly personal income in July 1998: 1,082.0 new rubles (Russian average: 891.7 new rubles)

Average monthly personal expenses in July 1998: 758.9 new rubles (Russian average: 684.9 new rubles)

Average monthly subsistence requirement in 1998: 505 new rubles (Russian average: 438 new rubles)

Consumer price index (as of July 1998): 135 (Russia overall = 100)

Budgetary revenues (1997): 5,056.5 billion rubles (Russia overall: 433,378.2 billion rubles)

Budgetary expenditures (1997): 5,448.9 billion rubles (Russia overall: 468,111.6 billion rubles)

Industrial production as percentage of all Russian production (Jan.–Aug. 1998): 0.85%

Proportion of loss-making enterprises (as of July 1998): 55.2% (Russia overall: 50.4%)

Number of enterprises with wage arrears (as of 1 Sept. 1998): 648 (0.48% of Russian total)

Agricultural production as percentage of all Russian production (1997): 0.74%

Number of private farms (as of 1 Jan. 1998): 1,061 (0.39% of Russian total)

Capital investment (1997): 2,963.7 billion rubles (Russia overall: 408,797 billion rubles)

Sources of investment (1997): federal budget: 18.1% (Russian average: 10.2%); regional budget: 10.0% (10.5%); extra-budgetary funds: 71.9% (79.3%)

Foreign investment (1997): 11,939,000 USD (Russia overall: 12,294,734,000 USD)

Number of joint ventures (1997): 140 (0.95% of Russian total)

Fixed capital investment in joint ventures and foreign companies (1997): 59,541 million rubles (Russia overall: 16,265.4 billion rubles)

Number of small businesses (as of 1 July 1998): 8,000 (0.92% of Russian total)

Number of enterprises privatized in 1997: 16 (0.58% of Russian total), including those which used to be municipal property: 100% (Russian average: 66.4%); regional property: 0% (20.0%); federal property: 0% (13.6%)

Number of telephones per 100 families (1997): in cities: 31.7 (Russian average: 49.2); in villages: 25.7 (19.8)

Brief Overview

The most important part of Khabarovsk Krai in Russia's Far East is the lower Amur River basin, but the krai also occupies a vast mountainous area along the coastline of the Sea of Okhotsk. The krai borders the Republic of Sakha (Yakutia), Amur and Magadan oblasts, Primorskii Krai, and China. There are also aboriginal peoples of the Manchu-Tungus language family here: Evenk and Even to the north, and Manchu peoples to the south of the Amur River. Some Nivkh (Gilyak), an indigenous fishing people, still live around the Amur delta. Taiga and tundra in the north, swampy forest in the central depression, and deciduous forest in the south are the natural vegetation in the area.

The krai's natural resources are poorly developed, though there are some deposits of coal and charcoal, tin, copper, silver, and gold. The region also has some oil and gas reserves, but they have not been exploited. Major regional industries are timber and fishing (including salmon) and, in the main cities, metallurgy, machine building, and chemicals. Komsomolsk-na-Amure is the iron and steel center of the Far East; a pipeline from northern Sakhalin supplies the petroleum-refining industry in the city of Khabarovsk.

Despite some wheat and soybean crops in the Amur basin, agriculture has not been highly developed, due to severe natural and climatic conditions. Local food production does not provide sufficiently for the local population.

The capital city, Khabarovsk, is at the junction of the Amur River and the Trans-Siberian Railroad, which makes it an important transportation center. The region also has the third-largest seaport in the Far East area—the port of Vanino.

Major foreign trade partners of the krai are Japan, which buys timber and petroleum products, the United States (petroleum products), and China (ferrous metals). The krai hopes to attract foreign investors to develop gold, silver, and other non-ferrous metal reserves, the forestry and timber industry, and seaport infrastructure.

According to a 1998 survey by *Ekspert* magazine, the krai ranked 29th among Russia's 89 regions in terms of investment potential and 64th in terms of investment risk. A 1998 survey by Bank Austria ranked the krai 35th in terms of investment climate.

Electoral History

2000 Presidential Election
Putin: 49.55%
Zyuganov: 28.05%
Zhirinovsky: 5.31%
Yavlinskii: 2.25%
Pamfilova: 1.58%
Tuleev: 1.23%
Turnout: 65.03% (Russia overall: 68.64%)

1999 Parliamentary Elections
Unity: 27.10%
Communist Party of the Russian Federation: 20.88%
Zhirinovsky Bloc: 9.22%
Union of Right Forces: 8.99%
Yabloko: 8.81%
Fatherland–All Russia: 5.33%
In single-mandate districts: 2 independent
Turnout: 58.23% (Russia overall: 61.85%)

1996 Gubernatorial Election
Ishaev (incumbent): 76.93%
Tsoi (State Duma deputy): 7.23%
Mantulov: 5.03%
Mironenko (LDPR): 1.26%
Yaroshenko: 0.89%
Pokusai (krai legislature deputy): 0.78%
Turnout: 48.93%%

1996 Presidential Election
Yeltsin: 39.01%/58.98% (first round/second round)
Zyuganov: 22.92%/33.72%
Lebed: 12.24%
Yavlinskii: 10.42%
Zhirinovsky: 8.65%
Turnout: 67.02%/66.05% (Russia overall: 69.67%/ 68.79%)

1995 Parliamentary Elections
Communist Party of the Russian Federation: 16.07%
Liberal Democratic Party of Russia: 12.25%
Party of Workers' Self-Government: 9.56%
Yabloko: 7.54%
Derzhava: 6.49%
Women of Russia: 5.84%
Our Home Is Russia: 3.97%
Communists–Workers' Russia: 3.91%

In single-mandate districts: 1 Communist Party of
the Russian Federation, 1 independent
Turnout: 64.45% (Russia overall: 64.37%)

1993 Constitutional Referendum
"Yes"—68.6% "No"—28.8%

1993 Parliamentary Elections
Liberal Democratic Party of Russia: 19.90%
Russia's Choice: 19.09%
Women of Russia: 12.91%
Communist Party of the Russian Federation: 12.07%
Party of Russian Unity and Concord: 7.53%
Yabloko: 7.27%
Democratic Party of Russia: 6.07%
Agrarian Party of Russia: 1.83%
In single-mandate districts: 1 Russia's Choice, 1
independent
Turnout: 46.13% (Russia overall: 54.34%)

1991 Presidential Election
Yeltsin: 59.75%
Ryzhkov: 18.10%
Zhirinovsky: 7.06%
Tuleev: 4.61%
Bakatin: 3.27%
Makashov: 3.21%
Turnout: 68.63% (Russia overall: 76.66%)

Regional Political Institutions

Executive:
Governor, 4-year term
Viktor Ivanovich Ishaev, elected December 1996
Ul. Karla Marksa, 56; Khabarovsk, 680000
Tel 7(421–2) 32–55–40;
Fax 7(421–2) 32–87–56
Federation Council in Moscow:
7(095) 292–80–56, 926–61–37

Legislative:
Unicameral
Zakonodatelnaya Duma—25 members, 4-year
term, elected December 1997
Chairman—Viktor Alekseevich Ozerov, elected
March 1994, December 1997

Regional Politics

Stable Reformer Amid Far Eastern Chaos

Viktor Ishaev is known as a pillar of stability standing against the stormy gales of Far Eastern politics in Russia. While Ishaev has governed Khabarovsk Krai since 1991, the region's western neighbor, Amur Oblast, has had six different governors, and its southern neighbor, Primorskii Krai, has been in a perpetual state of political controversy. Ishaev is frequently credited for keeping the krai economically and politically stable, especially in comparison to Primorskii Krai, which was plagued by an energy crisis, massive strikes, and a long-standing conflict between the krai governor and the mayor of its capital city.

Ishaev is enormously popular among his constituents. His success can be attributed to successful policies mixed with populist rhetoric. For his gubernatorial campaign, Ishaev adopted the popular slogan "My party is Khabarovsk Krai," fashioned to appeal to supporters of a wide range of political camps. Another successful campaign slogan Ishaev used was "I need a mandate of popular trust in order to speak with Moscow on equal terms." This statement subtly accuses the federal government of dismissing appointed officials who voice disagreement with it, thus necessitating the governor's popular election for truly effective governance. By making such statements, Ishaev tried to present himself as a truly democratic leader struggling with a badly structured system. Statements like this and the sentiments they expose characterize Ishaev's relationship to the center. The governor blames the federal government for many of the problems in Khabarovsk and other regions in the Far East.

Ishaev is well known in national politics for his active role in promoting development in the Far East and for his constant criticism of federal practices. The majority of his policies are directed toward helping Khabarovsk and the Far East become more prosperous and self-sufficient. Likewise, most of his grievances in fulfilling such initiatives highlight the lack of cooperation exhibited by the federal government.

Like many of his colleagues, Ishaev takes a tough line with the media. In July 1998 he ordered his subordinates to confiscate a cameraman's videotape at a public event. After viewing the tape, however, the authorities returned it.

Executive Platform: Democratic Regionalist

Ishaev mixes his support for market reforms with strong criticism of the federal government. Yeltsin appointed Ishaev governor of Khabarovsk Krai in October 1991; he won election to the post in December 1996, commanding 77 percent of the vote. Ishaev won a landslide victory because of the authoritative and effective way in which he guides the region. His style leaves little room for opposition. A member of Our Home Is Russia (NDR), Ishaev also lined up backing from the oppositionist National Patriotic Union of Russia (NPSR). He secured NPSR's support by promising to cooperate with the krai Duma and block any transfer of islands in the Amur River to China.

Ishaev is a strong regionalist whose interests and aims are always targeted on increasing Khabarovsk's stability and autonomy. In 1995 these sentiments developed into a rather radical proposal as Ishaev spoke in favor of creating a Far Eastern republic, with the goal of improving the region's economic position. Ishaev claimed that Khabarovsk sent 50 percent of its tax receipts to the federal budget, but the ethnic republics only sent 25 percent; thus, changing the status of Khabarovsk would serve the region's best interests. Ishaev has never pursued this idea, although he continues to criticize the federal government for ignoring its obligations to the Far East.

In 1999 Ishaev joined the All Russia party organized by Tatarstan President Mintimer Shaimiev and other governors.

Policies: Promoting Stability and Self-Sufficiency

Ishaev's main policy goal has been to foster economic and political stability in Khabarovsk. He has never advocated separating Khabarovsk from the Russian Federation, rather he hopes to build a better federation from stronger, more independent regions. Thus, he focuses on increasing Khabarovsk's self-sufficiency and reducing its reliance on the federal government. Ishaev is not afraid to play hardball with the center (see also Ties to Moscow).

Several of the governor's most noteworthy initia-

tives directly challenge Moscow's relationship with the region. Prior to the gubernatorial elections in 1996, he threatened to withhold payments to the federal budget if the government did not meet its financial obligations to the Far Eastern regions. In 1997 Ishaev slowed privatization by cutting 17 enterprises from the list of those to be privatized in 1998, complaining that the federal government was not sufficiently supportive of the national economy and was not paying enough attention to the needs of the regions. Ishaev claimed that several "banking and financial groups" were trying to take control of strategic properties in the military-industrial complex and were not working in the best interest of the country or the regions (*Segodnya*, 17 September 1997).

Following the financial crisis of August 1998, Ishaev announced that he would withhold transfers to the federal budget, complaining that Moscow owed the region more than $189 million. In addition to this measure, Ishaev also violated federal law in limiting food exports beyond the region's borders to ensure that the krai's population would have sufficient resources during the panic following the financial crisis. Among other conflicts with the federal government, Ishaev is greatly opposed to Moscow's proposals to introduce a border tax, claiming that it violates citizens' rights to enter and exit Russia freely. Ishaev's main concern was that a hefty tax would impact Khabarovsk's economy, which is heavily dependent on foreign trade.

Witnessing how economic hardship has devastated the political and social structures of other Far Eastern regions, Ishaev has prioritized building a healthy market economy. As a method to promote timely tax payments in Khabarovsk, Ishaev has established "obedient taxpayer" certificates, which entitle the bearer to freedom from a tax police audit for the following two years. Any legal entity that pays its taxes on time earns a certificate (*RFE/RL*, 17 August 1998). Another successful economic initiative was the construction of a bridge across the Amur River that connects the Jewish Autonomous Oblast, which is part of Khabarovsk, with the rest of the region.

Relationships Between Key Players

Of the 25-person Khabarovsk Krai legislature, only 8 members are from the Communist party, and the rest are prominent businessmen or politicians with a history in regional and local office. Ishaev apparently enjoys a relatively good relationship with the legislature, but the latter is not simply a tool of the governorship. On 7 July 1998 the body passed a resolution asking President Yeltsin to resign voluntarily. Although other regions passed similar pronouncements, Ishaev did not support measure.

Ties to Moscow: Constant Conflict with Federal Government

Ishaev is in constant conflict with the federal government for its failure to carry out multiple obligations to Khabarovsk and other regions (see also Policies). In particular, Ishaev has been highly critical of the federal government for not fulfilling President Boris Yeltsin's program for developing the Far East, which was promulgated during Yeltsin's 1996 presidential campaign visit to Khabarovsk. Ishaev, who is head of the Far East and Baikal interregional association, addressed the issue at a 19 November 1998 association meeting at which Yevgenii Primakov, who was prime minister at the time, was present. Ishaev stated that the federal government had provided only 3 percent of the funds needed for the program in 1998 and warned that if a new program was not developed, the Far East would be confronted with depopulation and the risk that its territory could be lost to other countries (*Segodnya*, 20 November 1998).

Ishaev also blames the federal government for the rise of separatist tendencies in Russia. He claims that the constitutional provision granting equal rights to all Russian regions is a farce because the center treats regions differently, depending on their relationship with Moscow bureaucrats. He asserts that the federal government has not settled its accounts with the krai and that federal authorities ruin all projects with which they are involved (*Izvestiya*, 5 March 1998).

In July 1996 Ishaev and then Prime Minister Viktor Chernomyrdin signed 11 power-sharing documents between Khabarovsk Krai and the federal government. The agreements discussed agriculture and industry, natural resources, developing the krai's northern areas, and defense issues. These agreements augmented the treaty signed by Ishaev and Yeltsin during the president's campaign visit in April 1996.

Relations with Other Regions: Active Far Eastern Leader

As the leader of the Far East and Baikal Association, Ishaev has been active in promoting Far Eastern interregional cooperation and development. Ishaev was a motivating force in getting the federal government to establish a development program for the Far East, and he has been extremely disappointed at Moscow's failure to support the program. To improve the situation in the Far East, Ishaev has suggested organizing a wholesale electricity market; reducing railroad tariffs; granting regions a greater share of the value-added tax, equity stake income, and customs duties; and cutting back on the number of federal offices in the area. Another goal of the Far East and Baikal association has been to increase economic cooperation with countries in the Asia-Pacific region.

In addition to his role in promoting the overall development of the Far East, Ishaev has also striven to develop direct relations between Khabarovsk and other Russian regions. In 1997 Ishaev and the governors of Sakhalin Oblast and Primorskii Krai, Igor Farkhutdinov and Yevgenii Nazdratenko, signed a joint treaty on economic cooperation until 2005. The agreement stated that the three regions would exploit the Sakhalin gas fields and make gas the primary fuel for Far Eastern power plants (*EWI RRR*, 3 July 1997).

Khabarovsk belongs to the Far East and Baikal interregional association, which also includes the republics of Buryatia and Sakha (Yakutia); Primorskii Krai; Amur, Kamchatka, Magadan, Chita, and Sakhalin oblasts; the Jewish Autonomous Oblast; and the Koryak and Chukotka autonomous okrugs.

Foreign Relations: Partnerships with Japan, China, and the United States

Ishaev has been active in increasing Khabarovsk's foreign ties in the economic, cultural, and educational fields, and has begun to develop international economic partnerships. He has signed agreements with Alaska and Japan's Hyogo prefecture to promote cooperation and develop a base for establishing economic contacts. He has also signed economic cooperation agreements with the Chinese provinces of Heilongjian and Liaonin and the Japanese prefectures of Aomori and Akita, as well as with the Korean province South Kensang and

Viktor Ivanovich Ishaev

16 April 1948—Born in the village Sergeevka in Kemerovo Oblast

1964–1971—Worked as an assembler and welder at the Khabarovsk shipbuilding factory

1971–1973—Served in the army

1979—Graduated from the Novosibirsk Institute of Water-Transport Engineers as an engineer-mechanic

1973–1988—Worked as a welder, head of shop planning bureau, head of supply department, deputy chief engineer, and deputy director at a shipbuilding factory

1988—Elected director of Khabarovsk Factory of Aluminum Construction

12 May 1990—Elected first deputy chairman of the Khabarovsk Krai executive committee, chief of economic management

24 October 1991—Appointed head of Khabarovsk Krai

12 December 1993—Elected to the first session of the Federation Council, serving on the Committee on International Affairs

10 January 1994—Halted the activities of the Khabarovsk Krai Council of People's Deputies

April 1995—Joined the organizational committee of Our Home Is Russia (NDR)

December 1995—Joined Vladimir Shumeiko's Reforms–New Course Movement

January 1996—Appointed to the Federation Council, remaining on the Committee on International Affairs

8 December 1996—Elected governor of Khabarovsk Krai

28 January–18 December 1997—Member of the government's Council for Issues of Social Development

September 1998—Appointed member of federal government presidium

Married, with a son and daughter

---

the Vietnamese region Haihyng. These agreements concern trade, exploiting natural resources, agriculture and fish industries, science and technology, transport, and communications. Khabarovsk has also been a part of the Far East's economic cooperation project with the Japanese island of Hokkaido. Khabarovsk also participates in the U.S. Regional Initiative, which focuses aid on Novgorod, Samara, Tomsk, Sakhalin, and Khabarovsk.

Not all of Ishaev's relations with foreign powers have been positive, however. Khabarovsk is in danger of losing some of its territory to the re-negotiation of the Russian-Chinese border. Even though Russia and China finally settled the majority of their border claims in April 1999, the fate of the Bolshoi Ussuriiskii and Tarabarovii islands remains undecided. The territory will remain under Russian juris-

diction until a decision can be made (Lateline News, www.lateline.muzi.net, 28 April 1999). In November 1996 Ishaev joined with the National Patriotic Union in rejecting the transfer of islands to China.

The governor has also had to deal with economic problems that have resulted from foreign ventures in the region. In 1997 Ishaev wrote to the president of South Korea to complain that the South Korean owners of Amurstal, the only Russian steel mill in the Far East, had not paid their workers in six months, causing the workers to begin a hunger strike.

Khabarovsk has also been involved in international ecological programs. In March 1997 Great Britain's Prince Philip visited Khabarovsk as the honorary president of the World Wide Nature Fund. The visit inspired Ishaev to set aside 10 percent of the krai's land for a nature preserve. In 1998 Khabarovsk was a recipient of a World Bank credit to carry out ecological programs in the forestry industry.

Attitudes Toward Business: Encourages FDI

As a way to strengthen Khabarovsk's economy, Ishaev encourages investment and business development in the region. In order to stimulate foreign investment over the past few years, Khabarovsk has introduced several regional tax breaks. Foreign investment is starting to play a greater role in the krai economy. There are more than 500 enterprises with foreign investment operating in Khabarovsk (www.geocities.com). The volume of foreign investment registered in the oblast exceeds $120 million dollars. About 30 percent of Khabarovsk's foreign investment comes from the United States, 21 percent from Japan, 9 percent from China, and 2 percent from Korea.

Internet Sites in the Region

http://www.adm.khv.ru/invest2.nsf/folders/home
This is the official site of the Khabarovsk Krai administration, featuring detailed information about the oblast's political structures, news, economy, international relations, and investment projects.

http://www.elect.khv.ru/
This site is devoted to the krai legislative assembly. It contains detailed information about the 1997 legislative elections and the Duma itself, including minutes from its meetings.

REPUBLIC OF KHAKASSIA

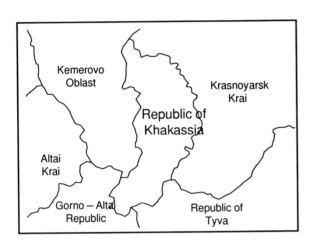

Territory: 61,900 km²
Population (as of 1 January 1998): 584,400
Distance from Moscow: 4,218 km

Major Cities:
Abakan, *capital* (pop. 166,500)
Chernogorsk (79,300)
Sayanogorsk (56,200)

Basic Facts

Population (as of 1 Jan. 1998): 584,000 (0.4% of Russian total)

Ethnic breakdown (1989 census): Russians 79.5%, Khakas 11.1%, Ukrainians 2.3%, Germans 2.0%

Urban population (as of 1 Jan. 1998): 70.8% (Russia overall: 73.1%)

Student population (as of 1 Sept. 1997): 136 per 10,000 (Russia overall: 208/10,000)

Pensioner population (1997): 23.29% (Russia overall: 25.96%)

Percent of population with higher education (1989 census): 8.0% (Russia overall: 11.3%)

Percent of population working in (1997): Industry: 26.9% (Russian average: 23.0%); Agriculture: 10.1% (13.7%); Trade: 15.2% (13.5%); Culture: 12.5% (13.3%)

Average monthly personal income in July 1998: 605.6 new rubles (Russian average: 891.7 new rubles)

Average monthly personal expenses in July 1998: 484.9 new rubles (Russian average: 684.9 new rubles)

Average monthly subsistence requirement in 1998: 473 new rubles (Russian average: 438 new rubles)

Consumer price index (as of July 1998): 105 (Russia overall = 100)

Budgetary revenues (1997): 1,268.1 billion rubles (Russia overall: 433,378.2 billion rubles)

Budgetary expenditures (1997): 1,430.7 billion rubles (Russia overall: 468,111.6 billion rubles)

Industrial production as percentage of all Russian production (Jan.–Aug. 1998): 0.27%

Proportion of loss-making enterprises (as of July 1998): 67.3% (Russia overall: 50.4%)

Number of enterprises with wage arrears (as of 1 Sept. 1998): 1,054 (0.78% of Russian total)

Agricultural production as percentage of all Russian production (1997): 0.54%

Number of private farms (as of 1 Jan. 1998): 1,072 (0.39% of Russian total)

Capital investment (1997): 975.8 billion rubles (Russia overall: 408,797 billion rubles)

Sources of investment (1997): federal budget: 10.0% (Russian average: 10.2%); regional budget: 12.2% (10.5%); extra-budgetary funds: 77.8% (79.3%)

Foreign investment (1997): 0 (Russia overall: 12,294,734,000 USD)

Number of joint ventures (1997): 9 (0.06% of Russian total)

Fixed capital investment in joint ventures and foreign companies (1997): 853 million rubles (Russia overall: 16,265.4 billion rubles)

Number of small businesses (as of 1 July 1998): 900 (0.1% of Russian total)

Number of enterprises privatized in 1997: 1 (0.04% of Russian total), including those which used to be municipal property: 0% (Russian average: 66.4%); regional property: 100% (20.0%); federal property: 0% (13.6%)

Number of telephones per 100 families (1997): in cities: 33.8 (Russian average: 49.2); in villages: 22.0 (19.8)

Brief Overview

Khakassia, with a territory of ca. 62,000 sq km, is located in the south of West Siberia, on the left bank of the Yenisei River. Until 1991 it was an autonomous oblast within Krasnoyarsk Krai. While in the beginning of the century the Khakas made up over two-thirds of the population, their current share is just over 10 percent, and the vast majority of the republic's population is Russian.

The republic is rich in raw materials: gold, coal, ferrous and non-ferrous metals, and marble. Coal and metal processing are the republic's major industries. Molybdenum, wolfram, and aluminum make up the majority of its exports. The republic houses the country's third-largest aluminum manufacturer, Sayansk Aluminum Factory (SaAZ), and the largest power plant, the Sayano-Shushenskaya Hydroelectric Station.

Despite its rich natural resources, the republican economy is underdeveloped—there are no major investment projects underway in the republic. According to a 1998 survey by *Ekspert* magazine, the republic's investment potential and risk had not changed by a single point since 1997. The region has little potential and has a risky investment environment; the republic ranks 73rd among Russia's regions in both categories. A 1998 survey by Bank Austria ranked the republic 43rd in terms of investment climate. Khakassia's population is the country's 10th poorest in terms of real per capita income, which in 1997 was only 9.47 percent of its 1991 level.

Electoral History

2000 Presidential Election
Putin: 42.45%
Zyuganov: 36.42%
Tuleev: 7.58%
Zhirinovsky: 4.51%
Yavlinskii: 3.25%
Turnout: 66.23% (Russia overall: 68.64%)

1999 Parliamentary Elections
Unity: 31.16%
Communist Party of the Russian Federation: 25.01%
Union of Right Forces: 9.72%
Zhirinovsky Bloc: 8.02%
Fatherland–All Russia: 5.02%
Women of Russia: 3.99%
Yabloko: 3.89%
In a single-mandate district: 1 independent
Turnout: 57.61% (Russia overall: 61.85%)

1996 Republican Executive Election
Lebed (State Duma deputy, Honor and Motherland): 42.10 %/71.85% (first round/second round)
Reznikov: 17.00%/19.77%
Smirnov (incumbent): 11.06%
Shpigalskikh (republican legislature deputy chairman): 5.88%
Shavyrkin: 4.98%
Bulakin (local administration head): 4.76%
Luzanov (local administration head): 3.76%
Plastunov: 2.03%
Turnout: 52.0%/46.34%

1996 Presidential Election
Yeltsin: 29.24%/47.18% (first round/second round)
Zyuganov: 35.48%/47.15%
Lebed: 12.53%
Zhirinovsky: 9.69%
Yavlinskii: 7.25%
Turnout: 65.84%/62.42% (Russia overall: 69.67%/ 68.79%)

1995 Parliamentary Elections
Communist Party of the Russian Federation: 21.57%
Liberal Democratic Party: 14.34%
Women of Russia: 6.51%
Russia's Democratic Choice: 6.02%
Communists–Workers' Russia: 5.97%
Congress of Russian Communities: 5.16%
Our Home Is Russia: 4.28%
Yabloko: 4.05%
Party of Workers' Self-Government: 3.73%
In a single-mandate district: 1 independent
Turnout: 57.57% (Russia overall: 64.37%)

1993 Constitutional Referendum
"Yes"—56.8%   "No"—40.3%

1993 Parliamentary Elections
Liberal Democratic Party of Russia: 27.45%
Russia's Choice: 15.35%

Communist Party of the Russian Federation: 10.89%
Women of Russia: 10.42%
Agrarian Party of Russia: 6.70%
Party of Russian Unity and Concord: 6.55%
Democratic Party of Russia: 5.56%
Yabloko: 3.85%
In a single-mandate district: 1 Russia's Choice
Turnout: 45.63% (Russia overall: 54.34%)

1991 Presidential Election
Yeltsin: 53.03%
Ryzhkov: 14.36%
Tuleev: 13.89%
Zhirinovsky: 9.97%
Bakatin: 2.64%
Makashov: 2.02%
Turnout: 72.89% (Russia overall: 76.66%)

Regional Political Institutions

Executive:
> Chairman of the Council of Ministers, 4-year term
> Aleksei Ivanovich Lebed, elected December 1996
> > Pr. Lenina, 67; Abakan, 662619;
> > Republic of Khakassia
> > Tel 7(390–22) 6–33–22;
> > Fax 7(390–22) 6–50–96
> > Federation Council in Moscow:
> > 7(095) 292–58–28, 926–65–11

Legislative:
> Unicameral
> Supreme Soviet—75 members, 4-year term,
> elected December 1996
> Chairman—Vladimir Nikolaevich Shtygashev,
> elected January 1997

Regional Politics

Younger Lebed Rules Neighboring Region

Although Aleksei Lebed may be best known as the younger brother of Krasnoyarsk Governor and former Russian Security Council Secretary Aleksandr Lebed, he has had a successful military and political career in his own right. Lebed is a retired colonel who served in Afghanistan, and was a member of the Russian State Duma before taking over the leadership of Khakassia. Aleksei Lebed is known popularly as *mladshii Lebed*—the "younger Lebed." Lebed says he doesn't mind this: "Being his brother has attracted me media interest" (*CSM*, 2 December 1998).

An interesting distinguishing factor between Aleksei and his older brother Aleksandr, born of a Ukrainian mother and Russian father, is that Aleksei considers himself an ethnic Ukrainian, while Aleksandr considers himself an ethnic Russian. Aleksei's sense of Ukrainian identity has helped to make him popular in Ukraine, where he was asked to run for president.

One reason why the younger Lebed remains in the elder's shadow could be that he has done little himself to attract attention. The most noteworthy event of his tenure thus far has been a series of audits conducted shortly after his election.

Unlike his brother, who had no connection to Krasnoyarsk before he ran for governor, Aleksei had served in Abakan, Khakassia's capital, for five years in the paratroops before becoming the republic's State Duma member and then executive.

Executive Platform: Distant from Moscow

Lebed was elected chairman of the Council of Ministers of the Republic of Khakassia on 22 December 1996, winning 71.85 percent of the vote in the election runoff. The republican electoral commission initially barred Lebed from the race because he had not yet lived in the republic for seven years, a requirement of the electoral law. He challenged this decision and was allowed to participate following a Russian Supreme Court decision in his favor. (Lebed's example did not set much of a precedent: Bashkortostan ignored the case in its subsequent regional elections.) Aleksandr Lebed came to Khakassia to campaign on his brother's behalf. Aleksei's electoral campaign was financed largely by the Sayansk Aluminum Factory, and several individuals connected with the factory subsequently joined Lebed's government. (See Relationships Between Key Players.)

Lebed believes that his military background gives him a wide set of experiences that help him to lead the region. He has been particularly critical of academics who have entered politics, like former acting Prime Minister Yegor Gaidar and former St. Petersburg Mayor Anatolii Sobchak, saying that they have as much understanding of the way the Russian economy works as do "American advisers" (Vladimir Tkachenko, "Aleksei Lebed," *Rossiiskii kto est´ kto*, no. 5, 1998, http://www.whoiswho.ru/). In his view it is the Russian governors who today are resurrecting the staggering economy.

Lebed supports his brother's national political aspirations, but he also joined Samara Governor Konstantin Titov's Voice of Russia movement.

Policies: Authoritative and Regulatory

Immediately following his election, Lebed began to audit the work of the previous administration. His investigation extended to an examination of the financial and economic activities of the republic's towns and districts as well. These investigations were often opposed by locals, particularly in two cities where armed gunmen led the audit. (See Relationships Between Key Players.)

In response to the financial crisis that struck the country in August 1998, Lebed announced that Khakassia would no longer make any contributions to the federal budget. He stated that the region was capable of surviving without transfers from Moscow, having paid more money in taxes than it had received in subsidies in recent years (*RFE/RL*, 31 August 1998). Such statements have little practical meaning since governors do not control tax flows.

Wage payments to public sector employees in the republic have run four to five months behind schedule. Lebed blames the problem on the Russian legislation that makes it impossible to collect taxes. He hopes to solve the problem by paying the workers with goods instead of money. However, the Sayano-Shushenskaya Hydroelectric station owes the republic more than 100 million rubles and has no products with which it can cover its debts.

Lebed seems sensitive to the non-Russian ethnic minorities in Khakassia. What little nationalist sentiment there was among the indigenous population grew out of student discussions at Leningrad State University. It has not been a local factor since 1991. Nevertheless, in July 1998 the republican government approved an education policy making the Khakas language a required subject in the republic's schools. The plan also proposed establishing courses in Khakas history and offering courses in the Chuvash and Polish languages in some schools (*RFE/RL*, 30 July 1998).

Relationships Between Key Players: Controversy with Sayansk Aluminum

Perhaps the defining event of Lebed's administration has been the ongoing controversy regarding his relationship with the Sayansk Aluminum Factory (SaAZ) which is part of Oleg Deripaska's Siberian Aluminum empire. SaAZ, the republic's largest enterprise and the third-largest aluminum producer in Russia, provided financial support for Lebed's electoral campaign. (Aleksandr Lebed also had enormous financial support from the Krasnoyarsk Aluminum Factory, but has since split with its leader, Anatolii Bykov.) Following his election, Lebed invited several individuals associated with SaAZ to join his government. Former deputy director Arkadii Sarkisyan became First Deputy Prime Minister responsible for economics, finance, mass media, and law-enforcement agencies, and former financial director Vladimir Popov became the Finance Minister. Lebed's close relationship with SaAZ has caused many to suggest that it is really the aluminum company and not Lebed controlling the republic. The fact that he has used his position to grant tax benefits to the firm contributes to this perception.

Related to the SaAZ issue is Lebed's relationship with the mayor of Sayanogorsk, the republic's second largest city, in which SaAZ is located. Mayor Sergei Bondarenko is a longtime opponent of SaAZ. Bondarenko claims that SaAZ does not honestly report its profits on the books, costing the city a sizable loss in taxes and thus hurting municipal services. Shortly after Lebed's election he ordered officers from the local branch of the Ministry of the Interior, armed with machine guns, to confiscate financial documents from the city. The mayor was outraged, especially because his administration was willing to comply with the audit. On the same day, Lebed ordered a similar forced examination of Chernogorsk, which also had agreed to the audit. Since then, Lebed has tried to have Mayor Bondarenko removed through a referendum.

Ties to Moscow: Slow Deterioration

Lebed's relations with Moscow have slowly deteriorated over time. During Yeltsin's standoff with the parliament in fall 1993, Lebed assured Khakas presidential representative Mikhail Mityukov of his loyalty to the president. However, since his elec-

Aleksei Ivanovich Lebed

14 April 1955—Born in Novocherkassk, Rostov Oblast

1976—Graduated from the Ryazan Aerial-Land Force Command School and moved on to serve in the 103 paratrooper division in Belarus

December 1979–1982—Served in Afghanistan as an intelligence commander and battalion commander

1982–1985—Served in the 76th paratrooper division in Pskov

1989—Graduated from the Frunze Military Academy and proceeded to serve in Abakan, Khakassia, Baku, Yerevan, and Dushanbe

May 1991—Became commander of the 300th parachute regiment in Kishinev, which was relocated to Abakan in 1993

17 December 1995—Elected to the State Duma from Khakassia as an independent and became a member of the Duma Committee for CIS Affairs

22 December 1996—Elected Chairman of the Council of Ministers of the Republic of Khakassia

January 1997—Joined the Federation Council and in **February** joined the Council's Committee on the Budget, Tax Policies, Finance, Currency, and Customs Regulations, and Bank Activities

Married, with a daughter, son, and granddaughter

---

tion, Lebed has not exerted energy in cultivating a relationship with the federal authorities. Lebed refused to sign the draft of a power-sharing agreement between the republic and the federal government that had been prepared by his predecessor. He stated that he intended to study the experiences of other republics and regions that had signed such agreements before preparing a new draft (*OMRI DD*, 18 February 1997). Such a draft has yet to be seen.

After the 17 August 1998 crisis began, Lebed ratcheted up his rhetoric against the president. On 26 August he addressed Yeltsin in a televised appearance, saying: "Your talent for command has surpassed that of Genghis Khan, Batu Khan, and Hitler, and in terms of your capacity for bringing ruin to [the country], you have left them all behind." (*EWI RRR*, 27 August 1998).

Lebed had no contact with President Yeltsin's representative in the region, Veniamin Anatolevich Striga, who once directed the local television station that ran extensive propaganda against Lebed (see Tkachenko). Lebed charged that by appointing such a representative Yeltsin's administration was alienating the region. In this vein he argued that the main source of separatist sentiment in the country was Moscow, not the regions.

The federal government did not have a favorable reaction to a stock issue in April 1998 by the Sayansk Aluminum Factory, with which Lebed is closely aligned. SaAZ reduced the British Trans World Group's share in the factory from 38 to 15 percent and the federal government's share from 15 to 6.5 percent. The Federal Property Fund has filed a protest with the Khakassia Property Fund, and Trans World is preparing to file a suit (*EWI RRR*, 25 June 1998).

Lebed has stated that he supports his brother's campaign for the Russian presidency. It is no surprise that he follows the elder Lebed's approach to dealing with the federal government and tends to lean on neighboring Krasnoyarsk Krai rather than Moscow to support his initiatives.

Relations with Other Regions: Close Ties to Krasnoyarsk

The relationship with Krasnoyarsk is key for Khakassia. Until 1991 Khakassia was an autonomous okrug that was part of Krasnoyarsk. Until the Lebeds took control of the two regions, relations had been relatively cool. As of late there has been some discussion of the republic rejoining the krai, although the likelihood of the younger brother ceding power to the elder is small. Nevertheless, the brothers Lebed have completed a series of economic agreements that further integrate their activities. One initiative is the "Bridge of Friendship," connecting the two regions at the Yenisei River.

Lebed also worked with Moscow Mayor Yurii Luzhkov to set up a marble factory, Sayanmramor, which supplied stone for the reconstruction of the Christ the Savior Cathedral in Moscow.

Khakassia belongs to the Siberian Accord Association, which includes the republics of Buryatia and Altai; Altai and Krasnoyarsk krais; Irkutsk, Novosibirsk, Omsk, Tomsk, Tyumen, and Kemerovo oblasts; and Agin-Buryat, Taimyr, Ust-Orda Buryat, Khanty-Mansi, Evenk, and Yamal-Nenets autonomous okrugs.

Foreign Relations: Favored in Ukraine

Unlike his brother, Aleksei Lebed has not gained much international attention. Nevertheless, he is quite popular in Ukraine. A few years ago Ukrainian politicians approached Lebed about running for president of Ukraine. He declined.

Attitudes Toward Business

There is little economic activity in Khakassia. The republic has no major investment projects underway and little foreign involvement. Khakassia, however, does have the largest deposit of jade in the former USSR, and it exports this material to Hong Kong and other parts of Asia.

The aluminum industry is important in both Khakassia and neighboring Krasnoyarsk Krai. The Sayansk Aluminum Factory is the basis of Siberian Aluminum. In spring 2000, this group joined with the business empires of Roman Abramovich and Boris Berezovskii to create Russian Aluminum, which controls 70 percent of Russian aluminum production, including Krasnoyarsk Aluminum Factory.

Internet Sites on the Region

http://www.whoiswho.ru/
In 1998, the *Rossiiskii kto est´ kto* on-line journal published a profile of Lebed.

KHANTY-MANSI AUTONOMOUS OKRUG

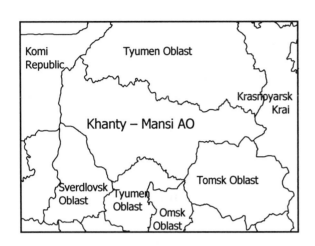

Territory: 523,100 km²
Population (as of 1 January 1998): 1,358,000
Distance from Moscow: 2,759 km

Major Cities:
Khanty-Mansiisk, *capital* (pop. 36,900)
Surgut (277,100)
Nizhnevartovsk (239,000)
Nefteyugansk (98,600)
Nyagan (59,800)
Kogalym (53,800)

Basic Facts

Population as of 1 January 1998: 1,358,000 (0.92% of Russian total)

Ethnic breakdown (1989 census): Russians 66.0%, Ukrainians 12.0%, Tatars 7.5%, Bashkirs 2.4%, Belarusans 2.3%, Chuvash 1.1%, Khanty 0.9%, Mansi 0.6%

Urban population (as of 1 Jan. 1998): 91.1% (Russia overall: 73.1%)

Student population (as of 1 Sept. 1997): 56 per 10,000 (Russia overall: 208/10,000)

Pensioner population (1997): 12.44% (Russia overall: 25.96%)

Percent of population with higher education (1989 census): 10.3% (Russia overall: 11.3%)

Average monthly personal income in July 1998: 2,514.4 new rubles (Russian average: 891.7 new rubles)

Average monthly personal expenses in July 1998: 1,011.4 new rubles (Russian average: 684.9 new rubles)

Average monthly subsistence requirement in 1998: 679 new rubles (Russian average: 438 new rubles)

Consumer price index (as of July 1998): 152 (Russia overall = 100)

Budgetary revenues (1997): 25,395.7 billion rubles (Russia overall: 433,378.2 billion rubles)

Budgetary expenditures (1997): 26,077.0 billion rubles (Russia overall: 468,111.6 billion rubles)

Industrial production as percentage of all Russian production (Jan.–Aug. 1998): 4.57%

Proportion of loss-making enterprises (as of July 1998): 54.3% (Russia overall: 50.4%)

Number of enterprises which have wage arrears (as of 1 Sept. 1998): 960 (0.71% of Russian total)

Agricultural production as percentage of all Russian production (1997): 0.20%

Number of private farms (as of 1 Jan. 1998): 720 (0.26% of Russian total)

Capital investment (1997): 31,927.3 billion rubles (Russia overall: 408,797 billion rubles)

Sources of investment (1997): federal budget: 1.5% (Russian average: 10.2%); regional budget: 18.5% (10.5%); extra-budgetary funds: 80.0% (79.3%)

Foreign investment (1997): 130,457,000 USD (Russia overall: 12,294,734,000 USD)

Number of joint ventures (1997): 81 (0.55% of Russian total)

Fixed capital investment in joint ventures and foreign companies (1997): 1,467,165 million rubles (Russia overall: 16,265.4 billion rubles)

Number of enterprises privatized in 1997: 37 (1.35% of Russian total), including those which used to be municipal property: 83.8% (Russian average: 66.4%); regional property: 0% (20.0%); federal property: 16.2% (13.6%)

Number of telephones per 100 families (1997): in cities: 49.6 (Russian average: 49.2); in villages: 16.2 (19.8)

Brief Overview

Khanty-Mansi Autonomous Okrug was established in December 1930 and is a part of Tyumen Oblast in Western Siberia. However, the 1993 Russian Constitution granted Khanty-Mansi Autonomous Okrug, along with all other autonomous okrugs, rights equal to those of an oblast. This ambiguity has produced considerable conflict between Tyumen Oblast and okrug authorities. The major bone of contention is control over Khanty-Mansi's extremely rich mineral resources: ferrous ores, charcoal, gold, diamonds, semiprecious stones and, most importantly, oil and gas.

Khanty-Mansi accounts for about 60 percent of Russia's oil extraction. It also possesses natural gas and other valuable deposits. Energy accounts for more than 90 percent of the okrug's overall output and makes it the second richest in the country. However, the energy industry contributes heavily to the level of air pollution in the area.

The okrug has a continental climate with long winters and short summers. Because of its flat landscape, plentiful precipitation, and frequent floods, almost half of the okrug's territory is covered with swamps. Forests, mostly of pine, fir, silver fir, and other conifers, fill out a third of the territory. More than 50 kinds of mammals, 200 kinds of birds, and 27 kinds of fish make up the okrug's diverse wildlife. Along with hunting, the okrug has well-developed fur-breeding: over 20 fur farms produce valuable fur animals, such as red, black, and polar fox. The okrug's agriculture, concentrated in cattle and reindeer breeding and fisheries, satisfies only 10–15 percent of local needs. Food products are the region's major import, while oil, oil products, and timber make up the majority of its exports.

According to a 1998 survey by *Ekspert* magazine, the okrug ranked 6th among Russia's 89 regions in terms of investment potential and 46th in terms of investment risk. A 1998 survey by Bank Austria ranked the okrug 53rd in terms of investment climate. The okrug's investment situation had significantly improved since 1997—it had the second-largest increase in investment potential in the country (23 points) and the second-largest decrease in risk (34 points).

Electoral History

2000 Presidential Election
Putin: 60.78%
Zyuganov: 21.25%
Yavlinskii: 6.86%
Zhirinovsky: 3.62%
Tuleev: 1.75%
Turnout: 68.19% (Russia overall: 68.64%)

2000 Gubernatorial Election
Filipenko (incumbent): 90.82%
Abramov: 1.04%
Kravets: 0.49%
Ostapenko: 0.37%
Turnout: 67.89%

1999 Parliamentary Elections
Unity: 29.20%
Communist Party of the Russian Federation: 15.49%
Union of Right Forces: 11.45%
Yabloko: 9.35%
Zhirinovsky Bloc: 8.34%
Fatherland–All Russia: 7.84%
In single-mandate districts: 2 independent
Turnout: 59.7% (Russia overall: 61.85%)

1996 Gubernatorial Election
Filipenko (incumbent): 71.49%
Korepanov (deputy governor): 11.18%
Turnout: 47.42%

1996 Presidential Election
Yeltsin: 52.53%/74.24% (first round/second round)
Lebed: 15.14%
Zyuganov: 12.82%/20.20%
Zhirinovsky: 7.59%
Yavlinskii: 6.61%
Turnout: 62.41%/60.95% (Russia overall: 69.67%/ 68.79%)

1995 Parliamentary Elections
Liberal Democratic Party of Russia: 15.28%
Our Home Is Russia: 14.08%
Party of Workers' Self-Government: 10.62%
Women of Russia: 8.78%
Communist Party of the Russian Federation: 7.96%
Yabloko: 5.68%
Congress of Russian Communities: 3.51%
Forward, Russia: 3.04%
Communists–Workers' Russia: 2.95%
Russia's Democratic Choice: 2.84%
Kedr: 2.68%
In single-mandate districts: 2 independent
Turnout: 54.67% (Russia overall: 64.37%)

1993 Constitutional Referendum
"Yes"—80.3% "No"—17.8%

1993 Parliamentary Elections
Russia's Choice: 23.66%
Liberal Democratic Party of Russia: 21.25%
Women of Russia: 12.20%
Party of Russian Unity and Concord: 9.52%
Yabloko: 8.24%
Democratic Party of Russia: 6.37%
Communist Party of the Russian Federation: 4.63%
Agrarian Party of Russia: 1.04%
In single-mandate districts: 1 independent, 1 Russia's
    Choice
Turnout: 38.91% (Russia overall: 54.34%)

1991 Presidential Elections
Yeltsin: 68.72%
Zhirinovsky: 9.67%
Ryzhkov: 8.12%
Tuleev: 3.81%
Bakatin: 3.76%
Makashov: 3.57%
Turnout: 64.54% (Russia overall: 76.66%)

Regional Political Institutions

Executive:
    Governor, 4-year term
    Aleksandr Vasilevich Filipenko, elected
    October 1996, reelected March 2000
        Dom Sovetov; Ul. Mira, 5;
        Khanty-Mansi, 626200;
        Khanty-Mansi AO, Tyumen Oblast
        Tel 7(346–71) 3–20–27, 3–20–95;
        Fax 7(346–71) 3–34–60
        Federation Council in Moscow:
        7(095) 292–58–65, 926–61–72

Legislative:
Unicameral
    Duma—23 members, 4-year term, elected
    October 1996
    Chairman—Sergei Semenovich Sobyanin, elected
    March 1994, November 1996

Regional Politics

Yeltsin Appointee with Separatist Interests

Aleksandr Filipenko, a strong lobbyist for his region, was elected governor of Khanty-Mansi Autonomous Okrug in October 1996, securing more than 70 percent of the vote. At the time of his election, Filipenko had been serving as governor for nearly five years, having been appointed to the post by President Yeltsin in December 1991. Filipenko faced no strong competition and had the unusual support of both the presidential administration and the Communist opposition. Filipenko was reelected with even greater support in March 2000, pulling in almost 91 percent of the vote.

In his role as regional executive, Filipenko is most well known for leading his okrug in attempts to secede from Tyumen Oblast, to which it is subordinate. Since Khanty-Mansi produces more than 60 percent of Russia's oil, it is one of Russia's few donor regions, and thus it is of great strategic importance to both Tyumen Oblast and the federal center.

Executive Platform: Greater Okrug Autonomy

Gaining greater autonomy for the okrug has been Filipenko's top priority in all of his electoral endeavors. In both his gubernatorial campaign and his campaign for election to the Federation Council in 1993, Filipenko stressed greater economic independence for the okrug. He believes that Khanty-Mansi's subordination to Tyumen Oblast violates the equal rights granted to the okrug as a subject of the Russian Federation.

Filipenko would like to see the okrug freed from its economic dependence on raw materials, and hopes that the construction and tourist industries will take root. The governor is interested in establishing tax and credit conditions to help stimulate enterprise production, and has spoken about financing employment programs for women and young people. Filipenko is pushing for measures to conserve the environment and ensure ecologically sound living conditions. He also is interested in protecting and preserving the cultures of the indigenous peoples of the north (Panorama Research Group, Labyrint Electronic Database, Moscow).

In 1999 Filipenko joined the All Russia party organized by Tatarstan President Mintimer Shaimiev and other governors.

Policies: Strong Social Sphere

Because of its vast oil wealth, Khanty-Mansi's budget is one of the richest in Russia. The region boasts sufficient means to support health, educational, cultural, and athletic institutions. Hospitals, schools, and enterprises for developing the region's natural resources are all being built (Panorama). Khanty-Mansi is also home to one of Russia's two battered women's shelters. The level of social defense for the inhabitants of the okrug is higher than the average Russian standard. One of Filipenko's social successes has been founding a university in the okrug.

Relationships Between Key Players

Filipenko is considered a relatively minor player in his region since most of the real power in Khanty-Mansi is wielded by Russia's influential oil companies. LUKoil, which draws its name from three okrug cities, is Russia's largest oil company and controls much of the local economy. Additionally, Yukos, which owns 51 percent of the voting shares in Yuganskneftegaz, located in the city of Nefteyugansk, has had a considerable impact on the region. The company has reduced wages by 30 percent and laid off approximately 15,000 people, reducing the workforce to 39,000. Locals often blame oligarch Mikhail Khodorkovskii, who controls Yukos, for the problems in Nefteyugansk. Yuganskneftegaz has also come into conflict with the Nefteyugansk local administration, which claims the company owes it back taxes. Former Nefteyugansk Mayor Vladimir Petukhov was assassinated in July 1998, a month after he led a demonstration that disrupted a meeting of Yukos shareholders. Viktor Tkachev was elected to replace Petukhov in February 1999, and was expected to reach a compromise with the company (*MT*, 2 March 1999).

Ties to Moscow: Donor Region

President Boris Yeltsin appointed Filipenko governor of Khanty-Mansi Autonomous Okrug in December 1991, and the presidential administration supported his candidacy in the 1996 gubernatorial elections. Nevertheless, Filipenko's conflicts with Tyumen Oblast (see Relations with Other Regions) have forced Moscow to intervene and mediate between the respective regions. Moscow tolerates this unrest most likely because of Khanty-Mansi's enormous wealth in natural resources.

In 1998, Filipenko began working to improve ties with the center. He and Russian Justice Minister Pavel Krasheninnikov signed an agreement aimed at increasing the compliance of the okrug's laws with Russian legislation. The two sides will share information to improve the quality of the okrug's legislation. They hope that their cooperation will be more productive than simply having the federal authorities criticize the regions for not complying with federal law (*NG*, 23 June 1998).

Khanty-Mansi is one of Russia's "donor" regions which contribute more to the federal budget than they receive in return. In November 1996 Filipenko joined other leaders from donor regions in sending a letter to the federal government calling for a change in policy toward economically advanced regions. The leaders suggested that all regions should receive equal treatment by the government, regardless of their status. The leaders proposed temporarily freezing mutual debts between fuel and energy companies and regions, tightening tax and payments discipline, and cutting energy and fuel prices.

Relations with Other Regions: Long-standing Conflict with Tyumen Oblast

Khanty-Mansi Autonomous Okrug is a federation subject that is also part of the territory of Tyumen Oblast. Yamal-Nenets Autonomous Okrug also has the same ambiguous status. Both of the okrugs have been trying to secede from Tyumen Oblast, primarily for economic reasons. Combined, Khanty-Mansi and Yamal-Nenets control 90 percent of Russia's natural gas and 60 percent of its oil reserves. Sixty percent of the money enterprises pay in taxes goes into okrug and local budgets, and the remaining 40 percent is split between the oblast (Tyumen) and federal budgets. If the okrugs were to successfully secede from Tyumen, then they could retain the additional 20 percent tax revenue.

Khanty-Mansi and Yamal-Nenets have tried to assert themselves in multiple ways, but the most noteworthy was their refusal to participate in the Tyumen Oblast gubernatorial elections in December 1996. Ultimately, Khanty-Mansi relented under persuasion from the federal government, and agreed to take part in the elections. However, only 15 percent of eligible voters from the okrug participated in the election, causing the results to be considered invalid since the 25 percent barrier was not reached. Thus, the okrug did not participate in the second round of voting. This did not affect the outcome of the elections, since the oblast amended its electoral law, eliminating a minimum voter turnout to validate elections. Filipenko was against the reelection of Tyumen Governor Leonid Roketskii because Roketskii had opposed the okrug's separatist tendencies.

Aleksandr Vasilevich Filipenko

31 May 1950—Born in the city of Karaganda in Kazakhstan

1967—Began working as a radio tuner at the Kirov Factory in Petropavlovsk, Kazakhstan

1973—Graduated from the Siberian Automobile and Roads Institute in Omsk as an engineer-bridge builder

1973–1977—Worked in Surgut, Khanty-Mansi Autonomous Okrug, as a construction foreman, engineer, and senior engineer

1977–1982—Worked as an instructor and manager of the construction department of the CPSU okrug committee

1982–1983—Deputy chairman of the Khanty-Mansi okrug executive committee

1983–1988—First secretary of the Berezovo CPSU district committee

1987—Graduated from the Sverdlovsk Higher Party School

1988–1989—Second secretary of the CPSU okrug committee

March 1989—Became chairman of the Khanty-Mansi okrug executive committee

March 1990—Elected to the Tyumen Oblast Council of People's Deputies and the Khanty-Mansi Autonomous Okrug Council of People's Deputies

May 1990—Elected chairman of the okrug executive committee

18 December 1991—Appointed governor of Khanty-Mansi Autonomous Okrug by presidential decree

12 December 1993—Elected to the Federation Council, where he served on the Committee for Federation Affairs, Federation Treaties, and Regional Politics until April 1994, when he joined the Committee for Northern Affairs and Indigenous Peoples

January 1996—Appointed to the second session of the Federation Council, serving on the Committee for Northern Affairs and Minority Peoples and the Mandate Committee

October 1996—Elected governor of Khanty-Mansi Autonomous Okrug

1996—Became a member of the advisory council for the All-Russian Bank for Regional Development

28 January 1997—Joined the government council on issues of social development

16 April 1997—Joined the presidential committee on improving legal cooperation between the federal and regional authorities

26 March 2000—Reelected governor of Khanty-Mansi AO

The issue of Khanty-Mansi and Yamal-Nenets independence from Tyumen Oblast was brought before the Constitutional Court in 1997. In July the Court handed down a decision skirting the issue by restating that the regions were simultaneously equal subjects of the federation and subordinate to Tyumen. Essentially, the okrugs have the right to secede at any time without the agreement of the oblast, yet the secession must be validated via federal constitutional law. The court also stated that the okrugs must participate in oblast legislative and gubernatorial elections; yet the powers of these institutions are defined by federal legislation, regional statutes, and bilateral treaties. Thus the court decision did not clarify the ambiguity of okrug-oblast relations nor settle the Khanty-Mansi versus Tyumen conflict. Filipenko has not directly challenged the court's decision, halting secessionist activities. A governors' council has been established as a forum for the heads of the two okrugs and Tyumen to address their problems. The okrug also signed an agreement to participate in the Tyumen legislative elections in December 1997.

Khanty-Mansi belongs to the Siberian Accord Association, which includes the republics of Buryatia, Gorno-Altai, and Khakassia; Altai and Krasnoyarsk krais; Irkutsk, Novosibirsk, Omsk, Tomsk, Tyumen, and Kemerovo oblasts; and Agin-Buryat, Taimyr, Ust-Orda Buryat, Evenk, and Yamal-Nenets autonomous okrugs.

Attitudes Toward Business: Member of Oil Board

Filipenko is on the board of directors of Surgutneftegaz, which provides 27 percent of the okrug's budget. Filipenko does not feel that this role causes any conflict of interest in political and economic spheres. He considers himself to represent the state on the board (*EWI RRR*, 23 October 1997).

The Samotlor oil field was once the Soviet Union's largest producer. Over the past 30 years it has provided 2.2 billion tons of oil, and it is estimated that an additional 1.5 billion tons remain in the ground. To extract the remaining oil, the Tyumen Oil Company in October 1998 agreed to work with Halliburton Energy Services. The project is expected to cost up to $10 billion. On 28 May 1999, Halliburton announced that the project was moving ahead (http://www.halliburton.com/news/hes_news/pr_hes_052899.htm).

KIROV OBLAST

Territory: 120,800 km²
Population (as of 1 January 1998):
1,613,000
Distance from Moscow: 896 km

Major Cities:
Kirov, *capital* (pop. 465,400)
Kirovo-Chepetsk (93,500)
Vyatskie Polyany (42,500)
Slobodskoi (35,100)
Kotelnich (31,400)
Omutninsk (28,900)

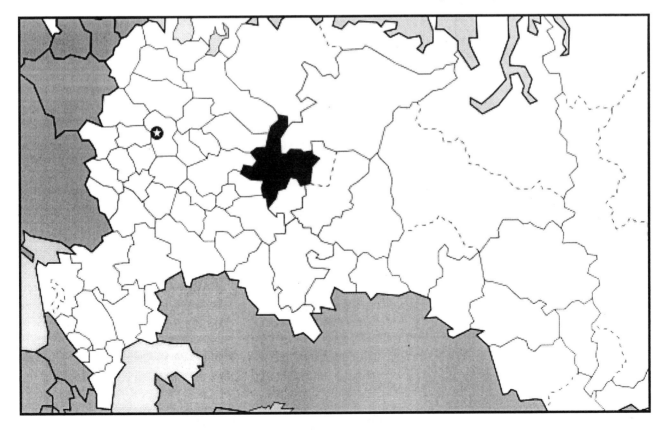

Basic Facts

Population (as of 1 Jan. 1998): 1,613,000 (1.10% of Russian total)

Ethnic breakdown (1989 census): Russians 90.4%, Tatars 2.7%, Marii 2.6%, Udmurts 1.4%, Ukrainians 1.1%

Urban population (as of 1 Jan. 1998): 70.8% (Russia overall: 73.1%)

Student population (as of 1 Sept. 1997): 114 per 10,000 (Russia overall: 208/10,000)

Pensioner population (1997): 27.28% (Russia overall: 25.96%)

Percent of population with higher education (1989 census): 7.9% (Russia overall: 11.3%)

Percent of population working in (1997): Industry: 26.8% (Russian average: 23.0%); Agriculture: 14.5% (13.7%); Trade: 14.7% (13.5%); Culture: 12.5% (13.3%)

Average monthly personal income in July 1998: 569.5 new rubles (Russian average: 891.7 new rubles)

Average monthly personal expenses in July 1998: 508.4 new rubles (Russian average: 684.9 new rubles)

Average monthly subsistence requirement in 1998: 430 new rubles (Russian average: 438 new rubles)

Consumer price index (as of July 1998): 81 (Russia overall = 100)

Budgetary revenues (1997): 2,837.8 billion rubles (Russia overall: 433,378.2 billion rubles)

Budgetary expenditures (1997): 3,150.8 billion rubles (Russia overall: 468,111.6 billion rubles)

Industrial production as percentage of all Russian production (Jan.–Aug. 1998): 0.62%

Proportion of loss-making enterprises (as of July 1998): 54.2% (Russia overall: 50.4%)

Number of enterprises which have wage arrears (as of 1 Sept. 1998): 1,829 (1.35% of Russian total)

Agricultural production as percentage of all Russian production (1997): 1.62%

Number of private farms (as of 1 Jan. 1998): 1,381 (0.50% of Russian total)

Capital investment (1997): 1,623.2 billion rubles (Russia overall: 408,797 billion rubles)

Sources of investment (1997): federal budget: 8.2% (Russian average: 10.2%); regional budget: 8.9% (10.5%); extra-budgetary funds: 82.9% (79.3%)

Foreign investment (1997): 827,000 USD (Russia overall: 12,294,734,000 USD)

Number of joint ventures (1997): 29 (0.20% of Russian total)

Fixed capital investment in joint ventures and foreign companies (1997): 2,822 million rubles (Russia overall: 16,265.4 billion rubles)

Number of small businesses (as of 1 July 1998): 4,100 (0.47% of Russian total)

Number of enterprises privatized in 1997: 17 (0.62% of Russian total), including those which used to be municipal property: 76.5% (Russian average: 66.4%); regional property: 5.9% (20.0%); federal property: 17.6% (13.6%)

Number of telephones per 100 families (1997): in cities: 39.5 (Russian average: 49.2); in villages: 17.9 (19.8)

Brief Overview

Kirov Oblast is located in the eastern part of the Eastern European plain, halfway between Moscow and the Ural Mountains. Due to a well-developed system of rivers and canals, it has transport links to harbors in the Baltic, Black, White, Azov, and Caspian seas. The region borders the republics of Udmurtia, Marii El, Tatarstan, and Komi, as well as Perm, Vologda, Kostroma, Arkhangelsk, and Nizhnii Novgorod oblasts. The oblast capital, Kirov (called Vyatka until 1934), was founded in 1374, and is located about 900 km northeast of Moscow.

Although in the past, the region was an agricultural area, it has now become a major industrial center. It is rich in mineral resources: ferrous and copper ores, oil, sands, and clays. It also houses the country's largest phosphorous field, and peat reserves exceed 300 million tons. Half of the oblast territory is covered with woods, which makes Kirov Oblast the country's fourth-largest timber cutting and fifth-largest timber working region. Local industry specializes in machine building, ferrous and non-ferrous metallurgy, chemicals, microbiology, timber working, cellulose, consumer goods, and food production. Though the soil is generally poor, it produces fairly good harvests of grain, potatoes, vegetables, and flax.

According to a 1998 survey by *Ekspert* magazine, the oblast is ranked 56th among Russia's 89 regions in terms of investment potential and 61st in terms of investment risk. A 1998 survey by Bank Austria ranked the oblast 64th in terms of investment climate.

Electoral History

2000 Presidential Election
Putin: 58.55%
Zyuganov: 27.22%
Yavlinskii: 3.68%
Zhirinovsky: 2.68%
Tuleev: 2.36%
Turnout: 72.59% (Russia overall: 68.64%)

2000 Gubernatorial Election
Sergeenkov (incumbent): 58.32%
Alpatov: 14.87%
Pervakov: 11.42%
Sharenkov: 4.36%
Kozunin: 2.16%
Turnout: 72.10%

1999 Parliamentary Elections
Unity: 33.41%
Communist Party of the Russian Federation: 22.77%
Union of Right Forces: 7.20%
Zhirinovsky Bloc: 6.03%
Yabloko: 5.04%
Fatherland–All Russia: 5.01%
In single-mandate districts: 2 independent
Turnout: 64.97% (Russia overall: 61.85%)

1996 Gubernatorial Election
Sergeenkov (State Duma deputy): 39.64%/50.46%
    (first round/second round)
Shtin: 30.54%/45.45%
Desyatnikov (incumbent): 18.20%
Polyantsev: 5.63%
Turnout: 50.7%/54.32%

1996 Presidential Election
Yeltsin: 31.24%/50.70% (first round/second round)
Zyuganov: 28.96%/41.57%
Lebed: 13.70%
Yavlinskii: 12.15%
Zhirinovsky: 8.62%
Turnout: 72.70%/69.86% (Russia overall: 69.67%/
    68.79%)

1995 Parliamentary Elections
Liberal Democratic Party of Russia: 17.05%
Communist Party of the Russian Federation: 14.78%
Agrarian Party of Russia: 9.54%
Women of Russia: 7.75%
Communists–Workers' Russia: 6.96%
Yabloko: 6.70%
Our Home Is Russia: 5.84%
Congress of Russian Communities: 3.38%
Party of Workers' Self-Government: 3.02%
In single-mandate districts: 1 Agrarian Party of
    Russia, 1 independent
Turnout: 68.82% (Russia overall: 64.37%)

1993 Constitutional Referendum
"Yes"—59.6% "No"—37.5%

1993 Parliamentary Elections
Liberal Democratic Party of Russia: 27.53%
Agrarian Party of Russia: 15.27%
Russia's Choice: 12.48%
Women of Russia: 9.96%

Communist Party of the Russian Federation: 8.74%
Yabloko: 7.54%
Party of Russian Unity and Concord: 5.34%
Democratic Party of Russia: 5.27%
In single-mandate districts: 1 Liberal Democratic
  Party of Russia, 1 independent
Turnout: 58.57% (Russia overall: 54.34%)

1991 Presidential Elections
Yeltsin: 50.94%
Bakatin: 14.68%
Ryzhkov: 9.70%
Tuleev: 8.39%
Zhirinovsky: 6.92%
Makashov: 2.99%
Turnout: 78.87% (Russia overall: 76.66%)

Regional Political Institutions

Executive:
  Governor, 4-year term
  Vladimir Nilovich Sergeenkov, elected
  October 1996, March 2000
    Ul. Derenyaeva, 34; Kirov, 610019
    Tel 7(833–2) 62–95–64; Fax 7(833–2)
    62–89–58
    Federation Council in Moscow:
    7(095) 292–04–27, 926–68–73

Legislative:
Unicameral
Oblast Duma—54 members, 4-year term, elected
  March 1997
Chairman—Mikhail Aleksandrovich Mikheev,
  elected April 1994, April 1997

Regional Politics

Communist Duma Deputy Ousts Reformer

Vladimir Sergeenkov was a member of the Popular
Power Duma faction when he was elected governor
of Kirov Oblast in October 1996. Sergeenkov, backed
by the Communist-led National Patriotic Union of
Russia (NPSR), earned 50.64 percent of the vote, defeating businessman Nikolai Shtin in the second
round. Incumbent Vasilii Desyatnikov did not even
manage to make it to the runoff. Sergeenkov was reelected in a first-round victory in March 2000, winning 58.32 percent of the vote.

Sergeenkov has enjoyed considerable support in Communist-dominated Kirov region. He favors generous
social security benefits for the population, and industrial development and defense conversion to replenish
the oblast economy. Sergeenkov has limited foreign
relations, but is trying to increase his ties to find additional trade markets for Kirov's timber products and
other manufactured goods, including in Iran.

Executive Platform: Renewed Socialism

Sergeenkov has described himself as an advocate of
renewed socialism (*Izvestiya*, 27 May 1998). Ideology aside, however, he is willing to do what it takes
to keep Kirov's economy functioning. In spring 1998,
he paid 20–25 percent of the population's wage arrears in food items to prevent rioting. Prior to the
August 1998 crisis, Sergeenkov advocated increasing the money supply to resolve Russia's economic
problems. He favors reinstating a state monopoly on
the sale of vodka and imposing high import tariffs on
chicken ("Bush legs") to protect domestic poultry
farmers. Sergeenkov, however, opposes mutual debt
cancellation among enterprises.

With an eye on the December 1999 parliamentary
and June 2000 presidential elections, Sergeenkov joined
Samara Governor Konstantin Titov's bloc of regional
leaders, Voice of Russia. However, when Putin's success was clear, he deftly switched sides and moved up
his election several months to secure a second term.

Policies: Defense Conversion and Timber Development

One of Sergeenkov's primary economic concerns is
the conversion of the region's defense enterprises to
profitable civilian output. Production in the defense
sector has dropped to less than one-sixth of its 1990
level, and state orders only make up 3.8 percent of
previous levels (www.kirov.region.ru). Nearly half of
all employees in the defense sector, 34,665 people,
have lost their jobs. In June 1998, Sergeenkov started
a two-year program for defense conversion. The
program's goal is to find organizational and financial
support on the regional and federal level for restructuring defense enterprises. If the program is carried
out as planned, the oblast anticipates an increase in
the volume of goods produced to 4.1 billion rubles by
the year 2000, sending 290 million rubles to the oblast
budget and creating more than 6,000 jobs. The greatest challenges confronting the program's success are

restructuring debts enterprises owe to the federal and local governments and securing loans.

Sergeenkov established a working group to investigate the millennium bug to make sure that the oblast was ready to deal with the Y2K problem (www.kirov.region.ru). Sergeenkov is also interested in developing Kirov's forestry industry. He is seeking markets in Asia and Europe, including Iran, where Sergeenkov believes there is a high demand for timber products. Sergeenkov hoped that foreign investment in Kirov Oblast would increase from 1.5 percent in 1997 to 15 percent in 1999.

Sergeenkov is very concerned about the social welfare of the region's inhabitants. In January 1999 he established a commission for developing a program providing hot meals for schoolchildren in needy families, using 80,000 rubles from the governor's charitable fund (www.kirov.region.ru).

In June 1999 the Kirov Oblast Duma amended the region's price policy to allow the administration to set prices for 22 types of food products, 3 industrial goods, and 7 services. The price controls cover essential food items, utilities, and public transportation.

Relationships Between Key Players: Communists Dominate

The Communist party dominates the Kirov political scene, providing Sergeenkov with considerable support for his initiatives. Communists are the best represented party in the oblast Duma elected in March 1997, holding about one-third of the seats. Farm directors hold 18 seats, enterprise directors 8, and other professionals, 12.

The city of Kirov received national attention in June 1998 when Sergei Bachinin, the controversial editor-in-chief of the *Vyatskii Nablyudatel* newspaper was hospitalized with a fractured skull after an alleged "biking incident." A year before, Bachinin had been taken into custody by local police as a "suspected drug dealer" and was subsequently found guilty of drug possession. His arrest occurred after the paper published articles critical of local authorities. The police appeared in his office, claiming that they had been sent to investigate a bomb scare and had found narcotics in their search. Bachinin's supporters believe that the police planted the evidence. Bachinin is a frequent critic of Sergeenkov and the Kirov city government and was the main opponent of current Kirov Mayor Vasilii Kiselev in the 1996 elections.

In 1997 there was a controversy in the oblast regarding the privatization of 38 percent of the Kirov-Chepetsk chemical plant. Residents protested the sale out of concern for the large deposits of radioactive and toxic waste on the land surrounding the plant. The privatization plan permitting the sale of this contaminated site was in direct violation of the law. Sergeenkov lobbied on the plant's behalf and addressed then Russian Prime Minister Viktor Chernomyrdin, suggesting that the maintenance of contaminated property should be handled by federal agencies (*EWI RRR*, 11 September 1997). The oblast procurator subsequently stopped privatization of the plant.

Ties to Moscow: Improved Relations

When Sergeenkov first came to power, relations with the federal government and president were tense, but various issues brought the governor and central powers together. The government sympathized with Sergeenkov's struggle against illegal woodcutters in the region, and sided with the governor during his conflict with the Kirov-Chepetsk chemical combine, when the oblast authorities demanded that their shares in the combine be returned. Relations between the governor and the federal government improved when former First Deputy Prime Minister Boris Nemtsov came to power.

Sergeenkov met with several members of former Prime Minister Yevgenii Primakov's cabinet, including Primakov himself. In February 1999 they met to discuss the problems confronting Kirov Oblast, particularly energy supply. Primakov supported Sergeenkov's interest in increasing the role of state management in privatized enterprises (www.kirov.region.ru). In December 1998, Sergeenkov met with then Minister of Trade Georgii Gabuniya and agreed on the preliminary text of a cooperation agreement between the ministry and the Kirov Oblast administration.

On 30 October 1997, Kirov signed a power-sharing agreement with the federal government.

Relations with Other Regions: Economic Ties with Komi

In the end of 1998 an exhibition of goods produced in Kirov Oblast was held in Syktyvkar, Komi Republic.

Vladimir Nilovich Sergeenkov

5 December 1938—Born in Kirov Oblast

1959—Graduated from the law department of Perm State University

1959–1962—Worked in Mordovia for the republican procurator

1962—Moved to party work, serving as the secretary of the district committee of the Komsomol, secretary of the CPSU district committee for the agro-industrial district of Mordovia, and eventually worked in the Saran city CPSU committee (until the early 1980s when he had a falling out with the republic's party leadership and returned to Kirov to work in academia)

1991—Head of the local Institute for Social-Economic Problems and a senior instructor at the Finance-Economics Institute

12 December 1993—Elected to the first session of the Federation Council

January 1994–January 1996—Deputy chair of the Federation Council Committee on Issues of Economic Reforms, Ownership, and Property Relations

17 December 1995—Elected to the State Duma, joining the Popular Power faction; served on the Duma Committee on Ownership, Privatization, and Economic Activities

20 October 1996—Elected governor of Kirov Oblast

26 March 2000—Reelected governor

Prior to the exhibition, the two regions had signed a cooperation agreement that subsequently doubled trade activity between Komi and Kirov.

Kirov belongs to the Northwest Regional Association, which includes the republics of Karelia and Komi; Arkhangelsk, Vologda, Kaliningrad, Leningrad, Murmansk, Novgorod, and Pskov oblasts; Nenets Autonomous Okrug; and the federal city of St. Petersburg.

Foreign Relations: Hoping to Export Defense Technology

In February 1999, a delegation from Iran visited the region. The delegation was particularly interested in the products of the local defense industry. Sergeenkov hopes to sell military goods and then invest the proceeds in high-technology production that will serve both military and civilian needs (*Izvestiya*, 11 March 1999).

In November 1998 chairman of the Swedish Business Club, Ulf Grenlund, visited several enterprises in the region. Sergeenkov hopes to develop trade relations with the group to increase commercial activity with Sweden.

Attitudes Toward Business: Strategy to Increase Output

Sergeenkov's two primary business goals are to further develop the oblast's timber industry and convert defense enterprises to manufacturing consumer goods. The Kirov Tire Factory is one regional enterprise that has undergone a successful conversion from the defense sector. The factory began producing tires for civilian vehicles in 1994. It has benefited from the Russian financial crisis, since the demand for domestic tires increased as imported tires became too expensive (*MT*, 25 February 1999).

Although Kirov has a strong industrial base, it lacks significant foreign capital. Nevertheless, some foreign businesses have shown an interest in Kirov, and Sergeenkov appears eager to work with them. In December 1998 a delegation from Siemens visited Kirov to discuss establishing a joint venture with the Kirskabel factory.

Internet Sites in the Region

http://kirov.region.ru

This is the oblast administration site, offering detailed information about the oblast, including welcoming remarks from Sergeenkov and press releases on the governor's activities.

KOMI REPUBLIC

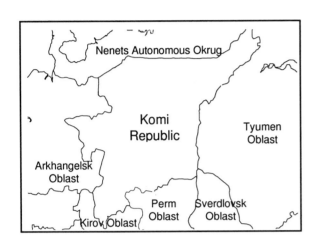

Territory: 415,900 km²
Population (as of 1 January 1998): 1,161,000
Distance from Moscow: 1,515 km

Major Cities:
Syktyvkar, *capital* (pop. 230,400)
Ukhta (103,700)
Vorkuta (96,200)
Pechora (61,800)

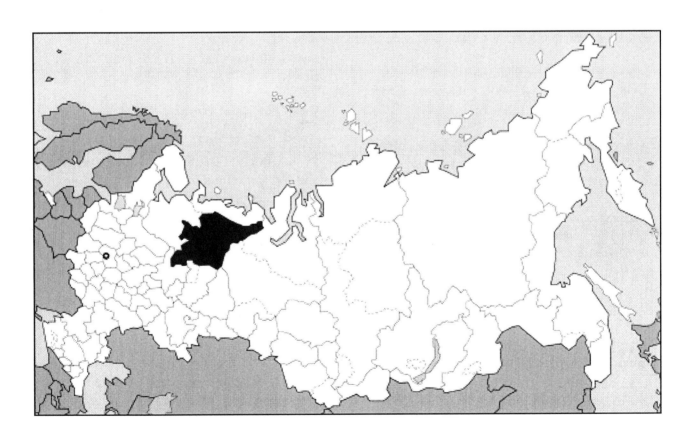

Basic Facts

Population (as of 1 Jan. 1998): 1,161,000
(0.79% of Russian total)

Ethnic breakdown (1989 census): Russians
57.7%, Komi 23.3%, Ukrainians 8.3%,
Belarusans 2.1%, Tatars 2.1%, Germans 1.0%

Urban population (as of 1 Jan. 1998): 74.3%
(Russia overall: 73.1%)

Student population (as of 1 Sept. 1997): 119
per 10,000 (Russia overall: 208/10,000)

Pensioner population (1997): 23.17% (Russia
overall: 25.96%)

**Percent of population with higher education
(1989 census):** 8.9% (Russia overall: 11.3%)

Percent of population working in (1997):
Industry: 24.9% (Russian average: 23.0%);
Agriculture: 5.2% (13.7%); Trade: 11.7%
(13.5%); Culture: 13.7% (13.3%)

**Average monthly personal income in July
1998:** 1,047.6 new rubles (Russian average:
891.7 new rubles)

**Average monthly personal expenses in July
1998:** 546.4 new rubles (Russian average: 684.9
new rubles)

**Average monthly subsistence requirement in
1998:** 460 new rubles (Russian average: 438 new
rubles)

Consumer price index (as of July 1998): 129
(Russia overall = 100)

Budgetary revenues (1997): 5,144.2 billion
rubles (Russia overall: 433,378.2 billion rubles)

Budgetary expenditures (1997): 6,436.3 billion
rubles (Russia overall: 468,111.6 billion rubles)

**Industrial production as percentage of all
Russian production (Jan.–Aug. 1998):** 0.89%

**Proportion of loss-making enterprises (as of
July 1998):** 64.5% (Russia overall: 50.4%)

**Number of enterprises which have wage
arrears (as of 1 Sept. 1998):** 1,372 (1.02% of
Russian total)

**Agricultural production as percentage of all
Russian production (1997):** 0.46%

Number of private farms (as of 1 Jan. 1998):
595 (0.22% of Russian total)

Capital investment (1997): 4,868.1 billion
rubles (Russia overall: 408,797 billion rubles)

Sources of investment (1997): federal budget:
13.4% (Russian average: 10.2%); regional
budget: 9.0% (10.5%); extra-budgetary funds:
77.6% (79.3%)

Foreign investment (1997): 31,062,000 USD
(Russia overall: 12,294,734,000 USD)

Number of joint ventures (1997): 46 (0.31%
of Russian total)

**Fixed capital investment in joint ventures
and foreign companies (1997):** 625,184 million
rubles (Russia overall: 16,265.4 billion rubles)

**Number of small businesses (as of 1 July
1998):** 4,700 (0.54% of Russian total)

Number of enterprises privatized in 1997: 26
(0.95% of Russian total), including those which
used to be municipal property: 100% (Russian
average: 66.4%); regional property: 0% (20.0%);
federal property: 0% (13.6%)

**Number of telephones per 100 families
(1997):** in cities: 55.2 (Russian average: 49.2);
in villages: 37.1 (19.8)

Brief Overview

Komi Republic is located on the northeast Russian plain and borders Arkhangelsk, Tyumen, Sverdlovsk, Perm, and Kirov oblasts. Over half of the population is Russian, while indigenous people, the Komi, make up less than one quarter of its citizens.

About two-thirds of the republic's territory is covered with forests, which make up about half of the country's north European forestry resources. The republic ranks 20th among Russia's 89 regions in terms of raw material deposits and 10th in terms of hydrocarbon reserves. It has reserves of gas, oil, coal, peat, ferrous, non-ferrous, and precious metals, and diamonds.

Fuel is the republic's largest industry, producing about 50 percent of the regional GDP, followed by forestry, timber working, pulp and paper manufacturing (16.4 percent of GDP), and the energy industry (16.2 percent). The mining industry is concentrated in the Pechora coal basin, which is unique for its coking coal. The Timan-Pechora basin is the center of the region's oil and gas industries. Highly developed industry causes significant air pollution in the region with over 750 kg of toxic wastes per capita.

Oil is the major export (63 percent of total exports), followed by coal (11 percent), paper (9 percent), processed timber (6 percent), and plywood (1 percent). Komi has trade partners in over 40 foreign countries. The republic's main customers include Germany, Hungary, the Czech Republic, Latvia, Italy, Poland, Belarus, and Ukraine. Major foreign investors come from Germany, the United States, Austria, Switzerland, Italy, and Great Britain. The largest joint ventures are: KomiArcticOil, NobelOil, and Parmaneft, which produce 25 percent of the entire republic's oil.

According to a 1998 survey by *Ekspert* magazine, the republic ranked 51st among Russia's 89 regions in terms of investment potential and 50th in terms of investment risk. A 1998 survey by Bank Austria ranked the republic 26th in terms of investment climate. Republican investment conditions improved between 1997 and 1998 with risk decreasing by 16 points and potential increasing by 9.

Electoral History

2000 Presidential Election
Putin: 59.91%
Zyuganov: 21.77%

Yavlinskii: 6.81%
Zhirinovsky: 3.22%
Tuleev: 2.68%
Turnout: 69.12% (Russia overall: 68.64%)

1999 Parliamentary Elections
Unity: 31.57%
Communist Party of the Russian Federation: 16.68%
Union of Right Forces: 9.95%
Yabloko: 8.91%
Zhirinovsky Bloc: 7.48%
Fatherland–All Russia: 5.61%
In a single-mandate district: 1 independent
Turnout: 59.26% (Russia overall: 61.85%)

1997 Republican Executive Election
Spiridonov (incumbent): 57.2%
Chistokhodova (State Duma deputy, KPRF): 19.8%
Turnout: 48.5%

1996 Presidential Election
Yeltsin: 40.48%/64.36% (first round/second round)
Lebed: 18.17%
Zyuganov: 16.32%/28.03%
Zhirinovsky: 9.82%
Yavlinskii: 9.44%
Turnout: 62.50%/60.48% (Russia overall: 69.67%/ 68.79%)

1995 Parliamentary Elections
Liberal Democratic Party of Russia: 17.51%
Communist Party of the Russian Federation: 13.05%
Our Home Is Russia: 12.86%
Women of Russia: 7.64%
Yabloko: 5.55%
Russia's Democratic Choice: 4.71%
Congress of Russian Communities: 3.87%
Party of Workers' Self-Government: 3.66%
In a single-mandate district: 1 independent
Turnout: 55.95% (Russia overall: 64.37%)

1993 Constitutional Referendum
"Yes"—62.2% "No"—35.4%

1993 Parliamentary Elections
Liberal Democratic Party of Russia: 24.31%
Russia's Choice: 21.83%
Women of Russia: 12.18%
Party of Russian Unity and Concord: 7.22%

Yabloko: 7.09%
Communist Party of the Russian Federation: 7.05%
Agrarian Party of Russia: 5.57%
Democratic Party of Russia: 5.26%
In single-mandate districts: 2 independent
From electoral associations: 1 Women of Russia
Turnout: 47.27% (Russia overall: 54.34%)

1991 Presidential Election
Yeltsin: 47.62%
Ryzhkov: 24.61%
Zhirinovsky: 8.78%
Tuleev: 6.95%
Bakatin: 4.88%
Makashov: 2.83%
Turnout: 68.82% (Russia overall: 76.66%)

Regional Political Institutions

Executive:

President, 4-year term
Yurii Alekseevich Spiridonov, elected May 1994,
November 1997
    Ul. Kommunisticheskaya, 8; Syktyvkar, 167010
    Tel 7(821–2) 28–51–05, 28–51–12;
    Fax 7(821–2) 21–43–84
    Federation Council in Moscow:
    7(095) 292–61–96, 926–67–32

Legislative:

Unicameral
State Council (*Gosudarstvennyi Sovet*)—50 members,
    4-year term, elected February 1999
Chairman—Vladimir Aleksandrovich Torlopov,
    elected February 1995, February 1999

Regional Politics

Powerful Autocrat in Northern Oil Region

Yurii Spiridonov has ruled over the Komi Republic since 1989 when he was elected first secretary of the republican branch of the CPSU. In May 1994 he was elected president of the republic. He won reelection in 1997, earning 62 percent of the vote. Spiridonov is one of the most autocratic executives in Russia's regions. Although Spiridonov has long claimed the right to appoint mayors in the republic, after a long battle the federal courts finally forced him to hold local elections in February 1999.

In spite of his autocratic form of governance, Spiridonov is a market reformer who had close relations with former Prime Minister Viktor Chernomyrdin and Unified Energy Systems head Anatolii Chubais. He consistently supported Russian President Boris Yeltsin and the federal government, but has always criticized the center's policies, in particular charging that Moscow neglects Russia's regions.

Spiridonov has prioritized developing Komi's economy, which is based primarily on natural resource extraction. The majority of exports from Komi are raw materials. In the late 1990s, 97–99 percent of the republic's exports came from the energy and forestry sectors. As a result, Komi is extremely vulnerable to price fluctuations. The worldwide drop in oil prices hurt Komi, forcing it to sell an additional 1 million tons of unprocessed oil in 1997.

Although the region has considerable hydrocarbon reserves, foreign oil companies generally prefer to transport the crude oil they extract from the region elsewhere for processing because it is too expensive to do it in Komi. Nevertheless, Komi has attracted quite a bit of foreign investment, although improved production-sharing legislation would probably bring more.

Executive Platform: Autocratic Reformer

Spiridonov is a very authoritative leader, not only in his manner of governing Komi but also in the way he challenges and criticizes federal authority. Although he generally supports the federal government, he frequently criticizes the center's actions, and many of Komi's policies and laws violate the Russian Constitution.

Like most other presidents of Russia's 21 ethnically defined republics, Spiridonov is persistent in demanding more freedom from the federal center. However, Spiridonov believes that all regions should enjoy equal rights and thus does not advocate special privileges for the republics. He basically supports a considerably decentralized federation with greater autonomy for all regions.

Spiridonov is an ethnic Russian and Russians are the ethnic majority, comprising 57.7 percent of Komi's population. Ethnic Komi make up 23.3 percent, Ukrainians 8.3 percent, and Tatars 2.1 percent. Accordingly, Spiridonov's motive for gaining regional autonomy is primarily economic rather than ethnic. His main economic priority is to seize control of economic issues from Moscow and place them under the control of the republic.

Although Spiridonov persistently challenges federal power, he is not a member of the anti-reform opposition. Spiridonov is a strong advocate for market reform, and Komi has been one of Russia's most successful regions in attracting foreign investment and developing joint ventures with foreign partners. Spiridonov was a strong supporter of former Prime Minister Viktor Chernomyrdin, who was active in lobbying regional interests on the federal level. Spiridonov belonged to Chernomyrdin's Our Home Is Russia (NDR) movement and was a member of its political council. Spiridonov was fully aware of the need to build relationships with influential leaders, and thus has continued to cultivate new ties in Moscow. In 1999 he participated in the regional founding conference of Moscow Mayor Yurii Luzhkov's Fatherland movement while voicing loyalty to Our Home Is Russia (NDR).

Policies: Strengthening Economy

The majority of Spiridonov's initiatives have focused on strengthening Komi's economy and making regional industries more self-sufficient. He is particularly active in attracting foreign investment to the region. Spiridonov has participated in various delegations addressing potential investors and has created a task force for establishing a free economic zone in Komi. Spiridonov has also participated in further developing certain sectors of Komi's economy, such as the timber industry.

One of Spiridonov's main economic and political concerns is the region's coal industry. Spiridonov, having both an education and fifteen years' work experience in the mining industry, has been active in trying to work with Komi's coal miners throughout their numerous strikes and protest movements. He tried to serve as a mediator between the federal government and the coal miners who were striking in front of the White House for about four months in summer and fall 1998. Komi miners in northern cities like Vorkuta seem to be in a constant state of protest to voice their grievances about wage arrears and poor working conditions. The region's miners spent nearly half of 1998 on strike. Spiridonov greatly sympathizes with the miners' plight and has pushed for a federal reform of the coal industry (see Ties to Moscow). Spiridonov has also met with virtually every high-level federal politician to discuss the miners' chronic problems. He feels that a federal ministry is neces-

sary to directly handle Russia's coal industry. He has also tried very hard to meet the striking miners' needs on the republican level. In 1998 Komi essentially forfeited any tax debts the mines had to the regional budget, and the republican government took out a $3.5 million loan from the Russian Savings Bank to aid the miners (*EWI RRR*, 4 June 1998).

Spiridonov has actively lobbied the federal government for aid in building the republican economy. At the end of 1998, Prime Minister Yevgenii Primakov signed into law a federal program for developing Komi's economic and social sphere, specifically providing for bauxite and manganese extraction and building new railroad links.

On 16 February 1999 Spiridonov issued a decree on improving conditions for small businesses in Komi. The decree requires all ministries and departments that regulate small businesses to coordinate their activities with the republican economics ministry. It also created an Interdepartmental Commission to remove administrative barriers blocking the development of small business. Republican and local governments can rent out state property on a competitive basis to individual entrepreneurs and small businesses that produce at least 75 percent of the goods and services they sell, and will also allow small businesses to donate property to the state in lieu of tax payments (*EWI RRR*, 25 February 1999).

In order to minimize the negative impact of Russia's financial crisis on Komi and reduce social tension in the region, Spiridonov developed a comprehensive economic strategy for 1999–2000 focusing on stabilizing the standard of living. In order to do this, he planned to increase government involvement in the management of state and municipal property, price control, foodstuffs supply, cash flows, salary payments, and industrial restructuring. In his fiscal policy he aimed to increase sources of budget revenues, strengthen financial control over monetary flows, and restructure republican debt obligations.

Relationships Between Key Players: Spiridonov Dominates

Spiridonov played an instrumental role in developing the structure of Komi's post-Soviet republican government. After Russian President Boris Yeltsin's face-off with the Duma in fall 1993, for fifteen months Spiridonov resisted Yeltsin's directive to dissolve the legislature. Instead he set up a directly elected executive office, to which he was easily elected in May 1994. Under Spiridonov's leadership in fall 1994, the republican Supreme Soviet adopted the Komi Law on Executive Authority, which created a structure of vertical authority with municipalities directly subordinate to the republican leader. This structure allowed the republican president to appoint Komi's local administration heads (mayors), violating the Russian Constitution.

In March 1997 the Komi Supreme Court ruled that republican laws on local self-government were in violation of federal laws and demanded that local elections be held by October 1997. This order was then delayed by another case brought before the Russian Constitutional Court. In January 1998 the Constitutional Court ruled that the Komi Constitution and Komi Law on Executive Authority violated the federal constitution and legislation. In spring 1998 the Russian Constitutional Court further limited Spiridonov's powers in Komi by ruling that officials employed in "state service" could not serve in regional legislative bodies. Eight State Council members were affected. Five resigned, and two left the government service. This court decision did not affect leaders of local administrations, since Komi law circumvents this issue by not defining their work as state service.

To better conform with federal legislation on local government, in June 1998 Komi adopted a law on local government stipulating that voters would elect town and raion councils that in turn would elect mayors, who would have been nominated by the republican president. Local self-government elections were finally held in February 1999. Spiridonov nominated mayoral candidates to the local legislatures, putting forth one candidate for each position. Thus, he essentially appointed the local executives. As this procedure still grants Spiridonov considerable power in determining local governments, the Russian Constitutional Court was continuing its review. Just a few days prior to the February elections, Spiridonov published a decree establishing a Coordinating Council, made up exclusively of high-ranking officials, to address issues regarding local government organization (*EWI RRR*, 11 February 1999).

Spiridonov enjoys wide support in Komi's State Council elected in February 1999, to which 20 of the region's 50 deputies were reelected. Thirteen heads of local administrations were elected, as well as several trade union leaders. The legislature has three major factions: Our Home Is Russia (16 members),

Fatherland (15 members), and rural deputies (7), all of which represent different groups within the "party of power." State Council Chairman Vladimir Torlopov has worked successfully with Spiridonov in the Federation Council and the two have cooperated in defining regional policy. Torlopov's apparent lack of political ambitions also contributes to his good relationship with Spiridonov, since the republican president does not view Torlopov as a threat to his power. Furthermore, the Komi State Council is a nonprofessional legislature that meets only twice a month, leaving Spiridonov's decisionmaking generally unfettered (*EWI RRR*, 21 May 1998).

Control of the legislature is extremely important in allowing Spiridonov to maintain his grip on the republic. Fearing that upcoming economic reforms including the ruble re-denomination in January 1998 would hurt his reelection chances, Spiridonov wanted to reschedule the executive elections, which had originally been set for May 1998, to an earlier date. However, a constitutional amendment was required to make such an adjustment. Thus, Spiridonov managed to convince an overwhelming majority of the State Council to support his request, and the elections were moved to November 1997 (*EWI RRR*, 21 May 1998).

Opposition in Komi to Spiridonov has been weak, primarily because opposition groups lack any tangible influence in the power structure. The lack of influence has caused several opposition groups to form alliances. One such alliance is the Transformation of the North movement, which brings together the People's Home of the Komi Republic; the Intelligentsia Congress of the Komi Republic; and the regional branches of Russia's Democratic Choice, Women of Russia, Our Home Is Russia, Democratic Russia, the Social-Democratic Party, and the Republican Party. Even this coalition can muster little influence.

Ties to Moscow: Critical of Moscow

Spiridonov claims that Moscow undermines Russian federalism. He believes that the center does not pay enough attention to the regions, and he complains that the 1998 federal tax reforms allow the federal government to grab those tax revenues that are easily collected, leaving the regions with the more difficult tax collection tasks and therefore less income. The distribution of tax revenues between the federal and republican governments has been an ongoing problem for Komi. In August 1997 Yeltsin issued a decree annulling Spiridonov's mandate setting up the non-commercial organization Northern Resources, which was collecting taxes in Komi. Spiridonov's decree had allowed Northern Resources to collect taxes through in-kind payments of goods or raw materials.

Spiridonov has also blasted the federal government for its management of the coal industry, which remains under Moscow's jurisdiction. Spiridonov has accused Moscow of ignoring the interests of Komi's Vorkuta territory, and giving preferential treatment to the Kuznetsk coal basin even though it cannot fulfill all of the country's coal needs. Production levels for Komi mines have been one-third of the Russian average while the mines' efficiency levels are higher than the national average (*PR*, 21 March 1998). Spiridonov argues that the country as a whole should devise a unified and cohesive coal policy and that new mines should be built as old mines are shut down.

In December 1998 Spiridonov met with then Prime Minister Yevgenii Primakov to discuss Spiridonov's suggestions for amending the federal tax code to address the special circumstances of the northern territories. At present, goods produced in the north are 35 percent more expensive than in the rest of Russia. There are several government-mandated employee benefits that increase costs, and on top of that, the government taxes these benefits. Spiridonov reported that Primakov was open to his suggestions and promised to amend the tax code.

Spiridonov is constantly looking for ways to evade Moscow's control. In 1996 when the federal authorities tried to enforce laws barring civil servants from participating in regional legislatures, Spiridonov had Komi's legal definition of civil servant changed so that it did not apply to appointed heads of administration (*Respublika*, April 1996). Many of these were members of the republican parliament, where they provided reliable support for Spiridonov.

Komi's federally appointed procurator also strives to keep Spiridonov in check. He requested that the republican Supreme Court examine Komi's law on foreign economic activities, claiming that the law contradicted federal statutes. The court ruled that the law was not in violation of the Russian Constitution or federal legislation on foreign economic relations.

The State Duma has been investigating the Komi government and State Council for alleged corruption and passing laws that violate the Russian Constitution. In particular, federal authorities were concerned about the privatization of Komineft and the transfer of the state share in Komineft to KomiTEK, a private organization that is alleged to have a very close alliance with Spiridonov. Some observers maintain that Spiridonov's close ties to the oil company help keep him in power.

Spiridonov was a firm supporter of former Prime Minister Viktor Chernomyrdin, and was disappointed that Chernomyrdin was not reconfirmed to replace Sergei Kirienko in September 1998. Spiridonov also holds Unified Energy System Chairman Anatolii Chubais in high regard. He has been critical of the State Duma, which he feels represents the interests of political parties rather than the regions. Spiridonov claims that the Duma is stuffed with politicians with an overly inflated sense of their own importance (*EWI RRR*, 19 November 1998).

Relations with Other Regions: Disagreement with Nenets

Spiridonov has been in a heated disagreement with neighboring Nenets Autonomous Okrug regarding the Timan-Pechora oil and gas fields that straddle the border of the two regions. There are several Komi-registered companies extracting resources from the fields in both regions that pay taxes only to Komi. The Nenets okrug is understandably bothered by the fact that a considerable amount of the natural resource extraction on its territory is not providing any revenue to the okrug budget. As a result, its administration has been trying to force Komi companies out.

The tension between the two regions grew in April 1998 when Nenets Governor Vladimir Butov presented a plan for building an oil transport terminal on the Barents Sea coast that would ship oil to customers in western Europe via the Barents Sea. At present, oil companies extracting hydrocarbons from the northern part of Timan-Pechora ship their oil via the Kharyaga-Usinsk pipeline, which runs through Komi. Komi's administration does not want to lose the tax revenues generated from the pipeline to Butov's proposed project.

LUKoil's decision to purchase KomiTEK may change the situation in the two regions, although it remains unclear what the exact changes will be. On 29 June 1999, the shareholders of LUKoil approved a plan for the company to purchase KomiTEK. LUKoil President Vagit Alekperov said that the purchase was important because it would allow LUKoil to begin

Yurii Alekseevich Spiridonov

1 November 1938—Born in the village Poltavka in Omsk Oblast

1961—Graduated from the Sverdlovsk Mining Institute

1982—Graduated from the Leningrad Higher Party School

1961–1975—Worked in mines in Magadan Oblast and the Komi Republic in the positions of mining foreman, section chief, and head engineer

1967—Joined the CPSU

1975–1984—Head of the Ukhta CPSU city committee, first secretary of the Usinsk CPSU city committee

January 1985—Elected second secretary and, in August 1989, first secretary of the Komi republican committee of the CPSU

21 January 1990—Elected to the USSR Congress of People's Deputies

April 1990—Elected Chairman of the Komi Supreme Soviet

12 December 1993—Elected to the Federation Council, joining the Committee on Northern Affairs and Indigenous Peoples

May 1994—Elected president of Komi Republic

30 November 1997—Reelected president of Komi Republic

20 May 1998—Confirmed a representative of the Russian Federation in the Congress of Local and Regional Powers of Europe

exploiting the enormous reserves of the Timan-Pechora oil basin. This region, rather than Western Siberia, will be the focus of LUKoil's strategy in the future. KomiTEK brings to the deal an infrastructure designed to produce 20–25 million tons of oil a year (*Vremya MN*, 30 June 1999).

Spiridonov has been close to Moscow Mayor Yurii Luzhkov and participated in an organizational meeting of Luzhkov's Fatherland movement in November 1998.

Komi belongs to the Northwest interregional association, which includes the Republic of Karelia; Arkhangelsk, Vologda, Kaliningrad, Kirov, Leningrad, Murmansk, Novgorod, and Pskov oblasts; Nenets Autonomous Okrug; and the city of St. Petersburg.

Foreign Relations: Aimed at Investment

Spiridonov actively seeks investment in Komi. In January 1998 he participated in the second annual U.S.-Russian Investment Symposium at Harvard University in Cambridge, Massachusetts. The main purpose was to make contacts and drum up support for investment in Komi's industries. In May 1998 Spiridonov visited France as part of a delegation led by Federation Council Speaker and Orel Governor

Yegor Stroev. Spiridonov's main goal was to acquaint French partners with Komi's economic potential. In August 1998 Spiridonov met with Iranian ambassador to Russia Makhdi Safari, and at the end of the year Spiridonov led a delegation to Iran to develop cooperative ties with the country. He hopes to increase trade with Iran, specifically in timber processing and oil.

Attitudes Toward Business: Promoters of Business and Industry

Komi has adopted a progressive law on foreign investment and launched an active marketing campaign focused on introducing Komi to foreigners, mostly through exhibits in European cities. In May 1998 Spiridonov spoke at the annual meeting of the UN Industrial Development Organization (UNIDO) in Vienna. UNIDO is opening an office in Komi's capital, Syktyvkar, and will cooperate with the republican government on various economic development projects.

The republic has attracted a considerable amount of foreign investment and has developed several joint ventures with foreign partners, particularly in the energy sector. There are eleven joint ventures involved in the Komi oil industry, accounting for 58.4 percent of all oil extracted in the republic. This is much higher than in other regions—in Russia as a whole only 5 percent of oil is extracted by joint ventures (*EWI RRR*, 13 August 1998). The largest joint ventures, most of which have Komineft as the Russian partner, are KomiArkticOil (Great Britain's British Gas), NobelOil (Switzerland's TVCOM), KomiQuest (Austria's Quest Petroleum), Severnaya Neft (TVCOM), Tebukneft (British and Cypriot companies), Bitran (Great Britain's Utro), and AmKomi (Ireland's Aminex). In spite of the success of joint ventures, the region's most prosperous oil enterprise is KomiTEK, which has a firm grasp on the work in Nenets Autonomous Okrug and the oil shelf in the Barents Sea and is rumored to have close ties with Spiridonov.

There are multiple development projects underway in the republic. One is the Belkomur railway, which connects Perm with Arkhangelsk through Syktyvkar, establishing a direct route to Arkhangelsk from the Urals. The railway's construction could be completed by 2014, but Komi and Arkhangelsk are trying to get the northern part of the railway finished in the next few years. One of the main obstacles to completing Belkomur is insufficient financial backing. Additional sources for financing must be found if the project is to be finished on schedule.

Another important project is the joint venture Leskom, owned by the republic's Komitrust and the Swiss Mariott Trading GA, which opened a timber-processing plant in Syktyvkar in 1998 and plans to produce up to 90,000 cubic meters of lumber annually. Spiridonov was on hand for the opening ceremony of the plant and spoke highly of its importance to the republic's economy (*PR*, 11 June 1998). The Leskom plant is the first foreign venture in the timber sector, and there is much hope that its organization and productivity will serve as an example to attract foreign money into Komi's timber industry.

The federal government is planning to develop the Middle Timan bauxite deposits in Komi. The bauxite will provide raw materials for the aluminum processing industry of Sverdlovsk Oblast, which has suffered since the collapse of the Soviet Union due to the high cost of importing raw materials. Hopefully the Middle Timan deposits can become the raw material base for aluminum producers in other parts of the country as well. This is one example of increased federal involvement in the region's economic development.

Internet Sites in the Region

http://www.govern.komi.ru/main.htm
This is the official website of the Komi Republic's administration. It includes basic information about Spiridonov, the republican assembly, institutes of higher education, and republican newspapers and journals.

KOMI-PERMYAK AUTONOMOUS OKRUG

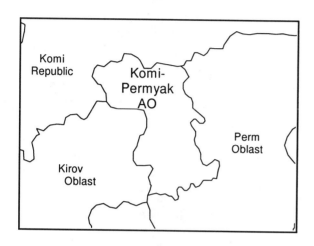

Territory: 32,900 km²
Population (as of 1 January 1998): 154,000
Distance from Moscow: 1,394 km

Major Cities:
Kudymkar, *capital* (pop. 34,200)

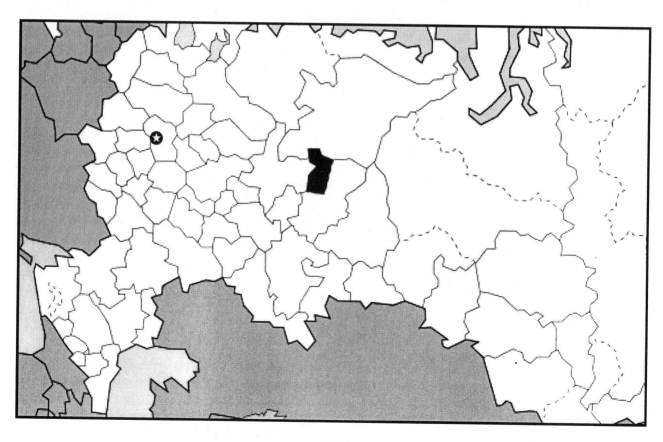

Basic Facts

Population (as of 1 Jan. 1998): 154,000 (0.10% of Russian total)

Ethnic breakdown (1989 census): Komi-Permyak 61.2%, Russians 34.9%

Urban population (as of 1 Jan. 1998): 31.2% (Russia overall: 73.1%)

Student population (as of 1 Sept. 1997): 11 per 10,000 (Russia overall: 208/10,000)

Pensioner population (1997): 27.27% (Russia overall: 25.96%)

Percent of population with higher education (1989 census): 4.3% (Russia overall: 11.3%)

Average monthly personal income in July 1998: 285.1 new rubles (Russian average: 891.7 new rubles)

Average monthly personal expenses in July 1998: 140.4 new rubles (Russian average: 684.9 new rubles)

Average monthly subsistence requirement in 1998: 326 new rubles (Russian average: 438 new rubles)

Consumer price index (as of July 1998): 85 (Russia overall = 100)

Budgetary revenues (1997): 248.7 billion rubles (Russia overall: 433,378.2 billion rubles)

Budgetary expenditures (1997): 308.0 billion rubles (Russia overall: 468,111.6 billion rubles)

Industrial production as percentage of all Russian production (Jan.–Aug. 1998): 0.009%

Proportion of loss-making enterprises (as of July 1998): 62.5% (Russia overall: 50.4%)

Number of enterprises which have wage arrears (as of 1 Sept. 1998): 394 (0.14% of Russian total)

Agricultural production as percentage of all Russian production (1997): 0.16%

Number of private farms (as of 1 Jan. 1998): 215 (0.08% of Russian total)

Capital investment (1997): 95.8 billion rubles (Russia overall: 408,797 billion rubles)

Sources of investment (1997): federal budget: 8.7% (Russian average: 10.2%); regional budget: 2.9% (10.5%); extra-budgetary funds: 88.4% (79.3%)

Number of telephones per 100 families (1997): in cities: 25.6 (Russian average: 49.2); in villages: 9.1 (19.8)

Brief Overview

Komi-Permyak Autonomous Okrug is located in northwest Perm Oblast, 150 km from the city of Perm. It borders the Republic of Komi, Kirov Oblast, and other parts of Perm Oblast.

The okrug is fairly rich in mineral resources, such as oil, charcoal, peat, and mineral waters. Additionally, the region may have gold and diamond deposits. However, forests are the okrug's major asset since over two-thirds of the territory is covered with woods. Forestry and timber-working are the region's major industries, while manufacturing accounts for over 50 percent of the total industrial output. Other important industries are machine building, chemicals, small-scale production, and food products. Local farmers specialize in cattle breeding; however, more than half of local agricultural products are exported outside the okrug unprocessed because the region lacks sufficient food-processing capabilities.

Timber is the major export and is shipped to Sweden, Finland, Germany, Kazakhstan, and Ukraine.

The region currently lacks rail service; however, the federal government plans to build a link connecting the Siberian Railroad with Arkhangelsk that would pass through Komi-Permyak.

According to a 1998 survey by *Ekspert* magazine, the okrug ranked 84th among Russia's 89 regions in terms of investment potential and 59th in terms of investment risk. A 1998 survey by Bank Austria ranked the okrug 79th in terms of investment climate. According to *Ekspert*, investment has become less risky since 1997—by 15 points.

Electoral History

2000 Presidential Election
Putin: 68.83%
Zyuganov: 19.91%
Zhirinovsky: 4.14%
Yavlinskii: 1.47%
Titov: 1.27%
Tuleev: 1.00%
Turnout: 70.13% (Russia overall: 68.64%)

1999 Parliamentary Elections
Unity: 26.75%
Communist Party of the Russian Federation: 17.02%
Zhirinovsky Bloc: 11.52%
Fatherland–All Russia: 8.10%
Union of Right Forces: 7.24%
Communists–Workers' Russia: 3.45%
Pensioners' Party: 3.29%
Our Home Is Russia: 2.80%
Women of Russia: 2.73%
Yabloko: 2.05%
In a single-mandate district: 1 independent
Turnout: 62.83% (Russia overall: 61.85%)

1996 Gubernatorial Election
Poluyanov (incumbent): 69.63%
Fedoseev (Constitutional Party of Russia): 15.26%
Golubkov: 3.95%
Turnout: 57.08%

1996 Presidential Election
Yeltsin: 53.29%/62.78% (first round/second round)
Zyuganov: 23.71%/32.58%
Zhirinovsky: 8.51%
Lebed: 5.45%
Yavlinskii: 3.00%
Turnout: 69.17%/68.55% (Russia overall: 69.67%/ 68.79%)

1995 Parliamentary Elections
Liberal Democratic Party of Russia: 21.69%
Communist Party of the Russian Federation: 12.27%
Our Home Is Russia: 9.56%
Women of Russia: 7.69%
Agrarian Party of Russia: 7.28%
Communists–Workers' Russia: 4.85%

Power to the People: 2.94%
Trade Unions and Industrialists of Russia—Union of Labor: 2.69%
Bloc of Ivan Rybkin: 2.17%
Forward, Russia: 2.05%
In a single-mandate district: 1 independent
Turnout: 62.34% (Russia overall: 64.37%)

1993 Constitutional Referendum
"Yes"—79.2% "No"—18.0%

1993 Parliamentary Elections
Liberal Democratic Party of Russia: 19.38%
Russia's Choice: 17.68%
Women of Russia: 13.52%
Agrarian Party of Russia: 12.22%
Party of Russian Unity and Concord: 11.33%
Communist Party of the Russian Federation: 6.76%
Democratic Party of Russia: 5.24%
Yabloko: 3.16%
In a single-mandate district: 1 Women of Russia
Turnout: 56.36% (Russia overall: 54.34%)

1991 Presidential Election
Yeltsin: 40.64%
Ryzhkov: 27.79%
Zhirinovsky: 9.11%
Makashov: 7.44%
Bakatin: 5.23%
Tuleev: 2.36%
Turnout: 82.90% (Russia overall: 76.66%)

Regional Political Institutions

Executive:
   Governor, 4-year term
   Nikolai Andreevich Poluyanov,
   elected November 1996
       Ul. 50–let Oktyabrya, 30; Kudymkar, 617240;
       Komi-Permyak Autonomous Okrug;
       Perm Oblast
       Tel 7(342–60) 2–09–03, 2–12–42;
       Fax 7 (342–60) 2–12–74
       Federation Council in Moscow:
       7(095) 229–26–89, 926–65–70

Legislative:
Unicameral
Legislative Assembly (*Zakonodatelnoe Sobranie*)—
   15 members, 4-year term, elected December 1997
Chairman—Ivan Vasilevich Chetin, elected March 1994, December 1997

Regional Politics

Colorless Leader in a Depressed Region

Nikolai Poluyanov was first appointed governor of Komi-Permyak Autonomous Okrug by President Boris Yeltsin in 1991. Poluyanov was popularly elected to the same post in November 1996, earning nearly 70 percent of the vote. Poluyanov has a long history in the regional political scene. He served in various okrug positions in the 1980s, and in March 1990 was elected to the Perm Oblast Legislative Assembly, winning reelection for another term in 1994. While serving in the Perm legislature, Poluyanov headed the Budget and Finance Committee.

Komi-Permyak is one of Russia's poorest regions. It is one of the most underdeveloped parts of European Russia, and its social provisions were far below other regions, even in the Soviet period. The life expectancies of residents of Komi-Permyak are 10–11 years lower than the Russian average, and the education level among most of the region's population is 2–3 years less than the average for Perm Oblast, of which Komi-Permyak is a constituent part (*EWI RRR*, 12 February 1998). The official unemployment rate is 18 percent, but it is considerably higher among young people. In recent years, the death rate has jumped dramatically, the birth rate decreased, and much of the working-age population has been leaving the region. According to okrug statistics in the first half of 1998 the mortality rate was one and a half times higher than the birth rate, and only 141 couples in a population of 150,000 decided to marry (*EWI RRR*, 22 October 1998).

Poluyanov himself is an ethnic Komi, a minority in the region. The okrug's largest ethnic group is Komi-Permyak, which comprises 61 percent of the region's population. The Komi-Permyak are related to the Komi-Zyryan and Udmurt ethnic groups. The rest of the population is primarily ethnic Russian. The Komi-Permyak are slowly shrinking in numbers. Emigration began in the 1960s, and since 1993 the group has exhibited a natural population decline (Michael McFaul and Nikolai Petrov, eds., *Politicheskii almanakh Rossii 1997*, v. 2, Moscow: Carnegie Endowment for International Peace, 1998, p. 1021).

Executive Platform

Poluyanov was a supporter of President Boris Yeltsin. He is reliant on large federal subsidies to maintain the region's already meager standard of living and thus engages in no real criticism of the federal government.

Policies: Helpless in Face of Economic Decline, Youth Flight

As part of his gubernatorial campaign, Poluyanov was able to secure 14 billion rubles from the Ministry of Finance to pay salaries and pensions (McFaul and Petrov, 1023). Aside from this measure, however, Poluyanov has failed to initiate any policies to effectively improve the situation in the okrug. The absence of effective state action is causing the okrug to fall into an even deeper depression. The economic situation in Komi-Permyak has been in a steady decline since the introduction of market economics in the early 1990s. The timber industry used to be the base of the okrug's economy, but now many of the region's timber enterprises have stopped operating due to low efficiency and a lack of investment capital, and those that are still working can barely get by. Collective farms are in serious debt, and their workers have not received cash salary payments for over four years. In 1998 in one of the okrug's six districts it had been over two years since anything was planted. Salary payment delays were about 6–8 months and pension arrears were 2–4 months. Pensioners constitute 21 percent of the okrug population and 70 percent of the rural population. Thus, pensioners served as the only real breadwinners in rural areas, and the flight of the working-age population offers little hope of a successful industrial renewal.

Relationships Between Key Players: Failure to Improve Drains Support

Although Poluyanov was elected with tremendous popular support, his failure to address the region's economic woes has caused his popularity to suffer. During the much anticipated 7 October 1998 nationwide protest demonstration, 800–1,000 people gathered in Kudymkar's central square. It was the first protest to take place in the region since 1989. The demonstration's participants voted almost unanimously for Poluyanov's resignation (*EWI RRR*, 22 October 1998). At the protest, Poluyanov made a speech announcing that production in the okrug had increased 102 percent over the previous year, which was refuted by several members of the crowd who stated that positive change could not be claimed when only six of the sixteen agricultural enterprises in the area were in operation.

Nikolai Andreevich Poluyanov

14 July 1952—Born in the village of Parfenovo-Demin in Komi-Permyak

1970–1972—Served in the army

1973—Graduated from the Perm Financial Technical College

1973–1983—Worked in financial organizations in Kudymkar

1979—Graduated from the economics department of Perm State University

1986—Deputy chair of the Komi-Permyak okrug agriculture committee

1988—Elected chair of the Kudymkar executive committee

March 1990—Elected to the Perm Oblast Soviet and in April became a member of the Presidium; also elected chair of the Kudymkar executive committee

14 December 1991—Appointed governor of Komi-Permyak Autonomous Okrug

March 1994—Elected to the Perm Oblast Assembly, where he headed the Budget and Finance Committee

1996—Joined the second session of the Federation Council, serving on the Committee for the Budget, Tax Policies, Finances, Currency, and Customs Regulations

17 November 1996—Elected governor of Komi-Permyak Autonomous Okrug

Married, with a son

Part of the okrug's problem lies in the fact that the old Soviet nomenklatura still runs the okrug's governing structures, or has only recently been pushed out. The okrug legislative assembly was elected in December 1997 after the old parliament had extended its mandate three times, more than any other Russian legislative institution. Only one incumbent, Speaker Ivan Chetin, was reelected to the assembly. The 15-person assembly has a strong representation of Agrarians.

Ties to Moscow: No Leverage

Poluyanov is in a very weak position in relation to the federal government since 83 percent of the okrug's budget comes from federal subsidies.

In May 1996 President Boris Yeltsin signed a power-sharing agreement with Perm Oblast and Komi-Permyak Autonomous Okrug.

Relations with Other Regions

Komi-Permyak, while a full subject of the Russian Federation, is also part of Perm Oblast. The okrug has good relations with the oblast, and has been highly supportive of Perm Governor Gennadii Igumnov.

Komi-Permyak belongs to the Urals Regional Association, which includes the republics of Bashkortostan and Udmurtia, and the Kurgan, Orenburg, Perm, Sverdlovsk, and Chelyabinsk oblasts.

Attitudes Toward Business

There are no investment projects in the okrug, and all housing construction has stopped.

KORYAK AUTONOMOUS OKRUG

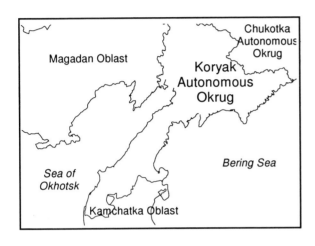

Territory: 301,500 km²
Population (as of 1 January 1998): 31,000
Distance from Moscow: 12,866 km

Major Cities:
Palana, *capital* (pop. 4,100)

Basic Facts

Population (as of 1 Jan. 1998): 31,000 (0.02% of Russian total)

Ethnic breakdown (1989 census): Russians 62%, Koryaks 16.5%, Ukrainians 7.3%, Chukchi 3.7%, Itelmens 3.0%, Evens 1.8%

Urban population (as of 1 Jan. 1998): 25.1% (Russia overall: 73.1%)

Pensioner population (1997): 19.35% (Russia overall: 25.96%)

Percent of population with higher education (1989 census): 10.7% (Russia overall: 11.3%)

Average monthly personal income in July 1998: 1,298.9 new rubles (Russian average: 891.7 new rubles)

Average monthly personal expenses in July 1998: 423.6 new rubles (Russian average: 684.9 new rubles)

Average monthly subsistence requirement in 1998: 1,497 new rubles (Russian average: 438 new rubles)

Consumer price index (as of July 1998): 304 (Russia overall = 100)

Budgetary revenues (1997): 316.6 billion rubles (Russia overall: 433,378.2 billion rubles)

Budgetary expenditures (1997): 652.8 billion rubles (Russia overall: 468,111.6 billion rubles)

Industrial production as percentage of all Russian production (Jan.–Aug. 1998): 0.02%

Proportion of loss-making enterprises (as of July 1998): 70.0% (Russia overall: 50.4%)

Number of enterprises which have wage arrears (as of 1 Sept. 1998): 67 (0.05% of Russian total)

Agricultural production as percentage of all Russian production (1997): 0.02%

Number of private farms (as of 1 Jan. 1998): 18 (0.007% of Russian total)

Capital investment (1997): 38.2 billion rubles (Russia overall: 408,797 billion rubles)

Sources of investment (1997): federal budget: 17.7% (Russian average: 10.2%); regional budget: 8.5% (10.5%); extra-budgetary funds: 73.8% (79.3%)

Foreign investment (1997): 1,438,000 USD (Russia overall: 12,294,734,000 USD)

Number of joint ventures (1997): 2 (0.01% of Russian total)

Fixed capital investment in joint ventures and foreign companies (1997): 25,892 million rubles (Russia overall: 16,265.4 billion rubles)

Number of telephones per 100 families (1997): in cities: 74.1 (Russian average: 49.2); in villages: 58.5 (19.8)

Brief Overview

Koryak Autonomous Okrug encompasses the northern section of the Kamchatka peninsula, the adjoining parts of the mainland, and Karaginskii Island. The okrug borders Magadan Oblast and Chukotka Autonomous Okrug. Koryak AO is one of the least developed and least populated regions in the country due to its severe climatic conditions and mountainous landscape.

The okrug is rich in gold, silver, platinum, tin, mercury, copper, chromium, coal, charcoal, and building materials. Fishing (including crab and salmon) is the major regional industry and contributes one-third of the okrug's GDP. Economic activity in the region also includes gold and coal mining, reindeer breeding, hunting, and food processing.

The okrug is among the poorest in the country: less than a quarter of its expenditures are covered by its own revenues. It ranks 4th from the bottom in terms of 1997 per capita income compared to 1991—5.61 percent.

According to a 1998 survey by *Ekspert* magazine, the okrug ranked 87th among Russia's 89 regions in terms of investment potential and 84th in terms of investment risk. A 1998 survey by Bank Austria ranked the okrug 83rd in terms of investment climate.

Electoral History

2000 Presidential Election
Putin: 61.12%
Zyuganov: 20.11%
Tuleev: 4.76%
Zhirinovsky: 4.66%
Yavlinskii: 4.19%
Turnout: 68.21% (Russia overall: 68.64%)

1999 Parliamentary Elections
Unity: 42.49%
Communist Party of the Russian Federation: 11.67%
Zhirinovsky Bloc: 8.29%
Yabloko: 6.34%
Union of Right Forces: 5.27%
Fatherland–All Russia: 4.16%
In a single-mandate district: 1 independent
Turnout: 69.20% (Russia overall: 61.85%)

1996 Gubernatorial Election
Bronevich (Kamchatka Oblast electoral commission chairwoman): 47.13%
Leushkin (incumbent): 25.58%
Savelev: 9.92%
Leginov: 1.84%
Vladimirova: 1.65%
Volkov: 1.50%
Turnout: 57.22%

1996 Presidential Election
Yeltsin: 45.99%/69.78% (first round/second round)
Lebed: 15.79%
Zyuganov: 14.97%/22.90%
Yavlinskii: 8.93%
Zhirinovsky: 6.50%
Turnout: 72.57%/67.86% (Russia overall: 69.67%/ 68.79%)

1995 Parliamentary Elections
Liberal Democratic Party of Russia: 13.14%
Communist Party of the Russian Federation: 10.00%
Yabloko: 9.40%

Women of Russia: 8.70%
Our Home Is Russia: 6.94%
Party of Workers' Self-Government: 5.51%
Communists–Workers' Russia: 3.90%
Kedr: 3.05%
Forward, Russia: 2.86%
Congress of Russian Communities: 2.74%
Russia's Democratic Choice: 2.49%
In a single-mandate district: 1 independent
Turnout: 65.90% (Russia overall: 64.37%)

1993 Constitutional Referendum
"Yes"—69.6% "No"—24.5%

1993 Parliamentary Elections
Liberal Democratic Party of Russia: 24.07%
Russia's Choice: 14.88%
Women of Russia: 12.51%
Yabloko: 11.92%
Party of Russian Unity and Concord: 9.58%
Democratic Party of Russia: 7.81%
Communist Party of the Russian Federation: 7.30%
Agrarian Party of Russia: 1.50%
In a single-mandate district: 1 independent
Turnout: 56.72% (Russia overall: 54.34%)

1991 Presidential Election
Yeltsin: 42.60%
Ryzhkov: 20.47%
Tuleev: 13.09%
Zhirinovsky: 10.79%
Bakatin: 4.21%
Makashov: 3.04%
Turnout: 80.09% (Russia overall: 76.66%)

Regional Political Institutions

Executive:
Governor, 4-year term
Valentina Tadeevna Bronevich, elected November 1996
Koryak Autonomous Okrug Administration; Porotov St., 22; Palana, 684620;
Koryak Autonomous Okrug, Kamchatka Oblast
Tel 7(415–43) 3–13–80;
Fax 7(415–43) 3–13–70, 3–21–07
Federation Council in Moscow:
7(095) 292–75–43, 926–69–53

Legislative:

Unicameral

Duma—12 members, 4-year term, elected November 1996

Chairman—Vladimir Nikolaevich Mizinin, elected December 1996

Regional Politics

First and Only Woman Executive

Valentina Bronevich was the first and only woman ever elected as governor in one of Russia's regions. Bronevich earned this honor on 17 November 1996 when she defeated incumbent Sergei Leushkin with 46 percent of the vote. Bronevich, who ran as an independent, secured her victory when another woman candidate, Nina Solodyakova, withdrew from the race the day before the election, throwing her support to Bronevich. This gave Bronevich the backing of the opposition umbrella group National Patriotic Union of Russia (NDSR) in addition to Vladimir Shumeiko's pro-Russia Reforms–New Course movement, which had supported her throughout her candidacy.

Bronevich assertively stands up for what she believes is right. She resigned from her position on the Koryak executive committee in 1990 because she did not agree with Leushkin's economic and social policy (*NG*, 12 November 1996). Bronevich is pro-reform, pro-Yeltsin, and highly supportive of the rights of indigenous peoples in the Koryak Autonomous Okrug. An ethnic Itelmen, she has articulated the interests of native peoples throughout her professional career. While working in Petropavlovsk-Kamchatskii, the capital of Kamchatka Oblast (of which the Koryak Autonomous Okrug is a part), Bronevich set up a legal center for the region's northern peoples. She also organized the publication of textbooks to teach school children their local languages, something she considers one of her main accomplishments (*OMRI RRR*, 20 November 1996).

Executive Platform: Strong Manager

Bronevich belongs to the group of governors elected in 1996 and described as "strong managers." The strong managers ran as independents, usually with support from the business community, and often, as in the case of Bronevich, backed by Vladimir Shumeiko's Reforms–New Course movement. The Kremlin secretly supported the strong managers, preferring governors who would be loyal to Anatolii Chubais, the presidential chief of staff at the time, to the incumbents who had been appointed under past chiefs of staff.

As a strong manager, Bronevich has stressed professionalism above political orientation (*NG*, 12 November 1996). Her primary interests are economic. Since her election, Bronevich has focused on improving the supply of food and fuel to remote parts of the okrug's eastern section, which suffers from severe climatic conditions and a poor communications infrastructure. The governor also has been intent on lowering the okrug's unemployment rate and the region's nearly exclusive dependence on federal subsidies.

Policies: Aimed at Self-Sufficiency

Bronevich's policies have exhibited two main goals: raising the Koryak AO to a position of greater self-sufficiency, and ensuring that the interests of the okrug's indigenous peoples receive top priority. The governor's plan for economic progress involves development and diversification of the region's manufacturing industry. This will increase the local population's share in the profits resulting from the exploitation of the okrug's natural resources. Bronevich would like to see growth in the okrug's fish industry, as well as further local development in fur and mineral enterprises. She is against offering tax incentives for business development, claiming that these policies, which were designed to help indigenous people, have been abused by foreign-owned companies and former state monopolies. Bronevich also wants to make certain that the rights of the indigenous peoples are considered when determining the development procedures for traditional hunting and herding grounds where mineral resources are found.

Ties to Moscow

Bronevich tended to side with Yeltsin on political issues, but has tried to decrease the okrug's economic dependence on the federal government. In spite of her efforts, the Koryak AO has not cleared its salary and pension debts.

Relations with Other Regions: Cooperation with Kamchatka

Bronevich is intent on keeping the Koryak AO within Kamchatka Oblast. The Koryak Okrug soviet tried to secede from Kamchatka in 1991, hoping to establish a Koryak republic within the RSFSR. The indigenous

Valentina Tadeevna Bronevich

25 January 1956—Born in the village Sopochnoe in the Tigilskii Raion of Koryak Autonomous Okrug

1978—Graduated with a law degree from Irkutsk State University

1978–1983—Worked as a lawyer for the Kamchatka Oblast Board of Attorneys in Petropavlovsk-Kamchatskii

1983–1990—Worked as a judge in Koryak AO, rising through the ranks to become assistant

chair of the okrug court and, ultimately, serving as chair of the okrug executive committee for four years

1990—Managed the department on affairs of northern peoples and national questions for the Kamchatka Oblast executive committee

1994–1996—Served as chair of the Kamchatka Oblast electoral committee

17 November 1996—Elected governor of Koryak AO

populations were hardly represented in the soviet, and thus Bronevich argued that secession would only lead to the creation of another expensive bureaucracy benefiting the old nomenklatura rather than the native peoples. The governor feels that the okrug would be better off deepening its ties with Kamchatka, particularly in the economic sphere. In May 1999 Bronevich signed a cooperation agreement with Kamchatka Oblast Governor Vladimir Biryukov.

The Koryak AO is a member of the Far East and Baikal Association, which is headed by Khabarovsk Krai Governor Viktor Ishaev. The association also includes the Buryatia and Sakha (Yakutia) republics; Primorskii Krai; Amur, Kamchatka, Magadan, Chita, and Sakhalin oblasts; the Jewish Autonomous Oblast; and Chukota Autonomous Okrug.

Foreign Relations: Focused on Asia

The Far East and Baikal Association, of which the Koryak AO is a member, agreed in April 1997 to co-

operate more closely with the Asian-Pacific Region (APR). The association wants to export machinery and raw materials to the APR and invite neighboring countries to participate in joint ventures to extract mineral resources from the region.

Attitudes Toward Business: Pro-Development, Anti–Tax Breaks

Although Bronevich wants to increase economic development in the Koryak AO, she has had little success in attracting investors to the region. The okrug is rich in natural and mineral resources, which Bronevich does not want to see turned over to monopolies. Her opposition to tax breaks most likely discourages potential investors. The governor would like the region's natives to reap the benefits of the okrug's natural resources, yet their poverty remains a formidable obstacle to enterprise development.

KOSTROMA OBLAST

Territory: 60,100 km²
Population (as of 1 January 1998):
797,000
Distance from Moscow: 372 km

Major Cities:
Kostroma, *capital* (pop. 288,500)
Bui (28,400)
Nerekhta (28,300)
Sharya (26,100)
Manturovo (20,900)
Galich (20,900)

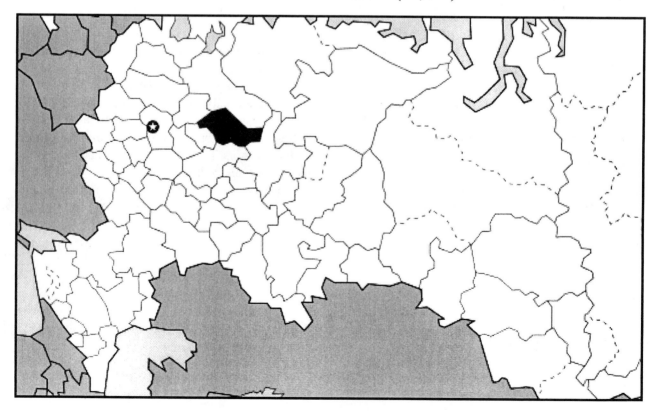

Basic Facts

Population (as of 1 Jan. 1998): 797,000 (0.54% of Russian total)

Ethnic breakdown (1989 census): Russians 96.3%, Ukrainians 1.2%

Urban population (as of 1 Jan. 1998): 65.5% (Russia overall: 73.1%)

Student population (as of 1 Sept. 1997): 164 per 10,000 (Russia overall: 208/10,000)

Pensioner population (1997): 28.98% (Russia overall: 25.96%)

Percent of population with higher education (1989 census): 8.4% (Russia overall: 11.3%)

Percent of population working in (1997): Industry: 23.7% (Russian average: 23.0%); Agriculture: 11.8% (13.7%); Trade: 13.2% (13.5%); Culture: 14.2% (13.3%)

Average monthly personal income in July 1998: 543.6 new rubles (Russian average: 891.7 new rubles)

Average monthly personal expenses in July 1998: 369.1 new rubles (Russian average: 684.9 new rubles)

Average monthly subsistence requirement in 1998: 330 new rubles (Russian average: 438 new rubles)

Consumer price index (as of July 1998): 90 (Russia overall = 100)

Budgetary revenues (1997): 2,723.1 billion rubles (Russia overall: 433,378.2 billion rubles)

Budgetary expenditures (1997): 2,937.5 billion rubles (Russia overall: 468,111.6 billion rubles)

Industrial production as percentage of all Russian production (Jan.–Aug. 1998): 0.31%

Proportion of loss-making enterprises (as of July 1998): 56.2% (Russia overall: 50.4%)

Number of enterprises which have wage arrears (as of 1 Sept. 1998): 978 (0.72% of Russian total)

Agricultural production as percentage of all Russian production (1997): 0.84%

Number of private farms (as of 1 Jan. 1998): 957 (0.35% of Russian total)

Capital investment (1997): 1,254.8 billion rubles (Russia overall: 408,797 billion rubles)

Sources of investment (1997): federal budget: 5.8% (Russian average: 10.2%); regional budget: 9.3% (10.5%); extra-budgetary funds: 84.9% (79.3%)

Foreign investment (1997): 30,000 USD (Russia overall: 12,294,734,000 USD)

Number of joint ventures (1997): 56 (0.38% of Russian total)

Fixed capital investment in joint ventures and foreign companies (1997): 5,463 million rubles (Russia overall: 16,265.4 billion rubles)

Number of small businesses (as of 1 July 1998): 3,100 (0.36% of Russian total)

Number of enterprises privatized in 1997: 1 (0.04% of Russian total), including those which used to be municipal property: 0% (Russian average: 66.4%); regional property: 0% (20.0%); federal property: 100% (13.6%)

Number of telephones per 100 families (1997): in cities: 35.7 (Russian average: 49.2); in villages: 24.0 (19.8)

Brief Overview

Kostroma Oblast is located in the center of European Russia and borders Yaroslavl, Vologda, Kirov, Ivanovo, and Nizhnii Novgorod oblasts.

The region is rich in raw materials, such as carbonate, clays, sands, and mineral waters. Its major industries are: energy, 80 percent of which is exported to other regions; machine building and metal-processing; forestry, timber working; and light and food industries. Regional enterprises manufacture equipment for the timber-working, metal-processing, and textile industries. They also produce road construction machines and other equipment. About 15percent of the oblast GDP comes from the timber industry, which manufactures plywood, cardboard, and paper. Forestry products are among the major export items of the oblast. Kostroma also exports equipment for various industries and jewelry.

According to a 1998 survey by *Ekspert* magazine, the oblast ranked 70th among Russia's 89 regions in terms of investment potential and 54th in terms of investment risk. Investment risk increased by 20 points since 1997, the country's ninth biggest increase. A 1998 survey by Bank Austria ranked the oblast 52nd in terms of investment climate.

Electoral History

2000 Presidential Election
Putin: 59.28%
Zyuganov: 25.84%
Yavlinskii: 3.79%
Zhirinovsky: 3.54%
Tuleev: 2.29%
Turnout: 71.49% (Russia overall: 68.64%)

1999 Parliamentary Elections
Unity: 35.00%
Communist Party of the Russian Federation: 21.03%
Zhirinovsky Bloc: 7.94%
Union of Right Forces: 6.73%
Fatherland–All Russia: 6.17%
Yabloko: 5.54%
In a single-mandate district: 1 independent
Turnout: 66.50% (Russia overall: 61.85%)

1996 Gubernatorial Election
Shershunov: 41.72%/64.10%
  (first round/second round)

Arbuzov (incumbent): 27.33%/30.74%
Romanov: 21.28%
Turnout: 58.14%/51.33%

1996 Presidential Election
Yeltsin: 28.02%/49.86% (first round/second round)
Zyuganov: 28.57%/42.70%
Lebed: 23.26%
Yavlinskii: 7.77%
Zhirinovsky: 7.62%
Turnout: 73.56%/69.76%
  (Russia overall: 69.67%/68.79%)

1995 Parliamentary Elections
Communist Party of the Russian Federation: 20.15%
Liberal Democratic Party of Russia: 11.45%
Our Home Is Russia: 8.65%
Agrarian Party of Russia: 6.98%
Women of Russia: 5.94%
Communists–Workers' Russia: 4.93%
Congress of Russian Communities: 4.75%
Yabloko: 4.44%
Derzhava: 4.24%
In a single-mandate district: 1 Agrarian Party of Russia
Turnout: 68.63% (Russia overall: 64.37%)

1993 Constitutional Referendum
"Yes"—56.8% "No"—41.1%

1993 Parliamentary Elections
Liberal Democratic Party of Russia: 26.12%
Russia's Choice: 14.59%
Agrarian Party of Russia: 11.89%
Women of Russia: 10.21%
Communist Party of the Russian Federation: 10.01%
Yabloko: 6.87%
Party of Russian Unity and Concord: 6.65%
Democratic Party of Russia: 5.70%
In a single-mandate district: 1 independent
Turnout: 59.69% (Russia overall: 54.34%)

1991 Presidential Election
Yeltsin: 49.80%
Ryzhkov: 22.20%
Tuleev: 7.46%
Zhirinovsky: 7.11%
Makashov: 4.48%
Bakatin: 4.07%
Turnout: 80.79% (Russia overall: 76.66%)

Regional Political Institutions

Executive:

Governor, 4-year term
Viktor Andreevich Shershunov,
elected December 1996

Kostroma Oblast Administration;
Ul. Dzerzhinskaya, 15; Kostroma, 15600
Tel 7(094–2) 31–34–72;
Fax 7(094–2) 31–33–95
Federation Council in Moscow:
7(095) 292–69–12, 926–67–46

Legislative:

Unicameral

Oblast Duma—21 members, 4–year term, elected
December 1996
Chairman—Andrei Ivanovich Bychkov, elected
March 1994, December 1996

Regional Politics

Anti-Nuclear Sentiment Benefits Communist Ruler

Viktor Shershunov was elected governor of Kostroma
Oblast in December 1996, unseating incumbent Valerii
Arbuzov with support from a wide variety of political
camps. Shershunov's victory is most appropriately
described as Arbuzov's defeat. The fate of Kostroma's
nuclear power plant served as the decisive issue in the
1996 gubernatorial election. In a referendum held on
the same day as the first round of the gubernatorial
elections, 87 percent of the participants cast ballots
against resuming construction at the plant, where work
had been temporarily halted after public protests. Turnout was 59 percent, well above the legally required 50
percent. Kostroma thus became the first Russian region to effectively stop work on potentially dangerous
nuclear projects through a referendum. Arbuzov had
been in favor of the plant's construction for the four
years prior to the referendum, greatly diminishing his
popularity (*OMRI RRR*, 20 November 1996).

Executive Platform: Seeks Greater Regional Economic Control

Viktor Shershunov was elected governor with the support of the opposition National Patriotic Union of Rus-

sia (NPSR). The local Communists, Aleksandr
Rutskoi's Derzhava, the Congress of Russian Communities, and Aleksandr Lebed's Honor and Motherland also supported his bid.

Shershunov's campaign platform focused on a variety of economic issues. He proposed confronting the
economic crisis in Kostroma by qualitatively changing the economic relations between the center and the
regions. His suggestions included increasing support
to local industries, changing federal and regional tax
policies, and increasing the oblast's control over the
use of its natural resources (*Vybory: Glav ispolnitel'noi
vlasti sub"ektov Rossiiskoi Federatsii 1995–1997*,
Moscow: Ves mir, 1997, 219). He argued that the
region's tax system needed to be completely over-
hauled. The taxes placed on enterprises are so unrea-
sonable that nearly all firms ignore them, which further
contributes to insufficient budget revenues.

Relationships Between Key Players

Most of the factories in the oblast capital are idle. Four-
fifths of the city's residents have garden plots which
provide their vegetables. Eighty percent of the transactions in the city are barter and even municipal governments accept payments in goods rather than money.
Half of the city residents pay little or no rent. Since
the collective farm and private farm structures in the
region have collapsed and fail to produce profits, pensioners have become the main income earners for rural families (Serge Schmemann, "How Can You Have
a Bust if You Never Had a Boom? The Precapitalist
Economy of the Russian Majority," The *New York
Times Magazine*, 27 December 1998, 28–32).

Shershunov appears to enjoy relatively good relations with the oblast legislature and the region's mayors. However, the city of Kostroma itself is deeply in
debt since most of its industry is not functioning. The
city's operating budget is 1.3 billion rubles a year, but
income in 1998 was just 525 million rubles. Payments
to city employees (policemen, bus drivers, teachers,
doctors, garbage collectors) are far behind schedule
(Schmemann, 28–32).

Ties to Moscow: Tense Relations

Shershunov openly opposed President Yeltsin during
his October 1993 stand-off with parliament, and stated
in his 1996 gubernatorial campaign that his position
had not changed (ITAR-TASS, 19 November 1996).

Viktor Andreevich Shershunov

16 November 1950—Born in the town of Lenger in the town of Khimkents Oblast of Kazakhstan; served in the Black Sea Fleet

1977—Graduated from Kazan State University with a degree in law and was commissioned to work in Kostroma

1977—Appointed investigator for the Galich interregional procurator's office

1978—Appointed senior investigator of the Sverdlovsk region for the Kostroma city procurator's office

1986—Named procurator of the Leninskii region for Kostroma city

1992—Elected deputy chairman of the Kostroma oblast soviet, and then first deputy chairman

1994—Began working for the Kostroma city administration; became chairman of the committee on legal affairs

1996—Selected as Chief of administrative-legal management for Kostroma city

1990—Elected to the oblast legislature and then selected as its deputy chairman

December 1996—Elected Kostroma Oblast governor with the support of the National Patriotic Union of Russia (NPSR)

Married, with three sons

Big soccer enthusiast and decorated classical wrestler

In June 1998 President Yeltsin visited Kostroma and promised to provide state support for the flax industry, but was harshly critical of Shershunov. When discussing the issue of stipends with students in Kostroma, Yeltsin questioned why the governor complained about arrears in pensions and stipends, yet was silent about the region's own debts. Kostroma is far behind in its contribution to pension funds. Yeltsin also criticized the region's farmers and industrialists for the low quality of their work and their numerous requests for government assistance (*MT*, 29 June 1998).

On 20 May, 1998 Yeltsin signed a power-sharing agreement with Kostroma.

Relations with Other Regions

Kostroma is a member of the Central Russia Association, which is headed by Kostroma's neighbor to the west—Yaroslavl Governor Anatolii Lisitsyn. The Central Russia Association also includes Bryansk, Vladimir, Ivanovo, Kaluga, Moscow, Ryazan, Smolensk, Tver, and Tula oblasts along with the city of Moscow.

Attitude Toward Business: Underdeveloped Potential

Given the depressed state of the local economy, the Kostroma authorities are generally open to business deals and are willing to allow outside investors access to currently idle factories and land. Labor and facilities are much cheaper than they would be in Moscow. As in most Russian cities, the main problem is a lack of capital.

There are two local success stories that benefit from direct foreign investment. Saint Springs, which sells bottled water on the domestic market, is a joint venture between the Kostroma branch of the Russian Orthodox Church and John King, a retired plastics manufacturer from California. They have had great success at selling their water to foreigners and locals who are afraid to drink tap water. Jeffrey Sweetbaum, another American, has invested $2 million in Fanplit, a plywood and particle board factory that has turned a profit from its exports (Schmemann, 31–32). Both manufacturers benefited from the 17 August crisis because their costs stayed the same while prices for imported competitors went up. As portfolio investors have mostly fled Russian markets, these small-scale direct foreign investments are likely to be the wave of the future.

In February 1998 the Centerneftegaz consortium was formed by Kostroma, Vologda, and Yaroslavl in conjunction with several regional companies to exploit the region's potential hydrocarbon resources. Gazprom holds a 23.5 percent stake in the project through a regional company, and the Central Fuel Company, controlled by the Moscow city government, owns 25 percent (*EWI RRR*, 14 May 1998).

Internet Sites in the Region

http://www.kostroma.ru
This site provides information about the history of the region its beautiful local monasteries and other attractions.

KRASNODAR KRAI

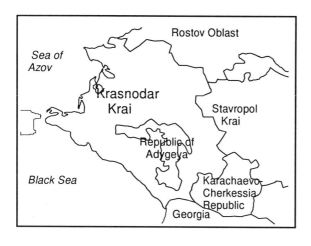

Territory: 76,000 km²
Population (as of 1 January 1998): 5,075,000
Distance from Moscow: 1,539 km

Major Cities:
Krasnodar, *capital* (pop. 646,200)
Sochi (334,700)
Novorossiisk (205,100)
Armavir (165,400)
Eisk (85,400)
Kropotkin (81,000)

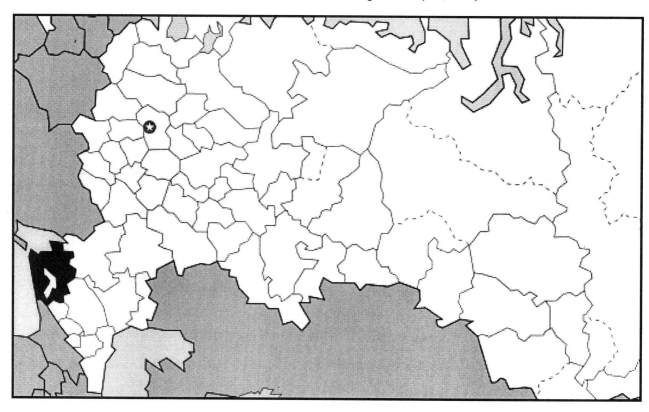

Basic Facts

Population (as of 1 Jan. 1998): 5,075,000 (3.45% of Russian total)

Ethnic breakdown (1989 census): Russians 84.6%, Ukrainians 3.9%, Armenians 3.7%

Urban population (as of 1 Jan. 1998): 53.7% (Russia overall: 73.1%)

Student population (as of 1 Sept. 1997): 120 per 10,000 (Russia overall: 208/10,000)

Pensioner population (1997): 26.9% (Russia overall: 25.96%)

Percent of population with higher education (1989 census): 9.2% (Russia overall: 11.3%)

Percent of population working in (1997): Industry: 16.6% (Russian average: 23.0%); Agriculture: 20.7% (13.7%); Trade: 13.9% (13.5%); Culture: 11.6% (13.3%)

Average monthly personal income in July 1998: 655.7 new rubles (Russian average: 897.1 new rubles)

Average monthly personal expenses in July 1998: 556.2 new rubles (Russian average: 684.9 new rubles)

Average monthly subsistence requirement in 1998: 369 new rubles (Russian average: 438 new rubles)

Consumer price index (as of July 1998): 92 (Russia overall = 100)

Budgetary revenues (1997): 8,340.2 billion rubles (Russia overall: 433,378.2 billion rubles)

Budgetary expenditures (1997): 8,437.8 billion rubles (Russia overall: 468,111.6 billion rubles)

Industrial production as percentage of all Russian production (Jan.–Aug. 1998): 0.91%

Proportion of loss-making enterprises (as of July 1998): 48.3% (Russia overall: 50.4%)

Number of enterprises which have wage arrears (as of 1 Sept. 1998): 1,619 (1.20% of Russian total)

Agricultural production as percentage of all Russian production (1997): 4.45%

Number of private farms (as of 1 Jan. 1998): 22,551 (8.22% of Russian total)

Capital investment (1997): 9,335.6 billion rubles (Russia overall: 408,797 billion rubles)

Sources of investment (1997): federal budget: 5.5% (Russian average: 10.2%); regional budget: 2.6% (10.5%); extra-budgetary funds: 91.9% (79.3%)

Foreign investment (1997): 15,272,000 USD (Russia overall: 12,294,734,000 USD)

Number of joint ventures (1997): 257 (1.74% of Russian total)

Fixed capital investment in joint ventures and foreign companies (1997): 248,004 million rubles (Russia overall: 16,265.4 billion rubles)

Number of small businesses (as of 1 July 1998): 24,600 (2.82% of Russian total)

Number of enterprises privatized in 1997: 121 (4.41% of Russian total), including those which used to be municipal property: 78.5% (Russian average: 66.4%); regional property: 5.0% (20.0%); federal property: 16.5% (13.6%)

Number of telephones per 100 families (1997): in cities: 40.7 (Russian average: 49.2); in villages: 21.4 (19.8)

Brief Overview

Krasnodar Krai lies in the western part of the North Caucasus. The region borders Rostov Oblast, Stavropol Krai, Karachaevo-Cherkessia, the Republic of Adygeya (which was an autonomous oblast within the krai until 1991), and Georgia (Abkhazia), and its coastline stretches along the Sea of Azov and the Black Sea to the Caucasus Mountains. The regional capital—Krasnodar (until 1920, Yekaterinodar)—located on the Kuban River, was founded in 1793 as a guard post of the Kuban Cossacks.

The region is the 16th largest in the country according to total reserves of various mineral resources, such as oil, gas, marble, limestone, iron ores, salt, and mineral and thermal waters. The northern two-thirds of the krai territory contain an extensive plain where the rich blackearth soil is used for intensive agriculture, which, along with the food-processing industry, dominates the regional economy and makes the region one of the country's most important "breadbaskets."

Oil and gas extraction, particularly on the Taman Peninsula, is also a significant contributor to the regional GDP. Other local industries include energy, chemicals, light industries, machine and equipment building, forestry, and timber working. The krai also has a well-developed transport infrastructure. The city of Krasnodar is an important railway junction, and there are large Black Sea ports at Novorossiisk and Tuapse.

According to a 1998 survey by *Ekspert* magazine, the krai ranked 13th among Russia's 89 regions in terms of investment potential and 25th in terms of investment risks. The survey noted that the investment situation in the krai had deteriorated since 1997: investment potential has decreased by 6 points (16th largest decrease in the country), while investment risk had grown by 27 points (5th largest). A 1998 survey by Bank Austria ranked the krai 12th in terms of investment climate.

Electoral History

2000 Presidential Election
Putin: 51.50%
Zyuganov: 37.39%
Yavlinskii: 3.40%
Zhirinovsky: 2.11%
Tuleev: 1.45%
Turnout: 66.02% (Russia overall: 68.64%)

1999 Parliamentary Elections
Communist Party of the Russian Federation: 36.81%
Unity: 27.81%
Union of Right Forces: 6.06%
Fatherland–All Russia: 4.99%
Zhirinovsky Bloc: 4.81%
Yabloko: 4.64%
In single-mandate districts: 4 Communist Party of the Russian Federation, 3 independent
Turnout: 58.46% (Russia overall: 61.85%)

1996 Gubernatorial Election
Kondratenko: 82.00%
Krokhmal: 7.18%
Yegorov (incumbent): 4.83%
Vavilov (krai legislature deputy, LDPR): 1.42%
Dyakonov (krai legislature deputy, Union of Kuban's Resurrection): 1.13%
Suslov: 0.32%
Pozdnyakov: 0.14%
Turnout: 48.63%

1996 Presidential Election
Zyuganov: 39.42%/52.48% (first round/second round)
Yeltsin: 26.26%/43.89%
Lebed: 17.49%
Zhirinovsky: 6.38%
Yavlinskii: 6.36%
Turnout: 67.19%/65.12% (Russia overall: 69.67%/ 68.79%)

1995 Parliamentary Elections
Communist Party of the Russian Federation: 24.39%
Liberal Democratic Party of Russia: 15.19%
Our Home Is Russia: 6.80%
Congress of Russian Communities: 6.55%
Communists–Workers' Russia: 6.46%
Yabloko: 6.39%
Party of Worker's Self-Government: 4.38%
Women of Russia: 2.99%
In single-mandate districts: 2 Communist Party of the Russian Federation, 3 Power to the People, 1 Union of Labor, 1 independent
Turnout: 60.53% (Russia overall: 64.37%)

1993 Constitutional Referendum
"Yes"—50.3% "No"—48.0%

1993 Parliamentary Elections
Liberal Democratic Party of Russia: 25.48%
Communist Party of the Russian Federation: 16.82%
Russia's Choice: 11.90%

Yabloko: 9.51%

Women of Russia: 8.57%

Agrarian Party of Russia: 7.59%

Party of Russian Unity and Concord: 7.51%

Democratic Party of Russia: 5.65%

In single-mandate districts: 1 Agrarian Party of Russia, 6 independent

From electoral associations: 1 Russia's Choice, 1 Agrarian Party of Russia

Turnout: 56.71% (Russia overall: 54.34%)

1991 Presidential Election

Yeltsin: 45.89%

Ryzhkov: 24.26%

Zhirinovsky: 12.87%

Tuleev: 6.82%

Bakatin: 3.46%

Makashov: 3.19%

Turnout: 72.83% (Russia overall: 76.66%)

Regional Political Institutions

Executive:

Governor, 4-year term

    Nikolai Ignatevich Kondratenko,

    elected December 1996

        Krasnodar Krai Administration; Ul. Krasnaya, 35; Krasnodar, 350014

        Tel 7(861–2) 62–57–16; Fax 7(861–2) 68–35–42

        Federation Council in Moscow: 7(095) 292–43–29, 926–65–91

Legislative:

Unicameral

Legislative Assembly (*Zakonodatelnoe Sobranie*)—50 members, 4-year term, elected December 1998

Chairman—Vladimir Andreevich Beketov, elected July 1995, December 1998

Regional Politics

Anti-Semitic Xenophobe Rules Krai

Governor Nikolai Kondratenko is famous in Russia and abroad for his ultra-nationalist and anti-Semitic speeches. In his region, however, he is seen as a charismatic figure. According to political scientist Arbakhan Magomedov: "His weekly live television call-in shows have become a tradition. His image as an honest and incorruptible leader attracts increasing

numbers of supporters from a variety of audiences. Local people see him as one of their own, who speaks the regional dialect and uses local aphorisms. The closest analogues to this patriarchal type of leadership are the leadership styles of Ulyanovsk Governor Yurii Goryachev and Belarusan President Aleksandr Lukashenko. Kondratenko is called *batka* (father) in the Kuban, just as Lukashenko is in Belarus" (Arbakhan Magomedov, "Krasnodar Krai: Nikolai Kondratenko's Regional Restoration," *Jamestown Foundation Prism*, 3 April 1998).

Kondratenko's speeches often describe his North Caucasus region as being overrun by foreigners, including Meskhetian Turks, Armenians, and Jews. In a 1998 address to an audience of young people, he used words such as *zhidy* (Yids/kikes), *zhidomasony* (Yid-Masons), *kosmopolity* (cosmopolitans), and *sionisty* (Zionists) 61 times (*Izvestiya*, 4 March 1998). Kondratenko has given the most nationalist and reactionary local Cossack groups the power to act as a police force.

Kondratenko makes at least a terminological distinction between Jews as a nationality and Zionism as an ideology. He blames Zionists for the collapse of the Soviet Union, the destruction of the Communist party, and the Chechen war. He divides the local media into two groups: "patriotic" and "Zionist." According to *Izvestiya*, the governor "is convinced of a global Jewish conspiracy and often discusses it privately" (*Izvestiya*, 4 March 1998). Surprisingly enough, in the category of Jews Kondratenko includes such diverse figures as Marshal Tukhachevskii, Margaret Thatcher, former CIA chief Allen Dulles, Leonid Brezhnev, and Mikhail Gorbachev. He has praised Stalin as someone who "knew Zionism well and fought against it" (*Izvestiya*, 28 May 1998).

Kondratenko puts his xenophobia into practice. In March 1998 he caused a scandal when he forced two employees of the U.S. National Democratic Institute to leave the krai. They were holding seminars on party building for members of the local branches of Yabloko, Our Home Is Russia, and Russia's Democratic Choice and conducting advocacy training for members of 25 local civic groups. In a radio broadcast Kondratenko claimed the lecturers were foreign intelligence agents (*KD*, 1 April 1998).

Kondratenko won the gubernatorial elections with the backing of a powerful coalition of leftist organizations called Fatherland (not to be confused with Moscow Mayor Yurii Luzhkov's movement, which has the same name). This party claimed over 60,000 active members (Magomedov). Kondratenko's predecessor and his main rival was Nikolai Yegorov, who had served as President Yeltsin's chief of staff in January–June 1996 and was then appointed governor after losing a Kremlin power struggle to Anatolii Chubais. In the first gubernatorial election held on 27 October 1996, Kondratenko outpolled Yegorov 57–25 percent, but the results were annulled on the grounds that turnout was below 50 percent. After the first round, the legislature lowered the minimum required turnout to 25 percent. Sensing imminent defeat, Yegorov attempted to postpone the vote by filing suit against the krai legislature and electoral commission. He also refused to allocate money for the new election from the krai budget. Yegorov was rarely seen in the krai during the 50 days before the repeat election. In the rematch held on 22 December, Kondratenko took 82 percent, handily defeating Yegorov, who managed only a meager 4.8 percent. Despite heavy snowfall in Krasnodar, turnout on 22 December was above 48 percent, up from 43 percent in October.

Executive Platform: Paranoid Reactionary

Kondratenko's permanent agenda includes "payment of wages, benefits, and pensions," "protection for local producers," and "the interests of the Kuban." He sees the region as engaged in a battle to thwart evil and punish the guilty (Magomedov). The gist of Kondratenko's "anti-crisis program" is that "the economic reforms conducted in Russia and in the Kuban between 1991 and 1996 were nothing other than a mechanism for destroying and strangling the domestic economy." Kondratenko has declared that "Russian government policy is a consistent policy of genocide against the citizens of Russia (above all, against ethnic Russians), carried out for the benefit, and under the direct supervision, of transnational imperialist forces."

Kondratenko has enjoyed the support of a wide range of nationalist-patriotic and Communist organizations, including the Communist Party of the Russian Federation (KPRF), the National Patriotic Union of Russia (NPSR), and Krasnodar's Fatherland coalition. Though Kondratenko was a faithful member of the Communist Party of the Soviet Union until it was banned in 1991, he did not join the KPRF. Nevertheless, when Gennadii Zyuganov and his nationalist and Agrarian allies negotiated the future make-up of a shadow government, Kondratenko was included in it. According to that March 1998 list, if the Communists

came to power, Kondratenko would be deputy prime minister in charge of the economy. He supported the Communists in the 1999 parliamentary elections.

Policies: Anti-Reform

In June 1997 Kondratenko signed a decree denouncing privatization in the region and ordering that it be reevaluated. According to Kondratenko, privatization resulted in the concentration of "national wealth in the hands of a small group of people, provoked numerous complaints from workers' collectives, . . . and exacerbated the economic crisis." Many regional enterprises were acquired by Moscow-based or foreign businesses, the governor claimed. Kondratenko ordered the creation of a commission that would search for legal violations in privatization deals and return illegally privatized property to the krai administration.

Kondratenko also intended to convince the federal government to transfer its shares of enterprises crucial for the krai's economy to the regional administration's ownership or management (*EWI RRR*, 3 July 1997).

The size of private land plots in Krasnodar Krai is kept small (*Izvestiya*, 21 August 1997). On one occasion Kondratenko declared that anyone who supported the unrestricted sale of land was a "Judas" opposing fundamental Russian values (*RFE/RL*, 19 February 1998).

Kondratenko dealt with the financial crisis following 17 August through traditional protectionist measures. Like many other governors, he attempted to limit the export of food beyond regional borders, defying federal law. Kondratenko then proceeded to evade a federal crackdown by forcing regional growers and food processors "voluntarily" to give first priority to supplying the krai market via a reserve food fund established by the governor.

Relationships Between Key Players: Controlled by "Fatherland"

Krasnodar Krai is called "the breadbasket of Russia" (Ukraine, which was "the breadbasket" of the Soviet Union, is now independent). It is also one of ten regions that provide 60 percent of all federal taxes (*OMRI DD*, 7 December 1996). However, Kondratenko's policies sometimes squander these riches. In August 1997, for example, Kondratenko issued a decree requiring growers to sell grain only at high prices that exceeded world levels. As a result, a lot of grain rotted in storage because it went unsold (*Ekspert*, 18 August 1997).

When Kondratenko won election, he immediately brought "his people" to power, appointing his fellow

Nikolai Ignatevich Kondratenko

16 February 1940—Born in a peasant family in Krasnodar Krai

1956–1959—Finished secondary school and worked at the Red Star collective farm and then as a secretary of the CPSU district committee

1959—Served in the army

1966—Graduated from the Agricultural University of Kuban

1966–1970—Worked as an agronomist, senior agronomist, and then deputy chairman of the Red Star collective farm

1970–1975—Second secretary of Dinskii CPSU District Committee

1975–1977—Instructor in Krasnodar Krai CPSU Committee

1977–1982—First secretary of Dinskii District CPSU Committee

1982–1984—Appointed general director of the North Caucasus Sugar-Processing Conglomerate (Krasnodar)

June 1987–1990—Elected chairman of the Krasnodar Krai CPSU Executive Committee

August 1991—During he coup, Kondratenko created a special institution that replicated the coup-makers' national institutions at the regional level. After the coup failed, Kondratenko was investigated, but the authorities eventually exonerated him.

1992–1996—Deputy director general of the company Reserve-Tobacco, deputy director of Kubangazprom, first deputy general director of the joint stock company Kuban of the conglomerate Krasnodarglavsnab, taught at the Agricultural University of Kuban

November 1992—Ran for a seat in the Russian Supreme Soviet, but the election results were annulled because of insufficient voter-turnout

April 1993—Elected to the Supreme Soviet, winning about 80 percent of the vote

December 1993—Elected to the Federation Council

Spring 1996—Worked as a representative for Gennadii Zyuganov during the presidential campaign

December 22, 1996—Elected governor, winning more than 80 percent of the vote

Fatherland members, former colleagues from Krasnodarglavsnab, and Cossack leaders as his deputies and aides. Kondratenko's main reason for firing all the people employed by his predecessor was that they "belonged to a team that had, directly or indirectly, supported the criminal policy that led to the pillaging of the Kuban" (Magomedov). Given his Communist affiliations, it is no surprise that many of the people who ruled in the region before 1991 returned to power. As political scientist Magomedov wittily noted, "these 'new old Russians' have replaced the 'new Russians,' who failed to take root in the territory."

In November 1998 the Krasnodar Krai Legislative Assembly elections brought 38 Fatherland members to the 50-member body. The remaining 12 spots were filled by one Yabloko member and eleven independents. Krasnodar Mayor Valerii Samoilenko, who campaigned with his own candidates strongly against Fatherland, said that the krai had acquired a "one-party parliament" to go with its one-party administration. He argued that since Krasnodar's party of power was in complete control of the krai government, it should accept responsibility for all of the krai's problems (*EWI RRR*, 3 December 1998). Though the previous krai legislature was also dominated by Kondratenko's leftist allies, the election results showed a sizable shift to the left in the region's voter preferences.

Ties to Moscow: Antagonistic

Kondratenko does not like the federal government and the feeling is mutual. Their positions have been so different that there was little chance for compromise. Many of the local elite shared Kondratenko's attitude to the federal government. For example, krai Deputy Prime Minister Nikolai Denisov called for defending the public against the "cosmopolitans around the Kremlin, who provide intellectual support for the policy of genocide against (ethnic) Russians and other peoples of Russia"(*Izvestiya*, 17 February 1998).

In the fall of 1997 Sergei Kovalev, Duma deputy and the leader of the human rights organization Memorial, launched a campaign against Kondratenko and the human rights violations he and his administration endorsed. He was especially concerned about the fate of numerous displaced persons from Chechnya and other regions who had settled in Krasnodar Krai. Meskhetian Turks were in the greatest danger, he feared. Meskhetians had been deported to Central Asia under Stalin, but after ethnic clashes in 1989 thousands of them were forced to leave Uzbekistan. In Krasnodar Krai there are some 12,000 Meskhetians and it is next to impossible for them to receive permanent residency permits (*propiski*) even though the Constitutional Court has ruled three times that the requirements for *propiski* were unconstitutional (*RFE/RL*, 17 December 1997). They also must pay to renew their registration with the police every 45 days (*RFE/RL*, 20 October 1997). They are frequently attacked by local Cossacks, though Kondratenko has described these incidents as nothing but fabrications. Kovalev also noted that the local media exacerbated the situation by portraying certain ethnic minorities, such as Meskhetians, as "criminal elements" (*RFE/RL*, 17 February 1998).

In spring 1998 a group of intellectuals issued a statement to the presidential administration declaring that Kondratenko's speeches showed him to be a fascist anti-Semite who promoted inter-ethnic violence. The Krasnodar Krai procurator's office refused to bring a criminal case against Kondratenko, arguing that it did not have enough evidence. Deputy General Procurator Rozanov explained that Kondratenko specifically criticized "Jews affiliated with the Zionist movement and not Jews in general" (*Izvestiya*, 28 July 1998).

Relations with Other Regions

Krasnodar belongs to the Association of Cooperation of Republics, Krais, and Oblasts of the North Caucasus.

The association includes the republics of Adygeya, Dagestan, Ingushetia, Kabardino-Balkaria, Karachaevo-Cherkessia, North Ossetia, and Kalmykia, Stavropol Krai; and Rostov Oblast.

Foreign Relations: Slavic Ties to Belarus and Ukraine

Kondratenko backs the establishment of a Russian-Belarusan union (*RFE/RL*, 21 May 1997). He also advocates closer ties to Ukraine (*NG*, 28 July 1998).

On one occasion Kondratenko warned the local population not to consume imported foodstuffs since, he said, the West had plotted the genocide of the Russian nation through poisoned foods.

Attitudes Toward Business

Despite Kondratenko's notoriety, visitors to the region claim that it is bustling with business activity and that flights between Krasnodar and Moscow are filled with Western businessmen. For example, the U.S. company Qualcomm won a $10 million contract to install a CDMA wireless telephone system in Krasnodar in January 1998 (*MT*, 14 January 1998).

Before the collapse of the ruble, tourism in the resort beach city of Sochi suffered because air tickets from Moscow to the city cost the same as tickets from Moscow to Greece (*FR*, 27 November 1997). Following 17 August, the situation changed considerably. Reports during the summer of 1999 suggested that many of the hotels in the city were sold out.

Knauf, a German construction materials firm, was granted control over the Kubanskii Gips factory in the town of Psebai by the Commission for the Protection of Investors' Rights. Knauf owned 50 percent of the shares of this factory, but when they tried to fire its director Alim Sergienko for corruption in 1996, Knauf was locked out. Knauf won repeated court decisions against Sergienko, but it did not help much. Sergienko used local Cossacks to throw out the German managers of the plant. In this battle Kondratenko of course took Sergienko's side, helping him to get rid of the "imperialists and colonizers." The governor blocked all of Knauf's efforts to repossess the plant. (For other reports on Knauf's difficulties in Russia, see the profile on Nizhnii Novgorod Oblast.)

Internet Sites in the Region

http://www.kuban.su/firminfo/raif/smi.htm
This site provides links to the major media in the region.

KRASNOYARSK KRAI

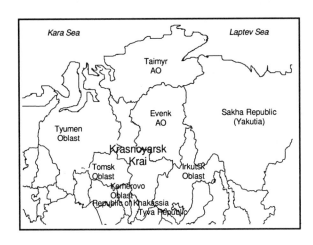

Territory: 2,339,700 km^2
Population (as of 1 January 1998):
3,080,000
Distance from Moscow: 3,955 km

Major Cities:
Krasnoyarsk, *capital* (pop. 875,100)
Norilsk (156,300)
Achinsk (122,700)
Kansk (108,100)
Zheleznogorsk (94,000)
Minusinsk (73,800)

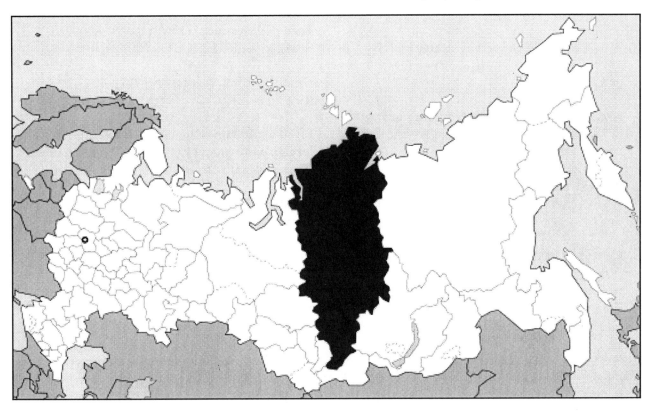

Basic Facts

Population (as of 1 Jan. 1998): 3,080,000 (2.09% of Russian total)

Ethnic breakdown (1989 census): Russians 87.5%, Ukrainians 3.5%, Tatars 1.6%, Germans 1.4%, northern peoples 0.5%

Urban population (as of 1 Jan. 1998): 74.2% (Russia overall: 73.1%)

Student population (as of 1 Sept. 1997): 222 per 10,000 (Russia overall: 208/10,000)

Pensioner population (1997): 22.6% (Russia overall: 25.96%)

Percent of population with higher education (1989 census): 9.8% (Russia overall: 11.3%)

Percent of population working in 1997: Industry: 28.1% (Russian average: 23.0%); Agriculture: 8.7% (13.7%); Trade: 13.3% (13.5%); Culture: 12.3% (13.3%)

Average monthly personal income in July 1998: 953.5 new rubles (Russian average: 891.7 new rubles)

Average monthly personal expenses in July 1998: 582.7 new rubles (Russian average: 684.9 new rubles)

Average monthly subsistence requirement in 1998: 437 new rubles (Russian average: 438 new rubles)

Consumer price index (as of July 1998): 135 (Russia overall = 100)

Budgetary revenues (1997): 10,620.0 billion rubles (Russia overall: 433,378.2 billion rubles)

Budgetary expenditures (1997): 11,725.1 billion rubles (Russia overall: 468,111.6 billion rubles)

Industrial production as percentage of all Russian production (Jan.–Aug. 1998): 2.71%

Proportion of loss-making enterprises (as of July 1998): 56.0% (Russia overall: 50.4%)

Number of enterprises which have wage arrears (as of 1 Sept. 1998): 1,864 (1.38% of Russian total)

Agricultural production as percentage of all Russian production (1997): 2.72%

Number of private farms (as of 1 Jan. 1998): 4,690 (1.7% of Russian total)

Capital investment (1997): 10,065.9 billion rubles (Russia overall: 408,797 billion rubles)

Sources of investment (1997): federal budget: 5.2% (Russian average: 10.2%); regional budget: 9.9% (10.5%); extra-budgetary funds: 84.9% (79.3%)

Foreign investment (1997): 379,997,000 USD (Russia overall: 12,294,734,000 USD)

Number of joint ventures (1997): 42 (0.29% of Russian total)

Fixed capital investment in joint ventures and foreign companies (1997): 13,249 million rubles (Russia overall: 16,265.4 billion rubles)

Number of small businesses (as of 1 July 1998): 12,900 (1.49% of Russian total)

Number of enterprises privatized in 1997: 48 (1.75% of Russian total), including those which used to be municipal property: 72.9% (Russian average: 66.4%); regional property: 12.5% (20.0%); federal property: 14.6% (13.6%)

Number of telephones per 100 families (1997): in cities: 29.5 (Russian average: 49.2); in villages: 16.9 (19.8)

Brief Overview

Krasnoyarsk Krai is the second-largest Russian region after Sakha (Yakutia), occupying an area of 2,339,700 sq km, which is nearly 14 percent of the country's total territory. It stretches 3,000 km from north to south. The krai lies in the middle of Siberia and borders Tyumen, Tomsk, Irkutsk, and Kemerovo oblasts; the republics of Khakassia, Tyva, and Sakha; and the Arctic Ocean in the north.

The krai was created in 1934 and then included the Taimyr and Evenk autonomous okrugs and Khakassia Autonomous Oblast. In 1991, Khakassia seceded and became a republic within the Russian Federation. Over 95 percent of the cities, a majority of the industrial enterprises, and all of the agriculture are concentrated in the south of the region. It is among the richest of Russia's regions in natural resources. Eighty percent of the country's nickel, 75 percent of its cobalt, 70 percent of its copper, 16 percent of its coal, and 10 percent of its gold are extracted in the region. Krasnoyarsk also produces 20 percent of the country's timber. It is one of a few Russian regions whose own budgetary revenues nearly cover its expenditures. In 1997, it raised 95.3 percent of its expenses by itself. The region's major industries are: non-ferrous metallurgy, energy, forestry, chemicals, and oil refining. Unfortunately, Krasnoyarsk's industry is damaging the environment: in 1998, according to a survey by *Ekspert* magazine, it had the second-worst air pollution in the country.

The region's main foreign trade partners are the Netherlands, the United States, Japan, France, Sweden, Italy, and South Korea. The krai ships metals and metal products, timber and cellulose, and fuel to them, while the main import item is aluminum ores for its processing industry.

According to the same survey by *Ekspert*, the region's investment potential, one of the best in the country, increased by 5 points from 1997 to 1998, and the krai was ranked 5th among Russia's 89 regions in terms of investment potential and 70th in terms of investment risk. The same year, the krai was 11th in the country according to direct foreign and capital investment in its economy—$23.1 million and 8.4 million rubles (0.59% and 2.42% of the country's total, respectively). A 1998 survey by Bank Austria ranked the krai 14th in terms of investment climate. However, at the end of 1998, Fitch ICBA gave the region its worst rating, putting it on the red list.

Electoral History

2000 Presidential Election
Putin: 48.36%
Zyuganov: 32.82%
Yavlinskii: 5.50%
Zhirinovsky: 4.24%
Tuleev: 2.75%
Turnout: 64.11% (Russia overall: 68.64%)

1999 Parliamentary Elections
Unity: 27.95%
Communist Party of the Russian Federation: 25.59%
Union of Right Forces: 8.36%
Zhirinovsky Bloc: 7.57%
Yabloko: 6.55%
Fatherland–All Russia: 4.00%
In single-mandate districts: 1 Communist Party of the Russian Federation, 1 Liberal Democratic Party of Russia, 2 independent
Turnout: 55.72% (Russia overall: 61.85%)

1998 Gubernatorial Election
Lebed: 45.11%/57.84% (first round/second round)
Zubov (incumbent): 35.40%38.70%
Turnout: 62.6%/63.83%

1996 Presidential Election
Yeltsin: 34.8%/53.43% (first round/second round)
Zyuganov: 28.52%/40.01%
Lebed: 13.87%
Yavlinskii: 10.01%
Zhirinovsky: 7.58%
Turnout: 70.20%/66.68% (Russia overall: 69.67%/ 68.79%)

1995 Parliamentary Elections
Communist Party of the Russian Federation: 18.84%
Liberal Democratic Party: 12.62%
Our Home Is Russia: 9.15%
Yabloko: 6.86%
Women of Russia: 5.78%
Congress of Russian Communities: 5.53%
Derzhava: 5.29%
Communists–Workers' Russia: 4.42%
Party of Workers' Self-Government: 3.75%
In single-mandate districts: 1 independent, 1 Agrarian Party of Russia, 1 Congress of Russian Communities, 1 Russia's Democratic Choice—United Democrats
Turnout: 64.66% (Russia overall: 64.37%)

1993 Constitutional Referendum

"Yes"—60.5% "No"—37.3%

1993 Parliamentary Elections

Liberal Democratic Party of Russia: 31.17%
Russia's Choice: 13.96%
Women of Russia: 9.28%
Communist Party of the Russian Federation: 9.06%
Agrarian Party of Russia: 7.84%
Yabloko: 7.29%
Party of Russian Unity and Concord: 6.56%
In single-mandate districts: 1 Liberal Democratic Party
   of Russia, 1 Agrarian Party of Russia, 2 independent
From electoral associations: 1 Russia's Choice, 1
   Liberal Democratic Party of Russia, 1 Democratic
   Party of Russia
Turnout: 52.17% (Russia overall: 54.34%)

1991 Presidential Election

Yeltsin: 60.06%
Ryzhkov: 15.41%
Zhirinovsky: 9.81%
Tuleev: 7.24%
Bakatin: 2.62%
Makashov: 1.75%
Turnout: 71.85% (Russia overall: 76.66%)

Regional Political Institutions

Executive:
Governor, 5-year term
   Aleksandr Ivanovich Lebed, elected May 1998
      Prospekt Mira, 110; 660009, Krasnoyarsk
      Tel 7 (391–2) 22–22–63; Fax 7 (391–2) 22–11–78

Legislative:
Unicameral
   Legislative Assembly (*Zakonodatelnoe Sobranie*)—
   42 members, 4-year term, elected December 1997
   Chairman—Aleksandr Victorovich Uss, elected
   January 1998

Regional Politics

Governor General with Presidential Ambitions

Lebed is the first national politician to seek a governorship as a platform to boost his career to the presidency. Many considered him a strong candidate to succeed Yeltsin if an angry protest vote swept aside more establishment politicians in Moscow. Lebed himself said that he would not run for the presidency unless he could first show real improvements in Krasnoyarsk, a goal he has not yet achieved. Lebed's decision to run for office in Krasnoyarsk was seen as a risk, since if he lost or was unable to address the problems of the region, it would damage his credentials in the presidential campaign. If he were to make the Krasnoyarsk economy boom, however, he would surely have improved his chances.

So far Lebed's record as governor is not very good, though it is true that many of the problems he now faces are not of his own making. He defeated incumbent Valerii Zubov, an ineffective academic, taking 57.84 percent in the runoff of their 1998 race. As governor, he cracked down on alleged corruption in the Zubov regime and fruitlessly tried to use price controls and export restrictions to deal with the financial crisis that began on 17 August. He is rarely in Krasnoyarsk, and after six months in office, entered into a bitter dispute with one of his key backers during the gubernatorial campaign. Unlike Moscow mayor Yurii Luzhkov, he has failed to build up a powerful network of allies among the country's other governors.

In his pre-gubernatorial, twenty-five-year military career Lebed won fame as the man who ended two wars. By his own account, he used force to end the conflict between ethnic Russians and Moldovans when he was serving as the commander of Russian troops in Trasndniester in 1992, and then applied reason to end the conflict in Chechnya in 1996. Now, he says, "I believe that only reason, not force, can settle conflicts and lay the basis for peace" (*EWI RRR*, 19 March 1998). Beyond his role as a peacemaker, Lebed has earned a reputation as a warrior against corruption who manages to keep his own hands clean and as a strong advocate of law and order. Although Lebed spent most of his career in the military, he has also demonstrated a strong ability to act independently, so it is not clear how much his military background determines his day-to-day decision making.

Executive Platform: Evolving Pragmatism Follows Early Experimentation

Although Lebed is one of Russia's most closely watched politicians, the specific planks of his platform are hard to define. Military analyst Pavel Felgengauer has commented, for example, that "his political and economic views are fluid, and his ideology appears to vary according to his audience" (*MT*, 21 May 1998). Since Lebed entered politics in 1995, most of his political alliances have turned sour. He no longer associates with the Congress of Russian Communities (KRO), the party on whose platform he ran in the 1995 State Duma elections.

Lebed is clear on several key points. He believes that the current attempts to build democracy in Russia are premature because the necessary preconditions for a democratic political system are not present (*KD*, 17 November 1998). He would much prefer to see the creation of a strong state. While he was secretary of the Security Council in the fall of 1996, he advised Yeltsin not to allow the election of the governors of Russia's regions (Aleksandr Lebed, *Ideologiya zdravogo smysla*, chapter 19, http://www.alebed.org). Although he is happy to use electoral mechanisms to advance his own career, he doubts that the introduction of real democracy will occur in his lifetime. In terms of reforming Russia's political institutions, he advocates the adoption of a new constitution that would make it easier for voters to remove presidents and legislators who no longer have the popular trust.

Lebed believes strongly in promoting law and order while cracking down on corruption and crime. He has argued for reinstating the death penalty in Russia and greatly expanding its use (Russia placed a moratorium on using the penalty when it joined the Council of Europe) (*Izvestiya*, 29 December 1998).

Lebed staunchly opposes the Communists as nothing but a return to the past, advocates of a policy that would not work in contemporary Russia. He supports the market and, after conducting a regional referendum, wants to introduce private property in land over a 10–15 year period. Russia's problems are not with market reforms as such, he contends, but the way that they were implemented. In general terms, he charges that former acting Prime Minister Yegor Gaidar and his associates were not thinking about human beings when they implemented their policies (Lebed, chapter 35). Further he charges that Russia only has a market economy for those at the top, in the sense that power and money go together, while most Russians have no access to the market.

Lebed argues that no single economic plan will work for all of Russia because the country is too big and cannot be controlled efficiently from Moscow. Nevertheless, one of his main themes is that Russia in general, and Krasnoyarsk as part of the larger country,

must rely on its own resources. He also consistently argues that the state should reduce the overall tax burden on businesses. Lebed maintains that a more rational federal tax policy would generate more money for the state and jobs for the unemployed. He also complains about the mutual debt problem. The Krasnoyarsk Krai administration owes 5 billion rubles, while others owe it 6 billion rubles. Much of the debt to the administration is owed by the federal government, which had failed to make arrangements to pay it off (NTV, 9 January 1999).

In terms of federalism, Lebed argues that Russia's most important task is to preserve the unity of the state (Lebed, chapter 16). He argues that Moscow should give the regions greater autonomy, but not to the point that they begin to set up their own armies.

Lebed has two political organizations, Honor and Motherland, and the Russian People's Republican Party (RNRP). Honor and Motherland was conceived as an organization that can gather and channel mass support, while the RNRP, as a more disciplined and professional party, will turn the ideas of the mass organization into concrete political action (A. M. Burovskii, *Lebed nad Yeniseem*, http://www.alebed.org/). According to A. M. Burovskii, the movement and the party provide the governor with a staff to maintain contacts with the wider population and carry out decisions. Lebed counts 32,000 members in the RNRP and more than 100,000 supporters of Honor and Motherland across Russia. However, given the numerous scandals surrounding Lebed's leadership of the krai, there are increasing divisions within the party.

Policies: Vague Economic Platform

In the economic program Lebed published during his gubernatorial campaign, he listed the krai's key problems as: increasing budget deficits, decreasing support for social services, a shrinking tax base, real money tax income comprising only 38.6 percent of the krai's overall income, regionally set property taxes that are too high, inefficient management of the krai's property, and little effective work to attract investment. He also pointed to the krai's delays in wage payments, debts to the pension fund, dangerous levels of unemployment, rising crime rate, inaccessible medical system, deteriorating levels of education, and widespread drunkenness and addiction to drugs. To fix these problems he called for bringing the region's large enterprises back to life, developing medium-sized and small businesses, and increasing the flow of real money into the budget ("Ekonomicheskaya programma kandidata na dolzhnost' gubernatora Krasnoyarskogo kraya Aleksandra Ivanovicha Lebedya," http://www.alebed.org). Unfortunately, he did not explain how he proposed to accomplish these tasks.

One of Lebed's key policy initiatives has been cracking down on corruption in the krai. In practical terms this means that he has investigated abuse of office by former Governor Zubov's staff and arrested many of Zubov's lieutenants. Among those arrested were former deputy governors Vladimir Kornev, Vladimir Kuzmin, and Valentina Cherezovaya, as well as a variety of other officials and businessmen (*EWI RRR*, 5 November 1998). Zubov has defended his former assistants and probably feared that he too would be arrested. Lebed could use the corruption crackdown to deflect attention from the region's economic problems.

In response to the financial crisis that began in August 1998, Lebed imposed a prohibition on "unwarranted" price increases in the region, capping them at 10 percent, and sought to prevent local producers from shipping their goods outside the region. The measures were ineffective and prices shot up dramatically.

Lebed has sought to bring a measure of fiscal austerity to the krai budget, proposing a balanced budget that would spend no more than the krai's projected income of 5.5 billion rubles in 1999. Staying within these limits would force Lebed to cut some of the social programs that he promised voters during his election campaign (*Vremya MN*, 20 November 1998). The 1998 budget, largely prepared by the Zubov team but signed by Lebed in June 1998, forecast an 18 percent deficit with revenues of 5.1 billion rubles and expenses of 6.0 billion rubles (*EWI RRR*, 25 June 1998).

Despite giving priority to the issue, Lebed has not been able to pay public sector salaries in the krai.

Relationships Between Key Players: Outsider Governor Losing Local Support

Lebed won the gubernatorial campaign by gaining the votes of less-educated rural voters (plus an overwhelming majority in Norilsk), while the majority of the urban electorate in Krasnoyarsk and the closed city of Zheleznogorsk (Krasnoyarsk-26) backed Zubov. Lebed had the support of the Rossiisskii Kredit bank and the region's local aluminum interests. Zubov, in turn, had the backing of Norilsk Nikel, in the north of the krai,

and its owner, Vladimir Potanin's Uneximbank. Lebed initially used his office to help the aluminum industry, providing it with cheap electricity.

Since Lebed was an outsider to Krasnoyarsk, he has relied on middle managers from Rossiiskii Kredit bank to staff key posts within his administration. These men generally flew in from Moscow on Monday and headed home for the weekend. Turnover among the officials was rapid. Locals deeply resented the outsiders and made fun of their ignorance about the krai. After Lebed's victory, the bank sent its personnel to Krasnoyarsk to give them some regional governing experience, with the expectation that Lebed would win the presidency and then need personnel to staff the federal ministries. Since the beginning of the August 1998 economic crisis, relations between Lebed and the bank became increasingly strained. The bank now has bigger problems than Krasnoyarsk Krai. Locals resent the fact that Lebed traveled frequently and involved himself in issues like the situation in the North Caucasus, far beyond the region's concern.

Itogi claimed that one of the most influential members of Lebed's staff was Deputy Governor Viktor Novikov, a mysterious individual who never gives interviews to the media. Novikov's philosophy is said to come from a mixture of ideas borrowed from the Black Hundreds, various mystics, and philosophers about the benefits of a strong state. He is said to be connected to key Lebed supporters such as Rossiiskii Kredit and magnate Boris Berezovskii (*Itogi*, 13 October 1998).

In December 1998, about six months into his term, Lebed suffered a major blow when one of his key supporters, Anatolii Bykov, turned against him. Bykov was the chairman of the Krasnoyarsk Aluminum Factory (KrAZ)—Russia's second-largest aluminum producer—a vice president of Rossiiskii Kredit, and a member of the Krasnoyarsk legislature. He provided crucial financial support for Lebed's election campaign. Bykov turned on Lebed because he believed that the governor was standing in the way of his attempts to gain cheaper electricity for his aluminum plant. Bykov is believed to have ties to the criminal world in Krasnoyarsk as well as to the chairman of the regional legislature, Aleksandr Uss, a former crime fighter who believed in using one criminal group against another. Bykov also controls the local TVK-6 television station. On 8 December 1998, Bykov claimed that Lebed had begun investigating KrAZ for criminal connections. After a loud scandal, in which Lebed was seen cursing on television, Prime Minister Yevgenii

Primakov stepped in to help Lebed. In April 1999 Deputy Minister of Internal Affairs Vladimir Kolesnikov announced that he was filing criminal charges against Bykov, who subsequently fled the country.

Bykov supported Lebed as governor so that Lebed would provide him low-priced inputs for the aluminum factory that drives much of the regional economy. In July 1998, when Lebed was close to Bykov, he appointed Nail Nasyrov, a KrAZ man, external manager of the Achinsk Alumina Combine (AGK). The plant provides raw material (alumina) to KrAZ and Bykov has fought hard to maintain control over it. Moreover, the city of Achinsk has 120,000 residents who depend on the plant for their livelihood (*MT*, 30 December 1998).During his falling out with Bykov, Lebed in December 1998 considered handing the plant back to Alfa Bank, which owns 12 percent of the plant's debts and is a competitor to Bykov. However, a last-minute compromise brought Lebed back to supporting Nasyrov. On 29 December 1998, a Chelyabinsk court ruled that Nasyrov would remain in charge for one more year. Nasyrov has been an effective manager who paid off many of the firm's debts (*EWI RRR*, 14 January 1999). However, Lebed's tense relations with Rossiiskii Kredit and Bykov may make him more willing to work with Alfa in the future.

KrAZ is also battling the national electricity monopoly, Unified Energy Systems, to gain control of the Krasnoyarsk hydroelectric dam. The aluminum smelter consumes huge amounts of electricity and controlling the dam would give it guaranteed access to cheap energy. It receives 80 percent of its electricity from the dam. When Lebed was elected governor, he helped Bykov gain access to the cheap electricity. It remains unclear how the conflict between Lebed and Bykov will affect the electricity producer (*MT*, 13 January 1999).

Also in dispute is the Borodinskii coal mine, the largest in Russia. In the fall of 1998, Lebed helped set up the Krasnoyarsk Fuel Company (KTK), which was allied with Bykov. That company gained control over the mine by buying the right to collect a 42-million-ruble debt from it and transferred it to an unidentified Novosibirsk firm. The Novosibirsk firm, presumably linked to Bykov, could bankrupt Borodinskii and try to grab its assets. Lebed used foul language in a televised meeting on 17 January 1999, berating KTK chief Marat Saitov and demanding that the mine be returned to the krai. Lebed was particularly angry about the deal because he had helped Bykov set up KTK in the first place. Lebed has ordered KTK banished from Krasnoyarsk (*MT*, 22 January 1999).

The other major plant in the krai is Norilsk Nikel, located in the far north, in Taimyr Autonomous Okrug, and controlled by Uneximbank. Lebed pressured the plant, which produces 13 percent of the world's nickel, to make good on its tax obligations to the krai. In November 1998 he required the plant to provide a promissory note for 60 million rubles in tax payments. He used the proceeds to cover some of the krai's salary arrears. He has also promised to help relocate 60,000 unemployed workers from the harsh arctic conditions in Norilsk to more hospitable southern regions. In March 1999 Lebed orchestrated another agreement among the city of Norilsk, Norilsk Nikel, Norilsk Combine, and the Norilsk Mining Company, stipulating that 80 percent of the income tax would stay in the okrug while only 20 percent would go to the krai. Lebed agreed to lobby for the interests of the plant in Moscow, and in exchange Norilsk Nikel would register all new subsidiaries in the krai.

Overall, there are 26,000 enterprises in Krasnoyarsk, yet 80 percent of the krai's income comes from taxes assessed on only nine of them. These plants employ just three percent of the region's workforce. The krai economy is closely connected to the export of raw materials. The region exports up to $2.5 billion worth of goods a year. Little is reinvested in Siberia, however, causing a general degradation of the regional economy (*EWI RRR*, 20 August 1998).

Chairman of the Krasnoyarsk Krai legislature Aleksandr Uss backed Zubov in the gubernatorial campaign and is not considered a Lebed ally. The regional parliament, which backed Bykov, is now also in opposition to Lebed. On 14 January 1999, 28 krai legislators sent Lebed a letter accusing him of failing to manage the krai's economy effectively. Among the signatories were Bykov and the former leader of Lebed's own Honor and Motherland faction, Viktor Zubarev. The legislature passed legislation that would make it possible to remove Lebed from office (*Izvestiya*, 19 December 1998).

Lebed requires all journalists covering his administration to be accredited and reserves the right to revoke their accreditation if he believes that the journalist is "incompetent" (*Izvestiya*, 18 September 1998). Newspapers like *MK v Krasnoyarske* and *Vechernii Krasnoyarsk* are critical of the governor. In January 1999 Lebed dismissed the director and chief editor of the Krasnoyarsk State Television and Radio Company, appointing one of his own men, Oleg Nelzin, to head the company.

Ties to Moscow: Critic of the Federal Government

Lebed consistently argues that the Kremlin has tried to concentrate too much power in the capital and that it should give the regions considerably more autonomy. He also believes that federal policy is not focused on helping the regions. In his view, the regions should only give Moscow responsibility for functions that they cannot perform, and the lion's share of tax revenues should stay in the regions (*KD*, 8 July 1998). He also bitterly complains that as much as 80 percent of the country's banking capital is concentrated in Moscow.

At a meeting of the Siberian Accord interregional association on 15 January 1999, Lebed said that the federal government should transfer ownership of factories, electricity generators, and coal mines to the regions, giving the regional leaderships significantly greater freedom from Moscow (*NG*, 16 January 1999). Lebed proposed subordinating the "approximately 90" regional branches of federal ministries working in the krai jointly to the governor as well as the federal government. Lebed warned that any attempt by the center to strengthen its ties to the regions would only increase separatist tendencies. Former Prime Minister Yevgenii Primakov responded, "We lost the Soviet Union, we are not going to lose Russia," and warned against separatism.

After placing third in the first round of the 1996 presidential elections, Lebed threw his support behind Yeltsin, helping him to defeat Zyuganov. He then served briefly as secretary of the Security Council, before Yeltsin fired him. By the end of 1998, he was calling for the president's resignation. He became a strong opponent of Yeltsin and his associates, labeling the federal leadership a "dictatorship of irresponsibility" (Lebed, chapter 45).

As an ally of Boris Berezovskii, Lebed backed the re-nomination of Viktor Chernomyrdin as prime minister after Yeltsin fired Sergei Kirienko in August 1998. However, he also supported the nomination of Kirienko's successor, Yevgenii Primakov, since he believed that Primakov would help prevent Russia from collapsing into chaos.

Lebed caused considerable irritation in Moscow on 24 July 1998 when he sent an open letter to then Prime Minister Kirienko stating that if the federal government did not pay the wages of the troops that control the silo-based nuclear arsenal in the region, Lebed would take them under the control of the regional administration. As early as 1997, former Governor Zubov had been paying the soldiers' salaries from the krai budget. Some speculated that if the soldiers decided to support the general, he would gain control of the nuclear weapons (*EWI RRR*, 30 July 1998). However, there is little evidence that Lebed has that kind of support among the armed forces.

Lebed criticized the power-sharing agreement signed between former Governor Zubov, the Taimyr and Evenk autonomous okrugs within Krasnoyarsk, and the federal government on 1 November 1997, claiming that it allows Moscow to rob the region (*EWI RRR*, 21 May 1998). Shortly after winning the governorship, he promised to renegotiate the deal. In the summer of 1998, he refused to sign a treaty with then First Deputy Prime Minister Boris Nemtsov, arguing that he and the federal government could not reach agreement (*KD*, 8 July 1998).

In looking for ways to keep Lebed in line, the Kremlin appointed Krasnoyarsk Mayor Petr Pimashkov to the presidential Council on Local Government (*Izvestiya*, 3 June 1998). During the campaign, Pimashkov supported Zubov, as did a majority of his constituents. At that time Lebed charged that the city unfairly soaked up money that belonged to the rest of the krai.

Relations with Other Regions: Little Support or Respect

Governor Lebed has enjoyed little respect in the Federation Council. Although his predecessor Zubov had been one of four deputy speakers in the upper chamber, the governors and regional legislative chairmen who make up the chamber filled the vacancy with Omsk Legislative Assembly Chairman Vladimir Varnavskii on 10 June 1998 rather than giving it to Lebed.

Lebed has little role to play in the Siberian Accord interregional association. When Lebed was elected governor, Novosibirsk Governor Vitalii Mukha chaired the association, but now it is led by Tomsk Governor Viktor Kress. Lebed had expressed an interest in taking over the association and making it work more effectively, but Mukha said that Lebed would first have to demonstrate that he could improve the situation in Krasnoyarsk before he could assume a leadership role in the Siberian organization (*NG*, 28 May 1998).

Lebed naturally has close ties with his younger brother Aleksei, who is the governor of Khakassia, a relatively poor republic just south of Krasnoyarsk. Aleksei provided financial support for Aleksandr's Krasnoyarsk campaign.

Aleksandr Ivanovich Lebed

20 April 1950—Born to a working-class family in Novocherkassk

1969–1973—Studied at the Ryazan Higher Air-Borne School

1972—Joined the Communist Party of the Soviet Union

1973–1981—Worked at the Ryazan military school

November 1981–July 1982—Commanded an airborne battalion in Afghanistan

1982–1985—Studied at the Frunze Military Academy

1985—Deputy commander, then commander of an airborne unit in Kostroma

1986–1988—Deputy commander of an airborne division in Pskov

1988–1991—Commander of the Tula airborne division which helped put down ethnic violence in Baku (November 1988) and Tbilisi (April 1989)

February 1991–June 1992—Served as deputy commander of the airborne forces in charge of military preparedness and education

1990—Elected as a delegate to the 28th CPSU Congress and the founding congress of the Russian Communist Party. Elected as a member of the hard-line Russian Communist Party Central Committee

August 1991—Apparently helped defend Yeltsin during the attempted hard-line Communist coup, though he claims that he did not take sides

23 June 1992—Arrived in Tiraspol as the commander of the 14th Russian Army and quickly used artillery bombardments to force the Moldovans to accept the Russian presence

June 1995—Discharged from the military by Yeltsin and quickly entered Russian politics

15 October 1995—Founded the Honor and Motherland (*Chest i rodina*) political movement

17 December 1995—Elected to the State Duma from a district in Tula. The party on whose list he ran, the Congress of Russian Communities, did not cross the 5 percent barrier.

16 June 1996—Took third place in the presidential elections, winning 14.7 percent of the votes.

18 June 1996—Appointed secretary of the Security Council and national security advisor to the president; resigned State Duma seat on 25 September

31 August 1996—Signed the Khasavyurt agreement with Aslan Maskhadov, effectively ending the fighting in the 1994–96 Chechen war and postponing a decision on Chechen independence for five years

17 October 1996—Fired as Security Council Secretary by Yeltsin

December 1996—Began setting up political party, the Russian People's Republican Party (*Rossiiskaya narodno-respublikanskaya partiya*)

26 April 1998—Won 44% of the vote in the first round of the Krasnoyarsk gubernatorial elections

17 May 1998—Elected governor of Krasnoyarsk, with 57.33% of the vote

Russian

Has three children, Aleksandr, Ivan, and Yekaterina

As a result of the role he played in ending the fighting between Russian and Chechen troops in 1996, Lebed developed a relationship with Chechen President Aslan Maskhadov. In July 1998 he issued a joint manifesto with Tatarstan President Mintimer Shaimiev, Chernomyrdin, and Berezovskii denouncing federal policy toward the troubled region. At the time, it seemed that the four might form a more permanent alliance, but they have done nothing collectively since issuing the statement. Lebed believed the Russian government should provide more support to Maskhadov to help him defeat his local enemies. By not doing so, he charged, that Russia was ceding its interests in Chechnya. Unlike Maskhadov, however, Lebed believes that Chechnya should remain a part of Russia.

Foreign Relations: Close Links with Belarus, Conflict with Ukraine

Lebed believes strongly in the close links between the Russian, Belarusan, and Ukrainian people. Ethnically, he is half-Russian and half-Ukrainian (his passport lists him as Russian, while his brother's passport lists Aleksei as Ukrainian). Although he recognizes that it is senseless to talk of recreating the former Soviet Union, he backs a Russia-Belarus Union, saying that the cost in money is less important than the "spiritual comfort of the nation"(Lebed, chapter 12). Lebed's use of force in Moldova when he commanded Russian troops there has given him the image of one who is not afraid to fight for the interests of Russians living outside of Russia's borders. He continues to stand up for the 25 million Russians living outside of Russia.

Lebed has complicated Russia's relationship with Ukraine because he wants Ukraine to pay $800–$1,000 a ton for dumping nuclear waste in the closed mountain city of Zheleznogorsk (Krasnoyarsk-26, pop. 100,000), rather than the $275/ton that Ukrainian and Russian producers are paying now. Until the Ukrainians agree to pay the higher price, he has blocked further shipments (*NG*, 11 January 1999). The facility is the only one in the world that can handle waste from RBMK-1000 plants which currently operate in Zaporozhe (Ukraine), St. Petersburg, Balakova, Tver, Kursk, and Smolensk. Lebed's actions alarmed residents of Zheleznogorsk because handling the waste provides one of their few sources of income (*KD*, 18 November 1998).

Lebed is much calmer than most Russian politicians about NATO's decision to open membership to the Czech Republic, Hungary, and Poland, arguing that they have always been part of Western society. However, he says it would be a different matter if the Baltic republics or Ukraine were to join (Lebed, chapter 22).

Lebed has visited the United States several times and has established a relationship with Texas Governor George W. Bush. He has called on the State Duma not to ratify the SALT II treaty, asking that Russia and the United States reduce their arsenal of nuclear weapons to 1,500–1,700 each rather than the 3,000–3,500 envisioned in the treaty (*RFE/RL*, 22 January 1999).

Attitudes Toward Business: Energetically Seeks Investment

Lebed energetically seeks foreign investment in his region, and often travels abroad to meet with potential partners. To make the region more attractive, he is trying to impose more discipline on the region's budget. He is also a vocal advocate for small businesses. However, the results have been meager. Japan's Marubeni, which has long been active in Krasnoyarsk, was the only major company to participate in Lebed's inauguration festivities.

Internet Sites in the Region

http://www.alebed.org
The home page of Lebed's Honor and Motherland organization and the Russian People's Republican Party provides updates of recent news. The site includes party activities and posts excerpts from the local press as well as press releases from the governor's press office. In the section titled "leader," an electronic version of Lebed's book *Ideologiya zdravogo smysla* is available. The site also has extensive information from the gubernatorial campaign, including the text of Lebed's campaign program.

http://www.geocities.com/CapitolHill/2568/ 1_lebed.html
Lebed lovers and haters will find an extensive list of links to Lebed material here.

http://www.krasnoyarsk.org
The web site of the former Krasnoyarsk governor Valerii Zubov, is not currently being updated.

KURGAN OBLAST

Territory: 71,000 km^2
Population (as of 1 January 1998): 1,106,000
Distance from Moscow: 1,973 km

Major Cities:
Kurgan, *capital* (pop. 366,500)
Shadrinsk (88,200)
Shumikha (21,300)
Kurtamysh (18,7000

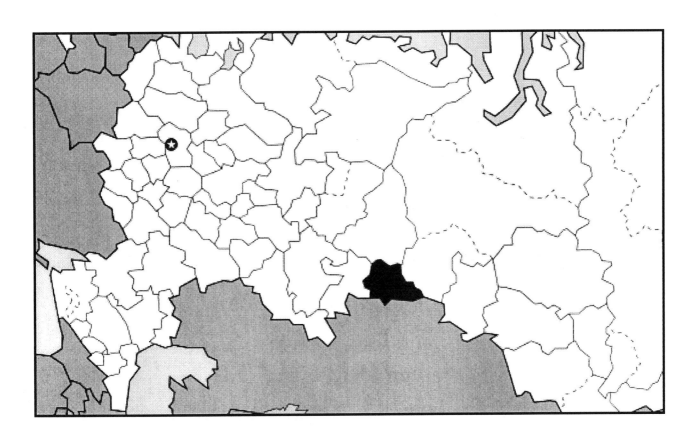

Basic Facts

Population (as of 1 Jan. 1998): 1,106,000 (0.75% of Russian total)

Ethnic breakdown (1989 census): Russians 91.4%, Tatars 2.0%, Bashkirs 1.6%, Kazakhs 1.4%, Ukrainians 1.3%

Urban population (as of 1 Jan. 1998): 55.6% (Russia overall: 73.1%)

Student population (as of 1 Sept. 1997): 128 per 10,000 (Russia overall: 208/10,000)

Pensioner population (1997): 26.31% (Russia overall: 25.96%)

Percent of population with higher education (1989 census): 7.2% (Russia overall: 11.3%)

Percent of population working in (1997): Industry: 20.0% (Russian average: 23.0%); Agriculture: 24.1% (13.7%); Trade: 11.4% (13.5%); Culture: 13.2% (13.3%)

Average monthly personal income in July 1998: 438.1 new rubles (Russian average: 891.7 new rubles)

Average monthly personal expenses in July 1998: 330.1 new rubles (Russian average: 684.9 new rubles)

Average monthly subsistence requirement in 1998: 328 new rubles (Russian average: 438 new rubles)

Consumer price index (as of July 1998): 88 (Russia overall = 100)

Budgetary revenues (1997): 1,651.1 billion rubles (Russia overall: 433,378.2 billion rubles)

Budgetary expenditures (1997): 2,018.1 billion rubles (Russia overall: 468,111.6 billion rubles)

Industrial production as percentage of all Russian production (Jan.–Aug. 1998): 0.37%

Proportion of loss-making enterprises (as of July 1998): 56.5% (Russia overall: 50.4%)

Number of enterprises which have wage arrears (as of 1 Sept. 1998): 2,829 (2.09% of Russian total)

Agricultural production as percentage of all Russian production (1997): 1.29%

Number of private farms (as of 1 Jan. 1998): 4,372 (1.59% of Russian total)

Capital investment (1997): 1,160.6 billion rubles (Russia overall: 408,797 billion rubles)

Sources of investment (1997): federal budget: 9.7% (Russian average: 10.2%); regional budget: 13.9% (10.5%); extra-budgetary funds: 76.4% (79.3%)

Foreign investment (1997): 4,000 USD (Russia overall: 12,294,734,000 USD)

Number of joint ventures (1997): 17 (0.12% of Russian total)

Fixed capital investment in joint ventures and foreign companies (1997): 670 million rubles (Russia overall: 16,265.4 billion rubles)

Number of small businesses (as of 1 July 1998): 3,700 (0.43% of Russian total)

Number of enterprises privatized in 1997: 1 (0.04% of Russian total), including those which used to be municipal property: 100% (Russian average: 66.4%); regional property: 0% (20.0%); federal property: 0% (13.6%)

Number of telephones per 100 families (1997): in cities: 32.5 (Russian average: 49.2); in villages: 24.9 (19.8)

Brief Overview

Kurgan Oblast is located in the southern part of the West Siberian plain in the Tobol River basin, bordering Chelyabinsk, Sverdlovsk, and Tyumen oblasts, and Kazakhstan. The oblast's capital, Kurgan, is linked to Yekaterinburg, Omsk, and Chelyabinsk by the Trans-Siberian railway, as well as to the shipping routes of the Ob-Irtysh system by the navigable Tobol River. The region lies on the route of major oil and gas pipelines connecting West Siberia to the European part of the country. Kurgan Oblast is not rich in mineral resources, though it has some reserves of iron ores, oil, and gas.

Once covered with steppe vegetation, most of the oblast is now used for agriculture. The main crop is spring wheat, but rye, oats, corn, and vegetables are also grown. Due to its traditional specialization in agriculture, the region has a strong food-processing industry.

Despite the agricultural focus, most of today's regional output comes from industry—mining, machine building, chemical and petrochemical industries, and production of construction materials, mostly concentrated in the cities of Kurgan and Shadrinsk. Parts of the oblast have suffered from radioactive contamination caused by nuclear accidents in adjacent Chelyabinsk Oblast.

A 1998 survey by *Ekspert* magazine ranked the oblast 62nd among Russia's 89 regions in terms of investment potential and 65th in terms of investment risk. Since 1997, the region had experienced the seventh largest investment potential growth (by 8 points) in the country, according to the same study. A 1998 survey by Bank Austria ranked the oblast 60th in terms of investment climate.

Electoral History

2000 Presidential Election
Putin: 48.39%
Zyuganov: 36.41%
Zhirinovsky: 4.63%
Yavlinskii: 3.16%
Tuleev: 2.11%
Turnout: 71.03% (Russia overall: 68.64%)

1999 Parliamentary Elections
Communist Party of the Russian Federation: 29.13%
Unity: 26.65%
Zhirinovsky Bloc: 8.88%

Union of Right Forces: 7.04%
Fatherland–All Russia: 6.16%
Yabloko: 3.89%
In a single-mandate district: 1 independent
Turnout: 65.56% (Russia overall: 61.85%)

1996 Gubernatorial Election
Bogomolov (oblast legislature chairman): 40.87%/ 66.29% (first round/second round)
Koltashev: 33.14%
Sobolev (incumbent): 12.92%
Turnout: 52.3%/43.56%

1996 Presidential Election
Zyuganov: 37.53%/50.52% (first round/second round)
Yeltsin: 29.25%/43.41%
Lebed: 11.14%
Zhirinovsky: 9.99%
Yavlinskii: 6.61%
Turnout: 74.02%/72.08% (Russia overall: 69.67%/ 68.79%)

1995 Parliamentary Elections
Communist Party of the Russian Federation: 22.20%
Liberal Democratic Party of Russia: 19.59%
Agrarian Party of Russia: 8.14%
Our Home Is Russia: 6.94%
Communists–Workers' Russia: 6.31%
Women of Russia: 3.55%
Party of Workers' Self-Government: 3.49%
Yabloko: 3.16%
In a single-mandate district: 1 independent
Turnout: 69.60% (Russia overall: 64.37%)

1993 Constitutional Referendum
"Yes"—56.1% "No"—41.1%

1993 Parliamentary Elections
Liberal Democratic Party of Russia: 23.72%
Women of Russia: 15.53%
Communist Party of the Russian Federation: 12.62%
Russia's Choice: 11.60%
Agrarian Party of Russia: 11.39%
Democratic Party of Russia: 7.35%
Party of Russian Unity and Concord: 5.58%
Yabloko: 4.00%
In single-mandate districts: 2 independent
From electoral associations: 1 Communist Party of the Russian Federation
Turnout: 61.21% (Russia overall: 54.34%)

1991 Presidential Election

Yeltsin: 52.26%

Ryzhkov: 25.07%

Zhirinovsky: 7.71%

Tuleev: 4.08%

Makashov: 3.26%

Bakatin: 2.38%

Turnout: 81.73% (Russia overall: 76.66%)

Regional Political Institutions

Executive:

Governor, 4-year term

Oleg Alekseevich Bogomolov, elected December 1996

Gogol St., 56; Kurgan, 640663

Tel 7(391–2) 2–25–34; Fax 7(352–22) 2–74–64

Federation Council in Moscow:

7(095) 292–07–18, 926–65–16,

Fax: 7(095) 292–59–36

Legislative:

Unicameral

Oblast Duma—33 members, 4-year term, elected November 1996

Chairman—Lev Grigorevich Yefremov, elected December 1996

Regional Politics

Governor Elected Without Opposition

Oleg Bogomolov was elected governor of Kurgan Oblast in December 1996. He ran unopposed in the second round since second-place finisher Anatolii Koltashev withdrew from the race. After Koltashev withdrew, third-place finisher incumbent Anatolii Sobolev, refused to compete in Koltashev's place. The regional electoral commission allowed Bogomolov to run unopposed provided that more people cast votes for rather than against him. The National Patriotic Union of Russia (NPSR) backed Bogomolov.

Executive Platform: Strong State Regulation

Bogomolov follows a basically Communist platform, though he also gave some support to Yeltsin. Bogomolov is opposed to selling land, in particular to foreigners, and prefers a strong state role in regulating economic activity. He was particularly supportive of

former Deputy Prime Minister (in charge of economic policy) Yurii Maslyukov, who served briefly under Prime Minister Yevgenii Primakov and once headed the USSR State Planning Committee.

Policies: Unsuccessful Protectionist

Kurgan is an economically depressed region. The drought of 1998 destroyed 60 percent of the region's crops. Most local industry is starved for investment. Furthermore, parts of the oblast have been ecologically damaged by radioactive contamination caused by nuclear accidents in neighboring Chelyabinsk.

Kurgan suffers from severe wage and pension arrears, primarily as a result of poor tax collection. Bogomolov blames these problems on the non-payment crisis and the tax system (Russian TV, 10 August 1998). However, several of Bogomolov's policies are not conducive to developing a healthy market system. In July 1997 he issued a decree limiting the sales of locally grown grain outside the oblast. The Kurgan Oblast court overturned the decree in December 1997, but many regional farmers had already suffered from it.

Relationships Between Key Players: Opposes Land Privatization

The Kurgan Oblast Duma has tried to pass a law permitting the buying and selling of land, but Bogomolov is strongly opposed to such a policy.

Ties to Moscow: Supports Leftists

Bogomolov, backed by the Communists in his gubernatorial bid, was generally supportive of Boris Yeltsin, although critical of some of the president's policies. He was opposed to the president's actions in fall 1993.

Bogomolov was very supportive of the appointment of Yurii Maslyukov and Viktor Gerashchenko as first deputy prime minister and chairman of the Central Bank in the Primakov cabinet. Bogomolov stresses that the federal government needs to work together with the regions in addressing the country's difficulties and taking the regions' concerns into consideration when formulating policy (*NG*, 22 September 1998).

Relations with Other Regions

Kurgan belongs to the Urals Regional Association, which includes the republics of Bashkortostan and Udmurtia; Komi-Permyak Autonomous Okrug; and Orenburg, Perm, Sverdlovsk, and Chelyabinsk oblasts.

Oleg Alekseevich Bogomolov

4 October 1950—Born in Kurgan Oblast

1972—Graduated from the Kurgan Machine Building Institute

1972–1975—Worked in the Kurgan Machine-Building Factory as an engineer-constructor and engineer for technical security

1975–1981—Commander of the Kurgan oblast student building detachment

1981–1988—Instructor of the Kurgan Oblast CPSU Committee, secretary of the party committee of Kurgantyazhstroi

1988–1990—Chair of the Oktyabr District Executive Committee

Spring 1990—Elected to the Kurgan Oblast soviet and the Oktyabr district soviet, serving as the latter's chairman from March 1991

October 1991—Chairman of the oblast soviet's Committee for Managing Municipal Property

February 1992—Elected chair of the Kurgan Oblast soviet

12 December 1993—Elected to the first session of the Federation Council, serving on the Committee for CIS Affairs

27 March 1994—Elected to the Kurgan Oblast Duma and on 12 April became chair

1995—Joined Vladimir Shumeiko's Reforms–New Course movement

January 1996—Appointed to the Federation Council and became the chair of the Committee for CIS Affairs

8 December 1996—Elected governor of Kurgan Oblast

18 December 1997—Joined the Government Council on Issues of Social Development

February 1998—Joined the Government Committee on CIS Affairs

Married, with two daughters

Foreign Relations: CIS Authority

Bogomolov, who chairs the Federation Council's Committee on CIS Affairs, backed the friendship and cooperation agreement between Russia and Ukraine ratified in February 1999. Moscow Mayor Yurii Luzhkov was the most vocal critic of the treaty in the Federation Council.

Attitudes Toward Business

Few Kurgan businesses have attracted outside investors. One exception is the textile company Lodiya, which has developed a successful venture with Britain's Nirman, exporting suits to the United States. It is using American equipment, which allows the company to make high-quality products.

Internet Sites in the Region

http://www.kurgan.ru/
This is the Kurgan Oblast official website, containing basic information about the oblast and its history, contact information for regional enterprises, listings of local media, and information on the oblast and city administrations.

KURSK OBLAST

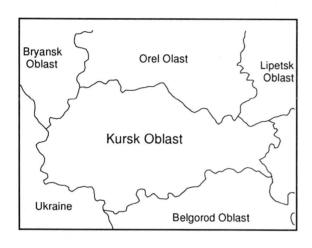

Territory: 29,800 km^2
Population (as of 1 January 1998):
1,336,000
Distance from Moscow: 536 km

Major Cities:
Kursk, *capital* (pop. 441,300)
Zheleznogorsk (96,300)
Kurchatov (48,000)
Lgov (24,100)
Shchigry (20,900)

Basic Facts

Population (as of 1 Jan. 1998): 1,336,000 (0.9% of Russian total)

Ethnic breakdown (1989 census): Russians 96.9%, Ukrainians 1.7%

Urban population (as of 1 Jan. 1998): 60.9% (Russia overall: 73.1%)

Student population (as of 1 Sept. 1997): 159 per 10,000 (Russia overall: 208/10,000)

Pensioner population (1997): 30.69% (Russia overall: 25.96%)

Percent of population with higher education (1989 census): 7.9% (Russia overall: 11.3%)

Percent of population working in 1997: Industry: 23.1% (Russian average: 23.0%); Agriculture: 19.7% (13.7%); Trade: 14.7% (13.5%); Culture: 11.6% (13.3%)

Average monthly personal income in July 1998: 614.4 new rubles (Russian average: 891.7 new rubles)

Average monthly personal expenses in July 1998: 442.6 new rubles (Russian average: 684.9 new rubles)

Average monthly subsistence requirement in 1998: 330 new rubles (Russian average: 438 new rubles)

Consumer price index (as of July 1998): 92 (Russia overall = 100)

Budgetary revenues (1997): 2,650.2 billion rubles (Russia overall: 433,378.2 billion rubles)

Budgetary expenditures (1997): 2,800.5 billion rubles (Russia overall: 468,111.6 billion rubles)

Industrial production as percentage of all Russian production (Jan.–Aug. 1998): 0.69%

Proportion of loss-making enterprises (as of July 1998): 53.9% (Russia overall: 50.4%)

Number of enterprises which have wage arrears (as of 1 Sept. 1998): 1,706 (1.26% of Russian total)

Agricultural production as percentage of all Russian production (1997): 1.53%

Number of private farms (as of 1 Jan. 1998): 1,448 (0.53% of Russian total)

Capital investment (1997): 2,585.9 billion rubles (Russia overall: 408,797 billion rubles)

Sources of investment (1997): federal budget: 5.7% (Russian average: 10.2%); regional budget: 9.2% (10.5%); extra-budgetary funds: 85.1% (79.3%)

Foreign investment (1997): 1,294,000 USD (Russia overall: 12,294,734,000 USD)

Number of joint ventures (1997): 37 (0.25% of Russian total)

Fixed capital investment in joint ventures and foreign companies (1997): 25,872 million rubles (Russia overall: 16,265.4 billion rubles)

Number of small businesses (as of 1 July 1998): 2,900 (0.33% of Russian total)

Number of enterprises privatized in 1997: 13 (0.47% of Russian total), including those which used to be municipal property: 61.5% (Russian average: 66.4%); regional property: 7.7% (20.0%); federal property: 30.8% (13.6%)

Number of telephones per 100 families (1997): in cities: 38.2 (Russian average: 49.2); in villages: 11.3 (19.8)

Brief Overview

Kursk Oblast is about 500 km south of Moscow on the Ukrainian border. In Russia it borders Belgorod, Voronezh, Lipetsk, Orel, and Bryansk oblasts. The oblast's administrative center dates to the 11th century. By the end of the 18th century it was the administrative center of Kursk Gubernia, and a century later it was an important industrial center with about 80 plants and factories processing raw materials—iron ores, peat, and construction materials.

The region, now ranked 13th in the country according to total reserves of mineral resources, has retained its industrial character and national importance. Major regional industrial enterprises include iron mining and enriching, machine building, chemicals and petrochemicals, and are located for the most part in the cities of Kursk and Zheleznogorsk. Kursk Oblast is also an important source of energy, which is generated from a large nuclear power station in the regional capital, for neighboring regions.

Once covered by forests, the oblast offers rich soil that is used for intensive farming—including grains, fruits, and vegetables—with the unfortunate consequence of severe soil erosion.

According to a 1998 survey by *Ekspert* magazine, the oblast ranked 33rd among Russia's 89 regions in terms of investment potential and 24th in terms of investment risk. A 1998 survey by Bank Austria ranked the oblast 55th in terms of investment climate.

Electoral History

2000 Presidential Election
Putin: 50.00%
Zyuganov: 39.70%
Yavlinskii: 2.47%
Zhirinovsky: 2.32%
Tuleev: 1.33%
Turnout: 72.08% (Russia overall: 68.64%)

1999 Parliamentary Elections
Communist Party of the Russian Federation: 31.95%
Unity: 31.46%
Fatherland–All Russia: 6.08%
Zhirinovsky Bloc: 5.57%
Union of Right Forces: 3.91%
Communists–Workers' Russia: 3.38%
Yabloko: 3.14%
In single-mandate districts: 1 Communist Party of the Russian Federation, 1 independent
Turnout: 63.18% (Russia overall: 61.85%)

1996 Gubernatorial Election
Rutskoi (Derzhava): 76.85%
Shuteev (incumbent): 17.55%
Molokoedov: 0.69%
Kureninov (Kursk Oblast People's Party of Russia): 0.62%
Turnout: 56.98%

1996 Presidential Election
Zyuganov: 51.13%/58.92% (first round/second round)
Yeltsin: 24.06%/36.24%
Lebed: 11.06%
Yavlinskii: 5.38%
Zhirinovsky: 3.89%
Turnout: 73.17%/70.50% (Russia overall: 69.67%/68.79%)

1995 Parliamentary Elections
Derzhava: 30.69%
Communist Party of the Russian Federation: 28.29%
Liberal Democratic Party of Russia: 6.08%
Our Home Is Russia: 5.15%
Communists–Workers' Russia: 3.63%
Agrarian Party of Russia: 3.34%
In single-mandate districts: 2 Communist Party of the Russian Federation
Turnout: 71.59% (Russia overall: 64.37%)

1993 Constitutional Referendum
"Yes"—43.1% "No"—55.3%

1993 Parliamentary Elections
Liberal Democratic Party of Russia: 33.48%
Communist Party of the Russian Federation: 20.03%
Agrarian Party of Russia: 11.46%
Russia's Choice: 10.64%
Women of Russia: 5.02%
Yabloko: 4.79%
Democratic Party of Russia: 4.41%
Party of Russian Unity and Concord: 4.11%
In single-mandate districts: 2 Communist Party of the Russian Federation
From electoral associations: 1 Communist Party of the Russian Federation, 1 Liberal Democratic Party of Russia, 1 Agrarian Party of Russia
Turnout: 64.67% (Russia overall: 54.34%)

1991 Presidential Election
Yeltsin: 54.16%
Ryzhkov: 21.03%
Zhirinovsky: 9.08%
Tuleev: 5.33%
Makashov: 3.58%
Bakatin: 2.30%
Turnout: 85.43% (Russia overall: 76.66%)

Regional Political Institutions

Executive:
Governor, 4-year term
    Aleksandr Vladimirovich Rutskoi,
    elected October 1996
        Kursk Oblast Administration; Dom Sovetov;
        Krasnaya Pl., 305002
        Tel 7(071–2) 22–62–62;
        Fax 7(071–2) 56–65–73
        Federation Council in Moscow:
        7(095) 292–63–76, 926–67–89

Legislative:
Unicameral
    Oblast Duma—45 members, 4-year term,
    elected December 1996
    Chairman—Viktor Dmitrievich Chernykh,
    elected January 1997

Regional Politics

Notorious Governor Rules His Own Fiefdom

Aleksandr Rutskoi is one of the most notorious governors in Russia. He is the first national politician to use his governorship as a secure power base. This group now includes Krasnoyarsk's Aleksandr Lebed and may grow in the future. A decorated Afghan war veteran, Rutskoi helped Yeltsin win the presidency in 1991 and then served as vice president. By 1993, however, he had turned on the president and led the rebellion against him in the September and October battle at the Russian White House.

Rutskoi rules Kursk Oblast as his personal fiefdom and appointed many of his family members to important positions, although several have since been arrested on various charges. He usually supports major initiatives of the federal government, apparently hoping that it will leave him alone. Rutskoi's personal empire includes a helicopter that is reportedly used to expedite the departure of federal officials or annoying

journalists. According to local lore, he has on occasion invited them for a ride and then dropped them off in the middle of nowhere.

Rutskoi also has a knowledge of age-old tricks to fool government officials. For instance, he reportedly ordered collective farmers to plow the ground near the main roads. Thus, in case inspectors arrive, the fields of Kursk Oblast look well tended.

He is also famous for his lavish parties. For example, he celebrated his 50th birthday in 1997 at the former estate of Princess Baryatinskii. Many representatives of Russia's political and cultural beau monde attended the event, including State Duma member Iosif Kobzon, film producer Nikita Mikhalkov, and former RSFSR Supreme Soviet Chairman Ruslan Khasbulatov. During the celebration, a helicopter hovering over the crowd dropped roses for his girlfriend (and now third wife), 23–year-old Irina Popova. Though Rutskoi was still married to another woman at the time, he claimed that he "has not had any close relations" with her for a long time (*KP*, 1 October 1997). Despite his reputation as a ladies' man, Rutskoi likes to cultivate the image of a very religious person. At his inauguration ceremony he swore an oath on both the constitution and the Bible. Before the beginning of the 1997–98 school year, he ordered the schools to begin teaching Bible lessons despite the objections of some teachers that Russia recognizes division between church and state.

Executive Platform: Neither Yeltsin nor Communists Support Him

Rutskoi began his political career in the late 1980s, when he participated in political activities organized by the pro-fascist Pamyat (Memory) (*RG*, 26 August 1995). In 1988 he joined the nationalist cultural society Fatherland and soon became its deputy chairman. However, at a crucial juncture, Rutskoi threw his support behind the democrats, creating the Communists for Democracy faction in the RSFSR Congress of People's Deputies to support Yeltsin. Seeking to win support from the nationalist end of the political spectrum, particularly from the military, Yeltsin chose Rutskoi as his running mate for the 1991 Russian presidential campaign. Rutskoi was Yeltsin's vice-president from June 1991 until fall 1993, but, he joined Khasbulatov and the parliamentary opposition to the president's reforms. Yeltsin dissolved the parliament and violence ensued. Rutskoi charged that Yeltsin and his entourage were singularly responsible for the deaths that took place at the White House during that "bloody autumn," and published a long book on that topic to support his claim (Aleksandr Rutskoi, *Krovavaya osen,* Moscow, 1995).

The democrats charged that Rutskoi was the man most responsible for the deaths because he led a band of Russian National Unity (RNE) extremists from the White House in an attack on the mayor's offices and the Ostankino TV center. He was jailed immediately after Yeltsin restored order, but released later under an amnesty passed by the newly elected Duma in February 1994.

Two months later, in April 1994, Rutskoi returned to politics by organizing his own political movement, Derzhava (Great Power). He sought a State Duma seat as the first candidate on the Derzhava party ticket, but Derzhava did not succeed in crossing the 5 percent barrier and did not win any seats in the lower house. In March 1996, Rutskoi and Derzhava officially joined the National Patriotic coalition which supported Zyuganov as its presidential candidate.

Rutskoi won the gubernatorial elections in Kursk by a wide margin in the fall of 1996, taking more than three-quarters of the vote. He won in the face of strong opposition from the local elite, who viewed Rutskoi as an outsider who would threaten their interests.

Upon election, he retired from the leadership of the Derzhava movement and the National Patriotic Union of Russia (NPSR). Derzhava is now headed by Konstantin Zatulin, an advisor to Moscow Mayor Yurii Luzhkov. By disengaging from the political parties, Rutskoi gave up one of his few tools of influence in Moscow. Meanwhile other governors were coming to realize the potential uses of regionally based parties, especially if they have the possibility of alliances with other regions and Moscow.

Despite his conflict with Yeltsin, Rutskoi did not maintain close ties with the Communist opposition. During his 1998 clash with the local procurator, Rutskoi named the local and national Communist Party organizations among his enemies (KD, 20 June 1998). Kursk Communists have accused him of creating a "lawless" situation in the region, and demand his voluntary resignation.

Policies: Self-Serving

Rutskoi's critics have described his policies as "egregious nepotism combined with authoritarian tactics in the tradition of Soviet-era Communist Party officials" (*RG*, 4 December 1997). Rutskoi appointed his youngest brother, Mikhail, a local policeman, as a oblast police chief. His other brother, Vladimir, became the head of the state-owned agricultural and food-processing company, Faktor. The governor's youngest son (from his second marriage), Aleksandr, began working at the Kurskneftekhim petrochemical factory, and thereafter the company enjoyed the oblast's favor. For example, the oblast signed over a 20-billion-ruble ($3.4 million) federal subsidy entirely to the plant. Rutskoi's son from his first marriage, Dmitrii, first served as his father's economic advisor, but later profitably participated in the privatization of the Kurskfarmatsia pharmaceutical company, eventually becoming its chief executive. This move blessed the company with lucrative government contracts. After Rutskoi took up with the 23-year-old Irina Popova, whom he presents as the oblast's first lady, her father was propelled to the post of deputy head of one of the local administrations.

The governor practiced this nepotism against the background of upbeat, if falsified, official reporting on the oblast's economic successes. Rutskoi's first annual report claimed successes on all fronts. But compared with impartial statistical data, the report's numbers seem carefully picked, ignoring dismal failures in some areas and exaggerating successes in others. Total wage arrears in the region are growing.

In the summer of 1998, the local procurator, Nikolai Tkachev, began to crack down on Rutskoi's cronyism. On 29 May the procurator charged Mikhail Rutskoi, the governor's brother, with abusing his office as deputy head of the Kursk Department of Internal Affairs, and he was fired on 10 June (*Izvestiya,* 16 and 17 June 1998). Additionally, the Arbitration Court declared the privatization of the firm Kurskfarmatsia by Rutskoi's son Dmitrii illegal (*KD,* 16 June 1998). On 15 June, Tkachev arrested two of Rutskoi's deputy governors—Yurii Kononchuk, who dealt with financing, banking, and investment, and Vladimir Bunchuk, who handled supplies, industry, and trade.

The conflict between Tkachev and Rutskoi began in 1996, when the Kursk elite opposed the election of Rutskoi as governor. After winning office, Rutskoi tried to have Tkachev removed, but Russian Procurator General Yurii Skuratov refused to sack him. In June 1998, Tkachev said that the governor's activity and the actions of his assistants were dangerous for the oblast and that investigating them was the main task of his office.

Aleksandr Vladimirovich Rutskoi

16 September 1947—Officially born in Kursk (the independent research of *Politicheskaya Sreda* showed that he actually studied there in secondary school for a couple of years, when his parents moved there, but never lived there afterward [*PS*, 24 April 1995]).

1965—Called up for military service; served in Germany

1971—Graduated from Barnaul Higher Military Pilot School

1980—Graduated from Yurii A. Gagarin Air Force Academy

1985—Began serving in Afghanistan, flew 428 missions overall

April 1986—His plane was shot down over Afghanistan and he was decorated as a Hero of the Soviet Union

4 August 1988—Plane again shot down; held as a POW

1989—Unsuccessfully ran for USSR Congress of People's Deputies

1990—Elected to RSFSR Congress of People's Deputies and Supreme Soviet

1990—Elected member of the RSFSR Communist Party Central Committee

1990—Graduated from General Staff Academy

31 March 1991—Founded Communists for Democracy faction in RSFSR Congress of People's Deputies to support Yeltsin

12 June 1991—Elected Russian vice president

6 August 1991—RSFSR Communist Party Central Committee excludes Rutskoi from membership

19–21 August 1991—Spent most of time in White House; flew to meet Gorbachev at Foros

4 October 1993—Arrested in White House and jailed after leading anti-Yeltsin rebellion

April 1994—Granted amnesty by the Duma and released from jail

April 1995—Derzhava founding congress

1996—Supported Gennadii Zyuganov for presidency

20 October 1996—Elected governor of Kursk with 76.85% of the vote

In the fall of 1999, the Kremlin secured the release of the two deputy governors and the retirement of the local procurator. (Skuratov himself would lose his post in April 2000.) Rutskoi in turn became an early backer of Unity.

Relationships Between Key Players: Hand-Picked, Faithful Supporters

Rutskoi blames all of Kursk's problems on the former governor, whom he has accused of wreaking more damage on the region than had Nazi invaders. When elected, Rutskoi hired many of his faithful supporters including several former members of the Communist nomenklatura from his Derzhava movement and those who backed him in his 1993 clash with President Boris Yeltsin. Some of them have local reputations for dishonesty.

The oblast administration not only refuses to cooperate with journalists but blatantly impedes free access to public information and tries to intimidate its most outspoken critics. An article in *Itogi* magazine described the widespread fear among civil servants and common people in Kursk of criticizing Rutskoi's policies (*Itogi*, 25 November 1997). The governor can exert considerable influence over his critics through his control of apartment rents, for example.

Not everybody in the region gives in to Rutskoi's coercion. The clash with Tkachev (see Policies) is evidence of an existing opposition.

Ties to Moscow

Rutskoi tries hard to look good in the Kremlin's eyes. Immediately after his election, he famously met with then presidential Chief of Staff Anatolii Chubais, once his arch-enemy, and declared that he supported the president's economic policy. He has prohibited anti-government trade union demonstrations in Kursk and declared his support for a November 1997 presidential decree on accord and reconciliation.

However, Rutskoi was not pleased when Yeltsin signed a decree on 18 December 1997 canceling several of the governor's directives. Yeltsin overturned Rutskoi's actions regulating the metals industry and the transfer of grain outside Kursk, pointing out that the governor had violated several federal laws and articles of the constitution (*RFE/RL*, 19 December 1997).

In the lead-up to the 2000 presidential elections, Rutskoi bet early on the winning horse, Vladimir Putin.

Relations with Other Regions

Rutskoi's former party, Derzhava, joined forces with Moscow Mayor Yurii Luzhkov's Fatherland political organization, but Rutskoi himself played an active role in the creation of the Kremlin's Unity bloc to compete in the 1999 Duma elections and the 2000 presidential elections. Derzhava has 51 regional branches, and representatives in the Voronezh and Tambov legislatures, and controls mayors' offices in Cherkessk (Karachaevo-Cherkessia) and Severodvinsk (Arkhangelsk) (*NG*, 4 July 1998).

Kursk Oblast is a member of the Black Earth Association, headed by Orel Governor and Federation Council Speaker Yegor Stroev. This organization also includes Voronezh, Belgorod, Lipetsk, Orel, and Tambov oblasts.

Attitudes Toward Business: State Monopolist

In August 1997 Rutskoi created the odd-sounding KGB—Kurskii Gubernskii Bank—and ordered all local enterprises (including private ones) to open accounts there while closing all accounts in other banks. All export-import transactions and investment projects were to go through this officially controlled institution. By issuing this order the governor sought complete control over the region's finances. However, the outrage of locals and of the federal government was great enough to make Rutskoi back down. The incident occurred just before the scheduled hearing of the "Kursk case" by the Anti-Monopoly Committee (*KD*, 25 June 1997). Rutskoi threatened that in the future, he would ally himself with other governors so he would have greater political support (*Izvestiya*, 17 July 1997). The governor's active policy of establishing monopolies has caused small and medium-sized businesses to leave the region (*MT*, 22 July 1997).

While production of most essential food items and goods has increased, power production has gone down, as has iron-ore mining. Like other governors seeking greater control over regional property, Rutskoi has seized control of half of the Mikhailovskii Iron Ore Works shares (*EWI RRR* 6 November 1997).

In agriculture, Rutskoi's incompetent management has been costly. The governor's agricultural policy consisted of taking out loans, using the oblast budget as collateral, and spending the money exclusively on the sowing campaign. At harvest time, there were no funds left for machine fuel, and farming enterprises could not repay their debts. To deal with this problem, Rutskoi forbade the debtors to export their produce outside Kursk Oblast, which compounded their losses (*Itogi*, 25 November 1997).

LENINGRAD OBLAST

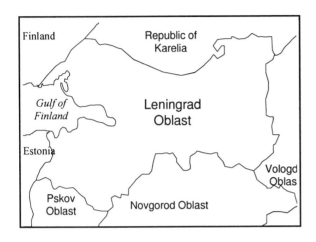

Territory: 85,900 km²
Population (as of 1 January 1998): 1,682,000
Distance from Moscow: 651 km

Note: These data include the population of St. Petersburg, but not its territory.

Major Cities:
Gatchina (82,000)
Vyborg (80,900)
Tikhvin (68,300)
Sosnovyi Bor (61,800)
Kirishi (56,300)

Basic Facts

Population (as of 1 Jan. 1998): 1,682,000 (1.14% of Russian total)

Ethnic breakdown (1989 census): Russians 90.9%, Ukrainians 3.0%, Belarusans 2.0%

Urban population (as of 1 Jan. 1998): 65.9% (Russia overall: 73.1%)

Student population (as of 1 Sept. 1997): 2 per 10,000 (Russia overall: 208/10,000)

Pensioner population (1997): 27.29% (Russia overall: 25.96%)

Percent of population with higher education (1989 census): 9.4% (Russia overall: 11.3%)

Percent of population working in (1997): Industry: 25.0% (Russian average: 23.0%); Agriculture: 11.5% (13.7%); Trade: 15.2% (13.5%); Culture: 11.2% (13.3%)

Average monthly personal income in July 1998: 615.0 rubles (Russian average: 891.7 new rubles)

Average monthly personal expenses in July 1998: 440.7 new rubles (Russian average: 684.9 new rubles)

Average monthly subsistence requirement in 1998: 440 new rubles (Russian average: 438 new rubles)

Consumer price index (as of July 1998): 93 (Russia overall = 100)

Budgetary revenues (1997): 3,342.6 billion rubles (Russia overall: 433,378.2 billion rubles)

Budgetary expenditures (1997): 3,789.1 billion rubles (Russia overall: 468,111.6 billion rubles)

Industrial production as percentage of all Russian production (Jan.–Aug. 1998): 0.92%

Proportion of loss-making enterprises (as of July 1998): 46.9% (Russia overall: 50.4%)

Number of enterprises which have wage arrears (as of 1 Sept. 1998): 711 (0.53% of Russian total)

Agricultural production as percentage of all Russian production (1997): 1.77%

Number of private farms (as of 1 Jan. 1998): 6,854 (2.5% of Russian total)

Capital investment (1997): 4,436.6 billion rubles (Russia overall: 408,797 billion rubles)

Sources of investment (1997): federal budget: 6.9% (Russian average: 10.2%); regional budget: 5.6% (10.5%); extra-budgetary funds: 87.5% (79.3%)

Foreign investment (1997): 170,357,000 USD (Russia overall: 12,294,734,000 USD)

Number of joint ventures (1997): 134 (0.9% of Russian total)

Fixed capital investment in joint ventures and foreign companies (1997): 252,941 million rubles (Russia overall: 16,265.4 billion rubles)

Number of small businesses (as of 1 July 1998): 12,100 (1.39% of Russian total)

Number of enterprises privatized in 1997: 13 (0.47% of Russian total), including those which used to be municipal property: 69.2% (Russian average: 66.4%); regional property: 15.4% (20.0%); federal property: 15.4% (13.6%)

Number of telephones per 100 families (1997): in cities: 53.4 (Russian average: 49.2); in villages: 25.2 (19.8)

Brief Overview

Leningrad Oblast is located in Russia's northwest. It borders the Republic of Karelia; Vologda, Novgorod, and Pskov oblasts; and Estonia and Finland. The region is famous for its numerous lakes, which number about 2,000 and take up about 15 percent of the oblast's total territory. The oblast also has many rivers, with a total length of 50,000 km, most of which are navigable.

The oblast is rich in raw materials, including peat, granite, limestone, clays, and sands. Regional industry focuses on fuel (40 percent of total industrial output), hydro-energy (13 percent), and timber and cellulose processing (11 percent). The oblast also has a significant agricultural sector which produces about a third of the region's GDP and is mostly composed of large cattle-breeding farms. The oblast is capable of supplying itself with nearly all food products except grain. It is also an important food supplier for St. Petersburg.

Leningrad Oblast has close commercial ties with over 20 foreign countries, including Finland, Germany, Belgium, Switzerland, and the United States. Foreign trade is made possible by two sea and two river harbors whose total capacity exceeds 7.5 million tons annually.

Despite a generally good legal environment, according to a 1998 survey by *Ekspert* magazine, regional investment potential had decreased by 8 points since 1997, the 6th largest decrease in the country, while investment risk decreased by 12 points (17th largest). The oblast then ranked 35th among Russia's 89 regions in terms of investment potential and 27th in terms of investment risk. A 1998 survey by Bank Austria ranked the oblast 18th in terms of investment climate.

Electoral History

2000 Presidential Election
Putin: 66.61%
Zyuganov: 18.97%
Yavlinskii: 5.10%
Zhirinovsky: 2.64%
Tuleev: 1.73%
Turnout: 66.67% (Russia overall: 68.64%)

1999 Parliamentary Elections
Unity: 30.00%
Communist Party of the Russian Federation: 17.64%
Fatherland–All Russia: 9.55%
Union of Right Forces: 8.41%
Zhirinovsky Bloc: 6.53%
Yabloko: 6.35%
In single-mandate districts: 1 Pensioners' Party, 1 Yedinstvo, 1 independent
Turnout: 49.94% (Russia overall: 61.85%)

1999 Gubernatorial Election
Serdyukov (incumbent): 30.30%
Gustov: 22.68%
Kovalev: 17.36%
Zubkov: 8.64%
Turnout: 41.73%

1999 Parliamentary Elections
Unity: 30.00%
Communist Party of the Russian Federation: 17.64%
Fatherland–All Russia: 9.55%
Union of Right Forces: 8.41%
Zhirinovsky Bloc: 6.53%
Yabloko: 6.35%
In single-mandate districts: 1 Pensioners' Party, 1 Unity, 1 unfilled
Turnout: 49.94% (Russia overall: 61.85%)

1996 Gubernatorial Election
Gustov: 53.37%
Belyakov (incumbent): 31.66%
Zolototrubov: 2.27%
Terentev (Russian Communist Workers' Party): 2.25%
Stepanov: 1.29%
Modestov (oblast legislature deputy): 1.16%
Istomin: 1.07%
Marychev: 0.46%
Turnout: 34.43%

1996 Presidential Election
Yeltsin: 37.46%/61.35% (first round/second round)
Zyuganov: 23.17%/32.30%
Lebed: 18.12%
Yavlinskii: 11.60%
Zhirinovsky: 4.29%
Turnout: 69.99%/69.20% (Russia overall: 69.67%/ 68.79%)

1995 Parliamentary Elections
Communist Party of the Russian Federation: 18.88%
Our Home Is Russia: 10.81%
Yabloko: 8.16%
Liberal Democratic Party of Russia: 8.01%
Communists–Workers' Russia: 6.18%
Women of Russia: 6.17%

Congress of Russian Communities: 5.91%
Party of Workers' Self-Government: 4.85%
Russia's Democratic Choice: 4.18%
In single-mandate districts: 1 Communist Party of the
　　Russian Federation, 1 Communists–Workers' Russia,
　　1 independent
Turnout: 61.79% (Russia overall: 64.37%)

1993 Constitutional Referendum
"Yes"—66.1% "No"—31.7%

1993 Parliamentary Elections
Liberal Democratic Party of Russia: 30.04%
Russia's Choice: 16.10%
Yabloko: 13.38%
Women of Russia: 9.39%
Communist Party of the Russian Federation: 8.55%
Party of Russian Unity and Concord: 5.29%
Democratic Party of Russia: 4.46%
Agrarian Party of Russia: 3.97%
In single-mandate districts: 1 Russian Movement for
　　Democratic Reform, 1 independent
From electoral associations: 1 Democratic Choice
Turnout: 50.42% (Russia overall: 54.34%)

1991 Presidential Election
Yeltsin: 49.64%
Ryzhkov: 15.77%
Zhirinovsky: 8.96%
Tuleev: 8.66%
Makashov: 7.31%
Bakatin: 4.00%
Turnout: 73.35% (Russia overall: 76.66%)

Regional Political Institutions

Executive:
　　Governor, 4–year term
　　Valerii Pavlovich Serdyukov, appointed acting gover-
　　nor September 1998; elected governor September 1999
　　　　Leningrad Oblast Administration;
　　　　Suvorovskii Prospekt, 67;
　　　　St. Petersburg, 193311
　　　　Tel. 7(812) 274–35–63, 315–86–65;
　　　　Fax 7(812) 271–56–27

Legislative:
　　Unicameral
　　Legislative Assembly (*Zakonodatelnoe Sobranie*)—
　　50 members, 4–year term, elected December 1997
　　Chairman—Vitalii Nikolaevich Klimov, elected
　　January 1998

Regional Politics

Acting Governor Beats Out Former Boss

Valerii Serdyukov was elected governor of Leningrad
Oblast on 19 September 1999 after having served as
the region's acting governor for a year. Leningrad
Oblast's former governor, Vadim Gustov, resigned his
position on 18 September 1998 when President Boris
Yeltsin appointed him to Prime Minister Yevgenii
Primakov's cabinet as first deputy prime minister in
charge of relations with the regions, the CIS, and youth.
Gustov was the only governor to take a position in
Primakov's government, although many had been offered posts. Seven months later, in April 1999, Yeltsin
fired Gustov shortly before he sacked the rest of the
Primakov cabinet. Gustov then announced his intention to return to regional politics and win back the
gubernatorial post in the oblast's September 1999 elections. Although the former governor was favored to
win the elections, he was unable to beat out his replacement, earning 23 percent of the vote while
Serdyukov pulled in 30 percent.

　　The last two months before the election were
marked by an intense battle between Gustov and
Serdyukov. Gustov had brought Serdyukov to work
in Leningrad Oblast from Vorkuta. Once Gustov left
for federal office Serdyukov decided to run for the
governor's seat, but Gustov's dismissal and return to
Leningrad politics complicated Serdyukov's plans.
Ultimately, Serdyukov decided to break his ties with
his former boss and campaign against him. Gustov
had offered to give Serdyukov the post of prime minister if he won the election, but Serdyukov was not
persuaded.

Executive Platform: Ports and Foreign Investment

When Serdyukov was first appointed acting governor
of Leningrad Oblast, he stated that his work would
not be anything new, but rather a continuation of the
policies and reforms initiated by Gustov
(www.lenobl.ru). The projects receiving Serdyukov's
top priority included paying pension and wage arrears,
stabilizing the oblast's economic situation, improving
the industrial and agricultural sectors, and completing
the construction of the three Baltic ports and the Philip
Morris tobacco factory.

　　Gustov had served as governor of Leningrad Oblast
for two years before joining the federal government.

He won election to the post with Communist support, yet he also won the endorsements of local trade unions, the local branch of Yabloko, and some chapters of Yegor Gaidar's Russia's Democratic Choice. Gustov also had the support of former St. Petersburg Mayor Anatolii Sobchak. As governor, Gustov pursued a policy amicable to businesses, a necessity as the oblast competed for foreign investment with St. Petersburg.

Policies: Leader Must Deal with Region's Effective Bankruptcy

Whoever rules Leningrad Oblast faces significant challenges. The oblast is effectively bankrupt and had a 50 percent budget deficit in 1998 (*KD*, 24 September 1998). Leningrad stopped making payments on its oblast obligations in December. A foreign bank syndicate that lent the oblast $50 million in May 1998 demanded the money back in May 1999, forcing the region to default on the debt temporarily. The procurator opened an investigation of how the borrowed money was used. Auditors charged that the funds went to restructure old, more expensive, debts, rather than new investment projects (*EWI RRR*, 22 December 1998).

Additionally, the region has not adopted an income tax, even though St. Petersburg imposed a 5 percent levy on 1 January 1999. On 29 December 1998, the oblast's legislative assembly rejected the idea in a 31–3 vote. Advocates of the tax said that it could raise 90 million rubles in new revenue annually, but opponents feared that it would bankrupt many local enterprises (*EWI RRR*, 14 January 1999).

While Gustov served as deputy prime minister, the oblast basically lived off his ability to arrange additional subsidies from Moscow. In the last quarter of 1998, the oblast received an unplanned subsidy of 80 million rubles, according to Vice-Governor for Finances Sergei Susekov (*EWI RRR*, 11 February 1999).

During his tenure as acting governor, Serdyukov prioritized social concerns and economic development in the oblast. He was particularly interested in promoting the region's timber industry. Serdyukov devoted considerable energy to increasing economic ties with Finland, the Baltic states, and CIS member states.

Relationships Between Key Players: Gustov Controlled Legislature

Leningrad Oblast elected its legislative assembly in December 1997. The legislature was close to Gustov because about 35 of the 50 candidates sponsored by

Gustov's Public Chamber Council of Leningrad Oblast were elected. All candidates from the Communists, Zhirinovsky's party, and Aleksandr Lebed's Honor and Motherland lost. Industrial enterprise directors held 26 of the seats (*EWI RRR*, 18 December 1997).

Along with the city of St. Petersburg, the Leningrad Oblast government owned a controlling stake in the Petersburg Television and Radio Company. Leningrad Oblast owned 13 percent while St. Petersburg owned 38 percent. The governments courted the Industrial Machines financial-industrial group to finance the broadcaster (*KD*, 25 February 1999).

Ties to Moscow: Mixed Results from Gustov's Federal Activities; Serdyukov Backs Putin

Although Gustov's brief tenure in the federal government provided Leningrad Oblast with a direct lobbyist for the region's interests and more immediate access to federal funds, the overall result of his participation in the cabinet was rather negative for Leningrad-Moscow relations. Gustov earned a bad reputation for spending a considerable amount of time lobbying on behalf of Leningrad Oblast's specific interests. Gustov managed to acquire influential enemies in the federal government, particularly in the Ministry of Finance. The ministry was obliged to deal with the multiple economic and financial problems Gustov left in the region, such as the May 1999 default on a $50 million foreign bank credit.

Gustov was considered ineffective during his brief tenure as first deputy prime minister. Since he was not backed by the resources of a specific ministry, Gustov had very little power. Russian President Boris Yeltsin dismissed Gustov partly because he believed that Gustov had allowed regional leaders such as Samara Governor Konstantin Titov and Moscow Mayor Yurii Luzhkov to form political blocs (*EWI RRR*, 29 April 1999). The development of such blocs made it increasingly difficult for the Kremlin to maintain control over the regions.

Serdyukov has established much better relations with the Kremlin, having declared his support for the Unity bloc before the 1999 parliamentary elections.

After his dismissal from the Primakov cabinet, Gustov returned to the Federation Council as the Leningrad Oblast representative. The upper house had never revoked Gustov's mandate after he joined the federal government, so he was able to pick up where he left off. Gustov was popularly elected to the Federation Council in 1993, then in 1996 as governor of Leningrad Oblast. Although he was an active member of the Council, Gustov argued that the body should be structured differently. He believed that the current system, which has deputies working only two or three days each month, impedes the Council's legislative work. Gustov advocated making half of the Council members full-time deputies chosen specifically for that job in regional elections, but allowing regional leaders to retain the right to become Council deputies (*RFE/RL*, 23 February 1998).

Leningrad Oblast signed a power-sharing agreement with the federal government on 13 June 1996.

Relations with Other Regions: Close to St. Petersburg

Leningrad Oblast's most important relationship is with the city of St. Petersburg. There has long been talk of merging the two regions into a single administrative unit ruled by one governor. However, such a merger has been politically impossible because it would have cost one leader his seat. An attempt to hold a referendum on the idea collapsed in November 1996. The possibility opened up again in September 1998, when Gustov resigned, creating an opportunity for merging the city and oblast without displacing a sitting governor, but the opportunity passed without a decision.

Both Gustov and Yeltsin supported the idea of a merger. St. Petersburg Governor Vladimir Yakovlev also supported the plan and was not put off by Leningrad Oblast's financial problems or the possibility that unification could potentially drive up unemployment rates in St. Petersburg. Backers of the idea argue that the separation of the city and oblast in 1931 has weakened them both economically. They also argue that a merger would save money by cutting the number of bureaucrats and reducing the number of bureaucratic procedures facing investors.

When he was still serving as acting governor, Serdyukov spoke in favor of the merger. But he stated that "unnecessary haste and zeal is intolerable" and that the territories should remain separate federation subjects until St. Petersburg Governor Yakovlev's term expired (www.lenobl.ru). However, Serdyukov's own gubernatorial ambitions called into question the sincerity of his support for a unified St. Petersburg and Leningrad Oblast.

Chairman of the Leningrad Oblast Legislative Assembly Vitalii Klimov believes that it will take two to five years to unite Leningrad Oblast with the city of St. Petersburg. The most difficult part of the merger process would be harmonizing the laws of the two regions. St. Petersburg has adopted more than 2,000 laws, while Leningrad Oblast has a somewhat smaller number. On 1 January 1999, St. Petersburg introduced a 5 percent sales tax, but Leningrad Oblast did not.

Leningrad Oblast belongs to the Northwest interregional association, which is led by St. Petersburg Governor Yakovlev. The association also includes the republics of Karelia and Komi; Arkhangelsk, Vologda, Kaliningrad, Kirov, Murmansk, Novgorod, and Pskov oblasts; and Nenets Autonomous Okrug.

Foreign Relations: Region Wants to Redirect Baltic Trade

Leningrad Oblast borders Estonia and Finland. However, the main foreign question in the region is building ports and then redirecting Russian trade from the Baltic countries through these ports. Leningrad Oblast hopes to construct three ports. In February 1999 then Prime Minister Yevgenii Primakov, accompanied by Gustov, visited St. Petersburg and said that he would support the ports (*MT*, 23 February 1999). Russia could save a $1 billion a year by exporting goods to the West from its own ports rather than paying shipping fees to the Baltic countries. Currently, the largest and most modern oil terminal along the former Soviet Baltic coast is at Ventspils in Latvia, having been built by Moscow in the 1960s. According to Ventspils' own statistics, published in *Delovoi Peterburg*, it exported 27 million tons of Russian oil and other fuels in 1996 (*EWI RRR*, 16 October 1997). If Russia succeeds in building the Leningrad Oblast ports, the Baltic countries would lose a considerable source of income.

Of the three ports the oblast is planning, the ports in Primorsk and Bukhta Batereinaya will be oil terminals, while the third at Ust-Luga is for coal, containers, grain, sugar, chemicals, cement, timber, and other dry cargo. The $3.7 billion Primorsk port has been bogged down as a result of financing difficulties and political in-fighting. The port would serve the unfinished Baltic pipeline system, sending Russian oil west. Unfortunately, the government currently does not have the money required to complete the pipeline. Also the Finns completed construction of a port at Porvoo in 1998, which is in direct competition to Primorsk. If and when funding becomes available, the construction is expected to take 10 years. Primorsk should eventually be able to handle 45 million tons of oil and petroleum products a year (*MT*, 23 February 1999). The Ust-Luga port is expected to cost $4 billion. Surgutneftegaz will be the owner of the port in Bukhta Batereinaya which when complete, will be the first privately constructed port in Russia (*EWI RRR*, 16 October 1997).

Some critics claim that the Leningrad ports may not be competitive with ports in the Baltic countries because those ports are farther west. Additionally, Oleg Bodurov, the head of the Green Cross environmental organization, has protested the construction of the three ports, claiming that they could destroy the ecosystems on three islands in the Gulf of Finland (*SPT*, 1–7 December 1997).

In July 1998, the residents of Ivangorod sent a petition to President Yeltsin asking him to let them unite with the Estonian city of Narva, which is just across the Narva River from Ivangorod. Unemployment in Ivangorod then was 20 percent and most of those with jobs had not been paid in months. Although more than 5 percent of the residents signed petitions for a referendum on the issue and to recall locally elected officials, the authorities did not set a date for the referendum as required by law. The governor's representative in the city said the protests were merely attempts to draw attention to the city's problems and that residents had no desire to join Estonia (*KD*, 16 July 1998).

Attitudes Toward Business: Successfully Competing with St. Petersburg

Leningrad Oblast has been successful in competing with St. Petersburg in attracting several large projects to the region. In 1998, it received $80 million in foreign investment. Among the projects currently under way:

- Ford Motor Company announced in June 1999 that it would build a $300 million automobile assembly plant in the region. The plans for the project finally went ahead following a delay caused by the August 1998 economic crisis (*EWI RRI*, 8 July 1999).

- International Paper bought a 90-percent stake in the Svetogorsk Paper Mill in the summer of 1998 from Tetra-Laval, which had bought the plant three years earlier and invested $127 million in it. In 1997, Svenski Cellulosa Akteibolaget bought a separate part of the mill for just over $26 million (*MT*, 18 July 1998).

- Caterpillar opened its $35 million road-building equipment plant in March 2000. The firm will use 80 percent local products to keep costs down (*MT*, 26 January 1999). The company is leasing 24 sq. hectares of land for 49 years, with an option to extend.

- Philip Morris opened its $330 million plant by in February 2000. It hopes to increase the production of domestically produced cigarettes (*KD*, 1 December 1998).

- Kres-Neva is building a $15 million factory for tobacco processing. Kres-Neva was established by the American firm Standard Commercial Corporation, which owns 20 tobacco processing factories around the world.

In addition to these projects, a group of 20 Finnish companies is planning to build a 40-hectare industrial park near the city of Svetogorsk. This project is the result of cooperation between Svetogorsk and the Finnish region of Imatra. The industrial park will specialize in producing food items using Finnish technology, imported equipment, and Russian raw materials. Companies involved in the project include Marli (juices), IDO, Ruokatalo (meat products), Nerpish (fish), NK Kylpylahuone (ceramics), VP-Kuljetus (transportation services), and Lemminkarinen (construction). The project will create 700 jobs, mostly held by Russians, with the exception of the top management positions, which will go to Finns.

Some foreign investors have had difficulty working in the region. Nimonor Investments Ltd. had to sell its stake in the Vyborg Cellulose and Paper Combine after Trade Union leader Osip Kikibush successfully prevented the investor's representatives from entering the factory grounds. The British company bought an 87-percent stake in the Leningrad Oblast plant for $30 million in November 1997. In March 1998, Kikibush's strike committee declared the factory "people's property." The British investors won a court order that was supposed to have been implemented by 16 August 1998, allowing them access to the plant. The court order was never implemented. Nimonor and representatives of the local administration claimed that the strike committee was closely connected to organized crime (*KD*, 12 March 1999). Ultimately, Nimonor sold its stake to the British firm Alsem for an undisclosed price (*EWI RRR*, 1 July 1999).

Valerii Pavlovich Serdyukov

9 November 1945—Born in the village of Khoroshevk in Gomel Oblast, Belarus; graduated from the Leningrad Mining Institute as a mining engineer, and later earned a graduate degree in economics

1962—Worked at Gomselmash

1967— Worked in the Vorkutaugol mines

1970—Took up party and Komsomol work, working his way up to first secretary of the Vorkuta city committee, a post which he held until 1990

1990—Became the Deputy General Director of Vorkutaugol

1996—Became Deputy Governor of Leningrad Oblast for Industry, fuel-energy, the timber complex, and the use of natural resources

18 September 1998—Appointed acting governor of Leningrad Oblast

19 September 1999—Elected governor of Leningrad Oblast

Enjoys playing chess and reading philosophy

Married, with two sons

Internet Sites in the Region

http://www.lenobl.ru/index.html
This is the official website of Leningrad Oblast, featuring news clippings archived back through 1998, texts of oblast laws, detailed information on investment projects in the oblast, and information on oblast political institutions.

http://www.taxpolice.spb.ru/
This is the website of the Leningrad Oblast tax police, featuring a blacklist of companies owing tax payments to the oblast budget.

http:// www.investor.spb.ru/eng/index.htm
This site features detailed information on investment projects in Leningrad Oblast and St. Petersburg.

LIPETSK OBLAST

Territory: 24,100 km²
Population (as of 1 January 1998):
1,248,000
Distance from Moscow: 508 km

Major Cities:
Lipetsk, *capital* (pop. 475,400)
Elets (120,000)
Gryazi (48,000)
Dankov (24,700)
Lebedyan (22,300)

Basic Facts

Population (as of 1 Jan. 1998): 1,248,000 (0.85% of Russian total)

Ethnic breakdown (1989 census): Russians 97.4%, Ukrainians 1.2%

Urban population (as of 1 Jan. 1998): 64.0% (Russia overall: 73.1%)

Student population (as of 1 Sept. 1997): 120 per 10,000 (Russia overall: 208/10,000)

Pensioner population (1997): 29.41% (Russia overall: 25.96%)

Percent of population with higher education (1989 census): 8.4% (Russia overall: 11.3%)

Percent of population working in (1997): Industry: 26.1% (Russian average: 23.0%); Agriculture: 15.8% (13.7%); Trade: 12.8% (13.5%); Culture: 11.0% (13.3%)

Average monthly personal income in July 1998: 707.7 new rubles (Russian average: 891.7 new rubles)

Average monthly personal expenses in July 1998: 511.2 new rubles (Russian average: 684.9 new rubles)

Average monthly subsistence requirement in 1998: 323 new rubles (Russian average: 438 new rubles)

Consumer price index (as of July 1998): 88 (Russia overall = 100)

Budgetary revenues (1997): 3,101.7 billion rubles (Russia overall: 433,378.2 billion rubles)

Budgetary expenditures (1997): 3,391.4 billion rubles (Russia overall: 468,111.6 billion rubles)

Industrial production as percentage of all Russian production (Jan.–Aug. 1998): 1.14%

Proportion of loss-making enterprises (as of July 1998): 42.3% (Russia overall: 50.4%)

Number of enterprises which have wage arrears (as of 1 Sept. 1998): 845 (0.63% of Russian total)

Agricultural production as percentage of all Russian production (1997): 1.35%

Number of private farms (as of 1 Jan. 1998): 1,437 (0.52% of Russian total)

Capital investment (1997): 2,497.3 billion rubles (Russia overall: 408,797 billion rubles)

Sources of investment (1997): federal budget: 8.4% (Russian average: 10.2%); regional budget: 18.6% (10.5%); extra-budgetary funds: 73.0% (79.3%)

Foreign investment (1997): 3,810,000 USD (Russia overall: 12,294,734,000 USD)

Number of joint ventures (1997): 34 (0.23% of Russian total)

Fixed capital investment in joint ventures and foreign companies (1997): 17,537 million rubles (Russia overall: 16,265.4 billion rubles)

Number of small businesses (as of 1 July 1998): 4,100 (0.47% of Russian total)

Number of enterprises privatized in 1997: 18 (0.66% of Russian total), including those which used to be municipal property: 69.2% (Russian average: 66.4%); regional property: 23.1% (20.0%); federal property: 7.7% (13.6%)

Number of telephones per 100 families (1997): in cities: 50.1 (Russian average: 49.2); in villages: 22.9 (19.8)

Brief Overview

Archeological research demonstrates that the territory now belonging to Lipetsk Oblast used to be the eastern boundary of Kievan Rus. In the beginning of the 18th century, Peter the Great ordered the construction of state-owed metal works to produce cannons, cannonballs, and other weapons for the newly created Russian fleet there when he learned of the large deposits of ferrous ores in the region. Modern Lipetsk Oblast, located 400 km southeast of Moscow in a basin of the upper Don River, was established in 1954. It was created from parts of Voronezh, Tambov, Orel, Ryazan, and Tula oblasts.

The oblast is highly industrialized with a high degree of air pollution as a side effect. It provides over 15 percent of the country's refrigerating equipment, 14 percent of its cast iron, 13 percent of its tractors, and 10 percent of steel smelting. Ferrous metallurgy is the oblast's major industry: its proportion of the regional GDP exceeds 60 percent, followed by machine building, metal processing, and the food industry (12 percent each). The oblast's largest enterprise, Novolipetsk Metallurgical Combine, is one of the most modern and technologically advanced enterprises in Russia, with exports to over 40 foreign countries.

According to a 1998 survey by *Ekspert* magazine, the oblast is ranked 43rd among Russia's 89 regions in terms of investment potential and 9th in terms of investment risk. A 1998 survey by Bank Austria ranked the oblast 33rd in terms of investment climate. It has become less risky to invest in regional economy due to investment risk decrease by 12 points since 1997.

Electoral History

2000 Presidential Election
Zyuganov: 47.41%
Putin: 40.86%
Yavlinskii: 3.09%
Zhirinovsky: 2.27%
Tuleev: 1.38%
Turnout: 69.72% (Russia overall: 68.64%)

1999 Parliamentary Elections
Communist Party of the Russian Federation: 39.02%
Unity: 19.09%
Fatherland–All Russia: 7.47%
Zhirinovsky Bloc: 5.65%
Union of Right Forces: 5.61%
Yabloko: 3.84%

In single-mandate districts: 1 Communist Party of the Russian Federation, 1 independent
Turnout: 61.51% (Russia overall: 61.85%)

1998 Gubernatorial Election
Korolev (oblast legislature chairman): 79.3%
Narolin (incumbent): 13.9%
Turnout: 57.0%

1996 Presidential Election
Zyuganov: 46.37%/56.30% (first round/second round)
Yeltsin: 25.08%/38.62%
Lebed: 13.16%
Yavlinskii: 5.56%
Zhirinovsky: 5.32%
Turnout: 70.85%/70.89% (Russia overall: 69.67%/68.79%)

1995 Parliamentary Elections
Communist Party of the Russian Federation: 28.96%
Liberal Democratic Party of Russia: 11.89%
Derzhava: 10.06%
Our Home Is Russia: 7.89%
Communists–Workers' Russia: 4.83%
Agrarian Party of Russia: 4.44%
Yabloko: 3.34%
Congress of Russian Communities: 3.14%
In single-mandate districts: 2 Communist Party of the Russian Federation
Turnout: 64.96% (Russia overall: 64.37%)

1993 Constitutional Referendum
"Yes"—41.4% "No"—56.3%

1993 Parliamentary Elections
Liberal Democratic Party of Russia: 31.70%
Communist Party of the Russian Federation: 14.27%
Russia's Choice: 12.93%
Agrarian Party of Russia: 12.24%
Women of Russia: 6.84%
Yabloko: 5.89%
Democratic Party of Russia: 5.09%
Party of Russian Unity and Concord: 4.69%
In single-mandate districts: 2 independent
Turnout: 59.95% (Russia overall: 54.34%)

1991 Presidential Election
Yeltsin: 61.94%
Ryzhkov: 16.03%

Zhirinovsky: 6.95%
Tuleev: 4.47%
Makashov: 3.38%
Bakatin: 2.84%
Turnout: 80.67% (Russia overall: 76.66%)

Regional Political Institutions

Executive:
Governor, 4-year term
Oleg Petrovich Korolev, elected April 1998
    Lipetsk Oblast Administration; Dom Sovetov;
    Sobornaya Pl., 1; Lipetsk, 398014
    Tel 7(074–2) 24–25–65; Fax 7(074–2) 72–24–26
    Federation Council in Moscow:
    7(095) 292–59–56, 292–57–88, 926–68–62

Legislative:
Unicameral
Council of People's Deputies—38 members, 4-year
term, elected June 1998
Chairman—Anatolii Ivanovich Savenkov, elected
June 1998

Regional Politics

"Orthodox Communist" Supported by Yabloko

Oleg Korolev, 46, the former chairman of the oblast legislature, won a crushing victory in the 12 April 1998 gubernatorial elections. Once labeled an "orthodox Communist" by former St. Petersburg Mayor Anatolii Sobchak, he had the support not only of the Communist Party but also the Lipetsk branch of Yabloko and at least 40 other local parties and movements. He gained some 79 percent of the vote, while incumbent Governor Mikhail Narolin trailed with slightly less than 14 percent. Narolin's backers included the local branches of Our Home Is Russia (NDR) and Vladimir Zhirinovsky's Liberal Democratic Party of Russia.

Korolev initially refused a 1997 suggestion from the local political and business elite that he run for governor. He suggested the mayor of Lipetsk as a candidate for this post. But when Narolin, the previous governor, decided to run, it was obvious that the mayor would not win against him. Thus the local elite turned to Korolev again, and this time he agreed (*RT*, 14 April 1998).

Executive Platform: Leftist

Korolev is hard to define politically. During his campaign, he expressed support for hard and soft-line Communists, Grigorii Yavlinskii's Yabloko, and even former First Deputy Prime Minster Anatolii Chubais. Communist Party leader Gennadii Zyuganov visited Lipetsk to campaign on behalf of Korolev. Candidate Korolev also boasted of his strong contacts in Moscow and his youth. The Communist State Duma member from the region, Vladimir Toporkov, withdrew from the race at the party's urging in support of Korolev.

When Korolev became chairman of the Lipetsk Council of People's Deputies in March 1994, his first step was to remove all the reform supporters from the legislative staff. He vigorously opposed the war in Chechnya and the way the privatization campaign was conducted. During the 1995 State Duma election campaign he openly declared his intention to vote for the opposition (*LI*, 15 December 1995). In the Federation Council, he supported reforms in the social sphere and measures to strengthen the Russian state. He also advocated developing strong local government. Although he avoided joining any political parties, in 1995 he was a member of Ivan Rybkin's "Concord" movement.

Policies

Korolev was not expected to introduce any major changes to the policies he inherited from his pro-Yeltsin predecessor (*EWI RRR*, 16 April 1998).

Relationships Between Key Players: Furious Battle over Steel Plant

Lipetsk is a relatively wealthy region that boasts free transportation and comparatively high salaries.

Ferrous metallurgy dominates the region's economy and the Novolipetsk Metallurgical Combine (NLMK) is the most important regional enterprise. NLMK's exports make up 97 percent of the oblast's total exports. The Novolipetsk plant is the most modern steel mill in Russia and the country's third-largest steel producer. It makes high-quality rolled-steel products. During the mid-1990s, the metal plant had been a case study of how directors abuse minority shareholders' rights. The main shareholders in the plant in 1997 were the Reforma group (comprising Uneximbank's MFK bank, Renaissance Capital's Sputnik Fund, and Cambridge Capital Management [CCM], a holding com-

Oleg Petrovich Korolev

23 February 1952—Born to a peasant family in Terbuni, Lipetsk Oblast, later graduating from Saratov University of Agriculture and the Rostov Party School

1973–1978—Forest warden of Dulgorokoe forest preserve, instructor of Dolgorukovskoe CPSU local committee, deputy chairman of "The Road to Communism" collective farm, and then the secretary of the local party bureau in Dolgorukovskoe raion

1978–1984—Chairman of "The Memory of Ilich" collective farm in Dolgorukovskoe raion

1985—Second secretary of the Dolgorukovskoe raion CPSU Committee

1987—First secretary of the Dobrinskii raion CPSU Committee

1989—Korolev was fired after his speech at a democratic conference in Luzhniki, Moscow; he then became the general-director of the enterprise "Lipetskvodomelioratsiya"

1990—Elected to the Lipetsk Oblast Soviet

1990–1992—Headed the Agrarian Committee of the Oblast Soviet

May 1992—Elected chairman of the Lipetsk Oblast Council of People's Deputies

22 September 1993—Small Soviet of Lipetsk Oblast ruled the Presidential Decree No 1400 (closing the Russian parliament) unconstitutional and confirmed its decision a month later

26 September 1993—Korolev convinced the Lipetsk Oblast Soviet to follow the orders of Vice-President Aleksandr Rutskoi and the decisions of the Supreme Soviet of Russian Federation

December 1993—Won a seat in the Federation Council with 27.4% of the vote; there he was a member of the Finance and Budget Committee, and then a member of the Committee for Agriculture

March 1994—Elected Chairman of the Lipetsk Oblast Deputies' Assembly

January 1996—Korolev joined the Federation Council as the oblast's legislative leader; with the endorsement of Yegor Stroev, he became one of four Federation Council Deputy Chairmen.

12 April 1998—Elected governor of Lipetsk Oblast with 79% of the vote

---

pany run by the U.S.-based Salomon Brothers); the UK's Trans World Group (TWG); and management, led by Chairman of the Board Vladimir Lisin. The Reforma group owned more than 42 percent of the stock, TWG held 38 percent, and management controlled 12 percent. Until December 1997, management teamed up with TWG to prevent Reforma from naming any members to the board of directors. However, in December, management switched sides, backing the Reforma group and effectively throwing out the TWG managers.

After defeating TWG, the members of the Reforma group then split. MFK-Renaissance and its allies now own 71 percent of the plant's stock (including a 36 percent share sold by Trans World), while CCM controls 17 percent. Other Western investors own the remaining 12 percent. The MFK-controlled board

decided on 27 January 1999 to sell an additional $150 million worth of stock, limiting buyers to current shareholders. To maintain the size of its stake, CCM would have to buy at least $25 million of the issue, *Kommersant Daily* (30 January 1999) reported. The newspaper also reported that CCM originally paid $1 million for its stake, so buying the new shares would be an enormous commitment, especially since the fund wrote off its Russian investments in 1998 as losses. MFK was expected to buy the shares if CCM did not.

Thanks to the deterioration in relations with TWG, Novolipetsk's exports began dropping at the end of 1997 because the plant had to find new export agents to sell its products abroad. The Russian business journal *Ekspert* claims that modernizing the plant will cost $600 million, a steep sum given the country's uncertain future. The plant was also one of the main losers when the United States slapped heavy import restrictions on Russian steel at the end of 1998. However, increased demand on the domestic and Asian markets has taken some of the sting out of this loss.

Ties to Moscow

Korolev has good relations with Federation Council Chairman Yegor Stroev and served as one of his four deputy chairmen in the parliament's upper chamber, handling issues related to the power ministries.

Relations with Other Regions

Lipetsk Oblast belongs to the Black Earth Association, which is headed by Orel Governor and Federation Council Speaker Yegor Stroev. The association also includes Voronezh, Belgorod, Kursk, Orel, and Tambov oblasts.

Foreign Relations

The Russian financial crisis that began 17 August 1998 benefited Russia's exporters by cutting the dollar price of domestically produced goods and services. However, these benefits may turn out to be too much of a good thing. Russian steel prices went so low toward the end of 1998 that U.S. producers asked the U.S. Department of Commerce to impose anti-dumping duties on Russian imports. In February 1999 the United States imposed harsh limits on the amount of hot-rolled steel Russia can sell on the U.S. market, effectively driving down 1999 sales to about 15 percent of 1998 sales. The EU has also imposed import quotas limiting the flow of Russian steel into Western Europe. One of the main targets of the U.S. duties is the Novolipetsk plant, leading Board of Directors Chairman Vladimir Lisin to complain that the issue was not dumping, but excluding Russia from the U.S. market.

Internet Sites in the Region

http://www.lipetsk.ru~adm1r/index.htm
This is the official server of the oblast administration.

MAGADAN OBLAST

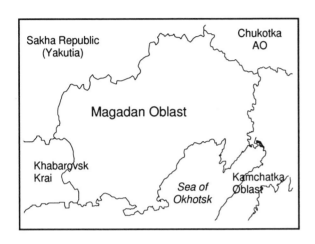

Territory: 461,400 km²
Population (as of 1 January 1998): 246,000
Distance from Moscow: 7,110 km

Major Cities:
Magadan, *capital* (pop. 121,500)

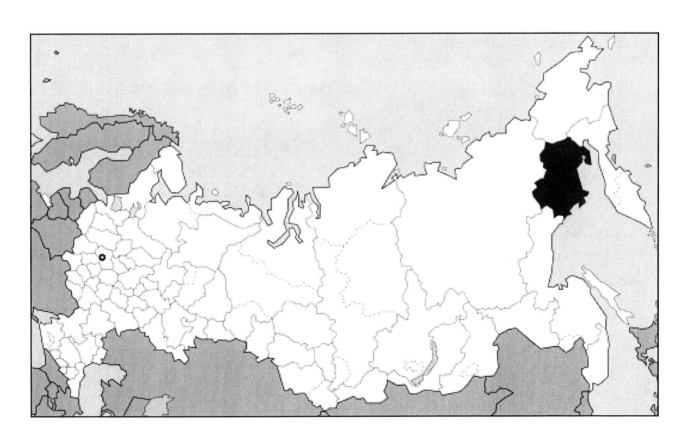

315

Basic Facts

Population (as of 1 Jan. 1998): 246,000 (0.17% of Russian total)

Ethnic breakdown (1989 census): Russians 72.4%, Ukrainians 15.5%, Belarusans 2.0%, Tatars 1.5%

Urban population (as of 1 Jan. 1998): 90.4% (Russia overall: 73.1%)

Student population (as of 1 Sept. 1997): 120 per 10,000 (Russia overall: 208/10,000)

Pensioner population (1997): 18.7% (Russia overall: 25.96%)

Percent of population with higher education (1989 census): 13.5% (Russia overall: 11.3%)

Percent of population working in (1997): Industry: 20.7% (Russian average: 23.0%); Agriculture: 5.0% (13.7%); Trade: 14.7% (13.5%); Culture: 13.4% (13.3%)

Average monthly personal income in July 1998: 1,546.4 new rubles (Russian average: 891.7 new rubles)

Average monthly personal expenses in July 1998: 777.8 new rubles (Russian average: 684.9 new rubles)

Average monthly subsistence requirement in 1998: 935 new rubles (Russian average: 438 new rubles)

Consumer price index (as of July 1998): 191 (Russia overall = 100)

Budgetary revenues (1997): 2,438.2 billion rubles (Russia overall: 433,378.2 billion rubles)

Budgetary expenditures (1997): 2,732.3 billion rubles (Russia overall: 468,111.6 billion rubles)

Industrial production as percentage of all Russian production (Jan.–Aug. 1998): 0.17%

Proportion of loss-making enterprises (as of July 1998): 64.0% (Russia overall: 50.4%)

Number of enterprises which have wage arrears (as of 1 Sept. 1998): 262 (0.19% of Russian total)

Agricultural production as percentage of all Russian production (1997): 0.09%

Number of private farms (as of 1 Jan. 1998): 299 (0.1% of Russian total)

Capital investment (1997): 1,378.9 billion rubles (Russia overall: 408,797 billion rubles)

Sources of investment (1997): federal budget: 5.7% (Russian average: 10.2%); regional budget: 3.3% (10.5%); extra-budgetary funds: 91.0% (79.3%)

Foreign investment (1997): 62,822,000 USD (Russia overall: 12,294,734,000 USD)

Number of joint ventures (1997): 22 (0.15% of Russian total)

Fixed capital investment in joint ventures and foreign companies (1997): 59,845 million rubles (Russia overall: 16,265.4 billion rubles)

Number of small businesses (as of 1 July 1998): 2,200 (0.25% of Russian total)

Number of enterprises privatized in 1997: 24 (0.87% of Russian total), including those which used to be municipal property: 87.5% (Russian average: 66.4%); regional property: 0% (20.0%); federal property: 12.5% (13.6%)

Number of telephones per 100 families (1997): in cities: 52.3 (Russian average: 49.2); in villages: 32.8 (19.8)

Brief Overview

Magadan Oblast is located in Russia's Far East, running north from its capital Magadan along the northern shore of the Sea of Okhotsk and eastward to the Taigonos Peninsula and the middle reaches of the Omolon River. The region borders the Republic of Sakha (Yakutia); Khabarovsk Krai; Kamchatka Oblast; and Chukotka Autonomous Okrug, which gained independence from Magadan Oblast in 1992.

Magadan is home to several indigenous ethnic groups, the most numerous of which are the Evens, who belong to the widespread Manchu-Tungus language family. Indigenous people traditionally live on reindeer breeding and fishing.

Apart from the swampy taiga along the coastline, most of the rugged mountainous area is covered by tundra on permafrost soil. The oblast is rich in various mineral resources and is ranked 10th in the country according to total raw materials. Mining, especially of gold, silver, tin, other non-ferrous metals, and coal, is the major regional industry, mainly located around the upper reaches of the Kolyma River. Magadan Oblast houses the country's largest gold and silver processing works, which belong to the Severovostokzoloto association. Due to intense processing of raw material, the region has the 18th most polluted air in the country with 211.6 kg of toxic waste per capita. Other regional industries are fishing, machine building, and agriculture. The oblast has close economic ties with such countries as Japan, South Korea, and the United States.

According to a 1998 survey by *Ekspert* magazine, the oblast is ranked 68th among Russia's 89 regions in terms of investment potential and 86th in terms of investment risks. The same survey reported that the region experienced the ninth largest decrease of investment potential in the country since 1997—by 7 points. A 1998 survey by Bank Austria ranked the oblast 27th in terms of investment climate.

Electoral History

2000 Presidential Election
Putin: 61.98%
Zyuganov: 22.52%
Zhirinovsky: 5.33%
Yavlinskii: 3.68%
Tuleev: 2.08%
Turnout: 64.46% (Russia overall: 68.64%)

1999 Parliamentary Elections
Unity: 42.95%
Communist Party of the Russian Federation: 18.86%
Zhirinovsky Bloc: 11.51%
Union of Right Forces: 6.60%
Yabloko: 3.92%
Fatherland–All Russia: 2.24%
In a single-mandate district: 1 independent
Turnout: 57.56% (Russia overall: 61.85%)

1996 Gubernatorial Election
Tsvetkov (State Duma deputy): 45.96%
Mikhailov (incumbent): 41.31%
Miroshnichenko: 2.00%
Turnout: 44.51%

1996 Presidential Election
Yeltsin: 36.93%/63.57% (first round/second round)
Lebed: 23.86%
Zyuganov: 16.04%/27.54%
Zhirinovsky: 10.91%
Yavlinskii: 6.15%
Turnout: 64.78%/62.27% (Russia overall: 69.67%/
    68.79%)

1995 Parliamentary Elections
Liberal Democratic Party of Russia: 22.32%
Communist Party of the Russian Federation: 12.57%
Our Home Is Russia: 8.16%
Yabloko: 7.63%
Party of Workers' Self-Government: 6.81%
Congress of Russian Communities: 5.44%
Women of Russia: 5.24%
Communists–Workers' Russia: 2.80%
In a single-mandate district: 1 independent
Turnout: 60.27% (Russia overall: 64.37%)

1993 Constitutional Referendum
"Yes"—67.2 "No"—30.8%

1993 Parliamentary Elections
Liberal Democratic Party of Russia: 29.21%
Yabloko: 16.45%
Russia's Choice: 14.39%
Women of Russia: 9.54%
Democratic Party of Russia: 7.31%
Communist Party of the Russian Federation: 5.99%
Party of Russian Unity and Concord: 5.11%
Agrarian Party of Russia: 1.11%
In a single-mandate district: 1 independent
Turnout: 46.86% (Russia overall: 54.34%)

1991 Presidential Elections

Yeltsin: 50.43%
Ryzhkov: 12.29%
Tuleev: 9.17%
Zhirinovsky: 9.01%
Makashov: 7.67%
Bakatin: 6.24%
Turnout: 85.43% (Russia overall: 76.66%)

Regional Political Institutions

Executive:

Governor, 4-year term
Valentin Ivanovich Tsvetkov, elected
November 1996
    Pl. Gorkogo, 6; Magadan, 685000
    Tel 7(413–22) 2–31–34;
    Fax 7(413–22) 2–04–25, 9–71–61
    Federation Council in Moscow:
    7(095) 292–80–54, 926–64–17

Legislative:

Unicameral
Oblast Duma—17 members, 4-year term, elected
May 1997
Chairman—Vladimir Alekseevich Pekhtin, elected
June 1997

Regional Politics

Former Duma Deputy Exerts
Tough Management in Far East

Valentin Tsvetkov was elected governor of Magadan
Oblast in November 1996, beating out incumbent
Viktor Mikhailov with a narrow 4 percent margin. Before moving into the political sphere, Tsvetkov worked
for 20 years in regional industry, ultimately becoming
the director of Magadannerud mining enterprise. Unlike many regional executives whose political careers
originated in local posts, Tsvetkov headed straight for
the national scene, serving in both chambers of the
federal parliament before becoming governor. He was
elected to the Federation Council in 1993, and then to
the Duma in 1995.

As governor of Magadan, Tsvetkov has focused on
the region's natural resource industries, specifically
gold mining and production. His desire to increase the
oblast's economic autonomy has led to some conflict
with the federal government. After great effort, in June

1999 Tsvetkov was finally able to establish a free economic zone in Magadan.

Tsvetkov has suggested the re-nationalization of
several unprofitable enterprises in the region, not because he believes that they will somehow bolster oblast
revenue, but rather to restructure or sell the companies so that they become profitable entities. Although
Magadan's economy is improving and several important initiatives are underway, the region is still reliant
on federal aid to deal with fuel and food shortages that
have threatened the population for the past several
winters. Thus, even though Tsvetkov has striven to
present a strong, self-reliant Magadan, he is still at the
mercy of the central government.

Executive Platform: Regionalist Reformer

Tsvetkov belongs to the group of governors elected in
1996 known as the "strong managers." The strong
managers ran as independents, campaigning primarily
on economic issues. Though an independent, Tsvetkov
was supported by a wide array of political parties in
his gubernatorial campaign. His proponents included
Vladimir Shumeiko's Reforms–New Course movement, Gennadii Zyuganov's National Patriotic Union
of Russia, Grigorii Yavlinskii's Yabloko party, and
Vladimir Zhirinovsky's Liberal Democratic Party of
Russia. Essentially, all groups wanting to oust incumbent Viktor Mikhailov stood behind Tsvetkov rather
than placing their own candidates in the race.

As a result of his eclectic support network, observers have pasted a number of labels on Tsvetkov. However, he is clearly a reformer and a regionalist. Most
of his attention has been devoted to Magadan's economic development, which he approaches in a very
business-like manner, clearly a carryover from his own
20-year career in business. A former member of the
Russian Regions Duma faction, Tsvetkov has been
intent on increasing Magadan's power in relation to
the center. He was highly critical of former Prime
Minister Viktor Chernomyrdin's government for its
failure to meet the regions' needs and its inability to
communicate effectively with regional leaders (*OMRI
RRR*, 11 December 1996). Rather than deal directly
with Chernomyrdin, Tsvetkov preferred to go to the
region's presidential representative with his concerns.

In the run-up to the 1999 State Duma elections,
Tsvetkov joined Samara Governor Konstantin Titov's
Voice of Russia regional party, then switched his support to the Kremlin's new Unity bloc.

Policies: Active Economic Restructuring

The majority of Tsvetkov's policies have been focused on Magadan's economic development. The governor has been heavily involved in trying to improve Magadan's energy situation, which has been problematic for several winters. He is interested in increasing the amount of hydroelectric energy used in the oblast to make energy prices more reasonable for consumers, who are expected to pay a larger share of their energy consumption in accordance with the on-going housing reform. Tsvetkov was active in planning the region's new oil-processing plant (see Attitudes Toward Business). He wanted a refinery capable of handling 50,000 tons of oil a year from Sakhalin, Alaska, and the United Arab Emirates (*RG*, 12 February 1998). The new plant should meet some of these needs.

Tsvetkov is extremely concerned about the region's natural resources and how they are being exploited. He feels that the absence of a sound legal framework governing the extraction of precious metals and gems has allowed the federal government to profit from resources that should belong primarily to the regions.

The issue of Magadan's gold mining industry has been a point of contention between Tsvetkov and the federal government (see Ties to Moscow). Tsvetkov considers Magadan's gold mining industry, which is the source of most of the region's revenue, to be a matter of life or death for the oblast. He was highly supportive of a new gold processing plant that opened in 1998 because it would create a bit of breathing space between the region's gold industry and the federal government. The new plant should also reduce the level of organized crime if all of its operations can be kept transparent (see Attitudes Toward Business). To address the issue of precious metals and gems on the federal level, in early 1998 the Federation Council established a precious metals commission, which is chaired by Tsvetkov.

The governor has been very active in dealing with the economic plight of several enterprises in the oblast. Unlike many other regional executives who continue to provide regional credits to unprofitable enterprises to keep them afloat and prevent unemployment, Tsvetkov takes a more far-sighted approach. Several enterprises in Magadan have been renationalized and then restructured into profitable enterprises or auctioned off. In July 1997 the Magadan Food Complex became the first enterprise to voluntarily sign its shares over to the oblast administration. The factory was in considerable debt and workers were owed several months' worth of back wages. Rather than subsidizing the unprofitable enterprise, the oblast administration helped refit the plant to produce quick-selling items so that the workers would not lose their jobs. Also in 1997 the Magadan Oblast Emergency Commission decided to renationalize the Magadan Marine Harbor. The port had profited from its monopolist position by increasing tariffs, thus raising the price of goods in Magadan and the neighboring Sakha Republic.

Ties to Moscow: Conflict over Oblast Gold

Tsvetkov remained loyal to President Boris Yeltsin and his administration even though he was highly critical of former Prime Minister Viktor Chernomyrdin. On 4 July 1997 Tsvetkov and President Yeltsin signed a power-sharing agreement between Magadan and the federal government. However, this agreement alone has not satisfied Tsvetkov's wishes regarding Magadan's authority over various aspects of the region's economy, thus causing tension and conflict.

In early 1998 Tsvetkov became involved in a serious dispute with the federal government over the oblast's gold. Then Russian Minister of Internal Affairs Anatolii Kulikov sent a letter to then Prime Minister Viktor Chernomyrdin accusing Tsvetkov of embezzling Russian gold. Shortly thereafter, over 170 kilograms of gold were seized from the Precious Metals Fund of Magadan Oblast. In response, Tsvetkov sent an open letter to the oblast legislature stating that federal law enforcement agencies took advantage of the absence of a proper legal framework for precious metal transactions to confiscate the Fund's property. He proceeded to accuse the police of leaving the gold miners to starve and the mines to collapse (*EWI RRR*, 29 January 1998). This incident was essentially the culmination of mounting tension regarding Magadan's precious metals. Furthermore, it exhibited the federal government's resistance to allowing Magadan to have additional control over its own gold resources, which was also manifested in opposition to various initiatives for changing the gold industry's structure in relation to the oblast. (See also Attitudes Toward Business.)

Ultimately, the tension between Tsvetkov and federal authorities cooled a bit, and in July 1998 Tsvetkov signed an agreement with then First Deputy Prime Minister Boris Nemtsov giving Magadan officials more freedom for distributing funds. In return, the oblast pledged to refrain from using commercial banks to handle budget funds, stop from using offsets to settle accounts between the government and enterprises, and introduce cost-cutting measures.

Tsvetkov had then hoped to make Magadan Oblast into a free economic zone with customs exemptions, but Nemtsov rejected such a proposal. However, in June 1999 Yeltsin signed a law setting up a 15-year special economic zone located in the city of Magadan aimed at creating favorable conditions for developing the region's natural resources and manufacturing sector. The zone frees industrialists from paying profit taxes and places them under a less strict customs regime (*RFR*, 9 June 1999).

Relations with Other Regions: Close to Ayatskov, Opposed to Stroev

Given his reputation as an advocate for regional authority, it is no surprise that Tsvetkov has generally good relations with other governors and sees the merit of working in coordination with them. Tsvetkov has cultivated relationships with several prominent regional executives. Saratov Governor Dmitrii Ayatskov, who is well known on the national political scene, has even placed Tsvetkov in the cabinet he would form if he were elected president of Russia.

In May 1998 Tsvetkov agreed to contribute funds to the Alliance Group, a foundation providing crisis support to enterprises in Russia and the CIS. The other member regions are Saratov, Leningrad, Novgorod, Murmansk, Irkutsk, Chita, Novosibirsk, Voronezh, Udmurtia, and Buryatia. The regional executives involved in the Alliance Group feel that close cooperation between regional administrations and enterprises provides the most effective crisis aid. Tsvetkov's own policies toward struggling enterprises in Magadan seem to exemplify this (see Policies).

Tsvetkov has a more difficult relationship with Federation Council Speaker Yegor Stroev. In 1997 Tsvetkov raised the question of replacing Stroev, claiming that Stroev had turned the Federation Council into an "appendage" of the presidency.

Magadan belongs to the Far East and Baikal Association, which brings together the republics of Buryatia and Sakha (Yakutia); Primorskii and Khabarovsk krais; Amur, Kamchatka, Chita, and Sakhalin oblasts; the Jewish Autonomous Oblast; and Koryak and Chukotka autonomous okrugs. One of the association's goals is to work more closely with the countries in the Asian-Pacific region, specifically regarding economic and business cooperation.

Foreign Relations: Economic Interests

Tsvetkov's foreign relations are primarily economic. There is considerable foreign investment in various oblast initiatives, and Tsvetkov would like to be able to trade Magadan's gold on the world market, but this requires approval from the federal government, which is unlikely.

In January 1998 Tsvetkov participated in the second annual U.S.-Russian Investment Symposium at Harvard University's Kennedy School of Government in Massachusetts, in hopes of networking and attracting investment to Magadan.

Attitudes Toward Business: Expanding Natural Resource Industries

Tsvetkov is very interested in developing the region's economy and expanding the natural resource industries. In early 1998 the federal government, the oblast administration, and Magadan's leading banks and corporations came together to form a financial-industrial company. The company focuses on controlling the gold, finances, and electricity production in the oblast.

The region has also launched several projects and initiatives likely to bolster local industries. In March 1998 Tsvetkov's administration and the Tyumen Oil Company signed an agreement to build an oil processing plant in Magadan to sell fuel products in the Far East. Tsvetkov claims that prices for the output will be 25 to 30 percent cheaper than those supplied by Sidanko, which already has facilities in the region.

In 1998 the Kolyma gold-processing plant opened its doors, receiving strong support from Tsvetkov, who considered the plant an important development for the oblast (*EWI RRR*, 12 February 1998). Deputy Prime Minister Boris Nemtsov was on hand for the grand opening, yet his appearance did not signify wholehearted federal support for the region's initiative. The new plant's existence questions the rationale of maintaining Goskhran, the federal agency responsible for precious metal extraction. The federal government has resisted regional attempts to reform the gold-mining sector. It refused to buy several tons of gold from the oblast in 1998, forcing the oblast to seek financial aid elsewhere for the gold's extraction. Fortunately, the French bank Société Generale loaned Magadan's gold miners $50 million to finance the mining season. This raised the question of whether or not the oblast can sell its gold on the world market, an initiative the federal government

Valentin Ivanovich Tsvetkov

27 August 1948—Born

1974—Graduated from the Zaporozhe Machine-Building Institute

1974–1980—Worked as a foreman, senior foreman, shop head, and department head at the Magadan Repair Factory

1980–1983—Deputy director of the Magadan Lumber Processing Combine

1983–1986—Deputy director and then director of the Magadannerud mining enterprise

1986–1994—General director of Magadannerud

12 December 1993—Elected to the Federation Council, and on 27 April 1994 became chair of the Committee on Northern Affairs and Indigenous Peoples

December 1995—Elected to the state Duma, joining the Committee on Natural Resources

3 November 1996—Elected governor of Magadan Oblast

Married, with one child

is not anxious to pursue. Tsvetkov claims that the federal government would prefer to see all gold-processing operations take place without the oblast government controlling the necessary natural and financial resources (*EWI RRR*, 12 February 1998).

In November 1997 the Dukat silver mine, which holds one of the largest silver deposits in the world, was auctioned to the Russian-Canadian enterprise Serebro Dukata, a joint venture between Canadian Pan-American Silver and Russian Geometall Plus. The mine, which had flourished in the 1980s, suffered a blow with the collapse of the Soviet Union when silver processing in Kazakhstan was no longer economically viable. It stood idle for a year as potential buyers shied away from the mine's mounting debts. Rather than allow the company to go bankrupt, Tsvetkov suggested that the company's workers voluntarily give up the mining license. He promised to ensure that the mine's new owner would fully pay back-wages and guarantee employment for the staff. The majority of the money paid by the winner in the auction has gone to paying wage arrears, and Serebro Dukata promised to keep on 90 percent of the staff. Serebro Dukata should have the mine in full operation by 2001.

REPUBLIC OF MARII EL

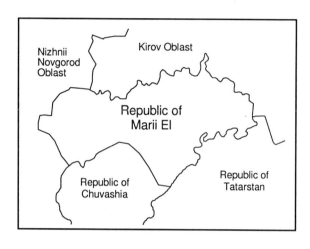

Territory: 23,200 km²
Population (as of 1 January 1998):
763,000
Distance from Moscow: 862 km

Major Cities:
Ioshkar-Ola, *capital* (pop. 250,600)
Volzhsk (61,800)
Kozmodemyansk (24,400)
Zvenigovo (14,400)

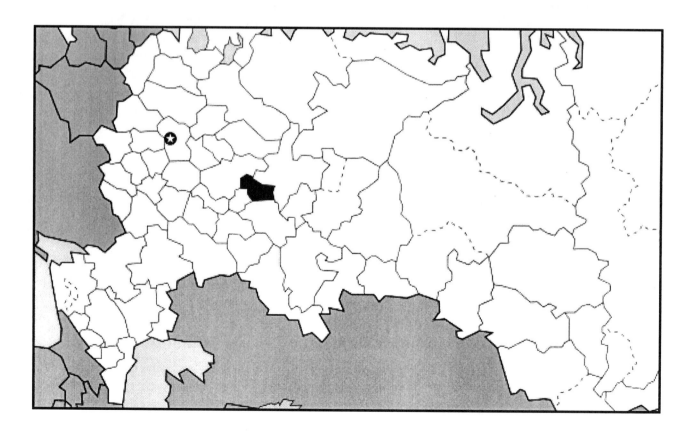

Basic Facts

Population (as of 1 Jan. 1998): 763,000 (0.52% of Russian total)

Ethnic breakdown (1989 census): Russians 47.5%, Marii 43.3%, Tatars 5.9%, Chuvash 1.2%

Urban population (as of 1 Jan. 1998): 61.9% (Russia overall: 73.1%)

Student population (as of 1 Sept. 1997): 202 per 10,000 (Russia overall: 208/10,000)

Pensioner population (1997): 24.64% (Russia overall: 25.96%)

Percent of population with higher education (1989 census): 9.7% (Russia overall: 11.3%)

Percent of population working in (1997): Industry: 23.1% (Russian average: 23.0%); Agriculture: 18.2% (13.7%); Trade: 13.3% (13.5%); Culture: 14.2% (13.3%)

Average monthly personal income in July 1998: 411.5 new rubles (Russian average: 891.7 new rubles)

Average monthly personal expenses in July 1998: 303.0 new rubles (Russian average: 684.9 new rubles)

Average monthly subsistence requirement in 1998: 394 new rubles (Russian average: 438 new rubles)

Consumer price index (as of July 1998): 78 (Russia overall = 100)

Budgetary revenues (1997): 1,204.8 billion rubles (Russia overall: 433,378.2 billion rubles)

Budgetary expenditures (1997): 1,436.4 billion rubles (Russia overall: 468,111.6 billion rubles)

Industrial production as percentage of all Russian production (Jan.–Aug. 1998): 0.19%

Proportion of loss-making enterprises (as of July 1998): 58.8% (Russia overall: 50.4%)

Number of enterprises which have wage arrears (as of 1 Sept. 1998): 1,327 (0.98% of Russian total)

Agricultural production as percentage of all Russian production (1997): 0.74%

Number of private farms (as of 1 Jan. 1998): 1,600 (0.58% of Russian total)

Capital investment (1997): 1,052.0 billion rubles (Russia overall: 408,797 billion rubles)

Sources of investment (1997): federal budget: 7.5% (Russian average: 10.2%); regional budget: 10.7% (10.5%); extra-budgetary funds: 81.8% (79.3%)

Foreign investment (1997): 987,000 USD (Russia overall: 12,294,734,000 USD)

Number of joint ventures (1997): 26 (0.18% of Russian total)

Fixed capital investment in joint ventures and foreign companies (1997): 5,966 million rubles (Russia overall: 16,265.4 billion rubles)

Number of small businesses (as of 1 July 1998): 2,700 (0.31% of Russian total)

Number of enterprises privatized in 1997: 3 (0.11% of Russian total), including those which used to be municipal property: 66.7% (Russian average: 66.4%); regional property: 0% (20.0%); federal property: 33.3% (13.6%)

Number of telephones per 100 families (1997): in cities: 61.7 (Russian average: 49.2); in villages: 18.2 (19.8)

Brief Overview

The Republic of Marii El is located almost in the middle of European Russia, in the basin of the Volga River. It is surrounded by the highly industrial regions of Tatarstan, Nizhnii Novgorod, Kirov, and Chuvashia. Woods, which cover over half of its territory, are the major wealth of the republic, which otherwise is poor in raw materials.

The republic's economy draws on both industry and agriculture. Major republican industries include: machine-building and metal processing (24 percent of GDP); food industry (20.4 percent); and forestry, lumber, and cellulose (13 percent each). About 8.5 percent of GDP comes from the defense sector, which employs about 35 percent of industrial workers. Republican agriculture specializes in the cultivation of grain, vegetables, and potatoes and the production of meat, milk, eggs, and wool.

The republic has attracted a considerable number of foreign investors from Italy, the United States, Germany, China, Bulgaria, India, and Turkey. However, it has become more dangerous to invest in the republican economy recently. From 1997 to 1998, the republic experienced the sixth-largest increase in investment risks in the country—by 27 points. According to a 1998 survey by *Ekspert* magazine, the republic is ranked 69th among Russia's 89 regions in terms of investment potential and 37th in terms of investment risks. A 1998 survey by Bank Austria ranked the republic 71st in terms of investment climate.

Electoral History

2000 Presidential Election
Putin: 44.51%
Zyuganov: 39.99%
Yavlinskii: 3.79%
Zhirinovsky: 2.78%
Tuleev: 2.48%
Turnout: 69.16% (Russia overall: 68.64%)

1999 Parliamentary Elections
Communist Party of the Russian Federation: 31.14%
Unity: 21.33%
Fatherland–All Russia: 8.96%
Union of Right Forces: 7.24%
Zhirinovsky Bloc: 6.90%
Yabloko: 4.68%
In a single-mandate district: 1 Communist Party of the Russian Federation
Turnout: 64.51% (Russia overall: 61.85%)

1996 Republican Presidential Election
Kislitsyn: 47.37%/58.89% (first round/second round)
Markelov (State Duma deputy): 29.21%/36.24%
Zotin (incumbent): 9.77%
Khlebnikov (republican deputy prime minister): 6.15%
Popov: 1.16%
Maksimov: 0.93%
Turnout: 67.4%/63.34%

1996 Presidential Election
Zyuganov: 43.44%/52.78% (first round/second round)
Yeltsin: 24.75%/40.74%
Lebed: 10.97%
Zhirinovsky: 7.43%
Yavlinskii: 7.37%
Turnout: 69.53%/68.77% (Russia overall: 69.67%/ 68.79%)

1995 Parliamentary Elections
Liberal Democratic Party of Russia: 20.72%
Communist Party of the Russian Federation: 18.51%
Agrarian Party of Russia: 9.41%
Our Home Is Russia: 5.01%
Women of Russia: 4.87%
Communists–Workers' Russia: 4.47%
Pamfilova–Gurov–Lysenko: 4.32%
Party of Workers' Self-Government: 3.56%
In a single-mandate district: 1 Agrarian Party of Russia
Turnout: 66.55% (Russia overall: 64.37%)

1993 Constitutional Referendum
"Yes"—50.7% "No"—46.0%

1993 Parliamentary Elections
Liberal Democratic Party of Russia: 24.47%
Agrarian Party of Russia: 14.17%
Communist Party of the Russian Federation: 12.55%
Russia's Choice: 11.42%
Women of Russia: 10.32%
Democratic Party of Russia: 6.62%
Party of Russian Unity and Concord: 6.49%
Yabloko: 4.51%
In single-mandate districts: 3 independent, 1 Yabloko
From electoral associations: 1 Party of Russian Unity and Concord
Turnout: 46.82% (Russia overall: 54.34%)

1991 Presidential Election
Yeltsin: 51.44%
Ryzhkov: 17.05%
Tuleev: 11.18%

Zhirinovsky: 6.58%

Makashov: 4.59%

Bakatin: 4.30%

Turnout: 76.51% (Russia overall: 76.66%)

Regional Political Institutions

Executive:
   President, 4-year term
   Vyacheslav Aleksandrovich Kislitsyn,
   elected January 1997
      Leninskii Prospect, 29; Ioshkar-Ola, 424001
      Tel 7(836–2) 63–04–08;
      Fax 7(836–2) 55–69–64

Legislative:
   Unicameral
   State Assembly (*Gosudarstvennoe Sobranie*)—
   67 members, 4-year term,
   elected October 1996 and January 1997
   Chairman—Mikhail Mikhailovich Zhukov,
    elected November 1996

Regional Politics

Communist Comes to Power Amid Election Controversy

Vyacheslav Kislitsyn rose to power in a bitter election controversy. In an attempt to ensure his reelection, former Marii El President Vladislav Zotin imposed a law requiring all candidates for the presidency to pass a test evaluating their proficiency in the republic's official language. Although such requirements are in violation of the Russian Constitution, several of the ethnically defined republics have adopted similar legislation. Zotin's plan was unsuccessful. Kislitsyn was the only candidate to pass an exam on the Marii El mountain languages, while the other candidates ignored the law. Zotin then tried to cancel elections two days before the first round. This decree was condemned by the Central Electoral Commission and overruled by the Marii El Supreme Court, but Zotin's supporters did not broadcast the court's decision in the local media. Nevertheless, this move worked against Zotin, who failed to make it to the runoffs. He won only 9 percent of the vote. Shortly after the vote, the Russian Procurator general's office opened a criminal case against Zotin for obstructing justice. In the end Kislitsyn took the presidency in January 1997 with the support of Gennadii Zyuganov's Communist Party, Grigorii Yavlinskii's Yabloko, and General Aleksandr Lebed.

Executive Platform: From Opposition to "Reformer"

Kislitsyn's political philosophy and loyalty are difficult to discern. He remained a member of the Communist Party after the dissolution of the Soviet Union and became president of Marii El on the KPRF ticket. However, following his election he became active in Viktor Chernomyrdin's Our Home Is Russia (NDR) movement and was elected to the NDR political council in April 1998, at the fifth NDR congress. In 1999 he joined reformist Samara Governor Konstantin Titov's Voice of Russia regional movement.

Policies: Pro-Investment, Anti-Crime

Kislitsyn's policies have been focused on promoting economic growth and industrial development in the region. In June 1997 Kislitsyn prepared a decree prohibiting the export of money and raw materials from the republic in order to stimulate the regional processing industry (*FI*, 10 June 1997). In fall 1997 Marii El introduced tax privileges for enterprises bringing investment into the region. If the volume of investment brought by a firm exceeds $100,000, then the enterprise is freed entirely from regional profit, property, and transportation taxes and the VAT for two years. Then for the following three years the firm is freed from 75 percent, 50 percent, and 25 percent of its tax obligations. Enterprises that bring in a smaller volume of investment are granted a 50 percent tax break for three years and a 25 percent break for two years (*FI*, 4 November 1997).

Kislitsyn introduced a number of measures to reduce crime in the republic. Shortly thereafter thieves broke into Kislitsyn's dacha and attempted to break into his daughter's apartment. The attacks were considered to be attempts by the president's opponents to put pressure on him (*EWI RRR*, 30 April 1997).

Relationships Between Key Players: Strong NDR Support

Following the October 1996 elections to the Marii El republican legislature, deputies affiliated with NDR held a majority of the seats, offering Kislitsyn a strong foundation of support. In the elections, mayors and executive branch officials won 18 of the 67 seats. Their victory violated both federal and republican law on the separation of the executive and legislative branches. The Russian Supreme Court ruled their election il-

Vyacheslav Aleksandrovich Kislitsyn

4 September 1948—Born in the Kosolapovo village of Marii El

1965—Graduated from a technical institute in Tomsk as an automotive worker

1969—Graduated from the Tomsk Railroad Institute with a degree in electrical technology

1969–1971—Served in the Soviet army

1972–1975—Chairman of district councils in Semenov and Znamen

1975–1978—Director of the Medvedev District public food association

1978—Graduated from the history department of the Marii El Pedagogical Institute

1978–1989—Management chairman of the Conqueror collective farm

August 1989—Elected chairman of the Medvedev District executive committee

1990—Finished a degree in law at the Moscow Higher Party School

1991—Elected head of administration of the Medvedev District

12 December 1993—Elected to the Federation Council, serving on the Committee for Science, Culture, and Education Issues

4 January 1997—Elected President of Marii El

Married, with a daughter

---

legal in October 1997, yet no changes were made in Marii El. Observers claim that the deputies have adopted several laws benefiting executive branch bureaucrats (*EWI RRR*, 11 December 1997).

Ties to Moscow: Generally Tolerated by the Kremlin

It is unclear where Kislitsyn stands in relation to the federal government. He was supported by Gennadii Zyuganov and the Communist Party in the 1996 republican presidential elections. However, after taking power, Kislitsyn joined the ranks of Our Home Is Russia, presumably to develop ties with the presidential administration. Moscow tends to leave Marii El alone as it does most republics that do not openly challenge the center's authority.

On 20 May 1998 Kislitsyn signed a power-sharing agreement with President Boris Yeltsin.

Relations with Other Regions: Conflict with Chuvashia

Marii El has been in a dispute with Chuvashia regarding $33,000 in annual tax revenues collected from the Volga River islands that lie between the two republics. The islands are generally believed to be part of Chuvashia, whose residents use the islands for growing hay. Marii El argues that the islands became part of its territory as a result of a 1925 All-Russian Central Executive Committee ruling, and thus asserts that all taxes from the islands should go into the Marii El treasury (*Izvestiya*, 16 June 1998).

Marii El belongs to the Greater Volga Association, which includes the republics of Tatarstan, Mordovia, and Chuvashia, and Astrakhan, Volgograd, Nizhnii Novgorod, Penza, Samara, Saratov, and Ulyanovsk oblasts.

Foreign Relations

In January 1999 Kislitsyn tried to sell the S-300 missile defense system to Kuwaiti Prime Minister Crown Prince Sheikh Saad Abdullah Salem Sabah. The system Kislitsyn allegedly tried to sell has exclusive classified technology intended for use only by the Russian military. Therefore, Kislitsyn's actions were in violation of federal and criminal laws. However, no action was taken against him (*RFE/RL*, 26 January 1999).

Attitudes Toward Business

In fall 1997 the republic approved several tax privileges for companies investing in the region. (See Policies.)

Internet Sites in the Region

http://www.mari.su/koi8/mariel/
This website offers basic information about Marii El, its cities, and the culture of the ethnic Marii, including information on the Marii language.

http://www.mari.su/index.html.ru
This website features basic information about Marii El and provides local news from Radio M. It has links to some other newspapers and contains considerable information about the internet in Russia.

http://www.yoshkar-ola.ru/union/ru/index.htm
This is the website for Ioshkar-Ola, the capital city of Marii El. It features links to some local newspapers including *Moskovskii Komsomolets*.

REPUBLIC OF MORDOVIA

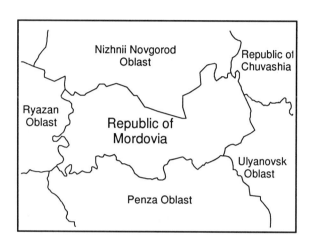

Territory: 26,200 km²
Population (as of 1 January 1998): 944,000
Distance from Moscow: 642 km

Major Cities:
Saransk, *capital* (pop. 318,100)
Ruzaevka (50,800)
Kovylkino (23,200)
Krasnoslobodsk (11,900)
Ardatov (10,100)

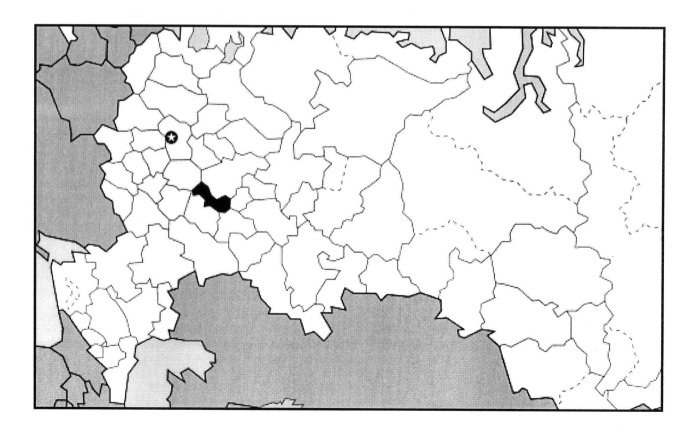

Basic Facts

Population (as of 1 Jan. 1998): 944,000 (0.64% of Russian total)

Ethnic breakdown (1989 census): Russians 60.8%, Mordvins 32.5%, Tatars 4.9%

Urban population (as of 1 Jan. 1998): 59.4% (Russia overall: 73.1%)

Student population (as of 1 Sept. 1997): 278 per 10,000 (Russia overall: 208/10,000)

Pensioner population (1997): 28.18% (Russia overall: 25.96%)

Percent of population with higher education (1989 census): 8.9% (Russia overall: 11.3%)

Percent of population working in (1997): Industry: 23.9% (Russian average: 23.0%); Agriculture: 17.3% (13.7%); Trade: 11.7% (13.5%); Culture: 12.3% (13.3%)

Average monthly personal income in July 1998: 446.7 new rubles (Russian average: 891.7 new rubles)

Average monthly personal expenses in July 1998: 340.6 new rubles (Russian average: 684.9 new rubles)

Average monthly subsistence requirement in 1998: 352 new rubles (Russian average: 438 new rubles)

Consumer price index (as of July 1998): 82 (Russia overall = 100)

Budgetary revenues (1997): 2,155.2 billion rubles (Russia overall: 433,378.2 billion rubles)

Budgetary expenditures (1997): 2,411.4 billion rubles (Russia overall: 468,111.6 billion rubles)

Industrial production as percentage of all Russian production (Jan.–Aug. 1998): 0.34%

Proportion of loss-making enterprises (as of July 1998): 56.6% (Russia overall: 50.4%)

Number of enterprises which have wage arrears (as of 1 Sept. 1998): 715 (0.53% of Russian total)

Agricultural production as percentage of all Russian production (1997): 0.98%

Number of private farms (as of Jan. 1998): 1,264 (0.46% of Russian total)

Capital investment (1997): 1,269.5 billion rubles (Russia overall: 408,797 billion rubles)

Sources of investment (1997): federal budget: 16.9% (Russian average: 10.2%); regional budget: 13.2% (10.5%); extra-budgetary funds: 69.9% (79.3%)

Foreign investment (1997): 1,690,000 USD (Russia overall: 12,294,734,000 USD)

Number of joint ventures (1997): 8 (0.05% of Russian total)

Fixed capital investment in joint ventures and foreign companies (1997): 7,695 million rubles (Russia overall: 16,265.4 billion rubles)

Number of small businesses (as of July 1998): 2,100 (0.24% of Russian total)

Number of enterprises privatized in 1997: 5 (0.18% of Russian total), including those which used to be municipal property: 40.0% (Russian average: 66.4%); regional property: 60.0% (20.0%); federal property: 0% (13.6%)

Number of telephones per 100 families (1997): in cities: 49.5 (Russian average: 49.2); in villages: 15.7 (19.8)

Brief Overview

The territory inhabited by the Mordvins became a part of what is now considered Russia in 1552, after the defeat of the Mongol horde. Mordvins, the titular nationality in the republic, now make up only one third of the republican population, while there are nearly twice as many Russians. The republic is located in the center of European Russia and borders Nizhnii Novgorod, Ryazan, Penza, and Ulyanovsk oblasts and Chuvashia.

The republic's natural endowment includes resources for the production of construction materials, particularly clay, sand, and cement. Half of the republic's GDP comes from machine building and metallurgy. The republic also is home to Russia's largest chemical and oil-processing enterprise, Rezinotekhnika, which manufactures over 15,000 products that are used for producing cars, electronic equipment, and machinery for the energy industry. Additionally, Mordovia boasts Europe's largest cement producer, Mordovtsement. Republican agriculture, which produces about 30 percent of the regional GDP, specializes in the cultivation of grain, potatoes, and vegetables, and in cattle breeding.

The republic has foreign trade with over 50 countries. It exports electronic and chemical equipment, medicines, automobiles and trucks, and timber. The republic has 22 joint ventures with partners from Ukraine, India, Hungary, Estonia, and other countries. Most of these enterprises specialize in commerce. The only industrial joint venture is a British-Russian brewery, Saranskaya Pivovarennaya Kompaniya.

According to a 1998 survey by *Ekspert* magazine, the republic ranked 60th among Russia's 89 regions in terms of investment potential and 22nd in terms of investment risks. The survey noted a 28-point decrease in investment risk (fifth largest in the country) since 1997. A 1998 survey by Bank Austria ranked the republic 69th in terms of investment climate.

Electoral History

2000 Presidential Election
Putin: 60.03%
Zyuganov: 30.79%
Zhirinovsky: 2.03%
Yavlinskii: 1.29%
Tuleev: 1.14%
Turnout: 79.42% (Russia overall: 68.64%)

1999 Parliamentary Elections
Fatherland–All Russia: 32.60%
Communist Party of the Russian Federation: 30.33%
Unity: 15.46%
Zhirinovsky Bloc: 4.93%
Union of Right Forces: 2.62%
Yabloko: 2.36%
In a single-mandate district: 1 Fatherland–All Russia
Turnout: 74.56% (Russia overall: 61.85%)

1998 Republican Executive Election
Merkushkin (incumbent): 93.1%
Sharov: 3.2%
Turnout: 75.7%

1996 Presidential Election
Zyuganov: 49.71%/47.74% (first round/second round)
Yeltsin: 24.14%/45.63%
Lebed: 10.64%
Zhirinovsky: 6.86%
Yavlinskii: 3.00%
Turnout: 70.17%/75.41% (Russia overall: 69.67%/ 68.79%)

1995 Parliamentary Elections
Communist Party of the Russian Federation: 22.84%
Our Home Is Russia: 19.56%
Liberal Democratic Party of Russia: 19.51%
Agrarian Party of Russia: 4.98%
Communists–Workers' Russia: 4.31%
Congress of Russian Communities: 3.46%
Derzhava: 2.52%
Yabloko: 2.41%
Women of Russia: 2.22%
In a single-mandate district: 1 independent
Turnout: 67.20% (Russia overall: 64.37%)

1993 Constitutional Referendum
"Yes"—36.2%   "No"—61.3%

1993 Parliamentary Elections
Liberal Democratic Party of Russia: 35.34%
Communist Party of the Russian Federation: 18.74%
Agrarian Party of Russia: 12.46%
Russia's Choice: 7.65%
Women of Russia: 6.14%
Yabloko: 5.39%
Democratic Party of Russia: 4.89%
Party of Russian Unity and Concord: 4.03%

In a single-mandate district: 1 Communist Party of the Russian Federation

From electoral associations: 1 Communist Party of the Russian Federation

Turnout: 62.13% (Russia overall: 54.34%)

1991 Presidential Election

Yeltsin: 61.63%

Ryzhkov: 12.32%

Tuleev: 7.73%

Zhirinovsky: 6.92%

Makashov: 5.52%

Bakatin: 2.41%

Turnout: 82.87% (Russia overall: 76.66%)

Regional Political Institutions

Executive:

President, 5-year term

Nikolai Ivanovich Merkushkin, elected February 1998

Ul. Sovetskaya, 35; Saransk, 430002

Tel 7(834–2) 17–54–71, 32–78–01;

Fax 7(834–2) 17–45–26

Federation Council in Moscow:

7(095) 292–46–55, 926–67–17

Legislative:

Unicameral

State Assembly (Gosudarstvennoe Sobranie)—75 members, 4-year term, elected November 1994 (in December 1995 extended term until 1999)

Chairman—Valerii Alekseevich Kechkin, elected October 1995

Regional Politics

Most Popular Executive Disqualifies Opponents

Nikolai Merkushkin has achieved one of the highest victory margins of any other Russian regional executive elected by popular mandate. He was elected President of Mordovia with 96.6 percent of the vote and a voter turnout of 75.6 percent. Merkushkin faced no real opposition in his electoral bid. His single opponent announced his support for Merkushkin's policies several times during the campaign, thus suggesting that his candidacy was simply a formality in order to validate the elections. Merkushkin minimized his chances of defeat by adding a clause to the electoral law disqualifying candidates whose signature lists supporting their candidacy contained more than 3 percent invalid signatures.

As a result, the republican Communist Party leader Yevgenii Kosterin was disqualified by the clause even though the 34,000 signatures he turned in were more than double the required 15,000 (*EWI RRR*, 19 February 1998). The clause is not in violation of federal legislation since federal law on voting rights does not discuss limits on the number of invalid signatures.

Merkushkin ran unsuccessfully for public office several times before winning the republican presidency. In 1990 he ran for the republican Supreme Soviet, in 1991 for the republican presidency, and in 1993 for the first session of the Federation Council. In 1994 he was elected to the republican State Assembly and served as its chairman until he was chosen as president of the republic in 1995. The republic had gone for over two years without a president since the position was abolished by the legislature in April 1993. Prior to this the post was held by Vasilii Guslyanikov.

Executive Platform: From Agrarian to Fatherland

Merkushkin is difficult to categorize politically. In 1993 he joined the Agrarian Party of Russia's republican council. Five years later he tied his fate to Moscow Mayor Yurii Luzhkov, joining Luzhkov's Fatherland movement. Clearly Merkushkin is able to win elections, though the way he managed the 1998 presidential campaign suggests that he is uneasy with the opposition in the region.

Merkushkin believes that the main priorities of the federal government in handling Russia's post–August 1998 crisis should be to support domestic producers and to cooperate with the regions in establishing anti-crisis measures (*NG*, 22 September 1998).

Policies: Pride in Vodka Imports

Merkushkin has restricted the import of vodka from other regions, and takes pride in himself for being the first regional leader to take such a measure. Yet he has also expressed an interest in westernizing the region's industry.

Relationships Between Key Players: Former Legislature Chair

Merkushkin is quite popular among the members of the republic's legislative assembly. He served as chairman of the assembly before it elected him republican president in September 1995 after the republic adopted a new constitution.

Ties to Moscow

Merkushkin has been on friendly terms with the Kremlin. After winning election to the republican presidency

Nikolai Ivanovich Merkushkin

5 February 1951—Born in the village of Novye Verkhi, Mordovia

Graduated from Mordovian State University and began work as a Komsomol functionary

1977–1987—Rose through the ranks to become the first secretary of the Mordovian Komsomol

1986–1990—First secretary of the Tengushevsk CPSU district committee

1990—Became second secretary of the Mordovian committee of the Communist Party

1992—Became chairman of the Mordovian State Property Fund

9 June 1993—Became co-chair of the Mordovian Economic Union

September 1993—Was invited to serve as a presidential representative, but refused

27 November 1994—Elected to the Mordovian Republican State Assembly

24 January 1995—Elected president of the Mordovian Republic State Assembly

September 1995—Elected president of the Republic of Mordovia

January 1996—Joined the second session of the Federation Council, serving as Deputy Chair of the Committee on Economic Policy

December 1997—Appointed Chairman of the Federation Council Committee for Regulations and Parliamentary Procedures

15 February 1998—Reelected president of the Republic of Mordovia

20 May 1998—Appointed to the Russian Federation representation to the Congress of Local and Regional Powers of Europe

in February 1998, Merkushkin received a message from Yeltsin congratulating him on his "convincing victory" (*RFE/RL*, 20 February 1998). The flagrant electoral violations that ensured Merkushkin's victory went unquestioned by the Russian president. This was consistent with Yeltsin's approach toward Russia's autonomous republics. As long as the republican leadership displayed a relatively supportive attitude toward the federal government and avoided overt separatist tactics, Yeltsin turned a blind eye to its domestic governance.

Merkushkin was offered a spot in former Prime Minister Sergei Kirienko's cabinet in spring 1998, but he rejected it.

Relations with Other Regions: Luzhkov Ally

Merkushkin is close to Moscow Mayor Yurii Luzhkov and participated in the establishment of his Fatherland party. Moscow buys more than half of Mordovia's output (*EWI RRR*, 19 February 1998). Mordovia has economic cooperation agreements with 11 regions: Moscow City, Astrakhan, Volgograd, Novosibirsk, Omsk, Orenburg, Sverdlovsk, Komi, Udmurtia, Khanty-Mansi,

and St. Petersburg. The agreements cover cooperation over a wide range of industries and sectors (*Ekonomika i Zhizn*, 4 February 1998).

Merkushkin is chair of the Greater Volga Association, so he was also automatically a member of the federal government presidium during the tenure of Prime Minister Yevgenii Primakov. He said that the meetings were "useful" although most observers described them as mere formalities. Other members of the association are the republics of Tatarstan, Chuvashia, and Marii El, and Astrakhan, Volgograd, Nizhnii Novgorod, Penza, Samara, Saratov, and Ulyanovsk oblasts.

Attitudes Toward Business

Merkushkin claims that he could revive Mordovia's economy if Western-standard technology was introduced into 10 to 15 of the region's major enterprises (*Ekonomika i Zhizn*, 4 February 1998).

Internet Sites in the Region

http://www.saransk.sitek.net/win/reclama/ogv.asp
This website offers contact information for republican and local officials.

MOSCOW CITY

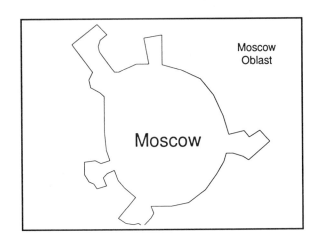

Moscow Oblast

Moscow

Territory: 1,200 km²
Population (as of 1 January 1998):
8,629,000

Major Cities:
Moscow, *capital* (pop. 8,298,900)
Zelenograd (205,800)

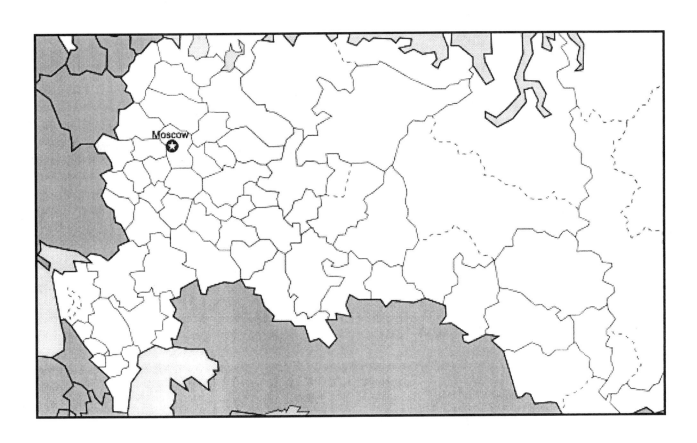

Basic Facts

Population (as of 1 Jan. 1998): 8,629,000 (5.87% of Russian total)

Ethnic breakdown (1989 census): Russians 89.7%, Ukrainians 2.9%, Jews 2.0%, Tatars 1.8%

Urban population (as of 1 Jan. 1998): 100% (Russia overall: 73.1%)

Student population (as of 1 Sept. 1997): 596 per 10,000 (Russia overall: 208/10,000)

Pensioner population (1997): 26.69% (Russia overall: 25.96%)

Percent of population with higher education (1989 census): 26.6% (Russia overall: 11.3%)

Percent of population working in 1997: Industry: 15.1% (Russian average: 23.0%); Agriculture: 0.2% (13.7%); Trade: 15.2% (13.5%); Culture: 20.3% (13.3%)

Average monthly personal income in July 1998: 3,777.3 new rubles (Russian average: 891.7 new rubles)

Average monthly personal expenses in July 1998: 3,103.8 new rubles (Russian average: 684.9 new rubles)

Average monthly subsistence requirement in 1998: 592 new rubles (Russian average: 438 new rubles)

Consumer price index (as of July 1998): 115 (Russia overall = 100)

Budgetary revenues (1997): 55,154.9 billion rubles (Russia overall: 433,378.2 billion rubles)

Budgetary expenditures (1997): 53,251.2 billion rubles (Russia overall: 468,111.6 billion rubles)

Industrial production as percentage of all Russian production (Jan.–Aug. 1998): 4.03%

Proportion of loss-making enterprises (as of July 1998): 31.7% (Russia overall: 50.4%)

Number of enterprises which have wage arrears (as of 1 Sept. 1998): 619 (0.46% of Russian total)

Capital investment (1997): 50,262.6 billion rubles (Russia overall: 408,797 billion rubles)

Sources of investment (1997): federal budget: 26.5% (Russian average: 10.2%); regional budget: 14.7% (10.5%); extra-budgetary funds: 58.8% (79.3%)

Foreign investment (1997): 8,475,664,000 USD (Russia overall: 12,294,734,000 USD)

Number of joint ventures (1997): 7,521 (51.05% of Russian total)

Fixed capital investment in joint ventures and foreign companies (1997): 5,858,222 million rubles (Russia overall: 16,265.4 billion rubles)

Number of small businesses (as of 1 July 1998): 176,200 (20.29% of Russian total)

Number of enterprises privatized in 1997: 175 (6.38% of Russian total), including those which used to be municipal property: 0% (Russian average: 66.4%); regional property: 83.4% (20.0%); federal property: 16.6% (13.6%)

Number of telephones per 100 families (1997): 100.8 (Russian average: 49.2)

Brief Overview

The capital city of the Russian Federation, Moscow is designated as a federal city along with St. Petersburg, giving it status equal to an oblast. Moscow is located in the central part of the East European plain, on the banks of Moscow River. It was first mentioned in historical annals in 1147, a date usually celebrated as Moscow's founding. During its early history, the city grew from a small settlement into the center of the increasingly powerful Moscow Principality. Its favorable location at an intersection of important trade routes encouraged growth. The military victories of Moscow princes over the Mongol and Lithuanian invaders in the 14th and 15th centuries strengthened the city's standing as the nucleus of a unified Russian state. Moscow remained the capital of Russia until Peter the Great moved his capital to the newly built St. Petersburg in 1712. However, Moscow retained its status as the "first" Russian capital and the country's political, economic, religious, and cultural center. The Soviet government moved the country's capital back to Moscow in 1918.

Moscow is one of the country's most advanced regions in economic terms. It has become the largest financial center of the country, housing over one thousand banks which control 60 percent of the capital in the entire country. Moscow has one of the best regional programs to support small businesses. About two-thirds of its 340,000 enterprises fall into this category and provide jobs for over 1.6 million people. It is also one of the richest regions in the country, with budgetary revenues exceeding expenditures.

Moscow attracts over two-thirds of all foreign investment in Russia. The most developed economic ties are with firms from Germany, Austria, the United States, Canada, and Italy. The city government actively works on several investment projects focusing particularly on housing construction, reconstruction of the city's center, and the development of communication and transportation infrastructures.

According to a 1998 survey by *Ekspert* magazine, the city ranked 1st among Russia's 89 regions in terms of investment potential and 2nd in terms of investment risk. A 1998 survey by Bank Austria ranked the city 1st in terms of investment climate.

Electoral History

2000 Presidential Election
Putin: 46.22%
Zyuganov: 19.16%
Yavlinskii: 18.57%
Govorukhin: 1.84%
Pamfilova: 1.83%
Tuleev: 1.61%
Zhirinovsky: 1.60%
Turnout: 66.94% (Russia overall: 68.64%)

1999 Parliamentary Elections
Fatherland–All Russia: 40.86%
Communist Party of the Russian Federation: 11.77%
Union of Right Forces: 11.49%
Yabloko: 9.53%
Unity: 6.95%
Zhirinovsky Bloc: 2.99%
In single-mandate districts: 9 Fatherland–All Russia, 1 Bloc of Nikolaev-Fedorov, 1 Yabloko, 4 independent
Turnout: 64.85% (Russia overall: 61.85%)

1999 Mayoral Election
Luzhkov (incumbent): 71.40%
Kirienko: 11.40%
Borodin: 6.10%
Turnout: 65.00%

1996 Presidential Election
Yeltsin: 61.16%/77.29% (first round/second round)
Zyuganov: 14.85%/17.93%
Lebed: 9.62%
Yavlinskii: 7.96%
Zhirinovsky: 1.46%
Turnout: 68.95%/70.38% (Russia overall: 69.67%/ 68.79%)

1996 Mayoral Election
Luzhkov (incumbent): 88.49%
Sergeeva (Moscow City legislature deputy): 4.94%
Krasnov: 3.31%
Filonenko: 0.26%
Turnout: 68.21%

1995 Parliamentary Elections
Our Home Is Russia: 19.05%
Yabloko: 14.94%
Communist Party of the Russian Federation: 14.84%
Russia's Democratic Choice: 11.55%
Congress of Russian Communities: 5.07%
Party of Workers' Self-Government: 4.45%
Forward, Russia: 3.36%
Liberal Democratic Party of Russia: 2.53%

Women of Russia: 2.45%

In single-mandate districts: 2 Russia's Democratic Choice, 1 Pamfilova–Gurov–Lysenko, 2 Forward, Russia!, 1 Common Cause, 1 Yabloko, 1 Party of Economic Freedom, 1 89 electoral bloc, 6 independent

Turnout: 62.83% (Russia overall: 64.37%)

1993 Constitutional Referendum

"Yes"—68.5%   "No"—29.4%

1993 Parliamentary Elections

Russia's Choice: 34.73%

Liberal Democratic Party of Russia: 12.82%

Yabloko: 12.08%

Communist Party of the Russian Federation: 11.03%

Party of Russian Unity and Concord: 6.48%

Democratic Party of Russia: 5.56%

Women of Russia: 4.35%

Agrarian Party of Russia: 1.43%

In single-mandate districts: 7 Russia's Choice, 1 Party of Economic Freedom, 1 Dignity and Charity, 1 Russian Movement for Democratic Reform, 5 independent

Turnout: 53.48% (Russia overall: 54.34%)

1991 Presidential Election

Yeltsin: 71.96%

Ryzhkov: 10.59%

Bakatin: 4.05%

Zhirinovsky: 4.01%

Makashov: 2.67%

Tuleev: 2.60%

Turnout: 66.79% (Russia overall: 76.66%)

Regional Political Institutions

Executive:

Mayor, 4-year term

Yurii Mikhailovich Luzhkov, elected June 1996

Ul. Tverskaya, 13; Moscow, 103032

Tel 7(095) 258–37–24

Fax 7(095) 234–32–95, 234–32–97

Legislative:

Unicameral

City Duma—35 members, 4-year term, elected December 1997

Chairman—Vladimir Mikhailovich Platonov, elected July 1998

Regional Politics

First Among Equals

Luzhkov is the model of the non-ideological governor who gets things done. He developed the slogan of being a "strong manager" (*khozyaistvennik*) rather than a "politician," and his example was soon copied by numerous other governors and gubernatorial candidates. His priority is rebuilding the city, with the most noticeable results apparent in the new look of Red Square and the Church of Christ the Savior (Andrey Fadin, "The Political Potential of the Mayor of Moscow," *Transition* 3:3, February 21, 1997, 33–35, and *Trud*, February 13, 1997).

Despite his authoritarian style of management, Luzhkov is wildly popular in the capital and was among the few serious contenders to replace President Boris Yeltsin in 2000 prior to Yeltsin's resignation in 1999. After taking over as mayor following the resignation of Gavriil Popov in June 1992, Luzhkov built up a popular base that allowed him to win 88.49 percent of the vote in his June 1996 election campaign (www.195.46.160.125/hist_96.htm). He was reelected in December 1999 with a strong showing of 71.4 percent of the vote.

While in the past Luzhkov was careful to support Yeltsin, as the June 2000 presidential elections approached, he planned his own presidential run. He founded the Fatherland party on 19 December 1998 and campaigned hard for the presidency. In the end he threw his support to the candidacy of former Prime Minister Yevgenii Primakov. As the election grew near it became clear that a Luzhkov-Primakov ticket would not be successful and they opted not to run in the race.

Luzhkov is a pragmatic nationalist. He initially took a hard-line stance on Chechnya, denouncing the Lebed-Maskhadov Khasavyurt accord, but then came out for Chechen independence. He courted nationalist support by demanding that Ukraine return Sevastopol and the rest of the Crimea peninsula to Russia.

Luzhkov's style of managerial authoritarianism has given him de facto control over the capital's mass media. Moscow newspapers are reluctant to criticize the mayor because his administration controls many of the buildings in which they are housed, as well as tax rates and communal services (*MT*, 4 December 1998). Moscow television stations, and particularly NTV, are inclined to give him favorable coverage because they are controlled by banks directly connected to the city budget. Thanks to the mayor's vigilance, no one has produced an investigation of the city's enormous business empire and how it was set up.

Human rights activists have accused Luzhkov of pursuing a racist policy against individuals of Caucasian descent, especially after a raid on a city mosque in September 1996. The Moscow government has refused to let people of all nationalities from the rest of the country move into the city without permits, even though this right is guaranteed in the Constitution. Nevertheless, Luzhkov has close personal relationships with key members of the major ethnic communities represented in the city and has taken a strong stand against extremist groups like the Russian National Unity (RNE).

Luzhkov worked in the Soviet chemicals industry until 1987, when Yeltsin tapped him to ensure the distribution of fruits and vegetables in the city. According to *Forbes*, "Luzhkov didn't so much end the corruption as manage it" (*Forbes*, 16 November 1998). In short, he made sure that the stores were well stocked, but did not ask questions about how the produce was delivered. Later he was put in charge of developing the city's small business network and worked hard to make sure that the city would get its share of the profits this sector produced. By the end of the Communist era, he was in charge of making the city work. Gavriil Popov, Moscow's first democratically elected mayor, took him on as his running mate. When Popov resigned in 1992, Luzhkov took over.

The crisis that began on 17 August 1998 threatened to tarnish Luzhkov's accomplishments in Moscow. However his failure to win the presidency in 2000 means that he will have to find a different outlet for his ambitions.

Executive Platform: Avowed Centrist

Luzhkov has defined himself as occupying the "left-center" in Russia's ideological spectrum. The platform of his Fatherland party supports a market economy, but with a strong role for the state. It seeks to address social problems while generally respecting individual freedom. It hopes to revive the defense sector and once again make Russia a strong and influential player on the international stage. Luzhkov claims it takes the best from the left and the right. Nevertheless, he was a strong critic of Yegor Gaidar, Anatolii Chubais, and other "young reformers" and in October 1998 began calling for them to be put on trial for the allegedly criminal way they privatized state property and for destroying the economy.

In the past, politicians espousing a centrist philosophy have had difficulty attracting much support in Russian politics. Russian centrist parties have tried to unite groups that do not really work well together or lack a coherent program. In either case, such an approach makes it difficult to generate excitement among voters (*NG*, 19 December 1998). When the party is organized around a strong political figure, it tends not to outlast the founder's own political career.

In laying the groundwork for the Fatherland party, former Security Council chairman Andrei Kokoshin led Luzhkov's brain trust in developing the party platform (*Itogi*, 21 December 1998). The key men behind the party initially were Congress of Russian Communities' leader Dmitrii Rogozin and Duma member Stepan Sulakshin, who came up with the idea that Luzhkov should define himself as part of the "left-center." Former presidential spokesman Sergei Yastrzhembskii handled public relations duties. Behind them was Vladimir Yevtushenkov, the head of the Moscow Sistema Corporation (see Relationships Between Key Players). *Kommersant* has charged that Yevtushenkov plays the same role with Luzhkov that former presidential bodyguard Aleksandr Korzhakov did with Yeltsin (*Kommersant Weekly*, 24 November 1998). In June 1999, Luzhkov named former Tax Minister Georgii Boos to head his campaign staff.

Luzhkov has cultivated alliances with Russia's regional elite (see Relations with Other Regions), trade unions, and moderate nationalists. In particular, this group included some factions inside Our Home Is Russia (such as former Duma faction leader Aleksandr Shokhin, who left the party in December 1998) and the non-Communist groups of the umbrella opposition National Patriotic Union (particularly Aleksei Podberezkin's Spiritual Heritage). He also set up alliances with several of Russia's small parties, including the Federation of Independent Trade Unions' Union of Labor (headed by Andrei Isaev), the Congress of Russian Communities (which backed Aleksandr Lebed in the 1995 Duma elections), Derzhava (the former party of Kursk Governor Aleksandr Rutskoi, now led by Luzhkov advisor Konstantin Zatulin), and Women of Russia. Luzhkov did not invite former ally Andrei Nikolaev and his Union of Popular Power and Labor to join Fatherland.

On 17 June Rogozin announced that the Congress of Russian Communities was leaving Fatherland. The Congress broke with Luzhkov because Rogozin did not support the party's efforts to merge with the All Russia regional bloc (*EWI RRR*, 15 July 1999).

Policies: Stresses Differences with Federal Policies

Although he remained loyal to Yeltsin in 1993 and 1996, Luzhkov has been a longtime critic of Yegor Gaidar and Anatolii Chubais. He blamed them for moving too quickly with economic reforms, cheating the people through voucher privatization, and selling state property at ridiculously low prices. Luzhkov conducted his own privatization policies in Moscow, the main aim of which was to consolidate his personal power.

Luzhkov regularly blasted the federal government's scheme of issuing GKOs, the now largely worthless Russian T-bills, saying that Russia was running its own pyramid scheme. Following the August 1998 crisis, Luzhkov joined many other governors in imposing price limits on some staple foods, despite federal objections. He favored renationalizing the country's vodka industry to generate more state revenue and wanted to bring down electricity, gas, and rail transport prices to make it cheaper to live and do business. At a 24 November 1998 meeting of the city government, he urged that the city remain committed to its plans to build new schools and medical clinics.

To pay for these programs, however, Luzhkov was forced to adopt some unpopular measures. In January 1999 he raised the price of monthly bus and metro passes by one third. The price of water rose 45 percent in December 1998, rents were set to go up 50 percent in April 1999, and electricity rates jumped 30 percent in July 1999 (Floriana Fossato, "Realist Luzhkov Versus Populist Luzhkov," *RFE/RL Newsline*, 1 December 1998).

Relationships Between Key Players: Luzhkov Controls Essentially Everything

Politically, Luzhkov dominates the city. The city Duma is chaired by Luzhkov ally Vladimir Platonov. In the 14 December 1997 elections, city voters handed Luzhkov a major victory by electing 26 of 35 candidates he supported for the 35-seat body. Only *Novaya Gazeta* journalist Yevgenii Bunimovich, who was backed by Yabloko, could be considered an opponent of the mayor. In general, the body carries out Luzhkov's wishes. However, toward the summer of 1999 Luzhkov and the city Duma came into conflict regarding the introduction of a sales tax in the city. Although both Luzhkov and the Duma favored establishing a sales tax, Luzhkov pushed

for a 5 percent rate, which the Duma considered too high. Ultimately the two sides concurred on a 4 percent rate, but the Duma managed to postpone its implementation, initiating the tax at a 2 percent rate on 1 July 1999 instead (*EWI RRR*, 27 May 1999). The new tax went into effect with little fuss.

Beyond his political monopoly, Luzhkov has a strong hand in the city economically. The Moscow city government owns stakes in more than 500 companies, including controlling interests in 260 firms (Bloomberg News Service, "Moscow Mayor Luzhkov Aims for Presidency: Bloomberg Profile," 20 December 1998). The city administration controls two big auto plants, an oil company, several large construction firms, part of the local phone and electric utilities, two fast food chains (including part of the local McDonald's), dozens of food processing plants, several big hotels, and hundreds of shops and restaurants (*Forbes*, 16 November 1998). The city government earns more than $1 billion a year from renting or selling its property. Nevertheless, many of the city-owned firms are unprofitable and a huge drain on public funds.

The Sistema company (founded in 1993) serves as the mayor's business manager. The same Yevtushenkov who played a major role in Fatherland and the mayor's presidential campaign is chairman of the board of directors. Sistema's holdings include telecommunications companies, high technology firms, Moscow's largest advertising agency, Intourist, Children's World department store, financial services, and the food industry.

Moscow benefits enormously from its status as Russia's capital. Many of Russia's most powerful companies and all the natural monopolies (Gazprom, Unified Energy Systems) pay their taxes in Moscow and much of the money remains there. This income gives Luzhkov the money he needs to finance many of his operations. Most of Russia's major banks were also based in Moscow, at least until the 17 August 1998 crisis hit. Moscow's ability to monopolize much of this money gave it enormous leverage over the rest of the country.

The mayor's major building project now is the Moscow City complex, designed to rival the City of London. However, since the financial crisis, the project has been in trouble, because it was largely backed by the bankrupt SBS-Agro bank. The huge new shopping complex under Manezh Square, where many of the store fronts were vacant in summer 1999, is also in jeopardy as is the alliance between ZIL and France's Renault. The city has loaned 240 million rubles to ZIL alone.

The Moscow mayor has an extensive media empire.

He has long enjoyed the support of *Moskovskii Komsomolets* and the media controlled by Media Most, including NTV, *Segodnya* newspaper, *Itogi* magazine, and others. Additionally, he has set up the TV-Center network, which went on the air in June 1997 and broadcasts to about 50 regions. Luzhkov's critics say that the station broadcasts only good news or no news about the mayor (*MT*, 4 December 1998). When the network ran into financial difficulties at the end of 1998, Luzhkov said that he would finance it from the city budget (*RFE/ RL*, 30 December 1998). In fall 1998 he set up the Metropolis publishing center which publishes *Metro* newspaper (distributed free of charge), the newspapers *Rossiya* (founded in March 1998), *Literaturnaia gazeta*, *Kultura*, and *Vechernyaya Moskva* (Laurie Belin, "Moscow Mayor's Media Empire Continues to Grow," *RFE/ RL Newsline*, 24 August 1998). Luzhkov also controls the Moskovskaya pravda printing press which prints 40 magazines and 128 newspapers, including *Moskovskii komsomolets*, *Novaya gazeta*, and *Segodnya* (*NYT*, 23 November 1998).

Media outlets financed by Boris Berezovskii, including Russian Public Television, Russia's top broadcaster, do provide critical coverage of the mayor and certainly helped to sink his presidential run. But most of the media hesitate to criticize Luzhkov because he controls the land under their offices and their apartments, and they could encounter numerous obstacles thrown up by the municipal authorities. Additionally, Luzhkov has won dozens of slander cases again different media outlets, another good reason for journalists not to dig too deeply into his affairs (*WP*, 6 December 1998 and *NG*, 12 November 1998).

Ties to Moscow: Distancing Himself from Yeltsin

The city of Moscow plays an enormous role in the affairs of the entire country, so its leader is automatically a figure of national prominence. It also has enormous economic heft since it contributes about 30 percent of Russia's taxes.

Luzhkov strongly supported Yeltsin's 1996 reelection campaign. But from the beginning of the crisis in August 1998, he called for Yeltsin to step down in an effort to speed up the timing of the next presidential elections. Some media even reported that the mayor circulated rumors that he never had good relations with Yeltsin (*Ekspert*, 26 October 1998). At Fatherland's founding congress, former presidential First Deputy Chief of Staff Oleg Sysuev said that the presidential administration supported Luzhkov's programmatic goals, but not his criticism of past federal policies (*Segodnya*, 21 December 1998). Sysuev was then working closely with Luzhkov's enemies Gaidar and Chubais to develop a new right-center party. Gaidar, Chernomyrdin, Chubais, Nemtsov, and Kirienko are among Luzhkov's harshest critics (*Izvestiya*, 22 December 1998).

In the summer of 1999, relations between Luzhkov and the Kremlin deteriorated into all-out war. With the appointment of Vladimir Putin as prime minister and Yeltsin's preferred successor, Luzhkov's national political prospects went into a steep decline. When Putin became president, Luzhkhov expressed his loyalty and the two did not attack each other.

In June 1998 Luzhkov signed a power-sharing treaty with the federal government.

Relations with Other Regions: Building Strong Horizontal Ties

Luzhkov has sought tirelessly to build ties with other governors and mayors across the country to advance his political and economic goals. Luckily for him, the attraction was mutual. Building alliances with Luzhkov could deliver lucrative benefits for Russia's other governors, since the city of Moscow is Russia's richest and most powerful region.

By the end of October 1998, Luzhkov had concluded economic cooperation agreements with 72 of the 88 other regions (*Ekspert*, 26 October 1998). Many of these treaties were designed to ensure that Moscow had sufficient supplies since it has few resources on its own. Some critics pointed out, however, that many of these agreements are not in Moscow's interests and were concluded for the purpose of currying support for the capital's mayor.

Luzhkov recruited many regional executives to join his Fatherland party including Novosibirsk's Vitalii Mukha, Nizhnii Novgorod's Ivan Sklyarov, Yaroslavl's Anatolii Lisitsyn, Arkhangelsk's Anatolii Yefremov, Mordovia's Nikolai Merkushkin, Moscow Oblast's Anatolii Tyazhlov, Udmurtia's Aleksandr Volkov, Murmansk's Yurii Yevdokimov, Komi's Yurii Spiridonov, and Karelia's Sergei Katanandov. Even governors who did participate covered their bases by working with a variety of other organizations. The All Russia regional movement organized by Tatarstan President Mintimer Shaimiev, and other regional leaders of several ethnically defined regions, formed a coalition with Fatherland for the December 1999 State Duma elections.

Samara Governor Konstantin Titov pointedly declined to join Fatherland and ultimately pursued his own unsuccessful run for the presidency.

Many governors owe Luzhkov favors because he helped them win election. For example, he strongly supported the campaigns of St. Petersburg Governor Vladimir Yakovlev and Nizhnii Novgorod Governor Ivan Sklyarov. Sometimes such efforts failed. Luzhkov campaigned for former Krasnoyarsk Governor Valerii Zubov, but Zubov was soundly defeated by Aleksandr Lebed in the spring of 1998.

Luzhkov also sought additional power in the Federation Council, as attempts in October 1998 to remove Speaker Yegor Stroev from his position attest (*Itogi,* 9 November 1998).

Luzhkov's main efforts to build ties with other governors are in the European part of Russia, and he is accordingly more popular there than in the Urals or Siberia. Luzhkov has particularly strong ties with the leaders of the Greater Volga interregional association. He has helped them by working out an aircraft construction deal with Ukraine in which Antonov planes will be built in Samara and Saratov oblasts and a tractor deal with Belarus that will bring business to Volgograd and Nizhnii Novgorod. Luzhkov has also built up ties with governors from agricultural regions by allowing them access to Moscow's huge consumer market. Each part of the city is assigned to particular regions which have the right to supply them. For example, the northern district of the city belongs to Bashkortostan and Kursk (*Itogi,* 9 November 1998). Such agreements have strengthened Luzhkov's ties with these governors.

Luzhkov is trying to impose strict discipline on Fatherland's regional branches in order to avoid the fate of Viktor Chernomyrdin's Our Home Is Russia, the former party of power that has essentially collapsed partly because it relied heavily on an unruly collection of regional elite. In particular, he has sought to prevent them from participating autonomously in elections. In December Yekaterinburg Mayor Arkadii Chernetskii suggested that such a requirement might prevent his Our Home–Our City movement from joining Fatherland. Chernetskii ultimately did decide to lead the Yekaterinburg Fatherland branch. Additionally, many opportunist politicians in the regions saw joining Luzhkov's new party as a way to advance their careers, making it difficult for Luzhkov to assemble the best personnel.

Many governors feared that if Luzhkov became

president he would strengthen the federal government, limiting many of the prerogatives the governors enjoyed under Yeltsin. Tatarstan's Shaimiev, for example, preferred former Prime Minister Yevgenii Primakov as a presidential candidate, clearly thinking he would be a less energetic and forceful leader than Luzhkov was likely to be.

Many people outside the capital see Moscow's success as the result of the city appropriating wealth that was originally generated in the regions. As a result, they view the city with some animosity.

Foreign Relations: A Strong Russia

Luzhkov is part of a broad consensus in Russia that wants to make the country a stronger player on the international stage. However, Luzhkov is not afraid to pursue foreign policies that differ from the official line of Russia's Ministry of Foreign Affairs. In particular, he claims that the Crimean peninsula belongs to Russia even though it is currently part of Ukraine. Luzhkov also supports some form of integration with Belarus, a policy that has different and changing degrees of support within the different departments of the federal government. The mayor planned a visit to Belarus in 1999.

While encouraging Western investment in Moscow, Luzhkov has blasted Western leaders for being too trusting of the "young reformers" in past Russian governments. Like many other Russian politicians, he is critical of NATO expansion, the Western use of force in Iraq, and NATO's intervention in the Kosovo conflict.

Luzhkov is working hard to build ties to the currently fashionable social-democratic leaders of Western Europe including British Prime Minister Tony Blair and German Chancellor Gerhard Schroeder. He visited both countries at the end of 1998.

Attitudes Toward Business: Strong Western Inflow Now a Liability

Before the crisis began, Moscow won 80 percent of foreign investment coming into Russia, a sum that amounted to $12 billion during Luzhkov's tenure. By the end of 1998, the city hosted some 5,000 foreign companies and joint ventures (*Forbes,* 16 November 1998).

Following the 1998 crisis, however, Moscow suffered more than other regions. Foreign investors are fleeing Russia in droves and much of the city's booming financial industry has collapsed. Moscow needed

Yurii Mikhailovich Luzhkov

21 September 1936—Born to a carpenter's family

1958—Graduated from the I. M. Gubkin Petrochemical and Gas Industrial Institute

1958–1964—Worked in a plastics laboratory

1964–1974—Headed a section of the USSR Chemical Industry Ministry

1968–1991—Member of the Communist Party of the Soviet Union

1974–1980—Director of a experimental design bureau in the USSR Chemical Industry Ministry

1975–1977—Member of the Babushkin Raion Council

1977–1990—Member of the Moscow City Council

1980–1986—General Director of the scientific-production association Neftekhimavtomatika (Automate Petrochemical)

1986–1987—Head of the Department of Science and Technology and a member of the USSR Ministry of Chemical Industry's collegium

1987–1990—First Deputy Chairman of the Moscow City executive committee, also chairman of the Moscow Agroindustrial Committee

1987–1990—Member of the RSFSR Supreme Soviet

1990–1991—Acting chairman of the city executive committee and then chairman

12 June 1991—Elected vice-mayor of Moscow with Mayor Gavriil Popov, also became prime minister of the Moscow government

August–December 1991—Deputy director of the Committee for operational management of the USSR economy

June 1992—Became mayor of Moscow and prime minister of the city government following Popov's resignation

April 1994—Appointed member of the Presidential Council

June 1996—Reelected mayor with 88.49% of the vote

19 December 1998—Founded Fatherland political party

December 1999—Reelected mayor with 71.5% of the vote

to come up with $210 million during 1999 to service its debts, though analysts said that the situation was not disastrous. Additionally, before the crisis, the city relied heavily on imported food. Since the value of the ruble plunged, Moscow had to find other sources.

Internet Sites in the Region

http://www.mos.ru/
This is the official server of the Moscow mayor's office. It is currently under construction.

http://www.duma.mos.ru/
The server of the Moscow City Duma provides exten-
sive information about the city's legislature as well as a searchable database of city legislation.

http://195.46.160.125/
This is the server of the Moscow City Electoral Commission. Besides data on local elections, it provides recent reports of the Central Electoral Commission.

http://www.luzhkov-otchestvo.ru/
This is the home page for Moscow Mayor Yurii Luzhkov's Fatherland. The site contains extensive information about the party, including the program, charter, leadership structure, regional branches, and materials from recent congresses.

MOSCOW OBLAST

Territory: 47,000 km²
Population (as of 1 January 1998): 6,564,000

Note: These data include the territory but exclude the population of Moscow City.

Major Cities:

Podolsk (195,400)
Lyubertsy (165,600)
Kolomna (151,900)
Mytishchi (155,400)
Elektrostal (148,000)

Serpukhov (136,900)
Khimki (134,500)
Korolev (134,000)
Balashikha (133,400)

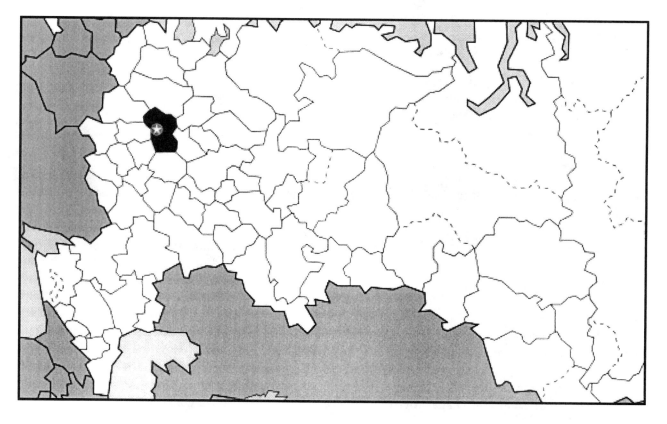

Basic Facts

Population (as of 1 Jan. 1998): 6,564,000 (4.46% of Russian total)

Ethnic breakdown (1989 census): Russians 93.5%, Ukrainians 2.8%

Urban population (as of 1 Jan. 1998): 79.7% (Russia overall: 73.1%)

Student population (as of 1 Sept. 1997): 127 per 10,000 (Russia overall: 208/10,000)

Pensioner population (1997): 27.35% (Russia overall: 25.96%)

Percent of population with higher education (1989 census): 14.8% (Russia overall: 11.3%)

Percent of population working in (1997): Industry: 23.5% (Russian average: 23.0%); Agriculture: 7.0% (13.7%); Trade: 14.6% (13.5%); Culture: 16.6% (13.3%)

Average monthly personal income in July 1998: 716.0 new rubles (Russian average: 891.7 new rubles)

Average monthly personal expenses in July 1998: 483.7 new rubles (Russian average: 684.9 new rubles)

Average monthly subsistence requirement in 1998: 413 new rubles (Russian average: 438 new rubles)

Consumer price index (as of July 1998): 108 (Russia overall = 100)

Budgetary revenues (1997): 16,160.9 billion rubles (Russia overall: 433,378.2 billion rubles)

Budgetary expenditures (1997): 17,174.2 billion rubles (Russia overall: 468,111.6 billion rubles)

Industrial production as percentage of all Russian production (Jan.–Aug. 1998): 2.07%

Proportion of loss-making enterprises (as of July 1998): 42.1% (Russia overall: 50.4%)

Number of enterprises which have wage arrears (as of 1 Sept. 1998): 1,575 (1.17% of Russian total)

Agricultural production as percentage of all Russian production (1997): 3.03%

Number of private farms (as of 1 Jan. 1998): 6,652 (2.43% of Russian total)

Capital investment (1997): 13,362.9 billion rubles (Russia overall: 408,797 billion rubles)

Sources of investment (1997): federal budget: 15.3% (Russian average: 10.2%); regional budget: 8.0% (10.5%); extra-budgetary funds: 76.7% (79.3%)

Foreign investment (1997): 74,475,000 USD (Russia overall: 12,294,734,000 USD)

Number of joint ventures (1997): 112 (0.76% of Russian total)

Fixed capital investment in joint ventures and foreign companies (1997): 347,076 million rubles (Russia overall: 16,265.4 billion rubles)

Number of small businesses (as of 1 July 1998): 35,600 (4.10% of Russian total)

Number of enterprises privatized in 1997: 95 (3.46% of Russian total), including those which used to be municipal property: 82.1% (Russian average: 66.4%); regional property: 4.2% (20.0%); federal property: 13.7% (13.6%)

Number of telephones per 100 families (1997): in cities: 50.1 (Russian average: 49.2); in villages: 19.0 (19.8)

Brief Overview

Moscow Oblast surrounds the capital and is located in the basins of the Moscow and Oka rivers and borders Kaluga, Smolensk, Tver, Yaroslavl, Vladimir, Ryazan and Tula oblasts.

The oblast's defining feature is its close integration with the City of Moscow, as well as a high level of industrialization. During the Soviet period, the oblast was one of the country's military industry centers. Now its GDP comes from machine building (30 percent of overall production), consumer goods production (24 percent), building materials manufacturing (16 percent), power generation (11 percent), and production of chemicals (8 percent). Some of the country's largest enterprises are located in the oblast, such as Energiya (aerospace), Energomash (machine building), and Elektrostal (steel).

The oblast houses over 20 percent of Russia's research institutions, which produce about a quarter of all research studies. Those facilities are largely a legacy of the region's military complex.

The region has legislation favorable for both domestic and foreign investment. Given its proximity to Moscow, the oblast is home to numerous joint ventures and other investment projects. According to a 1998 survey by *Ekspert* magazine, it had become less dangerous to invest in the oblast's economy since 1997: the oblast ranked 3rd among Russia's 89 regions in terms of investment potential and 14th in terms of investment risk. A 1998 survey by Bank Austria ranked the oblast 3rd in terms of investment climate.

Electoral History

2000 Presidential Election
Putin: 47.92%
Zyuganov: 27.94%
Yavlinskii: 10.31%
Zhirinovsky: 2.24%
Tuleev: 2.13%
Turnout: 64.69% (Russia overall: 68.64%)

1999/2000 Gubernatorial Election
Gromov (State Duma deputy): 20.90%/48.09% (first round/second round)
Seleznev (State Duma speaker): 27.52%/46.39%
Tikhonov: 14.34%
Tyazhlov (incumbent): 11.39%
Fedorov: 9.15%
Turnout: 62.19%/46.01%

1999 Parliamentary Elections
Fatherland–All Russia: 27.55%
Communist Party of the Russian Federation: 19.59%
Unity: 9.96%
Yabloko: 8.27%
Union of Right Forces: 8.21%
Zhirinovsky Bloc: 4.78%
In single-mandate districts: 4 Fatherland–All Russia, 2 Communist Party of the Russian Federation, 1 Russian Socialist Party, 4 independent
Turnout: 59.30% (Russia overall: 61.85%)

1996 Presidential Election
Yeltsin: 44.15%/64.20% (first round/second round)
Zyuganov: 24.05%/29.89%
Lebed: 15.07%
Yavlinskii: 7.87%
Zhirinovsky: 3.00%
Turnout: 70.46%/70.79% (Russia overall: 69.67%/68.79%)

1995 Gubernatorial Election
Tyazhlov (incumbent): 70.83%/43.33% (first round/second round)
Galchenko (oblast legislature deputy chairman): 21.41%/14.67%
Antonov (Communists–Agrarians–Socialists): 14.07%
Dorkin (local administration head): 5.74%
Kiselev (State Duma deputy, LDPR): 3.88%
Churilov: 3.45%
Turnout: 64.35%/29.59%

1995 Parliamentary Elections
Communist Party of the Russian Federation: 22.16%
Our Home Is Russia: 13.79%
Yabloko: 10.99%
Congress of Russian Communities: 6.82%
Liberal Democratic Party of Russia: 5.20%
Russia's Democratic Choice: 5.19%
Women of Russia: 4.31%
In single-mandate districts: 4 Communist Party of the Russian Federation, 2 Yabloko, 1 Russia's Democratic Choice, 1 Bloc of Ivan Rybkin, 1 Power to People, 2 independent
Turnout: 63.16% (Russia overall: 64.37%)

1993 Constitutional Referendum
"Yes"—61.0%   "No"—35.9%

1993 Parliamentary Elections
Liberal Democratic Party of Russia: 26.64%
Russia's Choice: 19.82%
Communist Party of the Russian Federation: 10.82%
Yabloko: 9.75%
Party of Russian Unity and Concord: 7.20%
Women of Russia: 6.69%
Democratic Party of Russia: 5.92%
Agrarian Party of Russia: 3.99%
In single-mandate districts: 2 Yabloko, 1 Russian
  Party of Free Labor, 1 Liberal Democratic Party
  of Russia, 6 independent
From electoral associations: 4 Liberal Democratic
  Party of Russia, 2 Agrarian Party of Russia,
  1 Democratic Party of Russia
Turnout: 54.77% (Russia overall: 54.34%)

1991 Presidential Election
Yeltsin: 62.47%
Ryzhkov: 13.54%
Zhirinovsky: 6.45%
Tuleev: 4.92%
Makashov: 3.87%
Bakatin: 3.45%
Turnout: 75.44% (Russia overall: 76.66%)

Regional Political Institutions

Executive:
  Governor, 4-year term
  Boris Vsevolodovich Gromov, elected January 2000
    Staraya Pl., 6; Moscow, 103070
    Tel 7(095) 206–60–93, 206–62–78;
    Fax 7(095) 928–98–12

Legislative:
  Unicameral
  Oblast Duma—50 members, 4-year term, elected
  December 1997
  Chairman—Aleksandr Yevgenevich Zharov, elected
  December 1997

Regional Politics

Former General Wins Heated Battle for Highly-Ranked Investment Region

Former General Boris Gromov, known for his role in leading the Soviet troops out of Afghanistan, was elected governor of Moscow Oblast on 9 January 2000.

Running on a centrist platform backed by Moscow Mayor Yurii Luzhkov, Gromov pushed out incumbent Anatolii Tyazhlov in the first round and was able to squeak by Communist State Duma Speaker Gennadii Seleznev in the second round with a victory margin of less than 2 percent. Tyazhlov had been a market reformer with close relations to both Russian President Boris Yeltsin and Luzhkov. He had offered strong incentives to investors, and successfully piggy-backed on Moscow City's success to win about 20 percent of Russia's foreign direct investment. Despite these successes, Tyazhlov had difficulties with an unruly local legislature, serious ecological problems, and a demanding population. These various stresses caused Tyazhlov's popularity to decline, making the region a lucrative target for such national figures as Gromov and Seleznev.

The 1999/2000 Moscow Oblast gubernatorial elections attracted considerable attention at the federal level due to both the national stature of the candidates and the movements supporting them. In addition to the support rendered to Gromov by Luzhkov and Fatherland–All Russia, both Yabloko and Union of Right Forces backed Gromov in the second round. Seleznev, however, received the endorsement of then Acting President Vladimir Putin in what was seen as a clear statement of opposition to Luzhkov.

Gromov made his career in the military, ultimately serving as the last Soviet commander in Afghanistan. He was elected to the USSR Congress of People's Deputies in 1989. He signed the notorious declaration "Word to the People," which served as the intellectual basis for the 1991 coup. However, during the event, he blocked the storming of the White House. At various times he served as first deputy minister of internal affairs and deputy defense minister. In 1995 he led the My Fatherland bloc in the State Duma elections. His party did not pass the five-percent barrier, but he won a single-member district seat from Saratov. In the Duma, he was a member of the Russian Regions faction.

Executive Platform: Emphasis on Social Issues

Throughout his political career Gromov has consistently been concerned with issues of social welfare, particularly regarding issues of importance to veterans and pensioners. He heads the veterans' association Boevoe Bratstvo, which brings together 60 organizations, including private enterprises, and participates in federal and regional programs. Its purpose is to provide assistance to veterans and the families of military personnel killed in the line of duty (Radio 1, 17 November 1999).

In his campaign platform Gromov spoke of raising the income levels of doctors, teachers, and other public sector workers in Moscow Oblast to those in Moscow City and securing subsidies from Moscow City to help improve the oblast's infrastructure. Gromov also emphasized support to small and medium-sized businesses, creating conditions for increasing salaries and pensions, ensuring social benefits, and improving health care and education in the region.

Gromov's predecessor, Tyazhlov, generally supported market reform. Under his leadership, Moscow Oblast became one of Russia's top investment regions, following only the cities of Moscow and St. Petersburg (T. Matiyasevich et al., *Russia: Regional Risk Rating*, Vienna: Bank Austria, 1998). Nevertheless, he felt that the government should more rigidly control the process of economic reform that is being carried out in the regions. Tyazhlov asserted that the federal government should more clearly divide economic responsibilities between the federal and oblast levels. He argued that establishing such boundaries would allow regional executives more control over oblast programs (NNS). Gromov has also advocated a stronger role for oblast authorities in carrying out economic reform.

Both Gromov and Tyazhlov belong to Moscow Mayor Yurii Luzhkov's Fatherland movement. Thus it seemed odd that the two would both compete in the region's gubernatorial elections with the party's endorsement. Tyazhlov was head of the Moscow Oblast branch of Fatherland, having left his position as chairman of the oblast branch of Our Home Is Russia. Gromov, however, had strong support within the national leadership of Fatherland, and was given the seventh spot on the Fatherland–All Russia 1999 State Duma party list, even though he had expressed his intention to compete in the Moscow Oblast gubernatorial elections on the same day.

Gromov was a strong critic of the 1994–96 Chechen war. He also opposed the September 1999 military offensive and supported using whatever means possible to extract Russian soldiers from this quagmire, including negotiations with the Chechen fighters. He believes that Chechnya is part of Russia, but that the military campaigns have only complicated the problem. Such statements are implicitly critical of Vladimir Putin, who stood behind the renewed use of force.

Policies

Tyazhlov's policies focused on developing Moscow Oblast's economy and creating conditions favorable for business development. To encourage foreign investment, Moscow Oblast grants special tax holidays to outside investors who bring in more than $1 million. Although Gromov also intends to support business development, his priority is improving the region's social infrastructure and developing closer ties to the Moscow city government.

Tyazhlov's tenure as governor was marked by several initiatives supporting small business. In March 1995 he signed a decree creating the Moscow Universal Leasing Company for developing small and medium-sized enterprises (NNS). In the fall of 1997 the Moscow Oblast Duma adopted a series of laws simplifying tax procedures for small businesses. Local tax agencies have the right to issue licenses that allow these small businesses to pay taxes at a special rate. Enterprises working in agriculture, health services, and education are exempt from paying the license fee. Additionally, in late 1997, the governor signed a directive allocating 300 million old rubles (approximately $50,000) to assist in the development of small and medium-sized businesses (*NG*, 18 November 1997). Oblast tax legislation provides benefits to foreign and domestic producers.

Relationships Between Key Players: Challenges Ahead

Given his narrow victory over Communist State Duma Speaker Gennadii Seleznev, Gromov will likely encounter difficulties dealing with the local opposition in the region, reducing his ability to govern effectively. Tyazhlov, whose political and economic position was essentially similar to Gromov's, had turbulent relations with the regional legislature. In the run-up to the 17 December 1997 legislative elections, Tyazhlov fought a bruising battle with his opposition to define how much power the regional legislature would have. Tyazhlov successfully backed a referendum held on election day that cut the power of the legislature by transforming 25 of the 50 members from full-time to part-time legislators. Until then, all deputies had served on a full-time basis, giving them ample opportunity to oppose the governor. With half the lawmakers forced to hold other jobs to support themselves, the legislature has fewer resources to oppose the governor's initiatives. The former Duma unsuccessfully fought the referendum in the courts, and on election day a majority of the voters backed the governor's position, limiting the Duma's power.

Although the Oblast Duma elected in December 1997 consisted almost entirely of reformers, the situation at the end of Tyazhlov's term was far from harmonious. Only 20 percent of those elected in December 1997 had served in the previous Duma, meaning that few of the deputies who had challenged Tyazhlov's authority remained. Ten of the 50 deputies are the directors of industrial enterprises. This increased number of businessmen in the Duma had inspired hope that these deputies would be more pragmatic than their predecessors. The situation seemed even more auspicious for Tyazhlov since his candidate Aleksandr Zharov was elected Duma chairman.

Despite Tyazhlov's apparent victory in the elections, the governor struggled with the Moscow Oblast Duma in adopting regional budgets. The assembly essentially split into two factions: for the social and economic rebirth of Moscow Oblast, which generally supported Tyazhlov, and Our Moscow Oblast, which was more leftist. The large deficits became the main obstacle to adopting both the 1998 and 1999 budgets. In May 1999 the Moscow Oblast Duma finally adopted its 1999 budget, providing for a 5.5 billion ruble deficit. This deficit greatly exceeded the 5 percent limit provided for by regional law. It also was designed with the expectation that regional debt should not exceed 30 percent of the budget's revenue, yet at the beginning of 1999 the region's debt was nearly 3 billion rubles, or more than 60 percent of the oblast's annual income. This situation demonstrates that the region's problems are so complex, even like-minded politicians have difficulty addressing major issues (*NG*, 28 May 1998).

Ties to Moscow: Lack of Support from Federal Leadership

Renowned for his leadership in Afghanistan and having remained vocal and visible on the federal political scene, Gromov is well known and respected among Russia's political elite. However, Acting President Vladimir Putin's support of Seleznev to counter Gromov in the second round of the Moscow Oblast gubernatorial elections is indicative that the region's relations with the Kremlin will not be as strong as during Tyazhlov's tenure. Yeltsin appointed Tyazhlov governor of Moscow Oblast in 1991 and Tyazhlov repeatedly expressed his loyalty to Yeltsin. In December 1995 Tyazhlov was one of the few governors Yeltsin let stand for election before the June 1996 presidential election. Until that time, most governors were appointed directly by the president. Letting Tyazhlov seek a popular mandate meant that Yeltsin felt that he was both politically reliable and capable of winning popular support among his constituents. During the 1996 presidential campaign, the governor headed up the local committee to support the president.

Putin's decision to support Seleznev rather than Gromov is related less to Gromov's personal background than to his alliance with Luzhkov. Putin chose to ally with the Communists because he felt Luzhkov was a more dangerous rival. It remains to be seen how Gromov's ties to Luzhkov will impact his relations with Putin and the federal government. Nevertheless, in spite of his relatively cool relationship with the central leadership, Gromov commands some influence in federal institutions, particularly in the State Duma, where he has several supporters. Following the first round of the elections, Gromov met with Patriarch of All Russia Aleksei II. The two discussed the situation in Chechnya and other problems concerning political and social life in Russia.

Relations with Other Regions: Close to Luzhkov

Like Tyazhlov, Gromov has close relations with Moscow Mayor Yurii Luzhkov, and received Luzhkov's endorsement for his electoral bid. For Moscow Oblast, whose economic and political life is intrinsically linked to Moscow City, maintaining good relations with the city's leadership is arguably more important than having close connections in the federal government. The oblast has clearly benefited from the strong relations its governors have had with Moscow City.

In February 1997 Tyazhlov signed an agreement with Luzhkov to increase the oblast's provision of food to the city. This agreement is primarily political since goods from other regions are often less expensive and of better quality than those from Moscow Oblast. A week before the agreement was signed, agricultural workers in the oblast had begun to collect signatures for a petition to recall Tyazhlov and his regional agricultural minister Yurii Korolev. Agricultural workers in the region blamed Tyazhlov and Korolev for the oblast's severe agricultural crisis. Thus the agreement between Luzhkov and Tyazhlov was signed with the intention of neutralizing the workers' dissatisfaction with the oblast's leadership. In return for this political favor, Luzhkov hoped to achieve his long-pursued goal of gaining control of the forests surrounding Moscow (*OMRI RRR*, 12 February 1997).

In August 1997 Tyazhlov and several other regional leaders signed an agreement calling for stronger co-operative relations between domestic industries and enterprises (*Novosti*, 30 August 1997). The goals of this agreement are to help Russian industries and products maintain a competitive edge with foreign industry and to increase inter-regional investment.

Moscow Oblast is a member of the Central Russia Association, which is headed by Yaroslavl Governor Anatolii Lisitsyn. The other member oblasts are Bryansk, Ivanovo, Kaluga, Kostroma, Ryazan, Smolensk, Tver, Tula, Vladimir, and the city of Moscow. Luzhkov holds considerable clout in the association and is considered its unofficial leader.

Attitudes Toward Business: Heavy Investment Region

Moscow Oblast is one of the most promising regions for business growth. During the last few years, regional output has risen and investment is continuing to increase. In 1998, Moscow Oblast attracted $637 million in direct foreign investment, almost ten times the figure for 1997 (*Ekspert*, 18 October 1999). At the end of 1997, Moscow Oblast had 31,200 small enterprises—33 percent in retail and food service, 21 percent in industrial production, 16.3 percent in construction, and 8.1 percent in research.

As of February 1998, 2,000 joint ventures were registered in the region, of which 500 are operating (Moscow Television, "Guberniya," 28 August 1998). A large part of this business activity can probably be attributed to the tax advantages which are offered to outside investors who bring in more than $1 million.

There are numerous Western investment projects underway in Moscow Oblast:

- Pepsico has opened a facility that has the capacity to produce 24,000 two–liter bottles an hour. It is the largest of five such facilities that the company has built in Russia in the last 25 years. Oblast officials say the plant has brought an additional $66 million worth of investment to the region.
- Mars candy has a plant in the city of Stupino.
- The Swedish company PLM opened a $125 million plant for producing beer and soda cans in the Naro-Fominsk district. The plant has a capacity of 1.75 billion cans per year. *Nezavisimaya Gazeta* claims that PLM hopes to

take advantage of local tax breaks to import an additional 1.75 billion cans with a 50 percent savings in tariffs (3 July 1998).
- Italy's Merloni Electrodomestici produces electric stoves and washing machines in Fryazino. The firm had a $300 million turnover in 1997, yet backed out of its investment project with Fryazino Experimental Factory in September 1998.
- Germany's Ehrmann is building a DM 60 million yogurt factory in Ramensk with expected completion in summer 1999. The factory will have the capacity to produce 30,000 tons a year.
- The Dutch company Campina, Ehrmann's main competitor, opened a factory in Stupino with a capacity of 50,000 tons of yogurt per year.
- Pakenso, a subsidiary of Finland's Enso, is building a packaging plant in Balabanov. The $40 million plant will have the capacity to produce 90 million square meters of corrugated cardboard per year.
- Bosch-Siemens Hausgerate GMBH makes gas stoves in Chernogolevsk, and sold DM 370 million worth of products in Russia in 1997.
- Sweden's Ericsson invested between $80 million and $100 million in Russia during 1998. The firm's primary investments are in production facilities in Moscow Oblast's Zelenograd, and in Nizhnii Novgorod.
- The French yogurt maker Danone is building a dairy plant and bakery in Moscow Oblast's Chekhov Raion. The plant will be able to produce 150,000 tons of yogurt and tvorog and 100,000 tons of confectionery products per year. Danone intends to invest $100 million in the plant over five years, and will buy only local ingredients.
- Canada's McDonald's has opened a restaurant in Odintsovo and several other oblast locations. More than $2 million was invested in each outlet.
- Global One's Russian subsidiary Global Odin (now fully owned by France Telecom), is building a model telephone infrastructure in Moscow Oblast.
- Switzerland's Nestlé planned to invest $20 million in the Nestlé-Zhukov Ice Cream joint venture in Moscow Oblast in 1999.
- Japan's NEC, with financial support from Sumitomo, opened a factory to produce digital telecommunications equipment at the Experimental Factory of the Russian Academy of Sciences in Chernogolevsk. The overall investment is worth $4 million.
- France's Formashe plans to build a $100 million cargo terminal at Sheremetyevo-2.

Boris Vsevolodovich Gromov

7 November 1943—Born in Saratov

1955–1962—Accepted to the Saratov Suvorov Military Training School and then transferred to the Kalinin Suvorov Military Training School from which he graduated.

1965—Graduated from the Leningrad Higher Military Training School

1967–1978—Served in the army as a commanding officer

1972—Graduated from the Frunze Academy

1978–1980—Division chief in the North Caucasus military district

November 1980–August 1982—Commander of infantry units in Afghanistan

1982–1984—Studied at the USSR Armed Forces Academy, where he earned a gold medal

March 1985–April 1986—Head of representatives from the general staff in Afghanistan

April 1986–June 1987—Commanded army in Belarus military district

June 1987–February 1989—Commanded 40th army in Afghanistan and served as the government representative of the Soviet military in Afghanistan

March 1988—Named Hero of the Soviet Union for his successful "Magistral" military operation

1989—Led Soviet troops out of Afghanistan

1989–1990—Commanded the Kiev Military District

1989—Elected to the USSR Congress of People's Deputies

December 1990–September 1991—USSR first deputy minister of internal affairs

1991—Participated in the Russian presidential elections as the vice presidential running mate of Nikolai Ryzhkov

November 1991—Appointed first deputy commander of Soviet ground forces

June 1992–March 1995—Russian deputy minister of defense

December 1995—Elected to the State Duma from Saratov and joined the Russian Regions faction

September 1999—Was included on the Fatherland–All Russia party list for in the State Duma election

9 January 2000—Elected governor of Moscow Oblast

Speaks English

Married, with 5 children

- Italy's Breda is working to produce passenger buses in the city of Yakhono.
- Coca-Cola is investing $60 million to build a distribution center in the city of Mytishchi.

Internet Sites in the Region

http://www.gromov.tsr.ru
Gromov's site provides visitors with the texts of various speeches Gromov has made, his opinions on various national and regional issues, and biographical information.

http://www.bisinfo.ru/moscow
This website offers contact information for the Moscow Oblast administration and the heads of the cities and districts in the oblast. It also provides the history of the oblast, some statistics, and information on regional tourist attractions.

http://www.bisinfo.ru/News.html
This website provides regional news as well as basic information on economics and business development in the oblast.

http://www.wild-east.de/firmen/reda/index.html
This is the home page for the Moscow Region Development Agency. It offers basic information on the oblast and discusses the Agency's services in regional economic development. This is an English language website that is clearly targeted at Western investors.

MURMANSK OBLAST

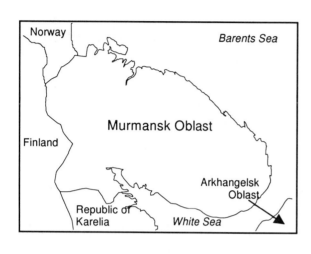

Territory: 144,900 km²
Population (as of 1 January 1998):
1,017,000
Distance from Moscow: 1,967 km

Major Cities:
Murmansk, *capital* (pop. 387,400)
Apatity (70,600)
Monchegorsk (59,800)
Severomorsk (57,100)
Kandalaksha (46,900)

Basic Facts

Population (as of 1 Jan. 1998): 1,017,000 (0.69% of Russian total)

Ethnic breakdown (1989 census): Russians 82.9%, Ukrainians 9.0%, Belarusans 3.3%, Tatars 1.0%

Urban population (as of 1 Jan. 1998): 91.8% (Russia overall: 73.1%)

Student population (as of 1 Sept. 1997): 100 per 10,000 (Russia overall: 208/10,000)

Pensioner population (1997): 22.5% (Russia overall: 25.96%)

Percent of population with higher education (1989 census): 13.9% (Russia overall: 11.3%)

Percent of population working in 1997: Industry: 29.2% (Russian average: 23.0%); Agriculture: 2.0% (13.7%); Trade: 13.3% (13.5%); Culture: 13.0% (13.3%)

Average monthly personal income in July 1998: 1,324.6 new rubles (Russian average: 891.7 new rubles)

Average monthly personal expenses in July 1998: 760.0 new rubles (Russian average: 684.9 new rubles)

Average monthly subsistence requirement in 1998: 592 new rubles (Russian average: 438 new rubles)

Consumer price index (as of July 1998): 124 (Russia overall = 100)

Budgetary revenues (1997): 4,561.4 billion rubles (Russia overall: 433,378.2 billion rubles)

Budgetary expenditures (1997): 4,924.1 billion rubles (Russia overall: 468,111.6 billion rubles)

Industrial production as percentage of all Russian production (Jan.–Aug. 1998): 0.84%

Proportion of loss-making enterprises (as of July 1998): 49.0% (Russia overall: 50.4%)

Number of enterprises which have wage arrears (as of 1 Sept. 1998): 439 (0.32% of Russian total)

Agricultural production as percentage of all Russian production (1997): 0.18%

Number of private farms (as of 1 Jan. 1998): 73 (0.03% of Russian total)

Capital investment (1997): 2,153.9 billion rubles (Russia overall: 408,797 billion rubles)

Sources of investment (1997): federal budget: 9.7% (Russian average: 10.2%); regional budget: 2.7% (10.5%); extra-budgetary funds: 87.6% (79.3%)

Foreign investment (1997): 3,165,000 USD (Russia overall: 12,294,734,000 USD)

Number of joint ventures (1997): 104 (0.7% of Russian total)

Fixed capital investment in joint ventures and foreign companies (1997): 20,419 million rubles (Russia overall: 16,265.4 billion rubles)

Number of small businesses (as of 1 July 1998): 3,900 (0.45% of Russian total)

Number of enterprises privatized in 1997: 0

Number of telephones per 100 families (1997): in cities: 53.5 (Russian average: 49.2); in villages: 25.6 (19.8)

Brief Overview

Murmansk Oblast occupies the Kola Peninsula, an extension of the Scandinavian Peninsula between the White Sea and the Barents Sea. It borders Norway and Finland to the west and Karelia to the south.

Apart from swampy forests in the south, the severely cold climate allows only tundra vegetation. The ice-free Barents Sea (benefiting from the influence of the Gulf Stream) provides the country with its only unrestricted access to the Atlantic. The oblast's northern seaports, including that of the capital of Murmansk (founded in 1916), have considerable national importance. A large portion of Russia's navy (the Northern Fleet) and commercial fleet is based on the Kola Peninsula, including nuclear submarines and icebreakers.

Though there is fishing and some forestry, the oblast's most important wealth lies in the mineral deposits of the Khibiny Mountains, with mining centers at Kirovsk and Apatity. Metallurgy is centered around Monchegorsk and Nikel, with its huge nickel smelters causing heavy air pollution.

According to a 1998 survey by *Ekspert* magazine, the oblast's investment potential had decreased by 5 points (the 19th greatest in the country), while investment risk increased by 13 points (the 15th largest) over the last year. However, several foreign businesses have made investments in the region. For instance, in February 1997 Pepsi-Cola General Bottlers chose the region as one of several locations for a $165 million investment project within the next three years. In 1998, Gazprom, Norway's Statoil, and Norsk Hydro signed an agreement for oil and gas exploration in the Barents Sea and the construction of new refineries in the area.

In April 1998, the regional administration announced that it would issue $100 million of Eurobonds in early 1999, but the 1998 financial crisis indefinitely postponed these plans.

According to a 1998 survey by *Ekspert* magazine, the oblast ranked 28th among Russia's 89 regions in terms of investment potential and 30th in terms of investment risk. A 1998 survey by Bank Austria ranked the oblast 31st in terms of investment climate.

Electoral History

2000 Presidential Election
Putin: 66.10%
Zyuganov: 15.64%
Yavlinskii: 7.04%

Zhirinovsky: 3.71%
Tuleev: 2.04%
Turnout: 69.38% (Russia overall: 68.64%)

2000 Gubernatorial Election
Yevdokimov (incumbent): 86.71%
Komarov: 3.38%
Isakov (LDPR): 2.19%
Ignatenko: 1.20%
Kening: 0.88%
Turnout: 69.11%

1999 Parliamentary Elections
Unity: 31.44%
Communist Party of the Russian Federation: 13.01%
Zhirinovsky Bloc: 11.21%
Yabloko: 10.01%
Union of Right Forces: 9.60%
Fatherland–All Russia: 7.90%
In single-mandate districts: 2 independent
Turnout: 60.43% (Russia overall: 61.85%)

1996 Gubernatorial Election
Yevdokimov: 20.10%/43.45% (first round/second round)
Komarov (incumbent): 31.09%/40.64%
Zub: 13.92%
Vorobev (LDPR): 10.15%
Kalaida (oblast legislature deputy): 7.14%
Lebedev (Yabloko): 4.93%
Myasnikov: 1.47%
Kirichenko: 0.91%
Turnout: 48.6%/44.64%

1996 Presidential Election
Yeltsin: 40.62%/70.13% (first round/second round)
Lebed: 25.43%
Zyuganov: 12.09%/21.88%
Yavlinskii: 9.68%
Zhirinovsky: 6.98%
Turnout: 59.59%/56.64% (Russia overall: 69.67%/ 68.79%)

1995 Parliamentary Elections
Liberal Democratic Party of Russia: 12.37%
Communist Party of the Russian Federation: 10.96%
Our Home Is Russia: 10.83%
Yabloko: 10.63%
Women of Russia: 7.03%

Congress of Russian Communities: 6.02%
Party of Workers' Self-Government: 5.19%
Russia's Democratic Choice: 4.57%
In single-mandate districts: 1 Our Home Is Russia,
  1 independent
Turnout: 60.94% (Russia overall: 64.37%)

1993 Constitutional Referendum
"Yes"—69.8%   "No"—28.1%

1993 Parliamentary Elections
Liberal Democratic Party of Russia: 24.26%
Russia's Choice: 23.47%
Yabloko: 14.25%
Women of Russia: 7.82%
Democratic Party of Russia: 6.97%
Party of Russian Unity and Concord: 6.44%
Communist Party of the Russian Federation: 5.67%
Agrarian Party of Russia: 1.30%
In single-mandate districts: 2 Russia's Choice
Turnout: 50.96% (Russia overall: 54.34%)

1991 Presidential Election
Yeltsin: 55.95%
Ryzhkov: 17.69%
Zhirinovsky: 9.0%4
Tuleev: 6.09%
Bakatin: 4.01%
Makashov: 2.06%
Turnout: 68.46% (Russia overall: 76.66%)

Regional Political Institutions

Executive:
  Governor, 4-year term
  Yurii Alekseevich Yevdokimov, elected December
  1996, reelected March 2000
    Leninskii Prospekt, 75; Murmansk, 183006
    Tel 7(815–2) 55–65–40;
    Fax 7(815–2) 55–55–03
    Federation Council in Moscow:
      7(095) 292–38–51, 926–64–05

Legislative:
  Unicameral
  Oblast Duma—25 members, 4-year term, elected
  December 1997
  Chairman—Pavel Aleksandrovich Sazhinov, elected
  March 1994, January 1998

Regional Politics

Former Lebed Ally Turns to Luzhkov

Yurii Yevdokimov is one of the few regional executives whose primary electoral support was drawn from the followers of former Russian Security Council Secretary and current Krasnoyarsk Krai Governor Aleksandr Lebed. Yevdokimov, who beat out incumbent Yevgenii Komarov in the runoff by 40 percent to win election as governor of Murmansk Oblast on 1 December 1996, was supported by numerous parties and movements besides Lebed's Honor and Motherland. The Communist-led National Patriotic Union of Russia (NPSR) was among them. The success of a Lebed ally in Murmansk was not surprising, given that Lebed himself had an excellent showing in the region in the 1996 Russian presidential election. In the first round, Lebed took 25 percent of Murmansk's vote, compared to the 12 percent earned by Communist candidate Gennadii Zyuganov.

However, in spite of capitalizing on Lebed's popularity as a springboard to the oblast's leadership, Yevdokimov is not a devoted Lebed follower. Although aspects of his style are similar to Lebed's, Yevdokimov does not necessarily defer to the former general on all issues. Unlike Lebed, Yevdokimov does not openly criticize the federal government, but prefers to keep a more indeterminate relationship to Moscow's powers. In 1999, Yevdokimov abandoned Lebed altogether in favor of Moscow Mayor Yurii Luzhkov. Yevdokimov joined Luzhkov's Fatherland political movement and started a regional branch of the party. Clearly, Yevdokimov is more interested in aligning with powerful and influential individuals than in sticking to any specific movement or ideology.

Likewise, the governor is concerned with his own popularity and the security of his position. To ensure his reelection, Yevdokimov moved up the region's gubernatorial election from December 2000 to March 2000 to coincide with the Russian presidential election. Leaving no time for opponents to campaign effectively, Yevdokimov soared to reelection, winning 86.71 percent of the vote.

Executive Platform: Moderate Reformer

Yevdokimov seems to be a moderate reformer. After his election, Yevdokimov announced his willingness to cooperate with the Northwest regional association, of which Murmansk is a member. He also stated his intention to continue the economic reforms started by Komarov, but planned to remove the bureaucrats who did not meet his moral and business standards. In this respect, Yevdokimov has remained true to his word, having passed several initiatives in support of small business development. The governor has also been active in trying to attract foreign investment to the region.

Policies: Business Oriented

The majority of Yevdokimov's policies are geared toward improving the region's economic situation. He has prioritized developing small business in Murmansk, and has played an active role in trying to help depressed industries and enterprises, such as Severonikel.

Yevdokimov is becoming more active on the international scene, specifically in the economic sphere. The governor has taken full advantage of his opportunities to network with foreign leaders, attending a G-8 meeting in May 1998.

Relationships Between Key Players

Of the 25 deputies elected to the Murmansk Oblast Duma in December 1997, there are two Communists, one member from Our Home Is Russia, and one from Yabloko.

Ties to Moscow: Keeps Neutral Stance

Yevdokimov has succeeded in keeping a low profile in regard to the federal government. He was chair of the Murmansk regional legislature in October 1993 when it was disbanded for not supporting President Boris Yeltsin in his battle against the Russian legislature. However, Yevdokimov has tried to disassociate himself from his belligerent role in the past. His 1996 election platform began with "I am far from the same person I was three years ago" (*OMRI RRR*, 8 January 1997), suggesting that he had turned over a new leaf in his view of Yeltsin. After becoming governor, Yevdokimov kept a rather neutral position in relation to Yeltsin, being neither a vocal opponent of the president nor an outspoken advocate of his policies.

In November 1997 Yevdokimov signed a power-sharing agreement with the federal government.

Relations with Other Regions: Support for Luzhkov

In November 1998 Yevdokimov attended an official meeting of the organizational committee of Moscow Mayor Yurii Luzhkov's new Fatherland political movement, (*EWI RRR*, 24 November 1998). Yevdokimov works actively with other regional executives in a variety of political and economic alliances. He is one of the founders of an association called the Alliance Group, which provides crisis support to struggling enterprises in Russia and the CIS. Other contributing regions are Saratov, Leningrad, Novgorod, Irkutsk, Magadan, Chita, Novosibirsk, and Voronezh. The Alliance Group believes that close cooperation between regional administrations and enterprises provides the most effective aid to firms on the verge of bankruptcy. Yevdokimov has tried to adopt a similar approach to dealing with such issues within Murmansk (see Attitudes Toward Business)

Murmansk belongs to the Northwest Association, which includes the republics of Karelia and Komi; Arkhangelsk, Vologda, Kaliningrad, Kirov, Leningrad, Novgorod, and Pskov oblasts; Nenets Autonomous Okrug; and the federal city St. Petersburg.

Foreign Relations: Ties to Scandinavia, Belarus

Yevdokimov has been actively trying to increase Murmansk's presence on the international scene. In May 1998 Yevdokimov accompanied Boris Yeltsin to participate in the G-8 meeting in Birmingham, England. Saratov Governor Dmitrii Ayatskov and Arkhangelsk Governor Anatolii Yefremov were also part of the delegation. The governors were hoping that their participation in the meeting would help attract foreign investment to their respective regions (*EWI RRR*, 21 May 1998).

In March 1998 Belarusan President Aleksandr Lukashenko visited Murmansk and met with Yevdokimov to discuss possible areas of cooperation. The same month, Yevdokimov visited the Troms region of Norway to discuss economic and cultural cooperation there (*RFE/RL*, 18 March 1998).

In September 1998 Yevdokimov requested food assistance for Murmansk from Finland, complaining that food shipments from central Russia had been reduced (*RFE/RL*, 8 September 1998). In this respect, Yevdokimov is beginning to look outward for assistance in order to reduce Murmansk's reliance on domestic services.

Attitudes Toward Business: Strengthening Small Business and Investment

Yevdokimov has some experience dealing with business and finance and thus it is no surprise that he has focused much of his attention on developing the

Yurii Alekseevich Yevdokimov

1 January 1946—Born in the city of Klevan, Ukraine

Graduated from an engineering-construction institute

1974—Headed a building combine and then began party work

1990–October 1993—Chairman of Murmansk Oblast executive committee

1993—Became the general director of the Murmansk branch of the financial corporation Sistema and chair of the Murmansk Union of Industrialists and Entrepreneurs

1 December 1996—Elected governor of Murmansk

June 1997–June 1998—Member of the Board of Directors of Norilsk Nikel

26 March 2000—Reelected governor

Married with two children

region's economic sector. Prior to becoming governor, Yevdokimov directed a regional branch of the Sistema financial organization, which is closely associated with Moscow Mayor Luzhkov. He also headed the Murmansk Oblast Union of Industrialists and Entrepreneurs. During his tenure as governor, Yevdokimov served on Norilsk Nikel's board of directors from June 1997 to June 1998. (Norilsk Nikel, located in Krasnoyarsk Krai, works closely with Murmansk's Severonikel.) The board removed Yevdokimov as well as the governors of Taimyr Autonomous Okrug and Krasnoyarsk Krai during the June 1998 shareholders meeting. The reasons for the governors' dismissal remain unclear.

Yevdokimov's efforts seemed to have paid off, at least before the August financial crisis. For the first half of 1998, foreign investment in Murmansk was $2.9 million, which was 6.7 times higher than the same period in 1997 (www.mstu.edu.ru). The majority of the region's investment comes from the Netherlands, which contributed $2.1 million in the first half of 1998. The region has passed laws on supporting small business, including a simplification of taxes for small enterprises. In 1997, one billion rubles from the oblast budget went to small business development (www.mstu.edu.ru).

One important issue concerning Murmansk's economic and business development has been the fate of Severonikel, which has been on the verge of bankruptcy because of its federal tax and pension debts. The plant's tax contributions make up 15 percent of the oblast budget and 70 percent of the Monchegorsk city budget. Severonikel has been suffering from the drop in the world price of the nickel, copper, cobalt, and platinum it produces. Yevdokimov worries that if the plant is ever declared bankrupt the oblast will lose a significant share of its income and will face higher unemployment. Oblast authorities and the state tax service are trying to save the plant (*EWI RRR*, 13 August 1998).

Among other economic and business developments in Murmansk, in March 1999 Yevdokimov signed a cooperation agreement with LUKoil President Vagit Alekperov. Murmansk will become a base region for LUKoil and Gazprom's exploration of the Barents Sea. Gazprom announced in June 1998 that it was interested in building a refinery in Murmansk to process oil extracted from the Pechora and Barents seas (*EWI RRR*, 4 June 1998).

Internet Sites in the Region

http://www.mstu.edu.ru/russian/region/
This is Yurii Yevdokimov's official site. The site offers several excellent resources, including detailed reports on Murmansk's economic and social situation for 1997 and 1998 and contact information for regional enterprises and officials.

NENETS AUTONOMOUS OKRUG

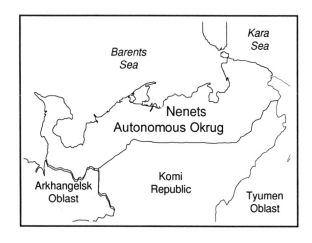

Territory: 176,700 km^2
Population (as of 1 January 1998): 47,000
Distance from Moscow: 2,230 km

Major Cities:
Naryan-Mar, *capital* (pop. 18,500)

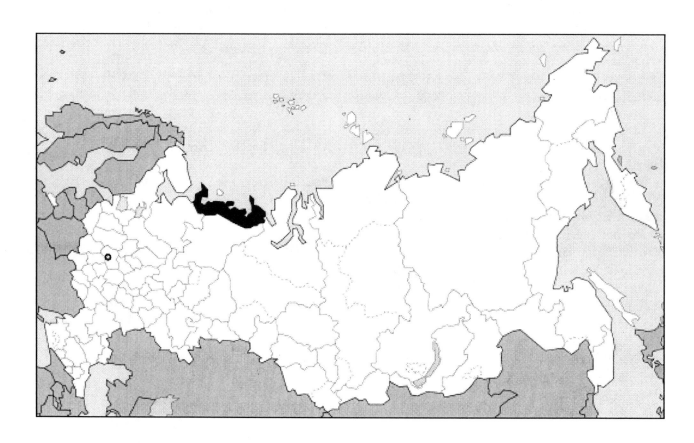

Basic Facts

Population (as of 1 Jan. 1998): 47,000 (0.03% of Russian total)

Ethnic breakdown (1989 census): Russians 65.6%, Nenets 11.4%, Komi 9.5%, Ukrainians 6.9%, Belarusans 2%

Urban population (as of 1 Jan. 1998): 59.4% (Russia overall: 73.1%)

Pensioner population (1997): 21.28% (Russia overall: 25.96%)

Percent of population with higher education (1989 census): 8.9% (Russia overall: 11.3%)

Average monthly personal income in July 1998: 1,178.1 new rubles (Russian average: 891.7 new rubles)

Average monthly personal expenses in July 1998: 528.8 new rubles (Russian average: 684.9 new rubles)

Average monthly subsistence requirement in 1998: 611 new rubles (Russian average: 438 new rubles)

Consumer price index (as of July 1998): 155 (Russia overall = 100)

Budgetary revenues (1997): 486.5 billion rubles (Russia overall: 433,378.2 billion rubles)

Budgetary expenditures (1997): 484.0 billion rubles (Russia overall: 468,111.6 billion rubles)

Industrial production as percentage of all Russian production (Jan.–Aug. 1998): 0.08%

Proportion of loss-making enterprises (as of July 1998): 44.4% (Russia overall: 50.4%)

Number of enterprises which have wage arrears (as of 1 Sept. 1998): 56 (0.04% of Russian total)

Agricultural production as percentage of all Russian production (1997): 0.02%

Number of private farms (as of 1 Jan. 1998): 14 (0.005% of Russian total)

Capital investment (1997): 197.4 billion rubles (Russia overall: 408,797 billion rubles)

Sources of investment (1997): federal budget: 18.2% (Russian average: 10.2%); regional budget: 13.9% (10.5%); extra-budgetary funds: 67.9% (79.3%)

Number of joint ventures (1997): 3 (0.02% of Russian total)

Fixed capital investment in joint ventures and foreign companies (1997): 24,588 million rubles (Russia overall: 16,265.4 billion rubles)

Number of telephones per 100 families (1997): in cities: 25.8 (Russian average: 49.2); in villages: 31.4 (19.8)

Brief Overview

Nenets AO is situated in the farthest northeastern section of the European part of the country and borders with the Komi Republic in the south and Arkhangelsk Oblast in the southeast. Seventy-five different ethnic groups reside in the okrug, including Russians, Nenets, and Komi. Most of the okrug's territory lies above the Arctic Circle.

The okrug is rich in raw materials. It has the third largest reserve of oil resources in the country. Major industries are: fuel and energy, timber working, and food processing. Most of the industry is concentrated in the okrug's main city, Naryan-Mar. Agriculture is mostly traditional: hunting, fishery, and reindeer herding.

According to a 1998 survey by *Ekspert* magazine, the okrug ranked 88th among Russia's 89 regions in terms of investment potential and 17th in terms of investment risk. A 1998 survey by Bank Austria ranked the okrug 76th in terms of investment climate.

Electoral History

2000 Presidential Election
Putin: 59.54%
Zyuganov: 20.82%
Yavlinskii: 5.03%
Zhirinovsky: 4.52%
Tuleev: 2.94%
Turnout: 73.97% (Russia overall: 68.64%)

1999 Parliamentary Elections
Unity: 19.55%
Fatherland–All Russia: 13.63%
Communist Party of the Russian Federation: 13.57%
Zhirinovsky Bloc: 10.67%
Yabloko: 7.16%
Union of Right Forces: 7.00%
Women of Russia: 6.89%
In a single-mandate district: 1 Fatherland–All Russia
Turnout: 73.98% (Russia overall: 61.85%)

1996 Gubernatorial Election
Butov (okrug legislature deputy): 48.46%/21.99%
    (first round/second round)
Khabarov (incumbent): 40.27%/40.64%
Komarovskii: 15.30%
Varankin: 5.48%
Ruzhnikov: 2.96%
Staich: 1.59%
Malashchenko: 1.25%
Turnout: 65.3%/62.14%

1996 Presidential Election
Yeltsin: 42.64%/61.54% (first round/second round)
Zyuganov: 18.37%/28.89%
Lebed: 11.98%
Zhirinovsky: 9.93%
Yavlinskii: 7.64%
Turnout: 72.80%/67.71% (Russia overall: 69.67%/
    68.79%)

1995 Parliamentary Elections
Liberal Democratic Party of Russia: 16.83%
Communist Party of the Russian Federation: 11.42%
Bloc of Ivan Rybkin: 10.45%
Women of Russia: 8.64%
Our Home Is Russia: 7.58%
Agrarian Party of Russia: 5.20%
Party of Workers' Self-Government: 4.47%

Yabloko: 4.08%
In a single-mandate district: 1 Bloc of Ivan Rybkin
Turnout: 74.73% (Russia overall: 64.37%)

1993 Constitutional Referendum
"Yes"—72.2%   "No"—24.8%

1993 Parliamentary Elections
Russia's Choice: 19.84%
Liberal Democratic Party of Russia: 19.15%
Women of Russia: 10.88%
Party of Russian Unity and Concord: 9.62%
Democratic Party of Russia: 7.36%
Yabloko: 6.65%
Communist Party of the Russian Federation:
    6.48%
Agrarian Party of Russia: 3.19%
In a single-mandate district: 1 Obnovlenie
Turnout: 63.00% (Russia overall: 54.34%)

1991 Presidential Election
Yeltsin: 46.08%
Ryzhkov: 26.42%
Zhirinovsky: 8.51%
Bakatin: 8.04%
Tuleev: 4.25%
Makashov: 2.42%
Turnout: 76.47% (Russia overall: 76.66%)

Regional Political Institutions

Executive:
    Governor, 4-year term
    Vladimir Yakovlevich Butov, elected
    December 1996
        Nenets Autonomous Okrug Administration;
        Naryan-Mar, 164700;
        Nenets Autonomous Okrug
        Tel 7(818–53) 4–22–69;
        Fax 7(095) 253–51–00
        Federation Council in Moscow:
        7(095) 292–69–01, 926–61–65

Legislative:
    Unicameral
    Deputy Assembly—15 members, 4-year term,
    elected December 1996
    Chairman—Vyacheslav Alekseevich Vyucheiskii,
    elected May 1994, December 1996

Regional Politics

Conflicts Prevent Development

A well-educated entrepreneur, Vladimir Butov, is a logical leader for the underdeveloped, but resource-rich Nenets Autonomous Okrug. However, the governor's attempts to protect local resources from exploitation by some domestic and foreign firms has embroiled him in a variety of disputes on local, regional, and international levels. Butov has stated that the Nenets Autonomous Okrug would not make a profit on its oil reserves before the year 2000 (*NV*, 13 February 1998). Given the roadblocks Butov has thrown up in front of the region's projects, however, 2000 was a very optimistic target.

Butov has made it abundantly clear that he wants the Nenets Okrug and its leader to be the primary beneficiary of its natural resource deposits, and seems to find the intentions of many regional and foreign investors unacceptable. However, for Butov to realize his own plans, greater support on all levels must be achieved. This is particularly true on the federal level, where Nenets lost a key ally when Prime Minister Viktor Chernomyrdin was dismissed.

Executive Platform: Protectionist, Strong Manager

Butov belongs to the group of governors described as "strong managers." These candidates ran as independents, usually with strong support from the business community. Although Moscow Mayor Yurii Luzhkov is the model, strong managers now govern in regions as diverse as Kaliningrad and Magadan oblasts, and Ust-Orda Buryat and Koryak autonomous okrugs. In December 1996, when Anatolii Chubais was presidential chief of staff, the Kremlin secretly offered electoral support to the "strong managers" against incumbents who had been appointed under previous chiefs of staff (*Segodnya*, 26 December 1996). The strong managers campaigned on economic issues. In Nenets, Butov's specific interests have been focused on further developing local oil reserves and promoting the okrug's share of the profits from these projects.

Policies: Blocking Deals Deemed Unfavorable to the Okrug

Butov is perhaps best known for blocking or opposing agreements rather than instituting policies. An entre-preneur with degrees in both economics and management, Butov's has focused on business issues. Butov has received considerable attention for his opposition to the Timan-Pechora Company project and for withdrawing Exxon's rights to develop the Tsentralnaya Khreiverskaya oil deposit. Rather than allowing foreign companies to capitalize on Nenets oil, Butov would like to see the creation of a local company to develop the okrug's natural resources. He is also pushing the federal government to build a northern pipeline through Nenets. Despite its potential wealth, the okrug lacks the resources to go it alone.

Relationships Between Key Players: Business Community Divided

Butov is a strong yet controversial leader and the business community is divided in its views of him. Butov avidly opposed the $40 million Timan-Pechora Company project championed by LUKoil and several foreign firms. However, he has the strong backing of the Arkhangelskgeoldobycha oil company, an influential firm that owns the exploration licenses to all 11 fields in the project (*NC*, Vol. 7, No. 16, 2).

Butov initially had relatively good relations with the okrug legislature, where he used to serve as a deputy. However, in December 1999, chairman Vyacheslav Vyucheiskii criticized Butov's handling of the okrug's finances. Butov failed in a subsequent attempt to remove Vyucheiskii.

Ties to Moscow: Chernomyrdin Sacking a Big Loss

Former Prime Minister Viktor Chernomyrdin supported several of Butov's efforts, particularly the construction of a northern pipeline through the okrug.

Butov and other leaders in the North kept up hopes of gaining allies in the federal government. During the brief reign of Sergei Kirienko, Komi Republic leader Yurii Spiridonov said that he, Butov, and Yamal-Nenets Governor Yurii Neelov intended to petition the young prime minister to keep Ramazan Abdulatipov in charge of the Russian Far North (*Respublika*, 31 March 1998). Their pleas to Kirienko fell on deaf ears, but former Prime Minister Yevgenii Primakov named Abdulatipov as his minister of nationality policies and Prime Minister Sergei Stepashin made him a minister without portfolio. This casual alliance between the governors was important given the several points of contention between Nenets and Komi (see Relations with Other Regions). It demonstrated that some regions are willing put aside their differences to cooperate in circumstances of mutual interest. In 1999, however, Butov backed the Kremlin's Unity ticket while Spiridonov backed Luzhkov's Fatherland.

Nenets, like many other regions, has not cleared its salary and pension debts. The governors blame the federal government for not sending enough subsidies, yet many of the regions are behind in their own payments (*Segodnya*, 13 January 1998).

Relations with Other Regions: Conflict with Neighbors

Nenets, under the leadership of Butov, is trying to assert its own interests and autonomy on the regional scene. In 1996 the Nenets legislature decided not to participate in the Arkhangelsk gubernatorial or legislative elections even though Nenets is formally a part of Arkhangelsk Oblast. (Under Russia's confusing 1993 constitution, autonomous okrugs are simultaneously independent regions and subordinate to the oblast and krais in which they are located.) This measure was taken as an attempt to increase Nenets' control over its natural resource revenues. By taking this action, Nenets followed the course of Khanty-Mansi and Yamal-Nenets autonomous okrugs, which have made attempts to secede from Tyumen Oblast.

Butov has also come into conflict with the neighboring Komi Republic over the Timan-Pechora oil and gas fields, which straddle the border separating the two regions. There are a considerable number of Komi-registered companies which extract resources from fields in both regions, yet pay taxes only to Komi. Thus, Nenets' natural resources are being exploited without providing any returns to the okrug's budget. As a result, the Nenets administration has been trying to push out the Komi companies (*EWI RRR*, 26 February 1998).

The conflict between Nenets and Komi intensified in the beginning of April 1998 when Butov presented a plan for establishing an oil transport terminal on the Barents Sea Coast. Butov suggested that in the future all the oil extracted in Nenets could be shipped through the Northern Sea Route (*Kommersant-Vlast*, 2 April 1998). Butov considers this project, called the Northern Gate, to be more attractive to investors than other alternatives. Presently, all oil extracted from the northern part of Timan-Pechora is shipped to central Russia via the Kharyaga-Usinsk pipeline, which runs through Komi. Komi is obviously against the construction of a northern pipeline. Former Prime Minister Chernomyrdin had vocally supported the construction of the northern pipeline route for Nenets oil, yet his dismissal has made it possible for other route proposals to be considered (*EWI RRR*, 7 May 1998).

Foreign Relations: Disputes with Investors

In August 1997, Butov withdrew Exxon's rights to develop the Tsentralnaya Khreiverskaya oil deposit, located in the Timan-Pechora basin to the south of the 11 fields set to be exploited by the Timan Pechora Company. This deposit is estimated to have 160 million metric tons of oil. Exxon, which was waiting for Duma approval for its production-sharing agreement, had not broken ground on the site. The agreement, which gave Exxon the tender to mine the deposit, stipulated that the Russian oil companies Rosneft, KomiTEK, and Arkhangelskgeoldobycha be included in Exxon's project, yet these companies believed that the deal gave too much to Exxon (*MT*, 21 August 1997). The Russian firms would hold only a 20 percent stake in the project, with the remaining stakes going to U.S. firms Exxon, Texaco, and to Amoco, and Norway's Norsk Hydro. Butov and the Nenets administration considered this insufficient to provide for Russia's national interests in the project, and objected to the consortium's plans of receiving the first profits only 12 years after developing the field (*EWI RRR*, 5 February 1998). The decision to withdraw Exxon's rights came six months after Nenets insisted that the terms of the agreement be revised.

Attitudes Toward Business

The governor's decision to withdraw Exxon's rights is not the only business conflict that has involved Butov and the oil industry. Nenets Autonomous Okrug possesses the third largest oil reserve in the country, thus it is not surprising that Butov has been at the head of several business discussions.

Butov opposed the $40 billion Timan-Pechora Company project. The Timan-Pechora Company united Exxon, Amoco, Texaco, Norsk Hydro, and Rosneft in a project to extract over 2.5 million barrels of reserves from the region (*NC*, Vol. 7, No. 16,2). Butov wanted the Russian companies' 20 percent share in the project (controlled by Rosneft) to be boosted to 51 percent, along with more rapid field exploration, tighter production deadlines, and a greater share of the profits (*NC*, Vol. 7, No. 16,2).

The governor, supported by the Arkhangelskgeol-

Vladimir Yakovlevich Butov

10 April 1958—Born in Novosibirsk to a family of workers

1975—Finished school and immediately began to work for a construction company in Novosibirsk

1976–1978—Served in the Navy; after completing his term of service, he worked as a rigger

1979—Moved to Nenets Autonomous Okrug and began to work as a tractor driver; in the following years he worked as a carpenter and a repairman for Buran snow-tractors

1988—Organized a cooperative

1992—Organized the industrial-commercial firm Ser-Vark and became the owner

1994—Earned a degree in economics

1995—Was elected a member of the Supreme Council of the United Russian Industrial Party (ROPP)

1996—Completed a degree in management

1994—Elected as a member of the okrug Legislative Assembly

13 December 1996—Elected Governor of the Nenets Autonomous Okrug

Married, with two sons

dobycha company, would prefer to abandon LUKoil's Timan-Pechora project and independently develop part of the contract zone (*NC*, Vol. 7, No. 16,2). Butov is working to create the Nenets Oil Company, which would be publicly held, with 25 percent of its stake distributed among the inhabitants of Nenets (*NV*, 13 February 1998).

Butov's opposition to the Timan-Pechora project prevented LUKoil from signing a deal with Western partners during the March 1998 Gore-Chernomyrdin Commission in Washington. However, LUKoil and Conoco signed an agreement to develop a 4,700 square km deposit in Conoco's Northern Territories project. They estimated that the deposit holds 135 million tons of oil and 63 billion cubic meters of natural gas (*KD*, 12 March 1998). LUKoil and Conoco plan to invest $2 billion in this project.

In December 1997 a consortium of ten Russian and Western oil companies proposed building a pipeline from the Timan-Pechora oil deposit to either Primorsk (Leningrad Oblast) or the Finnish port Porvoo. The consortium included Transneft, KomiTEK, Rosneft, Slavneft, Conoco, British Gas, Elf Neftegaz, Neste, Total, and Williams/IPL. Texaco and Exxon, although involved in the Timan-Pechora project, chose not to participate in the pipeline effort because they did not like either route (*EWI RRR*, 11 December 1997). With the potential to carry 30 million tons a year by 2010, this pipeline could generate considerable revenue (*RT*, 4 December 1998).

NIZHNII NOVGOROD OBLAST

Territory: 76,900 km²
Population (as of 1 January 1998): 3,697,000
Distance from Moscow: 439 km

Major Cities:
Nizhnii Novgorod, *capital* (pop. 1,364,200)
Dzerzhinsk (280,700)
Arzamas (111,400)
Sarov (83,400)
Pavlovo (71,100)
Kstovo (69,400)
Bor (64,400)

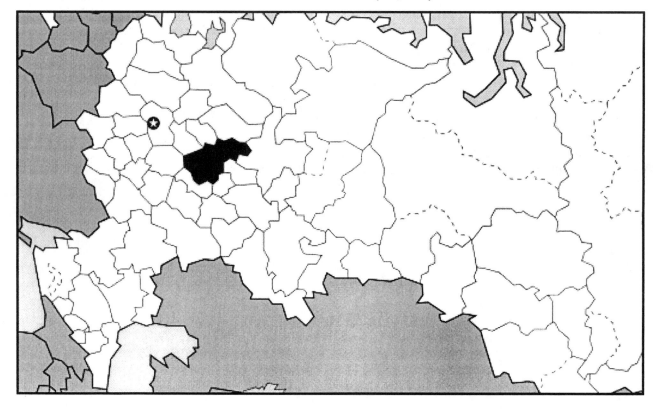

Basic Facts

Population (as of 1 Jan. 1998): 3,697,000 (2.51% of Russian total)

Ethnic breakdown (1989 census): Russians 94.6%, Tatars 1.6%, Mordvins 1%, Ukrainians 0.9%

Urban population (as of 1 Jan. 1998): 78.2% (Russia overall: 73.1%)

Student population (as of 1 Sept. 1997): 182 per 10,000 (Russia overall: 208/10,000)

Pensioner population (1997): 28.89% (Russia overall: 25.96%)

Percent of population with higher education (1989 census): 9.6% (Russia overall: 11.3%)

Percent of population working in 1997: Industry: 31.5% (Russian average: 23.0%); Agriculture: 8.8% (13.7%); Trade: 13.0% (13.5%); Culture: 13.3% (13.3%)

Average monthly personal income in July 1998: 627.4 new rubles (Russian average: 891.7 new rubles)

Average monthly personal expenses in July 1998: 495.3 new rubles (Russian average: 684.9 new rubles)

Average monthly subsistence requirement in 1998: 323 new rubles (Russian average: 438 new rubles)

Consumer price index (as of July 1998): 89 (Russia overall = 100)

Budgetary revenues (1997): 8,084.8 billion rubles (Russia overall: 433,378.2 billion rubles)

Budgetary expenditures (1997): 9,306.9 billion rubles (Russia overall: 468,111.6 billion rubles)

Industrial production as percentage of all Russian production (Jan.–Aug. 1998): 2.40%

Proportion of loss-making enterprises (as of July 1998): 41.5% (Russia overall: 50.4%)

Number of enterprises which have wage arrears (as of 1 Sept. 1998): 6,394 (4.73% of Russian total)

Agricultural production as percentage of all Russian production (1997): 1.85%

Number of private farms (as of 1 Jan. 1998): 3,546 (1.29% of Russian total)

Capital investment (1997): 7,619.7 billion rubles (Russia overall: 408,797 billion rubles)

Sources of investment (1997): federal budget: 5.2% (Russian average: 10.2%); regional budget: 15.8% (10.5%); extra-budgetary funds: 79.0% (79.3%)

Foreign investment (1997): 162,992,000 USD (Russia overall: 12,294,734,000 USD)

Number of joint ventures (1997): 133 (0.90% of Russian total)

Fixed capital investment in joint ventures and foreign companies (1997): 107,739 million rubles (Russia overall: 16,265.4 billion rubles)

Number of small businesses (as of 1 July 1998): 13,900 (1.60% of Russian total)

Number of enterprises privatized in 1997: 82 (2.99% of Russian total), including those which used to be municipal property: 39.1% (Russian average: 66.4%); regional property: 32.9% (20.0%); federal property: 28.0% (13.6%)

Number of telephones per 100 families (1997): in cities: 46.2 (Russian average: 49.2); in villages: 14.3 (19.8)

Brief Overview

Nizhnii Novgorod Oblast lies in European Russia occupying a territory of 74,800 sq km on both banks of the Middle Volga River and borders Kostroma, Kirov, Ryazan, Vladimir, and Ivanovo oblasts, and the republics of Marii El, Chuvashia, and Mordovia. The northern half contains a low plain, mostly covered by coniferous forest, while the southern half includes hills with deciduous trees and areas of forest steppe. From 1932 until 1990, the oblast and its capital were named Gorky in honor of the writer Maxim Gorky who was born there in 1868. The city was closed to foreign visitors because of its importance to the military-industrial complex.

The oblast's capital, Nizhnii Novgorod, located at the confluence of the Volga and Oka rivers, is the third largest city of the Russian Federation. It was established as a fort by Yurii Vsevolodovich, prince of Vladimir, in 1221. Due to its favorable geographical location, the city became a major trading center, which was famous for its annual fairs, held from 1817 until 1917, and renewed in 1991.

The region is highly industrialized, including machine building, ferrous metallurgy, chemicals, processing of agricultural and forestry products, and light manufacturing. In Soviet times, the oblast was one of the main centers of the defense industry. The Volga and its navigable tributaries, Oka and Sura, and a well-developed railroad and highway network provide excellent communications.

According to a 1998 survey by *Ekspert* magazine, the oblast is ranked 10th among Russia's 89 regions in terms of investment potential and 13th in terms of investment risk. A 1998 survey by Bank Austria ranked the oblast 6th in terms of investment climate.

Electoral History

2000 Presidential Election
Putin: 53.73%
Zyuganov: 32.72%
Yavlinskii: 3.91%
Zhirinovsky: 2.52%
Tuleev: 1.54%
Turnout: 65.54% (Russia overall: 68.64%)

1999 Parliamentary Elections
Communist Party of the Russian Federation: 24.41%
Unity: 19.84%

Union of Right Forces: 16.50%
Fatherland–All Russia: 6.76%
Zhirinovsky Bloc: 6.16%
Yabloko: 4.77%
In single-mandate districts: 1 Communist Party of the Russian Federation, 1 Union of Right Forces, 4 independent
Turnout: 57.56% (Russia overall: 61.85%)

1997 Gubernatorial Election
Sklyarov: 41.0%/52.2% (first round/second round)
Khodyrev (State Duma deputy): 37.8%/42.3%
Turnout: 39.9%/48.9%

1996 Presidential Election
Yeltsin: 34.83%/51.74% (first round/second round)
Zyuganov: 32.53%/42.35%
Lebed: 14.77%
Yavlinskii: 7.14%
Zhirinovsky: 5.43%
Turnout: 66.23%/65.35% (Russia overall: 69.67%/ 68.79%)

1995 Parliamentary Elections
Communist Party of the Russian Federation: 18.71%
Liberal Democratic Party of Russia: 12.07%
Yabloko: 10.56%
Our Home Is Russia: 10.47%
Women of Russia: 5.14%
Congress of Russian Communities: 4.88%
Communists–Workers' Russia: 4.45%
Agrarian Party of Russia: 3.12%
Party of Workers' Self-Government: 2.47%
In single-mandate districts: 2 Our Home Is Russia, 2 Communist Party of the Russian Federation, 1 Yabloko, 1 independent
Turnout: 62.43% (Russia overall: 64.37%)

1993 Constitutional Referendum
"Yes"—55.8%   "No"—41.3%

1993 Parliamentary Elections
Liberal Democratic Party of Russia: 19.91%
Russia's Choice: 13.96%
Yabloko: 12.23%
Communist Party of the Russian Federation: 11.58%
Women of Russia: 9.73%
Agrarian Party of Russia: 9.11%
Democratic Party of Russia: 7.08%

Party of Russian Unity and Concord: 5.65%
In single-mandate districts: 1 Yabloko, 4 12th December Union, 1 independent
From electoral associations: 1 Women of Russia, 1 Russia's Choice, 1 Democratic Party of Russia
Turnout: 52.88% (Russia overall: 54.34%)

1991 Presidential Election
Yeltsin: 69.93%
Ryzhkov: 12.25%
Tuleev: 4.33%
Zhirinovsky: 4.18%
Bakatin: 3.43%
Makashov: 2.78%
Turnout: 75.76% (Russia overall: 76.66%)

Regional Political Institutions

Executive:
Governor, 4-year term
Ivan Petrovich Sklyarov, elected July 1997
Kremlin, Corpus 5; Nizhnii Novgorod, 603082
Tel 7(831–2) 39–13–30;
Fax 7(831–2) 39–00–48
Federation Council in Moscow:
7(095) 292–64–47, 926–64–61

Legislative:
Unicameral
Legislative Assembly (Zakonodatelnoe Sobranie)—
45 members, 2–year term, elected March–November 1994, March 1998
Chairman—Anatolii Aleksandrovich Kozeradskii, elected 1994, April 1998

Regional Politics

Nizhnii Novgorod Mayor Replaces Nemtsov

Ivan Sklyarov, formerly mayor of Nizhnii Novgorod, succeeded Boris Nemtsov as governor of Nizhnii Novgorod Oblast in 1997. Nemtsov had come to power in late 1991, when Nizhnii Novgorod was a closed city with a large concentration of defense plants. During his tenure Nemtsov transformed the oblast into a showcase of reform and a model for Western aid projects, building a shining international reputation for a region that had formerly been known mainly as the location of dissident Andrei Sakharov's exile.

Despite steering the transition from communism and building a favorable reputation abroad, Nemtsov left a mixed legacy on the ground. Nizhnii Novgorod is the capital of an oblast boasting more joint ventures and greater hard currency turnover than oblasts with similar economic structures, such as Saratov and Samara. Nemtsov also managed to implement successful housing and privatization reforms. However, agricultural reform proved more troublesome, and the region has not been immune to the problem of wage and pension arrears plaguing the country. Prices for municipal services, transportation, and basic foodstuffs are among the highest in the country. Furthermore, it seems that the high level of foreign investment in the region was largely due to Nemtsov's personal charisma and contacts, and is not a result of strong regional policies. Nevertheless, Sklyarov has asserted himself over the region and managed to further its development even as he distanced himself from his famous predecessor.

Sklyarov gained popularity and stature in the region when, as mayor of Arzamas, he successfully helped the city recover from a devastating industrial explosion on 4 April 1988. His heroic actions in dealing with that emergency situation convinced many of his leadership skills.

Executive Platform: Pragmatic Reformer

Sklyarov considers himself a social democrat who rules in the style of Moscow Mayor Yurii Luzhkov. During the campaign when both men had a common enemy in Nemtsov, then serving as first deputy prime minister in the Russian government, Luzhkov was a strong supporter of Sklyarov's candidacy and the two spoke on a regular basis. Sklyarov admired Luzhkov's pragmatic approach to leadership, presenting himself as a manager rather than a politician. Thus it was no surprise that Sklyarov was one of the first governors to join Luzhkov's Fatherland party.

During the campaign, Sklyarov also had the backing of Yabloko's Grigorii Yavlinskii, Prime Minister Viktor Chernomyrdin's Our Home Is Russia, the Association of Industrialists and Entrepreneurs, and the oblast's Agro-Industrial Union. In the first round he just barely edged out Communist candidate Gennadii Khodyrev, 41–38 percent, with a 40 percent voter turnout. After Nemtsov returned to the region and campaigned for Sklyarov, voter participation jumped to 49 percent and Sklyarov easily won the race.

Sklyarov has adopted a critical stance toward his predecessor and questioned whether he alone was responsible for initiating and carrying out reforms in the region. Sklyarov was also offended that Nemtsov chose to join his campaign only at the end when his victory appeared imminent.

Sklyarov's attack on Nemtsov signaled a personal dispute with the former governor, rather than a move away from reform policies. Sklyarov continued many of Nemtsov's reforms and before the August 1998 crisis had been attracting more foreign investment to the region than was the case in the previous year. Sklyarov staunchly supports privatization. He rejects price regulation but is willing to index salaries in certain situations.

Sklyarov enthusiastically supports the construction of a new European transport route through Nizhnii Novgorod. In contrast to a place like Samara, which is seen as a gateway to the Urals, Nizhnii is too close to Moscow and is losing some of its importance as a transportation hub. Sklyarov hopes to further develop the oblast's transportation system for easier cargo shipment, and is providing business investment incentives and tax exemptions to achieve this goal.

Sklyarov does not endorse a strict adherence to principles of territorial integrity and feels that the administrative borders of the former USSR could be adjusted. Like Luzhkov, Sklyarov believes that the Kuril islands should remain in Russia's possession. He also argues that Crimea and Sevastopol are truly Russian territory and that Ukraine should return them. Additionally, the governor believes that the Latvian law on citizenship violates human rights standards. Sklyarov feels that Russia should defend through diplomatic and economic means the rights and interests of Russians living outside the country's borders as a result of the break-up of the USSR.

Policies: Populist and Pro-Investment

Sklyarov claims that the main accomplishments in his first few months as governor were floating a $100 million Eurobond issue, helping broker the signing of a nearly $1 billion joint venture contract between the Gorkii Automobile Factory (GAZ) and Italy's Fiat, and taking the first steps toward preventing the collapse of the Dzerzhinsk chemical industry (see Attitudes Toward Business).

In January 1998 Sklyarov issued a decree partially suspending a Constitutional Court ruling ordering all enterprises to pay their back taxes before paying back salaries. Sklyarov's decree, which concerned only re-

gional taxes paid to the regional budget, stated that companies must use only half of their income toward paying tax arrears and the other half may be put toward back wages. Industrialists supported Sklyarov's defiance of the federal court, arguing that his actions were rooted in the real state of affairs at the oblast's enterprises. Local banks, however, initially ignored the governor's decree because they were afraid to take his side in a dispute with the federal authorities. This caused Sklyarov to reinforce his original decree by publishing additional instructions, which had been coordinated in advance with local financial institutions and tax authorities.

Sklyarov offered a benefits package to local plants in 1998 if they continued to increase their output as they did in 1997. In order to receive the tax breaks, the firms had to demonstrate growth of more than 5 percent, preserve or increase the number of workers they employ, and pay wages and taxes on time. The benefits went mainly to large firms like GAZ, Norsi-Oil, and Pavlov Buses, and smaller firms like Sintez and Nizhfarm. The governor has also granted various tax breaks to foreign investors (see Attitudes Toward Business).

Relationships Between Key Players: Conflict with the Mayor

The 26 March 1998 mayoral elections in Nizhnii Novgorod led to nationwide controversy. The victor was local entrepreneur and erstwhile Nemtsov advisor Andrei Klimentev, who had two previous criminal convictions and was standing trial for charges of embezzlement. At the Kremlin's instigation, the election results were declared invalid and Klimentev was arrested and sentenced to six years in jail for misusing a state grant. Sklyarov blamed the scandal on imperfections in Russian electoral laws, which do not screen candidates for previous criminal convictions. Sklyarov indicated his support for the authorities' actions in canceling the elections, but also made clear that he was not involved in the whole process. What he did not admit to, however, was that the local "party of power" could not agree on a single candidate, and therefore two reform candidates split the vote, allowing Klimentev to win the elections with just a third of the ballots.

The repeat elections turned out to be a disappointment for Sklyarov. Yurii Lebedev, the former presidential representative in the region and one of Sklyarov's opponents in the gubernatorial election, ultimately was elected mayor on 11 October 1998. Sklyarov had supported Dmitrii Bednyakov, the former mayor whom Nemtsov had removed from power. Shortly after the election, the lines of dispute between Sklyarov and Lebedev were clear. Sklyarov wanted to use money from the relatively rich city of Nizhnii Novgorod to support social programs in the poorer parts of the oblast outside the capital. Lebedev, supporting the city's interests, would prefer to use the money to pay for programs aimed at improving the life of the city. Such conflicts between mayors and governors are common throughout Russia's regions.

One of the main points of contention between Sklyarov and Lebedev is the construction of a new hotel on the former site of the Hotel Moskva. Shortly after construction began in November 1997 an ancient burial ground was found on the site. Local and oblast authorities halted construction, wanting the project to be moved to another nearby site, which the project's backers, Spring Investments, a consortium including outside investors, refused to do (see Attitudes Toward Business). Shortly after his election, Lebedev gave his approval for the project to proceed, yet the oblast administration was still opposed to it. In December 1998 the oblast procurator, Vladimir Shevelev, ruled in favor of the hotel construction (*EWI RRR*, 12 November 1998 and 3 December 1998). However, as of May 1999, construction still had not resumed (*EWI RRI*, 27 May 1999).

The oblast legislative elections held on 26 March 1998 proved to be much more beneficial for Sklyarov. Of the 45 current deputies, 29 are government bureaucrats and industrial managers whose positions encourage loyalty to the governor. Sklyarov expressed satisfaction over the assembly's reelection of incumbent speaker Anatolii Kozeradskii and his deputy Aleksandr Listkov, stating that this leadership should promote stability. Nevertheless, Sklyarov has run into conflict with the Legislative Assembly. The budget committee requested that Sklyarov look into the loss of $6 million of the region's $100 million Eurobond credit due to incompetent fund management. Sklyarov's commission was accused of violating various loan requirements, including not holding a fair tender for managing the fund money and illegally using funds to buy stock in corporate securities for the oblast administration.

Ties to Moscow: Nemtsov-Based Personality Conflicts

Nemtsov's resignation from the Russian government at the end of August 1998, following the dismissal of his protégé Prime Minister Sergei Kirienko, presumably makes it easier for Sklyarov to deal with Moscow. While Kirienko and Nemtsov held federal office, Sklyarov's conflict with Nemtsov pitted him against the Moscow authorities. Sklyarov chose to join the ranks of other regional executives who placed responsibility for the economic and social hardship in the regions on the federal government. In particular, Sklyarov complained about Moscow's alcohol policies, claiming that raising duties and the minimum price for hard liquor caused the oblast multiple problems.

The controversial March 1998 mayoral election in Nizhnii Novgorod proved to be an important event in tipping the Moscow power balance in Sklyarov's favor. At first, Yeltsin reprimanded Sklyarov for not ensuring the observance of the electoral law. He then appeased Sklyarov by replacing his regional representative, Yurii Lebedev, with Aleksandr Kosarikov, a Sklyarov supporter. Lebedev, a Nemtsov ally, had served as acting governor during the period after Nemtsov accepted his federal post but before new elections could be held. Sklyarov had proposed appointing Kosarikov the previous year, but Nemtsov blocked the nomination.

Lebedev's subsequent election as mayor will complicate the situation for Sklyarov in asserting his authority over the region. The return of Kirienko in May 2000 as Putin's representative to the Volga Federal District also circumscribed Sklyarov's authority.

Nizhnii Novgorod signed a power-sharing agreement with Yeltsin in June 1996.

Relations with Other Regions: Strongly Backs Luzhkov

Sklyarov has been one of Moscow Mayor Yurii Luzhkov's most enthusiastic supporters. He presided over the meeting founding the Nizhnii Novgorod branch of Fatherland held on 10 February 1999, and it was assumed that Sklyarov would use his influence to provide key financial support from regional enterprises to Luzhkov's party.

Despite his ties with Sklyarov, Luzhkov has not always treated Nizhnii well. While trying to win support for Sklyarov's election, Luzhkov promised the workers of the Kaprolaktam factory in Dzerzhinsk that Moscow would buy water purifying agents and road salt from them. After Sklyarov's victory, Luzhkov cancelled Moscow's orders, complaining that the factory's products were of low quality and did not perform as expected. Dzerzhinsk's support for Sklyarov was based heavily on Luzhkov's promise.

Nizhnii Novgorod also has strong ties with neighboring Tatarstan. In January 1998 Tatarstan held a festival to boost economic ties with Nizhnii Novgorod. The two regions signed an economic cooperation agreement stipulating the implementation of about $20 million worth of business plans and an increase in trade turnover between Nizhnii Novgorod and Tatarstan by $250 million. The governments of the two regions, the Tatneft oil company, and the Norsi-Oil company signed an agreement in which Tatneft, which has plenty of oil but no processing facilities, would supply raw materials to Norsi, which has extensive processing facilities, but no sources of raw material on its own.

In September 1998 Sklyarov joined up with Samara Governor Konstantin Titov and St. Petersburg Governor Vladimir Yakovlev to coordinate efforts for confronting Russia's financial crisis. The three agreed not to compete with each other and thus not to develop new industries or production capacities when they could purchase the desired good from the other regions. They also decided to share their experiences in paying salaries and wages. The governors of donor regions also wanted the federal government to allow them to coordinate the local actions of the police, tax police, and bankruptcy agencies, all of which are under federal control.

Sklyarov is well respected in the Federation Council, which elected him chairman of the Committee on Regional Policy and Federal Relations in February 1998. Tatarstan President Mintimer Shaimiev was a strong supporter of Sklyarov's candidacy.

Nizhnii Novgorod belongs to the Greater Volga Association, which has a rotating leadership that is currently held by the president of Marii El. The association brings together the republics of Tatarstan, Mordovia, Chuvashia, and Marii El, and Astrakhan, Volgograd, Nizhnii Novgorod, Penza, Samara, Saratov, and Ulyanovsk oblasts. In March 1998 the association met to discuss the state of the petrochemical processing industry. The delegation heads signed a statement of intent to form a cartel agreement, coordinating price-setting, controlling competition among cartel members, and eliminating outside competition. This is one example of how the Greater Volga association presents a united front of regional participants. A June 1998 conference of the association, which was held in Nizhnii Novgorod, demonstrated that a collective approach put the regions in a better position to solve their

economic problems and perhaps to successfully lobby in Moscow.

Foreign Relations: Western Aid Recipient

Several international organizations have launched projects in Nizhnii Novgorod, attracted by the pro-reform image of former Governor Nemtsov. These include the International Finance Corporation, European Bank for Reconstruction and Development, Small Enterprise Equity Fund, British Know How Fund, Opportunity International, United States Peace Corps, Citizens Democracy Corps, and the American Business Center.

In October 1997 Sklyarov led a delegation of 150 oblast administration officials and businessmen to Dusseldorf, Germany, to participate in a fair on the region's economy.

In the fall of 1997 the World Bank lent Nizhnii Novgorod Oblast more than $15 million to buy 100 new electric buses and repair more than 150 electric trains and buses.

Attitudes Toward Business: Heavy Investment Region

Nizhnii Novgorod has been one of the most successful regions in attracting foreign investments, primarily due to the path-breaking efforts of former Governor Boris Nemtsov. Nemtsov's involvement played such a crucial role in developing the oblast's economic relations that many feared his move to national politics would cause foreign interest in the region to decline. However, during the first half of 1998, foreign investment in the oblast equaled $41 million, a $9 million increase over the same period in 1997 (during part of which Nemtsov was still in power). Sklyarov has taken an active role in furthering the region's economic development and bringing in foreign investment. Contracts and agreements involving both foreign and domestic firms that have been signed by Sklyarov and the oblast administration since he took the governor's seat include the following:

• Gorkii Automobile Factory (GAZ) and Italy's Fiat formed a joint venture, Nizhegorodmotors, with the European Bank for Reconstruction and Development. Overall investment in the project will total nearly $1 billion. Ultimately, GAZ plans to make 150,000 Fiat Sienas, Palios, and Mareas a year. The oblast legislature passed a law granting the joint venture a four-year tax holiday from the value-added tax and property and road taxes if foreign investment amounts to at least 40 percent of the company's charter capital. Production, however, has been delayed due to the Russian economic crisis as the project's partners prepare to lobby the oblast legislature to extend the tax break. GAZ is also planning a joint venture with Austria's Steyer to build a $260 million factory with the ability to produce 250,000 diesel engines a year. Given Russia's economic difficulties, it is not clear that there will be customers to buy the cars produced at the plant.

- Norsi-Oil signed a partnership agreement with Agip Petroli, part of Italy's ENI oil enterprise, to form a joint venture that will build modern gas stations in Nizhnii Novgorod. The first two gas stations will cost $2 million each, with the oblast donating the land, Agip contributing equipment, and Norsi supplying the stations with gasoline.

- Japan's Marubeni Corporation signed a five-year cooperation agreement with the oblast administration on developing the fuel and energy sectors. Marubeni also addressed opportunities for processing fuel oil at the Norsi-Oil facilities and a joint venture project involving GAZ. Sklyarov has stated that if Marubeni invests at least $250 million in the Nizhnii Novgorod economy, it will be granted sizable tax benefits.

- Sweden's Electrolux decided to invest $80 million over 5–6 years in a project to make domestic appliances. Initially, the new plant will assemble 300,000 new washing machines. Then production lines will be installed for washing machines, refrigerators, and gas stoves using parts manufactured by Russian producers.

- Japan's Mitsui will build a $150 million pharmaceutical factory in the city of Kotovo. The factory is expected to begin production in 2000, and plans to produce up to 68,000 tons of medicine annually, concentrating on cardiovascular medication.

- McDonald's has opened three restaurants in Nizhnii Novgorod and plans to open 10 more.

- Nizhnii Novgorod Oblast and Canada's Sinex are equal partners in an animal husbandry project that includes plans to increase facilities for artificial insemination.

- The oblast administration and the German company Ferrostahl AG launched a joint venture, which will open a cooperation office in the city of Essen. The Essen establishment will sell products made in Nizhnii factories, import German equipment, and form other cooperative ties.

- Coca-Cola has a bottling plant in the oblast.

- There are 13 investment projects worth $12 million with Dutch partners, including a water purification project, a carbon dioxide emission reduction project, and the construction of a wholesale trade center.

In addition to these projects, France's Peugeot, British Petroleum, and the American firm AFREX/ABC are also considering projects in the oblast.

The governor has other development ideas as well. He hopes to establish a new regional airline. Additionally, Sklyarov has asked his staff to explore the possibility of borrowing to save the Volga cellulose-paper company, whose drastic financial situation and frozen assets have threatened the budget of the city of Balakhna.

In spite of his successes in maintaining business development in the region, Sklyarov has become involved in some high-profile scandals that threaten the business environment as well. One such scandal is the controversy surrounding the Russian-American Spring Investments construction project. The investors, working with British Hotelier Sir Rocco Forte, want to build a new business-class hotel on a prime piece of downtown real estate that was discovered to contain an ancient mass burial site. Sklyarov and church representatives have opposed any construction on the site even though much of the city is built on old graveyards. In October 1998 Mayor Lebedev approved the project, a decision which was upheld by the oblast procurator in December 1998. By May 1999, however, construction work had not begun.

The Russian tax police also hounded Germany's Knauf, Europe's largest manufacturer of construction materials, which set up a joint venture with the Russian firm Avangard in Dzerzhinsk. During a tax audit in spring of 1998, the tax police found that Avangard-Knauf was not properly registered and demanded that the firms pay DM 18.5 million in fines, more than the company's three-year turnover. The figure also greatly exceeded Knauf's DM 8.5 investment.

After a long struggle, Knauf finally won a victory over the tax police on 29 March 1999. The case is no-

Ivan Petrovich Sklyarov

22 June 1948—Born in Evstratovka village Voronezh Oblast; Graduated from the Moscow Aviation Institute with a specialization in electro-mechanical engineering

1963–1967—Student at the Arzamas Instrument Making Technical School

1967–1971—Metal worker and technician at an Arzamas instrument making factory

1971–1973—Assistant secretary on the factory's Komsomol committee

1973–1974—Served in the Soviet Army

1974–1977—Secretary of the Arzamas instrument making factory Komsomol committee

1977–1981—Head of shop and head of factory production

1981–1985—Secretary and then first secretary of the Arzamas CPSU city committee

1985–1991—Chairman of the city executive committee and city council in Arzamas

1990—Elected to the RSFSR Congress of People's Deputies, member of the Agrarian faction

1990–1993—Member of the Russian Supreme Soviet

December 1991–April 1994—Vice-governor of Nizhnii Novgorod Oblast

April 1994—Appointed mayor of Nizhnii Novgorod

December 1995—Elected mayor of Nizhnii Novgorod

13 July 1997—Elected governor of Nizhnii Novgorod Oblast

18 February 1998—Elected chair of the Federation Council Committee on Regional Politics and Federal Relations

20 May 1998—Confirmed representative of the Congress on Local and Regional Governments of Europe

Loves running and walking

Married, with one daughter

---

table because Knauf found the resources and willpower to stand up to an opponent as powerful as the tax police, even after the lower court had ruled in favor of the tax police. Other investors had been watching the case to see how the foreigners would be treated. Knauf's battle secured it better treatment by the local authorities. On 19 April the oblast administration and Avangard-Knauf signed an agreement on social-economic cooperation according to which the authorities are even willing to provide some tax breaks to the plant (*EWI RRR*, 29 April 1999).

In addition to its tax troubles, the joint venture has experienced various difficulties including high transportation costs to bring in necessary raw materials and a lack of demand for its product on the local market, forcing the venture to ship its goods to Moscow, St. Petersburg, and even Germany, at high cost.

Internet Sites in the Region

http://www.xpress.inforis.nnov.su/n-nov/admin/
This site offers lots of useful information about the Nizhnii Novgorod Oblast administration. It includes information about the governor's activities, summaries of reports from the mass media, local press releases, and the texts of legislation and presidential decrees.

http://www.inforis.ru:8002/n-nov/admin/fino/hpage.html
This site is for the oblast property fund, displaying information about the fund and investment possibilities.

http://www.inforis.ru:8002/n-nov/admin/noks/mainoks.html
This is the home page for the Nizhnii Novgorod Oblast committee on state statistics.

http://www.inforis.ru:8002/n-nov/admin/email/ adresa.html
From this website you can access the e-mail addresses of oblast administrative bodies as well as the oblast's local and district leaders.

http://black.inforis.nnov.su/infobase/bases.ws?
This site provides information on oblast and local legislation and treaties. It includes the provisions of Nizhnii Novgorod's power-sharing agreement with Moscow and its various trade agreements with Tatarstan.

http://www.sci-nnov.ru/massmedia/papersnnpapers/
This site links to several regional newspapers, including access to back issues.

REPUBLIC OF NORTH OSSETIA-ALANIA

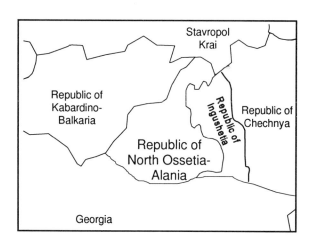

Territory: 8,000 km²
Population (as of 1 January 1998):
663,000
Distance from Moscow: 1,923 km

Major Cities:
Vladikavkaz, *capital* (pop. 309,800)
Mozdok (39,100)
Beslan (33,600)

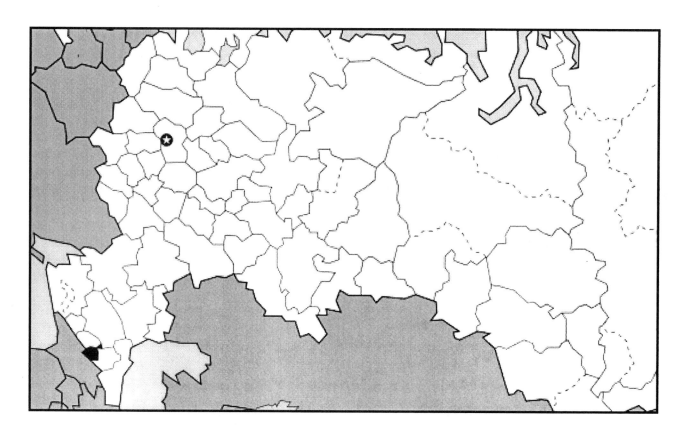

Basic Facts

Population (as of 1 Jan. 1998): 663,000 (0.45% of Russian total)

Ethnic breakdown (1989 census): Ossetians 53.0%, Russians 29.9%, Ingush 5.2%, Armenians 2.2%, Georgians 1.9%, Ukrainians 1.6%, Kumyks 1.5%

Urban population (as of 1 Jan. 1998): 68.9% (Russia overall: 73.1%)

Student population (as of 1 Sept. 1997): 315 per 10,000 (Russia overall: 208/10,000)

Pensioner population (1997): 27.75% (Russia overall: 25.96%)

Percent of population with higher education (1989 census): 13.3% (Russia overall: 11.3%)

Percent of population working in 1997: Industry: 20.4% (Russian average: 23.0%); Agriculture: 9.8% (13.7%); Trade: 12.3% (13.5%); Culture: 17.1% (13.3%)

Average monthly personal income in July 1998: 538.0 new rubles (Russian average: 891.7 new rubles)

Average monthly personal expenses in July 1998: 385.2 new rubles (Russian average: 684.9 new rubles)

Average monthly subsistence requirement in 1998: 404 new rubles (Russian average: 438 new rubles)

Consumer price index (as of July 1998): 93 (Russia overall = 100)

Budgetary revenues (1997): 1,317.4 billion rubles (Russia overall: 433,378.2 billion rubles)

Budgetary expenditures (1997): 1,484.3 billion rubles (Russia overall: 468,111.6 billion rubles)

Industrial production as percentage of all Russian production (Jan.–Aug. 1998): 0.08%

Proportion of loss-making enterprises (as of July 1998): 48.6% (Russia overall: 50.4%)

Number of enterprises which have wage arrears (as of 1 Sept. 1998): 582 (0.43% of Russian total)

Agricultural production as percentage of all Russian production (1997): 0.29%

Number of private farms (as of 1 Jan. 1998): 1,048 (0.38% of Russian total)

Capital investment (1997): 578.9 billion rubles (Russia overall: 408,797 billion rubles)

Sources of investment (1997): federal budget: 37.9% (Russian average: 10.2%); regional budget: 16.5% (10.5%); extra-budgetary funds: 45.6% (79.3%)

Number of joint ventures (1997): 8 (0.05% of Russian total)

Fixed capital investment in joint ventures and foreign companies (1997): 0 (Russia overall: 16,265.4 billion rubles)

Number of small businesses (as of 1 July 1998): 1,700 (0.20% of Russian total)

Number of telephones per 100 families (1997): in cities: 49.8 (Russian average: 49.2); in villages: 33.0 (19.8)

Brief Overview

The republic is located in the southeastern part of the North Caucasus and borders Stavropol Krai, Kabardino-Balkaria, Ingushetia, Chechnya, and Georgia. Unlike the majority of North Caucasian peoples who are Muslim, the majority of North Ossetians are Orthodox Christian.

Almost half of the republican territory is mountainous with peaks approaching 4,600–4,700 meters; plains make up the northern part of the republic. North Ossetia is fairly rich in mineral resources, boasting deposits of zinc, lead, tin, silver, granite, marble, and mineral waters. Additionally there may be oil within the republic's territory.

Almost half of the republican GDP (42.2%) comes from industry, followed by agriculture (23.8%), transportation and communication (18.1%), and construction (7.3%). Regional industries include non-ferrous metallurgy, machine building, metal processing, timber working, chemicals, small-scale production, glass, and food processing. The agricultural sector focuses on vegetables, fruit, grain, and grapes for wine making.

Almost all republican exports (90%) are raw materials. The region has economic contacts with over 30 foreign countries, among them Germany, Cyprus, Turkey, Bulgaria, China, Great Britain, Italy, Ukraine, Kazakhstan, and Lithuania.

According to a 1998 survey by *Ekspert* magazine, the republic ranked 67th among Russia's 89 regions in terms of investment potential and 74th in terms of investment risk. A 1998 survey by Bank Austria ranked the republic 78th in terms of investment climate.

Electoral History

2000 Presidential Election
Putin: 64.71%
Zyuganov: 28.46%
Zhirinovsky: 1.29%
Yavlinskii: 0.98%
Tuleev: 0.96%
Turnout: 70.95% (Russia overall: 68.64%)

1999 Parliamentary Elections
Communist Party of the Russian Federation: 42.13%
Fatherland–All Russia: 18.19%
Unity: 18.17%
Zhirinovsky Bloc: 4.29%
Communists–Workers' Russia: 2.62%
Union of Right Forces: 1.97%

Stalin's Bloc–For the USSR: 1.69%
Yabloko: 1.22%
In a single-mandate district: 1 Communist Party of the Russian Federation
Turnout: 53.93% (Russia overall: 61.85%)

1998 Republican Presidential Election
Dzasokhov (State Duma deputy): 76.1%
Galazov (incumbent): 9.7%
Turnout: 68.0%

1996 Presidential Election
Zyuganov: 62.33%/52.82% (first round/second round)
Yeltsin: 19.28%/43.00%
Lebed: 9.60%
Zhirinovsky: 3.23%
Yavlinskii: 1.80%
Turnout: 68.95%/70.44% (Russia overall: 69.67%/ 68.79%)

1995 Parliamentary Elections
Communist Party of the Russian Federation: 51.67%
Liberal Democratic Party of Russia: 10.22%
Our Home Is Russia: 5.97%
Communists–Workers' Russia: 4.64%
Congress of Russian Communities: 2.75%
Agrarian Party of Russia: 2.59%
Women of Russia: 2.17%
Derzhava: 2.02%
In a single-mandate district: 1 independent
Turnout: 62.97% (Russia overall: 64.37%)

1993 Constitutional Referendum
"Yes"—51.5%   "No"—45.5%

1993 Parliamentary Elections
Communist Party of the Russian Federation: 36.06%
Liberal Democratic Party of Russia: 17.47%
Russia's Choice: 7.81%
Democratic Party of Russia: 7.03%
Party of Russian Unity and Concord: 5.99%
Women of Russia: 5.94%
Yabloko: 5.04%
Agrarian Party of Russia: 3.94%
In a single-mandate district: 1 independent
Turnout: 59.81% (Russia overall: 54.34%)

1991 Presidential Elections

Ryzhkov: 41.86%

Yeltsin: 27.34%

Zhirinovsky: 11.16%

Makashov: 7.69%

Tuleev: 6.37%

Bakatin: 2.24%

Turnout: 84.01% (Russia overall: 76.66%)

Regional Political Institutions

Executive:

President, 4-year term

Aleksandr Sergeevich Dzasokhov, elected

January 1998

Svoboda St., 1; Vladikavkaz, 362038; Republic
of North Ossetia-Alania

Tel 7(867–2) 53–35–24;

Fax 7(867–2) 33–35–16

Legislative:

Unicameral

Parliament—75 members, 4-year term, elected
March 1995, April 1999

Chairman—Vyacheslav Semenovich Parinov,
elected June 1995, May 1999

Regional Politics

Elections Inspire Hope for Conflict Resolution

When Duma Deputy Aleksandr Dzasokhov was elected president of the Republic of North Ossetia-Alania on 18 January 1998, many hoped that a resolution to the conflict between North Ossetia and the Republic of Ingushetia would soon be found. One year later Dzasokhov and Ingushetia President Ruslan Aushev signed an agreement on repatriating refugees to the disputed region, but the situation in the region remains tense.

Although ethnic conflict plays a large role in North Caucasian history, the contemporary Ossetian-Ingush hostility is primarily a result of events from the Soviet period. In 1944 Stalin deported the entire populations of the Karachai, Balkar, Ingush, and Chechen national groups to areas in Central Asia, Kazakhstan, and Siberia, claiming that these groups had conspired with the Germans during World War II. At this time, the Soviet government granted North Ossetia the Ingush territory of the Prigorodnyi Raion.

In 1957 Khrushchev allowed the deported peoples to return to the North Caucasus, but did not return the Prigorodnyi Raion to the Ingush. Armed conflict between the two ethnic groups ensued, climaxing in the 1990s when Ingushetia separated from Chechnya and demanded the reacquisition of its former territory. In a week of extraordinary violence in October 1992, over 600 people were killed and thousands of homes were destroyed. As a result, tens of thousands of Ingush fled the region for Ingushetia. Meanwhile, more than 400,000 Ossetians have fled from conflict in Georgia to North Ossetia, and about 16,000 of them settled in abandoned Ingush homes in Prigorodnyi Raion. Thus the territorial conflict has been complicated by the fact that both republics need to accommodate masses of refugees, not to mention the effects of the war in Chechnya.

Despite this difficult context, North Ossetia was the first North Caucasian region to use elections as a tool for effecting political change. Dzasokhov won 76 percent of the vote, beating out incumbent Akhsarbeck Galazov, who received only 13 percent in the 1998 voting. During the campaign, he had the support of young people, veterans, the local intelligentsia, and half the members of the republican legislature. Reportedly, over two-thirds of the men serving in Russia's military, police, and border forces in the republic voted for him (*NG*, 20 January 1998). Our Home Is Russia supported Galazov, who had a good relationship with Moscow. Although Dzasokhov is officially a member of the Communist party, he rejected the support of the local branch of the party during the presidential elections because he wanted to be seen as a national leader, not as a Communist nominee (*Jamestown Foundation Prism*, No. 11, Part 3, 29 May 1998).

North Ossetia viewed the electoral results less as Dzasokhov's victory and more as Galazov's defeat. Galazov has been blamed for the region's economic difficulties and accused of financial mismanagement and possibly corruption (*Prism*, 29 May 1998). The collapse of the military-industrial complex has been particularly devastating to the republic, which is Russia's second most heavily militarized region. Moreover, Galazov was heavily criticized for failing to develop North Ossetia's industrial potential to meet modern needs.

Executive Platform: Honest Reformer

After his inauguration, Dzasokhov declared that his main two policy priorities were fighting crime and revitalizing the economy (*Prism*, 29 May 1998). He has increased police supervision in the republic, and intends to regularly publish budget information to prevent financial mismanagement.

In economic policy, Dzasokhov would like to legalize the region's underground vodka industry, put up to 70,000 unemployed workers to work in small businesses, and lobby heavily for federal support. He hopes to convince the Russian government to renovate the Georgian military highway and the Trans-Caucasus highway in order to increase freight traffic through the region. Additionally, he wants to establish relationships between North Ossetia's light industry and firms in Belarus and Bulgaria (*EWI RRR*, 29 January 1998).

Although Dzasokhov's role in national politics and ties to Moscow elites have made him an attractive leader to the impoverished region, his limited experience working locally creates doubts about whether or not he will be successful in controlling the republican executive branch.

In building a local base, Dzasokhov effectively used television to explain new policy initiatives and present himself directly to the people. Dzasokhov is popularly said to be an "honest politician" (Charles Blandy, "Prigorodnyy Rayon: The Continuing Dispute," Conflict Studies Research Center, September 1997)

In 1999 Dzasokhov joined the All Russia regional party headed by Tatarstan President Mintimer Shaimiev.

Policies: Ingush Negotiations

After his election, Dzasokhov helped expedite the return of Ingush refugees to the Pridorognyi Raion (for more on this topic, see Relations with Other Regions.

Relationships Between Key Players: Popular Politicians

Dzasokhov's cabinet is made up primarily of figures who are popular in the republic, giving his government the reputation of being less corrupt than its predecessor.

In October 1998 North Ossetia adopted a law on local government allowing Dzasokhov to appoint the republic's mayors, which is in direct violation of federal legislation stating that mayors must be elected. The presidential administration protested the law, but the Ministry of Regional Affairs and the procurator general chose not to take any action, claiming that there was no evidence that Dzasokhov had actually signed

the law. Dzasokhov claimed to have signed the law in late October while then Prime Minister Yevgenii Primakov was in town to meet with Chechen President Aslan Maskhadov. Dzasokhov claimed that the law was in accordance with federal legislation since he would select mayors from the elected members of local councils (*EWI RRR*, 19 November 1998). Tatarstan and Kabardino-Balkaria have similar practices for selecting local executives.

In April 1999 North Ossetia elected a new 75-person parliament. The republic's branch of the Communist party won the most seats of any political organization, 13. Enterprise directors, businessmen, and bankers won 39 seats. Seven ethnic Russians, one Armenian, and one Kumyk were elected to the assembly. Vyacheslav Parinov was reelected the parliament's speaker, a position he has held since 1995.

Ties to Moscow: Strong Connections with Federal Politicians

One of the complaints against former North Ossetian President Galazov was that he lacked sufficient ties to Moscow and thus could not protect the local business elite from the federal government's campaign against illegally imported alcohol from Georgia (*RT*, 17, 20 January 1998). Dzasokhov's better connections with Moscow, where he had served in the State Duma, and his desire to improve the region's economic situation were thus attractive to the republic's business community. Similarly, his diplomatic experience working as a Soviet ambassador in the Middle East and lack of involvement in the Ossetian-Ingush conflict raised hopes that Dzasokhov would help settle many of the problems in the North Caucasus.

Although Moscow supported Galazov during the elections, the presidential administration was on good terms with Dzasokhov. After the latter was elected, Yeltsin's then spokesman Sergei Yastrzhembskii said that Dzasokhov's pro-Moscow orientation was more important than his Communist association (*EWI RRR*, 21 May 1998).

Nevertheless, Dzasokhov is fed up with the manner in which Moscow handles North Caucasian affairs, which is one reason why he chose to leave national politics in favor of regional government. He believes that Moscow's policies have been ineffective, although he supports the negotiation-based approaches taken by Ivan Rybkin and Ramazan Abdulatipov as good examples (*Izvestiya*, 26 June 1998).

North Ossetia was one of the first regions to arrange a power-sharing agreement with Moscow, signing the treaty on 23 March 1995.

North Ossetia is unique in the North Caucasus because it is the only predominantly Orthodox Christian region, while the rest are dominated by Muslims. It is not clear, however, how this cultural link with Moscow has affected their relations, although it is generally assumed that it has played a role in Moscow's support of the Ossetians in the Ingush-Ossetian conflict.

Relations with Other Regions: Regional Diplomat

After his election, Dzasokhov immediately established a working relationship with Ingush President Ruslan Aushev. It is perhaps Dzasokhov's ability to negotiate with Aushev that sets him apart from his predecessor, who had strained relations with the Ingush president. Ingushetia welcomed Dzasokhov's election, since he had not played a part in the Ossetian-Ingush conflict and thus could move the negotiating process forward. Dzasokhov has been a strong advocate for repatriating Ingush refugees in the Prigorodnyi Raion and all other relevant areas. Relations between the two leaders suffered a setback in June 1998, when Aushev accused Dzasokhov of involvement in the kidnapping of six Ingush by Ossetians (*KD*, 11 June 1998). Yet, in January 1999 Aushev and Dzasokhov signed an agreement on refugee repatriation. A second agreement signed between the prime ministers of the two republics in March 1999 asserted that the refugees would return to their homes in Prigorodnyi Raion by December 1999. The refugees were to be given a choice of moving into their former apartments or receiving a plot of land in an Ingush region, and would be provided with security, credits for rebuilding their homes, and local aid in obtaining water, heat, and gas. It is unclear how many refugees actually returned. The Ingush claimed that 20,000 would seek repatriation, but the Ossetians believed this number was greatly exaggerated (*EWI RRR*, 4 March 1999).

Dzasokhov has also been active in trying to mediate the conflict between Russia and Chechnya (*Prism*, 29 May 1998). Moscow welcomed Dzasokhov's involvement, which supports the federal government's interest in involving the North Caucasus republics in working toward a solution to the Chechen problem.

North Ossetia belongs to the Association of Cooperation of Republics, Krais, and Oblasts of the Northern Caucasus, the poorest of Russia's eight regional associations. The association includes the republics of Adygeya, Dagestan, Ingushetia, Kabardino-Balkaria, Karachaevo-Cherkessia, and Kalmykia; Krasnodar and Stavropol krais; and Rostov Oblast.

North Ossetia has also participated in the North Caucasus Congress of Chambers of Industry and Trade. This congress involves chambers from Rostov, Krasnodar, Stavropol, Adygeya, Karachaevo-Cherkessia, and Dagestan. The main goal of this assembly is to influence federal investment priorities so that more emphasis is placed on developing the small business sector rather than continuing to support unprofitable enterprises in the state sector.

Foreign Relations: International Diplomat

Dzasokhov's long political and diplomatic career during the Soviet era allowed him to cultivate relationships with politicians who continue to play important roles in post-Soviet affairs. He is particularly close to Georgian President Eduard Shevardnadze and Azerbaijani President Heidar Aliev.

Immediately after his election, Dzasokhov met with the president of Georgia's South Ossetia, Ludwig Chibirov. The two leaders discussed regional integration and possibilities for increasing investment in South Ossetia, which receives hardly any funding from the central government in Georgia. Dzasokhov promised Chibirov that he would try to help expedite a solution to South Ossetia's ambiguous status within Georgia; however, he does not support the unification of the two Ossetias (*RFE/RL*, 28 January 1998). Dzasokhov met with Shevardnadze in May 1998 to discuss resolving the South Ossetian and other Caucasian conflicts. He backs Shevardnadze's proposal to establish a federation in Georgia and encouraged the leadership to give South Ossetia a generous degree of autonomy (*RFE/RL*, 14 May 1998).

Dzasokhov believes that cooperation between Russia, Georgia, Armenia, and Azerbaijan is necessary to successfully resolve conflicts in North Ossetia and other areas in the Caucasus (*NG*, 18 July 1998). He also considers it of vital importance for the Russian leadership to activate diplomatic contacts in the United States, Turkey, and Saudi Arabia.

Dzasokhov's vast experience and interest in foreign relations extend far beyond the needs of his small republic. He often expresses views on issues that have

Aleksandr Sergeevich Dzasokhov

3 April 1934—Born in Vladikavkaz

1957—Graduated from the North Caucasus Mining and Metallurgical Institute

1957—Joined the Communist Party

1957–1958—First secretary of the Ordzhonikidze Komsomol city committee

1958–1961—Chief manager of the Komsomol Central Committee

1961–1967—Worked for the Committee for Youth Organizations in the USSR in a variety of positions including chief secretary and first deputy chairman

1967–1986—Chief secretary, deputy, and first deputy chairman for the Soviet Committee for Solidarity with the Countries of Asia and Africa

1973—Defended his candidate's dissertation entitled "The Making of Young Independent States"

1986–1988—Soviet Ambassador to Syria

1988—Became first secretary of the North Ossetian regional committee of the CPSU

1989—Elected to the USSR Congress of People's Deputies and in February 1990 became the chairman of the Committee for International Affairs

June 1990—Participated in the 28th Party Congress of the CPSU, was elected a Politburo member and Central Committee secretary

1992—Elected to the Russian Congress of People's Deputies

12 December 1993—Elected to the Duma, serving from January 1994 to December 1995 on the Committee for International Affairs, and as chair of the Subcommittee on Problems with the UN and Other International Organizations

1995—Joined Regions of Russia movement

December 1995—Reelected to the Duma and became a member of the Committee for International Affairs

16 January 1996—Joined Nikolai Ryzhkov's Power to the People faction in the Duma

28 December 1996—Appointed by presidential decree to the Russian Federation Interdepartmental Commission for issues involving the Council of Europe

12 April 1997—Appointed by presidential decree to the Consultative Commission on the Charter for the Union of Belarus and Russia

16 April 1997—Chosen as head of the Russian delegation in the parliamentary assembly for the Council of Europe

18 January 1998—Elected president of the North Ossetia-Alania Republic

Ossetian

Married, with two sons

little relation to the governing of North Ossetia. However, his interest in international affairs and desire to be the top leader in the North Caucasus may cloud his ability to focus on matters more relevant to North Ossetia (*Prism*, 29 May 1998).

Attitudes Toward Business: Little Real Progress

Although Dzasokhov has expressed a serious commitment to revitalizing the republic's economy, he introduced few concrete measures to promote this goal. If Dzasokhov can succeed in stabilizing the region politically and reducing crime and corruption, he might find that the region has strong investment potential. North Ossetia is rich in mineral resources, possessing zinc, lead, tin, silver, granite, and marble deposits as well as mineral waters. Most of the republic's exports are raw materials. North Ossetia has economic contacts with over thirty countries including Germany, Cyprus, Turkey, Bulgaria, China, Great Britain, Italy, Ukraine, Kazakhstan, and Lithuania. Of course, violence and in-

stability throughout the region means that real investment is unlikely until these problems are resolved.

Internet Sites in the Region

http://www.mediaport.org/~osseet/ossetia.html
This English language website provides information about Ossetian culture, news, politics, etc. It offers a chat room, mailing list, and current stories on events in North and South Ossetia.

http://www.geocities.com/~kazik/mainpage.htm
This page offers basic information about North Ossetia's geography, history, and culture, in both English and Russian. It also displays several pictures of the region.

http://www.friends-partners.org/oldfriends/ossetia/index.html
This is an English-language website detailing North Ossetia's history and industry. It also includes an e-mail link to the region's administration: vgg@aprez.vladikavkaz.ru.

NOVGOROD OBLAST

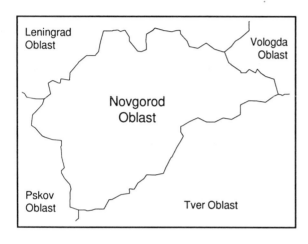

Territory: 55,300 km²
Population (as of 1 January 1998):
738,000
Distance from Moscow: 606 km

Major Cities:
Novgorod, *capital* (pop. 231,300)
Borovichi (61,500)
Staraya Russa (39,900)

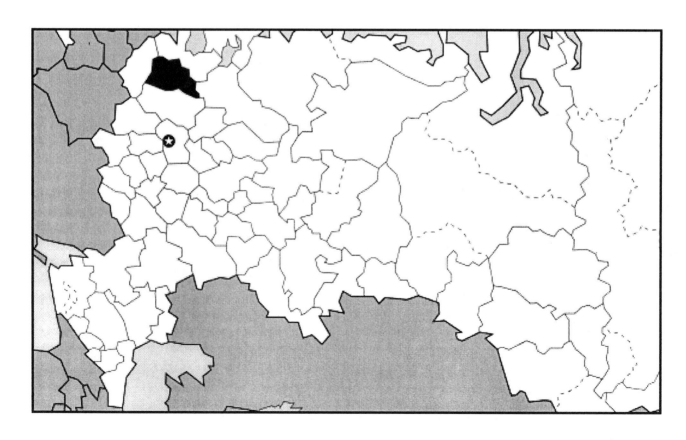

Basic Facts

Population (as of 1 Jan. 1998): 738,000 (0.50 of Russian total)

Ethnic breakdown (1989 census): Russians 94.7%, Ukrainians 1.9%

Urban population (as of 1 Jan. 1998): 71.2% (Russia overall: 73.1%)

Student population (as of 1 Sept. 1997): 178 per 10,000 (Russia overall: 208/10,000)

Pensioner population (1997): 29.67% (Russia overall: 25.96%)

Percent of population with higher education (1989 census): 8.8% (Russia overall: 11.3%)

Percent of population working in (1997): Industry: 24.1% (Russian average: 23.0%); Agriculture: 15.0% (13.7%); Trade: 11.5% (13.5%); Culture: 12.5% (13.3%)

Average monthly personal income in July 1998: 863.7 new rubles (Russian average: 891.7 new rubles)

Average monthly personal expenses in July 1998: 651.6 new rubles (Russian average: 684.9 new rubles)

Average monthly subsistence requirement in 1998: 385 new rubles (Russian average: 438 new rubles)

Consumer price index (as of July 1998): 94 (Russia overall = 100)

Budgetary revenues (1997): 1,762.8 billion rubles (Russia overall: 433,378.2 billion rubles)

Budgetary expenditures (1997): 1,845.2 billion rubles (Russia overall: 468,111.6 billion rubles)

Industrial production as percentage of all Russian production (Jan.–Aug. 1998): 0.38%

Proportion of loss-making enterprises (as of July 1998): 46.5% (Russia overall: 50.4%)

Number of enterprises which have wage arrears (as of 1 Sept. 1998): 528 (0.39% of Russian total)

Agricultural production as percentage of all Russian production (1997): 0.53%

Number of private farms (as of 1 Jan. 1998): 1,831 (0.67% of Russian total)

Capital investment (1997): 1,079.4 billion rubles (Russia overall: 408,797 billion rubles)

Sources of investment (1997): federal budget: 11.9% (Russian average: 10.2%); regional budget: 5.3% (10.5%); extra-budgetary funds: 82.8% (79.3%)

Foreign investment (1997): 94,270,000 USD (Russia overall: 12,294,734,000 USD)

Number of joint ventures (1997): 53 (0.36% of Russian total)

Fixed capital investment in joint ventures and foreign companies (1997): 53,104 million rubles (Russia overall: 16,265.4 billion rubles)

Number of small businesses (as of 1 July 1998): 2,700 (0.31% of Russian total)

Number of enterprises privatized in 1997: 32 (1.17% of Russian total), including those which used to be municipal property: 78.1% (Russian average: 66.4%); regional property: 15.6% (20.0%); federal property: 6.3% (13.6%)

Number of telephones per 100 families (1997): in cities: 42.6 (Russian average: 49.2); in villages: 20.2 (19.8)

Brief Overview

Novgorod Oblast is located in the northwest of Russia and borders Leningrad, Vologda, Tver, and Pskov oblasts. Its center, the city of Novgorod, is famous for its democratic traditions. The city was founded in 859 and almost immediately became an important trade center because of its strategic location at the crossroads of many commercial routes. For a long time, Novgorod was the only city governed by an assembly of its citizens, the *veche*, rather than by a king, as other cities and lands were at that time. Though the city also had a king, he was invited to rule by the veche and was merely a leader of the city army.

Today, the oblast still enjoys a favorable geographic location, being at the crossroads of many domestic and international trade routes, connecting Moscow, St. Petersburg, and the Baltic states. The region is fairly rich in mineral resources, including oil, diamonds, and peat. Among the major regional industries are: machine and equipment building, metallurgy, electronics, timber working, and cellulose.

According to a 1998 survey by *Ekspert* magazine, the oblast is ranked 66th among Russia's 89 regions in terms of investment potential and 5th in terms of investment risk. A 1998 survey by Bank Austria ranked the oblast 46th in terms of investment climate.

Electoral History

2000 Presidential Election
Putin: 64.86%
Zyuganov: 21.41%
Yavlinskii: 5.17%
Zhirinovsky: 2.54%
Tuleev: 1.52%
Turnout: 71.05% (Russia overall: 68.64%)

1999 Parliamentary Elections
Unity: 31.55%
Communist Party of the Russian Federation: 19.08%
Yabloko: 7.18%
Union of Right Forces: 7.04%
Zhirinovsky Bloc: 6.96%
Our Home Is Russia: 5.89%
Fatherland–All Russia: 5.83%
In a single-mandate district: 1 independent
Turnout: 63.99% (Russia overall: 61.85%)

1999 Gubernatorial Election
Prusak (incumbent): 91.56%
Peshkov: 1.62%
Demanov: 1.30%
Nefedov: 0.50%
Turnout: 50.16%

1996 Presidential Election
Yeltsin: 35.76%/59.14% (first round/second round)
Zyuganov: 23.76%/33.99%
Lebed: 18.52%
Yavlinskii: 11.03%
Zhirinovsky: 6.22%
Turnout: 71.86%/70.69% (Russia overall: 69.67%/68.79%)

1995 Gubernatorial Election
Prusak (incumbent): 56.17%
Kuznetsov: 8.94%
Gaidym (KPRF): 8.72%
Kondratev (LDPR): 8.13%
Ochin (State Duma deputy): 7.45%
Visloguzov: 1.15%
Aleksandrov: 0.76%
Murashov: 0.71%
Turnout: 67.38%

1995 Parliamentary Elections
Communist Party of the Russian Federation: 18.02%
Liberal Democratic Party of Russia: 12.13%
Our Home Is Russia: 10.51%
Women of Russia: 8.30%
Yabloko: 7.36%
Communists–Workers' Russia: 5.14%
Congress of Russian Communities: 3.89%
Party of Workers' Self-Government: 3.60%
In a single-mandate district: 1 independent
Turnout: 67.23% (Russia overall: 64.37%)

1993 Constitutional Referendum
"Yes"—61.6%   "No"—36.1%

1993 Parliamentary Elections
Liberal Democratic Party of Russia: 29.60%
Russia's Choice: 13.21%
Party of Russian Unity and Concord: 10.08%
Women of Russia: 9.52%
Communist Party of the Russian Federation: 9.25%
Yabloko: 7.61%

Agrarian Party of Russia: 6.91%

Democratic Party of Russia: 6.14%

In a single-mandate district: 1 Party of Russian Unity and Concord

From electoral associations: 1 Communist Party of the Russian Federation

Turnout: 58.06% (Russia overall: 54.34%)

1991 Presidential Election

Yeltsin: 46.65%

Ryzhkov: 21.32%

Tuleev: 9.46%

Zhirinovsky: 9.33%

Makashov: 4.72%

Bakatin: 3.95%

Turnout: 77.61% (Russia overall: 76.66%)

Regional Political Institutions

Executive:

Governor, 4–year term

Mikhail Mikhailovich Prusak, elected December 1995, reelected 1999

Pl. Sofiiskaya, 1; Novgorod, 173005

Tel 7(816–2) 27–47–79; 13–12–02

Fax 7(816–2) 13–13–30

Federation Council in Moscow:

7(095) 292–13–58, 926–63–72;

Fax: 7(095) 292–58–96

Legislative:

Unicameral

Oblast Duma—26 members, 4–year term, elected March 1997

Chairman—Anatolii Aleksandrovich Boitsev, elected March 1994, October 1997

Regional Politics

Russia's Top Investment Magnet

Mikhail Prusak has been one of the most successful regional executives in attracting foreign investment. In the seven years of his tenure in Novgorod Oblast, he has brought the region from 63rd place among Russia's 89 regions to the top six. He has turned the underdeveloped region into a hotspot where foreign capital makes up 80 percent of all investments. His successful reforms and business incentives have gained international attention and esteem.

Russian President Boris Yeltsin first appointed Mikhail Prusak governor of Novgorod Oblast in 1991. Prusak was elected to the post in December 1995, winning 56.2 percent of the vote and reelected in September 1999 with 91.6 percent. The primary reason Prusak was able to win such an overwhelming majority was because he managed to have the elections moved up by three months, drastically cutting short the time opponents had to conduct their campaigns. He was supported by Yabloko, the Fatherland–All Russia bloc, and Our Home Is Russia (NDR). He has been successful at getting along with just about everyone, regardless of their political coloring. Prusak admits: "I don't have any real opposition in Novgorod. In the 1995 elections, people from all parties voted for me: Communists, Zhirinovskyites, and members of Yabloko and Our Home Is Russia. Many elderly people were opposed, but once the factories were built and they saw that workers could support their families, they supported it [foreign investment]. Many people were greatly surprised by the high quality of the factories the foreigners built" (*EWI RRR*, 5 March 1998). However, a closer look at the political situation in the region suggests that Prusak is not really loved by all, but rather is so authoritative that others have to comply with him to some degree in order to work in the region.

Prusak is well known on the federal stage. He has been asked to join the federal government several times, but always refuses. Nevertheless, it is possible that he will seek federal office in the future and play a significant role in developing Russia's investment policies.

Executive Platform: Pro-Yeltsin, Pro-Business

Prusak was one of President Boris Yeltsin's most devoted allies. In many respects, Prusak epitomizes the reform ideal. He has instituted liberal market reforms, pushed through privatization, and has succeeded at giving his region one of the most attractive business climates in Russia. On the other hand, he has a very authoritarian style and it remains unclear how long his reforms will survive after he leaves office.

Prusak was a member of the pro-government Our Home Is Russia (NDR) and belonged to the movement's political council. Yet, Prusak prefered to work outside of party lines, and boasted of his popularity across ideological cleavages. Nevertheless, as the governors began to declare their political allegiances on the eve of the December 1999 State Duma elections, Prusak made clear that he still remained within NDR's ranks.

Policies: Targeted to Attract
Foreign Investment

Prusak's policy focus has been to attract foreign investment to Novgorod. The governor argues that investment was Novgorod's only hope since the region initially had such a low potential for succeeding in a market economy (*EWI RRR*, 5 March 1998). Prusak claims that the lack of tax legislation in Russia as a whole and the hesitancy exhibited by domestic investors to place money in Novgorod compelled the region to develop its own tax code within the framework of the Constitution and the laws that existed in 1992 (*EWI RRR*, 5 March 1998). Novgorod decided to free foreign investment projects from all regional and local taxes until the projects became profitable. Since regional and local taxes account for about 50 percent of all taxes payable by individuals and corporations, Novgorod's initiatives successfully attracted a number of foreign investors.

Another incentive adopted by Novgorod was to circumvent the absence of a land code permitting the sale or lease of land to foreigners by allowing Russian partners in joint ventures with foreigners to purchase land for a nominal sum. In order for a combined Russian-foreign firm to be registered as joint venture, the Russian partner must hold at least 2 percent of the stock. In instances when the foreign investor wanted to own 100 percent of a project, the oblast administration leased them the land for 49 years. Furthermore, in many instances when foreign investors found idle production facilities that they believed they could use, the oblast administration gave the respective land, buildings, and facilities to the enterprises to use for free (*EWI RRR*, 5 March 1998).

Prusak's primary weakness in regard to economic policy has been the lack of attention focused on attracting Russian investment to Novgorod. In 1993 Novgorod set up one of the first regional funds in Russia to competitively support small business initiatives. Small business now employs 21 percent of the region's working-age population (Nicolai N. Petro, "The Novgorod Region: A Russian Success Story," report prepared for The National Council for Eurasian and East European Research). However, this sector alone does not provide a sufficient domestic economic base. The oblast did adopt legislation in 1997 geared toward attracting domestic capital; however, the overwhelming majority of Novgorod's income comes from foreign ventures.

Relationships Between Key Players:
"Party of Business"

Prusak boasts that in his seven years as regional governor, the Novgorod legislature has never blocked one of his decisions and he has never vetoed a legislative decision (*EWI RRR*, 5 March 1998). He attributes this good relationship to the fact that all of the legislature's 27 members belong to the "party of business." Most of the legislative deputies are either heads of local administrations or directors of large enterprises. Prusak claims that the main reason why Novgorod is stable is that people can see the practical results of the administration's and legislature's work (*EWI RRR*, 5 March 1998).

Prusak has admitted some difficulties in working with Novgorod Mayor Aleksandr Korsunov, but feels that his situation is easier than in other regions since Korsunov also serves as his deputy. Both Prusak and Korsunov are members of Our Home Is Russia, and Korsunov is head of the movement's regional branch.

In spite of the generally stable support Prusak has experienced in Novgorod, he is clearly concerned about his losing influence in the region. In May 1999, at his suggestion, the Oblast Duma voted to move up gubernatorial elections in the region from December 1999, which would have coincided with the State Duma elections, to 5 September. This move gave Prusak a campaigning edge over the region's opposition, and it was clearly a strategic political tactic. Despite his fears Prusak won easily.

Ties to Moscow: Loyal

Prusak remained a loyal ally of President Yeltsin since first working on Yeltsin's presidential campaign team in spring and summer 1991, and continued to support Yeltsin throughout his presidential career. He easily transferred this loyalty to to Putin. Prusak is well known on the federal level and has been asked to join the federal government several times. He continues to turn down such offers, although it seems unlikely that the young governor will always limit himself to regional politics.

In spite of his loyalty to Yeltsin, Prusak became increasingly more critical of the federal government toward the end of the 1990s. He became more vocal in his disagreements following the dismissal of Viktor Chernomyrdin as Prime Minister in March 1998. Prusak felt that the Duma was forced to confirm Sergei Kirienko in Chernomyrdin's place. In reference to the perpetual "power vacuum" that he saw in Moscow, Prusak claimed that it was impossible to be a minister without first having been a governor and that the prime minister should have at least five years experience as a regional executive (*Ekspert*, 29 June 1998).

Prusak has suggested several amendments to the Constitution, particularly in relation to election procedures. He favored reinstating the position of vice president and advocated changing the Constitution so that the president would be elected indirectly by representatives of the regions rather than by the entire population. Prusak believed that this reform would make the president more responsive because he would need to answer to concrete individuals. However, Prusak did not feel that the Federation Council was the right body to conduct such an election.

Similarly, before Putin introduced such a reform, Prusak believed that governors should not be members of the Federation Council since governors are compromised into supporting President Yeltsin within the body to ensure that their regions continue to receive subsidies and transfers for salaries and pensions (*Ekspert*, 29 June 1998). Prusak argued that the way the State Duma is elected should also be changed. He believed that electing the Duma from party lists gave too much representation to Moscow. Rather, he prefered to elect the lower house from a pool of candidates with "legal education" in single-member districts (*EWI RRR*, 14 May 1998). Prusak has also suggested doing away with elections for regional and local leaders, instead advocating giving the president the right to appoint governors who would then appoint local leaders. Prusak argued that elections "continually destabilize the situation. Every time it's a shock to the state. Enormous amounts of money are spent, to no avail" (*RFE/RL*, 26 May 1998).

Novgorod's governor also made several suggestions regarding policy toward Russia's regions. First, he claimed that it was necessary for the federal government to transfer some of its powers to the regions. He also stated that ethnically defined republics should not be granted special privileges within the Russian Federation, but that all regions should play by the same rules. Prusak wanted republics to pay the same taxes as other regions and adopt legislation that was not in violation of the federal constitution (*Ekspert*, 29 June 1998). Prusak was highly critical of the institution of presidential representatives in each re-

gion, claiming that representatives only duplicate the work of governors and were therefore inefficient. In October 1998 he suggested that President Yeltsin appoint him as the presidential representative in Novgorod. The position was left vacant when the presidential representative Mikhail Dyagilev was appointed head of the local customs service. Yeltsin ultimately appointed someone else. Finally, Prusak disapproved of the size of the federal presence in Novgorod. He claimed that the oblast administration employed 500 people while federal bureaucrats numbered 7,000 (*EWI RRR*, 22 January 1998).

In spite of these criticisms, Prusak has been adamant in stressing that his reproaches are addressed to the system as a whole and not specific individuals. He repeatedly asserted his loyalty to Yeltsin, and continues to do so under Putin, who has implemented many of his ideas.

Relations with Other Regions: Close to Black Earth Regions

Although Prusak has good relationships with several regional executives, he claimed that there was no reason for governors to have business dealings with each other—that is the work of entrepreneurs. Nevertheless, Prusak is one of the founders of an association called the Alliance Group, which provides crisis support to struggling enterprises in Russia and the CIS. Other contributing regions are Saratov, Leningrad, Murmansk, Irkutsk, Magadan, Chita, Novosibirsk, and Voronezh. The Alliance Group feels that close cooperation between regional administrations and enterprises provides the most effective aid to firms on the verge of bankruptcy.

Novgorod belongs to both the Black Earth Association and the Northwest Association. The Black Earth Association, headed by Federation Council Speaker and Orel Oblast Governor Yegor Stroev, includes Voronezh, Belgorod, Kursk, Lipetsk, Orel, and Tambov oblasts. The Northwest Association consists of the republics of Karelia and Komi; Arkhangelsk, Vologda, Kaliningrad, Kirov, Leningrad, Murmansk, and Pskov oblasts; Nenets Autonomous Okrug; and the federal city St. Petersburg. Prusak claims that Novgorod is more active in the Black Earth Association because it sells fertilizer to places like Orel, Voronezh, Tambov, and Belgorod. Essentially, the region's interests relate more closely to the Black Earth region than to the Northwest (*EWI RRR*, 5 March 1998).

Mikhail Mikhailovich Prusak

23 February 1960—Born in Ivano-Frankivsk Oblast, Ukraine

1979—Graduated from the Kolomyisk Pedagogical Training School

1979–1980—Schoolteacher in Ivano-Frankivsk Oblast

1980–1982—Served in the Soviet army

1982–1986—Studied at the Komsomol's Higher School

November 1986—After graduating from the Komsomol's Higher School, he was sent to Novgorod, where he worked as the second and then first secretary of the Kholm district Komsomol committee

December 1988–December 1993—Director of the collective farm Trudovik

March 1989—Elected to the USSR Congress of People's Deputies as a Komsomol member, then elected to the Supreme Soviet

24 October 1991—Appointed governor of Novgorod Oblast

Summer 1993—Participated in the formation of the Party of Russian Unity and Concord (PRES), led by Sergei Shakhrai

12 December 1993—Elected to the first session of the Federation Council, serving on the Committee for CIS Affairs

27 February 1994—Elected to the PRES federal council presidium

1994—Graduated from the Academy of the National Economy

April 1995—Joined the organizing committee of Our Home Is Russia (NDR), and in May was elected to the NDR council

17 December 1995—Elected governor of Novgorod Oblast

January 1996—Appointed to the Federation Council, serving as the Chair of the Committee on International Affairs

September 1999—Reelected governor of Novgorod with 91.6% of the vote

Ukrainian

Married, with a daughter and son

Foreign Relations: Prominent Delegation Member

As chair of the Federation Council Committee on International Affairs, Prusak is better placed on the international scene than most other Russian regional executives. Prusak was part of the Russian delegation to the World Economic Forum at Davos in February 1998, and he participated in the Gore-Chernomyrdin summit talks in March 1998 as part of the U.S. Regional Initiative, which then focused aid on Novgorod, Samara, Sakhalin, and Khabarovsk. Prusak was also among the regional executives to meet with U.S. President Bill Clinton on his visit to Moscow in September 1998.

Novgorod has good relations with the Baltic countries, primarily because key transportation routes linking Russia to the Baltics run through Novgorod. The Baltics derive considerable income from transshipping Russian cargo.

Attitudes Toward Business: Pro-Investment

The entire focus of Prusak's tenure as governor of Novgorod Oblast has been to attract foreign investment to the region. He has been very successful in this regard. Among foreign firms producing in the region are Cadbury Schweppes, Stimorol, Pfleider, Sommer, and Pampers. Fiat, British Petroleum, Siemens, and

Coca-Cola are also heavily invested in Novgorod. Dresdner Bank and Bank Austria are active in the region, as well as several Russian banks. Novgorod is also home to several projects sponsored by the World Bank and EBRD. Due to the administration's successful approach, Novgorod has jumped to second place in Russia in terms of foreign investment per capita in the late 1990s, behind only Moscow, and third in terms of economic development. When Prusak first came to power, the region was ranked 63rd in Russia. In the late 1990s, more than half of Novgorod's industrial output was the result of foreign investment, and 80 percent of all overall investment in the oblast came from foreign sources (*EWI RRR*, 5 March 1998).

However, Novgorod has not been as successful at building up the region's domestic economic base. Prusak hopes that legislation adopted in 1997 intended to attract domestic capital will improve this situation. Nevertheless, there have been some successful Russian investment projects in Novgorod. The Moscow-based Cherkisov Meat Processing Factory built two plants in Novgorod, and Russia's largest refrigerated storage facility for meat is also located in Novgorod.

One of Novgorod's most successful enterprises is Acron, Russia's largest producer of nitrogen and com-pound fertilizers. The Acron Joint Stock Company emerged when the Azot Scientific-Industrial Association was privatized in 1992. Acron has gained a sound reputation as a supplier of mineral fertilizers on the international market. The firm is planning to diversify into various chemical and consumer products in order to guarantee its financial stability against fluctuations on the fertilizers market. Recently, Acron has taken part in the creation of the Nivy Nechernozemya holding company in alliance with producers of agricultural products and food and trade companies from different regions that purchase its mineral fertilizers. Prusak helped form the holding company, which has been praised by Federation Council Speaker and Orel Governor Yegor Stroev.

Internet Sites in the Region

http://www.region.adm.nov.ru/web.nsf
This is the official website of the Novgorod Oblast administration. It features basic information about the oblast and very specific information about its investment climate, projects, and laws concerning investment and business development. The site also links you to the region's major newspapers and journals.

NOVOSIBIRSK OBLAST

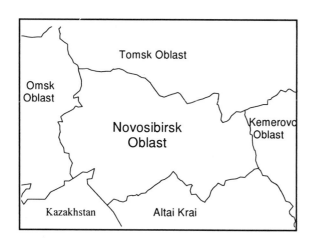

Territory: 178,200 km²
Population (as of 1 January 1998):
2,749,000
Distance from Moscow: 3,191 km

Major Cities:
Novosibirsk, *capital* (pop. 1,399,100)
Berdsk (85,600)
Iskitim (68,400)
Kuibyshev (52,500)

Basic Facts

Population (as of 1 Jan. 1998): 2,749,000 (1.87% of Russian total)

Ethnic breakdown (1989 census): Russians 92.0%, Germans 2.2%, Ukrainians 1.8%, Tatars 1.1%

Urban population (as of 1 Jan. 1998): 73.9% (Russia overall: 73.1%)

Student population (as of 1 Sept. 1997): 301 per 10,000 (Russia overall: 208/10,000)

Pensioner population (1997): 25.1% (Russia overall: 25.96%)

Percent of population with higher education (1989 census): 11.6% (Russia overall: 11.3%)

Percent of population working in (1997): Industry: 20.4% (Russian average: 23.0%); Agriculture: 13.3% (13.7%); Trade: 15.0% (13.5%); Culture: 16.0% (13.3%)

Average monthly personal income in July 1998: 832.9 new rubles (Russian average: 891.7 new rubles)

Average monthly personal expenses in July 1998: 868.5 new rubles (Russian average: 684.9 new rubles)

Average monthly subsistence requirement in 1998: 497 new rubles (Russian average: 438 new rubles)

Consumer price index (as of July 1998): 105 (Russia overall = 100)

Budgetary revenues (1997): 6,090.1 billion rubles (Russia overall: 433,378.2 billion rubles)

Budgetary expenditures (1997): 7,084.8 billion rubles (Russia overall: 468,111.6 billion rubles)

Industrial production as percentage of all Russian production (Jan.–Aug. 1998): 0.83%

Proportion of loss-making enterprises (as of July 1998): 49.7% (Russia overall: 50.4%)

Number of enterprises which have wage arrears (as of 1 Sept. 1998): 1,867 (1.38% of Russian total)

Agricultural production as percentage of all Russian production (1997): 2.28%

Number of private farms (as of 1 Jan. 1998): 4,822 (1.76% of Russian total)

Capital investment (1997): 4,735.9 billion rubles (Russia overall: 408,797 billion rubles)

Sources of investment (1997): federal budget: 16.1% (Russian average: 10.2%); regional budget: 8.7% (10.5%); extra-budgetary funds: 75.2% (79.3%)

Foreign investment (1997): 84,334,000 USD (Russia overall: 12,294,734,000 USD)

Number of joint ventures (1997): 185 (1.26% of Russian total)

Fixed capital investment in joint ventures and foreign companies (1997): 235,746 million rubles (Russia overall: 16,265.4 billion rubles)

Number of small businesses (as of 1 July 1998): 25,000 (2.35% of Russian total)

Number of enterprises privatized in 1997: 77 (2.8% of Russian total), including those which used to be municipal property: 66.2% (Russian average: 66.4%); regional property: 3.9% (20.0%); federal property: 29.9% (13.6%)

Number of telephones per 100 families (1997): in cities: 49.2 (Russian average: 49.2); in villages: 21.9 (19.8)

Brief Overview

Novosibirsk Oblast is located in the south of the West Siberian plain and borders Omsk, Tomsk, and Kemerovo oblasts, Altai Krai, and Kazakhstan. The oblast covers most of the Baraba lowland to the west of the middle Ob River, the north of which is in swampy taiga turning southward into forest steppe and steppe with numerous lakes. Most of the fertile steppe is under cultivation; rye, wheat, sunflowers, potatoes, and vegetables being the main crops.

The oblast is fairly rich in mineral resources such as peat, oil, marble, limestone, anthracite, and mineral and thermal waters. Additionally, the oblast has some gold, copper, and nickel reserves. Metallurgy and metal processing are the major regional industries, whose share in oblast industrial production amounts to 38 percent, followed by the food industry and energy complex (18 percent each). The oblast also has a high share of defense industry that began mostly during the evacuation of production facilities from western Russia during World War II. This sector is now making the difficult transition to civilian production. Former defense industry enterprises now manufacture AN-38 jets for civil aviation; space communication, electronic, and medical equipment; and consumer goods.

Novosibirsk hosts one of Russia's largest concentrations of scientific research facilities. Novosibirsk city and Akademgorodok, which lies to the south of the city on the shores of the Novosibirsk reservoir and is almost exclusively inhabited by scientists, are world-class scientific centers that house over a hundred research institutes specializing in almost all disciplines.

The oblast has attracted the attention of many foreign investors. Western countries, primarily France, Germany, Japan, and the United States, make up about 80 percent of the region's foreign trade.

According to a 1998 survey by *Ekspert* magazine, the oblast is ranked 19th among Russia's 89 regions in terms of investment potential and 63rd in terms of investment risk. A 1998 survey by Bank Austria ranked the oblast 19th in terms of investment climate.

Electoral History

2000 Presidential Election
Putin: 39.90%
Zyuganov: 38.27%
Yavlinskii: 7.92%
Tuleev: 5.39%
Zhirinovsky: 3.35%
Turnout: 65.17% (Russia overall: 68.64%)

1999/2000 Gubernatorial Election
Tolokonskii: 26.33%/44.32% (first round/second round)
Starikov: 20.87%/42.17%
Mukha (incumbent): 17.88%
Turnout: 64.00%/50.57%

1999 Parliamentary Elections
Communist Party of the Russian Federation: 28.31%
Unity: 20.40%
Yabloko: 9.82%
Union of Right Forces: 9.52%
Zhirinovsky Bloc: 6.83%
Fatherland–All Russia: 5.83%
In single-mandate districts: 2 Unity, 2 Communist Party of the Russian Federation
Turnout: 64.31% (Russia overall: 61.85%)

1996 Presidential Election
Zyuganov: 34.96%/48.90% (first round/second round)
Yeltsin: 25.61%/43.74%
Yavlinskii: 13.95%
Lebed: 10.00%
Zhirinovsky: 9.76%
Turnout: 71.18%/66.86% (Russia overall: 69.67%/ 68.79%)

1995 Gubernatorial Election
Mukha: 18.12%/54.04% (first round/second round)
Indinok (incumbent): 22.81%/37.24%
Manannikov: 17.49%
Starikov (Russian deputy economic minister: 16.92%
Loginov (State Duma deputy, LDPR): 15.58%
Frantsev: 2.24%
Isaev: 0.99%
Turnout: 67.39%/43.23%

1995 Parliamentary Elections
Communist Party of the Russian Federation: 21.26%
Liberal Democratic Party of Russia: 18.06%
Our Home Is Russia: 7.18%
Yabloko: 5.80%
Agrarian Party of Russia: 5.10%
Women of Russia: 4.52%

Party of Workers' Self-Government: 4.31%

Communists–Workers' Russia: 3.64%

In single-mandate districts: 1 Agrarian Party of Russia, 1 Liberal Democratic Party of Russia, 2 independent

Turnout: 66.69% (Russia overall: 64.37%)

1993 Constitutional Referendum

"Yes"—50.3%   "No"—47.4%

1993 Parliamentary Elections

Liberal Democratic Party of Russia: 25.64%

Yabloko: 12.23%

Russia's Choice: 12.06%

Communist Party of the Russian Federation: 11.44%

Agrarian Party of Russia: 8.69%

Women of Russia: 7.78%

Democratic Party of Russia: 7.25%

Party of Russian Unity and Concord: 5.61%

In single-mandate districts: 1 Russia's Choice, 1 Agrarian Party of Russia, 1 Dignity and Charity, 1 National Republican Party of Russia

Turnout: 51.04% (Russia overall: 54.34%)

1991 Presidential Elections

Yeltsin: 57.07%

Ryzhkov: 18.64%

Zhirinovsky: 7.92%

Tuleev: 6.96%

Bakatin: 3.13%

Makashov: 1.98%

Turnout: 73.57% (Russia overall: 76.66%)

Regional Political Institutions

Executive:

Governor, 4-year term

Viktor Aleksandrovich Tolokonskii,

elected, January 2000

Krasnyi Prospekt, 18; Novosibirsk, 630011

Tel 7(383–2) 23–08–62, 23–29–95;

Fax 7(383–2) 23–57–00

Legislative:

Unicameral

Oblast Council—49 members, 4-year term, elected December 1997

Chairman—Viktor Vasilevich Leonov, elected, January 1998

Regional Politics

Mayor Ousts Governor After Long-Running Battle

In the climax to one of Russia's most heated governor versus mayor battles, Novosibirsk Mayor Viktor Tolokonskii pushed incumbent Vitalii Mukha out of the governor's seat in the first round of Novosibirsk gubernatorial elections in December 1999 and went on to win a final victory in January 2000. Mukha's rating had dropped so far in the public polls that he did not even make it into the run-off. However, the leftist Tolokonskii's victory in a region with a consistently strong Communist representation was not entirely surprising.

Following his appointment as Novosibirsk governor in 1991, Mukha long held a revered place as an outspoken leader in Siberian politics. The former engineer and banker was twice dismissed by President Boris Yeltsin and staunchly defended regional interests throughout his tenures as governor and leader of the Siberian Accord Association. Once he had won an elected term, however, he gradually moved away from being a committed member of Yeltsin's opposition to establish a more centrist position, as a market reformer. In his reelection bid, Mukha was supported by former Prime Minister Yevgenii Primakov and the other leaders of the Fatherland–All Russia movement.

The results of the December 1999 elections show that the voters' desire for change, reflected in the defeat of the incumbent, had its limits as they elected the mayor rather than a relative outsider (Russian Deputy Economics Minister, Ivan Starikov, was Tolokonskii's opponent in the second round). The voters also confirmed their traditional sympathy for the left. Tolokonskii's main electorate was in the city. In the rural areas, where half of the population lives, Tolokonskii won votes only from those who believed that he promised to support the urban residents. During the second round of the voting all of the rightist parties in the region worked against Tolokonskii.

According to the local press, Tolokonskii has close ties to Boris Berezovskii and the Chernoi brothers of the Trans World Group, which once controlled much of Russia's aluminum sector. Lev Chernoi provided financial backing for his gubernatorial campaign. During his tenure, Governor Mukha drove them from control of the Novosibirsk Electrode Factory; with

Tolokonskii's victory, it is expected that they will be able to return.

Executive Platform: Leftist Who Prioritizes Social Benefits

However much Tolokonskii declares that he supports reforms, it is clear that he is a strong "statist" of the left who places social protections for the population above all other concerns. In his public statements, he stresses that he will pay off the oblast's onerous debts without harming the living standards of the population. The main thrust of his electoral program was generous social support for the region's poorest citizens. For example, Tolokonskii's Novosibirsk city 2000 budget raised spending on health care 4.5 times, and promised greater access to free education, and a wider variety of benefits. Local businesspeople were already used to the existing system and did not want to make any radical changes by electing Starikov to office.

Tolokonskii does not belong to any political party or movement. While Mukha was more focused on the real sector of the economy and attracting state orders and investment to regional industries, Tolokonskii concentrates more on trade and banking capital, according to an analysis in the Berezovskii-connected *Nezavisimaya gazeta* (30 November 1999).

Policies: Economic Development

Immediately after taking office Tolokonskii declared, "This year [2000] Novosibirsk Oblast should break out of its long depression." He identified paying wage arrears and restructuring the oblast's debt to financial institutions as his top priorities. When Tolokonskii took office there were several million rubles in wage arrears, with delays extending to 2–4 months in some parts of the oblast. In order to pay these salary debts, Tolokonskii promised that no less than 40 percent of the oblast's income would go to public sector salaries. While Tolokonskii feels that paying off the oblast's financial debt, which was listed as 2.2 billion rubles as of 1 January 2000, is crucial, he stressed that this issue would have to be resolved without threatening the budget's social expenditures.

When he was still mayor, Tolokonskii argued that every region should adopt a law clearly distinguishing between expenditures that should come out of oblast and local budgets (Radio Rossii, 12 March 1999). He argued that it was necessary for every city and rural jurisdiction to have a clear sense of its financial health. As mayor, Tolokonskii fought a pitched battle with Mukha over how the region's money would be used, seeking to block Mukha's attempts to increase oblast revenue at the expense of local budgets. As the oblast capital, Novosibirsk city was always particularly vulnerable to encroachments by the oblast government, losing one quarter of its tax income in the 1999 budget (*RRR*, 21 October 1999). Mukha was very critical of the city's 1998 budget, claiming that the city reduced revenue by giving tax breaks on nonresidential property and providing lower surcharges for heat and hot water than in the rest of the oblast (*RRR*, 7 April 1999). Now that Tolokonskii is governor, it is unclear if he will still favor the city's interests strongly over those of the oblast.

Despite his bitter battle with Mukha, Tolokonskii will inevitably continue some of the economic initiatives Mukha started. Mukha spent much of his time trying to improve Novosibirsk's economy and strengthen its business development. In 1999 Mukha approved a program providing state support for small businesses in Novosibirsk. There are 25,000 small businesses in the oblast. More than half are involved in trade and the food industry, while almost a third are in the productive sphere (www.adm.nso.ru). Mukha had personal experience with financial institutions, having worked as a banker from 1993 to 1995. In February 1997 the Novosibirsk Oblast legislature passed a law providing that only local banks would be allowed to work with budgetary funds. The status of "authorized" bank is granted for one year by the oblast's council and a special selection commission. This legislation allows regional authorities to have stricter control over transfers of budgetary funds within the oblast. Though as a mayor Tolokonskii was against granting regional officials sizable power over such funds, his opinion may change now that he is on the other side of the issue.

Relationships Between Key Players: Largely Communist

Former Governor Mukha had a good working relationship with the oblast legislature. Communists won 28 of the 49 seats in the legislature in December 1997. Fourteen of the 17 candidates Mukha unofficially backed were elected.

While it remains unclear how the legislators will work with Tolokonskii, the new governor is no stranger to conflict with the representative branch. As mayor of Novosibirsk Tolokonskii faced considerable problems following the December 1996 Novosibirsk city Council elections. The majority of the council's 24 deputies represented Vladimir Zhirinovsky's Liberal Democratic Party of Russia (LDPR) and the Communist Party, and were determined to limit Tolokonskii's influence in the city. According to the Novosibirsk city charter, the mayor is also the head of the council. The council's LDPR deputies tried to amend the city charter to remove Tolokonskii as the council head, but were unable to do so (Panorama).

Ties to Moscow: Difficult Under Mukha

Novosibirsk's relationship with the capital remained tenuous through most of the 1990s. Although it was Yeltsin who first appointed Mukha governor in 1991, he soon became one of the president's most vocal critics. In March 1993 the president released Mukha from office for two days but then reinstated him in the face of a large public protest. Mukha supported the opposition in Yeltsin's 1993 conflict with the parliament, and during the subsequent White House occupation, joined other Siberian leaders who threatened the Yeltsin government with a blockade of the Trans-Siberian railway. This move angered Yeltsin enough to fire Mukha again. Relations between Yeltsin and Mukha improved after Mukha won popular election to the governor's seat in December 1995. Yeltsin really had no choice but to compromise with the governor so as to curry favor in Novosibirsk, the unofficial capital of Siberia. Mukha also had to work with Yeltsin to win concessions from the federal government.

One of Moscow's tactics to counter powerful regional executives in the late 1990s was to build up the support of mayors. Tolokonskii benefited from this attention, and in November 1998 joined the Presidential Council for Local Self-Government.

With new executive leadership in place in both Novosibirsk and the federal government, it is unclear how center-periphery relations will develop.

Relations with Other Regions: Active in Siberian Politics

Tolokonskii, like Mukha, is an active leader in working with other Siberian regions. While Mukha was chairman of the Siberian Accord Association from February 1992 to January 1994 and December 1996 to June 1998, Tolokonskii was president of the Association of Siberian and Far Eastern Cities in 1994–1995 and was elected to this post again in 1998. The importance of Tolokonskii's role in this organization was only natural since Novosibirsk is considered the unofficial capital of Siberia. The new governor will likely play an important role in the Siberian Accord Association, which includes the republics of Gorno-Altai, Buryatia, and Khakassia; Krasnoyarsk and Altai krais; Irkutsk, Novosibirsk, Omsk, Tomsk, Tyumen, and Kemerovo oblasts; and Agin-Buryat, Taimyr, Ust-Orda Buryat, Khanty-Mansi, Evenk, and Yamal-Nenets autonomous okrugs.

Foreign Relations: Close Ties to Belarus

Mukha's closest foreign relations were with Belarus. In February 1998 Belarusan President Aleksandr Lukashenko visited Novosibirsk. In December 1998 Mukha led a delegation to Minsk to discuss developing commerce, scientific-technical, and cultural ties between enterprises and organizations in the oblast and Belarus (www.adm.nso.ru). Mukha also participated in the executive committee meeting of the Russian-Belarusan Union on 9 December 1998.

In 1997 a delegation from Novosibirsk visited China in hopes of establishing a representative office in Beijing. China is one of the region's main trading partners.

In June 1998 the Russian government approved a 10-year, $10 million EBRD credit to modernize the Tolmachevo airport in Novosibirsk. However, the federal government then seized control of the airport back from the region in February 1999 (*KD*, 16 February 1999).

Novosibirsk will house Russia's first Technical Support Center for the Control, Preservation, and Accounting of Nuclear Materials, a project sponsored by the Russian State Committee on Nuclear Supervision and the U.S. Department of Energy (*EWI RRR*, 8 January 1998).

Attitudes Toward Business: Attempts to Spur Growth

Mukha was active in promoting the region's economic development and trying to attract investment to it. Novosibirsk has the highest concentration of industry in Russia east of the Urals. The region has over 200 heavy industry plants and over 11,000 privatized en-

Viktor Aleksandrovich Tolokonskii

1953—Born in Novosibirsk

1974—Graduated from the Novosibirsk Economics Institute as an economist

1978—Earned a candidate of sciences degree in economics from Novosibirsk State University

1979–1981—Taught political economy at Novosibirsk State University and the Novosibirsk Economics Institute

1981–1991—Climbed the oblast political ladder, ultimately becoming deputy head of the economic planning administration

1991–1993—Deputy and then first deputy mayor of Novosibirsk

1993—Appointed mayor of Novosibirsk

1994—Elected Chairman of the Novosibirsk city council

1994–1995—President of the Association of Siberian and Far Eastern Cities

March 1996—Elected mayor of Novosibirsk

May 1997—Joined the Council on Local Self-Government in the Russian Federation

November 1998—Joined the Presidential Council on Local Self-Government

9 January 2000—Elected governor of Novosibirsk Oblast

Married, with a daughter and son

---

terprises. The largest enterprises are the Novosibirsk Metallurgical Plant, Novosibirsk Tin Smelting Plant, the Electrode Plant, Khimplast, and the Kuibyshev Chemical Plant.

Novosibirsk has nearly 400 joint ventures involving foreign partners, mostly from China, Korea, and Germany (www.ieie.nsc.ru). Among these enterprises are three popular fast-food outlets, Patio Pizza, Rostik's, and Grillmaster (all of which have suffered considerably since the financial crisis erupted in August 1998). Some other large-scale foreign investment projects include:

- A dry pet food plant built by the Mars Corporation in Novosibirsk.
- An agreement between Sibtekh Production Corporation and the South Korean firm LG to produce consumer electronic products in Novosibirsk.
- A Coca-Cola bottling facility in Novosibirsk. The plant is reportedly the first fully integrated system for producing, distributing, and sxelling a consumer product in Siberia.

Foreign direct investment has forced local industries to adapt to the new competitive market. One such example is Novosibirsk's Vinap, Europe's largest producer of alcoholic and non-alcoholic beverages, which has begun building a new production facility to increase its competitiveness with Coca-Cola and Pepsi. Another is the bankruptcy of the Vega company. In early 1998 the arbitrage court of Novosibirsk Oblast ordered an auction to sell the assets of the bankrupt company, which had been frozen for a year and a half. Vega, at one time the top producer of consumer electronics in Russia, suffered from poor restructuring as a privatized enterprise and was unable to compete with the higher-quality foreign imports flooding the Russian market. Various projects for revitalizing Vega were unsuccessful, including some supported by the oblast government. Mukha tried unsuccessfully to persuade Coca-Cola to put its production facilities on Vega's territory (*EWI RRR*, 5 February 1998).

Mukha was consistent in upholding his standards for effective market economics. In September 1997 the oblast administration reached an agreement with the oil company Sidanko for further developing the Verkh-Tarsk oil deposit. Sidanko had won a competition to develop the site in 1993, but did not meet the agreed upon schedule for investing in the deposit. Mukha then announced that the administration was considering filing a court case to revoke the company's license for developing the site, prompting the development of a new agreement.

Internet Sites in the Region

http://www.adm.nso.ru/
This is the official website of the Novosibirsk Oblast administration. It features detailed statistical information on regional economic, demographic, and social issues, up-to-date news clippings, and an archive of news articles.

OMSK OBLAST

Territory: 139,700 km^2
Population (as of 1 January 1998):
2,179,000
Distance from Moscow: 2,555 km

Major Cities:
Omsk, *capital* (pop. 1,159,200)
Isilkul (27,400)
Kalachinsk (25,900)

Basic Facts

Population (as of 1 Jan. 1998): 2,179,000 (1.48% of Russian total)

Ethnic breakdown (1989 census): Russians 80.3%, Germans 6.3%, Ukrainians 4.9%, Kazakhs 3.5%, Tatars 2.3%

Urban population (as of 1 Jan. 1998): 67.3% (Russia overall: 73.1%)

Student population (as of 1 Sept. 1997): 208 per 10,000 (Russia overall: 208/10,000)

Pensioner population (1997): 23.77% (Russia overall: 25.96%)

Percent of population with higher education (1989 census): 9.7% (Russia overall: 11.3%)

Percent of population working in (1997): Industry: 19.6% (Russian average: 23.0%); Agriculture: 16.1% (13.7%); Trade: 12.5% (13.5%); Culture: 12.9% (13.3%)

Average monthly personal income in July 1998: 753.7 new rubles (Russian average: 891.7 new rubles)

Average monthly personal expenses in July 1998: 619.4 new rubles (Russian average: 684.9 new rubles)

Average monthly subsistence requirement in 1998: 375 new rubles (Russian average: 438 new rubles)

Consumer price index (as of July 1998): 91 (Russia overall = 100)

Budgetary revenues (1997): 5,708.7 billion rubles (Russia overall: 433,378.2 billion rubles)

Budgetary expenditures (1997): 6,502.5 billion rubles (Russia overall: 468,111.6 billion rubles)

Industrial production as percentage of all Russian production (Jan.–Aug. 1998): 0.83%

Proportion of loss-making enterprises (as of July 1998): 63.1% (Russia overall: 50.4%)

Number of enterprises which have wage arrears (as of 1 Sept. 1998): 2,001 (1.48% of Russian total)

Agricultural production as percentage of all Russian production (1997): 2.26%

Number of private farms (as of 1 Jan. 1998): 7,435 (2.71% of Russian total)

Capital investment (1997): 3,475.7 billion rubles (Russia overall: 408,797 billion rubles)

Sources of investment (1997): federal budget: 9.4% (Russian average: 10.2%); regional budget: 12.7% (10.5%); extra-budgetary funds: 77.9% (79.3%)

Foreign investment (1997): 365,447,000 USD (Russia overall: 12,294,734,000 USD)

Number of joint ventures (1997): 104 (0.7% of Russian total)

Fixed capital investment in joint ventures and foreign companies (1997): 12,893 million rubles (Russia overall: 16,265.4 billion rubles)

Number of small businesses (as of 1 July 1998): 11,900 (1.37% of Russian total)

Number of enterprises privatized in 1997: 13 (0.47% of Russian total), including those which used to be municipal property: 23.1% (Russian average: 66.4%); regional property: 30.8% (20.0%); federal property: 46.1% (13.6%)

Number of telephones per 100 families (1997): in cities: 40.8 (Russian average: 49.2); in villages: 20.0 (19.8)

Brief Overview

Omsk Oblast lies on the West Siberian plain and borders Kazakhstan in the south, Tyumen Oblast in the west and north, and Novosibirsk and Tomsk oblasts in the east. Intensive development of Omsk Oblast began after Cossack Ataman Yermak's push into Siberia in the late 16th century. In 1716, the Omsk fortress was erected to protect Russia's southern borders. In the 17th through the 19th centuries, the Omsk region was a place of exile for various revolutionaries, including the Decembrists and participants in Polish uprisings against Russian czarism. In the beginning of this century, migrants from the European part of Russia and Ukraine started to settle in the oblast, boosting the local economy. In 1913, over a dozen European companies had branches in the oblast exporting leather and wool.

The region's industries are now concentrated in cities and towns along the Irtysh, Om, Tara, and Osha rivers and the Trans-Siberian railroad. The city of Omsk is the main industrial center, housing over half of the region's population and 90 percent of its industry. However, due to the city's poor ecological situation, further industrial development is almost impossible, a situation which is likely to stimulate the growth of other oblast towns. Energy and machine building, mostly concentrated in defense plants, are the main industries of the region. Their output totals 65 percent of overall production. However, most of the materials for the energy industry, mainly coal, used to come from neighboring Kazakhstan. Due to the increasing cost of importing coal, the oblast is trying to switch to gas-based energy, since it has some gas reserves of its own. Omsk city is one of the country's largest centers for oil processing and petrochemical industries—it houses the Siberian Oil Company (Sibneft), largely controlled by magnate Boris Berezovskii.

The oblast has ties with companies in over 50 countries, while its main business partners come from Cyprus, Germany, and China. Over half of the region's foreign exports go to third world countries. A survey by *Ekspert* magazine determined that Omsk Oblast had the third largest investment potential growth in the country in 1997. In 1998, the oblast ranked 26th among Russia's 89 regions in terms of investment potential and 49th in terms of investment risk. A 1998 survey by Bank Austria ranked the oblast 25th in terms of investment climate.

Electoral History

2000 Presidential Election
Zyuganov: 42.85%
Putin: 38.11%
Yavlinskii: 7.27%
Zhirinovsky: 3.27%
Tuleev: 2.21%
Turnout: 70.71% (Russia overall: 68.64%)

1999 Parliamentary Elections
Communist Party of the Russian Federation: 29.49%
Unity: 20.68%
Yabloko: 8.31%
Union of Right Forces: 7.99%
Zhirinovsky Bloc: 7.21%
Fatherland–All Russia: 6.86%
In single-mandate districts: 1 Communist Party of the Russian Federation, 2 independent
Turnout: 62.13% (Russia overall: 61.85%)

1999 Gubernatorial Election
Polezhaev (incumbent): 57.03%
Kravets (KPRF): 26.36%
Zakharov: 3.24%
Turnout: 51.25%

1996 Presidential Election
Zyuganov: 36.99%/47.51% (first round/second round)
Yeltsin: 32.80%/46.23%
Yavlinskii: 8.96%
Lebed: 8.37%
Zhirinovsky: 6.95%
Turnout: 73.78%/72.91% (Russia overall: 69.67%/68.79%)

1995 Gubernatorial Election
Polezhaev (incumbent): 59.62%
Lotkov (State Duma deputy): 13.75%
Gorynin: 8.79%
Pokhitailo (KPRF): 8.29%
Zakharchenko: 1.75%
Turnout: 68.73%

1995 Parliamentary Elections
Communist Party of the Russian Federation: 15.98%
Liberal Democratic Party of Russia: 15.91%

Power to the People: 8.44%
Our Home Is Russia: 6.53%
Women of Russia: 6.21%
Agrarian Party of Russia: 5.24%
Party of Workers' Self-Government: 5.13%
Communists–Workers' Russia: 4.89%
In single-mandate districts: 2 Power to the People, 1
   independent
Turnout: 68.40% (Russia overall: 64.37%)

1993 Constitutional Referendum
"Yes"—56.3%   "No"—41.1%

1993 Parliamentary Elections
Liberal Democratic Party of Russia: 21.19%
Russia's Choice: 16.95%
Communist Party of the Russian Federation:
   13.93%
Women of Russia: 10.72%
Agrarian Party of Russia: 8.53%
Democratic Party of Russia: 6.30%
Russian Movement for Democratic Reforms: 5.77%
Party of Russian Unity and Concord: 5.42%
Yabloko: 4.85%
In single-mandate districts: 2 independent, 1 Russian
   All-National Union
From electoral associations: 1 Russia's Choice
Turnout: 56.74% (Russia overall: 54.34%)

1991 Presidential Election
Yeltsin: 53.29%
Ryzhkov: 16.33%
Zhirinovsky: 13.46%
Tuleev: 6.77%
Bakatin: 3.07%
Makashov: 2.48%
Turnout: 79.44% (Russia overall: 76.66%)

Regional Political Institutions

Executive:
   Governor, 4-year term
   Leonid Konstantinovich Polezhaev, elected
   December 1995, reelected 1999
      Krasnyi Put, 1; Omsk-2, 644002
      Tel 7(381–2) 24–14–15, 24–40–11;
      Fax 7(381–2) 24–23–72
      Federation Council in Moscow:
      7 (095) 292–58–49, 926–63–11

Legislative:
   Unicameral
   Legislative Assembly (Zakonadatelnoe Sobranie)—
   30 members, 2-year term, elected March 1994, in 1996
   extended the term until March 1998, March 1998
   Chairman—Vladimir Alekseevich Varnavskii,
   elected 1994, March 1998

Regional Politics

Yeltsin Appointee in Constant Conflict

Leonid Polezhaev is one of the few regional executives appointed by President Boris Yeltsin in 1991 who is still in power. He subsequently won election to the post in December 1995, when Yeltsin permitted twelve of his appointees, whom he believed had a strong chance to win and loyally supported his policies, to hold gubernatorial elections before the 1996 presidential race. Polezhaev was reelected in September 1999 with 57.2 percent of the vote after he managed to have the elections moved up from December 1999 in order to curtail his opponents' ability to campaign. In particular, Polezhaev was concerned about the growing support for his rival, Omsk Mayor Valerii Roshchupkin, whose popularity as a gubernatorial candidate had been increasing throughout the region. By moving up the election Polezhaev was essentially able to remove Roshchupkin as a candidate by forcing the mayor to run for reelection to hold onto his post.

Although Polezhaev was able to win reelection, his tenure as governor has been marked by several conflicts. Polezhaev has constantly been at odds with the mayor of Omsk regarding tax revenues. He has also been accused of a conflict of interest regarding his role in the region's privatization projects. A perpetual struggle between regional and local authorities dominates the Omsk political scene.

Executive Platform: Shifting Alliances

Polezhaev was a loyal supporter of President Yeltsin. Yeltsin returned the trust by showing that he had enough confidence in Polezhaev's policies and popularity to allow him to run for election in 1995. Nevertheless, Polezhaev was critical of Yeltsin at many key points. He was strongly opposed to Yegor Gaidar's economic reforms and has tried to decrease the oblast's payments to the federal budget (Panorama Research Group, Labyrint Electronic Database, Moscow).

Polezhaev aligned with Viktor Chernomyrdin's Our Home Is Russia (NDR) at the movement's founding congress. He joined the movement's political council and in 1995 became chairman of the oblast branch of the movement. By 1998, his membership to the movement was essentially a formality as he seemed more interested in developing an alliance with Moscow Mayor Yurii Luzhkov (*EWI RRR*, 19 March 1998). However, he did not join Luzhkov's Fatherland movement, but opted instead for the All Russia party that allied with it. By late 1999 he backed the Kremlin's new Unity ticket.

Polezhaev is very interested in developing the oblast economy but has been criticized for focusing only on large industry and ignoring other aspects of development, specifically agriculture (Pete Glatter, "Omsk: The Oil Connection," unpublished manuscript, April 1998). The governor was personally involved in privatizing many enterprises in the region, often blurring his personal interests with his role as regional executive (see Attitudes Toward Business).

Policies: Budget Initiatives Violate Laws

Several of Polezhaev's fiscal proposals have been in violation of federal law. In 1993 the oblast legislature adopted Polezhaev's initiative to decrease the region's payments to the federal budget, a decision which was declared illegal by the local procurator (Panorama). Polezhaev attempted to narrow the 1997 oblast budget deficit by imposing duties on goods imported into the oblast, another violation of federal law. The duties included a 50 percent tax on imported alcoholic beverages and a 10 percent levy on sales of all imported food and non-food commodities.

In January 1997 the Omsk Oblast administration introduced a new economic policy that supported anticrisis programs for a limited number of large companies that were considered likely to benefit from restructuring. The program stipulated that the distribution of the local government's finances, tax benefits, and guarantees for credits from commercial banks would be based on the company's ability to generate profits from proposed investment projects. The oblast government was also given the right to seize part of a company's capital (*OMRI RRR*, 15 January 1997).

In December 1997 Polezhaev petitioned then Prime Minister Viktor Chernomyrdin to exclude the Omsk Transportation Machinery Plant from the federal privatization program and retain it as a state-owned enterprise (*EWI RRR*, 4 December 1997). The plant, which is Russia's largest producer of modern military tanks, has relied on commercial contracts in recent years.

In dealing with the immediate panic following the financial crisis that began on 17 August 1998, Polezhaev joined other regional leaders in claiming that he would withhold tax transfers to the federal budget. In general, though, the governors actually have little influence over the flow of tax revenue. He also introduced price controls to maintain a reasonable cost of living for oblast residents.

Relationships Between Key Players: Conflict with Omsk Mayor

Relations between the Omsk oblast and city assemblies as well as Polezhaev's relations with Omsk's mayors have always been strained. The primary reason for this tension has been competing economic interests that are loosely aligned with different regional and local authorities (Glatter, and Anne Le Huérou, "Pouvoirs Locaux et Pouvoirs Régionaux à Omsk," in ed. Marie Mendras, *Russie: Le Gouvernement des Provinces*, Geneva: Centre de Recherches Entreprises et Sociétés, 1997, 129–160). Polezhaev has close ties to many representatives of the former oblast nomenklatura who continue to hold important administrative posts in the oblast. He also has support of the influential financial institutions.

Polezhaev had a long-standing conflict with former Omsk Mayor Yurii Shoikhet. In January 1994 Shoikhet was removed from office by presidential decree for "destabilizing the political and economic situation in the city" (Panorama). It was popularly believed that Polezhaev took advantage of his close ties to the presidential administration to have Shoikhet dismissed.

Conflicting economic interests and a strong desire to protect their respective budgets have led to a vicious battle between Polezhaev and current Omsk Mayor Valerii Roshchupkin. Of the taxes collected in Omsk Oblast, 92 percent come from the capital city. Yet, the oblast administration has been contributing less to the city budget in recent years. Previously, 65 percent of the city's budget came from oblast revenues, now such transfers make up only 38 percent (*MT*, 3 November 1998). To increase the city's revenues; Roshchupkin has adopted a variety of tax initiatives, many of which are illegal. One of the most damaging taxes, adopted in 1996, forces all companies to pay a

2 percent tax on their turnover, rather than profits, to clean up the city. This tax inspired about 30 of Omsk's most prominent businesses to reregister just outside of the city's borders (*NG*, 29 May 1998). Many of these businesses have ties with the governor, which only served to further antagonize Roshchupkin. When Sibneft—the region's most important and influential enterprise—registered outside of the city, the mayor introduced a 35-ruble-per-ton tax on crude oil processed by the refinery, which then was contested in court. Roshchupkin complains that there is nothing he can do to boost the city's revenue since Polezhaev counters all of his measures by cutting transfers from the regional budget by the amount Omsk gains (*EWI RRR*, 5 November 1998).

In March 1999 Deputy Governor Andrei Golushko, who is responsible for the oblast's financial and economic policies, was wounded in an assassination attempt. There are several possible reasons why Golushko was targeted. Golushko had represented the oblast in its budgetary battles with the city of Omsk. Just days before the attack he had ordered the seizure of property from a local brewery and begun investigating a local vodka plant. Additionally, several days before the attack, Polezhaev had proposed to the Federation Council that the death penalty should be introduced for drug peddlers (*EWI RRR*, 25 March 1999).

The constant conflict between Omsk's local and regional powers, and the subsequent impact it has had on the region, has benefited the opposition. The number of Communists in both the oblast and city assemblies increased significantly in the April 1998 elections. Communists hold the majority in the Omsk city council.

The controversy regarding Sibneft's tax revenues is further complicated by the revenues' dwindling volume. The Omsk Oil Refinery, which is part of Sibneft, paid about $14–16 million a month to the city in taxes before it was incorporated into Sibneft at the end of 1995. The refinery would buy, process, and sell oil and then keep the profit. This process has changed since the refinery became part of Sibneft. Now, Sibneft pays the plant a fee for processing oil, which is much less profitable than actually buying and selling the oil. As a result, the refinery paid only $715,000 in taxes to the city for the last six months of 1998 (*MT*, 3 November 1998).

Ties to Moscow: Amicable Relations with Yeltsin

Although Polezhaev often criticized Yeltsin and the federal government, his overall relationship with the Russian president was good. Polezhaev supported Yeltsin in his 1993 stand-off with the parliament, and Yeltsin allowed Polezhaev to run for popular election in 1995, a year before most regional executives could do so. Omsk was also one of the first oblasts to sign a power-sharing agreement with the federal government, concluding the agreement in May 1996.

Polezhaev backed the dismissal of former Prime Minister Viktor Chernomyrdin in March 1998. He claimed that Chernomyrdin's government tried to live on domestic and foreign credit while selling off state property and failed to solve the problems confronting Russia's defense and agricultural industries (*EWI RRR*, 26 March 1998).

Relations with Other Regions: Former Leader of Siberian Accord

Polezhaev served as head of the Siberian Accord interregional association during 1995–96. He was generally criticized for his poor leadership, and the organization was considered ineffective during that period. Novosibirsk Governor Vitalii Mukha took over from Polezhaev in 1996, and then passed the mantle to Tomsk Governor Viktor Kress. Besides Omsk, the association includes the republics of Buryatia, Gorno-Altai, and Khakassia; Altai and Krasnoyarsk krais; and Irkutsk, Novosibirsk, Tomsk, Tyumen, and Kemerovo oblasts.

Foreign Relations: Historic Links to Kazakhstan

Omsk has historically played an influential role in relation to Kazakhstan, which is just south of the oblast. Polezhaev is a key figure in cross-border relations. In September 1998 he decreed that the most essential food products would be exported only with the permission of the state corporation Omsk Foodstuffs (*EWI RRR*, 4 February 1999). The measure, designed to prevent food shortages in the oblast, significantly limited exports of locally produced meat, dairy products, and vegetables (*OV*, 3 December 1998). However, the oblast procurator's office challenged the decree as contradicting federal anti-monopoly legislation and the national Constitution (*Orel-Ekspress*, No. 47, 1998).

In the end of 1998, Kazakhstan banned imports of Russian food products, thus shutting the border on the other side. In January 1999, Kazakhstan's authorities complained to the Russian government that food products imported from the eleven bordering Russian re-

Leonid Konstantinovich Polezhaev

30 January 1940—Born in Omsk

1965—Graduated from the Omsk Agricultural Institute

1965–1966—Worked in construction management for Tselinkraivodstroi

1966–1972—Head engineer of water management and deputy chief of agricultural management in Pavlodar

1972–1973—Manager of Irtyshsovkhozstroi

1973–1976—Manager of Pavlodarstroi

1976–1983—Head of construction of the Irtysh-Karaganda canal

1983–1987—First deputy chair of the Karaganda (Kazakhstan) Oblast executive committee

1986—Graduated from the CPSU Central Committee, Academy of General Sciences

1987—Became director of Omskvodstroi

1989—Director of economic management for the Omsk Oblast executive committee

March 1990—Elected to the Omsk Oblast Council of People's Deputies

31 March 1990—Elected chairman of the oblast executive committee

11 November 1991—Appointed governor of Omsk Oblast

12 December 1993—Elected to the Federation Council, where he served on the Committee for Federation Affairs, Federal Agreements, and Regional Policies

June 1995—Elected chairman of the Omsk regional branch of Our Home Is Russia (NDR)

17 December 1995—Elected governor of Omsk Oblast

January 1996—Joined the Federation Council Committee on Social Policies

September 1999—Reelected governor of Omsk Oblast with 57.2% of the vote

gions, including Omsk Oblast, had all but pushed Kazakhstan's own products out of the market in the country's northern regions. A cheaper ruble has made Russian imports cheaper as well, which Kazakhstan at first welcomed as a remedy against its own food shortages. In a congruent move, the Russian government revoked all customs reductions on food trade with other countries. Then Prime Minister Yevgenii Primakov required that firms have special licenses to export food—in a way, repeating Polezhaev's earlier policy. In the first part of 1999, all exports of Omsk food products had been halted.

Energy is another crucial issue in Omsk-Kazakhstani relations. Every year the oblast imports 8 million tons of coal from Kazakhstan (*EWI RRR*, 17 December 1998). Until now the two sides operated under a special agreement with Kazakhstan President Nursultan Nazarbaev, but now coal extraction in

Kazakhstan is run by Americans, who do not have much patience with Russian barter practices and the elaborate system of mutual debt cancellations that take the place of cash payments. Consequently, the oblast now must spend 2 billion rubles every year (or one quarter of the regional budget) to foot the energy bill, and this number is likely to grow in the future. Thus, switching to natural gas is a matter of life and death for Omsk Oblast.

Polezhaev stressed that supplying the oblast with gas was the only way to keep it afloat without hiking rents and utility prices for impoverished consumers. The oblast program provides for a gradual increase in gas consumption to 3.5 cubic meters a year. Over 100,000 residential apartments will be supplied with gas, and 1,600 kilometers of the gas pipeline network will stretch over the oblast. In February 1997 Polezhaev signed a five-year cooperation agreement with

Gazprom. The agreement obligated Gazprom to help 13 of the oblast's districts install a gas distribution network (*OMRI RRR*, 6 March 1997).

Such an aggressive gasification campaign should enable the oblast to cut its annual coal consumption by 105,000 tons, while fuel oil consumption will decrease by 193,000 tons. The oblast will save 75 million rubles, 65 million of which will be saved directly by the oblast budget. Many strata of the oblast population will benefit, specifically teachers, physicians, and other public sector employees, as well as the underprivileged.

Omsk city is one of the recipients of the World Bank's credits to Russia for improving public transportation systems (*EWI RRR*, 9 July 1998). Additionally, in April 1997 the European Bank for Reconstruction and Development gave the Omsk pasta factory a five-year, $2.229 million credit (*EWI RRR*, 24 April 1997).

Attitudes Toward Business: Oil Refinery Is Key

Polezhaev was one of the founders and the president of the joint-stock company Omsk Trading House (*Omskii Torgovyi Dom*) in the early 1990s. This trade cartel bought up several profitable enterprises, giving Polezhaev several conflicting interests. Yeltsin subsequently ordered Polezhanov to remove himself from the leadership of this commercial structure (Panorama).

The character of the oblast's economy is greatly determined by the economic health of the Omsk Oil Refinery. In 1995 it was the largest refinery in Russia and the third-largest in the world. Under Polezhaev's encouragement, the refinery was merged with Tyumen's Noyabrskneftegaz to form the Siberian Oil Company—Sibneft. Magnate Boris Berezovskii controls a 65 percent stake in the enterprise (Glatter). The company's tax debt received considerable attention at the end of 1997. At an 8 December meeting of the government's emergency commission for strengthening tax and budgetary discipline, chaired by Chubais, an enemy of Berezovskii, the commission threatened to seize the Omsk Oil Refinery's assets in order to pay its debts to the federal government. Polezhaev was highly critical of this proposal and appealed to Yeltsin. Instead, he suggested settling the refinery's $88 million debt through offsets since the center owed a significant sum to the Omsk regional utility, which owed the same amount to the refinery (*RFE/RL*, 15 December 1997). At a second meeting, on 17 December (chaired by then Prime Minister Viktor Chernomyrdin), the Omsk Oil Refinery was given until 25 December to pay off its debt in full. If it failed to meet the deadline, its property might be seized. The Omsk Oil Refinery managed to make the deadline, paying part in cash and part through offsets, which became outlawed a week later via presidential decree. However, the refinery still owed a massive sum in fines and penalties.

Polezhaev and the Omsk administration have been involved in a variety of complicated barter arrangements with Sibneft, which usually leave the administration at a disadvantage. As a result, Omsk is deeply in debt to Sibneft. The reason, the *Moscow Times* suggests, is that Runikom, a Sibneft intermediary that helps sell the firm's oil to CIS customers, employs the governor's son, Aleksei (*MT*, 3 November 1998).

Sweden's Volvo began producing buses in Omsk in August 1998. The factory ultimately hopes to produce 500 buses annually, using 80 percent Russian-produced parts, although the August economic crisis forced it to scale down its initial plans. The overall project is worth $16 million.

In December 1997 the West Siberian Investment Center, a non-profit organization offering information to investors, firms issuing stocks, and stock brokers, opened in Omsk.

Internet Sites in the Region

http://www.main.univer.omsk.su/omsk/index.win.html
This website offers detailed information about Omsk oblast and city. It features links to numerous firms in the oblast, including Sibneft, and provides information about political leaders and parties, banks, education, etc.

http://www.rmg.ru/note0818.html
This site offers information on the Omsk Oil Refinery.

OREL OBLAST

Territory: 24,700 km²
Population (as of 1 January 1998): 907,000
Distance from Moscow: 382 km

Major Cities:
Orel, *capital* (pop. 343,100)
Livny (57,300)
Mtsensk (51,100)

Basic Facts

Population (as of 1 Jan. 1998): 907,000 (0.62% of Russian total)

Ethnic breakdown (1989 census): Russians 97.0%, Ukrainians 1.3%

Urban population (as of 1 Jan. 1998): 63.2% (Russia overall: 73.1%)

Student population (as of 1 Sept. 1997): 243 per 10,000 (Russia overall: 208/10,000)

Pensioner population (1997): 29.66% (Russia overall: 25.96%)

Percent of population with higher education (1989 census): 8.8% (Russia overall: 11.3%)

Percent of population working in (1997): Industry: 22.5% (Russian average: 23.0%); Agriculture: 17.9% (13.7%); Trade: 14.2% (13.5%); Culture: 12.0% (13.3%)

Average monthly personal income in July 1998: 673.2 new rubles (Russian average: 891.7 new rubles)

Average monthly personal expenses in July 1998: 453.9 new rubles (Russian average: 684.7 new rubles)

Average monthly subsistence requirement in 1998: 358 new rubles (Russian average: 438 new rubles)

Consumer price index (as of July 1998): 91 (Russia overall = 100)

Budgetary revenues (1997): 2,221.1 billion rubles (Russia overall: 433,378.2 billion rubles)

Budgetary expenditures (1997): 2,260.1 billion rubles (Russia overall: 468,111.6 billion rubles)

Industrial production as percentage of all Russian production (Jan.–Aug. 1998): 0.29%

Proportion of loss-making enterprises (as of July 1998): 50.6% (Russia overall: 50.4%)

Number of enterprises which have wage arrears (as of 1 Sept. 1998): 743 (0.55% of Russian total)

Agricultural production as percentage of all Russian production (1997): 0.94%

Number of private farms (as of 1 Jan. 1998): 1,403 (0.51% of Russian total)

Capital investment (1997): 1,215.0 billion rubles (Russia overall: 408,797 billion rubles)

Sources of investment (1997): federal budget: 15.2% (Russian average: 10.2%); regional budget: 17.4% (10.5%); extra-budgetary funds: 67.4% (79.3%)

Foreign investment (1997): 39,662,000 USD (Russia overall: 12,294,734,000 USD)

Number of joint ventures (1997): 34 (0.23% of Russian total)

Fixed capital investment in joint ventures and foreign companies (1997): 71,025 million rubles (Russia overall: 16,265.4 billion rubles)

Number of small businesses (as of 1 July 1998): 2,700 (0.31% of Russian total)

Number of enterprises privatized in 1997: 1 (0.68% of Russian total), including those which used to be municipal property: 0% (Russian average: 66.4%); regional property: 100% (20.0%); federal property: 0% (13.6%)

Number of telephones per 100 families (1997): in cities: 43.6 (Russian average: 49.2); in villages: 15.5 (19.8)

Brief Overview

Orel Oblast is located in the center of European Russia. It borders Bryansk, Tula, Kaluga, Lipetsk, and Kursk oblasts. The region is rich in water resources: it has over 2,000 rivers, although none are suitable for navigation. The oblast is fairly poor in mineral resources.

Major industries include machine building (employing over 50 percent of the industrial labor force), ferrous and non-ferrous metallurgy, light industry, and food processing. The oblast has a well-developed agricultural sector and is among the top ten regions in per capita production of grains, milk, and meat. Orel Oblast exports a mere 5 percent of its industrial output and imports two-thirds of its energy as well as automobiles, food, and textiles. Coca-Cola has a major bottling facility in the region. In November 1997, a presidential decree permitted the oblast and several other federation subjects to issue Eurobonds.

According to a 1998 survey by *Ekspert* magazine, the oblast ranked 53rd among Russia's 89 regions in terms of investment potential and 34th in terms of investment risks. A 1998 survey by Bank Austria ranked the oblast 36th in terms of investment climate.

Electoral History

2000 Presidential Election
Putin: 45.84%
Zyuganov: 44.62%
Zhirinovsky: 2.41%
Yavlinskii: 1.90%
Tuleev: 1.31%
Turnout: 77.89% (Russia overall: 68.64%)

1999 Parliamentary Elections
Communist Party of the Russian Federation: 42.06%
Unity: 26.38%
Zhirinovsky Bloc: 5.52%
Union of Right Forces: 5.34%
Fatherland–All Russia: 4.11%
Yabloko: 2.49%
In a single-mandate district: 1 Communist Party of the Russian Federation
Turnout: 70.93% (Russia overall: 61.85%)

1997 Gubernatorial Election
Stroev (incumbent): 95.1%
Yenina: 2.8%
Turnout: 71.0%

1996 Presidential Election
Zyuganov: 54.25%/63.28% (first round/second round)
Yeltsin: 21.46%/32.05%
Lebed: 11.8%
Zhirinovsky: 4.41%
Yavlinskii: 3.89%
Turnout: 73.96%/72.74% (Russia overall: 69.67%/ 68.79%)

1995 Parliamentary Elections
Communist Party of the Russian Federation: 44.85%
Liberal Democratic Party of Russia: 9.48%
Our Home Is Russia: 5.08%
Communists–Workers' Russia: 3.88%
Agrarian Party of Russia: 3.62%
Women of Russia: 3.35%
Congress of Russian Communities: 3.23%
Derzhava: 2.82%
Yabloko: 2.78%
Party of Workers' Self-Government: 2.77%
Russia's Democratic Choice: 2.13%
In a single-mandate district: 1 Communist Party of the Russian Federation
Turnout: 70.47% (Russia overall: 64.37%)

1993 Constitutional Referendum
"Yes"—41.9%   "No"—56.4%

1993 Parliamentary Election
Liberal Democratic Party of Russia: 31.80%
Communist Party of the Russian Federation: 25.69%
Russia's Choice: 9.58%
Agrarian Party of Russia: 7.03%
Women of Russia: 6.04%
Democratic Party of Russia: 5.48%
Party of Russian Unity and Concord: 4.69%
Yabloko: 4.13%
In a single-mandate district: 1 independent
From electoral associations: 1 Communist Party of the Russian Federation, 1 Liberal Democratic Party of Russia
Turnout: 65.67% (Russia overall: 54.34%)

1991 Presidential Election

Yeltsin: 52.96%

Ryzhkov: 19.55%

Zhirinovsky: 9.30%

Makashov: 5.92%

Tuleev: 5.60%

Bakatin: 2.68%

Turnout: 82.43% (Russia overall: 76.66%)

Regional Political Institutions

Executive:

Governor, 5-year term

Yegor Semenovich Stroev, elected October 1997

Orel Oblast Administration; Lenin Square, 1;
Orel, 302000

Tel 7(086–2) 41–63–13, 41–25–73;

Fax 7(086–2) 41–25–30

Federation Council in Moscow:
7(095) 292–65–01, 292–5750

Fax: 7(095) 292–65–45

Legislative:

Unicameral

Council of People's Deputies—50 members, 4-year
term, elected 1994, March 1998

Chairman—Nikolai Andreevich Volodin, elected
1994, March 1998

Regional Politics

The Regions' National Leader

As the chairman of the Federation Council, the upper chamber of Russia's national parliament that is made up of regional executive and legislative leaders, Orel Oblast Governor Yegor Stroev is one of the most powerful and well-known figures in Russian politics. Leading the Federation Council makes Stroev one of the "Big Four" in Russian politics along with the president, the prime minister, and the Duma chairman. Stroev not only influences regional policy but has a strong voice in national and international matters as well. Thus Stroev vigorously opposed Putin's effort to reform the Federation Council in Summer 2000, an initiative likely to force Stroev from the national stage. In Orel, Stroev is a populist who has ensured low prices for necessary foodstuffs and the timely payment of salaries and pensions.

Stroev's political success can be attributed to his wide appeal. A former member of the Communist Party of the Soviet Union Politburo, Stroev has maintained close ties to the old guard. He is very popular among the region's Communists, and many claim that he would beat party leader Gennadii Zyuganov, an Orel native, if the two were to compete head-to-head in an election. (In the March 2000 presidential elections, Zyuganov narrowly lost to Vladimir Putin in Orel.) Unlike more orthodox Communists, however, Stroev adapted to the times. During the Yeltsin era he joined the pro-government Our Home Is Russia (NDR) movement, and supported the president on most policies.

Stroev's longtime role in national politics fostered several predictions that he would pursue the presidency in 2000. In October 1997, the governor of the neighboring Bryansk Oblast, Yurii Lodkin, claimed that Stroev could win the presidential election, but Stroev has always denied having higher ambitions (*EWI RRR*, 9 October 1997).

Executive Platform: Social Justice and Economic Management

Stroev was elected for a second term as governor on 26 October 1997, pulling in 95 percent of the vote. The only other candidate in the race, Vera Yenina, a soft-spoken local collective farm director, claimed that she would be happy if Stroev were reelected. Two other potential candidates from Zhirinovsky's Liberal Democratic Party of Russia, had been denied registration. This prompted accusations that Yenina participated only in order to ensure that the governor's reelection would be valid, since Russian elections require at least two candidates.

Stroev had won his first term as governor in an unusual April 1993 election. In his first gubernatorial campaign, Stroev stated that "there is only one way to overcome the chaos and social anarchy in Russia—to search once again for social justice and unity" (NNS). Stroev claims that the main task of governors is economic management, which must be carried out in an apolitical manner. He stresses the need to create a socially oriented economic system which is receptive to scientific and technological innovation and ensures a high standard of living for the Russian population (NNS). He believes that in 1992–93, Orel hurriedly privatized 92 percent of the agricultural enterprises and the service sector, causing a drop in production (Panorama Research Group, Labyrint Electronic Database, Moscow). He also criticized the Russian government for purchasing goods from other countries instead of from Russia's regions.

When Stroev was elected chairman of the Federation Council in January 1996, he stressed that his priorities would include issues of federalism, especially the lack of coordination among Russia's regions (*OMRI DD*, 24 January 1996).

Stroev believes that the president should be elected by a Constitutional Assembly or Assembly of Voters rather than via popular elections. He feels that elections are too expensive and could lead Russia to a civil war (*NG*, 31 October 1998).

Policies: Pioneer of Land Reform

One of Stroev's main economic goals has been to revitalize the region's agricultural sector. The reform process included three steps (*EWI RRR*, 26 March 1998). The first step was to distribute shares of farming enterprises to employees and provide a structure for consolidating the shares; the second stage integrated agricultural producers into diversified holding companies; and the third stage sought to develop investment projects. Stroev has emphasized that the most important goal of these reforms is to change popular attitudes toward owning property and make agricultural workers interested in developing their industry in the new market-based economy.

Orel is considered to be among the leading regions in land reform, having succeeded at establishing property rights through regional legislation. In October 1997 Stroev pushed forward land privatization in the Federation Council. He said that the upper house could pass the Land Code with provisions including private property for land, as well as rental and inheritance rights, as long as the state sells the land holdings at reasonable prices that are not artificially low (*NG*, 16 October 1997).

Stroev's popularity among his constituents flows largely from his attention to social concerns. He has succeeded in keeping prices reasonable and ensuring the timely payment of pensions and salaries. However, unlike many left-leaning governors, Stroev has not shied away from market reforms in order to reduce their unfortunate social consequences. Rather, Stroev has tried to strike a balance between the two. For example, in August 1997 he ordered a cut in local bread prices, which he justified in light of the surplus crop of grain for the season (*RFE/RL*, 27 August 1997). Thus, the producers were not deeply hurt and the poorer strata of society benefited.

Relationships Between Key Players

In the oblast's 1998 legislative elections, Communists took 11 of 50 seats, while the other elected candidates were independents. Given Stroev's successful experience working with both reformist and oppositionist political camps, he has a positive relationship with the new legislature.

In August 1997 Stroev emphasized that regional authorities should have a say over the distribution of timber, gas, and other natural resources located on their regions' territories (*RFE/RL*, 11 August 1997).

Ties to Moscow: Praised By Yeltsin

Despite his leftist leanings, Stroev was generally pro-Yeltsin, and was the first person to meet with him in 1995 following Yeltsin's long illness. In September 1997 Yeltsin visited Orel, praising Stroev for having brought "calm" and "prosperity" to the region (*RFE/RL*, 19 September 1997). Stroev is a member of the political council of Our Home Is Russia, but he is not an active participant in the movement and he maintained a neutral stance in the December 1999 parliamentary elections.

As Federation Council speaker, Stroev has a significant voice in the legislative branch of the federal government. He also is the leader of the Black Earth interregional association, giving him additional clout in the executive branch. In these various positions, Stroev straddles the interests of conservative and reformist politicians, as the Black Earth association includes some of Yeltsin's most outspoken enemies such as 1991 coup maker Tula Governor Vasilii Starodubtsev and Bryansk Governor Yurii Lodkin.

In July 1993 Stroev joined up with the governors of Belgorod, Voronezh, and Tambov oblasts and the chairmen of the oblast legislatures to appeal to President Yeltsin, Supreme Soviet Chairman Ruslan Khasbulatov, and Prime Minister Viktor Chernomyrdin. Their joint letter complained about the lack of available credit and technology for harvesting crops, and demanded credit, spare parts, and a purchase guarantee. The leaders also requested a change in all taxes on agricultural operations and the enactment of a decree by the Russian Congress of People's Deputies to revive the Russian village (Panorama).

In January 1997 Stroev proposed constitutional amendments to limit the powers allocated to the president. He suggested that the Duma should have the au-

Yegor Semenovich Stroev

25 February 1937—Born in Dudkin village in the Khotynetskii Raion of Orel Oblast

1954—Worked as a shepherd at the Progress Collective Farm, and then as a brigadier from 1956 to 1958, and as a production and agrarian assistant from 1958 to 1963

1958—Joined the CPSU and became the secretary of the party's collective farm bureau

1960—Graduated from the Tambov Agricultural Institute as an agronomist

1963–1965—Worked as assistant deputy of the Party committee, managing the ideological department

1965–1969—Secretary of the Khotynetskii Raion Party committee of Orel Oblast

1967–1969—Received a candidate of science degree from the CPSU Central Committee's Academy of General Sciences, defending a dissertation entitled "The Transformation of Socio-Economic Relations in the Countryside Under New Agricultural Conditions"

1969–1970—Second secretary of the Pokrovskii Raion Party committee of Orel Oblast

1970–1977—Chairman of the Pokrovskii Raion executive committee, and then first secretary of the CPSU Pokrovskii Raion committee

1973–1984—Secretary of the Orel oblast committee for agricultural issues

1984–1985—Inspector for the CPSU Central Committee

1985–1989—First secretary of the CPSU Orel Oblast committee

1986–1991—Member of the CPSU Central Committee, and secretary from 1989 to 1991, appointed by Mikhail Gorbachev

1989—Elected to the USSR Congress of People's Deputies

June 1990–August 1991—Member of the CPSU Politburo

April–August 1991—Chairman of the Central Committee commission on agrarian policy

1991–1993—Director of the All-Russian Scientific-Research Institute (VNII)

11 April 1993—Elected governor of Orel Oblast

12 December 1993—Elected to the Federation Council, serving on the Committee on the Budget, Finances, Currency and Credit Regulation, Money Emissions, Tax Policies, and Customs Regulation

1994—Earned a doctorate, with the dissertation "The Methodology and Practice of Agrarian Reforms"

March 1994—Joined the Realists, social-political union

April 1995—Elected a member of the Congress of Russian Communities' (KRO) National Committee

May 1995—Joined Our Home Is Russia (NDR)

13 June 1995—Became a member of the Committee for the Congress of Regional Powers of the Council of Europe

January 1996—Appointed to the Federation Council, and on 23 January, elected chairman

1996—Became vice chairman of the supervisory council for the All-Russian Bank for Regional Development

1996—Elected chairman for the Inter-Parliamentary Assembly (MPA) of the CIS

19 April 1997—Elected to the Political Council for NDR

26 October 1997—Reelected governor of Orel Oblast

thority to confirm deputy prime ministers and the Federation Council should be given the right to confirm the power ministers (*OMRI RRR*, 29 January 1997).

Additionally, Stroev is against the power-sharing agreements that Moscow has signed with the regions, stating that they are unconstitutional and widen the level of inequality among regions (*EWI RRR*, 30 October 1997). Stroev claims that the power-sharing agreements, which Moscow has signed with more than half of Russia's regions, contribute to the arbitrary nature of relations between the central and regional governments, and encourage relatively weak regions to be heavily dependent on the Kremlin (*RFE/RL*, 20 January 1998). Stroev is also critical of Moscow's attempts to blame regional leaders for failing to pay wage arrears since the federal government itself is behind in paying for state orders, hindering regions' ability to collect taxes (*RFE/RL*, 20 January 1998).

In spite of these criticisms of the central government, some governors considered removing Stroev from his position as speaker because they thought that he should be more critical of the Kremlin (*EWI RRR*, 2 July 1998).

Before Putin's move to restructure, Stroev stressed that in spite of the frequent disconnect between federal and regional leaders, the Federation Council could play a stabilizing role in the political process. Stroev believed that the Federation Council was well positioned for such a part because its members were both legislators who pass the laws and the administrators who must implement them (*OMRI RRR*, 29 January 1997).

The governor was a strong advocate of creating a consultative council that brings together the leaders of the executive branch, the speakers of both houses, Duma faction leaders, and other regional executives. He also believed that the Federation Council was an excellent forum for mediating disagreements between the lower house of the legislature and the executive branch (*OMRI RRR*, 29 January 1997).

Relations with Other Regions: Well Respected

As chairman of the Federation Council and the Black Earth Association, Stroev was well respected by his fellow governors. Nevertheless, within the corridors of the Federation Council there was often discontent with Stroev's management of the body, particularly his tendency to think of himself as first among equals, and what the other members feel is his lack of attention to their concerns. In the summer of 1999 some of

this grumbling became apparent when Ingushetia President Ruslan Aushev publicly denounced Stroev's decision to sharply limit the upper house's discussion of problems in his region.

The Black Earth Association includes Orel, Bryansk, Belgorod, Kursk, Lipetsk, Tula, Tambov, Novgorod, and Voronezh oblasts.

Foreign Relations

In April 1999 Stroev signed an agreement creating the Balkan Oil Consortium, a Russian-Bulgarian joint venture for developing projects in the Balkans. The consortium consists of Rosneft, Slavneft, Transneft, Stroitransgaz, Orel-Oil, the Bulgarian Petrol Holding Group, and Yukos Petroleum Bulgaria.

Attitudes Toward Business: Successful Reformer

Orel has been more successful at establishing free market institutions than other regions in central Russia. As of February 1997, only 8 percent of the oblast's enterprises were state owned, and approximately 50 businesses were joint ventures involving entrepreneurs from 25 foreign countries (*OMRI RRR*, 27 February 1997). The region's economic health has been attributed to Stroev's policies, which have provided some stability in the poor region.

Stroev's platform for economic revitalization has been more focused on the agricultural sector than on attracting investment and developing industries. Although the governor does not discourage such developments, he has done little to help stimulate their growth. Stroev unsuccessfully tried to gain ownership rights to the Polimer defense factory and 91 percent of the state-owned Tyumen Oil Company (*OMRI DD*, 18 February 1997). However, in September 1997, Orel officials signed a deal with a German company for a $64 million loan for grain production in the region (*RFE/RL* 19 September 1997). Additionally, Coca-Cola has a major bottling factory in the oblast, for which Stroev has been given tremendous credit.

In April 1999 Stroev signed a cooperation agreement with then Minister of Fuel and Energy Sergei Generalov and Transneft President Dmitrii Savelev. The agreement concerns various investment projects, including the construction of the Baltic Pipeline System and the resettlement of miners from northern Russian regions to Orel.

ORENBURG OBLAST

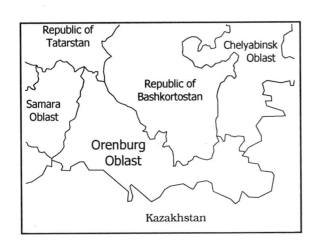

Territory: 124,000 km²
Population (as of 1 January 1998): 2,230,000
Distance from Moscow: 1,478 km

Major Cities:
Orenburg, *capital* (pop. 527,000)
Orsk (274,700)
Novotroitsk (109,800)
Buzuluk (86,000)
Buguruslan (54,400)

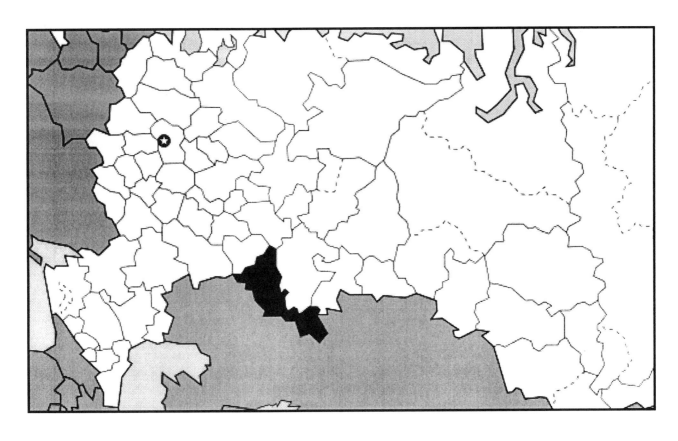

Basic Facts

Population (as of 1 Jan. 1998): 2,230,000 (1.52% of Russian total)

Ethnic breakdown (1989 census): Russians 72.2%, Tatars 7.3%, Kazakhs 5.1%, Ukrainians 4.7%, Mordvins 3.2%, Bashkirs 2.5%, Germans 2.2%, Chuvash 1.0%

Urban population (as of 1 Jan. 1998): 64.1% (Russia overall: 73.1%)

Student population (as of 1 Sept. 1997): 174 per 10,000 (Russia overall: 208/10,000)

Pensioner population (1997): 25.29% (Russia overall: 25.96%)

Percent of population with higher education (1989 census): 7.9% (Russia overall: 11.3%)

Percent of population working in 1997: Industry: 20.9% (Russian average: 23.0%); Agriculture: 19.1% (13.7%); Trade: 12.0% (13.5%); Culture: 11.7% (13.3%)

Average monthly personal income in July 1998: 586.1 new rubles (Russian average: 891.7 new rubles)

Average monthly personal expenses in July 1998: 391.1 new rubles (Russian average: 684.9 new rubles)

Average monthly subsistence requirement in 1998: 321 new rubles (Russian average: 438 new rubles)

Consumer price index (as of July 1998): 84 (Russia overall = 100)

Budgetary revenues (1997): 4,763.0 billion rubles (Russia overall: 433,378.2 billion rubles)

Budgetary expenditures (1997): 5,446.5 billion rubles (Russia overall: 468,111.6 billion rubles)

Industrial production as percentage of all Russian production (Jan.–Aug. 1998): 1.23%

Proportion of loss-making enterprises (as of July 1998): 49.8% (Russia overall: 50.4%)

Number of enterprises which have wage arrears (as of 1 Sept. 1998): 1,242 (0.92% of Russian total)

Agricultural production as percentage of all Russian production (1997): 2.11%

Number of private farms (as of 1 Jan. 1998): 7,116 (2.59% of Russian total)

Capital investment (1997): 5,804.9 billion rubles (Russia overall: 408,797 billion rubles)

Sources of investment (1997): federal budget: 3.8% (Russian average: 10.2%); regional budget: 9.6% (10.5%); extra-budgetary funds: 86.6% (79.3%)

Foreign investment (1997): 421,000 USD (Russia overall: 12,294,734,000 USD)

Number of joint ventures (1997): 54 (0.37% of Russian total)

Fixed capital investment in joint ventures and foreign companies (1997): 221,073 million rubles (Russia overall: 16,265.4 billion rubles)

Number of small businesses (as of 1 July 1998): 7,300 (0.84% of Russian total)

Number of enterprises privatized in 1997: 24 (0.87% of Russian total), including those which used to be municipal property: 45.9% (Russian average: 66.4%); regional property: 20.8% (20.0%); federal property: 33.3% (13.6%)

Number of telephones per 100 families (1997): in cities: 39.9 (Russian average: 49.2); in villages: 21.7 (19.8)

Brief Overview

Orenburg Oblast is located on the divide between Europe and Asia to the west of the Ural Mountains. It borders the republics of Bashkortostan and Tatarstan, Chelyabinsk and Samara oblasts, and Kazakhstan. Originally the territory of modern Orenburg Oblast was home to several nomadic tribes, including the Kalmyks, Scythians, and Tatars, who later moved westward. The Russian state took control of the region in the 16th and 17th centuries, though intensive migration to the area from the country's western territories began only in the 1830s. In 1743, the present oblast capital, Orenburg, was founded at the confluence of the Yaik and Sakmara rivers and immediately became the main administrative and trade center of the area.

Today the oblast is one of the country's most important industrial and agricultural regions. Its territory is rich in mineral resources: over 2,500 deposits of 75 different raw materials have been discovered and developed. Oil, charcoal, ferrous and non-ferrous metals are the key deposits. The oblast is second only to Yamal-Nenets in the extraction of gas. More than three-fourths of the oblast's output comes from industry, which is dominated by the fuel and energy sector, metallurgy, machine construction, and chemicals. The oblast is located at the crossroads of numerous railroads and highways making it an important transportation hub. The country's major gas and oil pipelines, connecting Siberian gas and oil fields to the European part of Russia and other European countries, cross its territory.

According to a 1998 survey by *Ekspert* magazine, the oblast ranked 25th among Russia's 89 regions in terms of investment potential and 28th in terms of investment risk. A 1998 survey by Bank Austria ranked the oblast 30th in terms of investment climate.

Electoral History

2000 Presidential Election
Putin: 45.22%
Zyuganov: 42.49%
Yavlinskii: 2.86%
Zhirinovsky: 2.82%
Titov: 1.99%
Tuleev: 1.72%
Turnout: 68.43% (Russia overall: 68.64%)

1999 Parliamentary Elections
Communist Party of the Russian Federation: 29.93%
Unity: 23.26%
Fatherland–All Russia: 6.74%
Union of Right Forces: 6.57%
Zhirinovsky Bloc: 6.22%
Yabloko: 4.07%
Our Home Is Russia: 4.07%
In single-mandate districts: 2 Communist Party of the Russian Federation, 1 independent
Turnout: 63.48% (Russia overall: 61.85%)

1999 Gubernatorial Election
Chernyshev: 23.86%/52.50%
Yelagin (incumbent): 33.45%/43.51% (first round/second round)
Turnout: 63.41%/47.87%

1996 Presidential Election
Zyuganov: 42.13%/53.94% (first round/second round)
Yeltsin: 25.96%/40.81%
Lebed: 13.62%
Zhirinovsky: 7.51%
Yavlinskii: 5.84%
Turnout: 70.29%/67.77% (Russia overall: 69.67%/68.79%)

1995 Gubernatorial Election
Yelagin (incumbent): 58.78%
Donkovtsev (Orenburg City mayor): 21.69%
Kalyuzhnyi (Derzhava): 7.79%
Pavlychev (local administration head): 4.43%
Mikhailov (Forward, Russia!): 1.62%
Turnout: 65.42%

1995 Parliamentary Elections
Communist Party of the Russian Federation: 23.60%
Our Home Is Russia: 12.28%
Liberal Democratic Party of Russia: 11.73%
Agrarian Party of Russia: 8.35%
Communists–Workers' Russia: 5.97%
Congress of Russian Communities: 3.98%
Yabloko: 3.98%
Women of Russia: 3.81%
In single-mandate districts: 1 Agrarian Party of Russia, 1 Yabloko, 1 Communist Party of the Russian Federation
Turnout: 65.01% (Russia overall: 64.37%)

1993 Constitutional Referendum
"Yes"—56.7%   "No"—41.0%

1993 Parliamentary Elections
Liberal Democratic Party of Russia: 22.55%
Agrarian Party of Russia: 17.79%
Communist Party of the Russian Federation: 13.20%
Russia's Choice: 13.16%
Women of Russia: 7.82%
Yabloko: 5.94%
Democratic Party of Russia: 5.82%
Party of Russian Unity and Concord: 5.59%
In single-mandate districts: 1 Yabloko, 1 Agrarian
   Party of Russia, 1 Communist Party of the
   Russian Federation
Turnout: 56.05% (Russia overall: 54.34%)

1991 Presidential Election
Yeltsin: 57.18%
Ryzhkov: 19.47%
Zhirinovsky: 8.17%
Tuleev: 4.46%
Makashov: 4.42%
Bakatin: 3.00%
Turnout: 79.23% (Russia overall: 76.66%)

Regional Political Institutions

Executive:
   Governor, 4-year term
   Aleksei Andreevich Chernyshev, elected December
   1999
      Dom Sovetov; Orenburg, 460015
      Tel 7(353–2) 77–69–31, 77–09–62;
      Fax 7(353–2) 77–38–02

Legislative:
   Unicameral
   Legislative Assembly (Zakonodatelnoe Sobranie)—
   47 members, 4-year term, elected March 1998
   Chairman—Valerii Nikolaevich Grigorev, elected
   March 1994, April 1998

Regional Politics

Popular Agrarian Ousts Yeltsin-Era Reformer

Aleksei Chernyshev's popular appeal among Orenburg's agricultural and industrial communities gave him the edge over Yeltsin appointee Vladimir Yelagin in the region's 1999 gubernatorial election. Chernyshev pulled past the incumbent in the election's second round, winning 52.8 percent of the vote. Yelagin was first appointed governor in October 1991 and was elected to the post in December 1995. However, though loyal to the president, his Moscow connections were not enough for Yelagin to spark substantial economic development in the region.

Though Orenburg has historically served as one of Russia's top industrial and agricultural centers, Yelagin did little to bolster these assets in capitalist Russia. The region has bountiful natural resources and is on an important transportation route. Yet, in spite of its seemingly strong potential, Orenburg has attracted very little investment and no major joint ventures with foreign partners.

Yelagin's failure to improve the region's economy through market reforms played directly into the hands of Chernyshev, a highly influential State Duma deputy belonging to the Agrarian faction. A native of Orenburg who served in local political structures until winning election to the federal parliament in 1990, Chernyshev is very familiar with the region's specific problems and concerns. His experience in the State Duma, as well as his close ties with the central leadership of the Communist Party, made him an attractive alternative for a population fed up with Yelagin's empty reform efforts.

Executive Platform: Communist Leader

Chernyshev is a visible leader of the Communists and Agrarians in Orenburg. He has good connections to Communist Party leader Gennadii Zyuganov and has considerable influence over the party's internal politics. While in the State Duma Chernyshev belonged to the Agrarian faction and was head of the Duma's Agrarian Committee from 1993 until he left the Duma to become governor. There he played a key role in preventing the adoption of legislation allowing the sale and purchase of arable land (see Stephen K. Wegren, *Agriculture and the State in Soviet and Post-Soviet Russia*, Pittsburgh: University of Pittsburgh Press, 1998, 166.)

Policies

One of Chernyshev's first moves as governor of Orenburg was to issue a decree improving the structure and reducing expenditures of administrative or-

Aleksei Andreevich Chernyshev

29 March 1939—Born in the village of Rybinko in Orenburg Oblast

Graduated from the engineering faculty of the Orenburg Agricultural Institute and the CPSU Central Committee's Academy of General Sciences

1962–1965—Worked on the Sovetskii collective farm

1965–1973—Chief engineer-mechanic and then head of agricultural production management of the Akbulakskii Raion

March 1973—Became first secretary of the Akbulakskii CPSU district committee

1978–1982—Director of the Orenburg Oblast agricultural administration, first deputy chairman of the oblast's agro-industrial complex council

1983–1991—Orenburg Oblast Committee second secretary

18 March 1990—Elected to the RSFSR Congress of People's Deputies, where he joined the Agrarian faction

12 December 1993—Elected to the State Duma, where he joined the Agrarian faction

January 1994–January 1995—First deputy chairman and then chairman of the Agrarian Committee

17 December 1995—Reelected to State Duma and Agrarian Committee chairmanship

27 December 1999—Elected governor of Orenburg Oblast

Married with a daughter

gans. The purpose of this decree was to put the region's 2000 budget in order. Oblast administration departments and committee heads of local administrations were given a week to reduce their expenditures by no less than 8 percent (*Ural Press*).

Relationships Between Key Players: Strong Communist Representation

Communists have strong grass-roots support on the Orenburg political scene, which clearly contributed to Chernyshev's success. Zyuganov was the region's choice in the 1996 presidential elections, and in March 1998 Communists increased their representation in the Orenburg Oblast legislature. The Communists won 16 seats in the 47-seat assembly, and Our Home Is Russia won only 10 seats. Chernyshev should have little difficulty passing his measures through the legislature.

Ties to Moscow

Yelagin and the rest of Orenburg's political elite successfully blocked the creation of a new "Gosneft" state oil company, which would have included the region's oil enterprise ONAKO. Yelagin, the Orenburg Legis-

lative Assembly, and ONAKO President Rem Khramov felt that ONAKO's inclusion in a state holding would negatively affect the company and the oblast's economic position since the enterprise's taxes, which make up one-fourth of the regional budget, would go to Moscow (*EWI RRR*, 6 May and 10 June).

On 30 January 1996 Yelagin and Yeltsin signed a power-sharing agreement between Orenburg Oblast and the Russian Federation.

Relations with Other Regions

Orenburg belongs to the Urals Regional Association, which also includes the republics of Bashkortostan and Udmurtia; the Komi-Permyak Autonomous Okrug; and Kurgan, Perm, Sverdlovsk, and Chelyabinsk oblasts.

Foreign Relations

In May 1998 Yelagin signed an agreement with Belarusan President Aleksandr Lukashenko to increase trade between Orenburg and Belarus by one third before the end of the year.

Orenburg was one of the cities participating in a 1996 World Bank project to foster housing privatization.

Attitudes Toward Business: Underdeveloped Potential

Although Yelagin was interested in further developing Orenburg's natural resources, he took few concrete measures to improve the region's market infrastructure and attract investment to the oblast.

Internet Sites in the Region

http://www.orenburg.ru/
This website offers basic information on the oblast and Orenburg city, including demographic and social statistics, data on regional enterprises, and tax policy texts.

PENZA OBLAST

Territory: 43,200 km²
Population (as of 1 January 1998):
1,549,000
Distance from Moscow: 709 km

Major Cities:
Penza, *capital* (pop. 529,000)
Kuznetsk (99,200)
Zarechnyi (63,700)
Kamenka (45,200)
Serdobsk (45,000)

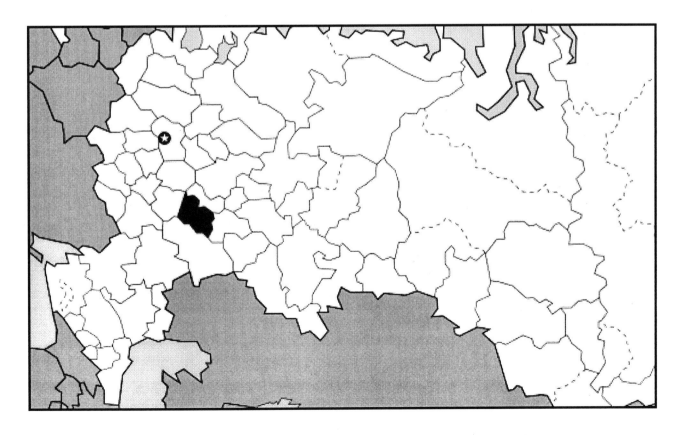

Basic Facts

Population (as of 1 Jan. 1998): 1,549,000 (1.05% of Russian total)

Ethnic breakdown (1989 census): Russians 86.2%, Mordvins 5.7%, Tatars 5.4%, Ukrainians 1.0%

Urban population (as of 1 Jan. 1998): 64.4% (Russia overall: 73.1%)

Student population (as of 1 Sept. 1997): 162 per 10,000 (Russia overall: 208/10,000)

Pensioner population (1997): 27.70% (Russia overall: 25.96%)

Percent of population with higher education (1989 census): 8.8% (Russia overall: 11.3%)

Percent of population working in (1997): Industry: 26.9% (Russian average: 23.0%); Agriculture: 17.7% (13.7%); Trade: 11.9% (13.5%); Culture: 13.0% (13.3%)

Average monthly personal income in July 1998: 402.3 new rubles (Russian average: 891.7 new rubles)

Average monthly personal expenses in July 1998: 300.1 new rubles (Russian average: 684.9 new rubles)

Average monthly subsistence requirement in 1998: 401 new rubles (Russian average: 438 new rubles)

Consumer price index (as of July 1998): 85 (Russia overall = 100)

Budgetary revenues (1997): 2,071.9 billion rubles (Russia overall: 433,378.2 billion rubles)

Budgetary expenditures (1997): 2,287.7 billion rubles (Russia overall: 468,111.6 billion rubles)

Industrial production as percentage of all Russian production (Jan.–Aug. 1998): 0.27%

Proportion of loss-making enterprises (as of July 1998): 53.3% (Russia overall: 50.4%)

Number of enterprises which have wage arrears (as of 1 Sept. 1998): 3,912 (2.89% of Russian total)

Agricultural production as percentage of all Russian production (1997): 1.19%

Number of private farms (as of 1 Jan. 1998): 2,062 (0.75% of Russian total)

Capital investment (1997): 1,959.7 billion rubles (Russia overall: 408,797 billion rubles)

Sources of investment (1997): federal budget: 7.1% (Russian average: 10.2%); regional budget: 9.9% (10.5%); extra-budgetary funds: 83.0% (79.3%)

Foreign investment (1997): 2,683,000 USD (Russia overall: 12,294,734,000 USD)

Number of joint ventures (1997): 18 (0.12% of Russian total)

Fixed capital investment in joint ventures and foreign companies (1997): 2,285 million rubles (Russia overall: 16,265.4 billion rubles)

Number of small businesses (as of 1 July 1998): 4,600 (0.53% of Russian total)

Number of enterprises privatized in 1997: 7 (0.26% of Russian total), including those which used to be municipal property: 42.8% (Russian average: 66.4%); regional property: 14.3% (20.0%); federal property: 42.9% (13.6%)

Number of telephones per 100 families (1997): in cities: 35.8 (Russian average: 49.2); in villages: 13.2 (19.8)

Brief Overview

Penza Oblast is located in the Middle Volga River area and borders Ulyanovsk, Saratov, Tambov, and Ryazan oblasts and the Republic of Mordovia.

The oblast has equally well-developed industrial and agricultural sectors. Machine building, chemicals, forestry, cellulose manufacturing, and electronics are the main industries. Grain, vegetables, sugar beets, and potatoes are the major agricultural products.

The oblast has an active foreign economic policy. Over 60 regional enterprises (mainly in the machine building, medical, and forestry industries) export their products to about 40 different countries. The main foreign trade partners of the oblast are companies from Germany, Great Britain, Austria, Switzerland, and Hong Kong.

According to a 1998 survey by *Ekspert* magazine, the oblast ranked 49th among Russia's 89 regions in terms of investment potential and 58th in terms of investment risk. A 1998 survey by Bank Austria ranked the oblast 59th in terms of investment climate.

Electoral History

2000 Presidential Election
Putin: 49.34%
Zyuganov: 38.34%
Yavlinskii: 3.20%
Zhirinovsky: 2.48%
Tuleev: 1.50%
Turnout: 70.01% (Russia overall: 68.64%)

1999 Parliamentary Elections
Unity: 29.31%
Communist Party of the Russian Federation: 28.93%
Fatherland–All Russia: 7.63%
Zhirinovsky Bloc: 5.70%
Union of Right Forces: 5.18%
Yabloko: 4.49%
In single-mandate districts: 1 Fatherland–All Russia, 1 In Support of the Army
Turnout: 63.38% (Russia overall: 61.85%)

1998 Gubernatorial Election
Bochkarev: 60.0%
Lyzhin (State Duma deputy): 10.0%
Kovlyagin (incumbent): 12.7%
Turnout: 49.8%

1996 Presidential Election
Zyuganov: 50.60%/58.95% (first round/second round)
Yeltsin: 20.81%/35.50%
Lebed: 12.06%
Yavlinskii: 6.93%
Zhirinovsky: 5.29%
Turnout: 74.92%/72.26% (Russia overall: 69.67%/68.79%)

1995 Parliamentary Elections
Communist Party of the Russian Federation: 37.33%
Liberal Democratic Party of Russia: 11.09%
Yabloko: 6.04%
Communists–Workers' Russia: 5.20%
Our Home Is Russia: 4.73%
Agrarian Party of Russia: 4.63%
Women of Russia: 3.15%
Derzhava: 3.10%
Party of Workers' Self-Government: 2.99%
Power to the People: 2.35%
Congress of Russian Communities: 2.29%
In single-mandate districts: 1 Communist Party of the Russian Federation, 1 Agrarian Party of Russia
Turnout: 70.51% (Russia overall: 64.37%)

1993 Constitutional Referendum
"Yes"—39.2%   "No"—59.0%

1993 Parliamentary Elections
Liberal Democratic Party of Russia: 32.56%
Communist Party of the Russian Federation: 19.49%
Agrarian Party of Russia: 10.40%
Russia's Choice: 8.56%
Women of Russia: 7.16%
Yabloko: 6.95%
Democratic Party of Russia: 4.71%
Party of Russian Unity and Concord: 4.69%
In single-mandate districts: 1 Yabloko, 1 Communist Party of the Russian Federation
Turnout: 62.64% (Russia overall: 54.34%)

1991 Presidential Election
Yeltsin: 61.28%
Ryzhkov: 15.06%
Zhirinovsky: 7.02%
Tuleev: 6.61%
Makashov: 3.72%
Bakatin: 1.97%
Turnout: 84.14% (Russia overall: 76.66%)

Regional Political Institutions

Executive:
  Governor, 5-year term
  Vasilii Kuzmich Bochkarev, elected April 1998
    Penza Oblast Administration; Dom Sovetov;
    Pl. im. Lenina ; Penza,440025
    Tel 7(841–2) 66–11–94, 66–83–50;
    Fax 7(841–2) 55–04–11

Legislative:
  Unicameral
  Legislative Assembly (Zakonodatelnoe Sobranie)—
  45 members, 4-year term, elected December 1997
  Chairman—Yurii Ivanovich Vechkasov, elected
  December 1997

Regional Politics

Businessman Comes to Power
in Communist Oblast

Vasilii Bochkarev won the 12 April 1998 gubernatorial elections in Penza with 59.5 percent of the vote. He is usually depicted as a "strong manager," though enemies describe Bochkarev as the "local Klimentev," referring to the Nizhnii Novgorod business who won that city's March 1998 mayoral elections even though he had a criminal record.

Bochkarev is obviously a wealthy man. All of his relatives, including his wife, are involved in business, but because they conduct their affairs outside his oblast, the procurator claimed no conflicts of interest. He is rumored to own property in Portugal. During the campaign, he controlled one of two local TV stations and had the support of several newspapers. In a region where $2 million is the normal campaign expenditure, his campaign cost an estimated $5–$6 million. Businessmen backed his candidacy, hoping he could spread his success throughout the oblast. However, as governor and a member of the Federation Council, some conflicts of interest between his need to rule impartially and his family's business interests seem possible (*EWI RRR*, 16 April 1998).

During the campaign, his supporters widely publicized the fact that wages, pensions, and child allowances were paid on time in the raion he once led. In the campaign, State Duma Deputy Yurii Lyzhin, the head of the regional Communist party, won 16 percent, and incumbent Governor Anatolii Kovlyagin placed third with 13 percent. The level of support for Lyzhin was extremely low in com-

parison with Communist presidential candidate Gennadii Zyuganov's strong showing in the 1996 presidential election in Penza. Zyuganov outpolled Yeltsin in the oblast by some 59–36 percent (*RFE/RL*, 14 April 1998).

Executive Platform

Bochkarev belonged to no political party when he ran for office. He campaigned as a pragmatist manager. In 1999 he signed on to the All Russia party.

Relationships Between Key Players

In spring 1999 the Penza Oblast Legislative Assembly approved a new law creating a Penza Oblast government, dividing the region's executive branch into two parts. The new model mirrors Russia's federal power arrangement, with the governor handling political issues and the government addressing social and economic concerns. The governor is in charge of making strategic decisions for strengthening and restoring the image of Penza Oblast in its relations with the federal government, other regions, and foreign states and businesses. He is also responsible for setting the strategy for oblast development and determining the key goals for the different members of the executive branch, including its relationship with the oblast legislature. The government focuses on stabilizing the oblast's socio-economic situation. The oblast government is now headed by a prime minister, Deputy Governor Aleksandr Dolganov, who controls eleven ministries. The governor has the right to name and remove the prime minister and his entire cabinet, but only with the approval of the oblast legislature.

The Communists won a third of the seats in the Penza legislative elections in December 1997, as well as ten additional sympathizers in the 45-seat assembly. Several current and past party leaders were elected. Neither Zhirinovsky's nor Lebed's parties succeeded in winning any seats.

Ties to Moscow

Moscow views Bochkarev as a dynamic ruler who has stimulated the growth of small-and medium-sized enterprises.

Relations with Other Regions

Penza belongs to the Greater Volga Association. The association, which has a rotating leadership, includes

Vasilii Kuzmich Bochkarev

1949—Born in the Ive village in Nizhnelomov raion of Penza Oblast

Graduated from Alatyr forest-technical school and Marii Polytechnical Institute as a builder

Headed the district executive committee of Zheleznodorozhnyi Raion in the city of Penza

1988–1998—Head of administration of the Zheleznodorozhnyi Raion in the city of Penza

1990—Elected to the RSFSR Congress of People's Deputies

April 1993—Unsuccessfully ran for the post of governor of Penza Oblast

January 1994—Elected a deputy of the Penza legislative assembly

12 April 1998—Elected governor of Penza Oblast

22 April 1998—Joined the Federation Council

Married

the republics of Tatarstan, Mordovia, Chuvashia, and Marii El, and Astrakhan, Volgograd, Nizhnii Novgorod, Samara, Saratov, and Ulyanovsk oblasts.

Foreign Relations

The oblast has an active foreign economic policy. Over 60 regional enterprises (mainly in the machine building, medical, and forestry industries) export their products to about 40 different countries. The main foreign trade partners of the oblast are companies from Germany, Great Britain, Austria, Switzerland, and Hong Kong.

The American Brenon Motors company has a long-term contract with Penza's fixture factory (*SPV*, No. 126, 4 July 1997).

PERM OBLAST

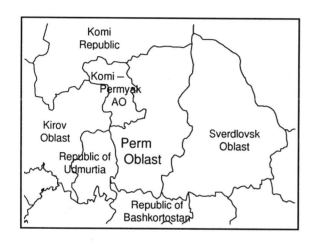

Territory: 160,600 km²
Population (as of 1 January 1998):
2,986,000
Distance from Moscow: 1,386 km

Major Cities:

Perm, *capital*
(pop. 1,022,700)
Berezniki (183,000)
Solikamsk (106,600)
Chaikovskii (89,800)

Kungur (76,000)
Lysva (75,900)
Chusovoi (54,700)
Krasnokamsk
(56,600)

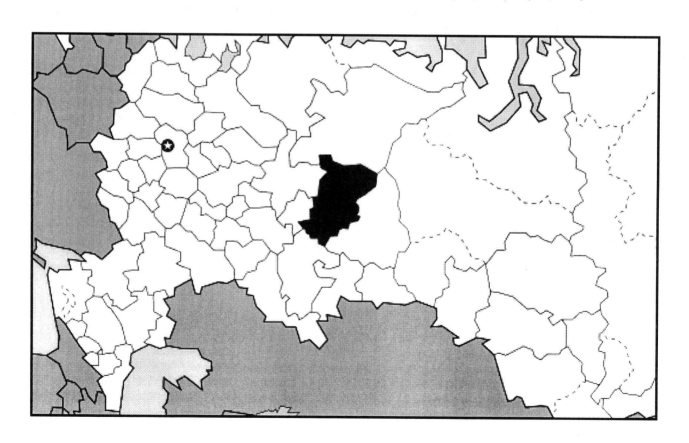

Basic Facts

Population (as of 1 Jan. 1998): 2,986,000 (2.03% of Russian total)

Ethnic breakdown (1989 census): Russians 85.9%, Tatars 5.2%, Bashkirs 1.8%, Ukrainians 1.6%, Udmurts 1.2%

Urban population (as of 1 Jan. 1998): 76.3% (Russia overall: 73.1%)

Student population (as of 1 Sept. 1997): 153 per 10,000 (Russia overall: 208/10,000)

Pensioner population (1997): 25.45% (Russia overall: 25.96%)

Percent of population with higher education (1989 census): 8.0% (Russia overall: 11.3%)

Percent of population working in (1997): Industry: 26.8% (Russian average: 23.0%); Agriculture: 9.4% (13.7%); Trade: 16.3% (13.5%); Culture: 13.4% (13.3%)

Average monthly personal income in July 1998: 929.4 new rubles (Russian average: 891.7 new rubles)

Average monthly personal expenses in July 1998: 643.0 new rubles (Russian average: 684.9 new rubles)

Average monthly subsistence requirement in 1998: 377 new rubles (Russian average: 438 new rubles)

Consumer price index (as of July 1998): 97 (Russia overall = 100)

Budgetary revenues (1997): 7,959.0 billion rubles (Russia overall: 433,378.2 billion rubles)

Budgetary expenditures (1997): 8,344.5 billion rubles (Russia overall: 468,111.6 billion rubles)

Industrial production as percentage of all Russian production (Jan.–Aug. 1998): 2.09%

Proportion of loss-making enterprises (as of July 1998): 48.5% (Russia overall: 50.4%)

Number of enterprises which have wage arrears (as of 1 Sept. 1998): 1,708 (1.26% of Russian total)

Agricultural production as percentage of all Russian production (1997): 1.86%

Number of private farms (as of 1 Jan. 1998): 3,506 (1.28% of Russian total)

Capital investment (1997): 7,850.3 billion rubles (Russia overall: 408,797 billion rubles)

Sources of investment (1997): federal budget: 8.1% (Russian average: 10.2%); regional budget: 5.9% (10.5%); extra-budgetary funds: 86.0% (79.3%)

Foreign investment (1997): 19,298,000 USD (Russia overall: 12,294,734,000 USD)

Number of joint ventures (1997): 100 (0.68% of Russian total)

Fixed capital investment in joint ventures and foreign companies (1997): 192,660 million rubles (Russia overall: 16,265.4 billion rubles)

Number of small businesses (as of 1 July 1998): 9,600 (1.11% of Russian total)

Number of enterprises privatized in 1997: 2 (0.07% of Russian total), including those which used to be municipal property: 100% (Russian average: 66.4%); regional property: 0% (20.0%); federal property: 0% (13.6%)

Number of telephones per 100 families (1997): in cities: 41.9 (Russian average: 49.2); in villages: 17.4 (19.8)

Brief Overview

Perm Oblast is located in the easternmost part of Europe, where the Russian plain meets the Ural Mountains. It occupies about one fifth of the entire Ural Mountains and borders Sverdlovsk and Kirov oblasts, as well as the republics of Bashkortostan, Komi, and Udmurtia.

The oblast's cpital, Perm, was founded in the late 18th century at the order of Catherine the Great and immediately became an important administrative center and the largest port in the Kama River basin. It was also one of the country's largest industrial centers: in the 19th century, the city housed over 130 industrial enterprises.

The oblast's territory is rich in mineral resources, including natural gas and oil. It also houses about 25 percent of the entire coal resources of the Ural economic region and is rich in ferrous and non-ferrous metals, including gold and platinum. The oblast has a diamond field, which is located in the Vishera River basin. Moreover, Perm Oblast is one of the richest timber regions in Europe.

Perm is now one of the three most industrially developed regions in the Ural area. Over one third of the regional GDP comes from the fuel and energy sector, followed by raw materials processing (20%) and machine building (16.1%). The latter is mostly concentrated in manufacturing military equipment and equipment for the oil, gas, mining, chemical, and timber-processing industries.

The oblast is located at the intersection of two railroads that connect it with European, Siberian and Far Eastern regions. A highly developed system of canals connects the oblast's major river, the Kama, with five seas—the Caspian, Baltic, Azov, White, and Black.

According to a 1998 survey by *Ekspert* magazine, the oblast ranked 8th among Russia's 89 regions in terms of investment potential and 31st in terms of investment risk. A 1998 survey by Bank Austria ranked the oblast 17th in terms of investment climate.

Electoral History

2000 Presidential Election
Putin: 60.79%
Zyuganov: 19.97%
Yavlinskii: 7.30%
Zhirinovsky: 3.47%
Tuleev: 1.74%
Turnout: 66.84% (Russia overall: 68.64%)

1999 Parliamentary Elections
Unity: 19.82%
Union of Right Forces: 15.24%
Communist Party of the Russian Federation: 14.15%
Fatherland–All Russia: 10.03%
Zhirinovsky Bloc: 7.51%
Yabloko: 6.97%
In single-mandate districts: 1 Fatherland–All Russia, 1 Union of Right Forces, 2 independent
Turnout: 58.06% (Russia overall: 61.85%)

1996 Gubernatorial Election
Igumnov (incumbent): 42.38%/63.86% (first round/ second round)
Levitan: 26.89%/29.08%
Ilinykh: 7.71%
Perkhun (KPRF): 4.89%
Parkhomenko (LDPR): 4.22%
Novikov (Russian Communist Workers' Party): 3.11%
Turnout: 44.2%39.35%

1996 Presidential Election
Yeltsin: 55.27%/70.84% (first round/second round)
Zyuganov: 16.12%/23.57%
Lebed: 9.69%
Yavlinskii: 7.21%
Zhirinovsky: 6.24%
Turnout: 66.55%/65.13% (Russia overall: 69.67%/ 68.79%)

1995 Parliamentary Elections
Liberal Democratic Party of Russia: 14.75%
Communist Party of the Russian Federation: 11.08%
Our Home Is Russia: 9.65%
Women of Russia: 8.21%
Russia's Democratic Choice: 5.78%
Yabloko: 5.59%
Party of Workers' Self-Government: 4.60%
Forward, Russia: 4.10%
In single-mandate districts: 1 Russia's Democratic Choice, 3 independent
Turnout: 58.58% (Russia overall: 64.37%)

1993 Constitutional Referendum
"Yes"—77.7%   "No"—19.7%

1993 Parliamentary Elections

Russia's Choice: 27.12%
Liberal Democratic Party of Russia: 14.81%
Women of Russia: 12.24%
Party of Russian Unity and Concord: 9.85%
Yabloko: 8.24%
Communist Party of the Russian Federation:
  6.91%
Democratic Party of Russia: 5.00%
Agrarian Party of Russia: 4.86%
In single-mandate districts: 1 Russia's Choice, 1
  Civic Union, 1 Communist Party of the Russian
  Federation, 1 independent
Turnout: 46.00% (Russia overall: 54.34%)

1991 Presidential Election

Yeltsin: 71.13%
Ryzhkov: 10.58%
Zhirinovsky: 4.99%
Bakatin: 4.54%
Makashov: 2.75%
Tuleev: 1.98%
Turnout: 73.48% (Russia overall: 76.66%)

Regional Political Institutions

Executive:
  Governor, 4-year term
  Gennadii Vyacheslavovich Igumnov,
  elected December 1996
    Ul. Kuibysheva, 14; Perm, 614006
    Tel 7(3422) 34–07–90, 90–16–00;
    Fax 7(3422) 34–89–52
    Federation Council in Moscow:
    7(095) 292–30–33, 926–68–20

Legislative:
  Unicameral
  Legislative Assembly (Zakonodatelnoe Sobranie)—
  40 members, 4-year term, elected December 1997
  Chairman—Yurii Germanovich Medvedev, elected
  January 1998

Regional Politics

Moderate Governor in a Peaceful Region

Gennadii Igumnov was elected governor of Perm
Oblast in December 1996, winning 64.6 percent of the
vote after having served in the position via appointment since January 1996. He had the support of President Boris Yeltsin's administration.

Igumnov has been a pragmatic leader for Perm. He prioritizes economic reform, and has successfully managed to direct policies that are supportive of business, while generally maintaining a comfortable living standard for Perm's residents. His moderate approach has allowed him to develop a wide support network among the region's political parties and key business leaders.

Executive Platform: Promoting Economic Reforms While Maintaining Living Standards

Igumnov has a rather low national stature in Russia largely because political stability and moderation define Perm's political climate (*EWI RRR*, 23 April 1998). The regional political elite favors a consensual approach to policymaking. Even though Perm maintained relatively strong support for President Yeltsin, who was often considered a 'native son' because he spent part of his life in the region's second largest city, Berezniki, Perm has never been among the leaders of economic reform. However, the region has never been an outsider either. Perm generally cultivates a moderately pro-reform image, avoiding extremes of any kind. The regional political elite is largely pragmatic, defining their main job as promoting economic reform while improving overall living standards. While the region and the federal government have some disagreements (especially over money and defense industry management), political leaders seek to avoid open conflict as much as possible.

Igumnov supported Yeltsin in his 1993 stand-off with the State Duma. In May 1997, he was elected to the 20-member presidium of Prime Minister Viktor Chernomyrdin's Our Home Is Russia (NDR). However, the party was not very active at the local level and Igumnov never set up an NDR faction in the local legislature although a majority of the deputies were loyal to him. In May 1999 Igumnov called upon the region's supporters of NDR and the regional blocs All Russia, Voice of Russia, and Fatherland to unite in order to serve as a more powerful force in the December 1999 State Duma elections.

Policies: Pro-Business Pragmatism

Politicians and businesspeople in Perm have agreed to work together to solve the problems facing business and preventing economic growth. For example, in 1994 the then newly elected regional assembly, with strong representation from the business sector, made reducing the profit tax from 22 percent (the maximum allowed by federal law) to 17.5 percent one of its first moves. During the 1997 gubernatorial elections, the regional business elite strongly backed the incumbent Igumnov in recognition of his popular authority and political management skills. Igumnov reciprocated by including people with a strong economic or business background on his new team, who, in combination with experienced but more conservative civil servants, provided a good balance between continuity and change. As Assembly member Andrei Klimov (who also has a strong business background) stressed in an interview, regional business people are one of the primary sources of political and social stability in the area. He believes they are far-sighted enough to be concerned not only with maximizing their own profits but with minimizing the risk of social protest, decreasing the level of crime, and providing better educational and cultural facilities.

Relationships Between Key Players: Consensus Decision Making

Conflict avoidance is the name of the game in relations between Governor Gennadii Igumnov and the regional assembly. The local authorities likewise maintain good working relations with almost all political parties in the region, from Yegor Gaidar's Russia's Democratic Choice to the Communist Party of the Russian Federation. The December 1997 regional assembly elections illustrated that pragmatic approach. In some districts, communists and democrats jointly backed the same candidates. Overall, candidates loyal to Igumnov in the United Democratic Forces of the Prikame bloc won 22 of the 40 seats (*EWI RRR*, 18 December 1997). During the elections for the speaker of the new assembly, Governor Igumnov asserted his willingness to work with either Yevgenii Sapiro (the incumbent speaker) or Yurii Medvedev (the director of the Gosznak factory), stressing that while personalities were important, regional interests should come first. Medvedev, who stood as an independent candidate, won a majority of the votes, and is the current speaker.

Perm Mayor Yurii Trutnev is a former president of one of the most successful companies in the region, the EKS International Trading Company, which is heavily involved in food supply and import operations.

Trutnev set up EKS in the early 1990s in a room rented from a Russian bathhouse. By 1997, the firm had 14,000 employees and 14 subsidiaries.

The regional authorities strongly support business and industrial development, and the governor's administration has cultivated strong links with the new business and managerial elites. For its part, the business elite actively engages in regional politics, with representatives in both the regional assembly and the city Duma as well as in the governor's and mayor's offices.

Despite the general unity among the business elite, there are cleavages among those who make their money from raw materials, manufacturing, trade, and banking. In 1997, the raw material interests were dominant and gained considerable influence over the region's elected officials by supplying generous campaign financing. The manufacturing elite is largely made up of the "red directors" who seek to reverse the course of reform and protect domestic industry. Their influence is minimal. Many of the traders have entered politics without giving up their primary occupation (*Zvezda*, 10 April 1997). Before the August 1998 economic collapse, local bankers were losing influence to their Moscow colleagues. With the Moscow banks now weakened, the Perm banks began to work together for their mutual salvation. To deal with the mutual debts problem, for example, in October 1998 several local banks set up a clearing center to service their financial obligations (*Kapital*, 23 September 1998).

Igumnov has faced some problems. Former Deputy Governor Leonid Valko was arrested in July 1998 for allegedly selling state flour and sugar and pocketing the proceeds. He is a longtime friend of Igumnov and the governor has defended him (*NG*, 15 July 1998).

The city is one of the most polluted in the country, and average life expectancy is only 52 years. On 14 December 1997 the city was supposed to hold a referendum on whether to allow the local Kirov defense plant to set up facilities to burn off the fuel from decommissioned strategic missiles. The courts cancelled the vote at the last minute, but strong local opposition forced project organizers to consider working in Udmurtia instead (*EWI RRR*, 18 December 1997).

Perm is generally politically stable at the mass as well as the elite level, with relatively few strikes and rallies. However, after some violence in April 1998, the number of protests grew. In May 1998, 100 coal miners blocked a major highway. In July 1998, about 300 pensioners spontaneously protested the one to-two month delays in their pension payments in front of the oblast administration building. The delays are relatively short compared to those in other regions (*EWI RRR*, 30 July 1998).

LUKoil is also an important force in Perm (see Foreign Relations). Local analysts believe that the head of the LUKoil-Perm subsidiary, Andrei Kuzyaev, will be a future governor of the region.

Ties to Moscow: Generally Good

Igumnov had good relations with the Yeltsin administration, and he was originally appointed to his job by the president.

Former Prime Minister Sergei Kirienko visited Perm in mid-August 1998, just a few days before announcing the devaluation of the ruble. He said nothing about the situation during his visit, calling into question the openness of his communications with the country's governors.

Perm Oblast and the Komi-Permyak Autonomous Okrug signed a power-sharing agreement with the federal government on 31 May 1996, just before the presidential elections.

Relations with Other Regions: Cooperation in Ethnic, Economic Issues

Perm has a large minority group of ethnic Tatars living on its territory. It has reached an agreement with the republic of Tatarstan over the treatment of these people.

Perm would benefit from the construction of a railroad link to Arkhangelsk through the Komi Republic. Komi leaders are working hard to make it a reality (*EWI RRR*, 11 June 1998).

Perm is a member of the Urals Regional Association, which is headed by one of Russia's most prominent regional leaders, Sverdlovsk Governor Eduard Rossel. It includes the republics of Bashkortostan and Udmurtia; Komi-Permyak Autonomous Okrug; and Kurgan, Orenburg, Sverdlovsk, and Chelyabinsk oblasts.

Foreign Relations: Extensive Economic Contacts

The region has strong potential to develop international links and increase foreign investment. The regional authorities try to attract foreign investment by giving companies tax holidays, inexpensive leases, and guarantees on some investments. In early 1998, for example, the regional administration signed a trade credit agreement with Germany to finance telecommunications projects in coordination with Alcatel. Perm is actively developing its already good telecommunications base, and the local Uralsvyazinform has become Russia's second largest regional telecom company in absolute terms.

The number of foreign companies and banks interested in the region has risen steadily. The Enterprise Support Center (established in 1995 with support from TACIS) provides consultation support to both domestic and foreign companies. In response to increasing demand, Lufthansa flies directly to Perm from Frankfurt. Perm's main partners include Germany, the UK, Denmark, and the United States. Direct investors range from the SUN Brewing group (in the beer industry) to Pratt & Whitney (aircraft jet engines production). A LUKoil-Permnefteorgsintez program unites 25 American and European companies for a variety of tasks, including design work and equipment provision. Among those involved are Foster Wheeler, Stratco, Texaco (U.S.), Comprismo (Netherlands), Haldor Topsoc (Denmark), Chemtech and Fisher Rosemount (Switzerland), and UOP Limited (UK). Perm is also developing new international ties in the fields of education (Oxford, Louisville), social issues, and environmental protection.

Attitudes Toward Business: Successfully Attracting Foreigners

One of the reasons Perm has maintained a stable political climate has been its relative success in adapting to market conditions. Foreign and domestic investors have shown considerable interest in Perm's industrial base.

A major battle has been brewing for control of Perm Motors, a maker of jet engines and gas-powered turbines. The major stockholders are Uneximbank-controlled Interros, and the U.S.'s Pratt & Whitney on one side and Gazprom on the other. By the end of 1998, they were battling each other by appointing and removing the board of directors (*EWI RRR*, 17 December 1998). Part of the problem is that the Perm city administration wants to be represented on the board. The plant is also suffering from large tax and wage arrears. Pratt & Whitney bought a 25 percent share in Perm Motors in September 1997 in exchange for a $120 million investment. By the end of 1998, the American firm had only invested $15 million and the next tranche was delayed indefinitely. Igumnov has worked assiduously to increase Gazprom's presence in the region, viewing the gas monopoly as a reliable source of income. In June 1999, he traveled to the

---

Gennadii Vyacheslavovich Igumnov

27 October 1936—Born in Gubakha, Perm Oblast

1956—Graduated from the Molotov River Training School

1956–1969—Held various positions in the mines in Kizel

1964—Graduated from the Kizel Mining Technical College

1969–1971—Head of the industrial transport division of the Kizel city CPSU committee

1971–1983—Chair of the Kizel city executive committee

1973—Graduated from the Moscow Higher School of Professional Advancement

1983–1990—Head of the organization-instruction division of the Perm Oblast executive committee

1990–1992—Head of a Perm Oblast Soviet department

1 January 1992–12 January 1996—First deputy governor of Perm Oblast

12 January 1996—Appointed governor of Perm Oblast

1996—Appointed to the Federation Council, serving on the Committee on Economic Policy

22 December 1996—Elected governor of Perm Oblast

United States. for negotiations with Pratt & Whitney's parent company, United Technologies.

In addition to the companies already mentioned, there are several other foreign firms working in the region:

- Germany's Stockhausen has invested in a plant, in conjunction with the Kirov enterprise, to make water purification equipment (*EWI RRR*, 29 October 1998).
- Kreditanstalt (Austria) effectively controls Russia's titanium and magnesium production with substantial holdings in the Solikamsk Magnesium Works, the Avisma Titanium Magnesium Combinate (both in Perm Oblast), and Sverdlovsk Oblast's Verkhne-Saldinsk Titanium Works. Other key players in this business are Minmet Financing (Switzerland) and Metallurg (U.S.). Titanium is particularly useful in building airplanes. In 1998 Boeing placed a $175 million five-year order from the Verkhne-Saldinsk Titanium Works. Some of the plant's other customers include Airbus Industries, General Electric (U.S.), and Pratt & Whitney

(U.S.). In 1997 Solikamsk signed a $90 million deal to provide magnesium alloys to General Motors (U.S.). It is now negotiating with Ford (U.S.), Mercedes-Benz, and Volkswagen (both Germany). Magnesium could be a serious competitor to aluminum in the future.
- Nestlé bought the Kamskaya Confectionery Factory in January 1998 and set aside $25 million to modernize it and another factory in Altai Krai.

Internet Sites in the Region

http://www.perm.ru/
This is the official site of the Perm Oblast administration. It features basic information about the oblast, its economy, business, investment, etc. and provides a list of useful contacts to enterprises in the region.

http://www.fas.org/spp/civil/russia/permmoto.htm
This is the site for the Perm Motors joint stock company, offering information about the company's history, projects, and so on.

PRIMORSKII KRAI

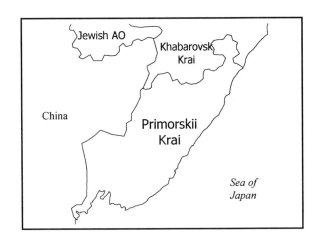

Territory: 165,900 km²
Population (as of 1 January 1998):
2,216,000
Distance from Moscow: 9,302 km

Major Cities:
Vladivostok, *capital* (pop. 615,800)
Nakhodka (160,300)
Ussuriisk (158,400)
Arsenev (68,200)
Artem (67,500)

Basic Facts

Population (as of 1 Jan. 1998): 2,216,000 (1.5% of Russian total)

Ethnic breakdown (1989 census): Russians 86.9%, Ukrainians 8.2%, Belarusans 1.0%

Urban population (as of 1 Jan. 1998): 78.2% (Russia overall: 73.1%)

Student population (as of 1 Sept. 1997): 200 per 10,000 (Russia overall: 208/10,000)

Pensioner population (1997): 21.21% (Russia overall: 25.96%)

Percent of population with higher education (1989 census): 12.8% (Russia overall: 11.3%)

Percent of population working in (1997): Industry: 19.6% (Russian average: 23.0%); Agriculture: 7.3% (13.7%); Trade: 19.9% (13.5%); Culture: 12.5% (13.3%)

Average monthly personal income in July 1998: 783.1 new rubles (Russian average: 891.7 new rubles)

Average monthly personal expenses in July 1998: 636.5 new rubles (Russian average: 684.9 new rubles)

Average monthly subsistence requirement in 1998: 510 new rubles (Russian average: 438 new rubles)

Consumer price index (as of July 1998): 132 (Russia overall = 100)

Budgetary revenues (1997): 6,437.8 billion rubles (Russia overall: 433,378.2 billion rubles)

Budgetary expenditures (1997): 7,183.7 billion rubles (Russia overall: 468,111.6 billion rubles)

Industrial production as percentage of all Russian production (Jan.–Aug. 1998): 0.98%

Proportion of loss-making enterprises (as of July 1998): 48.8% (Russia overall: 50.4%)

Number of enterprises which have wage arrears (as of 1 Sept. 1998): 965 (0.71% of Russian total)

Agricultural production as percentage of all Russian production (1997): 0.76%

Number of private farms (as of 1 Jan. 1998): 3,964 (1.12% of Russian total)

Capital investment (1997): 3,441.2 billion rubles (Russia overall: 408,797 billion rubles)

Sources of investment (1997): federal budget: 11.4% (Russian average: 10.2%); regional budget: 4.6% (10.5%); extra-budgetary funds: 84.0% (79.3%)

Foreign investment (1997): 94,526,000 USD (Russia overall: 12,294,734,000 USD)

Number of joint ventures (1997): 323 (2.19% of Russian total)

Fixed capital investment in joint ventures and foreign companies (1997): 523,384 million rubles (Russia overall: 16,265.4 billion rubles)

Number of small businesses (as of 1 July 1998): 10,100 (1.16% of Russian total)

Number of enterprises privatized in 1997: 16 (0.58% of Russian total), including those which used to be municipal property: 62.4% (Russian average: 66.4%); regional property: 6.3% (20.0%); federal property: 31.3% (13.6%)

Number of telephones per 100 families (1997): in cities: 36.1 (Russian average: 49.2); in villages: 19.2 (19.8)

Brief Overview

Primorskii Krai lies in the southern part of the Russian Far East, along the coast of the Sea of Japan. It borders China and North Korea in the west and southwest and Russia's Khabarovsk Krai in the north. Major regional industries include forestry, fishing, coal and rare metals extraction, non-ferrous metallurgy, machine building, and shipping. The krai is also one of the country's most important rice and soybean growers.

The krai is strategically important because of its location. Vladivostok and Nakhodka, the largest cities and main ports in the region, meet over 60 percent of the Far East's shipping needs. They, as well as some smaller harbors, host most of Russia's Pacific Fleet. Another city-port, Bolshoi Kamen, houses the Zvezda plant, which processes nuclear waste. Both Vladivostok and Nakhodka were closed to foreign visitors during the Soviet era. When they opened in the early 1990s, they experienced a boom in foreign investment. Nakhodka particularly benefited in the beginning since it was one of the first free economic zones in the country. However, its profitability dropped and in 1997 the local authorities declared that establishing the Nakhodka zone was a mistake.

While a variety of international companies have been active in the region, local enterprises have severely suffered from the country's long-lasting economic crisis. For example, in December 1998 the creditors of Dalenergo, a subsidiary of the Unified Energy System (EES) power utility and a monopolist on the local electricity market, voted to introduce external managers at the regional utility. The company's largest creditor, the coalmining company Primorskugol, sought Dalenergo's bankruptcy through the local arbitration court. Dalenergo's total debts to its creditors amounted to 4.7 billion rubles ($293 million).

According to a 1998 survey by *Ekspert* magazine, the krai ranked 23rd among Russia's 89 regions in terms of investment potential and 36th in terms of investment risk. A 1998 survey by Bank Austria ranked the krai 28th in terms of investment climate.

Electoral History

2000 Presidential Election
Putin: 40.16%
Zyuganov: 35.86%
Yavlinskii: 8.41%
Zhirinovsky: 5.92%
Tuleev: 2.62%
Turnout: 63.01% (Russia overall: 68.64%)

1999 Parliamentary Elections
Unity: 27.19%
Communist Party of the Russian Federation: 22.45%
Zhirinovsky Bloc: 10.09%
Yabloko: 6.78%
Union of Right Forces: 6.23%
Fatherland–All Russia: 5.89%
In single-mandate districts: 2 Communist Party of the Russian Federation, 1 unfilled
Turnout: 59.69% (Russia overall: 61.85%)

1999 Gubernatorial Election
Nazdratenko (incumbent): 66.98%
Kirilichev: 18.42%
Lukyanov: 2.86%
Bedernikov: 2.79%
Turnout: 60.60%

1996 Presidential Election
Yeltsin: 29.55%/52.26% (first round/second round)
Zyuganov: 24.56%/39.41%
Lebed: 19.47%
Zhirinovsky: 12.73%
Yavlinskii: 7.16%
Turnout: 66.13%/63.26% (Russia overall: 69.67%/68.79%)

1995 Gubernatorial Election
Nazdratenko (incumbent): 68.55%
Cherepkov: 17.24%
Gilgenberg: 4.10%
Vilchinskii (local administration head): 2.00%
Turnout: 62.25%

1995 Parliamentary Elections
Liberal Democratic Party of Russia: 20.12%
Communist Party of the Russian Federation: 18.50%
Yabloko: 9.56%
Women of Russia: 6.43%
Derzhava: 6.35%
Congress of Russian Communities: 5.11%
Communists–Workers' Russia: 3.96%
Our Home Is Russia: 3.45%
In single-mandate districts: 1 Communist Party of the Russian Federation, 1 Women of Russia, 1 independent
Turnout: 62.25% (Russia overall: 64.37%)

1993 Constitutional Referendum
"Yes"—69.7%   "No"—27.8%

1993 Parliamentary Elections
Liberal Democratic Party of Russia: 23.34%
Women of Russia: 15.27%
Russia's Choice: 14.09%
Communist Party of the Russian Federation:
    8.74%
Yabloko: 8.58%
Party of Russian Unity and Concord: 8.18%
Democratic Party of Russia: 7.32%
Agrarian Party of Russia: 2.52%
In single-mandate districts: 1 Yabloko, 1 Democratic
    Party of Russia, 1 independent
From electoral associations: 1 Democratic Party of
    Russia, 1 Liberal Democratic Party of Russia, 1
    Women of Russia
Turnout: 50.39% (Russia overall: 54.34%)

1991 Presidential Election
Yeltsin: 61.45%
Ryzhkov: 15.60%
Makashov: 5.54%
Zhirinovsky: 5.52%
Tuleev: 3.98%
Bakatin: 3.89%
Turnout: 71.65% (Russia overall: 76.66%)

Regional Political Institutions

Executive:
    Governor, 4-year term
    Yevgenii Ivanovich Nazdratenko, elected
    December 1995, reelected December 1999
        Ul. Svetlanskaya, 22; Vladivostok, 690110
        Tel. 7(423–2) 22–38–00;
        Fax 7(423–2) 22–52–77
        Federation Council in Moscow:
        7 (095) 292–14–83, 926–62–25

Legislative:
    Unicameral
    Krai Duma—39 members, 4-year term, elected
    December 1997
    Chairman—Sergei Viktorovich Zhekov, elected
    January 2000

Regional Politics

Populist Authoritarian Battles on All Fronts

One of Russia's most notorious governors, Yevgenii Nazdratenko has made a name for himself by taking on enemies at both the national and regional levels. Nazdratenko's conflicts with former Vladivostok Mayor Viktor Cherepkov and Anatolii Chubais are the most noteworthy. The presidential administration nearly succeeded at removing Nazdratenko from power in the spring of 1997, following an energy crisis that left Primorskii Krai's energy workers on strike and much of the population without electricity for 16 to18-hour-long stretches per day.

Nazdratenko has been accused of multiple crimes, ranging from general human rights violations to ordering the murder of Primorrybprom Director Andrei Zakharenko in 1995 (Panorama Research Group, Labyrint Electronic Database, Moscow). Nazdratenko combats this criticism by employing populist tactics to deflect attention from the poor state of affairs in the krai. He blames the federal and local governments for the region's multiple problems. Nazdratenko has also criticized the media for perpetrating a false image of the area, focusing only on the krai's energy problems and not on its successes at collecting taxes and paying pensions. Under the short-lived government of Yevgenii Primakov, the federal attacks on Nazdratenko came to an end and Nazdratenko seemed to be gaining power in Moscow. In response, Nazdratenko revealed his personal ambitions to hold higher office and offered to run for the vice presidency, assuming the constitution was changed to reestablish that office, on a ticket with former Prime Minister Yevgenii Primakov. Given his numerous suitors, Primakov declined to acknowledge Nazdratenko's offer.

With his early support for the pro-Kremlin Unity bloc organized in the fall of 1999, Nazdratenko undoubtedly hopes for better relations with Moscow.

Executive Platform: Independent Authoritarian

President Yeltsin appointed Nazdratenko governor of Primorskii Krai in May 1993 on the advice of major regional enterprise directors who had united in the Primorskii Shareholding Company of Commodity Producers (PAKT). The regional business elite then tried to present a united front to Moscow in the wake of privatization to prevent the center from snapping up regional property. Nazdratenko went on to win a popular election to the office in December 1995. He was reelected in December 1999, gathering 65 percent of the vote.

Although Nazdratenko supported Yeltsin personally—he supported the president's bid for reelection in 1996, and joined Our Home Is Russia in 1995—he opposed many initiatives carried out in the president's name. He was strongly opposed to the privatization campaign conducted by Anatolii Chubais, and believes that the entire energy complex should be nationalized. Nazdratenko is also against the buying and selling of land.

Nazdratenko's style of governance is highly authoritarian. He frequently comes into conflict with both Moscow and local politicians. Nazdratenko's policies often hurt the region. The most obvious example was the 1997 energy crisis, which was prolonged by Nazdratenko's refusal to cooperate with the federal authorities. Another example of Nazdratenko's political assertiveness is the conflict surrounding the Russian/Chinese border, the demarcation of which required the transfer of 1,500 hectares of Russian land, including land in Primorskii Krai, to China. In 1997 Nazdratenko organized a political party, the Party of Primore, which sought to conduct a referendum to ask Primorskii Krai voters whether Russian authorities should cede land to China. Nazdratenko feels that transferring land in the border region would hurt Russia's strategic position in the Asia-Pacific region. Yeltsin, in turn, requested that Nazdratenko stay out of the federal government's attempts to solve the border problem. Ultimately, the federal government went ahead with its plans despite Nazdratenko's complaints.

Policies: Strict Control

Nazdratenko's policies generally have focused on establishing strict control over most of the krai's affairs. Nazdratenko favors a strong law-and-order agenda and has initiated several administrative campaigns to combat poaching, illegal immigration, the drug mafia, and the smuggling of weapons and ammunition. In November 1994 Nazdratenko developed stricter regulations for registering foreign firms in the krai. He conducted a purge of the regional police, dismissing 1,073 officials. The governor also dismissed eleven heads of district governments for failing to keep sufficient control over the Chinese border.

Maintaining control over the disputed territory on the Russian/Chinese border was of political and economic importance for Nazdratenko. Politically,

Nazdratenko could win points by presenting himself as the defender of Russian territory. Economically, the more liberal border relations that have evolved between Russia and China since the collapse of the Soviet Union have caused a strain on Primorskii Krai's economy. Much of the trade that used to pass through the krai to Far Eastern ports is now being routed through China, and cheap imports from across the border have hurt local producers. Nazdratenko also had plans to increase the krai's territory by gaining control of the Kuril Islands. In July 1994 he sent a letter to Yeltsin requesting that the islands be placed under the authority of Vladivostok.

Nazdratenko is often in conflict with the federal authorities and is sometimes accused of harboring separatist tendencies. However, the governor appears to be working together with the government in combating the economic crisis following 17 August 1998. While many governors addressed the social panic by halting tax payments to the federal government and declaring states of emergency in their regions, Nazdratenko denounced such acts, stating that "such extremism may bring about irreversible consequences and may lead to the collapse of the state" (*EWI RRR*, 10 September 1998). He called on regional leaders to preserve Russia's unity.

Relationships Between Key Players: Perpetual Conflict with Cherepkov

The defining issue in Primorskii Krai's regional and local politics was the long-standing, bitter battle between Nazdratenko and former Vladivostok Mayor Viktor Cherepkov. In March 1994, Nazdratenko removed Cherepkov from office by force, claiming that the mayor had taken bribes, and replaced him with a loyal ally, Konstantin Tolstoshein. At the time, Yeltsin supported this move, but then Nazdratenko fell out with the federal government. Cherepkov proceeded to find allies among the Moscow "young reformers," particularly former Presidential Chief of Staff Anatolii Chubais, and when a court ruled that the mayor's removal was illegal, Yeltsin ordered Nazdratenko to reinstate Cherepkov in September 1996.

A year later the krai duma, backed by Nazdratenko, "temporarily" relieved Cherepkov of his duties, charging him with "unconstitutional activities," such as chronic strikes, chaos in the residential sector, and irregular water and energy supplies. Cherepkov ignored the krai duma's decision, which was revoked by a district court shortly after it was adopted. Then, in November 1997, Cherepkov announced his resignation from office, and proceeded to call a hunger strike that would end only when the krai officials he felt were responsible for the region's problems were punished. Though he had resigned, Cherepkov continued to remain in power while elections for mayor and city duma were repeatedly postponed. When mayoral elections were finally held in September 1998, Cherepkov decided to run again for the post. However, the electoral commission banned him from the race the night before the election was to take place. The majority of voters then voted "against all candidates," one of the choices appearing on Russian ballots, causing the election to be invalid. New elections were then set for January 1999.

In December 1998 Yeltsin signed a decree removing Cherepkov from office and authorizing Nazdratenko to appoint an acting mayor until the next mayoral election. The decree cited the fact that Cherepkov's term in office expired in July 1998, as well as requests by heads of local governments. In Cherepkov's place, Nazdratenko appointed the mayor's former deputy, Yurii Kopylov. Cherepkov refused to accept Yeltsin's decision, stating that the president did not have the right to remove an elected official from office. Cherepkov's supporters proceeded to barricade themselves in the mayor's offices for two weeks until they were removed by the police. The January mayoral elections were subsequently postponed until Vladivostok elected a duma and adopted a charter. City duma elections were held in January, and Cherepkov won a seat in the city's duma elections, yet was barred from taking office due to alleged violations in voting procedures, as were the majority of those who won seats. City duma elections were held again in May 1999, but insufficient voter turnout (only 7 percent) prevented the elections from being deemed valid. Ultimately, Cherepkov was elected to the state Duma in December 1999 and Kopylov was elected mayor in June 2000.

The conflict between these two powerful figures has made the region largely ungovernable, as they have constantly blocked each other's initiatives. Both individuals are extremely popular and stand as symbols for the different interests within the region. Their political battles are also fueled by Moscow, which uses the leaders' conflicts as an opportunity to further its own interests. At present, with Cherepkov down, Nazdratenko has been more successful at consolidating power in the region. He even succeeded in removeing krai duma Chairman Sergei Dudnik, who is the last vocal opponent Nazdratenko faces in the region's ruling elite.

The krai's Duma had been strongly loyal to Governor Nazdratenko, but the governor suffered a stinging defeat in the legislative elections held on 7 December 1997. The new Duma had more Cherepkov supporters and was chaired by Dudnik. Nevertheless, the elections have not really changed the balance of power in the region and Dudnik was forced out of the speakership in early 2000.

The most important issue in Primorskii Krai, affecting local, regional, and national level politics, is the ongoing energy crisis. The local electricity provider's failure to pay for coal deliveries caused large-scale strikes across the krai, leaving many residents without electricity. The electricity company cannot pay for the fuel it needs because its customers usually do not pay it for the energy they consume. Nazdratenko's inability to resolve the situation prompted federal authorities to try to remove him (see Ties to Moscow). Many striking miners demanded the resignations of both Nazdratenko and Cherepkov, asserting that their political feuding blocked any potential solutions. Nazdratenko, however, blamed the federal government for the region's energy problems, calling for lower energy rates and requesting an energy subsidy for the krai. As it is, Primorskii Krai receives the largest federal subsidy of any region. Nazdratenko has always been against the privatization of the fuel-energy sector, arguing that it is necessary for the state to oversee its activity. He feels that the energy crisis exemplifies why such regulation is necessary. In spring 1997 Nazdratenko signed an anti-crisis agreement with then-First Deputy Prime Minister Boris Nemtsov that called for an increase in energy prices for residential users to generate the revenue necessary to pay wage arrears to the krai's energy workers. Although this solution has been highly criticized, the widespread upheaval of 1997 was avoided in 1998 and 1999. In summer 2000, however, the crisis resumed when Dalenergo cut off electricity to large parts of Vladivostok, demanding that customers pay their bills.

Ties to Moscow: Fluctuate with Prime Minister

Nazdratenko has had a back-and-forth relationship with the federal government. His relations with Yeltsin were amicable—Nazdratenko was a strong supporter of Yeltsin in the 1996 elections—but it was the governor's associations with Yeltsin's aides that characterized the krai's relations to the center.

In September 1994 Yegor Gaidar, leader of the Russia's Choice Duma bloc, gave Yeltsin an appeal signed by the leaders of three other factions—Grigorii Yavlinskii (Yabloko), Boris Fedorov (Union of 12 December), and Sergei Shakhrai (PRES)—calling for gubernatorial elections in the krai to be suspended due to serious violations of human rights by the krai administration. This appeal was the beginning of the conflict between Nazdratenko and Gaidar. Nazdratenko also has very poor relations with Moscow's most controversial figure—Anatolii Chubais. He was strongly opposed to Chubais's privatization plans and resisted their implementation. Nazdratenko has been particularly opposed to the privatization of the energy sector and has come into conflict with Chubais multiple times because of this.

In May and June 1997 the federal government tried to remove Nazdratenko from office on the grounds that he had mismanaged the region so badly that it was on the verge of collapse. Moscow viewed the region's energy crisis as the prime example of such mismanagement. First Deputy Prime Minister Anatolii Chubais asked Nazdratenko to resign and Yeltsin transferred many of the governor's powers to the krai's presidential representative Viktor Kondratov, who was also the head of the regional branch of the Federal Security Service (FSB), essentially establishing presidential rule in the krai. Kondratov was given the right to coordinate all federal decrees regarding the regulation of the energy system, organize and monitor the use of federal money sent to the krai, and coordinate the activities of federal agencies. The president and First Deputy Prime Minister Boris Nemtsov hoped to hold new elections in the region. However, Moscow's plans fell through as governors of all political stripes, fearing encroachment on their own powers, rallied behind Nazdratenko, stating that they would refuse to vote him out of the Federation Council if Yeltsin tried to remove him as governor. Nazdratenko also responded by attacking the federal government in the media, blaming Primorskii Krai's economic difficulties on federal non-payments. Once the new krai duma was elected in December 1997, Kondratov requested that his extraordinary powers be rescinded, since the more reform-minded assembly could monitor the situation and more effectively counter Nazdratenko.

Since then Nazdratenko's relationship with the federal government has improved. The closer ties between Nazdratenko and the federal powers reflected in the change the center has shown in its approach toward Primorskii Krai, adopting and endorsing policies more favorable to Nazdratenko. In February 1999 Yeltsin dismissed Kondratov from his position as presidential rep-

resentative, and one month later he was also removed from his FSB post. In May Kondratov was appointed the FSB representative in Moldova, a clear demotion that reflected Nazdratenko's growing influence in Moscow power circles. In 1999–2000 Nazdratenko became an early supporter of the Kremlin's Unity bloc.

Unlike many other regions, Primorskii Krai has not signed a power-sharing agreement with the federal government. Nazdratenko is against such agreements, claiming that they are destroying the country (*Izvestiya*, 24 March 1999).

Relations with Other Regions: Cooperation in Far East

Nazdratenko's extensive battles with local and national level politicians appear to have isolated the governor in terms of relations with other regions. Nevertheless, in June 1997 Nazdratenko signed a joint treaty with the governors of Sakhalin Oblast and Khabarovsk Krai, Igor Farkhutdinov and Viktor Ishaev, on economic cooperation through 2005. The agreement provides that the three regions will jointly exploit the Sakhalin gas fields and make gas the major fuel for Far Eastern power plants.

Nazdratenko and Saratov Governor Dmitrii Ayatskov have discussed strengthening their economic ties and forming a political alliance. Although Ayatskov sent 40 train cars of grain to help feed miners in the city of Partizansk, it seems his interest in Primorskii Krai lies primarily in building up political support to bolster his own ambitions for national office.

Primorskii Krai belongs to the Far East and Baikal Association, which includes the republics of Buryatia and Sakha (Yakutia); Khabarovsk Krai; Amur, Chita, Kamchatka, Magadan, and Sakhalin oblasts; the Jewish Autonomous Oblast; and the Koryak and Chukotka autonomous okrugs.

Foreign Relations: Tension over Russian/Chinese Border

The majority of Nazdratenko's foreign relations are with Primorskii Krai's neighbors in the Asian-Pacific region. His greatest international concern is the krai's relations with China. The krai has an extensive border with China, which has caused multiple disputes over land, immigration, and illegal imports. Russia and China signed a preliminary border agreement in 1991, yet Nazdratenko has loudly protested the loss of 1,500 hectares, which he claims is damaging to Russia's strategic interests since it enables the Chinese to gain access to the ocean down the Tumen River between

Russia and North Korea. Nazdratenko has been opposed to the transfer of land to China from the beginning, and capitalized on this issue to curry popularity with local voters and distract public attention away from the region's ongoing energy crisis.

In late 1998 Nazdratenko accompanied then Prime Minister Yevgenii Primakov to the Asian Economic Forum in Malaysia. Nazdratenko's main interest in the forum was to address the issue of ownership of the Kuril Islands, which is disputed between Russia and Japan. He accused Russia's "young reformers" (meaning Anatolii Chubais and Boris Nemtsov) of betraying Russia's national interests by allowing Japanese fishermen to work in Russia's territorial waters without conditions or limitations (*EWI RRR*, 19 November 1998).

In spite of Nazdratenko's animosity toward Japan regarding the Kuril Islands dispute, the governor has appealed to Japan for assistance. In February 1998 Nazdratenko and Krai Duma Chairman Sergei Dudnik requested that the Japanese government extend a line of credit for salvaging nuclear waste from Pacific Fleet submarines. Russia lacks the finances to handle the waste, and Japan has already financed facilities for dealing with it. Among other relations with Asia, in March 1998 Nazdratenko called on residents in the Far East to offer humanitarian aid to combat food shortages in North Korea.

Belarusan President Aleksandr Lukashenko visited Vladivostok in February 1998 and stressed his hopes to strengthen the economic and cultural ties between Belarus and the Far East. Lukashenko expressed his strong support for Nazdratenko, saying that he has backed the governor on several political and economic issues. During this visit the possibility of trading Far Eastern fish for heavy trucks from Belarus was discussed. Having lost the strong backing of the Yeltsin administration, Lukashenko has sought to strengthen his ties with opposition-minded governors.

Nazdratenko also traveled to California's Silicon Valley to participate in the Gore-Chernomyrdin Commission's initiative to stimulate trade between the Russian Far East and the U.S. West Coast.

Attitudes Toward Business: Single-Minded Approach to Development

Business in Primorskii Krai is an important issue for Nazdratenko, since the region's economy has been suffering from a lack of business activity.

Nazdratenko is trying to revive business for the Trans-Siberian railroad, which terminates in Vladivostok. Activity on the railway has declined considerably in the post-Soviet period, with traffic dropping to a ninth of its former total. The lack of cargo on the railway has subsequently decreased the activity of Vladivostok's ports, leaving many workers unemployed. To address this problem, Nazdratenko is trying to lower the tariffs for using the railroad. He would also like to increase port activity by having the krai serve as a transit point for U.S. goods headed for northern China. Using such ports would reduce the distance to be traveled by 1,700 miles over Chinese ports.

Although Nazdratenko is concerned about economic activity and development in Primorskii Krai, he is very single-minded in his approach to attracting business activity. Nazdratenko has passed several initiatives to try and halt underground economic activity such as poaching, illegal imports, and drugs and weapons trade (see Policies). However, he has also essentially blocked a federal law that would simplify tax payments for small businesses in the region. According to the law, small businesses would pay one tax that would be based on the enterprises' results for the year, with two-thirds going to the krai and local governments and one-third going to the federal government. Yet, shortly after this law was passed, Nazdratenko decreed that the cost of a license to register for the tax would range from $6,700 to $42,000, a fee unaffordable to most small businesses. Licenses in other regions are considerably less expensive, and in Moscow they are free.

Nazdratenko has also taken actions to increase his control over the regional economy that have conflicted with the activities of foreign investors. In order to secure sufficient financing for the December 1999 gubernatorial elections, Nazdrentko tried to take control of the region's main shipping companies, Vostoktransflot (VTF) and Far East Shipping Company (DVMP or FESCO), in the summer of 1999. The governor has demanded that Andrew Fox, the chairman of the foreign investors in FESCO, who is also director of Tiger Securities and the honorary consul of Great Britain in Vladivostok, reduce the amount of control he and other foreign investors have over the company. Fox and his allies have sought to counter the governor's encroachments (see *EWI RRI*, 24 June 1999, and *EWI RRR*, 15 July 1999)

Yevgenii Ivanovich Nazdratenko

16 February 1949—Born on a ship traveling to avoid a tsunami in the northern Kuril Islands

1968–1970—Served in the Pacific Ocean Fleet

1970–1975—Worked for the Bor association and attended night courses at an industrial technical school

1975–1980—Mechanic and then section director for Bor

1980—Invited to work at the East artel, where he labored as a mechanic and then deputy chairman, becoming chairman in **1983**

1983—Graduated via correspondence courses from the Far East Technological Institute with a degree in economics

1990—The East artel was restructured into Far East Metal, and Nazdratenko became deputy director and then director until **1993**

18 March 1990—Elected to the RSFSR Congress of People's Deputies

May 1993—Appointed governor of Primorskii Krai

12 December 1993—Elected to the Federation Council, serving on the Committee for Security and Defense

1995—Joined Our Home Is Russia (NDR)

17 December 1995—Elected governor of Primorskii Krai

January 1996—Appointed to the second session of the Federation Council, again serving on the Committee for Security and Defense

19 December 1999—Reelected governor

Married, with two sons

Internet Sites in the Region

http://www.primorsky.ru/admin/general.htm
Nazdratenko's home page provides extensive information on official events in the region.

http://www.vl.vladnews.ru/
The *Vladivostok* newspaper available at this site provides daily coverage of events in the krai with a pro-Nazdratenko slant.

http://www.vlad.tribnet.com/
This is the English language *Vladivostok News*, a bi-weekly that has extensive business news.

PSKOV OBLAST

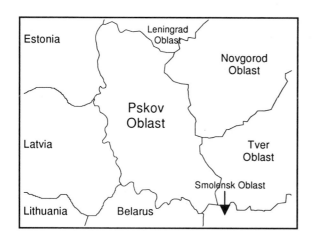

Territory: 55,300 km²
Population (as of 1 January 1998): 820,000
Distance from Moscow: 689 km

Major Cities:
Pskov, *capital* (pop. 203,900)
Velikie Luki (117,200)
Ostrov (29,800)

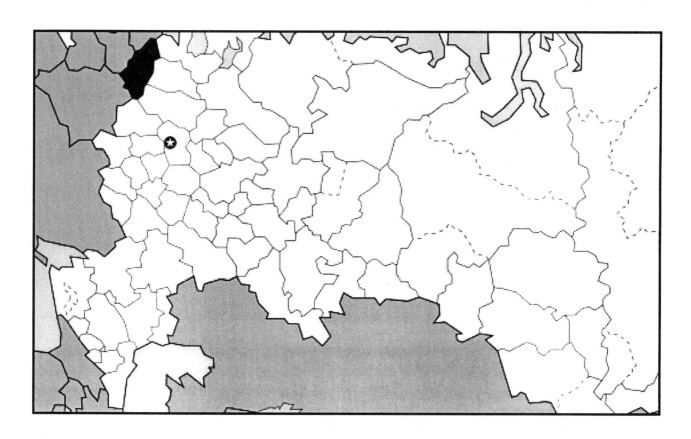

Basic Facts

Population (as of 1 Jan. 1998): 820,000 (0.56% of Russian total)

Ethnic breakdown (1989 census): Russians 94.3%, Ukrainians 1.8%, Belarusans 1.5%

Urban population (as of 1 Jan. 1998): 65.9% (Russia overall: 73.1%)

Student population (as of 1 Sept. 1997): 120 per 10,000 (Russia overall: 208/10,000)

Pensioner population (1997): 30.37% (Russia overall: 25.96%)

Percent of population with higher education (1989 census): 8.1% (Russia overall: 11.3%)

Percent of population working in (1997): Industry: 19.8% (Russian average: 23.0%); Agriculture: 15.1% (13.7%); Trade: 13.6% (13.5%); Culture: 12.7% (13.3%)

Average monthly personal income in July 1998: 524.8 new rubles (Russian average: 891.7 new rubles)

Average monthly personal expenses in July 1998: 356.9 new rubles (Russian average: 684.9 new rubles)

Average monthly subsistence requirement in 1998: 359 new rubles (Russian average: 438 new rubles)

Consumer price index (as of July 1998): 85 (Russia overall = 100)

Budgetary revenues (1997): 1,575.4 billion rubles (Russia overall: 433,378.2 billion rubles)

Budgetary expenditures (1997): 1,636.6 billion rubles (Russia overall: 468,111.6 billion rubles)

Industrial production as percentage of all Russian production (Jan.–Aug. 1998): 0.16%

Proportion of loss-making enterprises (as of July 1998): 49.4% (Russia overall: 50.4%)

Number of enterprises which have wage arrears (as of 1 Sept. 1998): 1,995 (1.48% of Russian total)

Agricultural production as percentage of all Russian production (1997): 0.77%

Number of private farms (as of 1 Jan. 1998): 2,977 (1.09% of Russian total)

Capital investment (1997): 866.4 billion rubles (Russia overall: 408,797 billion rubles)

Sources of investment (1997): federal budget: 15.1% (Russian average: 10.2%); regional budget: 4.8% (10.5%); extra-budgetary funds: 80.1% (79.3%)

Foreign investment (1997): 1,338,000 USD (Russia overall: 12,294,734,000 USD)

Number of joint ventures (1997): 77 (0.52% of Russian total)

Fixed capital investment in joint ventures and foreign companies (1997): 9,704 million rubles (Russia overall: 16,265.4 billion rubles)

Number of small businesses (as of 1 July 1998): 2,700 (0.31% of Russian total)

Number of enterprises privatized in 1997: 15 (0.55% of Russian total), including those which used to be municipal property: 73.3% (Russian average: 66.4%); regional property: 6.7% (20.0%); federal property: 20.0% (13.6%)

Number of telephones per 100 families (1997): in cities: 51.2 (Russian average: 49.2); in villages: 20.0 (19.8)

Brief Overview

Pskov is one of the oldest cities in Russia: it was first mentioned in written chronicles in 903, more than 200 years earlier than Moscow. Since the beginning of the 16th century, it was part of the Moscow Kingdom and, due to its favorable geographic and transportation location, grew to become one of the largest Russian cities of that era. In the 18th century, after St. Petersburg was constructed, Pskov's economic importance and prosperity declined. Now it is a poor region in St. Petersburg's shadow.

Pskov oblast is located on the northwestern Russian plain and borders Novgorod, Leningrad, Smolensk, and Tver oblasts as well as Belarus, Estonia, and Latvia. The region is rich in peat, sands, clays, timber, and fish. The two largest cities, Pskov and Velikie Luki, are home to two-thirds of the major industry. Major oblast industries are: machine building, metal processing, forestry, timber working, energy, small-scale production, and food processing. Since 1991, when the oblast became a border region, its importance in the country's foreign trade, particularly with the Baltic States, has significantly increased, and now about 10 percent of Russia's cargo export goes through Pskov Oblast.

According to a 1998 survey by *Ekspert* magazine, the oblast ranked 63rd among Russia's 89 regions in terms of investment potential and 39th in terms of investment risk. A 1998 survey by Bank Austria ranked the oblast 75th in terms of investment climate.

Electoral History

2000 Presidential Election
Putin: 62.55%
Zyuganov: 25.65%
Yavlinskii: 2.70%
Zhirinovsky: 2.69%
Tuleev: 2.27%
Turnout: 70.79% (Russia overall: 68.64%)

1999 Parliamentary Elections
Unity: 38.28%
Communist Party of the Russian Federation: 23.46%
Zhirinovsky Bloc: 6.98%
Fatherland–All Russia: 5.13%
Union of Right Forces: 4.97%
Yabloko: 3.24%
In a single-mandate district: 1 independent
Turnout: 66.27% (Russia overall: 61.85%)

1996 Gubernatorial Election
Mikhailov (State Duma deputy, LDPR): 22.71%/ 56.46% (first round/second round)
Tumanov (incumbent): 30.92%/36.89%
Sidorenko: 14.93%
Komar: 14.09%
Pushkarev: 10.94%
Osadchii (Pskov City legislature chairman): 1.20%
Zhukov: 0.83%
Turnout: 51.9%/60.16%

1996 Presidential Election
Zyuganov: 30.39%/48.08% (first round/second round)
Yeltsin: 24.81%/45.23%
Lebed: 23.56%
Zhirinovsky: 10.19%
Yavlinskii: 7.04%
Turnout: 75.57%/73.28% (Russia overall: 69.67%/ 68.79%)

1995 Parliamentary Elections
Communist Party of the Russian Federation: 22.65%
Liberal Democratic Party of Russia: 20.87%
Our Home Is Russia: 6.01%
Yabloko: 4.89%
Women of Russia: 4.78%
Communists–Workers' Russia: 4.59%
Party of Workers' Self-Government: 4.13%
Agrarian Party of Russia: 3.93%
Congress of Russian Communities: 3.62%
In a single-mandate district: 1 independent
Turnout: 73.42% (Russia overall: 64.37%)

1993 Constitutional Referendum
"Yes"—56.1%   "No"—42.4%

1993 Parliamentary Elections
Liberal Democratic Party of Russia: 43.01%
Russia's Choice: 10.13%
Communist Party of the Russian Federation: 9.50%
Agrarian Party of Russia: 8.94%
Women of Russia: 8.23%
Yabloko: 5.62%
Party of Russian Unity and Concord: 4.88%
Democratic Party of Russia: 4.06%
In a single-mandate district: 1 Liberal Democratic Party of Russia
Turnout: 68.27% (Russia overall: 54.34%)

1991 Presidential Elections

Yeltsin: 33.77%

Ryzhkov: 28.45%

Zhirinovsky: 14.83%

Tuleev: 9.41%

Makashov: 6.65%

Bakatin: 3.21%

Turnout: 82.57% (Russia overall: 76.66%)

Regional Political Institutions

Executive:

Governor, 4-year term

Yevgenii Eduardovich Mikhailov, elected
November 1996

Ul. Nekrasova, 23; Pskov, 180001

Tel 7(811–2) 222–03; Fax 7(811–2) 2–62–31

Federation Council in Moscow:
7(095) 292–59–10, 926–64–80

Legislative:

Unicameral

Assembly of deputies—2–year term, elected 1994,
March 1998

Chairman—Yurii Anisimovich Shmatov, elected
1994, April 1998

Regional Politics

Zhirinovsky Supporter on Baltic Border

Yevgenii Mikhailov was elected governor of Pskov
Oblast in November 1996, earning 56.5 percent of the
vote in the second round, ousting the incumbent
Vladislav Tumanov. He was the only Russian regional
executive belonging to Vladimir Zhirinovsky's Liberal Democratic Party of Russia (LDPR). The gubernatorial campaign was among the most heated in all
of Russia's regions. Moscow tried desperately to bolster Tumanov's popularity, even promising to allow
Pskov to keep 50 percent of the customs duties collected on its borders. The Communists joined the
LDPR in rallying behind Mikhailov, providing him
with a strong, widespread support base.

Although Mikhailov focused his efforts on promoting an economic development program, his campaign
nevertheless benefited from Zhirinovsky's flamboy-
ant presence. Prior to the election, Russian Public TV
(ORT) broadcast remarks Zhirinovsky made in the
Pechora district of Pskov, parts of which belonged to
Estonia prior to its inclusion in the USSR in 1940.

Zhirinovsky stated that on Estonian maps the district
was marked as belonging to Estonia and that the Esto-
nians would expel the Russian population if they re-
claimed the territory (*OMRI RRR*, 6 November 1996).
Comments such as these were compelling to the some
80,000 ethnic Russians who have immigrated to Pskov
from Latvia and Estonia.

Zhirinovsky's party has long been popular in Pskov.
The LDPR received 43 percent of the vote in the region in the 1993 Duma elections, and 21 percent in
1995. Zhirinovsky's nationalist appeals fall on fertile
ground in the region, which suffers from economic
depression, houses several military units, and shares a
contested border with both Latvia and Estonia.

Nevertheless, Mikhailov's tenure has not created the
kinds of tension with the Baltic states that one might
expect from the tenor of Zhirinovsky's statements.

Executive Platform: Pragmatist on LDPR Fringe

Until the rise of Putin, Mikhailov looked to Zhirinovsky
and the LDPR for support and guidance. In 1993 he became the deputy senior editor of Zhirinovsky's publicity
newspaper, *Pravda Zhirinovskogo*. He was elected to the
State Duma in 1993 and 1995, serving in the LDPR faction. He supported the party in the 1999 Duma elections.
When it was clear that Zhirinovsky was losing his popularity in 2000, Mikhailov left his party and appointed
himself as the head of the pro-Putin Unity branch in Pskov.

Although Mikhailov has benefited from Zhirinovsky's
popularity, his governing style does not draw on
Zhirinovsky's outrageous stunts. Mikhailov tends to focus more on regional issues. In his gubernatorial campaign Mikhailov stressed decreasing the region's
dependence on the federal government, proposing instead that the oblast attract resources from nongovern-
mental industrial and financial structures to improve its
oblast's economy (Michael McFaul and Nikolai Petrov,
eds., *Politicheskii Almanakh Rossii 1997*, Moscow:
Carnegie Endowment for International Peace, 1998,
789). His campaign slogan was "Clean hands, clear
goals," suggesting a more temperate approach than the
extremism Zhirinovsky is known for (Mikhail A.
Alekseev and Vladimir Vagin, "Russian Regions in Expanding Europe: The Pskov Connection," *Europe-Asia
Studies*, Vol. 51, No. 1, 1999, 45).

Nevertheless, Mikhailov did take advantage of his
affiliation with LDPR to promote his candidacy. One
of his most lucrative selling points was that by asso-

ciation with LDPR the leadership of Pskov would have increased opportunities for raising public and private funds for the region since Zhirinovsky had had a wide range of political and financial contacts (Alexseev and Vagin, p. 47).

Policies: Economic Development

The majority of Mikhailov's policies have been focused on decreasing Pskov's dependence on the federal government and developing the region's own areas of economic potential, specifically its advantageous geographical location en route to the Baltic states. Mikhailov hopes to establish an economic model similar to that of Moscow Oblast, centered on regional economic sustainability and lower taxes.

Ultimately, however, Mikhailov's key initiative was to create Pskovalko, an oblast-owned alcohol production monopoly that gave the oblast a lucrative stream of revenue. This initiative was heavily criticized by former Pskov city Mayor Aleksandr Prokofev, who claims that the enterprise simply gathered the existing tax-paying firms together, and it did not generate new revenue (*NG*, 23 June 1998).

Relationships Between Key Players: Lacks Support Among Other Regional Authorities

In spite of the LDPR's relative popularity in Pskov, Mikhailov does not enjoy much support in his region. The few LDPR members in his cabinet may be his only faithful supporters in the region. About 90 percent of Pskov's officials stayed on after Mikhailov's election. Moreover, the governor does not have strong support in the oblast legislative assembly, and is on poor terms with the Pskov city administration (McFaul and Petrov, eds., p. 790).

Pskov Mayor Aleksandr Prokofev, a democrat, complains that the oblast administration is taking increasingly more money from the city's budget. In 1996 the city's income was $45 million; in 1997 it fell to $40 million, and in 1998 it plummeted to $34.5 million. Prokofev has also accused Mikhailov of subordinating the city of Pskov to the LDPR party machine (*NG*, 23 June 1998). He argued that the Pskov city administration was essentially supporting the city's economy.

In February 2000 Pskov elected Mikhail Khoronen mayor. Pksov has a better relationship than he did with Prokofev.

Ties to Moscow: Dissatisfaction with Federal Support

Mikhailov's relationship with the federal center remains hard to define. Although he has not attracted much attention to his disagreements with the center, Mikhailov's tenure as governor has had its moments of confrontation. Mikhailov wants to decrease Pskov's economic reliance on the federal government, yet he is also confronted with the problem that many of Moscow's policies toward the Baltics are detrimental to Pskov's development. For example, the federal government charges all goods originating in or transported through Estonia into Pskov twice the import tariff charged on cargo not going through the Baltic states. This clearly affects Pskov's ability to capitalize from its cross-border activity. Mikhailov and local leaders in Pskov are also dissatisfied with Moscow's inefficiency in improving the customs and immigration control of the region's external border, complaining that the center built expensive facilities at checkpoints that did not need them rather than increasing control in areas where more supervision was required.

Relations with Other Regions

Pskov is a member of the North-West Association, which includes the republics of Karelia and Komi; Arkhangelsk, Vologda, Kaliningrad, Kirov, Leningrad, Novgorod, and Murmansk oblasts; Nenets Autonomous Okrug; and St. Petersburg.

Foreign Relations: Baltic Border Issues

Pskov's primary foreign relations concern the Baltic states, in part because there are territories in Pskov that have been the subject of border disputes between Russia and Latvia and Estonia, and also because Pskov's economic growth is closely linked to the Baltic states. Until 1997 Latvia refused to agree to any border with Russia that did not recognize the 1920 Riga Peace Treaty that gave Latvia 463 square miles of territory currently belonging to Pskov Oblast. Estonia also tried to make territorial claims in Pskov based on its own 1920 peace treaty with Russia. Pskov residents' fears over losing territory to the Baltic states contributed to LDPR's popularity in the region and Mikhailov's electoral success. In late 1996 and early 1997, the Baltic republics withdrew their claims to Pskov territory, but both sides remain suspicious of the others' intentions (*OMRI RRR*, 6 March 1997).

After winning election as Pskov governor, Mikhailov

Yevgenii Eduardovich Mikhailov

17 March 1963—Born in Arkhangelsk

1984—Graduated from the construction technical college in Velikie Luki, Pskov Oblast

1984–1986—Senior technician of the Velikie Luki branch of the Pskovgrazhdanproekt Institute

1986–1991—Earned an undergraduate degree from the history department at Moscow State University

1988–June 1991—Member of the CPSU

1990—Elected to the Moscow Council of People's Deputies, serving first on the culture committee and then as chair of the Committee for Budget-Financial Policies

May 1993—Joined Vladimir Zhirinovsky's Liberal Democratic Party of Russia (LDPR)

November 1993—Became deputy senior editor of the newspaper *Pravda Zhirinovskogo*

12 December 1993—Elected to the State Duma from the LDPR list

January 1994–December 1995—Served on the Duma Committee for the Budget, Taxes, Banks, and Finances

1994–1996—Pursued graduate studies in history at Moscow State University

17 December 1995—Reelected to the State Duma and again joined the Committee for the Budget, Taxes, Banks, and Finances

3 November 1996—Elected governor of Pskov Oblast

Married, with a son

promised to suppress "any specific encroachments on the territory of the oblast," and to prevent the "total disintegration of the Russian state" (Alekseev and Vagin, p. 45). In spite of such sentiments, Mikhailov's leadership has not caused relations between Pskov and the Baltics to worsen. In fact, it seems that Mikhailov's concerns regarding the "disintegration of the Russian state" may have more to do with the center's inability to establish good relations with the Baltic states than with tension between Pskov and its foreign neighbors. In March 1997 Mikhailov signed an agreement with Latvia to improve the ecology of the border regions by reducing the dumping of hazardous wastes into the local water supply, atmosphere, and soil.

Economically, Pskov has stood to benefit from its Baltic border. One of the successes of Mikhailov's predecessor Vladislav Tumanov was improving the effectiveness of the customs and immigration offices on the region's international border. By 1997 the customs office in the city of Pskov generated $5 million a year, which is more than any industrial manufacturer in the region. Mikhailov has continued to maintain a secure border and keep up the productivity of cross-border trade. Additionally, the majority of Pskov's joint ventures are with partners from Estonia and Latvia.

Mikhailov is a strong supporter of Slavic solidarity, and worked to heighten Pskov's relations with Belarus. He has a long-standing relationship with Belarusan President Aleksandr Lukashenko. In 1994 he was among the initiators of the Russia-Belarus parliamentary assembly. In December 1997 Mikhailov visited Minsk to discuss the possibility of setting up a Belarusan Trading House in Pskov and other issues of economic cooperation. Mikhailov feels that tighter political integration between Russia and Belarus is necessary in order to improve both states' economies (Alekseev and Vagin, p. 48).

In regards to Pskov's standing on the greater international scene, the region's cities Velikie Luki and Pskov are recipients of a World Bank loan for improving public transportation systems.

Attitudes Toward Business

One of Mikhailov's top priorities has been to make Pskov's economy more self-sufficient. Because federal subsidies are unreliable, Mikhailov has sought other alternatives to combat the region's economic depression. His most successful initiative has been to focus on the region's cross-border trade, which has proven to be Pskov's most reliable and prosperous source of income. The development of joint ventures and foreign-owned firms in the region has been slow, but steadily increasing. In 1997, 1,300 people were employed in foreign-owned and joint ventures, generating over $8.3 million in goods and services (Alekseev and Vagin, p. 51).

Internet Sites in the Region

http://www.ellink.ru/NP/
This is the site for the newspaper *Novosti Pskova*. It features the newspaper's most recent edition and archives dating back through December 1998. You can subscribe to receive *Novosti Pskova* via e-mail free of charge.

ROSTOV OBLAST

Territory: 100,800 km^2
Population (as of 1 January 1998): 4,404,000
Distance from Moscow: 1,226 km

Major Cities:
Rostov-na-Donu, *capital* (pop. 1,008,500)
Taganrog (288,600)
Shakhty (225,100)
Novocherkassk (186,100)
Volgodonsk (181,200)
Novoshakhtinsk (103,300)

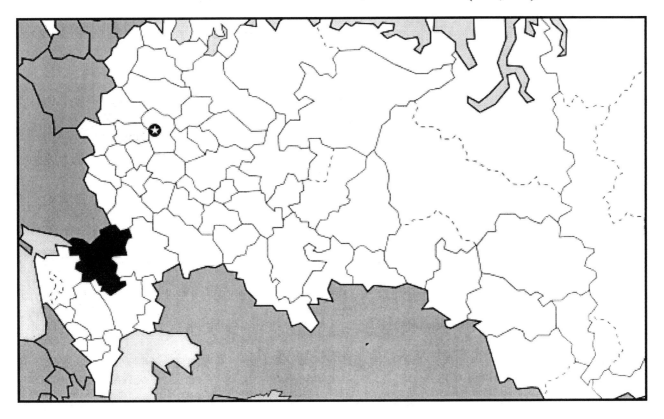

Basic Facts

Population (as of 1 Jan. 1998): 4,404,000 (3% of Russian total)

Ethnic breakdown (1989 census): Russians 89.6%, Ukrainians 4.2%, Armenians 1.5%

Urban population (as of 1 Jan. 1998): 67.8% (Russia overall: 73.1%)

Student population (as of 1 Sept. 1997): 224 per 10,000 (Russia overall: 208/10,000)

Pensioner population (1997): 28.43% (Russia overall: 25.96%)

Percent of population with higher education (1989 census): 10.6% (Russia overall: 11.3%)

Percent of population working in (1997): Industry: 22.6% (Russian average: 23.0%); Agriculture: 14.1% (13.7%); Trade: 15.7% (13.5%); Culture: 11.5% (13.3%)

Average monthly personal income in July 1998: 648.9 new rubles (Russian average: 891.7 new rubles)

Average monthly personal expenses in July 1998: 552.8 new rubles (Russian average: 684.9 new rubles)

Average monthly subsistence requirement in 1998: 311 new rubles (Russian average: 438 new rubles)

Consumer price index (as of July 1998): 81 (Russia overall = 100)

Budgetary revenues (1997): 5,887.0 billion rubles (Russia overall: 433,378.2 billion rubles)

Budgetary expenditures (1997): 6,491.9 billion rubles (Russia overall: 468,111.6 billion rubles)

Industrial production as percentage of all Russian production (Jan.–Aug. 1998): 1.18%

Proportion of loss-making enterprises (as of July 1998): 48.4% (Russia overall: 50.4%)

Number of enterprises which have wage arrears (as of 1 Sept. 1998): 2,406 (1.78% of Russian total)

Agricultural production as percentage of all Russian production (1997): 2.74%

Number of private farms (as of 1 Jan. 1998): 16,672 (6.08% of Russian total)

Capital investment (1997): 5,458.7 billion rubles (Russia overall: 408,797 billion rubles)

Sources of investment (1997): federal budget: 14.5% (Russian average: 10.2%); regional budget: 7.2% (10.5%); extra-budgetary funds: 78.3% (79.3%)

Foreign investment (1997): 25,209,000 USD (Russia overall: 12,294,734,000 USD)

Number of joint ventures (1997): 196 (1.33% of Russian total)

Fixed capital investment in joint ventures and foreign companies (1997): 75,325 million rubles (Russia overall: 16,265.4 billion rubles)

Number of small businesses (as of 1 July 1998): 27,300 (3.14% of Russian total)

Number of enterprises privatized in 1997: 74 (2.7% of Russian total), including those which used to be municipal property: 77.0% (Russian average: 66.4%); regional property: 6.8% (20.0%); federal property: 16.2% (13.6%)

Number of telephones per 100 families (1997): in cities: 35.9 (Russian average: 49.2); in villages: 19.5 (19.8)

Brief Overview

Rostov Oblast lies on the southern part of the East European plain, bounded by the Caucasus Mountains to the south and the Azov Sea to the west. It borders Voronezh and Volgograd oblasts, the Republic of Kalmykia, Stavropol and Krasnodar krais, and Ukraine. The oblast capital, Rostov-na-Donu, is located 1,226 km southeast of Moscow, on the Lower Don River. The Tatars held the region from 1237 until 1480. The territory came under Russian rule during the mid-16th century, except for the southern part, which remained Turkish as part of the Khanate of Crimea until the end of the 18th century. The Don Cossacks have long inhabited the territory of the oblast, and until 1937 the region bore the official name of the Don Cossack Armed Forces Oblast.

The region is rich in coal, including high-quality anthracite; gas; oil; and construction materials. It also has excellent soil for agriculture, as nearly two-thirds of its territory is made up of black soil that is up to 1.5 meters thick.

Industry and agriculture are almost equally developed, each contributing about 32 percent to 35 percent to the regional GDP. The remainder of domestic production comes from the construction sector (10 percent), transport and communications (5 to 6 percent), and trade (5 percent). Machine building and metal processing are the most important industries. It boasts some of Russia's leading enterprises among agricultural machines, helicopters, and biological defense equipment for atomic plants. The regional chemical industry is also of national significance. The oblast is the country's second largest supplier of agricultural products, mostly grain, sunflowers, and fruits and vegetables.

The oblast has close economic ties with over 70 foreign countries, including China, Italy, the Netherlands, Belgium, Bulgaria, Turkey, the United States, Cyprus, and Spain. It exports coal, fuel, equipment for the energy sector, and other machines and equipment, and imports mostly food products, including grains, such as wheat, corn, and rice.

According to a 1998 survey by *Ekspert* magazine, the oblast is ranked 14th among Russia's 89 regions in terms of investment potential and 16th in terms of investment risk. A 1998 survey by Bank Austria ranked the oblast 24th in terms of investment climate. Both investment potential and risk has dropped since 1997—by 8 (8th largest decline in the country) and 33 points (3rd largest), respectively.

Electoral History

2000 Presidential Election
Putin: 53.33%
Zyuganov: 32.54%
Yavlinskii: 5.18%
Zhirinovsky: 2.42%
Tuleev: 1.75%
Turnout: 71.71% (Russia overall: 68.64%)

1999 Parliamentary Elections
Unity: 30.78%
Communist Party of the Russian Federation: 28.48%
Fatherland–All Russia: 7.39%
Yabloko: 7.17%
Union of Right Forces: 5.96%
Zhirinovsky Bloc: 4.98%
In single-mandate districts: 2 Communist Party of the Russian Federation, 1 Yabloko, 4 independent
Turnout: 64.99% (Russia overall: 61.85%)

1996 Gubernatorial Election
Chub (incumbent): 62.15%
Ivanchenko (State Duma deputy, KPRF): 31.60%
Pyatikov: 1.61%
Turnout: 44.44%

1996 Presidential Election
Yeltsin: 29.08%/50.67% (first round/second round)
Zyuganov: 34.99%/44.17%
Lebed: 20.04%
Yavlinskii: 7.70%
Zhirinovsky: 4.61%
Turnout: 75.62%/73.03% (Russia overall: 69.67%/ 68.79%)

1995 Parliamentary Elections
Communist Party of the Russian Federation: 26.99%
Yabloko: 14.11%
Liberal Democratic Party of Russia: 10.25%
Congress of Russian Communities: 6.25%
Our Home Is Russia: 5.33%
Communists–Workers' Russia: 5.32%
Women of Russia: 4.16%
Party of Workers' Self-Government: 3.42%
Derzhava: 3.18%
In single-mandate districts: 2 Communist Party of the Russian Federation, 1 Agrarian Party of Russia, 1 Party of Russian Unity and Concord, 1 Yabloko, 2 independent
Turnout: 67.48% (Russia overall: 64.37%)

1993 Constitutional Referendum
"Yes"—50.3%   "No"—47.4%

1993 Parliamentary Elections
Liberal Democratic Party of Russia: 22.28%
Communist Party of the Russian Federation:
   17.31%
Russia's Choice: 12.30%
Party of Russian Unity and Concord: 12.11%
Women of Russia: 8.26%
Agrarian Party of Russia: 7.52%
Yabloko: 7.44%
Democratic Party of Russia: 6.24%
In single-mandate districts: 2 Communist Party of the
   Russian Federation, 1 Socialist Party, 3 indepen-
   dent
From electoral associations: 1 Democratic Choice, 1
   Party of Russian Unity and Concord
Turnout: 56.47% (Russia overall: 54.34%)

1991 Presidential Election
Yeltsin: 53.48%
Ryzhkov: 17.81%
Zhirinovsky: 11.63%
Tuleev: 6.47%
Makashov: 4.89%
Bakatin: 3.09%
Turnout: 77.34% (Russia overall: 76.66%)

Regional Political Institutions

Executive:
   Governor, 5-year term
   Vladimir Fedorovich Chub, elected September
   1996
      Rostov Oblast Administration; Sotsialisticheskaya
      Steet, 112; Rostov-na-Donu, 344050
      Tel 7(863–2) 66–78–10;
      Fax 7(863–2) 65–67–73
      Federation Council in Moscow:
      7(095) 292–08–05, 926–63–84

Legislative:
   Unicameral
   Legislative Assembly (Zakonodatelnoe Sobranie)—
   45 members, 2-year term, elected 1994, in 1996 ex-
   tended the term till 1998, March 1998
   Chairman—Aleksandr Vasilevich Popov, elected
   April 1994, April 1998

Regional Politics

Slow, Effective Administrator

Vladimir Fedorovich Chub is one of the few remaining governors who has served since October 1991. He was elected to the post in 1996. At the time, Rostov Oblast was the only region in Russia with a five-year gubernatorial term. Chub has taken to heart the famous Russian saying "the slower you go, the farther you will get," building a good reputation as an effective administrator in Russia without a noisy campaign drawing attention to himself.

Yeltsin originally gave Chub the position of governor as a reward for his loyalty during the August 1991 coup. On 20 August Chub called an emergency session of the Rostov City Council, of which he was then chairman, and declared that the putsch was unconstitutional and that only decrees of the Russian government and President Yeltsin were valid in the city.

While supporting Yeltsin now seems like an obvious thing to do, at the time it was quite gutsy. In his inaugural speech as governor, Chub promised to support local entrepreneurial activity, to revive the Don Cossack community, and to keep the local economy functioning.

Executive Platform: Pragmatic Democratic

Chub has always portrayed himself as a practical and professional man who could provide concrete benefits for his region. When he ran for office in the region's first gubernatorial elections, his main slogan was "Don't hope for a miracle (*na chudo*), vote for Chub (*za Chuba*)" (*KD*, 1 October 1996). He defeated his rival, Communist Leonid Ivanchenko, by a margin of 62 to 32 percent. Chub is a relative rarity in the region since neighboring Krasnodar, Stavropol, Voronezh, and Volgograd all have Communist governors. Communist party leader Gennadii Zyuganov blamed "massive falsification" for his candidate's loss, and Ivanchenko spent almost a year fruitlessly trying to prove that he had been cheated (*OMRI RRR*, 2 October 1996 and *Nashe vremya* [Rostov-na-Donu], 9 September 1997).

Chub quit the CPSU in 1991 and became a member of then Vice-President Rutskoi's People's Party of Free Russia. He then joined Our Home Is Russia (NDR). In April 1997, along with five other regional executives, was elected to the 20-member presidium of NDR's

Council. In 1999, he joined both Samara Governor Konstantin Titov's Voice of Russia movement and Moscow mayor Yurii Luzhkov -allied All Russia, then shifted to support the pro-Kremlin Unity bloc.

Policies: Moderate Reformer

Despite his loyalty to the president, Chub did not always support the economic policies of Yeltsin's governments. For instance, he criticized the cabinet of Prime Minister Yegor Gaidar, blaming it for the drop in the country's industrial output and the impoverishment of the population. He demanded more balanced economic policies and found the approach of Viktor Chernomyrdin more appropriate.

In Rostov, land privatization is happening spontaneously, as residents simply divide the soil among themselves while ignoring the legal nuances (*EWI RRR*, 15 January 1998). Even though these people do not technically own the land they are using, they are acting as if they do and are reaping rich rewards.

Like many other governors, Chub has tried to implement a protectionist policy on alcohol production, making it difficult for producers from outside Rostov to sell alcoholic beverages in the region. However, this policy was overturned by the local anti-monopoly committee (*KD*, 2 July 1997).

Relationships Between Key Players: Supportive Legislature

Governor Chub has a good working relationship with the chairman of the oblast's Legislative Assembly, Aleksandr Popov. Popov was originally elected in April 1994 and was able to hold on to his seat following the 29 March 1998 elections. Despite their close relationship, Chub and Popov have quite different styles. In contrast to Popov, Chub does not enjoying socializing and delegates most tasks that involve interacting with the public to his deputies.

Directors of industrial and agricultural enterprises representing the "pro-governor party of power" hold a strong majority in the assembly, about 30 of the 45 seats (*EWI RRR*, 9 April 1998). The Communists won only ten seats despite a visit by party leader Gennadii Zyuganov, and Yabloko won two seats. Vladimir Zhirinovsky's Liberal Democratic Party and the Cossacks did not gain any representation.

Chub also has a good relationship with Rostov Mayor Mikhail Chernyshev. On 27 May 1998, the mayors of Rostov Oblast's cities and raions formed the Rostov Oblast Association of Municipalities. The association elected Chernyshev, the driving force behind the new group, as its chairman. The local leaders hope that by forming an association they will have greater leverage over the Rostov Oblast administration. The association will also provide legal advice on questions of local government since many of the cities do not have the resources to obtain this kind of advice on their own. The association will have its own staff and secretary to provide leadership. The members even discussed the idea of turning the association into the upper house of the Rostov parliament, modeling themselves on the example of the Federation Council. Although the association gives Chernyshev greater clout, so far it has sought to work closely with the oblast administration (*Gorod N* [Rostov], 27 May–2 June 1998).

Despite Chub's overall popularity and close relationship with other local politicians, he faces a very vocal opposition. In November 1997 and January 1998 his Communist opponents initiated a referendum to call for the impeachment of the governor (*KD*, 14 January 1998).

To coopt the local Cossack population, Chub named Don Cossack Ataman Vyacheslav Khizhnyakov a deputy governor. The Don Cossacks were also officially inducted into state service in Rostov Oblast's Novocherkassk. They are involved in agricultural, border guard, police, and tax collection activities (*EWI RRR*, 17 July 1997). Chub tries to negotiate between different Cossack units and usually ignores their violent acts against non-Slavic groups of the population.

Ties to Moscow: Early Yeltsin Appointee

As one of Yeltsin's first gubernatorial appointees, Chub had close ties to the president. Chub and President Yeltsin signed a power-sharing treaty during the president's reelection campaign swing through the oblast on 11 June 1996 (*OMRI Daily Digest*, 12 July 1996).

In early 1998 Chub was one of the directors of the electricity monopoly Unified Energy System. The other regional leaders included in the board of directors were Chuvashia President Nikolai Fedorov and St. Petersburg Governor Vladimir Yakovlev (*RG*, 13 February 1998). Since then, the Federation Council has voted itself as owner of one third of the shares in the company, and the regions have received one third of the votes in the board of director's meeting. The votes are distributed among the regions according to how much electricity they consume. Chub no longer sits on the board.

Relations with Other Regions: Low-Profile Player in Caucasus

Despite Chub's relatively good reputation, he has not played a leading role among regional executives in the North Caucasus area. However, the oblast has at least one strong connection to St. Petersburg and Leningrad Oblast through a local brewery. In 1996 the shareholders of the Donskoe Pivo company approved a de facto acquisition of their plant by the Baltika beer factory. Representatives of Baltika, accompanied by the first deputy governor of Leningrad Oblast, attended the meeting. Baltika gained 60 percent of the Donskoe Pivo stock, in return for a $30 million investment in the technological restructuring of the Rostov brewery. The main reason for the merger was the numerous unsuccessful attempts by the previous management of Donskoe Pivo to keep the struggling brewery afloat. It faces severe competition from several other Volga beer producers. The new corporate entity planned to saturate the regional market with inexpensive but high-quality product and then move on to conquer Europe by the millennium (*EWI RRR*, 4 December 1997).

Rostov Oblast is a member of the Association of Cooperation of the Republics, Krais, and Oblasts of the Northern Caucasus. This group includes other predominantly agricultural and mountainous areas: the republics of Adygeya, Dagestan, Ingushetia, Kabardino-Balkaria, Karachaevo-Cherkessia, North Ossetia and Kalmykia, and Krasnodar and Stavropol krais.

The Rostov Chamber of Industry and Trade initiated the formation of the North Caucasus Congress of Chambers of Industry and Trade. Chambers from Krasnodar, Stavropol, Adygeya, Dagestan, Karachaevo-Cherkessia, and North Ossetia are participating. Their main goal is to change federal investment priorities. Now the vast majority of federal money goes into the state sector in an effort to support unprofitable enterprises with little noticeable result. Directors of the chambers want to see more federal money spent in an effort to increase the size of the small business sector.

Foreign Relations: Economic Ties with South Korea, Germany, Ukraine

Despite its enormous economic troubles, Rostov is one of the bright spots in the North Caucasus region.

Rostov's Krasnyi Aksai factory has begun selling Daewoo cars under the brand name Doninvest. In 1997, the factory sold 14,000 Nexias. In September 1998, Doninvest began assembling the Korean cars at the Taganrog Combine Factory. Despite Doninvest's ambitious plans, the plant has been a failure. After the crisis of 1998 most Russian consumers cannot afford to buy foreign make autos.

The South Korean Samsung Aerospace Industries has ordered a second Mi-26 helicopter, the largest transport helicopter in the world, from the Rostov Helicopter Factory. Samsung will help sell the aircraft in the Pacific region (*KD*, 18 September 1997).

The European Bank of Reconstruction and Development (EBRD) has paid $3 million for a 20 percent share of the Rostov Oblast Gloria Jeans, one of Russia's largest clothing manufacturers. The firm is using the money to establish itself as a recognized Russian brand name and plans to begin exporting to the European market. However, the company had to close its operations in St. Petersburg in 1998 after consumers there demonstrated little interest in buying the firm's products (*KD*, 8 July 1998). Visitors describe Vladimir Melnikov, Gloria's owner, as one of the most interesting entrepreneurs in Russia today.

The Coca-Cola plant in Rostov bought $8 million worth of equipment from the German firm Krones to produce Bon Aqua brand mineral water (*KD*, 26 February 1998).

Despite the arrest of employee Richard Bliss in December 1997 on charges of espionage in Rostov, Qualcomm signed an agreement with Rostov's Elektrosvyaz to build a mobile phone system. Rostov city is considered to have 100,000 potential customers, with 300,000 in the oblast. The three existing mobile telephone providers had signed up only 6,000–7,000 customers by the end of 1998. Qualcomm had licenses for up to 50,000 users (*Segodnya*, 10 December 1998).

In August 1997, South Korea's Daewoo Telecom signed a $2 million contract to build a new telephone station with Svyaz telecom in Volgodonsk. Though the deal was guaranteed by the city administration, Svyaz might not be able to fulfill its end of the bargain: the new telephone station, which was supposed to go into operation in March 1998, was not ready by the summer of 1998. The contract with Daewoo angered the oblast's monopolist, Roskomsvyaz (a partner of Germany's Siemens), which felt threatened by the South Korean competition. Roskomsvyaz took advantage of a legal loophole to get government telecom regulators to halt the construction of the phone station since Svyaz had failed to get the

---

Vladimir Fedorovich Chub

24 July 1948—Born in Pinsk, Belarus; his father was Belarusan, and his mother, Upper Don Cossack

1971—Graduated from Leningrad Institute of Water Transport Engineering

1971–1980—Worked at the Krasnyi Flot maintenance base for the RSFSR river fleet

1976—Joined the CPSU

1980–1983—Second Secretary of the CPSU committee of Rostov-na-Donu

1983–1985—Head engineer of the Volga-Don river fleet

1984—Graduated from the Main Party School

1985–1989—First Secretary of the CPSU Proletarskii District Committee of Rostov-na-Donu

1988–1990—Studied at the Academy of the National Economy via correspondence courses

1989–1991—Chairman of the Rostov-na-Donu city executive committee and the Council of People's Deputies

1991—Appointed Governor of Rostov Oblast

September 1996—Elected governor with 62% of the vote

Married, with children

---

monopolist's approval for this kind of work. Subsequently, 40 Svyaz employees, led by the director and the chief engineer, went on hunger strike. Svyaz representatives met with the head of the telecom regulatory agency in Rostov Oblast, but were unable to make any progress. The conflict has become a source of irritation not only for the city administration, but also for local consumers. Meanwhile, Svyaz met with another South Korean delegation on 22 May and is began incurring losses in its wait for a formal license to begin construction (*EWI RRR*, 4 July 1998).

The Rostov Oblast leadership has close ties to counterparts in neighboring Donetsk Oblast (Ukraine). There are many ethnic Ukrainians living in Rostov Oblast. In the spring of 1998 there was a meeting between the officials of the two regions. Then on 16 June 1998 there was an industrial fair in Donetsk, in which Rostov enterprises (Rostselmash, Priboi, etc.) exhibited their products (http://www.rostov.net/admrnd/).

Attitudes Toward Business: Ongoing Struggle over Rostselmash

The governor's support was crucial in some of the long-running battles over local businesses. The struggle for Rostselmash, the CIS's largest producer of grain harvesting machinery, is a good example. The giant factory was built in the 1920s and annual production reached 36,000 in the 1980s. The old director, Yurii Peskov, resisted the adoption of real reform at the plant, hoping that demand from CIS countries would increase as their old harvesters wore out. He was able to keep the plant alive mostly by winning subsidies from the federal government. However, Peskov was eased out in April 1996, and replaced by the plant's technical director, Vladimir Trinev. The new director then began to make enemies by firing workers and divesting subsidiaries and social welfare institutions. Chub eventually withdrew his support for the management, refusing to give more oblast guarantees for loans the plant was trying to raise. Trinev was ultimately jailed for financial violations at the plant. Chub also backed the proposal of the Federal Bankruptcy Administration (FUDN) to introduce temporary outside managers at the factory—as it has already done to good effect at the local Atommash nuclear power engineering plant and the Azov baby food combine (*EWI RRR*, 8 May 1997).

After standing idle for part of 1997, Rostselmash resumed production at the beginning of 1998 following an agreement with then Prime Minister Viktor Chernomyrdin to restructure the plant's 440 billion old ruble ($73 million) debt to federal and regional governments (former Prime Minister Yevgenii Primakov apparently confirmed the restructuring on

15 October 1998). Moreover, following a board meeting in June 1998, Chub and his administration gained control of Rostselmash. The previous board, which supported Trinev, opposed the oblast's attempts to take over the plant. In March 1999 the board replaced Trinev with Pavel Pokrovskii, who initially said that he would continue Trinev's policies. But he quickly turned against Trinev, blaming him for the plant's problems. At a subsequent board meeting, the conflict came out into the open. Pokrovskii was then able to increase the oblast administration's representation from two out of 11 seats to six out of 12.

In January 2000 the Moscow company Sodruzhestvo bought a quarter of Rostselmash's stock, apparently giving it control over the plant. Sodruzhestvo apparently has good relations with the oblast authorities and moved quickly to put in new management. The company is expected to provide capital to further revive Rostselmash.

Internet Sites in the Region

http://www.rostov.net/admrnd/
This is the official site of the Rostov Oblast administration. The governor's press service posts its press releases here. Readers can also find a lot of information on economic development in the region and investment projects.

http://www.rnd.runnet.ru/region/home.html
This is a home page devoted to the City of Rostov-na-Donu and Rostov Oblast on the server of Rostov State University. There is a lot of historical and cultural information about Rostov-na-Donu itself and other cities in the oblast, such as Taganrog, Tanais, Novocherkassk, and Starocherkassk.

http://www.icomm.ru/home/rostof/
This is the City of Rostov-na-Donu homepage with information about the mayor, city government, city duma, and municipal legislation.

RYAZAN OBLAST

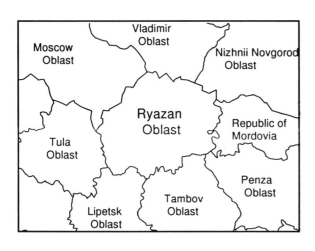

Territory: 39,600 km^2
Population (as of 1 January 1998):
1,307,000
Distance from Moscow: 196 km

Major Cities:
Ryazan, *capital* (pop. 530,600)
Kasimov (38,100)
Sasovo (33,100)
Skopin (28,000)
Ryazhsk (25,400)

Basic Facts

Population (as of 1 Jan. 1998): 1,307,000 (0.89% of Russian total)

Ethnic breakdown (1989 census): Russians 96.1%, Ukrainians 1.2%

Urban population (as of 1 Jan. 1998): 68.4% (Russia overall: 73.1%)

Student population (as of 1 Sept. 1997): 140 per 10,000 (Russia overall: 208/10,000)

Pensioner population (1997): 31.83% (Russia overall: 25.96%)

Percent of population with higher education (1989 census): 8.7% (Russia overall: 11.3%)

Percent of population working in (1997): Industry: 27.1% (Russian average: 23.0%); Agriculture: 13.9% (13.7%); Trade: 9.8% (13.5%); Culture: 12.9% (13.3%)

Average monthly personal income in July 1998: 534.0 new rubles (Russian average: 891.7 new rubles)

Average monthly personal expenses in July 1998: 343.7 new rubles (Russian average: 684.9 new rubles)

Average monthly subsistence requirement in 1998: 348 new rubles (Russian average: 438 new rubles)

Consumer price index (as of July 1998): 88 (Russia overall = 100)

Budgetary revenues (1997): 2,508.5 billion rubles (Russia overall: 433,378.2 billion rubles)

Budgetary expenditures (1997): 2,661.7 billion rubles (Russia overall: 468,111.6 billion rubles)

Industrial production as percentage of all Russian production (Jan.–Aug. 1998): 0.59%

Proportion of loss-making enterprises (as of July 1998): 53.2% (Russia overall: 50.4%)

Number of enterprises which have wage arrears (as of 1 Sept. 1998): 2,818 (2.08% of Russian total)

Agricultural production as percentage of all Russian production (1997): 1.49%

Number of private farms (as of 1 Jan. 1998): 2,364 (0.86% of Russian total)

Capital investment (1997): 1,720.7 billion rubles (Russia overall: 408,797 billion rubles)

Sources of investment (1997): federal budget: 8.6% (Russian average: 10.2%); regional budget: 13.9% (10.5%); extra-budgetary funds: 77.5% (79.3%)

Foreign investment (1997): 10,581,000 USD (Russia overall: 12,294,734,000 USD)

Number of joint ventures (1997): 36 (0.24% of Russian total)

Fixed capital investment in joint ventures and foreign companies (1997): 54,244 million rubles (Russia overall: 16,265.4 billion rubles)

Number of small businesses (as of 1 July 1998): 6,400 (0.74% of Russian total)

Number of enterprises privatized in 1997: 4 (0.15% of Russian total), including those which used to be municipal property: 0% (Russian average: 66.4%); regional property: 75.0% (20.0%); federal property: 25.0% (13.6%)

Number of telephones per 100 families (1997): in cities: 38.8 (Russian average: 49.2); in villages: 12.3 (19.8)

Brief Overview

The first state outpost on the territory of modern Ryazan Oblast was founded in the first half of the 12th century, before the founding of Moscow, and was called Ryazan Principality. In the early 16th century, it became a part of the centralized Moscow state. The oblast is located in the middle of the European Russia, southeast of Moscow, and borders Moscow, Tula, Lipetsk, Tambov, Penza, Vladimir and Nizhnii Novgorod oblasts and the Mordovian Republic.

The oblast is rich in mineral resources, including sands, clays, limestones, and peat; a quarter of its territory is covered with forests. Major regional industries are: energy, radio-electronics, machine building, metallurgy, and oil processing. Over 70 percent of regional output is produced in the city of Ryazan, which houses over 30 enterprises of different industries. The oblast's main exports are oil products, chemical fibers, textiles, and metals.

According to a 1998 survey by *Ekspert* magazine, the oblast ranked 44th among Russia's 89 regions in terms of investment potential and 43rd in terms of investment risk. A 1998 survey by Bank Austria ranked the oblast 45th in terms of investment climate. It had become much safer to invest in the oblast since investment risks had decreased by 18 points since 1997. However, the region's investment potential also decreased, though not as dramatically—only by 7 points over the same period.

Electoral History

2000 Presidential Election
Putin: 48.63%
Zyuganov: 36.33%
Yavlinskii: 4.18%
Zhirinovsky: 2.56%
Tuleev: 2.47%
Turnout: 68.97% (Russia overall: 68.64%)

1999 Parliamentary Elections
Communist Party of the Russian Federation: 29.94%
Unity: 23.05%
Fatherland–All Russia: 11.65%
Union of Right Forces: 6.36%
Zhirinovsky Bloc: 5.83%
Yabloko: 4.83%

In single-mandate districts: 2 Communist Party of the Russian Federation
Turnout: 62.18% (Russia overall: 61.85%)

1996 Gubernatorial Election
Lyubimov (Workers' Ryazan): 38.19%/56.06% (first round/second round)
Ivlev (acting governor): 29.55%/38.36%
Kalashnikov: 14.03%
Milekhin: 8.93%
Dorozhko: 2.33%
Turnout: 50.8%/49.43%

1996 Presidential Election
Zyuganov: 40.07%/51.62% (first round/second round)
Yeltsin: 24.70%/42.57%
Lebed: 19.81%
Yavlinskii: 5.60%
Zhirinovsky: 5.43%
Turnout: 73.47%/71.30% (Russia overall: 69.67%/68.79%)

1995 Parliamentary Elections
Communist Party of the Russian Federation: 30.97%
Liberal Democratic Party of Russia: 10.86%
Congress of Russian Communities: 7.23%
Our Home Is Russia: 6.81%
Agrarian Party of Russia: 5.28%
Communists–Workers' Russia: 5.15%
Yabloko: 4.16%
Women of Russia: 4.01%
In single-mandate districts: 1 Communist Party of the Russian Federation, 1 Agrarian Party of Russia
Turnout: 70.19% (Russia overall: 64.37%)

1993 Constitutional Referendum
"Yes"—49.5%   "No"—48.4%

1993 Parliamentary Elections
Liberal Democratic Party of Russia: 30.84%
Communist Party of the Russian Federation: 14.25%
Russia's Choice: 12.01%
Agrarian Party of Russia: 10.33%
Women of Russia: 7.43%
Democratic Party of Russia: 7.35%
Yabloko: 5.68%
Party of Russian Unity and Concord: 4.98%
In single-mandate districts: 1 Civic Union, 1 Agrarian Party of Russia

From electoral associations: 1 Communist Party of the Russian Federation
Turnout: 66.16% (Russia overall: 54.34%)

1991 Presidential Election
Yeltsin: 52.65%
Ryzhkov: 20.68%
Zhirinovsky: 9.00%
Tuleev: 5.65%
Makashov: 5.61%
Bakatin: 2.70%
Turnout: 81.48% (Russia overall: 76.66%)

Regional Political Institutions

Executive:
    Governor, 4–year term
    Vyacheslav Nikolaevich Lyubimov, elected December 1996
        Astrakhanskaya, 30; Ryazan, 390000
        Tel 7(091–2) 77–40–32;
        Fax 7(091–2) 44–25–68
        Federation Council in Moscow:
        7(095) 292–59–86, 926–66–12

Legislative:
    Unicameral
    Oblast Duma—36 members, 4–year term, elected March 1997
    Chairman—Vladimir Nikolaevich Fedotkin, elected April 1997

Regional Politics

Reviving Lenin's Tradition

Vyacheslav Nikolaevich Lyubimov's first initiative as the newly elected governor of Ryazan was to put Lenin's statue back in the center of the city. This initiative signaled Lyubimov's claim as one of Russia's most reactionary governors. Since taking power, he has not been able to improve the economy, and many of his faithful supporters have formed the Narodnoe delo movement to remove him from office following a variety of scandals.

During the summer of 1997, the governor allegedly built an apartment in Ryazan that cost taxpayers 2 billion rubles ($330,000). Then he tried to have the region's top judge and many other Moscow-appointed officials fired. He subsequently made questionable deals, trading vodka for medicine at prices that cost the oblast dearly, and purchasing coal from Tula Oblast at above-market prices. By late 1997, economic indicators were spiraling downward, spurring more anger toward the governor. Those seeking to remove him are willing to let him keep the apartment and his salary if he will step aside (*Novaya Gazeta*, 23 February 1998).

Lyubimov was elected to office in December 1996. With the support of the opposition National Patriotic Union of Russia (NPSR), he defeated incumbent Governor Igor Ivlev in a runoff by about 20 percent, receiving 58 percent of the vote.

Executive Platform: All Talk, Little Action

Lyubimov believes that Russia's economic difficulties require giving first priority to developing the agricultural-industrial complex. He vigorously opposed shock therapy and proposals promoting unrestricted sales of land. He speaks of the "active and reorganizing role" of the state in economic reforms and the need for "a greater degree of [state] monitoring in the economy."

Lyubimov has stated that "regardless of his political affiliations, every governor has to deal with economic problems first" (*NG*, 17 May 1997). However, according to an analysis on the anticommunist Radio Rossiya: "Lyubimov came to power without any economic agenda. His whole team was chosen on the basis of their faithful campaign support rather than for their professionalism. Lyubimov tried to bolster his popularity by criticizing the previous administration, often doing so without any particular reason" (Radio Rossiya, 8 January 1998).

Surprisingly, Lyubimov claims that he takes Nizhnii Novgorod, the archetype of market reforms, as a model for Ryazan (*NG*, 9 January 1997). This rhetoric is not borne out by real actions.

Relationships Between Key Players: Supportive Legislature, Oppositionist Court

President Yeltsin made a tactical error by replacing Ryazan Governor Gennadii Merkulov with his deputy in charge of agriculture, Igor Ivlev, a couple of months before the 8 December 1996 gubernatorial elections. Yeltsin did so in the hopes of repeating the success of the Saratov and Vologda elections, where newly appointed governors won by large margins.

At the time *Kommersant Daily* commented that this

"strategy was highly risky in the case of Ryazan," a region renown for its procommunist sentiments (*KD*, 17 October 1996). Merkulov was reasonably popular in the oblast at the time of his removal, particularly compared to Ivlev, who became an easy target for the Communist opposition. After the election, Yeltsin appointed Merkulov his representative in Ryazan, spurring the governor's opposition to write an open letter to Yeltsin, asking the president to transfer more responsibilities and powers to Merkulov to counter the leftist governor (*PG*, 13 June 1997).

Most of the other elected officials in the region are also Communists, including the Chairman of the Oblast Duma, Vladimir Fedotkin, who was elected to office in April 1997. Lyubimov and Fedotkin maintain friendly relations. In June 1998, they sent a letter to President Boris Yeltsin accusing the previous leaders of the region of corruption. In particular, they asked Yeltsin to sack Merkulov as his representative in the region (*Pravda*, 7 June 1998). In the same month, the Communist-dominated Oblast Duma sent an open letter to Yeltsin asking him to resign immediately (*PG*, 17 June 1998).

The judiciary has tried to block the implementation of the governor's policies. Accordingly, the governor has announced his desire to remove the top judge of the region, Oblast Court Chairman Anatolii Gostev. He lacks the power to do so, however, since judges are appointed by federal authorities in Moscow. Gostev's actions in the case of Mayor Mamatov's election (he was initially chosen by the city legislature in a controversial procedure, but then won a popular election in December 1996) and his efforts to prevent the governor's crackdown on the sale of alcohol produced outside the region only exacerbated the conflict (*NG Regiony*, 13 November 1997).

The local media are considered procommunist (*NG*, 9 January 1997).

Relations with Other Regions: Cooperation with Starodubtsev

Ryazan's leadership is a part of the Central Russia Association. The association also includes Bryansk, Vladimir, Ivanovo, Kaluga, Kostroma, Moscow, Smolensk, Tver, Tula, and Yaroslavl oblasts, along with the city of Moscow. Many of these areas have a relatively low level of industrial development and a low standard of living; they are often considered part of the "red belt," where opposition sentiment has traditionally been strong.

Lyubimov and Tula Governor Vasilii Starodubtsev signed a cooperation agreement in May 1997 (the so-called Lyubimov-Starodubtsev pact). The two governors agreed to provide mutual economic support and encourage trade links between their regions. Due to lack of money in the federal budget, the two regions have stopped receiving subsidies. This shortage of funds has forced them to combine their efforts in a search for alternative sources of investment for regional industries. They are also trying to rebuild their bilateral economic ties, which had been strong during the Soviet era. In addition to the economic issues, the treaty states that the Tula and Ryazan leaderships should develop a common strategy in their relations with the federal government (*NG*, 13 May 1997 and *Segodnya*, 14 May 1997). Despite the lofty ideals of the text, this agreement ended up costing the residents of Ryazan Oblast about 30 million rubles (then approximately $5 million). Ryazan paid this sum for extremely expensive but low-quality coal that Ryazan Oblast was obliged to buy under the terms of the deal (Radio Rossiya, 8 January 1998).

The Lyubimov administration weakened ties to other Russian regions by imposing a complicated system of inspections and quality checks on goods produced outside Ryazan. These protectionist measures, particularly ones aimed against alcohol produced outside Ryazan, chilled attempts to promote mutually beneficial trade (Radio Rossiya, 8 January 1998).

In October 1998 Lyubimov signed a cooperation agreement with Tambov Governor Aleksandr Ryabov. In the agreement, the two governors decided to eliminate middlemen in trade between the two regions. Middlemen regularly jack up the prices of goods considerably. The agreement also calls for collaboration in the areas of culture, science, and education. For example, Ryazan will help with engineering reforms in Tambov enterprises, and Tambov will supply Ryazan with receipt-issuing cash registers.

Foreign Relations

Foreign trade under Lyubimov dropped to half of the previous level, and investment projects shut down (Radio Rossiya, 8 January 1998).

Attitudes Toward Business: Ryazan Oil-Processing Plant Picking Up

Although the production of vodka has tripled, the economic situation in the region has plummeted (Radio Rossiya, 8 January 1998).

Vyacheslav Nikolaevich Lyubimov

17 January 1947—Born in Samodurovka, Tambov Oblast

1964—Graduated from Ryazan Polytechnic Trade School, later completing coursework at the Ryazan Agricultural Institute via correspondence and Gorkii (Nizhnii Novgorod) Higher Communist Party School, he earned a credentials as an economist-manager

1964—Started working at the Perm oil refinery

1966–1968—Served in the army

1968–1973—Worked at the Ryazan oil refinery

1973—Sent by the Komsomol to work at Ryazan GREZ, where he worked as a carpenter

1978–1987—Head of the management department, second and then first secretary of the Pronsk raion CPSU committee (Ryazan Oblast)

April 1987—Elected the first secretary of the Korableblinsky raion party committee; he also became a member of the Ryazan CPSU Oblast Committee and later served as the head of the Korableblinsky Raion soviet.

18 March 1990—Elected to the RSFSR Congress of People's Deputies winning 45.5% of the vote in the runoff

1991—Elected to the Supreme Soviet, where he served on the Chamber of Nationalities Council

1993—Joined the Communist Party of the Russian Federation (KPRF) and became one of its leaders in Ryazan Oblast

12 December 1993—Elected to the Federation Council

January 1994–January 1996—Deputy chairman of the Federation Council Agricultural Committee, a member of the Regulations and Parliamentary Procedures Commission

23 May 1995—Chosen from the Federation Council as an auditor for the Audit Chamber

22 December 1996—Elected governor of Ryazan Oblast

Although the region's industry is in generally bad shape, one bright spot is the Ryazan Oil Processing Plant (RNPZ). Paradoxically, it is the devastating economic crisis in the country that has helped the company begin a slow climb out of recession (*EWI RRR*, 3 December 1998). Sharply declining world prices for crude oil forced Russia's oil barons to look into processing their petroleum at home rather than exporting it. This was one of the few factors that helped the RNPZ, which was dying for inputs before 17 August 1998, to more than double its monthly volume of processed oil by the end of 1998.

In the beginning of 1998 the plant processed no more than 300,000 tons of oil a month, whereas now it turns out up to 800,000 tons. As the company restarts some of its previously dormant plant, output is expected to reach 1 million tons of oil a month. These numbers are quite telling, when one keeps in mind that the RNPZ's processing capacity is 18 million tons a year. In 1996 it had to reduce its operations by 45 percent compared to the previous year, and in the entire year of 1996 the plant managed to process a mere 4.12 million tons (*Rynok neftegazovogo oborudovaniya SNG*, 3–4 April 1997).

Another reason for the plant's success is the partnership it has developed recently with the Tyumen Oil Company (TNK), which both supplies the RNPZ with crude oil and helps sell the processed product. At the grand opening of the latest TNK gasoline station in Ryazan, the city's Mayor Pavel Mamatov said that the new enterprise benefits Ryazan in three ways: first, through the creation of well-built gas stations; second, through new jobs and more taxes for the local budget; and third, through high quality service to motorists.

The Ryazan Oil Processing Plant is also moving

ahead with creating new types of gasoline. Its latest series of fuels was deemed one of the 100 best consumer products in Russia. The plant's scientists have made considerable progress in creating an environmentally sound type of gasoline, labeled REK (Ryazan's ecological fuel). Soon the plant will be able to produce REK for the domestic market en masse. REK's specifications match, and at times exceed, European environmental quality standards. Additionally, oxidated additives make it a much more efficient type of car fuel. These developments will enable the RNPZ to reenter foreign markets, decreasing its dependency on the volatile domestic ones. The U.S. Export-Import Bank has provided a credit to help restructure the plant.

Internet Sites in the Region

http://www.adm1.ryazan.su/
The official page of the governor's office includes a weekly update from his press service, maps of the region, and some economic information.

http://www.virtual.ryazan.ru/
Virtual Ryazan is an on-line magazine. Local news.

http://www.riac.ryazan.su/pressa/pres1251.htm
Ryazan newspapers materials.

ST. PETERSBURG

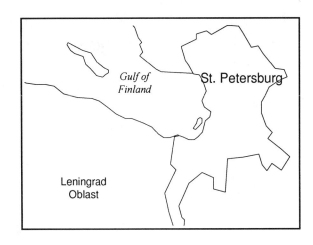

Territory: 600 km²
Population (as of 1 January 1998):
4,749,000
Distance from Moscow: 651 km

Major Cities:
St. Petersburg, *capital* (pop. 4,163,300)
Kolpino (142,500)
Pushkin (92,300)
Petrodvorets (80,400)

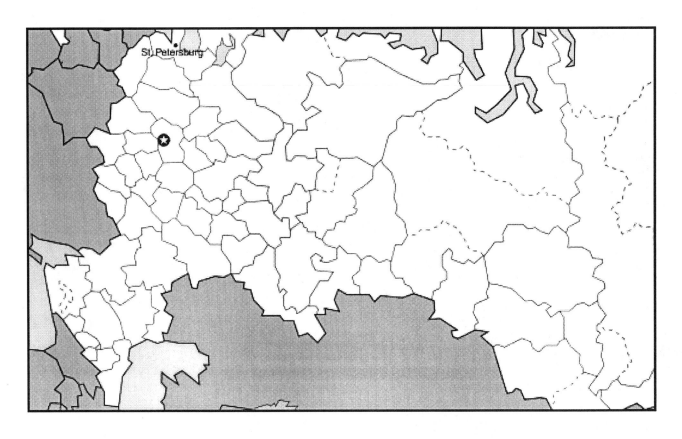

Basic Facts

Population (as of 1 Jan. 1998): 4,749,000 (3.23% of Russian total)

Ethnic breakdown (1989 census): Russians 89.1%, Ukrainians 3.0%, Jews 2.1%, Belarusans 1.9%

Urban population (as of 1 Jan. 1998): 100% (Russia overall: 73.1%)

Student population (as of 1 Sept. 1997): 489 per 10,000 (Russia overall: 208/10,000)

Pensioner population (1997): 26.11% (Russia overall: 25.96%)

Percent of population with higher education (1989 census): 22.0% (Russia overall: 11.3%)

Percent of population working in (1997): Industry: 22.7% (Russian average: 23.0%); Agriculture: 0.5% (13.7%); Trade: 16.0% (13.5%); Culture: 17.6% (13.3%)

Average monthly personal income in July 1998: 997.2 new rubles (Russian average: 891.7 new rubles)

Average monthly personal expenses in July 1998: 899.8 new rubles (Russian average: 684.9 new rubles)

Average monthly subsistence requirement in 1998: 512 new rubles (Russian average: 438 new rubles)

Consumer price index (as of July 1998): 96 (Russia overall = 100)

Budgetary revenues (1997): 13,597.9 billion rubles (Russia overall: 433,378.2 billion rubles)

Budgetary expenditures (1997): 14,085.4 billion rubles (Russia overall: 468,111.6 billion rubles)

Industrial production as percentage of all Russian production (Jan.–Aug. 1998): 2.32%

Proportion of loss-making enterprises (as of July 1998): 31.5% (Russia overall: 50.4%)

Number of enterprises which have wage arrears (as of 1 Sept. 1998): 603 (0.45% of Russian total)

Agricultural production as percentage of all Russian production (1997): 0%

Number of private farms (as of 1 Jan. 1998): 0

Capital investment (1997): 10,427.0 billion rubles (Russia overall: 408,797 billion rubles)

Sources of investment (1997): federal budget: 11.6% (Russian average: 10.2%); regional budget: 7.2% (10.5%); extra-budgetary funds: 81.2% (79.3%)

Foreign investment (1997): 233,983,000 USD (Russia overall: 12,294,734,000 USD)

Number of joint ventures (1997): 1,467 (9.96% of Russian total)

Fixed capital investment in joint ventures and foreign companies (1997): 2,260,306 billion rubles (Russia overall: 16,265.4 billion rubles)

Number of small businesses (as of 1 July 1998): 111,800 (12.87% of Russian total)

Number of enterprises privatized in 1997: 64 (2.33% of Russian total), including those which used to be municipal property: 0% (Russian average: 66.4%); regional property: 71.9% (20.0%); federal property: 28.1% (13.6%)

Number of telephones per 100 families (1997): in cities: 87.4 (Russian average: 49.2); in villages: 0 (19.8)

Brief Overview

St. Petersburg, Russia's second largest city, is located in the northwestern part of European Russia on the delta of the Neva River, where it flows into the Gulf of Finland. The city was founded as St. Petersburg in 1703 by Peter the Great and was made Russia's capital in 1712. At the beginning of World War I, the city was renamed Petrograd. It was the scene of the February and October revolutions in 1917. In March 1918, the capital was moved back to Moscow. In 1924, the city was renamed Leningrad. The city suffered a 900-day German siege during World War II (September 1941–January 1944). In June 1991, the citizens of Leningrad voted to change the city's name back to St. Petersburg. With its remarkable architecture, St. Petersburg is a major cultural center and boasts numerous educational institutions.

The city is famous for its seaport and highly concentrated military-industrial complex, which has degenerated since the collapse of the former Soviet Union resulting in many socioeconomic problems, such as high unemployment. Local government has been fairly successful in dealing with those problems, due to a significant inflow of both foreign and domestic investment. By 1999, 60 percent of the city's regional output came from the service sector, and only 30 percent from industry, marking a remarkable restructuring of city industry.

In February 1998, local authorities issued a series of tax breaks to lure investment. The benefits include reductions in city profit taxes if the profits are reinvested or used to pay bank credits for the initial investments. Additionally, investors who plowed more than $50 million into their projects between 1 January 1992 and 31 December 1999 are free from property tax through the year 2000. Those investing between $25 million and $50 million will pay only half of their property tax. These and other measures attracted significant foreign investment from many multinationals, but St. Petersburg has been nowhere near as successful as Moscow.

The city ranked 2nd among Russia's 89 regions in terms of investment potential and 1st in terms of investment risks, according to a 1998 survey by *Ekspert* magazine. A 1998 survey by Bank Austria ranked the city 2nd in terms of investment climate.

Electoral History

2000 Presidential Election

Putin: 62.41%
Zyuganov: 16.98%
Yavlinskii: 10.55%
Zhirinovsky: 1.87%
Tuleev: 1.47%
Turnout: 66.32% (Russia overall: 68.64%)

2000 Gubernatorial Elections

Yakovlev: 72.87%
Artemyev: 14.6%
Boldyrev: 3.78%
Turnout: 47.59 %

1999 Parliamentary Elections

Unity: 17.70%
Union of Right Forces: 17.40%
Fatherland–All Russia: 15.73%
Communist Party of the Russian Federation: 14.15%
Yabloko: 11.18%
Zhirinovsky Bloc: 4.23%
In single-mandate districts: 2 Union of Right Forces, 2 Fatherland–All Russia, 2 Yabloko, 2 independent
Turnout: 54.25% (Russia overall: 61.85%)

1996 Gubernatorial Election

Yakovlev (first deputy governor): 21.58%/47.49% (first round/second round)
Sobchak (incumbent): 29.02%/45.76%
Boldyrev: 17.09%
Sevenard (State Duma deputy): 10.02%
Belyakov (Leningrad Oblast governor): 9.82%
Belyaev: 4.47%
Khodyrev: 1.38%
Andreev (city legislature deputy): 1.09%
Turnout: 49.2%/44.20%

1996 Presidential Election

Yeltsin: 49.62%/73.86% (first round/second round)
Yavlinskii: 15.15%
Zyuganov: 14.94%/21.09%
Lebed: 14.01%
Zhirinovsky: 2.15%
Turnout: 62.06%/65.11% (Russia overall: 69.67%/ 68.79%)

1995 Parliamentary Elections

Yabloko: 16.03%
Communist Party of the Russian Federation: 13.21%
Our Home Is Russia: 12.78%
Russia's Democratic Choice: 12.37%

Party of Workers' Self-Government: 6.51%
Congress of Russian Communities: 5.13%
Communists–Workers' Russia: 3.79%
Liberal Democratic Party of Russia: 3.42%
Women of Russia: 2.75%
In single-mandate districts: 1 Russia's Democratic
    Choice, 5 Yabloko, 2 independent
Turnout: 60.52% (Russia overall: 64.37%)

1993 Constitutional Referendum
"Yes"—70.6%   "No"—28.0%

1993 Parliamentary Elections
Russia's Choice: 26.99%
Yabloko: 21.20%
Liberal Democratic Party of Russia: 18.02%
Communist Party of the Russian Federation:
    7.69%
Women of Russia: 5.04%
Democratic Party of Russia: 3.98%
Party of Russian Unity and Concord: 3.74%
Agrarian Party of Russia: 0.89%
In single-mandate districts: 4 Russia's Choice, 1 Free
    Democratic Party of Russia, 1 Russian National
    Unity, 3 independent
From electoral associations: 3 Yabloko, 2 Communist
    Party of the Russian Federation, 3 Liberal
    Democratic Party of Russia, 1 Democratic
    Party of Russia, 1 Russia's Choice
Turnout: 52.02% (Russia overall: 54.34%)

1991 Presidential Election
Yeltsin: 67.23%
Ryzhkov: 10.59%
Zhirinovsky: 5.65%
Makashov: 5.09%
Tuleev: 3.99%
Bakatin: 3.40%
Turnout: 65.11% (Russia overall: 76.66%)

Regional Political Institutions

Executive:
    Governor, 4-year term
    Vladimir Anatolevich Yakovlev, elected
    June 1996, reelected May 2000
        Smolnyi; 193060 Sankt-Peterburg
        Tel: 7(812) 271–74–13, 273–59–24;
        Fax 7(812) 276–18–27

Legislative:
    Unicameral
    Legislative Assembly (Zakonodatelnoe Sobranie)—
    50 members, 2–year term, elected March 1994, in
    1996 extended the term till 1998, December 1998
    Chairman—Sergei Tarasev, elected June 2000

Regional Politics

Hands-on Governor Replaces Intellectual in Second City

St. Petersburg is the only city in Russia besides Moscow to have the status of one of Russia's 89 regions. Governor Vladimir Yakovlev came to power in May 1996 at the crest of a wave of governors who presented themselves as good managers rather than supporting one or another ideology. While Anatolii Sobchak held the title "mayor," Yakovlev insisted on changing it to "governor" to better reflect his position as the head of one of Russia's 89 regions.

While Yakovlev's predecessor, the articulate law professor Anatolii Sobchak, used his international fame to serve as an ambassador for the city, Yakovlev focuses on nitty-gritty problems of making St. Petersburg work. The core of his electoral platform was rebuilding the city's crumbling infrastructure. He is a close ally of Moscow Mayor Yurii Luzhkov, who supported his candidacy. Unlike Luzhkov, however, Yakovlev has not been very successful in transforming the face of the city.

Having once served as Sobchak's assistant, Yakovlev is a member of the political elite rather than an outsider. According to NTV, he has close ties to the Moscow bankers and industrialists who backed Yeltsin's 1996 presidential campaign and supports their activities in St. Petersburg.

Yakovlev won a second term as St. Petersburg's governor on 14 May 2000. The governor's reelection bid was watched closely throughout the country, as it was the first regional election to take place following Vladimir Putin's election as Russia's president. Putin had worked with Yakovlev in Sobchak's administration, and the two became bitter rivals when Yakovlev defeated Sobchak in 1996. Putin served as Sobchak's campaign manager in that contest.

In 2000 Putin initially sought to prevent Yakovlev's reelection by backing the candidacy of Deputy Prime Minister Valentina Matvienko. However, Yakovlev's popularity in the city countered the weight of Putin's endorsement, and Matvienko's defeat appeared inevitable. Therefore, Putin recommended that she withdraw from the race a month before the election, leaving Yakovlev without any strong opposition. Putin suffered a clear setback because these events showed that he could not name the governor of his choice. However, they also showed that he was pragmatic enough to accept political realities.

Although Yakovlev was widely popular among the Petersburg population in 1999, he encountered strong opposition from the fractious political elite. This opposition came to a head when Yakovlev tried to move up the gubernatorial elections in order to ensure his victory. In autumn 1999 Yakovlev asked the St. Petersburg Legislative Assembly to move the election to December 1999, but the Yabloko and Boldyrev Bloc deputies boycotted the assembly to prevent a vote. The Legislative Assembly illegally passed Yakovlev's motion, but the Supreme Court overturned the decision. Another attempt to have the election coincide with the March presidential election was unsuccessful. Yakovlev was one of the few governors stymied by local opposition on this issue.

Executive Platform: Managerial Reformer

Like his predecessor, Yakovlev generally supports the introduction of market reforms in Russia. Sobchak, however, was an intellectual who wanted to emphasize the city's potential as a cultural, financial, and sports center. Yakovlev, whose background is more managerial, stresses industry, construction, and transportation. He has expressed support for medium-sized and small businesses and enthusiastically backs foreign investment. Upon election, his priority projects included constructing a new hockey stadium for the world championships in 2000; repairing St. Petersburg's decaying subway system, part of which had to be closed to repair leaks; building better highways, including a road circling the city; constructing a high-speed rail link to Moscow; and fixing up the city's housing stock (the field where he spent most of his career). Critics have blasted the stadium and high-speed rail link project as a waste of the city's funds.

During his 1996 electoral campaign Yakovlev formed a coalition with Yabloko, but that alliance has since fallen apart and the local branch of Yabloko is now one of his harshest critics. In 1999 Yakovlev became a leading force in the formation of the All Russia regional party. He was considered the second in charge, following Tatarstan President Mintimer Shaimiev.

Policies: Attention to the Details

Under Yakovlev, St. Petersburg has a balanced budget, collects all of its taxes, and enacted a stable tax policy that stimulates local business. The city has also avoided a large debt burden. Public sector employees receive their salaries on time and teachers have even won raises. Yakovlev thinks that the rest of the country should follow the city's policies by adopting a balanced, transparent budget and predictable tax policies, including an announcement that there will be no raises for 3–4 years and even some cuts in profit taxes. He also favors the reimposition of a state monopoly on the production, sale, and import of alcohol (*Izvestiya*, 16 September 1998).

In early 1998, the city adopted a strategic plan designed to create an attractive business climate, integrate the city in the global economy, improve the overall appearance and environment of the city, and develop a healthy social climate. The plan called for creating 200,000 jobs, increasing the population's real income by 15 percent, lengthening the average life span by three years, and increasing state revenue by 20 percent (www.stratplan.leontief.ru). Unfortunately, this plan never had a real impact on administration policy.

One of Yakovlev's early policies was to force city residents to pay higher prices for their apartment rents and use of municipal services. On 28 January 1997 he issued a decree implementing this plan. The move provoked the Communist Party into organizing a campaign to remove him from office. The Communist effort ultimately failed, but Yakovlev subsequently backed away from his reformist plans. Two deputy governors who were mainly responsible for the policy, Valentin Mettus and Yevgenii Oleinik, resigned in May 1997 in an effort by Yakovlev to cool public passions about the issue. By the end of the year, however, Yakovlev claimed that what had been implemented of his policies had brought in more revenue and increased competition to provide city services.

Yakovlev also made himself very unpopular during the early part of his tenure by imposing strict new leash laws on the city's dogs, placing additional restrictions on kiosk vendors, and reducing the number of tram lines (*Izvestiya*, 19 September 1997).

Relationships Between Key Players: Confrontation with the Old Legislature

St. Petersburg differs from most other Russian regions in that its legislature has traditionally been relatively strong and has opposed the governor on key issues.

Yakovlev came into conflict with the legislature shortly after his election, when it refused to approve his plans to reorganize and streamline the city's executive branch. Then, on 14 January 1998, the Legislative Assembly approved a new city charter that gave the legislature considerable power over the governor. Among other things, the charter assured that the legislators would serve in their duties full-time and prohibited the governor from engaging in commercial activities.

Yakovlev exacted his revenge when he won the legislature's approval to dump Speaker Yurii Kravtsov on 2 April 1998. Kravtsov's dismissal set the stage for the bitterly fought December 1998 city legislative elections.

In the first round of the voting, Yabloko's candidates proceeded to the runoffs in 23 of the 50 districts and seemed set to dominate the new legislature. Although Yabloko had backed Yakovlev in the 1996 gubernatorial elections, Yakovlev began to fear that the party would use its position to run its own candidate in the 2000 gubernatorial elections (*Ekspert*, 25 January 1999). Therefore, in the days before the runoff, he intensified a campaign of dirty tricks to prevent a Yabloko victory.

In the end, the city elected a highly fractionated legislature. Yakovlev controlled the largest bloc, with 18 deputies in the St. Petersburg Raions' faction. Yabloko ended up with only 8 seats. The Bloc of Yurii Boldyrev, whose leader had split from Yabloko several years earlier, initially had 15 seats, but then itself fractured, with at least three deputies splitting off to form the Industry faction (*EWI RRR*, 14 January 1999).

The city legislature only elected a speaker 18 months after it was seated, choosing the pro-Yakovlev deputy, Sergei Tarasev. Tarasev's victory was only possible in the wake of Yakovlev's decisive reelection victory.

Following the December 1998 elections to the city legislature, Yabloko broke its ties with Yakovlev, and the city's Yabloko leader Igor Artemev resigned his position as first deputy governor. Yabloko, by far the most popular party in St. Petersburg, had been the most powerful part of the coalition that elected Yakovlev as governor in 1996. Artemev had even dropped out of the race in favor of Yakovlev. Many considered him responsible for the successes of Yakovlev's first two years in office: the deficit-free budget, high international credit rating, and the timely payment of wages and pensions in the public sector. Artemev is now a critic of the administration who knows its workings

from the inside. Artemev objected to a number of Yakovlev's policies, including accepting a $200 million credit to build a high-speed train line to Moscow, a project that he claimed put the city on the verge of financial collapse; the governor's minimal support for neighborhood governments; the collapse of the city's television station; and the slow implementation of housing reform; dirty tricks during the campaign; and using the unsavory services of the notorious nationalist television journalist Aleksandr Nevzorov (*Izvestiya*, 19 January 1999). Yakovlev had appointed Nevzorov, who supported Gorbachev's use of force in the Baltic republics in 1991, his advisor in December 1997 (*NG*, 25 December 1997).

St. Petersburg has a system of 111 neighborhood councils that have been functioning since 8 February 1998. Voters showed little interest in the local councils, and elections in only one third of the districts were valid in the first vote in September 1997.

Against the background of these political battles and the August 1998 crisis in the Russian economy, Yakovlev has been trying to increase his hold over the city's economy. On 26 October 1998 he issued an order that four of the city's largest banks, Promstroibank, Baltoneksimbank, Petrovskii, and Sankt-Peterburg, give the administration a 25-percent-plus-one share of their stock to be held in trust in exchange for the right to continue working with city budget funds (and pension funds, in the case of Petrovskii). However, the scheme had little real impact because to carry out such a policy, the city would have had to set up a company with 1 million ECU in charter capital, a sum it did not have.

Yakovlev seeks to keep tight controls on the city media. He has been accused of searching journalists' homes, arranging for a critical newspaper (*MK v Petere*) to be bought by a friendly bank, and trying to shut down the city's Channel 5 TV station (*SPT*, 13–19 April 1998). In February 1999, journalists complained that it was increasingly difficult to publish articles critical of the governor in the city media (*Ekspert*, 8 February 1999).

Channel 5 used to broadcast nationally, but now its former frequency has been taken over by the national Kultura channel. Channel 5 still broadcasts locally and, until the 17 August crisis, its ownership was St. Petersburg (38%), Leningrad Oblast (13%), Promstroibank (17.5%), BaltUneksimbank (17.5%), and Menatep-St. Petersburg (14%). While the regional governments kept a 51 percent share, they anticipated major investments from the banks (*Segodnya*, 21 May 1998). However, after the crisis struck, the banks no longer had the capital to invest in the broadcaster, and the city administration began looking for new investors. One likely source may be the financial-industrial group Industrial Machines, a coalition of more than 100 industrial enterprises (*KD*, 25 February 1999).

St. Petersburg has witnessed a string of assassinations, including Deputy Governor and City Property Committee Chairman Mikhail Manevich on 18 August 1997 and State Duma member Galina Starovoitova on 20 November 1998. Neither case has been resolved, but the events have tarnished the city's image leading some to dub St. Petersburg Russia's "crime capital". Residents, however, protest that crime is no worse in the city than elsewhere in Russia.

Ties to Moscow: Increasing Demands for Money, Autonomy

Like many of his colleagues, Yakovlev wants to transfer more power from Moscow to the regions. In particular, he says that the federal government should hand over shares it owns in factories to regional governments because the federal government does not know enough about regional nuances to manage the shares effectively (*Interfaks-AiF*, 7–13 September 1998). In April 1997, Yakovlev (like many other governors), threatened to withhold tax payments to the federal government if Moscow did not make good on payments that it owed state organizations in the city (*KD*, 11 April 1997). In April 1998, in increasingly belligerent tones, he demanded that the federal government pay local defense enterprises for completed state orders (*KD*, 11 April 1998). At that time, the federal government owed the plants more than 1 billion rubles. Because the defense sector is so large in the city, the local economy relies heavily on its success.

As the leader of the Northwest interregional association, Yakovlev automatically won a seat in the federal government presidium in the fall of 1998.

Yakovlev also has a more sinister connection to Moscow. As St. Petersburg State University sociologist Daniel Tsygankov explained: Redistribution of power in St. Petersburg began during the May 1996 gubernatorial elections, when Moscow money was thrown into the race. Current Governor Vladimir Yakovlev never made his pro-Moscow leanings a secret during his campaign, and upon his election opened the city doors to greater influence from Moscow. Soon several real estate scandals involving Moscow financial interests came to light. The same Moscow financial circles were involved in dividing up TV Channel Five (the St. Petersburg broadcaster that has become Russia's new Culture network). Moreover, city residents still remember the affair with the transfer of city government accounts to BaltUneksim bank, a regional subsidiary of the [once] powerful Moscow-based Uneksim Bank (controlled by Vladimir Potanin). Furthermore, by September 1997 the city government had signed cooperation agreements with such Moscow banks as Inkombank, Menatep, Alfa-Bank and National Reserve Bank (*EWI RRR*, 18 December 1997).

Relations with Other Regions: Seeking Additional Territory

St. Petersburg's most important relationship is with Leningrad Oblast. There has long been talk of merging the two regions into one administrative unit ruled by one governor. However, such a merger has been politically impossible because it would have cost one leader his seat. An attempt to hold a referendum on the idea collapsed as recently as November 1996. However, the possibility opened up again on 18 September when Leningrad Oblast Governor Vadim Gustov took the position of first deputy prime minister in the Primakov government.

Both Gustov and Yeltsin supported the idea of a merger. Yakovlev also supports the plan and is not put off by the very poor financial condition of Leningrad Oblast, which had a 50 percent budget deficit in 1998 and is effectively bankrupt (*KD*, 24 September 1998). Backers of the idea argue that the separation of the city and oblast in 1931 weakened them both economically. They also argue that a merger will save money by cutting the number of bureaucrats and reducing the number of bureaucratic procedures facing investors. However, the electoral success of Gustov's successor, Valerii Serdyukov, in the September 1999 gubernatorial race in Leningrad Oblast reduces the possibility of a merger.

Chairman of the Leningrad Oblast Legislative Assembly Vitalii Klimov believed that it would take two to five years to unite Leningrad Oblast with the city of St. Petersburg. He said that the Leningrad legislators have long favored the merger and began preparations for a referendum of city and oblast residents in September 1998. The St. Petersburg legislators, who were reelected

Vladimir Anatolevich Yakovlev

25 November 1944—Born in Olekminsk (Sakha—Yakutia) while his mother (a native Leningrader) was there following her evacuation from the city during the Nazi siege. His father was a worker who died in 1954

1965–1968—Performed military service in the Transcaucasus Military District

1969—Joined the Communist Party of the Soviet Union and remained a member until 1991 when the party was disbanded

1974—Graduated from the North-West Correspondence Polytechnic Institute, specializing in construction. He also holds a Candidate's degree in Economics

—Worked as a skilled craftsman, senior engineer, director of a construction unit

—Deputy Chairman of the Dzerzhinskii Raion Executive Committee

June 1982—The Party fired him from the Executive Committee for using his position to buy a car for personal use. Following this punishment, he worked as a senior engineer in one of the city's large housing complexes

1982–1993—Worked as the head of a construction unit, and then the head engineer in a housing construction association

October 1993—Named Deputy Mayor under Mayor Anatolii Sobchak, and chaired the Commission on the City Economy

Spring 1994—Named First Deputy Mayor; chairman of the Committee for the Administration of Municipal Services

27 March 1996—Announced candidacy in the city's gubernatorial election, and ran an extremely bitter campaign against his boss Anatolii Sobchak, who demanded that he resign from office. To voters, he presented himself as the St. Petersburg version of Moscow Mayor Yurii Luzhkov

19 May 1996—Finished a surprising second in the first round of the gubernatorial elections in a field that originally included 14 candidates. He won 21.6% of the votes, while Sobchak took 29%

2 June 1996—Elected governor after defeating incumbent Mayor Sobchak in a runoff by a margin of 47.9% to 45.8% (the gap between them was only 27,000 votes)

August 1996—Elected leader of the North-West Regional Association of 9 Russian republics and regions

May 2000—Reelected governor of St. Petersburg

Yakovlev is married and has a grown son

in December, did not respond to their Leningrad colleagues. The most difficult part of the merger process would be harmonizing the laws of the two regions. St. Petersburg has adopted more than 2,000 laws, while Leningrad Oblast has a somewhat smaller number. On 1 January 1999, St. Petersburg introduced a 5 percent sales tax, but Leningrad Oblast did not. Another problem from St. Petersburg's point of view is that Leningrad Oblast is heavily Communist and could distort the city's generally liberal voting patterns.

On 23 September 1998, Yakovlev met with Samara Governor Konstantin Titov and Sverdlovsk Governor Eduard Rossel. They agreed not to compete with each other economically, shared experience on how to pay salaries and wages, and demanded that the federal government give them the ability to coordinate the local actions of the police, tax police, and bankruptcy agencies. The meeting was an early signal that some donor regions were getting together to press their demands against the federal government (*KD*, 24 September 1998). In general, St. Petersburg's important trading partners within Russia are Moscow, Pskov, Samara, Volgograd, Krasnodar, Voronezh and Tver (www.stratplan.leontief.ru).

In the Federation Council, Yakovlev has chaired the important Economic Policy Committee since December 1997. He has won the respect of his neighbors and they elected him the chairman of the Northwest interregional association, which includes Karelia, Komi, Arkhangelsk, Vologda, Kaliningrad, Kirov, Leningrad, Novgorod, Murmansk, Pskov, and the Nenets Autonomous Okrug.

Foreign Relations: Open for Business

St. Petersburg has developed its most important trading links with the Baltic republics, Finland, and other states in northern Europe. At least until August 1998, numerous shuttle traders hustled between the city and Helsinki, importing a wide variety of foreign products. Since then traffic has slowed.

Yakovlev has spoken up on some key issues of concern to the nationalist community, while edging away from others. In January 1997 Yakovlev joined then Nizhnii Novgorod Governor Boris Nemtsov and Moscow Mayor Yurii Luzhkov in declaring that Sevastopol belongs to Russia rather than Crimea. When many governors proposed boycotting Latvia in the spring of 1998 for abusing the rights of ethnic Russians, Yakovlev remained silent. St. Petersburg had $234 million in trade with Latvia in 1997, including $160 million in exports. Nevertheless, the St. Petersburg port competes with Latvian ports for business, so the relationship is not entirely friendly.

St. Petersburg's traditional role as a "window to the west" and its enormous cultural endowments mean that city leaders are constantly encouraging greater tourism. However, a lack of inexpensive hotels and the focus of most cultural programs during the White Nights period (June-July) means that in practice the city has not achieved its full potential.

Attitudes Toward Business:
Aggressively Seeking Investors

Yakovlev created a regional council on foreign investment on 10 February 1997, bringing together city administration officials and business leaders (www.government.spb.ru). The council met immediately after the August crisis began, to reassure investors. In February and July 1998, Yakovlev's government approved legislation providing tax holidays for companies making large investments ($50 million) in the city's economy. He also lowered property and other taxes and even pledged not to raise taxes for the three years following 1998. He particularly favors export-oriented production, import substitution (food and light industries), energy production, tourism, and the service sector. He has also simplified the registration process (*KD*, 21 February 1998 and *EWI RRR*, 22 December 1998).

In early 1998, St. Petersburg seemed to be losing the race for foreign investment to Leningrad Oblast, which was talking about building three new ports and was negotiating with Ford Motor Company to build an assembly plant. The crash of 17 August 1998 wrecked some of those plans, however, and St. Petersburg seems to be the more stable region.

Internet Sites in the Region

http://www.government.spb.ru/
This is the official website of the St. Petersburg government. It has extensive descriptions of Yakovlev's policy initiatives, including detailed information about the city budget.

http://www.stratplan.leontief.ru/windru.htm
St. Petersburg Leontief center helped prepared the city's spring 1998 strategic plan as well as other information about the city.

http://www.sptimes.ru/
The weekly English-language *St. Petersburg Times* has extensive information about the city.

http://www.politics.spb.ru
This site includes analyses of the latest developments in St. Petersburg politics.

SAKHA REPUBLIC (YAKUTIA)

Territory: 3,103,200 km^2
Population (as of 1 January 1998): 1,003,000
Distance from Moscow: 8,468 km

Major Cities:
Yakutsk, *capital* (pop. 195,700)
Neryungri (77,300)
Mirnyi (37,400)

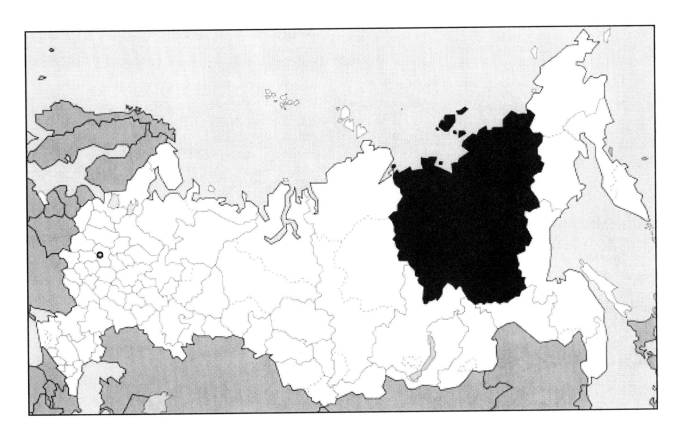

Basic Facts

Population (as of 1 Jan. 1998): 1,003,000 (0.68% of Russian total)

Ethnic breakdown (1989 census): Russians 50.3%, Yakuts 33.4%, Ukrainians 7.1%, Northern peoples 2.3%, Tatars 1.6%

Urban population (as of 1 Jan. 1998): 64.3% (Russia overall: 73.1%)

Student population (as of 1 Sept. 1997): 126 per 10,000 (Russia overall: 208/10,000)

Pensioner population (1997): 19.84% (Russia overall: 25.96%)

Percent of population with higher education (1989 census): 11.3% (Russia overall: 11.3%)

Percent of population working in (1997): Industry: 16.3% (Russian average: 23.0%); Agriculture: 10.5% (13.7%); Trade: 12.9% (13.5%); Culture: 17.3% (13.3%)

Average monthly personal income in July 1998: 1,417.8 new rubles (Russian average: 891.7 new rubles)

Average monthly personal expenses in July 1998: 761.5 new rubles (Russian average: 684.9 new rubles)

Average monthly subsistence requirement in 1998: 949 new rubles (Russian average: 438 new rubles)

Consumer price index (as of July 1998): 214 (Russia overall = 100)

Budgetary revenues (1997): 7,437.1 billion rubles (Russia overall: 433,378.2 billion rubles)

Budgetary expenditures (1997): 9,968.3 billion rubles (Russia overall: 468,111.6 billion rubles)

Industrial production as percentage of all Russian production (Jan.–Aug. 1998): 1.03%

Proportion of loss-making enterprises (as of July 1998): 64.1% (Russia overall: 50.4%)

Number of enterprises which have wage arrears (as of 1 Sept. 1998): 990 (0.73% of Russian total)

Agricultural production as percentage of all Russian production (1997): 0.77%

Number of private farms (as of 1 Jan. 1998): 3,901 (1.58% of Russian total)

Capital investment (1997): 5,451.1 billion rubles (Russia overall: 408,797 billion rubles)

Sources of investment (1997): federal budget: 4.1% (Russian average: 10.2%); regional budget: 15.2% (10.5%); extra-budgetary funds: 80.7% (79.3%)

Foreign investment (1997): 14,055,000 USD (Russia overall: 12,294,734,000 USD)

Number of joint ventures (1997): 30 (0.2% of Russian total)

Fixed capital investment in joint ventures and foreign companies (1997): 15,273 million rubles (Russia overall: 16,265.4 billion rubles)

Number of small businesses (as of 1 July 1998): 4,300 (0.50% of Russian total)

Number of enterprises privatized in 1997: 2 (0.07% of Russian total), including those which used to be municipal property: 0% (Russian average: 66.4%); regional property: 100% (20.0%); federal property: 0% (13.6%)

Number of telephones per 100 families (1997): in cities: 52.2 (Russian average: 49.2); in villages: 39.9 (19.8)

Brief Overview

The Sakha Republic (Yakutia) is the largest region in the Russian Federation (approximately the size of India). It lies in northern Siberia occupying the eastern half of the Central Siberian plateau and the East Siberian mountains, including the Kolyma Valley, stretching from the Arctic Ocean with the New Siberian Islands to the Patom and Stanovo Mountains. It borders Magadan, Irkutsk, Chita, and Amur oblasts, and Krasnoyarsk and Khabarovsk krais. Over half of the republic's inhabitants are Russians, while indigenous Yakuts, who call themselves the Sakha, make up one third of its population.

The republic is one of the most richly endowed parts of the world in terms of mineral resources. There are over 40,000 fields of over 100 various raw materials in Sakha, although only about 900 of them are being industrially exploited. The only resources being mined are ones that do not exist in other regions or are found only in small amounts. Sakha supplies 98 percent of Russia's natural diamonds and Almazy Rossii-Sakha (ALROSA) is the main distributor. Other important mineral resources include gold, tin, coal, natural gas, ferrous and non-ferrous metals, and timber.

According to a 1998 survey by *Ekspert* magazine, the republic ranked 18th among Russia's 89 regions in terms of investment potential and 72nd in terms of investment risk. A 1998 survey by Bank Austria ranked the republic 56th in terms of investment climate.

Electoral History

2000 Presidential Election

Putin: 52.50%
Zyuganov: 30.20%
Yavlinskii: 4.36%
Tuleev: 4.26%
Zhirinovsky: 2.96%
Turnout: 69.91% (Russia overall: 68.64%)

1999 Parliamentary Elections

Unity: 26.07%
Communist Party of the Russian Federation: 22.40%
Fatherland–All Russia: 10.03%
Union of Right Forces: 8.02%
Zhirinovsky Bloc: 6.12%
Yabloko: 3.38%
In a single-mandate district: 1 independent
Turnout: 64.00% (Russia overall: 61.85%)

1996 Republican Presidential Election

Nikolaev (incumbent): 58.96%
Alekseev (republican legislature deputy, NPSR): 25.46%
Osipov: 5.80%
Sannikov (republican legislature deputy, Democratic Yakutia): 1.98%
Arkhipov (Social-Democratic Party of Yakutia): 1.54%
Turnout: 64.66%

1996 Presidential Election

Yeltsin: 51.85%/64.65% (first round/second round)
Zyuganov: 20.55%/29.89%
Lebed: 12.61%
Yavlinskii: 4.68%
Zhirinovsky: 3.65%
Turnout: 71.94%/70.64% (Russia overall: 69.67%/68.79%)

1995 Parliamentary Elections

Communist Party of the Russian Federation: 17.61%
Our Home Is Russia: 13.75%
Power to the People: 7.48%
Women of Russia: 7.46%
Liberal Democratic Party of Russia: 6.80%
Congress of Russian Communities: 4.43%
Communists–Workers' Russia: 4.34%
Party of Workers' Self-Government: 3.84%
Yabloko: 3.63%
In a single-mandate district: 1 Power to the People
Turnout: 65.90% (Russia overall: 64.37%)

1993 Constitutional Referendum

"Yes"—52.4%   "No"—42.9%

1993 Parliamentary Elections

Liberal Democratic Party of Russia: 15.45%
Russia's Choice: 13.36%
Party of Russian Unity and Concord: 13.01%
Women of Russia: 11.44%
Agrarian Party of Russia: 10.51%
Communist Party of the Russian Federation: 10.19%
Yabloko: 7.04%
Democratic Party of Russia: 5.23%
In a single-mandate district: 1 independent
Turnout: 59.41% (Russia overall: 54.34%)

1991 Presidential Election

Yeltsin: 44.90%
Ryzhkov: 24.73%
Tuleev: 12.82%
Zhirinovsky: 6.68%
Bakatin: 3.72%
Makashov: 3.33%
Turnout: 76.65% (Russia overall: 76.66%)

Regional Political Institutions

Executive:

President, 5-year term
Mikhail Yefimovich Nikolaev, elected December 1996
   Ul. Kirova, 11; Yakutsk-22, 677022
   Tel 7(411–2) 43–50–50;
   Fax 7(411–2) 24–06–24
   Federation Council in Moscow:
   7(095) 292–58–81, 926–67–23

Legislative:

Bicameral
State Assembly (*Il Tumen*)—elected December 1997
Republican Chamber (Palata Respubliki)—35 members, 4-year term
Chairman—Vasilii Vasilevich Filippov, elected January 1998
House of Representatives (Palata Predstavitelei)—25 members, 4-year term
Chairman—Nikolai Ivanovich Solomov, elected January 1998

Regional Politics

Powerful Far Eastern President Gradually Losing Autonomy

Mikhail Nikolaev has ruled over the resource-rich Republic of Sakha (Yakutia) since he was first elected president of the republic in December 1991. Throughout his tenure, Nikolaev has succeeded in making Sakha one of the most autonomous of all the Russian regions. In the earlier part of his presidency, Nikolaev, an ethnic Yakut, spoke strongly in the language of people's rights. However, Nikolaev became much more conciliatory when the federal government gave him control over the republic's diamond resources.

Nearly all attention focused on Sakha is related to the region's vast mineral resources. Throughout most of his presidential career, Nikolaev has successfully used these resources as power levers when dealing with Moscow. From 1992 to 1997, Nikolaev controlled essentially all of the region's wealth through his exclusive control over Sakha's diamond industry, and during much of this period he managed to avoid paying taxes to the federal budget.

However, in 1997 the federal government decided to improve the situation and took back considerable control over Sakha's diamonds. The president has run into conflicts with the federal government regarding other issues as well, and it seems that the privileges Nikolaev enjoyed in the earlier part of his tenure are slowly slipping away. Increasingly difficult economic and social circumstances in the republic further complicate Nikolaev's position. In spring 1998 Sakha was devastated by floods caused by ice floes blocking the region's rivers. Twenty-two of Sakha's 35 regions were affected by the floods, which caused about $158 million in damages, representing about 20 percent of the republic's annual budget.

Executive Platform: Separatism As a Tool for Power

Nikolaev's platform has been greatly determined by his varying relationship with the federal government. Nikolaev generally had a good relationship with President Boris Yeltsin (see Ties to Moscow), which allowed him to secure a sizable amount of autonomy for the republican administration and privileges not afforded to other regions. When the situation was in his favor, Nikolaev supported Yeltsin. However, in instances when the federal government tried to exert more authority over the republic, Nikolaev immediately became more assertive in defending his republic's prerogatives.

In his 1991 presidential campaign, Nikolaev spoke in favor of state sovereignty for Yakutia within the Russian Federation. These policies prompted Moscow to make concessions, and ultimately the federal center granted Sakha considerable control over its diamond wealth. Sakha's autonomy within the federation continued to grow through a series of subsequent agreements. These successes placed Nikolaev in a favorable position for reelection in 1996. Nikolaev was largely popular at home for his ability to secure for the republic numerous powers normally reserved for federal control. Additionally, his diplomatic successes have given him a reputation as the guarantor of political stability.

However, Nikolaev's autonomy began slowly crumbling as Moscow demanded control over much of the region's resources and took back some of the rights it had granted to the republic (see Ties to Moscow). The region's revenue has declined sharply, the social situation is becoming more grave, and Nikolaev's tactics seem to have lost their ability to strike fear in the upper echelons of Russia's federal government.

Policies: Challenge Federal Doctrine

Nikolaev pays little heed to federal legislation when defining republican policy. There are many instances in which Sakha's regional laws do not coincide with federal norms. One such example is the law requiring the republican president to speak Yakut as well as Russian. Several other ethnic republics have similar laws. Even though the Russian Constitutional Court ruled that such requirements are illegal, no measures have been taken to prevent republics from continuing the practice. Another example was a decree Nikolaev issued in January 1995 freeing Sakha citizens from participating in military activities in Chechnya if they should be called for service.

Similarly, Nikolaev followed his own course of action in dealing with the financial crisis and subsequent panic that struck Russia in August 1998. Like several other regional executives, he instituted price controls on goods of basic necessity and held down the price of public transportation. Yet, Nikolaev also made an even bolder move and issued a decree blocking the sale of Sakha's gold to the Russian government (see Ties to Moscow).

In April 1997 Nikolaev signed a decree calling for stricter regulation of foreign activities in the republic. The decree states that all foreigners coming to Sakha are required to receive permission from local authorities and the republican interior ministry. The decree also stipulates that local businessmen using foreign labor must provide evidence that they will arrange accommodation for their workers and that the workers will leave the republic on the date stated in their contract. This move seemed a bit uncharacteristic of Nikolaev, who tends to welcome foreign partnerships and relations.

Nikolaev is also very concerned about environmental preservation and Sakha's ecology. During the Soviet era, Sakha was environmentally devastated by industrial pollution and underground nuclear testing, which have left the unpleasant consequences of radioactive permafrost. Nikolaev has been greatly opposed to rocket launches from the Svobodnyi cosmodrome in neighboring Amur Oblast because of environmentally damaging debris that lands on the republic's territory. In 1997 Sakha Deputy Prime Minister Yegor Borisov filed a suit against Russia's Military Space Forces over a rocket launch from the cosmodrome, claiming that the republic's demands that the launch be postponed until it received further safety guarantees were ignored. In 1996 Nikolaev promised to set aside more than one-fifth of the republic's territory as a nature reserve by the year 2000, and in 1997 the World Wildlife Fund allocated 500,000 Swiss francs to fund conservation projects in Sakha.

Relationships Between Key Players: Docile Legislature

In 1995 Nikolaev tried to have his presidential term extended until 2001 through a popular referendum. The republican assembly had agreed to hold the referendum after over 200,000 signatures were collected. However, when the idea was criticized as undemocratic, Nikolaev subsequently asked the assembly to cancel the decision.

In 1996 the president's analytical center wanted to replace the republic's constitution center staff claimed that it allowed the parliament to usurp the power of the president. The analysts wanted Nikolaev to disband the regional parliament and establish a Constitutional Assembly to adopt a new constitution, neither of which he did.

Ties to Moscow: Increased Tension

Nikolaev was a strong supporter of President Boris Yeltsin, particularly in comparison to the leaders of Russia's other republics. Observers have noted that in the early 1990s, the relations between the two men were very close on a personal level. Nikolaev's alliance with Yeltsin dates back to 1991 when he backed Yeltsin's campaign against Mikhail Gorbachev and directed the republic's diamond revenue to the Russian Federation rather than the Soviet government. Nikolaev also backed Yeltsin's 1993 decree disbanding the parliament. Yet, he was strongly opposed to adopting Russia's constitution by referendum, feeling that the regions should have ratified it. Later, however, the relationship between Nikolaev and Yeltsin began deteriorating as Moscow tried to exert additional control over the region.

Sakha signed multiple agreements in the early 1990s affording it additional rights not granted to other regions. The region's firm commitment to stay in the federation was sealed when Sakha signed a power-sharing agreement with the federal government on 29 June 1995. Over the years, Sakha had gained the right to collect federal taxes and distribute them for federal programs in the republic; the republic also maintains ownership of the republic's diamond resources and sells them abroad. Sakha was exempted from much of the state's privatization program, with local stores remaining state property. These multiple power privileges meant that Sakha was perhaps the most sovereign republic within the Russian Federation.

However, since 1997 the center has tried to reclaim many of the powers it granted to Sakha. Among the various controversial points are the financial relations between the republic's diamond company Almazy Rossii-Sakha (ALROSA) and the federal government. The 1992 agreement between Sakha and Moscow gave the republic the right to buy 20 percent of the diamonds produced in the republic at production cost, which is about 40 percent of world prices. Sakha then exported them, realizing considerable profits.

In spring 1997 then First Deputy Prime Minister Anatolii Chubais complained that Sakha had not transferred any diamond profits to the federal government. He was also bothered by the fact that Moscow received only a minuscule fraction of the money ALROSA made from its exports to South Africa's De Beers even though the federal government owned 32 percent of the company's stock. Shortly after, Yeltsin signed a decree revoking Sakha's supreme authority over the reserves. The decree permitted ALROSA to conclude a new agreement for exporting diamonds to De Beers, but reduced the region's benefits from the sales. Yeltsin's decree granted Sakha the right to buy only as many diamonds as the Russian president allowed and at prices established by the federal government. Therefore, Sakha essentially lost its authority over the resource that brings in 70 percent of the republic's revenue.

To prevent the federal government from taking over Sakha's gold, in August 1998 Nikolaev signed a decree blocking sales of the precious metal to the government. The decree stated that all firms mining gold in the republic had to furnish their gold to the republican government. Regional reserves would then be released after a decision from Sakha's committee on precious metals and gems. Nikolaev's move, taken at the height of the panic following Russia's August 1998 financial crisis, was an unsuccessful attempt to reestablish some leverage over Moscow. The decree caused panic among Sakha's mining firms since it essentially demanded that they break their contracts to sell gold to commercial banks. The Russian Finance ministry also was angered, since Sakha accounts for 17 percent of total gold production in Russia, and there was concern that Nikolaev might try to take similar control over Sakha's diamond reserve. On 10 January 1999 Yeltsin passed a decree suspending Nikolaev's decision.

In the fall of 1999, Nikolaev endorsed the pro-Kremlin Unity ticket.

Relations with Other Regions: Developing Cooperation

Nikolaev tends to steer a rather independent course, relying little on alliances with other regions. Sakha is, however, trying to increase its ties to particular regions, such as the Republic of Bashkortostan. A delegation of Sakha legislators visited the region in November 1998 and were received by Bashkortostan President Murtaza Rakhimov and members of the Bashkortostan State Council. The capital cities of Yakutsk and Ufa signed cooperation agreements, and the two republics hope to sign an agreement in the future. Bashkortostan had provided financial and technical assistance to Sakha following the floods that ravaged the republic in spring 1998.

Sakha belongs to the Far East and Baikal Association, which also includes the Republic of Buryatia; Primorskii and Khabarovsk krais; Amur, Kamchatka, Magadan, Chita, and Sakhalin oblasts; the Jewish Autonomous Oblast; and Koryak and Chukotka autonomous okrugs. One of the association's goals has been to develop stronger partnerships with Asian countries, particularly in the economic sphere.

Foreign Relations: Chairman of Northern Forum

Nikolaev's most intriguing foreign activity is his chairmanship of the Northern Forum, a non-profit organization that brings together the countries and peoples of Russia, Europe, and North America. Nikolaev and Sakha have been active in the Northern Forum's projects and organizational activities, sponsoring the Natural Processes and Mineral Resources project and hosting the Northern Forum's Russian Sub-Secretariat in Yakutsk (www.northernforum.org).

Mikhail Yefimovich Nikolaev

13 November 1937—Born in Sakha

1961—Graduated from Omsk Veterinary Institute and began working as a veterinarian, then switched to Komsomol work

1963—Joined the Communist Party

1969–1971—Studied at the Higher Party School of the CPSU Central Committee

1973—First secretary of the Verkhnevilyui CPSU district, committee

1975—Appointed deputy chair of the Sakha Council of Ministers

1979–1985—Agricultural minister for the Republic

1985–1989—Secretary of the Yakutsk oblast CPSU committee

8 December 1989—Elected chair of the Sakha Supreme Soviet Presidium

4 March 1990—Elected to the Sakha Congress of People's Deputies and the RSFSR Congress of People's Deputies

20 December 1991—Elected President of Sakha

12 December 1993—Elected to the first session of the Federation Council

January 1996—Appointed to the Federation Council and joined the Committee on Federation Affairs, Federal Agreements, and Regional Policies

22 December 1996—Reelected President of Sakha

Yakut

Aside from the Northern Forum, most of Sakha's international ties concern the diamond industry, which has been directly focused on relations with South Africa's De Beers. Yet, Sakha is trying to expand its diamond market to other regions. In June 1997 Nikolaev signed a cooperation agreement with Belarusan President Aleksandr Lukashenko, which was supposed to increase the supply of Sakha diamonds to the Belarusan diamond processing plant Kristall. In turn, Sakha would then receive trucks and tractors from Belarus. The status of this agreement given the federal government's increased control over Sakha diamonds is unclear.

Sakha has authorized its Forestry Department to lease 30 million cubic meters of wood in the Lenskii and Aldanskii raions of the republic. The government hopes to lease the land to countries like India, China, and Korea. Whoever leases the land will have the right to harvest its timber resources and secondary forest resources as well as cultivate bee hives, collect berries, nuts, mushrooms, moss, and medicinal herbs; hunt; and hold tourist activities. The proceeds will be invested in the local forestry complex and in ensuring the sustainability of the forest (*EWI RRI*, 20 May 1999).

Attitudes Toward Business:
Encourages Investment

Nikolaev is a strong advocate of business development and has actively worked to bring foreign investment to Sakha. In early 1997 Nikolaev issued a request for businessmen to invest money in Sakha's economy. The letter, which was published in *Rabochaya Tribuna*, stated that the republican government considered the creation of favorable conditions for businesses to be one of its primary goals. One such provision explained in the letter stated that the republican government was willing to guarantee the security of investments in top priority projects. In January 1998 Nikolaev participated in the second annual U.S.-Russian Investment Symposium at Harvard University in Massachusetts to try to attract investment to Sakha. Nikolaev was well received at the symposium when he noted, "I have come here not from a bandit Russia, but from a normal, democratic, developing Russia"(*EWI RRR*, 15 January 1998).

Business in Sakha mainly means diamonds, which, as mentioned above, is under greater scrutiny by the federal government. ALROSA's primary economic partnership has been with South Africa's De Beers. The relationship is so strong that in 1998 Alrosa issued Eurobonds backed by De Beers. In August 1998 ALROSA and De Beers renewed their contract, which had expired on 31 December 1997. The contract states that Alrosa will supply South Africa's De Beers with $550 million worth of diamonds annually for the next three years. For a while De Beers tried to encroach on ALROSA's Russian diamond monopoly, but has since ended the attempt.

Just weeks before the two firms signed the agreement, De Beers bought a 27 percent stake in Severalmaz, the firm that owns the rights to develop the Lomonosov diamond deposit in Arkhangelsk. The Lomonosov deposit could provide up to 25 percent of Russia's diamonds, and thus challenge ALROSA's monopoly status. Ultimately, De Beers backed out of the project selling ALROSA its stake.

Internet Sites in the Region

http://www.sakha.ru/
This is the official website of the Sakha republican administration. It offers some basic information about the republic, its government, natural resources, and universities.

http://www.yakutia.ru/~resp/n29032/n29032.html
This is the site of the newspaper *Yakutia*, featuring both the most recent issue and archives for the previous year.

SAKHALIN OBLAST

Territory: 87,100 km²
Population (as of 1 January 1998): 620,000
Distance from Moscow: 10,417 km

Major Cities:
Yuzhno-Sakhalinsk, *capital* (pop. 177,000)
Kholmsk (42,000)
Korsakov (39,700)
Okha (30,000)

Basic Facts

Population (as of 1 Jan. 1998): 620,000 (0.42% of Russian total)

Ethnic breakdown (1989 census): Russians 81.7%, Ukrainians 6.5%, Koreans 5.0%, Belarusans 1.6%, Tatars 1.5%

Urban population (as of 1 Jan. 1998): 86.3% (Russia overall: 73.1%)

Student population (as of 1 Sept. 1997): 63 per 10,000 (Russia overall: 208/10,000)

Pensioner population (1997): 23.23% (Russia overall: 25.96%)

Percent of population with higher education (1989 census): 11.2% (Russia overall: 11.3%)

Percent of population working in (1997): Industry: 22.8% (Russian average: 23.0%); Agriculture: 5.8% (13.7%); Trade: 15.8% (13.5%); Culture: 12.1% (13.3%)

Average monthly personal income in July 1998: 1,130.9 new rubles (Russian average: 891.7 new rubles)

Average monthly personal expenses in July 1998: 589.7 new rubles (Russian average: 684.9 new rubles)

Average monthly subsistence requirement in 1998: 731 new rubles (Russian average: 438 new rubles)

Consumer price index (as of July 1998): 183 (Russia overall = 100)

Budgetary revenues (1997): 2,782.6 billion rubles (Russia overall: 433,378.2 billion rubles)

Budgetary expenditures (1997): 3,045.1 billion rubles (Russia overall: 468,111.6 billion rubles)

Industrial production as percentage of all Russian production (Jan.–Aug. 1998): 0.28%

Proportion of loss-making enterprises (as of July 1998): 65.4% (Russia overall: 50.4%)

Number of enterprises which have wage arrears (as of 1 Sept. 1998): 575 (0.43% of Russian total)

Agricultural production as percentage of all Russian production (1997): 0.34%

Number of private farms (as of 1 Jan. 1998): 788 (0.29% of Russian total)

Capital investment (1997): 2,266.9 billion rubles (Russia overall: 408,797 billion rubles)

Sources of investment (1997): federal budget: 27.0% (Russian average: 10.2%); regional budget: 4.5% (10.5%); extra-budgetary funds: 68.5% (79.3%)

Foreign investment (1997): 52,743,000 USD (Russia overall: 12,294,734,000 USD)

Number of joint ventures (1997): 89 (0.06% of Russian total)

Fixed capital investment in joint ventures and foreign companies (1997): 162,264 million rubles (Russia overall: 16,265.4 billion rubles)

Number of small businesses (as of 1 July 1998): 4,000 (0.46% of Russian total)

Number of enterprises privatized in 1997: 8 (0.29% of Russian total), including those which used to be municipal property: 100% (Russian average: 66.4%); regional property: 0% (20.0%); federal property: 0% (13.6%)

Number of telephones per 100 families (1997): in cities: 45.6 (Russian average: 49.2); in villages: 32.2 (19.8)

Brief Overview

Sakhalin Oblast includes Sakhalin Island and the Kuril Islands chain, both of which lie off the coast of Khabarovsk Krai. The Kurils, forming the southern border of the Sea of Okhotsk, stretch from Kamchatka Peninsula to Hokkaido, Japan's northernmost island. Possession of the Kuril Islands has been a subject of dispute between Japan and Russia for more than three centuries. Japan held the southern Kuril Islands from 1855 until the end of World War II. Sakhalin was chiefly used as a prison colony by tsarist Russia: Japan won control over the southern half of the island in 1905, and lost it to the Soviet Union in 1945.

The region is rich in mineral resources, such as oil, gas, coal, and ferrous, non-ferrous, and precious metals. It also has access to abundant supplies of fish and other seafood. Over 80 percent of Sakhalin's regional GDP comes from the mining, forestry, timber working, cellulose, and fishing industries, as well as from exploration of the oil and gas field in the Sea of Okhotsk. The deposits are estimated to amount to 1.23 percent of the country's total hydrocarbon deposits. The Sakhalin-1 and Sakhalin-2 projects are among the few defined by production sharing agreements, which made them attractive for investment. Foreign companies such as Exxon, Mitsui, Mitsubishi, and Shell are involved in these projects. Many others have expressed interest in participating in other Sakhalin oil-and gas-related enterprises.

According to a 1998 survey by *Ekspert* magazine, the oblast ranked 65th among Russia's 89 regions in terms of investment potential and 67th in terms of investment risk. A 1998 survey by Bank Austria ranked the oblast 29th in terms of investment climate.

Electoral History

2000 Presidential Election
Putin: 46.73%
Zyuganov: 30.79%
Yavlinskii: 7.48%
Zhirinovsky: 5.62%
Tuleev: 2.78%
Turnout: 60.34% (Russia overall: 68.64%)

1999 Parliamentary Elections
Communist Party of the Russian Federation: 24.27%
Unity: 23.06%
Zhirinovsky Bloc: 10.60%
Union of Right Forces: 9.07%

Yabloko: 8.12%
Fatherland–All Russia: 4.89%
In a single-mandate district: 1 Communist Party of the Russian Federation
Turnout: 53.16% (Russia overall: 61.85%)

1996 Gubernatorial Election
Farkhutdinov (incumbent): 39.47%
Chernyi: 27.20%
Dolgikh: 9.44%
Bersenev: 7.21%
Litvin: 4.42%
Maksutov (oblast legislature chairman): 1.50%
Turnout: 33.69%

1996 Presidential Election
Yeltsin: 29.86%/53.38% (first round/second round)
Zyuganov: 26.91%/38.81%
Lebed: 18.67%
Yavlinskii: 9.24%
Zhirinovsky: 9.06%
Turnout: 63.46%/62.08% (Russia overall: 69.67%/ 68.79%)

1995 Parliamentary Elections
Communist Party of the Russian Federation: 24.61%
Liberal Democratic Party of Russia: 15.32%
Yabloko: 6.76%
Women of Russia: 6.14%
Party of Workers' Self-Government: 5.53%
Congress of Russian Communities: 4.78%
Communists–Workers' Russia: 4.51%
Our Home Is Russia: 4.08%
In a single-mandate district: 1 Communist Party of the Russian Federation
Turnout: 57.79% (Russia overall: 64.37%)

1993 Constitutional Referendum
"Yes"—62.4%   "No"—35.1%

1993 Parliamentary Elections
Liberal Democratic Party of Russia: 36.86%
Women of Russia: 10.43%
Russia's Choice: 9.60%
Communist Party of the Russian Federation: 8.91%
Party of Russian Unity and Concord: 8.35%
Yabloko: 7.62%
Democratic Party of Russia: 6.55%
Agrarian Party of Russia: 1.43%
In a single-mandate district: 1 independent
Turnout: 49.70% (Russia overall: 54.34%)

1991 Presidential Election

Yeltsin: 54.91%

Ryzhkov: 18.20%

Zhirinovsky: 8.12%

Tuleev: 5.49%

Bakatin: 5.05%

Makashov: 3.82%

Turnout: 69.96% (Russia overall: 76.66%)

Regional Political Institutions

Executive:

Governor, 4-year term

Igor Pavlovich Farkhutdinov, elected October 1996
    Kommunisticheskii Prospect, 39; Yuzhno-
    Sakhalinsk, 693011
    Tel 7(424–22) 42–14–02;
    Fax 7(424–22) 3–60–81
    Federation Council in Moscow:
    7(095) 292–66–29, 926–60–98

Legislative:

Unicameral

Oblast Duma—27 members, 4-year term, elected
October 1996

Chairman—Boris Nikitovich Tretyak, elected
November 1996

Regional Politics

Commanding Presence on Russian Island

Igor Farkhutdinov was first appointed governor of
Sakhalin Oblast in April 1995, and was popularly elected
to the post in October 1996. With more than twenty
years, experience in regional politics, Farkhutdinov was
serving as the mayor of the oblast's capital Yuzhno-
Sakhalinsk at the time he was appointed governor. President Boris Yeltsin tapped him to replace Yevgenii
Krasnoyarov, who had led the oblast since 1993 and
resigned under the cloud of allegations that he had misused federal aid to earthquake victims. Immediately after
Farkhutdinov's appointment, he was confronted with a
devastating natural disaster—an earthquake in the oblast
city of Neftegorsk, that killed nearly 2,000 people and
left many others homeless. The governor stepped up to
the challenge and was highly praised for his efforts in
handling the earthquake's aftermath.

Farkhutdinov's efficient and commanding approach to the Neftegorsk earthquake disaster set the

tone for his gubernatorial tenure. In many respects
Farkhutdinov is responsible for bringing the governance of Sakhalin under regional rather than federal
control. Immediately after being appointed governor,
Farkhutdinov petitioned the presidential administration to permit holding direct gubernatorial elections.
He has insisted that transactions between the federal
government and Sakhalin become more transparent,
and has even achieved more authority for distributing
funds in the region. Farkhutdinov has also demanded
that his input be considered regarding the fate of the
Kuril Islands, which presently are included in the
oblast's territory.

Farkhutdinov is also one of the key factors in the
region's relative success in attracting investors to develop its oil and gas deposits. Investors credit him with
helping to clear away obstacles to investments that have
hampered, similar projects in western Siberia.

Executive Platform: More Power to the Regions

Farkhutdinov is a regionalist who has strong reservations about the actions of the federal government. It is
important to him to ensure that the region's natural
resources are not unfairly exploited by the center. Yet,
Farkhutdinov is not a separatist. He supports a strong
federation with an equal balance of power between
the federal center and regions. Farkhutdinov has spoken in favor of reducing the number of Russian regions from the current 89 to a more manageable
number, an idea proposed by several prominent politicians, including Moscow Mayor Yurii Luzhkov.
Farkhutdinov stated that consolidating the existing
subjects would be "difficult and intricate," but necessary in order to keep Russia together as a whole (*EWI
RRR*, 25 September 1998).

Policies: Economic Authority

The majority of Farkhutdinov's policies have focused
specifically on the region's development and ensuring
that more powerful federal agencies and foreign companies do not capitalize on the region's resources at
the expense of Sakhalin. In August 1997 Farkhutdinov
announced that the oblast administration's Oversight
Department and the local branch of the Federal Security Service must approve all contracts with foreign
firms to develop the region's oil and gas resources.
Farkhutdinov adopted this measure because he believes
that Western investors are trying to take advantage of

Russia's poverty to gain social, political, economic, ecological, and geological information beyond what is necessary for their work (*EWI RRR*, 28 August 1997). The governor's interests in enacting such a decree lie in increasing the oblast's control over the income generated in developing its untapped natural resources. Despite its threatening nature, this decree did not pose large burdens on foreign investors working in the area.

Farkhutdinov has tried to take measures to guarantee that the Kuril Islands will remain a part of Sakhalin Oblast. In doing so, he is drafting a law on the oblast's borders and is trying to develop cooperative plans and projects with Japan (see Foreign Relations).

Relationships Between Key Players: Korean Relocation

The large Korean population residing in the oblast that was forcibly removed from their homeland to Sakhalin in the 1940s has been an important political issue for the oblast. Korea, Japan, and Sakhalin have been involved in trying to come up with a reasonable solution for relocating Koreans who would like to return to Korea. Only about 5,000 of the 31,000 Koreans still in the oblast have expressed an interest in emigrating.

Ties to Moscow: Asserts Regional Interests

Farkhutdinov has had friendly relations with the federal government, and in the lead-up to the 1999 parliamentary elections he endorsed the pro-Kremlin Unity ticket. However, he is very critical of the center's economic policies toward Sakhalin. Farkhutdinov believes that the federal government is collecting too much money from Sakhalin in the fees it charges for certain services and prices for natural monopolies. In May 1998 he ordered federal agencies to stop collecting money unless they were registered in the federal Justice Ministry and that all money already collected be turned over to the regional budget until it could be determined how the money was being spent. On 25 June 1998 the Sakhalin Oblast Duma passed a measure calling for President Boris Yeltsin to resign voluntarily. Ultimately, the conflict was resolved in July 1998 when Farkhutdinov signed an agreement with then Deputy Prime Minister Boris Nemtsov giving Sakhalin more authority for distributing funds.

Although Farkhutdinov strives to increase Sakhalin's authority and autonomy in relation to the center, he has called for federal assistance in dire instances, such as the devastating earthquake that shook Neftegorsk in May 1995. The governor looked to the federal government for help in resolving the coal miner blockade in July and August 1998 that left Sakhalin without sufficient electricity. The strike greatly damaged the oblast's economy, with electrical shortages forcing the shutdown of cold-storage units at the climax of the fishing season, destroying more than 100 tons of fish. The blockade was finally dispersed when then Deputy Prime Minister Boris Nemtsov agreed to provide federal funds to pay the miners' wage arrears.

On 29 May 1996 Farkhutdinov and then Prime Minister Viktor Chernomyrdin signed a power sharing agreement between Sakhalin Oblast and the Russian Federation. The agreement included land use, education, and international economic ties, as well as other issues.

Relations with Other Regions

Sakhalin belongs to the Far East and Baikal Association, which includes the republics of Buryatia and Sakha (Yakutia); Primorskii and Khabarovsk krais; Amur, Kamchatka, Magadan, and Chita oblasts; the Jewish Autonomous Oblast; and the Koryak and Chukotka autonomous okrugs. The association is trying to cooperate more closely with the countries in the Asian-Pacific region. They are, in particular, interested in broadening economic relations and developing joint ventures for extracting mineral resources in the Far East.

In 1997 Farkhutdinov signed a joint economic cooperation treaty with the governors of Khabarovsk and Primorskii krais, Viktor Ishaev and Yevgenii Nazdratenko. The agreement is in effect until 2005 and stipulates that the three regions will work together to exploit the Sakhalin gas fields and make gas the primary fuel for Far Eastern power plants (*EWI RRR*, 3 July 1997). In theory, these regions could benefit from the exploitation of Sakhalin oil and gas by providing equipment to the firms working on the deposits. In practice, however, few of the enterprises in the area produce equipment of high enough quality to work in the harsh conditions of the Sakhalin shelf.

Foreign Relations: Kuril Islands Conflict

The most significant international issue involving Sakhalin is the conflict regarding ownership of the Kuril Islands, which lie to the east of Sakhalin Island

Igor Pavlovich Farkhutdinov

16 April 1950—Born in Novosibirsk

1972—Graduated from the Krasnoyarsk Polytechnical Institute as an engineer-economist

1972–1977—Worked as an engineer, shift head, and head of shop at the electrical station in Sakhalin

1977–1980—First secretary of the Tymov district committee of the Sakhalin Oblast Komsomol

1980–1981—Head of the department of working and village youth of the Sakhalin CPSU Oblast Committee

1981–1985—Instructor for the department of party-organizational work for the Sakhalin oblast CPSU committee

1985–1991—Chair of the Nevel city executive committee of Sakhalin Oblast

1990—Elected to the Nevel city and Sakhalin Oblast Congresses of People's Deputies

1991–1995—Chair of the Yuzhno-Sakhalinsk city executive committee, mayor of Yuzhno-Sakhalinsk

April 1995—Appointed governor of Sakhalin Oblast

May 1995—Joined Our Home Is Russia (NDR)

January 1996—Appointed to the Federation Council, serving on the Committee for the Budget, Tax Policies, Finance, Currency and Customs Regulations

20 October 1996—Elected governor of Sakhalin Oblast

May 1997—Joined the Council for Local Self-Government in the Russian Federation

Married, with two sons

and north of the Japanese island Hokkaido. Possession of the Kuril Islands has been disputed between Japan and Russia for about three centuries, with current control belonging to Russia under the jurisdiction of Sakhalin Oblast. The Kuril territorial dispute was actually just part of a larger claim that included Sakhalin Island, most of which has been under Russian control since 1875. Disputes regarding the southern part of Sakhalin and the Kurils resulted in armed conflict in the nineteenth century, and further escalated given the territory's strategic importance in the twentieth century. Following World War II, the Soviet Union claimed the southern part of Sakhalin and the Kurils based on negotiations held during the 1945 Yalta conference. However, the Soviet Union and Japan have never officially signed a peace treaty, and thus Japan does not accept the Soviet, and now Russian, territorial claims as valid.

The Kurils lack the natural resource wealth found in the rest of the oblast, and the social welfare of the residents on the islands has deteriorated due to the dispute. Though the waters are filled with fish and crabs, profits from exploiting these resources are not sufficient to develop the islands, which remain mired in poverty. Some of the local administrators on the Kuril Islands have even appealed for Japanese help. In spite of the fact that the strategic importance and money-making potential of the territory has decreased, the long-standing conflict is the key issue inhibiting the development of better relations between Japan and Russia. The Kuril issue is addressed almost entirely on the federal level, with Sakhalin and Farkhutdinov commanding little influence on the islands' fate.

Farkhutdinov is determined to keep the Kurils in Sakhalin. In April 1998 he signed a statement declaring that the Kuril Islands belong to Russia and stated his intention to draft an oblast law on Sakhalin's border. This came out of concern that the federal government would return the islands to Japan. Shortly thereafter Deputy Prime Minister Nemtsov visited Sakhalin and assured the oblast that the federal government had no intention of returning the islands to Japan.

Even though Farkhutdinov is adamant about keeping the Kuril Islands in Sakhalin, he is interested in working together with Japan on mutually beneficial initiatives. In November 1998 he signed a cooperation agreement with Hokkaido. The governor said that the two regions would focus on developing geothermal energy sources around the Kuril Islands to be used as a power source. Farkhutdinov is also interested in removing the visa requirements between Sakhalin and Japan.

Attitudes Toward Business: Developing Natural Resources

Sakhalin is rich in natural resources, such as oil, gas, coal, precious metals, and fish. Farkhutdinov has been active in promoting exploratory and development work in these areas. His main concern regarding the region's natural resource industries has been to ensure that the oblast is the main beneficiary of the profits generated, rather than the Russian government or foreign companies. However, since Sakhalin lacks sufficient financial and technological resources to exploit its resources alone, it is reliant on the federal government and foreign investors for aiding its industrial growth. The region receives several million dollars annually in foreign direct investment (FDI), and in 1997 was in seventh place for FDI among Russia's 89 regions. In spring 1998 the Sakhalin Oblast administration joined several Russian and foreign financial institutions, including UNEKSIMbank and the EBRD, to open an export-import bank in the oblast. The bank's focus is financing promising investment projects in the oblast.

The main focus of most large-scale development activity has been the oil and gas field in the Sea of Okhotsk, which is estimated to contain 1.23 percent of Russia's total hydrocarbon deposits. Several projects for exploiting these resources are in the works, with two—Sakhalin-1 and Sakhalin-2—in the operational stage. Sakhalin-1 and Sakhalin-2 are expected to produce 400 million tons of oil and 700 billion cubic meters of gas over the next 40 years. The Sakhalin-1 consortium is made up of Exxon, Japan's Petroleum

Corporation, Itochu, and Marubeni. Rosneft was initially part of the group, but it dropped out in November 1998 due to its poor financial situation. Sakhalin-2 is under the leadership of Marathon, Mitsui, Mitsubishi, and Shell. Sakhalin-2 produced its first oil in 1999 and Sakhalin-1 expects to come online in 2001. Progress in Sakhalin-1 was slowed by difficulty privatizing Rosneft and then replacing it with different partners. The Sakhalin-1 consortium members have conducted negotiations with the Tokyo Electric Power Corporation and the Tokyo Gas Corporation to build a natural gas pipeline from the Sakhalin shelf to the Japanese city of Niigata. Sakhalin-3 is beginning exploratory work on the 7,000-square-kilometer Kirinskii block. Sakhalin-3, which is being developed by Mobil, Texaco, and Rosneft, is anticipated to yield more than $200 billion. This project won a production-sharing agreement in May 1999.

One of the main obstacles to Sakhalin's economic development is the fact that Russia's production sharing laws do not serve to attract investment. Few project proposals have received production sharing approval and many foreign investors refrain from participating in investment activities out of concern that their initial investments will not be recovered.

Amendments to the original 1995 production-sharing agreement in late 1998 and early 1999 improved the situation somewhat, encouraging many Western firms to conduct negotiations to strengthen their position in the country. However, investors still express strong reservations about Russia's overall business climate and the details of the country's investment legislation.

One of Sakhalin's indigenous peoples, the Nivkhi, have objected to Sakhalin's plans to develop offshore oil deposits, on environmental grounds. These objections have not caused any serious disruption to the oblast's development activities.

SAMARA OBLAST

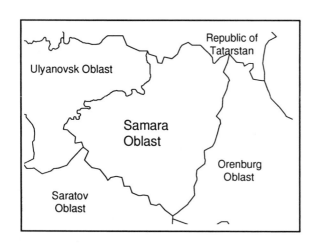

Territory: 53,600 km²
Population (as of 1 January 1998): 3,310,000
Distance from Moscow: 1,098 km

Major Cities:
Samara, *capital* (pop. 1,164,800)
Togliatti (715,100)
Syzran (187,200)
Novokuibyshevsk (115,800)
Chapaevsk (83,500)

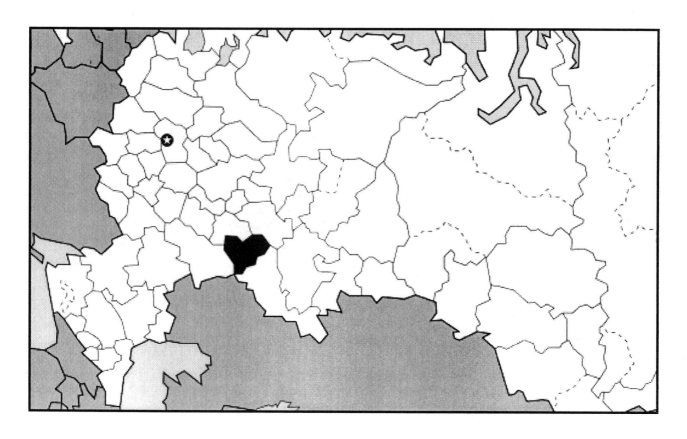

Basic Facts

Population (as of 1 Jan. 1998): 3,310,000 (2.25% of Russian total)

Ethnic breakdown (1989 census): Russians 83.4%, Chuvash 3.6%, Mordvins 3.6%, Tatars 3.5%, Ukrainians 2.5%

Urban population (as of 1 Jan. 1998): 80.5% (Russia overall: 73.1%)

Student population (as of 1 Sept. 1997): 218 per 10,000 (Russia overall: 208/10,000)

Pensioner population (1997): 25.65% (Russia overall: 25.96%)

Percent of population with higher education (1989 census): 11.2% (Russia overall: 11.3%)

Percent of population working in (1997): Industry: 30.8% (Russian average: 23.0%); Agriculture: 7.7% (13.7%); Trade: 11.7% (13.5%); Culture: 11.6% (13.3%)

Average monthly personal income in July 1998: 945.5 new rubles (Russian average: 891.7 new rubles)

Average monthly personal expenses in July 1998: 1,008.6 new rubles (Russian average: 684.9 new rubles)

Average monthly subsistence requirement in 1998: 406 new rubles (Russian average: 438 new rubles)

Consumer price index (as of July 1998): 107 (Russia overall = 100)

Budgetary revenues (1997): 9,845.4 billion rubles (Russia overall: 433,378.2 billion rubles)

Budgetary expenditures (1997): 9,920.0 billion rubles (Russia overall: 468,111.6 billion rubles)

Industrial production as percentage of all Russian production (Jan.–Aug. 1998): 3.25%

Proportion of loss-making enterprises (as of July 1998): 39.7% (Russia overall: 50.4%)

Number of enterprises which have wage arrears (as of 1 Sept. 1998): 1,005 (0.74% of Russian total)

Agricultural production as percentage of all Russian production (1997): 2.23%

Number of private farms (as of 1 Jan. 1998): 4,028 (1.47% of Russian total)

Capital investment (1997): 8,929.6 billion rubles (Russia overall: 408,797 billion rubles)

Sources of investment (1997): federal budget: 3.5% (Russian average: 10.2%); regional budget: 7.9% (10.5%); extra-budgetary funds: 88.6% (79.3%)

Foreign investment (1997): 25,280,000 USD (Russia overall: 12,294,734,000 USD)

Number of joint ventures (1997): 99 (0.67% of Russian total)

Fixed capital investment in joint ventures and foreign companies (1997): 295,995 million rubles (Russia overall: 16,265.4 billion rubles)

Number of small businesses (as of 1 July 1998): 21,700 (2.50% of Russian total)

Number of enterprises privatized in 1997: 51 (1.86% of Russian total), including those which used to be municipal property: 37.3% (Russian average: 66.4%); regional property: 47.0% (20.0%); federal property: 15.7% (13.6%)

Number of telephones per 100 families (1997): in cities: 37.6 (Russian average: 49.2); in villages: 22.4 (19.8)

Brief Overview

Samara Oblast, located in the lower Volga River area, covers a largely level plain on the Volga left bank and a small part of the hilly right bank. Samara borders Orenburg, Saratov, and Ulyanovsk oblasts, and the Republic of Tatarstan. The administrative center, Samara (named Kuibyshev between 1935 and 1991), was founded in 1586 as a fortress and is situated at the confluence of the Samara and Volga rivers. It has excellent links with European Russia and Siberia by train and along the Volga by ship.

The nearby natural oak woodlands and steppe have been plowed since the 18th century, leaving rich black soils that suffer severely from erosion. The oblast has some reserves of oil, gas, limestone, schist, and other raw materials. The region, is one of the most industrialized in the country and one of the wealthiest. It is ranked first in machinery production—70 percent of all the country's automobiles are produced by the Togliatti-based AvtoVAZ Company, which is also the largest tax debtor in the country. Samara is home to Russia's largest aluminum processing plant Sameko (Samara Metallurgical Plant). Other industries include chemicals and petrochemicals, non-ferrous metallurgy, metal processing, and defense production. The huge Zhiguli hydroelectric power station provides energy.

The oblast has adopted investment legislation that, along with the governor's policies, makes it very attractive for investment: investment risk had decreased by 21 points (the country's 8th biggest decrease) since 1997, according to the *Ekspert's* 1998 regional survey. The same study ranked Samara 4th according to direct foreign investment—62.1 million dollars in 1997 (1.59% of the country's total)—and 10th according to capital investment—8,511 billion old rubles in 1997 (2.47%). Pepsi International Bottlers, General Motors, Switzerland's Nestlé, France's Danone, and other multinational companies have invested in the region. The oblast has recently adopted a land code that, though prohibiting foreigners from buying land, allows them to enter into long-term leases.

According to a 1998 survey by *Ekspert* magazine, the oblast ranked 7th among Russia's 89 regions in terms of investment potential and 10th in terms of investment risk. A 1998 survey by Bank Austria ranked the oblast 5th in terms of investment climate.

Electoral History

2000 Gubernatorial Election
Titov: 53.25%
Tarkhov Alyans oil company vi ce president): 29.23%
Zvyagin: 9.09%
Nikitin: 1.96%

2000 Presidential Election
Putin: 40.86%
Zyuganov: 29.85%
Titov: 20.24%
Yavlinskii: 2.79%
Zhirinovsky: 1.75%
Tuleev: 1.07%
Turnout: 70.03% (Russia overall: 68.64%)

1999 Parliamentary Elections
Communist Party of the Russian Federation: 26.13%
Union of Right Forces: 22.13%
Unity: 19.98%
Zhirinovsky Bloc: 5.42%
Fatherland–All Russia: 4.86%
Yabloko: 3.57%
In single-mandate districts: 1 Communist Party of
   the Russian Federation, 1 Union of Right Forces,
   3 independent
Turnout: 61.97% (Russia overall: 61.85%)

1996 Gubernatorial Election
Titov (incumbent): 63.39%
Romanov (State Duma deputy, KPRF): 29.86%
Chupshev: 1.50%
Turnout: 50.73%

1996 Presidential Election
Yeltsin: 36.13%/51.95% (first round/second round)
Zyuganov: 35.17%/42.69%
Lebed: 11.65%
Yavlinskii: 6.16%
Zhirinovsky: 5.55%
Turnout: 69.85%/71.35% (Russia overall: 69.67%/
   68.79%)

1995 Parliamentary Elections
Communist Party of the Russian Federation: 22.27%
Liberal Democratic Party of Russia: 12.26%
Our Home Is Russia: 11.94%
Yabloko: 5.05%
Congress of Russian Communities: 4.37%
Women of Russia: 3.99%
Communists–Workers' Russia: 3.91%

Party of Workers' Self-Government: 3.61%

Forward, Russia: 3.24%

In single-mandate districts: 2 Communist Party of the Russian Federation, 2 Our Home Is Russia, 1 Agrarian Party of Russia

Turnout: 63.57% (Russia overall: 64.37%)

1993 Constitutional Referendum

"Yes"—55.4%   "No"—42.0%

1993 Parliamentary Elections

Liberal Democratic Party of Russia:
19.67%

Communist Party of the Russian Federation:
16.44%

Russia's Choice: 16.29%

Women of Russia: 10.09%

Yabloko: 8.75%

Democratic Party of Russia: 6.74%

Agrarian Party of Russia: 6.33%

Party of Russian Unity and Concord: 5.74%

In single-mandate districts: 1 Women of Russia, 4 independent

From electoral associations: 1 Russia's Choice, 1 Liberal Democratic Party of Russia, 1 Democratic Party of Russia

Turnout: 53.39% (Russia overall: 54.34%)

1991 Presidential Election

Yeltsin: 63.98%

Ryzhkov: 13.62%

Tuleev: 4.70%

Makashov: 4.49%

Zhirinovsky: 3.78%

Bakatin: 2.11%

Turnout: 85.43% (Russia overall: 76.66%)

Regional Political Institutions

Executive:
Governor, 4–year term
Konstantin Alekseevich Titov, elected December 1996
Ul. Molodogvardaya, 210; Samara, 443006
Tel 7(846–2) 32–22–68;
Fax 7(846–2) 32–13–40
Federation Council in Moscow:
7(095) 926–68–26, 292–12–83

Legislative:
Unicameral
Oblast Duma—25 members, 4–year term, elected December 1997
Chairman—Leon Iosifovich Kovalskii, elected December 1997

Regional Politics

Ambitious Market Reformer

After ruling Samara since 1991, Konstantin Titov resigned from the governorship following a devastating defeat in the 2000 presidential election. He took only about 1.5 percent of the national vote in the March poll. More ominously, he came in third in Samara Oblast, with 20.5 percent, trailing both Putin and the Communist candidate Zyuganov. The goal of the resignation was to move up the gubernatorial elections from December 2000 to 2 July, effectively ensuring another victory. Titov essentially renounced power only as a tactical move to strengthen his position. Despite his loss in the presidential campaign, he continued to have wide respect as governor and won a second term with more than 50 percent of the vote.

In running against Putin, Titov made a powerful enemy in the newly elected Russian president. During the campaign, he frequently denounced Putin's prosecution of the war in Chechnya. Titov ran as a newcomer in the national arena who would support a consistently liberal platform. However, when Titov announced his candidacy for the Russian presidency, his allies in the right-wing parties declined to endorse him and many shifted their support to Yeltsin's own choice, Putin.

Titov strongly backs market reform, claiming that his top goal is to build capitalism in Samara (www.adm. samara.ru). Titov wants to turn Samara into "Chicago-on-the Volga," a city with worldwide fame that is able to attract investors with little effort. The governor defines his management style as authoritarian and admires the political leadership of Peter Stolypin, Franklin Roosevelt, Winston Churchill, and Charles de Gaulle.

Titov won his first election to the post of governor in December 1996, defeating the leader of the Communist party oblast committee, Duma deputy Valentin Romanov, 62 to 31 percent. The future of the oblast's giant automobile producer, AvtoVAZ, which had a $2 billion debt to the federal government, was among the top issues in the elections. Both candidates were against the federal government's plans to bankrupt the plant that makes up to 70 percent of Russia's cars, but Titov's Moscow connections provided him with a better chance to lobby for AvtoVAZ's interests. Titov also increased his popularity by paying pensions on time and raising state employees' salaries 30 percent during the summer before elections.

Executive Platform: Powerful, Liberal Regionalism

Since leaving the Communist Party in 1991, Titov has belonged to several political organizations, usually backing those holding the most influence at a given time, yet avoiding communist and nationalist organizations. In 1992 he joined the newly formed Russian Movement for Democratic Reforms and became a member of its Political Council. After the movement's poor showing in the 1993 parliamentary elections Titov switched to Yegor Gaidar's Russia's Choice, which had the largest number of seats in the State Duma. In June 1995, at Gaidar's advice, he joined Prime Minister Viktor Chernomyrdin's Our Home Is Russia (NDR). He stayed with this movement until the beginning of 1999, serving as NDR deputy chairman and the head of the Samara regional branch, which is roughly the size of the oblast's Communist Party organization. On 28 January 1999, Titov announced the formation of his own bloc of regional leaders, called Voice of Russia (see Relations with Other Regions for details).

Titov is one of the most powerful regional executives on the national scene. He has been very influential among other regional executives, and has long figured among regional politicians with the potential to move to the federal level, a good example of the charismatic figures that have begun to characterize Russian regional leadership. Titov feels it is extremely important for Moscow to recognize the importance of Russia's regions when designing its policies. He has expressed this opinion multiple times in regard to seeking solutions for Russia's current economic and financial crisis.

Titov is willing to consider some changes in Russian borders, although he believes that the Kuril Islands should remain part of the country. He was one of the signatories of a letter supporting a Russian-Belarusan union in May 1997.

Policies: Successful Market Reforms

The majority of Titov's policies have been focused on advancing market reform and the construction of capitalism. He is against indexing salaries and regulating prices, and has been reasonably successful at transitioning his oblast to market economics without resorting to these tactics. As a governor who backed Gaidar's policies, Titov led Samara through an extensive privatization program. By June 1995, 80 percent of the former state enterprises had been sold and 61 percent of the region's workforce was employed in the private sector. As an incentive for investors, the oblast offers tax breaks and grants privileges to banks and other financial institutions that provide credit for investment projects.

In June 1998 the oblast Duma approved a law to legalize the purchase and sale of farmland. The law allows for land to be owned, inherited, and leased, and it can be confiscated if it is not used for its designated purpose or is exploited in a manner that is ecologically harmful. Titov is a strong supporter of the law, though he had hoped for legislation that would allow the sale of farmland to foreigners. Although foreigners cannot purchase land in the region, they are permitted to rent it.

Titov feels that boosting the economic performance of Russia's regions will be impossible if regional governments are not allocated a larger share of Russia's tax revenues. In accordance with his devotion to a liberalized economy, in April 1998 Titov spoke against a bill initiated in the Federation Council that would place the Central Bank under the control of the government and Duma.

Relationships Between Key Players: Opposition from Oblast Legislature, Mayor

In December 1997 elections were held for the oblast Duma. Prior to the elections, in October, Titov removed the head of the regional TV broadcasting company Samara, Anatolii Semenov, and replaced him with Aleksandr Knyazev, a famous tabloid journalist. Many viewed this as Titov's ploy to ensure that the candidates he preferred had good TV coverage before the oblast legislative elections. However, good television coverage was not enough to ensure a Titov-backed legislature. Only four deputies were reelected, which was a disappointment for Titov who had good relations with the former deputies. After the elections he expressed concern that the new legislature would be less likely to support his initiatives. Among the winners were Speaker Leon Kovalskii and Samara Mayor Georgii Limanskii, who won his mayoral seat without Titov's support. In 2000, Limanski considered running against Titov for the governor's seat, but ultimately decided he could not beat him.

The giant AvtoVAZ automobile plant dominates the

oblast economy and causes many of the region's problems. AvtoVAZ manufactures 70 percent of Russia's cars, yet also has incurred a debt of over $2 billion dollars to the federal government. The inefficient producer has also been plagued by a corrupt distribution system. Boris Berezovskii's Logovaz, AvtoVAZ's distributor, has eaten up profits on many of the cars produced. On 20 February 1999, as part of wider campaign against Berezovskii, the Russian general procurator announced that it was opening a corruption investigation against AvtoVAZ, many of whose directors allegedly received kickbacks from their arrangement with Berezovskii.

In August 1997 AvtoVAZ finally reached an agreement with its two largest creditors on paying back its debts over the next ten years. The shareholders agreed to give the federal government 51 percent of the plant's stock as collateral against its debt, and in turn the government would allow the firm to repay its debt over the next ten years. The stocks could be sold if AvtoVAZ missed two payments in a row. By August 1998, the plant was having difficulty making these payments, but the federal government is extremely unlikely to bankrupt the facility since it would throw thousands of people out of work. It is also unlikely to find a buyer for the plant's shares.

Titov has been very active in trying to save AvtoVAZ. In January 1998 General Motors' German division, Adam Opel AG, announced its decision to assemble cars at the AvtoVAZ Togliatti plant. The initial step would be to assemble 30,000 Opels a year and then increase production to 200,000 annually. The August 1998 crisis postponed the development of this project, however, and by summer 2000 GM still had no plans to move ahead.

Although the deal with Opel has been delayed, the crisis has generally been good for AvtoVAZ because it makes imported cars extremely expensive compared to the factory's own output. The plant produced 600,000 cars instead of the planned 720,000 in 1998 (1997 production was 749,500). Planned production for 1999 was 675,000 (*KD*, 20 January 1999). AvtoVAZ imports about 30 percent of its parts, so it cannot insulate itself completely from fluctuations in the exchange rate.

Titov has taken a personal role in the development of other oblast industrial sectors as well. He has extensive relations with the directors of enterprises involved in the oblast's military-industrial complex and the directors of new commercial structures, and devotes a lot of attention to the conversion of the region's defense enterprises. As of August 1998 the federal government owed Samara defense plants 769.4 million rubles. Titov encouraged defense plants to back

the newly formed national group, the League to Support Defense Enterprises, for lobbying the government to make good on its debts.

The governor is also building an oblast gold reserve in cooperation with Sakha (Yakutia). The reserve will be used as collateral for winning credits to increase the technological level of the oblast's enterprises.

Ties to Moscow: Yeltsin Supporter, Putin Challenger

Titov was a faithful Yeltsin supporter, providing him with excellent connections in the capital. During the August 1991 coup attempt against Gorbachev, Titov quit the Communist party and denounced the coup plotters. After the coup was defeated, Yeltsin named Titov to head the Samara Oblast administration.

In August 1997 Titov signed a power-sharing agreement with President Yeltsin. The agreement includes 13 supplemental protocols clarifying the political and economic relations between Samara and the federal government, including investment and banking policies. Titov claimed to be against the signing of such treaties in principle, yet concluded this agreement in hopes of ensuring good relations with Moscow.

Titov's close relationship with Yeltsin did not keep him from speaking his mind. Titov criticized the federal government on several occasions, finding particular fault with its lackluster support for domestic producers. In July 1998 Titov accused the federal government of instituting a dictatorship after it raised the value-added tax on necessities from 10 to 20 percent, ignoring the fact that both the Russian Duma and Federation Council were opposed to the idea. Titov appealed this action, and in October the Supreme Court ruled that it was unconstitutional.

Titov has also asserted that federal budget policies are reducing the economic potential of Russia's regions (*RFE/RL*, 17 December 1997). He and other governors have complained that the budget and new tax legislation proposed by the government for 1998 assigned all revenues from taxes that are easy to collect to the federal government, leaving the regional authorities to depend on revenue from taxes with difficult collection procedures. Additionally, Titov feels that Russia's donor regions, an elite group to which Samara belongs, should receive greater rights and benefits than recipient regions. Titov has tried for many years to extract greater contributions from the center.

Titov would also like to alter the structure of federal governance. He appealed many times to NDR leadership to initiate constitutional amendments to establish the position of a vice-president who would simultaneously head the Federation Council (*OMRI RRR*, 6 March 1997).

Even though Titov held a high position in NDR, he was extremely critical of Viktor Chernomyrdin. In May 1997 he claimed that Prime Minister Chernomyrdin was conducting a policy contradictory to Our Home Is Russia's platform and called for greater support for domestic producers and a simplification of the taxation system. Titov also stated that NDR's agenda was considerably less attractive to producers and entrepreneurs than ideas proposed by Aleksandr Lebed.

A year later, during the April 1998 congress of NDR, Titov suggested that the movement should consider nominating other candidates besides Chernomyrdin as president in 2000. When Chernomyrdin was nominated again to the post of prime minister in August 1998, Titov was skeptical of Chernomyrdin's ability to carry out an effective program for confronting the country's economic crisis. Accordingly, Titov was supportive of Yevgenii Primakov from his initial nomination to the post of prime minister in September 1998. There were many rumors that Titov would join Primakov's cabinet, yet Titov refuted all such discussion, announcing that he had no intention of becoming involved in national politics.

This was not Titov's first invitation to join the national political leadership. In March 1997, before engaging Boris Nemtsov to join his cabinet, Chernomyrdin offered the post of first deputy prime minister to Titov. Titov says that he rejected the offer because he had just won election as governor in December and wanted to continue working to increase investment in the region. He also stressed his important role as chairman of the Federation Council Budget Committee, which is charged with developing "normal financial relations between the center and the regions" (*OG*, 20–26 March 1998). If he joined the government, Titov would be compelled to defend the center's policies.

Titov rejected an offer to join the federal government a second time in August 1998, when Chernomyrdin was nominated once again to the post of prime minister. Before his nomination was rejected by the Duma, Chernomyrdin invited Titov and Krasnoyarsk Krai Governor Aleksandr Lebed to be deputy prime ministers in the new government.

In late March 2000, Titov announced his willingness to consider a federal post. As a Putin critic, however, Titov was considered unlikely to win an appointment in the new government (*RFE/RL Russian Election Report*, 7 April 2000).

Relations with Other Regions: Launches Own Party

Titov was one of the few governors to explicitly state that he was not going to join Moscow Mayor Yurii Luzhkov's Fatherland party. Titov said that he considered himself "right of center," while the mayor has backed a philosophy that was "left of center."

Instead, Titov announced the formation of his own regional bloc at a 28 January 1999 press conference. Thirty members of the Federation Council signed an appeal calling on the public to support the new group, provisionally called Voice of Russia, on 17 February. The governors who joined Titov were: Penza's Vasilii Bochkarev, Kaliningrad's Leonid Gorbenko, Perm's Gennadii Igumnov, Marii El's Vyacheslav Kislitsyn, Khakassia's Aleksei Lebed, Chukotka's Aleksandr Nazarov, Tver's Vladimir Platov, Vologda's Vyacheslav Pozgalev, Tyumen's Leonid Roketskii, Kirov's Vladimir Sergeenkov, Chelyabinsk's Petr Sumin, Kemerovo's Aman Tuleev, Magadan's Valentin Tsvetkov, and Rostov's Vladimir Chub. Additionally, fourteen regional legislative leaders signed on as well (*KD*, 19 February 1999).

The purpose of the bloc was to win seats in the December 1999 State Duma elections. Titov wanted the bloc to focus on issues of federalism, with the ultimate goal of improving the conditions of all Russian regions "to the level of Tatarstan." The text of the 17 February document criticized the current federal system as a unitary state in which the federal government robs the rich regions without giving the poor ones what they need. The current federal government does not work effectively in the regions, the statement argued, so the bloc hoped to fundamentally change the membership of the lower house. Since the bloc was not registered one year before the State Duma elections, however, it had to seek a partner that was registered in order to compete on the party list section of the ballot. Titov considered an alliance with Viktor Chernomyrdin's Our Home Is Russia, to which many of the governors belonged. (One of the main ideologists and organizers of the bloc was Aleksandr Shokhin, the former leader of the NDR State Duma faction.) Chernomyrdin, however, was skeptical of Titov's activities. The new bloc also contemplated alliances with Tatarstan President Mintimer Shaimiev and St. Petersburg Governor Vladimir Yakovlev's All

Russia movement and Moscow Mayor Yurii Luzhkov's Fatherland, but the latter two groups joined forces without Titov. Rapidly losing support, Titov led Voice of Russia into the Union of Right Forces, an electoral alliance built around the center-right bloc created by Yegor Gaidar, Anatolii Chubais, and Boris Nemtsov for the parliamentary elections. Titov's ambitions to hold national office suffered a devastating setback with his poor performance in the March 2000 presidential vote.

Voice of Russia's main financial backing came from Mikhail Khodorkovskii's Yukos and Oleg Deripaska's Siberian Aluminum. In June 1999 Titov convinced Khodorkovskii to transfer the registration of Yukos-RM, an oil refining subsidiary of the Yukos oil company, from Moscow to Samara. This meant that taxes generated by Yukos-RM would go to Samara rather than Moscow city. Khodorkovskii's move was viewed as entirely political, simultaneously strengthening Titov's position and weakening that of Moscow Mayor Yurii Luzhkov.

Samara belongs to the Greater Volga regional association, which includes the republics of Tatarstan, Mordovia, Chuvashia, and Marii El, and Astrakhan, Volgograd, Nizhnii Novgorod, Penza, Saratov, and Ulyanovsk oblasts. The Volga region is relatively prosperous, boasting three donor regions—Tatarstan, Nizhnii Novgorod, and Samara.

Foreign Relations: Recipient of EBRD, World Bank, and U.S. Loans

Titov has been active on the international scene, having had contact with many prominent foreign diplomats. In September 1997 German President Roman Hertzog traveled to Samara to participate in the oblast's Day of the German Economy Festival. Titov said that the event was aimed at consolidating the region's contacts with Germany (*RFE/RL*, 5 September 1997). U.S. Vice President Al Gore visited Samara in September 1997 when meeting with then Prime Minister Viktor Chernomyrdin. During his visit, Gore offered Samara Oblast a $10 million U.S. loan in 1998 for agricultural production and land reform (*KD*, 25 September 1997). Samara was one of four regions than included in the U.S.'s Regional Investment Initiative. Titov also met with U.S. President Bill Clinton on his September 1998 visit to Russia.

As a result of Titov's efforts, Samara has been the target of various foreign development projects. The oblast received a $33 million loan from the European Bank for Reconstruction and Development to purchase buses and renovate public transport and a similar loan from the World Bank for the same purpose.

In March 1999 Titov visited Ukraine to meet with Ukrainian President Leonid Kuchma. The two leaders discussed expanding economic cooperation between Russian and Ukrainian regions, focusing on projects such as Sea Launch, joint production of AN-70 and AN-140 airplanes, and agricultural cooperation.

Titov was one of the few regional leaders who publicly spoke out against sending Russian peacekeeping troops to Kosovo in June 1999. He argued that the mission would be too expensive and that Russia simply did not have the funds to cover the estimated $70 million in expenses.

Attitudes Toward Business: Successfully Promotes Active Western Involvement

Attracting investment and developing business have been among Titov's top priorities as governor. The oblast boasts two hundred investment projects, and Samara is ranked fifth in Russia for its volume of foreign investment. In December 1997 the Samara Oblast administration developed a draft law to support small business in the region. The bill defines procedures by which the administration can give small businesses buildings and land, allow them to participate in competitions for state orders, and protect them from unfair competition. The oblast also offers tax breaks as an incentive to financial institutions to offer credit to entrepreneurs (see Policies).

Numerous Western firms are active in the region. For example, Pepsi International Bottlers opened a $33 million bottling plant in Samara in June 1997. The plant has the largest capacity for non-alcoholic beverage production in the country. The Swiss company Nestlé owns two chocolate factories in the region, and in February 1999, announced plans to invest an additional $10 million.

Other Western companies in Samara include Boeing, Daimler-Benz, British Aerospace, Reynolds, Audi, Volvo, Opel, and Mitsubishi (*NG*, 10 February 1999).

In addition to the legislative initiatives designed to promote business, Titov has also encouraged the development of financial institutions to provide credits for enterprise growth. Five Samara banks, Inkombank, Sberbank, Rosestbank, Rossiiskii Kredit, and Samaraagrobank, are working together with the Euro-

Konstantin Alekseevich Titov

30 October 1944—Born in Moscow

1962–1963—Machine operator at an aviation factory

1968—Graduated from the Kuibyshev Aviation Institute as an engineer-mechanic in the technical operations of aviation motors

1968–1969—Worked as an aircraft mechanic

1968–1970—Member of the district executive committee and the city Komsomol committee

1969–1970—Deputy secretary of the Komsomol factory committee

1970—Joined the CPSU

1970–1973—Assistant manager of the student and young people's branch of the Kuibyshev Komsomol city committee

1973–1975—Secretary of the Komsomol committee at the Kuibyshev Planning Institute

1975–1978—Earned a candidate's degree in the economics and industry department of the Kuibyshev Planning Institute

1978–1987—Worked at the Kuibyshev Planning Institute, rising through the ranks to become the director of an economics laboratory

1987–1990—Assistant to the general director of economics at the Kuibyshev branch of the Soviet-Bulgarian enterprise, Informatika

March 1990—Elected to the Kuibyshev city council, and in April, elected chairman

31 August 1991—Appointed governor of Samara Oblast

1992—Joined the Russian Movement for Democratic Reforms and became a member of the Saratov regional council; in 1993 became a member of the movement's political council

1993—Joined Yegor Gaidar's Russia's Choice (later renamed Russia's Democratic Choice)

12 December 1993—Elected to the Federation Council, and from January 1994 to January 1996 served on the Committee for Federation Affairs, Federal Agreements, and Regional Policies

June 1994—Joined Russia's Democratic Choice's political council

April 1995—Joined Our Home Is Russia (NDR), and in May 1995 was elected first deputy chair

January 1996—Appointed to the Federation Council, serving as chair of the Budget Committee

1 December 1996—Elected governor of Samara Oblast

April 1998—Released from post as first deputy chair of NDR and elected deputy chair

28 January 1999—Organized Voice of Russia bloc

26 March 2000—Won 1.5% of vote in Russian presidential election

4 April 2000—Resigned governorship of Samara Oblast to seek reelection in gubernatorial vote moved up to 2 July 2000

2 July 2000—Elected governor of Samar Oblast

Loves soccer, hunting, art, music, and photography

Married with a son and grandson

pean Bank for Reconstruction and Development to give loans to small businesses in the region. This program has loaned more than $10 million to small businesses in the city of Samara and almost $9 million to businesses in the oblast.

Internet Sites in the Region

http://www.samara.ru/
The Samara server includes information on Governor Titov, the oblast's charter, statistical data on the region, comprehensive election analyses, administration phone numbers, and an interesting trip report by Webster University Professor Daniel C. Hellinger, who visited the city in the summer of 1996 to help Samara State University set up a legal studies program with funding from the Eurasia Foundation.

http://www.adm.samara.ru/index.asp
This website features the Samara Oblast administration, including an address by Governor Titov and detailed, up-to-date information about his policies, views, approaches, and addresses. Specific information is also available for other institutions in the oblast and details about regional life.

http://www.duma.sam-reg.ru/
This page belongs to the Samara Oblast Duma. It includes a listing of Duma members, committees and committee members, and laws passed since 1995.

http://www.vaz.tlt.ru/
This website belongs to the AvtoVAZ automobile manufacturer in Samara Oblast. It features detailed information about the firm's products as well as links to several major car manufacturers both in and outside of Russia.

SARATOV OBLAST

Territory: 100,200 km²
Population (as of 1 January 1998):
2,724,000
Distance from Moscow: 858 km

Major Cities:
Saratov, *capital* (pop. 883,900)
Balakovo (207,700)
Engels (188,600)
Balashov (95,700)
Volsk (66,700)
Rtishchevo (43,400)

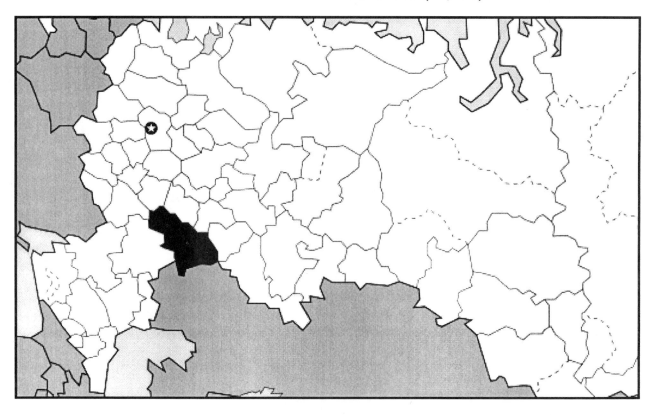

Basic Facts

Population (as of 1 Jan. 1998): 2,724,000 (1.85% of Russian total)

Ethnic breakdown (1989 census): Russians 85.6%, Ukrainians 3.8%, Kazakhs 2.7%, Tatars 2.0%

Urban population (as of 1 Jan. 1998): 73.2% (Russia overall: 73.1%)

Student population (as of 1 Sept. 1997): 222 per 10,000 (Russia overall: 208/10,000)

Pensioner population (1997): 26.28% (Russia overall: 25.96%)

Percent of population with higher education (1989 census): 11.0% (Russia overall: 11.3%)

Percent of population working in (1997): Industry: 21.6% (Russian average: 23.0%); Agriculture: 19.1% (13.7%); Trade: 12.0% (13.5%); Culture: 12.2% (13.3%)

Average monthly personal income in July 1998: 585.8 new rubles (Russian average: 891.7 new rubles)

Average monthly personal expenses in July 1998: 440.7 new rubles (Russian average: 684.9 new rubles)

Average monthly subsistence requirement in 1998: 359 new rubles (Russian average: 438 new rubles)

Consumer price index (as July 1998): 87 (Russia overall = 100)

Budgetary revenues (1997): 4,996.8 billion rubles (Russia overall: 433,378.2 billion rubles)

Budgetary expenditures (1997): 6,213.5 billion rubles (Russia overall: 468,111.6 billion rubles)

Industrial production as percentage of all Russian production (Jan.–Aug. 1998): 0.90%

Proportion of loss-making enterprises (as of July 1998): 41.2% (Russia overall: 50.4%)

Number of enterprises which have wage arrears (as of 1 Sept. 1998): 2,153 (1.59% of Russian total)

Agricultural production as percentage of all Russian production (1997): 2.55%

Number of private farms (as of 1 Jan. 1998): 8,834 (3.22% of Russian total)

Capital investment (1997): 5,313.5 billion rubles (Russia overall: 408,797 billion rubles)

Sources of investment (1997): federal budget: 10.4% (Russian average: 10.2%); regional budget: 26.7% (10.5%); extra-budgetary funds: 62.9% (79.3%)

Foreign investment (1997): 28,078,000 USD (Russia overall: 12,294,734,000 USD)

Number of joint ventures (1997): 57 (0.39% of Russian total)

Fixed capital investment in joint ventures and foreign companies (1997): 192,951 million rubles (Russia overall: 16,265.4 billion rubles)

Number of small businesses (as of 1 July 1998): 13,100 (1.51% of Russian total)

Number of enterprises privatized in 1997: 119 (4.34% of Russian total), including those which used to be municipal property: 79.0% (Russian average: 66.4%); regional property: 6.7% (20.0%); federal property: 14.3% (13.6%)

Number of telephones per 100 families (1997): in cities: 31.6 (Russian average: 49.2); in villages: 18.3 (19.8)

Brief Overview

Saratov Oblast is located on the southeastern Russian plain in the lower Volga River valley and borders Volgograd, Tambov, Penza, Samara, Voronezh, and Ulyanovsk oblasts and Kazakhstan. Most of the region's territory is steppe, with natural woods and parks occupying about 6 percent of oblast land.

The area is rich in mineral resources, boasting oil and gas fields, sands, mineral paints, cement, and other building materials. Saratov Oblast is a major industrial area of the Volga region and houses over 500 industrial enterprises that manufacture various products. The most developed sectors are machine building (high-tech electronics and equipment); the chemical and petrochemical industries; energy; and food processing. The cities of Saratov, Engels, and Balakovo are the major industrial centers. Saratov, which manufactures about 50 percent of the region's industrial products, is also an important scientific and cultural center—it has 13 institutions of higher education, including one of the oldest Russian universities and the third-largest conservatory.

According to a 1998 survey by *Ekspert* magazine, the oblast ranked 21st among Russia's 89 regions in terms of investment potential and 6th in terms of investment risk. A 1998 survey by Bank Austria ranked the oblast 21st in terms of investment climate.

Electoral History

2000 Presidential Election
Putin: 57.99%
Zyuganov: 28.36%
Yavlinskii: 3.78%
Zhirinovsky: 2.17%
Tuleev: 1.75%
Turnout: 74.95% (Russia overall: 68.64%)

2000 Gubernatorial Election
Ayatskov (incumbent): 67.32%
Karaulov: 9.66%
Tonakayan: 1.05%
Turnout: 75.13%

1999 Parliamentary Elections
Communist Party of the Russian Federation: 30.44%
Unity: 22.73%
Fatherland–All Russia: 8.39%
Union of Right Forces: 7.04%
Zhirinovsky Bloc: 5.53%
Our Home Is Russia: 5.33%
Yabloko: 4.28%
In single-mandate districts: 1 Fatherland–All Russia, 2 Communist Party of the Russian Federation, 1 Our Home Is Russia
Turnout: 68.99% (Russia overall: 61.85%)

1996 Gubernatorial Election
Ayatskov (incumbent): 80.19%
Gordeev (advisor to KPRF Central Committee chairman): 16.06%
Pavlov (Forward, Russia): 0.61%
Turnout: 56.53%

1996 Presidential Election
Zyuganov: 41.59%/49.94% (first round/second round)
Yeltsin: 28.38%/44.08%
Lebed: 12.76%
Zhirinovsky: 7.09%
Yavlinskii: 5.28%
Turnout: 73.46%/73.83% (Russia overall: 69.67%/ 68.79%)

1995 Parliamentary Elections
Communist Party of the Russian Federation: 28.26%
Liberal Democratic Party of Russia: 15.46%
Our Home Is Russia: 7.96%
Communists–Workers' Russia: 5.79%
Derzhava: 4.67%
Agrarian Party of Russia: 3.96%
Yabloko: 3.91%
Women of Russia: 3.73%
Russia's Democratic Choice: 3.10%
My Fatherland: 3.09%
In single-mandate districts: 3 Communist Party of the Russian Federation, 1 My Fatherland
Turnout: 68.07% (Russia overall: 64.37%)

1993 Constitutional Referendum
"Yes"—50.0%   "No"—48.0%

1993 Parliamentary Elections
Liberal Democratic Party of Russia: 26.63%
Communist Party of the Russian Federation: 15.28%
Russia's Choice: 12.30%
Women of Russia: 9.90%
Yabloko: 8.59%
Agrarian Party of Russia: 7.64%

Democratic Party of Russia: 6.45%

Party of Russian Unity and Concord: 5.68%

In single-mandate districts: 1 Russia's Choice, 1 Liberal Democratic Party of Russia, 1 Communist Party of the Russian Federation, 1 National Republican Party of Russia

From electoral associations: 1 Communist Party of the Russian Federation, 1 Russia's Choice

Turnout: 59.44% (Russia overall: 54.34%)

1991 Presidential Election

Yeltsin: 55.73%

Ryzhkov: 18.67%

Zhirinovsky: 7.91%

Tuleev: 7.16%

Makashov: 4.84%

Bakatin: 2.55%

Turnout: 79.02% (Russia overall: 76.66%)

Regional Political Institutions

Executive:

    Governor, 4-year term

    Dmitrii Fedorovich Ayatskov, elected

    September 1996, March 2000

        Moskovskaya Ul., 72; Saratov, 410042

        Tel 7(845–2) 72–20–86;

        Fax 7(845–2) 24–20–89

        Federation Council in Moscow:

        7(095) 292–68–32, 926–62–71

Legislative:

    Unicameral

    Oblast Duma—35 members, 5-year term, elected August–November 1997

    Chairman—Aleksandr Petrovich Kharitonov, elected June 1994, September 1997

Regional Politics

Reformer Seeks Media Attention via "Exotic" Initiatives

Dmitrii Ayatskov is one of Russia's most prominent regional leaders, winning national renown for promoting land reform and legalized prostitution. Despite his reformist ambitions, Ayatskov won a landslide victory in a region that until his election had generally voted for Communists. Former *Segodnya* journalist Tatyana

Malkina describes him as "smart, ambitious, business-like, charming and sexy" (NNS).

Ayatskov admits that his "exotic" initiatives (such as legalizing brothels, supplying bikes to local bureaucrats, and abolishing drunk tanks) were mostly just publicity stunts. "Otherwise nobody in Moscow would hear about Saratov," he claimed. "I didn't kill anybody, I didn't stage big scandals. I have my own tactics for drawing media attention to the region. Journalists would not be interested in merely reporting economic stories" (*MK*, 15 June 1998). Likewise, Ayatskov has won considerable media attention for his plans to go into space in 2001 to celebrate the 40th anniversary of Yurii Gagarin's historic first trip into orbit.

President Yeltsin originally appointed Ayatskov as governor in April 1996, replacing Yurii Belykh, who was dismissed in February for misuse of budgetary funds. Previously, Ayatskov was a deputy mayor of Saratov and deputy chairman of the city commission on combating crime. He quickly consolidated his power as governor and on 1 September 1996 won the first of Russia's approximately 50 gubernatorial races held that fall. Ayatskov defeated Communist Party (KPRF) challenger Anatolii Gordeev, an economics advisor to Gennadii Zyuganov, by a landslide margin of 81 to 16 percent despite Saratov's traditional preference for the reds. Zyuganov beat Yeltsin by more than five percent during the 1996 presidential elections in the region. Surprisingly, the local branch of the Agrarian Party and even some local Communist Party of the Russian Federation (KPRF) cells supported the incumbent. Ayatskov was reelected with a smaller victory margin in March 2000, winning 67.32 percent of the vote in early elections (moved up to coincide with the Russian presidential elections).

Executive Platform: Ambitious Leader and Reformer

Ayatskov made his name in Russian politics by actively advocating the buying and selling of land. While Yeltsin supported private ownership of land, the Communist-dominated State Duma has refused to pass a land code that would provide a federal legislative framework giving legal backing to this constitutionally guaranteed right. As a result, it has been up to regional leaders to implement their own policies in the vacuum created by the federal stand-off.

Additionally, Ayatskov advocates a drastic change in the tax code. He says that the current tax code is the main reason for the criminalization of the Russian economy. He favors greatly differentiating and decreasing the amount of taxes people pay. Ayatskov is a proponent of replacing the six land taxes in the draft federal tax code with a single tax. Advocates of the new system say its simplicity will make it easier to collect taxes and stimulate more efficient use of land. He firmly believes that the formation of a new middle class that includes the intelligentsia, skilled workers, and civil servants is very important for Russia (NNS).

Ayatskov addressed the citizens of his oblast with a text entitled "A Dictatorship of Law—for the Sake of a Worthy Life" through which he hoped to encourage people to obey the law (*Izvestiya*, 4 February 1998). Ayatskov pointed out that there is "too much democracy [in Russia right now]. Democracy goes as far as the poll box. After the last ballot is cast, it is time to use power."

Ayatskov has changed political affiliation several times seeking to curry favor with whoever is in power at the moment. Initially, Ayatskov was the chairman of the regional branch of the Reforms–New Course movement headed by former Federation Council Chairman Vladimir Shumeiko. When Yeltsin created the Our Home Is Russia (NDR) political movement to defend his interests in the 1995 State Duma campaign, he required all of his appointees to lead NDR's regional branches. In April 1997 Ayatskov joined the movement's political council.

Once Yeltsin announced his decision to dismiss Prime Minister Viktor Chernomyrdin on 23 March 1998, Ayatskov loudly declared his belief that Our Home Is Russia had little future if it was no longer the "party of power." Revealing an earthy side to his character, he remarked that Aleksandr Shokhin, then chairman of the NDR Duma faction, "soiled his pants" when he found out about the government's dismissal. At the time Ayatskov said that Chernomyrdin was not "a political corpse yet," but he might become one if he did not set NDR on a course that addressed popular concerns (*KD*, 3 April 1998).

On 28 April 1998, Ayatskov announced that he would found a new Landowners' political party since NDR did not have a strong local base and was not focused on solving Russia's most pressing social problems. He had hoped to attract votes beyond the two million in his oblast, arguing that the party would represent landowners, whom he claimed make up 80 percent of the electorate. Ayatskov also tried to build alliances with Moscow Mayor Yurii Luzhkov and with

Anatolii Chubais, Boris Nemtsov, and Yegor Gaidar, but nothing came of his overtures. These efforts were abandoned in 1999 as Ayatskov saw renewed opportunity in NDR.

In January 1999 Ayatskov hosted Chernomyrdin in Saratov and then asked for forgiveness for so harshly criticizing him at the subsequent meeting of the NDR political council. He became critical of the other alliances forming, calling Luzhkov's Fatherland a "haven for exhausted political material" and Samara Governor Konstantin Titov's Voice of Russia a "sham organization." In April 1999 Ayatskov was elected first deputy chairman of NDR, putting him in charge of the party's relations with other regions, the federal government, and the Federation Council. This appointment positioned Ayatskov to become prime minister if NDR leader Viktor Chernomyrdin had won the presidency. When he was courted by the Kremlin organizers of the new Unity bloc in the fall of 1999, Ayatskov declared his support for their efforts without withdrawing from NDR. Following Putin's rise to power, Ayatskou has loyally backed him.

Ayatskov makes little attempt to hide his ambitions to work at the federal level. Some local observers even believe that he is configuring the political situation in the region so that his successor will be dependent on him should he decide to work in Moscow.

Policies: Land Privatization and Prostitution

Ayatskov has rather mixed results in translating his generally liberal views into real policy. On 14 November 1997, he signed into force an oblast law to permit the buying and selling of land (*Segodnya*, 15 November 1997). The law allows Russian citizens to purchase land and foreigners to sign long-term (99 year) leases, although not actually to purchase land. Since the adoption of the law, Saratov has held a number of auctions, selling land parcels to the highest bidder. The now bankrupt SBS-Agro bank and the oblast administration's Radograd bank provided credits to individuals interested in purchasing land. Saratov has valued its land at an average of $1,000 per hectare. Oblast authorities believe that the region's land is worth about $10 billion (*KD*, 14 November 1997).

As Saratov has gained more experience with the auctions, however, it is becoming clear that there is little real demand for the region's agricultural land. The farmers who currently work the land simply don't have enough money to buy their land and others are not interested. The land law has not really had much positive influence on the oblast economy and the auctions have brought only a negligible amount of money into the oblast budget. Local experts also note that it is extremely difficult to implement the law in the absence of federal legislation (*EWI RRR*, 23 July 1998).

On 13 November the State Duma passed a measure (264–47, with 6 abstentions), asking the Saratov legislature to bring the new law into conformity with Russian legislation. The Duma claimed that only the federal government could pass measures regarding the buying and selling of land since the Constitution had given it the power to regulate Russia's unified market. Deputies from Our Home Is Russia, Yabloko, and the Russian Regions factions opposed the Duma majority. Ayatskov rebutted the allegations, asserting that the law is in full conformity with Russian legislation.

Ayatskov also gained national attention as a liberal when he declared that he would open Russia's first legal house of prostitution in Saratov. He supports legal prostitution in order to combat the spread of AIDS. Ayatskov said on 21 February 1998 that the Saratov legislature was drafting a bill that would permit the registration of brothels. Prostitutes would have to undergo regular medical examinations, and customers would have to practice "safe sex," he said. According to Ayatskov, such a law would also increase the oblast's revenues, since prostitutes would pay taxes "to the regional budget rather than to pimps" (*RFE/RL*, 23 February 1998).

Ayatskov and his administration have made a concerted effort to develop the region's oil industry. Proven reserves include 50 million tons of oil and 56 billion cubic meters of natural gas in Saratov Oblast. Experts believe Saratov also may hold as much as 1.977 million tons of oil and gas condensate. The region's oil industry is seeking $3 billion for the geological surveys necessary to locate and extract an additional 110 million tons of oil (*EWI RRR*, 26 February 1998).

In addition to promoting rather liberal reforms for the oblast's economic development, Ayatskov has in been successful in improving social conditions in the region. Housing construction in Saratov has been revitalized and the gasification of rural areas is nearly complete. An unprecedented number of schools and hospitals have been built in Saratov. Ayatskov brags that every fifth school built in Russia in 1998 was built in the oblast. He also takes pride in the fact that every school has a computer class (*KP*, 3 October 1998).

Following the August 1998 crisis, Saratov provided much-needed support to the region's pensioners, including free meals, groceries, and utility services (*KP*, 3 October 1998).

Ayatskov combines his liberal views in some areas with a strong penchant for order. Upon election, he removed half of the local raion administration chiefs, many of whom were charged with corruption. He set up a regional Security Council, the first such sub-national body in Russia. It handles questions concerning the vital interests of the oblast, including issues of state, economic, and ecological security, and individual rights, and tries to predict emergency situations and deal with their consequences (*OMRI DD*, 4 December 1996). Promoting professionalism, Ayatskov tested how well his assistants and other public sector employees know the Russian constitution and oblast charter. He fired civil servants who flunked the test.

Relationships Between Key Players: No Opposition

There is little political opposition in Saratov because there are no large Russian or foreign concerns with major political interests and the financial resources to sponsor lobbying efforts or establish coherent political organizations. Such groups are more commonly found in Moscow, Yekaterinburg, or Krasnoyarsk. As a result most people observe the rules of the game set by the authorities. Ayatskov has an air of extreme self-confidence in his governance. He once said, "You can call me the devil if you like, as long as I get things done. Yes, I don't need a nay-saying Duma, a disobedient mayor and a presidential representative spying through the keyhole" (*Russian Life*, June–July 1998).

Ayatskov is able to turn his ideas into policy largely because he managed to fill the regional legislature with members loyal to him. In the 31 August 1997 elections to the regional Duma, Communist candidates suffered a shocking defeat when they failed to win a single seat. Until that election, the Communists had dominated the oblast Duma. Immediately after his victory, Ayatskov told journalists that, now that he no longer faced opposition from the regional legislature, Saratov would become "a model of how power should be organized in Russia."

There is little criticism of Ayatskov in the media because journalists fear being declared persona non grata by the regional administration and cut off from official sources of information. Dissenting intellectuals generally avoid speaking out because reprisals could hurt their careers. However, speaking on condition of anonymity, they describe Ayatskov's style as authoritarian. Nevertheless, even the critics admit that Ayatskov may be just the type of leader Saratov needs because he has energy and gets things done (*Russian Life*, June–July 1998).

When Ayatskov was still the deputy mayor of Saratov he won the trust of local law enforcement agencies. Following Ayatskov's post-election purge, the heads of the raion administrations also back the governor. In the fall of 1997 Ayatskov issued an order prohibiting these local leaders from leaving town without notifying him.

In spite of his overwhelming power throughout the region, Ayatskov has run into conflict with the local council in Marx. In April 1999 Ayatskov forced Marx Mayor Ivan Kosyrev to resign from his position. The governor became dissatisfied with Kosyrev after Ayatskov's candidate lost a by-election to the Saratov Oblast Duma from the Marx district. A conflict then ensued between Kosyrev and Ayatskov regarding competing agricultural interests. According to the Saratov Oblast charter, mayors are elected by local councils from among their membership at the recommendation of the governor, and are dismissed by the councils at the governor's recommendation. The governor has the final word over dismissals, but the deputies make the ultimate decision over appointing the mayor. Initially, the local council refused to approve Kosyrev's dismissal, yet yielded to Ayatskov's pressure. However, to show their anger that Ayatskov was acting without taking their interests into account, the deputies refused to approve the governor's choice for mayor, agricultural enterprise director Nikolai Dorovskii. Instead they proposed two of their own candidates (*EWI RRR*, 15 April 1999).

Ties to Moscow: Yeltsin Protégé

Ayatskov maintained cordial relations with President Boris Yeltsin. He accompanied Yeltsin to the May 1998 G-8 conference in Birmingham, England. During the conference, Yeltsin introduced Ayatskov to U.S. President Bill Clinton as "the best governor" and the future president of Russia, but the governor said that he would not run until at least 2004 (*RFE/RL*, 11 February 1998).

Despite his connection to Yeltsin, Ayatskov tried to strengthen the position of the regions in relation to Moscow. On 4 July 1997 then Prime Minister Viktor Chernomyrdin signed a power-sharing agreement between the federal government and Saratov. However, Ayatskov has criticized the practice of concluding such treaties since he believes that they exacerbate inequalities among regions (*RFE/RL*, 22 May 1998).

Ayatskov is among the regional executives who had the greatest influence over the federal government during the government crisis that followed Yeltsin's decision to fire Chernomyrdin in April 1998 (*NG Regiony*, 19 May 1998). Newly appointed Prime Minister Sergei Kirienko apparently offered Ayatskov, and other regional executives, a job in the new cabinet, but none were interested in serving in any position other than as prime minister (*Itogi*, 18 May 1998).

Ayatskov also curried favor with the Yeltsin administration in his battle against the State Duma. He charged that the Duma electoral law did not guarantee equal rights for voters. Ayatskov said that he believed the proportional representation system used to elect half of the State Duma deputies was unconstitutional and should be abolished. Under the current electoral law, 225 out of the 450 Duma deputies are chosen by party lists from electoral blocs that receive at least 5 percent of the vote. The other 225 deputies are elected from single-member districts. If Duma elections were held only in single-member districts, regional leaders would have more influence over the results (*RFE/RL*, 27 January 1998). Yeltsin and many regional executives also believed that such a method would limit the number of Communists elected to the legislature.

Some of Ayatskov's critics accused him of obsequiousness before the commander-in-chief and excessive obedience to the president's team (*EWI RRR*, 23 July 1998). But Ayatskov does not always support the federal executive. In February 1998, for instance, he announced that the local airport would not accept special flights carrying federal officials to Saratov unless those flights had been cleared with him personally. He said that government ministers, State Duma deputies, and other high-ranking federal officials should coordinate with the governor in advance their visits to Saratov Oblast (*RFE/RL*, 11 February 1998).

Additionally, many of Ayatskov's initiatives have come into conflict with federal prerogatives. He has advocated closing the border with Kazakhstan because of the steady stream of arms, drugs, and illegally made vodka from there. Speaking out against hazing in the military, he demanded that young people from Saratov called to military service serve in units based in their

Dmitrii Fedorovich Ayatskov

9 November 1950—Born in Kalinino (before the October Revolution and after 1991—Stolypino) in Saratov Oblast

1965–1969—Farm mechanic and electrician at Kalinin collective farm

1969–1971—Served in the army in Poland

1977—Graduated from Saratov Agricultural Institute as a research agronomist

1977–1979—Head agronomist for the 1 May collective farm

1979–1980—Head agronomist for the Dawn of Communism collective farm

1980–1981—Construction foreman in Saratov

1981–1986—Head agronomist, foreman, and then deputy director of Tantal industrial enterprise in Saratov

1985—Graduated from Moscow Cooperative Institute (evening courses) as an economist

1986–1992—Worked as an economist, deputy director, and first deputy director of the poultry enterprise Saratovptitseprom (Saratovskoe after 1991)

6 June 1992—Appointed first deputy mayor of Saratov, a position he held until 1996

December 1993–1995—Member of the Federation Council; he was nominated from Saratov Oblast after a power struggle during which the mayor of Saratov, who was the first nominee, allegedly committed suicide

April 1996—Appointed Saratov Oblast governor by President Yeltsin

September 1996—Elected governor in popular elections, winning approximately 80% of the vote

26 March 2000—Reelected governor of Saratov Oblast with 67.3% of the vote

---

home region. Ayatskov wants to change his fiscal relationship with Moscow as well. He proposed not paying off the oblast's old debts since they were the result of specific conditions that favored ethnically defined republics while creating large tax burdens for predominantly ethnic Russian oblasts and krais.

Relations with Other Regions: Seeks Reform of Russian Federalism

Ayatskov is an outspoken critic of Russian federalism. On numerous occasions he has complained that Russia's krais and oblasts currently enjoy fewer rights than the country's republics. In an article published in *Nezavisimaya gazeta* on 11 February 1998, Ayatskov assailed various forms of "discrimination" against geographically based krais and oblasts, as opposed to republics, each of which represents a specific ethnic

group. He argued that the constitution guarantees equal rights for all regions and accused the Constitutional Court of "neglecting its duty" in interpreting the constitution.

Ayatskov has ruminated publicly about which regional leaders he would appoint as ministers if he were named prime minister. His choices include Orel Oblast Governor and Speaker of the Federation Council Yegor Stroev, Samara Oblast Governor Konstantin Titov, Mordovia President Nikolai Merkushkin, Magadan Oblast Governor Valentin Tsvetkov, former Leningrad Oblast Governor Vadim Gustov, St. Petersburg Governor Vladimir Yakovlev, Moscow Mayor Yurii Luzhkov, and President of the Kabardino-Balkar Republic Valerii Kokov.

Analysis of Ayatskov's choices of potential allies reveals several things. First, his "ideal" cabinet is composed of diverse and independent-minded regional leaders and would be a government of careful checks and balances on each individual's power. Reformers like Luzhkov and Titov balance the conservatives Stroev and Kokov. Tsvetkov is a counterbalance to the "rebellious" Primorskii Krai Governor Yevgenii Nazdratenko. The more compliant Merkushkin serves as an alternative to the overly independent Tatarstan President Mintimer Shaimiev.

Second, of the eight leaders of the regions in the Greater Volga Association, with whom Ayatskov works most closely, he favors only Konstantin Titov. Most Volga governors and presidents hold a grudge against Ayatskov for trying to position Saratov as the "capital of the Volga" and for making territorial claims against his neighbors. Ayatskov has suggested that Saratov take over parts of Volgograd to form a unified homeland for ethnic Germans. The land in question has valuable oil reserves, which have clearly sparked Ayatskov's interest. Titov, however, has expressed no anger against Ayatskov's regional "imperialism."

Foreign Relations: Cooperation Agreement with Kazakhstan

The Saratov Oblast government and the administration of Leninsk in Kazakhstan signed a cooperation agreement on 6 April. The agreement with Saratov envisages the establishment of a trade center in the Kazak city and the construction of housing in Saratov Oblast for Russians leaving the space center. Leninsk Mayor Gennadii Dmitrienko described it as the first direct agreement between Baikonur and one of Russia's regions.

Together with Moscow Mayor Yurii Luzhkov, Ayatskov called for measures against Latvia following the crisis in which Latvian police attacked Russian-speaking demonstrators in Riga in spring 1998.

Ayatskov supports increased Russian influence in Crimea and is working to achieve this goal by increasing the presence of Russian businessmen in this region and establishing more trade links between the Volga region and the Ukrainian autonomous republic (*EWI RRR*, 13 August 1998).

Attitudes Toward Business: Region Is Increasingly Attractive

Saratov rose from 69th to 10th place in the table of "investor-attractive" regions in Russia. There are plans for a new international airport and business center to be built in the region (*The Independent*, 18 June 1998).

The EBRD has launched a program to extract and process oil in Saratov.

Internet Sites in the Region

http://www.saratov.ru/gov/
Ayatskov appears to be a big fan of the Internet, and this site hosts the official home page of the Saratov Oblast government. It presents the latest regional news, full lists of the members of the government and Oblast duma, and the oblast's "transparent budget." You can also ask the governor questions.

http://www.infomost.ru/main/
This is the home of the regional information provider Volga Info-Most. It has a lot of useful information concerning the region's finances and economic opportunities, investment projects, etc.

http://www.saratov.su
This site provides general information about the city of Saratov and Saratov Oblast, raions of the region, neighboring regions, and links to the other regional websites.

SMOLENSK OBLAST

Territory: 49,800 km²
Population (as of 1 January 1998):
1,157,000
Distance from Moscow: 419 km

Major Cities:
Smolensk, *capital* (pop. 352,900)
Vyazma (60,400)
Roslavl (59,800)
Yartsevo (58,000)
Safonovo (54,500)

Basic Facts

Population (as of 1 Jan. 1998): 1,157,000 (0.79% of Russian total)

Ethnic breakdown (1989 census): Russians 94.1%, Belarusans 1.9%, Ukrainians 1.9%

Urban population (as of 1 Jan. 1998): 70.2% (Russia overall: 73.1%)

Student population (as of 1 Sept. 1997): 108 per 10,000 (Russia overall: 208/10,000)

Pensioner population (1997): 28.69% (Russia overall: 25.96%)

Percent of population with higher education (1989 census): 8.7% (Russia overall: 11.3%)

Percent of population working in 1997: Industry: 24.6% (Russian average: 23.0%); Agriculture: 14.9% (13.7%); Trade: 15.9% (13.5%); Culture: 12.2% (13.3%)

Average monthly personal income in July 1998: 663.5 new rubles (Russian average: 891.7 new rubles)

Average monthly personal expenses in July 1998: 472.1 new rubles (Russian average: 684.9 new rubles)

Average monthly subsistence requirement in 1998: 358 new rubles (Russian average: 438 new rubles)

Consumer price index (as of July 1998): 82 (Russia overall = 100)

Budgetary revenues (1997): 1,717.5 billion rubles (Russia overall: 433,378.2 billion rubles)

Budgetary expenditures (1997): 1,904.1 billion rubles (Russia overall: 468,111.6 billion rubles)

Industrial production as percentage of all Russian production (Jan.–Aug. 1998): 0.50%

Proportion of loss-making enterprises (as of July 1998): 52.9% (Russia overall: 50.4%)

Number of enterprises which have wage arrears (as of 1 Sept. 1998): 1,268 (0.94% of Russian total)

Agricultural production as percentage of all Russian production (1997): 0.96%

Number of private farms (as of 1 Jan. 1998): 2,553 (0.93% of Russian total)

Capital investment (1997): 1,056.2 billion rubles (Russia overall: 408,797 billion rubles)

Sources of investment (1997): federal budget: 19.4% (Russian average: 10.2%); regional budget: 2.7% (10.5%); extra-budgetary funds: 77.9% (79.3%)

Foreign investment (1997): 45,123,000 USD (Russia overall: 12,294,734,000 USD)

Number of joint ventures (1997): 31 (0.21% of Russian total)

Fixed capital investment in joint ventures and foreign companies (1997): 18,178 million rubles (Russia overall: 16,265.4 billion rubles)

Number of small businesses (as of 1 July 1998): 2,900 (0.33% of Russian total)

Number of enterprises privatized in 1997: 23 (0.84% of Russian total), including those which used to be municipal property: 73.9% (Russian average: 66.4%); regional property: 8.7% (20.0%); federal property: 17.4% (13.6%)

Number of telephones per 100 families (1997): in cities: 48.6 (Russian average: 49.2); in villages: 19.8 (19.8)

Brief Overview

Smolensk Oblast is located on the East European plain, at the conjunction of the Dnepr, Volga, and West Dvina rivers. It borders Tver, Moscow, Kaluga, Bryansk, and Pskov oblasts and Belarus. Smolensk, first mentioned in 863, was once the center of an independent Smolensk Kingdom. It was later part of Belarus, Lithuania, and Poland and became part of the Russian state in 1686.

Smolensk began industrializing in the early 17th century and developed a strong industrial base by 1900. Regional industries such as machine manufacturing, chemical and oil and processing, forestry and timber working, are based on local mineral resources. Those resources include peat, charcoal, and phosphorous. The oblast is home to one of the country's largest flax-processing enterprises as well as the Smolensk Nuclear Power Plant.

Almost all of the region's exports, including raw materials, machines, fertilizers, and processed diamonds, are shipped to Belgium, the United States, Germany, Italy, and France.

According to a 1998 survey by *Ekspert* magazine, the oblast ranked 50th among Russia's 89 regions in terms of investment potential and 52nd in terms of investment risk. A 1998 survey by Bank Austria ranked the oblast 49th in terms of investment climate. It became much safer to invest in the oblast since investment risks had decreased by 20 points since 1997. However, regional investment potential has also decreased, though not as drastically—only by 6 points.

Electoral History

2000 Presidential Election
Putin: 52.48%
Zyuganov: 34.78%
Yavlinskii: 3.27%
Zhirinovsky: 3.04%
Tuleev: 1.83%
Turnout: 67.68% (Russia overall: 68.64%)

1999 Parliamentary Elections
Communist Party of the Russian Federation: 31.48%
Unity: 26.75%
Zhirinovsky Bloc: 6.94%
Union of Right Forces: 6.57%
Fatherland–All Russia: 6.51%
Yabloko: 3.88%

In single-mandate districts: 2 Communist Party of the Russian Federation
Turnout: 59.08% (Russia overall: 61.85%)

1998 Gubernatorial Election
Prokhorov: 46.5%
Glushenkov (incumbent): 26.0%
Turnout: 39.6%

1996 Presidential Election
Zyuganov: 44.57%/56.25% (first round/second round)
Yeltsin: 21.98%/38.15%
Lebed: 15.92%
Zhirinovsky: 8.33%
Yavlinskii: 5.11%
Turnout: 72.88%/69.16% (Russia overall: 69.67%/ 68.79%)

1995 Parliamentary Elections
Communist Party of the Russian Federation: 31.89%
Liberal Democratic Party of Russia: 19.64%
Our Home Is Russia: 4.59%
Communists–Workers' Russia: 4.54%
Yabloko: 3.97%
Agrarian Party of Russia: 3.63%
Russia's Democratic Choice: 3.61%
Women of Russia: 3.32%
Congress of Russian Communities: 3.10%
In single-mandate districts: 2 Communist Party of the Russian Federation
Turnout: 68.55% (Russia overall: 64.37%)

1993 Constitutional Referendum
"Yes"—42.1%   "No"—56.2%

1993 Parliamentary Elections
Liberal Democratic Party of Russia: 32.63%
Communist Party of the Russian Federation: 16.15%
Agrarian Party of Russia: 13.05%
Russia's Choice: 11.39%
Women of Russia: 6.43%
Democratic Party of Russia: 5.74%
Yabloko: 4.69%
Party of Russian Unity and Concord: 4.09%
In single-mandate districts: 1 Communist Party of the Russian Federation, 1 Agrarian Party of Russia
From electoral associations: 1 Communist Party of the Russian Federation
Turnout: 65.07% (Russia overall: 54.34%)

1991 Presidential Election

Yeltsin: 37.57%

Ryzhkov: 33.52%

Zhirinovsky: 9.37%

Makashov: 6.92%

Tuleev: 6.79%

Bakatin: 2.70%

Turnout: 82.45% (Russia overall: 76.66%)

Regional Political Institutions

Executive:

Governor, 5-year term

Aleksandr Dmitrievich Prokhorov, elected

May 1998

Smolensk Oblast Administration; Dom Sovetov;

Smolensk, 214008

Tel 7(081–22) 3–63–08;

Fax 7(081–00) 3–68–51

Legislative:

Unicameral

Oblast Duma—30 members, 4-year term, elected

December 1997

Chairman—Vladimir Ivanovich Anisimov, elected

January 1998

Regional Politics

Kremlin Forced to Back Default Candidate

Aleksandr Prokhorov was elected governor on 17 May 1998, defeating incumbent Anatolii Glushenkov by a margin of 67–26 percent. Prokhorov, the former mayor of Smolensk, does not belong to a political party, but had the unusual backing of both the Communist Party and the presidential administration during the campaign. The Kremlin supported Prokhorov in an attempt to moderate his views since Glushenkov, who was endorsed by Our Home Is Russia, had no chance of winning reelection (*EWI RRR*, 21 May 1998). Prokhorov claims that he does not have any "special obligations" to the Communist Party, but wants the Kremlin to spend more money in order to improve the oblast's economy (*KD*, 19 May 1998). In the lead-up to the 1999 parliamentary elections, Prokhorov endorsed the Kremlin's new Unity bloc.

Both Prokhorov and Glushenkov reject new approaches to Smolensk's economic difficulties, preferring a more traditional approach (*Izvestiya*, 28 April 1998).

Policies: Establishing Order and Development

As mayor of Smolensk, Prokhorov was credited with establishing order in the city (*KW*, 11 August 1998). His greatest achievements were in commercial development. In 1997 Prokhorov reconstructed all of the city's markets and built many modern stores with improved designs and services. He also was successful at driving unregistered shuttle-traders from Belarus out of business (*EWI RRR*, 8 October 1998).

Prokhorov's improvements in the oblast's capital prompted some to compare him to Moscow Mayor Yurii Luzhkov (*KW*, 11 August 1998). Some claimed that he displayed "Luzhkov's character," treating Smolensk Oblast as his personal domain, while forcefully articulating the region's interests (*KW*, 11 August 1998). Similarly, his success as mayor led many people to believe that Prokhorov was connected to the local mafia.

Upon taking office as governor, Prokhorov decided to expand his reform of the retail trade sector throughout the entire oblast. He also hopes to capitalize on the road between Moscow and Minsk, which passes directly through the oblast and offers many attractive investment opportunities. Prokhorov is also taking measures to revitalize the region's flax industry. Smolensk has the capacity to conduct all stages of flax production, from growing to processing it. Although none of the governor's projects have been completed, his first few months were marked by strong initiatives.

In 1997 former Governor Glushenkov introduced an illegal tax on all vehicles that were not registered in the oblast, and established the Assistance Foundation in order to collect the tax. The Assistance Foundation built a series of checkpoints on all the highways crossing the region. Prokhorov criticized Glushenkov for the illegal tax during the electoral campaign, but he did not disband the Assistance Foundation after his election. Rather, he began to rebuild the highway with financial help from European institutions with the ultimate goal of making the highway a toll road so as to legalize this source of revenue for the oblast budget. On 11 May 2000 Putin issued a decree demanding that the oblast abolish the tax. Prokhorov also wants Gazprom and Russian oil companies to pay a tax to Smolensk for sending their products to Europe via the region.

Relationships Between Key Players: Business Based

Prokhorov has a good team of managers, which has contributed to his relative success thus far as gover-

Aleksandr Dmitrievich Prokhorov

22 April 1953—Born

1976—Graduated from the Smolensk branch of the Moscow Energy Institute

1976–1978—Engineer at the Smolensk Aviation Institute

1978–1986—Second, and then first secretary of the Smolensk city committee of the Komsomol

1986–1987—Manager of the industrial-transport department of the Promyshlenny district committee in Smolensk city

1987–1989—Assistant chairman of the Promyshlennyi district executive committee of the city of Smolensk

1989–1990—Second secretary of the Promyshlennyi CPSU district committee in Smolensk city

1990–1992—Chairman of the Promyshlennyi district executive committee in Smolensk city

1992–1996—Assistant chairman of the Smolensk City Council

1996–1997—Head of administration in the Promyshlennyi district of Smolensk city

1997—Elected mayor of Smolensk city

17 May 1998—Elected governor of Smolensk Oblast

Married

nor. After his victory, Prokhorov dismissed most of the administration staff and put twelve deputy-governors in place. There are no Communists in the regional government, although virtually all officials worked together previously in the Komsomol. The regional government defines itself as "pragmatic," drawing on common business interests and joint service in the Soviet-era youth league (*EWI RRR*, 8 October 1998). Prokhorov de facto controls the main regional newspapers, *Rabochii Put*, *Smolenskie Novosti*, and *Smolenskie Gubernskie Vedomosti*. He also has a good relationship with the oblast legislature, which is dominated by the Communists, who won a third of the seats in the December 1997 elections (*EWI RRR*, 30 April 1998).

Business and industrial players greatly influence the character of Smolensk local politics. Assassins murdered the general director of Smolensk's Kristall diamond enterprise, Aleksandr Shkadov, in August 1998, an event that provoked shock and outrage throughout the region. Shkadov was considered Prokhorov's "political godfather," and had enormous influence with the governor in the region (*Kommersant vlast*), 11 August 1998). Shkadov's official support of Prokhorov's electoral campaign certainly contributed to Prokhorov's victory. Moreover, Shkadov supposedly

had paid for Prokhorov's home in Smolensk and holidays in Greece. Many charged that his relationship with the governor gave the businessman too much political leverage.

Seventy percent of the budget's real money income comes from the Bacchus Complex, a conglomeration of spirit, liqueur, and vodka factories. It is the oblast's second largest taxpayer, but the largest, the Smolensk Nuclear Power Plant, pays mainly in promissory notes. Kristall pays taxes only to the federal government. Two weeks after his election, Prokhorov put a new director in charge of Bacchus, whose leadership is highly politicized. Furthermore, in a special session of the oblast Duma in July 1998, the regional legislators adopted a law limiting the import and sale of alcohol from outside the oblast.

Ties to Moscow

Smolensk has always been a "red" region lacking any real post-Soviet democratic development. The presidential administration endorsed Prokhorov's candidacy in an attempt to moderate his stand since his victory appeared imminent.

Prokhorov has suggested that Gazprom should pay for the presence of its pipelines in the oblast.

Relations with Other Regions

Smolensk is a member of the Central Russia Association, which is headed by Yaroslavl Governor Anatolii Lisitsyn. The association also includes Bryansk, Vladimir, Ivanovo, Kaluga, Kostroma, Moscow, Ryazan, Tver, and Tula oblasts, along with the city of Moscow.

Foreign Relations: Close to Neighboring Belarus

Smolensk maintains close ties to Belarus, and Prokhorov is a strong supporter of Belarusan President Aleksandr Lukashenko. In September 1998 the oblast administration announced its plans to establish closer ties to Belarus. Smolensk authorities intend to yield the flax sector to Belarusan enterprises to aid in reducing unemployment there. Additionally, they want to join Smolensk and Vitebsk (Belarus) university institutions into a single "Slavic University"(*EWI RRR*, 8 October 1998).

Prokhorov and his team are highly opposed to NATO expansion.

The governor has opened a trade representative offices for Smolensk in Minsk and Kiev.

Attitudes Toward Business: Pro-Investment

Prokhorov was very successful at building up Smolensk city, and hopes to develop the oblast in a similar fashion. He is interested in attracting investment to the region and revitalizing the flax industry.

Prokhorov hopes that the construction of a road connecting Moscow and Minsk, which will pass through Smolensk, will bring investment to the region. In July 1998, he met with Moscow Mayor Yurii Luzhkov to discuss this and other projects.

Internet Sites in the Region

http://www.smolensk.ru/
This website is the Smolensk city home page offering information about local businesses, education, attractions, etc. It includes a telephone directory of local officials.

STAVROPOL KRAI

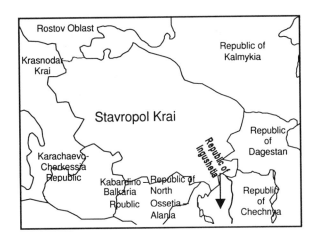

Territory: 66,500 km²
Population (as of 1 January 1998):
2,682,000
Distance from Moscow: 1,621 km

Major Cities:
Stavropol, *capital* (pop. 342,600)
Pyatigorsk (128,800)
Nevinnomyssk (132,400)
Kislovodsk (112,700)

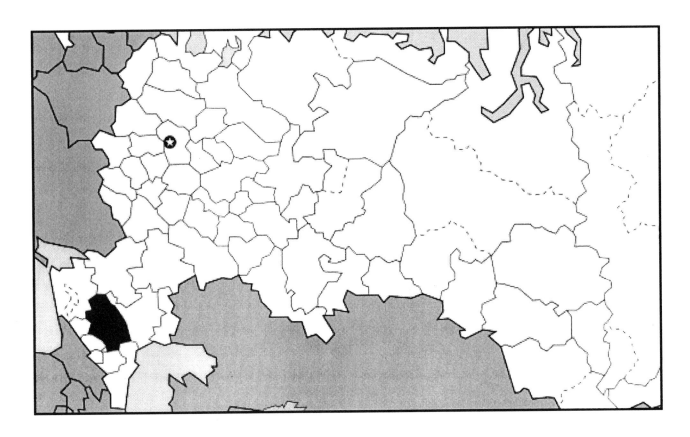

Basic Facts

Population (as of 1 Jan. 1998): 2,682,000 (1.82% of Russian total)

Ethnic breakdown (1989 census): Russians 84.0%, Armenians 2.9%, Ukrainians 2.6%, Dargins 1.3%, Greeks 1.1%

Urban population (as of 1 Jan. 1998): 54.0% (Russia overall: 73.1%)

Student population (as of 1 Sept. 1997): 135 per 10,000 (Russia overall: 208/10,000)

Pensioner population (1997): 26.06% (Russia overall: 25.96%)

Percent of population with higher education (1989 census): 9.7% (Russia overall: 11.3%)

Percent of population working in 1997 in: Industry: 17.3% (Russian average: 23.0%); Agriculture: 21.7% (13.7%); Trade: 16.8% (13.5%); Culture: 11.2% (13.3%)

Average monthly personal income in July 1998: 531.3 new rubles (Russian average: 891.7 new rubles)

Average monthly personal expenses in July 1998: 476.1 new rubles (Russian average: 684.9 new rubles)

Average monthly subsistence requirement in 1998: 369 new rubles (Russian average: 438 new rubles)

Consumer price index (as of July 1998): 85 (Russia overall = 100)

Budgetary revenues (1997): 3,793.9 billion rubles (Russia overall: 433,378.2 billion rubles)

Budgetary expenditures (1997): 4,036.7 billion rubles (Russia overall: 468,111.6 billion rubles)

Industrial production as percentage of all Russian production (Jan.–Aug. 1998): 0.57%

Proportion of loss-making enterprises (as of July 1998): 49.7% (Russia overall: 50.4%)

Number of enterprises which have wage arrears (as of 1 Sept. 1998): 1,859 (1.26% of Russian total)

Agricultural production as percentage of all Russian production (1997): 2.81%

Number of private farms (as of 1 Jan. 1998): 22,057 (8.04% of Russian total)

Capital investment (1997): 3,792.4 billion rubles (Russia overall: 408,797 billion rubles)

Sources of investment (1997): federal budget: 13.6% (Russian average: 10.2%); regional budget: 8.8% (10.5%); extra-budgetary funds: 77.6% (79.3%)

Foreign investment (1997): 36,376,000 USD (Russia overall: 12,294,734,000 USD)

Number of joint ventures (1997): 134 (0.91% of Russian total)

Fixed capital investment in joint ventures and foreign companies (1997): 147,780 million rubles (Russia overall: 16,265.4 billion rubles)

Number of small businesses (as of 1 July 1998): 15,200 (1.75% of Russian total)

Number of enterprises privatized in 1997: 13 (0.47% of Russian total), including those which used to be municipal property: 23.1% (Russian average: 66.4%); regional property: 30.8% (20.0%); federal property: 46.1% (13.6%)

Number of telephones per 100 families (1997): in cities: 57.3 (Russian average: 49.2); in villages: 24.2 (19.8)

Brief Overview

Stavropol Krai is located on the northern slope of the Caucasus Mountains and borders Rostov Oblast, Krasnodar Krai, and the republics of Kalmykia, Dagestan, Kabardino-Balkaria, Karachaevo-Cherkessia, North Ossetia–Alania, and Chechnya. Ethnic Russians make up the vast majority of the population, although 90 other ethnic groups are also represented.

The krai is fairly rich in mineral resources, including oil, gas, rare metals, and mineral waters. The region's spas are the most famous in Russia and federal legislation provides special ecological protection.

Over one-third of regional GDP comes from industry, 23 percent from agriculture, 14 percent from transportation and communications, and 13 percent from construction. Over 300 large industrial enterprises, mostly in machine building, chemicals, electronics, gas and oil processing, and light industries now operate in the region. The krai is one of the country's largest suppliers of grain.

According to a 1998 survey by *Ekspert* magazine, the krai ranked 31st among Russia's 89 regions in terms of investment potential and 29th in terms of investment risk. A 1998 survey by Bank Austria ranked the krai 41st in terms of investment climate.

Electoral History

2000 Presidential Election
Putin: 52.17%
Zyuganov: 36.43%
Yavlinskii: 3.02%
Zhirinovsky: 2.05%
Tuleev: 1.83%
Turnout: 68.02% (Russia overall: 68.64%)

1999 Parliamentary Elections
Communist Party of the Russian Federation: 31.23%
Unity: 28.29%
Fatherland–All Russia: 6.42%
Union of Right Forces: 5.68%
Zhirinovsky Bloc: 5.13%
Yabloko: 4.12%
In single-mandate districts: 2 Communist Party of the Russian Federation, 2 independent
Turnout: 59.70% (Russia overall: 61.85%)

1996 Gubernatorial Election
Chernogorov (State Duma deputy): 47.80%/55.10% (first round/second round)
Marchenko (incumbent, NDR): 37.63%/40.15%
Korobeinikov: 6.02%
Kulakovskii: 3.03%
Garanzha: 0.71%
Turnout: 45.1%/44.0%

1996 Presidential Election
Zyuganov: 43.93%/53.93% (first round/second round)
Yeltsin: 22.00%/40.93%
Lebed: 19.34%
Zhirinovsky: 6.19%
Yavlinskii: 4.10%
Turnout: 73.75%/71.65% (Russia overall: 69.67%/68.79%)

1995 Parliamentary Elections
Communist Party of the Russian Federation: 28.84%
Liberal Democratic Party of Russia: 13.06%
Congress of Russian Communities: 8.50%
Our Home Is Russia: 6.45%
Communists–Workers' Russia: 5.63%
Party of Workers' Self-Government: 3.50%
Women of Russia: 3.48%
Agrarian Party of Russia: 3.24%
Derzhava: 3.15%
Yabloko: 3.09%
In single-mandate districts: 3 Communist Party of the Russian Federation, 1 Bloc of Stanislav Govorukhin
Turnout: 67.21% (Russia overall: 64.37%)

1993 Constitutional Referendum
"Yes"—53.2% "No"—45.1%

1993 Parliamentary Elections
Liberal Democratic Party of Russia: 38.53%
Communist Party of the Russian Federation: 12.35%
Agrarian Party of Russia: 11.48%
Russia's Choice: 9.32%
Women of Russia: 6.93%
Party of Russian Unity and Concord: 6.19%
Yabloko: 5.13%
Democratic Party of Russia: 3.64%
In single-mandate districts: 1 Agrarian Party of Russia, 3 independent
From electoral associations: 1 Women of Russia, 1 Agrarian Party of Russia
Turnout: 63.77% (Russia overall: 54.34%)

1991 Presidential Election

Yeltsin: 46.04%
Ryzhkov: 21.84%
Zhirinovsky: 11.92%
Tuleev: 6.93%
Bakatin: 4.59%
Makashov: 4.37%
Turnout: 82.33% (Russia overall: 76.66%)

Regional Political Institutions

Executive:
> Governor, 4-year term
> Aleksandr Leonidovich Chernogorov,
> elected November 1996
>> Stavropol Krai Administration; Pl. Lenina, 1;
>> Stavropol, 355025
>> Tel 7(865–2) 35–11–72;
>> Fax 7(865–2) 35–22–52

Legislative:
> Unicameral
> State Duma—25 members, 4-year term,
> elected December 1997
> Chairman—Aleksandr Akimovich Shiyanov,
> elected December 1997

Regional Politics

North Caucasian Communist

Aleksandr Chernogorov, a career Communist, was elected governor on 17 November 1996 with the support of the opposition National Patriotic Union of Russia (NPSR), defeating pro-government incumbent Petr Marchenko in the second round of elections with 55 percent of the vote. Communist Party leader Gennadii Zyuganov even came to the oblast to campaign for him. Yet, Chernogorov's loyalty to the Communists is wavering. Although he supports leftist policies, his interests in maintaining good ties with Moscow and improving Stavropol's economy via capitalist reforms have alienated him from his traditional base.

Executive Platform: Backs a Communist Platform

In general terms, Chernogorov supports a Communist platform, favoring price controls and opposing the buy-ing and selling of land in the Federation Council. Despite these general oppositionist sympathies, however, Chernogorov has distanced himself from the Communists throughout his tenure as governor. After his election, he announced his intention to leave his positions as the krai's Communist Party leader and presidium member of the NPSR regional branch (KP, 30 November 1996). Chernogorov also announced that he would not blindly oppose the central government, but intended to work in cooperation with then Prime Minister Viktor Chernomyrdin and Gennadii Zyuganov (*OMRI RRR*, 4 December 1996). Since his election, the local communists have expressed dissatisfaction with Chernogorov's performance (*EWI RRR*, 25 September 1997).

Like the other oppositionist leaders in the North Caucasus, Chernogorov believes that the borders of the former USSR can change at the will of the people and feels that Russia should set aside its concerns over the country's territorial integrity and allow Chechnya to secede from the Federation (Panorama Research Group, Labyrint Electronic Database, Moscow). He has even expressed his disapproval of the Terek Cossacks' interest in returning to Stavropol the Naur and Shchelkov raions, which had been transferred to the Chechen-Ingush ASSR in 1958. Chernogorov believes that Stavropol has valid claims on the land, which is presently part of Chechnya, but also accepts Moscow's authority to rule on this issue (*RFE/RL* 10 June 1997).

Chernogorov hopes to establish concrete guidelines for developing Stavropol's economy and handling the military industrial complex (*SP*, 27 May 1997). He claims that the federal government works poorly with the regions, making it necessary for Stavropol to break from the center and become more self-sufficient. The governor complained that Moscow did not provide anything substantial for the krai in its 1998 budget, leaving Stavropol on its own for social programs (*SP*, 27 May 1997). Chernogorov feels that it is necessary to concentrate on attracting investments to help industry overcome its resource deficiency (*SP*, 27 May 1997). He asserts that every city should have a clear-cut program for enterprise development. Chernogorov and his administration expect local governments to take more initiative and responsibility in economic development. He claims that many local leaders are lost in the new economic situation and have practically given up on political solutions.

Policies: Krai Security

Stavropol borders on Chechnya and therefore suffers from the constant chaos in that region. In early 1999, the Federation Council recommended declaring a state of emergency in the region to deal with the increasing crime coming from Chechnya. Hundreds of krai residents are numbered among the missing, and at least 30 have been taken hostage (*EWI RRR*, 25 February 1999). Local police also began organizing citizen units to combat cross-border crime. Following the conviction of two women for a terrorist bombing in early 1999, the authorities introduced passport checks at the border. The women were tried for planting a bomb at the Pyatigorsk railway station in April 1997 that killed two people. Chechen field commanders threatened reprisals for the conviction, claiming that the women were innocent.

In April 1999 Chernogorov closed Stavropol's border with Chechnya. The measure was taken to secure the safety of the Stavropol border region, which has continually been subjected to acts of armed conflict, kidnappings, and murders involving Chechen assailants.

Stavropol Krai has moved into first place among Russian regions for the number of refugees on its territory. There were 70,000 officially registered forced migrants, including 40,000 from Chechnya, but the real number was estimated at 300,000–400,000. Additionally, Chernogorov has expressed concern over the 10,000 migrants that have entered the eastern part of the krai from Dagestan. Since the influx of these migrants there has been an increase in robberies, organized crime, and murders in the area, and it seems that ethnic tensions are mounting. Chernogorov is taking steps to increase security on the Stavropol-Dagestan border and has set up an ethnic council in Stavropol (*Izvestiya*, 25 April 1998).

Many are concerned that ethnic tensions will increase as migrants from unstable regions make their way into the krai. Although ethnic Russians make up 84 percent of the population of Stavropol, there are 90 other nationalities represented in the krai, and tense Cossack-Chechen relations could provoke aggravated conflict.

However, a more immediate concern is the strain the influx of migrants has had on the krai's social welfare structure. With the recent arrival of refugees and additional servicemen in the region, every fifth resident of Stavropol is not accounted for in the budget.

This additional strain on health care, education, and services for veterans and the handicapped threatens to lower the population's social welfare (*EWI RRR*, 25 February 1999).

In response to the Russian financial crisis in summer and fall 1998, Chernogorov signed a law prohibiting the export of food products from the region without the krai administration's approval and demanding that producers of "socially essential food products" sell them in the krai at rates approved by the authorities. Grain exports were limited to 6 percent of the krai's overall output.

Relationships Between Key Players: Oppositionist Parliament

Chernogorov has encountered considerable opposition governing in Stavropol. Although he was elected governor on the Communist party ticket, his support from the party has dwindled during his tenure. Therefore, even though Communists were elected to 11 of the 25 seats in the krai legislature in December 1997, this apparent success did not necessarily translate into a support network for Chernogorov. He has been involved in several conflicts with the krai duma. In November 1998 Chernogorov opposed the duma's proposed amendments to the krai charter because they would reduce his power substantially. Legislators likewise criticized Chernogorov for failing to draw up a law on the regional government structure. The krai duma also attacked Chernogorov and his administration for the lack of a firm anticrisis program following the economic and financial crisis of August 1998 (*EWI RRR*, 12 November 1998). However, it seems that popular support for communists throughout Stavropol Krai is also decreasing. Elections in April 1997 witnessed a considerable drop in the number of communist mayors and communists in local councils, with their representation dropping from 28.6 to 9.4 percent. Thus, Chernogorov's move away from the left could perhaps be working to his advantage in dealing with the rest of his constituents.

Chernogorov had also hoped to remove the local procurator, Yurii Lushnikov, yet was unable to do so since Moscow controls this office.

Ties to Moscow

Maintaining good relations with Moscow is important to Chernogorov, which perhaps explains his move away

Aleksandr Leonidovich Chernogorov

13 July 1959—Born in Vozdvizhenka village in the Apanasenkov raion of Stavropol krai

1971–1975—Worked as an assistant combine operator at the Krasnyi Manych collective farm

1975—Joined the Komsomol

1976–1981—Worked as a combine operator at Berezanskoe

1981—Graduated from the Kuban Agricultural Institute as an engineer-mechanic

1981–1982—Worked as an engineer-technician at the Saturn factory in Krasnodar

1982—Became the second secretary of the Kirov regional Komsomol committee in the city of Novopavlovsk

1982–1983—Instructor for the krai Komsomol committee and deputy director of the department for young workers and farmers

1983—Joined the CPSU

1983–1985—First secretary of the Izobilnen regional Komsomol committee

1985—Became a member of the krai committee

1985–1987—Member of the Presidium of Stavropol Trade Unions

1985–1990—Worked up to first secretary of the Stavropol Komsomol regional committee, joined the Komsomol Central Committee

1990–1994—Member of the Stavropol Krai Council of People's Deputies, where he served as chairman of the Committee on Youth Issues

1993—Graduated from the Russian Academy of Management

1994–1996—Senior instructor at the Stavropol Law University and law instructor at the Stavropol State Pedagogical University

1991–1993—Member of the Socialist Party of Laborers

1993—Joined the Communist Party of the Russian Federation (KPRF)

1994—Became secretary of the KPRF krai committee and the first secretary of the KPRF Stavropol city committee

17 December 1995—Elected to the State Duma from a single-member district, and became a member of the Committee for Legislative and Judicial Reforms

17 November 1996—Elected governor of Stavropol Krai

7 May 1997—Joined the Federal Commission on Problems in Chechnya

Married, with one daughter

from the Communists since his election. Nevertheless, Chernogorov chose to attend the Communist Party Congress in 1997. He was one of six governors who informed the presidential administration of their intention to attend the Communist Party Congress instead of NDR's. These governors also encouraged Moscow not to take their Communist affiliation too seriously (*EWI RRR*, 8 May 1997).

Relations with Other Regions

In May 1997 Chernogorov signed an agreement with the Congress of Russian Communities (KRO) aimed at resettling and employing over 30,000 ethnic Russians from Chechnya. In June 1997 Chernogorov and Chechen President Aslan Maskhadov signed a peace and cooperation agreement. Under the agreement, the two regions were to supply each other with goods and foodstuffs and their administrations would assist in establishing ties between regional enterprises (*KD*, 6 June 1997).

Chernogorov met with Aleksandr Lebed, now the governor of Krasnoyarsk Krai, in December 1997. Lebed stated that he had a favorable impression of the governor and that Chernogorov was a man open to compromise (*Segodnya*, 10 December 1997).

In January 1998 Stavropol participated in the North Caucasus Congress of Chambers of Industry and Trade. The Congress represents chambers from Rostov, Krasnodar, Adygeya, Dagestan, Karachaevo-Cherkessia, and North Ossetia. The main goal of the assembly is to convince the federal government to focus less on investing in the state sector and encourage the development of the small business sector.

Stavropol belongs to the Association of Cooperation of Republics, Krais, and Oblasts of the Northern Caucasus. The other members are the republics of Adygeya, Dagestan, Ingushetia, Kabardino-Balkaria, Karachaevo-Cherkessia, North Ossetia, and Kalmykia; Krasnodar Krai; and Rostov Oblast.

Attitudes Toward Business: In Search of Investors

Chernogorov is very interested in improving Stavropol's economy and restructuring regional enterprises to function under market conditions. He has assured industrialists of his interest in cooperative work. The governor believes that it has become necessary to determine which unprofitable businesses should be restructured, and which should be bankrupted (*SP*, 21 August 1997). He asserts that the slow rate with which this is being carried out is only aggravating the present situation and increasing the volume of enterprise debts. Chernogorov believes that a fundamental part of developing the krai's economy is raising the level of investment activity and creating conditions attractive to Russian investors (*SP*, 21 August 1997). Chernogorov has prepared a proposal to create an investment fund for the Stavropol Krai government and financial investors (*SP*, 21 August 1997).

Stavropol could benefit from a new Russian pipeline proposal that would enable Russia to transport oil from Azerbaijan without having to go through Chechnya.

SVERDLOVSK OBLAST

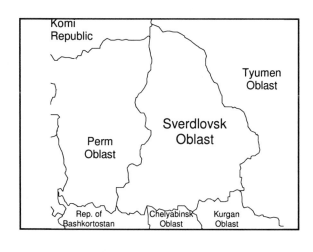

Territory: 194,800 km^2
Population (as of 1 January 1998):
4,656,000
Distance from Moscow: 1,667 km

Major Cities:
Yekaterinburg, *capital* (pop. 1,272,200)
Nizhnii Tagil (399,200)
Kamensk-Uralskii (192,100)
Pervouralsk (135,700)
Serov (100,000)
Asbest (81,700)

Basic Facts

Population (as of 1 Jan. 1998): 4,656,000 (3.17% of Russian total)

Ethnic breakdown (1989 census): Russians 88.7%, Tatars 3.9%, Ukrainians 1.8%

Urban population (as of 1 Jan. 1998): 87.5% (Russia overall: 73.1%)

Student population (as of 1 Sept. 1997): 208 per 10,000 (Russia overall: 208/10,000)

Pensioner population (1997): 26.59% (Russia overall: 25.96%)

Percent of population with higher education (1989 census): 9.1% (Russia overall: 11.3%)

Percent of population working in (1997): Industry: 32.2% (Russian average: 23.0%); Agriculture: 5.4% (13.7%); Trade: 13.9% (13.5%); Culture: 13.0% (13.3%)

Average monthly personal income in July 1998: 746.9 new rubles (Russian average: 891.7 new rubles)

Average monthly personal expenses in July 1998: 597.1 new rubles (Russian average: 684.9 new rubles)

Average monthly subsistence requirement in 1998: 471 new rubles (Russian average: 438 new rubles)

Consumer price index (as of July 1998): 98 (Russia overall = 100)

Budgetary revenues (1997): 11,825.1 billion rubles (Russia overall: 433,378.2 billion rubles)

Budgetary expenditures (1997): 12,124.4 billion rubles (Russia overall: 468,111.6 billion rubles)

Industrial production as percentage of all Russian production (Jan.–Aug. 1998): 3.59%

Proportion of loss-making enterprises (as of July 1998): 48.8% (Russia overall: 50.4%)

Number of enterprises which have wage arrears (as of 1 Sept. 1998): 1,752 (1.30% of Russian total)

Agricultural production as percentage of all Russian production (1997): 2.44%

Number of private farms (as of 1 Jan. 1998): 2,359 (0.86% of Russian total)

Capital investment (1997): 13,082.1 billion rubles (Russia overall: 408,797 billion rubles)

Sources of investment (1997): federal budget: 10.4% (Russian average: 10.2%); regional budget: 9.5% (10.5%); extra-budgetary funds: 80.1% (79.3%)

Foreign investment (1997): 70,556,000 USD (Russia overall: 12,294,734,000 USD)

Number of joint ventures (1997): 209 (1.42% of Russian total)

Fixed capital investment in joint ventures and foreign companies (1997): 438,122 million rubles (Russia overall: 16,265.4 billion rubles)

Number of small businesses (as of 1 July 1998): 25,900 (2.98% of Russian total)

Number of enterprises privatized in 1997: 135 (4.92% of Russian total), including those which used to be municipal property: 88.2% (Russian average: 66.4%); regional property: 4.4% (20.0%); federal property: 7.4% (13.6%)

Number of telephones per 100 families (1997): in cities: 41.5 (Russian average: 49.2); in villages: 18.9 (19.8)

Brief Overview

Sverdlovsk Oblast is located at the center of Russia, on the border dividing Europe and Asia. Its territory covers the eastern slopes of the Ural Mountains and the adjoining parts of the West Siberian lowland. Its central location makes it a highly developed rail, highway, and air transportation node. It shares a border with Tyumen, Kurgan, Chelyabinsk, and Perm oblasts and the republics of Bashkortostan and Komi.

Sverdlovsk Oblast is second only to Moscow Oblast in terms of industrial production and third in the proportion of expenditures covered by its own budgetary revenues (97.2 percent in 1997). It boasts major enterprises specializing in ferrous and non-ferrous metallurgy, electronics, chemicals, pharmaceuticals, and lumber processing. Sverdlovsk also excels in machine building, including the manufacture of equipment for the transportation, energy, mining, chemical, and metallurgical sectors. Sverdlovsk's land is rich in mineral resources which provide raw materials for the region's more than 2,500 processing enterprises. Sverdlovsk is also famous for mining precious stones and making jewelry. Highly developed industry causes serious air pollution in the region with about 300 kg of toxic wastes per capita.

According to a 1998 survey by *Ekspert* magazine, the oblast ranked 4th among Russia's 89 regions in terms of investment potential and 45th in terms of investment risk. A 1998 survey by Bank Austria ranked the oblast 7th in terms of investment climate.

Electoral History

2000 Presidential Election
Putin: 62.71%
Zyuganov: 17.05%
Yavlinskii: 7.77%
Zhirinovsky: 3.95%
Tuleev: 1.76%
Turnout: 62.09% (Russia overall: 68.64%)

1999 Parliamentary Elections
Unity: 25.47%
Union of Right Forces: 12.58%
Communist Party of the Russian Federation: 11.98%
Yabloko: 8.61%
Zhirinovsky Bloc: 7.24%
Fatherland–All Russia: 6.47%
Peace. Labor. May: 5.94%
In single-mandate districts: 1 Unity, 1 Our Home Is
    Russia, 1 Spiritual Heritage, 4 independent
Turnout: 52.10% (Russia overall: 61.85%)

1999 Gubernatorial Election
Rossel (incumbent): 38.80%/63.09%
Burkov (Sverdlovsk Oblast Legislative Assembly
    deputy): 18.36%/28.26%
Chernetskii (Yekaterinburg mayor): 15.49%
Kadochnikov: 9.64%
Kovpak: 8.81%
Belkova: 1.10%
Selivanov: 0.61%
Turnout: 40.93%/27.62%

1996 Presidential Election
Yeltsin: 59.45%/76.92% (first round/second round)
Lebed: 14.18%
Zyuganov: 11.66%/17.89%
Yavlinskii: 5.36%
Zhirinovsky: 4.88%
Turnout: 63.70%/65.02% (Russia overall: 69.67%/
    68.79%)

1995 Parliamentary Elections
Transformation of the Fatherland: 12.07%
Liberal Democratic Party of Russia: 9.20%
Our Home Is Russia: 8.32%
Communist Party of the Russian Federation: 8.25%
Yabloko: 6.65%
Women of Russia: 5.77%
Party of Workers' Self-Government: 5.74%
Russia's Democratic Choice: 4.87%
Communists–Workers' Russia: 4.83%
Congress of Russian Communities: 4.18%
In single-mandate districts: 4 independent, 1
    Yabloko, 1 Transformation of the Fatherland, 1
    Forward, Russia
Turnout: 53.13% (Russia overall: 64.37%)

1995 Gubernatorial Election
Rossel (ex-governor, oblast legislature chairman,
    Transformation of the Urals): 26.01%/59.86%
    (first round/second round)
Strakhov (incumbent): 23.44%/32.10%
Trushnikov (first deputy governor): 20.30%
Kadochnikov (KPRF): 8.06%
Gaisin: 4.89%
Kaletin: 2.99%
Zyablitsev: 2.75%
Martyanov (LDPR): 2.25%
Turnout: 37.0%/33.99%

1993 Constitutional Referendum
"Yes"—78.0%   "No"—19.7%

1993 Parliamentary Elections
Russia's Choice: 25.08%
Liberal Democratic Party of Russia: 17.64%
Party of Russian Unity and Concord: 9.76%
Women of Russia: 8.34%
Yabloko: 8.13%
Communist Party of the Russian Federation: 5.77%
Democratic Party of Russia: 5.48%
Agrarian Party of Russia: 3.95%
In single-mandate districts: 4 independent, 1 Party
    of economic Freedom, 1 Agrarian Party of Russia,
    1 Russia's Choice
From electoral associations: 1 Agrarian Party of Russia,
    1 Russia's Choice, 1 Liberal Democratic Party of Rus-
    sia, 1 Democratic Party of Russia
Turnout: 50.14% (Russia overall: 54.34%)

1991 Presidential Election
Yeltsin: 84.80%
Ryzhkov: 4.52%
Zhirinovsky: 4.43%
Makashov: 1.77%
Tuleev: 1.42%
Bakatin: 1.25%
Turnout: 78.86% (Russia overall: 76.66%)

Regional Political Institutions

Executive:
    Governor, 4-year term
    Eduard Ergartovich Rossel, elected August 1995,
    September, 1999
        Pl. Oktyabrskaya, 1; Yekaterinburg, 620031
        Tel. 7(343–2) 70–54–73, 70–54–68;
        Fax 7(343–2) 58–91–03
        Federation Council in Moscow:
        7(095) 292–61–02, 926–64–90

Legislative:
    Bicameral
    Legislative Assembly (*Zakonodatelnoe Sobranie*):
    Oblast Duma—14 members, 4-year term, elected
    April 1998
    Chair—Vyacheslav Sergeevich Surganov, elected
    1996, May 1998
    House of Representatives (*Palata Predstavitelei*)—
    21 members, 2–year term, May 1998
    Chair—Petr Yefimovich Golenishchev, elected
    May 1998

Regional Politics

Pro-Reform Regional Lobbyist

Unlike many other regional leaders, Sverdlovsk Governor Eduard Rossel is willing to share responsibility for the country's economic difficulties rather than simply blaming them all on the federal government. He believes that alongside developing the private sector, Russia should have a powerful state sector which produces 30–35 percent of GNP. He stresses that the state should support military enterprises and wants the government to print more money as a solution to its most pressing economic problems. Rossel is also ready to nationalize large enterprises that are poorly managed.

While he generally supports the overall course of reform and supported President Boris Yeltsin's 1996 reelection, Rossel has become one of the most visible spokesmen for regional interests in the country. In this role, he is in a strong position because of his long experience in power and the favorable economic situation in his region, both of which attract the interest of other regional leaders throughout the Urals and Siberia. Additionally, he is from Yeltsin's home region, and, although the two fought in the past, he enjoyed close ties to the president. While he is often at odds with Kremlin policy, his criticism of Moscow has not adversely affected the social and economic situation in Sverdlovsk. Despite his critical approach, however, he has not been able to develop a viable alternative plan for reform.

Rossel is the descendant of Germans who settled in the Volga region in the 18th century. His father and grandfather were executed in 1937, several months before Rossel's birth. His mother was then arrested and exiled to the northern Komi Republic four years later. Rossel was separated from his family for six years and rejoined them only when his mother was released at the end of the World War II. He worked in the mining industry for thirty years and by 1990 had risen to lead a regional construction division, Glavsreduralstroi. During those years, Rossel worked with Yeltsin, who was then first secretary of the Sverdlovsk Communist Party branch. Rossel notes that his relationship with Yeltsin was good, but did not go beyond business.

During the August 1991 putsch, Rossel denounced the coup plotters and actively supported Yeltsin. As a reward, the president appointed him Sverdlovsk governor despite the complaints of local democratic activists who labeled him a "red director." The local democrats claimed that Rossel secretly resisted reforms and would lobby for the interests of big businesses at the expense of common citizens. During his first two years in the office, Rossel remained loyal to the federal authorities. But he began to believe that Russia gave too many rights to its 21 ethnically defined republics while shortchanging the predominantly Russian oblasts and krais. In April 1993, he initiated a regional referendum which asked citizens whether they supported the idea of transforming Sverdlovsk Oblast into a Ural Republic, which would have the same privileges as the ethnic republics. Eighty percent of voters favored establishing the republic.

During Yeltsin's October 1993 tank battle with the Russian parliament, Rossel refused to explicitly support either side in the conflict but complied with all of Yeltsin's orders. Later that month, he announced the establishment of the Ural Republic, a move heavily criticized by the majority of Moscow politicians, including Prime Minister Viktor Chernomyrdin. Almost immediately after the republic had been proclaimed, Yeltsin sacked Rossel along with several governors who opposed presidential decrees during the conflict with the parliament.

Following his dismissal, Rossel did not join the Communist or nationalist opposition. He instead began to build an independent political party, Transformation of the Urals, which set up a national organization for the 1995 parliamentary elections (Transformation of the Fatherland). The party finished first in Sverdlovsk Oblast with 12 percent of the vote in the Duma race, but received less than 0.5 percent nationwide.

The party also endorsed Rossel for the August 1995 gubernatorial election, which he won, garnering more than 60 percent of the vote in the second round. He defeated the incumbent Aleksei Strakhov, whom Yeltsin had named to the post following Rossel's dismissal in 1993. Strakhov had the strong support of Chernomyrdin's Our Home Is Russia (NDR) and his defeat was seen at the time as a harbinger of Chernomyrdin's subsequent poor showing in the December 1995 parliamentary elections. Rossel was reelected on 12 September 1999, winning 63 percent of the vote in the second round of elections. In the runoff he faced the leader of the May movement, Aleksandr Burkov, who defeated five other candidates in the first round, including Rossel's main opponent and long-time rival, Yekaterinburg Mayor Arkadii Chernetskii.

Executive Platform: Lacks Alternatives to Government Policy

As an executive, Rossel is willing to experiment with radical ideas and does not expect the federal government to bail his region out of its problems. He has called on regional leaders to start working on regional anti-crisis programs rather than waiting for a nationwide plan prepared by the central government.

Despite his good intentions, Rossel's main failing as a regional spokesman is that he has not been able to generate a real alternative to the federal government's policies. On 22 May 1997 a number of leading economists and industrialists gathered in Yekaterinburg at his behest to discuss the economic situation in a forum billed as the Russian Davos. This was the second such gathering: the first "Russian Davos" (named after the annual meetings in the Swiss resort) took place in Yekaterinburg in May 1996, and was widely seen as a vote of support for Boris Yeltsin's election campaign from the political elite of the Urals.

The 1997 "Davos" adopted a more critical tone, but failed to produce a coherent alternative program. The proceedings of the meeting disappointed those observers of the Russian scene who hoped that regional elites would come up with a new set of policy initiatives which were more in tune with the economic situation beyond the Moscow beltway than the government's current policies. The speakers' evaluation of the country's problems was remarkably similar to the government's own analysis of the situation—from the crisis in tax revenues to the need to tighten regulation of the natural monopolies.

The meeting adopted a final document which called for the equivalent of a "New Deal" for Russia—a policy of active state intervention in industry to revive demand and solve the chronic problem of non-payments. The new policy should have a social democratic character "with Russian colors." Such a policy could provide the "national idea" around which healthy social forces might rally. (In July 1996 Boris Yeltsin called for intellectuals to come up with a new "national idea" to give Russia a sense of direction.)

The participants of the Yekaterinburg forum seemed to share the government's technocratic approach to policy making. While they acknowledged that there was something fundamentally wrong with the way political and economic institutions were working, they did not propose fundamental institutional reform, just new policy packages.

Policies: Enacting Greater State Control

Rossel has been extremely outspoken on financial issues. He thinks that the only way to impose order on the country's chaotic financial situation is for the state to take control of most financial flows. During the fall of 1998, he once again toyed with the idea of introducing his own currency in Sverdlovsk Oblast, the Urals franc, which had been used briefly in 1991, but backed down after realizing the idea was extremely impractical (*EWI RRR*, 22 October 1998). In October 1998, he also proposed banning the use of dollars in Russia and creating a gold-backed ruble. Again he had to withdraw these ideas in the face of loud public criticism.

In announcing proposals for his 1999 budget, Rossel broached the idea of abolishing several social benefits, and nationalizing several banks and industries. Critics have suggested that these proposals might only make the oblast's difficult economic situation even more dire.

In the Federation Council, Rossel has voted against the buying and selling of land.

Relationships Between Key Players: Back on Top

After dominating his region for much of the 1990s, Rossel seemed to be on the ropes through the first nine months of 1998. But the crisis of August 1998 gave him new energy to rebuild his image to prepare for the August 1999 gubernatorial elections. Rossel's main opponent in Sverdlovsk Oblast was Yekaterinburg Mayor Arkadii Chernetskii (for a detailed analysis of Rossel-Chernetskii relations, see *EWI RRR*, 25 June 1998). When Rossel won a second term and Chernetskii placed a distant third, Rossel's dominant position was assured. But Chernetskii also won reelection as Yekaterinburg mayor in December 1999, meaning their rivalry continued.

Chernetskii virtually disappeared from public view after the crisis began. The federal government's policies are now more in accord with Rossel's efforts to rebuild Sverdlovsk's productive enterprises than Chernetskii's focus on reviving the retail sector. Chernetskii criticized the oblast government for not spending enough on the population's social needs, a tactic that could backfire as it echoes the Communists' criticisms. Chernetskii was being criticized for being too obvious in his campaign and too critical without offering concrete ideas. The city's entrepreneurs criticized the way that his Our Home–Our City used their donations, while raion executives were concerned about Chernetskii's choice of a successor (*EWI RRR*, 5 November 1998).

Chernetskii has criticized Rossel for trying to take too much money from Yekaterinburg to pay for programs throughout the oblast. Yekaterinburg contributes two-thirds of the Sverdlovsk Oblast budget and then relies on oblast officials to give much of the money back in the form of programs. Of the 73 municipal jurisdictions in Sverdlovsk, only six generate more money than they need. Rossel has determined that each region must send 77 percent of the money it collects to the oblast, so the oblast leaders can decide how to spend the money. Chernetskii believes that the rural regions in the oblast should become more self-sufficient.

Rossel and Chernetskii have fought over many additional issues. Chernetskii tried to raise prices for renters living in municipal apartments and for municipal services during the first part of 1998. Rossel, however, rescinded these price increases. Chernetskii tried to introduce fee-based health care, but Rossel opposed such moves.

Rossel probably reached the nadir of his rule when his Transformation of the Urals party took only 9 percent of the party list vote in the April 1998 Sverdlovsk Oblast legislative elections. Chernetskii's Our Home–Our City won 21 percent and the combined Communists and Agrarians took 12 percent. The voters sent a strong message to Rossel protesting the large amounts he had spent rebuilding the governor's office and preparing for a Russian-French-German summit that was transferred to Moscow at the last moment. Nevertheless, Rossel's supporters won enough of the seats in the single-member districts so that his ally, Vyacheslav Surganov, was just able to retain his seat as the lower house's speaker. By the end of 1999, with the governor and mayor reelected, the voters had preserved the status quo for four more years.

Rossel's success in building his own regional political party has become a model for other regions. Rossel set up Transformation of the Urals (*Preobrazhenie Urala*) on 22 November 1993, after Yeltsin had fired him as governor. The party helped him win the gubernatorial elections in August 1995 and then won a majority of the seats in both houses of the newly created Legislative Assembly in the April 1996 elections. Although the party stumbled somewhat in the April 1998 legislative elections, the speakers of both houses of the regional legislature are also members of the party's political council. Since the regional leaders are all members of the same political organization, the key players can more easily coordinate their actions in governing the region and there is less tension between the executive and legislative branches than at the federal level.

Just as Yeltsin feared the growing influence of the increasingly assertive governors, Rossel has tried to limit the power of democratically elected local leaders. He devised a scheme of dividing the oblast into six administrative districts, which stand above the oblast's 73 municipal jurisdictions, to ensure that his policies are implemented on the ground. He plans to appoint the leaders of the districts who will coordinate the work of the democratically elected mayors and legislatures in the 73 districts (*UR*, 28 February 1997). Yekaterinburg Mayor Chernetskii opposed the plan because he feared that it would reduce his power. Yeltsin gave it his blessing even though he cracked down on other regions, like Udmurtia and Komi, where regional leaders have tried to appoint local leaders directly. When Putin came to power, he implemented a similar plan at the federal level.

The oblast's various media outlets are under the influence of the various politicians. Rossel controls Oblast TV and the *Transformation of the Urals* newspaper. The municipal TV station Channel 41 generally supports Mayor Chernetskii. Channel 4, Channel 51, Radio 101, Russian Radio, and the *Podrobnosti* newspaper are controlled by Moscow. State Duma member Yevgenii Zyablitsev's regional media empire includes Channel 10–Guberniya, NTT, Urals Center TV, and the newspaper *Novaya Khronika*. State Duma member Valerii Yazev owns the newspaper *Novaya Gorodskaya gazeta* and the Yava Publishing House. The newspaper *Uralskii Rabochii* has become a battleground for Rossel and Chernetskii. These media are engaged in constantly shifting ties of alliance, including a variety of secret dealings and public attacks on each other (*EWI RRR*, 21 January 1999).

Rossel has sought to increase his own political power by setting up an oblast-controlled bank. In late October 1998, he announced the formation of an oblast bank group including Uralpromstroibank, CSB-bank (a subsidiary of Menatep) and Uralsibsotsbank. Other banks can join the group by giving the oblast 50 percent of their stock. In return, they are given tax breaks and access to public funds (*KV*, 3 November 1999).

Rossel had tried a similar initiative in October 1997, when he sought to transform Inkor-bank into an oblast bank (*UR*, 25 October 1997 and *KD*, 28 October 1997). In April 1998, however, the federal government blocked him from using federal funds for this purpose. In these efforts Rossel is apparently following the example of Bashkortostan, which set up its own banking

system and then threw out the Moscow banks (*KD*, 4 April 1998).

In addition to trying to set up his own bank, in February 1999 Rossel issued a decree that prevents shareholders in important oblast companies from firing their directors without first gaining the governor's approval. The decree affects all firms that have "significance for the social-economic situation of the oblast" (*Izvestiya*, 16 February 1999).

Rossel has created some of his own personal problems. He has lied about the whereabouts of his daughter, who lives in Hamburg, Germany, where she works as a representative of the Interural company, which was set up in 1988 and has a monopoly on the export of all metal products from the oblast. Before the election, Rossel had claimed that she was living in Russia and afterward claimed that he had always maintained that she was in Germany. At a time when the oblast was having trouble paying many salaries, Rossel restored a beautiful lakeshore house as the governor's residence with a 17-million-ruble loan from GUTA-bank. He also blocked traffic from the area to ensure peace and quiet (*Profil*, 19 October 1998). In early 1999, the local legislature facetiously tried to put the property up for sale to recoup the state's investment.

Ties to Moscow: Critical of Federal Policies, but Good Relations with Yeltsin

Rossel often complains that the federal government does not take regional interests into account when it is formulating national policy. He believes that although the constitution gives regions considerable powers, regional leaders are unable to implement serious reforms because they lack financial resources, the distribution and allocation of which is a federal prerogative. As the leader of one of the few regions that makes a net contribution to the federal budget, he particularly objects to Moscow's practice of transferring money from rich to poor regions. He charges that this practice encourages poor regions to seek financial help from outside and gives them no incentive to solve problems on their own. Rossel strongly objects to policies of asymmetrical federalism in which the federal government gives special privileges to the ethnic republics that are not also extended to largely ethnic-Russian oblasts.

Rossel turned his philosophy into action by being the first governor of an oblast to sign a power-sharing treaty with the federal government, on 12 January

1996. Until Sverdlovsk Oblast gained such a treaty, the federal government had only signed them with ethnically defined republics. On the basis of the treaty, Rossel tried to introduce a variety of local taxes, including levies on imported chicken legs, alcohol produced outside the oblast, and passengers using the local airport. He claimed that the treaty gave him the right to levy these taxes, but the Constitutional Court ruled against him and the taxes were overturned (*Profil*, 19 October 1998).

Rossel is one of the numerous governors who denounced the federal government's 1999 draft budget as not providing enough support to the regions, while being based on unrealistic estimates about Russia's macroeconomic performance.

Rossel tenaciously defends the corporate interests of Russia's governors against encroachments by Moscow. He repeatedly denounced the federal government's 1997 campaign against Primorskii Krai Governor Yevgenii Nazdratenko. When the energy crisis became extreme in the Far East, Yeltsin first tried to remove Nazdratenko and then transferred many of his powers to a presidentially appointed representative. Rossel warned that such a precedent endangered all regional leaders because they could find themselves subject to similar sanctions.

The Kremlin ignores many of Rossel's criticisms because of Sverdlovsk Oblast's relative economic success. Rossel, unlike Moscow Mayor Yurii Luzhkov, who also frequently criticizes federal policies, does not have presidential ambitions. On the other hand, Rossel can deliver strong support to the president's chosen successor as long as the Kremlin continues to court him.

In the spring of 1997, Rossel turned down two offers to join the federal cabinet. Magnate Boris Berezovskii had hoped that he would serve as first deputy prime minister to balance out the power of the other first deputy prime minister, Anatolii Chubais, but Rossel rejected the offer, delivered through Yeltsin's daughter Tatyana. He also rejected an offer to head up the State Anti-monopoly Committee (*Profil*, 19 October 1998).

Relations with Other Regions: Favors Equal Rights for Oblasts, Republics

In trying to transform Sverdlovsk Oblast into the Ural Republic in 1993, Rossel made himself one of the most outspoken advocates of ending Russia's asymmetrical federalism and giving each region equal rights. Key leaders like Federation Council Speaker Yegor Stroev support similar plans, but powerful republican leaders like Tatarstan President Mintimer Shaimiev and Bashkortostan President Murtaza Rakhimov oppose them.

Moscow Mayor Yurii Luzhkov's Fatherland party initially sought to form an alliance in Sverdlovsk Oblast with Yekaterinburg Mayor Chernetskii's Our Home–Our City. However, Chernetskii severed ties when it became clear that Luzhkov wanted too much control over Our Home–Our City's future campaign activities (*EWI RRR*, 14 January 1999). The exit of Chernetskii created the potential for closer links between Rossel and Luzhkov.

Rossel has also been actively signing treaties with other regional leaders, most of which include barter deals involving the region's industrial output.

Foreign Relations: Actively Seeks New Ties

Rossel is working actively to restore links with the former Soviet republics that are now part of the CIS. The oblast has signed trade treaties with Georgia, Kazakhstan, Kyrgyzstan, Uzbekistan, and Armenia. Given the post-Soviet chaos, most of these ties have been lost. By the late 1990s, Sverdlovsk Oblast's trade was only 4 percent of what it had been with Georgia in 1991 (*EWI RRR*, 14 January 1999).

In December 1998, Rossel visited Iran, offering to build atomic and heat power stations, supply equipment for steel mills; deliver metal products; and develop a joint venture to make railroad cars. The two sides established four working groups to further develop links in specific sectors.

Attitudes Toward Business: Willing to Provide Investment Incentives

Governor Rossel has avidly courted foreign investment, although through 1998, foreigners had only invested a paltry $500 million in the region (*EWI RRR*, 22 December 1998). Rossel has pledged 10 percent of the oblast budget to pay back any investors who lose money at the fault of the oblast. So far it has not made any payouts. Rossel has also suggested that partially completed projects in the oblast be converted to foreign ownership, in exchange for the promise of future investments. In 1997, the Russian foreign ministry opened an investment promotion office in the region

Eduard Ergartovich Rossel

8 October 1937—Born in Bor (now Nizhnii Novgorod Oblast) to a family of Volga Germans. His father was shot before he was born and his mother was arrested 9 October 1941 and sent to a camp in Komi. She was reunited with her son six years later.

1962—Graduated from the Sverdlovsk Mining Institute, then worked for the institute as a junior researcher

1963–1975—Worked in the Tagilstroi trust (Nizhnii Tagil, Sverdlovsk Oblast), ultimately becoming the trust's senior engineer

1967–1991—Member of the Communist Party

1971—Completed a graduate program at the Urals Polytechnic Institute

1975–1983—Deputy director, then director, of the Tagiltyazhstroi combine

1983–January 1990—Deputy director of the territorial construction association, Glavsreduralstroi

January–April 1990—Director of Glavsreduralstroi

March 1990—Elected to the Sverdlovsk Oblast Council of People's Deputies

2 April 1990–October 1991—Elected chairman of the oblast executive committee

4 July 1990—Combined the post of chairman of the oblast council with his leadership of the oblast executive committee

August 1991—Backed Yeltsin's stand against the coup makers

18 October 1991—Appointed governor of Sverdlovsk Oblast by President Yeltsin

12 April 1993—Held an oblast referendum in which 80% of the population backed turning Sverdlovsk Oblast into the Ural Republic

October 1993—Effectively supported Yeltsin in battle against Russian parliament

27 October 1993—Sverdlovsk Oblast Council adopted constitution of the Ural Republic within the Russian Federation

9 November 1993—Yeltsin disbanded the Sverdlovsk Oblast Council

10 November 1993—Yeltsin replaced Rossel as governor with Aleksei Strakhov

11 November 1993—Rossel elected chairman of the Urals Interregional Association

November 1993—Founded the Transformation of the Urals political party

12 December 1993—Elected member of the Federation Council, served as a member of the Committee of Security and Defense

29 April 1994—Elected chairman of the Sverdlovsk Oblast Duma

13 August 1995—Elected governor after defeating Strakhov, who was backed by Our Home Is Russia

Fall 1995—Formed Transformation of the Fatherland political party for the 1995 State Duma elections, but won only 0.49% of the party list vote and one single-member district seat

January 1996—Reappointed to the Federation Council

14 January 1998—Survived assassination attempt

12 September 1999—Reelected governor with 63% of the vote (the first of its kind), and several countries have consulates there, including the U.S., UK, and China.

The oblast authorities are working on a series of tax concessions and free economic zones in the region to stimulate investment. These initiatives are based on the power-sharing agreement signed between the federal government and Sverdlovsk on 12 January 1996. The agreement gives Rossel the right to provide tax benefits and loan guarantees to foreign investors, create free trade zones, and develop local policies to attract capital. During a September 1997 trip to Japan, he promised to lower profit taxes for investors who bring in more than $10 million (*EWI RRR*, 2 October 1997).

In December 1998, Rossel advocated allowing foreign banks to operate in Russia so that citizens would be willing to take their money out of their mattresses and put it in savings accounts where it would stimulate investment.

Among the Western companies working in the region are Coca-Cola, Pepsi, DHL, Wrigley, Sprint, Ford, Rank Xerox, Asea Brown Boveri, Philips, Lufthansa, Siemens, Dresdner Bank, and Henkel.

Internet Sites in the Region

http://www.midural.ru/
This is the official website of the oblast administration. It has information about the governor, government, oblast legislature, and electoral commission. There are also daily press releases from the governor.

http://www.midural.ru/ek
This business-oriented site has information on 200 of the leading enterprises in the oblast An export map shows the products available for sale.

http://www.e-reliz.ru/govern/ru/default.htm
This is another official website, also with press releases from the governor.

http://www.politics.e-reliz.ru/politics/plso/parties/sites-1.asp
This site has links to all the political parties in the region.

http://www.ur.etel.ru
The *Uralskii rabochii* newspaper has extensive daily coverage of events in the region.

TAIMYR AUTONOMOUS OKRUG

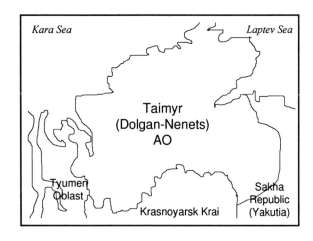

Territory: 862,100 km²
Population (as of 1 January 1998):
44,000
Distance from Moscow: 6,403 km

Major Cities:
Dudinka, *capital* (pop. 27,800)

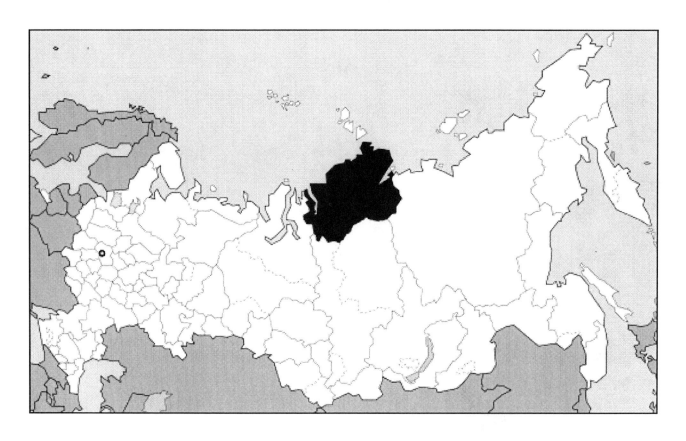

Basic Facts

Population (as of 1 Jan. 1998): 44,000 (0.03% of Russian total)

Ethnic breakdown (1989 census): Russians 67.1%, Dolgans 8.8%, Ukrainians 8.6%, Nenets 4.4%, Nganasans 1.5%, Germans 1.5%, Tatars 1.2%

Urban population (as of 1 Jan. 1998): 65.4% (Russia overall: 73.1%)

Pensioner population (1997): 18.18% (Russia overall: 25.96%)

Percent of population with higher education (1989 census): 11.0% (Russia overall: 11.3%)

Average monthly personal income in July 1998: 938.6 new rubles (Russian average: 891.7 new rubles)

Average monthly personal expenses in July 1998: 588.8 new rubles (Russian average: 684.9 new rubles)

Average monthly subsistence requirement in 1998: 810 new rubles (Russian average: 438 new rubles)

Consumer price index (as of July 1998): 223 (Russia overall = 100)

Budgetary revenues (1997): 465.7 billion rubles (Russia overall: 433,378.2 billion rubles)

Budgetary expenditures (1997): 470.9 billion rubles (Russia overall: 468,111.6 billion rubles)

Industrial production as percentage of all Russian production (Jan.–Aug. 1998): 0.001%

Proportion of loss-making enterprises (as of July 1998): 0% (Russia overall: 50.4%)

Number of enterprises which have wage arrears (as of 1 Sept. 1998): 27 (0.02% of Russian total)

Agricultural production as percentage of all Russian production (1997): 0.008%

Number of private farms (as of 1 Jan. 1998): 0 (0% of Russian total)

Capital investment (1997): 66.2 billion rubles (Russia overall: 408,797 billion rubles)

Sources of investment (1997): federal budget: 27.0% (Russian average: 10.2%); regional budget: 30.0% (10.5%); extra-budgetary funds: 43.0% (79.3%)

Number of telephones per 100 families (1997): in cities: 54.2 (Russian average: 49.2); in villages: 25.3 (19.8)

Brief Overview

Taimyr Autonomous Okrug is situated in the north of Krasnoyarsk Krai and borders Sakha (Yakutia), Evenk AO, and Yamal-Nenets AO. The okrug includes Taimyr Peninsula, which is the northernmost part of Eurasia and takes up almost half of the okrug's territory. The okrug is rich in water resources, and Taimyr Lake is the second largest lake in Siberia after Baikal. One tenth of the okrug's territory is occupied by three nature preserves—Taimyr, Putoran, and Big Arctic.

The okrug is rich in mineral resources, such as copper, nickel, gold, diamonds, coal, oil, and gas, but due to an extremely inclement climate most of the deposits are not being exploited. The mammoth Norilsk Metallurgical Works draws on the most valuable deposits of copper and nickel.

The investment situation in the okrug improved significantly toward the end of the decade. Investment potential grew by 6 points from 1997 to 1998, while investment risk decreased by 28 points over the same period. According to a 1998 survey by

Ekspert magazine, the okrug ranked 75th among Russia's 89 regions in terms of investment potential and 51st in terms of investment risk. A 1998 survey by Bank Austria ranked the okrug 80th in terms of investment climate.

Electoral History

2000 Presidential Election
Putin: 64.70%
Zyuganov: 14.85%
Yavlinskii: 5.90%
Zhirinovsky: 4.28%
Tuleev: 3.58%
Turnout: 64.42% (Russia overall: 68.64%)

1999 Parliamentary Elections
Unity: 35.20%
Zhirinovsky Bloc: 9.04%
Union of Right Forces: 8.17%
Yabloko: 8.04%
Communist Party of the Russian Federation: 7.57%
Pensioners' Party: 4.95%
Fatherland–All Russia: 4.01%
In a single-mandate district: 1 Our Home Is Russia
Turnout: 60.43% (Russia overall: 61.85%)

1996 Gubernatorial Election
Nedelin (incumbent): 65.70%
Subbotkin (okrug legislature deputy): 11.30%
Nechaev (okrug legislature deputy chairman): 7.88%
Turnout: 48.32%

1996 Presidential Election
Yeltsin: 49.47%/71.62% (first round/second round)
Lebed: 14.91%
Zyuganov: 12.08%/21.57%
Zhirinovsky: 10.07%
Yavlinskii: 6.47%
Turnout: 65.89%/61.74% (Russia overall: 69.67%/ 68.79%)

1995 Parliamentary Elections
Liberal Democratic Party of Russia: 15.40%
Our Home Is Russia: 13.84%
Women of Russia: 8.00%
Party of Workers' Self-Government: 6.80%
Yabloko: 6.14%
Communist Party of the Russian Federation: 6.12%

Congress of Russian Communities: 4.46%
Russia's Democratic Choice: 3.07%
In a single-mandate district: 1 independent
Turnout: 59.67% (Russia overall: 64.37%)

1993 Constitutional Referendum
"Yes"—79.4%　"No"—17.7%

1993 Parliamentary Elections
Russia's Choice: 27.99%
Liberal Democratic Party of Russia: 17.37%
Party of Russian Unity and Concord: 13.46%
Women of Russia: 9.64%
Yabloko: 7.85%
Democratic Party of Russia: 6.58%
Communist Party of the Russian Federation: 4.67%
Agrarian Party of Russia: 1.04%
In a single-mandate district: 1 independent
Turnout: 58.47% (Russia overall: 54.34%)

1991 Presidential Election
Yeltsin: 58.12%
Ryzhkov: 13.56%
Tuleev: 11.78%
Zhirinovsky: 8.91%
Bakatin: 2.60%
Makashov: 1.72%
Turnout: 75.00% (Russia overall: 76.66%)

Regional Political Institutions

Executive:
Governor, 4-year term
Gennadii Pavlovich Nedelin, elected December 1996
Ul. Sovetskaya, 35; Dudinka, 663210; Taimyr Autonomous Okrug, Krasnoyarsk Krai
Tel 7(391–11) 2–53–74, 2–11–60;
Fax 7(391–11) 2–56–93, 2–52–74
Federation Council in Moscow: 7(095) 292–56–30, 926–66–47

Legislative:
Unicameral
Duma—11 members, 2-year term, elected March 1995
Chairman—Aleksandr Ivanovich Zabeivorota, elected May 1995

Regional Politics

Yeltsin Appointee Still in Power

Gennadii Nedelin was elected governor of Taimyr Autonomous Okrug on 22 December 1996, receiving 64 percent of the vote. Nedelin had been serving as chief executive of the region since 1991, when Yeltsin appointed him to the post. Nedelin was a logical choice for Yeltsin. Not only had he spent nearly 30 years working in Komsomol and local political structures, Nedelin loyally backed Yeltsin during the August 1991 coup, ensuring that his decrees were carried out in the region.

Nedelin served for one year on the Board of Directors for Norilsk Nikel, the largest metal factory in Russia, which is located in Taimyr. The fate of Norilsk Nikel and the impact that the enterprise has on the okrug's inhabitants is the primary issue confronting the region. It also plays a determinant role in Taimyr's relations with Krasnoyarsk Krai, to which the okrug is subordinate.

Executive Platform

When Nedelin was appointed governor in 1991, he spoke in favor of increasing the rights of autonomous okrugs. Taimyr had exhibited some strong separatist tendencies, seeking independence from Kranoyarsk, yet Nedelin signed a power-sharing agreement with Moscow and Krasnoyarsk Krai in November 1997 (see Ties to Moscow).

Relationships Between Key Players

Norilsk Nikel, the largest metal factory in Russia, is located in Taimyr. The plant is controlled by Sergei Potanin's Interros (including Uneximbank), which bought a significant stake as part of the loans-for-shares scheme. The process by which the bank gained control of the company has been heavily criticized. The bank was allowed to organize the auction for the plant as well as compete in it. It paid the paltry price of $170.1 million after disqualifying a bid of $350 million. Upon taking control of Norilsk, Uneximbank fired the managers of the plant. (Joseph R. Blasi, Maya Kroumova, and Douglas Kruse, *Kremlin Capitalism: Privatizing the Russian Economy*, Ithaca: Cornell University Press, 1997).

During the Krasnoyarsk Krai gubernatorial campaign in spring 1998, Uneximbank backed incumbent Krasnoyarsk Governor Valerii Zubov against Lebed. Since most of the plant's workers voted for Lebed, there was presumably some disappointment with management.

Norilsk Nikel supplies 20 percent of the world's nickel and 5 percent of its copper. The factory produces about $2 billion worth of metals a year, 90 percent of which are exported. Dependence on world market prices for the supply of non-ferrous metals has hurt Norilsk residents considerably. Reduced world demand for nickel caused by the Asian economic crisis caused the price for the metal to drop from $8,000 a ton to $4,000 at the beginning of 1999. As a result, Norilsk Nikel planned to cut output by 7 percent in 1999 in an effort to bring the price back up. Experts believe that the plant produces between 180,000 and 200,000 tons of nickel a year. In 1998 the price drop cost the plant an estimated $600 million (*KD*, 16 February 1999).

Then First Deputy Prime Minister Yurii Maslyukov visited Norilsk on 23–24 October 1998 to investigate its status. Because of the plant's generally positive situation, there was no talk of re-nationalizing Norilsk during Maslyukov's visit, but that threat remains. The plant agreed to continue paying 1 billion to 1.4 billion rubles annually to maintain the region's social sphere, although Maslyukov agreed to help transfer these costs to the taxpayers. Maslyukov also agreed to give a state guarantee for a $500 million World Bank loan to move more than 40,000 residents from the arctic region where Norilsk is located to more hospitable parts of Russia. The plant currently owes $2.5 billion to its creditors, but Maslyukov promised to defend the current owners against any attacks on their property (*KD*, 27 October 1998).

On 11 November 1997, Norilsk Nikel gave ownership of the profitable Krasnoyarsk Non-Ferrous Metals Factory, Russia's largest producer of platinum, to the Krasnoyarsk Krai administration, to partially pay off its 1.7 billion ruble ($290,000) debt. This was the first time that a factory has handed over some of its assets to a regional government to pay off its tax debt. Norilsk Nikel will pay off the rest of its debts by giving some of its output to Krasnoyarsk factories. (*KD*, 13 November 1997).

Ties to Moscow: Longtime Yeltsin Ally

During the 1991 coup, Nedelin supported the President's actions and ensured that all of his decrees were transmitted over okrug radio.

Gennadii Pavlovich Nedelin

20 May 1938—Born in the village Klyucha in the Minusinskii raion of Krasnoyarsk Krai; he served for two years in the Soviet army, then graduated from the Technical School of Mechanization and then the Krasnoyarsk Agricultural Institute.

1963—Began working for the Komsomol, serving as a secretary for the Minusinskii Komsomol district committee, instructor for the Krasnoyarsk Komsomol krai committee, and then as the first secretary of the Minusinskii Komsomol district committee

1966–1971—Deputy chairman of the Minusinskii district executive committee

May 1971—Became deputy chairman of the Taimyr okrug executive committee

March 1990—Elected to the Krasnoyarsk Krai Council of People's Deputies

1990–1991—Elected assistant chairman and then chairman of the Taimyr okrug executive committee

18 December 1991—Appointed governor of Taimyr Autonomous Okrug

12 December 1993—Elected to the Federation Council

December 1996—Elected governor of Taimyr Autonomous Okrug and to the second session of the Federation Council, serving on the Committee for Northern Affairs and Minority Peoples

June 1997–June 1998—Member of the board of directors of Norilsk Nikel

Married, with three children

In November 1997 Nedelin signed a power-sharing agreement with Yeltsin and the governors of Krasnoyarsk Krai and the Evenk Autonomous Okrug. The treaty outlines the delineation of powers between the federal government, the krai, and the okrugs, which are constituent parts of the krai as well as equal subjects of the federation. However, when Krasnoyarsk Krai Governor Aleksandr Lebed was elected in April 1998, he expressed a strong desire to renegotiate the treaty (*EWI RRR*, 21 May 1998).

In December 1996 the State Duma approved a bill to stop Russia's autonomous okrugs from seceding from the krais and oblasts of which they are parts. At the time, Taimyr, Khanty-Mansi, Yamal-Nenets, and Nenets autonomous okrugs had wanted greater independence in order to gain control over the natural resources on their territories.

Relations with Other Regions: Negotiations with Krasnoyarsk

Norilsk residents' sense of abandonment by the rest of Krasnoyarsk Krai greatly contributed to Taimyr's desire to separate from the rest of Krasnoyarsk. At one point in 1997, tensions were so high that Norilsk refused to pay regional taxes, hurting the krai treasury and crippling wage and pension payments (*EWI RRR*, 11 December 1997). Toward the end of 1997 a compromise was reached that included reducing transportation costs for bringing agricultural products to the area.

Taimyr did not participate in the December 1997 elections for the Krasnoyarsk legislature; however, okrug residents did vote in the April 1998 elections for krai governor and elected members to the legislature at that time. Aleksandr Lebed was elected governor of Krasnoyarsk Krai, and the city of Norilsk, located in Taimyr, gave him over 86 percent of its vote, a record in this election (*EWI RRR*, 21 May 1998).

Shortly after taking office, Lebed set up three working groups in cooperation with the management of Norilsk Nikel, located in Taimyr. One group is examining ways to develop local industry by increasing the use of metals produced in Norilsk. The second group is exploring ways to move pensioners out of the region to warmer climates. The third group is addressing the financial relations between the krai, the city of Norilsk, and Taimyr (*EWI RRR*, 11 June 1998).

In March 1999 the city of Norilsk, Norilsk Nikel, Norilsk Combine, and the Norilsk Mining Company reached an agreement with Krasnoyarsk Krai Governor Aleksandr Lebed. The agreement stipulates that 80 percent of the income tax will stay in the okrug while only 20 percent will go to the krai. Lebed agreed to lobby Moscow in the interests of the plant, and in exchange Norilsk Nikel will register all new subsidiaries in the krai.

Taimyr is a member of the Siberian Accord Association, which is headed by Omsk Governor Leonid Polezhaev. The association is made up of the republics of Buryatia, Gorno-Altai, and Khakassia; Altai and Krasnoyarsk krais; Irkutsk, Novosibirsk, Omsk, Tomsk, Tyumen, and Kemerovo oblasts; and Agin-Buryat, Taimyr, Ust-Orda Buryat, Khanty-Mansi, Evenk, and Yamal-Nenets autonomous okrugs.

Attitudes Toward Business: Former Board Member of Norilsk Nikel

From June 1997 to June 1998 Nedelin served on the board of directors of Norilsk Nikel. During the annual shareholders' meeting in June 1998 the board removed Nedelin as well as the governors of Krasnoyarsk Krai and Murmansk Oblast.

TAMBOV OBLAST

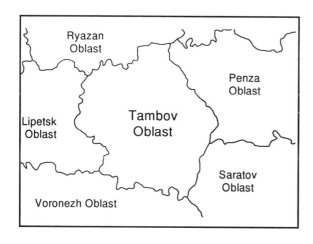

Territory: 34,300 km²
Population (as of 1 January 1998):
1,292,000
Distance from Moscow: 480 km

Major Cities:
Tambov, *capital* (pop. 315,900)
Michurinsk (120,000)
Morshansk (49,300)
Rasskazovo (48,900)

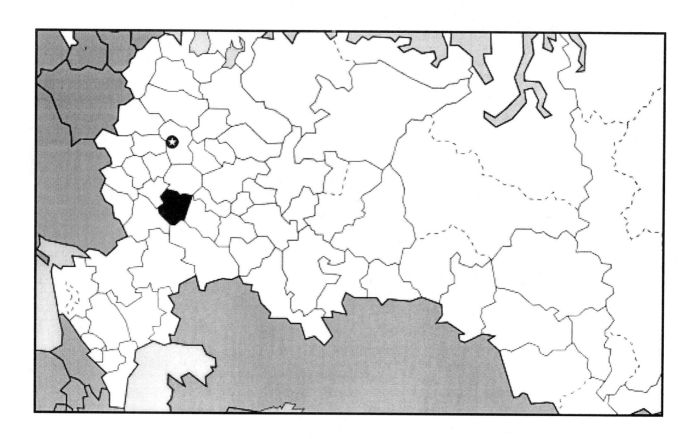

Basic Facts

Population (as of 1 Jan. 1998): 1,292,000 (0.88% of Russian total)

Ethnic breakdown (1989 census): Russians 97.2%, Ukrainians 1.0%

Urban population (as of 1 Jan. 1998): 58.2% (Russia overall: 73.1%)

Student population (as of 1 Sept. 1997): 159 per 10,000 (Russia overall: 208/10,000)

Pensioner population (1997): 30.42% (Russia overall: 25.96%)

Percent of population with higher education (1989 census): 8.0% (Russia overall: 11.3%)

Percent of population working in (1997): Industry: 20.1% (Russian average: 23.0%); Agriculture: 20.8% (13.7%); Trade: 13.1% (13.5%); Culture: 12.7% (13.3%)

Average monthly personal income in July 1998: 534.3 new rubles (Russian average: 891.7 new rubles)

Average monthly personal expenses in July 1998: 397.7 new rubles (Russian average: 684.9 new rubles)

Average monthly subsistence requirement in 1998: 276 new rubles (Russian average: 438 new rubles)

Consumer price index (as of July 1998): 77 (Russia overall = 100)

Budgetary revenues (1997): 2,013.6 billion rubles (Russia overall: 433,378.2 billion rubles)

Budgetary expenditures (1997): 2,132.0 billion rubles (Russia overall: 468,111.6 billion rubles)

Industrial production as percentage of all Russian production (Jan.–Aug. 1998): 0.30%

Proportion of loss-making enterprises (as of July 1998): 48.6% (Russia overall: 50.4%)

Number of enterprises which have wage arrears (as of 1 Sept. 1998): 2,358 (1.74% of Russian total)

Agricultural production as percentage of all Russian production (1997): 1.20%

Number of private farms (as of 1 Jan. 1998): 3,568 (1.30% of Russian total)

Capital investment (1997): 1,180.6 billion rubles (Russia overall: 408,797 billion rubles)

Sources of investment (1997): federal budget: 12.7% (Russian average: 10.2%); regional budget: 6.2% (10.5%); extra-budgetary funds:81.1% (79.3%)

Foreign investment (1997): 83,000 USD (Russia overall: 12,294,734,000 USD)

Number of joint ventures (1997): 13 (0.09% of Russian total)

Fixed capital investment in joint ventures and foreign companies (1997): 1,903 million rubles (Russia overall: 16,265.4 billion rubles)

Number of small businesses (as of 1 July 1998): 3,000 (0.35% of Russian total)

Number of enterprises privatized in 1997: 14 (0.51% of Russian total), including those which used to be municipal property: 50.0% (Russian average: 66.4%); regional property: 21.4% (20.0%); federal property: 28.6% (13.6%)

Number of telephones per 100 families (1997): in cities: 43.8 (Russian average: 49.2); in villages: 16.0 (19.8)

Brief Overview

Tambov Oblast is located in the center of the East European plain and borders Penza, Ryazan, Lipetsk, Voronezh, and Saratov oblasts. It has good transportation links and a favorable climate. Ten percent of the oblast territory is covered with woods. The oblast is rich in peat, mineral paints, phosphorus, sands, clays, zinc, titanium, and gold.

Tambov has well developed industrial and agricultural sectors. Its industry specializes in machine building and metal processing (22.6% of regional GDP), chemicals (19.1%), small-scale manufacturing, and food processing. Local farms produce grain, sugar beets, sunflowers, potatoes, and cattle.

The region imports coal, oil and petroleum products, ferrous metals, timber, and some construction materials. Major regional exports include: construction materials, equipment, mineral fertilizers, paints, grain, sugar, meat, milk, and butter. About 40 percent of the exports are shipped to western countries. The region has partnerships with companies from Finland, Sweden, the U.S., Germany, China, Croatia, the Czech Republic, Latvia, Kyrgyzstan, Belarus, and Ukraine. The oblast administration is seeking foreign investment in the regional food-processing industry, production of construction materials, and the truck-making industry.

According to a 1998 survey by *Ekspert* magazine, the oblast ranked 59th among Russia's 89 regions in terms of investment potential and 32nd in terms of investment risk. A 1998 survey by Bank Austria ranked the oblast 61st in terms of investment climate.

Electoral History

2000 Presidential Election
Putin: 48.13%
Zyuganov: 41.35%
Yavlinskii: 2.59%
Zhirinovsky: 2.26%
Tuleev: 1.47%
Turnout: 65.39% (Russia overall: 68.64%)

1999 Parliamentary Elections
Communist Party of the Russian Federation: 32.50%
Unity: 24.02%
Fatherland–All Russia: 6.28%
Zhirinovsky Bloc: 5.94%
Union of Right Forces: 4.32%

Yabloko: 3.84%
In single-mandate districts: 2 Communist Party of the Russian Federation
Turnout: 61.56% (Russia overall: 61.85%)

1999 Gubernatorial Election
Betin: 28.6%/50.34% (first round, second round)
Ryabov (incumbent): 27.7%/44.16%
Turnout: 59.8%/44.54%

1996 Presidential Election
Zyuganov: 52.26%/62.85 (first round, second round)
Yeltsin: 20.91%/32.57%
Lebed: 11.71%
Zhirinovsky: 6.11%
Yavlinskii: 4.63%
Turnout: 70.84%/68.09% (Russia overall: 69.67%/68.79%)

1995 Gubernatorial Election
Ryabov (oblast legislature chairman): 52.62%/36.80% (first round/second round)
Betin (incumbent): 43.48%/41.97%
Gorbunov: 7.34%
Baturov: 5.09%
Turnout: 68.89%/52.85%

1995 Parliamentary Elections
Communist Party of the Russian Federation: 40.31%
Liberal Democratic Party of Russia: 12.14%
Agrarian Party of Russia: 5.49%
Our Home Is Russia: 5.02%
Communists–Workers' Russia: 4.36%
Party of Workers' Self-Government: 3.26%
Women of Russia: 2.94%
Yabloko: 2.90%
Derzhava: 2.53%
In single-mandate districts: 2 Communist Party of the Russian Federation
Turnout: 68.60% (Russia overall: 64.37%)

1993 Constitutional Referendum
"Yes"—41.1%   "No"—56.8%

1993 Parliamentary Elections
Liberal Democratic Party of Russia: 35.32%
Communist Party of the Russian Federation: 16.86%
Agrarian Party of Russia: 9.83%
Russia's Choice: 9.27%

Women of Russia: 6.34%
Democratic Party of Russia: 5.86%
Yabloko: 5.32%
Party of Russian Unity and Concord: 5.19%
In single-mandate districts: 2 Communist Party of the
 Russian Federation
Turnout: 64.24% (Russia overall: 54.34%)

1991 Presidential Election
Yeltsin: 44.60%
Ryzhkov: 24.80%
Zhirinovsky: 12.15%
Tuleev: 7.44%
Makashov: 3.97%
Bakatin: 2.77%
Turnout: 81.90% (Russia overall: 76.66%)

Regional Political Institutions

Executive:
 Governor, 4-year term
 Oleg Ivanovich Betin, elected December 1999
  Tambov Oblast Administration;
  Ul. Internatsionalnaya, 14; Tambov, 392017
  Tel 7(075–2) 72–10–61;
  Fax 7(075–2) 72–25–18

Legislative:
 Unicameral
 Oblast Duma—50 members, 4-year term,
 elected December 1997
 Chairman—Vladimir Nikolaevich Karev,
 elected December 1997

Regional Politics

Former Reformist Governor Wins Back Old Post

Oleg Betin's victory in Tambov Oblast's 1999 gubernatorial election was noteworthy as it brought a former Yeltsin appointee who had failed to win popular election in 1995 back to power. In 1995 Betin faced Aleksandr Ryabov, who portrayed himself as a staunch Communist, opposed to Yeltsin's "anti-people regime." Ryabov accused Betin of blackmail and cynicism, and called for Yeltsin's resignation. Though support for the Communists carried Ryabov to the governor's office, it was unable to keep him there. During his tenure, he failed to win Yeltsin's support, cutting him off from the benefits high-level Kremlin access provides.

During Ryabov's 1995–1999 term, Betin remained both visible on the region's political scene and closely connected to Moscow, working as head of the Federal Treasury's regional branch in Tambov Oblast and then as presidential representative in the region. As the population began to chafe under Ryabov's Communist rule, Betin became a key player on the scene, ultimately avenging his 1995 loss by winning the 1999 electoral rematch.

Executive Platform: Reformist

After losing to Ryabov in the 1995 elections, Betin became one of the oblast's leading anti-Communist crusaders. In 1998 Betin formed the Za vozrozhdenie Tambovshchiny political movement, which sought to unite the disparate groups opposed to Ryabov (Panorama). Betin was particularly critical of Ryabov's approach to reforming the oblast economy "from above." Additionally he denounced the oblast's 1999 budget which he considered completely unrealistic.

In the 1999 State Duma elections Betin supported Moscow Mayor Yurii Luzhkov's Fatherland, and Luzhkov in turn offered Betin his support. Betin also had the support of Russian Prime Minister Vladimir Putin, who met with Betin on the eve of the elections. Betin announced his full support for Putin in the Russian presidential elections after Yeltsin's resignation (*KV*, 18 January 2000).

Relationships Between Key Players

In 1996 the region had the lowest per capita income in Central Russia.

Ties to Moscow

Under Ryabov's rule, credits from Moscow were scarce, apparently because of the governor's harsh criticism of federal policies. Relations with the center are likely to improve under Betin, who maintained close ties to Yeltsin that will likely carry over to his successor.

Relations with Other Regions

Tambov Oblast is a part of the Black Earth Association, headed by Orel Governor and Federation Council Speaker Yegor Stroev. This organization consists of Voronezh, Belgorod, Kursk, Lipetsk, Orel, and Tambov oblasts.

In October 1998 Ryabov signed a cooperation agreement with Ryazan Governor Vyacheslav Lyubimov. The agreement called for the elimination of middlemen in trade between the regions, complaining that

Oleg Ivanovich Betin

25 August 1950—Graduated from the Tambov Institute of Chemical and Mechanical Engineering and earned a candidate's degree in chemistry from the Moscow Physical-Chemical Institute

1981—Began party work for the oblast committee of the CPSU

1991–March 1995—Deputy Governor of Tambov Oblast

12 March 1995–Elected to the Our Home Is Russia council

24 March 1995–December 1995—Tambov Oblast Governor

December 1995—Lost gubernatorial election to Aleksandr Ryabov

1996—Assisted Boris Yeltsin in his presidential campaign

1996—Joined Tambov Oblast's branch of Ivan Rybkin's Socialist Party of Russia

1996–May 1998–Head of the Federal Treasury in Tambov Oblast

11 May 1998–December 1999—Presidential representative in Tambov Oblast

27 December 1999—Elected governor of Tambov Oblast

they needlessly raised the price of goods. The two regions also agreed to collaborate in the areas of culture, science, and education. Ryazan was to design reforms in Tambov enterprises, and Tambov would supply Ryazan with receipt-issuing cash registers. Betin will be unlikely to follow through on this agreement since he is aligned more closely with the Kremlin than the opposition.

Attitudes Toward Business

Ryabov's relations with the oblast's industrial and agricultural elite were difficult (Panorama). Many of the region's economic problems derive from the structure of its economy. Local industries do not manufacture products that enjoy strong market demand. Also, regional industries rely heavily on cheap sources of many of the materials that have been reoriented toward export over the last several years, such as oil, coal, metals, and timber.

Betin, who is well acquainted with the oblast's economy from his work in the oblast branch of the federal treasury, will likely be more successful at working with oblast businesses and developing the region's economy than his predecessor.

REPUBLIC OF TATARSTAN

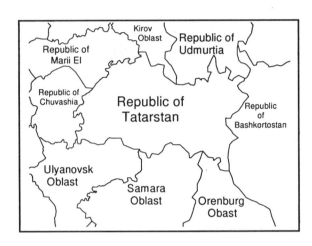

Territory: 68,000 km^2
Population (as of 1 January 1998):
3,774,000
Distance from Moscow: 797 km

Major Cities:
Kazan, *capital* (pop. 1,078,200)
Naberezhnye Chelny (525,100)
Nizhnekamsk (220,900)
Almetevsk (141,800)
Zelenodolsk (101,800)

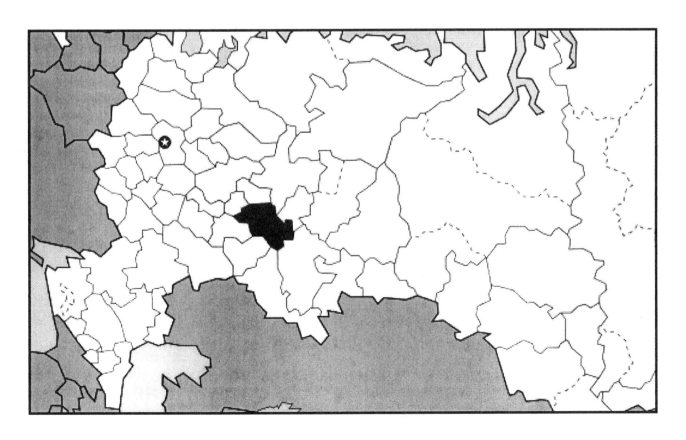

Basic Facts

Population (as of 1 Jan. 1998): 3,774,000 (2.57% of Russian total)

Ethnic breakdown (1989 census): Tatars 48.5%, Russians 43.3%, Chuvash 3.7%

Urban population (as of 1 Jan. 1998): 73.6% (Russia overall: 73.1%)

Student population (as of 1 Sept. 1997): 198 per 10,000 (Russia overall: 208/10,000)

Pensioner population (1997): 25.07% (Russia overall: 25.96%)

Percent of population with higher education (1989 census): 9.5% (Russia overall: 11.3%)

Percent of population working in (1997): Industry: 26.1% (Russian average: 23.0%); Agriculture: 13.8% (13.7%); Trade: 11.1% (13.5%); Culture: 14.1% (13.3%)

Average monthly personal income in July 1998: 686.3 new rubles (Russian average: 891.7 new rubles)

Average monthly personal expenses in July 1998: 561.2 new rubles (Russian average: 684.9 new rubles)

Average monthly subsistence requirement in 1998: 311 new rubles (Russian average: 438 new rubles)

Consumer price index (as of July 1998): 82 (Russia overall = 100)

Budgetary revenues (1997): 19,759.3 billion rubles (Russia overall: 433,378.2 billion rubles)

Budgetary expenditures (1997): 20,321.1 billion rubles (Russia overall: 468,111.6 billion rubles)

Industrial production as percentage of all Russian production (Jan.–Aug. 1998): 2.81%

Proportion of loss-making enterprises (as of July 1998): 43.5% (Russia overall: 50.4%)

Number of enterprises which have wage arrears (as of 1 Sept. 1998): 5,472 (4.05% of Russian total)

Agricultural production as percentage of all Russian production (1997): 4.08%

Number of private farms (as of 1 Jan. 1998): 1,078 (0.39% of Russian total)

Capital investment (1997): 13,272.9 billion rubles (Russia overall: 408,797 billion rubles)

Sources of investment (1997): federal budget: 2.2% (Russian average: 10.2%); regional budget: 12.7% (10.5%); extra-budgetary funds: 85.1% (79.3%)

Foreign investment (1997): 702,355,000 USD (Russia overall: 12,294,734,000 USD)

Number of joint ventures (1997): 133 (0.9% of Russian total)

Fixed capital investment in joint ventures and foreign companies (1997): 237,603 million rubles (Russia overall: 16,265.4 billion rubles)

Number of small businesses (as of 1 July 1998): 16,000 (1.84% of Russian total)

Number of enterprises privatized in 1997: 151 (5.5% of Russian total), including those which used to be municipal property: 80.8% (Russian average: 66.4%); regional property: 19.2% (20.0%); federal property: 0% (13.6%)

Number of telephones per 100 families (1997): in cities: 38.9 (Russian average: 49.2); in villages: 13.6 (19.8)

Brief Overview

Tatarstan is located in the east of European Russia, at the confluence of the middle Volga and the Kama rivers, and borders the republics of Bashkortostan and Chuvashia, and Orenburg, Samara, and Ulyanovsk oblasts. The Tatars, a Turkic-speaking people who constitute the second-largest ethnic group within Russia, have a widespread diaspora throughout the former Soviet Union. Only 25 percent of all Tatars live in Tatarstan, accounting for about half of the republic's population. Inhabiting the Eurasian steppes since ancient times, the Tatars built the Khanate of Kazan, one of the political units that emerged from the Mongol Empire, which ruled much of European Russia until the 15th century. In 1552, the Khanate was conquered by the Russians and became a part of the emerging Russian Empire. According to the 1992 constitution, today's Tatarstan is a "sovereign state, subject of international law, which builds its relations with Russia and other states on the basis of bilateral treaties."

Plains cover most of the republican territory, while the eastern lands rise with the Ural foothills. About one-fifth of the area is forested. The republic is rich in oil and natural gas (1.29 percent of the country's total reserves) and other mineral resources. Tatarstan has a highly developed industrial base and a stable agricultural sector. Major industries are oil and gas extraction and processing (70 percent of total industrial output); machine building, including airplanes, helicopters, automobiles, ships, and radios and electronic equipment (about 20 percent); and light and food industries (16 percent).

The republic trades with firms from over 60 foreign countries, particularly Germany, the United States, Hungary, Switzerland, Austria, China, and Turkey. Oil is Tatarstan's most significant export, while machines and equipment are the most significant import items. The republic has also attracted significant foreign investment. However, despite foreign investment and the republican authorities' initiatives, Tatarstan continues to struggle economically. All three major sectors of the regional economy—oil, defense, automobiles—have been experiencing severe hardship.

According to a 1998 survey by *Ekspert* magazine, the republic is ranked ninth among Russia's 89 regions in terms of investment potential and fourth in terms of investment risks. A 1998 survey by Bank Austria ranked the republic 11th in terms of investment climate.

Electoral History

2000 Presidential Election
Putin: 68.76%
Zyuganov: 19.95%
Yavlinskii: 3.08%
Tuleev: 2.15%
Zhirinovsky: 1.21%
Turnout: 79.84% (Russia overall: 68.64%)

1999 Parliamentary Elections
Fatherland–All Russia: 40.65%
Communist Party of the Russian Federation: 18.02%
Unity: 16.64%
Union of Right Forces: 5.16%
Zhirinovsky Bloc: 3.06%
Yabloko: 2.90%
In single-mandate districts: 3 Fatherland–All Russia,
    1 Russian All-People's Union, 1 independent
Turnout: 74.35% (Russia overall: 61.85%)

1996 Presidential Election
Yeltsin: 38.34%/61.45% (first round/second round)
Zyuganov: 38.10%/32.31%
Lebed: 7.38%
Yavlinskii: 6.90%
Zhirinovsky: 2.58%
Turnout: 73.74%/77.47% (Russia overall: 69.67%/
    68.79%)

1996 Republican Presidential Election
Shaimiev (incumbent): 97.14%
Turnout: 77.76%

1995 Parliamentary Elections
Our Home Is Russia: 28.62%
Communist Party of the Russian Federation: 15.42%
Communists–Workers' Russia: 7.35%
"Nur" Muslim Movement: 5.00%
Liberal Democratic Party of Russia: 4.84%
Yabloko: 4.07%
Women of Russia: 3.70%
Party of Workers' Self-Government: 3.37%
In single-mandate districts: 1 Agrarian Party of
    Russia, 1 Our Home Is Russia, 3 independent
Turnout: 59.21% (Russia overall: 64.37%)

1993 Constitutional Referendum
"Yes"—72.1%   "No"—24.2%

1993 Parliamentary Elections

Russia's Choice: 22.40%

Liberal Democratic Party of Russia: 22.00%

Yabloko: 11.55%

Communist Party of the Russian Federation: 9.38%

Party of Russian Unity and Concord: 8.54%

Women of Russia: 7.66%

Democratic Party of Russia: 5.42%

Agrarian Party of Russia: 2.12%

In single-mandate districts: 3 Party of Russian Unity and Concord, 1 Russia's Choice, 1 New Regional Policy

From electoral associations: 1 Yabloko

Turnout: 13.43% (Russia overall: 54.34%)

1991 Presidential Election

Yeltsin: 44.97%

Ryzhkov: 16.68%

Tuleev: 11.54%

Zhirinovsky: 9.37%

Makashov: 5.77%

Bakatin: 4.53%

Turnout: 36.59% (Russia overall: 76.66%)

Regional Political Institutions

Executive:

President, 5-year term

Mintimer Sharipovich Shaimiev, elected March 1996

Kremlin; Kazan, 420014

Tel 7(843–2) 32–70–01, 32–74–66;

Fax 7(834–2) 36–70–88

Moscow 7(095) 925–77–81

Legislative:

Unicameral

State Council (*Gosudarstvennyi Sovet*)—130 members, 5-year term, elected March 1995

Chairman—Farid Khairullovich Mukhametshin, elected May 1998

Regional Politics

Authoritarian Bargainer Wins Power from Moscow

Mintimer Shaimiev is one of the most outspoken and well-known regional executives in Russia. As president of an ethnic republic with a history of economic success, Shaimiev has played an active role in developing Russia's policies of "asymmetrical federalism." Shaimiev was the first regional executive to sign a power-sharing agreement with Moscow and win considerable autonomy from the federal center. Many other regions now want to win as much autonomy as Tatarstan achieved in its 1994 deal. In winning such concessions, Shaimiev did not shrink from making separatist threats against Moscow.

Since 1994, Shaimiev's authority within Tatarstan and among federal politicians has largely been due to his moderate nationality policy. Tatars make up 48 percent of the republic's population and ethnic Russians constitute 45.5 percent. Tatars have a long legacy in Russian history, descending from the Volga Bulgars. Kazan, the capital of Tatarstan, was also the head of the Mongol empire, the Kazan Khanate, of the 13th to 15th centuries. The president, an ethnic Tatar, tries to equally promote the interests of ethnic Russians and Tatars. The republic has two official languages, and Shaimiev has begun building a mosque next to a Russian Orthodox Church in the Kazan Kremlin.

One of Shaimiev's greatest challenges as president of Tatarstan is the region's decaying economy. The republic has had difficulty collecting sufficient income to meet its budgetary obligations. Many of the region's giant industrial plants are underutilized and direct investment is decreasing. In the late 1990s, sixty-five percent of all sales transactions in the republic were barter operations (*EWI RRR*, 23 April 1998). Moreover, Tatarstan has one of the worst records for wage and pension arrears in the country. The problem is particularly acute in the agricultural sector. In eight districts agrarian workers in April 1998 had not received their salaries since 1996, and in one district people were still waiting for 1995 wages (*EWI RRR*, 23 April 1998). The situation further deteriorated following the August 1998 financial crisis.

Executive Platform: Gradual Reformist

Shaimiev is a shrewd and highly authoritarian leader. He ran unopposed for the republican presidency twice, in 1991 and 1996, a violation of federal legislation. In November 1996 the republican constitution was amended to cancel the age limit for presidents and permit them to run for a third term in a row. Thus, Shaimiev will be able to stand for reelection again in 2001; however, this time the republican constitution says that he cannot run unopposed. Moscow generally turns a blind eye to these practices because it does not want to stir up new sources of trouble.

Shaimiev opposes radical economic reforms. He believes that reforms are useless if they cause people to suffer (Mary McAuley, *Russia's Politics of Uncertainty*, New York: Cambridge University Press, 1997, 89). He supported a more gradual transition to market economics including regulated prices and subsidizing collective farms. As a result, the development of private enterprise in the republic has been weak and there are virtually no private farmers (Panorama Research Group, Labyrint Electronic Database, Moscow). Prices were still regulated well into 1994, whereas much of the rest of Russia dropped price controls in 1992. Advocates of more rapid reform believe that Shaimiev's economic policy merely prolonged economic suffering in the republic. Shaimiev likes to avoid taking personal blame for the economic problems. Instead, he has been highly critical of his subordinates, blaming the republican government for Tatarstan's economic difficulties (*EWI RRR*, 23 April 1998).

In 1999 Shaimiev became the informal leader of a new inter-regional political movement, All Russia. The group brought together various regional executives, many from ethnic republics, who wanted a regional bloc to compete in the State Duma elections (see Relations with Other Regions).

Policies: Backs Land Sales, National Identity

In April 1998 the Tatarstan legislature adopted a law providing for the sale and purchase of land in the republic. Despite his opposition to other forms of market reform, Shaimiev was highly supportive of the law, stating that the future tax policy of the state was dependent on it (*EWI RRR*, 23 April 1998). The law is among the most liberal in Russia, permitting foreigners to buy land. Sales to foreigners, however, are restricted to purchases from the state, and therefore foreigners cannot buy land held in common by rural residents.

In April 1998 the Tatarstan State Council approved a controversial law on citizenship that allowed residents of the republic to be citizens of Tatarstan without being citizens of Russia. Shaimiev claimed that the law "is in full accordance with international law" (*RFE/RL*, 21 April 1998). This law was passed only a few months after many in the republic vocally denounced the introduction of new Russian Federation passports. The republican State Council ordered the

Tatarstan government not to issue the new passports, which did not mention the bearer's nationality or statehood, and were printed only in Russian. Shaimiev and the republican parliament felt that these omissions robbed Tatarstan of its status as an ethnic republic with two official languages and multiple nationalities. In mid-February 1999, Moscow and Kazan reached a compromise in which passports issued in the region would include a supplemental page in the local language that listed all the basic data of the bearer, including his nationality.

Following the beginning of the Russian financial crisis in August 1998, Shaimiev proposed several anticrisis measures in the republic. The government of Tatarstan imposed price controls on bread and dairy products for September and set an artificially low price for flour. The regional government also struck a deal with Moscow to free several food processing and light industrial enterprises from paying tax arrears to the federal budget in exchange for supplying 24 local enterprises to which federal agencies owed money with food and consumer goods (*EWI RRR*, 17 September 1998).

Relationships Between Key Players: Dominates Power Structure

Shaimiev has little opposition in Tatarstan. The State Council is almost completely subservient to the executive branch of power and generally rubber stamps Shaimiev's initiatives (*EWI RRR*, 6 November 1997). The State Council elected Farid Mukhametshin as its speaker in May 1998 at Shaimiev's recommendation. Mukhametshin served as speaker from 1991 to 1995 before being appointed republican prime minister, a post from which Shaimiev mysteriously removed him. Mukhametshin was elected to replace former speaker Vasilii Likhachev, who was appointed Russian ambassador to the European Union. Prior to his appointment, rumors circulated that the Tatarstan government hoped to remove Likhachev, an ethnic Russian, from the chair. Now, the top three political positions in Tatarstan—president, prime minister (Rustam Minnekhanov), and speaker of the legislature—are held by ethnic Tatars, a dominance that could cause concern for ethnic Russians.

Furthermore, Tatarstan allows the president to appoint mayors and local officials. This direct republican control of local government violates the Russian Constitution, yet federal authorities have not intervened on behalf of local government as they have in other republics such as Bashkortostan, Komi, and Udmurtia.

There are several small opposition groups in Tatarstan, but none have any real representation in the governing bodies and their ability to gather support outside the parliament is rather weak (*EWI RRR*, 6 November 1997).

Ties to Moscow: Simultaneously Supportive and Belligerent

Shaimiev seeks to develop close relationships with Russia's top federal leaders, yet simultaneously violates federal law and mandates. Shaimiev's style in dealing with Moscow is to offer just enough support to keep the federal authorities at a comfortable distance. Federal fears of provoking another Chechnya work to give Shaimiev extra breathing space.

Nevertheless, Shaimiev showed his support for Russian President Boris Yeltsin several times, calling him the "only leader capable of maintaining stability in Russia" (NNS). Yeltsin, likewise, was supportive of Shaimiev and ignored his multiple violations of federal law, fearing that a more nationalist Tatar leader could disrupt the peaceful relationship between the republic and the federal center.

Shaimiev has consistently tried to maintain good relations with whoever controls the federal government. When former Prime Minister Viktor Chernomyrdin was dismissed in March 1998 in favor of Sergei Kirienko, Shaimiev considered this a positive development, hailing the need for young leaders. Then, when Kirienko was removed in order to reinstate Chernomyrdin, Shaimiev was again supportive, noting that Chernomyrdin was a well-known politician with strong Duma support. Shaimiev was also thrilled with Yevgenii Primakov's appointment in September 1998 (*EWI RRR*, 17 September 1998). He furthered his support for Primakov by stating that the prime minister could keep the country in line as the next president if Yeltsin were to resign (*EWI RRR*, 22 October 1998). Shaimiev claimed that Primakov would be a good president because he was not a power-seeker, was willing to take on responsibility in a difficult time, was well known abroad, and would preserve democratic freedoms in Russia. In hope of a Primakov presidency, All Russia formed an alliance with Moscow Mayor Yurii Luzhkov and Primakov's Fatherland movement to back candidates in the 1999 parliamentary elections, but did not fare well against the Kremlin-backed Unity bloc.

Tatarstan regards itself as a subject of international law that yields some of its powers to the Russian Federation. Moscow considers Tatarstan one of its 89 constituent regions. Tatarstan was the first region to sign a power-sharing agreement with the federal government. The agreement was signed on 15 February 1994 and essentially gave Tatarstan control over all of the resources and economic assets located in the republic, as well as the right to conduct its own relations with foreign countries. Tatarstan does not pay the same level of taxes to Moscow as do the other regions, yet it also does not look to Moscow for as much economic aid.

Several laws and practices in Tatarstan violate federal laws and the Russian Constitution. According to federal legislation, all elections in Russia must have at least two registered candidates to be valid, yet until November 1996 Tatarstan's Constitution allowed any number of candidates to run. Thus, Shaimiev ran for the presidency of Tatarstan and won unopposed two times. Tatarstan also requires that presidential candidates speak the Tatar language as well as Russian. The Russian Constitutional Court ruled in April 1998 that the republics cannot require their presidential candidates to speak the titular language, yet Tatarstan is unlikely to obey this decision.

Relations with Other Regions: Leader of Ethnic Republics

Shaimiev is the most prominent leader of Russia's 21 ethnic republics. He is a vocal advocate of asymmetrical federalism, a policy which gives the republics much greater autonomy than the predominantly ethnic-Russian oblasts and krais. As a result, he is often the target of criticism by governors of ethnically Russian oblasts who believe all regions should be treated equally.

In April 1999 Shaimiev joined other governors in organizing the All Russia regional party, and is considered the movement's unofficial leader. Other regional executives who joined the party include St. Petersburg Governor Vladimir Yakovlev, Adygeya President Aslan Dzharimov, Astrakhan Governor Anatolii Guzhvin, Bashkortostan President Murtaza Rakhimov, Belgorod Governor Yevgenii Savchenko, Chelyabinsk Governor Petr Sumin, Chuvashia President Nikolai Fedorov, Ingushetia President Ruslan Aushev, Irkutsk Governor Boris Govorin, Khabarovsk Governor Viktor Ishaev, Khanty-Mansi Governor Aleksandr Filipenko, North Ossetia President Aleksandr Dzasokhov, Omsk Governor Leonid Polezhaev, Penza Governor Vasilii Bochkarev, and Rostov Governor Vladimir Chub. Shaimiev claimed that he did not want to be the movement's leader, fearing that it could affect his good relations with Moscow Mayor Yurii Luzhkov and Samara Governor Konstantin Titov, both of whom led other regional parties. He also was concerned that All Russia could earn a reputation as "Shaimiev's movement" in Tatarstan (*KD*, 22 April 1999). Shaimiev believed that the most important task was to bring together all of the different blocs that had been created so that votes would not be wasted since none of the parties could form a Duma majority working alone. All Russia and Luzhkov's Fatherland forged such an alliance for the 1999 State Duma elections.

In January 1998 Tatarstan hosted a festival to boost economic ties with Nizhnii Novgorod Oblast, resulting in an economic cooperation agreement between the two regions. The agreement provided for increased potential for joint ventures and economic cooperation. The main accomplishment of the festival was a quadrilateral agreement among the government of Tatarstan, the government of Nizhnii Novgorod Oblast, Tatneft oil, and the Norsi-Oil company (*EWI RRR*, 29 January 1998). Norsi's refineries are dependent on Tatneft for supplies of raw oil for processing.

In August 1997 Tatarstan signed an economic cooperation agreement with neighboring Bashkortostan. Immediately afterwards Bashkortostani President Murtaza Rakhimov suggested that the two republics could become a "unified state" (*RIA Novosti*, 29 August 1997). Shaimiev has not offered support for such a merger. Many Tatars complained when the Bashkortostani parliament adopted a language law on 21 January 1999 that recognized Bashkir and Russian as the republic's official languages, but not Tatar. In Bashkortostan, there are currently 2 million Russians, 1.2 million Tatars, and 900,000 Bashkirs (*EWI RRR*, 28 January 1999).

In May 1997 Shaimiev signed a cooperation agreement with Chechen President Aslan Maskhadov. In 1996 Shaimiev offered to serve as a mediator between Russian and Chechen forces. He argued that the federal government's inconsistent policies toward the rebel region were largely responsible for the war. In November 1998 Shaimiev defended Kalmykian President Kirsan Ilyumzhinov, who caused a stir by making comments of a strongly separatist nature.

In addition to these ties, Shaimiev has cultivated relationships with the heads of Moscow and St. Petersburg. In June 1996 Shaimiev signed a cooperation treaty with Moscow Mayor Yurii Luzhkov. As part of the treaty, Moscow reopened the Tatar cultural center

that closed in 1941, and agreed to provide accommodation for the republic's permanent representative in the city. In turn, Tatarstan agreed to cooperate with the Moscow Tire Factory in supplying rubber and tires to auto producers in both regions and Tatarstan also agreed to supply the raw materials for a new polypropylene factory in Moscow and buy the finished product (*OMRI DD*, 12 June 1996). In August 1996 Shaimiev signed a series of bilateral agreements on economic, scientific, and cultural cooperation with St. Petersburg Governor Vladimir Yakovlev.

Tatarstan belongs to the Greater Volga Association, which also includes the republics of Mordovia, Chuvashia, and Marii El, and Astrakhan, Volgograd, Nizhnii Novgorod, Penza, Samara, Saratov, and Ulyanovsk oblasts. In March 1998 members of the association met in Nizhnii Novgorod Oblast to discuss the petrochemical processing industry, resulting in a statement to form a cartel agreement. If the cartel is formed, its goals will be to coordinate price setting, control competition among cartel members, and eliminate outside competitors.

Foreign Relations: Agreements with Azerbaijan and Iran

Shaimiev actively tries to develop relations with foreign governments particularly states of the former Soviet Union. Most of his foreign relations concern the region's oil industry. In November 1996 Shaimiev made an official visit to Azerbaijan, during which he met Azerbaijani President Heidar Aliev and signed several economic agreements. Preceding this visit, Shaimiev traveled to Iran, where he met then President Ali Akbar Hashemi Rafsanjani. Tatarstan's First Deputy Prime Minister Ravil Muratov signed a trade agreement with the Iranian Trade Minister Yakhya al Eskhak regarding oil equipment, shipbuilding, and the TU-214 plane, which is manufactured in Tatarstan (*OMRI RRR*, 27 November 1996). Tatarstan and Pakistan signed a cooperation agreement to create a joint venture for producing Oka automobiles in Pakistan in May 1999.

In January 1998 a high-level delegation from Japan's Export-Import Bank visited Tatarstan. The bank's chief representative in Moscow, Kensaku Kumabe, who headed the delegation, clarified the necessary requirements for the inflow of Japanese capital to be increased. He stated that the bank was ready to consider proposals from Tatarstan's government (*EWI RRR*, 5 February 1998). In 1997 the republic's KamAZ truck manufacturer received a $150 million credit from the bank to help finance its modernization.

In November 1998 Tatarstan became the first Russian region to default on its foreign financial obligations. At the end of April 1998 the Dutch bank ING Barings granted Tatarstan a short-term $100 million credit with an annual interest rate set at LIBOR plus 9 percent, due on 25 November 1998 (*EWI RRR*, 3 December 1998). Following the default Standard & Poor's credit rating agency stripped Tatarstan of its international rating for long-term hard currency credits. The official position the republican government took regarding the default was surprising. Shaimiev stated that a solution for the default should be found on the federal level, and then the republic's own financial insolvency could be addressed (*RT*, 28 November 1998). He blamed the default on the fact that the financial crisis and subsequent devaluation of the ruble had tripled the ruble value of the republic's debt, and stated that Tatarstan could not agree to pay that much money.

Attitudes Toward Business: Pro-Investment, Struggling Sectors

Although Shaimiev has developed initiatives to encourage investment and business development in Tatarstan, the region continues to struggle economically. The three primary components influencing the region's industrial well-being are the oil industry, the defense complex, and the KamAZ automotive enterprise.

Tatneft, the region's key oil company, has been trying to further develop the region's oil industry and establish a vertically integrated system. Although Tatarstan has significant oil deposits, it lacks its own refineries to process the oil. Unfortunately for the republic, the oil found in Tatarstan is inferior to that found in other parts of Russia and Central Asia. In late 1997 Tatneft and Nizhnekamskneftekhim began construction on an oil processing plant in Nizhnekamsk so that Tatneft would be able to refine its oil. The overall cost of the project is $500–700 million, a large sum for the region's struggling industry. Since the region's oil fields have been heavily exploited, Tatarstan will need to develop other industries to secure long-term economic well-being.

In June 1999, Shaimiev secured the appointment of his most trusted associate, Tatarstan Prime Minister Rustam Minnekhanov, a close friend of the president's son, as the chairman of the Tatneft board of directors.

Minnekhanov immediately announced that the company would increase production from 23 to 30 million tons a year.

Tatarstan's defense sector once employed 60 percent of the republic's industrial workers, so the federal government's decision to scale back defense spending was a strong blow to the region. To make up for shrinking domestic orders, the republican government has been trying to increase its sales on the world market. Yet, none of the region's defense enterprises is licensed to sell abroad, a right held by the Russian state-owned Rosvooruzhenie. In 1998 Rosvooruzhenie finally opened an office in Kazan. Republican leaders hope the monopolist's presence will boost Tatarstan's presence on the foreign market.

One of Tatarstan's greatest economic challenges is the KamAZ truck factory located in Naberezhnye Chelny, the region's second largest city. KamAZ was the Soviet Union's largest truck manufacturer and one of the country's most productive enterprises. KamAZ was of even greater importance to Tatarstan, employing 150,000 people in 1993 and providing 20 percent of the republic's industrial output. However, KamAZ has experienced considerable difficulty under free market conditions. In the late 1990s, the enterprise has accumulated an enormous debt and is suffering from a severe decrease in demand. The cost of producing vehicles at KamAZ became much higher than the selling price. This situation came about in part because several firms have been receiving KamAZ trucks in barter exchanges and then selling them at very low prices to get cash, thus challenging any efforts KamAZ makes to sell trucks for a profit.

KamAZ's situation reached critical proportions in October 1996 when the Russian government announced its intentions to begin bankruptcy proceedings against the firm. Tatarstan refused to implement the decision, stating that it violated clauses of the region's power-sharing agreement with the federal government. The proceedings were eventually dropped. In 1997 the enterprise was restructured in an attempt to resolve its debt crisis, with the government of Tatarstan receiving 43 percent of the plant's shares. The republican government at this time also increased its influence in KamAZ when First Deputy Prime Minister of Tatarstan Ravil Muratov replaced Nikolai Bekh as chairman of the board of directors at Shaimiev's suggestion. Yet, these measures were not enough to solve KamAZ's problems. KamAZ was shut down for several months from November 1997 until

Mintimer Sharipovich Shaimiev

20 January 1937—Born in a village in the Anyakovo Aktanysh district of Tatarstan

1959—Graduated from the Kazan Agricultural Institute as an engineer-mechanic

1962–1967—Manager of the Menzelin district Selkhoztekhnik association

1963—Joined the CPSU

1967–1969—Worked as an instructor and assistant director of the agricultural department of the Tatarstani CPSU regional committee

1969–May 1983—Minister of water management for Tatarstan

May–November 1983—First deputy Chairman of the Tatarstan Council of Ministers

1983–1985—Secretary of the Tatarstan CPSU regional committee

1985–1989—Chairman of the Tatarstan Council of Ministers

July 1989—Elected to the USSR Congress of People's Deputies

1989–1990—First secretary of the Tatarstan CPSU regional committee

July 1990—Joined the CPSU Central Committee

1990–June 1991—Chairman of the Tatarstan Supreme Soviet

12 June 1991—Elected first President of Tatarstan

1994—Participated in a pilgrimage to Mecca as part of a government delegation

24 March 1996—Reelected President of Tatarstan

March 1997—Became the deputy chairman of the federal Commission on Problems in Chechnya

Tatar

---

late spring 1998. The plant was left idle since every truck produced incurred further losses.

In October 1998 then Russian Prime Minister Yevgenii Primakov restructured more than a billion dollars worth of KamAZ's debts so that creditors would receive enterprise shares rather than money. The governments of Russia and Tatarstan each own 25 percent of KamAZ's stock. KamAZ's other main creditors are the EBRD, Vneshtorgbank, Sberbank, and Tokobank.

KamAZ has not had much success with foreign partners. The American firm Kohlberg, Kravis & Roberts (KKR) had a three-year relationship with KamAZ comprising of a deal in which KKR would attract $3.5 billion in investment to KamAZ in exchange for 32 percent of the firm's stock. Yet, when the Tatarstan government increased its shares in the plant to 43 percent after KamAZ's ownership was restructured in 1997, it did not want to have such a large co-owner (*KD*, 8 August 1997). Furthermore, KKR was not hav-

ing much success attracting the necessary investments for KamAZ. In June 1997 the Japanese government agreed to provide $150 million in credit to KamAZ to modernize its production of diesel engines, yet this initiative alone was not sufficient for solving the enterprise's problems.

In June 1999, KamAZ decided to adopt a new approach. Having failed to solve any problems at the plant, Muratov stepped down as chairman of the board and Russian Economics Minister Andrei Shapovalyants stepped in to take his place. Both Shaimiev and KamAZ's main creditors hoped that Shapovalyants' access to federal funds would help turn the plant around. The 30 June shareholders' meeting reduced the size of the board from 23 members to13. Representatives of Russia and Tatarstan each hold five seats. The EBRD names two members and KKR names one (*EWI RRR*, 1 July 1999)

Tatarstan's major economic problems complicate

all efforts to attract direct investment and stimulate business. Tatarstan owes huge sums to Gazprom for gas deliveries. There have been several incidents in which Gazprom has cut off gas supplies to enterprises in the region, impeding industrial output. Nevertheless, Gazprom continues to engage in partnerships in the republic. In early 1998 Tatarstan signed a cooperation agreement with Gazprom. The government will help refurbish Gazprom facilities in Tatarstan and Gazprom will bring gas to rural areas in the republic (*EWI RRR*, 5 March 1998). This deal was signed in spite of Tatarstan's outstanding debt to the gas giant.

One relative success story in the region is the Yelabuga Automobile (YelAZ) plant's joint venture with General Motors (*EWI RRR*, 25 June 1998). In 1995, the two companies agreed to assemble Chevrolet Blazers from Brazilian-made kits. Plans called for making 50,000 vehicles a year, but by the summer of 1999, when the project was suspended, production never surpassed 1,600 (*EWI RRR*, 6 May 1999). On 22 June 1999, the plant began to assemble Opels from kits produced in Germany. The Russian government has awarded the enterprise considerable tax credits, over the 1997 protests of the IMF. In 1998 Tatarstan freed the plant from all local and republican taxes and lifted obligations to contribute to Tatarstan state non-budgetary funds.

In fall 1998 the government of Tatarstan unexpectedly tried to sell the Tatinkom Cellular Telephone company for $40 million to TAIF, a firm that employs Shaimiev's son (*EWI RRR*, 8 October 1998). The republican government founded the company in 1991 and invested $27 million in it, and Tatinkom became one of the government's most successful projects with a sizable profit margin. Thus, the sale of Tatinkom to TAIF's subsidiaries, TAIF-invest and TAIF-telekom, neither of which have much charter capital, did not seem to be in the republic's best interests. The deal was not authorized by the republican Securities Commission or the appropriate government agencies; no open tender was held, suggesting that the $40 million sale price was probably too low; and the contract does not require TAIF to pay the republic the entire price in cash. Subsequently, Shaimiev annulled the deal. This incident raised suspicions about Shaimiev's true interests in business development in the region.

Internet Sites in the Region

http://www.kcn.ru/tat ru/index.htm
This is the official site of the Tatarstan republican government. The site provides information on the region's politics, economics, culture, education, religion, etc. It offers the full text of Tatarstan's power-sharing agreement with Russia and the numerous agreements accompanying it. An English-language version of this site with some modifications can be found at http://www.kcn.ru/tat en/.

http://www.tatar.ru/tatarstan.html
This site offers basic information about the history, politics, and culture of Tatarstan.

http://www.vk.melt.ru/
This is the home page for the daily newspaper *Vechernii Kazan*, one of the republic's most prominent publications.

TOMSK OBLAST

Territory: 316,900 km²
Population (as of 1 January 1998):
1,073,000
Distance from Moscow: 3,500 km

Major Cities:
Tomsk, *capital* (pop. 477,700)
Seversk (118,600)
Strezhevoi (44,600)

Basic Facts

Population (as of 1 Jan. 1998): 1,073,000 (0.73% of Russian total)

Ethnic breakdown (1989 census): Russians 88.2%, Ukrainians 2.6%, Tatars 2.1%, Germans 1.6%, Belarusans 0.9%

Urban population (as of 1 Jan. 1998): 66.5% (Russia overall: 73.1%)

Student population (as of 1 Sept. 1997): 413 per 10,000 (Russia overall: 208/10,000)

Pensioner population (1997): 22.55% (Russia overall: 25.96%)

Percent of population with higher education (1989 census): 11.6% (Russia overall: 11.3%)

Percent of population working in (1997): Industry: 23.6% (Russian average: 23.0%); Agriculture: 8.0% (13.7%); Trade: 16.8% (13.5%); Culture: 14.3% (13.3%)

Average monthly personal income in July 1998: 803.4 new rubles (Russian average: 891.7 new rubles)

Average monthly personal expenses in July 1998: 507.1 new rubles (Russian average: 684.9 new rubles)

Average monthly subsistence requirement in 1998: 411 new rubles (Russian average: 438 new rubles)

Consumer price index (as of July 1998): 104 (Russia overall = 100)

Budgetary revenues (1997): 4,011.0 billion rubles (Russia overall: 433,378.2 billion rubles)

Budgetary expenditures (1997): 4,147.1 billion rubles (Russia overall: 468,111.6 billion rubles)

Industrial production as percentage of all Russian production (Jan.–Aug. 1998): 0.58%

Proportion of loss-making enterprises (as of July 1998): 62.7% (Russia overall: 50.4%)

Number of enterprises which have wage arrears (as of 1 Sept. 1998): 619 (0.46% of Russian total)

Agricultural production as percentage of all Russian production (1997): 0.82%

Number of private farms (as of 1 Jan. 1998): 1,991 (0.73% of Russian total)

Capital investment (1997): 4,232.2 billion rubles (Russia overall: 408,797 billion rubles)

Sources of investment (1997): federal budget: 19.0% (Russian average: 10.2%); regional budget: 9.1% (10.5%); extra-budgetary funds: 71.9% (79.3%)

Foreign investment (1997): 15,994,000 USD (Russia overall: 12,294,734,000 USD)

Number of joint ventures (1997): 74 (0.5% of Russian total)

Fixed capital investment in joint ventures and foreign companies (1997): 70,032 million rubles (Russia overall: 16,265.4 billion rubles)

Number of small businesses (as of 1 July 1998): 4,700 (0.54% of Russian total)

Number of enterprises privatized in 1997: 9 (0.33% of Russian total), including those which used to be municipal property: 55.6% (Russian average: 66.4%); regional property: 11.1% (20.0%); federal property: 33.3% (13.6%)

Number of telephones per 100 families (1997): in cities: 35.4 (Russian average: 49.2); in villages: 18.0 (19.8)

Brief Overview

Tomsk Oblast lies in the southeast of the West Siberian plain. The development of the territory which now belongs to the oblast began in the early 17th century. Tomsk itself was founded in 1604. Most of the oblast's 316,900 sq km territory is inaccessible because it is covered with taiga woods. The oblast borders Krasnoyarsk Krai, and Tyumen, Omsk, Novosibirsk, and Kemerovo oblasts.

Like its Siberian neighbors, Tomsk is rich in natural resources, particularly oil and gas (the region has the 11th largest hydrocarbon deposits in the country—1.13 percent of Russia's total), ferrous and non-ferrous metals, peat, and underground waters. Forests are also among the most significant assets of the oblast: about 20 percent of the West Siberian forest resources are located in Tomsk Oblast. Industry makes up about half of the regional GDP, while agriculture contributes 19 percent and construction 13 percent. Chemical and oil industries are the most developed in the region, followed by machine construction.

The oblast's major export items are: oil (62.1%), methanol (30.2%), and machines and equipment (4.8%). Oil extraction and timber production are the major business of the region's joint ventures.

According to a 1998 survey by *Ekspert* magazine, the region's investment potential had increased by 5 points since 1997 (the 14th largest increase in the country). The same survey reported that Tomsk received 1.45 percent of Russia's total capital investment in 1997 (20th largest), and that the oblast ranked 46th among Russia's 89 regions in terms of investment potential and 18th in terms of investment risk. A 1998 survey by Bank Austria ranked the oblast 23rd in terms of investment climate.

Electoral History

2000 Presidential Election
Putin: 52.52%
Zyuganov: 25.34%
Yavlinskii: 8.95%
Tuleev: 4.25%
Zhirinovsky: 3.36%
Turnout: 68.62% (Russia overall: 68.64%)

1999 Parliamentary Elections
Unity: 18.98%
Communist Party of the Russian Federation: 16.55%
Yabloko: 13.84%
Union of Right Forces: 11.58%
Zhirinovsky Bloc: 7.58%
Pensioners' Party: 6.53%
Fatherland–All Russia: 6.31%
In a single-mandate district: 1 independent
Turnout: 58.49% (Russia overall: 61.85%)

1999 Gubernatorial Election
Kress (incumbent): 72.90%
Deev: 13.90%
Chemeris: 4.80%
Turnout: 48.60%

1996 Presidential Election
Yeltsin: 34.95%/59.17% (first round/second round)
Zyuganov: 22.13%/33.69%
Lebed: 19.69%
Yavlinskii: 10.90%
Zhirinovsky: 7.11%
Turnout: 68.68%/65.92% (Russia overall: 69.67%/ 68.79%)

1995 Gubernatorial Election
Kress (incumbent): 52.09%
Koshel (LDPR): 15.52%
Tyutrin: 15.10%
Popadeikin: 9.61%
Turnout: 63.14%

1995 Parliamentary Elections
Communist Party of the Russian Federation: 18.77%
Liberal Democratic Party: 10.48%
Yabloko: 10.37%
Our Home Is Russia: 9.15%
Women of Russia: 6.91%
Congress of Russian Communities: 4.59%
Communists–Workers' Russia: 4.28%
Derzhava: 4.11%
Party of Workers' Self-Government: 3.50%
Russia's Democratic Choice: 3.09%
Agrarian Party of Russia: 2.23%
In a single-mandate district: 1 independent
Turnout: 62.95% (Russia overall: 64.37%)

1993 Constitutional Referendum
"Yes"—66.6%   "No"—30.7%

1993 Parliamentary Election
Russia's Choice: 22.06%
Liberal Democratic Party of Russia: 21.90%
Yabloko: 11.81%
Communist Party of the Russian Federation: 10.05%
Women of Russia: 8.86%
Democratic Party of Russia: 5.68%
Russian Movement for Democratic Reforms: 5.42%
Party of Russian Unity and Concord: 5.01%
Agrarian Party of Russia: 4.49%
In single-mandate districts: 2 Russia's Choice
From electoral associations: 1 Communist Party of the
    Russian Federation
Turnout: 46.00% (Russia overall: 54.34%)

1991 Presidential Election
Yeltsin: 61.12%
Ryzhkov: 14.70%
Tuleev: 9.20%
Zhirinovsky: 6.92%
Bakatin: 2.71%
Makashov: 1.53%
Turnout: 72.11% (Russia overall: 76.66%)

Regional Political Institutions

Executive:
    Governor, 4-year term
    Viktor Melkhiorovich Kress, elected
    December 1995, September 1999
        Pl. Lenina, 6; Tomsk, 634032
        Tel 7(382–2) 22–36–86, 22–28–13;
        Fax 7(382–2) 22–33–23
        Federation Council in Moscow:
        7 (095) 292–63–05, 926–67–96

Legislative:
    Unicameral
    Duma—42 members, 4-year term, elected
    December 1997
    Chairman—Boris Alekseevich Maltsev, elected
    April 1994, December 1997

Regional Politics

Highly Respected Siberian Leader

Viktor Kress is one of the most esteemed Siberian leaders, having served as a powerful force in regional politics for nearly ten years. An ethnic German (his family was sent to Siberia from Ukraine) like Sverdlovsk Governor Eduard Rossel, Kress was appointed to the governor's seat by President Boris Yeltsin in October 1991. He was one of twelve regional executives to stand for popular election before the 1996 presidential race. Kress was elected governor of Tomsk Oblast in December 1995, winning 51.9 percent of the vote, and was reelected in September 1999 with an even greater showing of support at 72.9 percent of the vote.

Kress took over the leadership of the Siberian Accord Interregional Association in July 1998, after serving for two years as the association's deputy chair.

Kress is one of the more thoughtful governors, having written two books in which he wrestles with the major problems facing the Russian Federation. Unlike many books by politicians that merely take credit for various policy accomplishments, Kress lays out a variety of issues and ruminates over common sensible solutions to them. He believes that it is useful to work openly, because the essence of political and economic reform is "changing the way people think" (Viktor Kress, *Russia's Difficult Time: A View from the Provinces*, Tomsk: Tsentr sotsial'nykh issledovani, 1998, www.tranet.trecom.tomsk.su). He argues that the German and Japanese miracles occurred because of the high levels of education in those societies. Russia and Tomsk meet this prerequisite, he believes. However, he warns that before setting to work, Russian policymakers must have a good sense of what they want to do (a task he addressed in writing his books). He also warns that Russia has an unjust society, with a huge divide between the center and the regions, the rich and the poor, and is plagued by corrupt officials. If the people do not understand what the reforms are about, they will not proceed, he suggests.

Executive Platform: Democratic Reformer

Kress is a democratic reformer committed to improving governing institutions and establishing a market economy. In 1995 Kress joined the pro-government Our Home Is Russia (NDR) faction at its founding congress and became a member of its political council. He held the first slot on the NDR regional party list for the 1995 parliamentary election, but withdrew after winning election as governor.

While accepting free markets, democracy, and freedom of conscience as the only solution to Russia's problems, the contemplative Kress warns that Russia need not repeat the mistakes of the West. There, he argues, fast economic growth led to ecological catastrophes, left little time for spiritual interests, depleted interpersonal relations, and encouraged a consumerist approach to life.

He feels that the aim of developing a new national idea is impossible since there are too many value systems among the population. Even the intellectual elite is too divided to come up with a common approach. He argues that there is nothing special in the Russian nation today in the sense that the Slavophiles had believed that there was. However, he proposes, patriotism, family, education, non-violence, and ecology could be the main values of the middle class which will inevitably rise up.

He proposes to minimize the level of state corruption by paying bureaucrats decent salaries so that they are not tempted to take bribes. He also wants to train a new generation of Russian managers who can deal with rapidly changing conditions.

Policies: Economic Development

Kress has been assertive in promoting policies for improving Tomsk's economy. The governor's administration decided to focus its energy on further developing the oblast's timber industry and small businesses in 1999–2000 (*EWI RRR*, 17 December 1998). As part of the oblast's plan for supporting small business, the administration plans to confiscate unused property from large enterprises and lease it to small businesses.

Following the financial crisis and subsequent panic that shook Russia in August 1998, Kress adopted the same course of action as many regional executives and threatened to stop paying taxes to the federal budget. He directed funds under his control, to pay employees in the state-financed universities and institutes (*EWI RRR*, 10 September 1998). Kress said that this measure was just temporary until the country's power vacuum was filled.

In the field of healthcare, Kress blames Russians' short anticipated lifespans on citizens' lifestyles rather than the economy. He wants to optimize public funds spent on healthcare by shortening hospital stays, improving the quality of care, increasing salaries for medical workers, improving out-patient services, and developing a system of family doctors who will work with patients from the time they are born.

In the housing sector, he wants to increase the share of municipal services paid for by residents but also cut the cost of providing the services by increasing competition among service providers. He would encourage people to economize by placing individual energy regulators in each apartment. However, housing costs should not be more than 25 percent of the family budget and he believes that the state should provide aid to the needy.

Tomsk is a large science center and the fate of the region's research institutes is of concern to the governor. He praises George Soros's foundations' support for fundamental research and says that Russia is doing well to follow this approach. Such foundations are a useful way of funding research because they do not support the interests of any particular institute, are competitive and open. He believes that Tomsk's future is connected to the development of its scientific establishments and technology-driven production. He is interested in establishing a venture capital fund to support technology-driven small businesses. The fund would help companies that market products based on the research of Tomsk institutes and would then benefit from any successes. He has even proposed letting them use the floor space of bankrupt factories.

Relationships Between Key Players: Legislature Dominated by Independents

The Tomsk oblast legislature is dominated by independents, many representing prominent businesses in the region, who won 30 of the legislature's 42 seats in the December 1997 elections. Communist-backed candidates won only five seats in the assembly. Such results suggest that Kress has a strong support network for his initiatives.

The region's economy is closely associated with the fate of the Eastern Oil Company (VNK), the oblast's largest tax payer. The large Russian oil company Yukos, which is controlled by Mikhail Khodorkovskii's Menatep bank, now owns it. Kress complains that the privatization process did not serve the oblast's interests because the company can now use various tricks to avoid paying taxes in Tomsk. He has also criticized the privatization process for allowing big businessmen to grab regional resources for much less than they are worth.

In 1998 Yukos and its subsidiary Eastern Oil Company were involved in a battle over Tomskneft with U.S. investor Kenneth Dart's Cyprus-based company

Acirota Ltd. Yukos owns 20 percent of Tomskneft, VNK owns 32 percent, Acirota owns 13.9 percent, and the rest belongs to 21,000 small shareholders. Acirota and its small shareholder allies charge that the VNK management had agreed to sell crude oil to Yukos at a fraction of the production cost. In 1998 Tomskneft extracted 10.5 million tons of oil (*EWI RRR*, 28 January 1999). Naturally, Yukos would sell it at the market price and pocket the profit. To make matters worse, Yukos did not even pay oblast taxes since it was not registered in Tomsk.

Acirota and Yukos held competing Tomskneft shareholders, meetings on 15 January 1999. Both meetings claimed to elect their own boards and define their own charters for Tomskneft. Russian courts ruled on 3 February that the Yukos meeting was valid, while the Acirota meeting was not (*MT*, 18 February 1999).

The federal government currently owns 36 percent of VNK. Tomsk leaders have been lobbying the feds to transfer these shares to the oblast, so far unsuccessfully.

Ties to Moscow: Good Relations with Yeltsin

Kress was on good terms with President Yeltsin. Yeltsin first appointed Kress to office in 1991, and then allowed him to stand for election in 1995—a year earlier than most other regional executives—because he was confident of Kress's chances for success and of his loyalty to the president. Kress, though supportive of Yeltsin, clearly showed that his deepest loyalty is to Tomsk and Siberia. He is not afraid to criticize the center and its initiatives.

In September 1998 Kress joined the federal government's presidium since he is the chair of the Siberian Accord Interregional Association. When first invited to join the presidium, Kress hoped to significantly transform center-periphery relations, particularly making financial relationships more transparent (*Novosti NSN*, 17 September 1998). However, the presidium is unlikely to have much influence over federal policy.

Relations with Other Regions: Chair of Siberian Accord

Kress has long been a visible leader in Siberian politics and is one of the most respected governors in the area. In July 1998 he was elected chair of the Siberian Accord Association. He had been serving as deputy chair of the organization since December 1996. The association includes the republics of Buryatia, Gorno-Altai, and Khakassia; Altai and Krasnoyarsk krais; Irkutsk, Novosibirsk, Omsk, Tomsk, Tyumen, and Kemerovo oblasts; and Agin-Buryat, Ust-Orda Buryat, Taimyr, Khanty-Mansi, Evenk and Yamal-Nenets autonomous okrugs.

Kress is trying to make the group a more influential organization. Prior to his election as association chairman, Kress described the organization as more of a political association than an economic one (*EWI RRR*, 22 January 1998). He said that the association could not focus entirely on economics because the members' interests are too different; it must work to bring together various approaches and concerns. The members of the association produce 70 percent of Russia's hard currency earnings and Kress wants the association to focus its efforts on improving Siberia's standard of living. The association will work to bring down the high rates charged by Russia's transportation, heat, and electricity monopolies.

Now the association can do little because most of its members have huge budget deficits and cannot invest in even the most favorable development projects. Moreover there are numerous conflicts of interests between the regions. It does not make sense, for example, to build international airports in Tomsk, Novosibirsk, and Kemerovo.

Kress argues that Moscow should not fear separatist tendencies from the association. A greater danger is the federal government's lack of a policy toward the associations, he argues.

Kress strongly believes that the federation should be reconstructed with equal rights for all regions. He asserts that many problems with Russia's federalism come from a system that mixes units based on ethnic and territorial criteria. Giving the ethnic republics more rights than the predominantly Russian oblasts and krais creates problems between center and regions, and between republics and oblasts. He argues that regions should not be sovereign, although many republican leaders do not accept this view. Kress points out that federations based on ethnicity tend to fall apart. In proposing that regions have equal rights, he realizes that it will be a difficult reform to achieve.

In marshalling this argument, he asserts that republics pay 5–16 percent of their collected taxes to the federal budget, while oblasts pay 40 percent. Taxpayers in the oblasts therefore pay for the social programs of the republics. He also complains that it is unfair

Viktor Melkhiorovich Kress

16 November 1948—Born in Kostroma Oblast

1971–1975—After graduating from the Novosibirsk Agricultural Institute he worked as an agronomist at the Kornilov collective farm

1975–1980—Director of the Rodina collective farm in Tomsk

1980–1986—Chair of oblast association Selkhozkhimiya, assistant head of agricultural management

1986–1987—Deputy director of the agro-industrial committee of Tomsk Oblast

1988–April 1990—First secretary of the CPSU Pervomai district committee

March 1990–1991—Chairman of oblast soviet

October 1991—Appointed governor of Tomsk Oblast

12 December 1993—Elected to the first session of the Federation Council, joining the Committee on the Budget, Finance, Currency and Credit Regulation, Monetary Emissions, Tax Policies, and Customs Regulations

17 December 1995—Elected governor of Tomsk Oblast

January 1996—Appointed to the Federation Council, serving on the Committee for Science, Culture, Education, Health, and Ecology

December 1996—Became the deputy chair of the Siberian Accord Association

July 1998—Elected chair of the Siberian Accord Association

September 1999—Reelected governor of Tomsk Oblast with 72.9% of the vote

German

that some regions have set up off-shore zones because then companies can avoid paying taxes in the region where they are working by registering in the zones. On a related issue, he complains that the city of Moscow siphons off much more than its fair share of tax revenue generated in Russia. Russia's natural monopolies (electricity, gas, railroads) work throughout the country, but pay taxes in Moscow. In 1997, Tomsk lost Tomsktransgaz, which paid huge sums to the city budget, to a newly created organization registered in Moscow Oblast. On top of this, he points out, the federal budget even transfers money to Moscow for services performed on behalf of the federal government. He wants the first step in reforming Russian federalism to be the adoption of a new tax code which is based on the principle that taxes should be paid where the primary economic activity is carried out.

He says that direct subsidies make up only 15–17 percent of the money that the center sends to the regions. There are seven different channels along which money flows from the center to the region and regions like to keep their true income secret. Kress argues for making the money flows more transparent.

Like Moscow Mayor Yurii Luzhkov and former Prime Minister Yevgenii Primakov, Kress feels that 89 regions is too many for an effective federation, especially when each region looks to the center for help. He believes that the number of administrative units will be reduced, but the process will take a long time. Unlike most regional executives, Kress is in favor of giving the president the ability to remove governors who overstep their bounds. Likewise he is in favor of giving governors similar rights to dismiss elected local officials (*EWI RRR*, 22 January 1998).

In March 1998 Kress met with other Siberian leaders including Novosibirsk Governor Vitalii Mukha and Altai Krai Governor Aleksandr Surikov to develop a program for overcoming Russia's economic crisis. Suggestions delivered to then Prime Minister Sergei Kirienko included introducing a zero tariff on basic cargo, pursuing anti-monopoly policies, developing protectionist trade policies for domestic producers, and strengthening government regulation of the foodstuffs market (*EWI RRR*, 16 April 1998).

Kress has also shown his willingness to work with neighboring Krasnoyarsk Krai Governor Aleksandr Lebed. Kress appeared at Lebed's inauguration in June 1998, delivering a speech highly critical of the federal government. Kress agreed with Lebed's campaign statements that Russia's financial system, laws, and policies were oriented toward helping Moscow at the expense of the regions. He called on Lebed to raise the Siberian Accord Association to a higher level of effectiveness and stressed that Lebed's combative style would be good for all of Siberia (*EWI RRR*, 11 June 1998).

Foreign Relations: Wants Foreign Investment

Kress has not developed an extensive foreign network, but has made some contacts in his endeavors to attract investment to Tomsk. In January 1998 the governor participated as a member of the Russian delegation to the second annual U.S.-Russian Investment Symposium at Harvard University's Kennedy School of Government in Massachusetts to work on attracting foreign investment to his region.

In October 1998 Kress met with Belarusan President Aleksandr Lukashenko to discuss increasing cooperation between Belarus and the Siberian Accord Association. Tomsk is also home to USAID and EBRD development programs. In 2000 it joined four other regions as part of the U.S. Regional Initiative.

Attitudes Toward Business: Pro-Business

Kress believes that economic salvation for Siberia will be increased export of oil, gas, and metals. Russia has so many of these resources, he argues, selling some will not compromise its territorial integrity (Kress). He complains that his region has not had the exposure of other regions which tend to be more favored by foreign companies. There is great potential in Tomsk, which is awash with forests, valuable mineral deposits, and considerable oil and gas resources. Yet, the region has not succeeded in securing a major foreign partner for any of its initiatives. There are several investment projects underway in Tomsk, including the construction of an airport with a runway capable of

supporting 747s; the building of an oil refinery; and various programs for developing the oblast's natural resources (www.tomsk.net).

In June 1997 the Tomsk oblast administration announced five projects aimed at attracting investment to the region (*EWI RRR*, 12 June 1997). The top two projects were for developing the region's gas fields and transporting gas to industrial and energy producing enterprises, and a project to attract capital for the construction of an oil processing plant. The other projects focused on the lumber industry, conversion of defense enterprises, and the construction of a titanium plant.

Kress strongly supports small business. He describes Russia's current system as oligarch capitalism in which a handful of financial-industrial groups control the economy. The only way to increase social support for reform is to give people their own property, and small business provides a good way to do this. He advocates creating information centers that help small businessmen defend themselves against difficult licensing procedures and the arbitrary actions of bureaucrats and criminals. Since the federal government has not done much to fill the gap, the regions must step in, he believes.

Internet Sites in the Region

http://www.tranet.trecom.tomsk.su/
This is the official site of the Tomsk administration. Readers can find Kress's second book, *Russia's Difficult Time: A View from the Provinces*, here. There is also an enormous amount of information about the region's economy, including small business, as well as the text of many of the region's laws. Links point to a press summary of regional newspapers and other sources of information in the region.

http://www.tomsk.net/who96/welcome.htm
This site is the Who's Who in Tomsk Oblast, offering detailed information on the oblast's banks, businesses, politicians, institutes of higher education, investment projects, etc. It includes a welcome by Governor Viktor Kress.

TULA OBLAST

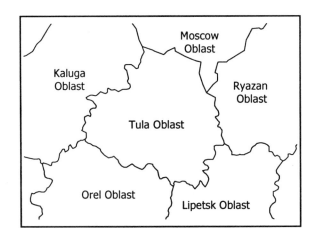

Territory: 25,700 km²
Population (as of 1 January 1998):
1,786,000
Distance from Moscow: 193 km

Major Cities:
Tula, *capital* (pop. 515,500)
Novomoskovsk (140,400)
Aleksin (70,600)
Shchelkino (65,300)
Uzlovaya (60,900)
Yfremov (54,900)

Basic Facts

Population (as of 1 Jan. 1998): 1,786,000 (1.21% of Russian total)

Ethnic breakdown (1989 census): Russians 95.4%, Ukrainians 2.0%

Urban population (as of 1 Jan. 1998): 81.4% (Russia overall: 73.1%)

Student population (as of 1 Sept. 1997): 116 per 10,000 (Russia overall: 208/10,000)

Pensioner population (1997): 34.15% (Russia overall: 25.96%)

Percent of population with higher education (1989 census): 9.3% (Russia overall: 11.3%)

Percent of population working in (1997): Industry: 29.3% (Russian average: 23.0%); Agriculture: 9.6% (13.7%); Trade: 16.3% (13.5%); Culture: 11.4% (13.3%)

Average monthly personal income in July 1998: 668.5 new rubles (Russian average: 891.7 new rubles)

Average monthly personal expenses in July 1998: 443.0 new rubles (Russian average: 684.9 new rubles)

Average monthly subsistence requirement in 1998: 328 new rubles (Russian average: 438 new rubles)

Consumer price index (as of July 1998): 86 (Russia overall = 100)

Budgetary revenues (1997): 3,008.2 billion rubles (Russia overall: 433,378.2 billion rubles)

Budgetary expenditures (1997): 3,764.1 billion rubles (Russia overall: 468,111.6 billion rubles)

Industrial production as percentage of all Russian production (Jan.–Aug. 1998): 0.85%

Proportion of loss-making enterprises (as of July 1998): 53.8% (Russia overall: 50.4%)

Number of enterprises which have wage arrears (as of 1 Sept. 1998): 4,448 (3.29% of Russian total)

Agricultural production as percentage of all Russian production (1997): 1.36%

Number of private farms (as of 1 Jan. 1998): 3,333 (1.22% of Russian total)

Capital investment (1997): 2,342.0 billion rubles (Russia overall: 408,797 billion rubles)

Sources of investment (1997): federal budget: 13.6% (Russian average: 10.2%); regional budget: 5.9% (10.5%); extra-budgetary funds: 80.5% (79.3%)

Foreign investment (1997): 35,649,000 USD (Russia overall: 12,294,734,000 USD)

Number of joint ventures (1997): 25 (0.17% of Russian total)

Fixed capital investment in joint ventures and foreign companies (1997): 161,027 million rubles (Russia overall: 16,265.4 billion rubles)

Number of small businesses (as of 1 July 1998): 7,500 (0.86% of Russian total)

Number of enterprises privatized in 1997: 13 (0.47% of Russian total), including those which used to be municipal property: 84.6% (Russian average: 66.4%); regional property: 15.4% (20.0%); federal property: 0% (13.6%)

Number of telephones per 100 families (1997): in cities: 47.7 (Russian average: 49.2); in villages: 20.2 (19.8)

Brief Overview

Tula Oblast lies to the south of Moscow in the Central Russian highland. It borders Moscow, Ryazan, Lipetsk, Orel, and Kaluga oblasts. The oblast's administrative center, Tula city, was first mentioned in 1146, a year before Moscow's founding. The oblast boasts rich charcoal deposits with supplies of rare, non-ferrous, and precious metals. The region has been famous for its armament, metallurgy, and samovar production since the times of Peter the Great.

Today, industry and agriculture are equally important for the regional economy. Chemical and petrochemical production is the leading industry (22.4 percent of industrial output), followed by machine building and metal processing (20.1 percent), ferrous metallurgy (16.5 percent), and food processing (11.1 percent). The largest regional enterprises produce mineral fertilizers, rubber, agricultural equipment, motor vehicles, and armaments, such as pistols and machine guns. The oblast also houses many defense industry enterprises which are now going through the process of conversion. Agricultural enterprises specialize in potatoes, sugar beets, dairy products, and livestock breeding.

The oblast's foreign contacts have been relatively poorly developed since the administration has not been welcoming to Western companies. Nevertheless, direct foreign investment in the oblast in 1997 was the 10th largest in the country and amounted to $31.3 million (0.8 percent of the Russian total), according to a survey by *Ekspert* magazine.

The oblast ranked 34th among Russia's 89 regions in terms of investment potential and 56th in terms of investment risk. A 1998 survey by Bank Austria ranked the oblast 22nd in terms of investment climate.

Electoral History

2000 Presidential Election
Putin: 48.01%
Zyuganov: 36.55%
Yavlinskii: 5.61%
Zhirinovsky: 2.31%
Tuleev: 1.72%
Turnout: 67.40% (Russia overall: 68.64%)

1999 Parliamentary Elections
Communist Party of the Russian Federation: 29.05%
Unity: 21.89%

Fatherland–All Russia: 9.27%
Union of Right Forces: 9.06%
Yabloko: 6.82%
Zhirinovsky Bloc: 5.45%
In single-mandate districts: 2 Communist Party of the Russian Federation, 1 independent
Turnout: 61.12% (Russia overall: 61.85%)

1997 Gubernatorial Election
Starodubtsev (KPRF): 62.82%
Sokolovskii: 15.08%
Sevryugin (incumbent): 4.76%
Tyaglivyi (Tula city mayor): 4.22%
Sergienko: 2.78%
Titkin: 2.54%
Mitin (first deputy governor): 1.25%
Turnout: 58.93%

1996 Presidential Election
Yeltsin: 29.96%/52.42% (first round/second round)
Zyuganov: 30.23%/41.13%
Lebed: 24.03%
Yavlinskii: 6.59%
Zhirinovsky: 4.58%
Turnout: 72.14%/71.08% (Russia overall: 69.67%/68.79%)

1995 Parliamentary Elections
Communist Party of the Russian Federation: 22.07%
Liberal Democratic Party of Russia: 13.19%
Our Home Is Russia: 10.33%
Congress of Russian Communities: 9.92%
Yabloko: 5.22%
Communists–Workers' Russia: 4.59%
Women of Russia: 4.23%
Agrarian Party of Russia: 3.74%
Party of Workers' Self-Government: 2.57%
In single-mandate districts: 1 Women of Russia, 1 Congress of Russian Communities, 1 independent
Turnout: 67.96% (Russia overall: 64.37%)

1993 Constitutional Referendum
"Yes"—56.6%   "No"—40.6%

1993 Parliamentary Elections
Liberal Democratic Party of Russia: 30.35%
Russia's Choice: 14.69%
Communist Party of the Russian Federation: 12.00%
Yabloko: 8.66%

Women of Russia: 8.24%
Agrarian Party of Russia: 6.56%
Party of Russian Unity and Concord: 6.32%
Democratic Party of Russia: 5.56%
In single-mandate districts: 1 independent, 1
    Russia's Choice, 1 Agrarian Party of Russia
From electoral associations: 1 Women of Russia
Turnout: 60.85% (Russia overall: 54.34%)

1991 Presidential Election

Yeltsin: 63.98%
Ryzhkov: 14.74%
Zhirinovsky: 6.19%
Tuleev: 5.89%
Makashov: 3.21%
Bakatin: 2.25%
Turnout: 78.22% (Russia overall: 76.66%)

Regional Political Institutions

Executive:
    Governor, 4-year term
    Vasilii Aleksandrovich Starodubtsev, elected
    March 1997
        Tula Oblast Administration;
        Leninskii Prospekt, 2; Tula, 300600
        Tel. 7 (0872) 27–84–36;
        Fax 7 (0872) 20–63–26

Legislative:
    Unicameral
    Oblast Duma—48 members, 4-year term, elected
    September 1996
    Chairman—Igor Viktorovich Ivanov, elected
    October 1996

Regional Politics

Coup-Maker Turned Red Governor

On 23 March 1997, Vasilii Aleksandrovich Starodubtsev, one of the infamous 1991 coup-makers and the leader of the Russian Agrarian Union, was elected governor of Tula Oblast. Starodubtsev believes that Lenin was "second only to Jesus Christ" and that the ideal society is something between capitalism and socialism.

From the very beginning of the electoral campaign, Starodubtsev was the clear front-runner among the eleven registered candidates: 40–45 percent of the vot-

ers consistently declared their support for him. Ultimately, he swept about 63 percent of the vote. He enjoyed strong support from local trade-union organizations (*TI*, 19 July 1997). One of the most important factors in his favor was the demographics of the local population. There is a significant proportion of elderly voters in most constituencies in the oblast. Moreover, since the Soviet era, Tula has been considered an important center for the defense industry, and many defense industry workers still live there. Most of these people tend to back the Communists or their affiliates.

Despite the hopes of his supporters, the new red governor has not improved the economic situation of the region and the situation has in fact deteriorated further. Additionally, the new governor has had to deal with corruption charges that surfaced not long after his victory. In the summer of 1999, many of the governor's opponents sent a letter to President Yeltsin asking him to remove Starodubtsev from office (*RFE/RL*, 9 July 1999). This letter was symbolic since Yeltsin did not have the power to remove the governor.

The enormous support for Starodubtsev grew out of a popular belief that he was a good manager. In June 1992, after he was released from prison for his participation in the coup, he took over as manager of the Lenin collective farm (*kolkhoz*) in Tula. His kolkhoz, often dubbed an "island of socialism," is regarded by many as one of the best in the oblast. Its employees have retained all the social benefits of the Soviet era, including free housing and health care. However, some reports claim that the average salary in the kolkhoz is only half the regional average and workers often leave the farm.

Critics accuse Starodubtsev of generating most of the kolkhoz's revenues from black-market vodka deals rather than its ostensible task of breeding animals. Despite these allegations, the oblast's numerous rural workers found Starodubtsev's program attractive. His focus on protecting domestic agricultural producers from imported goods appealed to the rural laborers who are hard hit by the country's economic slump. Only if the other candidates had been able to consolidate their efforts behind a single opponent would they have had a chance of preventing Starodubtsev from winning the race.

Executive Platform: Traditional Soviet

In August 1991, Starodubtsev, at that time a member of the USSR Congress of People's Deputies, joined the State Committee for the State of Emergency (GKChP), the group that carried out the unsuccessful coup against Soviet President Mikhail Gorbachev. He was arrested after the coup failed and was expelled from the Party "for organizing a coup d'etat" by the Presidium of the CPSU Central Control Commission. Starodubtsev never regretted taking part in the coup. In an interview with *Trud* shortly after the coup failed, he said: "The country was on the edge of a schism, and we tried to stop it. Unfortunately, we failed" (*RFE/RL*, 26 August, 1997).

Starodubtsev remains a strong opponent of the reformers. In 1997 he said that "every sane person would oppose the present government" (*NG*, 26 March 1997).

Starodubtsev rejects private land ownership and wants the federal government to adopt legislation to this end to prevent each region from adopting its own legislation. Starodubtsev was one of the founders of the Agrarian Party, whose State Duma faction was largely responsible for drafting the anti-privatization Land Code that was ultimately rejected by the president (*OMRI DD*, 26 March 1997). He is currently the chairman of the Agrarian Union of Russia, which formed part of the Agrarian Party electoral bloc in the December 1995 parliamentary elections. Starodubtsev was third on the federal list, but because the bloc failed to clear the 5 percent barrier, he did not win a seat in the Duma.

Starodubtsev is against privatization, but backs the "commercialization" of enterprises. His own prescriptions for reviving the country's economy consist of increasing state subsidies for the most important economic sectors and stopping raw materials exports.

Starodubtsev readily backed the 1997 "Freedom of Conscience" law, a measure designed primarily to protect the Russian Orthodox Church from having to compete for members with "foreign" religions seeking converts in Russia (Radio Rossiya, 26 July 1997). He himself is not religious, but is proud of helping to restore a church in his village during the Soviet era. He claims to practice yoga.

He is opposed to military reform measures aimed at reducing the officer corps (Radio Rossiya, 26 July 1997).

Starodubtsev criticizes barter trade with the countries of the former Soviet Union, pushing instead for them to buy goods at world prices. He believes that the government should monitor all internal and external trade.

Policies: Digging Deeper into Debt

Starodubtsev began his term as governor by sweeping out of office many of the affiliates of his predecessor, Nikolai Sevryugin, a pro-Yeltsin appointee who subsequently was put on trial for taking bribes (*Izvestiya*, 5 September 1997). He replaced the former bureaucrats with "reliable" members of the old Soviet nomenklatura. Most of them were already in their 60s, leading observers to dub the oblast's leadership "a typical gerontocracy."

Despite his campaign promises, Starodubtsev added an additional 400 billion old rubles ($68 million) to the oblast's existing 60 billion old ruble ($10 million) debt in the seven months after he was elected. In a November 1997 deal, he even mortgaged five local administration buildings, including the Tula White House, to Sberbank. The governor used the money to help the agrarian sector and pay off debts to civil servants. The overall oblast budget in 1997 was just over 700 billion old rubles ($120 million) (*KD*, 6 November 1997).

Although Starodubtsev is highly critical of his predecessor, he has continued some of his policies. For instance, he still engages in buying and selling nonferrous metals in volumes exceeding those allowed by the federal government and imposes protectionist restrictions on the sale of alcohol, favoring Tula producers over outsiders (MK [Tula], 19 August 1997).

Coal mining is one of the biggest problems facing Tula, inevitably drawing Starodubtsev into intense debates over the government's policies toward miners. During the August 1997 coal crisis, Starodubtsev invited the president to visit Tula but warned him that the coal policy proposed by First Deputy Prime Minister Anatolii Chubais threatened to cause severe unemployment in the oblast (*KD*, 26 August 1997). At that point Yeltsin told Chubais and other top government officials the same day that he shared Starodubtsev's concerns (*RFE/RL*, 26 August 1997).

In September 1997, the Tula administration gained a controlling stake in the local coal company that previously belonged to Rosugol. The acquisition gave the administration effective control over the local energy sector. Starodubtsev hoped to make coal mining more effective by "gradually shutting down" several mines (Radio Rossiya, 16 September 1997).

Taking a page from former General Secretary Nikita Khrushchev's book, Starodubtsev has backed a scheme to grow corn in the oblast. The 1998 crop was a failure, setting the region back $28 million, but the governor has said that he will try again (*KD*, 21 January 1999).

According to his income disclosure report for 1997, Starodubtsev received 94 million old rubles ($16,000) for his work at the Lenin State Farm, the Academy of Agricultural Sciences, the governor's office, and the Federation Council (*KD*, 25 March 1998).

Relationships Between Key Players: Covered in Corruption

From its consistent anti-Moscow voting, Tula has gained the reputation of a rebellious region. In the fall of 1997 the oblast elected Aleksandr Korzhakov to the State Duma. Korzhakov had served as President Yeltsin's chief bodyguard and confidant for ten years until an ugly falling-out before the presidential runoff in June 1996. This seat was previously held by General Aleksandr Lebed, who won it in December 1995 on an anti-Yeltsin platform.

The incumbent Sevryugin hardly presented much of an obstacle for Starodubtsev's gubernatorial campaign. As election day neared, all opinion polls showed that his approval rating was so low that he would be lucky to win 10 percent. During five and a half years in charge of the oblast, he proved unable to manage the region effectively and improve the standard of living. During his incumbency, the volume of industrial output dropped more than in Russia as a whole and at least one third of agricultural enterprises continued to lose money. The oblast, in which almost half of the population is retired and half of the territory was contaminated by radiation from Chernobyl, was suffering more than other regions from arrears in wages, pensions, and other social payments. Among Sevryugin's other problems was a popular conception that he frequently used state money for private purposes while in office. That assumption may prove to be true—just a couple of months after the elections, Sevryugin was arrested on charges of misusing budgetary funds, abusing his office, and taking a $100,000 bribe. The court ultimately postponed the trial because of Sevryugin's poor health.

Starodubtsev has not avoided corruption charges either. The Tula Oblast tax police have fined the collective farm he once headed 129 million rubles. The farm was charged with illegally trading spirits and pro-

ducing fake vodka. The farm had false contracts with foreign companies to supply them with 6.5 million liters of alcoholic beverages worth almost $9 million. However, the products were not exported outside Russia but sold in Tula and neighboring regions. Under Russian legislation, liquor producers must pay an 80 percent tax if their products are sold within the country, while exporters are freed from paying such charges. Starodubtsev immediately claimed that the case was spurred by the local vodka mafia as a reaction to his attempts to better regulate alcohol manufacturing in the oblast (*EWI RRR*, 3 July 1997).

Sergei Kazakov, the general director of a Gazprom subsidiary, was elected mayor of Tula in December 1997. He enjoyed the backing of the Communist Party and defeated incumbent Mayor Nikolai Tyaglivyi in a runoff, winning 67 percent of the vote, three times as many votes as his rival (*Izvestiya* and *RG*, 9 December 1997). He had the strong support of Starodubtsev (*KD*, 9 December 1997).

Ties to Moscow: Against Treaties

During his election campaign, Starodubtsev made it clear that he would work with the Yeltsin administration even though he did not support its policies (*OMRI DD*, 13 March 1997).

Starodubtsev believes that negotiated relations between the center and the region will ultimately lead to the destruction of the state (*EWI RRR*, 18 March 1999). He believes that it is impossible for regions with different and unequal rights and responsibilities, whose status is determined by treaties rather than the constitution, to exist in one federal state. Starodubtsev feels that it is not right that ethnic republics should have additional rights, freedoms, and economic privileges over primarily ethnic Russian regions.

Relations with Other Regions: Cooperation with Moscow and Ryazan

In August 1997 Starodubtsev and Moscow Mayor Yurii Luzhkov signed a cooperation agreement that will expire in 2000. Tula Oblast now has an official mission in the capital. Luzhkov said that he was especially interested in importing milk and meat from Tula Oblast, and that he would open several stores in the southern part of Moscow for Tula goods.

Starodubtsev and Ryazan Oblast Governor

Vasilii Aleksandrovich Starodubtsev

25 December 1931—Born in Volovchik, Lipetsk Oblast

1947—Collective farmer in Lipetsk Oblast

1949—Loader, production quality control specialist at the Osobstroi enterprise in Moscow Oblast

1951–1955—Military service

1955—Coal miner and mechanic-machinist in Mine No. 36 of the Stalinogorskugol trust in Novomoskovsk, Tula Oblast

1960—Joined the CPSU

1964—Became Chairman of the Lenin collective farm in Tula Oblast

1966—Graduated from the National Agricultural Correspondence Institute with a candidate's degree in agricultural science

1976—Named a Hero of Socialist Labor

1979—Nominated for the USSR State Prize

1986—Chairman of the Russian Council of Collective Farms

April 1990—Elected Chairman of the Agrarians (from 1992, the Agrarian Party of Russia).

June 1990—Elected chairman of the USSR Peasants' Union

1990—Opposed farm development projects at a special conference organized by Mikhail Gorbachev

1991—Worked in support of Nikolai Ryzhkov during the Russian presidential election campaign

August 1991—Helped lead the anti-Gorbachev coup; author of the "Save the Harvest" decree

February 1992—Became a member of the organizing committee of the Agrarian Party of Russia (APR)

7 June 1992—Released from prison and became the director of the Lenin collective farm, which by that time was a joint stock company

February 1993—Participated in the APR's first conference and was elected to the APR board

June 1993—Reelected Chairman of the Agrarian Union of Russia

December 1993—Elected to the Federation Council, where he was a member of the Agrarian Policy Committee

7 August 1996—At the organizing conference of the National Patriotic Union of Russia (NPSR), he was elected a member of the Coordinating Council and the Presidium of NPSR

23 March 1997—Elected governor of Tula Oblast

Vyacheslav Lyubimov signed a cooperation agreement in May 1997. The two governors, both elected to office in the early part of 1997 with the endorsement of the Communist Party, agreed to provide mutual economic support and encourage trade links between their regions. Due to a lack of money in the federal budget, the two regions have stopped receiving investment subsidies. This shortage of funds has forced them to combine their efforts in a search for alternative sources of investment for regional industries. They are also trying to rebuild their bilateral economic ties, which had been strong during the Soviet era. In addition to the economic issues, the treaty states that the Tula and Ryazan leaderships should develop a common strategy in their relations with the federal government (*NG*, 13 May 1997 and *Segodnya*, 14 May 1997).

Tula's leadership is a part of the Central Russia Association, headed by Yaroslavl Governor Anatolii

Lisitsyn. The association also includes Bryansk, Vladimir, Ivanovo, Kaluga, Kostroma, Moscow, Ryazan, Smolensk, and Tver oblasts, along with the city of Moscow.

Foreign Relations: Unfriendly to Western Investors

Tula has long been famous for its arms production and hopes to benefit from looser controls over weapons exports. Representatives of the British Special Forces were surprised at the high quality of the arms produced at the Tula Arms Factory during a September 1997 visit (*Izvestiya*, 24 September 1997). Otherwise foreign contacts are relatively poorly developed and the governor has not been very friendly to Western companies active in the region (see Attitudes Toward Business).

Attitudes Toward Business: Promotes Defense Industry

Starodubtsev strongly promotes the Tula defense industry. Tula was considered to be the center of the defense and arms industry during the Soviet era. After the collapse of the Soviet Union, the economic situation in the region deteriorated. The arms industry, however, is still competitive on the world market, particularly the Tula Arms Factory.

Defense industry workers in the region called off a strike in September 1997 after Starodubtsev signed a protocol agreeing to pay off wage arrears for 1996 and 1997 and resolving the workers' housing problems (*RIA Novosti*, 23 September 1997). The Splav and Machinery factories have signed long-term contracts with foreign companies (*MK*, 19 August 1997, 1–2).

In 1993 Procter & Gamble began investing in Novomoskovskbytkhim (NBKh), a cleaning supplies plant. P&G gained 90 percent of the factory's shares, but in 1997 a government auditor declared the privatization illegal, claiming that the factory had been federal government property and thus the regional administration had no right to privatize it. P&G also encountered problems with the factory's union as it tried to reduce its labor force. The company was ultimately forced to offer generous severance packages to entice employees to leave voluntarily (*MT*, 7 October 1997). In an attempt to improve relations with the administration, the Westerners sponsored the construction of a $2.5 million modern infectious disease unit in the Novomoskovsk city hospital in Tula Oblast (*Izvestiya*, 12 March 1998).

In March 1999 the American company Bestfoods opened a food production facility in Tula using 100 percent foreign capital. The factory plans to produce 300,000 tons of Hellmann's mayonnaise and 450 million tons of Knorr bouillon cubes, soups, and sauces annually.

TVER OBLAST

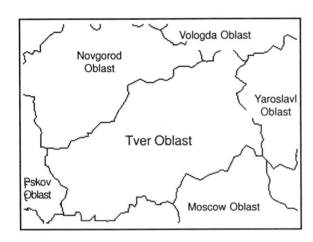

Territory: 84,100 km^2
Population (as of 1 January 1998):
1,633,000
Distance from Moscow: 167 km

Major Cities:
Tver, *capital* (pop. 451,800)
Rzhev (69,200)
Vyshnii Volochek (61,400)
Kimry (59,700)
Torzhok (50,500)
Konakovo (44,500)

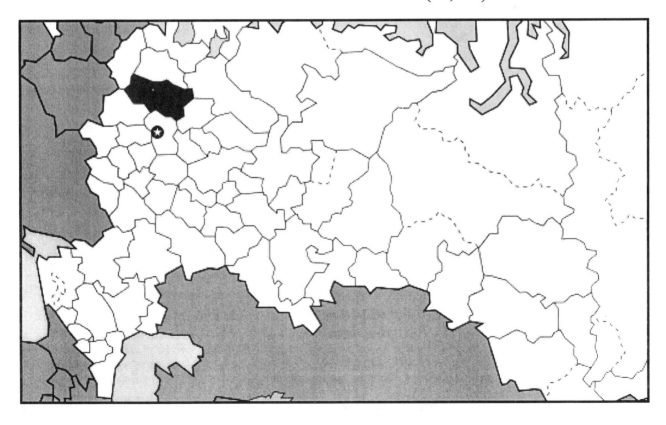

Basic Facts

Population (as of 1 Jan. 1998): 1,633,000 (0.14% of Russian total)

Ethnic breakdown (1989 census): Russians 93.5%, Ukrainians 1.7%, Karelians 1.4%

Urban population (as of 1 Jan. 1998): 73.2% (Russia overall: 73.1%)

Student population (as of 1 Sept. 1997): 122 per 10,000 (Russia overall: 208/10,000)

Pensioner population (1997): 29.88% (Russia overall: 25.96%)

Percent of population with higher education (1989 census): 8.8% (Russia overall: 11.3%)

Percent of population working in (1997): Industry: 27.0% (Russian average: 23.0%); Agriculture: 13.5% (13.7%); Trade: 13.2% (13.5%); Culture: 11.7% (13.3%)

Average monthly personal income in July 1998: 503.2 new rubles (Russian average: 891.7 new rubles)

Average monthly personal expenses in July 1998: 361.2 new rubles (Russian average: 684.9 new rubles)

Average monthly subsistence requirement in 1998: 335 new rubles (Russian average: 438 new rubles)

Consumer price index (as of July 1998): 82 (Russia overall = 100)

Budgetary revenues (1997): 3,005.2 billion rubles (Russia overall: 433,378.2 billion rubles)

Budgetary expenditures (1997): 3,438.6 billion rubles (Russia overall: 468,111.6 billion rubles)

Industrial production as percentage of all Russian production (Jan.–Aug. 1998): 0.67%

Proportion of loss-making enterprises (as of July 1998): 42.9% (Russia overall: 50.4%)

Number of enterprises which have wage arrears (as of 1 Sept. 1998): 1,444 (1.07% of Russian total)

Agricultural production as percentage of all Russian production (1997): 1.23%

Number of private farms (as of 1 Jan. 1998): 3,604 (1.31% of Russian total)

Capital investment (1997): 2,293.0 billion rubles (Russia overall: 408,797 billion rubles)

Sources of investment (1997): federal budget: 12.8% (Russian average: 10.2%); regional budget: 4.4% (10.5%); extra-budgetary funds: 82.8% (79.3%)

Foreign investment (1997): 6,048,000 USD (Russia overall: 12,294,734,000 USD)

Number of joint ventures (1997): 37 (0.25% of Russian total)

Fixed capital investment in joint ventures and foreign companies (1997): 3,139 million rubles (Russia overall: 16,265.4 billion rubles)

Number of small businesses (as of 1 July 1998): 3,600 (0.41% of Russian total)

Number of enterprises privatized in 1997: 90 (3.28% of Russian total), including those which used to be municipal property: 93.3% (Russian average: 66.4%); regional property: 1.1% (20.0%); federal property: 5.6% (13.6%)

Number of telephones per 100 families (1997): in cities: 26.6 (Russian average: 49.2); in villages: 15.7 (19.8)

Brief Overview

Tver Oblast (Kalinin Oblast until 1990) is located in the basin of the upper Volga River and borders Novgorod, Pskov, Vologda, Yaroslavl, Smolensk, and Moscow oblasts. The City of Tver was founded in the 12th century and around 1240 became the capital of the Great Tver Kingdom—one of the political and cultural centers of Russia at that time.

Many important trade routes linking Moscow and St. Petersburg cross the oblast, stimulating its industrial development. Forests cover half of the oblast's territory. It has over 600 lakes, including Seliger Lake, and over 800 rivers, including the upper Volga, Dnepr, and Western Dvina, with a total length of 17,000 km. The oblast is rich in raw materials, including peat, limestone, brick clays, gravel, and charcoal. It also has deposits of medicinal mineral waters.

Oblast industry is well diversified. Regional enterprises produce machines, equipment, synthetic fibers and leathers, glass, timber, and other goods. The Konakovo Hydroelectric Power Plant and the Kalinin Nuclear Plant are the oblast's largest industrial enterprises. Cattle breeding and flax dominate the oblast's agriculture, with over 30 percent of the country's flax grown in Tver Oblast.

Oblast legislation favors both domestic and foreign investors and includes special laws on domestic investment and several legislative provisions for foreign investment. According to a 1998 survey by *Ekspert* magazine, Tver ranked 38th among Russia's 89 regions in terms of investment potential and 8th in terms of investment risk. A 1998 survey by Bank Austria ranked the oblast 54th in terms of investment climate.

Electoral History

2000 Presidential Election
Putin: 57.71%
Zyuganov: 27.89%
Yavlinskii: 4.53%
Zhirinovsky: 2.59%
Tuleev: 2.32%
Turnout: 70.17% (Russia overall: 68.64%)

1999/2000 Gubernatorial Election
Platov (incumbent): 32.51%/46.55%
   (first round/second round)
Bayunov: 22.91%/46.02%
Potapov: 12.49%
Vinogradov: 5.95%
Popov: 5.49%
Turnout: 65.19%/53.03%

1999 Parliamentary Elections
Unity: 29.11%
Communist Party of the Russian Federation: 23.21%
Union of Right Forces: 8.75%
Fatherland–All Russia: 8.38%
Zhirinovsky Bloc: 6.45%
Yabloko: 5.52%
In single-mandate districts: 2 Communist Party of the
   Russian Federation
Turnout: 65.55% (Russia overall: 61.85%)

1996 Presidential Election
Yeltsin: 32.11%/50.16% (first round/second round)
Zyuganov: 33.59%/43.65%
Lebed: 17.14%
Yavlinskii: 6.95%
Zhirinovsky: 5.52%
Turnout: 74.23%/71.63% (Russia overall: 69.67%/
   68.79%)

1995 Gubernatorial Election
Platov (local administration head, People's Power):
   50.50%
Suslov (incumbent): 35.16%
Dontsov: 4.75%
Linov: 1.55%
Turnout: 71.32%

1995 Parliamentary Elections
Communist Party of the Russian Federation: 27.18%
Our Home Is Russia: 8.33%
Congress of Russian Communities: 8.01%
Liberal Democratic Party of Russia: 7.18%
Agrarian Party of Russia: 5.97%
Yabloko: 5.61%
Women of Russia: 4.65%
Communists–Workers' Russia: 4.49%
In single-mandate districts: 2 Communist Party of the
   Russian Federation
Turnout: 70.97% (Russia overall: 64.37%)

1993 Constitutional Referendum
"Yes"—50.2%   "No"—47.6%

1993 Parliamentary Elections
Liberal Democratic Party of Russia: 25.48%
Russia's Choice: 14.13%
Agrarian Party of Russia: 13.87%
Communist Party of the Russian Federation: 12.46%

Women of Russia: 7.72%

Democratic Party of Russia: 7.71%

Yabloko: 6.04%

Party of Russian Unity and Concord: 5.65%

In single-mandate districts: 2 Communist Party of the Russian Federation

From electoral associations: 1 Agrarian Party of Russia

Turnout: 63.92% (Russia overall: 54.34%)

1991 Presidential Election

Yeltsin: 43.67%

Ryzhkov: 24.82%

Zhirinovsky: 10.93%

Tuleev: 9.12%

Makashov: 4.07%

Bakatin: 3.55%

Turnout: 80.35% (Russia overall: 76.66%)

Regional Political Institutions

Executive:

Governor, 4-year term

Vladimir Ignatevich Platov, elected December 1995, January 2000

Tver Oblast Administration; Ul. Sovetskaya, 44; Tver, 170000

Tel 7(082–2) 33–10–51;

Fax 7(082–2) 42–55–08

Federation Council in Moscow: 7(095) 292–14–85, 926–65–19

Legislative:

Unicameral

Legislative Assembly (*Zakonodatelnoe Sobranie*)— 33 members, 4-year term, elected December 1997

Chairman—Vyacheslav Aleksandrovich Mironov, elected December 1997

Regional Politics

Democratic Governor in Red Belt Center

Vladimir Platov was elected governor of Tver Oblast in the region's first free elections on 17 December 1995, defeating incumbent Vladimir Suslov with over 50 percent of the vote. This victory in the heart of central Russia's red belt was a shock to many, and a signal that Tver was ready for change. Suslov had been the head of the Tver city Communist Party committee before perestroika, and was considered the favorite in the election, given his influence over the media and the support of the region's numerous Communists.

Platov's victory was his first successful bid in post-Soviet politics. He ran in the 1993 parliamentary elections on the party list for the Russian Movement of Democratic Reforms but did not win a seat because that party failed to cross the five-percent barrier. Platov also was originally on Yabloko's regional party list for the 1995 elections, but withdrew in order to pursue his gubernatorial campaign. In his race for governor, Platov had the support of the regional Power to the People movement (which he organized), Boris Fedorov's Forward, Russia!, Grigorii Yavlinskii's Yabloko, and other democratic groups.

Platov was elected to a second term on 9 January 2000, defeating Communist opponent Vladimir Bayunov by just over 3,000 votes in the election's second round. While Platov's victory ensured that the Communists will not control the region's highest post, the slim margin of victory presents Platov with a large number of problems. It is clear that Bayunov won support not only from raditional Communist/Agrarian electorate, but a much larger share of the population that is dissatisfied with the governor's policies.

Executive Platform: Liberal Economic Reforms

The governor is reform-minded, advocating a liberal political and economic platform. Platov believes that Russia should defend the rights and interests of ethnic Russians, regardless of where in the former Soviet Union they are located, and that this should be accomplished through diplomatic and economic measures (Panorama Research Group, Labyrint Electronic Database, Moscow). Platov was a member of the liberal Right Cause party headed by Yegor Gaidar, Boris Nemtsov, Anatolii Chubais, and Sergei Kirienko. He has also flirted with the other new regional parties, joining both Moscow Mayor Yurii Luzhkov's Fatherland movement at the Tver branch's founding congress and Samara Governor Konstantin Titov's Voice of Russia movement. However, his involvement in these groups seems to have been for the purpose of political positioning, to get a foot in all potentially powerful camps; in 1999 he ultimately endorsed Vladimir Putin's Unity party, and was the only governor included on the party list in the 1999 State Duma campaign.

Platov's main policy goals have been economic. He has repeatedly called Tver a "crisis region" plagued with a decline in production, lowered standards of living, and high unemployment. Platov would like to provide real economic autonomy for Tver and effective self-rule for its municipalities (*EWI RRR*, 18 September 1997). He believes that additional economic autonomy would help rejuvenate the region's industry. Over recent years Tver has lost nearly 65 percent of its total industry (*EWI RRR*, 28 August 1997). Unfortunately, the local banking sector has shown little interest in investing in industrial production.

Policies: Tax Incentives

In an attempt to implement regional economic autonomy, Platov tried to persuade the federal government and the oblast Legislative Assembly to experiment with allowing flexible business taxation within the region (*EWI RRR*, 18 September 1997). The regional authorities would pay a fixed sum of money to the federal budget, the amount that the federal government normally receives from oblast taxes, and then receive the right to establish their own tax policies within the region. This would allow the administration to set a flexible tax scale for different businesses. Moscow was unlikely to approve such a proposal, having had negative experiences with granting regions similar tax authority in 1993. Rather, Moscow proposed a program to revitalize various regional industries including the gas and energy sector, timber, and tourism. The federal government offered nearly 30 percent of the necessary funds to implement the program, but ultimately it never had the national importance the reformers hoped to achieve.

In 1996 the governor signed a regional law granting investors a five-year tax break on profit, property, and land taxes. The oblast government also has taken measures to provide shareholders with greater accountability over enterprise management (*EWI RRR*, 28 August 1997). Additionally, Platov authorized the establishment of the Institute for Executive Organizations, which is designed to assist enterprises with the development and execution of business plans, market research, and fundraising (*EWI RRR*, 28 August 1997). The oblast administration set aside $17 million from the oblast budget for the project. The governor intends for the fund to grow to $170 million over time (*EWI RRR*, 18 September 1997).

Platov, who has not had a drink of hard alcohol or smoked in over thirty years, has exhibited regional protectionism by restricting the import of vodka from other regions. He also prohibits the sale of hard alcohol in kiosks.

Platov's political strategy has been focused on consensus building. He seeks support from the entire spectrum of political and public organizations, all oblast municipalities, and all social groups. To improve relations with the oblast's municipalities, Platov created the Department of Territorial Monitoring, which organizes an exchange of information. The governor also supported the Legislative Assembly's decision to allow district executives to simultaneously serve in the Assembly.

In an attempt to increase his popular support, Platov dissolved the Power to the People movement, which had helped elect him to the post of governor. This measure was taken to disassociate the governor from any specific political camp and present him rather as a representative of everyone in the oblast (*EWI RRR*, 18 September 1997). Nevertheless, Platov was not very successful at creating such an image. In the spring of 1997 he established the Political Consultative Council of Public Organizations to help him face his strong Communist opposition in the oblast Legislative Assembly.

Relationships Between Key Players: Confronting Communist Challenges

After reform-minded Platov emerged victorious in the 1995 gubernatorial elections, his strong Communist opposition set out to block the new governor's initiatives in the region's Legislative Assembly (*EWI RRR*, 18 September 1997). The Communists also attacked the Tver branches of Yabloko and Our Home Is Russia (NDR). Although Our Home Is Russia usually backs democratic governors, in Tver specific political and economic interests have caused NDR to work against Platov.

To challenge the governor, the Legislative Assembly passed a law in March 1996 that defined impeachment procedures. The administration's lawyers immediately declared the law unconstitutional. However, the battle between the Communist opposition and Platov culminated in a May 1997 impeachment attempt. The Tver Regional Election Committee registered a group of 61 people trying to collect the necessary number of signatures to hold a referendum testing Platov's popularity (*EWI RRR*, 18 September 1997). The group wanted to hold Platov responsible for the pension and salary arrears in the region. The Communists wanted to replace Platov with either Tatyana Astrakhankina or Vladimir Bayunov. Interestingly, neither Yabloko nor NDR resisted the Communists' impeachment plans, in spite of the obvious harm the process could inflict on their respective political agendas.

Platov was able to halt the impeachment proceedings by appealing to the Tver Regional Court with the complaint that the Regional Election Committee had violated the impeachment law. The Court sided with the governor, declaring the registration of the impeachment group illegal.

In spite of these opposition attacks, in September 1997 Platov tried once again to develop a non-partisan political role by stating that he was ready to cooperate with all political parties and movements for the benefit of the region (*Veche Tveri*, 12 September 1997). Although this statement did not lead to any direct results, the December 1997 Legislative Assembly elections appeared to offer Platov a second chance for improved political consensus building. The majority of the new legislators elected were independents, including several businessmen and civil servants. These deputies likely back Platov on most matters.

In late 1998 and early 1999 Platov's administration faced the conviction of two of his deputies for taking bribes. Deputy Governor Anatolii Stepanov was sentenced to five years in jail for taking a bribe from Chechen businessman Ramzan Taramov in June 1998 (*EWI RRR*, 11 June 1998). Then on 25 January 1999, Deputy Governor Viktor Volkov was sentenced to nine years in jail for accepting a $250,000 bribe (*EWI RRR*, 4 February 1999). Some members of the oblast administration say that these arrests were politically motivated, resulting from a long-standing conflict between Platov and Tver Prosecutor Vladimir Parchevskii, whom Platov tried to replace (*KD*, 25 February 1998).

Ties to Moscow: Courted by Nemtsov and Chubais

Platov generally supported Yeltsin on political matters, including the decision to disband the parliament in 1993. Yet, Platov supports greater state control of the economy, specifically, regulating prices and indexing wages. On 13 June 1996 the governor signed a power-sharing agreement with Yeltsin. Nevertheless, Platov would like to see Tver gain greater economic autonomy from Moscow, particularly in regard to tax policy.

In May 1998 then Deputy Prime Minister Boris Nemtsov and Unified Energy System Director Anatolii Chubais offered Platov the position of industry and trade minister in then Prime Minister Sergei Kirienko's cabinet, which he refused (*EWI RRR*, 21 May 1998).

Relations with Other Regions

Tver belongs to the Central Russia Association, which is headed by Yaroslavl Governor Anatolii Lisitsyn. The association also includes Bryansk, Vladimir, Ivanovo, Kaluga, Kostroma, Ryazan, Smolensk, Moscow, and Tula oblasts as well as the city of Moscow.

Throughout Russia's 1998 financial crisis, Platov focused on increasing his ties with other regions to address the situation and aid the oblast's socio-economic development. He sends products like chicken meat and textiles to the Far North in barter deals to pay for Tver's use of natural gas (*EWI RRR*, 28 January 1999). In September 1998 he signed a cooperation treaty with Moscow Mayor Yurii Luzhkov.

Foreign Relations: World Bank Loan Recipient

Tver's foreign relations are entirely economic. Platov has prioritized attracting foreign investment, and several small foreign projects are underway in the region.

Tver's biggest project involves a loan from the World Bank. The World Bank is providing $30 million to finance a reform plan for the oblast's healthcare system. Tver must begin repaying the money in 2004 and finish by 2013, and the federal government will cover half of the costs (*EWI RRR*, 30 April 1998). The loan will be used for purchasing new ambulances, a dispatcher communications system, and medical and office equipment, and will fund the reconstruction of the prenatal care and delivery centers in the town of Rzhev.

Attitudes Toward Business: Successful at Attracting Investment

In August 1997 local and regional authorities joined representatives from the federal government and big industrial enterprises to discuss Tver's economic and social hardships. Several of the industries that were prominent in the region during the Soviet era such as flax, textiles, railroad car production, and electricity generation, are suffering considerably (*EWI RRR*, 4 September 1997). Forty-two percent of the region's factories are unprofitable, owing at least 9.5 billion rubles to creditors and 1.2 trillion to local, regional, and federal budgets. As a result, the banks are suffering since their customers cannot pay them. Three banks lost their licenses in 1997, and three-fourths of the re-

---

Vladimir Ignatevich Platov

23 October 1946—Born in Ovechkin village in the Sobin raion of Vladimir Oblast

1966—Graduated from the Vladimir Technical School for Aeromechanics with a degree in industrial enterprise electrical equipment

1967–1969—Served in the army in the Kuril islands

1967–1992—Worked at Bezhetskselmash Works in Bezhetsk, Kaliningrad, starting as an engineer and working his way up to director

1990—Left the Communist Party

1992–1995—Mayor of Bezhetsk and the Bezhetsk district of Tver Oblast

December 1993—Competed unsuccessfully in the State Duma elections on the Russian Movement of Democratic Reforms party ticket

1995—Organized the oblast Power to the People movement and stood as its candidate in the 1995 gubernatorial elections

17 December 1995—Elected governor of Tver Oblast

January 1996—Became a member of the Federation Council and its Committee on Social Policy

January 2000—Reelected governor of Tver Oblast by a slim margin

---

maining banks were experiencing difficulties at the end of 1997 (*EWI RRR*, 4 September 1997).

On the positive side, Platov is pro-business and has prioritized attracting investors and improving the region's industries in his economic platform. Foreign investment in the region is increasing. In the first half of 1997 it reached $11.6 million (*EWI RRR*, 4 September 1997). Some developments involving foreign investment include:

- A cooperation treaty between Tver and the Latvian port city Liepaja (*EWI RRR*, 11 December 1997)

- An agreement with the Swiss company Wifag to establish a publishing house involving Inkombank and the Union Bank of Switzerland (*EWI RRR*, 4 September 1997)

- A $10 million investment by the German brewery Holsten to modernize the equipment of Tver's brewery in exchange for up to 35 percent of its shares (*EWI RRR*, 26 November 1997)

- A trial contract between the Japanese firm Komazu and the Tver Excavator Factory to jointly produce oil refinery equipment (*EWI RRR*, 11 September 1997)

- A $5 million agreement between the Swedish businessman Per Erik Ariel and the local representative of the Federal Forestry Service to establish a lumber harvesting and wood processing plant in the Penov region (*EWI RRR*, 25 June 1998)

In March 1998 the Tver oblast administration and the Tver branch of the Russian State Transportation Company, Rossiya, were granted a license to use the Migalovo military airport for civilian purposes. The conversion project will cost $26 million (*EWI RRR*, 26 March 1998). The Rossiya Transportation Company expects to service 100 flights per day, primarily cargo traffic. Migalovo has a good location only a short distance from the main Moscow–St. Petersburg highway. The oblast administration also plans to establish a free economic zone around the airport which will grant lower customs tariffs to users. If successful, this project could provide Tver with a renewed industrial status as a transport center.

Gazprom has also expressed interest in several development projects in Tver. The gas pipeline project between Yamal-Nenets and Russia's western border will run through the oblast, and Gazprom plans to construct two underground gas storage tanks there (*EWI RRR*, 9 October 1997). Gazprom is also planning to build a $200 million gas pipeline that will connect Kaliningrad to the Tver Oblast city of Torzhok. The pipeline will run through Minsk, Vilnius, and Kaunas (*Energy and Politics*, 4 June 1998). In October 1998 Platov received a proposal from the leadership of the Siberian Trust Company, which handles Gazprom's affairs, to open a representative office in Tver. Additionally, geological surveys suggest that there could be gas deposits on Tver territory, prompting Platov to lobby Gazprom President Rem Vyakhirev to expand exploratory work in the region (*EWI RRR*, 9 October 1997).

Internet Sites in the Region

http://www/tver/ru/
This website offers a detailed look at the Tver city administration including the mayor, media, business, and investment.

TYUMEN OBLAST

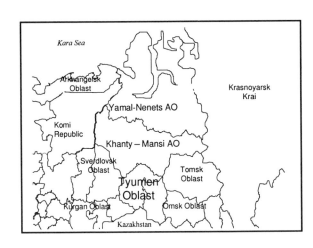

Territory: 1,435,200 km²
Population (as of 1 January 1998):
3,211,000
Distance from Moscow: 2,144 km

Major Cities:
Tyumen, *capital* (pop. 500,100)
Tobolsk (97,600)
Ishim (62,000)
Yalutorovsk (37,300)
Zavodoukovsk (25,900)

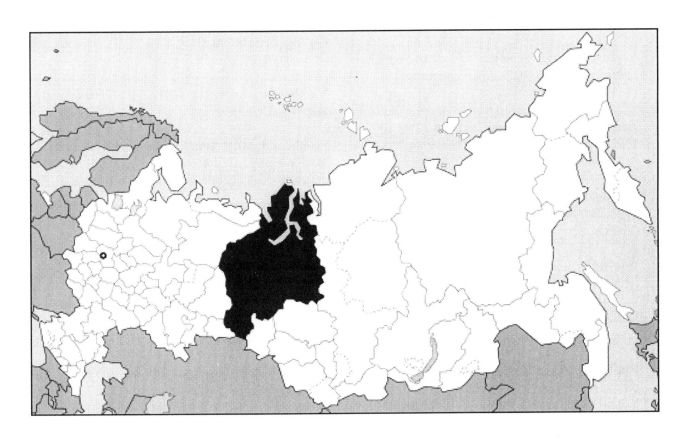

Basic Facts

Population (as of 1 Jan. 1998): 3,211,000 (2.19% of Russian total)

Ethnic breakdown (1989 census): Russians 83.5%, Tatars 7.7%, Ukrainians 2.2%, Germans 1.4%, Chuvash 1.1%

Urban population (as of 1 Jan. 1998): 76.1% (Russia overall: 73.1%)

Student population (as of 1 Sept. 1997): 155 per 10,000 (Russia overall: 208/10,000)

Pensioner population (1997): 16.5% (Russia overall: 25.96%)

Percent of population with higher education (1989 census): 10.2% (Russia overall: 11.3%)

Percent of population working in (1997): Industry: 18.1% (Russian average: 23.0%); Agriculture: 5.4% (13.7%); Trade: 11.7% (13.5%); Culture: 10.5% (13.3%)

Average monthly personal income in July 1998: 2,132.3 new rubles (Russian average: 891.7 new rubles)

Average monthly personal expenses in July 1998: 978.5 new rubles (Russian average: 684.9 new rubles)

Average monthly subsistence requirement in 1998: 596 new rubles (Russian average: 438 new rubles)

Consumer price index (as of July 1998): 122 (Russia overall = 100)

Budgetary revenues (1997): 45,266.6 billion rubles (Russia overall: 433,378.2 billion rubles)

Budgetary expenditures (1997): 46,881.4 billion rubles (Russia overall: 468,111.6 billion rubles)

Industrial production as percentage of all Russian production (Jan.–Aug. 1998): 7.13%

Proportion of loss-making enterprises (as of July 1998): 55.3% (Russia overall: 50.4%)

Number of enterprises which have wage arrears (as of 1 Sept. 1998): 3,244 (2.40% of Russian total)

Agricultural production as percentage of all Russian production (1997): 1.59%

Number of private farms (as of 1 Jan. 1998): 3,656 (1.33% of Russian total)

Capital investment (1997): 61,241.2 billion rubles (Russia overall: 408,797 billion rubles)

Sources of investment (1997): federal budget: 2.1% (Russian average: 10.2%); regional budget: 15.2% (10.5%); extra-budgetary funds: 82.7% (79.3%)

Foreign investment (1997): 222,550,000 USD (Russia overall: 12,294,734,000 USD)

Number of joint ventures (1997): 190 (1.29% of Russian total)

Fixed capital investment in joint ventures and foreign companies (1997): 1,704,269 million rubles (Russia overall: 16,265.4 billion rubles)

Number of small businesses (as of 1 July 1998): 16,700 (1.92% of Russian total)

Number of enterprises privatized in 1997: 58 (2.12% of Russian total), including those which used to be municipal property: 75.9% (Russian average: 66.4%); regional property: 8.6% (20.0%); federal property: 15.5% (13.6%)

Number of telephones per 100 families (1997): in cities: 44.8 (Russian average: 49.2); in villages: 21.4 (19.8)

Brief Overview

Stretching from the Ural Mountains in the west toward the lower reaches of the Yenisei River in the east and from the Kara Sea in the north to the Kazakh border in the south, Tyumen Oblast covers most of the West Siberian Plain (which is drained by the Ob and Irtysh rivers). In addition to Kazakhstan, it borders Komi Republic, Krasnoyarsk Krai, and Sverdlovsk, Kurgan, Omsk, Tomsk, and Arkhangelsk oblasts. The sparsely populated northern parts of the oblast are occupied by the Khanty-Mansi and Yamal-Nenets autonomous okrugs. The oblast administrative center, the city of Tyumen, is situated on the Trans-Siberian Railroad.

The oblast is extremely rich in raw materials. Tyumen Oblast (including Khanty-Mansi and Yamal-Nenets autonomous okrugs) is Russia's main oil and gas supplier (66 percent of the country's oil and 91 percent of its gas come from the region). Most of the oil and gas, however, as well as other raw materials, such as charcoal, peat, and gold, are located mostly on the territory of the okrugs, while the southern part of the oblast houses processing industries and agriculture. Forests cover more than a third of the oblast's territory, making the region the third largest producer of timber resources.

Ninety percent of regional GDP comes from the energy and fuel industry. Most of Russia's national oil and gas companies, such as LUKoil, Yukos, Sidanko, and Gazprom, operate in the region. The rest of the oblast's GDP comes from timber processing, machine building, petrochemical industries, and agriculture, and such traditional indigenous industries as fishing, hunting, and gathering.

The oblast maintains relations with over 50 countries. Most of the joint ventures established in the region either extract or process raw materials, particularly gas and oil.

Tyumen's investment climate has slightly improved in 1997: the oblast had the country's seventh biggest decrease of investment risks—by 35 points. According to a 1998 survey by *Ekspert* magazine, it is ranked 30th among Russia's 89 regions in terms of investment potential and 66th in terms of investment risk. A 1998 survey by Bank Austria ranked the oblast 4th in terms of investment climate.

Electoral History

2000 Presidential Election
Putin: 54.14%
Zyuganov: 28.79%
Yavlinskii: 4.96%
Zhirinovsky: 4.59%
Tuleev: 1.88%
Turnout: 66.45% (Russia overall: 68.64%)

1999 Parliamentary Elections
Unity: 27.78%
Communist Party of the Russian Federation: 19.11%
Communists–Workers' Russia: 8.97%
Zhirinovsky Bloc: 8.21%
Union of Right Forces: 7.41%
Yabloko: 5.88%
Fatherland–All Russia: 5.30%
In single-mandate districts: 2 independent
Turnout: 59.50% (Russia overall: 61.85%)

1996/1997 Gubernatorial Election
Roketskii (incumbent): 42.01%/58.83% (first round/ second round)
Atroshenko: 23.87%/32.94%
Raikov (State Duma deputy): 8.45%
Cherepanov (oblast legislature deputy, Russian Communist Workers' Party): 8.44%
Chertishchev: 7.62%
Bagin: 1.34%
Panteleev (Monarchist Party of Russia): 0.44%
Turnout: 30.3%/25.29%

1996 Presidential Election
Yeltsin: 39.07%/55.82% (first round/second round)
Zyuganov: 27.31%/38.16%
Lebed: 13.28%
Zhirinovsky: 9.38%
Yavlinskii: 5.70%
Turnout: 67.15%/67.19% (Russia overall: 69.67%/ 68.79%)

1995 Parliamentary Elections
Communist Party of the Russian Federation: 15.42%
Communists–Workers' Russia: 12.13%
Liberal Democratic Party of Russia: 11.15%
Our Home Is Russia: 9.48%

Party of Workers' Self-Government: 5.89%
Women of Russia: 5.51%
Yabloko: 4.42%
Power to the People: 3.07%
In single-mandate districts: 2 independent
Turnout: 61.25% (Russia overall: 64.37%)

1993 Constitutional Referendum
"Yes"—65.9%   "No"—31.3%

1993 Parliamentary Elections
Liberal Democratic Party of Russia: 21.03%
Women of Russia: 14.77%
Russia's Choice: 13.44%
Communist Party of the Russian Federation:
    11.03%
Agrarian Party of Russia: 10.57%
Party of Russian Unity and Concord: 6.72%
Democratic Party of Russia: 6.34%
Yabloko: 5.90%
In single-mandate districts: 2 independent
From electoral associations: 1 Liberal Democratic
    Party of Russia, 1 Democratic Party of Russia
Turnout: 48.22% (Russia overall: 54.34%)

1991 Presidential Election
Yeltsin: 56.28%
Ryzhkov: 18.26%
Zhirinovsky: 9.06%
Bakatin: 5.31%
Makashov: 4.77%
Tuleev: 3.01%
Turnout: 72.20% (Russia overall: 76.66%)

Regional Political Institutions

Executive:
    Governor, 4-year term
    Leonid Yulianovich Roketskii, elected January 1997
        Volodarskaya Ul., 45; Tyumen, 625004
        Tel 7(345–2) 26–77–20
        Federation Council in Moscow:
        7(095) 292–75–50, 926–65–81

Legislative:
    Unicameral
    Oblast Duma—25 members, 4-year term, elected
    December 1997
    Chairman—Sergei Yevgenevich Korepanov, elected
    January 1998

Regional Politics

*Experienced Leader Fights for
Territorial Integrity*

Leonid Roketskii, an ethnic Ukrainian, has been among
the top ranks of Tyumen Oblast since the end of the
Soviet period. He was appointed deputy governor in
1991, and became governor in 1993 when Russian
President Boris Yeltsin appointed then governor Yurii
Shafranik to serve as Russia's fuel and energy minister. Roketskii was elected governor on 12 January 1997
after defeating businessman Sergei Astroshenko by
over 20 percent in the runoff.

As the executive of one of the wealthiest Russian
regions, Roketskii has been confronted with intense
political battles that threaten the territorial integrity
and economic well-being of Tyumen. As the Khanty-
Mansi and the Yamal-Nenets autonomous okrugs, the
oblast's resource-rich northern territories, try to gain
independence from Tyumen, Roketskii is forced to
search for influential political allies and alternative
sources of financing for developing the southern part
of the oblast's economy and ensuring its stability.
Unlike the northern regions, which host the majority
of Russia's oil and gas reserves, the southern part of
Tyumen Oblast is a relatively poor agricultural region.

*Executive Platform: Member of NDR
and Voice of Russia*

Roketskii is reform minded, though his region is better known for political conflict than progressive reforms. In May 1995 Roketskii joined Our Home Is
Russia (NDR). The same year he also joined the Reforms–New Course movement led by Vladimir
Shumeiko. Former Prime Minister Viktor
Chernomyrdin was very supportive of Roketskii's gubernatorial campaign, giving Roketskii money to pay
back-wages prior to the elections.

As the 1999 elections gathered steam, Roketskii was
one of the few governors to remain loyal to Viktor
Chernomyrdin. However, he also sought to cover his
bets by signing on with Samara Governor Konstantin
Titov's Voice of Russia bloc as well.

*Policies: Preserving and Developing Regional
Government*

When he was first appointed governor in 1993,
Roketskii saw his three top priorities as developing

self-government in the region, reforming the agricultural sector, and preserving the region's territorial integrity by keeping the two northern autonomous okrugs within Tyumen Oblast (www.sibtel.ru).

Relationships Between Key Players: Low Legislative Support

In January 1998 the oblast duma elected Sergei Korepanov, former chairman of the Yamal-Nenets legislature, as its chairman. This move was considered the initial step in a Yamal-Nenets and Khanty-Mansi plan to try and remove Roketskii (*EWI RRR*, 22 January 1998). Since the two autonomous okrugs did not participate in Roketskii's election, the legislature could declare the election invalid and call for new elections. Fifteen of the 25 legislators backed Korepanov's candidacy, so it seems that support for Roketskii in the oblast duma is limited.

Ties to Moscow: Good Relations with Yeltsin

Roketskii's relations with the federal government have been amicable. Roketskii was generally supportive of President Boris Yeltsin, and is very close to former Prime Minister Viktor Chernomyrdin. Yeltsin supported Roketskii against the separatist Khanty-Mansi and Yamal-Nenets autonomous okrugs (see Relations with Other Regions), issuing a presidential decree in fall 1996 demanding that the regions participate in the Tyumen gubernatorial elections.

Nevertheless, Roketskii is not afraid to criticize federal policy. He was strongly opposed to the 1993 Russian draft constitution because it gave equal rights to the country's autonomous okrugs, including Khanty-Mansi and Yamal-Nenets, which are now simultaneously (and confusingly) subordinate and equal to Tyumen Oblast, thus reducing the oblast's power. Roketskii has also expressed frustration in dealing with the Kremlin in attracting foreign investment to his region (*EWI RRR*, 23 October 1997). He is also very critical of former Prime Minister Yevgenii Primakov's support for the idea of reducing the number of regions in Russia.

Relations with Other Regions: Conflict with Khanty-Mansi and Yamal-Nenets

The key issue for Tyumen Oblast is its relationship to Khanty-Mansi and Yamal-Nenets autonomous okrugs.

These two regions have the ambiguous status of simultaneously being equal subjects of the Russian Federation and subordinate to Tyumen Oblast. Tyumen is one of the wealthiest regions in Russia, yet the majority of this wealth lies in the two northern okrugs, which combined possess 90 percent of Russia's natural gas and 60 percent of its oil reserves. Without the okrugs, Tyumen's wealth drops considerably. Khanty-Mansi and Yamal-Nenets, headed by Aleksandr Filipenko and Yurii Neelov, respectively, have actively been trying to separate entirely from Tyumen's authority. As a result, Roketskii, Filipenko, and Neelov have been unable to come up with a charter for the oblast.

Because Roketskii opposes their separatist efforts, the two okrugs boycotted Tyumen's gubernatorial election, ignoring a presidential decree demanding their participation. To ensure that the elections would be valid, Tyumen lowered the level of necessary voter participation between electoral rounds so that a decent turnout in the southern part of the oblast would make up for the absence of votes in the okrugs. Thus, Roketskii was elected only by the very southern part of the oblast.

The Constitutional Court addressed the okrugs' demand for independence from Tyumen in 1997. The Court ruled that the regions were simultaneously equal subjects of the federation and subordinate to Tyumen, leaving the situation as ambiguous as before. The Court stated that the okrugs have the right to secede at any time without the oblast's agreement, but only if the secession is validated by federal constitutional law. Thus, this decision did little to solve the oblast-okrug conflict and relations between the respective regions remain tense and unresolved.

Tyumen Oblast belongs to the Siberian Accord Association, which includes the republics of Buryatia, Gorno-Altai, and Khakassia; Altai and Krasnoyarsk krais; Irkutsk, Novosibirsk, Omsk, Tomsk, and Kemerovo oblasts; and Agin-Buryat, Taimyr, Ust-Orda Buryat, Khanty-Mansi, Evenk, and Yamal-Nenets autonomous okrugs.

Foreign Relations

Roketskii is very interested in attracting foreign investment to the region, and has expressed frustration with Moscow's interference in this process. In late 1998 and early 1999, the federal government finally adopted amendments to the 1995 production sharing law, im-

Leonid Yulianovich Roketskii

15 March 1942—Born in Ternopol Oblast in Ukraine

1962–1966—Served in the Soviet Army

1970—Graduated from the Lviv Polytechnic Institute as an electrical engineer

1970–1988—Rose through multiple posts to become the chief engineer of the Surgutgazstra trust in Tyumen Oblast

1981—Appointed deputy chairman of the Surgut city executive committee

1988—Appointed chairman of the Surgut city executive committee

22 April 1990—Elected to the Tyumen Oblast Council of People's Deputies

May 1990—Elected chairman of the oblast executive committee and a member of the Tyumen CPSU oblast committee

November 1991—Appointed first deputy governor of Tyumen Oblast

20 February 1993—Appointed governor of Tyumen Oblast

12 December 1993—Elected to the first session of the Federation Council, where he served on the Committee for Federation Affairs, Federal Agreements, and Regional Policies

May 1995—Joined Our Home Is Russia

1995—Joined the Reforms–New Course movement

12 January 1997—Elected governor of Tyumen Oblast

January 1997—Appointed to the second session of the Federation Council, where he became deputy chair of the Committee on Budget, Tax Policies, Finance, Currency, and Customs Regulations

17 February 1999—Signed a declaration supporting Samara Governor Konstantin Titov's Voice of Russia

Ukrainian

Married, with a son and daughter

proving many of the deficiencies with this legislation. By the summer of 1999, large investors were negotiating to secure their positions, but mostly waiting until the results of the presidential elections were known before making any major investments.

Another problem is that when the price of oil fell on international markets, working in the difficult conditions of Western Siberia became unprofitable. Until there is a sustained price recovery, there is likely to be little foreign interest in the region.

Attitudes Toward Business: Encourages Investment

Many of Russia's major energy companies, including Gazprom and LUKoil, are based in Tyumen Oblast (including its two okrugs). One of the more interesting is the Tyumen Oil Company, of which Roketskii is the chairman of the board of directors. The Tyumen Oil Company was founded in 1995 when controlling shares of twelve major oil enterprises were grouped together. In 1997 Alfa bank gained control of the company, which has its main operating unit at Nizhnevartovsk. Although the new managers tried to cut costs, the company fell far behind schedule in making payments to the pension fund, threatening its privatized status. In April 1998 the company received a warning from then Prime Minister Sergei Kirienko that if it did not meet its payments on schedule, the state would take all possible legal measures against it, including annulling the privatization.

The Tyumen Oil Company (TNK), however, continues to grow. In March 1998 the company signed an agreement with the administration of Magadan Oblast to build an oil refinery in Magadan to sell fuel products in the Far East. It suffered a setback in the wake of the financial crisis in August 1998 when the French Société Générale froze its $75 million credit. Then, in October 1998, the Halliburton Energy Services agreed to work with the company to further develop the Samotlor oil field (located in Khanty-Mansi), once the Soviet Union's largest oil producer but heavily depleted over the years. The companies hope to produce up to 18 million tons of oil a year within a few years (*KD*, 22 October 1998).

The Tyumen Oil Company achieved great notoriety when it became embroiled in a conflict with BP Amoco. After BP Amoco bought a $57 million stake (10 percent) in Sidanko, TNK used its access to Russian courts to grab Sidanko's most valuable assets. At the peak of this battle in December 1999, the U.S. State Department put an unusual ban on a $500 million U.S. Export-Import Bank credit to TNK. Ultimately, BP Amoco and TNK worked out a compromise, and the State Department removed its ban in April 2000.

About $200 million from the ExIm credit will pay for a project to modernize the Ryazan Oil Processing Plant (RNPZ), allowing the company to increase its presence in Russia's gasoline market. By the summer of 1999, Tyumen Oil had 540 gas stations across Russia and planned to raise that number to 1,000 by 2001. During the same month Tyumen Oil signed an agreement with Coca-Cola so that Coca-Cola will be the sole distributor of soft drinks at the company's filling stations, which number 540 nationwide (*EWI RRR*, 27 May).

Among other projects concerning the energy industry, in February 1998 Gazprom signed a $500 million deal with Italy's Technimont to build a polymer plastics plant in Tobolsk, Tyumen Oblast. When the plant is complete it will be the largest of its kind in Russia.

Internet Sites in the Region

http://www.sibtel.ru/admin/index.htm
This is the official website of the Tyumen Oblast administration. It contains basic information on the governor, legislature, and region. It also features a detailed list of businesses in the region, including contact information.

http://www.rusline.com/oblast/tumen/locbus.html
This site provides contact information for businesses operating in Tyumen, including joint ventures.

REPUBLIC OF TYVA

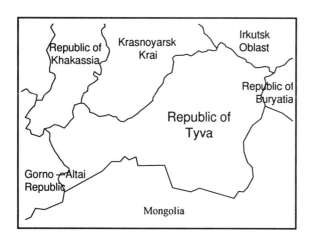

Territory: 170,500 km²
Population (as of 1 January 1998): 310,000
Distance from Moscow: 4,668 km

Major Cities:
Kyzyl, *capital* (pop. 97,300)
Ak-Dovurak (13,300)
Shagonar (9,100)

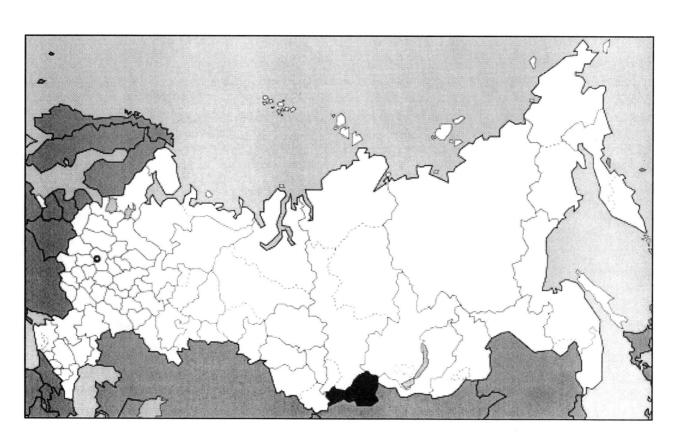

Basic Facts

Population (as of 1 Jan. 1998): 310,000 (0.21% of Russian total)

Ethnic breakdown: Tyvans 64.3%, Russians 32.0%

Urban population (as of 1 Jan. 1998): 47.5% (Russia overall: 73.1%)

Student population (as of 1 Sept. 1997): 118 per 10,000 (Russia overall: 208/10,000)

Pensioner population (1997): 22.26% (Russia overall: 25.96%)

Percent of population with higher education (1989 census): 15.9% (Russia overall: 11.3%)

Percent of population working in (1997): Industry: 9.3% (Russian average: 23.0%); Agriculture: 19.1% (13.7%); Trade: 15.3% (13.5%); Culture: 22.9% (13.3%)

Average monthly personal income in July 1998: 488.0 new rubles (Russian average: 891.7 new rubles)

Average monthly personal expenses in July 1998: 198.0 new rubles (Russian average: 684.9 new rubles)

Average monthly subsistence requirement in 1998: 568 new rubles (Russian average: 438 new rubles)

Consumer price index (as of July 1998): 126 (Russia overall = 100)

Budgetary revenues (1997): 682.9 billion rubles (Russia overall: 433,378.2 billion rubles)

Budgetary expenditures (1997): 1,326.5 billion rubles (Russia overall: 468,111.6 billion rubles)

Industrial production as percentage of all Russian production (Jan.–Aug. 1998): 0.02%

Proportion of loss-making enterprises (as of July 1998): 76.3% (Russia overall: 50.4%)

Number of enterprises which have wage arrears (as of 1 Sept. 1998): 393 (0.29% of Russian total)

Agricultural production as percentage of all Russian production (1997): 0.20%

Number of private farms (as of 1 Jan. 1998): 2,011 (0.73% of Russian total)

Capital investment (1997): 135.8 billion rubles (Russia overall: 408,797 billion rubles)

Sources of investment (1997): federal budget: 60.8% (Russian average: 10.2%); regional budget: 14.1% (10.5%); extra-budgetary funds: 25.1% (79.3%)

Foreign investment (1997): 0 (Russia overall: 12,294,734,000 USD)

Number of joint ventures (1997): 0

Fixed capital investment in joint ventures and foreign companies (1997): 0 (Russia overall: 16,265.4 billion rubles)

Number of small businesses (as of 1 July 1998): 500 (0.06% of Russian total)

Number of enterprises privatized in 1997: 3 (0.11% of Russian total), including those which used to be municipal property: 100% (Russian average: 66.4%); regional property: 0% (20.0%); federal property: 0% (13.6%)

Number of telephones per 100 families (1997): in cities: 38.2 (Russian average: 49.2); in villages: 9.2 (19.8)

Brief Overview

The Republic of Tyva is located in the middle of Asia, in the southern part of Eastern Siberia. Most of its land lies in the basin of the upper Yenisei River. It borders Krasnoyarsk and Altai krais, Irkutsk Oblast, the republics of Khakassia and Buryatia, and Mongolia. Until the 20th century, Tyva was to be a protectorate of neighboring states, and the first Tyvan nation-state, the People's Republic of Tannu-Tuva, was created in 1921. In 1944, it merged with the Soviet Union and became an autonomous oblast within the Russian Federation. By the beginning of the 1950s, the majority of the Tyvans' cattle-breeding homesteads were collectivized, a step that destroyed the people's traditional nomadic lifestyle.

The republic is rich in mineral resources, particularly coal, and rare and non-ferrous metals. Most of the population and industry is concentrated in the central area of the republic, which produces about 70 percent of the region's GDP. Because of its underdeveloped industry, Tyva has largely preserved a clean environment. The republic's numerous mineral water sources, salt lakes, and therapeutic mud baths are attractive tourist destinations.

Tyva is one of the poorest regions in the country. It is able to cover a mere 18 percent of its expenses with its own budgetary revenues. According to a 1998 *Ekspert* magazine survey, investing in the region was becoming increasingly risky. As a result, there have been no foreign economic activities in the region.

According to a 1998 survey by *Ekspert* magazine, the republic ranked 78th among Russia's 89 regions in terms of investment potential and 78th in terms of investment risk. A 1998 survey by Bank Austria ranked the republic 85th in terms of investment climate.

Electoral History

2000 Presidential Election
Putin: 62.41%
Zyuganov: 27.39%
Tuleev: 2.65%
Zhirinovskii: 1.79%
Yavlinskii: 1.57%
Turnout: 70.25% (Russia overall: 68.64%)

1999 Parliamentary Elections
Unity: 70.80%
Communist Party of the Russian Federation: 8.31%
Fatherland–All Russia: 2.88%
Zhirinovsky Bloc: 2.38%
Union of Right Forces: 1.64%
Communists–Workers' Russia: 1.46%
Yabloko: 1.27%
In a single-mandate district: 1 Unity
Turnout: 69.53% (Russia overall: 61.85%)

1997 Republican Presidential Election
Oorzhak (incumbent): 70.61%
Bicheldei (republican parliament speaker): 10.13%
Kashin (LDPR): 8.20%
Damba-Khuurak: 3.25%
Arakchaa (Socialist Party of Russia): 1.14%
Mongush: 1.07%
Kanzai (Republican Communist Organization): 0.70%
Turnout: 70.95%

1996 Presidential Election
Yeltsin: 59.93%/53.07% (first round/second round)
Zyuganov: 21.17%/32.11%
Lebed: 4.54%
Yavlinskii: 4.22%
Zhirinovsky: 3.02%
Turnout: 68.40%/67.50% (Russia overall: 69.67%/ 68.79%)

1995 Parliamentary Elections
Our Home Is Russia: 28.08%
Bloc of Ivan Rybkin: 12.06%
Communist Party of the Russian Federation: 11.45%
Agrarian Party of Russia: 8.67%
Communists–Workers' Russia: 5.57%
Liberal Democratic Party of Russia: 5.44%
Women of Russia: 3.24%
In a single-mandate district: 1 Our Home Is Russia
Turnout: 65.66% (Russia overall: 64.37%)

1993 Constitutional Referendum
"Yes"—29.9%   "No"—66.0%

1993 Parliamentary Elections
Party of Russian Unity and Concord: 48.38%
Liberal Democratic Party of Russia: 9.73%
Women of Russia: 9.00%
Communist Party of the Russian Federation: 8.40%
Russia's Choice: 6.15%

Agrarian Party of Russia: 5.56%
Democratic Party of Russia: 2.92%
Yabloko: 2.11%
In a single-mandate district: 1 independent
Turnout: 58.39% (Russia overall: 54.34%)

1991 Presidential Elections
Ryzhkov: 62.14%
Yeltsin: 15.25%
Tuleev: 10.08%
Zhirinovsky: 5.48%
Bakatin: 1.51%
Makashov: 1.31%
Turnout: 73.55% (Russia overall: 76.66%)

Regional Political Institutions

Executive:
   President, 5-year term
   Sherig-Ool Dizizhikovich Oorzhak, elected
   March 1997
      The Government Building; Ul. Chuldum, 18;
      Kyzyl, Republic of Tyva 667000;
      Tel 7(394–22) 3–69–12;
      Fax 7(394–22) 3–79–62
      Federation Council in Moscow:
      7(095) 292–75–27, 926–66–79

Legislative:
   Unicameral
   Verkhovnyi Khural—32 members, 4-year term,
   elected April 1998
   Chairman—Sholban Valerevich Kara-ool, elected
   June 1998

Regional Politics

Reformer Rules Siberian Region Famous for Its Singers

Sherig-Ool Dizizhikovich Oorzhak rules over one of the most isolated regions in Siberia. Tyva did not join the Soviet Union until 1944 when it became an autonomous okrug. In 1993 the region earned republican status. The republic has no rail lines and though it is possible to reach Tyva by plane, it is not particularly convenient.

Tyva is well known for a variety of unique characteristics. As an independent country, the region issued numerous postal stamps in the first half of the century that sparked interestd among collectors. It also won worldwide attention for its musical tradition of overtone throat singing, or *khoomei*. This type of singing requires producing two notes at once, one is a vibrating hum and the other is a quaver. One of the most famous khoomei groups, Huun-Huur-Tu, played with Frank Zappa during a visit to California in the mid-1990s (www.compulink.co.uk). In fact, music is Tyva's main export. The region also gained attention from the interest shown it by late physicist Richard Feynman.

Executive Platform: Socially Oriented Reformer

Oorzhak won the republic's first presidential elections in 1992, and then won reelection in 1997. In the first electoral round in 1997 he took over 70 percent of the vote, while his closest competitor took only 10 percent. Oorzhak ran on the Our Home Is Russia (NDR) party ticket, yet he is frequently described as a "leftist" since 75 percent of the regional budget goes to social programs. His most loyal electorate has been the rural areas of the republic and the ethnic Russian population.

Oorzhak, an ethnic Tyvan, feels strongly about protecting the equal rights of all nationalities. He encourages a revival of Tyvan history, customs, and traditions, but also considers it necessary to safeguard Russian culture. He has allocated funds for restoring the Russian Orthodox Church in the region (NNS). Oorzhak also actively speaks in favor of maintaining Russia's integrity. In December 1993, when the republic adopted a new constitution with a clause giving the region the right to secede, Oorzhak announced that Tyva had no intentions of leaving the Russian Federation. These active measures supporting the interests of the region's Russian minority have certainly contributed to Oorzhak's popularity among Russians.

Policies: Privatization and Anti-Crime

Oorzhak's policies tend to focus on supporting social programs. Yet, the president is supportive of market reforms. During his first term as president, Oorzhak carried out the privatization of small companies and supported transforming collective farms into small, private farms.

In March 1997 the Tyvan government created an anti-terrorist commission uniting representatives of various law enforcement and other government agencies aimed at fighting crime. The commission coordinates operations with border guards from Mongolia.

Sherig-ool Dizizhikovich Oorzhak

24 June 1942—Born in the Shekpeer village in Tyva

1962—Began working as a carpenter for the Selstraya enterprise

1962–1965—Served in the Soviet Army

1966—Worked as a physical education teacher

1971—Graduated from the Moscow Agricultural Institute and began work as an economist

1976—Became director of the Shekpeer collective farm

1980–1983—Elected chairman of the Barun-Zhemchug district soviet

1983–1986—First secretary of the Uluch-Zhemskii district CPSU committee

1985—Graduated from the Novosibirsk Higher Party School

1986—Head of the agrarian branch of the Tyva CPSU regional committee, and in April 1987 became secretary of issues involving the agro-industrial complex

1990–1992—Member of the RSFSR Congress of People's Deputies

1990–1992—Chairman of the Council of Ministers of Tyva

15 March 1992—Elected president of Tyva

12 December 1993—Elected to the first session of the Federation Council

1997—Reelected president of Tyva

Relationships Between Key Players: Trouble with Republican Capital

Relations between the administrations of the republic and its capital Kyzyl are tense. In September 1998 the city of Kyzyl asked to secede from Tyva and join neighboring Krasnoyarsk Krai. The acting mayor of Kyzyl argued that this threat was the only way to convince Tyva's government to pay its debts to the city (*RFE/RL*, 4 September 1998). The city has also had a difficult time electing a legislature. Insufficient voter turnout has been the main impediment in the past four attempts to elect the body. The most recent election was held in March 1999.

The electorate in Tyva tends to be more regionally than nationally focused. When the Russian Constitution was put to referendum in 1993, the Tyvan Constitution was also put up on the same day. Tyvans rejected the Russian Constitution, with only 29.7 percent voting in favor of it, but overwhelmingly accepted the republican constitution, with 62.2 percent backing it.

Ties to Moscow: Calm Relations

Oorzhak is on good terms with Moscow. He has guaranteed that the republic will not try to secede from the federation, and continually emphasizes maintaining Russia's integrity. In September 1997 the parliament in Tyva approved several amendments to the Tyvan Constitution, which had been adopted in 1993. The amendments served to rectify the 13 substantial contradictions between the republican constitution and that of the Russian Federation. The Tyvan Constitution previously granted the republic the right to have its own armed forces and to secede from the Russian Federation. Oorzhak backed removing these clauses so that the republican constitution would conform with the federal constitution.

Foreign Relations: Shares Border with Mongolia

Tyva shares a border with Mongolia and is working together with that state to combat crime.

The Dalai Lama visited the region in 1992.

Attitudes Toward Business: Pro-Investment

Oorzhak is very interested in increasing the republic's business development and investment potential. He attended the second annual U.S.-Russian Investment Symposium held at Harvard University's Kennedy School of Government in Massachusetts in January 1998 in hopes of making contacts and attracting investment to Tyva.

In August 1997 Mapo-Bank signed a deal with Tyva in which the bank agreed to invest in the republic's economy in return for access to the region's 200-ton gold deposits. Oorzhak hoped that the income from the gold sales would reduce the republic's dependence on federal subsidies (*KD*, 8 August 1997).

Internet Sites in the Region

http://www.feynman.com/Tyva/
This site is sponsored by the Friends of Tyva, an informal group of people interested in Tyva. It contains information on Tyvan culture and informal reports on various trips to the region.

http://www.region.rags.ru/texts/12.txt
This site features Tyva's constitution as adopted in 1996.

REPUBLIC OF UDMURTIA

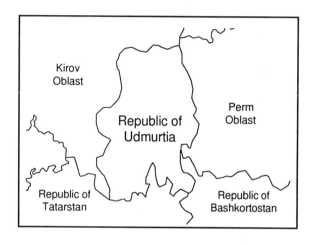

Territory: 42,100 km²
Population (as of 1 January 1998): 1,636,000
Distance from Moscow: 1,129 km

Major Cities:
Izhevsk, *capital* (pop. 654,100)
Sarapul (106,800)
Glazov (106,200)
Votkinsk (102,600)

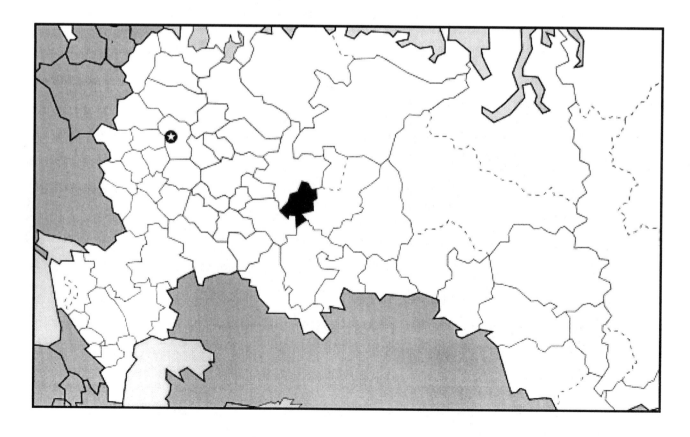

584

Basic Facts

Population (as of 1 Jan. 1998): 1,636,000 (1.11% of Russian total)

Ethnic breakdown (1989 census): Russians 58.9%, Udmurts 30.9%, Tatars 6.9%

Urban population (as of 1 Jan. 1998): 69.5% (Russia overall: 73.1%)

Student population (as of 1 Sept. 1997): 207 per 10,000 (Russia overall: 208/10,000)

Pensioner population (1997): 23.53% (Russia overall: 25.96%)

Percent of population with higher education (1989 census): 9.2% (Russia overall: 11.3%)

Percent of population working in (1997): Industry: 29.5% (Russian average: 23.0%); Agriculture: 13.5% (13.7%); Trade: 14.6% (13.5%); Culture: 12.7% (13.3%)

Average monthly personal income in July 1998: 557.8 new rubles (Russian average: 891.7 new rubles)

Average monthly personal expenses in July 1998: 446.1 new rubles (Russian average: 684.9 new rubles)

Average monthly subsistence requirement in 1998: 403 new rubles (Russian average: 438 new rubles)

Consumer price index (as of July 1998): 87 (Russia overall = 100)

Budgetary revenues (1997): 4,578.8 billion rubles (Russia overall: 433,378.2 billion rubles)

Budgetary expenditures (1997): 5,018.1 billion rubles (Russia overall: 468,111.6 billion rubles)

Industrial production as percentage of all Russian production (Jan.–Aug. 1998): 0.86%

Proportion of loss-making enterprises (as of July 1998): 48.0% (Russia overall: 50.4%)

Number of enterprises which have wage arrears (as of 1 Sept. 1998): 2,104 (1.56% of Russian total)

Agricultural production as percentage of all Russian production (1997): 1.22%

Number of private farms (as of 1 Jan. 1998): 3,559 (1.30% of Russian total)

Capital investment (1997): 4,115.7 billion rubles (Russia overall: 408,797 billion rubles)

Sources of investment (1997): federal budget: 2.3% (Russian average: 10.2%); regional budget: 7.7% (10.5%); extra-budgetary funds: 90.0% (79.3%)

Foreign investment (1997): 10,010,000 USD (Russia overall: 12,294,734,000 USD)

Number of joint ventures (1997): 49 (0.33% of Russian total)

Fixed capital investment in joint ventures and foreign companies (1997): 42,016 million rubles (Russia overall: 16,265.4 billion rubles)

Number of small businesses (as of 1 July 1998): 7,100 (0.82% of Russian total)

Number of enterprises privatized in 1997: 17 (0.62% of Russian total), including those which used to be municipal property: 94.1% (Russian average: 66.4%); regional property: 5.9% (20.0%); federal property: 0% (13.6%)

Number of telephones per 100 families (1997): in cities: 48.8 (Russian average: 49.2); in villages: 21.5 (19.8)

Brief Overview

Udmurtia is located to the west of the Urals Mountains and borders Kirov and Perm oblasts, Tatarstan, and Bashkortostan. The republic is rich with oil, peat, and clays, while annual oil and gas extraction reaches 10 million tons and 60 million cubic meters, respectively. Since the 17th century, Udmurtia has developed a unique industrial complex, which produces an extensive arsenal of weapons. In the beginning of the 1990s, the military industry, which makes up a quarter of the republic's industrial complex, produced about 80 percent of its GDP. With the defense industry now in decline, the republic is suffering severe economic difficulties. Other industries include oil extraction and processing, ferrous metallurgy, automobile construction, and chemicals. The republic is now seeking foreign investment with its rich mineral resources, well-developed industry, and highly-trained personnel. Udmurtia places a priority on investing in the oil industry, exporting machines, and converting military plants to high-tech civilian pursuits.

According to a 1998 survey by *Ekspert* magazine, the republic ranked 37th among Russia's 89 regions in terms of investment potential and 77th in terms of investment risk. A 1998 survey by Bank Austria ranked the republic 32nd in terms of investment climate.

Electoral History

2000 Presidential Election
Putin: 61.01%
Zyuganov: 24.83%
Zhirinovsky: 3.05%
Tuleev: 2.85%
Yavlinskii: 2.78%
Turnout: 70.21% (Russia overall: 68.64%)

1999 Parliamentary Elections
Unity: 36.60%
Communist Party of the Russian Federation: 18.75%
Zhirinovsky Bloc: 8.55%
Fatherland–All Russia: 7.98%
Union of Right Forces: 6.95%
Women of Russia: 3.13%
Yabloko: 2.71%
In single-mandate districts: 1 Communist Party of the Russian Federation, 1 independent
Turnout: 61.75% (Russia overall: 61.85%)

1996 Presidential Election
Yeltsin: 36.81%/52.83% (first round/second round)
Zyuganov: 30.47%/40.73%
Lebed: 11.52%
Yavlinskii: 9.23%
Zhirinovsky: 5.99%
Turnout: 64.12%/64.27% (Russia overall: 69.67%/68.79%)

1995 Parliamentary Elections
Communist Party of the Russian Federation: 14.92%
Liberal Democratic Party of Russia: 9.51%
Women of Russia: 8.46%
Communists–Workers' Russia: 8.42%
Agrarian Party of Russia: 7.54%
Our Home Is Russia: 6.37%
Congress of Russian Communities: 5.89%
Yabloko: 4.38%
Russia's Democratic Choice: 3.77%
Party of Workers' Self-Government: 2.91%
In single-mandate districts: 2 independent
Turnout: 57.64% (Russia overall: 64.37%)

1993 Constitutional Referendum
"Yes"—55.7%   "No"—41.3%

1993 Parliamentary Elections
Liberal Democratic Party of Russia: 17.59%
Russia's Choice: 16.19%
Women of Russia: 14.70%
Communist Party of the Russian Federation: 11.14%
Agrarian Party of Russia: 11.07%
Yabloko: 8.18%
Party of Russian Unity and Concord: 7.00%
Democratic Party of Russia: 5.34%
In single-mandate districts: 2 independent
From electoral associations: 1 Liberal Democratic Party of Russia, 1 Women of Russia
Turnout: 44.23% (Russia overall: 54.34%)

1991 Presidential Election
Yeltsin: 51.87%
Ryzhkov: 17.39%
Tuleev: 9.79%
Bakatin: 7.69%
Zhirinovsky: 4.24%
Makashov: 3.13%
Turnout: 74.39% (Russia overall: 76.66%)

Regional Political Institutions

Executive:

Chairman of Udmurtia's State Council, 4-year term
Aleksandr Aleksandrovich Volkov, elected April
1995, April 1999
Pl. 50-letiya Oktyabrya, 15; Izhevsk, 426074;
Republic of Udmurtia
Tel 7(341–2) 75–39–80, 75–48–01;
Fax 7(341–2) 75–29–87
Federation Council in Moscow:
292–59–01, 926–64–36
Chairman of the Republican Government—Nikolai
Alekseevich Ganza, appointed April 1999

Legislative:

Unicameral
State Council (Gosudarstvennyi sovet)—100
members, 4-year term
Chairman—Aleksandr Aleksandrovich Volkov,
elected April 1995, April 1999

Regional Politics

Authoritative Chairman of Defense Region

Aleksandr Volkov became chairman of Udmurtia's State
Council in April 1995 and was reelected to the post four
years later in April 1999 until 2000. Udmurtia was the
only Russian region with a parliamentary style of government. Volkov long sought to adopt a presidential system. He tried to persuade the State Council to hold a
referendum on introducing a presidency in 1997, but
was unable to muster enough support. The republic had
a referendum on the question in May 1995 before Volkov
came to power, but it did not pass. Only 26 March 2000
did such a referendum succeed. Then 69 percent of the
population voted to amend the constitution after federal legislation adopted in 1997 made it mandatory.

Volkov's most blatant "power grab" was the April
1996 law dismissing popularly elected mayors. Volkov
encouraged the State Council to adopt such a measure
so that he would have direct control over the mayors.
This plan backfired and the Russian Constitutional
Court demanded that Volkov reinstate the elected officials. He refused to implement the court's decision for
two months, ultimately succumbing to pressure from
Russian President Boris Yeltsin.

Udmurtia is home to a unique industrial base that
has evolved since the 17th century. The region was an
important part of the Soviet military-industrial complex,
producing SS-20 and SS-25 missiles and Kalashnikov
machine guns. The heavy concentration of defense enterprises has hurt Udmurtia in Russia's new economy.
As a result, Volkov has prioritized defense conversion
and new business development in the region.

Executive Platform: Moderate Reformer

In general Volkov can be described as a reformer. He
supported Russian President Boris Yeltsin on the federal level, even though he criticized Yeltsin's policies
and stood up to presidential decrees. An obstacle to
Volkov's adopting a completely reformist platform has
been Udmurtia's heavy industrial base. In the early
1990s, the defense sector constituted 80 percent of its
industrial output, making Udmurtia extremely dependent on the federal government. Due to this burden
Volkov's policies have taken a slightly oppositionist
coloring at times. For example, in 1994 he spoke in
favor of introducing fixed prices for fuel and increasing state orders for military industrial products (Panorama Research Group, Labyrint Electronic Database,
Moscow). Subsequently, Volkov focused on energy issues and developing new enterprises in the regions.

In December 1998 he joined Moscow Mayor Yurii
Luzhkov's Fatherland movement and became the head
of its Udmurtia branch.

Policies

Many of the republic's economic difficulties have resulted from the collapsing defense industry. By mid-
1999, only 35 percent of the factories in this sector
were functioning. Volkov blamed the federal government for this problem, claiming that the federal policy
toward the defense sector has been poorly thought-
out. He has called on the center to decide which factories to close and which to fund more fully.

Volkov has also stressed developing the republic's oil
and automobile industries. Volkov's goal is to attract $200
million worth of investment for the local oil industry (*EWI
RRR*, 1 July 1999). Taxes from the oil sector make up
approximately 30 percent of the budget.

In December 1998 the Udmurtia State Council adopted
a 4 percent republican sales tax on purchases of expensive furniture, stereo equipment, clothing, prepared foods,
jewelry, furs, video equipment, tourist agency services,
hotel rooms, first-class train tickets, and airline tickets.
The republican budget receives 40 percent of the tax revenue and local governments take in 60 percent. The tax
is expected to bring in 200 million rubles per year.

Relationships Between Key Players: Conflict with Izhevsk Mayor

Udmurtia was the last Russian region to use a parliamentary rather than presidential system. Volkov has employed a variety of stratagems to increase his powers within this system. In March 1995, before Volkov became chair of the State Council, Udmurtia held a referendum about introducing the presidency in the republic, but it did not pass. Volkov tried to reintroduce the idea two years later and created a public movement in support of the proposal, yet he was unable to gather enough support in the State Council to put the issue on the parliament's agenda. Volkov hoped to use the increased powers of the presidency to improve his position vis-à-vis several republican rivals. Volkov had a long-standing conflict with former republican Prime Minister Pavel Vershinin, who refused to support the establishment of the presidency (*EWI RRR*, 5 June 1997). Similarly, the additional power afforded a president would have benefited Volkov in his dispute with Izhevsk Mayor Anatolii Saltykov. Udmurtiya ultimately introduced the presidency in 2000.

Volkov has long been at odds with Saltykov, who was elected mayor of Udmurtia's capital Izhevsk in 1994. In an attempt to remove Saltykov from power, in April 1996 Volkov urged the State Council to adopt a law dissolving popularly elected local governments and replaced them with his appointees. Volkov forced Saltykov from office in October. In January 1997 the Russian Constitutional Court ruled that the law was in violation of federal legislation, yet the State Council continued to implement it. President Yeltsin issued two decrees ordering the State Council to abide by the court decision before it finally annulled the law and allowed Saltykov to resume his post. In April 1998 Anatolii Saltykov was reelected mayor of Izhevsk, defeating Volkov ally Valerii Zagainov. The Izhevsk city council elected at the same time is dominated by big businessmen.

The conflict between Volkov and Saltykov is also related to the friction between the region's defense enterprises and new businesses. The defense sector relies heavily on budgetary subsidies. Enterprise directors in the military-industrial complex turned to Saltykov to lobby on their behalf. Volkov has supported the new entrepreneurs who were also looking for a powerful advocate in the political sphere. The April 1996 law abolishing local self-government placed local institutions under republican control and thus would have given the republican administration exclusive control over Udmurtia's assets and allowed it to allocate budgetary funds in a manner favorable to its political supporters. Thus, defense enterprises felt threatened and put pressure on Moscow to overturn the republican law.

After dismissing local governments in October 1996, Volkov cracked down on media in the region. Having heard reports critical of his actions, Volkov cancelled broadcasts and removed journalists from their jobs. He claimed that this was necessary to prevent unjustified criticism of weak local industries (*OMRI DD*, 31 October 1996).

The opposition Volkov faces in dealing with Saltykov is countered by the support he enjoys in the State Council elected in April 1999. Eighty-five of the Council's 100 deputies voted for the prime minister Volkov had recommended. Moscow Mayor Yurii Luzhkov's Fatherland holds the largest faction in the Council with 44 seats. Only 7 Communists were elected to the Council. Fifty-five of the members are local industrial directors.

The destruction of nuclear and chemical weapons, many of which were produced in the republic and are still stored there, is an extremely important issue for the region. In January 1999, 94.6 percent of the electorate in the city of Votkinsk voted against building a plant for burning off rocket fuel from decommissioned intercontinental ballistic missiles. The plant would have been sponsored by the United States government and would have been built by the U.S.'s Lockheed Martin. Originally the missiles were going to be destroyed at the Kirov plant in Perm, but public outrage caused the project to be moved to Votkinsk, where the missiles were produced.

The city of Kizner is planning to destroy chemical weapons from the local stockpile which holds 14.2 percent of Russia's chemical arsenal. Kizner's Mayor Vladimir Alekseev agreed to have the weapons destroyed on site and hopes to receive sizable federal compensation to use for building housing, hospitals, and roads (*Izvestiya*, 30 May 1998).

Ties to Moscow

Although Volkov was generally supportive of Yeltsin, he was not afraid to criticize the president. He was opposed to Yeltsin's actions in fall 1993 and became an active critic of the federal government's policies in 1994. In particular, he felt that the state should introduce fixed prices for fuel and increase state orders for defense products, which make up a quarter of the region's industry (Panorama Research Group). As a result of Volkov's persistence, President Boris Yeltsin signed a decree relieving all major enterprises in Udmurtia of taxes for six months following March 1994.

In October 1995 Udmurtia signed a power-sharing agreement with the federal government outlining the division of state property, budget relations, law and order, defense industries, the use of oil and forest resources, and environmental protection.

Relations with Other Regions:
Cooperates with Luzhkov

In October 1997 Volkov signed a cooperation agreement with Moscow Mayor Yurii Luzhkov focusing primarily on Udmurtia's oil reserves and heavy industrial enterprises. They signed additional agreements in April 1999 just prior to the Udmurtia State Council elections, in which Fatherland-backed candidates won nearly half of the seats. In December 1998 Volkov joined Luzhkov's Fatherland movement and became head of the republican branch.

Volkov is a member of the Alliance Group, a foundation providing crisis support to enterprises in Russia and other CIS countries. The Alliance Group was founded by Saratov, Leningrad, Novgorod, Murmansk, Irkutsk, Magadan, Chita, Novosibirsk, and Voronezh oblasts and the republics of Buryatia and Udmurtia.

Udmurtia belongs to the Urals Regional Association, which includes the Republic of Bashkortostan, Komi-Permyak Autonomous Okrug, and Kurgan, Orenburg, Perm, Sverdlovsk, and Chelyabinsk oblasts.

Foreign Relations

In September 1998 Volkov met with Belarusan President Aleksandr Lukashenko and Prime Minister Syarhey Linh.

Attitudes Toward Business: Seeking Investment

Volkov has concentrated on making Udmurtia's industrial base more profitable by seeking foreign investors

and export markets. The republic attracts up to $60 million a year in foreign investment. Udmurtia's industrial base is highly concentrated in the defense sector. In 1993 Udmurtia became the first region to receive an export license for military products and in June 1997 the Russian arms exporter Rosvooruzhenie opened its first representative office in Izhevsk for exporting arms produced in the region. In October 1997 the republican enterprise Izhmash signed an agreement with the U.S. firm Smith & Wesson to produce each other's products. Izhmash was to produce guns designed by Smith & Wesson and Smith & Wesson would assemble Saiga-12 hunting rifles and Bizon-2 pistols (*KD*, 24 October 1997).

Udmurtia's industrial base has also served to attract investment from foreign carmakers. The automotive sector once made up 30 percent of the republican budget, yet in 1999 it was contributing only 4 percent. Republican authorities had hoped to attract an outside investor, such as the Czech Republic's Skoda, but the plans did not materialize.

In May 1998 the Chepetsk Mechanical Plant formed a joint venture with the U.S. firm OBC for making batteries for electric car engines. All of the enterprise's output is to be exported to the U.S. (*Segodnya*, 19 May 1998). In March 1999 Izhmash signed an agreement with the American company KMW stating that KMW would adapt Izhmash engines for compatibility with Nissan, Toyota, and General Motors vehicles (*MN*, 30 March 1999).

In 1996–97 the American company Samson International Ltd. won an international competition for the right to develop 12 oil deposits in Udmurtia using production-sharing agreements. However, development has been postponed because the federal government has not adopted adequate production-sharing legislation. Volkov wants to work with Samson in spite of the delay, anticipating that the republican budget will gain $4–5 million annually as a result. Due to the absence of favorable production-sharing legislation, Samson has suggested going ahead with the project on the basis of leasing agreements. Samson aimed to drill 20–25 wells by the end of 1999 and begin producing 300,000 tons of oil per year within 15–18 months (*Biznes-Novosti Urala*, 22 February 1999).

Udmurtia has an extremely modern telephone system, which relies on a 63-percent digital network. The only Russian region with a more modern system is Tula.

Aleksandr Aleksandrovich Volkov

25 December 1951—Born in Bryansk

1969—Began working at the Chepetsk construction company, where he rose through the ranks to become head of construction

1970—Graduated from the Bryansk Construction Technical College as an industrial and civil engineer

1978—Graduated from the Perm Polytechnic Institute as an engineer-builder

1986–1988—Chairman of the Executive Committee of the Glasov City Council

1989—Became first chairman of the Udmurtia State Planning Committee

1990–1993—Deputy chairman of the Udmurtia Council of Ministers, simultaneously serving as chairman of the State Committee for Architecture and Construction

26 June 1993—Appointed chairman of the Udmurtia Council of Ministers

12 December 1993—Elected to the Federation Council, joining the Committee on the Budget, Finance, Currency and Credit Regulations, Monetary Emissions, Tax Policies, and Customs Regulations

January 1995—Elected to the Udmurtia State Council and became chairman at the first session in April 1995

1996—Member of the Federation Council Committee on Economic Policy

20 April 1999—Reelected chairman of the Udmurtia State Council

Married, with two children

Internet Sites in the Region

http://www.udm.ru/
This site offers basic information about Udmurtia, its history, business, economy, industry, and culture.

http://www.izhcom.ru/
This site provides useful information and links to various services in Udmurtia.

ULYANOVSK OBLAST

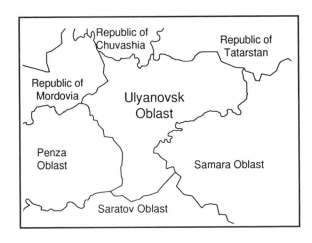

Territory: 37,300 km^2
Population (as of 1 January 1998):
1,483,000
Distance from Moscow: 893 km

Major Cities:
Ulyanovsk, *capital* (pop. 674,100)
Dmitrovgrad (136,700)
Inza (22,900)
Barysh (21,500)

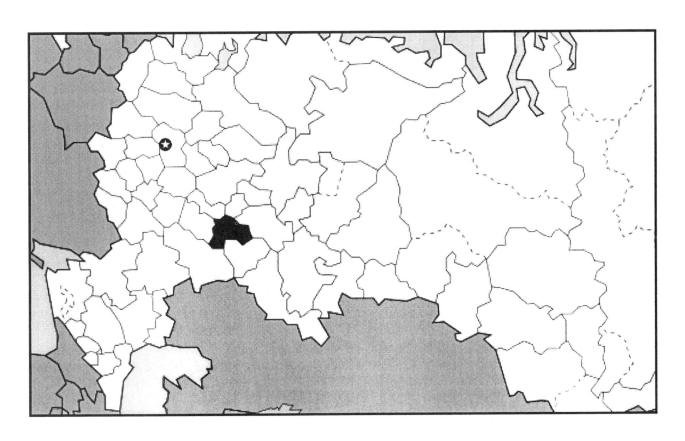

Basic Facts

Population (as of Jan. 1, 1998): 1,483,000 (1.01% of Russian total)

Ethnic breakdown (1989 census): Russians 72.8%, Tatars 11.4%, Chuvash 8.4%, Mordvins 4.4%, Ukrainians 1.3%

Urban population (as of Jan. 1, 1998): 73.0% (Russia overall: 73.1%)

Student population (as of Sept. 1, 1997): 167 per 10,000 (Russia overall: 208/10,000)

Pensioner population (1997): 25.29% (Russia overall: 25.96%)

Percent of population with higher education (1989 census): 8.9% (Russia overall: 11.3%)

Percent of population working in 1997: Industry: 29.4% (Russian average: 23.0%); Agriculture: 14.1% (13.7%); Trade: 11.8% (13.5%); Culture: 12.3% (13.3%)

Average monthly personal income in July 1998: 565.6 new rubles (Russian average: 891.7 new rubles)

Average monthly personal expenses in July 1998: 486.6 new rubles (Russian average: 684.9 new rubles)

Average monthly subsistence requirement in 1998: 277 new rubles (Russian average: 438 new rubles)

Consumer price index (as of July 1998): 78 (Russia overall = 100)

Budgetary revenues (1997): 2,492.5 billion rubles (Russia overall: 433,378.2 billion rubles) Budgetary expenditures (1997): 3,019.8 billion rubles (Russia overall: 468,111.6 billion rubles)

Industrial production as percentage of all Russian production (Jan.–Aug. 1998): 0.74%

Proportion of loss-making enterprises (as of July 1998): 58.8% (Russia overall: 50.4%)

Number of enterprises which have wage arrears (as of Sept. 1, 1998): 1,320 (0.98% of Russian total)

Agricultural production as percentage of all Russian production (1997): 1.24%

Number of private farms (as of Jan. 1, 1998): 2,117 (0.77% of Russian total)

Capital investment (1997): 1,996.3 billion rubles (Russia overall: 408,797 billion rubles)

Sources of investment (1997): federal budget: 6.4% (Russian average: 10.2%); regional budget: 10.1% (10.5%); extra-budgetary funds: 77.1% (79.3%)

Foreign investment (1997): 2,364,000 USD (Russia overall: 12,294,734,000 USD)

Number of joint ventures (1997): 21 (0.14% of Russian total)

Fixed capital investment in joint ventures and foreign companies (1997): 71,166 million rubles (Russia overall: 16,265.4 billion rubles)

Number of small businesses (as of July 1, 1998): 4,600 (0.53% of Russian total)

Number of enterprises privatized in 1997: 33 (1.20% of Russian total), including those which used to be municipal property: 97.0% (Russian average: 66.4%); regional property: 0% (20.0%); federal property: 3.0% (13.6%)

Number of telephones per 100 families (1997): in cities: 34.8 (Russian average: 49.2); in villages: 15.3 (19.8)

Brief Overview

Ulyanovsk Oblast is located in the basin of the Volga River about 900 km from Moscow. It borders Samara, Saratov, and Penza oblasts, and the republics of Mordovia, Chuvashia, and Tatarstan.

Ulyanovsk, which bore the name Simbirsk until 1924, was founded in 1648 as a military fortress. In 1796 it became the center of Simbirsk Gubernia, an administrative unit in Czarist Russia. Simbirsk is the hometown of Vladimir Lenin (Ulyanov).

In the nineteenth century, the city became one of the country's trade centers. Today, the region has a highly developed machine-building industry, which manufactures cars, planes, and agricultural and chemical equipment. There are also strong light and food industries. Regional agriculture specializes in cultivating grain, potatoes, vegetables, sugar beets, and sunflowers.

According to a 1998 survey by *Ekspert* magazine, the oblast ranked 42nd among Russia's 89 regions in terms of investment potential and 20th in terms of investment risk. A 1998 survey by Bank Austria ranked the oblast 50th in terms of investment climate.

Electoral History

2000 Presidential Election
Putin: 47.45%
Zyuganov: 38.27%
Titov: 3.39%
Yavlinskii: 2.97%
Zhirinovsky: 2.41%
Tuleev: 2.03%
Turnout: 70.11% (Russia overall: 68.64%)

1999 Parliamentary Elections
Communist Party of the Russian Federation: 33.03%
Unity: 23.92%
Fatherland–All Russia: 9.18%
Union of Right Forces: 7.11%
Zhirinovsky Bloc: 6.21%
Yabloko: 3.77%
In single-mandate districts: 1 Fatherland–All Russia, 1 independent
Turnout: 63.56% (Russia overall: 61.85%)

1996 Gubernatorial Election
Goryachev (incumbent): 42.48%
Kruglikov (State Duma deputy, KPRF)): 33.71%

Semashin: 7.63%
Bartkaitis: 5.63%
Cheburov: 3.45%
Chinov: 0.33%
Turnout: 50.13%

1996 Presidential Election
Zyuganov: 45.83%/56.28% (first round/second round)
Yeltsin: 23.78%/37.83%
Lebed: 12.34%
Zhirinovsky: 7.38%
Yavlinskii: 5.91%
Turnout: 71.05%/69.37% (Russia overall: 69.67%/ 68.79%)

1995 Parliamentary Elections
Communist Party of the Russian Federation: 37.16%
Liberal Democratic Party of Russia: 13.26%
Women of Russia: 7.82%
Communists–Workers' Russia: 4.84%
Our Home Is Russia: 4.70%
Party of Workers' Self-Government: 3.05%
Agrarian Party of Russia: 2.94%
Yabloko: 2.89%
Congress of Russian Communities: 2.62%
Russia's Democratic Choice: 2.59%
In single-mandate districts: 1 Women of Russia, 1 independent
Turnout: 66.35% (Russia overall: 64.37%)

1993 Constitutional Referendum
"Yes"—50.0%   "No"—47.7%

1993 Parliamentary Elections
Liberal Democratic Party of Russia: 24.57%
Communist Party of the Russian Federation: 17.50%
Agrarian Party of Russia: 13.98%
Russia's Choice: 12.23%
Women of Russia: 8.04%
Party of Russian Unity and Concord: 6.17%
Democratic Party of Russia: 5.52%
Yabloko: 4.78%
In single-mandate districts: 2 independent
Turnout: 58.01% (Russia overall: 54.34%)

1991 Presidential Election
Yeltsin: 52.83%
Ryzhkov: 23.37%

Tuleev: 7.77%
Zhirinovsky: 6.65%
Makashov: 3.22%
Bakatin: 2.76%
Turnout: 78.40% (Russia overall: 76.66%)

Regional Political Institutions

Executive:
   Governor, 4-year term
   Yurii Frolovich Goryachev, elected December 1996
      Ulyanovsk Oblast Administration;
      Leninskaya Ploshchod, 1; Ulyanovsk, 432700
      Tel 7(842–2) 41–20–78, 41–25–06;
      Fax 7(842–2) 41–48–12
      Federation Council in Moscow:
        7(095) 292–80–65, 926–69–61

Legislative:
   Unicameral
   Legislative Assembly (Zakonodatelnoe Sobranie)—
   25 members, 4-year term elected December 1995
   Chairman—Sergei Nikolaevich Ryabukhin, elected
   January 1996, January 2000

Regional Politics

Old-Style Politician Initially Appointed by Yeltsin

Despite his explicit old-style attitudes and resistance to most reforms, Goryachev was appointed governor by President Yeltsin in 1992. For Yeltsin this was an act of desperation after the local elite had made it impossible for Yeltsin's first appointee to govern (*JFP*, 20 February 1998).

Goryachev is difficult to categorize politically. On the one hand, he is famous for having established a socialist stronghold in Ulyanovsk Oblast. The All-Russian Coordinating Council, seeking to elect pro-Yeltsin governors, did not back his 1996 gubernatorial campaign. On the other hand, though having claimed to be an "old" communist, he did not join the Communist Party after its re-establishment in 1993 and supported Yeltsin's reelection, reason enough for the Communists to endorse their own candidate in the gubernatorial elections. Ultimately, Goryachev's 1996 campaign was backed by Grigorii Yavlinskii's Yabloko and the local branch of Our Home Is Russia (NDR) even though NDR's national leadership refused to help

him. Goryachev's foremost promoter may have been Aleksandr Lebed, who once considered him as a potential candidate for the post of Russian prime minister during his 1996 presidential campaign. Since his election, Goryachev has been trying to take over Ulyanovsk's leftist camp, initiating his own leftist Ulyanovsk Patriotic Union, which has gathered a sizable following in the region.

In February 1999, Goryachev changed the oblast charter so that he could run for a third term in 2000 (*EWI RRR*, 18 February 1999).

Executive Platform: Social Welfare at Cost of Progress

Goryachev's economic policy demonstrates that social welfare has been his main priority. Rather than proceed with market reforms that would devastate the populace, the governor maintained Soviet-style economic policies as long as he could. Until June 1996, he preserved a food rationing coupon system. Prices for basic foodstuffs were lifted only after his 1996 electoral victory, and some subsidies still remain for the lowest strata of society. The pace of privatization in his oblast is one of the slowest in the country. Among other measures, Goryachev's administration has levied special taxes on local enterprises to finance a so-called "stability fund" earmarked for social issues.

At first Goryachev's plan to cushion Ulyanovsk from shock therapy seemed successful, keeping food prices among the lowest in the country, and maintaining pension payments. However, the residual effects of Goryachev's socialist economic policies are slowly seeping their way into Ulyanovsk Oblast. Prices of consumer goods are comparable with those in neighboring regions, yet salaries remain relatively low, suggesting that the standard of living in the region is below that of its neighbors. The region has a weak market infrastructure and low business activity (*JFP*, 20 February 1998). Rather than encourage small business development, the oblast administration supports a network of state-controlled commercial outlets. As a result, the number of supermarkets, department stores, and shops are low compared to neighboring regions, and there is a poorer variety of goods (*JFP*, 20 February 1998). Thus, the popular support Goryachev gained by maintaining a higher standard of living during the economic crisis of shock therapy may wane as conditions in the oblast fail to improve.

Goryachev carefully limits free speech in the region.

Approximately 1,000 people staged a protest in support of freedom of speech in the city of Ulyanovsk in January 1998. The participants demanded that the oblast government respect the public's constitutional rights and liberties. One complaint is that the oblast has unconstitutionally denied the public access to information such as budgetary expenditures (*EWI RRR*, 29 January 1998). Additionally, publications loyal to the governor receive $1.3 million in public funding annually, and local courts frequently rule in Goryachev's favor when he sues journalists for libel (*EWI RRR*, 29 January 1998 and *RFE/RL*, 29 January 1998).

In May 1999 Goryachev and Chairman of the Ulyanovsk Oblast Legislative Assembly Sergei Ryabukhin announced that they had not joined any of the new political parties emerging in preparation for the State Duma elections and did not intend to do so. They claimed that the only political organization that they considered themselves members of is the Ulyanovsk Patriotic Union (USP), a leftist organization (originally the USP had the same acronym as the Communist Party of the Soviet Union—KPSS, standing for the Congress of Patriots for Social Justice). However, according to Our Home Is Russia (NDR), Goryachev was elected to the movement's political council with his consent and has not announced his intention to leave. Similarly, both Goryachev and Ryabukhin appear on the list of initiators for Samara Governor Konstantin Titov's Voice of Russia movement.

Policies: Tight Control over Enterprises

Goryachev seeks to maintain tight control over the region's enterprises. In January 1999, the oblast's chief economist announced that the oblast will seek to acquire a controlling stake in the region's major enterprises (*EWI RRR*, 28 January 1999). Largely, this was to be done through a "tax debt for shares" swap, whereby enterprises will transfer some of their shares to the oblast instead of paying mounting tax arrears.

At the beginning of 1999, there were 180 enterprises in the oblast with partial state ownership. Of those, the state owns over 51 percent of the shares in 21 cases, over 25 percent in 85 cases, and over 20 percent in 29 cases. As of 1998, fully or partially privatized enterprises accounted for 92 percent of all production in the oblast. The oblast administration is hoping to augment its revenue stream with dividends from the industrial shares.

Relationships Between Key Players: Communist Stronghold

Ulyanovsk has one of the most conservative leaderships in all of the Russian regions. The Communists dominate the oblast legislature, and Goryachev maintains strong ties with it. Goryachev is the leader of the Ulyanovsk Patriotic Union, which over the past several months has become the dominant force of the oblast's leftist camp, and is likely to replace the local Communist Party as the region's primary leftist organization. The oblast Communist organization, led by State Duma Deputy Aleksandr Kruglikov, was left out of the USP alliance, having not been allowed to participate in the party's founding congress (*EWI RRR*, 19 November 1998). The Communist-run local government also has close relations with the regional economic elite. Government officials and economic managers are drawn from the same pool of individuals (*JFP*, 20 February 1998).

At the end of 1998, the Ulyanovsk City Duma won a court case against the oblast and forced the oblast to stop sending it unfunded mandates (*EWI RRR*, 14 January 1999). The oblast had required the city to make child support payments, but had not provided enough funds to do so. The city of Ulyanovsk received only 5.3 million rubles from the oblast in 1998, whereas servicing the child support allowance program required at least 64 million rubles.

This ruling had several important ramifications. First, it allowed the city to demand that courts reconsider previous cases in which Ulyanovsk was found liable for child support. Second, lower-level courts will not be able to force the city to pay in cases like this, since the oblast court has established that the city is not responsible. Third, the city can now demand reimbursement from the oblast for all the payments it had to make on the claims. Fourth, oblast legislators will be much more cautious in the future not to delegate government responsibilities to municipalities. Finally, trying this case in court has set an important precedent for the resolution of disputes between different levels of government. Now every municipality in the oblast can go to court to protect the integrity of its budget.

Nevertheless, in spite of the 1998 precedent, Ulyanovsk's 1999 budget, which planned for a 27.3 percent deficit, repeated the oblast's attack on local governments by recommending that local budgets

Yurii Frolovich Goryachev

11 November 1938—Born in the village Novo-Osorgino, Kamyshlinskii Raion, Kuibyshev Oblast (since 1991, Samara Oblast)

1960—Joined the CPSU

1961—Graduated from the Ulyanovsk Agricultural Institute

1961—Worked as head of the interregional veterinary-bacteriological laboratory in Novospasskoe

1961–1965—Worked as a Komsomol functionary

1974—Graduated from the Higher Party School under the CPSU Central Committee

1965–1987—First secretary of the Ulyanovsk Oblast Komsomol Committee, secretary of the Kuzovatovo CPSU Oblast Committee

1987–1990—Chairman of the Ulyanovsk Executive Committee and a member of the CPSU Oblast Committee

4 March 1990—Elected to the Ulyanovsk Oblast Soviet and to the RSFSR Congress of People's Deputies

April 1990—Elected chairman of the Ulyanovsk Oblast Soviet and first secretary of the Ulyanovsk CPSU Oblast Committee

July 1990—Became a member of the Central Committee of the CPSU; remained on the Committee until he left the party in August 1991

9 January 1992—Appointed governor by President Yeltsin

12 December 1993—Elected to the Federation Council, where he served as a member of the Committee on Science, Culture, and Education

January 1996—Member of the Federation Council, where he served on the Committee for Science, Culture, Education, Health Care, and Ecology

22 December 1996—Elected governor in the first round, defeating Duma Deputy Aleksandr Kruglikov by a margin of 8.5 percent

Married, with two sons and a grandson.

---

cover funds that the oblast can no longer provide for. Ulyanovsk Mayor Vitalii Marusin was greatly displeased with the budget since the oblast had transferred obligations but not finances to the local level. The city authorities are suing the oblast over articles of the budget that they charge illegally take away city income or give the city responsibilities for which it cannot pay.

Goryachev has considerable control over the oblast media, using them as a tool to trumpet his accomplishments and downplay his administration's shortcomings. The media tend to blame the various inadequacies of Goryachev's policies on Moscow or the Ulyanovsk city administration (*EWI RRR*, 22 December 1998). The

governor's tightening control over the media is likely related to his waning popularity in the face of upcoming gubernatorial elections in 2000.

Ties to Moscow: Fence-Post Squatter

Goryachev maintains a rather ambiguous relationship with the federal government. Goryachev remained neutral during the 1991 coup attempt. In January 1993 Yeltsin offered Goryachev the post of deputy prime minister responsible for agriculture, but Goryachev refused. Goryachev has stated that he is against "democratic" reforms, claiming that "meetings and discussions won't increase meat or sugar production" (*JFP*, 20 February 1998). Yet, after signing a power-sharing agreement with Yeltsin on 30 October 1997, Goryachev stated that Ulyanovsk "would continue to implement the new democratic market reforms with a strong commitment to maintaining a high level of social security and preserving the living standard of the population" (*EWI RRR*, 26 November 1997). Through these remarks, Goryachev tried to demonstrate that he has some liberal tendencies. Yet, the governor was adamantly against shock therapy, and called Gaidar's team the "hoorah-reformists" (an insult which, incidentally, did not include Yeltsin) (*JFP*, 20 February 1998).

Goryachev's relationship to the center has affected the amount of subsidies the oblast receives. Thus, in spite of Ulyanovsk's economic problems, it receives less government support than other pro-Yeltsin regions with healthier economies.

In April 1997 the Duma instructed the state's Audit Chamber to examine the Ulyanovsk Oblast administration for allegations of corruption and misuse of federal funds (*RFE/RL*, 25 April 1997).

Relations with Other Regions: Potential Lebed Ally

Current Krasnoyarsk Krai governor Aleksandr Lebed showed his support for Goryachev while Lebed was campaigning for president in 1996.

Ulyanovsk belongs to the Greater Volga regional association, which is headed by Samara Oblast Governor Konstantin Titov. The other members of the association are the republics of Tatarstan, Mordovia, Chuvashia, and Marii El, and Astrakhan, Volgograd, Nizhnii Novgorod, Penza, Samara, and Saratov oblasts.

Attitudes Toward Business: Supportive But Not Active

Although Goryachev is not anti-business, he has done little to initiate business development. As a result, Ulyanovsk boasts few small and medium sized businesses. Additionally, the region's aircraft and automobile industries are in very poor shape. The Ulyanovsk Automobile Factory has not signed a deal with a foreign investor as others have. In April 1998 the oblast Legislative Assembly sent a letter to the president, the National Security Council, and the Federation Council petitioning the federal authorities to refrain from buying foreign aircraft (*EWI RRR*, 2 April 1998). The largest Russian aircraft manufacturer, Aviastar, is located in Ulyanovsk, and has suffered a serious decline due to lack of demand. Even Aeroflot does not want to buy its low-quality airplanes.

Various investment projects involving American banks and companies have been discussed. Goryachev has expressed his support for such development (*UP*, 4 October 1997, 4). Still, he has not actively pursued investors, and his traditional economic approaches probably intimidate entrepreneurs.

Nevertheless, the Volzhanka confectionery factory was the first Russian food enterprise to receive the ISO-9000 certificate for international standards, which could be an economic asset for the region (Mayak Radio Station, "Biznes-Klub," 17 September 1997).

Internet Sites in the Region

http://www.st.simbirsk.su/rcons/index.pl
This website displays all of the legislation passed in Ulyanovsk from 1992 to 1997. It also features a search engine.

UST-ORDA BURYAT AUTONOMOUS OKRUG

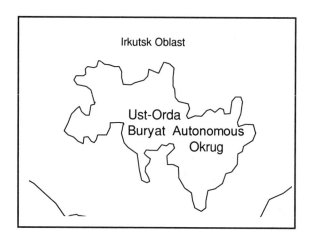

Irkutsk Oblast

Ust-Orda Buryat Autonomous Okrug

Territory: 22,400 km²
Population (as of 1 January 1998): 144,000
Distance from Moscow: 5,111 km

Major Cities:
Ust-Ordynskii, *capital*

Basic Facts

Population (as of 1 Jan. 1998): 144,000 (0.10% of Russian total)

Ethnic breakdown (1989 census): Russians 56.7%, Buryats 35.7%, Tatars 3.3%, Ukrainians 1.9%

Urban population (as of 1 Jan. 1998): 0% (Russia overall: 73.1%)

Pensioner population (1997): 22.22% (Russia overall: 25.96%)

Percent of population with higher education (1989 census): 7.1% (Russia overall: 11.3%)

Average monthly personal income in July 1998: 239.5 new rubles (Russian average: 891.7 new rubles)

Average monthly personal expenses in July 1998: 137.1 new rubles (Russian average: 684.9 new rubles)

Average monthly subsistence requirement in 1998: 362 new rubles (Russian average: 438 new rubles)

Consumer price index (as of July 1998): 127 (Russia overall = 100)

Budgetary revenues (1997): 256.8 billion rubles (Russia overall: 433,378.2 billion rubles)

Budgetary expenditures (1997): 290.5 billion rubles (Russia overall: 468,111.6 billion rubles)

Industrial production as percentage of all Russian production (Jan.–Aug. 1998): 0.004%

Proportion of loss-making enterprises (as of July 1998): 58.3% (Russia overall: 50.4%)

Number of enterprises which have wage arrears (as of 1 Sept. 1998): 132 (0.10% of Russian total)

Agricultural production as percentage of all Russian production (1997): 0.44%

Number of private farms (as of 1 Jan. 1998): 776 (0.28% of Russian total)

Capital investment (1997): 92.0 billion rubles (Russia overall: 408,797 billion rubles)

Sources of investment (1997): federal budget: 11.5% (Russian average: 10.2%); regional budget: 38.7% (10.5%); extra-budgetary funds: 49.8% (79.3%)

Number of telephones per 100 families (1997): in cities: 29.2 (Russian average: 49.2); in villages: 14.7 (19.8)

Brief Overview

The okrug is located in the southern part of Irkutsk Oblast to the west of Lake Baikal. Its population includes 79 different ethnic groups.

The okrug is rich in coal, gypsum, and clay. Oil and gas fields have been discovered but remain unexplored. Major regional industries are gypsum and coal extraction and forestry and timber working. However, only 5 percent of the local population are employed in industry, with the others involved in agriculture.

Investing in the okrug has become more dangerous as of late. Regional investment risk increased by 14 points in 1997. According to a 1998 survey by *Ekspert* magazine, the okrug ranked 83rd among Russia's 89 regions in terms of investment potential and 71st in terms of investment risk. A 1998 survey by Bank Austria ranked the okrug 82nd in terms of investment climate.

Electoral History

2000 Presidential Election
Putin: 56.80%
Zyuganov: 31.30%
Tuleev: 4.31%
Zhirinovsky: 2.54%
Yavlinskii: 1.27%
Turnout: 71.52% (Russia overall: 68.64%)

1999 Parliamentary Elections
Unity: 35.71%
Communist Party of the Russian Federation: 25.40%
Fatherland–All Russia: 7.43%
Zhirinovsky Bloc: 5.73%
Union of Right Forces: 3.63%
Communists–Workers' Russia: 3.29%
Women of Russia: 3.10%
Our Home Is Russia: 2.73%
Pensioners Party: 2.29%
Yabloko: 1.26%
In a single-mandate district: 1 independent
Turnout: 68.20% (Russia overall: 61.85%)

1996 Gubernatorial Election
Maleev: 37.74%
Batagaev (incumbent): 26.84%
Ivanov: 25.70%
Nazarov: 1.73%
Byvaltsev (deputy governor): 0.78%
Turnout: 56.98%

1996 Presidential Election
Yeltsin: 36.99%/48.67% (first round/second round)
Zyuganov: 40.01%/47.00%
Lebed: 8.54%
Zhirinovsky: 4.56%
Yavlinskii: 3.96%
Turnout: 71.14%/71.99% (Russia overall: 69.67%/68.79%)

1995 Parliamentary Elections
Communist Party of the Russian Federation: 22.80%
Agrarian Party of Russia: 19.08%
Our Home Is Russia: 9.28%
Women of Russia: 8.78%
Communists–Workers' Russia: 8.32%
Liberal Democratic Party of Russia: 7.18%

Party of Workers' Self-Government: 2.11%
Yabloko: 2.05%
In a single-mandate district: 1 Our Home Is Russia
Turnout: 70.14% (Russia overall: 64.37%)

1993 Constitutional Referendum
"Yes"—79.5%   "No"—18.8%

1993 Parliamentary Elections
Agrarian Party of Russia: 25.28%
Liberal Democratic Party of Russia: 14.35%
Party of Russian Unity and Concord: 13.25%
Women of Russia: 12.34%
Communist Party of the Russian Federation: 11.86%
Russia's Choice: 10.02%
Democratic Party of Russia: 3.58%
Yabloko: 2.14%
In a single-mandate district: 1 independent
Turnout: 69.73% (Russia overall: 54.34%)

1991 Presidential Election
Yeltsin: 32.37%
Ryzhkov: 24.28%
Tuleev: 19.18%
Zhirinovsky: 12.93%
Bakatin: 3.93%
Makashov: 2.81%
Turnout: 83.72% (Russia overall: 76.66%)

Regional Political Institutions

Executive:
    Governor, 4-year term
    Valerii Gennadevich Maleev, elected November 1996
        Ust-Orda Buryat Autonomous Okrug
        Administration; Pl. Sovetov;
        Ust-Orda, 666110; Ust-Orda Buryat Autonomous
        Okrug, Irkutsk Oblast
        Tel 7(395–41) 2–10–62;
        Fax 7(395–41) 2–25–93
        Federation Council in Moscow:
            7(095) 292–68–21, 926–66–35

Legislative:
    Unicameral
    Duma—19 members, 4-year term
    Chairman—Leonid Aleksandrovich Khutanov,
        elected 1994, December 1996

Regional Politics

Young Manager Moves from Farms to Politics

The 32-year-old Valerii Maleev won 38 percent of the vote in his 17 November 1996 election to defeat incumbent Aleksei Batagaev, making him the youngest member of the Federation Council. Maleev is known for his youthful energy and effective management skills. In 1991, at the age of 27, Maleev became the director of the Kamensk collective farm, which was on the verge of collapse. Maleev successfully revived the farm, in part by diversifying its output to include processed grains. His accomplishments at Kamen inspired a local newspaper to call the farm an "island of prosperity" (*VSP*, 13 November 1996). Local observers see Maleev as a "farmer by birth, but a new sort of farmer who is well educated and keeps state interests in mind" (*VSP*, 13 November 1996).

For Ust-Orda Buryat AO, which is a small, completely rural region, relations with Irkustsk are key. In 1996 the okrug signed a power-sharing agreement with the federal government and the administration of Irkutsk Oblast, of which it is a part.

Executive Platform: Strong Manager

Maleev belongs to the group of regional administrators elected in 1996 described as "strong managers." The strong managers ran as independents, usually with support from the business community. Maleev's campaign was financed by the East Siberian Coal Company (headed by Maleev's cousin), and the local branch of Our Home Is Russia (NDR) offered organizational support. The Kremlin secretly offered support to these candidates since the incumbent governors had been appointed under past chiefs of staff and the chief staff Anatolii Chubais wanted governors sympathetic to his interests.

The main campaign issues in the okrug election were stopping the fall in living standards and further developing the okrug's relationships with the federal government and Irkutsk Oblast. Thus, Maleev's experience in both collective farm management and regional politics most certainly contributed to his electoral success.

Maleev attributes Russia's agrarian crisis to the economic ignorance of farm directors, who lack necessary managerial skills. He believes that the best way to address this problem is setting up a knowledgeable staff that can work individually with each manager to help him find a profitable market niche (*EWI RRR*, 21 January 1999).

Ties to Moscow: Cooperates with Center

Although Maleev ran as an independent in the gubernatorial elections, he promised to cooperate with Moscow after his victory.

In February 1997 Russian Justice Minister Valentin Kovalev notified Maleev that the Ust-Orda Buryat administration was violating federal law by not sending its decrees to the ministry for legal examination (*RV*, 27 February 1997). Although the Justice Ministry estimates that between one third and one half of regional laws violate federal legislation, Maleev was only one of six regional executives to receive such a warning then. Despite numerous complaints about this problem, Moscow did little to improve the situation until Putin came to power.

On 27 May 1996 Yeltsin signed a power-sharing agreement with Ust-Orda Buryat AO and Irkutsk Oblast. Yeltsin championed this unprecedented trilateral agreement which outlined the division of powers and responsibilities between Moscow, Irkutsk, and Ust-Orda Buryat (*RFE/RL*, 28 May 1996). The treaty was a significant accomplishment for Russian federal politics, which has managed to leave the status of autonomous okrugs and their relationship to oblasts ambiguous. Two similar agreements, between Perm and Komi-Permyak Autonomous Okrug, and Krasnoyarsk and Taimyr and Evenk autonomous okrugs, have followed this example.

Relations with Other Regions: Buryat Solidarity

Ust-Orda Buryat is just one of three regions home to Buryats. Ust-Orda Buryat and Agin-Buryat autonomous okrugs were separated from the Buryat-Mongol ASSR (the present-day Republic of Buryatia) in 1937 when the Soviet federal leadership reduced the Buryat-Mongol titular territory in an attempt to suppress supposed nationalist sentiment (Ian Bremmer and Ray Taras, eds., *New States, New Politics: Building the Post-Soviet Nations*, New York: Cambridge University Press, 1997, 209). During glasnost Buryatia demanded that its pre-1937 borders be restored, but it eventually recognized the constitutional status of the two autonomous okrugs.

In 1991 an all-Buryat congress was held in the capital of Buryatia, Ulan-Ude, resulting in the creation of an all-Union association of Buryat culture. The goal of

Valerii Gennadevich Maleev

28 May 1964—Born in the village Kamensk in the Bokhan raion of Irkutsk Oblast

1986—Graduated from two faculties of the Irkutsk Agricultural Institute, in wildlife and biology; also earned a degree from the Academy of Economics

1987–1996—Worked as bookkeeper, agronomist, head zoologist, deputy, and then from 17

December 1991 as director of the Kamen collective farm

1991—Elected deputy of the Ust-Orda Buryat Legislative Assembly

17 November 1996—Elected governor of Ust-Orda Buryat Autonomous Okrug

Married, with two sons

---

the association is to establish a national-cultural autonomy to consolidate the Buryat people (*RFE/RL*, 25 February 1991).

Ust-Orda Buryat is part of Irkutsk Oblast and maintains strong ties with it. Irkutsk Oblast consumes 90 percent of the okrug's products. Because of Irkutsk's relative economic strength, the okrug's economy is better off than either the republic of Buryatia or the Agin-Buryat Autonomous Okrug. Irkutsk Governor Boris Govorin has described Maleev as "a truly honest manager, who is both young and energetic. He understands agricultural problems and can solve them" (*EWI RRR*, 21 January 1999).

The okrug is a member of the Siberian Accord Association, which is made up of the republics of Buryatia, Gorno-Altai, and Khakassia, Altai and Krasnoyarsk krais; Irkutsk, Novosibirsk, Tomsk, Tyumen, and Kemerovo oblasts; and Agin-Buryat, Taimyr, Khanty-Mansi, Evenk, and Yamal-Nenets autonomous okrugs.

VLADIMIR OBLAST

Territory: 29,000 km^2
Population (as of 1 January 1998): 1,631,000
Distance from Moscow: 190 km

Major Cities:
Vladimir, *capital* (pop. 336,100)
Kovrov (162,400)
Murom (142,200)
Gus-Khrustalnyi (74,000)
Aleksandrov (66,100)

Basic Facts

Population (as of 1 Jan. 1998): 1,631,000 (1.11% of Russian total)

Ethnic breakdown (1989 census): Russians 95.8%, Ukrainians 1.3%

Urban population (as of 1 Jan. 1998): 80.4% (Russia overall: 73.1%)

Student population (as of 1 Sept. 1997): 111 per 10,000 (Russia overall: 208/10,000)

Pensioner population (1997): 29.00% (Russia overall: 25.96%)

Percent of population with higher education (1989 census): 9.2% (Russia overall: 11.3%)

Percent of population working in (1997): Industry: 35.0% (Russian average: 23.0%); Agriculture: 7.5% (13.7%); Trade: 15.1% (13.5%); Culture: 11.8% (13.3%)

Average monthly personal income in July 1998: 526.5 new rubles (Russian average: 891.7 new rubles)

Average monthly personal expenses in July 1998: 368.3 new rubles (Russian average: 684.9 new rubles)

Average monthly subsistence requirement in 1998: 342 new rubles (Russian average: 438 new rubles)

Consumer price index (as of July 1998): 88 (Russia overall = 100)

Budgetary revenues (1997): 3,005 billion rubles (Russia overall: 433,378.2 billion rubles)

Budgetary expenditures (1997): 3,122.3 billion rubles (Russia overall: 468,111.6 billion rubles)

Industrial production as percentage of all Russian production (Jan.–Aug. 1998): 0.71%

Proportion of loss-making enterprises (as of July 1998): 47.8% (Russia overall: 50.4%)

Number of enterprises which have wage arrears (as of 1 Sept. 1998): 1,914 (1.42% of Russian total)

Agricultural production as percentage of all Russian production (1997): 0.90%

Number of private farms (as of 1 Jan. 1998): 2,328 (0.85% of Russian total)

Capital investment (1997): 2,219.5 billion rubles (Russia overall: 408,797 billion rubles)

Sources of investment (1997): federal budget: 5.5% (Russian average: 10.2%); regional budget: 2.1% (10.5%); extra-budgetary funds: 92.4% (79.3%)

Foreign investment (1997): 20,632,000 USD (Russia overall: 12,294,734,000 USD)

Number of joint ventures (1997): 85 (0.58% of Russian total)

Fixed capital investment in joint ventures and foreign companies (1997): 128,291 million rubles (Russia overall: 16,265.4 billion rubles)

Number of small businesses (as of 1 July 1998): 6,600 (0.76% of Russian total)

Number of enterprises privatized in 1997: 5 (0.18% of Russian total), including those which used to be municipal property: 60.0% (Russian average: 66.4%); regional property: 40.0% (20.0%); federal property: 0% (13.6%)

Number of telephones per 100 families (1997): in cities: 32.7 (Russian average: 49.2); in villages: 13.2 (19.8)

Brief Overview

Vladimir Oblast is located in the middle of European Russia, about 200 km east of Moscow. The oblast acquired its present borders in 1944, uniting parts of Moscow, Ivanovo, and Gorkii (currently, Nizhnii Novgorod) oblasts.

The oblast is now one of the most economically developed areas of the Central Economic Region. In terms of industrial output, the oblast ranks among Russia's top twenty regions. Its nine major plants manufacture over 30,000 different products, which are exported to over 70 foreign countries as well as other regions of the Russian Federation. Machine building is the major regional industry and its output makes up more than 40 percent of total regional production. Unlike most of the other oblasts in this economic region, Vladimir Oblast does not have a high concentration of industrial enterprises in the regional capital of Vladimir. Its industrial enterprises are dispersed throughout many cities, towns, and even villages.

According to a 1998 survey by *Ekspert* magazine, the oblast ranked 32nd among Russia's 89 regions in terms of investment potential and 11th in terms of investment risk. A 1998 survey by Bank Austria ranked the oblast 51st in terms of investment climate.

Electoral History

2000 Presidential Election
Putin: 53.16%
Zyuganov: 30.73%
Yavlinskii: 5.07%
Zhirinovsky: 2.83%
Tuleev: 2.14%
Turnout: 67.03% (Russia overall: 68.64%)

1999 Parliamentary Elections
Unity: 25.05%
Communist Party of the Russian Federation: 23.54%
Fatherland–All Russia: 9.48%
Union of Right Forces: 8.67%
Zhirinovsky Bloc: 6.83%
Yabloko: 5.85%
In single-mandate districts: 1 Communist Party of the Russian Federation, 1 independent
Turnout: 58.96% (Russia overall: 61.85%)

1996 Gubernatorial Election
Vinogradov (oblast legislature chairman): 62.20%
Vlasov (incumbent): 21.71%
Yegorov: 3.95%
Sokolov (first deputy governor): 3.13%
Shergin (Yabloko): 1.80%
Turnout: 44.19%

1996 Presidential Election
Yeltsin: 30.89%/51.56% (first round/second round)
Zyuganov: 29.87%/41.86%
Lebed: 19.91%
Yavlinskii: 7.39%
Zhirinovsky: 6.71%
Turnout: 70.47%/65.34% (Russia overall: 69.67%/ 68.79%)

1995 Parliamentary Elections
Communist Party of the Russian Federation: 20.72%
Liberal Democratic Party of Russia: 14.70%
Our Home Is Russia: 12.25%
Yabloko: 6.53%
Women of Russia: 5.16%
Congress of Russian Communities: 4.56%
Communists–Workers' Russia: 3.68%
Party of Workers' Self-Government: 3.33%
In single-mandate districts: 1 Communist Party of the Russian Federation, 1 Agrarian Party of Russia
Turnout: 66.36% (Russia overall: 64.37%)

1993 Constitutional Referendum
"Yes"—58.1%   "No"—39.3%

1993 Parliamentary Elections
Liberal Democratic Party of Russia: 29.49%
Russia's Choice: 16.92%
Women of Russia: 9.65%
Communist Party of the Russian Federation: 9.55%
Yabloko: 7.73%
Agrarian Party of Russia: 7.36%
Party of Russian Unity and Concord: 6.42%
Democratic Party of Russia: 5.47%
In single-mandate districts: 2 Agrarian Party of Russia
From electoral associations: 1 Women of Russia, 1 independent
Turnout: 60.47% (Russia overall: 54.34%)

1991 Presidential Election

Yeltsin: 61.43%
Ryzhkov: 13.81%
Zhirinovsky: 7.51%
Tuleev: 6.21%
Makashov: 3.53%
Bakatin: 3.21%
Turnout: 79.91% (Russia overall: 76.66%)

Regional Political Institutions

Executive:

Governor, 4-year term
Nikolai Vladimirovich Vinogradov, elected
December 1996
    Oktyabrskii Prospekt, 21; Vladimir, 600000
    Tel 7(092–2) 33–15–52;
    Fax 7(092–2) 25–34–45
    Federation Council in Moscow:
    7(095) 292–57–65, 926–64–57

Legislative:

Unicamerl
Legislative Assembly (*Zakonodatelnoe
Sobranie*)—37 members, 4-year term, elected
December 1996
Chairman—Vitalii Yakovlevich Kotov, elected
December 1997

Regional Politics

Contemporary Communist in Russia's Red Belt

Nikolai Vinogradov seems to value Vladimir's position in central Russia's "red belt" over its location in Russia's Golden Ring. Rather than capitalizing on the region's enormous tourist potential, Vinogradov has been focused on reconciling his communist faith and the oblast's need to advance in market development. The governor considers himself a proponent of market economics and a Communist. "I don't see any contradiction whatsoever in this," he claims (*Izvestiya*, 10 December 1997). Communist Party leader Gennadii Zyuganov described Nikolai Vinogradov as "young," "energetic," and "contemporary" (*OMRI RRR*, 18 September 1996). Perhaps it is Vinogradov's goal of synthesizing his communist beliefs with current market development that makes him a "contemporary" Communist.

Executive Platform: Shoveling Away Obstacles

Vinogradov was elected governor in December 1996, winning out over incumbent Yurii Vlasov (the youngest governor in Russia when appointed in 1991 at age 30). Vinogradov's victory resulted in part from poor politicking on the part of the region's democrats. In addition to Vlasov, three other pro-Yeltsin candidates participated in the race, weakening the solidarity of the democratic vote. Nevertheless, a unified democratic front would not have prevented Vinogradov's 62 percent landslide, an unusually high victory margin for Russia's fragmented multiple-party elections. The main reason for Vinogradov's strong support was probably his predecessor's inability to address the region's poor economic health. In 1996 Vladimir was one of the thirteen Russian regions with an unemployment rate double the national average. Clearly, the electorate had been dissatisfied with Yeltsin's young reformer and wanted to return to the security and stability that had been guaranteed in the Communist past.

Upon election, Vinogradov set a number of goals for his term. In the first year he wanted to "shovel away the economic and social obstacles" blocking "harmony in the work of the apparatus and cooperation with trade industries" (*Rabochaya Tribuna*, 25 March 1997). Finding solutions to concrete problems was his stated goal for the second year of the term.

Policies: Tax Incentives and Economic Restructuring

The governor's policy plans have been focused primarily on improving the region's economic health by revitalizing its depressed industries. The main problem, according to Vinogradov, is that the enterprises have no money and are thus unable to restructure themselves sufficiently to become profitable in the new market economy (*Rabochaya Tribuna*, 25 March 1997). The governor's policies represent his self-proclaimed character, offering a mix of pro-market reforms and more traditional communist views. Vinogradov's approach has generally been based on offering tax incentives in order to attract investors to the bankrupt enterprises. Several agreements have been signed according to this principle.

The initial tax incentive the administration offered to regional enterprises granted property tax allowances on a case-by-case basis. Although there was great concern that this would significantly reduce tax revenues from enterprises, which contribute heavily to the oblast budget, these tax breaks have accomplished their goal of further stimulating production (*Rabochaya Tribuna*, 25 March 1997).

Vinogradov has approved tax credits for enterprises working in the fields of mechanical engineering, construction, metallurgy, chemical and gas technology, glass, and timber, and also for several light industries (Prime-TASS, No. 27, 1997). He also offers tax incentives to foreign investors (*Izvestiya*, 10 December 1997).

In June 1997 Vinogradov issued a decree that provided for a public credit-financial mechanism for house building from 1997 to 2000. Primary funding consisted of 3.5 million rubles from the oblast budget with supplementary sources from bank credits, industrial enterprises, and insurance funds (*FI*, 3 June 1997).

The governor has also been working on a more conservative project that would grant the oblast administration shares of enterprises located in the region. Vinogradov explained his intentions for such a project: to prevent enterprise shares from being traded on the market where they could be sold for significantly less than their actual value (*Rabochaya Tribuna*, 25 March 1997). Yet, this plan is more than an altruistic mechanism to preserve the sanctity of Vladimir's enterprises. The advantages it offers to the oblast administration cannot be ignored. The plan would raise the administration's revenues, helping to cover the losses resulting from the aforementioned tax breaks. Although it has not been made clear whether or not the suggested shares would have voting rights, this situation would undoubtedly provide the oblast administration with considerable leverage over regional enterprises.

Relationships Between Key Players: Supportive Legislature

Vinogradov enjoys support from the oblast legislature, which he formerly headed. On 25 February 1998 legislation was passed to provide for the use of regional and local funds to support small business. Entrepreneurs who create jobs are granted credits and tax breaks (*RT*, 27 February 1998). This legislation further promotes Vinogradov's program for reviving the region's industries via tax incentives.

The governor opposed Vladimir Mayor Vladimir Shamov's attending the Congress of Municipalities in June 1998.

Ties to Moscow: Strives for Good Relations

The governor strives to keep good relations with Moscow in spite of his Communist membership. This desire is presumably what prompted him to join Viktor Chernomyrdin's Our Home Is Russia (NDR) in 1995. Several other Communist governors also chose to back NDR while Chernomyrdin's power was at its peak in order to establish better ties with the presidential administration. Nevertheless, Vinogradov's loyalty lies with the KPRF, as evidenced in April 1997 when he chose to attend the Communists' annual congress over that of NDR. Vinogradov was one of nine governors present at the congress. Yet, he demonstrated a sense of diplomacy (or simply an attempt to remain in good standing with the men in power) by informing the presidential administration of his decision to attend the opposition congress and encouraged it not to take his Communist affiliation too seriously (*MN*, No. 18, 1997).

Relations with Other Regions

Vladimir is a member of the Central Russia Association, which is headed by Yaroslavl Governor Anatolii Lisitsyn. The other member oblasts involved are Bryansk, Ivanovo, Kaluga, Kostroma, Moscow, Ryazan, Smolensk, Tver, Tula, and the city of Moscow. Vinogradov is a strong supporter of the association and feels that organizations of this sort offer a good forum for addressing inter-regional interests and problems (*Rabochaya Tribuna*, 25 March 1997).

In an October 1997 meeting of the Central Russia Association, Vinogradov expressed concern about the military-industrial complex (*Vspole*, 1 November 1997). Vladimir Oblast has a large defense sector and thus is interested in capitalizing on the complex's conversion potential. Other regional leaders supported Vinogradov, and the association hopes to win greater federal support.

Attitudes Toward Business: Pro-Market

Vinogradov considers himself a proponent of market reforms and has offered several tax incentives to promote investment in the oblast's industries. Yet, these incentives have not spawned any major joint-venture projects. The oblast ranks among Russia's top twenty regions in terms of industrial output, manufacturing over

Nikolai Vladimirovich Vinogradov

22 April 1947—Born in the city of Vladimir, capital of Vladimir Oblast

Graduated from the Moscow Engineering-Construction Institute as an engineer construction technician

Graduated from the CPSU Central Committee's Academy of General Sciences as a political scientist

1960–1977—Worked in a Vladimir factory as a reinforced-concrete construction specialist, rising through the positions of foreman, engineer, and chief factory engineer

1977—Began working on the party staff

1978–1983—Instructor and deputy manager of the construction department of the CPSU's Vladimir Oblast Committee

1983–1985—Second secretary of the CPSU's Vladimir City Committee

1985–1987—First secretary of the CPSU's Kolchugin City Committee

1987–1989—Instructor in the department of organizational-party work for the CPSU Central Committee

1989–1991—Second secretary of the CPSU's Vladimir Oblast Committee

1991–1993—First deputy general director of Vladimirglavsnab and deputy association director for Inmekhstrom (Investment in Mechanics, Construction, and Materials)

1993–1995—Member of the KPRF Central Committee

27 March 1994—Elected to the oblast Legislative Assembly, and on April 11 elected chairman

1995—Joined Our Home Is Russia (NDR)

January 1996—Appointed to the Federation Council and became a member of the Committee on Budget, Tax Policies, Finances, Currency, and Customs Regulation

8 December 1996—Elected governor of Vladimir Oblast

Speaks English

30,000 different products that are exported to more than 70 foreign countries (*EWI RRR*, 11 December 1997). Nevertheless, Vladimir's functioning industries are not sufficient to ensure the oblast's economic health.

During the first half of 1997, immediately after Vinogradov was elected governor, foreign investment in Vladimir Oblast fell to less than 25 percent of what it had been in the first half of 1996. The drop was due partially to the German government's decision to significantly curtail its Transform consulting program and ATH's (Malta) decision to reduce its investments in the Vladimir Truck Factory (*EWI RRR*, 28 August 1997). The only major foreign project in Vladimir Oblast involves the German chocolate company Stollwerk. Stollwerk opened a confectionery factory in the city Pokrov on 15 July 1997, providing 300 new jobs. The factory took one year to build and cost DM35 million.

In January 1998 the governor signed an agreement with Rostekstil, Russia's largest textile producer and seller, to revive Vladimir's textile industry. According to the agreement, Rostekstil will supply an undefined amount of materials and orders to the oblast's factories and will receive various tax reductions in return (*KD*, 13 January 1998). This agreement is important to Vladimir since the textile industry makes up a majority of the oblast's output.

In April 1998 a trade mission of American Chamber of Commerce member companies, including Honeywell, AM Cosmetics, British Petroleum, Euro Swiss International, Rosinter, and Holding Capital Group visited Vladimir to investigate trade and investment opportunities in the region. The mission resulted in the signing of a cooperation agreement between the American Chamber of Commerce in Russia, the Vladimir Oblast Administration and the Vladimir Chamber of Commerce and Industry (Work of the Chamber, May–June 1998).

Internet Sites in the Region

http://www.vladimir.ru/home.html

This website offers little of value, given that most of its features are under construction or have been moved to an unstated location.

VOLGOGRAD OBLAST

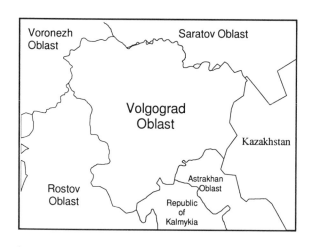

Territory: 113,900 km²
Population (as of 1 January 1998):
2,701,000
Distance from Moscow: 1,073 km

Major Cities:
Volgograd, *capital* (pop. 998,800)
Volzhskii (288,400)
Kamyshin (128,800)

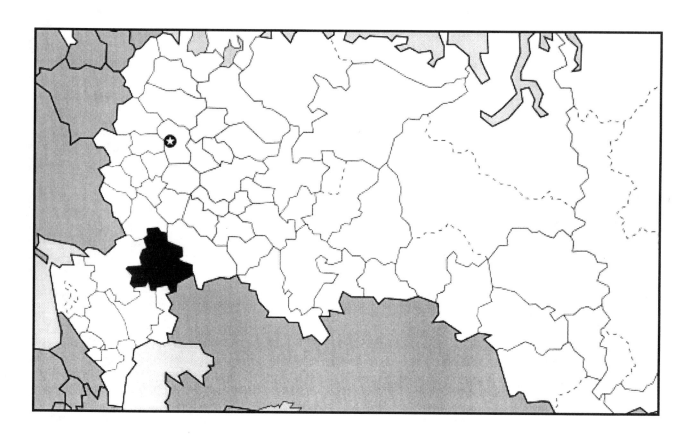

610

Basic Facts

Population (as of 1 Jan. 1998): 2,701,000 (1.84% of Russian total)

Ethnic breakdown (1989 census): Russians 89.1%, Ukrainians 3.0%, Kazakhs 1.6%, Germans 1.1%, Tatars 1.0%

Urban population (as of 1 Jan. 1998): 74.3% (Russia overall: 73.1%)

Student population (as of 1 Sept. 1997): 175 per 10,000 (Russia overall: 208/10,000)

Pensioner population (1997): 26.92% (Russia overall: 25.96%)

Percent of population with higher education (1989 census): 9.7% (Russia overall: 11.3%)

Percent of population working in (1997): Industry: 22.1% (Russian average: 23.0%); Agriculture: 15.3% (13.7%); Trade: 16.3% (13.5%); Culture: 10.6% (13.3%)

Average monthly personal income in July 1998: 601.6 new rubles (Russian average: 891.7 new rubles)

Average monthly personal expenses in July 1998: 486.8 new rubles (Russian average: 684.9 new rubles)

Average monthly subsistence requirement in 1998: 387 new rubles (Russian average: 438 new rubles)

Consumer price index (as of July 1998): 88 (Russia overall = 100)

Budgetary revenues (1997): 4,532.6 billion rubles (Russia overall: 433,378.2 billion rubles)

Budgetary expenditures (1997): 4,830.1 billion rubles (Russia overall: 468,111.6 billion rubles)

Industrial production as percentage of all Russian production (Jan.–Aug. 1998): 1.25%

Proportion of loss-making enterprises (as of July 1998): 50.9% (Russia overall: 50.4%)

Number of enterprises which have wage arrears (as of 1 Sept. 1998): 5,412 (4.00% of Russian total)

Agricultural production as percentage of all Russian production (1997): 2.36%

Number of private farms (as of 1 Jan. 1998): 13,264 (4.84% of Russian total)

Capital investment (1997): 5,068.1 billion rubles (Russia overall: 408,797 billion rubles)

Sources of investment (1997): federal budget: 8.1% (Russian average: 10.2%); regional budget: 11.4% (10.5%); extra-budgetary funds: 80.5% (79.3%)

Foreign investment (1997): 38,755,000 USD (Russia overall: 12,294,734,000 USD)

Number of joint ventures (1997): 145 (0.98% of Russian total)

Fixed capital investment in joint ventures and foreign companies (1997): 381,298 million rubles (Russia overall: 16,265.4 billion rubles)

Number of small businesses (as of 1 July 1998): 13,500 (1.55% of Russian total)

Number of enterprises privatized in 1997: 48 (1.75% of Russian total), including those which used to be municipal property: 79.2% (Russian average: 66.4%); regional property: 8.3% (20.0%); federal property: 12.5% (13.6%)

Number of telephones per 100 families (1997): in cities: 41.8 (Russian average: 49.2); in villages: 20.7 (19.8)

Brief Overview

Large numbers of migrants moved to the plain between the Volga and Don rivers in the 18th century. The new residents included Ukrainians, Russians from western parts of the country, and Germans. The town of Tsaritsyn, which started as a fortress in a line of other forts on Russia's southern border, evolved into a large transportation hub. In the end of the last century, it also became one of the country's industrial centers. In 1925 Tsaritsyn was renamed Stalingrad, a name that became famous during World War II when the Soviet Army had its first significant victory over the Nazis there. The city and oblast were named Volgograd in 1961 when the dictator fell out of favor.

The oblast is part of the Volga economic region and borders Voronezh, Saratov, Astrakhan, and Rostov oblasts, the Republic of Kalmykia, and Kazakhstan. It is rich in raw materials, including oil, gas, salts, and phosphors. Though oil extraction has gradually decreased over the last few years, the oblast still ranks 15th among the country's 89 regions in terms of oil production. The region has a highly developed industrial base, including machine building, oil and chemical industries, ferrous metallurgy, and light and food industries. Industry makes up 75 percent of the region's GDP. Tractors, pipes, and steel are the oblast's major products. Raw oil, oil products, ferrous metals, aluminum, chemical products, machines, and equipment are the major exports. Though the region has an extremely unfavorable climate for agriculture, the oblast grows wheat, corn, rice, grapes, tomatoes, fruits and vegetables.

According to a 1998 survey by *Ekspert* magazine, the oblast ranked 22nd among Russia's 89 regions in terms of investment potential and 12th in terms of investment risk. A 1998 survey by Bank Austria ranked the oblast 13th in terms of investment climate.

Electoral History

2000 Presidential Election
Putin: 53.47%
Zyuganov: 33.94%
Yavlinskii: 3.76%
Zhirinovsky: 2.34%
Tuleev: 1.83%
Turnout: 68.41% (Russia overall: 68.64%)

1999 Parliamentary Elections
Communist Party of the Russian Federation: 29.73%
Unity: 28.86%
Union of Right Forces: 8.46%
Zhirinovsky Bloc: 6.17%
Fatherland–All Russia: 6.04%
Yabloko: 4.07%
In single-mandate districts: 1 Communist Party of the Russian Federation, 1 Agrarian Party of Russia, 2 independent
Turnout: 58.81% (Russia overall: 61.85%)

1996 Gubernatorial Election
Maksyuta (Volgograd city legislature chairman): 28.51%/50.96% (first round/second round)
Shabunin (incumbent): 37.64%/44.15%
Chekhov (Volgograd city mayor): 25.22%
Terentev: 2.11%
Molchanov (LDPR): 1.09%
Turnout: 60.1%/46.14%

1996 Presidential Election
Zyuganov: 40.04%/44.21% (first round/second round)
Yeltsin: 28.59%/44.21%
Lebed: 13.65%
Zhirinovsky: 6.55%
Yavlinskii: 6.43%
Turnout: 71.88%/69.49% (Russia overall: 69.67%/68.79%)

1995 Parliamentary Elections
Communist Party of the Russian Federation: 28.13%
Liberal Democratic Party of Russia: 14.72%
Our Home Is Russia: 9.14%
Yabloko: 6.72%
Party of Workers' Self-Government: 4.88%
Communists–Workers' Russia: 4.23%
Congress of Russian Communities: 3.97%
Agrarian Party of Russia: 3.48%
Women of Russia: 3.37%
Russia's Democratic Choice: 2.23%
In single-mandate districts: 3 Communist Party of the Russian Federation, 1 Agrarian Party of Russia
Turnout: 65.13% (Russia overall: 64.37%)

1993 Constitutional Referendum
"Yes"—47.4%   "No"—49.9%

1993 Parliamentary Elections
Liberal Democratic Party of Russia: 27.67%
Communist Party of the Russian Federation:
  14.42%
Russia's Choice: 11.86%
Agrarian Party of Russia: 10.90%
Yabloko: 9.53%
Women of Russia: 7.59%
Party of Russian Unity and Concord: 5.84%
Democratic Party of Russia: 5.19%
In single-mandate districts: 3 independent,
  1 Yabloko
From electoral associations: 2 Agrarian Party of
  Russia, 1 Communist Party of the Russian
  Federation, 1 Russia's Choice, 1 Women of
  Russia
Turnout: 53.46% (Russia overall: 54.34%)

1991 Presidential Election
Yeltsin: 55.69%
Ryzhkov: 16.85%
Zhirinovsky: 9.07%
Tuleev: 5.70%
Bakatin: 3.83%
Makashov: 3.19%
Turnout: 73.26% (Russia overall: 76.66%)

Regional Political Institutions

Executive:
  Governor, 4-year term
  Nikolai Kirillovich Maksyuta, elected
  December 1996
    Pr. im. V.I. Lenina, 9; Volgograd 98, 400008
    Tel 7 (844–2) 33–66–88;
    Fax 7 (844–2) 93–62–12
    Federation Council in Moscow:
    7 (095) 292–13–98, 926–61–39

Legislative:
  Unicameral
  Oblast Duma—16 members, 4-year term,
   elected March 1997
  Chairman—Viktor Ivanovich Pripisnov, elected
  December 1998

Regional Politics

Communist Rules the Buckle of the Red Belt

Nikolai Maksyuta was elected governor of Volgograd Oblast on 29 December 1996, defeating incumbent Governor Ivan Shabunin by a 7 percent margin. Maksyuta was supported by the Communist-led National Patriotic Union of Russia (NPSR). His victory was a surprise to many, since Shabunin's reelection seemed inevitable. Shabunin had been a Yeltsin appointee in the early 1990's, but the presidential administration then chose to support Volgograd Mayor Yurii Chekhov as a better alternative in the 1996 elections. However, Shabunin refused to yield to Moscow's new man of choice. This dispute resulted in a split democratic vote, allowing Maksyuta and the Communists to slip into power. Maksyuta's victory, and the election of a Communist duma in 1998, reconfirmed Volgograd's nickname as the "buckle of the red belt."

Executive Platform: Effective Management Takes Precedence over Communism

Although Maksyuta ran for governor on the Communist Party ticket, he does not display unfaltering devotion to the party, giving effective governance priority instead. When elected governor, Maksyuta seemed unprepared to assume leadership. It took a few months for him to appoint a staff, which ultimately proved to be a mix of old party bureaucrats and holdovers from the Shabunin's administration. Despite the fact that Maksyuta worked as an aide to Communist candidate Gennadii Zyuganov in 1996, Maksyuta approached governance cautiously, choosing not to implement the party's recommendations immediately. This approach inspired criticism from Communist Party members. Nevertheless, Maksyuta started his gubernatorial career by establishing himself as friendly toward business.

After his first year in office, Maksyuta had managed to establish himself among the Volgograd political and business elite. He has been fighting to ensure that the region receives a large share of the contracts from the federal budget for rebuilding Chechnya.

The agricultural districts in the city were very supportive of Maksyuta's gubernatorial bid. Subsequently, he voted against the sale of land in the Federation Council.

Policies: Conservative Protectionism

Like many other governors, Maksyuta immediately adopted protectionist measures following the ruble's devaluation and the subsequent panic in August and September 1998. Authorities in Volgograd prohibited the transport of food across the oblast's borders to ensure that the region did not run out of necessary foodstuffs. Maksyuta believes that these measures stabilized the situation in the oblast.

On 22 January 1998 Maksyuta signed a decree that effectively limits public subsidies to publications that are wholly or partially owned by the regional authorities. The editor of the local independent newspaper *Inter*, Yefim Shusterman, charged that the governor had given himself almost complete control of the media before the next elections. However, there are several independent media outlets in the region.

In June 1999 Maksyuta shut down many scrap metal dealers who collect non-ferrous metals from the population. The high prices the dealers were paying for the metal had encouraged many people to steal expensive, still-functioning equipment from their enterprises. The situation had become so extreme that municipal authorities could not mount the copper wires for a new trolleybus line until the night before it was to open for fear that the wire would be stolen (*EWI RRR*, 17 June 1999).

In August 1998 Maksyuta asked Yeltsin to declare Volgograd a disaster area because of the devastating drought the region suffered that year.

Relationships Between Key Players: Communists Control Majority in Oblast Legislature

Following elections on 13 December 1998, the Communists control 23 of the 32 seats in the Volgograd Oblast Duma, giving them a 74 percent majority. At the beginning of 1999, they elected Communist Viktor Pripisnov, a professor at the Agricultural Academy, as the Duma's new chairman. Pripisnov replaced Our Home Is Russia activist Leonid Semergei, who was an apolitical figure.

Volgograd Mayor Yurii Chekhov considers himself the natural leader of the democratic opposition to Communist rule in the region. He will face mayoral elections in fall 1999 and he is certain his main opponent will be a Communist. He has expressed considerable concern that if living standards for the local population continue to drop, the Volgograd Duma will seek out "enemies" responsible for the problems (*GV*, 16 December 1998).

Maksyuta has demonstrated his priority of effective governance over party loyalty in his relations with the Communist mayor of Volzhskii, Anatolii Shiryaev. Volzhskii is the second largest city in the oblast, and has been an economic basket case since Shiryaev came to power in late 1996. The situation in Volzhskii has tarnished Volgograd Oblast's reputation on the federal level, and Maksyuta has been hoping to find a way to have the mayor legally removed from office.

Maksyuta has not been particularly popular with the Communist Party's oblast leadership. Volgograd State Duma Member Alevtina Aparina had criticized Maksyuta for not appointing enough Communists to high positions. Maksyuta would rather appoint competent professionals than party bureaucrats.

Ties to Moscow: Suspicions that Communist Loyalties Cut Federal Subsidies

Maksyuta has been trying to build a good relationship with the federal authorities. In May 1997, having chosen to attend the annual KPRF congress instead of Our Home Is Russia's meeting, Maksyuta informed the presidential administration of his intention to attend the opposition congress. He and the other five governors who contacted the administration also urged it not to take their affiliation with the opposition too seriously.

Similarly, Maksyuta had backed Kirienko as a compromise candidate in April 1998, feeling that it was necessary to support him for the sake of political stability. Maksyuta and Kemerovo Governor Aman Tuleev published an open letter to Gennadii Zyuganov asking Zyuganov to back Kirienko's confirmation.

Newspapers in Volgograd frequently address the issue of inequality in providing federal transfers to Russia's regions. Volgograd receives considerably less in terms of federal subsidies than its neighboring regions on the Volga. Many people assert that the federal government intentionally blacklists the oblast because of Maksyuta's Communist Party affiliation. The district heads of Volgograd's rural areas have expressed similar complaints, claiming that their region received funds from the federal budget until Maksyuta came to power.

Relations with Other Regions: Challenging Kalmykia's Off-Shore Zone

In June 1998 Maksyuta denounced next-door-neighbor Kalmykia's off-shore zone. Companies working in the zone do not need to pay most local and republican taxes, thus inspiring many Volgograd firms to reregister in Kalmykia to lighten their tax burden. Maksyuta claims that Volgograd lost $28 million in tax revenues in just the first five months of 1998 because of the zone. In June the Volga regional airline discontinued service and reregistered as Volga Air-Express in Kalmykia, costing Volgograd additional revenue. Maksyuta announced that he is prepared to pressure enterprises to return to Volgograd, possibly resorting to economic sanctions, such as raising fees for land, water, and other necessary resources.

Astrakhan and Volgograd oblasts are trying to encourage greater interregional trade, though the effort has not turned a profit yet. The cooperation began after Astrakhan Governor Anatolii Guzhvin and Maksyuta signed a treaty promoting trade at a midnight airport meeting during the summer of 1998 when they were returning from a Federation Council session in Moscow. The two governors sat together on the flight, an opportunity that gave them their first chance to speak about common interests, according to reports in Volgograd newspapers. Guzhvin had to change planes in Volgograd so the governors decided not to wait until the next meeting in Moscow, but to sign an agreement in the airport. Since then both governors have encouraged local producers, primarily of food products, to sell in the neighboring region. Guzhvin has pushed Astrakhan producers to sell rice in Volgograd at prices lower than they charge at home (*DP*, November 1998, no. 47). Volgograd businessmen believe that the initial efforts have little more than publicity value.

Volgograd is a member of the Greater Volga Association, which also includes the republics of Tatarstan, Mordovia, Chuvashia, and Marii El, and Astrakhan, Nizhnii Novgorod, Penza, Samara, Saratov, and Ulyanovsk oblasts.

Foreign Relations: In Favor of Russian-Belarusan Union

Maksyuta was one of fourteen signatories to a 1997 letter supporting a Russian-Belarusan union. (Other signatories included the leaders of Krasnodar, Amur, Samara, and Kalmykia.) Additionally, in December 1998, Maksyuta turned down an invitation to Kazakhstan to instead visit Belarusan President Aleksandr Lukashenko in Minsk. Lukashenko is a much higher priority for a governor from the "Red

Belt" than Kazakhstan President Nursultan Nazarbaev. In May 1999 Lukashenko returned the gesture and visited Volgograd. Lukashenko would be one of the strongest leaders of the leftist camp if Russia and Belarus go ahead with a much-discussed reunification (*EWI RRR*, 14 January 1999). There were also purely economic reasons for such a choice, however. For instance, the Volgograd and Minsk tractor plants traditionally co-operated with common part suppliers during the Soviet era. Now some of those plants are in Russia (for example, the Volgograd Tractor Parts Plant), while others are in Belarus.

In early 1999 Belarus established a trade house in Volgograd to make it easier for Belarus and Volgograd to engage in barter trade. According to Trade House Executive Director Vladimir Sitnikov, barter offers a way to overcome broken ties and mutual debt (*GV*, 4 February 1999). For example, vegetable oil from Uryupinsk (Volgograd Oblast) is sent to Belarus in exchange for tractor parts from Minsk (Belarus brand tractors are widely used in Volgograd agriculture). In the city of Volzhskii, the Povolzhe brewery can purchase forage corn in Volgograd Oblast and exchange it in Belarus for barley, which is in demand in the Lower Volga region. Numerous other plants are involved in the deals. Most of Volgograd's exports to Belarus are semi-finished, while Belarus sends technologically advanced equipment to Volgograd. Sitnikov believes that because imports have become too expensive for most Russian consumers, relatively cheap and reasonably good quality consumer goods such as Belarusan refrigerators and knitted wear will sell well.

Attitudes Toward Business: Seeking Foreign Customers

One of the great success stories in the region is the Volzhskii Pipe Plant (VTZ). In January 1999 it won a tender offered by the Caspian Pipeline Consortium to supply pipelines for the project connecting Kazakhstan's Tengiz oil field to the Novorossiisk port terminal. VTZ will supply 60 percent of the pipes, while the Italian firm ILVA will provide the remaining 40 percent. VTZ's contract with the consortium is worth $86.6 million. The contract secures 5,000 jobs for 18 months (*EWI RRR*, 14 January 1999). In spring 1998, the plant won a contract from Exxon.

In May 1998, the federal government had tried to bankrupt VTZ in a rather mysterious move. Seven months later, in January 1999, VTZ Director Vitalii

---

Nikolai Kirillovich Maksyuta

26 May 1947—Born in Kirovograd Oblast, Ukraine

1965—Entered the Nikolaev Shipbuilding Institute, ultimately graduating as an engineer-mechanic

1971—Began working in Volgograd as a master's assistant, ultimately moving up to become the general director of the Volgograd Shipbuilding Factory

2 September 1994—Elected to the Volgograd City Duma, and became the chairman

29 December 1996—Elected Governor of Volgograd Oblast in the second electoral round, winning 50.95 percent of the vote

5 March 1998—Joined the Federation Council's Budget Committee

Married, with two children

Sadykov explained that the Vyksunskii Metallurgical Plant (Nizhnii Novgorod Oblast), one of VTZ's main rivals, initiated the bankruptcy procedures to weaken its opponent. At that time, Nizhnii had the support of several key members of the federal government, including then Prime Minister Sergei Kirienko and then First Deputy Prime Minister Boris Nemtsov.

There are several other projects currently underway in Volgograd. In 1997 the Volgograd Tractor Plant won a tender issued by the Iraqi Agriculture Ministry to provide tractors for Iraq, and the Volgograd Shipbuilding Factory is working on a flotilla of ten super tankers for LUKoil. The ships will have the capacity of 3,800 tons in rivers and 6,400 tons in the ocean. The overall contract is worth $100 million and is expected to be completed by 2001.

There is also great potential for further exploiting and developing industries focused on Volgograd's natural resources. Oil production is an extremely important part of the oblast economy. Volgograd oil is the cheapest to produce in Russia, since oil men do not have to face the Siberian cold as they do in Khanty-Mansi or the off-shore wells of Sakhalin Oblast. Volgograd's largest oil firm, Nizhnevolzhskneft, contributes approximately 15 percent of the oblast's budget. Additionally, Nizhnevolzhskneft will be developing the technology for exploiting Iraq's Western Kurna field, one of the world's largest oil deposits.

Volgograd also has the world's largest bischofite field, containing an estimated 500 billion tons of the mineral, which is a rich source of magnesium. It is believed that investments in bischofite extraction may be more profitable than investing in the oil industry. Bischofite is used in the pharmaceutical industry and as a fertilizer. Yet, the most promising use for bischofite is as a source of rare chemical elements. However, several investment projects to develop this field have fallen through, including projects involving U.S. and German firms.

Maksyuta has also proceeded with the project initiated by his predecessor Ivan Shabunin of constructing a new bridge across the Volga. The bridge is expected to boost the regional economy by providing better transport links for farm goods and by attracting tourism. Yet, even more importantly, crossing Volgograd and Rostov oblasts is the shortest way to travel from Central Asia to Ukraine and Europe, so the new bridge will attract traffic that currently moves along a northern route via Moscow. However, money for completing this project is not secure. Moscow has been financing construction, but this funding may cease. Regional authorities are hoping to attract private investment.

Maksyuta has been active in trying to establish credit support for business development in the region. In 1997 Maksyuta signed cooperation agreements with Gazprom and a regional branch of Moscow's Inkombank. The agreements provided for increased gas supplies to the oblast and credits to state enterprises. In May 1997 Rossiiskii Kredit bank signed an agreement with the oblast to invest money into the region, particularly in the chemical and refining industries. The bank also agreed to assist in attracting foreign investment and help distribute regional securities. Additionally, in January 1998 the Volgograd Oblast administration established the Sfera firm to serve as a mediator between potential investors and the enterprise or project being invested in. Sfera provides investors with shares of enterprises, which were being held by the oblast government, as security for their investments.

Internet Sites in the Region

http://www.volgograd.ru/eng/index.htm

Hosted by the American Business Center and the Volgograd Internet Service provider, this site provides extensive information about the region.

VOLOGDA OBLAST

Territory: 145,700 km²
Population (as of 1 January 1998):
1,339,000
Distance from Moscow: 497 km

Major Cities:
Vologda, *capital* (pop. 300,100)
Cherepovets (322,000)
Sokol (45,900)
Velikii Ustyug (35,800)

Basic Facts

Population (as of 1 Jan. 1998): 1,339,000 (0.91% of Russian total)

Ethnic breakdown (1989 census): Russians 96.5%, Ukrainians 1.4%

Urban population (as of 1 Jan. 1998): 68.3% (Russia overall: 73.1%)

Student population (as of 1 Sept. 1997): 159 per 10,000 (Russia overall: 208/10,000)

Pensioner population (1997): 27.26% (Russia overall: 25.96%)

Percent of population with higher education (1989 census): 8.2% (Russia overall: 11.3%)

Percent of population working in 1997: Industry: 29.7% (Russian average: 23.0%); Agriculture: 11.0% (13.7%); Trade: 12.2% (13.5%); Culture: 11.9% (13.3%)

Average monthly personal income in July 1998: 757.5 new rubles (Russian average: 891.7 new rubles)

Average monthly personal expenses in July 1998: 501.3 new rubles (Russian average: 684.9 new rubles)

Average monthly subsistence requirement in 1998: 411 new rubles (Russian average: 438 new rubles)

Consumer price index (as of July 1998): 95 (Russia overall = 100)

Budgetary revenues (1997): 3,531.8 billion rubles (Russia overall: 433,378.2 billion rubles)

Budgetary expenditures (1997): 3,926.7 billion rubles (Russia overall: 468,111.6 billion rubles)

Industrial production as percentage of all Russian production (Jan.–Aug. 1998): 1.56%

Proportion of loss-making enterprises (as of July 1998): 36.6% (Russia overall: 50.4%)

Number of enterprises which have wage arrears (as of 1 Sept. 1998): 1,167 (0.86% of Russian total)

Agricultural production as percentage of all Russian production (1997): 1.19%

Number of private farms (as of 1 Jan. 1998): 1,507 (0.55% of Russian total)

Capital investment (1997): 2,837.0 billion rubles (Russia overall: 408,797 billion rubles)

Sources of investment (1997): federal budget: 6.6% (Russian average: 10.2%); regional budget: 7.1% (10.5%); extra-budgetary funds: 86.3% (79.3%)

Foreign investment (1997): 10,727,000 USD (Russia overall: 12,294,734,000 USD)

Number of joint ventures (1997): 52 (0.35% of Russian total)

Fixed capital investment in joint ventures and foreign companies (1997): 73,899 million rubles (Russia overall: 16,265.4 billion rubles)

Number of small businesses (as of 1 July 1998): 4,000 (0.46% of Russian total)

Number of enterprises privatized in 1997: 113 (4.12% of Russian total), including those which used to be municipal property: 91.1% (Russian average: 66.4%); regional property: 2.7% (20.0%); federal property: 6.2% (13.6%)

Number of telephones per 100 families (1997): in cities: 37.0 (Russian average: 49.2); in villages: 20.0 (19.8)

Brief Overview

Vologda Oblast is situated in the northern part of European Russia and borders Leningrad, Novgorod, Tver, Kostroma, Yaroslavl, Kirov, and Arkhangelsk oblasts and the Republic of Karelia. Its administrative center, Vologda, is 500 km (300 miles) northeast of Moscow on the Vologda River, a tributary of the Sukhona River. Vologda is an important rail junction with lines to Moscow, St. Petersburg, Arkhangelsk, and Kirov, as well as the Urals and Siberia.

The oblast is extremely rich in forestry resources, so the timber industry naturally dominates the regional economy. The oblast also houses significant peat, limestone, salt, and gravel fields. Other main industries include metallurgy and chemicals in Cherepovets, which is one of the most important industrial centers in the country, and machine building and engineering in Vologda. Highly developed industry is a source of serious air pollution in the oblast. In 1997, Vologda was listed as the region with the eighth worst air pollution, with over 500 kg toxic wastes per capita.

Vologda Oblast is one of the largest exporters in the northern economic region. Its main exports are ferrous metals (75.3%), products of the chemical and petrochemical industry (19.1%), and timber (3.1%). The oblast trades and has established joint ventures with companies from over 80 foreign countries, including Finland, Sweden, Switzerland, Germany, and the United States.

According to a 1998 survey by *Ekspert* magazine, the oblast ranked 45th among Russia's 89 regions in terms of investment potential and 12th in terms of investment risk. Vologda's investment situation had significantly improved since 1997: investment potential had grown by eight points (6th largest growth in the country) and risk had decreased by 36 points (best). A 1998 survey by Bank Austria ranked the oblast 20th in terms of investment climate.

Electoral History

2000 Presidential Election
Putin: 66.91%
Zyuganov: 19.00%
Yavlinskii: 3.84%
Zhirinovsky: 2.99%
Tuleev: 1.81%
Turnout: 71.02% (Russia overall: 68.64%)

1999 Parliamentary Elections
Unity: 30.59%
Communist Party of the Russian Federation: 14.88%
Union of Right Forces: 9.28%
Zhirinovsky Bloc: 9.24%
Fatherland–All Russia: 6.73%
Yabloko: 4.68%
In single-mandate districts: 2 independent
Turnout: 63.83% (Russia overall: 61.85%)

1999 Gubernatorial Election
Pozgalev: 82.97%
Karonnov: 8.20%
Turnout: 60.00%

1996 Gubernatorial Election
Pozgalev (incumbent): 80.69%
Surov (oblast legislature deputy): 4.21%
Beznin (Union of Patriotic Forces): 3.22%
Podgornov: 3.18%
Kiselev (oblast legislature deputy, Honor and Motherland): 2.74%
Shteingart: 0.29%
Turnout: 44.73%

1996 Presidential Election
Yeltsin: 45.17%/63.97% (first round/second round)
Zyuganov: 18.66%/28.49%
Lebed: 17.63%
Zhirinovsky: 7.12%
Yavlinskii: 5.92%
Turnout: 69.03%/67.41% (Russia overall: 69.67%/68.79%)

1995 Parliamentary Elections
Liberal Democratic Party of Russia: 14.36%
Communist Party of the Russian Federation: 12.09%
Our Home Is Russia: 10.69%
Women of Russia: 6.69%
Agrarian Party of Russia: 6.17%
Yabloko: 5.53%
Russia's Democratic Choice: 4.99%
Communists–Workers' Russia: 4.71%
Congress of Russian Communities: 4.36
In single-mandate districts: 1 Communist Party of the Russian Federation, 1 independent
Turnout: 64.16% (Russia overall: 64.37%)

1993 Constitutional Referendum
"Yes"—68.2%   "No"—29.4%

1993 Parliamentary Elections
Liberal Democratic Party of Russia:
    29.66%
Russia's Choice: 16.51%
Agrarian Party of Russia: 15.21%
Women of Russia: 9.59%
Yabloko: 5.84%
Communist Party of the Russian Federation:
    5.19%
Party of Russian Unity and Concord: 5.18%
Democratic Party of Russia: 4.36%
In single-member districts: 1 Agrarian Party of
    Russia, 1 independent
From electoral associations: 1 Liberal Democratic
    Party of Russia
Turnout: 59.98% (Russia overall: 54.34%)

1991 Presidential Election
Yeltsin: 53.78%
Ryzhkov: 20.7%
Zhirinovsky: 7.8%
Tuleev: 6.01%
Bakatin: 4.00%
Makashov: 2.91%
Turnout: 77.38% (Russia overall: 76.66%)

Regional Political Institutions

Executive:
    Governor, 4-year term
    Vyacheslav Yevgenevich Pozgalev, elected
    October 1996, December 1999
        Ul. Gertsena, 2; Vologda, 160000
        Tel 7(817–2) 72–23–80, 72–07–64;
        Fax 7(817–2) 25–15–54
        Federation Council in Moscow:
        7(095) 292–69–36, 926–66–42

Legislative:
    Unicameral
    Legislative Assembly (*Zakonodatelnoe
    Sobranie*)—30 members, 4-year term on
    2–year rotation, elected 1996, March 1998
    Chairman—Gennadii Timofeevich Khripel,
    elected April 1998

Regional Politics

Popular Reformer

Vyacheslav Pozgalev was appointed governor of
Vologda Oblast in March 1996 and was elected to the
post shortly after, winning an overwhelming majority
of the vote. He was reelected in December 1999 with
even stronger support, taking 83 percent of the vote.
Pozgalev was a logical choice for President Boris
Yeltsin, who wanted to ensure that his appointee would
stand a good chance at winning popular election.
Pozgalev was well liked in Vologda long before he
became the region's top executive. Before moving into
politics, Pozgalev was the general director of the
Cherepovets Metallurgical Combine (also known as
Severstal) and was subsequently elected mayor of
Cherepovets, Vologda's largest industrial center.

Pozgalev describes his gubernatorial duties as com-
bining the Soviet-era posts of first secretary of the
Communist Party and chairman of the regional execu-
tive committee, since these two jobs brought together
the responsibilities for political and economic issues.
Politically, Pozgalev has tried to focus on making
Vologda attractive to investors and to avoid scandals.
He has been rather successful at attaining these goals.

Though a vocal liberal reformer, Pozgalev tries to
present himself less as an effective politician and more
as a man of the people. He claims that he has never
been motivated by power. Rather, his interest in politics resulted from his own questions as to why the enormously talented Russian population should live under
such horrible conditions (www.ns.vologda.ru).
Pozgalev claims that power is simply an instrument
for achieving his goals, and his main goal is to improve the lives of Vologda's inhabitants. To demonstrate
his lack of ambition, Pozgalev has written a book entitled *I Don't Want to be President.*

Executive Platform: Liberal, Gaidar Supporter

Pozgalev is a liberal market reformer. He was a strong
supporter of President Boris Yeltsin and was appointed
governor of Vologda by Yeltsin after the dismissal of
Nikolai Podgornov on corruption charges (see Relationships Between Key Players). Pozgalev, who was
serving in the Federation Council at the time of his
appointment, quickly became extremely popular as the
region's top executive. Just six months after his appointment, in October 1996, Pozgalev won election to
the post, earning 80.76 percent of the vote. The two

other contenders took in less than eight percent of the total vote.

Pozgalev supports former acting Prime Minister Yegor Gaidar. In 1993–94 Pozgalev belonged to Gaidar's Russia's Choice movement, and participated in Gaidar's efforts to establish a right-center political bloc in the late 1990s.

Pozgalev has spoken up in defense of women in politics, calling it very unfortunate that women are generally excluded from the upper echelons of Russia's heirarchy politics (www.ns.vologda.ru). The governor also feels very strongly about preserving freedom of speech in the media. He says that the foundation of journalism should be the public's trust (www.ns.vologda.ru*)*.

In 1999 Pozgalev joined Samara Governor Konstantin Titov's Voice of Russia movement.

Policies: Economic and Investment Development

Vologda has experienced considerable economic growth since Pozgalev took over as governor. Pozgalev attributes the region's improvements to the state control of specific industries. The governor and regional legislature have also prioritized attracting investment to the region. In 1997 the Vologda Legislative Assembly passed a law providing for tax breaks and state guarantees for investors, and support for long-term projects (www.ns.vologda.ru).

One economic sector Pozgalev has been very involved in is the region's agricultural industry. In August 1998 Vologda was bombarded with three times the average monthly rainfall over a ten-day period, creating devastating flood conditions. To protect Vologda farmers from losing everything, Pozgalev instituted extraordinary measures to minimize the devastation. He mobilized Vologda's students, public sector employees, and unemployed to bring in the crops since the flood conditions left tractors unusable. The government also blocked any attempts to repossess agricultural equipment for debts and made it illegal to switch off gas and electricity to farms for unpaid bills (*Izvestiya*, 28 August 1998).

Pozgalev has also been active in fighting corruption in Vologda. In November 1997 he took personal responsibility for the Vologda Property Fund, firing the director who had allegedly set inflated salaries for the Fund's management. He then requested that the procurator investigate the situation to determine if there was any criminal wrongdoing. The Vologda Property Fund is one of the few that is not subordinate to the federal government (*EWI RRR*, 20 November 1997).

Relationships Between Key Players: Former Governor Removed for Corruption

Pozgalev became governor of Vologda after the removal of former Governor Nikolai Podgornov. Yeltsin removed Podgornov from office on 23 March 1996 following an *Izvestiya* report detailing the governor's alleged criminal actions. He was subsequently put on trial for abusing office by spending over $3 million of state money on his family and friends and for taking bribes. Most of the charges against Podgornov were ultimately dropped, and he was quickly amnestied for the convictions that stuck.

Pozgalev seems to enjoy considerable support in the regional legislature. Vologda's legislature mostly includes independents, who back Pozgalev's relatively liberal initiatives.

However, Pozgalev's popularity among his constituents may be waning. In January 1999 teachers in the region began gathering signatures to remove him from office. They stated that the governor had made numerous empty promises without accomplishing anything (*Izvestiya*, 22 January 1999). The teachers had not been paid since summer of 1998, and at the time of the January strike were owed 100 million rubles.

Ties to Moscow: Close with Yeltsin

Pozgalev was on good terms with Moscow and rarely challenged Yeltsin's authority. On 4 July 1997 Pozgalev signed a power-sharing agreement with Yeltsin.

Relations with Other Regions: Titov, Gaidar Ally

Like many other governors who were not sure how the 1999 State Duma electoral campaign would evolve, Pozgalev built alliances with at least two political camps. He was on close terms with Gaidar's Right Cause and also signed on to support Samara Governor Konstantin Titov's regional bloc, Voice of Russia.

Pozgalev has also developed a good relationship with Moscow Mayor Yurii Luzhkov. Luzhkov provided Vologda with funds from the Moscow city budget to make repairs after the devastating floods of August 1998. As a gesture of appreciation, Pozgalev awarded Luzhkov the Order of Ded Moroz, the Russian Santa Claus. At a Moscow public holiday celebration in December 1998 Luzhkov suggested an opinion that Ded Moroz was from the Vologda city of Velikii Ustyug, which is the snowiest city in all of Russia.

Vologda is a member of the Northwest interregional association. The association includes the republics of

Vyacheslav Yevgenevich Pozgalev

15 November 1946—Born to a military family based in Korea

1970—Graduated from the Leningrad Electro-Technical Institute as an electromechanical engineer

1970–1990—Rose through the ranks to become general director of the Cherepovets Metallurgical Combine (Severstal)

1989—Elected to the Cherepovets city council and chair of the city executive committee

1991—Elected mayor of Cherepovets

1993–1994—Member of Russia's Choice

1993–1996—Member of the first session of the Federation Council, serving on the Committee for the Budget, Finances, Currency and Credit Regulations, Monetary Emissions, Tax Policies, and Customs Regulations

23 March 1996—Appointed governor of Vologda Oblast

6 October 1996—Elected governor of Vologda Oblast

April 1998—Joined the Board of Directors of Severstal

December 1999—Reelected governor of Vologda Oblast with 83% of the vote

Married, with a daughter

Karelia and Komi; Vologda, Arkhangelsk, Kaliningrad, Kirov, Leningrad, Murmansk, Novgorod, and Pskov oblasts; Nenets Autonomous Okrug; and the city of St. Petersburg. The region also has good trade relations with the prominent agricultural regions in southern Russia, such as Tambov, Voronezh, Rostov, Orel, Saratov, Stavropol, and Krasnoyarsk.

Foreign Relations: Problems Exporting Steel

Vologda houses one of Russia's three top steelmakers, Severstal in Cherepovets. With a management whose average age is about 30, the recently restructured plant produces some of the cheapest hot- and cold-rolled coil steel in the world. In 1998, Russia's major steel exporters (Severstal, Magnitogorsk in Chelyabinsk Oblast, and Novolipetsk in Lipetsk Oblast) earned $1–1.5 billion selling to the U.S., with Severstal's share being more than a third. About 40 percent of Russian exports went to the U.S. in 1998.

In November 1998, however, the United States began investigating whether Russia was dumping steel on the U.S. market. Finally in February 1999, the Americans imposed harsh limits on what Russia could sell in the U.S., effectively driving down 1999 sales to about 15 percent of what they were in 1998. The American politicians were responding to complaints from domestic steelmakers that Russian imports were

costing America jobs. Severstal General Director Aleksei Mordashev described the limits as a "death sentence" for the plant, which has no outside strategic investor (*MT*, 24 February 1999). The EU has long blocked Russian steel imports. Only a revival of orders in the domestic or Asian market could offset the loss of the U.S. market for companies like Severstal.

Two of the oblast's cities, Vologda and Cherepovets, are recipients of a World Bank loan for improving their public transport systems.

Attitudes Toward Business: Promoting Industrial Growth

As the former director of Severstal, Pozgalev has successfully pushed for legislation and government support for projects that attract investment to Vologda. There are 174 joint ventures registered in the region. More than half of these firms have partners from Finland, Sweden, Switzerland, Germany, and the U.S.

Internet Sites in the Region

http://ns.vologda.ru/~avo/toc.html
This is the website of the Vologda Oblast administration. It contains detailed information about the oblast's history and economy, including information on investment and business development.

VORONEZH OBLAST

Territory: 52,400 km^2
Population (as of 1 January 1998):
2,486,000
Distance from Moscow: 587 km

Major Cities:
Voronezh, *capital* (pop. 903,700)
Borisoglebsk (65,700)
Rossosh (63,400)
Liski (55,700)

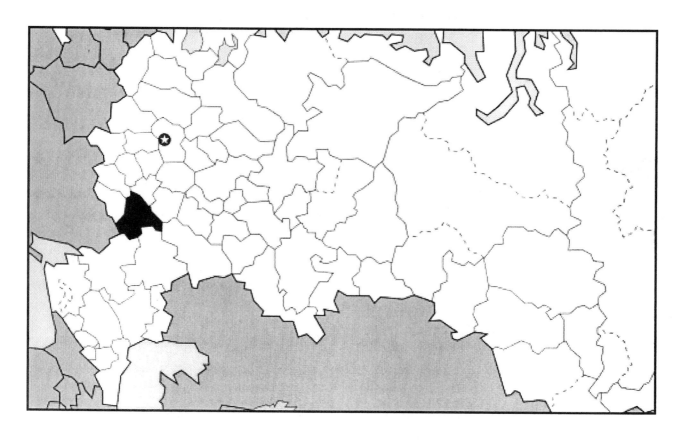

Basic Facts

Population (as of 1 Jan. 1998): 2,486,000 (1.69% of Russian total)

Ethnic breakdown (1989 census): Russians 93.4%, Ukrainians 5.0%

Urban population (as of 1 Jan. 1998): 62.1% (Russia overall: 73.1%)

Student population (as of 1 Sept. 1997): 215 per 10,000 (Russia overall: 208/10,000)

Pensioner population (1997): 30.85% (Russia overall: 25.96%)

Percent of population with higher education (1989 census): 10.4% (Russia overall: 11.3%)

Percent of population working in (1997): Industry: 22.1% (Russian average: 23.0%); Agriculture: 17.4% (13.7%); Trade: 13.5% (13.5%); Culture: 12.6% (13.3%)

Average monthly personal income in July 1998: 593.9 new rubles (Russian average: 891.7 new rubles)

Average monthly personal expenses in July 1998: 431.2 new rubles (Russian average: 684.9 new rubles)

Average monthly subsistence requirement in 1998: 332 new rubles (Russian average: 438 new rubles)

Consumer price index (as of July 1998): 89 (Russia overall = 100)

Budgetary revenues (1997): 3,710.0 billion rubles (Russia overall: 433,378.2 billion rubles)

Budgetary expenditures (1997): 3,659.5 billion rubles (Russia overall: 468,111.6 billion rubles)

Industrial production as percentage of all Russian production (Jan.–Aug. 1998): 0.76%

Proportion of loss-making enterprises (as of July 1998): 47.9% (Russia overall: 50.4%)

Number of enterprises which have wage arrears (as of 1 Sept. 1998): 1,627 (1.20% of Russian total)

Agricultural production as percentage of all Russian production (1997): 2.26%

Number of private farms (as of 1 Jan. 1998): 3,267 (1.19% of Russian total)

Capital investment (1997): 3,133.2 billion rubles (Russia overall: 408,797 billion rubles)

Sources of investment (1997): federal budget: 8.0% (Russian average: 10.2%); regional budget: 9.8% (10.5%); extra-budgetary funds: 82.24% (79.3%)

Foreign investment (1997): 1,109,000 USD (Russia overall: 12,294,734,000 USD)

Number of joint ventures (1997): 56 (0.38% of Russian total)

Fixed capital investment in joint ventures and foreign companies (1997): 9,207 million rubles (Russia overall: 16,265.4 billion rubles)

Number of small businesses (as of 1 July 1998): 9,400 (1.08% of Russian total)

Number of enterprises privatized in 1997: 11 (0.40% of Russian total), including those which used to be municipal property: 100% (Russian average: 66.4%); regional property: 0% (20.0%); federal property: 0% (13.6%)

Number of telephones per 100 families (1997): in cities: 53.0 (Russian average: 49.2); in villages: 21.5 (19.8)

Brief Overview

Voronezh Oblast is located in the center of the East European plain, in the basin of the middle Don River. It is part of the Black Earth economic region and borders Rostov, Volgograd, Saratov, Tambov, Lipetsk, Kursk, and Belgorod oblasts, and Lugansk Oblast in Ukraine.

The city of Voronezh was founded in 1585 as one of the fortresses on the southern frontier of the recently centralized Russian state. The region started to industrialize in the 19th century, although even now it remains a mostly agricultural area with fertile black earth soil covering about 75 percent of its territory. Major regional industries include aircraft building; radio-electronics; manufacturing equipment for the chemical, mining, and agricultural sectors; rubber and automobile tires; and food processing. The oblast produces 99 percent of Russia's equipment for packaging dried food products, 54 percent of grain-sorting machines, and 44 percent of its VCRs. Philips had been a major foreign investor, but pulled out when the market for Russian televisions collapsed.

The oblast's territory is rich in non-ore raw materials such as clays, mineral ochre, limestone, chalk, granite, and sands. Forests cover about one-tenth of the land.

According to a 1998 survey by *Ekspert* magazine, the oblast ranked 27th among Russia's 89 regions in terms of investment potential and 35th in terms of investment risk. A 1998 survey by Bank Austria ranked the oblast 40th in terms of investment climate.

Electoral History

2000 Presidential Election
Putin: 56.70%
Zyuganov: 31.73%
Zhirinovsky: 2.99%
Yavlinskii: 2.88%
Tuleev: 1.35%
Turnout: 70.58% (Russia overall: 68.64%)

1999 Parliamentary Elections
Unity: 32.66%
Communist Party of the Russian Federation: 29.97%
Zhirinovsky Bloc: 7.35%
Fatherland–All Russia: 5.42%
Union of Right Forces: 4.99%

Yabloko: 2.96%
In single-mandate districts: 1 Congress of Russian Communities, 1 In Support of the Army, 1 Communist Party of the Russian Federation, 1 independent
Turnout: 63.59% (Russia overall: 61.85%)

1996 Gubernatorial Election
Shabanov (oblast legislature chairman): 48.97%
Tsapin (incumbent): 41.02%
Kotlyar: 1.76%
Kobylkin (State Duma deputy): 1.66%
Matveev: 1.60%
Turnout: 52.56%

1996 Presidential Election
Zyuganov: 45.48%/57.64% (first round/second round)
Yeltsin: 22.65%/36.97%
Lebed: 17.46%
Zhirinovsky: 5.84%
Yavlinskii: 4.43%
Turnout: 71.85%/68.84% (Russia overall: 69.67%/ 68.79%)

1995 Parliamentary Elections
Communist Party of the Russian Federation: 26.82%
Liberal Democratic Party of Russia: 14.42%
Our Home Is Russia: 6.88%
Congress of Russian Communities: 5.85%
Communists–Workers' Russia: 5.66%
Yabloko: 4.44%
Agrarian Party of Russia: 4.33%
Bloc of Ivan Rybkin: 3.15%
Derzhava: 3.01%
In single-mandate districts: 3 Communist Party of the Russian Federation, 1 Bloc of Ivan Rybkin
Turnout: 67.97% (Russia overall: 64.37%)

1993 Constitutional Referendum
"Yes"—44.4%   "No"—53.9%

1993 Parliamentary Elections
Liberal Democratic Party of Russia: 30.63%
Communist Party of the Russian Federation: 14.54%
Agrarian Party of Russia: 11.99%
Russia's Choice: 11.91%
Yabloko: 7.84%
Democratic Party of Russia: 7.23%
Women of Russia: 5.96%

Party of Russian Unity and Concord: 4.02%
In single-mandate districts: 1 Russia's Choice, 1 Renewal, 2 independent
From electoral associations: 1 Russia's Choice,
    1 Democratic Party of Russia, 1 Liberal Democratic Party of Russia
Turnout: 59.92% (Russia overall: 54.34%)

1991 Presidential Elections
Yeltsin: 57.38%
Ryzhkov: 18.06%
Zhirinovsky: 9.20%
Tuleev: 4.55%
Makashov: 4.04%
Bakatin: 3.83%
Turnout: 80.68% (Russia overall: 76.66%)

Regional Political Institutions

Executive:
    Governor, 4-year term
    Ivan Mikhailovich Shabanov, elected
    December 1996
        Voronezh Oblast Administration;
        Leninskaya Ploshchod, 1; Voronezh, 394015
        Tel 7(073–2) 55–27–37;
        Fax 7(073–2) 55–38–78
        Federation Council in Moscow:
        7(095) 292–57–94, 926–65–74

Legislative:
    Unicameral
    Oblast Duma—45 members, 4-year term,
    elected March 1997
    Chairman—Anatolii Semenovich Goliusov,
    elected April 1997

Regional Politics

Southern Leader Once Soft on Chauvinism

Although Ivan Shabanov claims he is open to foreign investment, the region has not provided friendly ground. The administration has already taken over a local television picture tube joint venture that had been run with Philips. Moreover, the governor, who won his seat in the December 1996 elections with Communist support, apparently has ties to the extreme branch of the Russian nationalist movement. On 22

June 1997 activists from Russian National Unity (Russkoe Natsionalnoe Edinstvo—RNE) joined the regular police force in patrolling the streets of Voronezh. According to *Nezavisimaya Gazeta*, the activists' presence signaled the administration's benign approach toward chauvinism. The RNE was also able to hold a 1997 conference in the Oblast Duma building (*NG*, 18 October 1997).

Executive Platform: Communist Oppositionist

Shabanov is a member of the Communist Party of the Russian Federation (KPRF). During the 1993 confrontation between Yeltsin and the Russian Supreme Soviet in Moscow, Shabanov supported opposition leaders Vice President Aleksandr Rutskoi and Supreme Soviet Speaker Ruslan Khasbulatov. Shabanov vigorously opposed the ratification of the 1993 Constitution that dramatically strengthened Yeltsin's powers. He argued that the new basic law did not secure the separation of powers and limited the rights of the regions (*EWI RRR*, 26 March 1998).

During 1993–94, Shabanov regularly criticized the government and its policies on Voronezh TV. Though Communist Party leader Gennadii Zyuganov visited the region in 1996 to campaign for Shabanov, the more orthodox faction within the KPRF believed he compromised too much with the presidential administration (*OMRI RRR*, 11 September 1996). In May 1995, Shabanov joined the Concord movement headed by then-State Duma speaker Ivan Rybkin. Rybkin established this party at Yeltsin's order to create an "opposition movement" that could be controlled by the Kremlin. It quickly collapsed because of the obvious contradiction in its goals. Shabanov was also the head of his own pre-election party—Power to the People. As the chairman of the Oblast Duma (a post he held from April 1994 until he was elected governor), Shabanov opposed the policies of Aleksandr Kovalev, the governor of Voronezh at the time. He declared unconstitutional Yeltsin's decree postponing the gubernatorial elections in most of Russia's regions until the end of 1996. Shabanov proposed early elections in December 1995 along with the elections to the State Duma, while the then-governor of Voronezh Oblast Kovalev sought further delays in the regional and local elections.

Shabanov won the 8 December 1996 gubernatorial election with the support of the Communist-led National Patriotic Union of Russia (NPSR) and the Agrarian Party, receiving 49 percent of the vote. While the city of Voronezh supported his more liberal opponent, Shabanov's main constituencies were in the surrounding countryside and among veterans' organizations. Local observers pointed out that he was "more popular for his roots than his political views" (Helen Roos, "December Gubernatorial Election in Voronezh Oblast," unpublished paper).

In addition to his overall opposition to the Yeltsin program, Shabanov strongly objected to Anatolii Chubais's privatization scheme. In stark contrast to Saratov Governor Dmitrii Ayatskov, he also opposes the adoption of a land code that would allow the unrestricted buying and selling of land. When he was the chairman of the regional legislature, it adopted a law against "speculative land deals" (*Molodoi Kommunar*, 28 May 1996).

Despite his leftist leanings, Shabanov once noted that he supported the rise of regional leaders like former First Deputy Prime Minister Boris Nemtsov, despite his liberal philosophy. He explained that he hoped "government policy would now take better account of regional interests" (*OMRI DD*, 21 March 1997).

Policies: Often Resorts to Ineffective Anti-Market Mechanisms

In response to the financial crisis of August 1998, Shabanov issued a decree setting a price ceiling for 25 "socially significant goods," primarily food items. He also forbade many local producers from exporting their products outside the oblast. The initial reaction by many producers to this decree was to withhold their products from the market and wait until the currency stabilized so that they would know how to set their prices to ensure a profit. Thus initially goods disappeared, and when they returned to the market, their prices were much higher than the governor's target levels. Overall, the attempt to ensure the supply of goods through administrative means proved ineffective.

In addition to imposing price caps and export restrictions, Shabanov tried to blame all the problems on Moscow. During the 7 October 1998 day of national protest sponsored by the Independent Federation of Trade Unions and Communist Party, Shabanov led a crowd of 25,000 protesters to the city's central Lenin Square. The protest was one of the largest in Russia on a day that was marked by generally tepid

turnout. Shabanov's strongly anti-Moscow rhetoric was broadcast by the networks across the country. In particular, he resorted to the populist demand of reversing the government's privatization program.

Just a few weeks later, it became clear that Shabanov's efforts were not working. Although no one had denounced him at the 7 October meeting, by the end of October, smaller crowds were beginning to meet in Voronezh's Lenin Square, to blame Shabanov himself for the oblast's problems.

In some areas Shabanov is pragmatic enough to avoid implementing Communist ideals. He took the unpopular move of abolishing college students' free access to public transportation. This privilege still exists in the majority of Russian cities (*RG*, 29 October 1997). However, he did not touch pension benefits, since senior citizens make up the base of his electoral support. KPRF regional secretary Ruslan Gostev argues that the governor is not very consistent in his agenda, so there is no significant progress in either economic or social spheres (*RG*, 30 October 1997).

Relationships Between Key Players: Key Offices Dominated by Communists or the Governor's Allies

In late 1998 and early 1999, Shabanov began to create an oblast government which would handle the day-to-day issues of making the regional economy work. The new structure allows Shabanov to concentrate on larger strategic issues and conveniently pass the blame for any regional difficulties on to the new oblast prime minister. In setting up the government, the governor sought to show that he is taking decisive action to deal with the region's economic problems and distance himself from the scandal caused by the arrest of several of his deputies by federal authorities in the fall of 1998 (see Ties to Moscow). Despite the changes, Shabanov and his two vice governors, "Gray Cardinals" Aleksandr Merkulov and Vladimir Korneev, are still at the top of the oblast's political hierarchy (*EWI RRR*, 4 February 1999).

On 16 January 1999, the Voronezh Oblast Duma approved the controversial Aleksandr Sisoev as the new oblast prime minister. Sisoev was not Shabanov's first choice for the position. Vasilii Avdeev, the head of Anna raion, rejected the proposal immediately after it was offered to him. Shabanov's second choice, Viktor Shevtsov, the head of Liski raion, fought to give the future cabinet more power, especially in the field of economics and finance, but when this effort failed, he also declined to serve (*Bereg*, 22 January 1999).

Sisoev has a checkered past. In 1994 he won election to the Voronezh Oblast Duma, where he served as deputy speaker. During his tenure he became involved in a scandal connected with the distribution of selective tax cuts to regional enterprises. In early 1998 the leaders of the Oblast Duma initiated the tax cuts for several enterprises without notifying the deputies in the regional legislature. Sisoev signed most of these decrees. The local media then assumed that Shabanov was using this channel to pay off the sponsors of his electoral campaign (*Novaya Gazeta v Voronezhe*, 19 January 1999). This particular incident shows the extent of the governor's confidence in Sisoev and Sisoev's loyalty to the governor.

The legitimacy of the new government is questionable. Oblast Procurator Aleksandr Frolov has noted that the Oblast Duma has adopted 21 laws that do not comply with federal legislation.

The Chairman of the Oblast Duma is Anatolii Goliusov, elected March 1997. Since most members of the regional legislature are current or former members of the Communist Party, relations between the governor and the regional legislature are cooperative.

In March 1999 Shabanov dismissed Vice-Governor Vladimir Anischev, the region's representative to Moscow. Anischev's dismissal occurred after the vice-governor gave a particularly angry interview to *Komsomolskaya pravda*, in which he said that he was fed up with the Communist rhetoric in the administration. He proclaimed that if he were governor, "I would fire everybody—from the highest officials to the janitors." The incident gave the region a public relations black eye.

In an outburst of anger on 20 April 1999 the Voronezh City Council impeached Voronezh Mayor Aleksandr Tsapin and named his replacement, Vasilii Kochergin. Tsapin was elected mayor in December 1995 but abandoned the post in September 1996 when Yeltsin appointed him governor just two months before the gubernatorial elections were held. He ran in that contest against Shabanov in December 1996 but lost. He was not out of work long, however. The city council assumed the power of electing the mayor and it unanimously voted for Tsapin.

The April 1999 conflict began when council members Oleg Berg and Galina Kudryavtseva suggested examining the status of council members who hold more than one office in the government. Seven deputies holding positions in the city administration fell into this category. The deputies in question left the chamber and the remaining legislators voted to remove them from office, effectively reducing the number of city council members from 33 to 26, leaving a majority comprised of Communist Party members, businessmen, and independents. The new majority proceeded to change the city charter to simplify the process of impeaching the mayor and subsequently removed Tsapin. Shabanov intervened to resolve the conflict, winning badly-needed popularity points. Ultimately it was agreed that all decisions made on 20 April should be annulled and a final decision would be made by the Russian Supreme Court. Shabanov took some responsibility for the mess, claiming that he was partly to blame because he did not play a larger role in Voronezh's city politics (*EWI RRR*, 6 May 1999).

Around the same time that this scandal was unfolding, Shabanov was trying to push for further reforms in the Voronezh political structures. He sent out official letters addressed to all the local governments in the oblast proposing that raion governments be renamed councils of people's deputies, which would elect raion heads from among their members. Rather than persuading the Oblast Duma to abolish local governments—a move that could possibly be declared unconstitutional—Shabanov asked that the local councils delegate him the power to nominate candidates to the executive positions. As of June 1999 half of the oblast's 32 raions had amended their charters and agreed to the new system. Shabanov hoped to extend this system to elect mayors of local municipalities and ultimately would like to form an upper chamber in the oblast legislature that would consist of the same raion heads he would be appointing. This body would have the power to elect the governor, essentially allowing Shabanov to remain in power as long as he wished.

One issue raising a lot of controversy in Voronezh is the construction of the Voronezh Thermal Nuclear Power Station (VAST), an experimental project that was defeated via popular referendum in 1990. Yet, in spite of the popular opposition to this project, the oblast administration has consistently pushed for the project's revival. The Moscow-based Rosenergoatom, which deals with the economic activities of the Ministry of Atomic Energy, told the oblast administration that it would cover the expenses required to complete the power station. In May 1998 Rosenergoatom General Director Yevgenii

Ignatenko signed a cooperation agreement with Shabanov, and Mayor Tsapin promised Ignatenko that he would handle all legal issues so that VAST construction could resume as soon as possible. The public remains opposed to the project, and it appears unlikely that Rosenergoatom will have sufficient funds to complete it (*EWI RRR*, 12 November 1998).

Ties to Moscow: Called on Yeltsin to Resign

Despite the general weakness of the country's federal institutions under Yeltsin, the local branches of the federal law enforcement agencies have launched an anticorruption campaign against the Shabanov administration. By the beginning of December 1998, the federal authorities had arrested six high-ranking oblast administration officials, including three deputy governors and the manager of the oblast's business affairs (*Izvestiya*, 27 November 1998). Shabanov has not provided a substantive rebuttal to the arrests. If the center decides to pursue a more aggressive policy against the regions, it may choose to use a similar technique in cracking down on other rebellious governors.

Shabanov is one of the vocal opposition governors who called on President Yeltsin to resign.

Relations with Other Regions

Shabanov has a close working relationship with Moscow Mayor Yurii Luzhkov. In 1997 the Moscow Department of Food Provision agreed to pay 6 million rubles in advance for the delivery of dry milk, sunflower oil, apples, and wheat from Voronezh Oblast (Radio Rossii, 29 July 1997).

Against the background of threats by Chechen terrorist Salman Raduev to blow up the Voronezh railway station, Shabanov tried to maintain good relations with Chechen President Aslan Maskhadov. In May 1997 Voronezh sent two train cars of corn, potatoes, and sunflowers to Chechnya as humanitarian aid (*Izvestiya*, 17 May 1997).

Voronezh Oblast leadership is a part of the Black Earth Association, headed by Orel Governor and Federation Council Speaker Yegor Stroev. This organization consists of Voronezh, Belgorod, Kursk, Lipetsk, Orel, and Tambov oblasts.

Foreign Relations: Opening Doors to Foreign Assistance

In February 1999 Shabanov signed a 5–year interregional cooperation agreement with Lugansk Oblast (Ukraine) Governor Aleksandr Yefremov. Although Lugansk and Voronezh are contiguous, the volume of trade between the two regions had dropped 25 percent in the previous two years. The agreement is aimed at increasing economic, scientific, and technical cooperation, but also envisions cooperation in the spheres of ecology, youth, and student exchanges.

The EU's TACIS program and two U.S. AID technical assistance projects are underway in the region. Voronezh is also a part of the Federal Project for Agricultural Reform Support (ARIS), financed by the World Bank.

Attitudes Toward Business: Problems with Philips

Voronezh Oblast does not provide welcoming conditions for western business. In one exemplary case, the Voronezh mayor is working to "regionalize" the city's private pharmacies. The clear purpose of his move is to give the city control over the large revenue streams generated by this industry (*EWI RRR*, 1 September 1998).

In words, at least, Shabanov welcomes foreign investment. But the Dutch firm Philips' project failed amid bitter accusations between the investors and the regional administration. Philips bought Voronezh's VELT factory for $2 million in 1995 and spent $60 million of an originally planned $210 million investment trying to modernize it (*KD*, 2 July 1997). After the plant had stood idle for more than a year and workers went unpaid, the Voronezh Oblast administration accused Philips of using its ownership of the plant to inhibit Russian television production and flood the market with imports (*KD*, 7 May 1997). Indeed, the domestic Russian television manufacturing market has effectively collapsed because it remains cheaper to import TVs rather than make them in Russia. Philips has now effectively walked away from its investment, and the oblast government has taken over its shares.

The oblast received some good news on this front when then First Deputy Prime Minister Vadim Gustov visited Voronezh on 11 January 1999 to help revive

Ivan Mikhailovich Shabanov

18 October 1939—Born in Nizhnyaya Baygora, Voronezh Oblast

1964–1965—Served in the army

Graduated from the Voronezh Agricultural Institute and then graduated from the CPSU Central Committee's Academy of Social Sciences, where he received a candidate's degree in history. His dissertation was entitled "Forms and Methods of Strengthening Party Discipline."

1966—Joined the Communist Party and worked as a member of the oblast party staff for 18 years

1982–1988—Served as the chairman of the Voronezh Oblast Executive Committee

1988–1991—Served as the first secretary of the CPSU's oblast committee

1990—Elected to the Oblast Soviet

April 1990—Elected chairman of the Oblast Soviet

August 1991—Temporarily unemployed following banning of the Communst Party

December 1993—Unsuccessfully ran for the Federation Council

27 March 1994—Elected to the Voronezh Legislative Council

April 1994—Elected chairman of the Voronezh Legislative Council

January 1996—Ex officio joined the Federation Council, where he serves as deputy chairman of the Committee on Security and Defense

8 December 1996—Elected governor of Voronezh Oblast

production at VELT. Gustov promised about 14.5 million rubles in capital investments in the near future and said that VELT would produce its first 10,000 tubes in March 1999. He pledged an additional investment of about 70 million rubles, claiming that by the end of the year, production should reach 40,000 tubes a month. Russia and Belarus launched a joint project at the end of 1998 to stimulate domestic television production in plants in Novgorod and Belarus (*EWI RRR*, 12 November 1998). VELT is to supply picture tubes to the TV makers. However, the show of support from the federal government was not sufficient for Philips, and in March 1999 the company sold VELT to the Voronezh Oblast administration for 1 ruble. In June 1999, the Shabanov administration apparently found investment from the Prague Bank, which will deliver $100 million with the goal of increasing production to 25,000 tubes a year.

Despite the problems with Philips, the American firm Lucent Technologies and the Russian firm Svyazstroi-1 opened a $14 million fiber optic cable factory in Voronezh in February 1999 (*Segodnya*, 19 February 1999).

Internet Sites in the Region

http://www.vorstu.ac/engl/delov/invest.html
This web page is devoted to foreign investment. Though there is some general information about ongoing investment projects, many of the data are probably inflated.

http://www.city.vrn.ru/content.html
The city administration's official site provides considerable statistical information on the local economy. There is also some information about banking opportunities and current investment projects.

YAMAL-NENETS AUTONOMOUS OKRUG

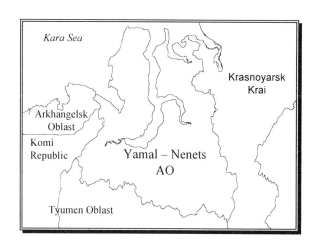

Territory: 750,300 km²
Population (as of 1 January 1998): 497,000
Distance from Moscow: 2,436 km

Major Cities:
Salekhard, *capital* (pop. 31,400)
Noyabrsk (98,600)
Novyi Urengoi (91,900)
Nadym (48,300)

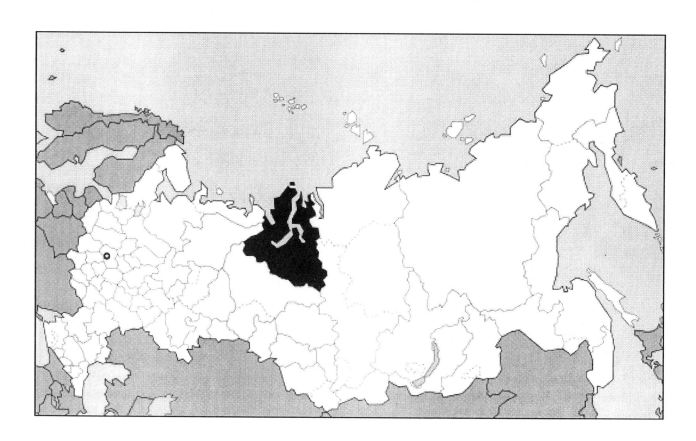

Basic Facts

Population (as of 1 Jan. 1998): 497,000 (0.34% of Russian total)

Ethnic breakdown (1989 census): Russians 79.2%, Ukrainians 17.7%, Tatars 5.3%, Nenets 4.0%, Belarusans 2.7%, Khanty 1.5%, Bashkirs 1.3%, Komi 1.2%, Moldovans 1.1%

Urban population (as of 1 Jan. 1998): 82.9% (Russia overall: 73.1%)

Pensioner population (1997): 11.47% (Russia overall: 25.96%)

Percent of population with higher education (1989 census): 12.5% (Russia overall: 11.3%)

Average monthly personal income in July 1998: 3,124.3 new rubles (Russian average: 891.7 new rubles)

Average monthly personal expenses in July 1998: 890.3 new rubles (Russian average: 684.9 new rubles)

Average monthly subsistence requirement in 1998: 800 new rubles (Russian average: 438 new rubles)

Consumer price index (as of July 1998): 187 (Russia overall = 100)

Budgetary revenues (1997): 14,147.9 billion rubles (Russia overall: 433,378.2 billion rubles)

Budgetary expenditures (1997): 14,691.2 billion rubles (Russia overall: 468,111.6 billion rubles)

Industrial production as percentage of all Russian production (Jan.–Aug. 1998): 2.17%

Proportion of loss-making enterprises (as of July 1998): 67.1% (Russia overall: 50.4%)

Number of enterprises which have wage arrears (as of 1 Sept. 1998): 439 (0.32% of Russian total)

Agricultural production as percentage of all Russian production (1997): 0.04%

Number of private farms (as of 1 Jan. 1998): 36 (0.01% of Russian total)

Capital investment (1997): 24,050.7 billion rubles (Russia overall: 408,797 billion rubles)

Sources of investment (1997): federal budget: 2.1% (Russian average: 10.2%); regional budget: 11.3% (10.5%); extra-budgetary funds: 86.6% (79.3%)

Foreign investment (1997): 38,145,000 USD (Russia overall: 12,294,734,000 USD)

Number of joint ventures (1997): 12 (0.08% of Russian total)

Fixed capital investment in joint ventures and foreign companies (1997): 95,050 million rubles (Russia overall: 16,265.4 billion rubles)

Number of enterprises privatized in 1997: 6 (0.22% of Russian total), including those which used to be municipal property: 100% (Russian average: 66.4%); regional property: 0% (20.0%); federal property: 0% (13.6%)

Number of telephones per 100 families (1997): in cities: 45.6 (Russian average: 49.2); in villages: 14.7 (19.8)

Brief Overview

The Yamal-Nenets Autonomous Okrug was created in December 1930. Half of it is located above the polar circle in the West Siberian lowland between the polar Urals and the Yenisei River basin. The okrug borders Nenets, Khanty-Mansi, Taimyr, and Evenk autonomous okrugs and Komi Republic. The okrug has about 300,000 lakes and 48,000 rivers.

Extensive oil and gas deposits were discovered in the 1950s. They now amount to almost half of the country's total reserves. The region produces 90 percent of Russia's gas and 12 percent of its oil and gas condensates. These raw materials account for 90 percent of the okrug's output. The region also contains deposits of manganese, phosphorus, and rare earth and valuable metals. Moreover, the okrug has a fairly well developed forestry and timber-working industry; timber resources exceed 110 million cubic meters. As a result of intense industry, the okrug has the worst air pollution in the country, with over a ton of toxic wastes per capita.

About a dozen indigenous peoples live in Yamal-Nenets, although they constitute only about 10 percent of its population. They are mostly employed in the traditional industries of fishing, reindeer breeding, and hunting.

The okrug had the largest investment potential growth in the country since 1997—by 26 points—and had ranked 17th among Russia's 89 regions in terms of investment potential and 75th in terms of investment risk, according to a 1998 *Ekspert* magazine survey. A 1998 survey by Bank Austria ranked the okrug 58th in terms of investment climate.

Electoral History

2000 Presidential Election
Putin: 59.11%
Zyuganov: 20.25%
Yavlinskii: 8.81%
Zhirinovsky: 3.59%
Tuleev: 2.00%
Turnout: 68.84% (Russia overall: 68.64%)

2000 Gubernatorial Election
Neelov (incumbent): 87.93%
Tatarchuk: 1.94%
Todyrko: 1.52%
Turnout: 68.61%

1999 Parliamentary Elections
Unity: 20.03%
Communist Party of the Russian Federation: 13.48%
Our Home Is Russia: 12.65%
Union of Right Forces: 12.48%
Yabloko: 9.99%
Zhirinovsky Bloc: 7.91%
Fatherland–All Russia: 6.87%
In a single-mandate district: 1 Our Home Is Russia
Turnout: 59.82% (Russia overall: 61.85%)

1996 Gubernatorial Election
Neelov (incumbent): 68.88%
Goman (State Duma deputy): 22.77%
Kudryavtsev: 1.95%
Kryuk: 0.50%
Turnout: 49.12%

1996 Presidential Election
Yeltsin: 55.26%/79.28% (first round/second round)
Lebed: 15.76%
Zyuganov: 9.18%/15.18%
Zhirinovsky: 7.57%
Yavlinskii: 6.25%
Turnout: 63.73%/66.09% (Russia overall: 69.67%/ 68.79%)

1995 Parliamentary Elections
Our Home Is Russia: 23.05%
Liberal Democratic Party of Russia: 14.95%
Party of Workers' Self-Government: 11.05%
Women of Russia: 6.62%
Yabloko: 6.23%
Communist Party of the Russian Federation: 5.63%
Congress of Russian Communities: 3.67%
Forward, Russia: 3.01%
In a single-mandate district: 1 independent
Turnout: 61.02% (Russia overall: 64.37%)

1993 Constitutional Referendum
"Yes"—78.7%, "No"—19.3%

1993 Parliamentary Elections
Liberal Democratic Party of Russia: 19.57%
Russia's Choice: 19.37%
Women of Russia: 19.12%
Yabloko: 9.11%
Party of Russian Unity and Concord: 7.83%
Democratic Party of Russia: 6.69%

Communist Party of the Russian Federation:
  3.99%
Agrarian Party of Russia: 1.14%
In a single-mandate district: 1 independent
From electoral associations: 1 Women of Russia
Turnout: 46.94% (Russia overall: 54.34%)

1991 Presidential Election
Yeltsin: 67.91%
Zhirinovsky: 10.46%
Ryzhkov: 8.33%
Tuleev: 5.17%
Bakatin: 3.59%
Makashov: 2.41%
Turnout: 69.02% (Russia overall: 76.66%)

Regional Political Institutions

Executive:
  Governor, 4year term
  Yurii Vasilevich Neelov,
    elected October 1996, reelected 2000
    Respublika Ul., 72; Salekhard, 626608;
    Yamal-Nenets Autonomous Okrug
    Tel 7(345–91) 4–46–02, 4–00–66;
    Fax 7(345–91) 4–52–89
    Federation Council in Moscow:
    7(095) 292–63–54, 926–65–71

Legislative:
  Unicameral
  State Duma—21 members, 4-year term,
  elected April 1996
  Chairman—Andrei Viktorovich Artyukhov,
  elected January 1998

Regional Politics

Governor of Strategic Region Central to Numerous Political Battles

Yurii Neelov has a long history in Siberian politics. He entered politics through Komsomol activity and worked his way up to become governor of one of Russia's wealthiest regions. Yamal-Nenets ranks among Russia's few donor regions—regions whose contributions to the federal budget exceed their returns from it. It holds 90 percent of Russia's natural gas reserves, and is also home to sizable oil and precious metal deposits.

Neelov was appointed governor of Yamal-Nenets Autonomous Okrug in 1994, won election to the post in October 1996, and was reelected in March 2000. Although Neelov had worked for many years in Tyumen Oblast politics, on becoming governor of the okrug, he immediately took up the Yamal-Nenets secessionist cause. The okrug is located on the territory of Tyumen Oblast, yet the power relationship between these two administrative units is extremely contentious and Yamal-Nenets has been trying to sever its subordination to the oblast since 1990.

As governor of such a geopolitically important region, one would expect Neelov to wield considerable political clout. However, it seems that thus far his power lies in choosing which individuals in Moscow he will follow.

Executive Platform: Okrug Domination of Natural Resource Wealth

Neelov is clearly interested in capitalizing on the vast natural resources located in Yamal-Nenets, and ensuring that as much wealth as possible remains in the region. This is why Neelov has been so forceful in seeking Yamal-Nenets's independence from Tyumen (see Relations with Other Regions). He has also been critical of Moscow's role in the region's economy, asserting that the capital has made it difficult for the okrug to attract investment to develop its natural resources.

Neelov believes that the federal government abuses its power to suppress the initiatives and activities of the regions. He believes that it was these motives that prompted the federal government's attempt to remove Primorskii Krai Governor Yevgenii Nazdratenko from power in 1997 (*Segodnya*, 4 July 1997).

Policies: Expanding Energy Industries

Neelov has been focused on developing and expanding the okrug's energy industries. During the Soviet period, Yamal-Nenets was treated merely as a source of natural resources, and thus lacked other forms of industry. As a result, the region relies on imports of manufactured goods and foodstuffs from other regions. Neelov is intent on establishing relationships with other regions in Russia without going through Moscow as a middleman (see Relations with Other Regions).

Neelov is also cracking down on energy enterprises forcing them to pay their debts to the okrug budget (see Attitudes Toward Business).

Ties to Moscow: Asserting Region's Interests

Since Yamal-Nenets is a donor region, the federal government tends to tolerate its deviances more than those committed by regions with less wealth. Although Neelov presumably has decent relations with the federal authorities, he has asserted himself against Moscow on several occasions. In fall 1996 the governor violated a presidential decree that ordered Yamal-Nenets to hold its gubernatorial election on the same day as Tyumen Oblast. Neelov went ahead and held the Yamal-Nenets election before Tyumen's and further announced that the okrug would permit voting for the Tyumen Oblast governor to be conducted on the okrug's territory only after a power-sharing agreement with the oblast had been signed. An agreement was not arranged, and Yamal-Nenets followed through with its threat to boycott Tyumen's elections (see Relations with Other Regions).

Former Prime Minister Viktor Chernomyrdin is a popular figure in Yamal-Nenets. Before joining the federal government in 1992 Chernomyrdin headed Gazprom, the largest employer in the resource-rich region. After being dismissed as prime minister in March 1998, Chernomyrdin had planned to run for a vacant State Duma seat from the region. However, he decided against running, announcing that he would pursue a never realized bid for the presidency in 2000.

Relations with Other Regions: Long-standing Conflict with Tyumen

Yamal-Nenets Autonomous Okrug falls into the ambiguous situation of being both a subject of the Russian Federation, thus receiving equal status with all other subjects before the federal center, and a subordinate of Tyumen Oblast. Khanty-Mansi Autonomous Okrug has the same status. Together, the two okrugs control 90 percent of Russia's natural gas and 60 percent of its oil reserves. Of the tax money collected from okrug enterprises, 60 percent goes to okrug and local budgets and the remaining 40 percent is divided between the Tyumen and federal budgets. If Yamal-Nenets and Khanty-Mansi were to successfully secede from Tyumen, as they have been attempting through various political initiatives, then the 20 percent of taxes that goes to Tyumen would remain in okrug budgets.

Yamal-Nenets's attempts at seceding from Tyumen

Oblast began in 1990, when the okrug declared that the territory was an independent subject of the Russian Soviet Republic, but would remain part of Tyumen until the existence of a Yamal-Nenets republic was constitutionally recognized. Such recognition was never achieved.

The most noteworthy secessionist activity undertaken by Yamal-Nenets since Neelov came to power in 1994 was the region's refusal to participate in Tyumen Oblast's gubernatorial elections in 1996. Neelov ignored both presidential decrees and visits from Kremlin emissaries demanding that the region participate. Both Neelov and Khanty-Mansi Governor Aleksandr Filipenko were opposed to the candidacy of Tyumen Governor Leonid Roketskii, who strongly rejects any loosening of okrug-oblast relations. However, Tyumen changed its electoral law, requiring no minimum voter turnout for an election to be valid; thus, Roketskii was reelected even without the support of the two okrugs.

In July 1997 the Constitutional Court ruled on the relationship between Yamal-Nenets and Khanty-Mansi autonomous okrugs and Tyumen Oblast. However, the court's ruling simply restated the existing ambiguities. It defended the constitutional provision that the okrugs have equal rights with the oblast in relations with the center, other federation subjects, and foreign states, and can secede from the oblast at any time. However, for a secessionist attempt to be validated, it must be approved by a constitutional law. The court stated that the okrugs must participate in elections to the oblast's executive and legislative institutions, yet the powers of these institutions are defined by federal legislation, regional statutes, and bilateral treaties.

Both Yamal-Nenets and Khanty-Mansi participated in the December 1997 Tyumen Oblast Legislative Assembly elections. This decision appears to be less a change of heart than a change in separatist tactics. Nine directors of oil and gas companies, who rely heavily on okrug leadership to pursue their business interests, were elected to the oblast duma. In January 1998 the Tyumen Oblast Duma elected Sergei Korepanov as its chairman. Korepanov had previously served as chairman of the Yamal-Nenets legislature, and thus his rise to power in oblast politics has been interpreted as the first move in an attempt by Yamal-Nenets and Khanty-Mansi to remove Tyumen Governor Roketskii. Fifteen of the twenty-five legislators supported Korepanov's candidacy.

Yurii Vasilevich Neelov

24 June 1952—Born in the city of Salekhard, the capital of Yamal-Nenets

1974—Graduated from the Tyumen Industrial Institute as an engineer-mechanic

1991—Graduated from the Management Academy in Moscow

1974–1976—Worked as a mechanic and then as director of a motor pool at a Salekhard aviation enterprise

1976—Turned to party work, serving as an instructor for the Yamal-Nenets Okrug Komsomol Committee

1977—Became the first secretary of the Priural District Komsomol Committee

1978–1982—Second and then first secretary of the Okrug Komsomol Committee

1982—Became the secretary of the Salekhard Komsomol City Committee

1983—Appointed first secretary of the Tyumen Oblast Komsomol Committee

1986—Became the second secretary of the Surgut CPSU City Committee

1987—Became the chairman of the Surgut CPSU District Committee

1989—Elected to the USSR Congress of People's Deputies

1990–1991—Chairman of the Surgut district Council of People's Deputies

1992–1994—Deputy governor of Tyumen Oblast

12 February 1994—Appointed acting governor of Yamal-Nenets Autonomous Okrug, and was confirmed as governor on 3 August

6 March 1994—Elected to the Federation Council, where he became a member of the Committee for Federation Affairs, Federal Agreements, and Regional Policies

January 1996—Appointed to the new session of the Federation Council and joined the Committee on Northern Affairs and Indigenous Peoples

13 October 1996—Elected governor of Yamal-Nenets Autonomous Okrug

26 March 2000—Reelected governor of Yamal-Nenets Autonomous Okrug

Married, with a son

Neelov's interest in gaining greater independence for Yamal-Nenets is also related to his interests in developing relations with other regions independent of Moscow's or Tyumen's interference. Neelov has been successful at using the region's natural resources to establish economic ties with manufacturing and agricultural regions. In December 1997 Yamal-Nenets and Orel Oblast signed a cooperation agreement calling on Yamal-Nenets to build an oil-processing plant in Orel. In return, Orel will provide foodstuffs for pensioners in the region. In June 1998 Neelov signed an agreement with Chuvashia's President Nikolai Fedorov to increase trade between the two regions. Again, the trade transactions will be conducted through barter, swapping Yamal-Nenets's energy sources for Chuvash foodstuffs and manufactured goods.

Yamal-Nenets belongs to the Siberian Accord Association, which includes the republics of Buryatia, Gorno-Altai, and Khakassia; Altai and Krasnoyarsk krais; Irkutsk, Novosibirsk, Omsk, Tomsk, Tyumen, and Kemerovo oblasts; and Agin-Buryat, Taimyr, Ust-Orda Buryat, Khanty-Mansi, and Evenk autonomous okrugs.

Attitudes Toward Business: Close to Gazprom

Clearly Yamal-Nenets's greatest economic asset, and thus the main focus of its business initiatives, is its vast gas and oil resources. The okrug produces 90 percent of Russia's gas. The wealth afforded to this donor region due to its energy industries has also been the source of nearly all of Neelov's conflicts with the federal government and Tyumen Oblast (see Relations with Other Regions).

Neelov has been very active in building relationships with Russia's energy companies, particularly Gazprom. In November 1997 the okrug administration and Gazprom signed an accord obliging the company to pay the okrug government $51 million per month during 1998, up from $31 million the previous year. The agreement also allowed the okrug to sell $375 million worth of gas and oil on its own.

In January 1997 the okrug administration signed a cooperation agreement with the oil company Rosneft for structuring their mutual debts. The agreement provided that Rosneft would pay its debt to Yamal-Nenets by supplying oil and oil products to the okrug, and the government would in turn grant the company tax and investment benefits to make it easier for the company to obtain licenses for developing oil deposits in the region. The okrug signed a similar agreement with the oil company Sibneft. In summer 1997 Neelov withdrew a gas extraction license from the region's largest gas company, Norilskgazprom, which had incurred a debt of over $12 million to the okrug budget.

Although international investment activity in the okrug remains low compared to Russia's other resource-rich regions, Yamal-Nenets is developing foreign economic relations. Until the August 1998 crash, the oblast had been planning a $450 million Eurobond issue managed by Lehman Bankhaus, the German branch of America's Lehman Brothers investment bank. The bank has also lent the okrug $100 million.

YAROSLAVL OBLAST

Territory: 36,400 km^2
Population (as of 1 January 1998):
1,435,000
Distance from Moscow: 282 km

Major Cities:
Yaroslavl, *capital* (pop. 618,800)
Rybinsk (244,400)
Tutaev (45,700)
Pereslavl-Zalesskii (44,900)
Uglich (38,400)
Rostov (36,300)

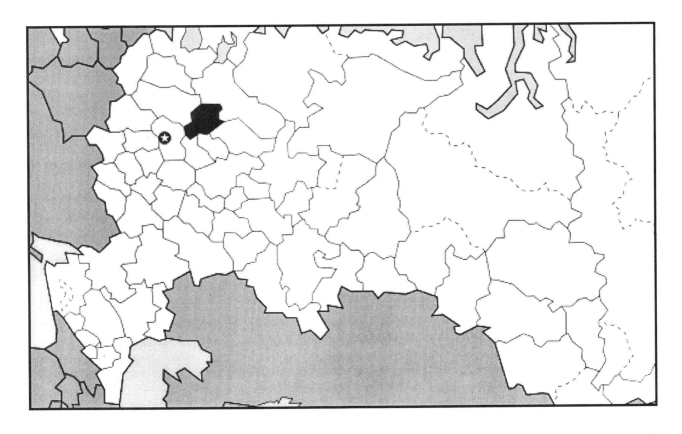

Basic Facts

Population (as of 1 Jan. 1998): 1,435,000 (0.98% of Russian total)

Ethnic breakdown (1989 census): Russians 96.4%, Ukrainians 1.3%, Tatars 0.5%, Belarusans 0.4%

Urban population (as of 1 Jan. 1998): 80.4% (Russia overall: 73.1%)

Student population (as of 1 Sept. 1997): 165 per 10,000 (Russia overall: 208/10,000)

Pensioner population (1997): 29.55% (Russia overall: 25.96%)

Percent of population with higher education (1989 census): 9.5% (Russia overall: 11.3%)

Percent of population working (1997): Industry: 32.2% (Russian average: 23.0%); Agriculture: 8.2% (13.7%); Trade: 15.2% (13.5%); Culture: 11.6% (13.3%)

Average monthly personal income in July 1998: 692.9 new rubles (Russian average: 891.7 new rubles)

Average monthly personal expenses in July 1998: 525.2 new rubles (Russian average: 684.9 new rubles)

Average monthly subsistence requirement in 1998: 377 new rubles (Russian average: 438 new rubles)

Consumer price index (as of July 1998): 94 (Russia overall = 100)

Budgetary revenues (1997): 4,005.6 billion rubles (Russia overall: 433,378.2 billion rubles)

Budgetary expenditures (1997): 4,372.8 billion rubles (Russia overall: 468,111.6 billion rubles)

Industrial production as percentage of all Russian production (Jan.–Aug. 1998): 0.89%

Proportion of loss-making enterprises (as of July 1998): 38.0% (Russia overall: 50.4%)

Number of enterprises which have wage arrears (as of 1 Sept. 1998): 2,901 (2.15% of Russian total)

Agricultural production as percentage of all Russian production (1997): 1.01%

Number of private farms (as of 1 Jan. 1998): 2,235 (0.81% of Russian total)

Capital investment (1997): 2,381.9 billion rubles (Russia overall: 408,797 billion rubles)

Sources of investment (1997): federal budget: 4.4% (Russian average: 10.2%); regional budget: 10.0% (10.5%); extra-budgetary funds: 85.6% (79.3%)

Foreign investment (1997): 24,833,000 USD (Russia overall: 12,294,734,000 USD)

Number of joint ventures (1997): 78 (0.53% of Russian total)

Fixed capital investment in joint ventures and foreign companies (1997): 51,883 million rubles (Russia overall: 16,265.4 billion rubles)

Number of small businesses (as of 1 July 1998): 8,400 (0.97% of Russian total)

Number of enterprises privatized in 1997: 83 (3.03% of Russian total), including those which used to be municipal property: 68.7% (Russian average: 66.4%); regional property: 19.3% (20.0%); federal property: 12.0% (13.6%)

Number of telephones per 100 families (1997): in cities: 42.0 (Russian average: 49.2); in villages: 19.5 (19.8)

Brief Overview

Yaroslavl Oblast, which is located in the central part of the East European plain just northeast of Moscow and borders Tver, Moscow, Ivanovo, Vladimir, Kostroma, and Vologda oblasts, formed an autonomous economic unit sometime in the 17th century. During the rule of Peter the Great, the first large manufacturing plants producing flax and silk fabrics appeared in the area, already famous for its textile and tannery craftsmen. Most of the textiles produced in the region were exported to Europe. In the 1870s, the first heavy industrial enterprises, particularly metal processing and machine building, were founded in the region. Intensive industrialization of the oblast was carried out during the first five-year plans of the Soviet Union, giving the oblast specialization in oil processing, the chemical industry, and machine building. This economic development rapidly urbanized the oblast, 60 percent of whose population resides in two cities—Yaroslavl and Rybinsk.

Due to unfavorable soil and climate conditions, regional agriculture mostly specializes in flax, vegetables, and cattle breeding, rather than the cultivation of grain.

Currently, the oblast has highly developed automobile, electro-technical, shipbuilding, fuel, chemical, and timber-working industries. However, the over 200 large enterprises in the region are highly dependent on outside supplies since the oblast lacks an endowment of mineral resources. On the other hand, over two thirds of its production is exported to the country's other regions. Lately, the oblast has also established economic ties with foreign companies, mostly from Germany, Holland, Finland, the United States, and some countries in Latin America and Eastern Europe.

According to a 1998 survey by *Ekspert* magazine, the oblast ranked 36th among Russia's 89 regions in terms of investment potential and 7th in terms of investment risk. A 1998 survey by Bank Austria ranked the oblast 34th in terms of investment climate.

Electoral History

2000 Presidential Election

Putin: 63.52%
Zyuganov: 20.38%
Yavlinskii: 4.85%
Zhirinovsky: 3.00%
Tuleev: 2.03%
Turnout: 72.16% (Russia overall: 68.64%)

1999 Parliamentary Elections

Unity: 30.86%
Communist Party of the Russian Federation: 16.02%
Union of Right Forces: 10.22%
Fatherland–All Russia: 7.51%
Zhirinovsky Bloc: 7.27%
Yabloko: 5.76%
In single-mandate districts: 1 Russian All-People's Union, 1 independent
Turnout: 68.74% (Russia overall: 61.85%)

1999 Gubernatorial Election

Lisitsyn (incumbent): 63.26%
Vakhrukov: 14.30%
Kornilov: 10.94%
Sorokin: 2.10%
Turnout: 59.40%

1996 Presidential Election

Yeltsin: 32.93%/60.56% (first round/second round)
Lebed: 31.00%
Zyuganov: 18.20%/31.51%
Yavlinskii: 8.32%
Zhirinovsky: 4.84%
Turnout: 72.14%/70.26% (Russia overall: 69.67%/ 68.79%)

1995 Gubernatorial Election

Lisitsyn (incumbent): 51.81%
Kornilov: 33.10%
Turnout: 68.65%

1995 Parliamentary Elections

Communist Party of the Russian Federation: 14.53%
Yabloko: 11.69%
Liberal Democratic Party of Russia: 9.89%
Our Home Is Russia: 8.68%
Women of Russia: 6.11%
Congress of Russian Communities: 5.68%
Derzhava: 4.74%
In single-mandate districts: 1 Yabloko, 1 Power to the People
Turnout: 68.27% (Russia overall: 64.37%)

1993 Constitutional Referendum

"Yes"—64.6%   "No"—32.8%

1993 Parliamentary Elections

Russia's Choice: 22.31%
Liberal Democratic Party of Russia: 21.66%
Women of Russia: 11.01%
Communist Party of the Russian Federation:
8.14%
Agrarian Party of Russia: 7.51%
Yabloko: 7.34%
Party of Russian Unity and Concord: 6.29%
Democratic Party of Russia: 5.72%
In single-mandate districts: 2 independent
From electoral associations: 1 Russia's Choice
Turnout: 59.26% (Russia overall: 54.34%)

1991 Presidential Election

Yeltsin: 54.80%
Ryzhkov: 18.23%
Tuleev: 7.76%
Zhirinovsky: 7.22%
Bakatin: 4.22%
Makashov: 3.99%
Turnout: 75.20% (Russia overall: 76.66%)

Regional Political Institutions

Executive:

Governor, 4-year term
Anatolii Ivanovich Lisitsyn, elected
December 1995, December 1999
Sovetskaya Ploshchad, 3; Yaroslavl, 150000
Tel 7(085–2) 22–23–28;
Fax 7(085–2) 32–84–14
Federation Council in Moscow:
7(095) 292–18–93, 926–68–33

Legislative:

Unicameral
Oblast Duma—50 members, 4-year term,
elected February 1996, March 2000
Chairman—Andrei Krutikov, elected June 2000

Regional Politics

Yeltsin-Appointee Still in Office

Anatolii Lisitsyn is one of the few governors still serving today who was originally appointed by President Boris Yeltsin in 1991. Lisitsyn won popular election to the post in December 1995 and was reelected in December 1999 in a strong victory, pulling in 65 percent of the vote. Like most of the politicians who came to power in the heady days as Russia was asserting itself on the rubble of the collapsing Soviet Union, Lisitsyn espouses a strongly liberal policy.

Despite his success staying in office during the turbulent first years of Russian statehood, Lisitsyn did not make his early career in politics. The governor worked in a furniture-making factory in Rybinsk for twenty-five years before moving to administrative work in 1987. He had begun working at the company at the age of 16 as a manual laborer and ultimately rose to become the enterprise director. Perhaps it is this personal success that inspires Lisitsyn's optimism and confidence in Yaroslavl's future and its economic potential.

Lisitsyn boasts that tourists find Yaroslavl to be the "pearl" of Russia's Golden Ring (www.adm.yar.ru), but believes that the oblast can offer much more to foreigners than a peaceful taste of Russian history. There is extensive foreign investment in the region's industrial base. However, the governor's economic policies are somewhat muddled. The region's economy survives more by relying on the industrial base built during the Soviet era than on a clear plan for marching into the future.

Executive Platform: Yeltsin-Style Reformer

Lisitsyn remained loyal to Yeltsin and his program of reform after the president appointed him governor in December 1991. Yeltsin gave Lisitsyn a mandate to clear the regional government of Communist apparatchiks and replace them with liberal supporters, a task the new governor fulfilled with relish (Jeffrey W. Hahn, "The Development of Local Legislatures in Russia: The Case of Yaroslavl," in Jeffrey W. Hahn, ed., *Democratization in Russia: The Development of Legislative Institutions*, Armonk: M.E. Sharpe, 1996, 175). His efforts won him the support of the Democratic Russia movement, the liberal movement that originally helped boost Yeltsin into power. In 1992 he was not afraid to express his support for Yegor Gaidar's economic proposals. In December 1993 Lisitsyn faithfully backed Gaidar's Russia's Choice bloc in the first State Duma elections. In April 1995 he obligingly joined Our Home Is Russia (NDR). Since then he has championed liberal reformers, such as Anatolii Chubais and Boris Nemtsov (*Izvestiya*, 21 March 1997). In December 1998 he joined Moscow Mayor Yurii Luzhkov's

Fatherland movement, but ultimately dropped out of that party before the December 1999 parliamentary elections, declaring himself an independent.

Lisitsyn believes that Western investment is crucial for boosting the Russian economy, particularly in the Central region which relies primarily on industrial enterprises. Lisitsyn backs industrial restructuring, and with his approval, Yaroslavl Oblast has embarked on several joint venture plans backed by funds secured from foreign businesses and banks.

Policies: Business and Investment

Lisitsyn's goal in policy development has been to foster conditions that invite business development and attract investors. In 1997 investors were offered significant business incentives when they were freed from local taxes on income, property, and highway use (*FI*, 28 May 1998).

Despite his support of free-market approaches, the governor is not afraid to use state influence to build the regional economy. The oblast authorities want to create a system for formulating oblast orders focused on securing the needs of the state, developing a program for reforming enterprises, and improving state control over the natural monopolies (gas, electricity, railroads), of which the government is a major shareholder (*FI*, 28 May 1998).

Although Lisitsyn and his supporters have displayed a strong interest in business and economic development, observers have noted that the various goals of developing an independent export base, advancing an investment program, and supporting agriculture, are more like "competing ideas and intentions" than a coherent economic policy (*FI*, 28 May 1998). The administration's policy needs to be more focused to produce significant effects. The maintenance of Yaroslavl's economic security relies almost entirely on its existing industrial plants. As long as these plants continue to function and attract domestic and foreign investment, the oblast will maintain its standard of living. However, the administration lacks clear vision for the future.

On 5 January 1999, Yaroslavl introduced a five percent sales tax in the region. Lisitsyn and Yaroslavl Mayor Viktor Volonchunas strongly supported the new tax, although local businessmen were ardently opposed. The governor claims that the tax is necessary to provide the region with funds to cover its social obligations. He had tried to introduce a sales tax in the

fall of 1997, but the tax was declared illegal at that time (*NG*, 25 February 1999). There were also difficulties implementing the tax in 1999.

Relationships Between Key Players: Strong Legislative Support

Lisitsyn enjoys a legislature supportive of his political and economic interests. The chairman of the Yaroslavl Duma Andrei Krutikov is the governor's ally. His predecessor, Sergei Vakhrukov, had worked with the governor for several years. He entered the political scene at about the same time as Lisitsyn, and served as deputy-governor of the oblast until February 1996. Lisitsyn helped Vakhrukov achieve the chairmanship by encouraging enterprise directors to support him.

In September 1996 Lisitsyn founded and headed the Governor's Council, which consists of representatives from the primary political parties (except the Communists). This council included Vakhrukov (*LG*, 3 October 1996).

Ties to Moscow: Belarus Came Between Lisitsyn and Yeltsin

Yaroslavl's economy is not self-sufficient, making it greatly dependent on the federal government. This relationship is likely to worsen since Moscow has demanded that it be paid in cash, while the region functioned heavily on cash surrogates and barter payments (59 percent of the oblast's income came in non-cash payments) (*EWI RRR*, 4 June 1998). Despite close ties to Yeltsin, Lisitsyn steered his own course on relations with Belarus (see Foreign Ties).

Until the 1998 crisis the most successful commercial banks in Yaroslavl were branches of powerful Moscow banks (*FI*, 28 May 1998). These banks offered credits to many of the agricultural and industrial enterprises in Yaroslavl. The Moscow banks divided the oblast into functional spheres of influence. The bank Menatep provided loans to the oil industry; Most-Bank concentrated on tourism, financing the construction of a luxury hotel; and Petrovskii took the lead in developing pension funds (*FI*, 28 May 1998).

On 30 October, 1997 Yaroslavl signed a power-sharing agreement with Moscow.

Relations with Other Regions

Lisitsyn has won the respect of the other governors in the Central economic region and they have elected him the president of the Central Russia inter-regional association, a position he has held since 1995. The association includes Bryansk, Vladimir, Ivanovo, Kaluga, Kostroma, Moscow, Ryazan, Smolensk, Tver, and Tula oblasts and the city of Moscow. Moscow plays an important role in the association, with Mayor Yurii Luzhkov considered the association's informal leader.

Lisitsyn also has some common interests with Moscow. Luzhkov has proposed transferring shares in leading defense industries to Moscow (including some based in Yaroslavl Oblast) in exchange for tax breaks and reduced energy charges (*RFE/RL*, 20 March 1998). This initiative would be quite beneficial to Yaroslavl's industries and could help foster the type of investment desired by Lisitsyn. Lisitsyn joined Luzhkov's Fatherland movement at the founding congress, established a Yaroslavl branch in December 1998, but dropped out before the 1999 elections to avoid the appearance that he was seeking another job if he lost the governor's race.

Foreign Relations: Belarus and Latvian Controversies

Lisitsyn is certainly not reserved about promoting Yaroslavl's international interests, even when they conflict with Kremlin priorities. In October 1997 Yeltsin prevented Belarus President Aleksandr Lukashenko from visiting the region since Lukashenko was then holding Pavel Sheremet, a Belarusan citizen working as a correspondent for Russian television, in jail for his critical reporting. The cancellation of Lukashenko's visit infuriated Lisitsyn, who regarded the meeting with the Belarusan president as an "exceptional necessity" for discussing important economic concerns (*FI*, 28 May 1998). Trade between Yaroslavl and Belarus amounted to $147 million annually. Approximately one third of the products from Yaroslavl's four main diesel factories (which employ approximately 100,000 people) are exported to Belarus (*FI*, 28 May 1998). Since Russian customers often pay in kind (if they pay at all), Belarusan credit provides Yaroslavl with a source of hard currency which can in turn be used to pay back wage arrears and taxes (*FI*, 28 May 1998).

When Lukashenko was finally able to visit the region on 23 May 1998, he signed an agreement to increase economic cooperation between Belarus and Central Russia. Lukashenko courted the regional leaders in hopes of using them as leverage against powerful individuals in the federal government who opposed an economic union between Belarus and Russia (*RFE/RL*, 25 May 1998). Lisitsyn supported the merger.

Lisitsyn initiated a boycott of Latvian goods on 7 April 1998 in response to the Latvian authorities' decision to disperse a 3 March demonstration of Russian-speaking pensioners in Riga. However, the boycott is largely symbolic since Yaroslavl stores sell few Latvian goods and Yaroslavl continues to export several million dollars worth of oil to Latvia a year. Yaroslavl has no plans to end this trade, a move that would greatly endanger the region's economic welfare.

Attitudes Toward Business: Successful at Attracting Investment

Lisitsyn encourages investment in the key sectors of Yaroslavl's industry. He has suggested further developing the diesel engine industry, transportation, and local natural resources such as peat, salt, and building materials that contribute more than half of the oblast's revenues (www.adm.yar.ru). Lisitsyn claims that from 1995 to 1997 Yaroslavl has attracted more than $800 million in investments. In 1997, the oblast received $95.9 million, making it the third most attractive region after Moscow and Moscow Oblast (www.adm.yar.ru).

There are currently more than 30 major investment projects in the oblast. The largest joint venture underway is the reconstruction of the Slavneft-Yaroslav-nefteogrsintez oil refinery, a part of the federal "Fuel and Energy" program aimed at improving the quality of oil refining technology. This project was funded by the company's own resources and by a $200 million credit from the Bank of New York under a guarantee of the Export-Import Bank of the United States. The Slavneft project is vital to the economic growth of Yaroslavl Oblast since one third of the oblast's budget comes from the factory's taxes. Despite Slavneft's prominent role in the oblast, its head office is in Moscow and thus a significant amount of the taxes it pays go to the capital rather than the oblast (*FI*, 28 May 1998). A credit line has also been opened with the Export-Import bank of Japan for $240 million. Support for this project is to be provided by the Japanese firms Mitsui and Toyo Engineering and the German firm Tyson (www.adm.yar.ru).

The American firm General Electric is interested in working with Yaroslavl's Rybinsk Factory to produce equipment for the energy industry. The firm, which makes most of its money building aircraft engines, is hiring new engineers, scientists, and designers to increase its ability to compete in the energy equipment sector. Among the key hires was the director of indus-

Anatolii Ivanovich Lisitsyn

26 June 1947—Born in the village of Bolshie Smenki of Kalininskaya (now Tver) Oblast

1977—Graduated from Leningrad's Forestry Academy as an engineer-technician

1963–1987—Worked for the Rybinsk furniture-making company Svoboda, rising through the ranks from a carpenter to enterprise director

1987—Became chairman of the Central Regional Executive Committee for Rybinsk and the first deputy chairman of the Rybinsk City Executive Committee

March 1990—Elected to the Yaroslavl Oblast Soviet and the Rybinsk City Soviet

May 1990–December 1991—Chairman of the Rybinsk City Executive Committee

August 1991—Left the CPSU

December 1991—Appointed by Yeltsin as acting governor of Yaroslavl

10 October 1992—Appointed governor

25 April 1993—Won a seat in the Russian Congress of People's Deputies in a by-election

10 December 1993—Elected to the Federation Council and served on the Committee for International Affairs

April 1995—Joined Viktor Chernomyrdin's Our Home Is Russia (NDR)

May 1995—Became member of NDR Political Committee

1995—Elected president of the Central Russia inter-regional association

17 December 1995—Elected governor in a popular election, receiving 52% of the vote

January 1996—Appointed to the Federation Council and became a member of the Committee on International Affairs

December 1999—Reelected governor of Yaroslavl Oblast with 63% of the vote

trial gas turbines, Aleksandr Snitko, the former deputy general designer at Perm's Aviadvigatel, one of Russia's largest producers of aircraft engines, gas turbines, and ships. In 1997 the company was profitable and increased production. It now employs 23,000 workers.

Kodak is involved in an extensive investment project in the town of Pereslavl-Zalesskii. The Slavich plant has the capacity to cut and package paper and develop and process film. The goal is to be able to manufacture paper for color photographs by the year 2000 (*RT*, 20 March 1998). Eventually, Kodak intends to spend more than $15 million in its Yaroslavl business developments (www.adm.yar.ru).

In addition to these projects, an agreement between the Russian Federation and the World Bank provided Yaroslavl with $2.5 million to develop asbestos-free gaskets in automobile engines (www.adm.yar.ru), and Volvo has discussed the possibility of assembling buses at the Tutaev Motor Works (*RT*, 24 February 1998). Yaroslavl has also established economic ties with foreign companies from Germany, Holland, Finland, the United States, and some Latin American and Eastern European countries (*EWI RRR*, 18 December 1997).

Internet Sites in the Region

http://www.adm.yar.ru/
This is the website for Yaroslavl Oblast, containing information about Lisitsyn, the economy, investment, politics, law, and many other aspects of regional life. This site also offers highlights of regional news.

http://www.adm.yar.ru/inv/investm.htm
This website features an address by Lisitsyn, which details prominent investment projects in Yaroslavl Oblast. It offers considerable information about international investment ventures and proposals for projects aimed at attracting domestic funds.

Selected Bibliography

Reference Works

Afanas'ev, M., G. Bylov, A. Zhuravlev, A. Lavrov, N. Merzlyakova, Ye. Skatershchikova, L. Smirnyagin, and N. Filippova. *Rossiiskie regiony nakanune vyborov-95*. Moscow: Yuridicheskaya literatura, 1995.

Central Electoral Commission. *Vybory deputatov Gosudarstvennoi Dumy 1995*. Moscow:Ves' mir, 1996.

Central Electoral Commission. *Vybory glav ispolnitel'noi vlasti sub"ektov Rossiiskoi Federatsii 1995–1997*. Moscow: Ves' mir, 1997.

Central Electoral Commission. *Vybory v zakonodatel'nye (predstavitel'nye) organy gosudarstvennoi vlasti sub'ektov Rossiiskoi Federatsii 1995–1997*. Moscow: Ves'' mir, 1998.

Filyukova N. Sh. *Spravochnik regiony Rossii*. Moscow: Staviya, 1998.

Goskomstat. *Regiony Rossii*. Moscow, 1998.

Goskomstat. *Sotsial'no-ekonomicheskoe polozhenie Rossii: ianvar-avgust 1998 goda*. Moscow, 1998.

Itogi vyborov 17 dekabrya 1995 goda po regionam. Moscow: Panorama, 1996.

Lysenko, V., L. Lysenko, V. Oldakovskaya, N. Zubarenko, O. Ryzhkina, and A. Bakanina. *Vlast'. Gubernatory Rossii. Kratkii biograficheskii spravochnik.*. Moscow: Institut sovremennoi politiki, 1996.

Matiyasevich, T., N. Mogel, S.A. Nagaev, M. Rossmann, L.I. Smirnych, and A. Woergoetter. *Russia: Regional Risk Rating*. Vienna: Bank Austria, 1998.

McFaul, Michael, and N. Petrov. *Politicheskii al'manakh Rossii 1997*. Moscow: Carnegie Center, 1998.

Panorama Research Group, Labyrint Electronic Database, Moscow.

Territorial Administration of the President of the Russian Federation. *Rossiiskie regiony posle vyborov-96*. Moscow: Yuridicheskaya literatura, 1997.

Periodicals

Boston Globe
Bryanskii Rabochii
Christian Science Monitor
Delovoe Povolzhie
EastWest Institute Russian Regional Report
Ekspert
Finansovaya Rossiya
Finansovye Izvestiya
Forbes
Gorodskie Vesti
Itogi
Ivanovskaya Gazeta
Izvestiya
Jamestown Foundation Prism
Kommersant Daily
Kommersant Vlast
Komsomolskaya Pravda
Lipetskie Izvestiya
Literaturnaya Gazeta
Moscow Times
Moskovskie Novosti
Moskovskii Komsomolets
Naryana Vynder
Nefte Compass
New York Times
Nezavisimaya Gazeta
NG Regiony
Novye Izvestiya
Obshchaya Gazeta
Omskii Vestnik
Open Media Research Institute Daily Digest
Open Media Research Institute Russian Regional Report
Panorama Respubliki
Politicheskaya Sreda
Priokskaya Gazeta
Profil
Rabochii Krai
Radio Free Europe/Radio Liberty Newsline
Radio Free Europe/Radio Liberty Russian Federation Report
Respublika Tatarstan
Rossiiskaya Gazeta
Rossiiskie Vesti
Russkii Telegraf
Sankt-Peterburgskie Vedomosti
Segodnya
Sovetskaya Rossiya
St. Petersburg Times
Stavropolskaya Pravda
Tulskie Izvestiya
Ulyanovskaya Pravda
Uralskii Rabochii
Vechernyaya Ufa
Vesti
Vostochno-Sibirskaya Pravda
Vremya MN
Washington Post

INDEX OF PROPER NAMES

This index includes all names of persons, companies, organizations, political parties, cities, and countries appearing in the text of this book, as well as cross-references to regions mentioned outside of their individual chapters.